Schaefer Online Learning Center Website

Visit the Online Learning Center with PowerWeb, a companion website for *Sociology*, 9/e that offers students and instructors a variety of resources and activities (www.mhhe.com/schaefer9).

VIDEO CLIPS

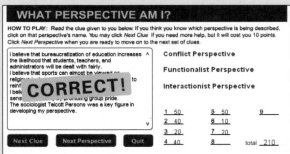

INTERACTIVE QUIZZES

WHAT PERSPECTIVE AM I? QUIZ

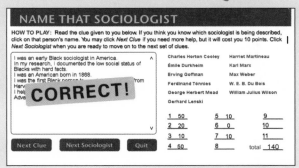

NAME THAT SOCIOLOGIST QUIZ

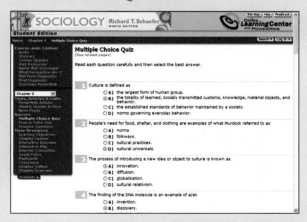

SOCIAL POLICY EXERCISES

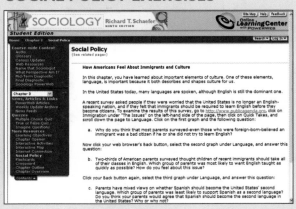

INTERACTIVE MAPS & ACTIVITIES

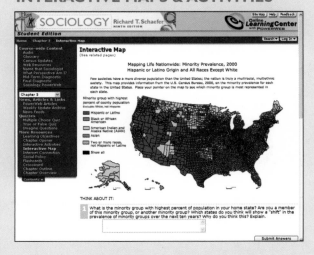

IMPORTANT

HERE IS YOUR REGISTRATION CODE TO ACCESS MCGRAW-HILL PREMIUM CONTENT AND MCGRAW-HILL ONLINE RESOURCES

For key premium online resources you need THIS CODE to gain access. Once the code is entered, you will be able to use the web resources for the length of your course.

Access is provided only if you have purchased a new book.

If the registration code is missing from this book, the registration screen on our website, and within your WebCT or Blackboard course will tell you how to obtain your new code. Your registration code can be used only once to establish access. It is not transferable.

To gain access to these online resources

1. **USE** your web browser to go to: **http://www.mhhe.com/schaefer9**

2. **CLICK** on "First Time User"

3. **ENTER** the Registration Code printed on the tear-off bookmark on the right

4. After you have entered your registration code, click on "Register"

5. **FOLLOW** the instructions to setup your personal UserID and Password

6. **WRITE** your UserID and Password down for future reference. Keep it in a safe place.

If your course is using WebCT or Blackboard, you'll be able to use this code to access the McGraw-Hill content within your instructor's online course.

To gain access to the McGraw-Hill content in your instructor's WebCT or Blackboard course simply log into the course with the user ID and Password provided by your instructor. Enter the registration code exactly as it appears to the right when prompted by the system. You will only need to use this code the first time you click on McGraw-Hill content.

These instructions are specifically for student access. Instructors are not required to register via the above instructions.

*The **McGraw·Hill** Companies*

 Higher Education

Thank you, and welcome to your
McGraw-Hill Online Resources.

0-07-294077-8 SCHAEFER: SOCIOLOGY, 9/E

C3DF-004Y-QOH7-CLTW-MFUL

REGISTRATION CODE
REGISTRATION CODE

REGISTRATION CODE
REGISTRATION CODE

The McGraw·Hill Companies **Higher Education**

SOCIOLOGY

Sociology Around the World

The countries that are identified on this map are cited in the book, either in the context of research studies or in relevant statistical data. Refer to the subject index for specific page references.

NINTH EDITION

SOCIOLOGY

Richard T. Schaefer
DePaul University

Boston   Burr Ridge, IL   Dubuque, IA   Madison, WI   New York   San Francisco   St. Louis
Bangkok   Bogotá   Caracas   Kuala Lumpur   Lisbon   London   Madrid   Mexico City
Milan   Montreal   New Delhi   Santiago   Seoul   Singapore   Sydney   Taipei   Toronto

Higher Education

SOCIOLOGY

Published by McGraw-Hill, a business unit of The McGraw-Hill Companies, Inc., 1221 Avenue of the Americas, New York, NY 10020. Copyright © 2005, 2003, 2001, 1998, 1995, 1992, 1989, 1986, 1983, by The McGraw-Hill Companies, Inc. All rights reserved. No part of this publication may be reproduced or distributed in any form or by any means, or stored in a database or retrieval system, without the prior written consent of The McGraw-Hill Companies, Inc., including, but not limited to, in any network or other electronic storage or transmission, or broadcast for distance learning. Some ancillaries, including electronic and print components, may not be available to customers outside the United States.

This book is printed on acid-free paper.

domestic   2 3 4 5 6 7 8 9 0 DOW/DOW 0 9 8 7 6 5 4
international   1 2 3 4 5 6 7 8 9 0 DOW/DOW 0 9 8 7 6 5 4 3

ISBN   0-07-288692-7 (student edition)
ISBN   0-07-294173-1 (annotated instructor's edition)

Publisher :   *Phillip A. Butcher*
Sponsoring editor: *Sherith Pankratz*
Director of development and media technology: *Rhona Robbin*
Senior marketing manager: *Daniel M. Loch*
Producer, media technology: *Jessica Bodie Richards*
Project manager: *Diane M. Folliard*
Senior production supervisor: *Carol A. Bielski*
Design manager: *Laurie J. Entringer*
Supplement producer: *Marc Mattson*
Photo research coordinator: *Nora Agbayani*
Photo researchers: *Deborah Bull and Jennifer Sanfilippo*
Art editor: *Emma Ghiselli*
Cover and interior design: *Laurie J. Entringer*
Typeface: *10/12 Minion*
Compositor: *Prographics*
Printer: *R. R. Donnelley/Willard*

The cover symbolizes the vibrant, rich, and fascinating diversity of social behavior presented in this book. Professor Schaefer urges readers to become "attentive observers of how people in groups interact and function . . . aware of people's different needs and interests—and perhaps more ready to work for the common good, while still recognizing the individuality of each person."

Library of Congress Cataloging-in-Publication Data

Schaefer, Richard T.
    Sociology / Richard T. Schaefer.—9th ed., annotated instructor's ed.
       p. cm
    Includes bibliographical references and index.
    ISBN 0-07-288692-7 (student ed. : alk. paper) — ISBN 0-07-294173-1 (annotated instructor's ed. : alk. paper)
    1. Sociology. 2. Social problems. 3. United States—Social policy. I. Title.
HM586.S33 2005
2003061500

INTERNATIONAL EDITION ISBN 0-07-111192-1
Copyright © 2005. Exclusive rights by The McGraw-Hill Companies, Inc., for manufacture and export. This book cannot be re-exported from the country to which it is sold by McGraw-Hill. The International Edition is not available in North America.

www.mhhe.com

Dedication

To my son, Peter

About the Author

Taking Sociology To Work

RICHARD T. SCHAEFER: Professor, DePaul University
B.A. Northwestern University
M.A., Ph.D. University of Chicago

Growing up in Chicago at a time when neighborhoods were going through transitions in ethnic and racial composition, Richard T. Schaefer found himself increasingly intrigued by what was happening, how people were reacting, and how these changes were affecting neighborhoods and people's jobs. His interest in social issues caused him to gravitate to sociology courses at Northwestern University, where he eventually received a B.A. in sociology.

"Originally as an undergraduate I thought I would go on to law school and become a lawyer. But after taking a few sociology courses, I found myself wanting to learn more about what sociologists studied, and fascinated by the kinds of questions they raised." This fascination led him to obtain his M.A. and Ph.D. in sociology from the University of Chicago. Dr. Schaefer's continuing interest in race relations led him to write his master's thesis on the membership of the Ku Klux Klan and his doctoral thesis on racial prejudice and race relations in Great Britain.

Dr. Schaefer went on to become a professor of sociology. He has taught introductory sociology for over 30 years to students in colleges, adult education programs, nursing programs, and even a maximum-security prison. Dr. Schaefer's love of teaching is apparent in his interaction with his stu-

dents. "I find myself constantly learning from the students who are in my classes and from reading what they write. Their insights into the material we read or current events that we discuss often become part of future course material and sometimes even find their way into my writing."

Dr. Schaefer is author of the fifth edition of *Sociology: A Brief Introduction* (McGraw-Hill, 2004) and of *Sociology Matters* (McGraw-Hill, 2004). Dr. Schaefer is also the author of *Racial and Ethnic Groups*, now in its ninth edition, and *Race and Ethnicity in the United States*, third edition. His articles and book reviews have appeared in many journals, including *American Journal of Sociology*; *Phylon: A Review of Race and Culture*; *Contemporary Sociology*; *Sociology and Social Research*; *Sociological Quarterly*; and *Teaching Sociology*. He served as president of the Midwest Sociological Society in 1994–1995.

Dr. Schaefer's advice to students is to "look at the material and make connections to your own life and experiences. Sociology will make you a more attentive observer of how people in groups interact and function. It will also make you more aware of people's different needs and interests—and perhaps more ready to work for the common good, while still recognizing the individuality of each person."

Contents in Brief

List of Chapter-Opening Excerpts xviii
List of Boxes xx
List of Social Policy Sections xxii
List of Maps xxiv
Preface xxv

1 The Sociological Perspective

1 Understanding Sociology 1

2 Sociological Research 27

2 Organizing Social Life

3 Culture 56

4 Socialization 79

5 Social Interaction and Social Structure 101

6 Groups and Organizations 125

7 The Mass Media 147

8 Deviance and Social Control 169

3 Social Inequality

9 Stratification and Social Mobility in the United States 197

10 Social Inequality Worldwide 224

11 Racial and Ethnic Inequality 248

12 Stratification by Gender 280

13 Stratification by Age 302

4 Social Institutions

14 The Family and Intimate Relationships 322

15 Religion 349

16 Education 373

17 Government and Politics 395

18 The Economy and Work 413

19 Health and Medicine 436

5 Changing Society

20 Communities and Urbanization 459

21 Population and the Environment 483

22 Collective Behavior and Social Movements 504

23 Social Change and Technology 525

Glossary 547
References 558
Acknowledgments 590
Photo Credits 594
Name Index 597
Subject Index 607

Contents

List of Chapter-Opening Excerpts   xviii

List of Boxes   xx

List of Social Policy Sections   xxii

List of Maps   xxiv

Preface   xxv

Part I   The Sociological Perspective

1 UNDERSTANDING SOCIOLOGY   1

WHAT IS SOCIOLOGY?   3

The Sociological Imagination   3

Photo Essay: Are You What You Own?   4

Sociology and the Social Sciences   6

Sociology and Common Sense   7

WHAT IS SOCIOLOGICAL THEORY?   7

THE DEVELOPMENT OF SOCIOLOGY   9

Early Thinkers   9

Émile Durkheim   10

Max Weber   10

Karl Marx   11

Modern Developments   12

MAJOR THEORETICAL PERSPECTIVES   13

Functionalist Perspective   13

Conflict Perspective   14

Interactionist Perspective   16

The Sociological Approach   17

APPLIED AND CLINICAL SOCIOLOGY   17

Research in Action: Looking at Sports from Three Theoretical Perspectives   19

DEVELOPING A SOCIOLOGICAL IMAGINATION   20

Theory in Practice   20

Research in Action   20

The Significance of Social Inequality   20

Sociology in the Global Community: Women in Public Places Worldwide   21

Speaking across Race, Gender, and National Boundaries   21

Social Policy throughout the World   22

APPENDIX: CAREERS IN SOCIOLOGY   25

2 SOCIOLOGICAL RESEARCH   27

WHAT IS THE SCIENTIFIC METHOD?   29

Defining the Problem   30

Reviewing the Literature   32

Formulating the Hypothesis   32

Collecting and Analyzing Data   33

Developing the Conclusion   34

In Summary: The Scientific Method   34

MAJOR RESEARCH DESIGNS   35

Surveys   35

Research in Action: Framing Survey Questions about Interracial Friendships   36

Observation   37

Experiments   38

Use of Existing Sources   39

ETHICS OF RESEARCH   40

Sociology on Campus: Does Hard Work Lead to Better Grades?   41

The Right to Know versus the Right to Privacy   42

Preserving Confidentiality   43

Neutrality and Politics in Research   43

TECHNOLOGY AND SOCIOLOGICAL RESEARCH   44

Taking Sociology to Work: Paul Donato, Chief Research Officer, Nielsen Media Research   45

SOCIAL POLICY AND SOCIOLOGICAL RESEARCH: Studying Human Sexuality   46

APPENDIX I: USING STATISTICS, TABLES, AND GRAPHS   50

APPENDIX II: WRITING A RESEARCH REPORT   52

2 Organizing Social Life

3 CULTURE   56

CULTURE AND SOCIETY   58

DEVELOPMENT OF CULTURE AROUND THE WORLD   59

Cultural Universals   59

Innovation   60

Globalization, Diffusion, and Technology   60

Sociology in the Global Community: Life in the Global Village   61

Sociobiology   62

ELEMENTS OF CULTURE   63

Language   63

Norms   66

Sanctions   67

Values   67

CULTURE AND THE DOMINANT IDEOLOGY   69

CULTURAL VARIATION   69

Aspects of Cultural Variation   69

Sociology on Campus: A Culture of Cheating?   70

Attitudes toward Cultural Variation   72

SOCIAL POLICY AND CULTURE: Bilingualism   74

4 SOCIALIZATION   79

THE ROLE OF SOCIALIZATION   81

Social Environment: The Impact of Isolation   81

The Influence of Heredity   83

THE SELF AND SOCIALIZATION   84

Sociological Approaches to the Self   84

Psychological Approaches to the Self   86

Sociology on Campus: Impression Management by Students   87

SOCIALIZATION AND THE LIFE COURSE   88

The Life Course   88

Anticipatory Socialization and Resocialization   90

AGENTS OF SOCIALIZATION   91

Family   91

Sociology in the Global Community: Raising Amish Children   92

School   93

Peer Group   94

Mass Media and Technology   95

Workplace   95

The State   96

SOCIAL POLICY AND SOCIALIZATION: Child Care around the World   97

5 SOCIAL INTERACTION AND SOCIAL STRUCTURE   101

SOCIAL INTERACTION AND REALITY   103

Defining and Reconstructing Reality   103

Negotiated Order   104

ELEMENTS OF SOCIAL STRUCTURE   105

Statuses   105

Social Roles   106

Social Inequality: Disability as a Master Status   107

Groups   109

Social Networks and Technology   110

Research in Action: Social Networks among Low-Income Women   111

Social Institutions   112

SOCIAL STRUCTURE IN GLOBAL PERSPECTIVE 114

Durkheim's Mechanical and Organic Solidarity 115

Tönnies's *Gemeinschaft* and *Gesellschaft* 115

Lenski's Sociocultural Evolution Approach 117

SOCIAL POLICY AND SOCIAL STRUCTURE: The AIDS Crisis 119

6 GROUPS AND ORGANIZATIONS 125

UNDERSTANDING GROUPS 127

Types of Groups 127

Research in Action: Pizza Delivery Employees as a Secondary Group 128

Studying Small Groups 130

UNDERSTANDING ORGANIZATIONS 132

Formal Organizations and Bureaucracies 132

Characteristics of a Bureaucracy 133

Research in Action: Bureaucracy and Its Consequences at NASA 135

Bureaucracy and Organizational Culture 136

Sociology in the Global Community: Amway the Chinese Way 137

Voluntary Associations 138

Organizational Change 139

TECHNOLOGY'S IMPACT ON THE WORKPLACE 140

Telecommuting 140

Electronic Communication 140

SOCIAL POLICY AND ORGANIZATIONS: The State of the Unions 141

7 THE MASS MEDIA 147

SOCIOLOGICAL PERSPECTIVES ON THE MEDIA 149

Functionalist View 149

Conflict View 153

Social Inequality: The Color of Network TV 156

Feminist View 157

Interactionist View 158

THE AUDIENCE 159

Who Is in the Audience? 159

The Segmented Audience 160

Audience Behavior 160

THE MEDIA INDUSTRY 161

Media Concentration 161

The Media's Global Reach 162

Sociology in the Global Community: Al Jazeera Is on the Air 163

SOCIAL POLICY AND THE MASS MEDIA: Media Violence 164

8 DEVIANCE AND SOCIAL CONTROL 169

SOCIAL CONTROL 171

Conformity and Obedience 172

Informal and Formal Social Control 174

Law and Society 175

DEVIANCE 176

What Is Deviance? 176

Sociology on Campus: Binge Drinking 177

Photo Essay: Who Is Deviant? 178

Explaining Deviance 181

Social Inequality: Discretionary Justice 187

CRIME 188

Types of Crime 188

Taking Sociology to Work: Tiffany Zapata-Mancilla, Victim Witness Specialist, Cook County State's Attorney's Office 189

Crime Statistics 191

SOCIAL POLICY AND SOCIAL CONTROL: Gun Control 192

3 Social Inequality

Part

9 STRATIFICATION AND SOCIAL MOBILITY IN THE UNITED STATES 197

UNDERSTANDING STRATIFICATION 199

Systems of Stratification 199

Sociology in the Global Community: Under Pressure: The Caste System in India 201

Perspectives on Stratification 203

Is Stratification Universal? 205

STRATIFICATION BY SOCIAL CLASS 208

Measuring Social Class 208

Wealth and Income 210

Poverty 211

Research in Action: When Jobs Disappear 214

Life Chances 215

SOCIAL MOBILITY 216

Open versus Closed Stratification Systems 216

Types of Social Mobility 216

Social Mobility in the United States 217

SOCIAL POLICY AND STRATIFICATION: Rethinking Welfare in North America and Europe 219

10 SOCIAL INEQUALITY WORLDWIDE 224

STRATIFICATION IN THE WORLD SYSTEM 227

The Legacy of Colonialism 229

Multinational Corporations 230

Modernization 232

STRATIFICATION WITHIN NATIONS: A COMPARATIVE PERSPECTIVE 234

Distribution of Wealth and Income 234

Prestige 234

Social Inequality: Stratification in Japan 235

Social Mobility 235

Sociology in the Global Community: The Informal Economy 237

CASE STUDY: STRATIFICATION IN MEXICO 238

Race Relations in Mexico: The Color Hierarchy 238

The Status of Women in Mexico 239

Mexico's Economy and Environment 240

The Borderlands 240

SOCIAL POLICY AND SOCIAL INEQUALITY WORLDWIDE: Universal Human Rights 243

11 RACIAL AND ETHNIC INEQUALITY 248

MINORITY, RACIAL, AND ETHNIC GROUPS 250

Minority Groups 250

Race 251

Ethnicity 253

Research in Action: Prejudice against Arab Americans and Muslim Americans 254

PREJUDICE AND DISCRIMINATION 254

Prejudice 255

Discriminatory Behavior 257

The Privileges of the Dominant 257

Institutional Discrimination 258

STUDYING RACE AND ETHNICITY 259

Functionalist Perspective 260

Conflict Perspective 260

Taking Sociology to Work: Prudence Hannis, Researcher and Community Activist, Quebec Native Women 261

Interactionist Perspective 261

PATTERNS OF INTERGROUP RELATIONS 262

Amalgamation 263

Assimilation 263

Segregation 263

Pluralism 264

RACE AND ETHNICITY IN THE UNITED STATES 264

Racial Groups 264

Ethnic Groups 270

Social Inequality: The Latino Middle Class 271

SOCIAL POLICY AND RACE AND ETHNICITY: Global Immigration 274

12 STRATIFICATION BY GENDER 280

SOCIAL CONSTRUCTION OF GENDER 282

Gender Roles in the United States 283

Cross-Cultural Perspective 285

EXPLAINING STRATIFICATION BY GENDER 286

The Functionalist View 286

The Conflict Response 286

The Feminist Perspective 287

The Interactionist Approach 288

WOMEN: THE OPPRESSED MAJORITY 288

Sexism and Sex Discrimination 288

Research in Action: Communication Differences between Female and Male Physicians 289

Sociology in the Global Community: The Head Scarf and the Veil: Complex Symbols 290

Sexual Harassment 291

The Status of Women Worldwide 291

Women in the Workforce of the United States 292

Women: Emergence of a Collective Consciousness 294

MINORITY WOMEN: DOUBLE JEOPARDY 296

SOCIAL POLICY AND GENDER STRATIFICATION:
The Battle over Abortion from a Global
Perspective 297

13 STRATIFICATION BY AGE 302

AGING AND SOCIETY 304

EXPLAINING THE AGING PROCESS 305

Functionalist Approach: Disengagement Theory 305

*Sociology in the Global Community: Aging Worldwide;
Issues and Consequences 306*

Interactionist Approach: Activity Theory 306

The Conflict Approach 308

ROLE TRANSITIONS THROUGHOUT THE LIFE
COURSE 308

*Taking Sociology to Work: A. David Roberts,
Social Worker 309*

Sociology on Campus: Adult Students 310

The Sandwich Generation 311

Adjusting to Retirement 312

Death and Dying 313

AGE STRATIFICATION IN THE UNITED
STATES 314

The "Graying of America" 314

Wealth and Income 315

Ageism 316

Competition in the Labor Force 316

The Elderly: Emergence of a Collective
Consciousness 317

SOCIAL POLICY AND AGE STRATIFICATION:
The Right to Die Worldwide 318

4 Social Institutions

14 THE FAMILY AND INTIMATE RELATIONSHIPS 322

GLOBAL VIEW OF THE FAMILY 324

Composition: What Is the Family? 324

Kinship Patterns: To Whom Are We Related? 325

Authority Patterns: Who Rules? 326

STUDYING THE FAMILY 327

Functionalist View 327

Conflict View 327

Sociology in the Global Community: Domestic Violence 328

Interactionist View 328

Feminist View 328

MARRIAGE AND FAMILY 329

Courtship and Mate Selection 330

Variations in Family Life and Intimate Relationships 331

Child-Rearing Patterns in Family Life 333

Photo Essay: What Is a Family? 334

DIVORCE 338

Statistical Trends in Divorce 338

Factors Associated with Divorce 339

Impact of Divorce on Children 339

DIVERSE LIFESTYLES 339

Research in Action: The Lingering Impact of Divorce 340

Cohabitation 340

Remaining Single 341

Lesbian and Gay Relationships 342

Marriage without Children 343

SOCIAL POLICY AND THE FAMILY:
Reproductive Technology 344

15 RELIGION 349

DURKHEIM AND THE SOCIOLOGICAL APPROACH TO RELIGION 351

WORLD RELIGIONS 353

THE ROLE OF RELIGION 354

The Integrative Function of Religion 355

Religion and Social Support 355

Photo Essay: Why Do Sociologists Study Religion? 356

Religion and Social Change 358

Social Inequality: The Stained Glass Ceiling 359

Religion and Social Control: A Conflict View 359

RELIGIOUS BEHAVIOR 360

Belief 360

Ritual 360

Experience 361

RELIGIOUS ORGANIZATION 362

Ecclesiae 362

Research in Action: Doing Religion 363

Denominations 363

Sects 364

New Religious Movements or Cults 365

Comparing Forms of Religious Organization 366

CASE STUDY: RELIGION IN INDIA 367

The Religious Tapestry in India 367

Religion and the State in India 368

Religion and Society in India 368

SOCIAL POLICY AND RELIGION: RELIGION IN THE SCHOOLS 369

16 EDUCATION 373

SOCIOLOGICAL PERSPECTIVES ON EDUCATION 375

Functionalist View 375

Taking Sociology to Work: Ray Zapata, Business Owner and Former Regent, Texas State University 379

Conflict View 379

Interactionist View 382

Sociology on Campus: The Debate over Title IX 383

SCHOOLS AS FORMAL ORGANIZATIONS 384

Bureaucratization of Schools 384

Teachers: Employees and Instructors 385

Student Subcultures 385

Research in Action: Violence in the Schools 386

TRENDS IN CONTEMPORARY EDUCATION 388

Testing 389

Homeschooling 389

SOCIAL POLICY AND EDUCATION: School Choice Programs 390

17 GOVERNMENT AND POLITICS 395

POWER AND AUTHORITY 397

Power 397

Sociology in the Global Community: Terrorist Violence 398

Types of Authority 399

POLITICAL BEHAVIOR 400

Political Socialization 400

Participation and Apathy 401

Women in Politics 402

Research in Action: Why Don't Young People Vote? 403

MODELS OF POWER STRUCTURE IN THE UNITED STATES 404

Social Inequality: Gender Quotas at the Ballot Box 405

Power Elite Models 405

Pluralist Model 407

POLITICAL ACTIVISM ON THE INTERNET 408

SOCIAL POLICY AND THE GOVERNMENT: Campaign Financing 409

18 THE ECONOMY AND WORK 413

ECONOMIC SYSTEMS 415

Capitalism 415

Socialism 417

The Informal Economy 418

CASE STUDY: CAPITALISM IN CHINA 418

Social Inequality: Working Women in Nepal 419

The Road to Capitalism 419

The Chinese Economy Today 420

Chinese Workers in the New Economy 420

ASPECTS OF WORK 421

Occupations and Professions 421

Work and Alienation: Marx's View   422

Worker Satisfaction   423

THE CHANGING ECONOMY   425

The Changing Face of the Workforce   425

Deindustrialization   426

Taking Sociology to Work: Richard J. Hawk, Vice President and Financial Consultant, Smith Barney   428

The Contingent Workforce   428

The Impact of New Technology   429

Sociology in the Global Community: The Worldwide Jobs– Skills Mismatch   430

SOCIAL POLICY AND THE ECONOMY: Affirmative Action   431

19 HEALTH AND MEDICINE   436

CULTURE AND HEALTH   438

SOCIOLOGICAL PERSPECTIVES ON HEALTH AND ILLNESS   438

Functionalist Approach   439

Conflict Approach   440

Interactionist Approach   441

Social Inequality: To Inform or Not to Inform? How Race and Ethnicity Affect Views of Patient Autonomy   442

Labeling Approach   442

SOCIAL EPIDEMIOLOGY AND HEALTH   443

Social Class   444

Research in Action: The Nun Study   445

Race and Ethnicity   445

Gender   447

Age   447

HEALTH CARE IN THE UNITED STATES   448

A Historical View   449

Physicians, Nurses, and Patients   449

Alternatives to Traditional Health Care   450

Taking Sociology to Work: Erika Miles, Director, Health Programs, CVS.com   451

The Role of Government   451

MENTAL ILLNESS IN THE UNITED STATES   452

Theoretical Models of Mental Disorders   453

Patterns of Care   454

SOCIAL POLICY AND HEALTH: Financing Health Care Worldwide   455

Part 5   Changing Society

20 COMMUNITIES AND URBANIZATION   459

HOW DID COMMUNITIES ORIGINATE?   461

Early Communities   461

Preindustrial Cities   462

Industrial and Postindustrial Cities   463

URBANIZATION   463

Functionalist View: Urban Ecology   464

Conflict View: New Urban Sociology   467

Photo Essay: How Do Communities Change?   468

TYPES OF COMMUNITIES   470

Central Cities   470

Sociology in the Global Community: Squatter Settlements   471

Suburbs   474

Rural Communities   475

Research in Action: Store Wars   476

SOCIAL POLICY AND COMMUNITIES: Seeking Shelter Worldwide   477

21 POPULATION AND THE ENVIRONMENT   483

DEMOGRAPHY: THE STUDY OF POPULATION   485

Malthus's Thesis and Marx's Response   487

Studying Population Today   487

Taking Sociology to Work: Kelsie Lenor Wilson-Dorsett, Deputy Director, Department of Statistics, Government of Bahamas   488

Elements of Demography   488

WORLD POPULATION PATTERNS   490

Demographic Transition   490

The Population Explosion   492

Sociology in the Global Community: Population Policy in China   493

FERTILITY PATTERNS IN THE UNITED STATES 493

The Baby Boom 493

Stable Population Growth 494

POPULATION AND MIGRATION 494

International Migration 494

Internal Migration 495

THE ENVIRONMENT 496

Environmental Problems: An Overview 496

Functionalism and Human Ecology 498

Conflict View of Environmental Issues 499

Environmental Justice 499

SOCIAL POLICY AND POPULATION:
World Population Policy 500

22 COLLECTIVE BEHAVIOR AND SOCIAL MOVEMENTS 504

THEORIES OF COLLECTIVE BEHAVIOR 506

Emergent-Norm Perspective 506

Value-Added Perspective 507

Assembling Perspective 508

FORMS OF COLLECTIVE BEHAVIOR 509

Crowds 509

Disaster Behavior 510

Fads and Fashions 511

Panics and Crazes 512

Rumors 512

Publics and Public Opinion 513

Social Movements 513

Sociology on Campus: Antiwar Protests 516

Sociology in the Global Community: A New Social Movement in Rural India 518

COMMUNICATIONS TECHNOLOGY AND COLLECTIVE BEHAVIOR 518

SOCIAL POLICY AND SOCIAL MOVEMENTS:
Lesbian and Gay Rights 519

23 SOCIAL CHANGE AND TECHNOLOGY 525

THEORIES OF SOCIAL CHANGE 527

Evolutionary Theory 527

Functionalist Theory 528

Conflict Theory 529

Global Social Change 529

RESISTANCE TO SOCIAL CHANGE 530

Economic and Cultural Factors 530

Sociology in the Global Community: Social Change in South Africa 531

Resistance to Technology 532

TECHNOLOGY AND THE FUTURE 533

Computer Technology 533

Biotechnology 534

Technological Accidents 536

Research in Action: The Human Genome Project 537

TECHNOLOGY AND SOCIETY 538

Culture and Social Interaction 538

Social Control 539

Stratification and Inequality 540

SOCIAL POLICY AND TECHNOLOGY:
Privacy and Censorship in a Global Village 542

Glossary 547

References 558

Acknowledgments 590

Photo Credits 594

Name Index 597

Subject Index 607

Chapter-Opening Excerpts

Every chapter in this textbook begins with an excerpt from one of the works listed below. These excerpts convey the excitement and relevance of sociological inquiry and draw readers into the subject matter for each chapter.

Chapter 1

Nickel and Dimed: On (Not) Getting By in America by Barbara Ehrenreich   2

Chapter 2

Streetwise: Race, Class, and Change in an Urban Community by Elijah Anderson   28

Chapter 3

Cultures@Silicon Valley by J. A. English-Lueck   57

Chapter 4

Black Picket Fences: Privilege and Peril Among the Black Middle Class by Mary Pattillo-McCoy   80

Chapter 5

"Pathology of Imprisonment" by Philip Zimbardo   102

Chapter 6

The McDonaldization of Society by George Ritzer   126

Chapter 7

Media Unlimited: How the Torrent of Images and Sounds Overwhelms Our Lives by Todd Gitlin   148

Chapter 8

Wallbangin': Graffiti and Gangs in L.A. by Susan A. Phillips   170

Chapter 9

No Shame in My Game: The Working Poor in the Inner City by Katherine S. Newman   198

Chapter 10

Nike Culture by Robert Goldman and Stephen Papson   225

Chapter 11

Asian American Dreams: The Emergence of an American People by Helen Zia   249

Chapter 12

The Beauty Myth: How Images of Beauty Are Used Against Women by Naomi Wolf   281

Chapter 13

Tuesdays with Morrie: An Old Man, a Young Man, and Life's Greatest Lesson by Mitch Albom   303

Chapter 14

The War Against Parents by Sylvia Ann Hewlett and Cornel West   323

Chapter 15

For This Land: Writings on Religion in America by Vine Deloria Jr.   350

Chapter 16

Savage Inequalities: Children in America's Schools by Jonathan Kozol   374

Chapter 17

Diversity in the Power Elite: Have Women and Minorities Reached the Top? by Richard L. Zweigenhaft and G. William Domhoff   396

Chapter 18

The End of Work: The Decline of the Global Labor Force and the Dawn of the Post-Market Era by Jeremy Rifkin   414

Chapter 19

The Scalpel and the Silver Bear: The First Navajo Woman Surgeon Combines Western Medicine and Traditional Healing by Lori Arviso Alvord, M.D., and Elizabeth Cohen Van Pelt   437

Chapter 20

Sidewalk by Mitchell Duneier   460

Chapter 21

A New Species of Trouble: The Human Experience of Modern Disasters by Kai Erikson   484

Chapter 22

Smart Mobs by Howard Rheingold   505

Chapter 23

Ruling the Waves: Cycles of Discovery, Chaos, and Wealth from the Compass to the Internet by Debora L. Spar   526

Boxed Features

Sociology in the Global Community

1-2   Women in Public Places Worldwide   21
3-1   Life in the Global Village   61
4-2   Raising Amish Children   92
6-3   Amway the Chinese Way   137
7-2   Al Jazeera Is on the Air   163
9-2   Under Pressure: The Caste System in India   201
10-1   The Informal Economy   237
12-2   The Head Scarf and the Veil: Complex Symbols   290
13-1   Aging Worldwide: Issues and Consequences   306
14-1   Domestic Violence   328
17-1   Terrorist Violence   398
18-2   The Worldwide Jobs–Skills Mismatch   430
20-1   Squatter Settlements   471
21-1   Population Policy in China   493
22-2   A New Social Movement in Rural India   518
23-1   Social Change in South Africa   531

Research in Action

1-1   Looking at Sports from Three Theoretical Perspectives   19

2-1   Framing Survey Questions about Interracial Friendships   36
5-2   Social Networks among Low-Income Women   111
6-1   Pizza Delivery Employees as a Secondary Group   128
6-2   Bureaucracy and Its Consequences at NASA   135
9-1   When Jobs Disappear   214
11-1   Prejudice against Arab Americans and Muslim Americans   254
12-1   Communication Differences between Female and Male Physicians   289
14-2   The Lingering Impact of Divorce   340
15-2   Doing Religion   363
16-2   Violence in the Schools   386
17-2   Why Don't Young People Vote?   403
19-2   The Nun Study   445
20-2   Store Wars   476
23-2   The Human Genome Project   537

Social Inequality

5-1   Disability as a Master Status   107
7-1   The Color of Network TV   156
8-1   Discretionary Justice   187
10-2   Stratification in Japan   235
11-2   The Latino Middle Class   271

15-1   The Stained Glass Ceiling   359

17-3   Gender Quotas at the Ballot Box   405

18-1   Working Women in Nepal   419

19-1   To Inform or Not to Inform? How Race and Ethnicity Affect Views of Patient Autonomy   442

Richard J. Hawk, Vice President and Financial Consultant, Smith Barney   428

Erika Miles, Director, Health Programs, CVS.com   451

Kelsie Lenor Wilson-Dorsett, Deputy Director, Department of Statistics, Government of Bahamas   488

Taking Sociology to Work

Paul Donato, Chief Research Officer, Nielsen Media Research   45

Tiffany Zapata-Mancilla, Victim Witness Specialist, Cook County State's Attorney's Office   189

Prudence Hannis, Researcher and Community Activist, Quebec Native Women   261

A. David Roberts, Social Worker   309

Ray Zapata, Business Owner and Former Regent, Texas State University   379

Sociology on Campus

2-2   Does Hard Work Lead to Better Grades?   41

3-2   A Culture of Cheating?   70

4-1   Impression Management by Students   87

8-1   Binge Drinking   177

13-2   Adult Students   310

16-1   The Debate over Title IX   383

22-1   Antiwar Protests   516

Social Policy Sections

Chapter 2

Social Policy and Sociological Research: Studying Human Sexuality   46

Chapter 3

Social Policy and Culture: Bilingualism   74

Chapter 4

Social Policy and Socialization: Child Care around the World   97

Chapter 5

Social Policy and Social Structure: The AIDS Crisis   119

Chapter 6

Social Policy and Organizations: The State of the Unions   141

Chapter 7

Social Policy and the Mass Media: Media Violence   164

Chapter 8

Social Policy and Social Control: Gun Control   192

Chapter 9

Social Policy and Stratification: Rethinking Welfare in North America and Europe   219

Chapter 10

Social Policy and Social Inequality Worldwide: Universal Human Rights   243

Chapter 11

Social Policy and Race and Ethnicity: Global Immigration   274

Chapter 12

Social Policy and Gender Stratification: The Battle over Abortion from a Global Perspective   297

Chapter 13

Social Policy and Age Stratification: The Right to Die Worldwide   318

Chapter 14

Social Policy and the Family: Reproductive Technology   344

Chapter 15

Social Policy and Religion: Religion in the Schools   369

Chapter 16

Social Policy and Education: School Choice Programs   390

Chapter 17

Social Policy and the Government: Campaign Financing   409

Chapter 18

Social Policy and the Economy: Affirmative Action   431

Chapter 19

Social Policy and Health: Financing Health Care Worldwide   455

Chapter 20

Social Policy and Communities: Seeking Shelter Worldwide   477

Chapter 21

Social Policy and Population: World Population Policy 500

Chapter 22

Social Policy and Social Movements: Lesbian and Gay Rights 519

Chapter 23

Social Policy and Technology: Privacy and Censorship in a Global Village 542

Maps

Mapping Life Nationwide

Educational Level and Household Income in the United States   31

States with Official English Laws   75

Union Membership in the United States   142

The Status of Medical Marijuana   175

Active Hate Groups in the United States, 2002   256

Census 2000: The Image of Diversity   265

Restrictions on Public Funding for Abortion   298

Twenty-six Floridas by 2025   315

Unmarried-Couple Households by State   341

Largest Religious Groups in the United States by County, 2000   364

High School Exit Examination Requirements by State, 2002   389

Availability of Physicians by State   447

Where Americans Moved in the 1990s   496

Mapping Life Worldwide

Languages of the World   64

The Geography of People Living with HIV/AIDS, 2002   120

Gross National Income per Capita, 2002   228

The Borderlands   241

The Global Divide on Abortion   299

Religions of the World   352

Urbanization around the World, 2003   465

World Population, 2003   486

Without a doubt, you have thought about sociological issues before opening this book. Have you or a childhood friend ever spent time in day care? Are your parents or a friend's parents divorced? Do you know someone who owns a gun? Is plagiarism a problem on your campus? Have you participated in an antiwar protest? Chances are you have been touched by most or all of these issues. If you are like most students, you've also spent a great deal of time thinking about your future career. If you major in sociology, what occupations can you choose from?

These are just some of the topics of immediate personal interest that are dealt with in this book. Sociologists also address broader issues, from bilingual education to the existence of slavery in the 21st century. Sociology includes the study of immigration, homelessness, overpopulation, and the process and problems of growing old in different cultures. In the aftermath of September 11, 2001, sociology has been called on to explain the social consequences of the attacks—how people coped following the disasters, how they reacted to minority group members, how rumors spread through the mass media. These issues, along with many others, are of great interest to me, but it is the sociological explanations for them that I find especially compelling. The introductory sociology class provides the ideal laboratory in which to study our own society and those of our global neighbors.

After more than 30 years of teaching sociology to students in colleges, adult education programs, nursing programs, an overseas program based in London, and even a maximum-security prison, I am firmly convinced that the discipline can play a valuable role in teaching critical thinking skills. Sociology can help students to better understand the workings of their own lives as well as of their society and other cultures. The distinctive emphasis on social policy found in this text shows students how to use the sociological imagination in examining such public policy issues as sexual harassment, the AIDS crisis, welfare reform, the death penalty, and privacy and censorship in an electronic age.

My hope is that, through their reading of this book, students will begin to think like sociologists and will be able to use sociological theories and concepts in evaluating human interactions and institutions. From the introduction of the concept of sociological imagination in Chapter 1—which draws on a study that a colleague and I conducted of the food bank system of the United States—this text stresses the distinctive way in which sociologists examine and question even the most familiar patterns of social behavior.

The first eight editions of *Sociology* have been well received; the book is currently used in more than 500 colleges and universities. *Sociology,* Ninth Edition, brings the research into the 21st century and introduces a number of features designed to appeal to today's students. One thing that remains unchanged, however, is the steady focus on three especially important points:

- **Comprehensive and balanced coverage of theoretical perspectives throughout the text.** Chapter 1 introduces, defines, and contrasts the functionalist, conflict, and interactionist perspectives. We explore their distinctive views of such topics as social institutions (Chapter 5), deviance (Chapter 8), the family (Chapter 14), education (Chapter 16), and health and medicine (Chapter 19). In addition, the feminist perspective is introduced in Chapter 1. Other theoretical approaches particular to certain topics are presented in later chapters.
- **Strong coverage of issues pertaining to gender, age, race, ethnicity, and class in all chapters.** Examples of such coverage include social policy sections on bilingualism (Chapter 3), welfare (Chapter 9), immigration (Chapter 11), and affirmative action (Chapter 18); a chapter opener on the "beauty myth" (Chapter 12); boxes on urban poverty and joblessness (Chapter 9), prejudice against Arab Americans and Muslim Americans (Chapter 11), domestic violence (Chapter 14), and squatter

settlements (Chapter 20); and sections on the social construction of race (Chapter 11), gender equity in education (Chapter 16), and the contingent or temporary workforce (Chapter 18).

- **Use of cross-cultural material throughout the text.** Chapter 10 treats the topic of stratification from a global perspective. This chapter introduces world systems analysis, dependency theory, and modernization theory, and examines multinational corporations and the global economy. Every chapter presents global material and makes use of cross-cultural examples. Among the topics examined are:

  Neglect of children in Eastern European orphanages (Chapter 4)

  The global "McDonaldization of society" (Chapter 6)

  The status of women around the world (Chapter 12)

  Issues of aging around the world (Chapter 13)

  Transmission of cultural values through education (Chapter 16)

  Affirmative action in South Africa, Malaysia, and Brazil (Chapter 18)

  Homelessness worldwide (Chapter 20)

  Population policy in China (Chapter 21)

  The global disconnect in technology (Chapter 23)

I take great care to introduce the basic concepts and research methods of sociology and to reinforce this material in all chapters. The most recent data are included, making this book more current than all previous editions.

 SPECIAL FEATURES

Integrated Learning System

The text, its accompanying Reel Society Interactive Movie CD-ROM, and the Online Learning Center website work together as an integrated learning system to bring the theories, research findings, and basic concepts of sociology to life for students. Offering a combination of print, multimedia, and web-based materials, this comprehensive system meets the needs of instructors and students with a variety of teaching and learning styles. The material that follows describes the many features of the text, CD-ROM, and Online Learning Center, as well as the supplementary materials that support those resources.

Poster Art

Each chapter opens with a reproduction of a poster or piece of graphic art that illustrates a key theme or concept of the chapter. Accompanying captions help readers to grasp the relevance of the artwork to the chapter.

Chapter Opener

The chapter openers convey the excitement and relevance of sociological inquiry by means of lively excerpts from writings of sociologists and others who explore sociological topics. These openers are designed to expose students to vivid writing on a broad range of topics and to stimulate their sociological imaginations. For example, Chapter 1 opens with Barbara Ehrenreich's account of her experiment in survival as a low-wage worker, drawn from her best-selling book *Nickel and Dimed*. Chapter 3 begins with J. A. English-Lueck's sketch of a typical morning for an immigrant software engineer in California's multicultural Silicon Valley. Chapter 5 opens with a description of Philip Zimbardo's now-classic mock prison study. And in the opening to Chapter 21, Kai Erikson reflects on the connection between population, the economy, and environmental disasters.

Chapter Overview

The opener is followed by a chapter overview that provides a bridge between the opening excerpt and the content of the chapter. In addition, the overview poses questions and describes the content of the chapter in narrative form.

Key Terms

I have given careful attention to presenting understandable and accurate definitions of each key term. These terms are highlighted in bold italics when they are introduced. A list of key terms and definitions in each chapter—with page references—follows the end of the chapter. In addition, the glossary at the end of the book includes the definitions of the textbook's key terms and the page references for each term.

Research in Action

These sections present sociological findings on topics such as divorce, school violence, political apathy among young people, and prejudice against Arab Americans and Muslim Americans.

Sociology in the Global Community

These sections provide a global perspective on topics such as aging, domestic violence, terrorism, and the jobs-skills mismatch.

Social Inequality

These sections illustrate various types of social stratification. Featured topics include discretionary justice, the Latino middle class, and the "stained glass ceiling" that hovers over female clergy.

Taking Sociology to Work

These sections profile individuals who majored in sociology and use its principles in their work. While these people are employed in a variety of occupations and professions, they share a conviction that their background in sociology has been valuable in their careers.

Sociology on Campus

New to this edition, these sections apply the sociological perspective to issues of immediate interest to today's students. Title IX, plagiarism, and antiwar protests are among the featured topics.

Illustrations

The photographs, cartoons, figures, and tables are closely linked to the themes of the chapters. The maps, titled Mapping Life Nationwide and Mapping Life Worldwide, show the prevalence of social trends. A world map highlighting those countries used as examples in the text appears on pages ii–iii.

Photo Essays

Five new photo essays enliven the text. Each begins with a question that is intended to prompt students to see some part of everyday life with new eyes—those of a sociologist. For instance, the essay in Chapter 1 asks "Are You What You Own?" and the essay in Chapter 8 asks "Who Is Deviant?" The photos and captions that follow suggest the answer to the question.

Social Policy Sections

The social policy sections that close all but one of the chapters play a critical role in helping students to think like sociologists. They apply sociological principles and theories to important social and political issues being debated by policymakers and the general public. New to this edition is a section on gun control (Chapter 8). All the social policy sections now present a global perspective.

Cross Reference Icons

When the text discussion refers to a concept introduced earlier in the book, an icon in the margin points the reader to the exact page.

Chapter Summaries

Each chapter includes a brief numbered summary to aid students in reviewing the important themes.

Critical Thinking Questions

After the summary, each chapter includes critical thinking questions that will help students analyze the social world in which they participate. Critical thinking is an essential element in the sociological imagination.

Internet Connection Exercises

Exercises in each chapter take students online to analyze social issues relevant to chapter topics. Throughout the text an icon signals where more information and/or updates are available on the book's website.

Endpapers

The front endpapers feature a visual guide to the Reel Society Interactive Movie CD-ROM available with this book, and also showcase several components of the Online Learning Center website. The back endpapers feature two summary tables: one that highlights the book's coverage of race, class, and gender and another that summarizes its applications of sociology's major theoretical approaches.

 WHAT'S NEW IN THE NINTH EDITION?

The most important changes in this edition include the following (refer as well to the chapter-by-chapter list of changes on pages xxviii–xxxii and to the *Visual Preview* on pages xxxvi–xli):

Content

- Two new case studies, added to a third that has been significantly revised, provide a closer look at the social worlds of three different countries, illustrating the impact of globalization on each. In Chapter 10, "Stratification in Mexico" discusses the economic importance of the "migradollars" Mexican immigrants to the United States send home to their families. In Chapter 15, "Religion in India" takes a closer look at several religions, their role in Indian politics, and their social effects. In Chapter 18, "Capitalism in China" describes China's transition from managed socialism to a more open system that embraces free enterprise and investment by multinational corporations.

- "Sociology on Campus" boxes apply the sociological perspective to several issues of immediate interest to today's students.

- Five new chapter-opening excerpts, drawn from sociological writings, convey the excitement and relevance of sociological inquiry: *Cultures@silicon valley* by J. A. English-Lueck (Chapter 3), *Media Unlimited* by Todd Gitlin (Chapter 7), *Wallbangin': Graffiti and Gangs in L.A.* by Susan A. Phillips (Chapter 8), *No Shame in My Game* by Katherine S. Newman (Chapter 9), and *Smart Mobs* by Howard Rheingold (Chapter 22).

- Material in several chapters provides a sociological analysis of the aftermath of September 11, 2001. Topics covered include the impact of regime change in Iraq and other countries, disaster behavior research conducted at Ground Zero, continuing distrust of Muslim and Arab Americans, and the issue of the individual's right to privacy versus government's need for intelligence on terrorist activities.

Pedagogy

- Additional summary tables help to pull together coverage of the major theoretical perspectives.
- Reel Society icons highlight related material on the Reel Society Interactive Movie CD-ROM, available with this book.
- Four new U.S. maps illustrate important sociological trends and developments.

Supplements

- **Reel Society: An Interactive Movie CD-ROM**
  This disk features an interactive movie that demonstrates the sociological imagination through the use of actors and scenarios involving campus life. The program allows students to interact with the concepts described in the textbook in a relevant and meaningful context. Students are asked to take on the role of one of the characters and influence key plot turns by making choices for the character. A wide variety of issues and perspectives

(such as culture, socialization, deviance, inequality, race and ethnicity, social institutions, and social change) are addressed in order to relate major sociological concepts and theories to the students' lives. There are also interactive quiz questions on the CD. This CD-ROM, a breakthrough in the use of media to teach introductory sociology students, can serve as an integral companion to the book. An instructor's guide to using the CD-ROM is available with the CD, as well as on the Instructor's Resource CD-ROM.

- New Online Learning Center website features include interactive quizzes, video clips with accompanying essay questions, interactive maps, two interactive games (Name That Sociologist and What Perspective Am I?), diagnostic midterm and final exams, links to additional information about the chapter-opening excerpts and their authors, and SurveyMaker, software that allows students to construct and electronically disseminate their own polls for class research projects.

- A 60-minute VHS videotape features brief clips (5–10 minutes each) from *NBC News* and the *Today Show* that dramatize sociological concepts, serve as lecture launchers, and generate class discussion. This videotape is accompanied by a guide that is available on the Online Learning Center website (www.mhhe.com/schaefer9).

This edition has been thoroughly updated. It includes the most recent data and research findings, many of which were published in the last three years. Recent data from the Census Bureau, Bureau of Labor Statistics, Current Population Reports, the Population Reference Bureau, the World Bank, the United Nations Development Programme, and the Centers for Disease Control have been incorporated.

A more complete, chapter-by-chapter listing of the most significant new material in this edition follows.

 WHAT'S NEW IN EACH CHAPTER?

Chapter 1: Understanding Sociology

- Expanded, reader-friendly introduction to the definition of sociology.
- New examples of the sociological imagination.
- Two-page photo essay: "Are You What You Own?"
- Discussion of approaches to the death penalty in different social sciences, with figure.
- Feminist view incorporated with the conflict perspective.

- Discussion (in the interactionist section) of tattoo symbols of the terrorist attacks of September 11, 2001.

Chapter 2: Sociological Research

- Chapter-opening poster: "There Are Still Traditional Families."
- Sociology on Campus box: "Does Hard Work Lead to Better Grades?" with two-part graph.
- Two-part Mapping Life Nationwide map: "Educational Levels and Household Income in the United States."
- Updated social policy section on the study of human sexuality, with discussions of *(a)* recent attempts to deny funding for NIH research on sexuality and *(b)* changing sexual behavior in China, with photo.
- Appendix on statistical measures—percentage, mean, median, mode—with two-part figure and table: "Percentage of Respondents for or against Legalization of Marijuana."

Chapter 3: Culture

- Chapter-opening excerpt from *Cultures@silicon valley* by J. A. English-Lueck.
- Sociology in the Global Community box: "Life in the Global Village."
- Sociology on Campus box: "A Culture of Cheating?"
- Discussion of the trend toward observance of Christmas in non-Christian societies as an example of globalization, with photo.
- Expanded section on nonverbal communication, with examples of cultural differences in touching and hand signals and illustrative photo.
- Discussion of the Phishhead subculture, with table.

Chapter 4: Socialization

- Summary table: "Theoretical Approaches to Development of the Self."
- Discussion of the gender gap in technological training.
- Discussion of gender differences in high school students' paths to popularity, with table.

Chapter 5: Social Interaction and Social Structure

- Revised Research in Action box: "Social Networks among Low-Income Women."

- Discussion of *diwaniyas,* traditional Kuwaiti men's groups.
- Table illustrating texting lingo.
- Updated discussion of electronic networking among U.S. soldiers and their families.
- Discussion of national sense of purpose developed after September 11, 2001, through patriotic demonstrations.
- Section on Dukheim's concepts of mechanical and organic solidarity.
- Thoroughly updated social policy section on the AIDS crisis.

Chapter 6: Groups and Organizations

- Chapter-opening poster: "Are You In?"
- Sociology in the Global Community box: "Amway the Chinese Way."
- Research in Action box: "Bureaucracy and Its Consequences at NASA."
- Section on focus groups, with photo.
- Discussion of bureaucratic failure to share information among U.S. intelligence agencies prior to the September 11, 2001, attacks, in section on Weber's five characteristics of bureaucracy.
- Example of Enron Corporation's failure in section on bureaucracy and organizational culture.
- Updated Mapping Life Nationwide Map: "Union Membership in the United States."
- Discussion of the establishment of the Department of Homeland Security, with attendant restrictions on unionization and collective bargaining.

Chapter 7: The Mass Media

- Chapter-opening excerpt from Todd Gitlin's *Media Unlimited: How the Torrent of Images and Sounds Overwhelms Our Lives.*
- Discussion of the status conferral function of Internet searches, with figure.
- Section on the promotion of consumption as a media function.
- Updated discussion of minority stereotyping and lack of roles for Blacks and Hispanics on network TV.
- Expanded discussion of the reliance of U.S. media on overseas markets.
- Discussion of the increase in local TV programming in other nations.
- Discussion of the feminist perspective on pornography.
- Discussion of the functions and dysfunctions of the Internet.

- New Sociology in the Global Community box: "Al Jazeera Is on the Air"
- Expanded discussion of video and Internet violence.

Chapter 8: Deviance and Social Control

- Chapter-opening poster: KISS plugging chocolate milk.
- Chapter-opening excerpt from Susan A. Phillips's *Wallbangin': Graffiti and Gangs in L.A.*
- Mapping Life Nationwide map: "The Status of Medical Marijuana."
- Two-page photo essay: "Who Is Deviant?"
- New figure: "Race and the Death Penalty," in Social Inequality box on discretionary justice.
- Discussion of increased formal social control in the United States following terrorist attacks of September 11, 2001.
- Social Policy section: "Gun Control," with photo and cartoon.

Chapter 9: Stratification and Social Mobility in the United States

- Chapter-opening excerpt from Katherine S. Newman, *No Shame in My Game.*
- Sociology in the Global Community box: "Under Pressure: The Caste System in India."
- Section on the estate system.
- Section on the interactionist view of stratification (Thorstein Veblen, conspicuous consumption and conspicuous leisure).
- Summary table: "Major Perspectives on Social Stratification."
- Section on the intersection of class, race, and gender, with photo.
- Updated social policy section on welfare in North America and Europe, with new cartoon.

Chapter 10: Social Inequality Worldwide

- Chapter-opening poster stressing the exploitation of child labor in developing countries.
- Thoroughly updated case study on stratification in Mexico.
- Thoroughly updated social policy section on universal human rights, including new coverage of *(a)* increased surveillance following the terrorist attacks of September 11, 2001, and *(b)* the practice of genital mutilation.

Chapter 11: Racial and Ethnic Inequality

- Chapter-opening poster: "Have You Ever Seen a Real Indian?"
- Table: "Racial and Ethnic Groups in the United States, 2000."
- Updated discussion of hate crimes.
- Updated Mapping Life Nationwide map: "Active Hate Groups in the United States, 2002."
- Updated Research in Action box, "Prejudice against Arab Americans and Muslim Americans," with new cartoon.
- Section on the privileges of the dominant.
- Discussion of discriminatory effects of the Aviation and Transportation Security Act.
- New Taking Sociology to Work box: "Prudence Hannis, Researcher and Community Activist, Quebec Native Women."
- Discussion of racial profiling.

Chapter 12: Stratification by Gender

- Chapter-opening poster: "The Anatomically Correct Oscar."
- Updated discussion of gender roles in children's books.
- Discussion of stay-at-home fathers.
- Discussion of males' underperformance in school.
- Research in Action box: "Communication Differences between Female and Male Physicians."
- Updated table: "U.S. Women in Selected Occupations, 2001."
- Discussion of the *glass escalator* (rapid promotion of men in female-dominated occupations).
- Revised social policy section on abortion.

Chapter 13: Stratification by Age

- Chapter-opening poster: "Towards a Society for All Ages."
- Sociology on Campus box: "Adult Students," with graph.
- Discussion of Senate Subcommittee on Aging's panel on media portrayal of older people.
- Discussion of public opinion surveys regarding euthanasia.

Chapter 14: The Family and Intimate Relationships

- Discussion of households in which women earn more money than their husbands.

- Summary table: "Four Major Perspectives on the Family."
- Photo essay: "What Is a Family?"
- Discussion of foster children.
- Discussion of frequency of cohabitation among racial and ethnic groups.
- Mapping Life Nationwide map: "Unmarried-Couple Households by State."

Chapter 15: Religion

- Photo essay: "Why Do Sociologists Study Religion?"
- Mapping Life Nationwide map: "Largest Religious Groups in the United States by County."
- Case study: "Religion in India," with photograph.
- Updated social policy section, "Religion in the Schools," with new cartoon.

Chapter 16: Education

- Sociology on Campus box: "The Debate over Title IX."
- Updated discussion of high-stakes testing, with Mapping Life Nationwide Map: "High School Exit Examination Requirements by State."
- Updated social policy section on school choice programs.

Chapter 17: Government and Politics

- Chapter-opening poster: "Get off your seat and VOTE."
- Extension of Weber's conceptualization of power to globalization and the rise of multinational corporations.
- Research on civic education and its effects on later political participation.
- Discussion of the interlocking membership of the boards of directors, Fortune 1,000 corporations.
- Updated social policy section on campaign financing, with new cartoon.

Chapter 18: The Economy and Work

- Discussion of the destabilizing effect of increased demand for the metal coltan on the Democratic Republic of the Congo (an example of a harmful effect of globalization).
- Case study: "Capitalism in China," with cartoon and photo.
- Taking Sociology to Work box: "Richard J. Hawk, Vice President and Financial Consultant, Smith Barney."

- Section on the impact of new technology, including a discussion of the widening wage gap.
- Updated social policy section on affirmative action, including *(a)* discussion of the June 2003 Supreme Court decision on the University of Michigan programs and *(b)* discussion of affirmative action programs in other countries, including Malaysia and Brazil.

Chapter 19: Health and Medicine

- Discussion of the interactionist perspective on how medical students learn to play the role of physician.
- Discussion of World Health Organization's study of folk medicines, with photo of street vendor selling home remedies.

Chapter 20: Communities and Urbanization

- Chapter-opening poster: "You Won't See Them; The Cold Will."
- Photo essay: "How Do Communities Change?"
- Discussion of the arrival of big-city problems in rural communities.

Chapter 21: Population and the Environment

- Chapter-opening poster: German environmental protest.
- Taking Sociology to Work box: "Kelsie Lenor Wilson-Dorsett, Deputy Director, Department of Statistics, Government of Bahamas."
- Updated Sociology in the Global Community box: "Population Policy in China."
- Discussion of new study on the relationship between siting of environmental hazards and segregation in nearby schools.

Chapter 22: Collective Behavior and Social Movements

- Chapter-opening excerpt from Howard Rheingold, *Smart Mobs*.
- Sociology on Campus box: "Antiwar Protests."
- Summary table: "Contributions to Social Movement Theory."
- Updated social policy section on lesbian and gay rights, including *(a)* discussion of the 2003 Supreme Court decision overturning laws against homosexual

relations, *(b)* graph showing the change in public opinion on the legality of homosexual relations, and *(c)* updated coverage of corporate policy regarding discrimination against gays and lesbians.

Chapter 23: Social Change and Technology

- Chapter-opening poster: Clonaid.
- Updated Sociology in the Global Community box: "Social Change in South Africa."
- Discussion of biotechnology as a manifestation of the medicalization of society.
- Discussion of sex selection in connection with in vitro fertilization.
- Research in Action box: "The Human Genome Project."
- Condensed and updated social policy section on privacy and censorship, including *(a)* new opening on electronic surveillance, *(b)* discussion of the Patriot Act, and *(c)* updated discussion of government censorship of Internet sites.

SUPPORT FOR INSTRUCTORS AND STUDENTS

PRINT RESOURCES

Annotated Instructor's Edition

An annotated instructor's edition (AIE) of the text, prepared by Lynn Newhart of Rockford College in Illinois, offers page-by-page annotations to assist instructors in using textbook material.

Study Guide

The study guide, prepared by Rebecca Matthews of the University of Iowa, includes standard features such as detailed key points, definitions of key terms, multiple-choice questions, fill-in questions, and true–false questions. All study guide questions are keyed to specific pages in the textbook, and page references are provided for key points and definitions of key terms.

In addition to the questions in the study guide, students can test their mastery of the subject matter by taking the quizzes on the Reel Society CD-ROM and on the Online Learning Center website. Students therefore have three different sets of questions to draw on for review.

Primis Customized Readers

An array of first-rate readings are available to adopters in a customized electronic database. Some are classic articles from the sociological literature; others are provocative pieces written especially for McGraw-Hill by leading sociologists.

McGraw-Hill Dushkin

Any of the Dushkin publications can be packaged with this text at a discount: Annual Editions, Taking Sides, Sources, Global Studies. For more information, please visit the website at **http://www.dushkin.com.**

Digital and Video Resources

VHS Videotapes

Two VHS videotapes (90 minutes and 60 minutes) feature brief clips (5–10 minutes each) from *NBC News* and the *Today Show* that dramatize sociological concepts, serve as lecture launchers, and generate class discussion. Each is accompanied by a guide that is available on the Online Learning Center website (www.mhhe.com/ schaefer9).

PageOut: The Course Website Development Center

All online content for *Sociology,* Ninth Edition, is supported by WebCT, eCollege.com, Blackboard, and other course management systems. Additionally, McGraw-Hill's PageOut service is available to get you and your course up and running online in a matter of hours, at no cost. PageOut was designed for instructors just beginning to explore web options. Even the novice computer user can create a course website with a template provided by McGraw-Hill (no programming knowledge necessary). To learn more about PageOut, ask your McGraw-Hill representative for details, or visit www.mhhe.com/ pageout.

Reel Society: *An Interactive Movie CD-ROM*

This disk features an interactive movie that demonstrates the sociological imagination through the use of actors and scenarios involving campus life. The program allows students to interact with the concepts described in the textbook in a relevant and meaningful context. Students are asked to take on the role of one of the characters and influence key plot turns by making choices for the character. A wide variety of issues and perspectives (such as culture, socialization, deviance, inequality, race and ethnicity, social institutions, and social change) are addressed in order to relate major sociological concepts and theories to the students' lives. There are also interactive quiz questions on the CD. This CD-ROM, a breakthrough in the use of media to teach introductory sociology students, can serve as an integral companion to the book. An instructor's guide to using the CD-ROM, written by Rebecca Matthews of the University of Iowa, is available with the CD, as well as on the Instructor's Resource CD-ROM.

John Tenuto of College of Lake County (in Illinois) served as the academic consultant throughout the development of this program. The script for Reel Society was reviewed by the following instructors: Jan Abu Shakrah, Portland Community College; Grant Farr, Portland State University; Rebecca Matthews, University of Iowa; Kenneth L. Stewart, Angelo State University (in Texas); and Cheryl Tieman, Radford University (in Virginia). In addition, students from George Mason University in Virginia offered their reactions to the script during a focus group.

There are several ways for instructors and students to use *Reel Society*. Students can follow the storyline from start to finish or choose only those scenes for a given chapter or topic. In either case, the movie segments are augmented by a robust array of review and assessment features including self-quizzes. Instructors are provided with their own version of *Reel Society* that allows them to choose which of the program's review features to show in class, if any. Additional quizzes and critical thinking activities are located on the *Reel Society* website, and instructors will find test questions related to the movie on the Instructor's Resource CD-ROM.

Online Learning Center Website

The Online Learning Center website that accompanies this text (www.mhhe.com/schaefer9) offers a rich array of resources for instructors and students, most of which were developed by Lynn Newhart of Rockford College in Illinois. Here you will find the author's audio introductions to each chapter, as well as interactive quizzes and maps, social policy exercises, PowerPoint slides, Census 2000 updates, chapter glossaries, vocabulary flash cards, PowerWeb, video clips, additional information about the chapter-opening excerpts and their authors, news updates, and other resources. New Online Learning Center website features include interactive quizzes, video clips with accompanying essay questions, interactive maps, two interactive games (Name That Sociologist and What Perspective Am I?), diagnostic midterm and final exams, links to additional information about the chapter-opening excerpts and their authors, and SurveyMaker, software that allows students to construct and electronically disseminate their own polls for class research projects. It's also possible to link directly to Internet sites from the Online Learning Center. And you can use any of the material from the Online Learning Center in a course website that you create using PageOut.

PowerWeb

PowerWeb is a resource for the introductory course that is fully integrated with the Online Learning Center website. PowerWeb content is password-protected on the Online Learning Center and includes referenced course-specific web links and articles, student study tools, weekly updates, and additional resources.

In addition to the PowerWeb site for sociology, a special PowerWeb site on violence and terrorism is available from a link on the Online Learning Center. Created in response to the events of September 11, 2001, and their aftermath, this unique website helps instructors and students to integrate coverage of terrorism into their courses. Not just another long list of URLs, the site includes the full texts of thought-provoking articles on terrorism from the scholarly and popular press, as well as weekly updates and a 24-hour newsfeed.

Accompanying both the PowerWeb site for sociology and the site for violence and terrorism are correlation guides that link relevant articles to specific chapters in the textbook, and provide suggested questions and activities. These correlation guides can be found on the Online Learning Center website. For further information about PowerWeb, visit the following site: www.dushkin.com/powerweb/pwwl.mhtml.

PowerPoint Slides

Adopters of *Sociology* can also receive a set of more than 500 PowerPoint slides developed especially for this edition by Richard T. Schaefer and Anne Sachs. The slides are included on the Instructor's Resource CD-ROM (described below) and in the Instructor's Edition of the Online Learning Center website. The set includes bulleted lecture points, graphs, and maps. Instructors are welcome to generate overhead transparencies from the slides if they wish to do so.

Instructor's Resource CD-ROM with Computerized Test Bank

This CD-ROM includes the contents of the Instructor's Resource Manual, Test Banks I and II in computerized and Word formats, the instructor's guide to the Reel Society CD, and PowerPoint slides for instructors' convenience in customizing multimedia lectures. The Instructor's Resource Manual, prepared by Richard T. Schaefer and Clayton Steenberg of Arkansas State University, provides sociology instructors with detailed chapter outlines, learning objectives, additional lecture ideas (among them, alternative social policy issues), class discussion topics, essay questions, topics for student research (along with suggested research materials for each topic), and suggested additional readings. Media materials are suggested for each chapter, including videotapes and films. The test banks were written by Clayton Steenberg of Arkansas State University. Multiple-choice and true–false questions are included for each chapter; they will be useful in testing students on basic sociological concepts, application of theoretical perspectives, and recall of important factual information. Correct answers and page references are provided for all questions.

Primis Online

Professors can customize this book by selecting from it only those chapters they want to use in their courses. Primis Online allows users to choose and change the order of chapters, as well as to add readings from McGraw-Hill's vast database of content. Both custom-printed textbooks and electronic eBooks are available. To learn more, contact your McGraw-Hill sales representative, or visit our website at www.mhhe.com/primis/online.

 ACKNOWLEDGMENTS

Betty Morgan played an integral role in the preparation of the Ninth Edition, and collaborated with me on several earlier editions. Virginia Joyner assisted with two chapters in the present volume and worked with me as well on parts of previous editions. Their efforts have greatly enhanced my presentation of the sociological imagination.

I deeply appreciate the contributions to this book made by my editors. Rhona Robbin, director of development and media technology at McGraw-Hill, has continually and successfully challenged me to make each edition better than its predecessor.

I have received strong support and encouragement from Phillip Butcher, publisher; Sherith Pankratz, sponsoring editor; and Dan Loch, senior marketing manager. Additional guidance and support were provided by Amy Shaffer, editorial coordinator; Diane Folliard, project manager; Laurie Entringer, designer; Jessica Bodie, media producer; Nora Agbayani, Deborah Bull, and Jen Sanfilippo, photo editors; Emma Ghiselli, art editor; and Elsa Peterson and Judy Brody, permissions editors. I would like to express appreciation to DePaul University student Todd Fuist for his assistance with the preparation of material for this book.

I would also like to acknowledge the contributions of the following individuals: Lynn Newhart of Rockford College in Illinois for her work on the annotated instructor's edition and the Online Learning Center; Clayton Steenberg of Arkansas State University for his work on the Instructor's Resource Manual and the test banks; Rebecca Matthews of the University of Iowa for her work on the study guide; Thom Holmes of McGraw-Hill and John Tenuto of Lake County College in Illinois for their work on the Reel Society CD-ROM; and Rebecca Matthews of the University of Iowa for her work on the instructor's guide to accompany the Reel Society CD-ROM, and on a series of exam questions based on Reel Society scenarios.

As is evident from these acknowledgments, the preparation of a textbook is truly a team effort. The most valuable member of this effort continues to be my wife, Sandy. She provides the support so necessary in my creative and scholarly activities.

I have had the good fortune to be able to introduce students to sociology for many years. These students have been enormously helpful in spurring on my own sociological imagination. In ways I can fully appreciate but cannot fully acknowledge, their questions in class and queries in the hallway have found their way into this textbook.

Richard T. Schaefer
www.schaefersociology.net
schaeferrt@aol.com

As a full-service publisher of quality educational products, McGraw-Hill does much more than just sell textbooks to your students. We create and publish an extensive array of print, video, and digital supplements to support instruction on your campus. Orders of new (versus used) textbooks help us to defray the cost of developing such supplements, which is substantial. Please consult your local McGraw-Hill representative to learn about the availability of the supplements that accompany Sociology. *If you are not sure who your representative is, you can find him or her by using the Rep Locator at www.mhhe.com.*

Academic Reviewers

This edition continues to reflect many insightful suggestions made by reviewers of the first eight hardcover editions and the five paperback brief editions. The current edition has benefited from constructive and thorough evaluations provided by sociologists from both two-year and four-year institutions.

Jan Abu Shakrah
Portland Community College

Therese Baker-Degler
California State University–San Marcos

Stanley Baran
Bryant University

Denise Cobb
University of Arkansas–Little Rock

Kelly Dagan
Illinois College

Estelle Disch
University of Massachusetts–Boston

Robyn Driskell
Baylor University

Kathleen French
Kapiolani Community College

Jennifer F. Hamer
Wayne State University

Chad M. Hanson
Casper College

Brooke Harrington
Brown University

Jeremy Hein
University of Wisconsin–Eau Claire

William Hoynes
Vassar College

Robert O. Keel
University of Missouri–St. Louis

Jerome Koch
Texas Tech University

Martin Marger
Michigan State University

Matthew Oware
DePauw University

Ralph Pyle
Michigan State University

Paul D. Roof
College of Charleston

Jim Thomas
Northern Illinois University

Leona Tompkin
University of Toledo

Melissa J. Wilde
Indiana University

J. Russell Willis
Grambling State University

A Visual Preview of the Ninth Edition

The ninth edition of *Sociology* continues its tradition of teaching students how to think critically about society and their own lives from a wide range of classical and contemporary sociological perspectives.

Intriguing Book Excerpts

Chapter openers convey the excitement and relevance of sociological inquiry by means of lively excerpts from writings of sociologists and others who explore sociological topics.

Book Excerpt Links to Chapters

Chapter overviews provide a bridge between the chapter-opening excerpt and the content of the chapter.

New Sociology on Campus Boxes

These boxes on topics such as cheating, binge drinking, the debate over Title IX, and antiwar protests apply a sociological perspective to several issues of immediate interest to today's students.

New Country Case Studies

Two new case studies and one updated case provide a closer look at the social worlds of three countries, illustrating the impact of globalization on each. These cases explore stratification in Mexico (Chapter 10), religion in India (Chapter 15), and capitalism in China (Chapter 18).

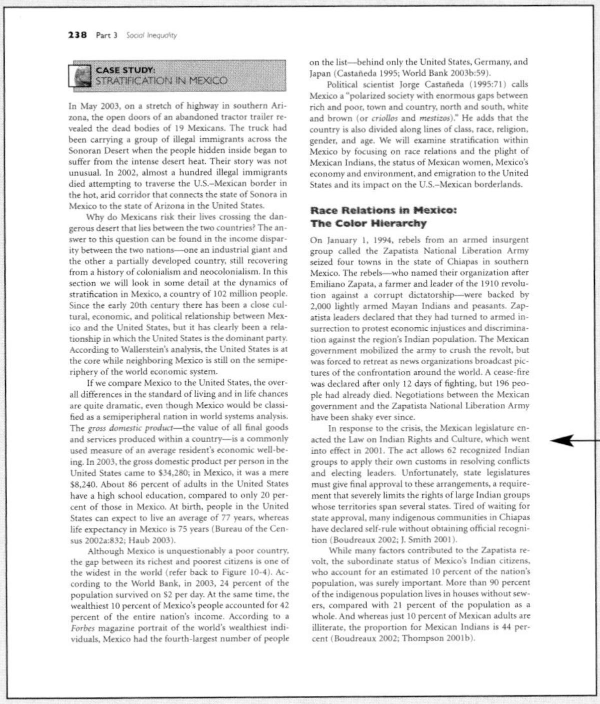

238 Part 3 *Social Inequality*

CASE STUDY:
STRATIFICATION IN MEXICO

In May 2003, on a stretch of highway in southern Arizona, the open doors of an abandoned tractor trailer revealed the dead bodies of 19 Mexicans. The truck had been carrying a group of illegal immigrants across the Sonoran Desert when the people hidden inside began to suffer from the intense desert heat. Their story was not unusual. In 2002, almost a hundred illegal immigrants died attempting to traverse the U.S.–Mexican border in the hot, arid corridor that connects the state of Sonora in Mexico to the state of Arizona in the United States.

Why do Mexicans risk their lives crossing the dangerous desert that lies between the two countries? The answer to this question can be found in the income disparity between the two nations—one an industrial giant and the other a partially developed country, still recovering from a history of colonialism and neocolonialism. In this section we will look in some detail at the dynamics of stratification in Mexico, a country of 102 million people. Since the early 20th century there has been a close cultural, economic, and political relationship between Mexico and the United States, but it has clearly been a relationship in which the United States is the dominant party. According to Wallerstein's analysis, the United States is at the core while neighboring Mexico is still on the semiperiphery of the world economic system.

If we compare Mexico to the United States, the overall differences in the standard of living and in life chances are quite dramatic, even though Mexico would be classified as a semiperipheral nation in world systems analysis. The *gross domestic product*—the value of all final goods and services produced within a country—is a commonly used measure of an average resident's economic well-being. In 2003, the gross domestic product per person in the United States came to $34,280; in Mexico, it was a mere $8,240. About 86 percent of adults in the United States have a high school education, compared to only 20 percent of those in Mexico. At birth, people in the United States can expect to live an average of 77 years, whereas life expectancy in Mexico is 75 years (Bureau of the Census 2002a:832; Haub 2003).

Although Mexico is unquestionably a poor country, the gap between its richest and poorest citizens is one of the widest in the world (refer back to Figure 10-4). According to the World Bank, in 2003, 24 percent of the population survived on $2 per day. At the same time, the wealthiest 10 percent of Mexico's people accounted for 42 percent of the entire nation's income. According to a *Forbes* magazine portrait of the world's wealthiest individuals, Mexico had the fourth-largest number of people on the list—behind only the United States, Germany, and Japan (Castañeda 1995; World Bank 2003b:59).

Political scientist Jorge Castañeda (1995:71) calls Mexico a "polarized society with enormous gaps between rich and poor, town and country, north and south, white and brown (or *criollos* and *mestizos*)." He adds that the country is also divided along lines of class, race, religion, gender, and age. We will examine stratification within Mexico by focusing on race relations and the plight of Mexican Indians, the status of Mexican women, Mexico's economy and environment, and emigration to the United States and its impact on the U.S.–Mexican borderlands.

Race Relations in Mexico: The Color Hierarchy

On January 1, 1994, rebels from an armed insurgent group called the Zapatista National Liberation Army seized four towns in the state of Chiapas in southern Mexico. The rebels—who named their organization after Emiliano Zapata, a farmer and leader of the 1910 revolution against a corrupt dictatorship—were backed by 2,000 lightly armed Mayan Indians and peasants. Zapatista leaders declared that they had turned to armed insurrection to protest economic injustices and discrimination against the region's Indian population. The Mexican government mobilized the army to crush the revolt, but was forced to retreat as news organizations broadcast pictures of the confrontation around the world. A cease-fire was declared after only 12 days of fighting, but 196 people had already died. Negotiations between the Mexican government and the Zapatista National Liberation Army have been shaky ever since.

In response to the crisis, the Mexican legislature enacted the Law on Indian Rights and Culture, which went into effect in 2001. The act allows 62 recognized Indian groups to apply their own customs in resolving conflicts and electing leaders. Unfortunately, state legislatures must give final approval to these arrangements, a requirement that severely limits the rights of large Indian groups whose territories span several states. Tired of waiting for state approval, many indigenous communities in Chiapas have declared self-rule without obtaining official recognition (Boudreaux 2002; J. Smith 2001).

While many factors contributed to the Zapatista revolt, the subordinate status of Mexico's Indian citizens, who account for an estimated 10 percent of the nation's population, was surely important. More than 90 percent of the indigenous population lives in houses without sewers, compared with 21 percent of the population as a whole. And whereas just 10 percent of Mexican adults are illiterate, the proportion for Mexican Indians is 44 percent (Boudreaux 2002; Thompson 2001b).

Stratification in Mexico

This case study explores the social factors that contribute to social inequality in Mexico.

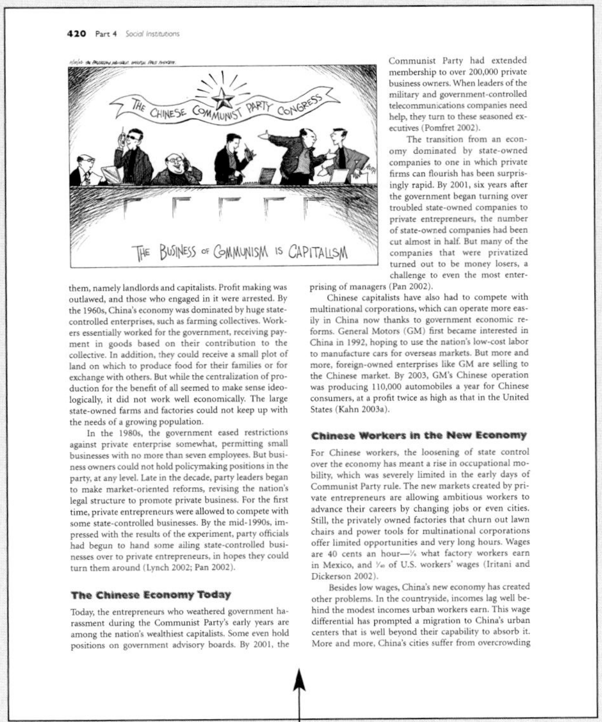

420 Part 4 *Social Institutions*

them, namely landlords and capitalists. Profit making was outlawed, and those who engaged in it were arrested. By the 1960s, China's economy was dominated by huge state-controlled enterprises, such as farming collectives. Workers essentially worked for the government, receiving payment in goods based on their contribution to the collective. In addition, they could receive a small plot of land on which to produce food for their families or for exchange with others. But while the centralization of production for the benefit of all seemed to make sense ideologically, it did not work well economically. The large state-owned farms and factories could not keep up with the needs of a growing population.

In the 1980s, the government eased restrictions against private enterprise somewhat, permitting small businesses with no more than seven employees. But business owners could not hold policymaking positions in the party, at any level. Late in the decade, party leaders began to make market-oriented reforms, revising the nation's legal structure to promote private business. For the first time, private entrepreneurs were allowed to compete with some state-controlled businesses. By the mid-1990s, impressed with the results of the experiment, party officials had begun to hand some ailing state-controlled businesses over to private entrepreneurs, in hopes they could turn them around (Lynch 2002; Pan 2002).

The Chinese Economy Today

Today, the entrepreneurs who weathered government harassment during the Communist Party's early years are among the nation's wealthiest capitalists. Some even hold positions on government advisory boards. By 2001, the Communist Party had extended membership to over 200,000 private business owners. When leaders of the military and government-controlled telecommunications companies need help, they turn to these seasoned executives (Pomfret 2002).

The transition from an economy dominated by state-owned companies to one in which private firms can flourish has been surprisingly rapid. By 2001, six years after the government began turning over troubled state-owned companies to private entrepreneurs, the number of state-owned companies had been cut almost in half. But many of the companies that were privatized turned out to be money losers, a challenge to even the most enterprising of managers (Pan 2002).

Chinese capitalists have also had to compete with multinational corporations, which can operate more easily in China now thanks to government economic reforms. General Motors (GM) first became interested in China in 1992, hoping to use the nation's low-cost labor to manufacture cars for overseas markets. But more and more, foreign-owned enterprises like GM are selling to the Chinese market. By 2003, GM's Chinese operation was producing 110,000 automobiles a year for Chinese consumers, at a profit twice as high as that in the United States (Kahn 2003a).

Chinese Workers in the New Economy

For Chinese workers, the loosening of state control over the economy has meant a rise in occupational mobility, which was severely limited in the early days of Communist Party rule. The new markets created by private entrepreneurs are allowing ambitious workers to advance their careers by changing jobs or even cities. Still, the privately owned factories that churn out lawn chairs and power tools for multinational corporations offer limited opportunities and very long hours. Wages are 40 cents an hour—$\frac{1}{6}$ what factory workers earn in Mexico, and $\frac{1}{40}$ of U.S. workers' wages (Iritani and Dickerson 2002).

Besides low wages, China's new economy has created other problems. In the countryside, incomes lag well behind the modest incomes urban workers earn. This wage differential has prompted a migration to China's urban centers that is well beyond their capability to absorb it. More and more, China's cities suffer from overcrowding

Capitalism in China

This case study explores the social impact of the transition from socialism to a capitalist economy in China.

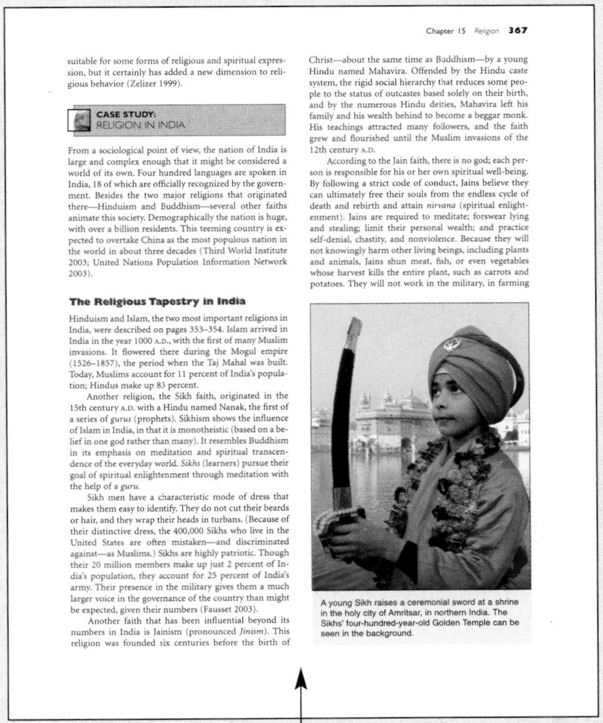

Chapter 15 *Religion* **367**

suitable for some forms of religious and spiritual expression, but it certainly has added a new dimension to religious behavior (Zelizer 1999).

CASE STUDY:
RELIGION IN INDIA

From a sociological point of view, the nation of India is large and complex enough that it might be considered a world of its own. Four hundred languages are spoken in India, 18 of which are officially recognized by the government. Besides the two major religions that originated there—Hinduism and Buddhism—several other faiths animate this society. Demographically the nation is huge, with over a billion residents. This teeming country is expected to overtake China as the most populous nation in the world in about three decades (Third World Institute 2003; United Nations Population Information Network 2003).

The Religious Tapestry in India

Hinduism and Islam, the two most important religions in India, were described on pages 353–354. Islam arrived in India in the year 1000 A.D., with the first of many Muslim invasions. It flowered there during the Mogul empire (1526–1857), the period when the Taj Mahal was built. Today, Muslims account for 11 percent of India's population; Hindus make up 83 percent.

Another religion, the Sikh faith, originated in the 15th century A.D. with a Hindu named Nanak, the first of a series of *gurus* (prophets). Sikhism shows the influence of Islam in India, in that it is monotheistic (based on a belief in one god rather than many). It resembles Buddhism in its emphasis on meditation and spiritual transcendence of the everyday world. *Sikhs* (learners) pursue their goal of spiritual enlightenment through meditation with the help of a *guru*.

Sikh men have a characteristic mode of dress that makes them easy to identify. They do not cut their beards or hair, and they wrap their heads in turbans. (Because of their distinctive dress, the 400,000 Sikhs who live in the United States are often mistaken—and discriminated against—as Muslims.) Sikhs are highly patriotic. Though their 20 million members make up just 2 percent of India's population, they account for 25 percent of India's army. Their presence in the military gives them a much larger voice in the governance of the country than might be expected, given their numbers (Fausset 2003).

Another faith that has been influential beyond its numbers in India is Jainism (pronounced *Jinism*). This religion was founded six centuries before the birth of Christ—about the same time as Buddhism—by a young Hindu named Mahavira. Offended by the Hindu caste system, the rigid social hierarchy that reduces some people to the status of outcastes based solely on their birth, and by the numerous Hindu deities, Mahavira left his family and his wealth behind to become a beggar monk. His teachings attracted many followers, and the faith grew and flourished until the Muslim invasions of the 12th century A.D.

According to the Jain faith, there is no god; each person is responsible for his or her own spiritual well-being. By following a strict code of conduct, Jains believe they can ultimately free their souls from the endless cycle of death and rebirth and attain *nirvana* (spiritual enlightenment). Jains are required to meditate; forswear lying and stealing; limit their personal wealth; and practice self-denial, chastity, and nonviolence. Because they will not knowingly harm other living beings, including plants and animals, Jains shun meat, fish, or even vegetables whose harvest kills the entire plant, such as carrots and potatoes. They will not work in the military, in farming

A young Sikh raises a ceremonial sword at a shrine in the holy city of Amritsar, in northern India. The Sikhs' four-hundred-year-old Golden Temple can be seen in the background.

Religion in India

This case study takes a closer look at several religions, their role in Indian politics, and their social effects.

"Sociology in the Global Community" Boxes

These boxes provide a global perspective on topics such as terrorist violence, the worldwide jobs–skills mismatch, and life in the global village.

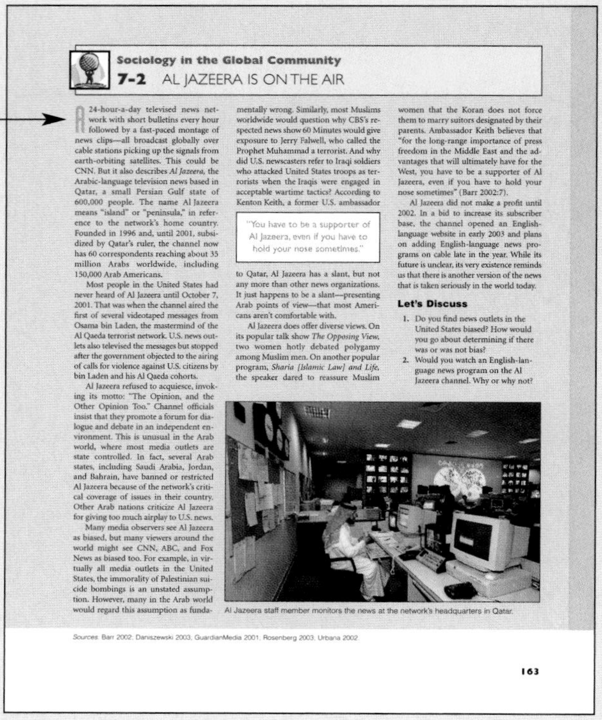

Sociology in the Global Community
7-2 AL JAZEERA IS ON THE AIR

A 24-hour-a-day televised news network with short bulletins every hour followed by a fast-paced montage of news clips—all broadcast globally over cable stations picking up the signals from earth-orbiting satellites. This could be CNN. But it also describes *Al Jazeera*, the Arabic-language television news based in Qatar, a small Persian Gulf state of 600,000 people. The name Al Jazeera means "island" or "peninsula," in reference to the network's home country. Founded in 1996 and, until 2001, subsidized by Qatar's ruler, the channel now has 60 correspondents reaching about 35 million Arabs worldwide, including 150,000 Arab Americans.

Most people in the United States had never heard of Al Jazeera until October 7, 2001. That was when the channel aired the first of several videotaped messages from Osama bin Laden, the mastermind of the Al Qaeda terrorist network. U.S. news outlets also televised the messages but stopped after the government objected to the airing of calls for violence against U.S. citizens by bin Laden and his Al Qaeda cohorts.

Al Jazeera refused to acquiesce, invoking its motto: "The Opinion, and the Other Opinion Too." Channel officials insist that they promote a forum for dialogue and debate in an independent environment. This is unusual in the Arab world, where most media outlets are state controlled. In fact, several Arab states, including Saudi Arabia, Jordan, and Bahrain, have banned or restricted Al Jazeera because of the network's critical coverage of issues in their country. Other Arab nations criticize Al Jazeera for giving too much airplay to U.S. news.

Many media observers see Al Jazeera as biased, but many viewers around the world might see CNN, ABC, and Fox News as biased too. For example, in virtually all media outlets in the United States, the immorality of Palestinian suicide bombings is an unstated assumption. However, many in the Arab world would regard this assumption as fundamentally wrong. Similarly, most Muslims worldwide would question why CBS's respected news show 60 Minutes would give exposure to Jerry Falwell, who called the Prophet Muhammad a terrorist. And why did U.S. newscasters refer to Iraqi soldiers who attacked United States troops as terrorists when the Iraqis were engaged in acceptable wartime tactics? According to Kenton Keith, a former U.S. ambassador to Qatar, Al Jazeera has a slant, but not any more than other news organizations. It just happens to be a slant—presenting Arab points of view—that most Americans aren't comfortable with.

"You have to be a supporter of Al Jazeera, even if you have to hold your nose sometimes."

Al Jazeera does offer diverse views. On its popular talk show *The Opposing View*, two women hotly debated polygamy among Muslim men. On another popular program, *Sharia [Islamic Law] and Life*, the speaker dared to reassure Muslim women that the Koran does not force them to marry suitors designated by their parents. Ambassador Keith believes that "for the long-range importance of press freedom in the Middle East and the advantages that will ultimately have for the West, you have to be a supporter of Al Jazeera, even if you have to hold your nose sometimes" (Barr 2002:7).

Al Jazeera did not make a profit until 2002. In a bid to increase its subscriber base, the channel opened an English-language website in early 2003 and plans on adding English-language news programs on cable late in the year. While its future is unclear, its very existence reminds us that there is another version of the news that is taken seriously in the world today.

Let's Discuss

1. Do you find news outlets in the United States biased? How would you go about determining if there was or was not bias?
2. Would you watch an English-language news program on the Al Jazeera channel. Why or why not?

Al Jazeera staff member monitors the news at the network's headquarters in Qatar.

Sources: Barr 2002; Daniszewski 2003; GuardianMedia 2001; Rosenberg 2003; Urbana 2002.

163

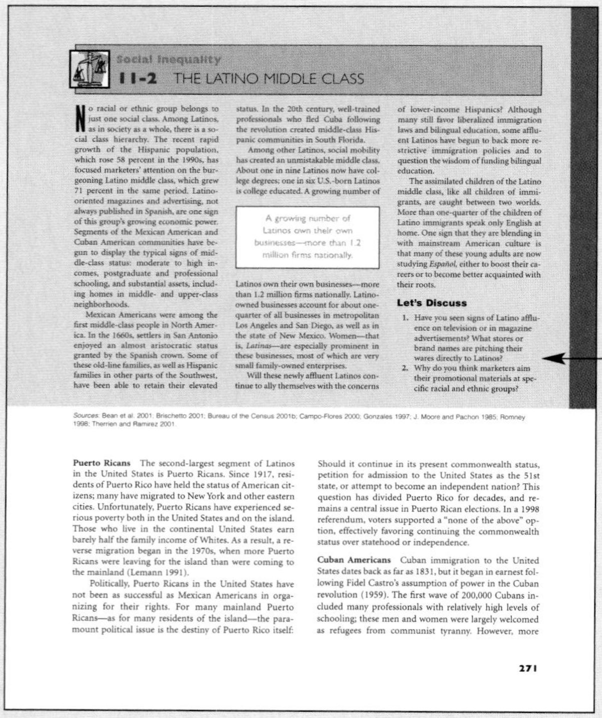

Social Inequality
11-2 THE LATINO MIDDLE CLASS

No racial or ethnic group belongs to just one social class. Among Latinos, as in society as a whole, there is a social class hierarchy. The recent rapid growth of the Hispanic population, which rose 58 percent in the 1990s, has focused marketers' attention on the burgeoning Latino middle class, which grew 71 percent in the same period. Latino-oriented magazines and advertising, not always published in Spanish, are one sign of this group's growing economic power. Segments of the Mexican American and Cuban American communities have begun to display the typical signs of middle-class status: moderate to high incomes, postgraduate and professional schooling, and substantial assets, including homes in middle- and upper-class neighborhoods.

Mexican Americans were among the first middle-class people in North America. In the 1660s, settlers in San Antonio enjoyed an almost aristocratic status granted by the Spanish crown. Some of these old-line families, as well as Hispanic families in other parts of the Southwest, have been able to retain their elevated status. In the 20th century, well-trained professionals who fled Cuba following the revolution created middle-class Hispanic communities in South Florida.

Among other Latinos, social mobility has created an unmistakable middle class. About one in nine Latinos now have college degrees; one in six U.S.-born Latinos is college educated. A growing number of Latinos own their own businesses—more than 1.2 million firms nationally. Latino-owned businesses account for about one-quarter of all businesses in metropolitan Los Angeles and San Diego, as well as in the state of New Mexico. Women—that is, *Latinas*—are especially prominent in these businesses, most of which are very small family-owned enterprises.

A growing number of Latinos own their own businesses—more than 1.2 million firms nationally.

Will these newly affluent Latinos continue to ally themselves with the concerns of lower-income Hispanics? Although many still favor liberalized immigration laws and bilingual education, some affluent Latinos have begun to back more restrictive immigration policies and to question the wisdom of funding bilingual education.

The assimilated children of the Latino middle class, like all children of immigrants, are caught between two worlds. More than one-quarter of the children of Latino immigrants speak only English at home. One sign that they are blending in with mainstream American culture is that many of these young adults are now studying *Español*, either to boost their careers or to become better acquainted with their roots.

Let's Discuss

1. Have you seen signs of Latino affluence on television or in magazine advertisements? What stores or brand names are pitching their wares directly to Latinos?
2. Why do you think marketers aim their promotional materials at specific racial and ethnic groups?

Sources: Bean et al. 2001; Brischetto 2001; Bureau of the Census 2001b; Campo-Flores 2000; Gonzales 1997; J. Moore and Pachon 1985; Romney 1998; Therrien and Ramirez 2001.

Puerto Ricans The second-largest segment of Latinos in the United States is Puerto Ricans. Since 1917, residents of Puerto Rico have held the status of American citizens; many have migrated to New York and other eastern cities. Unfortunately, Puerto Ricans have experienced serious poverty both in the United States and on the island. Those who live in the continental United States earn barely half the family income of Whites. As a result, a reverse migration began in the 1970s, when more Puerto Ricans were leaving for the island than were coming to the mainland (Lemann 1991).

Politically, Puerto Ricans in the United States have not been as successful as Mexican Americans in organizing for their rights. For many mainland Puerto Ricans—as for many residents of the island—the paramount political issue is the destiny of Puerto Rico itself: Should it continue in its present commonwealth status, petition for admission to the United States as the 51st state, or attempt to become an independent nation? This question has divided Puerto Rico for decades, and remains a central issue in Puerto Rican elections. In a 1998 referendum, voters supported a "none of the above" option, effectively favoring continuing the commonwealth status over statehood or independence.

Cuban Americans Cuban immigration to the United States dates back as far as 1831, but it began in earnest following Fidel Castro's assumption of power in the Cuban revolution (1959). The first wave of 200,000 Cubans included many professionals with relatively high levels of schooling; these men and women were largely welcomed as refugees from communist tyranny. However, more

271

"Social Inequality" Boxes

These boxes on topics such as the Latino middle class, discretionary justice, disability as a master status, and stratification in Japan highlight an important area of analysis for sociologists today.

"Research in Action" Boxes

These boxes present sociological findings on topics such as prejudice against Arab Americans and Muslim Americans, the lingering impact of divorce, and social networks among low-income women.

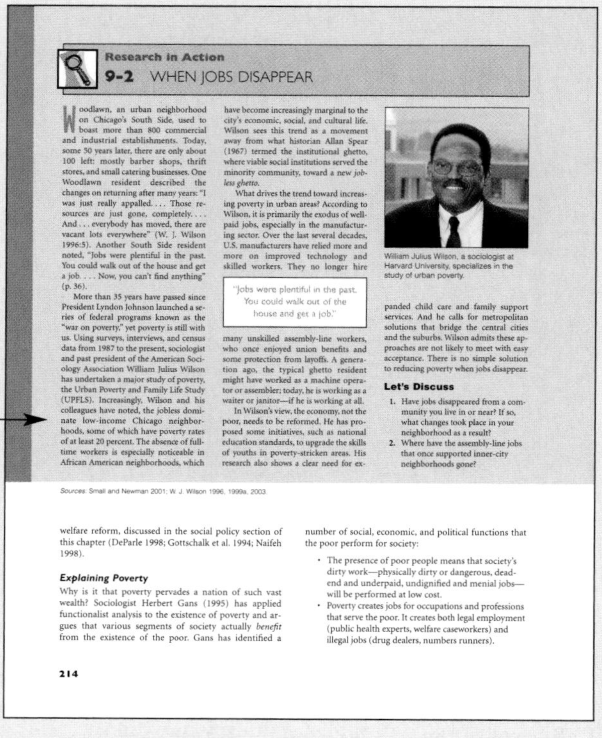

Research in Action
9-2 WHEN JOBS DISAPPEAR

Woodlawn, an urban neighborhood on Chicago's South Side, used to boast more than 800 commercial and industrial establishments. Today, some 50 years later, there are only about 100 left: mostly barber shops, thrift stores, and small catering businesses. One Woodlawn resident described the changes on returning after many years: "I was just really appalled. . . . Those resources are just gone, completely. . . . And . . . everybody has moved, there are vacant lots everywhere" (W. J. Wilson 1996:5). Another South Side resident noted, "Jobs were plentiful in the past. You could walk out of the house and get a job. . . . Now, you can't find anything" (p. 36).

More than 35 years have passed since President Lyndon Johnson launched a series of federal programs known as the "war on poverty," yet poverty is still with us. Using surveys, interviews, and census data from 1987 to the present, sociologist and past president of the American Sociology Association William Julius Wilson has undertaken a major study of poverty, the Urban Poverty and Family Life Study (UPFLS). Increasingly, Wilson and his colleagues have noted, the jobless dominate low-income Chicago neighborhoods, some of which have poverty rates of at least 20 percent. The absence of full-time workers is especially noticeable in African American neighborhoods, which have become increasingly marginal to the city's economic, social, and cultural life. Wilson sees this trend as a movement away from what historian Allan Spear (1967) termed the institutional ghetto, where viable social institutions served the minority community, toward a new *jobless ghetto*.

What drives the trend toward increasing poverty in urban areas? According to Wilson, it is primarily the exodus of well-paid jobs, especially in the manufacturing sector. Over the last several decades, U.S. manufacturers have relied more and more on improved technology and skilled workers. They no longer hire many unskilled assembly-line workers, who once enjoyed union benefits and some protection from layoffs. A generation ago, the typical ghetto resident might have worked as a machine operator or assembler; today, he is working as a waiter or janitor—if he is working at all.

"Jobs were plentiful in the past. You could walk out of the house and get a job."

In Wilson's view, the economy, not the poor, needs to be reformed. He has proposed some initiatives, such as national education standards, to upgrade the skills of youths in poverty-stricken areas. His research also shows a clear need for expanded child care and family support services. And he calls for metropolitan solutions that bridge the central cities and the suburbs. Wilson admits these approaches are not likely to meet with easy acceptance. There is no simple solution to reducing poverty when jobs disappear.

William Julius Wilson, a sociologist at Harvard University, specializes in the study of urban poverty.

Let's Discuss

1. Have jobs disappeared from a community you live in or near? If so, what changes took place in your neighborhood as a result?
2. Where have the assembly-line jobs that once supported inner-city neighborhoods gone?

Sources: Small and Newman 2001; W. J. Wilson 1996, 1999a, 2003.

welfare reform, discussed in the social policy section of this chapter (DeParle 1998; Gottschalk et al. 1994; Naifeh 1998).

Explaining Poverty

Why is it that poverty pervades a nation of such vast wealth? Sociologist Herbert Gans (1995) has applied functionalist analysis to the existence of poverty and argues that various segments of society actually *benefit* from the existence of the poor. Gans has identified a number of social, economic, and political functions that the poor perform for society:

- The presence of poor people means that society's dirty work—physically dirty or dangerous, dead-end and underpaid, undignified and menial jobs—will be performed at low cost.
- Poverty creates jobs for occupations and professions that serve the poor. It creates both legal employment (public health experts, welfare caseworkers) and illegal jobs (drug dealers, numbers runners).

214

New Revealing Photo Essays

Five photo essays stimulate students' sociological imagination. Each begins with a question that is intended to prompt students to see some part of everyday life with new eyes—those of a sociologist. The accompanying photos and captions suggest the answer to the question.

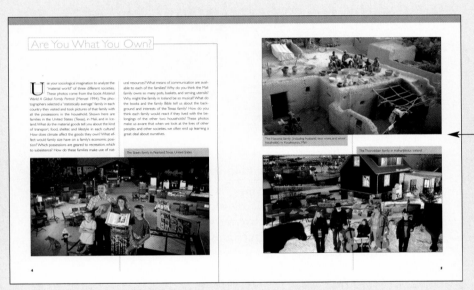

Are You What You Own?

This photo essay invites students to analyze the "material world" of three different societies.

Who is Deviant?

This photo essay helps students to understand that deviance is a social construction.

"Use Your Sociological Imagination" Sections

These sections within each chapter pose questions designed to stimulate students' sociological imagination to help them figure out how major concepts and issues apply to their own lives.

Demographic Map Program

Two kinds of maps—"Mapping Life Nationwide" and "Mapping Life Worldwide"—are featured throughout the text. Interactive versions of many of these maps with accompanying questions appear on the book's Online Learning Center website.

"Think About It" Caption Feature

These captions, which accompany many of the book's maps, graphs, and tables, encourage students to think critically about information presented in illustrative materials.

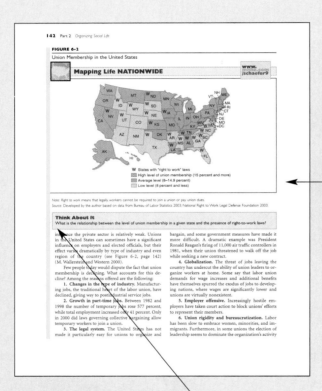

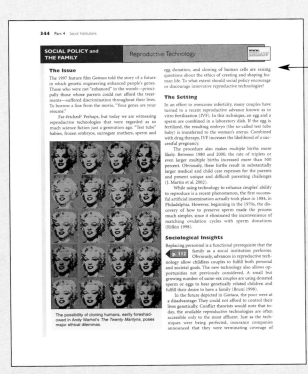

Analytical Social Policy Sections

These discussions, a hallmark of this text, provide a sociological perspective on contemporary social issues such as gun control, global immigration, and affirmative action. Providing a global view of the issues, these sections are organized around a consistent heading structure and include questions designed to stimulate critical thinking about the issues being explored.

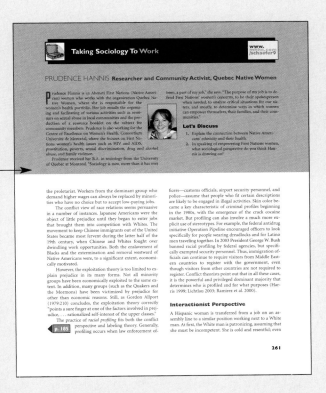

Motivational "Taking Sociology to Work" Boxes

"Taking Sociology to Work" boxes underscore the value of an undergraduate degree in sociology through profiles of individuals who majored in sociology and use its principles in their work.

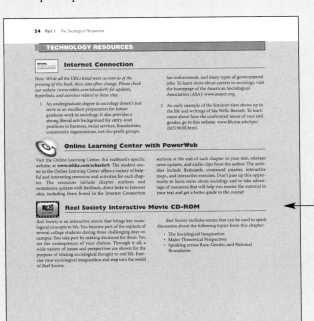

Meaningful Technology Resources

These resources include Internet exercises, brief descriptions of specific content on the Online Learning Center website, and a listing of relevant topics that are explored on the *Reel Society* Interactive Movie CD-ROM.

chapter 1

UNDERSTANDING SOCIOLOGY

Sociology is a field of study that encompasses a wide range of subjects, from important social issues to aspects of contemporary culture—such as comic books. The comic books shown above fill stalls that line the streets near the railroad station in Bombay, India. At first glance, they seem very different from comic books sold in the United States, but closer inspection reveals common themes—romance, mystery, action, adventure, and crime.

What Is Sociology?

What Is Sociological Theory?

The Development of Sociology

Major Theoretical Perspectives

Applied and Clinical Sociology

Developing a Sociological Imagination

Appendix: Careers in Sociology

Boxes

SOCIOLOGY IN THE GLOBAL COMMUNITY: Women in Public Places Worldwide

RESEARCH IN ACTION: Looking at Sports from Three Theoretical Perspectives

1

I am, of course, very different from the people who normally fill America's least attractive jobs, and in ways that both helped and limited me. Most obviously, I was only visiting a world that others inhabit full-time, often for most of their lives. With all the real-life assets I've built up in middle age—bank account, IRA, health insurance, multiroom home—waiting indulgently in the background, there was no way I was going to "experience poverty" or find out how it "really feels" to be a long-term low-wage worker. My aim here was much more straightforward and objective—just to see whether I could match income to expenses, as the truly poor attempt to do every day....

In Portland, Maine, I came closest to achieving a decent fit between income and expenses, but only because I worked seven days a week. Between my two jobs, I was earning approximately $300 a week after taxes and paying $480 a month in rent, or a manageable 40 percent of my earnings. It helped, too, that gas and electricity were included in my rent and that I got two or three free meals each weekend at the nursing home. But I was there at the beginning of the off-season. If I had stayed until June 2000 I would have faced the Blue Haven's summer rent of $390 a week, which would of course have been out of the question. So to survive year-round, I would have had to save enough, in the months between August 1999 and May 2000, to accumulate the first month's rent and deposit on an actual apartment. I think I could have done

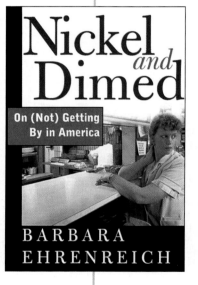

this—saved $800 to $1,000—at least if no car trouble or illness interfered with my budget. I am not sure, however, that I could have maintained the seven-day-a-week regimen month after month or eluded the kinds of injuries that afflicted my fellow workers in the housecleaning business.

In Minneapolis—well, here we are left with a lot of speculation. If I had been able to find an apartment for $400 a month or less, my pay at Wal-Mart—$1,120 a month before taxes—might have been sufficient, although the cost of living in a motel while I searched for such an apartment might have made it impossible for me to save enough for the first month's rent and deposit. A weekend job, such as the one I almost landed at a supermarket for about $7.75 an hour, would have helped, but I had no guarantee that I could arrange my schedule at Wal-Mart to reliably exclude weekends. If I had taken the job at Menards and the pay was in fact $10 an hour for eleven hours a day, I would have made about $440 a week after taxes—enough to pay for a motel room and still have something left over to save up for the initial costs of an apartment. But were they really offering $10 an hour? And could I have stayed on my feet eleven hours a day, five days a week? So yes, with some different choices, I probably could have survived in Minneapolis. But I'm not going back for a rematch. *(Ehrenreich 2001:6, 197–198)* ■ ◎

Additional information about this excerpt can be found on the Online Learning Center at **www.mhhe.com/schaefer9.**

In her undercover attempts to survive as a low-wage worker in two different cities in the United States, journalist Barbara Ehrenreich revealed patterns of human interaction and used methods of study that foster sociological investigation. This excerpt from her book *Nickel and Dimed: On (Not) Getting By in America* describes how she left a comfortable home and assumed the identity of a divorced, middle-aged housewife with no college degree and little working experience. She set out to get the best-paying job and the cheapest living quarters she could find to see whether she could make ends meet. Months later, physically exhausted and demoralized by demeaning work rules, Ehrenreich confirmed what she suspected before she began: getting by in this country as a low-wage worker is a losing proposition.

Ehrenreich's study focused on an unequal society, which is a central topic in sociology. Social inequality has a pervasive influence on human interactions and institutions. Certain groups of people control scarce resources, wield power, and receive special treatment. The poster that opens this chapter illustrates another common focus of sociologists—the elements of culture that define a society. In India, comic books are a very popular form of media that reflect central cultural values.

While it might be interesting to know how one individual is affected by the need to make ends meet or even by the contents of an adventure comic, sociologists consider how entire groups of people are affected by these kinds of factors and how society itself might be altered by them. Sociologists then are not concerned with what one individual does or does not do, but with what people do as members of a group or in interactions with one another, and what that means for the individuals and for society as a whole.

As a field of study, sociology is extremely broad in scope. You will see throughout this book the range of topics sociologists investigate—from suicide to TV viewing habits, from Amish society to global economic patterns, from peer pressure to pickpocketing techniques. Sociology looks at how others influence our behavior, how major social institutions like the government, religion, and the economy affect us, and how we ourselves affect other individuals, groups, and even organizations.

This chapter will explore the nature of sociology as a field of inquiry and an exercise of the "sociological imagination." How did sociology develop? In what ways does it differ from other social sciences? Why should we use our sociological imagination?

We'll look at the discipline as a science and consider its relationship to other social sciences. We'll meet three pioneering thinkers—Émile Durkheim, Max Weber, and Karl Marx—and examine the theoretical perspectives that grew out of their work. Next we will look at the uses of both applied and clinical sociology. Finally, we will consider the ways sociology helps us to develop our sociological imagination. ■

WHAT IS SOCIOLOGY?

"What has sociology got to do with me or with my life?" As a student, you might well have asked this question when you signed up for your introductory sociology course. To answer that, consider these points: Are you influenced by what you see on television? Do you use the Internet? Did you vote in the last election? Are you familiar with binge drinking on campus? Do you use alternative medicine? These are just a few of the everyday life situations described in this book that sociology can shed light on, revealing patterns and meanings. But, as the opening excerpt indicates, sociology also looks at large social issues. We use sociology to investigate why thousands of jobs have moved from the United States to developing nations, what social forces promote prejudice, what leads someone to join a social movement and work for social change, how access to computer technology can reduce social inequality, and why relationships between men and women in Seattle differ from those in Singapore.

Sociology is, very simply, the systematic study of social behavior and human groups. It focuses on social relationships, how these relationships influence people's behavior, and how societies, the sum total of these relationships, develop and change.

The Sociological Imagination

In attempting to understand social behavior, sociologists rely on an unusual type of creative thinking. A leading sociologist, C. Wright Mills, described such thinking as the

Are You What You Own?

Use your sociological imagination to analyze the "material world" of three different societies. These photos come from the book *Material World: A Global Family Portrait* (Menzel 1994). The photographers selected a "statistically average" family in each country they visited and took pictures of that family with all the possessions in the household. Shown here are families in the United States (Texas), in Mali, and in Iceland. What do the material goods tell you about the kind of transport, food, shelter, and lifestyle in each culture? How does climate affect the goods they own? What effect would family size have on a family's economic position? Which possessions are geared to recreation, which to subsistence? How do these families make use of natural resources? What means of communication are available to each of the families? Why do you think the Mali family owns so many pots, baskets, and serving utensils? Why might the family in Iceland be so musical? What do the books and the family Bible tell us about the background and interests of the Texas family? How do you think each family would react if they lived with the belongings of the other two households? These photos make us aware that when we look at the lives of other peoples and other societies, we often end up learning a great deal about ourselves.

The Skeen family in Pearland, Texas, United States

The Natoma family (including husband, two wives, and wives' housholds) in Kouakourou, Mali

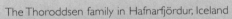

The Thoroddsen family in Hafnarfjördur, Iceland

sociological imagination—an awareness of the relationship between an individual and the wider society. This awareness allows all of us (not just sociologists) to comprehend the links between our immediate, personal social settings and the remote, impersonal social world that surrounds us and helps to shape us. Barbara Ehrenreich certainly used her sociological imagination in her study of low-wage workers (Mills [1959] 2000a).

A key element in the sociological imagination is the ability to view one's own society as an outsider would, rather than only from the perspective of personal experiences and cultural biases. Consider something as simple as sporting events. On college campuses, thousands of students cheer well-trained football players. In Bali, Indonesia, dozens of spectators gather around a ring to cheer on well-trained roosters engaged in cockfights. In both instances, the spectators debate the merits of their favorites and bet on the outcome of the events. Yet what is considered a normal sporting event in one part of the world is considered unusual in another part.

The sociological imagination allows us to go beyond personal experiences and observations to understand broader public issues. Divorce, for example, is unquestionably a personal hardship for a husband and wife who split apart. However, C. Wright Mills advocated using the sociological imagination to view divorce not simply as an individual's personal problem but rather as a societal concern. Using this perspective, we can see that an increase in the divorce rate actually redefines a major social institution—the family. Today's households frequently include stepparents and half-siblings whose parents have divorced and remarried.

The sociological imagination is an empowering tool. It allows us to look beyond a limited understanding of human behavior to see the world and its people in a new way and through a broader lens than we might otherwise use. It may be as simple as understanding why a roommate prefers country music to hip-hop, or it may open up a whole different way of understanding whole populations in the world. For example, in the aftermath of the terrorist attacks on the United States on September 11, 2001, many citizens wanted to understand how Muslims throughout the world perceived their country, and why. From time to time this textbook will offer you the chance to exercise your own sociological imagination in a variety of situations. We'll begin with one that may be close to home for you.

Use Your Sociological Imagination www.mhhe.com/schaefer9

You attend a rock concert one night and a religious service the next morning. What differences would you see in how the two audiences behaved and in how they responded to the leader? What might account for these differences?

Sociology and the Social Sciences

Is sociology a science? The term *science* refers to the body of knowledge obtained by methods based on systematic observation. Just like other scientific disciplines, sociology engages in organized, systematic study of phenomena (in this case, human behavior) in order to enhance understanding. All scientists, whether studying mushrooms or murderers, attempt to collect precise information through methods of study that are as objective as possible. They rely on careful recording of observations and accumulation of data.

Of course, there is a great difference between sociology and physics, between psychology and astronomy. For this reason, the sciences are commonly divided into natural and social sciences. *Natural science* is the study of the physical features of nature and the ways in which they interact and change. Astronomy, biology, chemistry, geology, and physics are all natural sciences. *Social science* is the study of the social features of humans and the ways they interact and change. The social sciences include sociology, anthropology, economics, history, psychology, and political science.

These social science disciplines have a common focus on the social behavior of people, yet each has a particular orientation. Anthropologists usually study past cultures and preindustrial societies that continue today, as well as the origins of humans. Economists explore the ways in which people produce and exchange goods and services, along with money and other resources. Historians are concerned with the peoples and events of the past and their significance for us today. Political scientists study international relations, the workings of government, and the exercise of power and authority. Psychologists investigate personality and individual behavior. So what do *sociologists* focus on? They study the influence that society has on people's attitudes and behavior and the ways in which people interact and thereby shape society. Humans are social animals; therefore, sociologists scientifically examine our social relationships with others.

Let's consider how the different social sciences might approach the hotly debated issue of the death penalty. Historians would be interested in the development of the use of capital punishment from colonial days to the present. Economists might conduct research that compares the costs of incarcerating a person for life to the expense of conducting the appeals that automatically come with death penalty cases. Psychologists would look at individual cases and assess the impact of the death penalty on the families of both the victim and the death row inmate. Political scientists would study the different stances taken by elected officials and the implications of their stands for their reelection campaigns.

And what approach would sociologists take? They might look at how race and ethnicity affect the outcome of death penalty cases. According to a study released in 2002, more than 80 percent of death penalty cases in the United States involve White victims, even though only 50 percent of all murder victims nationally are White (see Figure 1-1). It appears that the race of the victim influences whether a defendant will be charged with capital murder (that is, murder punishable by death) and whether he or she will eventually receive the death penalty. Thus, the criminal justice system seems more intent on giving out harsh punishments when the victims are White than when they are minorities.

Sociologists put their sociological imagination to work in a variety of areas—including aging, the family, human ecology, and religion. Throughout this textbook, you will see how sociologists develop theories and conduct research to study and better understand societies. And you will be encouraged to use your sociological imagination to examine the United States (and other societies) from the viewpoint of a respectful but questioning outsider.

Sociology and Common Sense

Sociology focuses on the study of human behavior. Yet we all have experience with human behavior and at least some knowledge of it. All of us might well have theories about why people become homeless, for example. Our theories and opinions typically come from "common sense"—that is, from our experiences and conversations, from what we read, from what we see on television, and so forth.

In our daily lives, we rely on common sense to get us through many unfamiliar situations. However, this commonsense knowledge, while sometimes accurate, is not always reliable, because it rests on commonly held beliefs rather than on systematic analysis of facts. It was once considered common sense to accept that the earth was flat—a view rightly questioned by Pythagoras and Aristotle. Incorrect commonsense notions are not just a part of the distant past; they remain with us today.

In the United States, "common sense" tells us that an "epidemic" of teen pregnancies accounts for most unwed births today, creating a drag on the welfare system. "Common sense" tells us that people panic when faced with natural disasters, such as floods and earthquakes, or even in the wake of tragedies such as the attacks on New York City and Washington, D.C., on September 11, 2001. However, these particular "commonsense" notions—like the notion that the earth is flat—are untrue; neither of them is supported by sociological research. The proportion of unwed mothers in their teens is declining; in fact, women who are *not* in their teens account for most of the unwed mothers (Martin et al. 2002).

Disasters do not generally produce panic. In the aftermath of disasters and even explosions, greater social organization and structure emerge to deal with a community's problems. In the United States, for example, an emergency operations group often coordinates public services and even certain services normally performed by the private sector, such as food distribution. Decision making becomes more centralized in times of disaster.

Like other social scientists, sociologists do not accept something as a fact because "everyone knows it." Instead, each piece of information must be tested and recorded, then analyzed in relationship to other data. Sociologists rely on scientific studies in order to describe and understand a social environment. At times, the findings of sociologists may seem like common sense because they deal with familiar facets of everyday life. The difference is that such findings have been *tested* by researchers. Common sense now tells us that the earth is round. But this particular commonsense notion is based on centuries of scientific work upholding the breakthrough made by Pythagoras and Aristotle.

WHAT IS SOCIOLOGICAL THEORY?

Why do people commit suicide? One traditional commonsense answer is that people inherit the desire to kill themselves. Another view is that sunspots drive people to take their own lives. These explanations may not

FIGURE I-I

Race of Victims in Death Penalty Cases

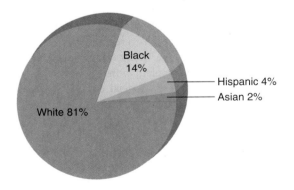

White 81%

Black 14%

Hispanic 4%
Asian 2%

Note: Data are for all death penalty cases from 1976 through August 7, 2003. Percentage exceeds 100 due to rounding error.

Source: Death Penalty Information Center 2003

The death penalty is more likely to be imposed when the victim is White. Nationally, 50 percent of all murder victims are White, but in cases tried under the death penalty, the percentage of White victims is more than 80 percent.

Do disasters produce panic or an organized, structured response? Common sense might tell us the former, but, in fact, disasters bring out a great deal of structure and organization to deal with their aftermath. When the September 11, 2001, terrorist attack destroyed New York City's emergency command center, officials quickly set up this one to direct the search and recovery effort.

seem especially convincing to contemporary researchers, but they represent beliefs widely held as recently as 1900.

Sociologists are not particularly interested in why any one individual commits suicide; they are more concerned with identifying the social forces that systematically cause some people to take their own lives. In order to undertake this research, sociologists develop a *theory* that offers a general explanation of suicidal behavior.

We can think of theories as attempts to explain events, forces, materials, ideas, or behavior in a comprehensive manner. Within sociology, a **theory** is a set of statements that seeks to explain problems, actions, or behavior. An effective theory may have both explanatory and predictive power. That is, it can help us see the relationships among seemingly isolated phenomena as well as understand how one type of change in an environment leads to other changes.

The World Health Organization (2002) estimated that 815,000 people committed suicide in the world in 2000. More than a hundred years earlier a sociologist tried to look at suicide data scientifically. Émile Durkheim ([1897] 1951) developed a highly original theory about the relationship between suicide and social factors. He was primarily concerned not with the personalities of individual suicide victims, but rather with suicide rates and how they varied from country to country. As a result, when he looked at the number of reported suicides in France, England, and Denmark in 1869, he also noted the total population of each country in order to determine the rate of suicide in each nation. He found that whereas England had only 67 reported suicides per million inhabitants, France had 135 per million and Denmark had 277 per million. The question then became: "Why did Denmark have a comparatively high rate of reported suicides?"

Durkheim went much deeper into his investigation of suicide rates, and the result was his landmark work *Suicide,* published in 1897. Durkheim refused to automatically accept unproved explanations regarding suicide, including the beliefs that cosmic forces or inherited tendencies caused such deaths. Instead, he focused on social factors, such as the cohesiveness or lack of cohesiveness of religious, social, and occupational groups.

Durkheim's research suggested that suicide, while a solitary act, is related to group life. Protestants had much higher suicide rates than Catholics did; the unmarried had much higher rates than married people did; soldiers were more likely to take their lives than civilians were. In addition, there seemed to be higher rates of suicide in times of peace than in times of war and revolution, and in times of economic instability and recession rather than in times of prosperity. Durkheim concluded that the suicide rates of a society reflected the extent to which people were or were not integrated into the group life of the society.

Émile Durkheim, like many other social scientists, developed a *theory* to explain how individual behavior can be understood within a social context. He pointed out the influence of groups and societal forces on what had always been viewed as a highly personal act. Clearly, Durkheim offered a more *scientific* explanation for the causes of suicide than that of sunspots or inherited tendencies. His theory has predictive power, since it suggests that suicide rates will rise or fall in conjunction with certain social and economic changes.

Of course, a theory—even the best of theories—is not a final statement about human behavior. Durkheim's theory of suicide is no exception. Sociologists continue to examine factors that contribute to differences in suicide rates around the world and to a particular society's rate of suicide. For example, although the overall rate of suicide in New Zealand is only marginally higher than in the United States, the suicide rate among young people is 41 percent higher in New Zealand. Sociologists and psychiatrists from that country suggest that their remote, sparsely populated society maintains exaggerated standards of masculinity that are especially difficult for young males. Gay adolescents who fail to conform to their peers' preference for sports are particularly vulnerable to suicide (Shenon 1995; for a critique of Durkheim's work, see Douglas 1967).

Use Your Sociological Imagination | www. mhhe.com /schaefer9

If you were Durkheim's successor in his research on suicide, how would you proceed to investigate the factors that may explain the increase in suicide rates among young people in the United States today?

THE DEVELOPMENT OF SOCIOLOGY

People have always been curious about sociological matters—such as how we get along with others, what we do for a living, and whom we select as our leaders. Philosophers and religious authorities of ancient and medieval societies made countless observations about human behavior. They did not test or verify these observations scientifically; nevertheless, these observations often became the foundation for moral codes. Several of the early social philosophers predicted that a systematic study of human behavior would one day emerge. Beginning in the 19th century, European theorists made pioneering contributions to the development of a science of human behavior.

Early Thinkers

Auguste Comte

The 19th century was an unsettling time in France. The French monarchy had been deposed earlier in the revolution of 1789, and Napoleon had subsequently suffered defeat in his effort to conquer Europe. Amid this chaos, philosophers considered how society might be improved. Auguste Comte (1798–1857), credited with being the most influential of these philosophers of the early 1800s, believed that a theoretical science of society and systematic investigation of behavior were needed to improve society. He coined the term *sociology* to apply to the science of human behavior.

Writing in the 1800s, Comte feared that the excesses of the French Revolution had permanently impaired France's stability. Yet he hoped that the study of social behavior in a systematic way would eventually lead to more rational human interactions. In Comte's hierarchy of sci-

Harriet Martineau, an early pioneer of sociology, studied social behavior both in her native England and in the United States.

ences, sociology was at the top. He called it the "queen" and its practitioners "scientist-priests." This French theorist did not simply give sociology its name; he also presented a rather ambitious challenge to the fledgling discipline.

Harriet Martineau

Scholars were able to learn of Comte's works largely through translations by the English sociologist Harriet Martineau (1802–1876). But Martineau was a pathbreaker in her own right as a sociologist. She offered insightful observations of the customs and social practices of both her native Britain and the United States. Martineau's book *Society in America* ([1837] 1962) examines religion, politics, child rearing, and immigration in the young nation. Martineau gives special attention to social class distinctions and to such factors as gender and race.

Martineau's writings emphasized the impact that the economy, law, trade, health, and population could have on the social problems of contemporary society. She spoke out in favor of the rights of women, the emancipation of slaves, and religious tolerance. Deafness later in life did not keep her from being an activist. In Martineau's (1876) view, intellectuals and scholars should not simply offer observations of social conditions; they should *act* on their convictions in a manner that will benefit society. That is why Martineau conducted research on the nature of female employment and pointed to the need for further investigation of this important issue (Hill and Hoecker-Drysdale 2001).

Herbert Spencer

Another important early contributor to the discipline of sociology was Herbert Spencer (1820–1903). A relatively prosperous Victorian Englishman, Spencer (unlike Martineau) did not feel compelled to correct or improve society; instead, he merely hoped to understand it better. Drawing on Charles Darwin's study *On the Origin of Species,* Spencer applied the concept of evolution of the species to societies in order to explain how they change, or evolve, over time. Similarly, he adapted Darwin's evolutionary view of the "survival of the fittest" by arguing that it is "natural" that some people are rich while others are poor.

Spencer's approach to societal change was extremely popular in his own lifetime. Unlike Comte, Spencer suggested that since societies are bound to change eventually, one need not be highly critical of present social arrangements or work actively for social change. This viewpoint appealed to many influential people in England and the United States who had a vested interest in the status quo and were suspicious of social thinkers who endorsed change.

Émile Durkheim

Émile Durkheim made many pioneering contributions to sociology, including his important theoretical work on suicide. The son of a rabbi, Durkheim (1858–1917) was educated in both France and Germany. He established an impressive academic reputation and was appointed as one of the first professors of sociology in France. Above all, Durkheim will be remembered for his insistence that behavior must be understood within a larger social context, not just in individualistic terms.

As one example of this emphasis, Durkheim ([1912] 2001) developed a fundamental thesis to help explain all forms of society through intensive study of the Arunta, an Australian tribe. He focused on the functions that religion performed for the Arunta and underscored the role that group life plays in defining what we consider religious. Durkheim concluded that, like other forms of group behavior, religion reinforces a group's solidarity.

Another of Durkheim's main interests was the consequences of work in modern societies. In his view, the growing division of labor in industrial societies as workers became much more specialized in their tasks led to what he called anomie. **Anomie** refers to the loss of direction that a society feels when social control of individual

behavior has become ineffective. The state of anomie occurs when people have lost their sense of purpose or direction, often during a time of profound social change. In a period of anomie, people are so confused and unable to cope with the new social environment that they may resort to taking their own lives.

Durkheim was concerned about the dangers that alienation, loneliness, and isolation might pose for modern industrial societies. He shared Comte's belief that sociology should provide direction for social change. As a result, he advocated the creation of new social groups—between the individual's family and the state—which would ideally provide a sense of belonging for members of huge, impersonal societies. Unions would be an example of such a group.

Like many other sociologists, Durkheim did not limit his interests to one aspect of social behavior. Later in this book, we will consider his thinking on crime and punishment, religion, and the workplace. Few sociologists have had such a dramatic impact on so many different areas within the discipline.

Max Weber

Another important early theorist was Max Weber (pronounced "VAY-ber"). Born in Germany, Weber (1864–1920) studied legal and economic history, but he gradually developed an interest in sociology. Eventually, he became a professor at various German universities. Weber taught his students that they should employ **Verstehen,** the German word for "understanding" or "insight," in their intellectual work. He pointed out that we cannot analyze our social behavior by the same type of objective criteria we use to measure weight or temperature. To fully comprehend behavior, we must learn the subjective meanings people attach to their actions—how they themselves view and explain their behavior.

For example, suppose that a sociologist was studying the social ranking of individuals in a fraternity. Weber would expect the researcher to employ *Verstehen* to determine the significance of the fraternity's social hierarchy for its members. The researcher might examine the effects of athleticism or grades or social skills or seniority on standing within the fraternity. He or she would seek to learn how the fraternity members relate to other members of higher or lower status. While investigating these questions, the researcher would take into account people's emotions, thoughts, beliefs, and attitudes (L. Coser 1977).

We also owe credit to Weber for a key conceptual tool: the ideal type. An **ideal type** is a construct, or made-up model, that serves as a measuring rod against which actual cases can be evaluated. In his own works, Weber identified various characteristics of bureaucracy as an ideal type (discussed in detail in Chapter 6). In presenting

FIGURE 1-2

Early Social Thinkers

	Émile Durkheim 1858–1917	**Max Weber 1864–1920**	**Karl Marx 1818–1883**
Academic training	Philosophy	Law, economics, history, philosophy	Philosophy, law
Key works	1893—*The Division of Labor in Society* 1897—*Suicide: A Study in Sociology* 1912—*Elementary Forms of Religious Life*	1904–1905—*The Protestant Ethic and the Spirit of Capitalism* 1922—*Wirtschaft und Gesellschaft*	1848—*The Communist Manifesto* 1867—*Das Kapital*

this model of bureaucracy, Weber was not describing any particular business, nor was he using the term *ideal* in a way that suggested a positive evaluation. Instead, his purpose was to provide a useful standard for measuring how bureaucratic an actual organization is (Gerth and Mills 1958). Later in this textbook, we use the concept of *ideal* type to study the family, religion, authority, and economic systems as well as to analyze bureaucracy.

Although their professional careers coincided, Émile Durkheim and Max Weber never met and probably were unaware of each other's existence, let alone ideas. This was certainly not true of the work of Karl Marx. Durkheim's thinking about the impact of the division of labor in industrial societies was related to Marx's writings, while Weber's concern for a value-free, objective sociology was a direct response to Marx's deeply held convictions. Thus, it is not surprising that Karl Marx is viewed as a major figure in the development of sociology as well as several other social sciences (see Figure 1-2).

Karl Marx

Karl Marx (1818–1883) shared with Durkheim and Weber a dual interest in abstract philosophical issues and the concrete reality of everyday life. Unlike the others, Marx was so critical of existing institutions that a conventional academic career was impossible, and he spent most of his life in exile from his native Germany.

Marx's personal life was a difficult struggle. When a paper that he had written was suppressed, he fled to France. In Paris, he met Friedrich Engels (1820–1895), with whom he formed a lifelong friendship. They lived at a time when European and North American economic life was increasingly being dominated by the factory rather than the farm.

While in London in 1847, Marx and Engels attended secret meetings of an illegal coalition of labor unions, known as the Communist League. The following year, they prepared a platform called *The Communist Manifesto*, in which they argued that the masses of people with no resources other than their labor (whom they referred to as the *proletariat*) should unite to fight for the overthrow of capitalist societies. In the words of Marx and Engels:

> The history of all hitherto existing society is the history of class struggles. . . . The proletarians have nothing to lose but their chains. They have a world to win. WORKING MEN OF ALL COUNTRIES UNITE! (Feuer 1989:7, 41)

After completing *The Communist Manifesto*, Marx returned to Germany, only to be expelled. He then moved to England, where he continued to write books and essays. Marx lived there in extreme poverty. He pawned most of his possessions, and several of his children died of malnutrition and disease. Marx clearly was an outsider in British society, a fact that may well have colored his view of Western cultures.

In Marx's analysis, society was fundamentally divided between classes that clash in pursuit of their own class interests. When he examined the industrial societies

A postage stamp honored social reformer Jane Addams, an early pioneer both in sociology and in the settlement house movement.

of his time, such as Germany, England, and the United States, he saw the factory as the center of conflict between the exploiters (the owners of the means of production) and the exploited (the workers). Marx viewed these relationships in systematic terms; that is, he believed that an entire system of economic, social, and political relationships maintained the power and dominance of the owners over the workers. Consequently, Marx and Engels argued that the working class needed to *overthrow* the existing class system. Marx's influence on contemporary thinking has been dramatic. His writings inspired those who were later to lead communist revolutions in Russia, China, Cuba, Vietnam, and elsewhere.

Even apart from the political revolutions that his work fostered, Marx's significance is profound. Marx emphasized the *group* identifications and associations that influence an individual's place in society. This area of study is the major focus of contemporary sociology. Throughout this textbook, we will consider how membership in a particular gender classification, age group, racial group, or economic class affects a person's attitudes and behavior. In an important sense, we can trace this way of understanding society back to the pioneering work of Karl Marx.

Modern Developments

Sociology today builds on the firm foundation developed by Émile Durkheim, Max Weber, and Karl Marx. However, the discipline of sociology has certainly not remained stagnant over the last hundred years. While Euro-

peans have continued to make contributions to the discipline, sociologists from throughout the world and especially the United States have advanced sociological theory and research. Their new insights have helped us to better understand the workings of society.

Charles Horton Cooley

Charles Horton Cooley (1864–1929) was typical of the sociologists who came to prominence in the early 1900s. Cooley was born in Ann Arbor, Michigan, and received his graduate training in economics but later became a sociology professor at the University of Michigan. Like other early sociologists, he had become interested in this "new" discipline while pursuing a related area of study.

Cooley shared the desire of Durkheim, Weber, and Marx to learn more about society. But to do so effectively, Cooley preferred to use the sociological perspective to look first at smaller units—intimate, face-to-face groups such as families, gangs, and friendship networks. He saw these groups as the seedbeds of society in the sense that they shape people's ideals, beliefs, values, and social nature. Cooley's work increased our understanding of groups of relatively small size.

Jane Addams

In the early 1900s, many leading sociologists in the United States saw themselves as social reformers dedicated to systematically studying and then improving a corrupt society. They were genuinely concerned about the lives of immigrants in the nation's growing cities, whether these immigrants came from Europe or from the rural American South. Early female sociologists, in particular, often took active roles in poor urban areas as leaders of community centers known as *settlement houses.* For example, Jane Addams (1860–1935), an active member of the American Sociological Society, cofounded the famous Chicago settlement, Hull House.

Addams and other pioneering female sociologists commonly combined intellectual inquiry, social service work, and political activism—all with the goal of assisting the underprivileged and creating a more egalitarian society. For example, working with the Black journalist and educator Ida Wells-Barnett, Addams successfully prevented racial segregation in the Chicago public schools. Addams's efforts to establish a juvenile court system and a women's trade union also reveal the practical focus of her work (Addams 1910, 1930; Deegan 1991; Lengermann and Niebrugge-Brantley 1998).

By the middle of the 20th century, however, the focus of the discipline had shifted. Sociologists for the most part restricted themselves to theorizing and gathering information; the aim of transforming society was left to social workers and activists. This shift away from social reform was accompanied by a growing commitment to scientific methods of research and to value-free interpretation of data. Not all sociologists were happy with this emphasis. A new organization, the Society for the Study of Social Problems, was created in 1950 to deal more directly with social inequality and other social problems.

Robert Merton

Sociologist Robert Merton (1910–2003) made an important contribution to the discipline by successfully combining theory and research. Born to Slavic immigrant parents in Philadelphia, Merton subsequently won a scholarship to Temple University. He continued his studies at Harvard, where he acquired his lifelong interest in sociology. Merton's teaching career was based at Columbia University.

Merton (1968) produced a theory that is one of the most frequently cited explanations of deviant behavior. He noted different ways in which people attempt to achieve success in life. In his view, some may deviate from the socially agreed-on goal of accumulating material goods or the socially accepted means of achieving this goal. For example, in Merton's classification scheme, "innovators" are people who accept the goal of pursuing material wealth but use illegal means to do so, including robbery, burglary, and extortion. Merton based his explanation of crime on individual behavior that has been influenced by society's approved goals and means, yet it has wider applications. It helps to account for the high crime rates among the nation's poor, who may see no hope of advancing themselves through traditional roads to success. Chapter 8 discusses Merton's theory in greater detail.

Merton also emphasized that sociology should strive to bring together the "macro-level" and "micro-level" approaches to the study of society. *Macrosociology* concentrates on large-scale phenomena or entire civilizations. Émile Durkheim's cross-cultural study of suicide is an example of macro-level research. More recently, macrosociologists have examined international crime rates (see Chapter 8), the stereotype of Asian Americans as a "model minority" (see Chapter 11), and the population patterns of Islamic countries (see Chapter 21). By contrast, *microsociology* stresses study of small groups and often uses experimental study in laboratories. Sociological research on the micro level has included studies of how divorced men and women disengage from significant social roles (see Chapter 5); of how conformity can influence the expression of prejudiced attitudes (see Chapter 8); and of how a teacher's expectations can affect a student's academic performance (see Chapter 16).

Today sociology reflects the diverse contributions of earlier theorists. As sociologists approach such topics as divorce, drug addiction, and religious cults, they can draw on the theoretical insights of the discipline's pioneers. A careful reader can hear Comte, Durkheim, Weber, Marx, Cooley, Addams, and many others speaking through the pages of current research. Sociology has also broadened beyond the intellectual confines of North America and Europe. Contributions to the discipline now come from sociologists studying and researching human behavior in other parts of the world. In describing the work of today's sociologists, it is helpful to examine a number of influential theoretical approaches (also known as *perspectives*).

MAJOR THEORETICAL PERSPECTIVES

Sociologists view society in different ways. Some see the world basically as a stable and ongoing entity. They are impressed with the endurance of the family, organized religion, and other social institutions. Some sociologists see society as composed of many groups in conflict, competing for scarce resources. To other sociologists, the most fascinating aspects of the social world are the everyday, routine interactions among individuals that we sometimes take for granted. These three views, the ones most widely used by sociologists, are the functionalist, conflict, and interactionist perspectives. Together, these approaches will provide an introductory look at the discipline.

Functionalist Perspective

Think of society as a living organism in which each part of the organism contributes to its survival. This view is the *functionalist perspective,* which emphasizes the way that parts of a society are structured to maintain its stability.

Talcott Parsons (1902–1979), a Harvard University sociologist, was a key figure in the development of functionalist theory. Parsons had been greatly influenced by the work of Émile Durkheim, Max Weber, and other European sociologists. For over four decades, Parsons dominated sociology in the United States with his advocacy of functionalism. He saw any society as a vast network of connected parts, each of which helps to maintain the system as a whole. The functionalist approach holds that if an aspect of social life does not contribute to a society's stability or survival—if it does not serve some identifiably useful function or promote value consensus among members of a society—it will not be passed on from one generation to the next.

Let's examine prostitution as an example of the functionalist perspective. Why is it that a practice so widely condemned continues to display such persistence and vitality? Functionalists suggest that prostitution satisfies needs of patrons that may not be readily met through more socially acceptable forms such as courtship or marriage. The "buyer" receives sex without any responsibility for procreation or sentimental attachment; at the same time, the "seller" makes a living through this exchange.

Such an examination leads us to conclude that prostitution does perform certain functions that society seems to need. However, this is not to suggest that prostitution is a desirable or legitimate form of social behavior. Functionalists do not make such judgments. Rather, advocates of the functionalist perspective hope to explain how an aspect of society that is so frequently attacked can nevertheless manage to survive (Davis 1937).

Manifest and Latent Functions

Your college catalog typically states various functions of the institution. It may inform you, for example, that the university intends to "offer each student a broad education in classical and contemporary thought, in the humanities, in the sciences, and in the arts." However, it would be quite a surprise to find a catalog that declared, "This university was founded in 1895 to keep people between the ages of 18 and 22 out of the job market, thus reducing unemployment." No college catalog will declare that this is the purpose of the university. Yet societal institutions serve many functions, some of them quite subtle. The university, in fact, *does* delay people's entry into the job market.

Robert Merton (1968) made an important distinction between manifest and latent functions. *Manifest functions* of institutions are open, stated, conscious functions. They involve the intended, recognized consequences of an aspect of society, such as the university's role in certifying academic competence and excellence. By contrast, latent functions are unconscious or unintended functions and may reflect hidden purposes of an institution. One *latent function* of universities is to hold down unemployment. Another is to serve as a meeting ground for people seeking marital partners.

Dysfunctions

Functionalists acknowledge that not all parts of a society contribute to its stability all the time. A *dysfunction* refers to an element or a process of society that may actually disrupt a social system or lead to a decrease in stability.

We view many dysfunctional behavior patterns, such as homicide, as undesirable. Yet we should not automatically interpret dysfunctions as negative. The evaluation of a dysfunction depends on one's own values or, as the saying goes, on "where you sit." For example, the official view in prisons in the United States is that inmate gangs should be eradicated because they are dysfunctional to smooth operations. Yet some guards have actually come

to view prison gangs as functional for their jobs. The danger posed by gangs creates a "threat to security," requiring increased surveillance and more overtime work for guards as well as requests for special staffing to address prison gang problems (Scott 2001).

Conflict Perspective

Where functionalists see stability and consensus, conflict sociologists see a social world in continual struggle. The *conflict perspective* assumes that social behavior is best understood in terms of conflict or tension between competing groups. Such conflict need not be violent; it can take the form of labor negotiations, party politics, competition between religious groups for members, or disputes over the federal budget.

Throughout most of the 1900s, the functionalist perspective had the upper hand in sociology in the United States. However, the conflict approach has become increasingly persuasive since the late 1960s. The widespread social unrest resulting from battles over civil rights, bitter divisions over the war in Vietnam, the rise of the feminist and gay liberation movements, the Watergate political scandal, urban riots, and confrontations at abortion clinics offered support for the conflict approach—the view that our social world is characterized by continual struggle between competing groups. Currently, the discipline of sociology accepts conflict theory as one valid way to gain insight into a society.

The Marxist View

As we saw earlier, Karl Marx viewed struggle between social classes as inevitable, given the exploitation of

On the face of it, prison gangs may seem dysfunctional since they pose a threat to security. But prison guards consider these gangs functional for their jobs because they may require overtime, higher pay, and increased staffing.

workers under capitalism. Expanding on Marx's work, sociologists and other social scientists have come to see conflict not merely as a class phenomenon but as a part of everyday life in all societies. In studying any culture, organization, or social group, sociologists want to know who benefits, who suffers, and who dominates at the expense of others. They are concerned with the conflicts between women and men, parents and children, cities and suburbs, and Whites and Blacks, to name only a few. Conflict theorists are interested in how society's institutions—including the family, government, religion, education, and the media—may help to maintain the privileges of some groups and keep others in a subservient position. Their emphasis on social change and redistribution of resources makes conflict theorists more "radical" and "activist" than functionalists (Dahrendorf 1959).

An African American View: W. E. B. Du Bois

One important contribution of conflict theory is that it has encouraged sociologists to view society through the eyes of those segments of the population that rarely influence decision making. Some early Black sociologists, including W. E. B. Du Bois (1868–1963), conducted research that they hoped would assist the struggle for a racially egalitarian society. Du Bois believed that knowledge was essential in combating prejudice and achieving tolerance and justice. Sociology, Du Bois contended, had to draw on scientific principles to study social problems such as those experienced by Blacks in the United States. In addition, Du Bois made a major contribution to sociology through his in-depth studies of urban life—both White and Black.

Du Bois had little patience for theorists such as Herbert Spencer who seemed content with the status quo. He advocated basic research on the lives of Blacks that would separate opinion from fact. In this way he documented their relatively low status in Philadelphia and Atlanta. Du Bois believed that the granting of full political rights to Blacks was essential to their social and economic progress in the United States. Many of his ideas challenging the status quo did not find a receptive audience within either the government or the academic world. As a result, Du Bois became increasingly involved with organizations whose members questioned the established social order, and he helped to found the National Association for the Advancement of Colored People, better known as the NAACP (Lewis 1994, 2000).

The addition of diverse views within sociology in recent years has led to some valuable research, especially for African Americans. For many years, African Americans were understandably wary of participating in medical research studies, because those studies had been used for such purposes as justifying slavery or determining the

W. E. B. Du Bois challenged the status quo in both academic and political circles. The first Black person to receive a doctorate from Harvard University, Du Bois later helped organize the National Association for the Advancement of Colored People (NAACP).

impact of untreated syphilis. Now, however, African American sociologists and other social scientists are working to involve Blacks in useful ethnic medical research in such areas as diabetes and sickle cell anemia, two disorders that strike Black populations especially hard (Young, Jr., and Deskins, Jr. 2001).

The Feminist View

Sociologists began embracing the feminist perspective in the 1970s, although it has a long tradition in many other disciplines. The *feminist view* sees inequity in gender as central to all behavior and organization. Because it clearly focuses on one aspect of inequality, it is often allied with the conflict perspective. Proponents of the feminist perspective tend to focus on the macro level, just as conflict theorists do. Drawing on the work of Marx and Engels, contemporary feminist theorists often view women's subordination as inherent in capitalist societies. Some radical feminist theorists, however, view the oppression of women as inevitable in *all* male-dominated societies, whether labeled *capitalist, socialist,* or *communist.*

An early example of this perspective (long before the label came into use by sociologists) shows up in the life and writings of Ida Wells-Barnett (1862–1931). Following her groundbreaking publications in the 1890s on the practice of lynching Black Americans, she became an advocate in the women's rights campaign, especially the struggle to win the vote for women. Like feminist theorists who succeeded her, Wells-Barnett used her analysis of society as a means of resisting oppression. In her case, she researched what it meant to be African American, a woman in the United States, and a Black woman in the United States (Wells-Barnett 1970).

Feminist scholarship in sociology has broadened our understanding of social behavior by taking it beyond the White male point of view. For example, a family's social standing is no longer defined solely by the husband's position and income. Feminist scholars have not only challenged stereotyping of women; they have argued for a gender-balanced study of society in which women's experiences and contributions are as visible as those of men (England 1999; Komarovsky 1991; Tuchman 1992).

The feminist perspective has given sociologists new views of familiar social behavior. For example, past research on crime rarely considered women, and when it did, the studies tended to focus on "traditional" crimes by women like shoplifting. Such a view tended to ignore the role that women play in all types of crime as well as the disproportionate role that they play as *victims* of crime. Research conducted by Meda Chesney-Lind and Noelie Rodriguez (1993) showed that nearly all women in prison had suffered physical and/or sexual abuse when they were young; half had been raped. Contributions by both feminist and minority scholars have enriched all the sociological perspectives.

Use Your Sociological Imagination   www.mhhe.com/schaefer9

Imagine that you are a sociologist who uses the conflict perspective to study various aspects of our society. How do you think you would interpret the practice of prostitution? Contrast this view with the functionalist perspective. Do you think your comments would differ if you took the feminist view, and if so, how?

Interactionist Perspective

Workers interacting on the job, encounters in public places like bus stops and parks, behavior in small groups—these are all aspects of microsociology that catch the attention of interactionists. Whereas functionalist and conflict theorists both analyze large-scale societywide patterns of behavior, the ***interactionist perspective*** generalizes about everyday forms of social interaction in order to explain society as a whole. In the 1990s, for example, the workings of juries became a subject of public scrutiny. High-profile trials ended in verdicts that left some people shaking their heads. Long before jury members were being interviewed on their front lawns following trials, interactionists tried to better understand behavior in the small-group setting of a jury deliberation room.

Interactionism is a sociological framework for viewing human beings as living in a world of meaningful objects. These "objects" may include material things, actions, other people, relationships, and even symbols.

The interactionist perspective is sometimes referred to as the *symbolic interactionist perspective,* because interactionists see symbols as an especially important part of human communication. Members of a society share the social meanings of symbols. In the United States, for example, a salute symbolizes respect, while a clenched fist signifies defiance. However, another culture might use different gestures to convey a feeling of respect or defiance. These types of symbolic interaction are classified as forms of ***nonverbal communication,*** which can include many other gestures, facial expressions, and postures.

Symbols in the form of tattoos took on special importance in the aftermath of September 11, 2001. Tattoo parlors in lower Manhattan were overwhelmed with requests from various groups for designs that carried symbolic significance for them. New York City firefighters asked for tattoos with names of their fallen colleagues; police officers requested designs incorporating their distinctive NYPD shield; recovery workers at Ground Zero sought tattoos that incorporated the image of the giant steel cross, the remnant of a massive cross-beam in a

Ida Wells-Barnett explored what it meant to be female and Black living in the United States. Her work established her as one of the earliest feminist theorists.

World Trade Center building. Through symbols, such as these tattoos, people communicate their values and beliefs to those around them (Scharnberg 2002).

While functionalist and conflict approaches were initiated in Europe, interactionism developed first in the United States. George Herbert Mead (1863–1931) is widely regarded as the founder of the interactionist perspective. Mead taught at the University of Chicago from 1893 until his death. His sociological analysis, like that of Charles Horton Cooley, often focused on human interactions within one-to-one situations and small groups. Mead was interested in observing the most minute forms of communication—smiles, frowns, nodding of one's head—and in understanding how such individual behavior was influenced by the larger context of a group or society. Despite his innovative views, Mead only occasionally wrote articles, and never a book. He was an extremely popular teacher, and most of his insights have come to us through edited volumes of lectures that his students published after his death.

As Mead's teachings have become more well known, sociologists have expressed greater interest in the interactionist perspective. Many have moved away from what may have been an excessive preoccupation with the large-scale (macro) level of social behavior and have redirected their attention toward behavior that occurs in small groups (micro level).

Erving Goffman (1922–1982) popularized a particular type of interactionist method known as the **dramaturgical approach,** which examines people as if they were theatrical performers. The dramaturgist compares everyday life to the setting of the theater and stage. Just as actors project certain images, all of us seek to present particular features of our personalities while we hide other qualities. Thus, in a class, we may feel the need to project a serious image; at a party, we want to look relaxed and friendly.

The Sociological Approach

Which perspective should a sociologist use in studying human behavior? Functionalist? Conflict? Interactionist? In fact, sociologists make use of all the perspectives summarized in Table 1-1 (page 18), since each offers unique insights into the same issue. We gain the broadest understanding of our society, then, by drawing on all the major perspectives, noting where they overlap and where they diverge.

Although no one approach is correct by itself, and sociologists draw on all of them for various purposes, many sociologists tend to favor one particular perspective over others. A sociologist's theoretical orientation influences his or her approach to a research problem in important ways—including the choice of what to study, how to study it, and what questions to pose (or not to

pose). (See Box 1-1 on page 19 for an example of how a researcher would study sports from different perspectives.) In the next part of this chapter, we will see how sociologists have used their discipline for practical applications. Bear in mind, though, that for whatever purpose sociologists work, their research will always be guided by their theoretical viewpoint. Research results, like theories, shine a spotlight on one part of the stage, leaving others in relative darkness.

APPLIED AND CLINICAL SOCIOLOGY

Many early sociologists—notably, Jane Addams, W. E. B. Du Bois, and George Herbert Mead—were strong advocates for social reform. They wanted their theories

Interactionists would be interested in the social significance of team mascots and symbols. This Native American is protesting the use of the word *Indians* by a major league baseball team. By making up other team names that other groups might find offensive, he invites you to put yourself in his shoes.

Table 1-1	Comparing Major Theoretical Perspectives		
	Functionalist	**Conflict**	**Interactionist**
View of society	Stable, well integrated	Characterized by tension and struggle between groups	Active in influencing and affecting everyday social interaction
Level of analysis emphasized	Macro	Macro	Micro analysis as a way of understanding the larger macro phenomena
Key concepts	Manifest functions Latent functions Dysfunction	Inequality Capitalism Stratification	Symbols Nonverbal communication Face-to-face interaction
View of the individual	People are socialized to perform societal functions	People are shaped by power, coercion, and authority	People manipulate symbols and create their social worlds through interaction
View of the social order	Maintained through cooperation and consensus	Maintained through force and coercion	Maintained by shared understanding of everyday behavior
View of social change	Predictable, reinforcing	Change takes place all the time and may have positive consequences	Reflected in people's social positions and their communications with others
Example	Public punishments reinforce the social order	Laws reinforce the positions of those in power	People respect laws or disobey them based on their own past experience
Proponents	Émile Durkheim Talcott Parsons Robert Merton	Karl Marx W. E. B. Du Bois Ida Wells-Barnett	George Herbert Mead Charles Horton Cooley Erving Goffman

and findings to be relevant to policymakers and to people's lives in general. For instance, Mead was the treasurer of Hull House for many years, where he applied his theory to improving the lives of those who were powerless (especially immigrants). He also served on committees dealing with Chicago's labor problems and public education. Today, *applied sociology* is the use of the discipline of sociology with the specific intent of yielding practical applications for human behavior and organizations.

Often, the goal of such work is to assist in resolving a social problem. For example, in the last 35 years, eight presidents of the United States have established commissions to delve into major societal concerns facing our nation. Sociologists are often asked to apply their expertise to studying such issues as violence, pornography, crime, immigration, and population. In Europe, both academic

and governmental research departments are offering increasing financial support for applied studies.

An example of applied sociology is the growing local community research movement. Sociologists at DePaul University in Chicago and their students have been examining the impact of the opening of a Motorola cellular phone plant with 5,000 employees in the small town of Harvard, Illinois. This rural, agriculture-based community has only 6,500 residents and is 80 miles from Chicago (well outside the suburban fringe). Some residents of Harvard viewed the arrival of Motorola as a great boost to the local economy, but others were fearful of the power of a Fortune 500 company. In studying the social and economic impact of Motorola on Harvard, the DePaul researchers were interested not only in the influence a huge corporation could have on a town but in whether the lifestyle of a rural Illinois community could

1-1 LOOKING AT SPORTS FROM THREE THEORETICAL PERSPECTIVES

We watch sports. Talk sports. Spend money on sports. Some of us live and breathe sports. Because sports occupy much of our time and directly or indirectly consume and generate a great deal of money, it should not be surprising that sports have sociological components that can be analyzed by the various theoretical perspectives.

Functionalist View

In examining any aspect of society, functionalists emphasize the contribution it makes to overall social stability. Functionalists regard sports as an almost religious institution that uses ritual and ceremony to reinforce the common values of a society:

- Sports socialize young people into such values as competition and patriotism.
- Sports help to maintain people's physical well-being.
- Sports serve as a safety valve for both participants and spectators, who are allowed to shed tension and aggressive energy in a socially acceptable way.
- Sports "bring together" members of a community (supporting local athletes and teams) or even a nation (as seen during World Cup matches and the Olympics) and promote an overall feeling of unity and social solidarity.

Conflict View

Conflict theorists argue that the social order is based on coercion and exploitation. They emphasize that sports reflect and even exacerbate many of the divisions of society:

- Sports are a form of big business in which profits are more important than the health and safety of the workers (athletes).
- Sports perpetuate the false idea that success can be achieved simply through hard work, while failure should be blamed on the individual alone (rather than on injustices in the larger social system). Sports serve as an "opiate" that encourages people to seek a "fix" or temporary "high" rather than focus on personal problems and social issues.

> Despite their differences, functionalists, conflict theorists, and interactionists would all agree that there is much more to sports than exercise or recreation.

- Sports maintain the subordinate role of Blacks and Latinos, who toil as athletes but are less visible in supervisory positions as coaches, managers, and owners.
- Gender expectations encourage female athletes to be passive and gentle, qualities that do not support the emphasis on competitiveness in sports.

Interactionist View

In studying the social order, interactionists are especially interested in shared understandings of everyday behavior. Interactionists examine sports on the micro level by focusing on how day-to-day social behavior is shaped by the distinctive norms, values, and demands of the world of sports:

- Sports often heighten parent–child involvement; they may lead to parental expectations for participation and (sometimes unrealistically) for success.
- Participation in sports provides friendship networks that can permeate everyday life.
- Despite class, racial, and religious differences, teammates may work together harmoniously and may even abandon previous stereotypes and prejudices.
- Relationships in the sports world are defined by people's social positions as players, coaches, and referees—as well as by the high or low status that individuals hold as a result of their performances and reputations.

Despite their differences, functionalists, conflict theorists, and interactionists would all agree that there is much more to sports than exercise or recreation. They would also agree that sports and other popular forms of culture are worthy subjects of serious study by sociologists.

Let's Discuss

1. Have you experienced or witnessed discrimination in sports based on gender or race? How did you react? Has the representation of Blacks or women on teams been controversial on your campus? In what ways?
2. Which perspective do you think is most useful in looking at the sociology of sports? Why?

Sources: Acosta and Carpenter 2001; Edwards 1973; Eitzen 2003; Fine 1987.

influence the corporation. The scheduled closure of the plant in 2003, just nine years after it opened, will have yet another impact on the town.

This study also shows how a rural community is connected to a global economy. Nationwide in 2001, Motorola cut 40,000 jobs but at the same time poured $3.4

billion into operations in China, making the company the largest foreign investor in that country. This means that sociologists have to consider events in Hunan and Sichuan provinces of China in order to understand what is happening in Illinois (Chandler 2001; Koval et al. 1996; Long 2002).

Growing interest in applied sociology has led to such specializations as medical sociology and environmental sociology. The former includes research on how health care professionals and patients deal with disease. As one example, medical sociologists have studied the social impact of the AIDS crisis on families, friends, and communities (see Chapter 5). Environmental sociologists examine the relationship between human societies and the physical environment. One focus of their work is the issue of "environmental justice" (see Chapter 21), which has been raised because researchers and community activists have found that hazardous waste dumps are especially likely to be found in poor and minority neighborhoods (M. Martin 1996).

The growing popularity of applied sociology has led to the rise of the specialty of clinical sociology. Louis Wirth (1931) wrote about clinical sociology more than 60 years ago, but the term itself has become popular only in recent years. While applied sociology may simply evaluate social issues, *clinical sociology* is dedicated to facilitating change by altering social relationships (as in family therapy) or restructuring social institutions (as in the reorganization of a medical center).

The Sociological Practice Association was founded in 1978 to promote the application of sociological knowledge to intervention for individual and social change. This professional group has developed a procedure for certifying clinical sociologists—much as physical therapists or psychologists are certified. In 1999 a new journal was published called *Sociological Practice: A Journal of Clinical and Applied Sociology.*

Applied sociologists generally leave it to others to act on their evaluations. By contrast, clinical sociologists take direct responsibility for implementation and view those with whom they work as their clients. This specialty has become increasingly attractive to sociology graduate students because it offers an opportunity to apply intellectual learning in a practical way. Up to now, a shrinking job market in the academic world has made such alternative career routes appealing.

Applied and clinical sociology can be contrasted with *basic* (or *pure*) *sociology,* which seeks a more profound knowledge of the fundamental aspects of social phenomena. This type of research is not necessarily meant to generate specific applications, although such ideas may result once findings are analyzed. When Durkheim studied suicide rates, he was not primarily interested in discovering

a way to eliminate suicide. In this sense, his research was an example of basic rather than applied sociology.

Use Your Sociological Imagination www.mhhe.com /schaefer9

What issues facing your local community would you like to address with applied sociological research?

DEVELOPING A SOCIOLOGICAL IMAGINATION

In this book, we will be illustrating the sociological imagination in several different ways—by showing theory in practice and research in action; by exploring the significance of social inequality; by speaking across race, gender, and national boundaries; and by highlighting social policy throughout the world.

Theory in Practice

We will illustrate how the major sociological perspectives are helpful in understanding today's issues, whether it be capital punishment or the AIDS crisis. Sociologists do not necessarily declare "Here I am using functionalism," but their research and approaches do tend to draw on one or more theoretical frameworks, as will become clear in the pages to follow.

Research in Action

Sociologists actively investigate a variety of issues and social behavior. We have already seen that such research might involve the meaning of suicide and decision making in the jury box. Often the research has direct applications to improving people's lives, as in the case of increasing the participation of African Americans in diabetes testing. Throughout the rest of the book, the research performed by sociologists and other social scientists will shed light on group behavior of all types.

The Significance of Social Inequality

Who holds power? Who doesn't? Who has prestige? Who lacks it? Perhaps the major theme of analysis in sociology today is *social inequality,* a condition in which members of society have differing amounts of wealth, prestige, or power. Barbara Ehrenreich's research among low-wage workers uncovered aspects of social inequality. Whether using the functionalist or feminist perspective, focusing on Arizona or Afghanistan, considering a garden club or the global marketplace, sociologists often see behavior as shaped by social inequality.

Sociology in the Global Community

1-2   WOMEN IN PUBLIC PLACES WORLDWIDE

By definition, a public place, such as a sidewalk or a park, is open to all persons. Even some private establishments, such as restaurants, are intended to be open to people as a whole. Yet sociologists and other social scientists have found that societies define access to these places differently for women and men.

In many Middle Eastern societies, women are prohibited from public places and are restricted to certain places in the house. In such societies, the coffeehouse and the market are considered male domains. Some other societies, such as Malagasy, strictly limit the presence of women in public places yet allow women to conduct the haggling that is a part of shopping in open-air markets. In some West African societies, women actually control the marketplace. In various eastern European countries and Turkey, women appear to be free to move about in public places, but the coffeehouse remains the exclusive preserve of males. Contrast this with coffeehouses in North America, where women and men mingle freely and even engage each other in conversation as total strangers.

While casual observers may view both private and public space in the United States as gender-neutral, private all-male clubs do persist, and even in public spaces women experience some inequality. Erving Goffman, an interactionist, conducted classic studies of public spaces. He found them to be settings for routine interactions, such as "helping" encounters when a person is lost and asks for directions. But sociologist Carol Brooks Gardner has offered a feminist critique of Goffman's work: "Rarely does Goffman emphasize the habitual dispro-

> Women are well aware that a casual helping encounter with a man in a public place can too easily lead to undesired sexual queries or advances.

portionate fear that women can come to feel in public toward men, much less the routine trepidation that ethnic and racial minorities and the disabled can experience" (1989:45). Women are well aware that a casual helping encounter with a man in a public place can too easily lead to undesired sexual queries or advances.

Whereas Goffman suggests that street remarks about women occur rarely—and that they generally hold no unpleasant

or threatening implications—Gardner (1989:49) counters that "for young women especially, . . . appearing in public places carries with it the constant possibility of evaluation, compliments that are not really so complimentary after all, and harsh or vulgar insults if the woman is found wanting." She adds that these remarks are sometimes accompanied by tweaks, pinches, or even blows, unmasking the latent hostility of many male-to-female street remarks.

According to Gardner, many women have a well-founded fear of the sexual harassment, assault, and rape that can occur in public places. She concludes that "public places are arenas for the enactment of inequality in everyday life for women and for many others" (1989:56).

Let's Discuss

1. How would a coffeehouse in Turkey differ from one in Seattle, Washington? What might account for these differences?
2. Do you know a woman who has encountered sexual harassment in a public place? How did she react? Has her social behavior changed as a result of the experience?

Sources: Cheng and Liao 1994; Gardner 1989, 1990, 1995; Goffman 1963b, 1971; Rosman and Rubel 1994.

Some sociologists, seeking to understand the effect of inequality, often make the case for social justice. W. E. B. Du Bois ([1940] 1968:418) noted that the greatest power in the land is not "thought or ethics, but wealth." As we have seen, the contributions of Karl Marx, Jane Addams, and Ida Wells-Barnett also focused on social inequality and social justice. Joe Feagin (2001) echoed this sentiment for the overarching importance of social inequality in his recent presidential address to the American Sociological Association.

Throughout, this book will highlight the work of sociologists on social inequality. Many chapters also feature a box with this theme.

Speaking across Race, Gender, and National Boundaries

Sociologists include both men and women, people from a variety of ethnic, national, and religious origins. In their work, sociologists seek to draw conclusions that speak to all people—not just the affluent or powerful. This is not always easy. Insights into how a corporation can increase its profits tend to attract more attention and financial support than do, say, the merits of a needle exchange program for low-income inner-city residents. Yet sociology today, more than ever, seeks to better understand the experiences of all people. In Box 1-2 (page 21), we look at how a woman's role in public places is defined differently from that of a man in different parts of the world.

Social Policy throughout the World

One important way we can use the sociological imagination is to enhance our understanding of current social issues throughout the world. Beginning with Chapter 2, each chapter will conclude with a discussion of a contemporary social policy issue. In some cases, we will examine a specific issue facing national governments. For example, government funding of child care centers will be discussed in Chapter 4, Socialization; immigration policies in Chapter 11, Racial and Ethnic Inequality; and religion in schools in Chapter 15, Religion. These social policy sections will demonstrate how fundamental sociological concepts can enhance our critical thinking skills and help us to better understand current public policy debates taking place around the world.

In addition, sociology has been used to evaluate the success of programs or the impact of changes brought about by policymakers and political activists. For example, Chapter 10, Social Inequality Worldwide, includes a discussion of research on the effectiveness of welfare reform experiments. Such discussions underscore the many practical applications of sociological theory and research.

Sociologists expect the next quarter of a century to be perhaps the most exciting and critical period in the history of the discipline. This is because of a growing recognition—both in the United States and around the world—that current social problems *must* be addressed before their magnitude overwhelms human societies. We can expect sociologists to play an increasing role in the government sector by researching and developing public policy alternatives. It seems only natural for this textbook to focus on the connection between the work of sociologists and the difficult questions confronting the policymakers and people of the United States.

CHAPTER RESOURCES

Summary

Sociology is the systematic study of social behavior and human groups. In this chapter, we examine the nature of sociological theory, the founders of the discipline, theoretical perspectives of contemporary sociology, applications of sociology, and ways to exercise the "sociological imagination."

1. The *sociological imagination* is an awareness of the relationship between an individual and the wider society. It is based on the ability to view our own society as an outsider might, rather than from the perspective of our limited experiences and cultural biases.

2. In contrast to other *social sciences,* sociology emphasizes the influence that groups can have on people's behavior and attitudes and the ways in which people shape society.

3. Knowledge that relies on "common sense" is not always reliable. Sociologists must test and analyze each piece of information that they use.

4. Sociologists employ *theories* to examine the relationships between observations or data that may seem completely unrelated.

5. Nineteenth-century thinkers who contributed sociological insights included Auguste Comte, a French philosopher; Harriet Martineau, an English sociologist; and Herbert Spencer, an English scholar.

6. Other important figures in the development of sociology were Émile Durkheim, who pioneered work on suicide; Max Weber, who taught the need for "insight" in intellectual work; and Karl Marx, who emphasized the importance of the economy and of conflict in society.

7. In the 20th century, the discipline of sociology is indebted to the U.S. sociologists Charles Horton Cooley and Robert Merton.

8. *Macrosociology* concentrates on large-scale phenomena or entire civilizations, whereas *microsociology* stresses study of small groups.

9. The *functionalist perspective* of sociology emphasizes the way that parts of a society are structured to maintain its stability.

10. The *conflict perspective* assumes that social behavior is best understood in terms of conflict or tension between competing groups.

11. The *interactionist perspective* is primarily concerned with fundamental or everyday forms of interaction, including symbols and other types of nonverbal communication.

12. Sociologists make use of all three perspectives, since each offers unique insights into the same issue.

13. *Applied* and *clinical sociology* aim for practical applications to human behavior and organizations. By contrast, *basic sociology* seeks only to gain a deeper knowledge of the fundamental aspects of social phenomena.

14. This textbook makes use of the sociological imagination by showing theory in practice and research in action; by focusing on the significance of social inequality; by speaking across race, gender, and national boundaries; and by highlighting social policy around the world.

Critical Thinking Questions

1. What aspects of the social and work environment in a fast-food restaurant would be of particular interest to a sociologist because of his or her "sociological imagination"?

2. What are the manifest and latent functions of a health club?

3. How might the interactionist perspective be applied to a place where you have been employed or to an organization you joined?

Key Terms

Anomie   The loss of direction felt in a society when social control of individual behavior has become ineffective. (page 10)

Applied sociology   The use of the discipline of sociology with the specific intent of yielding practical applications for human behavior and organizations. (18)

Basic sociology   Sociological inquiry conducted with the objective of gaining a more profound knowledge of the fundamental aspects of social phenomena. Also known as *pure sociology*. (20)

Clinical sociology   The use of the discipline of sociology with the specific intent of altering social relationships or restructuring social institutions. (20)

Conflict perspective   A sociological approach that assumes that social behavior is best understood in terms of conflict or tension between competing groups. (14)

Dramaturgical approach   A view of social interaction in which people are seen as theatrical performers. (17)

Dysfunction   An element or a process of society that may disrupt a social system or lead to a decrease in stability. (14)

Feminist view   A sociological approach that views inequity in gender as central to all behavior and organization. (15)

Functionalist perspective   A sociological approach that emphasizes the way that parts of a society are structured to maintain its stability. (13)

Ideal type   A construct or model for evaluating specific cases. (10)

Interactionist perspective   A sociological approach that generalizes about everyday forms of social interaction in order to explain society as a whole. (16)

Latent function   Unconscious or unintended function; hidden purpose. (14)

Macrosociology   Sociological investigation that concentrates on large-scale phenomena or entire civilizations. (13)

Manifest function   Open, stated, and conscious function. (14)

Microsociology   Sociological investigation that stresses study of small groups and often uses laboratory experimental studies. (13)

Natural science   The study of the physical features of nature and the ways in which they interact and change. (6)

Nonverbal communication   The sending of messages through the use of posture, facial expressions, and gestures. (16)

Science   The body of knowledge obtained by methods based on systematic observation. (6)

Social inequality   A condition in which members of society have differing amounts of wealth, prestige, or power. (20)

Social science   The study of social features of humans and the ways they interact and change. (6)

Sociological imagination   An awareness of the relationship between an individual and the wider society. (6)

Sociology   The systematic study of social behavior and human groups. (3)

Theory   In sociology, a set of statements that seeks to explain problems, actions, or behavior. (8)

Verstehen   The German word for "understanding" or "insight"; used to stress the need for sociologists to take into account the subjective meanings people attach to their actions. (10)

TECHNOLOGY RESOURCES

 ## Internet Connection

Note: While all the URLs listed were current as of the printing of this book, these sites often change. Please check our website (www.mhhe.com/schaefer9) for updates, hyperlinks, and exercises related to these sites.

1. An undergraduate degree in sociology doesn't just serve as an excellent preparation for future graduate work in sociology. It also provides a strong liberal arts background for entry-level positions in business, social services, foundations, community organizations, not-for-profit groups, law enforcement, and many types of governmental jobs. To learn more about careers in sociology, visit the homepage of the American Sociological Association (ASA): www.asanet.org.

2. An early example of the feminist view shows up in the life and writings of Ida Wells-Barnett. To learn more about how she confronted issues of race and gender, go to this website: www.lib.niu.edu/ipo/iht319630.html.

 ## Online Learning Center with PowerWeb

Visit the Online Learning Center, this textbook's specific website, at **www.mhhe.com/schaefer9**. The student center in the Online Learning Center offers a variety of helpful and interesting resources and activities for each chapter. The resources include chapter outlines and summaries, quizzes with feedback, direct links to Internet sites, including those found in the Internet Connection sections at the end of each chapter in your text, relevant news updates, and audio clips from the author. The activities include flashcards, crossword puzzles, interactive maps, and interactive exercises. Don't pass up this opportunity to learn more about sociology and to take advantage of resources that will help you master the material in your text and get a better grade in the course!

 ## Reel Society Interactive Movie CD-ROM

Reel Society is an interactive movie that brings key sociological concepts to life. You become part of the exploits of several college students during three challenging days on campus. You take part by making decisions for them. You see the consequences of your choices. Through it all, a wide variety of issues and perspectives are shown for the purpose of relating sociological thought to real life. Exercise your sociological imagination and step into the world of *Reel Society*.

Reel Society includes scenes that can be used to spark discussion about the following topics from this chapter:

• The Sociological Imagination
• Major Theoretical Perspectives
• Speaking across Race, Gender, and National Boundaries

CAREERS IN SOCIOLOGY

An undergraduate degree in sociology doesn't just serve as excellent preparation for future graduate work in sociology. It also provides a strong liberal arts background for entry-level positions in business, social services, foundations, community organizations, not-for-profit groups, law enforcement, and many types of governmental jobs. A number of fields—among them marketing, public relations, and broadcasting—now require investigative skills and an understanding of diverse groups found in today's multiethnic and multinational environment. Moreover, a sociology degree requires accomplishment in oral and written communication, interpersonal skills, problem solving, and critical thinking—all job-related skills that may give sociology graduates an advantage over those who pursue more technical degrees (Benner and Hitchcock 1986; Billson and Huber 1993).

Consequently, while few occupations specifically require an undergraduate degree in sociology, such academic training can be an important asset in entering a wide range of occupations (American Sociological Association, 1993, 2002). Just to bring this home, a number of chapters highlight a real-life professional who describes how the study of sociology has helped in his or her career. Look for the "Taking Sociology to Work" boxes.

The accompanying figure summarizes sources of employment for those with BA or BS degrees in sociology. It shows that the areas of human services, the not-for-profit sector, business, and government offer major career opportunities for sociology graduates. Undergraduates who know where their career interests lie are well advised to enroll in sociology courses and specialties best suited for those interests. For example, students hoping to become health planners would take a class in medical sociology; students seeking employment as social science research assistants would focus on courses in statistics and methods. Internships, such as placements at city planning agencies and survey research organizations, afford another way for sociology students to prepare for careers. Studies show that students who choose an internship placement have less trouble finding jobs, obtain better jobs, and enjoy greater job satisfaction than students without internship placements (Salem and Grabarek 1986).

Occupational Fields of Sociology BA/MA Graduates

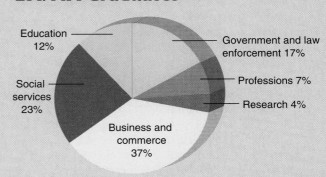

Source: Schaefer, 1998b.

Many college students view social work as the field most closely associated with sociology. Traditionally, social workers received their undergraduate training in sociology and allied fields such as psychology and counseling. After some practical experience, social workers would generally seek a master's degree in social work (MSW) to be considered for supervisory or administrative positions. Today, however, some students choose (where it is available) to pursue an undergraduate degree in social work (BSW). This degree prepares graduates for direct service positions such as caseworker or group worker.

Many students continue their sociological training beyond the bachelor's degree. More than 250 universities in the United States have graduate programs in sociology that offer PhD and/or master's degrees. These programs differ greatly in their areas of specialization, course requirements, costs, and research and teaching opportunities available to graduate students. About 55 percent of the graduates are women (American Sociological Association 2004; Spalter-Roth and Lee 2000).

Higher education is an important source of employment for sociologists with graduate degrees. About 83 percent of recent PhD recipients in sociology sought employment in colleges and universities. These sociologists teach not only majors committed to the discipline but also students hoping to become doctors, nurses, lawyers, police officers, and so forth (Spalter-Roth et al. 2000).

For sociology graduates interested in academic careers, the road to a PhD (or doctorate) can be long and difficult. This degree symbolizes competence in original research; each candidate must prepare a book-length study known as a dissertation. Typically, a doctoral student in sociology will engage in four to seven years of intensive work, including the time required to complete the dissertation. Yet even this effort is no guarantee of a job as a sociology professor.

The good news is that over the next 10 years, the demand for instructors is expected to increase because of high rates of retirement among faculty from the baby-boom generation, as well as the anticipated slow but steady growth in the college student population in the United States. Nonetheless, anyone who launches an academic career must be prepared for considerable uncertainty and competition in the college job market (American Sociological Association 2002; Huber 1985).

Of course, not all people working as sociologists teach or hold doctoral degrees. Take government, for example. The Census Bureau relies on people with sociological training to interpret data for other government agencies and the general public. Virtually every agency depends on survey research—a field in which sociology students can specialize—in order to assess everything from community needs to the morale of the agency's own workers. In addition, people with sociological training can put their academic knowledge to effective use in probation and parole, health sciences, community development, and recreational services. Some people working in government or private industry have a master's degree (MA or MS) in sociology; others have a bachelor's degree (BA or BS).

Currently, about 22 percent of the members of the American Sociological Association use their sociological skills outside the academic world, whether in social service agencies or in marketing positions for business firms. A renewed interest in applied sociology has led to the hir-

Sociology students put in many years and a great deal of work on the way to a PhD. Fortunately, the job market for instructors is looking better than in years past as the size of the college student population steadily grows.

ing of an increasing number of sociologists with graduate degrees by businesses, industry, hospitals, and nonprofit organizations. Studies show that many sociology graduates are making career changes from social service areas to business and commerce. As an undergraduate major, sociology is excellent preparation for employment in many parts of the business world (American Sociological Association 2001).

Whether you take a few courses in sociology or actually complete a degree, you will benefit from the critical thinking skills developed in this discipline. Sociologists emphasize the value of being able to analyze, interpret, and function within a variety of working situations; this is an asset in virtually any career. Moreover, given rapid technological change and the expanding global economy, all of us will need to adapt to substantial social change, even in our own careers. Sociology provides a rich conceptual framework that can serve as a foundation for flexible career development and can assist you in taking advantage of new employment opportunities (American Sociological Association 1995, 2002).

SOCIOLOGICAL RESEARCH

The data social scientists collect often confirm what most people think, but sometimes—as this billboard, which appeared in 1992, suggests—it causes us to think more deeply about our society.

What Is the Scientific Method?

Major Research Designs

Ethics of Research

Technology and Sociological Research

Social Policy and Sociological Research: Studying Human Sexuality

Appendix I: Using Statistics, Tables, and Graphs

Appendix II: Writing a Research Report

Boxes

RESEARCH IN ACTION: Framing Survey Questions about Interracial Friendships

SOCIOLOGY ON CAMPUS: Does Hard Work Lead to Better Grades?

TAKING SOCIOLOGY TO WORK: Paul Donato, Chief Research Officer, Nielsen Media Research

Because public interactions generally matter for only a few crucial seconds, people are conditioned to rapid scrutiny of the looks, speech, public behavior, gender, and color of those sharing the environment.... [T]he central strategy in maintaining safety on the streets is to avoid strange black males....

Many blacks perceive whites as tense or hostile to them in public. They pay attention to the amount of eye contact given. In general, black males get far less time in this regard than do white males. Whites tend not to "hold" the eyes of a black person. It is more common for black and white strangers to meet each other's eyes for only a few seconds, and then to avert their gaze abruptly. Such behavior seems to say, "I am aware of your presence," and no more. Women especially feel that eye contact invites unwanted advances, but some white men feel the same and want to be clear about what they intend. This eye work is a way to maintain distance, mainly for safety and social purposes. Consistent with this, some blacks are very surprised to find a white person who holds their eyes longer than is normal according to the rules of the public sphere. As one middle-aged white female resident commented:

Just this morning, I saw a [black] guy when I went over to Mr. Chow's to get some milk at 7:15. You always greet people you see at 7:15, and I looked at him and smiled. And he said "Hello" or "Good morning" or something. I smiled again. It was clear that he saw this as surprising. . . .

Many people, particularly those who see themselves as more economically privileged than others in the community, are careful not to let their eyes stray, in order to avoid an uncomfortable situation. As they walk down the street they pretend not to see other pedestrians, or they look right at them without speaking, a behavior many blacks find offensive....

Moreover, whites of the Village often scowl to keep young blacks at a social and physical distance. As they venture out on the streets of the Village and, to a lesser extent, of Northton, they may plant this look on their faces to ward off others who might mean them harm. Scowling by whites may be compared to gritting [looking "tough"] by blacks as a coping strategy. At times members of either group make such faces with little regard for circumstances, as if they were dressing for inclement weather. But on the Village streets it does not always storm, and such overcoats repel the sunshine as well as the rain, frustrating many attempts at spontaneous human communication. *(Anderson 1990: 208, 220–221)* ■ 🔄

Additional information about this excerpt can be found on the Online Learning Center at **www.mhhe.com/schaefer9.**

This study of "eye work" was part of extensive research into life on the street that sociologist Elijah Anderson conducted in two adjacent neighborhoods of Philadelphia—"the Village," a racially mixed area with mixed incomes, and "Northton," mostly Black and low-income. Anderson became intrigued with the nature of social interaction between strangers on the street shortly after moving into the Village community in 1975. Over the next 14 years he undertook a formal study. Using the interactionist perspective, he focused on how such a diverse group of people related to one another in everyday life. In particular, he was interested in their "public behavior," including the way they used eye contact in their daily encounters.

Like any good scientist, Anderson was thorough in his research. He interviewed residents, videotaped street scenes, took extensive notes, photographed settings, and hung out for hours at a time in the local bars, laundromats, and corner stores in the course of his observations. As a Black man, he was also able to draw on his own experiences with the Whites in his neighborhood. Anderson systematically traced how social changes—including gentrification of previously low-income areas, increasing drug use and crime, and declining city services—affected social relations and the ways people negotiated public spaces. Three of his books, *A Place on the Corner* (1978), *Streetwise* (1990), and *Code of the Streets* (1999), came out of this research, and he hopes other researchers will make use of his database for their own studies.

Effective sociological research can be quite thought-provoking. It may suggest many new questions about social interactions that require further study, such as why we make assumptions about people's intentions based merely on their gender or age or race. In some cases, rather than raising additional questions, a study will simply confirm previous beliefs and findings.

This chapter will examine the research process used in conducting sociological studies. How do sociologists go about setting up a research project? And how do they ensure that the results of the research are reliable and accurate? Can they carry out their research without stepping on the rights of those they study?

We will first look at the steps that make up the scientific method used in research. Then we will take a look at various techniques commonly used in sociological research, such as experiments, observations, and surveys. We will pay particular attention to the ethical challenges sociologists face in studying human behavior and to the debate raised by Max Weber's call for "value neutrality" in social science research. We will also examine the role that technology plays in research today. The social policy section considers the difficulties in researching the controversial subject of human sexuality.

Whatever the area of sociological inquiry and whatever the perspective of the sociologist—whether functionalist, conflict, interactionist, or any other—there is one crucial requirement: imaginative, responsible research that meets the highest scientific and ethical standards. ▪

WHAT IS THE SCIENTIFIC METHOD?

Like all of us, sociologists are interested in the central questions of our time. Is the family falling apart? Why is there so much crime in the United States? Is the world lagging behind in its ability to feed the population? Such issues concern most people, whether or not they have academic training. However, unlike the typical citizen, the sociologist has a commitment to use the *scientific method* in studying society. The scientific method is a systematic, organized series of steps that ensures maximum objectivity and consistency in researching a problem.

Many of us will never actually conduct scientific research. Why, then, is it important that we understand the scientific method? The answer is that it plays a major role in the workings of our society. Residents of the United States are constantly bombarded with "facts" or "data." A television news report informs us that "one in every two marriages in this country now ends in divorce," yet Chapter 14 will show that this assertion is based on misleading statistics. Almost daily, advertisers cite supposedly scientific studies to prove that their products are superior. Such claims may be accurate or exaggerated. We can better evaluate such information—and will not be fooled so easily—if we are familiar with the standards of

FIGURE 2-1

The Scientific Method

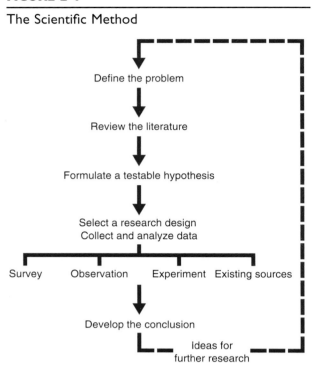

The scientific method allows sociologists to objectively and logically evaluate the data they collect. Their findings can suggest further ideas for sociological research.

scientific research. These standards are quite stringent, and demand as strict adherence as possible.

The scientific method requires precise preparation in developing useful research. Otherwise, the research data collected may not prove accurate. Sociologists and other researchers follow five basic steps in the scientific method: (1) defining the problem, (2) reviewing the literature, (3) formulating the hypothesis, (4) selecting the research design and then collecting and analyzing data, and (5) developing the conclusion (see Figure 2-1). We'll use an actual example to illustrate the workings of the scientific method.

Defining the Problem

Does it "pay" to go to college? Some people make great sacrifices and work hard to get a college education. Parents borrow money for their children's tuition. Students work part-time jobs or even take full-time positions while attending evening or weekend classes. Does it pay off? Are there monetary returns for getting that degree?

The first step in any research project is to state as clearly as possible what you hope to investigate—that is, *define the problem.* In this instance, we are interested in knowing how schooling relates to income. We want to find out the earnings of people with different levels of formal schooling. Early on, any social science researcher must develop an *operational definition* of each concept being studied. An **operational definition** is an explanation of an abstract concept that is specific enough to allow a researcher to assess the concept. For example, a sociologist interested in status might use membership in exclusive social clubs as an operational definition of status. Someone studying prejudice might consider a person's unwillingness to hire or work with members of minority groups as an operational definition of prejudice. In our example, we need to develop two operational definitions—education and earnings—in order to study whether it "pays" to get an advanced educational degree.

Initially, we will take a functionalist perspective (although we may end up incorporating other approaches). We will argue that opportunities for more earning power are related to level of schooling, and that schools prepare students for employment.

It seems reasonable to assume that these Columbia University graduates will earn more income than high school graduates. But how would you go about testing that hypothesis?

FIGURE 2-2

Educational Level and Household Income in the United States

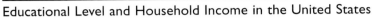

Mapping Life NATIONWIDE

www.
mhhe.com
/schaefer9

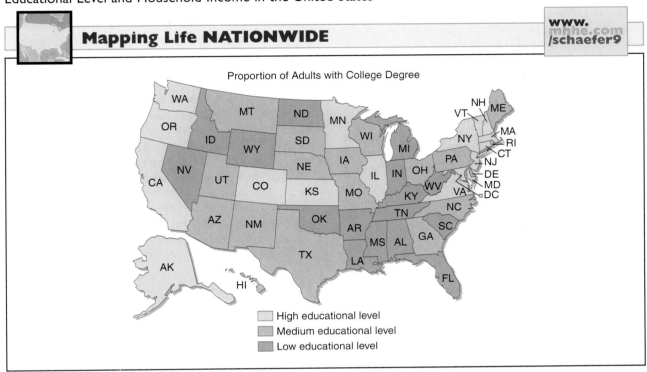

Proportion of Adults with College Degree

High educational level
Medium educational level
Low educational level

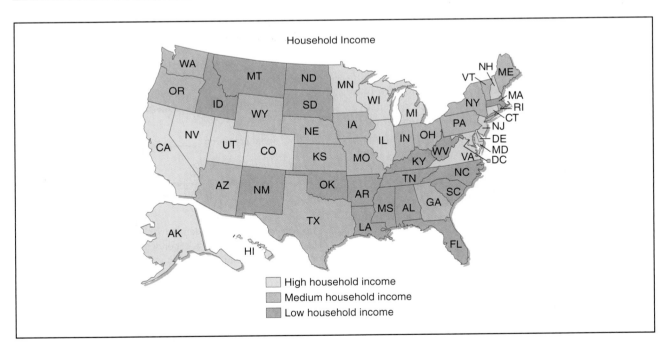

Household Income

High household income
Medium household income
Low household income

In general, states with high educational levels (top) also have high household incomes (bottom).

Notes: Education data are for 2000. Cutoffs for high/medium and medium/low educational levels were 27 percent and 23 percent of the population with a college degree, respectively; median for the entire nation was 25.6 percent. Income data are 2000-2001 2-year average medians. Cutoffs for high/medium and medium/low household income levels were $44,000 and $39,000, respectively; national median household income was $42,695.

Source: Bureau of the Census 2002a:141; DeNavas-Walt and Cleveland 2002:11.

Reviewing the Literature

By conducting a *review of the literature*—relevant scholarly studies and information—researchers refine the problem under study, clarify possible techniques to be used in collecting data, and eliminate or reduce avoidable mistakes. In our example, we would examine information about the salaries for different occupations. We would see if jobs that require more academic training are better rewarded. It would also be appropriate to review other studies on the relationship between education and income.

The review of the literature would soon tell us that many other factors besides years of schooling influence earning potential. For example, we would learn that the children of rich parents are more likely to go to college than those from modest backgrounds, so we might consider the possibility that these parents may later help their children secure better-paying jobs.

We might also look at macro-level data, such as state-by-state comparisons of income and educational levels. In one macro-level study based on census data, researchers found that in states whose residents have a relatively high level of education, household income levels are high as well (see Figure 2-2, page 31). This finding suggests that schooling may well be related to income, though it does not speak to the micro-level relationship we are interested in. That is, we want to know whether *individuals* who are well educated are also well paid.

Formulating the Hypothesis

After reviewing earlier research and drawing on the contributions of sociological theorists, the researchers may then *formulate the hypothesis*. A **hypothesis** is a speculative statement about the relationship between two or more factors known as variables. Income, religion, occupation, and gender can all serve as variables in a study. We can define a **variable** as a measurable trait or characteristic that is subject to change under different conditions.

Researchers who formulate a hypothesis generally must suggest how one aspect of human behavior influences or affects another. The variable hypothesized to cause or influence another is called the **independent variable**. The second variable is termed the **dependent variable** because its action "depends" on the influence of the independent variable.

Our hypothesis is that the higher one's educational degree, the more money one will earn. The independent variable that is to be measured is the level of education. The variable that is thought to "depend" on it—income—must also be measured.

Identifying independent and dependent variables is a critical step in clarifying cause-and-effect relationships.

As shown in Figure 2-3, **causal logic** involves the relationship between a condition or variable and a particular consequence, with one event leading to the other. For instance, being less integrated into society may be directly related to, or produce a greater likelihood of, suicide. Similarly, the time students spend reviewing material for a quiz may be directly related to, or produce a greater likelihood of, getting a high score on the quiz.

A **correlation** exists when a change in one variable coincides with a change in the other. Correlations are an indication that causality *may* be present; they do not necessarily indicate causation. For example, data indicate that working mothers are more likely to have delinquent children than are mothers who do not work outside the home. But this correlation is actually caused by a third variable: family income. Lower-class households are more likely to have a full-time working mother; at the same time, reported rates of delinquency are higher in this class than at other economic levels. Consequently, while

FIGURE 2-3

Causal Logic

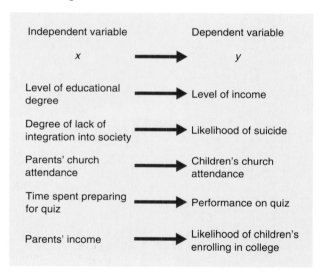

In *causal logic* an independent variable (often designated by the symbol *x*) influences a dependent variable (generally designated as *y*); thus, *x* leads to *y*. For example, parents who attend church regularly (*x*) are more likely to have children who are churchgoers (*y*). Notice that the first two pairs of variables are taken from studies already described in this textbook.

Think About It
Identify two or three dependent variables that might be influenced by this independent variable: number of alcoholic drinks ingested.

having a mother who works outside the home is correlated with delinquency, it does not *cause* delinquency. Sociologists seek to identify the *causal* link between variables; this causal link is generally described in the hypothesis.

Collecting and Analyzing Data

How do you test a hypothesis to determine if it is supported or refuted? You need to collect information, using one of the research designs described later in the chapter. The research design guides the researcher in collecting and analyzing data.

Selecting the Sample

In most studies, social scientists must carefully select what is known as a *sample*. A *sample* is a selection from a larger population that is statistically representative of that population. There are many kinds of samples, but the one social scientists use most frequently is the random sample. In a *random sample,* every member of an entire population being studied has the same chance of being selected. Thus, if researchers want to examine the opinions of people listed in a city directory (a book that, unlike the telephone directory, lists all households), they might use a computer to randomly select names from the directory. The results would constitute a random sample. The advantage of using specialized sampling techniques is that sociologists do not need to question everyone in a population.

It is all too easy to confuse the careful scientific techniques used in representative sampling with the many *nonscientific* polls that receive much more media attention. For example, television viewers and radio listeners are often encouraged to e-mail their views on today's headlines or on political contests. Such polls reflect nothing more than the views of those who happened to see the television program (or hear the radio broadcast) and took the time, perhaps at some cost, to register their opinions. These data do not necessarily reflect (and indeed may distort) the views of the broader population. Not everyone has access to a television or radio, time to watch or listen to a program, or the means and/or inclination to send e-mail. Similar problems are raised by the "mail-back" questionnaires found in many magazines and by "mall intercepts" in which shoppers are asked about some issue. Even when these techniques include answers from tens of thousands of people, they will be far less accurate than a carefully selected representative sample of 1,500 respondents.

For the purposes of our research example, we will use information collected in the General Social Survey (GSS). Since 1972, the National Opinion Research Center

(NORC) has conducted this national survey 23 times, most recently in 2002. A representative sample of the adult population is interviewed on a variety of topics for about one and a half hours. The author of this book examined the responses of the 1,875 people interviewed in 2002 concerning their level of education and income.

Ensuring Validity and Reliability

The scientific method requires that research results be both valid and reliable. *Validity* refers to the degree to which a measure or scale truly reflects the phenomenon under study. *Reliability* refers to the extent to which a measure produces consistent results. A valid measure of income depends on gathering accurate data. Various studies show that people are reasonably accurate in reporting how much money they earned in the most recent year. One problem of reliability is that some people may not *disclose* accurate information, but most do. In the General Social Survey, only 5 percent of the respondents refused to give their income or indicated they did not know what their income was. That means 95 percent of the respondents gave their income, which we can assume is reasonably accurate (given their other responses about occupation and years in the labor force).

"And don't waste your time canvassing the whole building, young man. We think alike."

When conducting a study, researchers must draw their sample carefully so that it is representative of the general population.

Table 2-1	**Education and Income**				
	Income by Education (Percentage of Graduates in Each Income Group)				
Income Group	**Less Than High School Education**	**High School Diploma**	**Associate's Degree**	**BA/BS**	**Graduate Degree**
Under $15,000	50%	31%	11%	17%	11%
$15,000–24,999	25	22	18	12	8
$25,000–34,999	14	26	32	22	17
$35,000–59,999	7	15	18	23	25
$60,000 and over	4	6	21	26	39
Total	100%	100%	100%	100%	100%

Source: Author's analysis of General Social Survey 2002 in J. A. Davis et al. 2003.

Developing the Conclusion

Scientific studies, including those conducted by sociologists, do not aim to answer all the questions that can be raised about a particular subject. Therefore, the conclusion of a research study represents both an end and a beginning. It terminates a specific phase of the investigation, but should also generate ideas for future study.

Supporting Hypotheses

In our example, we find that the data support our hypothesis: People with more formal schooling *do* earn more money. Those with a high school diploma earn more than those who failed to complete high school, but those with an associate's degree earn more than high school graduates. The relationship continues through more advanced levels of schooling, so that those with graduate degrees earn the most (see Table 2-1).

The relationship is not perfect. Obviously, some people who drop out of high school end up with high incomes, whereas some with advanced degrees have modest incomes, as shown in Figure 2-4. A successful entrepreneur, for example, might not have much formal schooling, and a holder of a doctorate degree may choose to work for a low-paying nonprofit institution. Sociologists are interested in both the general pattern that emerges from their data and exceptions to the pattern.

Sociological studies do not always generate data that support the original hypothesis. In many instances, a hypothesis is refuted, and researchers must reformulate their conclusions. Unexpected results may also lead sociologists to reexamine their methodology and make changes in the research design.

Controlling for Other Factors

A *control variable* is a factor that is held constant to test the relative impact of the independent variable. For example, if researchers wanted to know how adults in the United States feel about restrictions on smoking in public places, they would probably attempt to use a respondent's smoking behavior as a control variable. That is, how do smokers versus nonsmokers feel about smoking in public places? The researchers would compile separate statistics on how smokers and nonsmokers feel about antismoking regulations.

Our study of the influence of education on income suggests that not everyone enjoys equal educational p. 20–21 opportunities, a disparity that is one of the causes of social inequality. Since education affects a person's income, we may wish to call on the conflict perspective to explore this topic further. What impact does a person's race or gender have? Is a woman with a college degree likely to earn as much as a man with similar schooling? Later in this textbook we will consider these other factors and variables. We will examine the impact that education has on income, while controlling for variables such as gender and race.

In Summary: The Scientific Method

Let us briefly summarize the process of the scientific method through a review of the example. We *defined a*

Doonesbury

BY GARRY TRUDEAU

Think About It
What would constitute a less biased question for a survey on smoking?

problem (the question of whether it pays to get a higher educational degree). We *reviewed the literature* (other studies of the relationship between education and income) and *formulated a hypothesis* (the higher one's educational degree, the more money one will earn). We *collected and analyzed the data,* making sure the sample was representative and the data were valid and reliable.

Finally, we *developed the conclusion:* The data do support our hypothesis about the influence of education on income.

MAJOR RESEARCH DESIGNS

An important aspect of sociological research is deciding *how* to collect the data. A **research design** is a detailed plan or method for obtaining data scientifically. Selection of a research design is often based on the theories and hypotheses the researcher starts with (Merton 1948). The choice requires creativity and ingenuity, because it directly influences both the cost of the project and the amount of time needed to collect the data. Research designs that sociologists regularly use to generate data include surveys, observation, experiments, and existing sources.

Surveys

Almost all of us have responded to surveys of one kind or another. We may have been asked what kind of detergent we use, which presidential candidate we intend to vote for, or what our favorite television program is. A **survey** is a study, generally in the form of an interview or

FIGURE 2-4

Impact of a College Education on Income

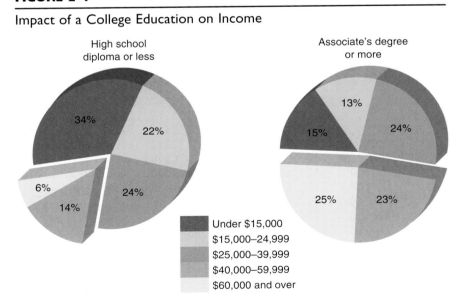

Source: Author's analysis of General Social Survey 2002 in J. A. Davis et al. 2003.

Fifty-six percent of people with a high school diploma or less (left) earn under $25,000 a year, while only 20 percent earn $40,000 or more. In contrast, 48 percent of those with an associate's degree or higher (right) earn $40,000 or more, while only 28 percent earn less than $25,000.

D o White people really have close Black friends, and vice versa? Many surveys have attempted to gauge the amount of White–Black interaction. But unless the questions are phrased carefully, it is possible to overestimate "racial togetherness."

Sociologist Tom Smith, who heads up the respected General Social Survey, no-

> Unless the questions are phrased carefully, it is possible to overestimate just how much "racial togetherness" is taking place.

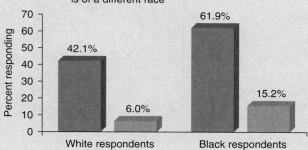

■ Percent who say they have a close friend who is Black or White

■ Percent who name a close friend who is of a different race

Source: T. Smith 1999.

ticed that a high proportion of Whites and African Americans indicate they have close friends of the other race. But is this statement in fact true? When Smith and his fellow researchers analyzed data from the 1998 General Social Survey, they found that response rates varied according to how the question was phrased.

For example, when asked whether any of the friends they feel close to was Black, 42.1 percent of Whites said "yes." Yet when asked to give the names of friends they feel close to, only 6 percent of Whites listed a close friend of a different race or ethnicity. The accompanying figure shows the results for both White and Black respondents.

Let's Discuss

1. Why do you think people responded so differently to these two questions? How would you frame a question to get an accurate picture of interracial friendships?

2. Do you have close friends of another race? If asked to list your close friends, would you list someone of a different race?

Source: T. Smith 1999.

questionnaire, that provides researchers with information about how people think and act. Among the United States' best-known surveys of opinion are the Gallup poll and the Harris poll. As anyone who watches the news during presidential campaigns knows, these polls have become a staple of political life.

When you think of surveys, you may recall seeing many "person on the street" interviews on local television news shows. Although such interviews can be highly entertaining, they are not necessarily an accurate indication of public opinion. First, they reflect the opinions of only those people who happen to be at a certain location. Such a sample can be biased in favor of commuters, middle-class shoppers, or factory workers, depending on which street or area the newspeople select. Second, television in-

terviews tend to attract outgoing people who are willing to appear on the air, while they frighten away others who may feel intimidated by a camera. As we've seen, a survey must use precise, representative sampling if it is to genuinely reflect a broad range of the population.

In preparing to conduct a survey, sociologists must not only develop representative samples; they must exercise great care in the wording of questions. An effective survey question must be simple and clear enough for people to understand. It must also be specific enough so that there are no problems in interpreting the results. Open-ended questions ("What do you think of the programming on educational television?") must be carefully phrased to solicit the type of information desired. Box 2-1 illustrates the different results that different phrasing of a question can produce. Surveys can be indispensable sources of information, but only if the sampling is done properly and the questions are worded accurately and without bias.

There are two main forms of surveys: the ***interview,*** in which a researcher obtains information through face-to-face or telephone questioning, and the ***questionnaire,*** in which the researcher uses a printed or written form to obtain information from a respondent. Each of these has its own advantages. An interviewer can obtain a higher response rate because people find it more difficult to turn down a personal request for an interview than to throw away a written questionnaire. In addition, a skillful interviewer can go beyond written questions and probe for a subject's underlying feelings and reasons. On the other hand, questionnaires have the advantage of being cheaper, especially in large samples.

Studies have shown that the characteristics of the interviewer have an impact on survey data. For example, women interviewers tend to receive more feminist responses from female subjects than do male researchers, and African American interviewers tend to receive more detailed responses about race-related issues from Black subjects than do White interviewers. The possible impact of gender and race indicates again how much care social research requires (D. Davis 1997; Huddy et al. 1997).

The survey is an example of ***quantitative research,*** which collects and reports data primarily in numerical form. Most of the survey research discussed so far in this book has been quantitative. While this type of research can make use of large samples, it can't offer great depth and detail on a topic. That is why researchers also make use of ***qualitative research,*** which relies on what is seen in field and naturalistic settings, and often focuses on small groups and communities rather than large groups or whole nations. The most common form of qualitative research is observation, which we consider next. Throughout this book you will find examples of both quantitative and qualitative research, since both are used widely. Some sociologists prefer one type of research to the other, but we learn most when we draw on many different research designs and do not limit ourselves to a particular type of research.

Observation

As we saw in the chapter opening, Elijah Anderson gathered his information on street life in Philadelphia through *observing* everyday interactions of the residents. Investigators who collect information through direct participation and/or closely watching a group or community are engaged in ***observation.*** This method allows sociologists to examine certain behaviors and communities that could not be investigated through other research techniques.

An increasingly popular form of qualitative research in sociology today is ethnography. ***Ethnography*** refers to efforts to describe an entire social setting through extended systematic observation. Typically, the description emphasizes how the subjects themselves view their social setting. Anthropologists rely heavily on ethnography. Much as an anthropologist seeks to understand the people of some Polynesian island, the sociologist as ethnographer seeks to understand and present an entire way of life in some setting. Anderson's study involved understanding not just the behavior of pedestrians but all facets of life in two urban neighborhoods (P. Adler and Adler 2003).

In some cases, the sociologist actually joins a group for a period of time to get an accurate sense of how it operates. This appoach is called *participant observation.* In the study of low-wage workers described in Chapter 1, as well as in Anderson's study of "eye work," the researcher was a participant observer.

During the late 1930s, in a classic example of participant-observation research, William F. Whyte moved into a low-income Italian neighborhood in Boston. For nearly four years, he was a member of the social circle of "corner boys" that he describes in *Street Corner Society.* Whyte revealed his identity to these men and joined in their conversations, bowling, and other leisure-time activities. His goal was to gain greater insight into the community that these men had established. As Whyte (1981) listened to Doc, the leader of the group, he "learned the answers to questions I would not even have had the sense to ask if I had been getting my information solely on an interviewing basis" (p. 303). Whyte's work was especially valuable, since at the time the academic world had little direct knowledge of the poor, and tended to rely for information on the records of social service agencies, hospitals, and courts (Adler and Johnson 1992).

The initial challenge that Whyte faced—and that every participant observer encounters—was to gain acceptance into an unfamiliar group. It is no simple matter for a college-trained sociologist to win the trust of a religious cult, a youth gang, a poor Appalachian community, or a circle of skid row residents. It requires a great deal of patience and an accepting, nonthreatening type of personality on the part of the observer.

Observation research poses other complex challenges for the investigator. Sociologists must be able to fully understand what they are observing. In a sense, then, researchers must learn to see the world as the group sees it in order to fully comprehend the events taking place around them.

Does arresting someone for domestic assault deter the person from committing future incidents of violence? Researchers in Miami, Florida, studied this question in the field by making use of control and experimental groups.

This raises a delicate issue. If the research is to be successful, the observer cannot allow the close associations or even friendships that inevitably develop to influence the subjects' behavior or the conclusions of the study. Anson Shupe and David Bromley (1980), two sociologists who have used participant observation, have likened this challenge to that of walking a tightrope. Even while working hard to gain acceptance from the group being studied, the participant observer *must* maintain some degree of detachment.

The feminist perspective in sociology has drawn attention to a shortcoming in ethnographic research. For most of the history of sociology, studies were conducted on male subjects or about male-led groups and organizations, and the findings were generalized to all people. For example, for many decades studies of urban life focused on street corners, neighborhood taverns, and bowling alleys—places where men typically congregated. Although the insights gained were valuable, they did not give a true impression of city life because they overlooked the areas where women were likely to gather, such as playgrounds, grocery stores, and front stoops. The feminist perspective focuses on these arenas. Feminist researchers also tend to involve and consult their subjects more than other researchers, and they are more oriented to seeking change, raising consciousness, and trying to affect policy. In addition, feminist researchers are particularly open to a multidisciplinary approach, such as making use of historical evidence or legal studies as well as feminist theory (T. Baker 1999; L. Lofland 1975; Reinharz 1992).

Experiments

When sociologists want to study a possible cause-and-effect relationship, they may conduct experiments. An *experiment* is an artificially created situation that allows the researcher to manipulate variables.

In the classic method of conducting an experiment, two groups of people are selected and matched for

How do people respond to being observed? Evidently these employees at the Hawthorne plant enjoyed the attention paid them when researchers observed them at work. No matter what variables were changed, the workers increased their productivity, even when the level of lighting was *reduced*.

similar characteristics, such as age or education. The researchers then assign the subjects to one of two groups: the experimental or the control group. The ***experimental group*** is exposed to an independent variable; the ***control group*** is not. Thus, if scientists were testing a new type of antibiotic drug, they would administer that drug to an experimental group but not to a control group.

Sociologists don't often rely on this classic form of experiment, because it generally involves manipulating human behavior in an inappropriate manner, especially in a laboratory setting. However, they do try to re-create experimental conditions in the field. For example, they may compare children's academic performance in two schools with different curricula. Another area of investigation that has led to several experimental studies in the field is police action in domestic assault cases. Emergency calls to a household where domestic violence is occurring account for a significant part of a police officer's work. Sociologists Anthony Pate and Edwin Hamilton (1992) studied cases in Dade County (Miami) Florida in which officers did or did not arrest the violent suspect, and then looked at the effect of the arrest or nonarrest on future incidents of assault in the household. In other words, they compared cases in which no arrest was made (the control group) with incidents in which the suspect was arrested (experimental group). They found that an arrest did have a deterrent effect if the suspect was employed. Pate and Hamilton concluded that while an arrest may be a sobering experience for any individual, the impact of being taken to a police station is greater if a person is employed and is forced to explain what is happening in his or her personal life to a boss.

In some experiments, just as in observation research, the presence of a social scientist or other observer may affect the behavior of the people being studied. The recognition of this phenomenon grew out of an experiment conducted during the 1920s and 1930s at the Hawthorne plant of the Western Electric Company. A group of researchers set out to determine how to improve the productivity of workers at the plant. The investigators manipulated such variables as the lighting and working hours to see what impact the changes had on productivity. To their surprise, they found that *every* step they took seemed to increase productivity. Even measures that seemed likely to have the opposite effect, such as reducing the amount of lighting in the plant, led to higher productivity.

Why did the plant's employees work harder even under less favorable conditions? Their behavior apparently was influenced by the greater attention being paid to them in the course of the research, and by the novelty of being subjects in an experiment. Since that time, sociologists have used the term ***Hawthorne effect*** in referring to

subjects of research who deviate from their typical behavior because they realize that they are under observation (S. Jones 1992; Lang 1992; Pelton 1994).

Use Your Sociological Imagination www.mhhe.com/schaefer9

You are a researcher interested in the effect of TV watching on schoolchildren's grades. How would you go about setting up an experiment to measure this effect?

Use of Existing Sources

Sociologists do not necessarily need to collect new data in order to conduct research and test hypotheses. The term ***secondary analysis*** refers to a variety of research techniques that make use of previously collected and publicly accessible information and data. Generally, in conducting secondary analysis, researchers utilize data in ways that were unintended by the initial collectors of information. For example, census data are compiled for specific uses by the federal government, but are also valuable to marketing specialists in locating everything from bicycle stores to nursing homes.

Sociologists consider secondary analysis to be *nonreactive*, since it does not influence people's behavior. As an example, Émile Durkheim's statistical analysis of suicide neither increased nor decreased human self-destruction. Researchers, then, can avoid the Hawthorne effect by using secondary analysis.

There is one inherent problem, however: the researcher who relies on data collected by someone else may not find exactly what is needed. Social scientists

Content analysis of recent films finds this unstated message: smoking is cool. In this still from the 2001 movie *Bridget Jones's Diary*, Renee Zellweger enjoys a cigarette. If the movie industry is made aware of the frequency of such scenes and the message they send to young viewers, perhaps executives will try to alter the message.

Table 2-2	**Existing Sources Used in Sociological Research**

Most Frequently Used Sources

Census data

Crime statistics

Birth, death, marriage, and divorce statistics

Other Sources

Newspapers and periodicals

Personal journals, diaries, e-mail, and letters

Records and archival material of religious organizations, corporations, and other organizations

Transcripts of radio programs

Videotapes of motion pictures and television programs

Webpages

Song lyrics

Scientific records (such as patent applications)

Speeches of public figures (such as politicians)

Votes cast in elections or by elected officials on specific legislative proposals

Attendance records for public events

Videotapes of social protests and rallies

Literature, including folklore

studying family violence can use statistics from police and social service agencies on *reported* cases of spouse abuse and child abuse. But how many cases are not reported? Government bodies have no precise data on *all* cases of abuse.

Many social scientists find it useful to study cultural, economic, and political documents, including newspapers, periodicals, radio and television tapes, the Internet, scripts, diaries, songs, folklore, and legal papers, to name some examples (see Table 2-2). In examining these sources, researchers employ a technique known as ***content analysis,*** which is the systematic coding and objective recording of data, guided by some rationale.

Using content analysis, Erving Goffman (1979) conducted a pioneering exploration of how advertisements portrayed women as inferior to men. The ads typically showed women as being subordinate to or dependent on others, or as being instructed by men. They engaged in caressing and touching gestures more than men. Even when presented in leadership-type roles, women were likely to be shown in seductive poses, or gazing out into space.

Today, researchers analyzing the content of films are finding an increase in smoking in motion pictures, despite increased public health concerns. For example, a 1999 content analysis showed that tobacco use appeared in 89 percent of the 200 most popular movie rentals. This type of content analysis can have clear social policy implications if it draws the attention of the motion picture industry to the message it may be delivering (especially to young people), that smoking is acceptable, even desirable (Kang 1997; D. Roberts et al. 1999).

Often, research designs mix different techniques. In the study described in Box 2-2, the researchers combined survey research with existing sources to investigate the relationship between college students' behavior and their academic achievement.

ETHICS OF RESEARCH

A biochemist cannot inject a drug into a human being unless it has been thoroughly tested and the subject agrees to the shot. To do otherwise would be both

Does a serious work ethic pay off in better grades? Sociologist William Rau wanted to answer that question. Working with Ann Durand, a former student who is now employed in the research department of State Farm Insurance Companies, Rau devised a research study. The dependent variable was easy to measure—the two could use an already existing data source, students' grade point averages (GPAs), as their operational definition. But how could they measure the independent variable, a student's work ethic?

After considering many possibilities, the two researchers decided to focus on students' drinking behavior and study habits. They developed a scale comprised of a series of items on which students rated their drinking and studying behavior. At one extreme were many hours of daily studying and abstention from drinking. At the other extreme were fre-

quent drinking—even on weekdays—and infrequent studying, usually cramming just before tests. The operational definition of students' work ethic became students' self-reports of their drinking and studying behavior in response to a series of questions.

Rau and Durand administered their

> Generally, students who drank less and studied more performed better.

behavior scale to 255 students and then compared the scores on the scale to students' GPAs. The results were fairly striking. Generally, those students who drank less and studied more than others performed better academically, as measured by their GPAs. The researchers had been careful to control for students' ability lev-

els using two more existing sources of data, students' class ranks in high school and their scores on college entrance exams. These sources indicated that the abstainers had not arrived at college better prepared than other students. Hard work really *does* pay off in better grades.

Let's Discuss

1. Where does your own drinking and studying behavior fall on Rau and Durand's behavior scale? What is your GPA? Is your academic achievement consistent with your drinking and studying behavior?

2. What other ways of measuring a student's work ethic could the researchers have considered? Can you think of any other variable besides a student's ability level that might have distorted the study's results?

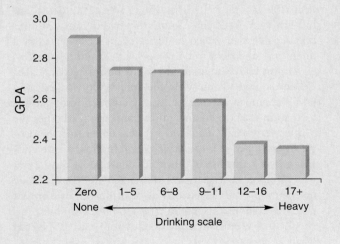

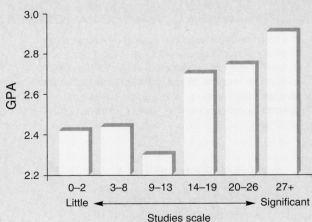

Source: Rau and Durand 2000.

unethical and illegal. Sociologists must also abide by certain specific standards in conducting research, called a ***code of ethics.*** The professional society of the discipline, the American Sociological Association (ASA), first published the Code of Ethics in 1971 and revised it most recently in 1997. It puts forth the following basic principles:

1. Maintain objectivity and integrity in research.

2. Respect the subject's right to privacy and dignity.

3. Protect subjects from personal harm.

4. Preserve confidentiality.

5. Seek informed consent when data are collected from research participants or when behavior occurs in a private context.

Are some people who die in single-occupant car crashes actually suicides? One sociological study of possible "autocides" concluded that at least 12 percent of such accident victims did in fact commit suicide. But the study also raised some ethical questions concerning the right to know and the right to privacy.

6. Acknowledge research collaboration and assistance.
7. Disclose all sources of financial support (American Sociological Association 1997).

These basic principles probably seem clear-cut. How could they lead to any disagreement or controversy? Yet many delicate ethical questions cannot be resolved simply by reading these seven principles. For example, should a sociologist who is engaged in participant-observation research always protect the confidentiality of subjects? What if the subjects are members of a religious cult allegedly engaged in unethical and possibly illegal activities? What if the sociologist is interviewing political activists and is questioned by government authorities about the research?

Because most sociological research uses *people* as sources of information—as respondents to survey questions, subjects of observation, or participants in experiments—these sorts of questions are important. In all cases, sociologists need to be certain they are not invading their subjects' privacy. Generally, they do so by assuring subjects of anonymity and by guaranteeing the confidentiality of their personal information. In addition, research proposals that involve human subjects must now be overseen by a review board, whose members seek to ensure that subjects are not placed at an unreasonable level of risk. If necessary, the board may ask researchers to revise their research designs to conform to the code of ethics. We can appreciate the ethical problems researchers confront by considering a study done by William Zellner in the 1970s, described in the following section. This study raised some serious concerns about the extent to which sociologists can threaten people's right to privacy.

The Right to Know versus the Right to Privacy

A car lies at the bottom of a cliff, its driver dead. Was this an accident or a suicide? Sociologist William Zellner (1978) wanted to learn if fatal car crashes are sometimes suicides disguised as accidents in order to protect family and friends (and perhaps to collect otherwise unredeemable insurance benefits). Such acts of "autocide" are by nature covert. Zellner found that research on automobile accidents in which fatalities occur poses an ethical dilemma—the right to know versus the right to privacy.

In his efforts to assess the frequency of such suicides, Zellner sought to interview the friends, co-workers, and family members of the deceased. He hoped to obtain information that would allow him to ascertain whether the deaths were accidental or deliberate. Zellner told the people he approached for interviews that his goal was to contribute to a reduction of future accidents by learning about the emotional characteristics of accident victims. He made no mention of his suspicions of autocide, out of fear that potential respondents would refuse to meet with him.

Zellner eventually concluded that at least 12 percent of all fatal single-occupant crashes are suicides. This information could be valuable to society, particularly since some of the probable suicides actually killed or critically injured innocent bystanders in the process of taking their own lives. Yet the ethical questions still must be faced. Was Zellner's research unethical because he misrepresented his motives and failed to obtain his subjects' informed consent? Or was his deception justified by the social value of his findings?

The answers to these questions are not immediately apparent. Zellner appeared to have admirable motives and took great care in protecting his subjects' confidentiality. He did not reveal the names of suspected suicides to insurance companies, though he did recommend that the insurance industry drop double indemnity (payment of twice the person's life insurance benefits in the event of an accidental death).

Zellner's study raised an additional ethical issue: the possibility of harm to those who were interviewed. Subjects were asked if the deceased had "talked about suicide" or spoken of feeling "bad or useless." Could these questions have led people to guess Zellner's true intentions? Perhaps, but according to Zellner, none of the informants voiced such suspicions. More seriously, might the study have caused the bereaved subjects to *suspect* suicide— when before the survey they had accepted the deaths as accidental? Again, there is no evidence to suggest this, but we cannot be sure.

Given our uncertainty about this last question, was the research justified? Was Zellner taking too big a risk in asking the friends and families if the deceased victims had spoken of suicide before their death? Does the right to know outweigh the right to privacy in this type of situation? And who has the right to make such a judgment? In practice, as in Zellner's study, it is the *researcher,* not the subjects of inquiry, who makes the critical ethical decisions. Therefore, sociologists and other investigators bear the responsibility for establishing clear and sensitive boundaries for ethical scientific investigation.

Preserving Confidentiality

Like journalists, sociologists occasionally find themselves subject to questions from law enforcement authorities because of knowledge they have gained in conducting research. This uncomfortable situation raises profound ethical questions.

In May 1993, Rik Scarce, a doctoral candidate in sociology at Washington State University, was jailed for contempt of court. Scarce had declined to tell a federal grand jury what he knew—or even whether he knew anything—about a 1991 raid on a university research laboratory by animal rights activists. At the time, Scarce was conducting research for a book about environmental protestors, and knew at least one suspect in the break-in. Curiously, although he was chastised by a federal judge, Scarce won respect from fellow prison inmates, who regarded him as a man who "wouldn't snitch" (Monaghan 1993:A8).

The American Sociological Association supported Scarce's position when he appealed his sentence. Scarce maintained his silence. Ultimately the judge ruled that nothing would be gained by further incarceration, and Scarce was released after serving 159 days in jail. In January 1994, the U.S. Supreme Court declined to hear Scarce's case on appeal. The Court's failure to consider his case led Scarce (1994, 1995) to argue that federal legislation is needed to clarify the rights of scholars and members of the press to preserve the confidentiality of research subjects.

Neutrality and Politics in Research

The ethical considerations of sociologists lie not only in the methods they use but also in the way they interpret results. Max Weber ([1904] 1949) recognized that personal values would influence the questions that sociologists select for research. In his view, that was perfectly acceptable, but under no conditions could a researcher allow his or her personal feelings to influence the *interpretation* of data. In Weber's phrase, sociologists must practice **value neutrality** in their research.

As part of this neutrality, investigators have an ethical obligation to accept research findings even when the data run counter to their own personal views, to theoretically based explanations, or to widely accepted beliefs. For example, Émile Durkheim challenged popular conceptions when he reported that social (rather than supernatural) forces were an important factor in suicide.

Some sociologists believe that neutrality is impossible. At the same time, Weber's insistence on value-free sociology may lead the public to accept sociological conclusions without exploring researchers' biases. Drawing on the conflict perspective, Alvin Gouldner (1970), among others, has suggested that sociologists may use objectivity as a justification for remaining uncritical of existing institutions and centers of power. These arguments are attacks not so much on Weber himself as on the way his goals have been misinterpreted. As we have seen, Weber was quite clear that sociologists may bring values to their subject matter. In his view, however, they must not confuse their own values with the social reality under study (Bendix 1968).

Let's consider what might happen when researchers bring their own biases to the investigation. A person investigating the impact of intercollegiate sports on alumni contributions, for example, may focus only on the highly visible revenue-generating sports of football and basketball, and neglect the so-called "minor sports," such as tennis or soccer, which are more likely to involve women athletes. Despite the early work of W. E. B. Du Bois and Jane Addams, sociologists still need to be reminded that the discipline often fails to adequately consider all people's social behavior.

In her book *The Death of White Sociology* (1973) Joyce Ladner called attention to the tendency of mainstream sociology to treat the lives of African Americans as a social

p. 8

A homeless woman living in Chicago. Sociologist Peter Rossi came under attack by the Chicago Coalition for the Homeless for finding in a carefully researched study that the city's homeless population was far below the Coalition's estimate. The Coalition accused Rossi of hampering their efforts at social reform.

problem. More recently, feminist sociologist Shulamit Reinharz (1992) has argued that sociological research should be not only inclusive but open to bringing about social change and to drawing on relevant research by nonsociologists. Both Reinharz and Ladner maintain that researchers should always analyze whether women's unequal social status has affected the study in any way. For example, one might broaden the study of the impact of education on income to consider the implications of the unequal pay status of men and women. The issue of value neutrality does not mean that sociologists can't have opinions, but it does mean that they must work to overcome any biases, however unintentional, that they may bring to their analysis of the research.

Peter Rossi (1987) admits to having liberal inclinations that direct him to fields of study. Yet, in line with Weber's view of value neutrality, Rossi's commitment to rigorous research methods and objective interpretation of data has sometimes led him to controversial findings that are not necessarily supportive of his own liberal values. For example, his measure of the extent of homelessness in Chicago in the mid-1980s fell far below the estimates of the Chicago Coalition for the Homeless. Coalition members bitterly attacked Rossi for hampering their social reform efforts by minimizing the extent of homelessness. Rossi (1987:79) concluded that "in the short term, good social research will often be greeted as a betrayal of one or another side to a particular controversy."

TECHNOLOGY AND SOCIOLOGICAL RESEARCH

Advances in technology have affected all aspects of our lives, and sociological research is no exception. The increased speed and capacity of computers are enabling

Computers have vastly extended the range and capability of sociological research, both by allowing large amounts of data to be stored and analyzed and by facilitating communication with other researchers via websites, newsgroups, and e-mail.

PAUL DONATO Chief Research Officer, Nielsen Media Research

For more than two decades, Paul Donato has been active in media research, both at home and abroad, and in both the print and electronic communication industries. In his current position he oversees research in television ratings, those vital figures that help executives determine how much commercials should sell for on various television programs. A typical work day takes him from client meetings to administrative work and staff management.

Donato began his study of sociology in the late 1960s and early 1970s, "a particularly interesting time for me from a social policy point of view—for studying what was happening in the streets." His undergraduate sociology degree and his master's in methodological research, both from the State University of New York at Stony Brook, introduced him to conflict theory, systems theory, functional and qualitative analysis, communications and management theory, and critical analysis—all of which he says are relevant to his career. Although Donato acknowledges that you can't manage from a book, he thinks it helps to at least be informed about issues before you have to face them.

Donato credits exposure to various ideological perspectives in sociology for his success in the emerging markets abroad, particularly those undergoing political instability. "Most people think we only care about the United States. So anything that you understand about other people's culture, society, ideologies, and politics immediately establishes credibility as you build a business relationship."

Donato's advice to students: "Set objectives for yourself in your study of sociology. Look at the content of your courses and try to figure out the connections with what you think you want to be doing 10 years later."

Let's Discuss

1. Using your sociological imagination, describe what sorts of information a sociologist might glean from an analysis of TV ratings.
2. Do you know what you want to be doing 10 years from now? If so, what connections, if any, do you see between your career choice and the study of sociology?

---

sociologists to handle larger and larger sets of data. In the recent past, only people with grants or major institutional support could easily work with census data. Now anyone with a desktop computer and modem can access census information and learn more about social behavior. Moreover, data from foreign countries concerning crime statistics and health care are sometimes as available as information from the United States.

Researchers usually rely on computers to deal with quantitative data—that is, numerical measures—but electronic technology is also assisting us with qualitative data, such as information obtained in observational research. Numerous software programs such as Ethnograph and NUD*IST allow the researcher not only to record observations but also to identify common behavioral patterns or similar concerns expressed in interviews. For example, after observing students in a college cafeteria over several weeks and putting your observations into the computer, you could group all your observations according to certain variables, such as "sorority" or "study group."

The Internet affords an excellent opportunity to communicate with fellow researchers as well as to locate useful information on social issues that has been posted on websites. It would be impossible to calculate all the sociological postings on websites or Internet mailing lists. Of course, you need to apply the same critical scrutiny to Internet material that you would to any printed resource.

How useful is the Internet for conducting survey research? That is still unclear. It is relatively easy to send out a questionnaire or post one on an electronic bulletin board. This is an inexpensive way to reach large numbers of potential respondents and get a quick response. However, there are some obvious dilemmas. How do you protect a respondent's anonymity? How do you define the potential audience? Even if you know to whom you sent the questionnaire, the respondents may forward it to others.

Web-based surveys are still in their early stages. Even so, the initial results are promising. For example, Inter-Survey has created a pool of Internet respondents, initially selected by telephone, to serve as a diverse and representative sample. Using similar methods to locate 50,000 adult respondents in 33 nations, the National Geographic Society conducted an online survey that focused on migration and regional culture. Social scientists are closely monitoring these new approaches to gauge how they might revolutionize one type of research design (Bainbridge 1999; Morin 2000).

This new technology is exciting, but there is one basic limitation to the methodology: Internet surveying works only with those who are online, who have access to the Internet. For some market researchers, such a limitation is acceptable. For example, if you were interested in the willingness of Internet users to order books or make

travel reservations online, limiting the sample population to those who are already online makes sense. However, if you were surveying the general public about their plans to buy a computer in the coming year or their views on a particular candidate, your online research would need to be supplemented by more traditional sampling procedures, such as mailed questionnaires.

Sociological research relies on a number of tools, from observational research and use of existing sources to the latest technology. We turn now to a research study that used a survey of the general population to learn more about a particular social behavior—human sexuality.

SOCIAL POLICY and SOCIOLOGICAL RESEARCH | Studying Human Sexuality |

The Issue

Reality TV shows often feature an attempt to create a relationship or even a marriage between two strangers. In a picturesque setting, an eligible bachelor or bride interviews potential partners—all of them good looking—and gradually eliminates those who seem less promising. The questions that are posed on camera can be explicit. "How many sexual partners have you had?" "How often would you be willing to have sex?"

The Kaiser Family Foundation conducts a study of sexual content on television every two years. The latest report, released in 2003, shows that more than two-thirds of all shows on TV include some sexual content, up from about half of all shows four years earlier (Figure 2-5). Media representations of sexual behavior are important because surveys of teens and young adults tell us that television is a top source of information and ideas about sex for them; it has more influence than schools, parents, or peers.

In this age of devastating sexually transmitted diseases, there is no time more important to increase our scientific understanding of human sexuality. As we will see, however, this is a difficult topic to research because of all the preconceptions, myths, and beliefs people bring to the subject of sexuality. How does one carry out scientific research on such a controversial and personal topic?

The Setting

Sociologists have little reliable national data on patterns of sexual behavior in the United States. Until recently, the only comprehensive study of sexual behavior was the famous two-volume Kinsey Report prepared in the

FIGURE 2-5

Percent of Television Shows That Contain Sexual Content

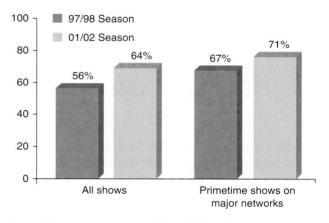

Source: Kaiser Family Foundation 2001:2, 2003:38, 40.

1940s (Kinsey et al. 1948, 1953). Although the Kinsey Report is still widely quoted, the volunteers interviewed for the report were not representative of the nation's adult population. Every two years the general public is interviewed as a part of the federally funded General Social Survey, which provides some useful information on sexual attitudes. For instance, Figure 2-6 shows how attitudes about premarital sexual behavior have changed since the early 1970s.

In part, we lack reliable data on patterns of sexual behavior because it is difficult for researchers to obtain accurate information about this sensitive subject. Moreover, until AIDS emerged in the 1980s, there was little

FIGURE 2-6

Views on Sex before Marriage

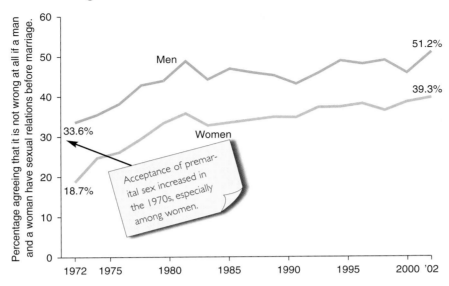

Source: Author's analysis of General Social Surveys, 1972–2002; see J. A. Davis et al. 2003.

scientific demand for data on sexual behavior, except for specific concerns such as contraception. Finally, even though the AIDS crisis has reached dramatic proportions (as will be discussed in the social policy section of Chapter 5), government funding for studies of sexual behavior is controversial. Because the General Social Survey concerns sexual attitudes rather than behavior, its funding has not been jeopardized.

Sociological Insights

The controversy surrounding research on human sexual behavior raises the issue of value neutrality, which becomes especially delicate when one considers the relationship of sociology to the government. The federal government has become the major source of funding for sociological research. Yet Max Weber urged that sociology remain an autonomous discipline, and not become unduly influenced by any one segment of society. According to Weber's ideal of value neutrality, sociologists must remain free to reveal information that is embarrassing to the government or, for that matter, is supportive of government institutions. Thus, researchers who are investigating a prison riot must be ready to examine objectively not only the behavior of inmates but also the conduct of prison officials before and during the outbreak.

Conflict theorists and feminists, among others, have been critical of some research that claims to be objective. In turn, their research is occasionally criticized

for not sufficiently addressing Weber's principle of value neutrality. In any case, maintaining objectivity may be difficult if sociologists fear that findings which are critical of government institutions will jeopardize their chances of obtaining federal support for new research projects.

Although the American Sociological Association's *Code of Ethics* requires sociologists to disclose all funding sources, it does not address the issue of whether sociologists who accept funding from a particular agency may also accept the agency's perspective on what needs to be studied. Lewis Coser (1956:27) has argued that as sociologists in the United States have increasingly turned from basic sociological research to research that has applications in government agencies and the private sector, "they have relinquished to a large extent the freedom to choose their own problems, substituting the problems of their clients for those which might have interested them on purely theoretical grounds." Viewed in this light, government funding of sociological studies raises troubling questions for those who cherish Weber's ideal of value neutrality in research. As we will see in the next section, applied sociological research on human sexuality has run into barriers constructed by government funding agencies.

Policy Initiatives

In 1987 the National Institute of Child Health and Human Development sought proposals for a national survey of sexual behavior. Sociologists responded with various plans that a review panel of scientists approved for funding. However, in 1991, led by Senator Jesse Helms and other conservatives, the U.S. Senate voted 66–34 to forbid funding any survey on adult sexual practices. Helms appealed to popular fears by arguing that such surveys were intended to "legitimize homosexual lifestyles" and to support "sexual decadence." Two years earlier, a similar debate in Great Britain had led to the denial of government funding for a national sex survey (A. Johnson et al. 1994; Laumann et al. 1994a:36).

Despite the vote by the U.S. Senate, sociologists Edward Laumann, John Gagnon, Stuart Michaels, and Robert Michael developed the National Health and Social Life Survey (NHSLS) to better understand the sexual practices of adults in the United States. The researchers raised $1.6 million of *private* funding to make their study possible (Laumann et al. 1994a, 1994b).

The researchers made great efforts to ensure privacy during the NHSLS interviews, as well as confidentiality and security in maintaining data files. Perhaps because of this careful effort, the interviewers did not typically experience problems getting responses, even though they were asking people about their sexual behavior. All interviews were conducted in person, although a confidential form included questions about sensitive subjects such as family income and masturbation. The researchers used several techniques to test the accuracy of subjects' responses, such as asking redundant questions at different times and in different ways during the 90-minute interview. These careful procedures helped to establish the validity of the NHSLS findings.

Research dealing with human sexuality continues to receive special scrutiny by Congress. In July 2003, by a vote of 212 to 210, the House of Representatives narrowly defeated an effort to block funding for a series of grants approved by the National Institutes of Health. The four grants were earmarked for the collection of data on sexual risk taking, the sexual habits of older men, drug use and HIV-related behavior, and bisexuality. Even after final approval by the scientific community, then, proposals to investigate human sexuality may run into political interference (Associated Press 2003).

Despite these political battles, the authors of the NHSLS believe that their research is important. They argue that using data from their survey allows us to more easily address public policy issues such as AIDS, sexual harassment, rape, welfare reform, sex discrimination, abortion, teenage pregnancy, and family planning.

This sexually provocative billboard in Beijing advertises South Korean cell phones. Increasingly, multinational companies are turning to sex to sell sophisticated consumer products to younger-generation Chinese.

Moreover, the research findings help to counter some "commonsense" notions. For instance, contrary to the popular beliefs that women regularly use abortion for birth control, and that poor teens are the most likely socioeconomic group to have abortions, researchers found that three-fourths of all abortions are the first for the woman, and that well-educated and affluent women are more likely to have abortions than poor teens (Sweet 2001).

Scholars in China, aware of the NHSLS, have begun to collaborate with sociologists in the United States on a similar study in China. The data are just now being analyzed, but responses thus far indicate dramatic differences in the sexual behavior of people in their 20s, compared to that reported at the same age by people who are now in their 50s. Younger-generation Chinese are more active sexually and have more partners than their parents did. Partly in response to these preliminary results, the Chinese Ministry of Health has sought U.S. assistance on HIV/AIDS prevention and research (Braverman 2002).

Let's Discuss

1. Why is human sexuality a difficult subject to research? Would you feel comfortable answering questions about your own sex life?

2. How does value neutrality become an important issue in research sponsored by the government?

3. Describe the efforts that the NHSLS researchers made to ensure that their study was confidential and that the results were reliable and valid. If you were to conduct a survey of people in your community who engage in premarital sex, how would you set it up?

USING STATISTICS, TABLES, AND GRAPHS

In their effort to better understand social behavior, sociologists rely heavily on numbers and statistics. How large is the typical household today, compared to the typical household of 1980? If a community were to introduce drug education into its elementary schools, what would be the cost per pupil? Such questions, and many others, are most easily answered in numerical terms.

The most common summary measures used by sociologists are percentages, means, modes, and medians. A **percentage** shows a portion of 100. Use of percentages allows us to compare groups of different sizes. For example, if we were comparing financial contributors to a town's Baptist and Roman Catholic churches, the absolute numbers of contributors in each group could be misleading if there were many more Baptists than Catholics in the town. Through use of percentages, we could obtain a more meaningful comparison, showing the proportion of persons in each group who contribute to churches.

The **mean,** or *average,* is a number calculated by adding a series of values and then dividing by the number of values. For example, to find the mean of the numbers 5, 19, and 27, we add them together (for a total of 51), divide by the number of values (3), and discover that the mean is 17.

The **mode** is the single most common value in a series of scores. Suppose we were looking at the following scores on a 10-point quiz:

10	7
10	7
9	7
9	6
8	5
8	

The mode—the most frequent score on the quiz—is 7. While the mode is easier to identify than other summary measures, it tells sociologists little about all the other values. Hence, you will find much less use of the mode in this book than of the mean and the median.

The **median** is the midpoint or number that divides a series of values into two groups of equal numbers

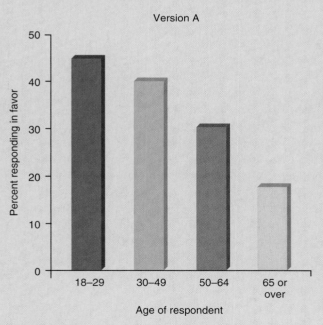

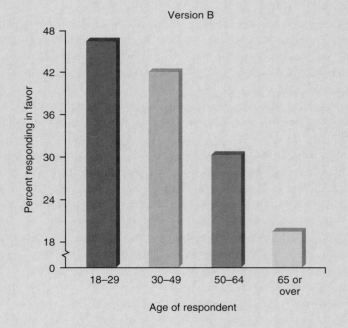

Source: General Social Survey in J. A. Davis et al. 2003.

of values. For the quiz just discussed, the median, or central value, is 8. The mean, or average, would be 86 (the sum of all scores) divided by 11 (the total number of scores), or 7.8.

In the United States, the median household income for the year 2001 was $42,228; this indicates that half of all households had incomes above $42,228, while half had lower incomes (DeNavas-Walt and Cleveland 2002). In many respects, the median is the most characteristic value. While it may not reflect the full range of scores, it does approximate the typical value in a set of scores, and is not affected by extreme scores.

Some of these statistics may seem confusing at first. But think how difficult it is to comb an endless list of numbers to identify a pattern or central tendency. Percentages, means, modes, and medians are essential time-savers in sociological research and analysis.

Tables allow social scientists to display data and make it easier for them to develop conclusions. A ***cross-tabulation*** is a type of table that illustrates the relationship between two or more characteristics.

During 2002, the National Opinion Research Center interviewed 847 people in the United States, ages 18 and over. Each respondent was interviewed and asked: "Do you think the use of marijuana should be made legal or not?" There is no way that, without some type of summary, analysts could examine hundreds of individual responses and reach firm conclusions. However, through use of the cross-tabulation presented in the accompanying table, we can quickly see that older people are less likely to favor legalization of marijuana than are younger people.

Percentage of Respondents for or against Legalization of Marijuana

Age of Respondent	For	Against
18–29 years	46%	54%
30–49 years	42	58
50–64 years	30	70
65 years and older	19	81

Source: General Social Survey in J. A. Davis et al. 2003.

Graphs, like tables, can be quite useful for sociologists. And illustrations are often easier for the general public to understand, whether they are in newspapers or in PowerPoint presentations. Still, as with all data, we need to be careful how they are presented. For example, the two bar graphs on page 50 present the same data concerning legalization of marijuana as in the table. Yet the differences in attitudes between the age groups seem much more striking in version B than in version A. Both figures are accurate, but because the vertical axis in B uses a different scale, it appears as if virtually no older respondents favored legalization. In reality, about one in five did, compared to a bit more than two of five of the youngest respondents.

WRITING A RESEARCH REPORT

Let's say that you have decided to write a report on cohabitation (unmarried couples living together). How do you go about doing the necessary library research? Students must follow procedures similar to those used by sociologists in conducting original research. First, you must define the problem that you wish to study—perhaps in this case, how much cohabitation occurs and what its impact is on marital happiness later. The next step is to review the literature, which generally requires library research.

The following steps will be helpful in finding information:

1. Check this textbook and other textbooks that you own. Don't forget to begin with the materials closest at hand, including CD-ROMs and sites on the Internet.

2. Use the library catalog. Computerized library systems now access not only the college library's collection but also books and magazines from other libraries available through interlibrary loans. These systems allow you to search for books by author or title. You can use title searches to locate books by subject as well. For example, if you search the title base for the keyword *cohabitation,* you will learn where books with that word somewhere in the title are located in the library's book stacks. Near these books will be other works on cohabitation that may not happen to have that word in the title. You may also want to search other related keywords, such as *unmarried couples.*

3. Investigate using computerized periodical indexes if available in your library. *Sociological Abstracts* online covers most sociological writing since 1974. A recent search of just this one database found more than 896 articles having either *unmarried couples* or *cohabitation* as keywords. Some dealt with laws about cohabitation while others focused on trends in other countries. If you limited your topic to same-sex couples, you would find 45 articles. Other electronic databases cover general-interest periodicals *(Time, Ms., National Review,*

Atlantic Monthly, and so forth), reference materials, or newspapers. These electronic systems may be connected to a printer, allowing you to produce your own printout complete with bibliographic information and sometimes even complete copies of articles.

4. Examine government documents. The United States government, states and cities, and the United Nations publish information on virtually every subject of interest to social science researchers. Publications of the Census Bureau, for example, include tables showing the number of unmarried couples living together and some social characteristics of these households. Many university libraries have access to a wide range of government reports. Consult the librarian for assistance in locating such materials.

5. Use newspapers. Major newspapers publish indexes annually or even weekly that are useful in locating information about specific events or issues. Academic Universe News is an electronic index to U.S. and international newspapers.

6. Ask people, organizations, and agencies concerned with the topic for information and assistance. Be as specific as possible in making requests. You might receive very different information on the issue of cohabitation from talking with marriage counselors and with clergy from different religions.

7. If you run into difficulties, consult the instructor, teaching assistant, or reference librarian at your college library.

Once you have completed all research, the task of writing the report can begin. Here are a few tips:

- Be sure the topic you have chosen is not too broad. You must be able to cover it adequately in a reasonable amount of time and a reasonable number of pages.
- Develop an outline for your report. You should have an introduction and a conclusion that relate

to each other—and the discussion should proceed logically throughout the paper. Use headings within the paper if they will improve clarity and organization.

- Do not leave all the writing until the last minute. It is best to write a rough draft, let it sit for a few days, and then take a fresh look before beginning revisions.
- If possible, read your paper *aloud.* Doing so may be helpful in locating sections or phrases that don't make sense.

Remember that you *must* cite all information you have obtained from other sources. If you use an author's exact words, it is essential that they be placed in quotation marks. Even if you reworked someone else's ideas, you must indicate the source of these ideas.

Some professors may require that students use footnotes in research reports. Others will allow students to employ the form of referencing used in this textbook, which follows the format of the American Sociological Association (ASA). If you see "(Merton 1968:27)" listed after a statement or paragraph, it means that the material has been quoted from page 27 of a work published by Merton in 1968 and listed in the reference section at the back of this textbook. (You can also consult the "Preparation checklist for ASA manuscripts," under "Publications," at the ASA website: www.asanet.org.)

CHAPTER RESOURCES

Summary

Sociologists are committed to the use of the scientific method in their research efforts. In this chapter, we examined the basic principles of the scientific method and studied various techniques used by sociologists in conducting research.

1. There are five basic steps in the **scientific method:** defining the problem, reviewing the literature, formulating the hypothesis, collecting and analyzing the data, and developing the conclusion.
2. Whenever researchers wish to study abstract concepts, such as intelligence or prejudice, they must develop workable **operational definitions.**
3. A **hypothesis** usually states a possible relationship between two or more variables.
4. By using a **sample,** sociologists avoid having to test everyone in a population.
5. According to the scientific method, research results must possess both **validity** and **reliability.**
6. An important part of scientific research is devising a plan for collecting data, called a **research design**. Sociologists use four major research designs: surveys, observation, experiments, and existing sources.
7. The two principal forms of **survey** research are the **interview** and the **questionnaire.**

8. **Observation** allows sociologists to study certain behaviors and communities that cannot be investigated through other research methods.
9. When sociologists wish to study a cause-and-effect relationship, they may conduct an **experiment.**
10. Sociologists also make use of existing sources in **secondary analysis** and **content analysis.**
11. The **Code of Ethics** of the American Sociological Association calls for objectivity and integrity in research, respect for the subject's privacy, and confidentiality.
12. Max Weber urged sociologists to practice **value neutrality** in their research by ensuring that their personal feelings do not influence the interpretation of data.
13. Technology today plays an important role in sociological research, whether it be a computer database or information from the Internet.
14. Despite failure to obtain government funding, researchers developed the National Health and Social Life Survey (NHSLS) to better understand the sexual practices of adults in the United States.

Critical Thinking Questions

1. Suppose that your sociology instructor has asked you to do a study of homelessness. Which research technique (survey, observation, experiment, or existing sources) would you find most useful? How would you use that technique to complete your assignment?

2. How can a sociologist genuinely maintain value neutrality while studying a group that he or she finds repugnant (for example, a White supremacist organization, a satanic cult, or a group of convicted rapists)?

3. Why is it important for sociologists to have a code of ethics?

Key Terms

Causal logic   The relationship between a condition or variable and a particular consequence in which one event leads to the other. (page 32)

Code of ethics   The standards of acceptable behavior developed by and for members of a profession. (41)

Content analysis   The systematic coding and objective recording of data, guided by some rationale. (40)

Control group   The subjects in an experiment who are not introduced to the independent variable by the researcher. (39)

Control variable   A factor that is held constant to test the relative impact of an independent variable. (34)

Correlation   A relationship between two variables in which a change in one coincides with a change in the other. (32)

Cross-tabulation   A table that shows the relationship between two or more variables. (51)

Dependent variable   The variable in a causal relationship that is subject to the influence of another variable. (32)

Ethnography   The study of an entire social setting through extended systematic observation. (37)

Experiment   An artificially created situation that allows the researcher to manipulate variables. (38)

Experimental group   The subjects in an experiment who are exposed to an independent variable introduced by a researcher. (39)

Hawthorne effect   The unintended influence that observers of experiments can have on their subjects. (39)

Hypothesis   A speculative statement about the relationship between two or more variables. (32)

Independent variable   The variable in a causal relationship that causes or influences a change in a second variable. (32)

Interview   A face-to-face or telephone questioning of a respondent to obtain desired information. (37)

Mean   A number calculated by adding a series of values and then dividing by the number of values. (50)

Median   The midpoint or number that divides a series of values into two groups of equal numbers of values. (50)

Mode   The single most common value in a series of scores. (50)

Observation   A research technique in which an investigator collects information through direct participation and/or closely watching a group or community. (37)

Operational definition   An explanation of an abstract concept that is specific enough to allow a researcher to assess the concept. (30)

Percentage   A portion of 100. (50)

Qualitative research   Research that relies on what is seen in field or naturalistic settings more than on statistical data. (37)

Quantitative research   Research that collects and reports data primarily in numerical form. (37)

Questionnaire   A printed or written form used to obtain desired information from a respondent. (37)

Random sample   A sample for which every member of the entire population has the same chance of being selected. (33)

Reliability   The extent to which a measure provides consistent results. (33)

Research design   A detailed plan or method for obtaining data scientifically. (35)

Sample   A selection from a larger population that is statistically representative of that population. (33)

Scientific method   A systematic, organized series of steps that ensures maximum objectivity and consistency in researching a problem. (29)

Secondary analysis   A variety of research techniques that make use of previously existing and publicly accessible information and data. (39)

Survey   A study, generally in the form of an interview or questionnaire, that provides researchers with information concerning how people think and act. (35)

Validity   The degree to which a scale or measure truly reflects the phenomenon under study. (33)

Value neutrality   Max Weber's term for objectivity of sociologists in the interpretation of data. (43)

Variable   A measurable trait or characteristic that is subject to change under different conditions. (32)

TECHNOLOGY RESOURCES

 Internet Connection

Note: While all the URLs listed were current as of the printing of this book, these sites often change. Please check our website (www. mhhe.com/schaefer9) for updates, hyperlinks, and exercises related to these sites.

1. An important aspect of sociological research is deciding how to collect data. Research designs that sociologists regularly use to generate data include surveys, observation, experiments, and existing

sources. To learn more about surveys, visit the Gallup poll homepage at www.gallup.com.

2. The Substance Abuse and Mental Health Services Administration (SAMHSA) conducts a national household survey on drug abuse. Read about Ecstasy use among adolescents and young adults by linking to www.samhsa.gov/oas/2k3/ecstasy/ecstasy.cfm.

 Online Learning Center with PowerWeb

When you visit the student center of the Online Learning Center, one of the Internet exercises for this chapter gives you the opportunity to become a sociological researcher, by taking Goffman's research into cyberspace. You will conduct a content analysis of two popular magazines

directed toward women and two popular magazines for men. You will be asked to look at the colors, models, clothing, and topics and analyze them from a sociological viewpoint. After this learning experience, you will never look at magazines the same way again!

 Reel Society Interactive Movie CD-ROM

Reel Society includes scenes that can be used to spark discussion about the following topics from this chapter:

- The Scientific Method
- Neutrality and Politics in Research

CULTURE

LA AND THE SOUTH PACIFIC // UNITED

THREE DAILY NONSTOPS TO THE SOUTH PACIFIC.

Each culture has its own forms of individual expression, as this billboard for United Airlines illustrates. The young woman from Los Angeles shows off her tongue stud while the South Pacific islander displays a ceremonial tattooed face.

Culture and Society

Development of Culture
around the World

Elements of Culture

Culture and the Dominant Ideology

Cultural Variation

Social Policy and Culture: Bilingualism

Boxes

SOCIOLOGY IN THE GLOBAL COMMUNITY: Life in
the Global Village

SOCIOLOGY ON CAMPUS: A Culture of Cheating?

Asok is a software engineer in one of the showcase companies in Silicon Valley, a gleaming edifice of glass and tile. He and his wife were born in India. Like many of his network of friends, he went to Stanford University to pursue a graduate degree and found work in a large company. He stayed in that company for three years, coding, learning American ways, and discovering that political hierarchies in American workplaces are very different from those he had known in India. Eager and enthusiastic, he put his heart and soul into his first project. His teammates were like family. They worked long hours together, eighty to a hundred hours per week in the crunch times. They went to Burgess Park for picnics, and loaned each other money. It was a heady experience. Suddenly, the product on which his project was based was canceled. His group was broken up and his teammates were distributed among a number of other projects. . . .

Priyesh and his wife, Sima, old friends of Asok's, are having breakfast. Sima tells Priyesh that her relatives were asking if they will go back to India soon. They shake their heads, wondering why they would want to go back. She says, "I do not miss India . . . anything Indian I want I have it right here—grocery stores, temples, cultural programs, Hindu magazines. There are three movie theaters in the Bay Area showing Hindi movies seven days a week. I only miss my family." Priyesh reflects that here in Silicon Valley he can have all the good parts of India—the people and cul-

cultures@siliconvalley

j.a.english-lueck

ture—without having to put up with a decaying bureaucracy and failing infrastructure. They argue gently about whether they really live in an Indian world. She points out that while many of their friends are Indian, including a recently immigrated cousin, Priyesh still has to work with many non-Indians.

Sima adds that she has to interact with very different cultures in their son's preschool—where they celebrate Chinese New Year and Cinco de Mayo. She pauses and then notes that it isn't really too different from interacting with all the different religions and cultures back in India. Priyesh scoffs at the whole problem. All these cultural differences don't matter to him. When he is at work, it is the technology that matters. . . .

Priyesh goes back into his home office. He makes a practice of telecommuting every day from about six to nine o'clock in the morning. . . . He can, at the very least, spend those hours reviewing his e-mail. He gets from fifty to one hundred e-mails each day. Many are work-related, but others connect him to mailing lists of people who are interested in technology stock investment, or people who like to play Indian music or tennis. They will send each other quick messages to set up meeting times or to announce the arrival of a particular artist. He also stays in touch with his family in India with e-mail, since that is the most convenient way to communicate across time zones. *(English-Lueck 2002:1–3)* ■ ◉

Additional information about this excerpt can be found on the Online Learning Center at **www.mhhe.com/schaefer9.**

In this excerpt from the book *Cultures@Silicon Valley* by Jan English-Lueck, an anthropologist describes the daily lives of some typical residents of California's world-famous center for cutting-edge technologies. English-Lueck is a professor and chair of the Department of Anthropology at San Jose State University. Fascinated by the mix of cultures and entrepreneurism that powers her region's high-tech economy, she has spent 10 years doing ethnographic research on the software engineers who immigrate from India and Ireland to work in the corporations that invented the Information Age. She sees the community as a microcosm of globalization, where new technologies intersect with international business interests and a multicultural, transnational workforce.

The Silicon Valley culture revealed by English-Lueck's painstaking research is a many-layered mosaic of ethnic traditions, corporate values, consumerism, and global mass media. The well-educated immigrants who staff Silicon Valley's software development departments maintain close-knit ethnic networks, which provide a sense of stability that is lacking in their high-risk business. They accept the corporate profit motive, which means that their jobs are only as secure as the prospects for the new technologies they develop. They consider the demands of learning to live with people of other nationalities a worthwhile exchange for the comfort and efficiency of life in a developed country.

And they allow the high-tech gadgets they create to alter the way they live their lives, changing the ways they work and communicate with others.

Though the high-tech industry has suffered in the recent economic recession, immigrants are still drawn to Silicon Valley, and the corporations that reside there are still developing new technologies with which to integrate diverse cultures. In the future, the United States will continue to rely on talented people from around the world to fuel its expanding economy. In our rapidly globalizing culture, then, understanding other cultures is vital to our national well-being. How does our culture change as we encounter cultures very different from our own? What accounts for cultural variation between and within societies? In this chapter we will see just how basic the study of culture is to sociology. We will examine the meaning of culture and society, as well as the development of culture from its roots in the prehistoric human experience to the technological advances of today. We will define and explore the major aspects of culture, including language, norms, sanctions, and values. We will see how cultures develop a dominant ideology, and how functionalist and conflict theorists view culture. Our discussion will focus both on general cultural practices found in all societies and on the wide variations that can distinguish one society from another. In the social policy section we will look at the conflicts in cultural values that underlie current debates over bilingualism. ■

CULTURE AND SOCIETY

Culture is the totality of learned, socially transmitted customs, knowledge, material objects, and behavior. It includes the ideas, values, customs, and artifacts (for example, DVDs, comic books, and birth control devices) of groups of people. Patriotic attachment to the flag of the United States is an aspect of culture, as is a national passion for the tango in Argentina.

Sometimes people refer to a particular person as "very cultured" or to a city as having "lots of culture." That use of the term *culture* is different from our use in this textbook. In sociological terms, *culture* does not refer solely to the fine arts and refined intellectual taste. It consists of *all* objects and ideas within a society, including ice

cream cones, rock music, and slang words. Sociologists consider both a portrait by Rembrandt and the work of graffiti spray painters to be aspects of a culture. A tribe that cultivates soil by hand has just as much of a culture as a people that relies on computer-operated machinery. Each people has a distinctive culture with its own characteristic ways of gathering and preparing food, constructing homes, structuring the family, and promoting standards of right and wrong.

The fact that you share a similar culture with others helps to define the group or society to which you belong. A fairly large number of people are said to constitute a **society** when they live in the same territory, are relatively independent of people outside their area, and participate in a common culture. The city of Los Angeles is more populous than many nations of the world, yet sociologists do not consider it a society in its own right. Rather, they see it as part of—and dependent on—the larger society of the United States.

A society is the largest form of human group. It consists of people who share a common heritage and culture. Members of the society learn this culture and transmit it from one generation to the next. They even preserve their distinctive culture through literature, art, video recordings, and other means of expression. If it were not for the social transmission of culture, each generation would have to reinvent television, not to mention the wheel.

Having a common culture also simplifies many day-to-day interactions. For example, when you buy an airline ticket, you know you don't have to bring along hundreds of dollars in cash. You can pay with a credit card. When you are part of a society, you take for granted many small (as well as more important) cultural patterns. You assume that theaters will provide seats for the audience, that physicians will not disclose confidential information, and that parents will be careful when crossing the street with young children. All these assumptions reflect basic values, beliefs, and customs of the culture of the United States.

Language is a critical element of culture that sets humans apart from other species. Members of a society generally share a common language, which facilitates day-to-day exchanges with others. When you ask a hardware store clerk for a flashlight, you don't need to draw a picture of the instrument. You share the same cultural term for a small, portable battery-operated light. However, if you were in England and needed this item, you would have to ask for an "electric torch." Of course, even within the same society, a term can have a number of different meanings. In the United States, *grass* signifies both a plant eaten by grazing animals and an intoxicating drug.

DEVELOPMENT OF CULTURE AROUND THE WORLD

We've come a long way from our prehistoric heritage. The human species has produced such achievements as the ragtime compositions of Scott Joplin, the poetry of V. S. Naipaul, the paintings of Vincent van Gogh, the novels of Jane Austen, and the films of Akira Kurosawa. As we begin a new millennium, we can transmit an entire book around the world via the Internet, clone cells, and prolong lives through organ transplants. We can peer into the outermost reaches of the universe and analyze our innermost feelings. In all these ways, we are remarkably different from other species of the animal kingdom.

Cooking is a cultural universal. Both the Cambodian woman and the Moroccan women in these photos show a preference for food grilled on skewers.

Cultural Universals

All societies have developed certain common practices and beliefs, known as ***cultural universals.*** Many cultural universals are, in fact, adaptations to meet essential human needs, such as people's need for food, shelter, and clothing. Anthropologist George Murdock (1945:124) compiled a list of cultural universals, including athletic sports, cooking, funeral ceremonies, medicine, marriage, and sexual restrictions.

The cultural practices Murdock listed may be universal, but the manner in which they are expressed varies from culture to culture. For example, one society may let its members choose their own marriage partners. Another may encourage marriages arranged by the parents.

Not only does the expression of cultural universals vary from one society to another; it may also change dramatically over time within a society. Each generation, and each year for that matter, most human cultures change and expand through the processes of innovation and diffusion.

Innovation

The process of introducing a new idea or object to a culture is known as *innovation.* Innovation interests sociologists because of the social consequences that introducing something new can have in any society. There are two forms of innovation: discovery and invention. A *discovery* involves making known or sharing the existence of an aspect of reality. The finding of the DNA molecule and the identification of a new moon of Saturn are both acts of discovery. A significant factor in the process of discovery is the sharing of newfound knowledge with others. By contrast, an *invention* results when existing cultural items are combined into a form that did not exist before. The bow and arrow, the automobile, and the television are all examples of inventions, as are Protestantism and democracy.

In Vietnam, Santa Claus rides a bicycle loaded with gifts. The observance of Western holidays in non-Western countries is one sign of globalization.

Globalization, Diffusion, and Technology

The Christmas season is in full swing, and the city is aglow with evergreen wreaths, snowmen, and silvery bells. On the street, shoppers hurry past bakery windows stocked with tempting holiday confections. Handel's *Messiah* is being performed tonight at the music hall. No, this isn't New York, London, or Berlin; it's Beijing. China, the country that exports many of the toys that end up under the Christmas tree in the United States, has caught the holiday spirit. But you won't find many manger scenes here, where those who take the message of Christmas seriously are still persecuted. For the Chinese, Christmas is merely a chic Western custom, a welcome chance to relax with family and friends (Marquand 2002).

Not just in China, but in Vietnam, South Korea, and the Philippines, the observance of Western holidays is one more sign of the rapidly escalating *globalization* of culture today. *Globalization* is the worldwide integration of government policies, cultures, social movements, and financial markets through trade and the exchange of ideas. While public discussion of globalization is relatively recent, intellectuals have been pondering its social consequences for a long time. Karl Marx and Friedrich Engels warned in *The Communist Manifesto* (written in 1848) of

a world market that would lead to production in distant lands, sweeping away existing working relationships.

Today, developments outside a country are as likely to influence people's lives as changes at home. For example, though much of the world was already in recession by September 2001, the terrorist attacks on New York and Washington, D.C., caused an immediate decline in international tourism, which lasted for at least two years. The effects have been felt by people far removed from the United States, including African game wardens and Asian taxi drivers. Some observers see globalization and its effects as the natural result of advances in communications technology, particularly the Internet and satellite transmission of the mass media. Others view it more critically, as a process that allows multinational corporations to expand unchecked. We will examine this issue more fully in Box 3-1 (Chase-Dunn et al. 2000; Feketekuty 2001; Feuer 1959; Pearlstein 2001; Ritzer 2004).

As the observance of Western holidays shows, more and more cultural expressions and practices are crossing national borders and having an effect on the traditions and customs of the societies exposed to them. Sociologists use the term *diffusion* to refer to the process by which a cultural item spreads from group to group or society to society. Diffusion can occur through a variety of means, among them exploration, military conquest, missionary work, the influence of the mass media, tourism, and the Internet.

Sociology in the Global Community

3-1 LIFE IN THE GLOBAL VILLAGE

Imagine a "borderless world" in which culture, trade, commerce, money, and even people move freely from one place to another. Popular culture is widely shared, whether it be Japanese sushi or U.S. running shoes, and the English speaker who answers questions on the telephone about your credit card account is as likely to be in India or Ireland as in the United States. In this world, even the sovereignty of nations is at risk, challenged by political movements and ideologies that span nations.

There is no need to imagine this world, for we are already living in the age of globalization. African tribal youngsters wear Michael Jordan T-shirts, Thai teens dance to techno music, Burmese entrepreneurs conduct commerce on cell phones, U.S. supermarkets sell Pokemon cards, and ethnic accessories have become a fashion statement in the United States.

How did we get to this point? First, sociologists take note of advances in communication technology. Satellite TV, cell phones, the Internet, and the like allow information to flow freely across the world and serve to link global markets. Second, corporations in the industrial nations have become multinational, with both factories and markets in developing countries. Business leaders welcome the opportunity to sell consumer goods in populous countries such as China and India. Finally, these multinational firms have cooperated with global financial institutions, organizations, and governments to promote free trade—unrestricted or lightly restricted commerce across national borders.

Globalization is not universally welcomed. Many critics see the dominance of "businesses without borders" as benefiting the rich, particularly the very wealthy in industrial countries, at the ex-

pense of the poor in less developed nations. They consider globalization to be a successor to the imperialism and colonialism that oppressed Third World nations for centuries.

Another criticism of globalization comes from people who feel overwhelmed by global culture. Decision makers are likely to be far removed culturally and spatially from the daily lives of individuals. And when cultural change can come from any part of the global village, no single style can dominate a local community for long. Embedded in the concept of globalization is the notion of cultural domination of developing nations by more affluent nations. Simply put, people lose their traditional values

> Even James Bond movies and Britney Spears may be seen as threats to native cultures, if they dominate the media at the expense of local art forms.

and begin to identify with the culture of the dominant nations. They may discard or neglect their native language and dress as they attempt to copy the icons of mass-market entertainment and fashion. Even James Bond movies and Britney Spears may be seen as threats to native cultures, if they dominate the media at the expense of local art forms. As Sembene Ousmane, one of Africa's most prominent writers and filmmakers, noted, "[Today] we are more familiar with European fairy tales than with our own traditional stories" (World Development Forum 1990:4).

Some societies try to protect themselves from the invasion of too much culture from other countries, especially the economically dominant United States. In

Brazil, for example, a toy manufacturer has challenged Barbie's popularity by designing a doll named Susi that looks more like Brazilian girls. Susi has a slightly smaller chest, much wider thighs, and darker skin than Barbie. Her wardrobe includes the skimpy bikinis favored on Brazilian beaches as well as a soccer shirt honoring the national team. Brazilians have responded: In Brazil, five Susi dolls are sold for every two Barbies.

Of course, globalization has its positive side too. Many developing nations are taking their place in the world of commerce and bringing in much needed income. The communications revolution helps people to stay connected and gives them access to knowledge that can improve living standards and even save lives. For example, people suffering from illnesses are now accessing treatment programs that were developed outside their own nation's medical establishment. The key seems to be finding a balance between the old ways and the new—becoming modernized without leaving meaningful cultural traditions behind.

Let's Discuss

1. How are you affected by globalization? What items of popular culture do you enjoy that come from other nations? Which aspects of globalization do you find advantageous and which do you find objectionable?

2. How would you feel if the customs and traditions you grew up with were replaced with the culture or values of another country? How might you try to protect your culture?

Sources: Austin 2002; Delawala 2003; Dodds 2000; Downie 2000; Giddens 1991; Hansen 2001; Hirst and Thompson 1996; Ritzer 2004; Sernau 2001.

Sociologist George Ritzer (2000) coined the term "McDonaldization of society" to describe how the principles of fast-food restaurants developed in the United States have come to dominate more and more sectors of societies throughout the world. For example, hair salons and medical clinics now take walk-in appointments. In Hong Kong, sex selection clinics offer a menu of items, from fertility enhancement to methods of increasing the likelihood of having a child of the desired sex. Religious groups—from evangelical preachers on local stations or websites to priests at the Vatican Television Center—use marketing techniques similar to those that are used to sell "happy meals."

McDonaldization is associated with the melding of cultures, so that we see more and more similarities in cultural expression. In Japan, for example, African entrepreneurs have found a thriving market for hip-hop fashions popularized by teens in the United States. In Austria, the McDonald's organization itself has drawn on the Austrians' love of coffee, cake, and conversation to create the McCafe, a new part of its fast-food chain. Many critical observers believe that McDonaldization and globalization serve to dilute the distinctive aspects of a society's culture (Alfino et al. 1998; Ritzer 2002).

Technology in its many forms has increased the speed of cultural diffusion and broadened the distribution of cultural elements. Sociologist Gerhard Lenski has defined **technology** as "information about how to use the material resources of the environment to satisfy human needs and desires" (Nolan and Lenski 1999:41). Today's technological developments no longer need to await publication in journals with limited circulation. Press conferences, often carried simultaneously on the Internet, trumpet the new developments.

Technology not only accelerates the diffusion of scientific innovations but also transmits culture. Later, in Chapter 23, we will discuss the concern in many parts of the world that the English language and North American culture dominate the Internet and World Wide Web. Such control, or at least dominance, of technology influences the direction of diffusion of culture. Websites cover even the most superficial aspects of U.S. culture but offer little information about the pressing issues faced by citizens of other nations. People all over the world find it easier to visit electronic chat rooms about daytime television soaps like *All My Children* than to learn about their own government's policies on day care or infant nutrition.

Sociologist William F. Ogburn (1922) made a useful distinction between the elements of material and nonmaterial culture. **Material culture** refers to the physical or technological aspects of our daily lives, including food items, houses, factories, and raw materials. **Nonmaterial culture** refers to ways of

pp. 4–5

using material objects and to customs, beliefs, philosophies, governments, and patterns of communication. Generally, the nonmaterial culture is more resistant to change than the material culture. Consequently, Ogburn introduced the term **culture lag** to refer to the period of maladjustment when the nonmaterial culture is still struggling to adapt to new material conditions. For example, the ethics of using the Internet, particularly issues concerning privacy and censorship, have not yet caught up with the explosion in Internet use and technology (see the social policy section in Chapter 23).

Use Your Sociological Imagination www.mhhe.com/schaefer9

If you grew up in your parents' generation—without computers, e-mail, the Internet, pagers, and cell phones—how would your daily life differ from the one you lead today?

Sociobiology

While sociology emphasizes diversity and change in the expression of culture, another school of thought, *sociobiology,* stresses the universal aspects of culture. **Sociobiology** is the systematic study of how biology affects human social behavior. Sociobiologists assert that many of the cultural traits humans display, such as the almost universal expectation that women will be nurturers and men will be providers, are not learned but are rooted in our genetic makeup.

Sociobiology is founded on the naturalist Charles Darwin's (1859) theory of evolution. In traveling the world, Darwin had noted small variations in species—in the shape of a bird's beak, for example—from one location to another. He theorized that over hundreds of generations, random variations in genetic makeup had helped certain members of a species to survive in a particular environment. A bird with a differently shaped beak might have been better at gathering seeds than other birds, for instance. In reproducing, these lucky individuals had passed on their advantageous genes to succeeding generations. Eventually, given their advantage in survival, individuals with the variation began to outnumber other members of the species. The species was slowly adapting to its environment. Darwin called this process of adaptation to the environment through random genetic variation *natural selection.*

Sociobiologists apply Darwin's principle of natural selection to the study of social behavior. They assume that particular forms of behavior become genetically linked to a species if they contribute to its fitness to survive (van den Berghe 1978). In its extreme form, sociobiology suggests that *all* behavior is the result of genetic or biological factors and that social interactions play no role in shaping people's conduct.

Sociobiologists do not seek to describe individual behavior on the level of "Why is Fred more aggressive than Jim?" Rather, they focus on how human nature is affected by the genetic composition of a *group* of people who share certain characteristics (such as men or women, or members of isolated tribal bands). In general, sociobiologists have stressed the basic genetic heritage that *all* humans share and have shown little interest in speculating about alleged differences between racial groups or nationalities (E. Wilson 1975, 1978).

Some researchers insist that intellectual interest in sociobiology will only deflect serious study of the more significant influence on human behavior, the social environment. Yet Lois Wladis Hoffman (1985), in her presidential address to the Society for the Psychological Study of Social Issues, argued that sociobiology poses a valuable challenge to social scientists to better document their own research. Interactionists, for example, could show how social behavior is not programmed by human biology, but instead adjusts continually to the attitudes and responses of others.

Certainly most social scientists would agree that there is a biological basis for social behavior. But there is less support for the extreme positions taken by certain advocates of sociobiology. Like interactionists, conflict theorists and functionalists believe that people's behavior rather than their genetic structure defines social reality. Conflict theorists fear that the sociobiological approach could be used as an argument against efforts to assist disadvantaged people, such as schoolchildren who are not competing successfully (Guterman 2000; Segerstråle 2000; E. Wilson 2000).

ELEMENTS OF CULTURE

Each culture considers its own distinctive ways of handling basic societal tasks to be "natural." But, in fact, methods of education, marital ceremonies, religious doctrines, and other aspects of culture are learned and transmitted through human interaction within specific societies. Parents in India are accustomed to arranging marriages for their children; parents in the United States leave marital decisions up to their offspring. Lifelong residents of Naples consider it natural to speak Italian; lifelong residents of Buenos Aires feel the same way about Spanish. Let's take a look at the major aspects of culture that shape the way the members of a society live: language, norms, sanctions, and values.

Language

The English language makes extensive use of words dealing with war. We speak of "conquering" space, "fighting" the "battle" of the budget, "waging war" on drugs, making a "killing" on the stock market, and "bombing" an examination; something monumental or great is "the bomb." An observer from an entirely different and warless culture could gauge the importance that war and the military have had in our lives simply by recognizing the prominence that militaristic terms have in our language. On the other hand, in the Old West, words such as *gelding, stallion, mare, piebald,* and *sorrel* were all used to describe one animal—the horse. Even if we knew little of this period of history, we could conclude from the list of terms that horses were important in this culture. Similarly, the Slave Indians of northern Canada, who live in a frigid climate, have 14 terms to describe ice, including 8 for different kinds of "solid ice" and others for "seamed ice," "cracked ice," and "floating ice." Clearly, language reflects the priorities of a culture (Basso 1972; Haviland 2002).

Language is, in fact, the foundation of every culture. **Language** is an abstract system of word meanings and symbols for all aspects of culture. It includes speech, written characters, numerals, symbols, and nonverbal gestures and expressions. Figure 3-1 (page 64) shows where the major languages of the world are spoken.

Because language is the foundation of every culture, the ability to speak other languages is crucial to intercultural relations. Throughout the Cold War era, beginning in the 1950s and continuing well into the 1970s, the U.S. government encouraged the study of Russian by developing special language schools for diplomats and military advisors who dealt with the Soviet Union. And following September 11, 2001, the nation recognized how few skilled translators it had for Arabic and other languages spoken in Muslim countries. Language quickly became a key not only to tracking potential terrorists, but to building diplomatic bridges with Muslim countries willing to help in the war against terrorism.

While language is a cultural universal, striking differences in the use of language are evident around the world. This is the case even when two countries use the same spoken language. For example, an English-speaking person from the United States who is visiting London might be puzzled the first time an English friend says "I'll ring you up." The friend means "I'll call you on the telephone."

Sapir-Whorf Hypothesis

Language does more than simply describe reality; it also serves to *shape* the reality of a culture. For example, most people in the United States cannot easily make the verbal distinctions concerning ice that are possible in the Slave Indian culture. As a result, they are less likely to notice such differences.

The **Sapir-Whorf hypothesis,** named for two linguists, describes the role of language in shaping our

FIGURE 3-I

Languages of the World

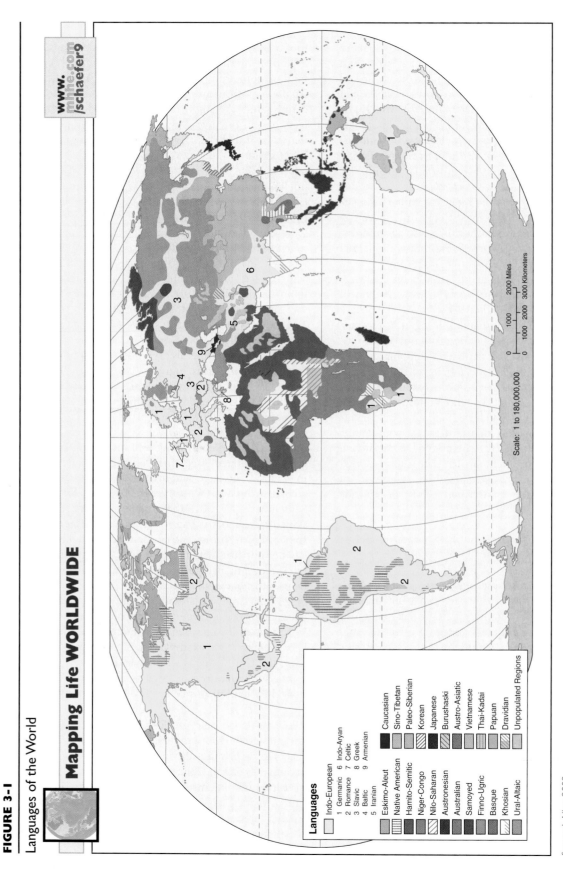

Mapping Life WORLDWIDE

www.
mhhe.com
/schaefer9

Languages

Indo-European	6 Indo-Aryan
1 Germanic	7 Celtic
2 Romance	8 Greek
3 Slavic	9 Armenian
4 Baltic	
5 Iranian	

Eskimo-Aleut
Native American
Hamito-Semitic
Niger-Congo
Nilo-Saharan
Austronesian
Australian
Samoyed
Finno-Ugric
Basque
Khoisan
Ural-Altaic

Caucasian
Sino-Tibetan
Paleo-Siberian
Korean
Japanese
Burushaski
Austro-Asiatic
Vietnamese
Thai-Kadai
Papuan
Dravidian
Unpopulated Regions

Scale: 1 to 180,000,000

Source: J. Allen 2003.

Think About It

Why do you think people in the United States are much less likely to master more than one language than people in other parts of the world?

interpretation of reality. According to Sapir and Whorf, since people can conceptualize the world only through language, language *precedes* thought. Thus, the word symbols and grammar of a language organize the world for us. The Sapir-Whorf hypothesis also holds that language is not a given. Rather, it is culturally determined, and encourages a distinctive interpretation of reality by focusing our attention on certain phenomena.

In a literal sense, language may color how we see the world. Berlin and Kay (1991) have noted that humans possess the physical ability to make millions of color distinctions, yet languages differ in the number of colors they recognize. The English language distinguishes between yellow and orange, but some other languages do not. In the Dugum Dani language of New Guinea's West Highlands, there are only two basic color terms—*modla* for "white" and *mili* for "black." By contrast, there are 11 basic terms in English. Russian and Hungarian, though, have 12 color terms. Russians have terms for light blue and dark blue, while Hungarians have terms for two different shades of red.

Feminists have noted that gender-related language can reflect—although in itself it does not determine—the traditional acceptance of men and women in certain occupations. Each time we use a term such as *mailman, policeman,* or *fireman,* we are implying (especially to young children) that these occupations can be filled only by males. Yet many women work as *letter carriers, police officers,* and *firefighters*—a fact that is being increasingly recognized and legitimized through the use of such nonsexist language.

Language can also transmit stereotypes related to race. Look up the meanings of the adjective *black* in dictionaries published in the United States. You will find *dismal, gloomy* or *forbidding, destitute of moral light* or *goodness, atrocious, evil, threatening, clouded with anger.* By contrast, dictionaries list *pure* and *innocent* among the meanings of the adjective *white.* Through such patterns of language, our culture reinforces positive associations with the term (and skin color) *white* and negative associations with *black.* Is it surprising, then, that a list preventing people from working in a profession is called a *blacklist,* while a lie that we think of as somewhat acceptable is called a *white lie?*

Language can shape how we see, taste, smell, feel, and hear. It also influences the way we think about the people, ideas, and objects around us. Language communicates a culture's most important norms, values, and sanctions to people. That's why the introduction of a new language into a society is such a sensitive issue in many parts of the world (see the social policy section of this chapter).

Hand signals have different meanings in different cultures. U.S. film critic Roger Ebert uses the thumbs-up sign to recommend a new movie, but in Australia his gesture would be seen as offensive rather than complimentary (Passero 2002).

Nonverbal Communication

If you don't like the way a meeting is going, you might suddenly sit back, fold your arms, and turn down the corners of your mouth. When you see a friend in tears, you may give a quick hug. After winning a big game you probably high-five your teammates. These are all examples of *nonverbal communication,* the use of gestures, facial expressions, and other visual images to communicate.

We are not born with these expressions. We learn them, just as we learn other forms of language, from people who share our same culture. This is as true for the basic expressions of happiness and sadness as it is for more complex emotions such as shame or distress (Fridlund et al. 1987).

Like other forms of language, nonverbal communication is not the same in all cultures. For example, sociological research at the micro level documents that people from various cultures differ in the degree to which they touch others during the course of normal social interactions. Even experienced travelers are sometimes caught off guard by these differences. In Saudi Arabia, a middle-aged man may want to hold hands with a partner after closing a business deal. The gesture, which would shock an American businessman, is considered a compliment in that culture. The meaning of hand signals is another form of nonverbal communication that can differ from one culture to the next. In Australia, the thumbs-up sign is considered rude (Passero 2002).

Norms

"Wash your hands before dinner." "Thou shalt not kill." "Respect your elders." All societies have ways of encouraging and enforcing what they view as appropriate behavior while discouraging and punishing what they consider to be improper behavior. *Norms* are the established standards of behavior maintained by a society.

For a norm to become significant, it must be widely shared and understood. For example, in movie theaters in the United States, we typically expect that people will be quiet while the film is shown. Of course, the application of this norm can vary, depending on the particular film and type of audience. People viewing a serious artistic film will be more likely to insist on the norm of silence than those watching a slapstick comedy or horror movie.

Types of Norms

Sociologists distinguish between norms in two ways. First, norms are classified as either formal or informal. *Formal norms* generally have been written down and specify strict punishments for violators. In the United States, we often formalize norms into laws, which are very precise in defining proper and improper behavior. Sociologist Donald Black (1995) has termed *law* "governmental social control," establishing laws as formal norms enforced by the state. Laws are just one example of formal norms. The requirements for a college major and the rules of a card game are also considered formal norms.

By contrast, *informal norms* are generally understood but are not precisely recorded. Standards of proper dress are a common example of informal norms. Our society has no specific punishment or sanction for a person who comes to school, say, wearing a monkey suit. Making fun of the nonconforming student is usually the most likely response.

Norms are also classified by their relative importance to society. When classified in this way, they are known as *mores* and *folkways*.

Mores (pronounced "MOR-ays") are norms deemed highly necessary to the welfare of a society, often because they embody the most cherished principles of a people. Each society demands obedience to its mores; violation can lead to severe penalties. Thus, the United States has strong mores against murder, treason, and child abuse, which have been institutionalized into formal norms.

Folkways are norms governing everyday behavior. Folkways play an important role in shaping the daily behavior of members of a culture. Society is less likely to

formalize folkways than mores, and their violation raises comparatively little concern. For example, walking up a "down" escalator in a department store challenges our standards of appropriate behavior, but it will not result in a fine or a jail sentence.

In many societies around the world, folkways exist to reinforce patterns of male dominance. Various folkways reveal men's hierarchical position above women within the traditional Buddhist areas of southeast Asia. In the sleeping cars of trains, women do not sleep in upper berths above men. Hospitals that house men on the first floor do not place women patients on the second floor. Even on clotheslines, folkways dictate male dominance: women's attire is hung lower than that of men (Bulle 1987).

> **Use Your Sociological Imagination** www.mhhe.com/schaefer9
>
> You are a high school principal. What norms would you want to govern the students' behavior? How might these norms differ from those appropriate for college students?

Acceptance of Norms

People do not follow norms, whether mores or folkways, in all situations. In some cases, they can evade a norm because they know it is weakly enforced. It is illegal for U.S. teenagers to drink alcoholic beverages, yet drinking by minors is common throughout the nation. (In fact, teenage alcoholism is a serious social problem.)

In some instances, behavior that appears to violate society's norms may actually represent adherence to the norms of a particular group. Teenage drinkers are conforming to the standards of their peer group when they violate norms that condemn underage drinking. Similarly, business executives who use shady accounting techniques may be responding to a corporate culture that demands the maximization of profits at any cost, including the deception of investors and government regulatory agencies.

Norms are violated in some instances because one norm conflicts with another. For example, suppose that you live in an apartment building and one night hear the screams of the woman next door, who is being beaten by her husband. If you decide to intervene by ringing their doorbell or calling the police, you are violating the norm of "minding your own business," while at the same time following the norm of assisting a victim of violence.

Even when norms do not conflict, there are always exceptions to any norm. The same action, under different circumstances, can cause one to be viewed as either a hero or a villain. Secretly taping telephone conversations is normally considered illegal and abhorrent. However, it

Cockfighting, anyone? It's legal only in New Mexico, Louisiana, and Oklahoma (shown here), but practiced behind closed doors elsewhere in the nation. What does this situation tell us about social norms?

can be done with a court order to obtain valid evidence for a criminal trial. We would heap praise on a government agent who used such methods to convict an organized crime figure. In our culture, we tolerate killing another human being in self-defense, and we actually reward killing in warfare.

Acceptance of norms is subject to change as the political, economic, and social conditions of a culture are transformed. For example, traditional norms in the United States once called for a woman to marry, rear children, and remain at home if her husband could support the family without her assistance. However, those norms have been changing in recent decades, in part as a result of the feminist movement (see Chapter 12). As support for traditional norms weakens, people feel free to violate them more frequently and openly, and are less likely to be punished for doing so.

Sanctions

Suppose that a football coach sends a 12th player onto the field. Imagine a college graduate showing up in shorts for a job interview at a large bank. Or consider a driver who neglects to put any money into a parking meter. These people have violated widely shared and understood norms. So what happens? In each of these situations, the person will receive sanctions if his or her behavior is detected.

Sanctions are penalties and rewards for conduct concerning a social norm. Note that the concept of *reward* is included in this definition. Conformity to a norm can lead to positive sanctions such as a pay raise, a medal, a word of gratitude, or a pat on the back. Negative sanctions include fines, threats, imprisonment, and stares of contempt.

Table 3-1 (page 68) summarizes the relationship between norms and sanctions. As you can see, the sanctions that are associated with formal norms (those that are written down and codified) tend to be formal as well. If a coach sends too many players onto the field, the team will be penalized 15 yards. The driver who fails to put money in the parking meter will receive a ticket and have to pay a fine. But sanctions for violations of informal norms can vary. The college graduate who goes to the bank interview in shorts will probably lose any chance of getting the job; on the other hand, he or she might be so brilliant that bank officials will overlook the unconventional attire.

The entire fabric of norms and sanctions in a culture reflects that culture's values and priorities. The most cherished values will be most heavily sanctioned; matters regarded as less critical, on the other hand, will carry light and informal sanctions.

Values

Though we each have our own personal set of standards—which may include caring or fitness or success in business—we also share a general set of objectives as members of a society. Cultural *values* are these collective conceptions of what is considered good, desirable, and proper—or bad, undesirable, and improper—in a culture. They indicate what people in a given culture prefer as well as what they find important and morally right (or wrong). Values may be specific, such as honoring one's parents and owning a home, or they may be more general, such as health, love, and democracy. Of course, the members of a society do not uniformly share its values. Angry political debates and billboards promoting conflicting causes tell us that much.

Values influence people's behavior and serve as criteria for evaluating the actions of others. The values, norms, and sanctions of a culture are often directly related. For example, if a culture highly values the institution of marriage, it may have norms (and strict sanctions)

Table 3-1	Norms and Sanctions	
Norms	**Sanctions**	
	Positive	**Negative**
Formal	Salary bonus	Demotion
	Testimonial dinner	Firing from a job
	Medal	Jail sentence
	Diploma	Expulsion
Informal	Smile	Frown
	Compliment	Humiliation
	Cheers	Belittling

that prohibit the act of adultery or make divorce difficult. If a culture views private property as a basic value, it will probably have stiff laws against theft and vandalism.

The values of a culture may change, but most remain relatively stable during any one person's lifetime. Socially shared, intensely felt values are a fundamental part of our lives in the United States. Sociologist Robin Williams (1970) has offered a list of basic values. It includes achievement, efficiency, material comfort, nationalism, equality, and the supremacy of science and reason over faith. Obviously, not all 290 million people in this country agree on all these values, and we should not look on such a list as anything more than a starting point in defining the national character. Nevertheless, a review of 27 different attempts to describe the "American value system," including the works of anthropologist Margaret Mead and sociologist Talcott Parsons, revealed an overall similarity to the values identified by Williams (Devine 1972).

Each year more than 283,000 entering college students at 437 of the nation's four-year colleges fill out a questionnaire surveying their attitudes. Because this survey focuses on an array of issues, beliefs, and life goals, it is commonly cited as a barometer of the nation's values. The respondents are asked what values are personally important to them. Over the last 33 years, the value of "being very well-off financially" has shown the strongest gain in popularity; the proportion of first-year college students who endorse this value as "essential" or "very important" rose from 44 percent in 1967 to 72 percent in 2002 (see Figure 3-2). In contrast, the value that has shown the most striking decline in endorsement by students is "developing a meaningful philosophy of life." While this value was the most popular in the 1967 survey,

endorsed by more than 80 percent of the respondents, it had fallen to ninth place on the list by 2002, when it was endorsed by less than 40 percent of students entering college.

During the 1980s and 1990s, support for values having to do with money, power, and status grew. At the same time, support for certain values having to do with social awareness and altruism, such as "helping others," declined. According to the 2002 nationwide survey, only 40 percent of first-year college students stated that "influencing social values" was an "essential" or "very important" goal. The proportion of students for whom "helping to promote racial understanding" was an essential or very important goal reached a record high of 42 percent in 1992, but fell to 32 percent in 2002. Like other aspects of culture, such as language and norms, a nation's values are not necessarily fixed.

Recently, cheating has become a hot issue on college campuses. Professors who take advantage of computerized services than can identify plagiarism, such as the search engine Google, have been shocked to learn that many of the papers their students hand in are plagiarized in whole or in part. Box 3-2 on page 70 examines the shift in values that underlies this decline in academic integrity.

FIGURE 3-2

Life Goals of First-Year College Students in the United States, 1966–2002

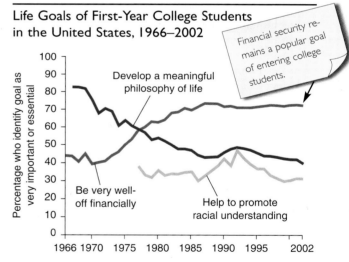

Sources: UCLA Higher Education Research Institute, as reported in Astin et al. 1994; Sax et al. 2002:33.

Think About It

Why do you think values have shifted among college students in the last few decades? Which of these values is important to you? Have your values changed since September 11, 2001?

Another value that has begun to change recently, not just among students but among the public in general, is the right to privacy. Americans have always valued their privacy and resented government intrusions into their personal lives. In the aftermath of the terrorist attacks of September 11, 2001, however, many citizens called for greater protection against the threat of terrorism. In response, the U.S. government broadened its surveillance powers and increased its ability to monitor people's behavior without court approval. We will discuss the ambivalence Americans felt about increased government surveillance and the threat it posed to people's privacy in the social policy section in Chapter 23.

CULTURE AND THE DOMINANT IDEOLOGY

Both functionalist and conflict theorists agree that culture and society are in harmony with each other, but for different reasons. Functionalists maintain that stability requires a consensus and the support of society's members; consequently, there are strong central values and common norms. This view of culture became popular in sociology beginning in the 1950s. It was borrowed from British anthropologists who saw all cultural traits as working toward stabilizing a culture. From a functionalist perspective, a cultural trait or practice will persist if it fulfills functions that society seems to need or contributes to overall social stability and consensus. This view helps to explain why widely condemned social practices such as prostitution continue to survive.

pp. 13–14

Conflict theorists agree that a common culture may exist, but they argue that it serves to maintain the privileges of certain groups. Moreover, while protecting their own self-interests, powerful groups may keep others in a subservient position. The term ***dominant ideology*** describes the set of cultural beliefs and practices that help to maintain powerful social, economic, and political interests. This concept was first used by Hungarian Marxist Georg Lukács (1923) and Italian Marxist Antonio Gramsci (1929), but it did not gain an audience in the United States until the early 1970s. In Karl Marx's view, a capitalist society has a dominant ideology that serves the interests of the ruling class.

From a conflict perspective, the dominant ideology has major social significance. Not only do a society's most powerful groups and institutions control wealth and property; even more important, they control the means of producing beliefs about reality through religion, education, and the media. Feminists would also argue that if all of a society's most important institutions tell women that they should be subservient to men, this dominant ideology will help to control women and keep them in a subordinate position (Abercrombie et al. 1980, 1990; Robertson 1988).

A growing number of social scientists believe it is not easy to identify a "core culture" in the United States. For support, they point to the lack of consensus on national values, the diffusion of cultural traits, the diversity within our culture, and the changing views of young people (look again at Figure 3-2). Yet there is no way of denying that certain expressions of values have greater influence than others, even in so complex a society as the United States (Abercrombie et al. 1980, 1990; Archer 1988; Wuthnow and Witten 1988).

CULTURAL VARIATION

Each culture has a unique character. Inuit tribes in northern Canada—wrapped in furs and dieting on whale blubber—have little in common with farmers in Southeast Asia, who dress for the heat and subsist mainly on the rice they grow in their paddies. Cultures adapt to meet specific sets of circumstances, such as climate, level of technology, population, and geography. This adaptation to different conditions shows up in differences in all elements of culture, including norms, sanctions, values, and language. Thus, despite the presence of cultural universals such as courtship and religion, there is still great diversity among the world's many cultures. Moreover, even *within* a single nation, certain segments of the populace develop cultural patterns that differ from the patterns of the dominant society.

Aspects of Cultural Variation

Subcultures

Rodeo cowboys, residents of a retirement community, workers on an offshore oil rig, street gangs—all are examples of what sociologists refer to as *subcultures*. A **subculture** is a segment of society that shares a distinctive pattern of mores, folkways, and values that differs from the pattern of the larger society. In a sense, a subculture can be thought of as a culture existing within a larger, dominant culture. The existence of many subcultures is characteristic of complex societies such as the United States.

Members of a subculture participate in the dominant culture while at the same time engaging in unique and distinctive forms of behavior. Frequently, a subculture will develop an ***argot***, or specialized language, that distinguishes it from the wider society. For example, if you were to join a band of pickpockets you would need to learn

On November 21, 2002, after issuing several warnings, officials at the U.S. Naval Academy seized the computers of almost 100 midshipmen suspected of downloading movies and music illegally from the Internet. Officers at the school may have taken the unusually strong action to avoid liability on the part of the U.S. government, which owns the computers students were using. But across the nation, college administrators have been trying to restrain students from downloading pirated entertainment for free. The practice is so widespread, it has been slowing down the high-powered computer networks colleges and universities depend on for research and admissions.

Illegal downloading is just one aspect of the growing problem of copyright violation, both on campus and off. Now that college students can use personal computers to surf the Internet, most do their research online. Apparently, the temptation to cut and paste passages from website postings and pass them off as one's own is irresistible to many. Surveys done by the Center for Academic Integrity show that from 1999 to 2001, the percentage of students who approve of this type of plagiarism rose from 10 percent to 41 percent. At the same time, the percentage who consider cutting and pasting from the Internet to be a serious form of cheating fell from 68 percent to 27 percent.

Other forms of cheating are becoming rampant, as well. The Center for Academic Integrity estimates that at most schools, more than three quarters of the students engage in some form of cheating. Students not only cut passages from the Internet and paste them into their papers without citing the source; they share questions and answers on exams, collaborate on assignments they are supposed to do independently, and even falsify the results of their laboratory experiments. Worse, many professors have become inured to the problem and have ceased to report it.

To address what they consider an alarming trend, many schools are rewrit-

> Cheating is considerably less common at schools with honor codes than at schools without honor codes.

ing or adopting new academic honor codes. According to the Center for Academic Integrity, cheating on tests and papers is considerably less common at schools with honor codes than at schools without honor codes. Cornell, Duke, and Kansas State University are just three of a growing number of schools that are instituting or strengthening their honor codes in an attempt to curb student cheating.

This renewed emphasis on honor and integrity underscores the influence of cultural values on social behavior. Observers contend that the increase in student cheating reflects widely publicized instances of cheating in public life, which have served to create an alternative set of values in which the means justifies the ends. When young people see sports heroes, authors, entertainers, and corporate executives exposed for cheating in one form or another, the message seems to be, "Cheating is OK, as long as you don't get caught." More than proctoring of exams or reliance on search engines to identify plagiarism, then, educating students about the need for academic honesty seems to reduce the incidence of cheating. "The feeling of being treated as an adult and responding in kind," says Professor Donald McCabe of Rutgers University, "it's clearly there for many students. They don't want to violate that trust."

Let's Discuss

1. Do you know anyone who has engaged in Internet plagiarism? What about cheating on tests or falsifying laboratory results? If so, how did the person justify these forms of dishonesty?
2. Even if cheaters aren't caught, what negative effects does their academic dishonesty have on them? What effects does it have on students who are honest? Could an entire college or university suffer from students' dishonesty?

Sources: Argetsinger and Krim 2002; Center for Academic Integrity 2003; R. Murray Thomas 2003; Zernike 2002.

---

what the dip, dish, and tailpipe are expected to do (see Figure 3-3).

Argot allows insiders, the members of the subculture, to understand words with special meanings. It also establishes patterns of communication that outsiders can't understand. Sociologists associated with the interactionist perspective emphasize that language and symbols offer a powerful way for a subculture to feel cohesive and maintain its identity.

Music fans often form subcultures dedicated to a particular type of music or musician. Recently a subculture called Phishheads, after the Vermont jam rock band Phish, has emerged. Reminiscent of the Deadheads who once devoted themselves to the Grateful Dead, Phishheads have constructed a way of life that revolves entirely around Phish recordings and concerts. As Table 3-2 (page 72), drawn from www.pholktales.com, shows, Phishheads use the Internet to maintain their identity.

Subcultures develop in a number of ways. Often a subculture emerges because a segment of society faces problems or even privileges unique to its position. Subcultures may be based on common age (teenagers or old

Cultures vary in their taste for films. Europeans and North Americans enjoyed the exotic aspects of *Crouching Tiger, Hidden Dragon* (shown here), but it was not well received in China. Audiences there found it slow-paced, and they were especially annoyed by the clumsy Mandarin spoken by actors more used to Cantonese roles.

and technological. This group included primarily political radicals and "hippies" who had "dropped out" of mainstream social institutions. These young men and women rejected the pressure to accumulate more and more cars, larger and larger homes, and an endless array of material goods. Instead, they expressed a desire to live in a culture based on more humanistic values, such as sharing, love, and coexistence with the environment. As a political force, this subculture opposed the United States' involvement in the war in Vietnam and encouraged draft resistance (Flacks 1971; Roszak 1969).

When a subculture conspicuously and deliberately opposes certain aspects of the larger culture, it is known as a *counterculture.* Countercultures typically thrive among the young, who have the least investment in the existing culture. In most cases, a 20-year-old can adjust to new cultural standards more easily than someone who has spent 60 years following the patterns of the dominant culture (Zellner 1995).

In the wake of the terrorist attacks of September 11, 2001, people around the United States learned of the existence of terrorist groups operating as a counterculture within their country. This was a situation that

people), region (Appalachians), ethnic heritage (Cuban Americans), occupation (firefighters), or beliefs (deaf activists working to preserve deaf culture). Certain subcultures, such as computer hackers, develop because of a shared interest or hobby. In still other subcultures, such as that of prison inmates, members have been excluded from conventional society and are forced to develop alternative ways of living.

Functionalist and conflict theorists agree that variation exists within a culture. Functionalists view subcultures as variations of particular social environments and as evidence that differences can exist within a common culture. However, conflict theorists suggest that variations often reflect the inequality of social arrangements within a society. A conflict perspective would view the challenge to dominant social norms by African American activists, the feminist movement, and the disability rights movement as a reflection of inequity based on race, gender, and disability status. Conflict theorists also argue that subcultures sometimes emerge when the dominant society unsuccessfully tries to suppress a practice, such as the use of illegal drugs.

Countercultures

By the end of the 1960s, an extensive subculture had emerged in the United States, composed of young people turned off by a society they believed was too materialistic

FIGURE 3-3

The Argot of Pickpockets

Source: Gearty 1996.

Table 3-2	**Are You a Phishhead?**

You know you are a Phishhead

—When someone asks you what type of music you listen to, you say Phish

—While pledging a fraternity during hell week, your only rule as punishment is not to talk about Phish the whole time

—You have 35 emails from friends after Phish is on the Simpsons.

—You stare at Ebay for a good while contemplating the $700 seats to Worcester (concert).

—It doesn't matter how late, or early you are phor something . . . you're sittin in that car till the song's over.

—You are the only phan at school, but it doesn't matter because it makes your passion that much more intense

—Your parents stop asking you if you are getting a job this summer and instead ask which tour you will be on

—Because you listen to them only

Source: Selected by the author from Pholktales 2003.

generations have lived with in Northern Ireland, Israel and the Palestinian territory, and many other parts of the world. Terrorist cells worldwide are not necessarily fueled only by outsiders. Frequently people become disenchanted with the policies of their own country, and a few take very violent steps.

Culture Shock

Anyone who feels disoriented, uncertain, out of place, even fearful, when immersed in an unfamiliar culture may be experiencing **culture shock.** For example, a resident of the United States who visits certain areas in China and wants local meat for dinner may be stunned to learn that the specialty is dog meat. Similarly, someone from a strict Islamic culture may be shocked upon first seeing the comparatively provocative dress styles and open displays of affection that are common in the United States and various European cultures.

All of us, to some extent, take for granted the cultural practices of our society. As a result, it can be surprising and even disturbing to realize that other cultures do not follow our "way of life." The fact is that customs that seem strange to us are considered normal and proper in other cultures, which may see our own mores and folkways as odd.

Use Your Sociological Imagination   www. mhhe.com /schaefer9

You arrive in a developing African country as a Peace Corps volunteer. What aspects of a very different culture do you think would be the hardest to adjust to? What might the citizens of that country find shocking about your culture?

Attitudes toward Cultural Variation

Ethnocentrism

Many everyday statements reflect our attitude that our own culture is best. We use terms such as *underdeveloped,* *backward,* and *primitive* to refer to other societies. What "we" believe is a religion; what "they" believe is superstition and mythology.

"IT'S ENDLESS. WE JOIN A COUNTER-CULTURE; IT BECOMES THE CULTURE. WE JOIN ANOTHER COUNTER-CULTURE; IT BECOMES THE CULTURE . . ."

Cultures change. Fashions we once regarded as unacceptable—such as men wearing earrings and people wearing jeans in the workplace—or associated with fringe groups (such as men and women with tattoos) are now widely accepted. Countercultural practices are sometimes absorbed by mainstream culture.

It is tempting to evaluate the practices of other cultures on the basis of our own perspectives. Sociologist William Graham Sumner (1906) coined the term ***ethnocentrism*** to refer to the tendency to assume that one's culture and way of life represent the norm or are superior to all others. The ethnocentric person sees his or her own group as the center or defining point of culture and views all other cultures as deviations from what is "normal." Westerners who think cattle are to be used for food might look down on India's Hindu religion and culture, which views the cow as sacred. Or people in one culture may dismiss as unthinkable the mate selection or child-rearing practices of another culture.

Conflict theorists point out that ethnocentric value judgments serve to devalue groups and to deny equal opportunities. Psychologist Walter Stephan notes a typical example of ethnocentrism in New Mexico's schools. Both Hispanic and Native American cultures teach children to look down when they are being criticized by adults, yet many "Anglo" (non-Hispanic White) teachers believe that you should look someone in the eye when you are being criticized. "Anglo teachers can feel that these students are being disrespectful," notes Stephan. "That's the kind of misunderstanding that can evolve into stereotype and prejudice" (Goleman 1991:C8).

Functionalists, on the other hand, point out that ethnocentrism serves to maintain a sense of solidarity by promoting group pride. Denigrating other nations and cultures can enhance our own patriotic feelings and belief that our way of life is superior. Yet this type of social stability is established at the expense of other peoples. Of course, ethnocentrism is hardly limited to citizens of the United States. Visitors from many African cultures are surprised at the disrespect that children in the United States show their parents. People from India may be repelled by our practice of living in the same household with dogs and cats. Many Islamic fundamentalists in the Arab world and Asia view the United States as corrupt, decadent, and doomed to destruction. All these people may feel comforted by membership in cultures that in their view are superior to ours.

Cultural Relativism

While ethnocentrism evaluates foreign cultures using the familiar culture of the observer as a standard of correct behavior, ***cultural relativism*** views people's behavior from the perspective of their own culture. It places a priority on understanding other cultures, rather than dismissing them as "strange" or "exotic." Unlike ethnocentrism, cultural relativism employs the kind of value neutrality in scientific study that Max Weber saw as so important.

p. 43

Cultural relativism stresses that different social contexts give rise to different norms and values. Thus, we must examine practices such as polygamy, bullfighting, and monarchy within the particular contexts of the cultures in which they are found. While cultural relativism does not suggest that we must unquestionably *accept* every cultural variation, it does require a serious and unbiased effort to evaluate norms, values, and customs in light of their distinctive culture.

An interesting extension of cultural relativism is referred to as *xenocentrism*. **Xenocentrism** is the belief that the products, styles, or ideas of one's society are inferior to those that originate elsewhere. In a sense, it is a reverse ethnocentrism. For example, people in the United States often assume that French fashions or Japanese electronic devices are superior to our own. Are they? Or are people unduly charmed by the lure of goods from exotic places? Such fascination with overseas products can be damaging to competitors in the United States. Some U.S. companies have responded by creating products that *sound* European, such as Häagen-Dazs ice cream (made in Teaneck, New Jersey). Conflict theorists are most likely to consider the economic impact of xenocentrism in the developing world. Consumers in developing nations frequently turn their backs on locally produced goods and instead purchase items imported from Europe or North America (W. Wilson et al. 1976).

How one views a culture—whether from an ethnocentric point of view or through the lens of cultural relativism—has important consequences in the area of social policy. A hot issue today is the extent to which a nation should accommodate nonnative language speakers by sponsoring bilingual programs. We'll take a close look at this issue in the next section.

The Issue

In Sri Lanka, Tamils seek to break away from the Sinhalese-speaking majority. Romanian radio announces that in areas where 20 percent of the people speak Hungarian, bilingual road and government signs will be posted. In schools from Miami to Boston to Chicago, administrators strive to deliver education to their Creole-speaking Haitian students. All over the world, nations face the challenge of how to deal with residential minorities who speak a language different from that of the mainstream culture.

Bilingualism refers to the use of two or more languages in a particular setting, such as the workplace or schoolroom, treating each language as equally legitimate. Thus, a teacher of bilingual education may instruct children in their native language while gradually introducing them to the language of the host society. If the curriculum is also bicultural, it will teach children about the mores and folkways of both the dominant culture and the subculture. To what degree should schools in the United States present the curriculum in a language other than English? This issue has prompted a great deal of debate among educators and policymakers.

The Setting

Languages know no political boundaries. Despite the portrayal of dominant languages in Figure 3-1 (page 64), minority languages are common in many nations. For example, Hindi is the most widely spoken language in India, and English is used widely for official purposes, but 18 other languages are officially recognized in this nation of about 1 billion people. According to the Census 2000, 45 million residents of the United States over the age of five—that's about 18 percent of the population—speak a language other than English as their primary language. Indeed, 50 different languages are each spoken by at least 200,000 residents of this country (Bureau of the Census 2001a).

Schools throughout the world must deal with incoming students speaking many languages. Do bilingual programs in the United States help these children to learn English? It is difficult to reach firm conclusions because bilingual programs in general vary so widely in their quality and approach. They differ in the length of the transition to English and in how long they allow students to remain in bilingual classrooms. Moreover, results have been mixed. In the years since California effectively dismantled its bilingual education program, reading and math scores of students with limited English proficiency rose dramatically, especially in the lower grades. Yet a major overview of 11 different studies on bilingual education found that children with limited English who are taught using at least some of their native language perform significantly better on standardized tests than similar children who are taught only in English (Foreman 2002; Greene 1998; Pyle 1998; Steinberg 2000).

Sociological Insights

For a long time, people in the United States demanded conformity to a single language. This demand coincides with the functionalist view that language serves to unify members of a society. Immigrant children from Europe and Asia—including young Italians, Jews, Poles, Chinese, and Japanese—were expected to learn English once they entered school. In some cases, immigrant children were actually forbidden to speak their native languages on school grounds. There was little respect granted to immigrants' cultural traditions; a young person would often be teased about his or her "funny" name, accent, or style of dress.

Recent decades have seen challenges to this pattern of forced obedience to our dominant ideology. Beginning in the 1960s, active movements for Black pride and ethnic pride insisted that people regard the traditions of *all* racial and ethnic subcultures as legitimate and important. Conflict theorists explain this development as a case of subordinated language minorities seeking opportunities of self-expression. Partly as a result of these challenges, people began to view bilingualism as an asset. It seemed to provide a sensitive way of assisting millions of non–English-speaking people in the United States to *learn* English in order to function more effectively within the society.

The perspective of conflict theory also helps us to understand some of the attacks on bilingual programs. Many of them stem from an ethnocentric point of view, which holds that any deviation from the majority is bad. This attitude tends to be expressed by those who wish to stamp out foreign influence wherever it occurs, especially in our schools. It does not take into account that success in bilingual education may actually have beneficial results, such as decreasing the number of high school dropouts and increasing the number of Hispanics in colleges and universities.

Policy Initiatives

Bilingualism has policy implications largely in two areas: efforts to maintain language purity and programs to enhance bilingual education. Nations vary dramatically in their tolerance for a variety of languages. China continues to tighten its cultural control over Tibet by extending instruction of Mandarin, a Chinese dialect, from high school into the elementary schools, which will now be bilingual along with Tibetan. Even more forceful is Indonesia, which has a large Chinese-speaking minority; public display of Chinese-language signs or books is totally banned. By contrast, nearby Singapore establishes English as the medium of instruction but allows students to take their mother tongue as a second language, be it Chinese, Malay, or Tamil (M. Farley 1998).

French speakers in Quebec are zealous about protecting the prevalence of their language in the Canadian province. These French Pokémon cards were a response to intense lobbying efforts.

In many nations, language dominance is a regional issue—for example, in Miami or along the border of Texas, where Spanish speaking is prevalent. A particularly virulent bilingual hot spot is Quebec, the French-speaking province of Canada. The Québécois, as they are known, represent 83 percent of the province's

FIGURE 3-4

States with Official English Laws

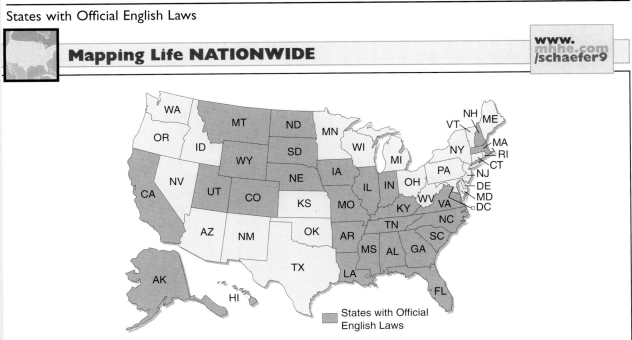

Source: U.S. English 2002.

population, but only 25 percent of Canada's total population. A law implemented in 1978 mandated education in French for all Quebec's children except those whose parents or siblings had learned English elsewhere in Canada. While special laws like this one have advanced French in the province, dissatisfied Québécois have tried to form their own separate country. In 1995, the people of Quebec voted to remain united with Canada by only the narrowest of margins (50.5 percent). Language and language-related cultural areas both unify and divide this nation of 32 million people (Krauss 2003; Schaefer 2004).

Policymakers in the United States have been somewhat ambivalent in dealing with the issue of bilingualism. In 1965, the Elementary and Secondary Education Act (ESEA) provided for bilingual, bicultural education. In the 1970s, the federal government took an active role in establishing the proper form for bilingual programs. However, more recently, federal policy has been less supportive of bilingualism, and local school districts have been forced to provide an increased share of funding for their bilingual programs. Yet bilingual programs are an expense that many communities and states are unwilling to pay for and are quick to cut back. In 1998, voters in California approved a proposition that all but eliminated bilingual education: it requires instruction in English for 1.4 million children who are not fluent in the language.

In the United States, repeated efforts have been made to introduce a constitutional amendment declaring English the official language of the nation. A major force behind efforts to restrict bilingualism is U.S. English, a nationwide organization founded in 1983 that now claims to have 1.7 million members. Its adherents say they feel like strangers in their own neighborhoods, aliens in their own country. By contrast, Hispanic leaders see the U.S. English campaign as a veiled expression of racism.

Despite such challenges, U.S. English seems to be making headway in its efforts to oppose bilingualism. By 2003, 27 states had declared English to be their official language (see Figure 3-4 on page 75). The actual impact of these measures, beyond their symbolism, is unclear.

Let's Discuss

1. How might someone with an ethnocentric point of view see bilingualism?
2. Describe how conflict theorists would explain recent developments in bilingual programs in the United States.
3. Have you attended a school with a number of students for whom English is a second language? Did the school set up a special bilingual program? Was it effective? What is your opinion of such programs?

CHAPTER RESOURCES

Summary

Culture is the totality of learned, socially transmitted customs, knowledge, material objects, and behavior. This chapter examines the basic elements that make up a culture, social practices common to all cultures, and variations that distinguish one culture from another.

1. A shared culture helps to define the group or society to which we belong.
2. Anthropologist George Murdock compiled a list of *cultural universals,* or general practices found in every culture, including courtship, family, sports, language, medicine, religion, and sexual restrictions.
3. Human culture is constantly expanding through the process of *innovation,* which includes both *discovery* and *invention.*
4. *Diffusion*—the spread of cultural items from one place to another—has fostered *globalization.* But

people resist ideas that seem too foreign, as well as those they perceive as threatening to their own values and beliefs.

5. *Language,* an important element of culture, includes speech, written characters, numerals, and symbols, as well as gestures and other forms of nonverbal communication. Language both describes culture and shapes it.
6. Sociologists distinguish between *norms* in two ways, classifying them either as *formal* or *informal* or as *mores* or *folkways.*
7. The more cherished *values* of a culture will receive the heaviest *sanctions;* matters that are regarded as less critical will carry light sanctions.
8. The *dominant ideology* of a culture is the set of cultural beliefs and practices that help to maintain powerful social, economic, and political interests.

9. In a sense, a *subculture* can be thought of as a culture that exists within a larger, dominant culture. *Countercultures* are subcultures that deliberately oppose aspects of the larger culture.

10. People who measure other cultures by the standard of their own engage in *ethnocentrism. Cultural relativism* is the practice of viewing people from the perspective of their own culture.

11. The social policy of *bilingualism* calls for the use of two or more languages, treating each as equally legitimate. It is supported by those who want to ease the transition of non-native language speakers into a host society, but opposed by those who adhere to a single cultural tradition and language.

Critical Thinking Questions

1. Select three cultural universals from George Murdock's list (see page 59) and analyze them from a functionalist perspective. Why are these practices found in every culture? What functions do they serve?

2. Drawing on the theories and concepts presented in this chapter, apply sociological analysis to one subculture with which you are familiar. Describe the norms, values, argot, and sanctions evident in that subculture.

3. In what ways is the dominant ideology of the United States evident in the nation's literature, music, movies, theater, television programs, and sporting events?

Key Terms

Argot   Specialized language used by members of a group or subculture. (page 69)

Bilingualism   The use of two or more languages in a particular setting, such as the workplace or schoolroom, treating each language as equally legitimate. (74)

Counterculture   A subculture that deliberately opposes certain aspects of the larger culture. (71)

Cultural relativism   The viewing of people's behavior from the perspective of their own culture. (73)

Cultural universal   A common practice or belief found in every culture. (59)

Culture   The totality of learned, socially transmitted customs, knowledge, material objects, and behavior. (58)

Culture lag   A period of maladjustment when the nonmaterial culture is still struggling to adapt to new material conditions. (62)

Culture shock   The feeling of surprise and disorientation that people experience when they encounter cultural practices that are different from their own. (72)

Diffusion   The process by which a cultural item spreads from group to group or society to society. (60)

Discovery   The process of making known or sharing the existence of an aspect of reality. (60)

Dominant ideology   A set of cultural beliefs and practices that help to maintain powerful social, economic, and political interests. (69)

Ethnocentrism   The tendency to assume that one's own culture and way of life represent the norm or are superior to all others. (73)

Folkway   A norm governing everyday behavior whose violation raises comparatively little concern. (66)

Formal norm   A norm that has been written down and that specifies strict punishments for violators. (66)

Globalization   The worldwide integration of government policies, cultures, social movements, and financial markets through trade and the exchange of ideas. (60)

Informal norm   A norm that is generally understood but is not precisely recorded. (66)

Innovation   The process of introducing a new idea or object into a culture through discovery or invention. (60)

Invention   The combination of existing cultural items into a form that did not exist before. (60)

Language   An abstract system of word meanings and symbols for all aspects of culture; includes gestures and other nonverbal communication. (63)

Law   Governmental social control. (66)

Material culture   The physical or technological aspects of our daily lives. (62)

Mores   A norm deemed highly necessary to the welfare of a society. (66)

Nonmaterial culture   Ways of using material objects, as well as customs, beliefs, philosophies, governments, and patterns of communication. (62)

Norm   An established standard of behavior maintained by a society. (66)

Sanction   A penalty or reward for conduct concerning a social norm. (67)

Sapir-Whorf hypothesis   A hypothesis concerning the role of language in shaping our interpretation of reality. It holds that language is culturally determined. (63)

Society A fairly large number of people who live in the same territory, are relatively independent of people outside it, and participate in a common culture. (58)

Sociobiology The systematic study of how biology affects human social behavior. (62)

Subculture A segment of society that shares a distinctive pattern of mores, folkways, and values that differs from the pattern of the larger society. (69)

Technology Information about how to use the material resources of the environment to satisfy human needs and desires. (62)

Value A collective conception of what is considered good, desirable, and proper—or bad, undesirable, and improper—in a culture. (67)

Xenocentrism The belief that the products, styles, or ideas of one's society are inferior to those that originate elsewhere. (73)

TECHNOLOGY RESOURCES

Internet Connection

Note: While all the URLs listed were current as of the printing of this book, these sites often change. Please check our website (www.mhhe.com/schaefer9) for updates, hyperlinks, and exercises related to these cites.

1. Nonverbal communication is an important element in all cultures. The art of Chinese dance traces its origins to a period before the appearance of the first written Chinese characters. Learn about the history, meaning, and culture of the art of

Chinese dance by visiting www.houstoncul.org/culdir/danc/danc.htm.

2. Body tattooing has recently become quite popular in mainstream American culture. However, this form of body art has long been popular worldwide. The British Tattoo History Museum maintains an interesting website on the history of tattoo. Explore the history of tattoo by visiting www.tattoo.co.uk/index.htm.

Online Learning Center with PowerWeb

In this chapter, you have learned that language is the foundation of every culture. For a long time, people in the United States demanded conformity to a single language. More recently, however, we have seen challenges to this forced obedience to our dominant ideology. One of the interactive exercises in the student center of the Online Learning Center (**www.mhhe.com/schaefer9**) will only let you use a "foreign" language to do the activity. You will be taught a simple language called Pig Latin. Give it a try, and see whether or not you feel competent completing the exercise in this "foreign" language.

Reel Society Interactive Movie CD-ROM

Reel Society includes scenes that can be used to spark discussion about the following topics from this chapter:

- Cultural Universals
- Norms

4

SOCIALIZATION

Schools can sometimes be stressful arenas of socialization. The poster shown above informs schoolchildren in Japan that they can call a hotline and receive advice concerning stress, bullying by classmates, and corporal punishment from their teachers.

The Role of Socialization

The Self and Socialization

Socialization and the Life Course

Agents of Socialization

Social Policy and Socialization: Child Care around the World

Boxes

SOCIOLOGY IN THE GLOBAL COMMUNITY: Raising Amish Children

SOCIOLOGY ON CAMPUS: Impression Management by Students

Charisse...is sixteen and lives with her mother and younger sister, Deanne, across the street from St. Mary's Catholic Church and School. Charisse's mother is a personnel assistant at a Chicago university, and is taking classes there to get her bachelor's degree. Mr. Baker is a Chicago firefighter. While her father and mother are separated, Charisse sees her father many times a week at the afterschool basketball hour that he supervises at St. Mary's gym. He and Charisse's mother are on very good terms, and Charisse has a loving relationship with both parents. Mr. Baker is as active as any parent could be, attending the father/daughter dances at Charisse's high school, never missing a big performance, and visiting his daughters often.

Charisse and her sister are being raised by the neighborhood family in addition to their biological parents. "We [are] real close. Like all our neighbors know us because my dad grew up over here. Since the '60s." Charisse is a third-generation Grovelandite just like Neisha Morris. Her grandparents moved into Groveland with Charisse's then-teenage father when the neighborhood first opened to African Americans.... Now Charisse is benefiting from the friends her family has made over their years of residence in Groveland, especially the members of St. Mary's church, who play the role of surrogate parents. When Charisse was in elementary school at St. Mary's, her late paternal grandmother was the school secretary, and so the Baker girls were always under the watchful

eye of their grandmother as well as the staff, who were their grandmother's friends. And in the evenings Charisse's mother would bring her and her sister to choir practice, where they accumulated an ensemble of mothers and fathers.

After St. Mary's elementary school, Charisse went on to St. Agnes Catholic High School for girls, her father's choice. St. Agnes is located in a suburb of Chicago and is a solid, integrated Catholic school where 100 percent of the girls graduate and over 95 percent go on to college....

Most of Charisse's close friends went to St. Mary's and now go to St. Agnes with her, but her choice of boyfriends shows modest signs of rebellion.... Many of Charisse's male interests are older than she, and irregularly employed—although some are in and out of school. She meets many of them hanging out at the mall. One evening, members of the church's youth choir sat around talking about their relationships. Charisse cooed while talking about her present boyfriend, who had just graduated from high school but did not have a job and was uncertain about his future. But in the middle of that thought, Charisse spontaneously changed her attentions to a new young man that she had just met. "Charisse changes boyfriends like she changes her clothes," her sister joked, indicating the impetuous nature of adolescent relationships. *(Pattillo-McCoy 1999:100–102)* ■ 🖎

Additional information about this excerpt can be found on the Online Learning Center at **www.mhhe.com/schaefer9**.

his excerpt from *Black Picket Fences: Privilege and Peril among the Black Middle Class* describes the upbringing of a young resident of Groveland, a close-knit African American community in Chicago. The author, sociologist Mary Pattillo-McCoy, became acquainted with Charisse while living in the Groveland neighborhood, where she was doing ethnographic research. Charisse's childhood is similar to that of other youths in many respects. Regardless of race or social class, a young person's development involves a host of influences, from parents, grandparents, and siblings to friends and classmates, teachers and school administrators, neighbors and churchgoers—even youths who frequent the local mall. Yet in some ways, Charisse's development is specifically influenced by her race and social class. Contact with family and community members, for instance, has undoubtedly prepared her to deal with prejudice and the absence of positive images of African Americans in the media.

Sociologists, in general, are interested in the patterns of behavior and attitudes that emerge *throughout* the life course, from infancy to old age. These patterns are part of the lifelong process of **socialization,** in which people learn the attitudes, values, and behaviors appropriate for members of a particular culture. Socialization occurs through human interactions. We learn a great deal from those people most important in our lives—immediate family members, best friends, and teachers. But we also learn from people we see on the street, on television, on the Internet, and in films and magazines. From a microsociological perspective,

socialization helps us to discover how to behave "properly" and what to expect from others if we follow (or challenge) society's norms and values. From a macrosociological perspective, socialization provides for the transmission of a culture from one generation to the next, and thereby for the long-term continuance of a society.

Socialization also shapes our self-images. For example, in the United States, a person who is viewed as "too heavy" or "too short" does not conform to the ideal cultural standard of physical attractiveness. This kind of unfavorable evaluation can significantly influence the person's self-esteem. In this sense, socialization experiences can help to shape our personalities. In everyday speech, the term **personality** is used to refer to a person's typical patterns of attitudes, needs, characteristics, and behavior.

How much of a person's personality is shaped by culture, as opposed to inborn traits? In what ways does socialization continue into adulthood? Who are the most powerful agents of socialization? In this chapter we will examine the role of socialization in human development. We will begin by analyzing the interaction of heredity and environmental factors. We pay particular attention to how people develop perceptions, feelings, and beliefs about themselves. The chapter will also explore the lifelong nature of the socialization process, as well as important agents of socialization, among them the family, schools, peers, and the media. Finally, the social policy section will focus on the socialization experience of group child care for young children. ■

THE ROLE OF SOCIALIZATION

What makes us who we are? Is it the genes we are born with? Or the environment in which we grow up? Researchers have traditionally clashed over the relative importance of biological inheritance and environmental factors in human development—a conflict called the *nature versus nurture* (or *heredity versus environment*) debate. Today, most social scientists have moved beyond this debate, acknowledging instead the *interaction of* these variables in shaping human development. However,

we can better appreciate how heredity and environmental factors interact and influence the socialization process if we first examine situations in which one factor operates almost entirely without the other (Homans 1979).

Social Environment: The Impact of Isolation

In the 1994 movie *Nell,* Jodie Foster played a young woman hidden from birth by her mother in a backwoods cabin. Raised without normal human contact, Nell crouches like an animal, screams wildly, and speaks or sings in a language all her own. This movie was drawn from the actual account of an emaciated 16-year-old boy who mysteriously appeared in 1828 in the town square of Nuremberg, Germany (Lipson 1994).

The Case of Isabelle

Some viewers may have found the story of Nell difficult to believe, but the painful childhood of Isabelle was all too real. For the first six years of her life, Isabelle lived in almost total seclusion in a darkened room. She had little contact with other people, with the exception of her mother, who could neither speak nor hear. Isabelle's mother's parents had been so deeply ashamed of Isabelle's illegitimate birth that they kept her hidden away from the world. Ohio authorities finally discovered the child in 1938, when Isabelle's mother escaped from her parents' home, taking her daughter with her.

When she was discovered at age six, Isabelle could not speak. She could merely make various croaking sounds. Her only communications with her mother were simple gestures. Isabelle had been largely deprived of the typical interactions and socialization experiences of childhood. Since she had actually seen few people, she initially showed a strong fear of strangers and reacted almost like a wild animal when confronted with an unfamiliar person. As she became accustomed to seeing certain individuals, her reaction changed to one of extreme apathy. At first, observers believed that Isabelle was deaf, but she soon began to react to nearby sounds. On tests of maturity, she scored at the level of an infant rather than a six-year-old.

Specialists developed a systematic training program to help Isabelle adapt to human relationships and socialization. After a few days of training, she made her first attempt to verbalize. Although she started slowly, Isabelle quickly passed through six years of development. In a little over two months, she was speaking in complete sentences. Nine months later, she could identify both words and sentences. Before Isabelle reached the age of nine, she was ready to attend school with other children. By her 14th year, she was in sixth grade, doing well in school, and emotionally well-adjusted.

Yet, without an opportunity to experience socialization in her first six years, Isabelle had been hardly human in the social sense when she was first discovered. Her inability to communicate at the time of her discovery—despite her physical and cognitive potential to learn—and her remarkable progress over the next few years underscore the impact of socialization on human development (K. Davis 1940, 1947).

Isabelle's experience is important for researchers because it is one of few cases of children reared in total isolation. Unfortunately, however, there are many cases of children raised in extremely neglectful social circumstances. Recently, attention has focused on infants and young children in orphanages in the formerly communist countries of Eastern Europe. For example, in Romanian orphanages, babies lie in their cribs for 18 or 20 hours a day, curled against their feeding bottles and receiving little adult care. Such minimal attention continues for the first five years of their lives. Many of them are fearful of human contact and prone to unpredictable antisocial behavior. This situation came to light as families in North America and Europe began adopting thousands of these children. The adjustment problems for about 20 percent of them were often so dramatic that the adopting families suffered guilty fears of being ill-fit adoptive parents. Many of them have asked for assistance in dealing with the children. Slowly, efforts are being made to introduce the deprived youngsters to feelings of attachment that they have never experienced before (Groza et al. 1999; Talbot 1998).

Increasingly, researchers are emphasizing the importance of early socialization experiences for children who grow up in more normal environments. We now know that it is not enough to care for an infant's physical needs; parents must also concern themselves with children's social development. If, for example, children are discouraged from having friends, they will miss out on social interactions with peers that are critical for emotional growth.

Primate Studies

Studies of animals raised in isolation also support the importance of socialization in development. Harry Harlow (1971), a researcher at the primate laboratory of the University of Wisconsin, conducted tests with rhesus monkeys that had been raised away from their mothers and away from contact with other monkeys. As was the case with Isabelle, the rhesus monkeys raised in isolation were fearful and easily frightened. They did not mate, and the females who were artificially inseminated became abusive mothers. Apparently, isolation had had a damaging effect on the monkeys.

A creative aspect of Harlow's experimentation was his use of "artificial mothers." In one such experiment, Harlow presented monkeys raised in isolation with two substitute mothers—one cloth-covered replica and one covered with wire that had the ability to offer milk. Monkey after monkey went to the wire mother for the life-giving milk, yet spent much more time clinging to the more motherlike cloth model. It appears that the infant monkeys developed greater social attachments from their need for warmth, comfort, and intimacy than from their need for milk.

While the isolation studies discussed above may seem to suggest that heredity can be dismissed as a factor in the social development of humans and animals, studies of twins provide insight into a fascinating interplay between hereditary and environmental factors.

Use Your Sociological Imagination www.mhhe.com/schaefer9

What events in your life have had a strong influence on who you are?

The Influence of Heredity

Identical twins Oskar Stohr and Jack Yufe were separated soon after their birth and raised on different continents in very different cultural settings. Oskar was reared as a strict Catholic by his maternal grandmother in the Sudetenland of Czechoslovakia. As a member of the Hitler Youth movement in Nazi Germany, he learned to hate Jews. By contrast, his brother Jack was reared in Trinidad

Harry Harlow with one of his rhesus monkeys, gazing at its surrogate wire mother.

by the twins' Jewish father. Jack joined an Israeli kibbutz (a collective settlement) at age 17 and later served in the Israeli army. But when the twins were reunited in middle age, some startling similarities emerged: They both wore wire-rimmed glasses and mustaches. They both liked spicy foods and sweet liqueurs, were absent-minded, flushed the toilet before using it, stored rubber bands on their wrists, and dipped buttered toast in their coffee (Holden 1980).

The twins also differed in many important respects: Jack was a workaholic; Oskar enjoyed leisure-time activities. Whereas Oskar was a traditionalist who was domineering toward women, Jack was a political liberal much more accepting of feminism. Finally, Jack was extremely proud of being Jewish, while Oskar never mentioned his Jewish heritage (Holden 1987).

Oskar and Jack are prime examples of the interplay of heredity and environment. For a number of years, the Minnesota Twin Family Study has been following pairs of identical twins reared apart to determine what similarities, if any, they show in personality traits, behavior, and intelligence. Preliminary results from the available twin studies indicate that *both* genetic factors *and* socialization experiences are influential in human development. Certain characteristics, such as temperaments, voice patterns, and nervous habits, appear to be strikingly similar even in twins reared apart, suggesting that these qualities may be linked to hereditary causes. However, identical twins reared apart differ far more in their attitudes, values, chosen mates, and even drinking habits; these qualities, it would seem, are influenced by environmental factors. In examining clusters of personality traits among such twins, researchers have found marked similarities in their tendency toward leadership or dominance, but significant differences in their need for intimacy, comfort, and assistance.

Researchers have also been impressed with the similar scores on intelligence tests of twins reared apart in *roughly similar* social settings. Most of the identical twins register scores even closer than those that would be expected if the same person took a test twice. At the same time, however, identical twins brought up in *dramatically different* social environments score quite differently on intelligence tests—a finding that supports the impact of socialization on human development (McGue and Bouchard 1998; Minnesota Twin Family Study 2001).

We need to be cautious when reviewing the studies of twin pairs and other relevant research. Widely broadcast findings have often been based on extremely small samples and preliminary analysis. For example, one study (not involving twin pairs) was frequently cited as confirming genetic links with behavior. Yet the researchers had to retract their conclusions after they increased the sample and re-classified two of the original cases. After these changes, the initial findings were no longer valid.

Critics add that the studies on twin pairs have not provided satisfactory information concerning the extent to which separated identical twins may have had contact with each other, even though they were "raised apart." Such interactions—especially if they were extensive—could call into question the validity of the twin studies. As this debate continues, we can certainly anticipate numerous efforts to replicate the research and clarify the interplay between hereditary and environmental factors in human development (Horgan 1993; Kelsoe et al. 1989; Leo 1987; Plomin 1989; Wallis 1987).

Children imitate the people around them, especially family members they continually interact with, during the *preparatory stage* described by George Herbert Mead.

THE SELF AND SOCIALIZATION

We all have various perceptions, feelings, and beliefs about who we are and what we are like. How do we come to develop these? Do they change as we age?

We were not born with these understandings. Building on the work of George Herbert Mead (1964b), sociologists recognize that we create our own designation: the self. The *self* is a distinct identity that sets us apart from others. It is not a static phenomenon, but continues to develop and change throughout our lives.

Sociologists and psychologists alike have expressed interest in how the individual develops and modifies the sense of self as a result of social interaction. The work of sociologists Charles Horton Cooley and George Herbert Mead, pioneers of the interactionist approach, has been especially useful in furthering our understanding of these important issues (Gecas 1982).

p. 17

Sociological Approaches to the Self

Cooley: Looking-Glass Self

In the early 1900s, Charles Horton Cooley advanced the belief that we learn who we are by interacting with others. Our view of ourselves, then, comes not only from direct contemplation of our personal qualities but also from our impressions of how others perceive us. Cooley used the phrase **looking-glass self** to emphasize that the self is the product of our social interactions with other people.

The process of developing a self-identity or self-concept has three phases. First, we imagine how we present ourselves to others—to relatives, friends, even strangers on the street. Then we imagine how others evaluate us (attractive, intelligent, shy, or strange). Finally, we develop some sort of feeling about ourselves, such as respect or shame, as a result of these impressions (Cooley 1902; M. Howard 1989).

A subtle but critical aspect of Cooley's looking-glass self is that the self results from an individual's "imagination" of how others view him or her. As a result, we can develop self-identities based on *incorrect* perceptions of how others see us. A student may react strongly to a teacher's criticism and decide (wrongly) that the instructor views the student as stupid. This misperception can easily be converted into a negative self-identity through the following process: (1) the teacher criticized me, (2) the teacher must think that I'm stupid, (3) I *am* stupid. Yet self-identities are also subject to change. If the student receives an A at the end of the course, he or she will probably no longer feel stupid.

Mead: Stages of the Self

George Herbert Mead continued Cooley's exploration of interactionist theory. Mead (1934, 1964a) developed a useful model of the process by which the self emerges, defined by three distinct stages: the preparatory stage, the play stage, and the game stage.

The Preparatory Stage. During the *preparatory stage,* children merely imitate the people around them, especially family members with whom they continually interact. Thus, a small child will bang on a piece of wood while a parent is engaged in carpentry work, or will try to throw a ball if an older sibling is doing so nearby.

As they grow older, children become more adept at using symbols to communicate with others. *Symbols* are the gestures, objects, and language that form the basis of human communication. By interacting with relatives and friends, as well as by watching cartoons on television and looking at picture books, children in the preparatory stage begin to understand the use of symbols. Like spoken languages, symbols vary from culture to culture and even between subcultures. Raising one's eyebrows may mean astonishment in North America, but in Peru it means "money" or "pay me," while in the Pacific island nation of Tonga it means "yes" or "I agree" (Axtell 1990).

The Play Stage. Mead was among the first to analyze the relationship of symbols to socialization. As children develop skill in communicating through symbols, they gradually become more aware of social relationships. As a result, during the *play stage,* they begin to pretend to be other people. Just as an actor "becomes" a character, a child becomes a doctor, parent, superhero, or ship captain.

Mead, in fact, noted that an important aspect of the play stage is role playing. *Role taking* is the process of mentally assuming the perspective of another and responding from that imagined viewpoint. For example, through this process, a young child will gradually learn when it is best to ask a parent for favors. If the parent usually comes home from work in a bad mood, the child will wait until after dinner, when the parent is more relaxed and approachable.

The Game Stage. In Mead's third stage, the *game stage,* the child of about eight or nine years old no longer just plays roles, but begins to consider several actual tasks and relationships simultaneously. At this point in development, children grasp not only their own social po-sitions, but also those of others around them—just as in a football game the players must understand their own and everyone else's positions. Consider a girl or boy who is part of a scout troop out on a weekend hike in the mountains. The child must understand what he or she is expected to do, but also must recognize the responsibilities of other scouts as well as the leaders. This is the final stage of development under Mead's model; the child can now respond to numerous members of the social environment.

Mead uses the term **generalized other** to refer to the attitudes, viewpoints, and expectations of society as a whole that a child takes into account in his or her behavior. Simply put, this concept suggests that when an individual acts, he or she takes into account an entire group of people. For example, a child will not act courteously merely to please a particular parent. Rather, the child comes to understand that courtesy is a widespread social value endorsed by parents, teachers, and religious leaders.

At the game stage, children can take a more sophisticated view of people and the social environment. They now understand what specific occupations and social positions are and no longer equate Mr. Williams only with the role of "librarian" or Ms. Sanchez only with "principal." It has become clear to the child that Mr. Williams can be a librarian, a parent, and a marathon runner at the same time and that Ms. Sanchez is one of many principals in our society. Thus, the child has reached a new level

Double Dutch jump roping contests require contestants to carry out several tasks at once and to understand the roles of others—characteristics of the *game stage* outlined by George Herbert Mead.

of sophistication in observations of individuals and institutions.

Mead: Theory of the Self

Mead is best known for his theory of the self. According to Mead (1964b), the self begins at a privileged, central position in a person's world. Young children picture themselves as the focus of everything around them, and find it difficult to consider the perspectives of others. For example, when shown a mountain scene and asked to describe what an observer on the opposite side of the mountain might see (such as a lake or hikers), young children describe only objects visible from their own vantage point. This childhood tendency to place ourselves at the center of events never entirely disappears. Many people with a fear of flying automatically assume that if any plane goes down, it will be the one they are on. And who reads the horoscope section in the paper without looking at their own horoscope first? Why else do we buy lottery tickets, if we do not imagine ourselves winning?

Nonetheless, as people mature, the self changes and begins to reflect greater concern about the reactions of others. Parents, friends, co-workers, coaches, and teachers are often among those who play a major role in shaping a person's self. Mead used the term **significant others** to refer to those individuals who are most important in the development of the self. Many young people, for example, find themselves drawn to the same kind of work their parents engage in (Schlenker 1985).

In some instances, studies of significant others have generated controversy among researchers. For example, some researchers have contended that African American adolescents are more "peer-oriented" than their White counterparts because of presumed weaknesses in Black families. However, investigations indicate that these hasty conclusions were based on limited studies focusing on less affluent Blacks. In fact, there appears to be little difference in who African Americans and Whites from similar economic backgrounds regard as their significant others (Giordano et al. 1993; Juhasz 1989).

 Use Your Sociological Imagination www.mhhe.com/schaefer9

Who have been your significant others? Are you someone else's significant other?

Goffman: Presentation of the Self

How do we manage our "self"? How do we display to others who we are? Erving Goffman, a sociologist associated with the interactionist perspective, suggested that many of our daily activities involve attempts to convey impressions of who we are. His observations help us to understand the sometimes subtle yet critical ways in which we learn to present ourselves socially.

Early in life, the individual learns to slant his or her presentation of the self in order to create distinctive appearances and satisfy particular audiences. Goffman (1959) referred to this altering of the presentation of the self as **impression management.** Box 4-1 describes an everyday example of this concept—the way students behave after receiving their exam grades. In analyzing such everyday social interactions, Goffman makes so many explicit parallels to the theater that his view has been termed the **dramaturgical approach.** According to this perspective, people resemble performers in action. For example, a clerk may try to appear busier than he or she actually is if a supervisor happens to be watching. A customer in a singles' bar may try to look as if he or she is waiting for a particular person to arrive.

Goffman (1959) has also drawn attention to another aspect of the self—**face-work.** How often do you initiate some kind of face-saving behavior when you feel embarrassed or rejected? In response to a rejection at the singles' bar, a person may engage in face-work by saying, "There really isn't an interesting person in this entire crowd." We feel the need to maintain a proper image of the self if we are to continue social interaction.

In some cultures, people engage in elaborate deceptions to avoid losing face. In Japan, for example, where lifetime employment has until recently been the norm, "company men" thrown out of work by a deep economic recession may feign employment, rising as usual in the morning, donning suit and tie, and heading for the business district. But instead of going to the office, they congregate at places such as Tokyo's Hibiya Library, where they pass the time by reading before returning home at the usual hour. Many of these men are trying to protect family members, who would be shamed if neighbors discovered the family breadwinner was unemployed. Others are deceiving their wives and families as well (H. W. French 2001).

Goffman's work on the self represents a logical progression of sociological studies begun by Cooley and Mead on how personality is acquired through socialization and how we manage the presentation of the self to others. Cooley stressed the process by which we come to create a self; Mead focused on how the self develops as we learn to interact with others; Goffman emphasized the ways in which we consciously create images of ourselves for others.

Psychological Approaches to the Self

Psychologists have shared the interest of Cooley, Mead, and other sociologists in the development of the self.

4-1 IMPRESSION MANAGEMENT BY STUDENTS

When you get an exam back, you probably react differently with fellow classmates depending on the grades that you and they earned. This is all part of *impression management*, as sociologists Daniel Albas and Cheryl Albas have demonstrated. The two explored the strategies college students use to create desired appearances after receiving their grades on exams. Albas and Albas divided these encounters into three categories: those between students who have all received high grades (Ace–Ace encounters); those between students who have received high grades and those who have received low or even failing grades (Ace–Bomber encounters); and those between students who have all received low grades (Bomber–Bomber encounters).

Ace–Ace encounters occur in a rather open atmosphere, because there is comfort in sharing a high mark with another high achiever. It is even acceptable to violate the norm of modesty and brag when among other Aces, since as one student admitted, "It's much easier to admit a high mark to someone who has done better than you, or at least as well."

Ace–Bomber encounters are often sensitive. Bombers generally attempt to avoid such exchanges, because "you . . . emerge looking like the dumb one" or "feel like you are lazy or unreliable." When forced into interactions with Aces, Bombers work to appear gracious and congratulatory. For their part, Aces offer sympathy and support to the dissatisfied Bombers, and even rationalize their own "lucky" high scores. To help Bombers save face, Aces may emphasize the difficulty and unfairness of the examination.

> When forced into interactions with Aces, Bombers work to appear gracious and congratulatory.

Bomber–Bomber encounters tend to be closed, reflecting the group effort to wall off the feared disdain of others. Yet, within the safety of these encounters, Bombers openly share their disappointment and engage in expressions of mutual self-pity that they themselves call "pity parties." They devise face-saving excuses for their poor performances, such as "I wasn't feeling well all week" or "I had four exams and two papers due

that week." If the grade distribution in a class includes particularly low scores, Bombers may blame the professor, attacking him or her as a sadist, a slave driver, or simply an incompetent.

As is evident from these descriptions, students' impression management strategies conform to society's informal norms regarding modesty and consideration for less successful peers. In classroom settings, as in the workplace and in other types of human interactions, efforts at impression management are most intense when status differentials are pronounced, as in encounters between the high-scoring Aces and the low-scoring Bombers.

Let's Discuss

1. How do you react with those who have received higher or lower grades than you? Do you engage in impression management? How would you like others to react to your grade?
2. What social norms govern students' impression management strategies?

Source: Albas and Albas 1988.

Early work in psychology, such as that of Sigmund Freud (1856–1939), stressed the role of inborn drives—among them the drive for sexual gratification—in channeling human behavior. More recently, psychologists such as Jean Piaget have emphasized the stages through which human beings progress as the self develops.

Like Charles Horton Cooley and George Herbert Mead, Freud believed that the self is a social product, and that aspects of one's personality are influenced by other people (especially one's parents). However, unlike Cooley and Mead, he suggested that the self has components that work in opposition to each other. According to Freud, our natural impulsive instincts are in constant conflict with societal constraints. Part of us seeks limitless pleasure, while another part favors rational behavior. By interacting with others, we learn the expectations of society and then select behavior most appropriate to our own culture. (Of course, as Freud was well aware, we sometimes distort reality and behave irrationally.)

Research on newborn babies by the Swiss child psychologist Jean Piaget (1896–1980) has underscored the importance of social interactions in developing a sense of self. Piaget found that newborns have no self in the sense of a looking-glass image. Ironically, though, they are quite self-centered; they demand that all attention be directed toward them. Newborns have not yet separated themselves from the universe of which they are a part. For these babies, the phrase "you and me" has no meaning; they understand only "me." However, as they mature, children are gradually socialized into social

Body painting is a ritual marking the passage to puberty among young people in Liberia, in western Africa.

the ability to think more abstractly. When children learn the rules of a game such as checkers or jacks, they are learning to obey societal norms. Those under eight years old display a rather basic level of morality: rules are rules, and there is no concept of "extenuating circumstances." However, as they mature, children become capable of greater autonomy, and begin to experience moral dilemmas and doubts as to what constitutes proper behavior.

According to Jean Piaget, social interaction is the key to development. As they grow older, children pay increasing attention to how other people think and why they act in particular ways. In order to develop a distinct personality, each of us needs opportunities to interact with others. As we saw earlier, Isabelle was deprived of the chance for normal social interactions, and the consequences were severe (Kitchener 1991).

We have seen that a number of thinkers considered social interaction the key to the development of an individual's sense of self. As is generally true, we can best understand this topic by drawing on a variety of theory and research. Table 4-1 summarizes the rich literature, both sociological and psychological, on the development of the self.

 SOCIALIZATION AND THE LIFE COURSE

The Life Course

Among the Kota people of the Congo in Africa, adolescents paint themselves blue. Mexican American girls go on a daylong religious retreat before dancing the night away. Egyptian mothers step over their newborn infants seven times, and students at the Naval Academy throw their hats in the air. These are all ways of celebrating *rites of passage,* a means of dramatizing and validating changes in a person's status. The Kota rite marks the passage to adulthood. The color blue, viewed as the color of death, symbolizes the death of childhood. Hispanic girls celebrate reaching womanhood with a *quinceañera* ceremony at age 15. In the Cuban American community of Miami, the popularity of the *quinceañera* supports a network of party planners, caterers, dress designers, and the Miss Quinceañera Latina pageant. For thousands of years, Egyptian mothers have welcomed their newborns to the world in the Soboa ceremony by stepping over the seven-day-old infant seven times. And Naval Academy seniors celebrate their graduation from college by hurling their hats skyward (D. Cohen 1991; Garza 1993; McLane 1995; Quadagno 2002).

These specific ceremonies mark stages of development in the life course. They indicate that the socialization

relationships, even within their rather self-centered world.

In his well-known **cognitive theory of development,** Piaget (1954) identified four stages in the development of children's thought processes. In the first, or *sensorimotor,* stage, young children use their senses to make discoveries. For example, through touching they discover that their hands are actually a part of themselves. During the second, or *preoperational,* stage, children begin to use words and symbols to distinguish objects and ideas. The milestone in the third, or *concrete operational,* stage is that children engage in more logical thinking. They learn that even when a formless lump of clay is shaped into a snake, it is still the same clay. Finally, in the fourth, or *formal operational,* stage, adolescents become capable of sophisticated abstract thought, and can deal with ideas and values in a logical manner.

Piaget suggested that moral development becomes an important part of socialization as children develop

Table 4-1	Theoretical Approaches to Development of the Self	
Scholar	**Key Concepts and Contributions**	**Major Points of Theory**
Charles Horton Cooley 1864–1929 sociologist (USA)	Looking-glass self	Stages of development not distinct; feelings toward ourselves developed through interaction with others
George Herbert Mead 1863–1931 sociologist (USA)	The self Generalized other Significant others	Three distinct stages of development; self develops as children grasp the roles of others in their lives
Erving Goffman 1922–1982 sociologist (USA)	Impression management Dramaturgical approach Face-work	Self developed through the impressions we convey to others and to groups
Sigmund Freud 1856–1939 psychotherapist (Austria)	Psychotherapy	Self influenced by parents and by inborn drives, such as the drive for sexual gratification
Jean Piaget 1896–1980 child psychologist (Switzerland)	Cognitive theory of development	Four stages of cognitive development; moral development linked to socialization

Freshman cadets at the Virginia Military Institute crawl up a muddy hill in the school's gritty indoctrination into strict military discipline, a rite of passage at the school.

process continues through all stages of the human life cycle. Sociologists and other social scientists use the life-course approach in recognition that biological changes mold but do not dictate human behavior from birth until death.

In the culture of the United States, each individual has a "personal biography" that is influenced by events both in the family and in the larger society. While the completion of religious confirmations, school graduations, marriage, and parenthood can all be regarded as rites of passage in our society, people do not necessarily experience them at the same time. The timing of these events depends on such factors as one's gender, economic background, place of residence (central city, suburb, or rural area), and even time of birth.

We encounter some of the most difficult socialization challenges (and rites of passage) in the later years of life. Assessing one's accomplishments, coping with declining physical abilities, experiencing retirement, and facing the inevitability of death may lead to painful adjustments. Old age is further complicated by the negative way that many societies, including the United States, view and treat the elderly. The common stereotypes of the elderly as helpless and dependent may well weaken an older person's self-image. However, as we will explore more fully in Chapter 13, many older people continue to lead active, productive, fulfilled lives—whether in the paid labor force or as retirees.

Prisons are centers of resocialization, where people are placed under pressure to discard old behavior patterns and accept new ones. These prisoners are learning to use weights to release tension and exert their strength—a socially acceptable method of handling antisocial impulses.

Use Your Sociological Imagination www.mhhe.com/schaefer9

What was the last rite of passage you participated in? Was it formal or informal?

Anticipatory Socialization and Resocialization

The development of a social self is literally a lifelong transformation that begins in the crib and continues as one prepares for death. Two types of socialization occur at many points throughout the life course: anticipatory socialization and resocialization.

Anticipatory socialization refers to the processes of socialization in which a person "rehearses" for future positions, occupations, and social relationships. A culture can function more efficiently and smoothly if members become acquainted with the norms, values, and behavior associated with a social position before actually assuming that status. Preparation for many aspects of adult life begins with anticipatory socialization during childhood and adolescence, and continues throughout our lives as we prepare for new responsibilities.

You can see the process of anticipatory socialization take place when high school students start to consider what colleges they may attend. Traditionally, this meant looking at publications received in the mail or making campus visits. However, with new technology, more and more students are using the Web to begin their college experience. Colleges are investing more time and money in developing attractive websites through which students can take "virtual" campus walks and hear audio clips of everything from the college anthem to a sample zoology lecture.

Occasionally, assuming a new social or occupational position requires us to *unlearn* a previous orientation. *Resocialization* refers to the process of discarding former behavior patterns and accepting new ones as part of a transition in one's life. Often resocialization occurs during an explicit effort to transform an individual, as happens in reform schools, therapy groups, prisons, religious conversion settings, and political indoctrination camps. The process of resocialization typically involves considerable stress for the individual—much more so than socialization in general, or even anticipatory socialization (Gecas 1992).

Resocialization is particularly effective when it occurs within a total institution. Erving Goffman (1961) coined the term *total institutions* to refer to institutions, such as prisons, the military, mental hospitals, and convents, that regulate all aspects of a person's life under a single authority. Because the total institution is generally cut off from the rest of society, it provides for all the needs of its members. Quite literally, the crew of a merchant vessel at sea becomes part of a total institution. So elaborate are its requirements, so all-encompassing its activities, a total institution often represents a miniature society.

Goffman (1961) has identified four common traits of total institutions:

- All aspects of life are conducted in the same place under the control of a single authority.
- Any activities within the institution are conducted in the company of others in the same circumstances—for example, army recruits or novices in a convent.
- The authorities devise rules and schedule activities without consulting the participants.
- All aspects of life within a total institution are designed to fulfill the purpose of the organization. Thus, all activities in a monastery might be centered on prayer and communion with God. (Davies 1989; P. Rose et al. 1979)

People often lose their individuality within total institutions. For example, a person entering prison may experience the humiliation of a ***degradation ceremony*** as he or she is stripped of clothing, jewelry, and other personal possessions. From this point on, scheduled daily routines allow for little or no personal initiative. The individual becomes secondary and rather invisible in the overbearing social environment (Garfinkel 1956).

AGENTS OF SOCIALIZATION

As we have seen, the culture of the United States is defined by rather gradual movements from one stage of socialization to the next. The continuing and lifelong socialization process involves many different social forces that influence our lives and alter our self-images.

The family is the most important agent of socialization in the United States, especially for children. We'll also give particular attention in this chapter to five other agents of socialization: the school, the peer group, the mass media, the workplace, and the state. The role of religion in socializing young people into society's norms and values will be explored in Chapter 15.

Family

Children in Amish communities are raised in a highly structured and disciplined manner. But they are not immune to the temptations posed by their peers in the non-Amish world—"rebellious" acts such as dancing, drinking, and riding in cars. Still, Amish families don't get too concerned; they know the strong influence they ultimately exert over their offspring (see Box 4-2, page 92). The same is true for the family. It is tempting to say that the "peer group" or even the "media" really raise kids these days, especially when the spotlight falls on young people involved in shooting sprees and hate crimes. Almost all available research, however, shows that the role of the family in socializing a child cannot be overestimated (W. Williams 1998; for a different view see J. Harris 1998).

The lifelong process of learning begins shortly after birth. Since newborns can hear, see, smell, taste, and feel heat, cold, and pain, they are constantly orienting themselves to the surrounding world. Human beings, especially family members, constitute an important part of their social environment. People minister to the baby's needs by feeding, cleansing, carrying, and comforting the baby.

Cultural Influences

As both Charles Horton Cooley and George Herbert Mead noted, the development of the self is a critical aspect of the early years of one's life. But how children develop this sense of self can vary from one society to another. For example, parents in the United States would

never think of sending six-year-olds to school unsupervised. But this is the norm in Japan, where parents push their children to commute to school on their own from an early age. In cities like Tokyo, first-graders must learn to negotiate buses, subways, and long walks. To ensure their safety, parents carefully lay out rules: never talk to strangers; check with a station attendant if you get off at the wrong stop; if you miss your stop stay on to the end of the line, then call; take stairs, not escalators; don't fall asleep. Some parents equip the children with cell phones or pagers. One parent acknowledges that she worries, "but after they are 6, children are supposed to start being independent from the mother. If you're still taking your child to school after the first month, everyone looks at you funny" (Tolbert 2000:17).

While we consider the family's role in socialization, we need to remember that children do not play a passive role. They are active agents, influencing and altering the families, schools, and communities of which they are a part (Corsaro 1997).

The Impact of Race and Gender

In the United States, social development includes exposure to cultural assumptions regarding gender and race. African American parents, for example, have learned that children as young as two years old can absorb negative

Entrepreneur Yla Eason poses with the ethnic dolls her company creates and merchandises. Young girls learn about themselves and their social roles by playing with dolls.

Jacob is a typical teenager in his Amish community in Lancaster County, Pennsylvania. At 14 he is in his final year of schooling. Over the next few years he will become a full-time worker on the family farm, taking breaks only for three-hour religious services each morning. When he is a bit older, Jacob may bring a date to a community "singing" in his family's horse-drawn buggy. But he will be forbidden to date outside his own community and can marry only with the deacon's consent. Jacob is well aware of the rather different way of life of the "English" (the Amish term for non-Amish people). One summer, late at night, he and his friends hitchhiked to a nearby town to see a movie, breaking several Amish taboos. His parents learned of his adventure, but like most Amish they are confident that their son will choose the Amish way of life. What is this way of life, and how can his parents be so sure of its appeal?

Jacob and his family live in a manner very similar to their ancestors, members of the conservative Mennonite church who migrated to North America from Europe in the 18th and 19th centuries. Schisms in the church after 1850 led to a division between those who wanted to preserve the "old order" and those who favored a "new order" with more progressive methods and organization. Today the old order Amish live in about 50 communities in the United States and Canada. Estimates put their number at about 80,000, with approximately 75 percent living in three states—Ohio, Pennsylvania, and Indiana.

The old order Amish live a simple life and reject most aspects of modernization and contemporary technology. That's why they spurn conveniences such as electricity, automobiles, radio, and television. The Amish maintain their own schools and traditions, and do not want their children socialized into many norms and values of the dominant culture of the United States. Those who stray

> The old order Amish live a "simple" life and reject most aspects of modernization and contemporary technology.

too far from Amish mores may be excommunicated and shunned by all other members of the community—a practice of social control called *Meiding*. Sociologists sometimes use the term "secessionist minorities" to refer to groups like the Amish, who reject assimilation and coexist with the rest of society primarily on their own terms.

The socialization of Amish youths pushes them to forgo movies, radio, television, cosmetics, jewelry, musical instruments of any kind, and motorized vehicles. Yet, like Jacob did, Amish youths often test their subculture's boundaries during a period of discovery called *rumspringe*, a term that means "running around." Amish young people attend barn dances where taboos like drinking, smoking, and driving cars are commonly broken. Parents often react by looking the other way, sometimes literally. For example, when they hear radio sounds from a barn or a motorcycle entering their property in the middle of the night, they don't immediately investigate and punish their offspring. Instead, they pretend not to notice, secure in the comfort that their children almost always return to the traditions of the Amish lifestyle. Research shows that only about 20 percent of Amish youths leave the fold, generally to join a more liberal Mennonite group. Rarely does a baptized adult ever leave. The socialization of Amish youths moves them gently but firmly into becoming Amish adults.

Let's Discuss

1. What makes Amish parents so sure that their children will choose to remain in the Amish community?
2. If you lived in an Amish community, how would your life differ from the way it is now? In your opinion, what advantages and disadvantages would that lifestyle have?

Sources: Meyers 1992; Remnick 1998b; Zellner 2001.

messages about Blacks in children's books, toys, and television shows—all of which are designed primarily for White consumers. At the same time, African American children are exposed more often than others to the inner-city youth gang culture. Because most Blacks, even those who are middle class, live near very poor neighborhoods, children such as Charisse (see the chapter opening excerpt) are susceptible to these influences, despite their parents' strong family values (Linn and Poussaint 1999; Pattillo-McCoy 1999).

The term **gender roles** refers to expectations regarding the proper behavior, attitudes, and activities of males and females. For example, we traditionally think of "toughness" as masculine—and desirable only in men—while we view "tenderness" as feminine. As we will see in Chapter 12, other cultures do not necessarily assign these qualities to each gender in the way that our culture does.

As the primary agents of childhood socialization, parents play a critical role in guiding children into those gender roles deemed appropriate in a society. Other adults, older siblings, the mass media, and religious and educational institutions also have a noticeable impact on a child's socialization into feminine and masculine norms. A culture or subculture may require that one sex or the other take primary responsibility for socialization of children, economic support of the family, or religious or intellectual leadership.

Interactionists remind us that socialization concerning not only masculinity and femininity, but also marriage and parenthood, begins in childhood as a part of family life. Children observe their parents as they express affection, deal with finances, quarrel, complain about in-laws, and so forth. This represents an informal process of anticipatory socialization. The child develops a tentative model of what being married and being a parent are like. (We will explore socialization for marriage and parenthood more fully in Chapter 14.)

Typically, parents are thought to have a positive effect on their children's socialization. But that is not always the case. A survey of nearly 600 teens in New York, Texas, Florida, and California indicated that 20 percent had shared drugs other than alcohol with their parents, and about 5 percent were actually introduced to drugs by their mothers or fathers. Approximately 1.5 million children under the age of 18, or 2 percent of all U.S. youths, have a parent in a state or federal prison at some time during the year. Whether positive or negative, socialization within the family is a powerful process (Leinwand 2000; Mumola 2000).

School

Where did you learn the national anthem? Who taught you about the heroes of the American Revolution? Where were you first tested on your knowledge of your culture? Like the family, schools have an explicit mandate to socialize people in the United States—and especially children—into the norms and values of our culture.

As conflict theorists Samuel Bowles and Herbert Gintis (1976) have observed, schools in this country foster competition through built-in systems of reward and punishment, such as grades and evaluations by teachers. Consequently, a child who is working intently to learn a new skill can sometimes come to feel stupid and unsuccessful. However, as the self matures, children become capable of increasingly realistic assessments of their intellectual, physical, and social abilities.

Functionalists point out that schools, as agents of socialization, fulfill the function of teaching children the values and customs of the larger society. Conflict theorists agree, but add that schools can reinforce the divisive aspects of society, especially those of social class. For example, higher education in the United States is costly despite the existence of financial aid programs. Students from affluent backgrounds have an advantage in gaining access to universities and professional training. At the same time, less affluent young people may never receive the preparation that would qualify them for the best-paying and most prestigious jobs. The contrast between the functionalist and conflict views of education will be discussed in more detail in Chapter 16.

In teaching students the values and customs of the larger society, schools in the United States have traditionally socialized children into conventional gender roles. Professors of education Myra Sadker and David Sadker (1985:54; 1995) note that "although many believe that classroom sexism disappeared in the early '70s, it hasn't." A report released by the American Association of University Women, which summarized numerous studies of girls in school, concluded that girls in U.S. schools face some special challenges.

According to this report, schools are making progress toward equitable treatment of boys and girls, but

Despite equal opportunity in high school, boys are more likely than girls to pursue advanced training in computer science. The technical know-how they gain gives them an edge later on in life.

Table 4-2	High School Popularity			
What makes high school girls popular?		**What makes high school boys popular?**		
According to college men:	**According to college women:**	**According to college men:**	**According to college women:**	
1. Physical attractiveness 2. Grades/intelligence 3. Participation in sports 4. General sociability 5. Popularity with boys	1. Grades/intelligence 2. Participation in sports 3. General sociability 4. Physical attractiveness 5. Clothes	1. Participation in sports 2. Grades/intelligence 3. Popularity with girls 4. General sociability 5. Car	1. Participation in sports 2. Grades/intelligence 3. General sociability 4. Physical attractiveness 5. School clubs/government	

Note: Students at the following universities were asked in which ways adolescents in their high schools had gained prestige with their peers: Cornell University, Louisiana State University, Southeastern Louisiana University, State University of New York at Albany, State University of New York at Stony Brook, University of Georgia, and the University of New Hampshire.

Source: Suitor et al. 2001:445.

concerns remain. Girls excel in writing, foreign languages, and literature, but they lag well behind boys in technological training, which is currently much in demand in the labor force. Boys outnumber girls 3 to 1 in taking Advanced Placement tests in computer science, for example. Particularly significant, according to the report, is the fact that girls are more vulnerable than boys to sexual violence and harassment both at home and at school, which certainly threatens their success in formal schooling (American Association of University Women 1998).

In other cultures as well, schools serve socialization functions. Until the otherthrow of Saddam Hussein in 2003, the sixth-grade textbooks used in Iraqi schools concentrated almost entirely on the military and its values of loyalty, honor, and sacrifice. Children were taught that their enemies were Iran, the United States, Israel and its supporters, and NATO, the European military alliance. Within months of the regime's fall, the curriculum had been rewritten to remove indoctrination on behalf of Hussein, his army, and his Baath Socialist Party (Marr 2003).

Peer Group

Ask 13-year-olds who matters most in their lives and they are likely to answer "friends." As a child grows older, the family becomes somewhat less important in social development. Instead, peer groups increasingly assume the role of Mead's significant others. Within the peer group, young people associate with others who are approximately their own age, and who often enjoy a similar social status.

Peer groups can ease the transition to adult responsibilities. At home, parents tend to dominate; at school,

the teenager must contend with teachers and administrators. But within the peer group, each member can assert himself or herself in a way that may not be possible elsewhere. Nevertheless, almost all adolescents in our culture remain economically dependent on their parents, and most are emotionally dependent as well.

Peers can be the source of harassment as well as support. This problem has received considerable attention in Japan, where bullying in school is a constant fact of life. Groups of students act together to humiliate, disgrace, or torment a specific student, a practice known in Japan as *ijime*. Most students go along with the bullying out of fear that they might be the target sometime. In some cases the *ijime* has led to a child's suicide. In 1998, the situation became so desperate that a volunteer association set up a 24-hour telephone hotline in Tokyo just for children (see the chapter-opening poster). The success of this effort convinced the government to sponsor a nationwide hotline system (Matsushita 1999; Sugimoto 1997).

Gender differences are noteworthy among adolescents. Boys and girls are socialized by their parents, peers, and the media to identify many of the same paths to popularity, but to different degrees. Table 4-2 compares male and female college students' reports of how girls and boys they knew become popular in high school. The two groups named many of the same paths to popularity, but gave them a different order of importance. While neither men nor women named sexual activity, drug or alcohol use as one of the top five paths, college men were much more likely than women to mention those behaviors as a means to becoming popular, for both boys and girls.

The social grouping of adolescents also varies by gender. Males are more likely to spend time in *groups* of males, whereas females are more likely to interact with a *single* other female. This pattern reflects differences in levels of emotional intimacy; teenage males are less likely to develop strong emotional ties than are females. Instead, males are more inclined to share in group activities. These patterns are evident among adolescents in many societies besides the United States (Dornbusch 1989).

Mass Media and Technology

In the last 80 years, media innovations—radio, motion pictures, recorded music, television, and the Internet—have become important agents of socialization. Television, in particular, is a critical force in the socialization of children in the United States. Remarkably, 32 percent of children in the United States under the age of 7 have their own television, and 53 percent of all children ages 12 to 18 have their own sets. As Figure 4-1 shows, young people in the United States spend an average of 5.5 hours per day with some form of media, mostly television. Little wonder that the American Academy of Pediatrics has urged parents not to allow children under two years old to watch television. Parents should also avoid using any kind of media as an electronic baby-sitter, and should try to create an "electronic media–free" environment in their children's rooms (Rideout et al. 1999). The impact of the media and related technology on socialization will be covered in detail in Chapter 7.

Television, however, is not always a negative socializing influence. Television programs and even commercials can introduce young people to unfamiliar lifestyles and cultures. Not only do children in the United States learn about life in "faraway lands," but inner-city children learn about the lives of farm children, and vice versa. The same goes for children living in other countries.

Sociologists and other social scientists have also begun to consider the impact of technology on socialization, especially as it applies to family life. The Silicon Valley Cultures Project studied families in California's Silicon Valley (a technological corridor) for 10 years, beginning in 1991. Although these families may not be typical, they probably represent a lifestyle that more and more households will approximate as time goes by. This study has found that technology in the form of e-mail, webpages, cellular phones, voice mail, digital organizers, and pagers is allowing householders to let outsiders do everything from grocery shopping to carpooling. The researchers are also finding that families are socialized into multitasking (doing more than one task at a time) as the social norm; devoting one's full attention to one task—even eating or driving—is less and less common on a typical day (Silicon Valley Cultures Project 2003).

Workplace

Learning to behave appropriately within an occupation is a fundamental aspect of human socialization. In the United States, working full-time confirms adult status; it indicates that one has passed out of adolescence. In a sense, socialization into an occupation can represent both a harsh reality ("I have to work in order to buy food and pay the rent") and the realization of an ambition ("I've always wanted to be an airline pilot") (W. Moore 1968:862).

It used to be that going to work began with the end of our formal schooling, but that is no longer the case, at least not in the United States. More and more young people work today, and not just for a parent or relative. Adolescents generally seek jobs in order to make spending money; 80 percent of high school seniors say that little or none of what they earn goes to family expenses. And these teens rarely look on their employment as a means of exploring vocational interests or getting on-the-job training.

Some observers feel that the increasing number of teenagers who are working earlier in life and for longer hours are now finding the workplace almost as important

FIGURE 4-1

Media Usage, Ages 2–18

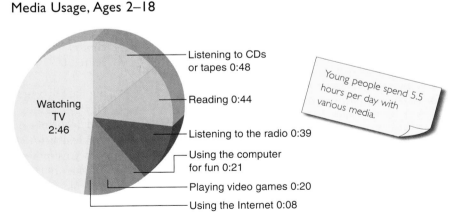

Source: Based on Rideout et al. 1999.

> **Think About It**
> How does your use of the media compare to these national averages?

This boy's day doesn't end when school lets out. So many teenagers now work after school, the workplace has become another important agent of socialization for that age group.

an agent of socialization as school. In fact, a number of educators complain that student time at work is adversely affecting schoolwork. The level of teenage employment in the United States is the highest among industrial countries, which may provide one explanation for why U.S. high school students lag behind those in other countries on international achievement tests.

Socialization in the workplace changes when it involves a more permanent shift from an after-school job to full-time employment. Occupational socialization can be most intense during the transition from school to job, but it continues throughout one's work history. Technological advances may alter the requirements of the position and necessitate some degree of resocialization. Today, men and women change occupations, employers, or places of work many times during their adult years. Occupational socialization continues, then, throughout a person's years in the labor market.

College students today recognize that occupational socialization is not socialization into one lifetime occupation. They anticipate going through a number of jobs. A survey of college students and recent graduates found that 78 percent plan to stay with their first employer for no longer than three years. One out of every four antici-

pates staying with a first employer only one year (Jobtrak.com 2000a).

The State

Social scientists have increasingly recognized the importance of the government as an agent of socialization because of its growing impact on the life course. Traditionally, family members have served as the primary caregivers in our culture, but in the twentieth century, the family's protective function was steadily transferred to outside agencies such as hospitals, mental health clinics, and insurance companies. The state runs many of these agencies or licenses and regulates them (Ogburn and Tibbits 1934).

In the past, heads of households and local groups such as religious organizations influenced the life course most significantly. However, today national interests are increasingly influencing the individual as a citizen and an economic actor. For example, labor unions and political parties serve as intermediaries between the individual and the state.

The state has had a noteworthy impact on the life course by reinstituting rites of passage that had disappeared from agricultural societies and during periods of early industrialization. For example, government regulations stipulate the ages at which a person may drive a car, drink alcohol, vote in elections, marry without parental permission, work overtime, and retire. These regulations do not constitute strict rites of passage: most 18-year-olds choose not to vote, and most people choose their age of retirement without reference to government dictates. Still, the state shapes the socialization process by regulating the life course to some degree and by influencing our views of appropriate behavior at particular ages (Mayer and Schoepflin 1989).

In the social policy section that follows, we will see that government is now under pressure to become a provider of child care, which would give it a new and direct role in the socialization of infants and young children.

SOCIAL POLICY and SOCIALIZATION	Child Care around the World	

The Issue

The rise in single-parent families, increased job opportunities for women, and the need for additional family income have all propelled an increasing number of mothers of young children into the paid labor force of the United States. In 2002, 55 percent of women who had given birth the previous year were back in the labor force. Who, then, takes care of the children of these women during work hours?

For 35 percent of all preschoolers with employed mothers, the solution has become group child care programs. Day care centers have become the functional equivalent of the nuclear family, performing some of the nurturing and socialization functions previously handled only by family members. But how does group day care compare to care in the home? And what is the state's responsibility to assure high-quality care (Fields 2003; K. Smith 2000)?

The Setting

Few people in the United States or elsewhere can afford the luxury of having a parent stay at home, or of paying for high-quality live-in child care. For millions of mothers and fathers, finding the right kind of child care is a challenge to parenting and to the pocketbook.

Researchers have found that high-quality child care centers do not adversely affect the socialization of children; in fact, good day care benefits children. The value of preschool programs was documented in a series of studies conducted in the United States by the National Institute of Child Health and Human Development. Researchers found no significant differences in infants who had received extensive nonmaternal care compared with those who had been cared for solely by their mothers. They also reported that more and more infants in the United States are being placed in child care outside the home, and that overall, the quality of these arrangements is better

than has been found in previous studies. It is difficult, however, to generalize about child care, since there is so much variability among day care providers, and even among policies from one state to another (M. Gardner 2001; NICHD 1998).

Sociological Insights

Studies that assess the quality of child care outside the home reflect the micro level of analysis and the interest of interactionists in the impact of face-to-face interaction. These studies also explore macro-level implications for the functioning of social institutions like the family. But some of the issues surrounding day care have also been of interest to those who take the conflict perspective.

In the United States, high-quality day care is not equally available to all families. Parents in wealthy neighborhoods have an easier time finding day care than those in poor or working-class communities. Finding *affordable* child care is also a problem. Viewed from a conflict perspective, child care costs are an especially serious burden for lower-class families. The poorest families spend 25 percent of their income for preschool child care, while families who are *not* poor pay only 6 percent or less of their income for day care.

People in Sweden pay higher taxes than U.S. citizens, but they have access to excellent preschool day care at little or no cost.

Feminists echo the concern of conflict theorists that high-quality child care receives little government support because it is regarded as "merely a way to let women work." Nearly all child care workers (97 percent) are women; many find themselves in low-status, minimum-wage jobs. Typically, food servers, messengers, and gas station attendants make more money than child care workers, most of whom earn less than $8.00 per hour. Not surprisingly, turnover among employees in child care centers runs at about 30 percent per year (Bureau of the Census 2001a:380; Clawson and Gerstel 2002).

Policy Initiatives

Policies regarding child care outside the home vary throughout the world. Most developing nations do not have the economic base to provide subsidized child care. Working mothers rely largely on relatives or take their children to work. Even those industrial countries with elaborate programs of subsidized child care occasionally fall short of the need for high-quality supervised child care.

When policymakers decide that child care is desirable, they must determine the degree to which taxpayers should subsidize it. In Sweden and Denmark, one-third to one-half of children under age three were in government-subsidized child care full-time in 2001. In the United States, where government subsidies are very lim-

ited, the total cost of child care can easily run between $5,000 and $10,000 per family per year (Mencimer 2002).

We have a long way to go in making high-quality child care more affordable and accessible, not just in the United States but throughout the world. In an attempt to reduce government spending, France is considering cutting back the budgets of subsidized nurseries, even though waiting lists exist and the French public heartily disapproves of cutbacks. In Germany, reunification has reduced the options previously open to East German mothers, who had become accustomed to government-supported child care (Hank 2001; L. King 1998).

Experts in child development view such reports as a vivid reminder of the need for greater government and private-sector support for child care.

Let's Discuss

1. Were you ever in a day care program? Do you recall the experience as good or bad? In general, do you think it is desirable to expose young children to the socializing influence of day care?
2. In the view of conflict theorists, why does child care receive little government support?
3. Should the costs of day care programs be paid by government, by the private sector, or entirely by parents?

CHAPTER RESOURCES

Summary

Socialization is the process in which people learn the attitudes, values, and actions appropriate for members of a particular culture. This chapter examined the role of socialization in human development; the way in which people develop perceptions, feelings, and beliefs about themselves; the lifelong nature of the socialization process; and the important agents of socialization.

1. Socialization affects the overall cultural practices of a society; it also shapes the images that we hold of ourselves.
2. Heredity and environmental factors interact in influencing the socialization process.
3. In the early 1900s, Charles Horton Cooley advanced the belief that we learn who we are by interacting with others, a phenomenon he called the *looking-glass self.*

4. George Herbert Mead, best known for his theory of the *self,* proposed that as people mature, their selves begin to reflect their concern about reactions from others—both *generalized others* and *significant others.*
5. Erving Goffman has shown that in many of our daily activities, we try to convey distinct impressions of who we are, a process called *impression management.*
6. Socialization proceeds throughout the life course. Some societies mark stages of development with formal *rites of passage.* In the culture of the United States, significant events such as marriage and parenthood serve to change a person's status.
7. As the primary agents of socialization, parents play a critical role in guiding children into those *gender roles* deemed appropriate in a society.

8. Like the family, schools in the United States have an explicit mandate to socialize people—especially children—into the norms and values of our culture.
9. Peer groups and the mass media, especially television, are important agents of socialization for adolescents.
10. Socialization in the workplace begins with part-time employment while we are in school and continues when we work full-time and change jobs throughout our lives.
11. The state shapes the socialization process by regulating the life course and influencing our views of appropriate behavior at particular ages.
12. As more and more mothers of young children have entered the labor market, the demand for child care has increased dramatically, posing policy questions for many nations around the world.

Critical Thinking Questions

1. Should social research be conducted on issues such as the influence of heredity and environment, even though many investigators believe that this type of analysis is potentially detrimental to large numbers of people?
2. Drawing on Erving Goffman's dramaturgical approach, discuss how the following groups engage in impression management: athletes, college instructors, parents, physicians, and politicians.
3. How would functionalists and conflict theorists differ in their analysis of socialization by the mass media?

Key Terms

Anticipatory socialization   Processes of socialization in which a person "rehearses" for future positions, occupations, and social relationships. (page 90)

Cognitive theory of development   Jean Piaget's theory that children's thought progresses through four stages of development. (88)

Degradation ceremony   An aspect of the socialization process within some total institutions, in which people are subjected to humiliating rituals. 91)

Dramaturgical approach   A view of social interaction in which people are seen as theatrical performers. (86)

Face-work   The efforts people make to maintain the proper image and avoid public embarrassment. (86)

Gender role   Expectations regarding the proper behavior, attitudes, and activities of a male or female. (91)

Generalized other   The attitudes, viewpoints, and expectations of society as a whole that a child takes into account in his or her behavior. (85)

Impression management   The altering of the presentation of the self in order to create distinctive appearances and satisfy particular audiences. (86)

Looking-glass self   A concept that emphasizes the self as the product of our social interactions with others. (84)

Personality   A person's typical patterns of attitudes, needs, characteristics, and behavior. (81)

Resocialization   The process of discarding former behavior patterns and accepting new ones as part of a transition in one's life. (90)

Rite of passage   A ritual marking the symbolic transition from one social position to another. (88)

Role taking   The process of mentally assuming the perspective of another and responding from that imagined viewpoint. (85)

Self   A distinct identity that sets us apart from others. (84)

Significant other   An individual who is most important in the development of the self, such as a parent, friend, or teacher. (86)

Socialization   The lifelong process in which people learn the attitudes, values, and behaviors appropriate for members of a particular culture. (81)

Symbol   A gesture, object, or word that forms the basis of human communication. (85)

Total institution   An institution that regulates all aspects of a person's life under a single authority, such as a prison, the military, a mental hospital, or a convent. (90)

TECHNOLOGY RESOURCES

Internet Connection

Note: While all the URLs listed were current as of the printing of this book, these sites often change. Please check our website (www.mhhe.com/schaefer9) for updates, hyperlinks, and exercises related to these sites.

1. In this chapter, you have learned that the Amish maintain their own schools and traditions, and do not want their children socialized into many norms and values of the dominant culture of the United States. Amish net (http://Amish.net/lifestyle.asp) helps the public to understand the Amish lifestyle. Visit the site to learn more about this lifestyle.

2. Erving Goffman coined the term *total institutions* to refer to institutions that regulate all aspects of a person's life under a single authority, such as prisons, the military, mental hospitals, and convents. During World War II, the United States government forced 120,000 people of Japanese ancestry to live in internment camps. To learn more about these camps as total institutions, link to www.lib.utah.edu/spc/photo/9066/9066.htm.

Online Learning Center with PowerWeb

The development of the social self is literally a lifelong transformation that begins in the crib and continues throughout one's life course. One type of socialization that can occur at some point in the life course is resocialization. *Resocialization* refers to the process of discarding former behavior patterns and accepting new ones as part of a transition in one's life. One of the Internet activities in the student center of the Online Learning Center (**www.mhhe.com/schaefer9**) gives you a glimpse into the resocialization experienced by those in concentration camps. Spend time learning about the Holocaust and life in concentration camps through the video, photographs, and stories.

SOCIAL INTERACTION AND SOCIAL STRUCTURE

Social Interaction and Reality

Elements of Social Structure

Social Structure in Global Perspective

Social Policy and Social Structure: The AIDS Crisis

Boxes

SOCIAL INEQUALITY:
Disability as a Master Status

RESEARCH IN ACTION:
Social Networks among Low-Income Women

If this picture offends you, we apologize. If it doesn't, perhaps we should explain. Because, although this picture looks innocent enough, to the Asian market, it symbolizes death. But then, not everyone should be expected to know that.

That's where we come in. Over the last 7 years Intertrend has been guiding clients to the Asian market with some very impressive results. Clients like California Bank & Trust, Disneyland, GTE, JCPenney, Nestlé, Northwest Airlines, Sempra Energy, The Southern California Gas Company and Western Union have all profited from our knowledge of this country's fastest growing and most affluent cultural market. And their success has made us one of the largest Asian advertising agencies in the country.

We can help you as well. Give us a call or E-mail us at jych@intertrend.com. We can share some more of our trade secrets. We can also show you how we've helped our clients succeed in the Asian market. And that's something that needs no apology.

InterTrend Communications
19191 South Vermont Ave., Suite 400
Torrance, CA 90502
310.324.6313   fax 310.324.6848

OOOOPS.

In our social interaction with other cultures it is important to know what social rules apply. In Japan, for example, it is impolite to leave your chopsticks sticking up in the rice bowl—a symbol of death for the Japanese and an insult to their dead ancestors. This poster was created by an advertising agency that promises to steer its U.S. clients clear of such gaffes.

The quiet of a summer Sunday morning in Palo Alto, California, was shattered by a screeching squad car siren as police swept through the city picking up college students in a surprise mass arrest. Each suspect was charged with a felony, warned of his constitutional rights, spread-eagled against the car, searched, handcuffed and carted off in the back seat of the squad car to the police station for booking.

After being fingerprinted and having identification forms prepared for his "jacket" (central information file), each prisoner was left isolated in a detention cell to wonder what he had done to get himself into this mess. After a while, he was blindfolded and transported to the "Stanford County Prison." Here he began the induction process of becoming a prisoner—stripped naked, skin searched, deloused, and issued a uniform, bedding, soap and towel. By late afternoon when nine such arrests had been completed, these youthful "first offenders" sat in dazed silence on the cots in their barren cells.

These men were part of a very unusual kind of prison, an experimental or mock prison, created by social psychologists for the purpose of intensively studying the effects of imprisonment upon volunteer research subjects. When we planned our two-week long simulation of prison life, we were primarily concerned about understanding the process by which people adapt to the novel and alien environment in which those called "prisoners" lose their liberty, civil rights, independence and privacy, while those called "guards" gain social power by accepting the responsibility for controlling and managing the lives of their dependent charges. . . .

Our final sample of participants (10 prisoners and 11 guards) were selected from over 75 volunteers recruited through ads in the city and campus newspapers. . . . Half were randomly assigned to role-play being guards, the others to be prisoners. Thus, there were no measurable differences between the guards and the prisoners at the start of this experiment. . . .

At the end of only six days we had to close down our mock prison because what we saw was frightening. It was no longer apparent to most of the subjects (or to us) where reality ended and their roles began. The majority had indeed become prisoners or guards, no longer able to clearly differentiate between role playing and self. There were dramatic changes in virtually every aspect of their behavior, thinking and feeling. In less than a week the experience of imprisonment undid (temporarily) a lifetime of learning; human values were suspended, self-concepts were challenged and the ugliest, most base, pathological side of human nature surfaced. We were horrified because we saw some boys (guards) treat others as if they were despicable animals, taking pleasure in cruelty, while other boys (prisoners) became servile, dehumanized robots who thought only of escape, of their own individual survival, and of their mounting hatred for the guards. *(Zimbardo et al. 1974:61, 62, 63; Zimbardo 1972:4)* ■ ◉

Additional information about this excerpt can be found on the Online Learning Center at **www.mhhe.com/schaefer9.**

I n this study directed and described by social psychologist Philip Zimbardo, college students adopted the patterns of social interaction expected of guards and prisoners when they were placed in a mock prison. Sociologists use the term *social interaction* to refer to the ways in which people respond to one another, whether face to face or over the telephone or on the computer. In the mock prison, social interactions between guards and prisoners were highly impersonal. The guards addressed the prisoners by number rather than name, and they wore reflective sunglasses that made eye contact impossible.

As in many real-life prisons, the simulated prison at Stanford University had a social structure in which guards held virtually total control over prisoners. The term *social structure* refers to the way in which a society is organized into predictable relationships. The social structure of Zimbardo's mock prison influenced how the guards and prisoners interacted. Zimbardo (2003:546) notes that it was a real prison "in the minds of the jailers and their captives." His simulated prison experiment, first conducted more than 30 years ago, has subsequently been repeated (with similar findings) both in the United States and in other countries. In fact, in 2002 the British Broadcasting Company (BBC) created a reality-based television program called *The Experiment,* in which, over the objections of Zimbardo and other scholars, producers tried to re-create the mock prison experiment. Fortunately, the presence of TV cameras mitigated the harsh treatment of prisoners.

The closely linked concepts of social interaction and social structure are central to sociological study. Sociologists scrutinize patterns of behavior to understand and accurately describe the social interactions of a community or society and the social structure in which they take place. Who determines how we should behave with one another? Is it possible to redefine or change that "social reality"? How do we acquire our social roles, and how do they affect our interactions? These topics are closely related to socialization (see Chapter 4), the process through which people learn the attitudes, values, and behaviors appropriate to their culture.

This chapter begins by considering how social interaction shapes the way we view the world around us. We will focus next on the five basic elements of social structure: statuses, social roles, groups, social networks, and social institutions. Groups are important because much of our social interaction occurs in them. Social institutions such as the family, religion, and government are a fundamental aspect of social structure. We will contrast the functionalist, conflict, and interactionist approaches to the study of social institutions. We will also examine the typologies developed by Émile Durkheim, Ferdinand Tönnies, and Gerhard Lenski for comparing modern societies with simpler forms of social structure. The social policy section will consider the AIDS crisis and its implications for social institutions throughout the world. ■

SOCIAL INTERACTION AND REALITY

When someone in a crowd shoves you, do you automatically push back? Or do you consider the circumstances of the incident and the attitude of the instigator before you react? Chances are you do the latter. According to sociologist Herbert Blumer (1969:79), the distinctive characteristic of social interaction among people is that "human beings interpret or 'define' each other's actions instead of merely reacting to each other's actions." In other words, our response to someone's behavior is based on the *meaning* we attach to his or her actions. Reality is shaped by our perceptions, evaluations, and definitions.

These meanings typically reflect the norms and values of the dominant culture and our socialization experiences within that culture. As interactionists emphasize, the meanings that we attach to people's behavior are shaped by our interactions with them and with the larger society. Social reality is literally constructed from our social interactions (Berger and Luckmann 1966).

Defining and Reconstructing Reality

How do we define our social reality? As an example, consider something as simple as how we regard tattoos. Even as recently as a few years ago, most of us in the United States considered tattoos weird or kooky. We associated

Symbols of status and power, such as this judge's robes, tend to reinforce the position of the dominant groups in society. When such symbols are associated with a member of a racial minority, they challenge prevailing racial stereotypes, changing what the interactionist William I. Thomas called "the definition of the situation."

meaning that that person or situation has for them. For example, in Philip Zimbardo's mock prison experiment, student "guards" and "prisoners" accepted the definition of the situation (including the traditional roles and behavior associated with being a guard or prisoner) and acted accordingly.

As we have seen throughout the last 50 years—first in the civil rights movement of the 1960s and since then among such groups as women, the elderly, gays and lesbians, and people with disabilities—an important aspect of the process of social change involves redefining or reconstructing social reality. Members of subordinate groups challenge traditional definitions and begin to perceive and experience reality in a new way. For example, the world champion boxer Muhammad Ali began his career as the creation of a White male syndicate, which sponsored his early matches when he was known as Cassius Clay. Soon, however, the young boxer rebelled against those who would keep him or his race down. He broke the old stereotypes of the self-effacing Black athlete. He insisted on his own political views (including refusing to serve in the Vietnam War), his own religion (Black Muslim), and his own name (Muhammad Ali). Not only did Ali change the world of sports; he also had a hand in altering the world of race relations (Remnick 1998a).

Viewed from a sociological perspective, then, Ali was redefining social reality by looking much more critically at the racist thinking and terminology that restricted him and other African Americans.

Negotiated Order

As we have just seen, people can reconstruct social reality through a process of internal change, taking a different view of everyday behavior. Yet people also reshape reality by *negotiating* changes in patterns of social interaction. The term *negotiation* refers to the attempt to reach agreement with others concerning some objective. Negotiation does not involve coercion; it goes by many names, including *bargaining, compromising, trading off, mediating, exchanging, "wheeling and dealing,"* and *collusion*. It is through negotiation as a form of social interaction that society creates its social structure (A. Strauss 1977; see also Fine 1984).

Negotiation occurs in many ways. As interactionists point out, some social situations, such as buying groceries, involve no mediation, while other situations require negotiation. For example, we may negotiate with others regarding time ("When should we arrive?"), space ("Could we meet at your house?"), or even the assignment of places in line while waiting for concert tickets. In traditional societies, impending marriage often leads to negotiations between the families of the bride and

them with fringe countercultural groups, such as punk rockers, bike gangs, and skinheads. Among many people, a tattoo elicited an automatic negative response. Now, however, so many people have tattoos—including society's trendsetters and major sports figures—and the ritual of getting a tattoo has become so legitimized, the mainstream culture regards tattoos differently. At this point, as a result of increased social interaction with tattooed people, tattoos look perfectly at home to us in a number of settings.

The ability to define social reality reflects a group's power within a society. In fact, one of the most crucial aspects of the relationship between dominant and subordinate groups is the ability of the dominant or majority group to define a society's values. Sociologist William I. Thomas (1923), an early critic of theories of racial and gender differences, recognized that the "definition of the situation" could mold the thinking and personality of the individual. Writing from an interactionist perspective, Thomas observed that people respond not only to the objective features of a person or situation but also to the groom. For example, anthropologist Ray Abrahams (1968) has described how the Labwor people of Africa arrange for livestock to go from the groom's to the bride's family at the time of marriage. In the view of the Labwor, such bargaining over an exchange of cows and sheep culminates not only in a marriage, but more important, in the linking of two clans or families.

While such family-to-family bargaining is common in traditional cultures, negotiation can take much more elaborate forms in modern industrial societies. Consider college financial aid programs. From a sociological perspective, such programs are formal norms (reflected in established practices and procedures for granting aid to college students). Yet the programs undergo revision through negotiated outcomes involving many interests, including foundations, banks, the admissions office, and the faculty. On an individual level, the student applicant will mediate with representatives of the college financial aid office. Changes in the individual's situation will occur through such negotiations (Maines 1977, 1982; J. Thomas 1984).

Negotiations underlie much of our social behavior. Because most elements of social structure are not static, they are subject to change through bargaining and exchanging. Sociologists use the term *negotiated order* to underscore the fact that the social order is continually being constructed and altered through negotiation. **Negotiated order** refers to a social structure that derives its existence from the social interactions through which people define and redefine its character.

We can add negotiation to our list of cultural universals because all societies provide guidelines or norms in which negotiations take place. The recurring role of negotiation in social interaction and social structure will be apparent as we examine the major elements of social structure (Strauss 1977).

p. 59

ELEMENTS OF SOCIAL STRUCTURE

We can examine predictable social relationships in terms of five elements: statuses, social roles, groups, social networks, and social institutions. These elements make up social structure just as a foundation, walls, and ceilings make up a building's structure. The elements of social structure are developed through the lifelong process of socialization, described in Chapter 4.

Statuses

We normally think of a person's "status" as having to do with influence, wealth, and fame. However, sociologists use the term **status** to refer to any of the full range of so-

FIGURE 5-1

Social Statuses

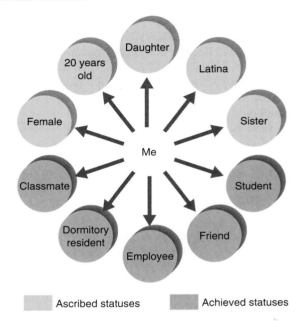

Ascribed statuses ⬤ Achieved statuses ⬤

> **Think About It**
> The young woman in this figure—"me"—occupies many positions in society, each of which involves distinct statuses. How would you define your statuses? Which have the most influence in your life?

cially defined positions within a large group or society—from the lowest to the highest position. Within our society, a person can occupy the status of president of the United States, fruit picker, son or daughter, violinist, teenager, resident of Minneapolis, dental technician, or neighbor. A person can hold a number of statuses at the same time.

Ascribed and Achieved Status

Sociologists view some statuses as *ascribed,* while they categorize others as *achieved* (see Figure 5-1). An **ascribed status** is assigned to a person by society without regard for the person's unique talents or characteristics. Generally, this assignment takes place at birth; thus, a person's racial background, gender, and age are all considered ascribed statuses. Though these characteristics are biological in origin, they are significant mainly because of the *social* meanings they have in our culture. Conflict theorists are especially interested in ascribed statuses, since they often confer privileges or reflect a person's membership in a subordinate group. The social meanings of race and ethnicity, gender, and age will be analyzed more fully in Chapters 11–13.

In most cases, we can do little to change an ascribed status. But we can attempt to change the traditional constraints associated with such statuses. For example, the Gray Panthers—an activist political group founded in 1971 to work for the rights of older people—have tried to modify society's negative and confining stereotypes of the elderly (see Chapter 13). As a result of their work and that of other groups supporting older citizens, the ascribed status of "senior citizen" is no longer as difficult for millions of older people.

An ascribed status does not necessarily have the same social meaning in every society. In a cross-cultural study, sociologist Gary Huang (1988) confirmed the long-held view that respect for the elderly is an important cultural norm in China. In many cases, the prefix "old" is used respectfully: calling someone "old teacher" or "old person" is like calling a judge in the United States "your honor." Huang points out that positive age-seniority language distinctions are uncommon in the United States; consequently, we view the term *old man* as more of an insult than a celebration of seniority and wisdom.

Unlike ascribed statuses, an ***achieved status*** comes to us largely through our own efforts. Both "bank president" and "prison guard" are achieved statuses, as are "lawyer," "pianist," "sorority member," "convict," and "social worker." We must do something to acquire an achieved status—go to school, learn a skill, establish a friendship, invent a new product. But as we will see in the next section, our ascribed status heavily influences our achieved status. Being male, for example, would decrease the likelihood that we would consider being a child care worker.

Master Status

Each person holds many different and sometimes conflicting statuses; some may connote higher social position and some, lower position. How, then, do others view one's overall social position? According to sociologist Everett Hughes (1945), societies deal with inconsistencies by agreeing that certain statuses are more important than others. A ***master status*** is a status that dominates others and thereby determines a person's general position in society. For example, Arthur Ashe, who died of AIDS in 1993, had a remarkable career as a tennis star, but at the end of his life, his status as a well-known personality with AIDS may have outweighed his statuses as a retired athlete, author, and political activist. Throughout the world, many people with disabilities find that their status as "disabled" receives undue weight, overshadowing their actual ability to perform successfully in meaningful employment (see Box 5-1).

Our society gives such importance to race and gender that they often dominate our lives. These ascribed statuses frequently influence our achieved status. The

African American activist Malcolm X (1925–1965), an eloquent and controversial advocate of Black power and Black pride during the early 1960s, recalled that his feelings and perspectives changed dramatically while in eighth grade. When his English teacher, a White man, advised him that his goal of becoming a lawyer was "no realistic goal for a nigger" and encouraged him instead to become a carpenter, Malcolm X (1964:37) found that his position as a Black man (ascribed status) was an obstacle to his dream of becoming a lawyer (achieved status). In the United States, the ascribed statuses of race and gender can function as master statuses that have an important impact on one's potential to achieve a desired professional and social status.

Social Roles

What Are Social Roles?

Throughout our lives, we acquire what sociologists call *social roles*. A ***social role*** is a set of expectations for people who occupy a given social position or status. Thus, in the United States, we expect that cab drivers will know how to get around a city, that receptionists will be reliable in handling phone messages, and that police officers will take action if they see a citizen being threatened. With

Who do you see in this photo: a food service worker, an elderly food service worker, or an elderly woman? Our achieved and ascribed statuses determine how others see us.

5-1 DISABILITY AS A MASTER STATUS

When officials in New Hampshire required a handicap access ramp for a mountain shelter, they were ridiculed for wasting taxpayers' money. Who could climb a mountain in a wheelchair? critics asked. In the summer of 2000 that challenge impelled several intrepid climbers, some in wheelchairs, to make a 12-hour trek over rocks and rough trail so that they could enter the shelter in triumph. As a result of such feats, stereotypes about the disabled are gradually falling away. But the status of "disabled" still carries a stigma.

Throughout history and around the world, people with disabilities have often been subjected to cruel and inhuman treatment. For example, in the 20th century, the disabled were frequently viewed as subhuman creatures who were a menace to society. In Japan more than 16,000 women with disabilities were involuntarily sterilized with government approval from 1945 to 1995. Sweden recently apologized for the same action taken against 62,000 of its citizens in the 1970s.

Such blatantly hostile treatment of people with disabilities generally gave way to a *medical model,* in which the disabled are viewed as chronic patients. Increasingly, however, people concerned with the rights of the disabled have criticized this model as well. In their view, it is the unnecessary and discriminatory barriers present in the environment—both physical and attitudinal—that stand in the way of people with disabilities, more than any biological limitations do. Applying a *civil rights model,* activists emphasize that those with disabilities face widespread prejudice, discrimination, and segregation. For example, most voting places are inaccessible to wheelchair

users and fail to provide ballots that can be used by those unable to read print.

Drawing on the earlier work of Erving Goffman, contemporary sociologists have suggested that society has attached a stigma to many forms of disability, and that this stigma leads to prejudicial treatment. People with disabilities frequently observe that the nondisabled see them only as blind, wheelchair users, and so forth, rather than as complex human beings with individual strengths and weaknesses, whose blindness or use of a wheelchair is merely one aspect of their lives. A review of studies of people with disabilities disclosed that most academic

> In Japan more than 16,000 women with disabilities were involuntarily sterilized with government approval from 1945 to 1995.

research on the subject does not differentiate gender, thereby perpetuating the view that a disability overrides other personal characteristics. Consequently, disability serves as a master status.

Without question, people with disabilities occupy a subordinate position in the United States. But in 1970, a strong political movement for disability rights emerged across the nation. Women and men involved in this movement are working to challenge negative views of disabled people and to modify the social structure by reshaping laws, institutions, and environments so that people with disabilities can be fully integrated into mainstream society.

Discrimination against the disabled occurs around the world. Despite a regulation in China that universities may not reject students because of a physical disability, many universities do just that. In fact, in the last five years, the dozens of universities in Beijing alone have accepted only 236 students with *any* kind of disability, however minor. It appears that bias against the disabled runs deep in China, and many universities use a mandate to nurture physical development as an excuse to keep out the disabled.

Kenya's constitution outlaws discrimination on the basis of many characteristics, including race, sex, tribe, place of origin, creed, and religion, but not on the basis of disability. The African nation of Botswana, on the other hand, has plans to assist its disabled, most of whom live in rural areas and need special services for mobility and economic development. In many countries, disability rights activists are targeting issues essential to overcoming this master status and to becoming a full citizen, including employment, housing, education, and access to public buildings.

Let's Discuss

1. Does your campus present barriers to disabled students? If so, what kind of barriers—physical, attitudinal, or both? Describe some of them.

2. Why do you think nondisabled people see disability as the most important characteristic of a disabled person? What can be done to help people see beyond the wheelchair and the seeing-eye dog?

Sources: Albrecht et al. 2001; Goffman 1963a; D. Murphy 1997; *Newsday* 1997; Rosenthal 2001; J. Shapiro 1993; Waldrop and Stern 2003; Willet and Deegan 2000.

each distinctive social status—whether ascribed or achieved—come particular role expectations. However, actual performance varies from individual to individual. One secretary may assume extensive administrative responsibilities, while another may focus on clerical duties. Similarly, in Philip Zimbardo's mock prison experiment, some students were brutal and sadistic guards, but others were not.

Police officers may face role strain when they try to develop positive community relations but still maintain an authoritative position.

Roles are a significant component of social structure. Viewed from a functionalist perspective, roles contribute to a society's stability by enabling members to anticipate the behavior of others and to pattern their own actions accordingly. Yet social roles can also be dysfunctional if they restrict people's interactions and relationships. If we view a person *only* as a "police officer" or "supervisor," it will be difficult to relate to him or her as a friend or neighbor.

Role Conflict

Imagine the delicate situation of a woman who has worked for a decade on an assembly line in an electrical plant, and has recently been named supervisor of her unit. How is this woman expected to relate to her long-time friends and co-workers? Should she still go out to lunch with them, as she has done almost daily for years? Is it her responsibility to recommend the firing of an old friend who cannot keep up with the demands of the assembly line?

Role conflict occurs when incompatible expectations arise from two or more social positions held by the same person. Fulfillment of the roles associated with one status may directly violate the roles linked to a second status. In the example just given, the newly promoted supervisor will most likely experience a sharp conflict between her social and occupational roles.

Role conflicts call for important ethical choices. So, the new supervisor will have to make a difficult decision about how much allegiance she owes her friend and how much she owes her employers, who have given her supervisory responsibilities.

Another type of role conflict occurs when individuals move into occupations that are not common among people with their ascribed status. Male preschool teachers and female police officers experience this type of role conflict. In the latter case, female officers must strive to reconcile their workplace role in law enforcement with the societal view of a woman's role, which does not embrace many skills needed in police work. And while female police officers encounter sexual harassment, as women do throughout the labor force, they must also deal with the "code of silence," an informal norm that precludes their implicating fellow officers in wrongdoing (C. Fletcher 1995; S. Martin 1994).

Use Your Sociological Imagination www.mhhe.com/schaefer9

If you were a male nurse, what aspects of role conflict would you need to consider? Now imagine you are a professional boxer and a woman. What conflicting role expectations might that involve? In both cases, how well do you think you would handle role conflict?

Role Strain

Role conflict describes the situation of a person dealing with the challenge of occupying two social positions simultaneously. However, even a single position can cause problems. Sociologists use the term *role strain* to describe the difficulty that arises when the same social position imposes conflicting demands and expectations.

In the chapter opening example, social psychologist Philip Zimbardo unexpectedly experienced role strain. He initially saw himself merely as a college professor directing an imaginative experiment in which students played the roles of either guard or inmate. However, he soon found that as a professor, he is also expected to look after the welfare of students, or at least not to endanger them. Eventually he resolved the role strain by making the difficult decision to terminate the experiment. Twenty-five years later, in a television interview, he was still reflecting on the challenge of his role (CBS News 1998).

Role Exit

Often, when we think of assuming a social role, we focus on the preparation and anticipatory socialization a person undergoes for that role. Such is true if a person is about to become an attorney, a chef, a spouse, or a parent. Yet until recently, social scientists have given little attention to the adjustments involved in *leaving* social roles.

Sociologist Helen Rose Fuchs Ebaugh (1988) developed the term *role exit* to describe the process of disengagement from a role that is central to one's self-identity and establishment of a new role and identity. Drawing on interviews with 185 people—among them ex-convicts, divorced men and women, recovering alcoholics, ex-nuns, former doctors, retirees, and transsexuals—Ebaugh (herself a former nun) studied the process of voluntarily exiting from significant social roles.

Ebaugh has offered a four-stage model of role exit. The first stage begins with *doubt.* The person experiences frustration, burnout, or simply unhappiness with an accustomed status and the roles associated with the social position. The second stage involves a *search for alternatives.* A person who is unhappy with his or her career may take a leave of absence; an unhappily married couple may begin what they see as a temporary separation.

The third stage of role exit is the *action stage* or *departure.* Ebaugh found that the vast majority of her respondents could identify a clear turning point that made them feel it was essential to take final action and leave their job, end their marriage, or engage in another type of role exit. Twenty percent of respondents saw their role exit as a gradual, evolutionary process that had no single turning point.

The last stage of role exit involves the *creation of a new identity.* Many of you participated in a role exit when you made the transition from high school to college. You left behind the role of offspring living at home and took on the role of a somewhat independent college student living with peers in a dorm. Sociologist Ira Silver (1996) has studied the central role that material objects play in this transition. The objects students choose to leave at home (like stuffed animals and dolls) are associated with their prior identities. They may remain deeply attached to those objects, but do not want them to be seen as part of their new identities at college. The objects they bring with them symbolize how they now see themselves and how they wish to be perceived. CDs and wall posters, for example, are calculated to say, "This is me."

Groups

In sociological terms, a **group** is any number of people with similar norms, values, and expectations who interact with one another on a regular basis. The members of a women's basketball team, a hospital's business office, a synagogue, or a symphony orchestra constitute a group. However, the residents of a suburb would not be considered a group, since they rarely interact with one another at one time.

This college student in India decorated his dorm room with photos of beautiful women and fast cars. They may signify his attempt to create a new identity, the final stage in his exit from the role of high school student living at home.

Every society is composed of many groups in which daily social interaction takes place. We seek out groups to establish friendships, to accomplish certain goals, and to fulfill the social roles we have acquired. In Kuwait, men gather in groups called *diwaniyas,* which means "little guest house" in Arabic. Hundreds of these gatherings take place every night. *Diwaniyas* may be centered around a family, but are just as likely to be organized around a business, specific occupation, or politics. Men gather to exchange gossip or ideas in these groups, which range in size from 5 or 6 members to well over 100. Meetings can last an hour in the early evening or stretch well into the night. *Diwaniyas* have a rich history in Kuwait, going back over 200 years. Recently a handful of *diwaniyas* has begun to allow women to attend—a major departure from custom for this type of social group. We'll explore the various types of groups in which people interact in detail in Chapter 6, where we will also examine sociological investigations of group behavior (Marshall 2003).

Groups play a vital part in a society's social structure. Much of our social interaction takes place within groups and is influenced by their norms and sanctions. Being a teenager or a retired person takes on special meanings when you interact within groups designed for people with that particular status. The expectations associated with many social roles, including those accompanying the statuses of brother, sister, and student, become more clearly defined in the context of a group.

New technology has broadened the definition of groups to include those who interact electronically. Not all the "people" with whom we converse online are real. At some websites, *chatterbots*—fictitious correspondents created by artificial intelligence programs—respond to questions as if a human were replying. While answering product or service-related questions, the chatterbot may begin "chatting" with an online consumer about family or the weather. Ultimately, such conversations may develop into a chat group that includes other online correspondents, both real and artificial. New groups organized around old interests, such as antique collection or bowling, have already arisen from this type of virtual reality (Van Slambrouck 1999).

For the human participant, such online exchanges offer a new opportunity to alter one's image— what Goffman (1959) refers to as impression management. How might you present yourself to an online discussion group?

Even though you may not be totally sure whom you are "talking to" online, the Internet has added a massive new dimension to social interaction.

Social Networks and Technology

Groups do not merely serve to define other elements of the social structure, such as roles and statuses; they also link the individual and the larger society. We all belong to a number of different groups, and through our acquaintances make connections with people in different social circles. These connections are known as a ***social network***—that is, a series of social relationships that links a person directly to others, and through them indirectly to still more people. Social networks may constrain people by limiting the range of their interactions, yet networks may also empower people by making available to them vast resources (Lin 1999).

Involvement in social networks—commonly known as *networking*—is especially valuable in finding employment. Albert Einstein was successful in finding a job only when a classmate's father put him in touch with his future employer. These kinds of contacts—even those that are weak and distant—can be crucial in establishing social networks and facilitating the transmission of information.

In the workplace, networking pays off more for men than for women because of the traditional presence of men in leadership positions. A 1997 survey of executives found that 63 percent of men use networking to find new jobs, compared to 41 percent of women. Thirty-one percent of the women use classified advertisements to find jobs, compared to only 13 percent of the men. Still, women at all levels of the paid labor force are beginning to make effective use of social networks. A study of women who were leaving the welfare rolls to enter the paid workforce found that networking was an effective tool in their search for employment. Informal networking also helped them to locate child care and better housing—keys to successful employment. As Box 5-2 shows, even women of modest means can make effective use of social networks (Carey and McLean 1997; Henly 1999).

With advances in technology, we can now maintain social networks electronically; we don't need face-to-face contacts anymore. It is not uncommon for those looking for employment or for others with common interests to turn to the Internet. Many high school students get a first look at their future college via a webpage. And a survey of college students found that 79 percent consider the quality of an employer's website important in deciding whether or not to apply for a job there (Jobtrak.com 2000b).

Sociologist Manuel Castells (1997, 1998, 2000) views these emerging electronic social networks as fundamental

Research in Action

5-2 SOCIAL NETWORKS AMONG LOW-INCOME WOMEN

While sociologists have rightly paid a good deal of attention to "old-boy networks," they have been displaying growing interest in the social networks created by women. Research shows that such social networks are not limited to professional women "doing lunch" to trade inside tips or identify prospective clients. Networking is popular among women of much more modest means as well.

Sociologist Pierrette Hondagneu-Sotelo conducted observation research and interviews among Hispanic women (primarily Mexican immigrants) who live in San Francisco and are employed as domestic workers in middle- and upper-class homes. These women engage in what sociologist Mary Romero has called "job work." That is, the domestic worker has several employers and cleans each home on a weekly or biweekly basis for a flat rate of pay for the work completed (in Spanish, *por el trabajo*) as opposed to being paid an hourly rate (*por la hora*). Job work typically involves low pay, no reimbursement for transportation costs, and no health care benefits.

At first glance, we might expect that women engaged in such job work would be isolated from each other, since they work alone. However, Hondagneu-Sotelo found that these Hispanic women have created strong social networks. Through

interactions in various social settings—such as picnics, baby showers, church events, and informal gatherings at women's homes—they share such valuable information as cleaning tips, remedies for work-related physical ailments, tactics for negotiating better pay and gratuities, and advice on how to leave undesirable jobs.

Sociologists Silva Domínguez and Celeste Watkins did fieldwork among low-income women in Boston. They found that many of the younger mothers relied

> Women who were part of networks definitely had greater resources than more isolated women.

heavily on family-based social networks. The two researchers also documented the strength of friendship-based and institution-based networks. The latter included ties to social service providers, which have often been overlooked in similar studies. Ties to service providers are particularly important where family-based and friendship-based networks are unavailable or ineffective. Domínguez and Watkins found that providers offered the mothers help in the form of child care, emotional support, and small loans.

In the past, some sociologists have suspected that these low-income women's networks might help members simply to survive, rather than to improve their lives. Too often, they feared, network members would get drawn into time-consuming relationships with women who are experiencing even worse problems than their own. Yet Domínguez and Watkins found that women who were part of networks definitely had greater resources than more isolated women. Networks allowed many of the women they studied to advance both socially and economically.

Let's Discuss

1. Do you belong to an informal social network? If so, describe the members and the purpose of your network. Do the members all live near one another, or are they far-flung? How do you keep in touch? What kinds of help do you give one another?

2. Has helping a network member who is in trouble ever consumed a lot of your time and energy? If so, explain the circumstances. On balance, is your membership in the network worthwhile, despite the time and effort it requires?

Sources: Domínguez and Watkins 2003; Hondagneu-Sotelo 2001; Romero 1988.

to new organizations and the growth of existing businesses and associations. One such network, in particular, is changing the way people interact. "Texting" refers to the exchange of wireless e-mails over cell phones. It began first in Asia in 2000 and has now taken off in North America and Europe. Initially, texting was popular among young users, who sent shorthand messages such as "WRU" and "CU2NYT" (see Table 5-1, page 112). But now the business world has seen the advantages of transmitting e-mails via cell phones or handheld PalmPilots. However, sociologists caution that

such devices create a workday that never ends, and that increasingly people are busy checking their digital devices rather than actually conversing with those around them (Rosen 2001).

In 2003, the deployment of U.S. troops in the Middle East increased many people's reliance on e-mail. Today, digital photos and sound files accompany e-mail messages between soldiers and their families and friends. Well-established networks have developed to help those who are novices at electronic communication to connect to the Internet.

Table 5-1	RU Ready for Texting Lingo?
Lingo	**Meaning**
@ wrk	At work
A3	Anytime, anywhere, anyplace
Abt 2	About to
AFAIR	As far as I remember
AML	All my love
A/S	Age/Sex?
AWCIGO	And where can I get one?
AYT	Are you there?
CU2NYT	See you tonight
Grr	I'm angry
RUF2T	Are you free to talk?
RUMF	Are you male or female?
UOK	Are you OK?
WRU	Where are you?

If you were deaf, what impact might instant messaging over the Internet have on you?

Social Institutions

The mass media, the government, the economy, the family, and the health care system are all examples of social institutions found in our society. ***Social institutions*** are organized patterns of beliefs and behavior centered on basic social needs, such as replacing personnel (the family) and preserving order (the government).

A close look at social institutions gives sociologists insight into the structure of a society. Consider religion, for example. The institution of religion adapts to the segment of society that it serves. Church work has very different meanings for ministers who serve a skid row area or a suburban middle-class community. Religious leaders assigned to a skid row mission will focus on tending to the ill and providing food and shelter. In contrast, clergy in affluent suburbs will be occupied with counseling those considering marriage and divorce, arranging youth activities, and overseeing cultural events.

Functionalist View

One way to understand social institutions is to see how they fulfill essential functions. Anthropologist David F. Aberle and his colleagues (1950) and sociologists Raymond Mack and Calvin Bradford (1979) have identified five major tasks, or functional prerequisites, that a society or relatively permanent group must accomplish if it is to survive:

1. *Replacing personnel.* Any group or society must replace personnel when they die, leave, or become incapacitated. This task is accomplished through such means as immigration, annexation of neighboring groups of people, acquisition of slaves, or normal sexual reproduction. The Shakers, a religious sect that came to the United States in 1774, are a conspicuous example of a group that has *failed* to replace personnel. Their religious beliefs commit the Shakers to celibacy; to survive, the group must recruit new members. At first, the Shakers proved quite successful in attracting members, reaching a peak of about 6,000 members in the United States during the 1840s. As of 2001, however, the only Shaker community left in this country was a farm in Maine with six members (Associated Press 2001).

2. *Teaching new recruits.* No group or society can survive if many of its members reject the group's established behavior and responsibilities. Thus, finding or producing new members is not sufficient; the group or society must also encourage recruits to learn and accept its values and customs. This learning can take place formally, within schools (where learning is a manifest function) or informally, through interaction and negotiation in peer groups (where instruction is a latent function).

3. *Producing and distributing goods and services.* Any relatively permanent group or society must provide and distribute desired goods and services to its members. Each society establishes a set of rules for the allocation of financial and other resources. The group must satisfy the needs of most members to some extent, or it will risk the possibility of discontent and ultimately disorder.

4. *Preserving order.* The native people of Tasmania, a large island just south of Australia, are now extinct. During the 1800s, they were destroyed by the hunting parties of European conquerors, who looked upon the Tasmanians as half-human. This annihilation underscores a critical function of every group or society—preserving order and protecting itself from attack. Because the Tasmanians

were unable to defend themselves against the more developed European technology of warfare, an entire people was wiped out.

5. *Providing and maintaining a sense of purpose.* People must feel motivated to continue as members of a group or society in order to fulfill the previous four requirements. After the September 11, 2001, attacks on New York City and Washington, D.C., memorial services and community gatherings across the nation allowed people to affirm their allegiance to their country and bind up the psychic wounds inflicted by the terrorists. Patriotism, then, assists some people in developing and maintaining a sense

This memorial service in New York City for the victims of the September 11, 2001, terrorist attack incorporated many patriotic elements, all of which helped to maintain a sense of purpose in extremely difficult times.

of purpose. For others, tribal identities, religious values, or personal moral codes are especially meaningful. Whatever the motivator, in any society there remains one common and critical reality: If an individual does not have a sense of purpose, he or she has little reason to contribute to a society's survival.

This list of functional prerequisites does not specify *how* a society and its corresponding social institutions will perform each task. For example, one society may protect itself from external attack by amassing a frightening arsenal of weaponry, while another may make determined efforts to remain neutral in world politics and to promote cooperative relationships with its neighbors. No matter what its particular strategy, any society or relatively permanent group must attempt to satisfy all these functional prerequisites for survival. If it fails on even one condition, as the Tasmanians did, the society runs the risk of extinction.

Conflict View

Conflict theorists do not concur with the functionalist approach to social institutions. Although proponents of both perspectives agree that institutions are organized to meet basic social needs, conflict theorists object to the implication that the outcome is necessarily efficient and desirable.

From a conflict perspective, the present organization of social institutions is no accident. Major institutions,

such as education, help to maintain the privileges of the most powerful individuals and groups within a society, while contributing to the powerlessness of others. To give one example, public schools in the United States are financed largely through property taxes. This arrangement allows more affluent areas to provide their children with better-equipped schools and better-paid teachers than low-income areas can afford. As a result, children from prosperous communities are better prepared to compete academically than children from impoverished communities. The structure of the nation's educational system permits and even promotes such unequal treatment of schoolchildren.

Conflict theorists argue that social institutions such as education have an inherently conservative nature. Without question, it has been difficult to implement educational reforms that promote equal opportunity—whether bilingual education, school desegregation, or mainstreaming of students with disabilities. From a functionalist perspective, social change can be dysfunctional, since it often leads to instability. However, from a conflict view, why should we preserve the existing social structure if it is unfair and discriminatory?

Social institutions also operate in gendered and racist environments, as conflict theorists, as well as feminists and interactionists, have pointed out. In schools, offices, and government institutions, assumptions about what people can do reflect the sexism and racism of the larger society. For instance, many people assume that women cannot make tough decisions—even those in the top

Social institutions affect the way we behave. How might the worshipers at this mosque in Egypt interact differently in school or the workplace?

echelons of corporate management. Others assume that all Black students at elite colleges represent affirmative action admissions. Inequality based on gender, economic status, race, and ethnicity thrives in such an environment—to which we might add discrimination based on age, physical disability, and sexual orientation. The truth of this assertion can be seen in routine decisions by employers on how to advertise jobs, as well as whether to provide fringe benefits such as child care and parental leave.

Use Your Sociological Imagination

Do you think social networks might be more important for a migrant worker in California than for someone with political and social clout? Why or why not?

Interactionist View

Social institutions affect our everyday behavior, whether we are driving down the street or waiting in a long shopping line. Sociologist Mitchell Duneier (1994a, 1994b)

studied the social behavior of the word processors, all women, who work in the service center of a large Chicago law firm. Duneier was interested in the informal social norms that emerged in this work environment and the rich social network these female employees created.

The Network Center, as it is called, is merely a single, windowless room in a large office building where the law firm occupies seven floors. This center is staffed by two shifts of word processors, who work either from 4:00 P.M. to midnight or from midnight to 8:00 A.M. Each word processor works in a cubicle with just enough room for her keyboard, terminal, printer, and telephone. Work assignments for the word processors are placed in a central basket and then completed according to precise procedures.

At first glance, we might think that these women labor with little social contact, apart from limited breaks and occasional conversations with their supervisor. However, drawing on the interactionist perspective, Duneier learned that despite working in a large office, these women find private moments to talk (often in the halls or outside the washroom) and share a critical view of the law firm's attorneys and day-shift secretaries. Indeed, the word processors routinely suggest that their assignments represent work that the "lazy" secretaries should have completed during the normal workday. Duneier (1994b) tells of one word processor who resented the lawyers' superior attitude and pointedly refused to recognize or speak with any attorney who would not address her by name.

Interactionist theorists emphasize that our social behavior is conditioned by the roles and statuses that we accept, the groups to which we belong, and the institutions within which we function. For example, the social roles associated with being a judge occur within the larger context of the criminal justice system. The status of "judge" stands in relation to other statuses, such as attorney, plaintiff, defendant, and witness, as well as to the social institution of government. Although courts and jails have great symbolic importance, the judicial system derives its continued significance from the roles people carry out in social interactions (Berger and Luckmann 1966).

SOCIAL STRUCTURE IN GLOBAL PERSPECTIVE

Modern societies are complex, especially when compared with earlier social arrangements. Sociologists Émile Durkheim, Ferdinand Tönnies, and Gerhard Lenski have developed ways to contrast modern societies with simpler forms of social structure.

Durkheim's Mechanical and Organic Solidarity

In his *Division of Labor* ([1893] 1933), Durkheim argued that social structure depends on the division of labor in a society—in other words, on the manner in which tasks are performed. Thus, a task such as providing food can be carried out almost totally by one individual, or it can be divided among many people. The latter pattern is typical of modern societies, in which the cultivation, processing, distribution, and retailing of a single food item are performed by literally hundreds of people.

In societies in which there is minimal division of labor, a collective consciousness develops that emphasizes group solidarity. Durkheim termed this collective frame of mind **mechanical solidarity,** implying that all individuals perform the same tasks. In this type of society, no one needs to ask, "What do your parents do?" since all are engaged in similar work. Each person prepares food, hunts, makes clothing, builds homes, and so forth. Because people have few options regarding what to do with their lives, there is little concern for individual needs. Instead, the group will is the dominating force in society. Both social interaction and negotiation are based on close, intimate, face-to-face social contacts. Since there is little specialization, there are few social roles.

As societies become more advanced technologically, greater division of labor takes place. The person who cuts down timber is not the same person who puts up your roof. With increasing specialization, many different tasks must be performed by many different individuals—even in manufacturing a single item, such as a radio or stove. In general, social interactions become less personal than in societies characterized by mechanical solidarity. We begin relating to others on the basis of their social positions ("butcher," "nurse") rather than their distinctive human qualities. Because the overall social structure of the society continues to change, statuses and social roles are in perpetual flux.

Once society becomes more complex and there is greater division of labor, no individual can go it alone. Dependence on others becomes essential for group survival. In Durkheim's terms, mechanical solidarity is replaced by **organic solidarity,** a collective consciousness resting on the need a society's members have for one another. Durkheim chose the term *organic solidarity* because in his view, individuals become interdependent in much the same way as organs of the human body.

Tönnies's Gemeinschaft and Gesellschaft

Ferdinand Tönnies (1855–1936) was appalled by the rise of an industrial city in his native Germany during the late 1800s. In his view, this city marked a dramatic change from the ideal of a close-knit community, which Tönnies termed a *Gemeinschaft,* to that of an impersonal mass society, known as a *Gesellschaft* (Tönnies [1887] 1988).

The **Gemeinschaft** (pronounced guh-MINE-shoft) community is typical of rural life. It is a small community in which people have similar backgrounds and life experiences. Virtually everyone knows one another, and social interactions are intimate and familiar, almost as among kinfolk. In this community there is a commitment to the larger social group and a sense of togetherness among members. People relate to others in a personal way, not just as "clerk" or "manager." With this more personal interaction comes less privacy, however: we know more about everyone.

Social control in the *Gemeinschaft* community is maintained through informal means such as moral persuasion, gossip, and even gestures. These techniques

In small communities like this one in South America, people maintain social control through informal means such as gossip. Tönnies referred to this type of community as a *Gemeinschaft.*

"I'd like to think of you as a person, David, but it's my job to think of you as personnel."

In a *Gesellschaft*, people are likely to relate to one another in terms of their roles rather than their individual backgrounds.

work effectively because people genuinely care about how others feel about them. Social change is relatively limited in the *Gemeinschaft*; the lives of members of one generation may be quite similar to those of their grandparents.

In contrast, the **Gesellschaft** (pronounced guh-ZELL-shoft) is an ideal community that is characteristic of modern urban life. In this community most people are strangers who feel little in common with other residents. Relationships are governed by social roles that grow out of immediate tasks, such as purchasing a product or arranging a business meeting. Self-interest dominates, and there is little consensus concerning values or commitment to the group. As a result, social control must rest on more formal techniques, such as laws and legally defined punishments. Social change is an important aspect of life in the *Gesellschaft*; it can be strikingly evident even within a single generation.

Table 5-2 summarizes the differences between the *Gemeinschaft* and the *Gesellschaft* described by Tönnies. Sociologists have used these terms to compare social structures that stress close relationships with those that emphasize less personal ties. It is easy to view the *Gemeinschaft* with nostalgia, as a far better way of life than the "rat race" of contemporary existence. However, the more intimate relationships of the *Gemeinschaft* come at a price. The prejudice and discrimination found there can be quite confining; ascribed statuses such as family background often outweigh a person's unique talents and achievements. In addition, the *Gemeinschaft* tends to distrust individuals who seek to be creative or just to be different.

Table 5-2	**Comparison of *Gemeinschaft* and *Gesellschaft***
Gemeinschaft	***Gesellschaft***
Rural life typifies this form.	Urban life typifies this form.
People share a feeling of community that results from their similar backgrounds and life experiences.	People have little sense of commonality. Their differences appear more striking than their similarities.
Social interactions, including negotiations, are intimate and familiar.	Social interactions, including negotiations, are likely to be impersonal and task-specific.
People maintain a spirit of cooperation and unity of will.	Self-interest dominates.
Tasks and personal relationships cannot be separated.	The task being performed is paramount; relationships are subordinate.
People place little emphasis on individual privacy.	Privacy is valued.
Informal social control predominates.	Formal social control is evident.
People are not very tolerant of deviance.	People are more tolerant of deviance.
Emphasis is on ascribed statuses.	More emphasis is put on achieved statuses.
Social change is relatively limited.	Social change is very evident, even within a generation.

Think About It
How would you classify the communities with which you are familiar? Are they more *Gemeinschaft* or *Gesellschaft*?

Table 5-3	Stages of Sociocultural Evolution	
Societal Type	**First Appearance**	**Characteristics**
Hunting-and-gathering	Beginning of human life	Nomadic; reliance on readily available food and fibers
Horticultural	About 10,000 to 12,000 years ago	More settled; development of agriculture and limited technology
Agrarian	About 5,000 years ago	Larger, more stable settlements; improved technology, increased crop yields, and specialization of labor
Industrial	1760–1850	Reliance on mechanical power and new sources of energy; centralized workplaces; economic interdependence; formal education
Postindustrial	1960s	Reliance on services, especially the processing and control of information; expanded middle class
Postmodern	Latter 1970s	High technology; mass consumption of consumer goods and media images; cross-cultural integration

Lenski's Sociocultural Evolution Approach

Sociologist Gerhard Lenski takes a very different view of society and social structure. Rather than distinguishing between two opposite types of society, as Tönnies did, Lenski sees human societies as undergoing a process of change according to a dominant pattern, known as *sociocultural evolution.* This term refers to the "process of change and development in human societies that results from cumulative growth in their stores of cultural information" (Lenski et al. 1995:75).

In Lenski's view, a society's level of technology is critical to the way it is organized. Lenski defines **technology** as "information about the ways in which the material resources of the environment may be used to satisfy human needs and desires" (Nolan and Lenski 1999:414). The available technology does not completely define the form that a particular society and its social structure take. Nevertheless, a low level of technology may limit the degree to which a society can depend on such things as irrigation or complex machinery. As technology advances, Lenski writes, a community evolves from a preindustrial to an industrial and finally a postindustrial society.

Preindustrial Societies

How does a preindustrial society organize its economy? If we know that, we can categorize the society. The first type of preindustrial society to emerge in human history was the *hunting-and-gathering society,* in which people simply rely on whatever foods and fibers are readily available. Technology in such societies is minimal. Organized in

groups, people move constantly in search of food. There is little division of labor into specialized tasks.

Hunting-and-gathering societies are composed of small, widely dispersed groups. Each group consists almost entirely of people who are related to one another. As a result, kinship ties are the source of authority and influence, and the social institution of the family takes on a particularly important role. Tönnies would certainly view such societies as examples of the *Gemeinschaft.*

Social differentiation within the hunting-and-gathering society is based on ascribed statuses such as gender, age, and family background. Since resources are scarce, there is relatively little inequality in terms of material goods. By the close of the 20th century, the last hunting-and-gathering societies had virtually disappeared (Nolan and Lenski 1999).

Horticultural societies, in which people plant seeds and crops rather than merely subsist on available foods, emerged about 10,000 to 12,000 years ago. Members of horticultural societies are much less nomadic than hunters and gatherers. They place greater emphasis on the production of tools and household objects. Yet technology remains rather limited within horticultural societies, whose members cultivate crops with the aid of digging sticks or hoes (Wilford 1997).

The last stage of preindustrial development is the *agrarian society,* which emerged about 5,000 years ago. As in horticultural societies, members of agrarian societies are engaged primarily in the production of food. However, the introduction of new technological innovations such as the plow allows farmers to dramatically increase their crop yields. They can cultivate the same fields over generations, allowing the emergence of still larger settlements.

The agrarian society continues to rely on the physical power of humans and animals (as opposed to mechanical power). Nevertheless, its social structure has more carefully defined roles than that of horticultural societies. Individuals focus on specialized tasks, such as the repair of fishing nets or blacksmith work. As human settlements become more established and stable, social institutions become more elaborate and property rights take on greater importance. The comparative permanence and greater surpluses of an agrarian society allow members to create artifacts such as statues, public monuments, and art objects and to pass them on from one generation to the next.

Table 5-3 on page 117 summarizes Lenski's stages of sociocultural evolution, as well as the stages that followed.

Industrial Societies

Although the industrial revolution did not topple monarchs, it produced changes every bit as significant as those resulting from political revolutions. The industrial revolution, which took place largely in England during the period 1760 to 1830, was a scientific revolution focused on the application of nonanimal (mechanical) sources of power to labor tasks. An *industrial society* is a society that depends on mechanization to produce its goods and services. Industrial societies rely on new inventions that facilitate agricultural and industrial production, and on new sources of energy, such as steam.

As the industrial revolution proceeded, a new form of social structure emerged. Many societies underwent an irrevocable shift from an agrarian-oriented economy to an industrial base. No longer did an individual or a family typically make an entire product. Instead, specialization of tasks and manufacturing of goods became increasingly common. Workers, generally men but also women and even children, left their family homesteads to work in central locations such as factories.

The process of industrialization had distinctive social consequences. Families and communities could not continue to function as self-sufficient units. Individuals, villages, and regions began to exchange goods and services and to become interdependent. As people came to rely on the labor of members of other communities, the family lost its unique position as the source of power and authority. The need for specialized knowledge led to more formalized schooling, and education emerged as a social institution distinct from the family.

Postindustrial and Postmodern Societies

When Lenski first proposed the sociocultural evolutionary approach in the 1960s, he paid relatively little atten-

tion to how maturing industrialized societies may change with the emergence of even more advanced forms of technology. More recently, he and other sociologists have studied the significant changes in the occupational structure of industrial societies as they shift from manufacturing to service economies. In the 1970s sociologist Daniel Bell wrote about the technologically advanced *postindustrial society,* whose economic system is engaged primarily in the processing and control of information. The main output of a postindustrial society is services rather than manufactured goods. Large numbers of people become involved in occupations devoted to the teaching, generation, or dissemination of ideas (D. Bell 1999).

Bell views the transition from industrial to postindustrial society as a positive development. He sees a general decline in organized working-class groups and a rise in interest groups concerned with national issues such as health, education, and the environment. Bell's outlook is functionalist, because he portrays the postindustrial society as basically consensual. As organizations and interest groups engage in an open and competitive process of decision

In a postmodern society, people consume goods and media images en masse. In Paris, Disneyworld is popularizing U.S. media images abroad, illustrating another characteristic of postmodern societies—globalization—in the process.

making, Bell believes, the level of conflict between diverse groups will diminish, strengthening social stability.

Conflict theorists take issue with Bell's functionalist analysis of the postindustrial society. For example, Michael Harrington (1980), who alerted the nation to the problems of the poor in his book *The Other America,* questioned the significance that Bell attached to the growing class of white-collar workers. Harrington conceded that scientists, engineers, and economists are involved in important political and economic decisions, but he disagreed with Bell's claim that they have a free hand in decision making, independent of the interests of the rich. Harrington followed in the tradition of Marx by arguing that conflict between social classes will continue in the postindustrial society.

Sociologists have recently gone beyond discussion of the postindustrial society to the ideal of the postmodern society. A ***postmodern society*** is a technologically sophisticated society that is preoccupied with consumer goods and media images (Brannigan 1992). Such societies consume goods and information on a mass scale. Postmodern theorists take a global perspective, noting the ways that culture crosses national boundaries. For example, residents of the United States may listen to reggae music from Jamaica, eat sushi and other Japanese foods, and wear clogs from Sweden (Lyotard 1993).

The emphasis of postmodern theorists is on observing and describing newly emerging cultural forms and patterns of social interaction. Within sociology, the postmodern view offers support for integrating the insights of various theoretical perspectives—functionalism, conflict theory, feminist theory, interactionism, and labeling theory—while also incorporating other contemporary approaches. Feminist sociologists argue optimistically that with its indifference to hierarchies and distinctions, the postmodern society will discard traditional values of male dominance in favor of gender equality. Yet others contend that despite new technologies, postindustrial and postmodern societies can be expected to display the same

problems of inequality that plague industrial societies (Ritzer 1995; Sale 1996; Smart 1990; B. Turner 1990; van Vucht Tijssen 1990).

Durkheim, Tönnies, and Lenski present three visions of society's social structure. While they differ, each is useful, and this textbook will draw on all three. The sociocultural evolutionary approach emphasizes a historical perspective. It does not picture different types of social structures coexisting within the same society. Consequently, one would not expect a single society to include hunters and gatherers along with a postmodern culture. In contrast, Durkheim's and Tönnies's theories allow for the existence of different types of community—such as a *Gemeinschaft* and a *Gesellschaft*—in the same society. Thus, a rural New Hampshire community located 100 miles from Boston can be linked to the city by modern information technology. The main difference between these two theories is a matter of emphasis. While Tönnies emphasized the overriding concern in each type of community—one's own self-interest or the well-being of the larger society—Durkheim emphasized the division (or lack of division) of labor.

The work of these three thinkers reminds us that a major focus of sociology has been to identify changes in social structure and the consequences for human behavior. At the macro level, we see society shifting to more advanced forms of technology. The social structure becomes increasingly complex, and new social institutions emerge to assume some functions that once were performed by the family. On the micro level, these changes affect the nature of social interactions between people. Each individual takes on multiple social roles, and people come to rely more on social networks and less on kinship ties. As the social structure becomes more complex, people's relationships become more impersonal, transient, and fragmented.

In the social policy section that follows we will examine the impact of the AIDS crisis on the social structure and social interaction in the United States and other nations.

SOCIAL POLICY and SOCIAL STRUCTURE

The AIDS Crisis

The Issue

In his novel *The Plague,* Albert Camus (1948:34) wrote, "There have been as many plagues as wars in history, yet always plagues and wars take people equally by surprise." Regarded by many as the distinctive plague of the modern era, AIDS certainly caught major social in-

stitutions—particularly the government, the health care system, and the economy—by surprise when it initially was noticed by medical practitioners in the 1970s. It has since spread around the world. While encouraging new therapies have been developed to treat people, there is currently no way to eradicate AIDS by medical

FIGURE 5-2

The Geography of People Living with HIV/AIDS, 2002

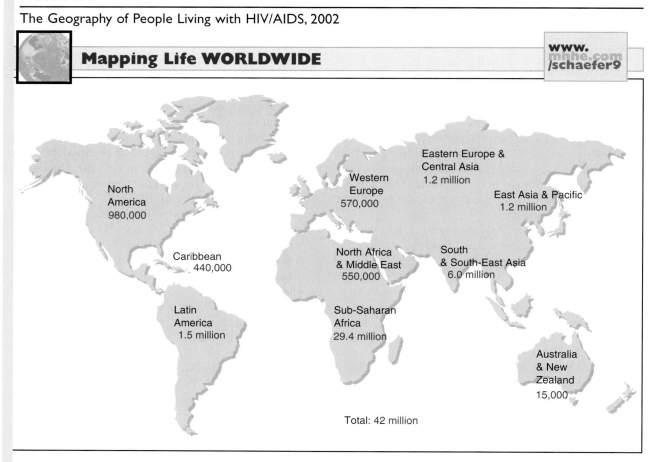

Mapping Life **WORLDWIDE**

www.mhhe.com/schaefer9

North America
980,000

Western Europe
570,000

Eastern Europe & Central Asia
1.2 million

East Asia & Pacific
1.2 million

Caribbean
440,000

North Africa & Middle East
550,000

South & South-East Asia
6.0 million

Latin America
1.5 million

Sub-Saharan Africa
29.4 million

Australia & New Zealand
15,000

Total: 42 million

Source: UNAIDS 2002:34.

means. Therefore, it is essential to protect people by reducing the transmission of the fatal virus. But how is that to be done, and whose responsibility is it? What role do social institutions have in preventing the spread of AIDS?

The Setting

AIDS is the acronym for *acquired immune deficiency syndrome.* Rather than being a distinct disease, AIDS is actually a predisposition to disease that is caused by a virus, the human immunodeficiency virus (HIV). This virus gradually destroys the body's immune system, leaving the carrier vulnerable to infections such as pneumonia that those with healthy immune systems can generally resist. Transmission of the virus from one person to another appears to require either intimate sexual contact or exchange of blood or bodily fluids (whether from contaminated hypodermic needles or syringes, transfusions of infected blood, or transmission

from an infected mother to her child before or during birth). Health practitioners pay particular attention to methods of transmitting HIV because there is no cure or vaccine for AIDS at this time.

The first cases of AIDS in the United States were reported in 1981. While the numbers of new cases and deaths have recently shown some evidence of decline, an estimated 950,000 people were living with AIDS or HIV by early 2003, of whom over a fourth did not yet know they were infected. Women account for a growing proportion of new cases. Racial and ethnic minorities account for 74 percent of all new cases. Worldwide, AIDS is on the increase, with an estimated 42 million people infected and over 3 million dying annually (see Figure 5-2). AIDS is not evenly distributed; those areas least equipped to deal with it—the developing nations of sub-Saharan Africa—face the greatest challenge (Centers for Disease Control and Prevention 2003; Maugh 2003; UNAIDS 2002).

Sociological Insights

Dramatic crises like the AIDS epidemic are likely to bring about certain transformations in a society's social structure. From a functionalist perspective, if established social institutions cannot meet a crucial need, new social networks are likely to emerge to perform that function. In the case of AIDS, self-help groups—especially in the gay communities of major cities—have organized to care for the sick, educate the healthy, and lobby for more responsive public policies.

The label of "person with AIDS" or "HIV-positive" often functions as a master status. People who have AIDS or are infected with the virus actually face a powerful dual stigma. Not only are they associated with a lethal and contagious disease, but they have a disease that disproportionately afflicts already stigmatized groups, such as gay males and intravenous drug users. This linkage with stigmatized groups delayed recognition of the severity of the AIDS epidemic; the media took little interest in the disease until it seemed to be spreading beyond the gay community.

Viewed from a conflict perspective, policymakers were slow to respond to the AIDS crisis because those in high-risk groups—gay men and IV drug users—were comparatively powerless. Furthermore, a study done in 2002 documented the fact that female and minority groups are less likely than others to receive experimental treatments for the HIV infection (Gifford et al. 2002).

On the micro level of social interaction, observers widely forecast that AIDS would lead to a more conservative sexual climate—among both homosexuals and heterosexuals—in which people would be much more cautious about becoming involved with new partners. Yet it appears that many sexually active people in the United States have not heeded precautions about "safe sex." Data from studies conducted in the early 1990s indicated a growing complacency about AIDS, even among those most vulnerable (*AIDS Alert* 1999).

Another interactionist concern is the tremendous impact that taking the appropriate medication has on one's daily routine. Tens of thousands of AIDS patients are having to reorder their lives around their medical regimens. Even infected patients without the symptoms of AIDS find the concentrated effort that is needed to fight the disease—taking 95 doses of 16 different medications every 24 hours—extremely taxing. Think for a moment about the effect such a regimen would have on your own life, from eating and sleeping to work, study, child care, and recreation.

Thanks to new medications, people who suffer from AIDS are living longer than they did in the past. Keeping track of all the pills they must take to stay alive is no easy task, however.

Policy Initiatives

AIDS has struck all societies, but not all nations can respond in the same manner. Studies done in the United States show that people with the virus and with AIDS who receive appropriate medical treatment are living longer than in the past. This advance may put additional pressure on policymakers to address the issues raised by the spread of AIDS. In his 2003 State of the Union message, President George W. Bush pledged a dramatic increase in assistance to those fighting the battle against AIDS globally, pushing the cost of the effort beyond the $1 billion mark.

In some nations, cultural practices may prevent people from dealing with the AIDS epidemic realistically. They may be less likely to take the necessary preventive measures, including more open discussion of sexuality, homosexuality, and drug use. Prevention has shown signs of working among target groups, such as drug users, pregnant women, and gay men and lesbians, but preventative initiatives are few and far between in developing nations. The prescribed treatment to reduce mother-to-baby transmission of AIDS in a pregnant woman costs about $1,000. This is many times the average annual income in much of the world where the risk of AIDS is greatest, such as Africa, which accounts for 77 percent of the world's AIDS deaths. Even more costly is the medication for adult patients with HIV (UNAIDS 2002:36).

The high cost of drug treatment programs has generated intensive worldwide pressure on the major pharmaceutical companies to lower their prices to patients in developing nations, especially in sub-Saharan Africa. In 2001, bowing to this pressure, several of the companies agreed to make the combination therapies available at cost. Even at these much lower prices, however, less than 5 percent of those sick enough to need treatment were receiving it a year later, in 2002. In many nations, social institutions simply are not equipped to distribute medicine to those who need it (McNeil 2002).

Let's Discuss

1. Do the people you know take fewer risks sexually because of the danger of becoming infected with the AIDS virus? If not, why not?

2. Look at the map in Figure 5-2. Why do you think North Africa and the Middle East had only 550,000 people living with AIDS in 2002, while sub-Saharan Africa had 29.4 million? List as many factors as you can that might account for the disparity in numbers.

3. Aside from the obvious humanitarian reasons, why should the United States help developing countries in the fight against AIDS?

CHAPTER RESOURCES

Summary

Social interaction refers to the ways in which people respond to one another. *Social structure* refers to the way in which a society is organized into predictable relationships. This chapter examines the basic elements of social structure: statuses, social roles, groups, networks, and institutions.

1. We shape our social reality based on what we learn through our social interactions. Social change comes from redefining or reconstructing social reality. Sometimes change results from *negotiation.*

2. An *ascribed status* is generally assigned to a person at birth, whereas an *achieved status* is attained largely through one's own effort.

3. In the United States, ascribed statuses, such as race and gender, can function as *master statuses* that have an important impact on one's potential to achieve a desired professional and social status.

4. With each distinctive status—whether ascribed or achieved—come particular *social roles,* the set of expectations for people who occupy that status.

5. Much of our patterned behavior takes place within *groups* and is influenced by the norms and sanctions established by groups. Groups serve as links to *social networks* and their vast resources.

6. The mass media, the government, the economy, the family, and the health care system are all examples of *social institutions* found in the United States.

7. One way to understand social institutions is to ask how they fulfill essential functions, such as replacing personnel, training new recruits, and preserving order.

8. Conflict theorists argue that social institutions help to maintain the privileges of the powerful while contributing to the powerlessness of others.

9. Interactionist theorists emphasize the idea that our social behavior is conditioned by the roles and statuses that we accept, the groups to which we belong, and the institutions within which we function.

10. Émile Durkheim thought that social structure depends on the division of labor in a society. According to Durkheim's theory, societies with minimal division of labor have a collective consciousness called *mechanical solidarity;* those with greater division of labor show an interdependence called *organic solidarity.*

11. Ferdinand Tönnies distinguished the close-knit community of *Gemeinschaft* from the impersonal mass society known as *Gesellschaft.*

12. Gerhard Lenski thinks that a society's social structure changes as its culture and technology become more sophisticated, a process he calls *sociocultural evolution.*

13. The AIDS crisis has changed our society's social structure, prompting the creation of new networks to care for the ill and educate the healthy. Policymakers were slow to respond to the crisis at first because the high-risk groups the disease affected were relatively powerless.

Critical Thinking Questions

1. People in certain professions seem particularly susceptible to role conflict. For example, journalists commonly experience role conflict during disasters, crimes, and other distressing situations. Should they offer assistance to the needy or cover breaking news? Select two other professions and discuss the role conflicts people in them might experience.

2. The functionalist, conflict, and interactionist perspectives can all be used in analyzing social institutions. What are the strengths and weaknesses in each perspective's analysis of social institutions?

3. In what ways does HIV serve to underscore issues of race, class, and gender in the United States today?

Key Terms

Achieved status   A social position that is attained by a person largely through his or her own efforts. (page 106)

Agrarian society   The most technologically advanced form of preindustrial society. Members are engaged primarily in the production of food, but increase their crop yield through technological innovations such as the plow. (116)

Ascribed status   A social position that is assigned to a person by society without regard for the person's unique talents or characteristics. (105)

Gemeinschaft   A close-knit community, often found in rural areas, in which strong personal bonds unite members. (115)

Gesellschaft   A community, often urban, that is large and impersonal, with little commitment to the group or consensus on values. (116)

Group   Any number of people with similar norms, values, and expectations who interact with one another on a regular basis. (109)

Horticultural society   A preindustrial society in which people plant seeds and crops rather than merely subsist on available foods. (116)

Hunting-and-gathering society   A preindustrial society in which people rely on whatever foods and fibers are readily available in order to survive. (116)

Industrial society   A society that depends on mechanization to produce its goods and services. (118)

Master status   A status that dominates others and thereby determines a person's general position in society. (106)

Mechanical solidarity   A collective consciousness that emphasizes group solidarity, characteristic of societies with minimal division of labor. (115)

Negotiated order   A social structure that derives its existence from the social interactions through which people define and redefine its character. (105)

Negotiation   The attempt to reach agreement with others concerning some objective. (104)

Organic solidarity   A collective consciousness that rests on mutual interdependence, characteristic of societies with a complex division of labor. (115)

Postindustrial society   A society whose economic system is engaged primarily in the processing and control of information. (118)

Postmodern society   A technologically sophisticated society that is preoccupied with consumer goods and media images. (119)

Role conflict   The situation that occurs when incompatible expectations arise from two or more social positions held by the same person. (108)

Role exit   The process of disengagement from a role that is central to one's self-identity and establishment of a new role and identity. (108)

Role strain   The difficulty that arises when the same social position imposes conflicting demands and expectations. (108)

Social institution   An organized pattern of beliefs and behavior centered on basic social needs. (112)

Social interaction   The ways in which people respond to one another. (103)

Social network   A series of social relationships that links a person directly to others, and through them indirectly to still more people. (110)

Social role   A set of expectations for people who occupy a given social position or status. (106)

Social structure   The way in which a society is organized into predictable relationships. (103)

Sociocultural evolution   The process of change and development in human societies that results from cumulative growth in their stores of cultural information. (116)

Status   A term used by sociologists to refer to any of the full range of socially defined positions within a large group or society. (105)

Technology   Information about how to use the material resources of the environment to satisfy human needs and desires. (116)

TECHNOLOGY RESOURCES

Internet Connection

*Note: While all the URLs listed were current as of the printing of this book, these sites often change. Please check our website (**www.mhhe.com/schaefer9**) for updates, hyperlinks, and exercises related to these sites.*

1. This chapter opens with a discussion of a study conducted by Philip Zimbardo. The study, known as the Stanford Prison experiment, provides a revealing glimpse into social interaction and social structure. The Stanford Prison experiment website (**www.prisonexp.org**) presents a slide show and discussions of the experiment.

2. Our lives are both enriched and complicated by the vast array of social roles we play. This chapter reveals how the variety of roles we play makes us susceptible to role conflict and role strain. See how these terms can be applied to the social life of any of the former presidents of the United States by logging onto the White House website at (**www. whitehouse.gov/history/presidents**). There you will find biographies and links on presidents from Washington to Bush.

Online Learning Center with PowerWeb

Try the crossword puzzle in the student center of the Online Learning Center (**www.mhhe.com/schaefer9**). Working this crossword puzzle is a great way to see how familiar you are with the important terms and concepts related to social interaction and social structure. It's also an enjoyable way to review for exams.

6

GROUPS AND ORGANIZATIONS

Understanding Groups

Understanding Organizations

Technology's Impact on the Workplace

Social Policy and Organizations: The State of the Unions

Boxes

SOCIOLOGY IN THE GLOBAL COMMUNITY: Amway the Chinese Way

RESEARCH IN ACTION: Pizza Delivery Employees as a Secondary Group

RESEARCH IN ACTION: Bureaucracy and Its Consequences at NASA

Groups come in all sizes and cover a broad array of interests. This poster is directed to a group of people interested in a marketplace featuring fashions for young men. It asks: "Are you in?"

ay Kroc, the genius behind the franchising of McDonald's restaurants, was a man with big ideas and grand ambitions. But even Kroc could not have anticipated the astounding impact of his creation. McDonald's is the basis of one of the most influential developments in contemporary society. Its reverberations extend far beyond its point of origin in the United States and in the fast-food business. It has influenced a wide range of undertakings, indeed the way of life, of a significant portion of the world. And that impact is likely to expand at an accelerating rate.

However, this is not a book about McDonald's, or even about the fast-food business.... Rather, McDonald's serves here as the major example, the paradigm, of a wide-ranging process I call *McDonaldization*.... As you will see, McDonaldization affects not only the restaurant business but also education, work, health care, travel, leisure, dieting, politics, the family, and virtually every other aspect of society. McDonaldization has shown every sign of being an inexorable process, sweeping through seemingly impervious institutions and regions of the world....

Other types of businesses are increasingly adapting the principles of the fast-food industry to their needs. Said the vice chairman of Toys 'R' Us, "We want to be thought of as a sort of McDonald's of toys."... Other chains with similar ambitions include Jiffy Lube, AAMCO Transmissions, Midas Muffler &

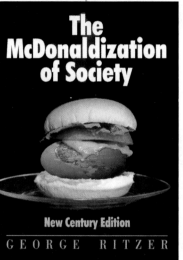

The McDonaldization of Society

New Century Edition

GEORGE RITZER

Brake Shops, Hair Plus, H&R Block, Pearle Vision Centers....

Other nations have developed their own variants of this American institution.... Paris, a city whose love for fine cuisine might lead you to think it would prove immune to fast food, has a large number of fast-food croissanteries; the revered French bread has also been McDonaldized. India has a chain of fast-food restaurants, Nirula's, that sells mutton burgers (about 80% of Indians are Hindus, who eat no beef) as well as local Indian cuisine. Mos Burgers is a Japanese chain with over fifteen hundred restaurants that, in addition to the usual fare, sell Teriyaki chicken burgers, rice burgers, and "Oshiruko with brown rice cake." Russkoye Bistro, a Russian chain, sells traditional Russian fare such as pirogi (meat and vegetable pies), blini (thin pancakes), Cossack apricot curd tart, and, of course, vodka....

McDonald's is such a powerful model that many businesses have acquired nicknames beginning with Mc. Examples include "McDentists" and "McDoctors," meaning drive-in clinics designed to deal quickly and efficiently with minor dental and medical problems; "McChild" care centers, meaning child care centers such as Kinder-Care; "McStables," designating the nationwide race horse–training operation of Wayne Lucas; and "McPaper," designating the newspaper *USA TODAY*. (Ritzer 2000:1–4, 10) ■ ◎

Additional information about this excerpt can be found on the Online Learning Center at **www.mhhe.com/schaefer9**.

In this excerpt from *The McDonaldization of Society,* sociologist George Ritzer contemplates the enormous influence of a well-known fast-food organization on modern-day culture and social life. Ritzer defines *McDonaldization* as "the process by which the principles of the fast-food restaurant are coming to dominate more and more sectors of American society as well as the rest of the world" (Ritzer 2000:1). In his book, he shows how the business principles on which the fast-food industry is founded—efficiency, calculability, predictability, and control—have changed not only the way Americans do business and run their organizations, but the way they live their lives. Today, busy families rely on the takeout meals served up by fast-food establishments, and McDonald's has become a regular meeting place for social groups from adolescents to senior citizens.

Despite the runaway success of McDonald's and its imitators, and the advantages these enterprises bring to millions of people around the world, Ritzer is critical of their effect on society. The waste and environmental degradation created by billions of disposable containers and the dehumanized work routines of fast-food crews are two of the disadvantages he cites in his critique. Would the modern world be a better one, Ritzer asks, if it were less McDonaldized?

This chapter considers the impact of groups and organizations on social interaction. Do we behave differently in large groups than in small ones? How do we make large organizations manageable? What effect are social changes today having on the structure of groups? The chapter begins by noting the distinctions between various types of groups, with particular attention given to the dynamics of small groups. We will examine how and why formal organizations came into existence and describe Max Weber's model of the modern bureaucracy. We'll also look at technology's impact on the organization of the workplace. The social policy section will focus on the status of organized labor unions today.

UNDERSTANDING GROUPS

Most of us use the term *group* loosely to describe any collection of individuals, whether three strangers sharing an elevator or hundreds attending a rock concert. However, in sociological terms a *group* is any number of people with similar norms, values, and expectations who interact with one another on a regular basis. College sororities and fraternities, dance companies, tenants' associations, and chess clubs are all considered examples of groups. The important point is that members of a group share some sense of belonging. This characteristic distinguishes groups from mere *aggregates* of people, such as passengers who happen to be together on an airplane flight, or from *categories* of people, those who share a common feature (such as being retired) but otherwise do not act together.

Consider the case of a college a cappella singing group. It has agreed-on values and social norms. All members want to improve their singing skills and schedule lots of performances. In addition, like many groups, the singing ensemble has both a formal and an informal structure. The members meet regularly to rehearse; they choose leaders to run the rehearsals and manage their affairs. At the same time, some group members may take on unofficial leadership roles by coaching new members in singing techniques and performing skills.

The study of groups has become an important part of sociological investigation because they play such a key role in the transmission of culture. As we interact with others, we pass on our ways of thinking and acting—from language and values to ways of dressing and leisure activities.

Types of Groups

Sociologists have made a number of useful distinctions between types of groups—primary and secondary groups, in-groups and out-groups, and reference groups.

Primary and Secondary Groups

Charles Horton Cooley (1902) coined the term *primary group* to refer to a small group characterized by intimate, face-to-face association and cooperation. The members of a street gang constitute a primary group; so do members of a family living in the same household, as well as a group of "sisters" in a college sorority.

Primary groups play a pivotal role both in the socialization process (see Chapter 4) and in the development of

We all tend to take pizza delivery for granted. We may not even take note of the person who brings the pizza to our door. But sociologists Patrick Kinkade and Michael Katovich did. Using an interactionist perspective, they explored the social relationships that developed among urban pizza delivery drivers as they socialized during work, while waiting for orders, and after work in bars. In fact, one of the researchers spent 18 months as a pizza delivery person at three locales in Ft. Worth, Texas. What they found was that pizza deliverers form a tight network based on the ordinary transactions and the occasional dangerous interactions of their profession.

Within their culture, the pizza delivery drivers take risks and receive minimal rewards. While attacks on them are usually publicized, they are not documented statistically. But the drivers themselves are well aware of the possible dangers and talk to one another a great deal about them. During the observation period, two drivers were robbed and eight others were "tailed," resulting in four automobile accidents.

The researchers found that the world of this secondary group is "hypermasculine," with racist and sexist overtones. The drivers uniformly characterized the

dangers to their safety as coming from members of racial and ethnic communities, even when there was no evidence of this. The drivers also regularly boasted of their sexual prowess and told and retold accounts of sexual favors they received from customers.

Among the 106 drivers studied by the researchers, five types emerged:

- *The comedian.* This individual uses humor to neutralize or trivialize the anxiety of making runs into neighbor-

> Within their culture, the pizza delivery drivers take risks and receive minimal rewards.

hoods perceived as high-risk.
- *The adventurer.* The adventurer claims to invite problems and actually looks forward to testing himself in dangerous situations.
- *The denier.* This individual attempts to neutralize anxiety by suggesting a problem does not exist or is exaggerated.
- *The fatalist.* This person recognizes and admits the risk of danger but simply accepts it without making any effort to neutralize it.

- *The pro.* The pro generally has had a long history in the delivery business, having worked for several pizza services, often serving as an assistant manager, if not a manager, at one of the other stores.

In general, the researchers found through observation and interview that urban pizza deliverers derive more satisfaction from their secondary group membership than from monetary rewards. Group membership and identity, therefore, are very important. The study shows how people, especially in urban environments, make use of secondary groups to carve out a niche in the larger social world. They accept their identity as a delivery person and assume a particular type that they feel comfortable with.

Let's Discuss

1. Think about a secondary group to which you belong. Can you identify any common role types? If so, describe them.
2. If you were to do research like that of Kinkade and Katovich, what group would you choose to study? What research techniques would you use?

Source: Kinkade and Katovich 1997.

roles and statuses (see Chapter 5). Indeed, primary groups can be instrumental in a person's day-to-day existence. When we find ourselves identifying closely with a group, it is probably a primary group.

We also participate in many groups that are not characterized by close bonds of friendship, such as large college classes and business associations. The term *secondary group* refers to a formal, impersonal group in which there is little social intimacy or mutual understanding (see Table 6-1). The distinction between primary and secondary groups is not always clear-cut. Some social clubs may become so large and impersonal that they no longer function as primary groups.

Secondary groups often emerge in the workplace among those who share special understandings about their occupation. Almost all of us have come into contact with people who deliver food. Using observation research, two sociologists have given us new understanding of the secondary group ties that emerge in this occupation (see Box 6-1).

In-Groups and Out-Groups

A group can hold special meaning for members because of its relationship to other groups. People in one group sometimes feel antagonistic to or threatened by another group, especially if that group is perceived as being different culturally or racially. Sociologists identify these "we" and "they" feelings by using two terms first employed by William Graham Sumner (1906): *in-group* and *out-group*.

An **in-group** can be defined as any group or category to which people feel they belong. Simply put, it comprises everyone who is regarded as "we" or "us." The in-group may be as narrow as a teenage clique or as broad as an entire society. The very existence of an in-group implies that there is an **out-group** viewed as "they" or "them." An out-group is a group or category to which people feel they do *not* belong.

In-group members typically feel distinct and superior, and see themselves as better than people in the out-group. Proper behavior for the in-group is simultaneously viewed as unacceptable behavior for the out-group. This double standard enhances the sense of superiority. Sociologist Robert Merton (1968) describes this process as the conversion of "in-group virtues" into "out-group vices." We can see this differential standard operating in worldwide discussions of terrorism. When a group or a nation takes aggressive actions, it usually justifies them as necessary, even if civilians are hurt and killed. Opponents are quick to label such actions with the emotion-laden term of *terrorist* and appeal to the world community for condemnation. Yet these same people may themselves retaliate with actions that hurt civilians, which the first group will then condemn.

Conflict between in-groups and out-groups can turn violent on a personal as well as a political level. In 1999 two disaffected students at Columbine High School in Littleton, Colorado, launched an attack on the school that left 15 students and teachers dead, in-

"So long, Bill. This is my club. You can't come in."

An exclusive social club is an in-group whose members consider themselves superior to others.

cluding themselves. The gunmen, members of an out-group that other students referred to as the Trenchcoat Mafia, apparently resented taunting by an in-group referred to as the Jocks. Similar episodes have occurred in schools across the nation, where rejected adolescents, overwhelmed by personal and family problems, peer group pressure, academic responsibilities, or media images of violence, have struck out against more popular classmates.

In-group members who actively provoke out-group members may have their own problems, including limited time and attention from working parents. Sociologists David Stevenson and Barbara Schneider (1999), who studied 7,000 teenagers, found that despite many opportunities for group membership, young people spend an average of three and a half hours alone every day. While youths may claim they want privacy, they also crave attention, and striking out at members of an in-group or out-group, be they the wrong gender, race, or friendship group, seems to be one way to get it.

| **Use Your Sociological Imagination** | www.mhhe.com/schaefer9 |

Try putting yourself in the shoes of an out-group member. What does your in-group look like from that perspective?

Table 6-1	Comparison of Primary and Secondary Groups	
Primary Group	**Secondary Group**	
Generally small	Usually large	
Relatively long period of interaction	Relatively short duration, often temporary	
Intimate, face-to-face association	Little social intimacy or mutual understanding	
Some emotional depth in relationships	Relationships generally superficial	
Cooperative, friendly	More formal and impersonal	

George Clooney in the motion picture *The Perfect Storm.* Warner Brothers changed the movie's final scene when focus groups reacted negatively to the original ending, which featured the doomed fisherman's final thoughts.

Focus Groups

Another type of group includes people who do not interact on a regular basis. *Focus groups* are composed of 10 to 15 people assembled by a researcher to discuss a predetermined topic, such as a new consumer product or community needs. Guided by a moderator, the members, who are selected to be representative of the general public, offer their own opinions on the topic and react to other members' views. Focus group members are usually paid for their participation, and realize that their views are being recorded.

Focus groups were first developed by Robert Merton (1987) and his colleagues at Columbia University in the early 1940s, to evaluate the relative effectiveness of radio advertising. Today, advertisers and corporations rely heavily on this research method, which Merton called the *focused interview.* While the corporate world has been the principal user of focus groups over the last six decades, sociologists have recently returned to the method to investigate community opinion and workplace morale. They use the information they receive from the groups to design more extensive qualitative or quantitative research.

Reference Groups

Both in-groups and primary groups can dramatically influence the way an individual thinks and behaves. Sociologists call any group that individuals use as a standard for evaluating themselves and their own behavior a *reference group.* For example, a high school student who aspires to join a social circle of hip-hop music devotees will pattern his or her behavior after that of the group. The student will begin dressing like these peers, listening to the same tapes and CDs, and hanging out at the same stores and clubs.

Reference groups have two basic purposes. They serve a normative function by setting and enforcing standards of conduct and belief. The high school student who wants the approval of the hip-hop crowd will have to follow the group's dictates to at least some extent. Reference groups also perform a comparison function by serving as a standard against which people can measure themselves and others. An actor will evaluate himself or herself against a reference group composed of others in the acting profession (Merton and Kitt 1950).

Reference groups may help the process of anticipatory socialization. For example, a college student majoring in finance may read the *Wall Street Journal,* study the annual reports of corporations, and listen to midday stock market news on the radio. Such a student is using financial experts as a reference group to which he or she aspires.

Often, two or more reference groups influence us at the same time. Our family members, neighbors, and co-workers all shape different aspects of our self-evaluation. In addition, reference group attachments change during the life cycle. A corporate executive who quits the rat race at age 45 to become a social worker will find new reference groups to use as standards for evaluation. We shift reference groups as we take on different statuses during our lives.

Studying Small Groups

Sociological research on the micro level and research from the interactionist perspective usually focus on the study of small groups. The term *small group* refers to a group small enough for all members to interact simultaneously—that is, to talk with one another or at least be well acquainted. Certain primary groups, such as families, may also be classified as small groups. However, many small groups differ from primary groups in that they do not necessarily offer the intimate personal relationships characteristic of primary groups. For example, a manufacturer may bring together its seven-member regional sales staff twice a year for an intensive sales conference. The salespeople, who live in different cities and rarely see one another, constitute a small secondary group, not a primary group.

We may think of small groups as being informal and unpatterned; yet, as interactionist researchers have revealed, there are distinct and predictable processes at work in the functioning of small groups. A long-term ethnographic study of street gangs in Chicago revealed an elaborate structure resembling that of a family business. A street gang there is composed of several geographically based units called sets, each of which possesses a leader, lower-ranking officers, and a rank-and-file membership. Besides staffing the economic network of the drug trade, gang members develop relationships with tenant leaders in public housing projects and participate in nondelinquent social activities important to the maintenance of their authority in the neighborhood (Venkatesh 2000).

Size of a Group

At what point does a collection of people become too large to be called a small group? That is not clear. In a group with more than 20 members, it is difficult for individuals to interact regularly in a direct and intimate manner. But even within a range of 2 to 20 people, group size can substantially alter the quality of social relationships. For example, as the number of group participants increases, the most active communicators become even more active relative to others. Therefore, a person who

dominates a group of 3 or 4 members will be relatively more dominant in a 15-person group.

Group size also has noticeable social implications for members who do not assume leadership roles. In a larger group, each member has less time to speak, more points of view to absorb, and a more elaborate structure to function in. At the same time, an individual has greater freedom to ignore certain members or viewpoints than he or she would in a smaller group. It is harder to disregard someone in a 4-person workforce than someone in an office with 30 employees, harder to disregard someone in a string quartet than someone in a college band with 50 members.

German sociologist Georg Simmel (1858–1918) is credited as the first sociologist to emphasize the importance of interactive processes within groups and note how they change as the group's size changes. The simplest of all social groups or relationships is the **dyad,** or two-member group. A wife and a husband constitute a dyad, as does a business partnership or a singing duo. In a dyad, one is able to achieve a special level of intimacy that cannot be duplicated in larger groups. However, as Simmel ([1917] 1950) noted, a dyad, unlike any other group, can be destroyed by the loss of a single member. Therefore, the threat of termination hangs over a dyadic relationship perhaps more than over any other type.

Obviously, the introduction of one additional person to a dyad dramatically transforms the character of the small group. The dyad now becomes a three-member group, or **triad.** The new member has many ways of interacting with and influencing the dynamics of the group. The new person may play a *unifying* role within a triad. When a married couple has its first child, the baby may serve to bind the group closer together. A newcomer may also play a *mediating* role within a three-person group. If two roommates in an apartment are perpetually sniping at each other, the third roommate may attempt to remain on good terms with both and arrange compromise solutions to problems. Finally, a member of a triad can choose to employ a *divide-and-rule* strategy. This is the case, for example, with a coach who hopes to gain greater control over two assistants by making them rivals (Nixon 1979).

Coalitions

As groups grow to the size of triads or larger, we can expect coalitions to

Groups come in all types and sizes. The members of this Manchester, Vermont, group belong to a national club of antique bicycle buffs called the Wheelmen. They take their Victorian-era bicycles out for rides, and often dress in period costume from the late 1800s, as shown here.

develop. A *coalition* is a temporary or permanent alliance geared toward a common goal. Coalitions can be broad-based or narrow, and can take on many different objectives. Sociologist William Julius Wilson (1999b) has described community-based organizations in Texas that include Whites and Latinos, working class and affluent, who have banded together to work for improved sidewalks, better drainage systems, and comprehensive street paving. Out of this type of coalition building, Wilson hopes, will emerge better interracial understanding.

Some coalitions are intentionally short lived. Short-term coalition building is a key to success in popular TV programs like *Survivor*. In *Survivor I,* broadcast in 2000, the four members of the "Tagi alliance" banded together to vote fellow castaways off the island. The political world is also the scene of many temporary coalitions. For example, in 1997 big tobacco companies joined with antismoking groups to draw up a settlement for reimbursing states for tobacco-related medical costs. Soon after the settlement was announced the coalition members returned to their decades-long fight against each other (Pear 1997).

The effects of group size and coalitions on group dynamics are but two of the many aspects of the small group that sociologists have studied. Another aspect, conformity and deviance, is examined in Chapter 8. Although it is clear that small-group encounters have a considerable influence on our lives, we are also deeply affected by much larger groupings of people, as we'll see in the next section.

In *Survivor 6*, "The Amazon," producers pitted men against women in a mock competition for survival. Short-term coalition building has been a key to success in this popular reality TV series.

UNDERSTANDING ORGANIZATIONS

Formal Organizations and Bureaucracies

As contemporary societies have shifted to more advanced forms of technology and their social structures have become more complex, our lives have become increasingly dominated by large secondary groups referred to as *formal organizations*. A *formal organization* is a group designed for a special purpose and structured for maximum efficiency. The U.S. Postal Service, McDonald's, the Boston Pops orchestra, and the college you attend are all examples of formal organizations. Though organizations vary in their size, specificity of goals, and degree of efficiency, they are all structured to facilitate the management of large-scale operations. They also have a bureaucratic form of organization (described in the next section).

In our society, formal organizations fulfill an enormous variety of personal and societal needs and shape the lives of every one of us. In fact, formal organizations have become such a dominant force that we must create organizations to supervise other organizations, such as the Securities and Exchange Commission (SEC) to regulate brokerage companies. While it sounds much more exciting to say that we live in the "computer age" than to say that ours is the "age of formal organization," the latter is probably a more accurate description of our times (Azumi and Hage 1972; Etzioni 1964).

Ascribed statuses such as gender, race, and ethnicity can influence how we see ourselves within formal organizations. For example, a study of women lawyers in the nation's largest law firms found significant differences in these women's self-images, depending on the relative presence or absence of women in positions of power. In firms in which fewer than 15 percent of partners were women, the female lawyers were likely to believe that "feminine" traits were strongly devalued and that masculinity was equated with success. As one female attorney put it, "Let's face it: this is a man's environment, and it's sort of Jock City, especially at my firm." Women in firms where female lawyers were better represented in positions of power had a stronger desire for and higher expectations of promotion (Ely 1995:619).

Characteristics of a Bureaucracy

A **bureaucracy** is a component of formal organization that uses rules and hierarchical ranking to achieve efficiency. Rows of desks staffed by seemingly faceless people, endless lines and forms, impossibly complex language, and frustrating encounters with red tape—all these unpleasant images have combined to make *bureaucracy* a dirty word and an easy target in political campaigns. As a result, few people want to identify their occupation as "bureaucrat," despite the fact that all of us perform various bureaucratic tasks. Elements of bureaucracy enter into almost every occupation in an industrial society.

Max Weber ([1922] 1947) first directed researchers to the significance of bureaucratic structure. In an important sociological advance, Weber emphasized the basic similarity of structure and process found in the otherwise dissimilar enterprises of religion, government, education, and business. Weber saw bureaucracy as a form of organization quite different from the family-run business. For analytical purposes, he developed an *ideal type* of bureaucracy that would reflect the most characteristic aspects of all human organizations. By **ideal type** Weber meant a construct or model that could serve as a standard for evaluating specific cases. In actuality, perfect bureaucracies do not exist; no real-world organization corresponds exactly to Weber's ideal type.

Weber proposed that whether the purpose is to run a church, a corporation, or an army, the ideal bureaucracy displays five basic characteristics. A discussion of those characteristics, as well as the dysfunctions of a bureaucracy, follows. Table 6-2 (page 134) summarizes the discussion.

1. Division of Labor. Specialized experts perform specific tasks. In your college bureaucracy, the admissions officer does not do the job of registrar; the guidance counselor doesn't see to the maintenance of buildings. By working at a specific task, people are more likely to become highly skilled and carry out a job with maximum efficiency. This emphasis on specialization is so basic a part of our lives that we may not realize that it is a fairly recent development in Western culture.

The downside of division of labor is that the fragmentation of work into smaller and smaller tasks can divide workers and remove any connection they might feel to the overall objective of the bureaucracy. In *The Communist Manifesto* (written in 1848), Karl Marx and Friedrich Engels charged that the capitalist system reduces workers to a mere "appendage of the machine"

Whistle-blower Colleen Rowley, an FBI agent, tried unsuccessfully to bring her superiors' attention to a French Moroccan who had signed up for pilot training at a local flight school, keen to operate a 747. The man later used his training to crash a hijacked jet into the World Trade Center. Rowley was photographed as she testified before the Senate Judiciary Committee in June 2002.

(Feuer 1959). Such a work arrangement, they wrote, produces extreme **alienation**—a condition of estrangement or dissociation from the surrounding society. According to both Marx and conflict theorists, restricting workers to very small tasks also weakens their job security, since new employees can be easily trained to replace them.

Although division of labor has certainly enhanced the performance of many complex bureaucracies, in some cases it can lead to **trained incapacity;** that is, workers become so specialized that they develop blind spots and fail to notice obvious problems. Even worse, they may not care about what is happening in the next department. Some observers believe that such developments have caused workers in the United States to become less productive on the job.

In some cases, the bureaucratic division of labor can have tragic results. In the wake of the coordinated attacks on the World Trade Center and the Pentagon on September 11, 2001, Americans wondered aloud how the FBI and CIA could have failed to detect the terrorists' elaborately planned operation. The problem, in part, turned out to be the division of labor between the FBI, which focuses on domestic matters, and the CIA, which operates overseas. Officials at these intelligence-gathering organizations, both of which are huge bureaucracies, are well known for jealously guarding information from one

Table 6-2	Characteristics of a Bureaucracy		
		Negative Consequence	
Characteristic	**Positive Consequence**	**For the Individual**	**For the Organization**
Division of labor	Produces efficiency in large-scale corporation	Produces trained incapacity	Produces a narrow perspective
Hierarchy of authority	Clarifies who is in command	Deprives employees of a voice in decision making	Permits concealment of mistakes
Written rules and regulations	Let workers know what is expected of them	Stifle initiative and imagination	Lead to goal displacement
Impersonality	Reduces bias	Contributes to feelings of alienation	Discourages loyalty to company
Employment based on technical qualifications	Discourages favoritism and reduces petty rivalries	Discourages ambition to improve oneself elsewhere	Fosters Peter principle

another. Subsequent investigations revealed that they knew about Osama bin Laden and his al-Qaeda terrorist network in the early 1990s. Unfortunately, five federal agencies—the CIA, FBI, National Security Agency, Defense Intelligence Agency, and National Reconnaissance Office—failed to share their leads on the network. Although the hijacking of the four commercial airliners used in the massive attacks may not have been preventable, the bureaucratic division of labor definitely hindered efforts to defend against terrorism, and actually undermined U.S. national security.

2. Hierarchy of Authority. Bureaucracies follow the principle of hierarchy; that is, each position is under the supervision of a higher authority. A president heads a college bureaucracy; he or she selects members of the administration, who in turn hire their own staff. In the Roman Catholic Church, the pope is the supreme authority; under him are cardinals, bishops, and so forth.

3. Written Rules and Regulations. What if your sociology professor gave your classmate an A for having such a friendly smile? You might think that wasn't fair, that it was against the rules.

Rules and regulations, as we all know, are an important characteristic of bureaucracies. Ideally, through such procedures, a bureaucracy ensures uniform performance of every task. This prohibits your classmate from receiving an A for a nice smile, because the rules guarantee that all students will receive essentially the same treatment.

Through written rules and regulations, bureaucracies generally offer employees clear standards for an

adequate (or exceptional) performance. In addition, procedures provide a valuable sense of continuity in a bureaucracy. Individual workers will come and go, but the structure and past records give the organization a life of its own that outlives the services of any one bureaucrat.

Of course, rules and regulations can overshadow the larger goals of an organization and become dysfunctional. What if a hospital emergency room physician failed to treat a seriously injured person because he or she had no valid proof of U.S. citizenship? If blindly applied, rules no longer serve as a means to achieving an objective, but instead become important (and perhaps too important) in their own right. Robert Merton (1968) used the term ***goal displacement*** to refer to overzealous conformity to official regulations.

4. Impersonality. Max Weber wrote that in a bureaucracy, work is carried out *sine ira et studio,* "without hatred or passion." Bureaucratic norms dictate that officials perform their duties without the personal consideration of people as individuals. Although this is intended to guarantee equal treatment for each person, it also contributes to the often cold and uncaring feeling associated with modern organizations. We typically think of big government and big business when we think of impersonal bureaucracies. But today even small firms have telephone systems that greet callers with an electronic menu.

5. Employment Based on Technical Qualifications. Within the ideal bureaucracy, hiring is based on technical qualifications rather than on favoritism, and performance is measured against specific standards.

6-2 BUREAUCRACY AND ITS CONSEQUENCES AT NASA

In February 2003, the space shuttle *Columbia* disintegrated as it reentered the atmosphere. Seven astronauts died in the accident, which was blamed at first on a piece of foam that had struck the spacecraft's wing during liftoff. But by August, the *Columbia* Accident Investigation Board (2003) had identified a second cause: NASA's bureaucratic organizational culture.

The board's blistering report cited NASA's emphasis on bureaucratic rules and regulations at the expense of astronauts' safety. Though engineers had voiced safety concerns over the years, especially after the shuttle *Challenger's* explosion in 1986, their memos rarely reached the top of NASA's hierarchy, where costs and scheduling were considered paramount. In fact, the organization's culture discouraged the expression of safety concerns (Vaughan 1996, 1999).

> NASA's culture discouraged the expression of safety concerns.

When engineers tried to obtain special images of the *Columbia's* wing during its last flight so they could check for damage, managers denied their request.

Part of the problem was that over the years, foam had fallen during liftoff without disastrous results. Officials had come to expect a shower of debris during a launch, and to speak of it as an "acceptable risk." Even after the investigation of the *Challenger* explosion condemned this attitude, NASA's organizational culture did not change. As any member of a large organization knows, bureaucracy has a life of its own.

Let's Discuss

Do you know anyone who was injured by a bureaucratic organizational culture? Explain what happened from a sociological point of view.

Written personnel policies dictate who gets promoted, and people often have a right to appeal if they believe that particular rules have been violated. Such procedures protect bureaucrats against arbitrary dismissal, provide a measure of security, and encourage loyalty to the organization.

In this sense, the "impersonal" bureaucracy can be considered an improvement over nonbureaucratic organizations. College faculty members, for example, are ideally hired and promoted according to their professional qualifications, including degrees earned and research published, and not because of whom they know. Once they are granted tenure, their jobs are protected against the whims of a president or dean.

Although any bureaucracy ideally will value technical and professional competence, personnel decisions do not always follow this ideal pattern. Dysfunctions within bureaucracy have become well publicized, particularly because of the work of Laurence J. Peter. According to the **Peter principle,** every employee within a hierarchy tends to rise to his or her level of incompetence (Peter and Hull 1969). This hypothesis, which has not been directly or systematically tested, reflects a possible dysfunctional outcome of structuring advancement on the basis of merit. Talented people receive promotion after promotion until, sadly, some of them finally achieve positions that they cannot handle with their usual competence (Blau and Meyer 1987).

The five characteristics of bureaucracy, developed by Max Weber more than 80 years ago, describe an ideal type rather than offer a precise definition of an actual bureaucracy. Not every formal organization will possess all five of Weber's characteristics. In fact, wide variation exists among actual bureaucratic organizations.

Bureaucratization as a Process

Have you ever had to speak to 10 or 12 individuals in a corporation or government agency just to find out which official has jurisdiction over a particular problem? Ever been transferred from one department to another until you finally hung up in disgust? Sociologists have used the term **bureaucratization** to refer to the process by which a group, organization, or social movement becomes increasingly bureaucratic.

Normally, we think of bureaucratization in terms of large organizations. But bureaucratization also takes place within small-group settings. Sociologist Jennifer Bickman Mendez (1998) studied domestic houseworkers employed in central California by a nationwide franchise. She found that housekeeping tasks were minutely defined, to the point that employees had to follow 22 written steps for cleaning a bathroom. Complaints and special requests went not to the workers, but to an office-based manager.

The impersonality and inefficiency of a bureaucracy can have tragic results, as Box 6-2 shows.

Oligarchy: Rule by a Few

Conflict theorists have examined the bureaucratization of social movements. German sociologist Robert Michels (1915) studied socialist parties and labor unions in Europe before World War I and found that such organizations were becoming increasingly bureaucratic. The emerging leaders of these organizations—even some of the most radical—had a vested interest in clinging to power. If they lost their leadership posts, they would have to return to full-time work as manual laborers.

Through his research, Michels originated the idea of the **iron law of oligarchy,** which describes how even a democratic organization will eventually develop into a bureaucracy ruled by a few (called an oligarchy). Why do oligarchies emerge? People who achieve leadership roles usually have the skills, knowledge, or charismatic appeal (as Weber noted) to direct, if not control, others. Michels argued that the rank and file of a movement or organization look to leaders for direction and thereby reinforce the process of rule by a few. In addition, members of an oligarchy are strongly motivated to maintain their leadership roles, privileges, and power.

Michels's insights continue to be relevant today. Contemporary labor unions in the United States and Western Europe bear little resemblance to those organized spontaneously by exploited workers. Conflict theorists have pointed to the longevity of union leaders, who are not always responsive to the needs and demands of the membership, and seem more concerned with maintaining their own positions and power. (The policy section at the end of this chapter focuses on the status of labor unions today.)

Bureaucracy and Organizational Culture

How does bureaucratization affect the average individual who works in an organization? The early theorists of formal organizations tended to neglect this question. Max Weber, for example, focused on the management personnel within bureaucracies, but had little to say about workers in industry or clerks in government agencies.

According to the **classical theory** of formal organizations, also known as the **scientific management approach,** workers are motivated almost entirely by economic rewards. This theory stresses that only the physical constraints on workers limit their productivity. Therefore, workers may be treated as a resource, much like the machines that began to replace them in the twentieth century. Under the scientific management approach, management attempts to achieve maximum work efficiency through scientific planning, established performance standards, and careful supervision of workers and

A former employee of Enron Corporation, a high-flying energy trading company, removes her belongings from the building following mass layoffs in 2002. Informal interactions among some top executives who had engaged in deceptive accounting practices ultimately led to the company's collapse.

production. Planning involves efficiency studies, but not studies of workers' attitudes or job satisfaction.

Not until workers organized unions—and forced management to recognize that they were not objects—did theorists of formal organizations begin to revise the classical approach. Along with management and administrators, social scientists became aware that informal groups of workers have an important impact on organizations (Perrow 1986). An alternative way of considering bureaucratic dynamics, the **human relations approach,** emphasizes the role of people, communication, and participation within a bureaucracy. This type of analysis reflects the interest of interactionist theorists in small-group behavior. Unlike planning under the scientific management approach, planning based on the human relations perspective focuses on workers' feelings, frustrations, and emotional need for job satisfaction.

The gradual move away from a sole focus on the physical aspects of getting the job done—and toward the concerns and needs of workers—led advocates of the human relations approach to stress the less formal aspects of bureaucratic structure. Informal groups and social networks within organizations develop partly as a result of people's ability to create more direct forms of communication than under the formal structure. Charles Page (1946) has used the term *bureaucracy's other face* to refer to the unofficial activities and interactions that are such a basic part of daily organizational life. As Box 6-3 shows, some direct merchandising companies have capitalized on the existence of informal groups and social networks to build their organizations—though in China

Sociology in the Global Community

6-3   AMWAY THE CHINESE WAY

Amway began in 1959, when two young men in Michigan began a person-to-person merchandise marketing system. Today, more than 3.6 million individuals in 80 countries distribute Amway cosmetics, food supplements, and home care products. Distributors will often gather friends and neighbors at a party designed to persuade them to buy the company's products, or better yet, to become distributors themselves. Distributors' ability to line up customers who become distributors themselves, and in turn line up still more customers and distributors, has been critical to the company's success. Thus, primary group ties have become the tool of a large, bureaucratic business organization.

Amway entered China in 1995, followed closely by rival direct sellers like Avon and Mary Kay. China's more than 1 billion residents, combined with its growing acceptance of capitalistic business practices, made it an attractive market for these Western merchandisers. And Amway's emphasis on building sales networks through relatives and friends seemed a perfect fit for Chinese culture, in which personal recommendations are considered especially persuasive. After

just two years, Amway had 80,000 distributors in China. But in 1998, the Chinese government suddenly outlawed Amway's operation, accusing the company of fostering "weird cults, triads, superstitious groups, and hooliganism."

What had happened? Apparently Amway's success had produced a host of copycats, some of them con artists peddling dubious merchandise. Government officials complained, too, about the promotional hoopla at Amway's sales meet-

> To do business globally, Amway has successfully reinvented its business model.

ings, which featured songs, sloganeering, and other Western-style activities designed to encourage organizational bonding. To the Chinese, these innocuous activities suggested a cult-like fervor.

Facing the loss of their Chinese investments, Amway and other direct marketers asked the U.S. trade representative to intervene. After intense pressure, the Chinese government agreed to a partial reversal of the ban on direct selling. Un-

der new regulations issued in 1998, Amway, Avon, and Mary Kay are permitted to sell their products through conventional retail outlets. They can also employ salespeople to go door to door, but they cannot receive any income from signing up new distributors. Despite this handicap, China is now Amway's fourth largest market worldwide. In 2002 sales were four times what they were before the government ban on direct selling. To do business globally, Amway has successfully reinvented its business model.

Let's Discuss

1. Have you ever bought merchandise from a direct seller like Amway, perhaps at a party? If so, who introduced you to the organization? Were you comfortable with its merchandising methods? Explain.

2. Can you think of another kind of bureaucratic organization, other than a business, that exploits its members' ties to primary groups in order to grow? Analyze the organization and its operating methods from a sociological point of view.

Sources: Amway 1999, 2003; Chang 2003; Hill 2003; Wonacott 2001.

they have run into trouble with the formal government bureaucracy.

A series of classic studies illustrates the value of the human relations approach. The Hawthorne studies alerted sociologists to the fact that research subjects may p. 39 alter their behavior to match the experimenter's expectations. The major focus of the Hawthorne studies, however, was the role of social factors in workers' productivity. One aspect of the research investigated the switchboard-bank wiring room, where 14 men were making parts of switches for telephone equipment. The researchers discovered that these men were producing far below their physical capabilities. This discovery was especially surprising because they would earn more money if they produced more parts.

What accounted for such an unexpected restriction of output? The men feared that if they produced switch parts at a faster rate, their pay rate might be reduced, or some of them might lose their jobs. As a result, this group of workers established their own (unofficial) norm for a proper day's work. They created informal rules and sanctions to enforce it. Yet management was unaware of these practices, and actually believed that the men were working as hard as they could (Roethlisberger and Dickson 1939; for a different perspective, see Vallas 1999).

Today, research on formal organizations is following new avenues. First, the proportion of women and minority group members in high-level management positions is still much lower than might be expected, given their numbers in the labor force. Researchers are now beginning to look at the impact this gender and racial/ethnic

The AARP is a voluntary association of people aged 50 and older, both retired and working, that advocates for the needs of older Americans. A huge organization, it has been instrumental in maintaining Social Security benefits to retirees. Here AARP volunteers staff a phone bank in an effort to get out the vote in Des Moines, Iowa.

imbalance may have on managerial judgment, both formal and informal. Second, a company's power structure is only partly reflected in its formal organizational charts. In practice, core groups tend to emerge to dominate the decision-making process. Very large corporations—say, a General Electric or a Procter & Gamble—may have hundreds of interlocking core groups, each of which plays a key role in its division or region (Kleiner 2003).

Voluntary Associations

In the mid-19th century, the French writer Alexis de Tocqueville noted that people in the United States are "forever forming associations." By 2003, there were more than 444,000 voluntary associations in a national database. **Voluntary associations** are organizations established on the basis of common interest, whose members volunteer or even pay to participate. The Girl Scouts of America, the American Jewish Congress, the Kiwanis Club, and the League of Women Voters are all considered voluntary associations; so, too, are the American Association of Aardvark Aficionados, the Cats on Stamps Study Group, the Mikes of America, the New York Corset Club, and the William Shatner Fellowship (Gale 2003).

The categories of "formal organization" and "voluntary association" are not mutually exclusive. Large voluntary associations such as the Lions Club and the Masons have structures similar to those of profit-making corporations. At the same time, certain formal organizations,

such as the Young Men's Christian Association (YMCA) and the Peace Corps, have philanthropic and educational goals usually found in voluntary associations. The Democratic Party and the United Farm Workers union are considered examples of voluntary associations. Even though membership in a political party or union can be a condition of employment and therefore not genuinely voluntary, political parties and labor unions are usually included in discussions of voluntary associations.

Participation in voluntary associations is not unique to the United States. This textbook's author attended a carnival in London featuring bungee-jumping, at which participants were expected to jump from a height of 180 feet. Skeptics were given assurances of the attraction's safety by being told that the proprietor belonged to a voluntary association: the British Elastic Rope Sports Association. An analysis of 15 industrial nations, including the United States, showed that active memberships in voluntary associations typically increased during the 1980s and 1990s. Only relatively inactive memberships in religious organizations and labor unions have showed a decline. On the whole, then, voluntary associations are fairly healthy (Baer et al. 2000).

Voluntary associations can provide support to people in preindustrial societies. During the post–World War II period, migration from rural areas of Africa to the cities was accompanied by a growth in voluntary associations, including trade unions, occupational societies, and mutual aid organizations developed along old tribal ties. As people moved from the *Gemeinschaft* of the countryside **p. 115** to the *Gesellschaft* of the city, these voluntary associations provided immigrants with substitutes for the extended groups of kinfolk in their villages (Little 1988).

Voluntary associations in the United States are largely segregated by gender. Half of them are exclusively female, and one-fifth are all-male. Because the exclusively male associations tend to be larger and more heterogeneous, in terms of the background of members, all-male associations hold more promise for networking than all-female groups. Although participation varies across the population of the United States, most people belong to at least one voluntary association (see Figure 6-1), while more than one-fourth maintain three or more memberships.

The importance of voluntary associations—and especially of their unpaid workers (or volunteers)—is increasingly being recognized. Traditionally, we have devalued unpaid work, even though the skill levels, experience, and training demands are often comparable with those of wage labor. Viewed from a conflict perspective, the critical difference has been that women perform a substantial amount of volunteer work. Feminists and conflict theorists agree that like the unpaid child care and household labor of homemakers, the effort of volunteers has too often been ignored by scholars—and awarded too little respect by the larger society—because it is viewed as "women's work." Failure to recognize women's volunteerism obscures a critical contribution women make to a society's social structure (Daniels 1987, 1988).

Organizational Change

Just as individuals and relationships change, so too do organizations, both formal and voluntary. The most obvious changes often involve personnel: a new president of the United States is elected, an executive is fired, a star athlete retires. However, sociologists are most interested in how the organization itself changes.

These changes often relate to other social institutions, particularly the government, whose regulatory statutes, licensing procedures, tax laws, and contracting for goods and services directly influence the structure of formal organizations. For example, government policies relating to affirmative action (see Chapter 18) and disability rights (see Chapter 5) influence the internal decisions of organizations, and may even require the hiring of new personnel.

FIGURE 6-1

Membership in Voluntary Associations in the United States

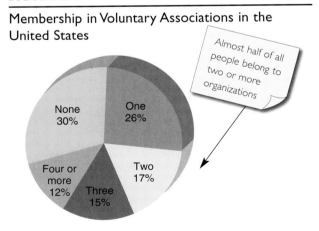

Almost half of all people belong to two or more organizations

Source: J. Davis and Smith 2001:347.

Think About It
How many voluntary associations do you belong to? What functions do they serve?

In addition, an organization's goals may change over time along with its leaders and structure. A church starts a basketball league; an oil company purchases a movie studio; a chewing tobacco firm begins to manufacture ballpoint pens. Such actions take place when an organization decides that its traditional goals are no longer adequate. It must then modify its previous objectives or cease to exist.

Goal Multiplication

If an organization concludes that its goals must change, it will typically establish additional goals or expand its traditional objectives. For example, in the 1970s many colleges began continuing education programs to meet the needs of potential students who held full-time jobs and wished to take classes at night. In the 1980s, colleges opened their campuses to the Elderhostel organization, enabling older people to live and learn along with much younger college students.

Goal multiplication takes place when an organization expands its purposes, generally as a result of changing social or economic conditions that threaten the organization's survival. The YMCA has practiced such goal multiplication. Reflecting its name, the Young Men's Christian Association had a strong evangelistic focus during its beginnings in the United States in the 1850s. Earlier, YMCAs provided Bible study and tent revival meetings. However, in the early 1900s, the YMCA began to diversify its appeal by offering gymnasium facilities and residence quarters. Gradually, women, Lutherans, Roman Catholics, Jews, and the "unchurched" were accepted and even recruited as members.

The most recent phase of goal multiplication at the YMCA began in the 1960s. In large urban areas, the organization became involved in providing employment training and juvenile delinquency programs. As a result, the YMCA received substantial funding from the federal government. This was a dramatic change for an organization whose income had previously come solely from membership fees and charitable contributions. The YMCA's impressive range of activities currently includes social service programs for the disabled, day care centers, fitness classes for office workers, residence dormitories for college students and single adults, "learning for living" classes for adults, and senior citizens' facilities (Schmidt 1990).

These transitions in the YMCA were not always smooth. At times, major contributors and board members withdrew support because of opposition to organizational changes; they preferred the YMCA to remain as it had been. However, the YMCA has survived and grown by expanding its goals from evangelism to general community service (Etzioni 1964; Zald 1970).

More and more people are becoming telecommuters, employees who work at home while linked to the office through computer terminals, phones, and fax machines. Telecommuting is one sign of the impact of new technologies on the workplace.

Goal Succession

Unlike goal multiplication, ***goal succession*** occurs when a group or organization has either realized or been denied its goal. If the group is to continue, it must identify an entirely new objective. Cases of goal succession are rare because most organizations never fully achieve their goals. Those that do, such as a committee supporting a victorious candidate for public office, usually dissolve.

Sociologist Peter Blau (1964), who coined the term *succession of goals,* noted that organizations do not necessarily behave in a rigid manner when their goals are achieved or become irrelevant. Rather, they may shift to new objectives. A case in point is the Foundation for Infantile Paralysis, organized in 1938. For some time, the foundation's major goals were to support medical research on polio and to provide assistance for victims of the disease. However, in 1955 the Salk vaccine was found to be an effective protection against paralytic polio, leaving the foundation, so to speak, unemployed. Suddenly, a vast network of committed staff members and volunteers was left without a clear rationale for existence. The group might have disbanded at that point, but instead it selected a new goal—combating arthritis and birth defects—and in 1958 took on the new name of March of Dimes Birth Defects Foundation (Etzioni 1964; Sills 1957).

TECHNOLOGY'S IMPACT ON THE WORKPLACE

In 1968, Stanley Kubrick's motion picture *2001: A Space Odyssey* dazzled audiences with its futuristic depiction of travel to Jupiter. We have now passed 2001, but have not yet explored Jupiter. What about the portrayal of computers in *2001*? In the movie, a mellow-voiced computer named HAL is at first very efficient and helpful to the crew—only to try to take over the ship later. Today, computers can successfully compete against chess champions, but they are as far short of achieving the artificial intelligence of HAL as earthlings are of accomplishing manned travel to Jupiter.

Still, the computer is a commanding presence in our lives, and in the workplace in particular. It is not just that the computer makes tedious, routine tasks easier, such as electronically correcting the spelling of documents. It has affected the workplace in far more dramatic ways (Liker et al. 1999).

Telecommuting

Increasingly, workers are turning into *telecommuters* in many industrial countries. ***Telecommuters*** are employees who work full-time or part-time at home rather than in an outside office, and who are linked to their supervisors and colleagues through computer terminals, phones, and fax machines (see Chapter 18). One national survey showed that next to on-site day care, most office workers want virtual offices that allow them to work off-site. Not surprisingly, the number of telecommuters increased from 8.5 million in 1995 to 28 million in 2001 (Donald B. Davis and Polonko 2001).

What are the social implications of this shift toward the virtual office? From an interactionist perspective, the workplace is a major source of friendships; restricting face-to-face social opportunities could destroy the trust that is created by "handshake agreements." Thus, telecommuting may move society further along the continuum from *Gemeinschaft* to *Gesellschaft*. On a more positive note, telecommuting may be the first social change that pulls fathers and mothers back into the home rather than pushing them out. The trend, if it continues, should also increase autonomy and job satisfaction for many employees (Castells 2001b; DiMaggio et al. 2001).

Use Your Sociological Imagination

If your first full-time job after college involved telecommuting, what do you think would be the advantages and disadvantages of working out of a home office? Do you think you would be satisfied as a telecommuter? Why or why not?

Electronic Communication

Electronic communication in the workplace has generated some heat lately. On the one hand, e-mailing is a convenient way to push messages around, especially with the CC (carbon copy) button. It's democratic, too: lower-status employees are more likely to participate in e-mail discussion than in face-to-face communications, giving organizations the benefit of their experience and views. But e-mailing is almost too easy to use. At Computer Associates, a software company, people were e-mailing colleagues in the next cubicle. To deal with the electronic chaos, the company's CEO took the unusual step of banning all e-mails from 9:30 to 12 and 1:30 to 4. Other companies have limited the number of CCs that can be sent and banned systemwide messages (Gwynne and Dickerson 1997; DiMaggio et al. 2001).

There are other problems with e-mail. It doesn't convey body language, which in face-to-face communication

can soften insensitive phrasing and make unpleasant messages (such as a reprimand) easier to take. It also leaves a permanent record, which can be a problem if messages are written thoughtlessly. In an antitrust case that the federal government brought against Microsoft in 1998, the prosecutors used as evidence e-mail sent to and from Microsoft's CEO Bill Gates. Finally, as will be discussed in detail in Chapter 23, companies can monitor e-mail as a means of "watching" their employees. Dartmouth professor Paul Argenti advises those who use e-mail, "Think before you write. The most important thing to know is what not to write" (Gwynne and Dickerson 1997:90).

SOCIAL POLICY and ORGANIZATIONS

The State of the Unions

www.mhhe.com/schaefer9

The Issue

How many people do you know who belong to a labor union? Chances are you can name a lot fewer people than someone could 50 years ago. In 1954, unions represented 39 percent of workers in the private sector of the U.S. economy; in 2001, they represented only 14 percent (AFL-CIO 2001). What has happened to diminish the importance of organized labor today? Have unions outlived their usefulness in a rapidly changing global economy that is dominated by the service sector?

The Setting

Labor unions consist of organized workers who share either the same skill (as in electronics) or the same employer (as in the

Members of the South Florida Carpenters union join together to support one another and demonstrate their strength. In recent decades economic change has eliminated many union jobs, reducing unions' membership and weakening their bargaining power.

case of postal employees). Unions began to emerge during the Industrial Revolution in England, in the 1700s. Groups of workers banded together to extract concessions from employers (e.g., safer working conditions, a shorter work week), as well as to protect their positions. They frequently tried to protect their jobs by limiting entry to their occupation based on gender, race, ethnicity, citizenship, age, and sometimes rather arbitrary meas-

ures of skill levels. Today we see less of this protection of special interests, but individual labor unions are still the target of charges of discrimination, as are employers.

The power of labor unions varies widely in different countries. In some, such as Britain and Mexico, unions play a key role in the foundation of governments. In others, such as Japan and Korea, their role in politics is very limited, and even their ability to

FIGURE 6-2

Union Membership in the United States

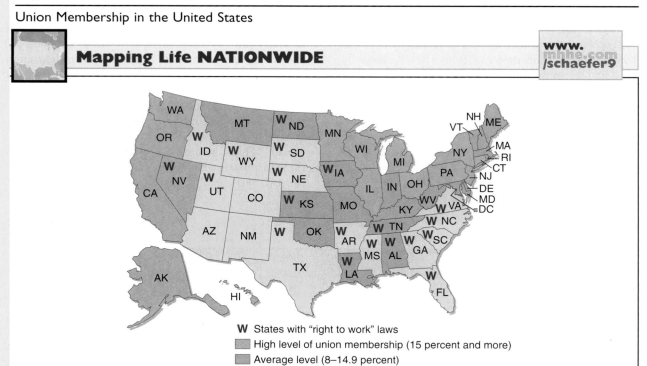

Mapping Life NATIONWIDE

www.
mhhe.com
/schaefer9

W States with "right to work" laws

High level of union membership (15 percent and more)

Average level (8–14.9 percent)

Low level (8 percent and less)

Note: Right to work means that legally, workers cannot be required to join a union or pay union dues.

Source: Developed by the author based on data from Bureau of Labor Statistics 2003; National Right to Work Legal Defense Foundation 2003.

Think About It

What is the relationship between the level of union membership in a given state and the presence of right-to-work laws?

influence the private sector is relatively weak. Unions in the United States can sometimes have a significant influence on employers and elected officials, but their effect varies dramatically by type of industry and even region of the country (see Figure 6-2) (M. Wallerstein and Western 2000).

Few people today would dispute the fact that union membership is declining. What accounts for this decline? Among the reasons offered are the following:

1. Changes in the type of industry. Manufacturing jobs, the traditional heart of the labor union, have declined, giving way to postindustrial service jobs.

2. Growth in part-time jobs. Between 1982 and 1998 the number of temporary jobs rose 577 percent, while total employment increased only 41 percent. Only in 2000 did laws governing collective bargaining allow temporary workers to join a union.

3. The legal system. The United States has not made it particularly easy for unions to organize and

bargain, and some government measures have made it more difficult. A dramatic example was President Ronald Reagan's firing of 11,000 air traffic controllers in 1981, when their union threatened to walk off the job while seeking a new contract.

4. Globalization. The threat of jobs leaving the country has undercut the ability of union leaders to organize workers at home. Some say that labor union demands for wage increases and additional benefits have themselves spurred the exodus of jobs to developing nations, where wages are significantly lower and unions are virtually nonexistent.

5. Employer offensive. Increasingly hostile employers have taken court action to block unions' efforts to represent their members.

6. Union rigidity and bureaucratization. Labor has been slow to embrace women, minorities, and immigrants. Furthermore, in some unions the election of leadership seems to dominate the organization's activity

(AFL-CIO 2001; Clawson and Clawson 1999; Cornfield 1991; Greenhouse 2000a; Migration News 2001).

Perhaps as a result of all these factors, confidence in unions is low. Only 1 out of 10 persons in the United States expresses a great deal of confidence in unions—more than for major corporations and government, but far less than for educational and religious institutions and the military (Bureau of the Census 2001a:249).

Sociological Insights

Both Marxists and functionalists would view unions as a logical response to the emergence of impersonal, large-scale, formal, and often alienating organizations. This view certainly characterized the growth of unions in major manufacturing industries with a sharp division of labor. However, as manufacturing has declined, unions have had to look elsewhere for growth (Cornfield 1991).

Today labor unions in the United States and Europe bear little resemblance to those early unions organized spontaneously by exploited workers. In line with the oligarchic model developed by Robert Michels (see page 136), unions have become increasingly bureaucratized under a self-serving leadership. Conflict theorists would point out that the longer union leaders are in office, the less responsive they are to the needs and demands of the rank and file, and the more concerned they are with maintaining their own positions and power. Yet research shows that under certain circumstances, union leadership can change significantly. Smaller unions are vulnerable to changes in leadership, as are unions whose membership shifts in composition from predominantly White to African American or Latino (Cornfield 1991; Form 1992).

Many union employees encounter role conflict. For example, they may agree to provide a needed service and then organize a "strike" to withhold it. Role conflict is

p. 108

especially apparent in the so-called helping occupations: teaching, social work, nursing, law enforcement, and firefighting. These workers may feel torn between carrying out their professional responsibilities and enduring working conditions they find unacceptable (Aronowitz and Di Fazio 1994).

Policy Initiatives

U.S. law grants workers the right to self-organize via unions. But the United States is unique among industrial democracies in allowing employers to actively oppose their employees' decision to organize (Comstock and Fox 1994).

A major barrier to union growth exists in the 20 states that have so-called right-to-work laws (see Figure 6-2). In these states, workers cannot be *required* to join or pay dues or fees to a union. The very term *right to work* reflects the anti-union view that a worker should not be forced to join a union, even if that union may negotiate on his or her behalf and achieve results that benefit that worker. This situation is unlikely to change. That is, right-to-work states will remain so; those without such laws typically have a strong union tradition or restrict union activities in other ways (National Right to Work Legal Defense Foundation 2001).

On the national level, union power is waning. In the security buildup that followed the terrorist attacks of September 11, 2001, federal officials created many new jobs and reorganized existing agencies into the Department of Homeland Security. In doing so, they specified that some 170,000 workers would not have collective bargaining rights, and that 56,000 newly federalized airport security screeners could not be unionized. Though these stipulations may or may not stand up to legal challenges, many observers see them as another sign of increasingly anti-union sentiment at all levels of government (Borosage 2003).

In Europe, labor unions tend to play a major role in political elections. (The ruling party in Great Britain, in fact, is called the Labour Party.) Although unions in the United States play a lesser political role, they have recently faced attacks for their large financial contributions to political campaigns. Debate over campaign finance reform in Congress in 2001 raised the question of whether labor unions should be able to use dues to support a particular candidate or promote a position via "issue ads" that favor one particular party, usually the Democrats.

Let's Discuss

1. What kinds of unions are represented on your college campus? Have you been aware of union activity? Has there been any opposition to the unions on the part of the administration?

2. Do you think nurses should be allowed to strike? Why or why not? How about teachers or police officers?

3. If a union is working on behalf of all the workers of a company, should all the employees be required to join the union and pay dues? Why or why not?

Summary

Social interaction among human beings is necessary to the transmission of culture and the survival of every society. This chapter examines the social behavior of *groups, formal organizations,* and *voluntary associations.*

1. When we find ourselves identifying closely with a group, it is probably a *primary group.* A *secondary group* is more formal and impersonal.
2. People tend to see the world in terms of *in-groups* and *out-groups,* a perception often fostered by the very groups to which they belong.
3. *Reference groups* set and enforce standards of conduct and serve as a source of comparison for people's evaluations of themselves and others.
4. Interactionist researchers have noted distinct and predictable processes in the functioning of *small groups.* The simplest group is a *dyad,* composed of two members. *Triads* and larger groups increase the ways of interacting and allow for *coalitions* to form.
5. As societies have become more complex, large *formal organizations* have become more powerful and pervasive.
6. Max Weber argued that in its ideal form, every *bureaucracy* has five basic characteristics: division of

labor, hierarchical authority, written rules and regulations, impersonality, and employment based on technical qualifications.

7. Bureaucracy can be understood both as a process and as a matter of degree. Thus, an organization may be more or less bureaucratic than other organizations.
8. When leaders of an organization build up their power, the result can be *oligarchy* (rule by a few).
9. The informal structure of an organization can undermine and redefine official bureaucratic policies.
10. People join *voluntary associations* for a variety of purposes—for example, to share in joint activities or to get help with personal problems.
11. An organization's goals may change over time, either through the addition of goals *(goal multiplication)* or through the replacement of old goals with new ones *(goal succession).*
12. Technology has transformed workplace organizations through *telecommuting* and electronic communication.
13. *Labor unions* are on the decline because of major shifts in the economy.

Critical Thinking Questions

1. Think about how behavior is shaped by reference groups. What different reference groups have shaped your outlook and your goals at different periods in your life? How have they done so?
2. Are primary groups, secondary groups, in-groups, out-groups, and reference groups likely to be found within a formal organization? What functions do these groups serve for a formal organization? What dysfunctions might occur as a result of their presence?

3. Max Weber identified five basic characteristics of bureaucracy. Select an actual organization familiar to you (for example, your college, a workplace, or a religious institution or civic association you belong to) and apply Weber's five characteristics to that organization. To what degree does it correspond to Weber's ideal type of bureaucracy?

Key Terms

Alienation   A condition of estrangement or dissociation from the surrounding society. (page 133)

Bureaucracy   A component of formal organization that uses rules and hierarchical ranking to achieve efficiency. (133)

Bureaucratization   The process by which a group, organization, or social movement becomes increasingly bureaucratic. (135)

Classical theory   An approach to the study of formal organizations that views workers as being motivated almost entirely by economic rewards. (136)

Coalition   A temporary or permanent alliance geared toward a common goal. (132)

Dyad   A two-member group. (131)

Focus group   A group of 10 to 15 people assembled by a researcher to discuss a predetermined topic, guided by a moderator. (130)

Formal organization   A group designed for a special purpose and structured for maximum efficiency. (132)

Goal displacement   Overzealous conformity to official regulations of a bureaucracy. (134)

Goal multiplication   The process through which an organization expands its purpose. (139)

Goal succession   The process through which an organization identifies an entirely new objective because its traditional goals have been realized or denied. (139)

Group   Any number of people with similar norms, values, and expectations who interact with one another on a regular basis. (127)

Human relations approach   An approach to the study of formal organizations that emphasizes the role of people, communication, and participation within a bureaucracy and tends to focus on the informal structure of the organization. (136)

Ideal type   A construct or model that serves as a standard for evaluating specific cases. (133)

In-group   Any group or category to which people feel they belong. (129)

Iron law of oligarchy   A principle of organizational life under which even democratic organizations will develop into bureaucracies ruled by a few individuals. (135)

Labor union   Organized workers who share either the same skill or the same employer. (141)

McDonaldization   The process by which the principles of the fast-food restaurant industry have come to dominate certain sectors of society, both in the United States and throughout the world. (127)

Out-group   A group or category to which people feel they do not belong. (129)

Peter principle   A principle of organizational life according to which each individual within a hierarchy tends to rise to his or her level of incompetence. (135)

Primary group   A small group characterized by intimate, face-to-face association and cooperation. (127)

Reference group   Any group that individuals use as a standard for evaluating themselves and their own behavior. (130)

Scientific management approach   Another name for the *classical theory* of formal organizations. (136)

Secondary group   A formal, impersonal group in which there is little social intimacy or mutual understanding. (128)

Small group   A group small enough for all members to interact simultaneously—that is, to talk with one another or at least be well acquainted. (130)

Telecommuter   An employee who works full-time or part-time at home rather than in an outside office and who is linked to supervisor and colleagues through computer terminals, phone lines, and fax machines. (140)

Trained incapacity   The tendency of workers in a bureaucracy to become so specialized that they develop blind spots and fail to notice obvious problems. (133)

Triad   A three-member group. (131)

Voluntary association   An organization established on the basis of common interest, whose members volunteer or even pay to participate. (138)

TECHNOLOGY RESOURCES

Internet Connection

Note: While all the URLs listed were current as of the printing of this book, these sites often change. Please check our website (www.mhhe.com/schaefer9) for updates, hyperlinks, and exercises related to these sites.

1. One of Max Weber's most important contributions to sociology has been his examination of bureaucracies. To learn more about his influence, log on to the Dead Sociologists' Society, a website developed by Larry R. Ridener (www2.pfeiffer.edu/~lridener/DSS/deadsoc.html).

2. The opening excerpt for this chapter discusses the concept of McDonaldization, introduced by sociologist George Ritzer. In a recent commentary, Ritzer discussed the McDonaldization of society and introduced another concept, "vertical McDonaldization." Read his comments by logging on to: (www.philly.com/mld/inquirer/news/editorial/5361977.htm).

Online Learning Center with PowerWeb

The focus of this chapter has been groups and organizations. Everyone is a member of an "in-group," and most people have also been members of an "out-group." Visit the student center in the Online Learning Center (**www.mhhe.com/schaefer9**) and link to the first Interactive Activity, called "In-Groups," "Out-Groups," and "Un-words." For this activity, you will be asked to discuss your experiences as a member of an in-group and an out-group. You can also do the word scramble, which contains key words or phrases from this chapter.

chapter

7

THE MASS MEDIA

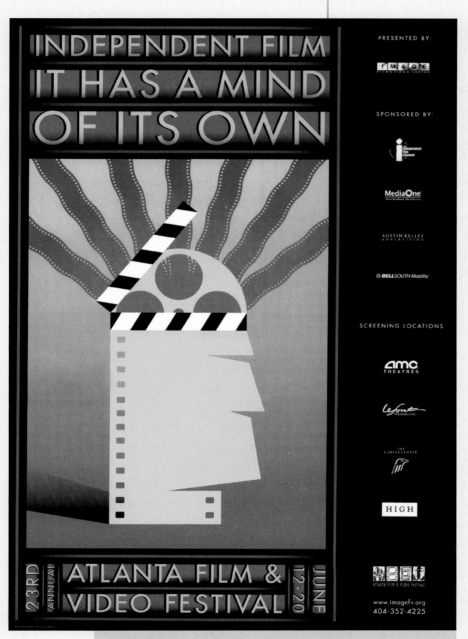

Sociological Perspectives on the Media

The Audience

The Media Industry

Social Policy and Mass Media: Media Violence

Boxes

SOCIOLOGY IN THE GLOBAL COMMUNITY: Al Jazeera Is on the Air

SOCIAL INEQUALITY: The Color of Network TV

Movies have long been an influential form of mass media in both reflecting and creating social mores. Sociologists are interested in the influence of other types of mass media as well, including television, newspapers, magazines, and online content.

Everywhere, the media flow defies national boundaries. This is one of its obvious, but at the same time amazing, features. A global torrent is not, of course, the master metaphor to which we have grown accustomed. We're more accustomed to Marshall McLuhan's *global village*. Those who resort to this metaphor casually often forget that if the world is a global village, some live in mansions on the hill, others in huts. Some dispatch images and sounds around town at the touch of a button; others collect them at the touch of *their* buttons. Yet McLuhan's image reveals an indispensable half-truth. If there is a village, it speaks American. It wears jeans, drinks Coke, eats at the golden arches, walks on swooshed shoes, plays electric guitars, recognizes Mickey Mouse, James Dean, E.T., Bart Simpson, R2-D2, and Pamela Anderson. . . .

Entertainment is one of America's top exports. In 1999, in fact, film, television, music, radio, advertising, print publishing, and computer software together were the top export, almost $80 billion worth, and while software alone accounted for $50 billion of the total, some of that category also qualifies as entertainment—video games and pornography, for example. Hardly anyone is exempt from the force of American images and sounds. . . . American popular culture is the nemesis that hundreds of millions—perhaps billions—of people love, and love to hate. The antagonism and the dependency are inseparable, for the media flood—essentially American in its origin, but virtually unlimited in its

reach—represents, like it or not, a common imagination.

How shall we understand the Hong Kong T-shirt that says "I Feel Coke"? Or the little Japanese girl who asks an American visitor in all innocence, "Is there really a Disneyland in America?" (She knows the one in Tokyo.) Or the experience of a German television reporter sent to Siberia to film indigenous life, who after flying out of Moscow and then traveling for days by boat, bus, and jeep, arrives near the Arctic Sea where a tribe of Tungusians live known to ethnologists for their bear-skin rituals. In the community store sits a grandfather with his grandchild on his knee. Grandfather is dressed in traditional Tungusian clothing. Grandson has on his head a reversed baseball cap. . . .

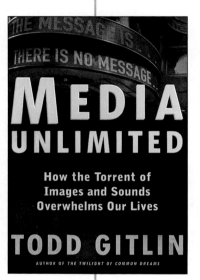

The misleadingly easy answer to the question of how American images and sounds became omnipresent is: American imperialism. But the images are not even faintly force-fed by American corporate, political, or military power. The empire strikes from inside the spectator as well as from outside. This is a conundrum that deserves to be approached with respect if we are to grasp the fact that Mickey Mouse and Coke are everywhere recognized and often enough *enjoyed*. In the peculiar unification at work throughout the world, there is surely a supply side, but there is not only a supply side. Some things are true even if multinational corporations claim so: there is demand. (*Gitlin 2001:176–179*) ■ 🎧

Additional information about this excerpt can be found on the Online Learning Center at **www.mhhe.com/schaefer9.**

148

In his book *Media Unlimited: How the Torrent of Images and Sounds Overwhelms Our Lives*, sociologist Todd Gitlin focuses on what he calls "the obvious but hard-to-grasp truth . . . that living with the media is today one of the main things Americans and many other human beings do" (2001:5). We immerse ourselves in images and sounds. And, as he noted in the opening excerpt, media entertainment is one of the top exports from the United States to the rest of the world.

By *mass media* sociologists refer to the print and electronic instruments of communication that carry messages to often widespread audiences. Print media include newspapers, magazines, and books; electronic media include radio, television, motion pictures, and the Internet. Advertising, which falls into both categories, is also a form of mass media.

The pervasiveness of the mass media in society is obvious. Consider a few examples. TV dinners were invented to accommodate the millions of "couch potatoes" who won't miss their favorite television programs. Today *screen time* encompasses not just television viewing but also playing video games and surfing the Internet. Candidates for political office rely on their media consultants to project a winning image both in print and in the electronic media. World leaders use all forms of media for political advantage, whether it is to gain territory or to make a successful bid for hosting the Olympics. AIDS education projects in parts of Africa and Asia owe much of their success to media campaigns. During the 2003 Iraqi war both the British and U.S. governments allowed 500 journalists to be embedded in frontline troops as a means of "telling their story."

Few aspects of society are as central as the mass media. Through the media we expand our understanding of people and events beyond what we experience in person. The media inform us about different cultures and lifestyles and about the latest forms of technology. For sociologists, the key questions are how do the mass media affect our social institutions and how do they influence our social behavior? They want to know: Why are the media so influential? Who benefits from media influence, and why? How do we maintain cultural and ethical standards in the face of negative media images?

In this chapter, we will consider the ways sociologists help us to answer these questions. First, we will take a look at how proponents of the various sociological perspectives view the media. Then we will examine just who makes up the media's audience as well as how the media operate, especially in their global reach. In the social policy section we will consider whether violence shown in the media breeds violent behavior in their audience. ▪

SOCIOLOGICAL PERSPECTIVES ON THE MEDIA

The penetration of mass media into people's homes has been dramatic over the last sixty years. As Figure 7-1 on the next page shows, the percentage of homes with televisions rose from less than 10 percent in 1950 to close to 100 percent in 2000. In what follows we'll examine the impact of the mass media from the points of view of the proponents of major sociological perspectives.

Functionalist View

One obvious function of mass media is to entertain. Except for clearly stated news or educational programming, we often think the explicit purpose of the mass media is to occupy our leisure time—from comics and crossword puzzles in newspapers to the latest music releases playing on the radio or the Internet. While this is true, we may be overlooking other important functions of the mass media. They also socialize us, enforce social norms, confer status, promote consumption, and keep us informed about our social environment. An important dysfunction of the mass media is that they may act as a narcotic, desensitizing us to events (Lazarsfeld and Merton 1948; Wright 1986).

Agent of Socialization

The media increase social cohesion by presenting a more or less standardized, common view of culture through mass communication. Sociologist Robert Park (1922) studied how newspapers helped immigrants to the United States adjust to their environment by changing

FIGURE 7-1

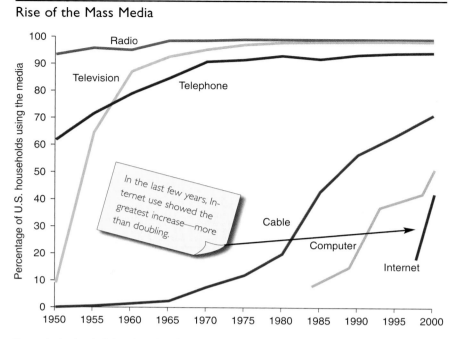

Rise of the Mass Media

In the last few years, Internet use showed the greatest increase—more than doubling.

Source: Author's calculations based on Bureau of the Census 1975:43, 783, 796; 2000a:567; Newburger 2001; Television Bureau of Advertisers 2001.

Think About It
Why do you think more households today have a television than a telephone?

their customary habits and teaching them the opinions held by people in their new home country. The mass media unquestionably play a significant role in providing a collective experience for members of a society. Think about how the mass media "bring together" members of

p. 95

a community or even a nation by showing important events and ceremonies (such as inaugurations, press conferences, parades, state funerals, and the Olympics) and by covering disasters (such as the 1995 bombing in Oklahoma City, the terrorist attacks on New York City and Washington, D.C., in 2001, and the loss of the space shuttle *Columbia* in 2003).

Which media outlets did people turn to in the aftermath of the 2001 tragedy? Television and the telephone were the primary means by which people in the United States bonded. But the Internet also played a prominent role. About half of all Internet users—more than 53 million people—received some kind of news about the attacks online. Nearly three-fourths of Internet users communicated via e-mail to show patriotism, to discuss events with family and friends, or to reconnect with friends. More than a third of Internet users read or posted material in online forums. In the first 30 days alone, the Library of Congress collected in one Internet site more

than half a million pages having to do with the terrorist attacks. As a Library director noted, "The Internet has become for many the public commons, a place where they can come together and talk" (D. L. Miller and Darlington 2002; Mirapaul 2001:E2; Rainie 2001).

Not everyone applauds the socialization function of the mass media. Many people worry about the effect of using television as a baby-sitter or the impact of violent programming on viewer behavior (see the social policy section). Some people adopt a blame-the-media mentality, holding the media accountable for anything that goes wrong, especially with young people.

Enforcer of Social Norms

The media often reaffirm proper behavior by showing what happens to people who act in a way that violates societal expectations. These messages are conveyed when the bad guy gets clobbered in cartoons or is thrown in jail on *Law and Order,* for example. Yet the media also sometimes glorify disapproved behavior, whether it is physical violence, disrespect to a teacher, or drug use.

The media play a critical role in shaping perceptions about the risks of substance use, although not necessarily in a positive fashion. Increases in substance use among youth during the 1990s were linked to a decline in warning and antidrug messages from the media; the proliferation of pro-use messages from the entertainment industry; and high levels of tobacco and alcohol product advertising and promotion. Media research using content analysis shows that in the 200 most popular movie rentals in 1996 and 1997, alcohol use appeared in 93 percent, tobacco use in 89 percent, and illicit drug use in 22 percent, with marijuana and cocaine use depicted most often. Analysis of the 1,000 most popular songs during the same period showed that 27 percent referred to either alcohol or illicit drugs. In 1999, 44 percent of entertainment programs aired by the four major television networks portrayed tobacco use in at least one episode (Ericson 2001; D. F. Roberts et al. 1999).

In 1997, a federal law required the television networks to provide one free minute for every minute the government bought for a public service announcement with an antidrug message. The networks subsequently

FIGURE 7-2

Tracking the Ebbs and Flows of Popularity for Some of the World's Biggest Celebrities, 2002

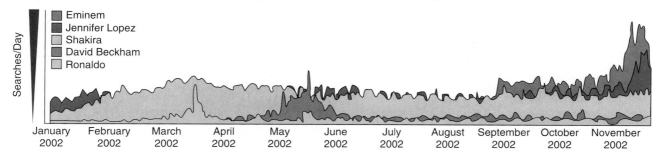

Source: Google Inc. 2003.

This graph charts the number of Google searches for five celebrities made by Google users around the world in 2002.

made an agreement with the government to drop the free minutes in exchange for embedding aggressive antidrug messages in their programs, such as *ER, The Practice,* and *Sabrina the Teenage Witch.* Some people objected, saying that the networks were evading their legal responsibility in using the public airwaves, but criticism really mounted when word got out that the government agency overseeing drug policy was screening scripts in advance and even working on the story lines of shows. Many critics felt this represented a slippery slope that could open the way for government to plant messages in the media

on other topics as well, such as abortion or gun control (Albiniak 2000).

Conferral of Status

The mass media confer status on people, organizations, and public issues. Whether it is an issue such as the homeless or a celebrity such as Cameron Diaz, the media single out one from thousands of other similarly placed issues or people to become significant. Table 7-1 (page 152) shows how certain public figures are prominently featured on weekly magazine covers. Obviously, *People* magazine alone was not responsible for making Princess Diana into a worldwide figure, but collectively all the media outlets created a notoriety that Princess Victoria of Sweden, for one, did not enjoy.

The print media constitute just one way we confer celebrity status on individuals. Another way we confer status is by seeking out information about people on the Internet. At the end of 2002, Google, a major search engine, summarized the trends of more than 55 billion searches conducted by Google users from many different countries over the course of the year (Google Inc. 2003). These kinds of summaries are valuable sources of information for sociologists and other researchers who want to track trends, determine who is hot (and who is not), and compare how interests vary by region and country. Figure 7-2 tracks the global trends for hits

Mass media can serve to reinforce proper behavior. But they can also endorse illicit activity, such as drag racing down city streets, as shown in this still from the 2003 movie *2 Fast 2 Furious.*

Table 7-1		Status Conferred by Magazines			
Rank/Person	**Number of Times on Cover of *Time***	**Rank/Person**	**Number of Times on Cover of *People***	**Rank/Person**	**Number of Times on Cover of *Ebony***
1. Richard Nixon	59	1. Princess Diana	52	1. Muhammad Ali	15
2. Ronald Reagan	34	2. Julia Roberts	27	1. Michael Jackson	15
3. Bill Clinton	29	3. Elizabeth Taylor	15	3. Whitney Houston	14
4. Dwight Eisenhower	22	4. Michael Jackson	14	4. Janet Jackson	12
4. Lyndon Johnson	22	5. Madonna	13	5. Halle Berry	11
4. Gerald Ford	22	5. Jackie Onassis	13	5. Diahann Carroll	11
7. Jimmy Carter	19	5. Sarah Ferguson	13	5. Lena Horne	11
8. George H. W. Bush	18	5. Cher	13	5. Sidney Poitier	11
9. Jesus Christ	17	9. John Travolta	9	9. Bill Cosby	10
9. Henry Kissinger	17	9. Princess Caroline (Monaco)	9	10. Sammy Davis, Jr.	9
9. John F. Kennedy	17				

Source: Author's content analysis of primary cover subject for full run of the periodicals beginning with *Time* March 3, 1923; *People* March 4, 1974; *Ebony* November 1945 through September 15, 2003.

Think About It

How do the magazines differ in the types of people they feature on their covers? Which type do you think enjoys the most status? Why?

on five major celebrities—singers and movie stars Eminem and Jennifer Lopez, soccer stars David Beckham (United Kingdom) and Ronaldo (Brazil), and singer Shakira. The means may have changed since the first issue of *Time* magazine hit the stands in 1923, but the media still confer status. In today's world it is often by electronic means.

Promoting Consumption

Twenty-thousand commercials a year—that is the number the average child in the United States watches on television, according to the American Academy of Pediatrics. Young people cannot escape commercial messages promoting consumption. They show up on high school scoreboards, at rock concerts, and as banners on webpages. They are even embedded in motion pictures (remember Reese's Pieces in 1982's *E.T.: The Extra-Terres-*

trial?). This *product placement* is nothing new. In 1951 *The African Queen* prominently displayed Gordon's Gin aboard the boat on which Katherine Hepburn and Humphrey Bogart were adrift. But commercial promotion has become far more common today. Moreover, through their media advertising companies attempt to develop brand or logo loyalty at younger and younger ages, with the hope of creating a lifelong consumer (Lasn 2003; Quart 2003).

Media advertising has several clear functions: it supports the economy, provides information about products, and underwrites the cost of media. In some cases, advertising becomes a part of the entertainment industry itself. A national survey showed that 14 percent of those viewing the 2003 Super Bowl did so *only* for the commercials. Yet related to these functions are dysfunctions. Media advertising contributes to a consumer culture that creates "needs" and raises unrealistic expectations of what is required to be happy or satisfied. Moreover, because the media depend heavily on advertising revenue, advertisers are able to influence media content. For example, Ford Motor Company sponsored *Time*'s special issue "Heroes for the Planet," which conveniently neglected to identify even one clean-air environmentalist (FAIR 2001; Horwitz 2003).

Surveillance of the Social Environment

The *surveillance function* refers to the collection and distribution of information concerning events in the social environment. The media collect and distribute facts about a variety of events, including stock market quotations and tomorrow's weather, as well as election campaigns, play openings, sports events, and international conflicts.

But what exactly constitutes a fact? Who gets portrayed as a hero, a villain, a patriot, a terrorist? The media generally define these for the audience, using a definition that reflects the values and orientation of the decision makers within media organizations.

Product placement plays an increasing part in the revenue of motion pictures. A scene from *Austin Powers: The Spy Who Shagged Me* (1999) doubles as a commercial for Starbucks coffee.

Use Your Sociological Imagination   www.mhhe.com/schaefer9

You are a news junkie. Where would you gather your facts or information? Is it more likely to be from newspapers, tabloids, magazines, TV newscasts, or the Internet? Why would you choose that medium?

Dysfunctional Media: The Narcotizing Effect

In addition to the functions previously noted, the media perform a *dysfunction,* as identified by sociologists Paul Lazarsfeld and Robert Merton (1948). They created the term *narcotizing dysfunction* to refer to the phenomenon whereby the media provide such massive amounts of information that the audience becomes numb and generally fails to act on the information, regardless of how compelling the issue. Interested citizens may take in the information, but they may make no decision or take no action.

Consider how often the media initiate a great outpouring of philanthropic support for natural disasters or family crises documented on local news stations. But then

what happens? Research shows that as the tragedy is prolonged, viewer fatigue begins. The mass media audience becomes numb, desensitized to the suffering, and even starts to conclude that a solution to the crisis has been found (Moeller 1999).

The media's narcotizing dysfunction was identified over 50 years ago, when just a few homes had television and well before the advent of electronic media. At that time, sociologists felt this dysfunction was going largely unnoticed, but today it is common to point out the ill effects of addiction to television or the Internet, especially among young people.

Conflict View

Conflict theorists emphasize that the media reflect and even exacerbate many of the divisions of our society and world, including those based on gender, race, ethnicity, and social class. They point in particular to the media's ability to decide what gets transmitted through gatekeeping.

Gatekeeping

What story is placed on page 1 of the morning newspaper? Which motion picture plays three screens at the local cineplex rather than one? What picture is not released

Television programmers have capitalized on the appeal of "reality" shows (such as *Survivor*) to young viewers. *The Bachelor* is one that made it through the gatekeeping process. In this series, a bevy of young women seek the attention of a bachelor, who, week by week, eliminates candidates until one is left.

at all? What news makes it onto the evening broadcast? Lurking behind these decisions is usually the presence of powerful figures, such as publishers, editors, and other media moguls.

The mass media constitute a form of big business in which profits are generally more important than the quality of the product (programming). Within the mass media, a relatively small number of people control what eventually reaches the audience, a process known as *gatekeeping.* This term describes how material must travel through a series of checkpoints (or gates) before it reaches the public. A select few decide what images to bring to a broad audience. In many countries the government plays a gatekeeping role. A study for the World Bank found that in 97 countries, 60 percent of the top five TV stations and 72 percent of the largest radio stations are government-owned (World Bank 2001:183).

Gatekeeping prevails in all kinds of media. In the recording industry, gatekeepers may reject a popular local band because it competes with a group already on their label. Or, even if the band gets recorded, radio station programmers may reject it because it does not fit their station's "sound." Television network programmers may keep a pilot for a new TV series off the air because the gatekeepers believe it does not appeal to their target audience (which is sometimes determined by the advertising sponsors). Similar decisions are made by gatekeepers in the publishing industry (J. R. Wilson and Wilson 2001).

Gatekeeping is not as dominant in at least one form of mass media—the Internet. You can send virtually any message to electronic bulletin boards. You can create a webpage or a blog (weblog) to advance any argument you might wish, including one that insists the earth is flat. The Internet is a means to quickly disseminate information (or misinformation) without going through any significant gatekeeping process.

Nevertheless, the Internet is not totally without restrictions. Laws in many nations try to regulate content on such issues as gambling, pornography, and even political views. Popular Internet service providers will terminate accounts for offensive behavior. After the terrorist attack in 2001, eBay did not allow people to sell parts of the World Trade Center on its online auction. The World Bank study found that 17 countries place significant controls on Internet content. China routinely blocks search engines like Google and AltaVista from accessing names of groups or individuals critical of the government (Ni 2000; World Bank 2001b:187).

Critics of the content of mass media argue that the gatekeeping process reflects a desire to maximize profits. Why else, they argue, would movie star Julia Roberts make the cover of *Time* magazine rather than Palestinian leader Yasir Arafat? We will consider later in this chapter the role that corporate structure plays in the content and delivery of mass media. Another criticism of the gatekeeping process is that what content makes it through the gates does not reflect the diversity of the audience, as we will now see.

Dominant Ideology: Constructing Reality

Conflict theorists argue that the mass media serve to maintain the privileges of certain groups. Moreover, while protecting their own interests, powerful groups may limit the representation of others in the media. The term *dominant ideology* describes a set of cultural beliefs p. 69 and practices that help to maintain powerful social, economic, and political interests. The media transmit messages that virtually define what we regard as the real world, even though these images are frequently at wide variance from what the larger society experiences.

Mass media decision makers are overwhelmingly White, male, and wealthy. It may come as no surprise, then, that the media tend to ignore the lives and ambitions of subordinate groups, among them working-class people, African Americans, Hispanics, gays and lesbians, people with disabilities, overweight people, and older people. Even worse, the content may create false images or *stereotypes* of these groups that become accepted as accurate portrayals of reality. *Stereotypes* are unreliable generalizations about all members of a group that do not recognize individual differences within the group.

Television content is a prime example of ignoring reality. How many characters who are overweight can you name? Even though in real life one out of every four women is obese (30 or more pounds over a healthy body weight), only 3 out of 100 TV characters are portrayed as obese. Heavyset men and women on television programs have fewer romances, talk less about sex, eat more often, and are the object of ridicule more often than their thin counterparts (Hellmich 2001).

Minority groups are often stereotyped in TV shows. Almost all the leading roles are cast as White, even in urban-based programs such as *Friends,* which is situated in ethnically diverse New York City. Blacks on television tend to be featured mainly in crime-based dramas; Latinos are virtually ignored. Box 7-1 (page 156) discusses the distorted picture of society presented on prime-time television programs.

Another concern about the media from the conflict perspective is that television distorts the political process. Until the campaign finance system is truly reformed and enforced, candidates with the most money (often backed by powerful lobbying groups) will be able to buy exposure to voters and saturate the air with commercials attacking their opponents.

When media executives seek the assistance of the powerful, the influence of the dominant ideology can be especially explicit. Filmmakers who want their motion pictures about the military to look authentic often seek assistance from Pentagon consultants, but sometimes the government refuses to cooperate because it feels the military is portrayed in an unfavorable way. In some cases, the Hollywood film industry actually *changes* the movie in order to gain access to military bases and military equipment (Robb 2001; Suid 2002).

For example, when Paramount Pictures sought military assistance for *The Sum of All Fears,* the 2002 film about nuclear terrorism, it had to make some changes to the screenplay. The original script called for a U.S. carrier to be destroyed by cruise missiles, but Pentagon officials were troubled by the idea that an aircraft carrier could be portrayed as so vulnerable. No problem. The screenplay was revised so that the carrier stayed intact while only some flight operations were destroyed. This kind of exploitation in the making of war movies is mutual: the producers get authentic military hardware and technical assistance at minimal cost, while the military gets to promote a positive image, which attracts recruits and larger defense budgets (Seelye 2002).

Dominant Ideology: Whose Culture?

Globalization projects the dominating reach of the U.S. media into the rest of the world. Movies produced in the United States account for 65 percent of the global box office. Magazines as diverse as *Cosmopolitan* and *Reader's Digest* sell two issues abroad for every one they sell in the pp. 60–62 United States. These media cultural exports undermine the distinctive traditions and art forms of other societies and encourage their cultural and economic dependence on the United States. Countries throughout the world decry U.S. exports, from films to language to Bart Simpson. In the opening essay for this chapter, Todd Gitlin describes American popular culture as something that "people love, and love to hate" (2001:177; Farhi and Rosenfeld 1998).

The U.S. media economy has come to rely on the overseas market. Many motion pictures, such as *Star Wars: Attack of the Clones, A.I., Moulin Rouge,* and *Ice Age,* have brought in more revenue abroad than at home. Hollywood

Making movies about governmental agencies or the military is a lot easier when the filmmakers can count on the cooperation of the government. *Apollo 13,* which glorified NASA's space program, easily won government approval. But *G. I. Jane,* featuring Demi Moore as a Navy SEAL who bucks high-ranking military and government officials, did not get approved.

Before the 2002 fall television season, executives of the major TV networks once again renewed their commitment to diversify both who is on television and who is responsible for the content. It proved to be a tough commitment to keep. Only two of the 26 new fall series had even one minority person in a leading role. Furthermore, a Directors Guild of America report indicated that of all 826 episodes of the 40 most popular series in 2001, 80 percent were directed by White males and 11 percent by White females. That left only 9 percent directed by Blacks, Latinos, or Asian Americans, who collectively account for more than 25 percent of television viewers.

When minority actors do appear on television and other forms of media, their roles tend to reinforce the stereotypes associated with their ethnic or racial group. Gifted Hispanic character actress Lupe Ontiverus has played the role of maid 150 times. Latinas are now featured as maids on *Will and Grace* (Rosario), *Dharma and Greg* (Celia), and even the animated *King*

of the Hill (Lupino), to name just three television shows.

In the 1999–2000 season, the leading characters in all 26 new prime-time series were White; network gatekeepers seemed surprised by the news. Producers, writers, executives, and advertisers blamed one another for the oversight. Television programming was dictated by advertisers, a

> Marc Hirshfeld, an NBC executive, claims some White producers have told him they don't know how to write for Black characters.

former executive claimed; if advertisers said they wanted blatantly biased programming, the networks would provide it. Jery Isenberg, chairman of the Caucus for Producers, Writers & Directors, blamed the networks, saying that writers would produce a series about three-headed Martians if the networks told them to.

Beyond these excuses, real reasons can be found for the departure from the diversity exhibited in past shows and seasons. In recent years, the rise of more networks, cable TV, and the Internet has fragmented the broadcast entertainment market, siphoning viewers away from the general-audience sitcoms and dramas of the past. Both the UPN and WB networks produce situation comedies and even full nights geared toward African American audiences. With the proliferation of cable channels such as Black Entertainment Television (BET) and the Spanish-language Univision, and websites that cater to every imaginable taste, there no longer seems to be a need for broadly popular series such as *The Cosby Show*, the tone and content of which appealed to Whites as well as Blacks in a way the newer series do not. The result of these sweeping technological changes has been a sharp divergence in viewer preference.

Meanwhile, the mainstream network executives, producers, and writers remain overwhelmingly White. Most of them live

Sources: Bielby and Bielby 2002; Braxton and Calvo 2002; Children Now 2002; Directors Guild of America 2002; A. Hoffman 1997; Navarro 2002; Poniewozik 2001; Soriano 2001; D. B. Wood 2000.

even prepares trailers tailored to resonate with the local culture. For example, *Moulin Rouge* trailers in the United States showed Nicole Kidman locked in a swirling, sensual dance with her lover. In Japan, where tragic love is considered noble and honorable, the trailers featured Kidman taking her final breath with a heartsick young man sobbing at her side. Some Hollywood movies, however, are so insensitive they cannot benefit from any amount of impression management. The James Bond movie *Die Another Day* featured a crazed North Korean colonel, a character even many *South* Koreans found unacceptable; a small boycott greeted its 2003 release in Seoul (Brooke 2003a; Eller and Muñoz 2002).

We risk being ethnocentric, however, if we overstress U.S. dominance. For example *Survivor, Who Wants to Be a Millionaire,* and *Iron Chef,* immensely popular TV programs in the United States, came from Sweden, Britain, and Japan, respectively. The steamy telenovelas of Mexico

and other Spanish-speaking countries owe very little of their origin to soap operas on U.S. television. Unlike motion pictures, television is gradually moving away from U.S. domination and is more likely to be locally produced. A 2001 survey found that 71 percent of the top 10 programs in 60 countries were local productions. The United States is still a major global player, but the days when U.S. studios called all the shots abroad are gone (Kapner 2003).

Nations that feel a loss of identity may try to defend against the cultural invasion from foreign countries, especially the economically dominant United States. Many developing nations have long argued for a greatly improved two-way flow of news and information between industrialized nations and developing nations. They complain that the news from the Third World is scant, and what news there is reflects unfavorably on the developing nations. For example, what do you know about

A rare sight on television: In UPN's *The Parkers*, almost all leading roles are played by African Americans.

far from ethnically and racially diverse inner-city neighborhoods and tend to write and produce stories about people like themselves. Marc Hirshfeld, an NBC executive, claims some White producers

have told him they don't know *how* to write for Black characters. Stephen Bochco, producer of *NYPD Blue,* is a rare exception. His series *City of Angels* featured a mostly non-White cast, like the people Bochco grew up with in an inner-city neighborhood.

In the long run, media observers believe, the major networks will need to integrate the ranks of gatekeepers before they achieve true diversity in programming. Adonis Hoffman, director of the Corporate Policy Institute, has urged network executives to throw open their studios and boardrooms to minorities. Hoffman thinks such a move would empower Black writers and producers to present a true-to-life portrait of African Americans. There are some signs of agreement from the networks. According to Doug Herzog, president of Fox Entertainment, real progress means incorporating diversity from within.

Why should it matter that minority groups aren't visible on major network television, if they are well represented on

other channels such as UPN, WB, BET, and Univision? The problem is that Whites as well as minorities see a distorted picture of their society every time they turn on network TV. In Hoffman's words, "African Americans, Latinos and Asians, while portrayed as such, are not merely walk-ons in our society—they are woven into the fabric of what has made this country great" (A. Hoffman 1997:M6).

Let's Discuss

1. Do you watch network TV? If so, how well do you think it represents the diversity of U.S. society?
2. Have you seen a movie or TV show recently that portrayed members of a minority group in a sensitive and realistic way—as real people rather than as stereotypes or token walk-ons? If so, describe the show.

South America? Most people in the United States will mention the two topics that dominate the news from countries south of the border: revolution and drugs. Most know little else about the continent. To remedy this imbalance, a resolution to monitor the news and content that cross the borders of developing nations was passed by the United Nations Educational, Scientific, and Cultural Organization (UNESCO) in the 1980s. The United States disagreed with the proposal, which became one factor in the U.S. decision to withdraw from UNESCO back in the mid-1980s (Dominick 2002).

Feminist View

Feminists share the view of conflict theorists that the mass media stereotype and misrepresent social reality. The media powerfully influence how we look at men and women, and, according to this view, their images of the

sexes communicate unrealistic, stereotypical, and limiting perceptions. Here are three problems feminists believe arise from media coverage (J. T. Wood 1994):

1. Women are underrepresented, which suggests that men are the cultural standard and women are insignificant.

2. Men and women are portrayed in ways that reflect and perpetuate stereotypical views of gender. It is women, for example, who are shown in peril, needing to be rescued by a male, and rarely the reverse.

3. Depictions of male–female relationships emphasize traditional sex roles and normalize violence against women.

Educators and social scientists have long noted the stereotypical depiction of women and men in the mass media. Women are often portrayed as shallow and obsessed with beauty. Women are more likely than men to be shown unclothed or in danger or even physically

Oscar winner Halle Berry played the role of a savvy CIA spy called Jinx in the 2002 James Bond movie *Die Another Day.* But even when women play strong, no-nonsense roles, their status as sex object is not far removed.

victimized. Responding to the way advertising and the entertainment media make objects of women and even dehumanize them, Jean Kilbourne argues in her writings and film documentaries that "we [women] are the product." Feminist Vivian Gornick asserts that the depiction of women in the media reflects "innumerable small murders of the mind and spirit [that] take place daily" (1979:ix; Cortese 1999; Goffman 1979; Kilbourne 2000a, 2000b).

A continuing, troubling issue for feminists and society as a whole is pornography. Feminists tend to be very supportive of freedom of expression and self-determination, qualities denied to women more often than to men. Yet pornography presents women as sex objects and seems to make it acceptable to view all women that way. The concerns with pornography are not limited to this type of objectification and imagery as well as the implicit endorsement of violence against women that the imagery often entails. The industry that creates adult, risqué images for videos, DVDs, and the Internet is largely unregulated, putting its own performers at risk. A 2002 health survey of triple-X, as the porn industry refers to itself, found 40 percent of actors and actresses with at least one sexually transmitted disease compared to 0.1 percent of the general population. The short career span of these women (and men) is usually about 18 months, but the profits for the industry are continuous and enormous (Huffstutter 2003).

As in other areas of sociology, feminist researchers caution against assuming that what holds true for men's media behavior is true for everyone. Researchers, for example, have studied the different ways that women and men approach the Internet. According to 2001 data, women's use of the Internet is increasing faster than men's. Women are also more likely to regard e-mail as a means of maintaining contact with friends and relatives. Their use of websites differs in fundamental ways from the way men use them. Women are more likely to seek health and religious information, research new jobs, and play games online. Men are more likely to use the web to get news, shop, seek financial information, and participate in online auctions (Fox and Rainie 2001; Rainie and Kohut 2000).

Interactionist View

Interactionists are especially interested in shared understandings of everyday behavior. They examine the media on the micro level to see how they shape day-to-day social behavior. Scholars increasingly point to the mass media as the source of major daily activity; some argue that television serves virtually as a primary group for many individuals who share TV viewing. Other mass-media participation is not necessarily face to face. For example, we usually listen to the radio or read the newspaper as a solitary activity, although it is possible to share that event with others (Cerulo et al. 1992; Waite 2000).

Friendship networks can emerge from shared viewing habits or from recollection of a cherished television series from the past. Family members and friends often gather for parties centered on the broadcasting of popular events such as the Super Bowl or the Academy Awards. And, as we've noted, television often serves as a baby-sitter or a playmate for many children and even for infants.

The power of the mass media encourages political leaders and entertainment figures to carefully manipulate their images through public appearances called photo opportunities, or photo ops. By embracing symbols (posing with celebrities or in front of prestigious landmarks), participants in these staged events attempt to convey self-serving definitions of social reality (M. Weinstein and D. Weinstein 2000).

The rise of the Internet facilitates new forms of communication and social interaction. Grandparents can now keep up with their grandchildren via e-mail. Gay and lesbian teens have online resources for getting support and information. People can even find their lifetime partners through computer dating services.

Early users of the Internet established a subculture with specific norms and values. These pioneers generally resented formal rules for Internet communication, believed that access to information should be free and unlimited, and distrusted efforts to centralize control of the Internet. The subculture of early Internet users also developed argot terms, such as *flaming* (hurling abuse online), *chat rooms* (bulletin boards for people with common interests), and *hacking* (using one's personal computer to break into others' electronic files).

One troubling issue has been raised about day-to-day life on the Internet. What, if anything, should be done about use of the Internet by terrorists and other extremist groups who exchange messages of hatred and even bomb-making recipes? What, if anything, should be done about the issue of sexual expression on the Internet? How can children be protected from it? Should there be censorship of "hot chat" and X-rated film clips? Or should there be complete freedom of expression? The impact of technological change on issues of privacy and censorship will be examined in Chapter 23.

While many people in the United States embrace the Internet, we should note that information is not evenly dis-

Colorful U.S. and British flags provided a striking "photo op" for President George Bush and British Prime Minister Tony Blair at a time when they were drumming up support for the war in Iraq in April 2003.

tributed throughout the population. The same people, by and large, who experience poor health and have few job opportunities also have been left off the information highway.

The interactionist perspective also helps us to understand more about one important aspect of the entire mass media system—the audience. How do we actively participate in media events? How do we construct with others the meaning of media messages?

THE AUDIENCE

One night a few years ago, I was watching "my" Chicago Bulls make yet another bid for the NBA championship. Michael Jordan made a spectacular steal and went on to score a game-winning basket. I shouted, but what I remember most were the cheers I heard from others in Chicago through the open window. Earlier that year my son was watching *Beverly Hills 90210* in his college dorm room. One of the characters revealed that she was going to attend my son's university. He and his friends screamed when they heard this, and simultaneously they heard cheers all across the campus. In a very unusual way we had both been reminded that we are part of a larger audience.

Who Is in the Audience?

Sociologists distinguish the mass media from other social institutions by the necessary presence of an audience. It can be an identifiable, finite group, such as an audience at a jazz club or a Broadway musical. Or it can be much larger and undefined, such as the viewer audience for VH-1 on television or the people who read the same issue of *USA Today*. The audience may be a secondary group gathered in a large auditorium, or it may be a primary group, such as a mother and her son watching the latest Disney video at home.

We can look at the audience from the level of both *microsociology* and *macrosociology*. At the micro level, we would consider how the audience members interacting among themselves would respond to the media or, in the case of live performances, would perhaps influence the performers. At the macro level, we would examine broader societal consequences of the media, such as early childhood education through programming like *Sesame Street*.

Even if the audience is spread out over a wide geographic area and the members don't know one another, we would still find that the audience is somewhat distinctive in terms of age, gender, income, political party, formal schooling, race, and ethnicity. People in the audience for a ballet, for example, would differ substantially from those who listen to alternative music.

Some audiences are distinctive. For example, an audience for a gospel concert is likely to be predominantly Black, but you would find mostly Whites in the audience for a White pop singer.

Use Your Sociological Imagination www.
mhhe.com
/schaefer9

Think about the last time you were part of an audience. How similar or different were the other audience members from yourself, from what you could observe? What might account for whatever similarities or differences you noticed?

The Segmented Audience

Once a media outlet, such as a radio station or a magazine, has identified its audience, it targets that group. The media are increasingly marketing themselves to a *particular* audience. To some degree, this specialization is driven by advertising. Advertising media specialists have sharpened their ability, through survey research, to identify particular target audiences. As a result, Nike would be much more likely to promote a new line of golf clubs on the Golf Cable Channel, for example, than it would on an episode of *Frasier*. The many more choices that the growing Internet and satellite broadcast channels offer audiences also foster specialization. Members of these audiences are more likely to *expect* content geared to their own interests.

This specialized targeting of audiences has led some scholars to ponder whether there is still a "mass" in mass media. Are viewing audiences so segmented that there are fewer and fewer large collective audiences? That is not yet clear. Even though we seem to be in an age of *personal* computers and *personal* digital assistants (PDAs), large formal organizations still do transmit public messages that reach a sizable, heterogeneous, and scattered audience (Dominick 2002).

Audience Behavior

Sociologists have long researched how audiences interact with one another and how they then share information after the media event. The role of audience members as opinion leaders particularly intrigues social researchers. An **opinion leader** is someone who, through day-to-day personal contacts and communication, influences the opinions and decisions of others. A movie or theater critic functions as an opinion leader. Sociologist Paul Lazarsfeld and his colleagues (1948) pioneered the study of opinion leaders in their research on voting behavior in the 1940s. They found that opinion leaders encourage their relatives, friends, and co-workers to think positively about a particular candidate, perhaps pushing them to listen to the politician's speeches or read the campaign literature.

Today, film critics often attribute the success of low-budget independent movies to word of mouth. This is another way of stating that the mass media influence opinion leaders who, in turn, influence still others. The audience, then, is not a group of passive people but of active consumers who often are impelled to interact with others about the media event (Croteau and Hoynes 2000; C. R. Wright 1986).

Despite the role of opinion leaders, members of an audience do not all interpret media in the same way. Often their response is influenced by their social characteristics such as occupation, race, education, and income. Take the example of the televised news coverage of the riots in Los Angeles in 1992. These riots were an angry response to the acquittal of two White police officers accused of severely beating a Black motorist. Sociologist Darnell Hunt (1997) was interested in finding out how the social composition of audience members would affect how they interpreted the news coverage. He gathered 15 groups from the Los Angeles area, with group members equally divided among Whites, African Americans, and Latinos. He showed each group a 17-minute film clip from the televised coverage of the riots and asked the group members to discuss how they would describe what they just saw to a 12-year-old. In analyzing the group discussions, Hunt found that although gender and class did not cause respondents to vary their answers by much, race did.

Hunt went beyond noting simple racial differences in perceptions; he also analyzed how the differences were manifested. For example, Black viewers were much more likely than Latinos or Whites to refer to the events in terms of "us" and "them" in the group discussion. Another difference was that Black and Latino viewers were more animated and critical than the White groups as they watched the film segment. White viewers tended to be quiet, still, and unquestioning, suggesting that they were more comfortable with the news coverage than the Blacks or Hispanics. (In Chapter 22 we will consider in greater detail the behavior of mass audiences.)

THE MEDIA INDUSTRY

"My Heart Will Go On," the hit song from the movie *Titanic,* was a real crowd pleaser. But how did this song come into being? That requires looking at the music industry from what researchers call the *production perspective.* It emphasizes the media production process rather than the specific media product. So while music may be the apparent medium, the process requires the contribution of a songwriter, a performer, a movie soundtrack producer, a music video director, advertisers, and promoters, to name just a few participants in the music industry (Croteau and Hoynes 2001, 2003).

Media Concentration

Who owns this production process in the media? Ownership is getting more and more centralized. Even though there continue to be thousands of independent media outlets in every state, the clear trend has been toward centralization. A handful of multinational corporations dominate the publishing, broadcasting, and film industries, although they may be hard to identify since global conglomerates operate under many different product names. Walt Disney alone owns 16 television channels that reach 140 countries. Media outlets are likely to get even more concentrated if a 2003 ruling by the Federal Communications Commission (FCC) is allowed to stand. The ruling relaxed restrictions on owning more than one media outlet in the same market area (Carter and Rutenberg 2003; Rutenberg 2002).

A prime example of media concentration was the merger in 2001 of AOL and Time Warner, creating a new corporation that permeates almost every media sector. The AOL network, along with its Netscape Internet browser, operates the most popular Internet sites and boasts more than 37 million online subscribers worldwide. Time Warner is the largest U.S. magazine publisher based on advertising dollars. AOL Time Warner subsidiaries Warner Brothers and New Line Cinema rank among the top 10 motion picture producers. Warner Music Group artists accounted for 38 of the top 200 best-selling albums and 16 percent of all U.S. album sales in 2000. Time Warner Cable provides many of the most popular cable channels, including HBO, TBS, CNN, TNT, and Nickelodeon. The WB network broadcasts such successful series as *Smallville* and *The Gilmore Girls* (K. L. Alexander 2001; AOL Time Warner 2003; *New York Times* 2001; J. L. Roberts 2001).

And AOL Time Warner is only *one* media giant. Add to the list Walt Disney (which includes ABC, ESPN, and Lifetime networks), Rupert Murdoch's News Corporation of Australia (Fox Network Television, book publishers, numerous newspapers and magazines, including *TV Guide,* and 20th Century Fox), Sony of Japan (Columbia Pictures, IMAX, CBS Records, and Columbia Records), and Viacom (Paramount, MTV, CBS, UPN, Black Entertainment Television, Simon and Schuster, and Blockbuster). This concentration of media giants fosters considerable cross-promotion. For example, the release of the Warner Brothers film *Harry Potter and the Sorcerer's Stone* in 2001 was heavily promoted by both CNN and *Time* magazine. In fact, *Time* managed to devote six pages to the film's release in the midst of the war in Afghanistan and even placed Harry Potter in a conspicuous insert on a cover featuring President George W. Bush.

Similar concerns are raised about the situation in such countries as China, Cuba, Iraq, and North Korea, where the ruling party owns and controls the media. The difference, which is considerable, is that the gatekeeping process in the United States is in the hands of private individuals who desire to maximize profits. In the other countries, the gatekeeping process lies with political leaders who desire to maintain control of the government.

We should note that there is one significant exception to the centralization and concentration of the media—the Internet. Currently the web is fairly accessible through independent outlets, giving access to millions of producers of media content. Obviously, the producer needs to be technologically proficient and must have access to a computer, but compared to other media outlets, the Internet is readily available thus far. Media conglomerates, well aware of the Internet's potential, are already delivering their well-produced, sophisticated material via the web. Still, for now, the Internet allows the individual to become a media entrepreneur with a potential audience of millions.

FIGURE 7-3

Media in Selected Countries

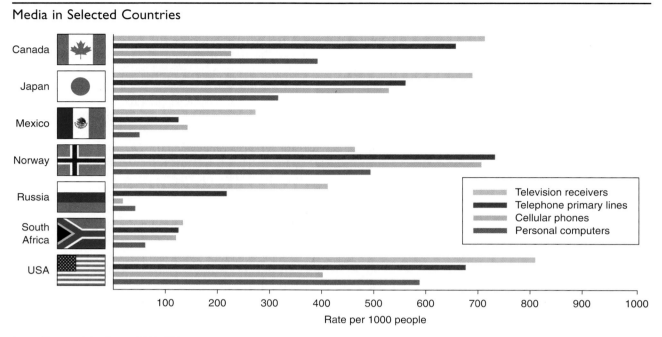

Source: Bureau of the Census 2001a:858.

The Media's Global Reach

Has the rise of the electronic media created a "global village"? Canadian linguist Marshall McLuhan predicted this result some 40 years ago. Today, physical distance is no longer a barrier, and instant messaging is possible across the world. The mass media have indeed begun to create a global village in terms of communication. As Figure 7-3 shows, not all countries are equally connected, but the progress is staggering when we consider that voice transmission was just beginning 100 years ago (McLuhan 1964; McLuhan and Fiore 1967).

Sociologist Todd Gitlin considers "global torrent" a more apt metaphor for the media's reach than "global village," as we saw in this chapter's opening essay. The media permeate all aspects of everyday life. Take advertising, for example. Consumer goods are vigorously marketed worldwide, from advertisements on baggage carriers at airports to imprints on the sand of beaches. Little wonder that people around the world develop loyalty to a brand and are as likely to sport a logo of Nike, Coca-Cola, or Harley-Davidson as they are of their favorite soccer or baseball team (Gitlin 2001; Klein 1999).

A very visible part of the media, whether it be print or electronic, is news. Most people in the United States, however, have had little familiarity with news outlets outside their own country, with the possible exception of the British-based Reuters news service and BBC News. Like so many other things, that all changed after September

11, 2001. An Arab news network took center stage, as Box 7-2 shows.

The key to creating a truly global network that reaches directly into workplaces, schools, and homes is the introduction of the Internet in the mass media. Much of the online global transmission today is limited to print

Television was introduced in the remote Asian kingdom of Bhutan in 1997. Oprah Winfrey's show was beamed into the living room of this Bhutanese household on their first day of owning a television. What are the advantages of bringing communications technology to a previously isolated nation? What are the disadvantages?

Sociology in the Global Community

7-2   AL JAZEERA IS ON THE AIR

A 24-hour-a-day televised news network with short bulletins every hour followed by a fast-paced montage of news clips—all broadcast globally over cable stations picking up the signals from earth-orbiting satellites. This could be CNN. But it also describes *Al Jazeera*, the Arabic-language television news network based in Qatar, a small Persian Gulf state of 600,000 people. The name Al Jazeera means "island" or "peninsula," in reference to the network's home country. Founded in 1996 and, until 2001, subsidized by Qatar's ruler, the channel now has 60 correspondents reaching about 35 million Arabs worldwide, including 150,000 Arab Americans.

Most people in the United States had never heard of Al Jazeera until October 7, 2001. That was when the channel aired the first of several videotaped messages from Osama bin Laden, the mastermind of the Al Qaeda terrorist network. U.S. news outlets also televised the messages but stopped after the government objected to the airing of calls for violence against U.S. citizens by bin Laden and his Al Qaeda cohorts.

Al Jazeera refused to acquiesce, invoking its motto: "The Opinion, and the Other Opinion Too." Channel officials insist that they promote a forum for dialogue and debate in an independent environment. This is unusual in the Arab world, where most media outlets are state controlled. In fact, several Arab states, including Saudi Arabia, Jordan, and Bahrain, have banned or restricted Al Jazeera because of the network's critical coverage of issues in their country. Other Arab nations criticize Al Jazeera for giving too much airplay to U.S. news.

Many media observers see Al Jazeera as biased, but many viewers around the world might see CNN, ABC, and Fox News as biased too. For example, in virtually all media outlets in the United States, the immorality of Palestinian suicide bombings is an unstated assumption. However, many in the Arab world would regard this assumption as fundamentally wrong. Similarly, most Muslims worldwide would question why CBS's respected news show *60 Minutes* would give exposure to Jerry Falwell, who called the Prophet Muhammad a terrorist. And why did U.S. newscasters refer to Iraqi soldiers who attacked United States troops as terrorists when the Iraqis were engaged in acceptable wartime tactics? According to Kenton Keith, a former U.S. ambassador

> "You have to be a supporter of Al Jazeera, even if you have to hold your nose sometimes."

to Qatar, Al Jazeera has a slant, but not any more than other news organizations. It just happens to be a slant—presenting Arab points of view—that most Americans aren't comfortable with.

Al Jazeera does offer diverse views. On its popular talk show *The Opposing View*, two women hotly debated polygamy among Muslim men. On another popular program, *Sharia [Islamic Law] and Life*, the speaker dared to reassure Muslim women that the Koran does not force them to marry suitors designated by their parents. Ambassador Keith believes that "for the long-range importance of press freedom in the Middle East and the advantages that will ultimately have for the West, you have to be a supporter of Al Jazeera, even if you have to hold your nose sometimes" (Barr 2002:7).

Al Jazeera did not make a profit until 2002. In a bid to increase its subscriber base, the channel opened an English-language website in early 2003 and plans on adding English-language news programs on cable late in the year. While its future is unclear, its very existence reminds us that there is another version of the news that is taken seriously in the world today.

Let's Discuss

1. Do you find news outlets in the United States biased? How would you go about determining if there was or was not bias?
2. Would you watch an English-language news program on the Al Jazeera channel? Why or why not?

Al Jazeera staff member monitors the news at the network's headquarters in Qatar.

Sources: Barr 2002; Daniszewski 2003; MediaGuardian 2001; Rosenberg 2003; Urbana 2002.

and pictures, but the capacity to send audio and video via the Internet will increasingly reach into every part of the world. Social interaction will then truly take place on a global stage.

The Internet also has facilitated other forms of communication. Reference materials and data banks can now be made accessible across national boundaries. Information related to international finance, marketing, trade, and manufacturing is literally a keystroke away. We also can see the emergence of truly world news outlets and the promotion of a world music that is not clearly identifiable with any single culture. Even the most future-oriented thinker would find the growth in the reach of the mass media in postindustrial and postmodern societies remarkable (Castells 2000, 2001b; Croteau and Hoynes 2001, 2003).

The lack of one national home for the various forms of mass media points to a potential dilemma for users. People are concerned that unhealthy influences and even crime are taking place in today's electronic global village and that there are few, if any, controls to prevent them. For example, the leaders of Bhutan worry about the impact that newly introduced television programming is having on their culture and their people. Similarly, industrial countries, including the United States, are concerned about everything from video poker to pornography to hacking industrial and government agency information databanks on the electronic highways. In the policy section that follows, we consider how violence portrayed in the media can have an undesirable influence on society.

SOCIAL POLICY and the MASS MEDIA — Media Violence

The Issue

A film depicts the story of 42 ninth-graders abducted to a remote island and forced to play the ultimate game of Survivor: Kill or be killed until only one is left. In gruesome detail, the movie portrays teachers doing away with students, young girls murdering shy admirers, and popular students killing rivals with hatchets and grenades, poison and machine guns. The film, *Battle Royale,* by renowned Japanese director Kinji Fukasaku, shows a Japan that is falling apart in the early 21st century. Millions are out of work, bureaucrats have lost control, and the government is convinced that its deadly game is the only way to teach rampaging juveniles a lesson (Magnier 2001).

What effect does this movie and hundreds of others like it have on audiences? Portrayal of violence is not limited to motion pictures, but is common in television, on Internet sites, and in video games as well. The *Grand Theft Auto III (GTA3)* video game sold 7 million copies in 2002; it is a virtual urban war game. Companion Internet sites to *GTA3* encourage players to run over pedestrians, shoot the paramedics who show up, and loot the bodies for spare change. The 2003 sequel, *Vice City,* set in Miami around 1986, features gun-toting thugs, killings, and hijackings, with rocket launchers and Molotov cocktails (Grossman 2002).

Does violence in the media lead people, especially youth, to become more violent? This question has been raised since the early days of comic books when POW!

and SPLAT! were accompanied by vivid pictures of fights. Today the mass media show far more violent and gruesome scenes. Table 7-2 gives an idea of how much violence shows up on television and in motion pictures. Content analyses of television programming show that the media have gradually become more violent, even in programs targeted to children (Parents Television Council 2001a, 2001b).

The Setting

We spend a great deal of time with the media. According to a communications industry study, we spend 10 hours every day with television, videotaped movies, computer games, radio, and other media outlets. At the end of a week, the time averages more than 69 hours—far more than a full workweek (Bureau of the Census 2001a:704).

But does this mean that watching hours of mass media with violent images causes one to behave differently? This research question is exceedingly complex since many social factors influence behavior. The most comprehensive analysis of more than 200 studies on media violence and aggressive behavior found that exposure to violence causes short-term increases in the aggressive behavior of youth. Another more recent study found that less television and other media exposure is related to less observed physical aggression. But in such research findings it is important to recognize that other factors besides the media are also related to aggressive

Table 7-2	Violence in the Media, 1998–1999		
Medium	**Acts of Violence**	**Acts of Serious Violence**	**Violent Acts per Episode/Movie**
Television	3,381	1,754	12 (6 serious)
Broadcast and cable movies	865	485	17 (10 serious)
Theatrical release movies	2,319	1,377	46 (28 serious)

Note: Content analysis of television season covers all major broadcast and cable systems in the 1998–1999 television season. Movie releases refer to the top 50 grossing motion pictures in 1998. Serious violence refers to FBI index offenses.

Source: Lichter et al. 1999.

behavior. Witnessing and experiencing violence within one's own home and encouragement by others have also been shown to be related to violent behavior (J. Johnson et al. 2002; Paik and Comstock 1994; T. N. Robinson et al. 2001; U.S. Surgeon General 2001).

Sociological Insights

The controversy surrounding violence and the media raises basic questions about the function of the media. If some of its functions are to entertain, socialize, and enforce social norms, how can violence be a part of that message, especially when the offender rarely pays any apparent consequences for violent behavior?

Even if a viewer does not necessarily become more violent from watching violent images, there could be a desensitization taking place. Using the premise of the narcotizing dysfunction, one might suggest that extended exposure to violent imagery leads to an increased tolerance and acceptance of violence in others.

Both conflict and feminist theorists are troubled that the victims depicted in violent imagery are often those who are given less respect in real life: women, children, the poor, racial minorities, citizens of foreign countries, and even the physically disabled. The media routinely portray rapes in a way that further devalues women. Many women are cast as prostitutes in even well-regarded motion pictures, from Federico Fellini's *Nights of Cabiria* (1956) to Jodie Foster in *Taxi Driver* (1976) to Julia Roberts in *Pretty Woman* (1990) to Elisabeth Shue in *Leaving Las Vegas* (1995).

Interactionists are especially interested in finding out if violence in media may then become a script for real-life behavior. Aggression is a product of socialization, and people may model themselves after the violent behavior they see, especially if the situations approximate their lives. Battling dinosaurs in *Jurassic Park* or the Green Goblin in *Spider-Man* is one thing, but what

if the violence represents only a slight adjustment to normal behavior? For example, in the 1995 film *The Program,* Touchstone Films ordered the removal of a scene in which high school football players prove their manhood by lying in the middle of a highway at night. This action came after several deaths had occurred when young men tried to prove their own manhood by imitating the scene.

Policy Initiatives

Policymakers have responded to the links between violence depicted in the media and real-life aggression on two levels. In public statements, politicians are quick to call for more family-oriented, less violent content, but on the legislative level, policymakers are reluctant to engage in what could be regarded as censorship. They encourage the media industries to regulate themselves.

The U.S. Surgeon General's 2001 report on youth violence recommended that parents use V-chip technology, which screens the television programs their children can watch. Yet despite parental concerns, a 2001 national study showed that only 17 percent of parents use the chip to block programs with sexual or violent

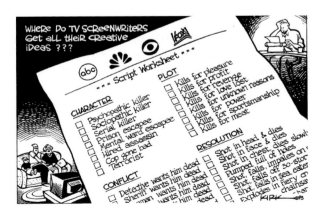

content. In general, most observers agree that parents should play more of a role in monitoring their children's media consumption (Kaiser Family Foundation 2001; U.S. Surgeon General 2001).

Often government studies are initiated by violent events we desperately wish to explain. The 2001 Surgeon General's report on youth violence came out of the 1999 Columbine High School shooting in Colorado. Canada launched a serious look at media violence following a 1989 incident at a Montreal university in which 14 young women were shot to death. A senseless beating of a five-year-old girl by three friends in Norway in 1994 led that country to look at violence in the media. In all these cases, initial calls for stiff government regulation eventually gave way to industry self-regulation and greater adult involvement in young people's viewing patterns (Bok 1998; Health Canada 1993).

Much of our knowledge of media violence comes from the study of children who watch traditional television. Some more recent studies have tried to assess the impact of video games. But we should not lose sight of the fact that media outlets are becoming increasingly diverse, especially with the role the Internet now plays in the delivery of media content. Much of this new content holds great promise for broadening educational horizons, but, unfortunately, these new easily obtainable outlets also offer an unending diet of violence (A. Alexander and Hanson 2001:44).

Let's Discuss

1. Do you know of anyone whose behavior has become more aggressive from exposure to violence in the media? How is this aggression expressed? Do you notice any changes in your own behavior?
2. To what extent should government act as a media censor, especially in regard to violent content directed to young people?
3. What role do you think parents should have in monitoring their children's media diet? Will you limit the hours your children can access media outlets? What alternative activities might children be offered?

CHAPTER RESOURCES

Summary

The **mass media** refer to the print and electronic instruments of communication that carry messages to often widespread audiences. They pervade all areas of society, from entertainment to education to politics. This chapter examines how the mass media affect our social institutions and influence our social behavior.

1. From the functionalist perspective, the media entertain, socialize, enforce social norms, confer status, promote consumption, and keep us informed (the **surveillance function**). They can be dysfunctional to the extent that they desensitize us to events (the **narcotizing dysfunction**).
2. Conflict theorists see the media as reflecting and even deepening divisions in society through **gatekeeping,** controlling the material that reaches the public, and by spreading the **dominant ideology,** which defines reality and overwhelms local cultures.
3. Feminist theorists point out that media images of the sexes communicate unrealistic, stereotypical, limiting, and sometimes violent perceptions of women.

4. Interactionists examine the media on the micro level to see how they shape day-to-day social behavior, such as shared TV viewing and staged public appearances intended to convey self-serving definitions of reality.
5. The mass media require the presence of an audience—whether it is small and defined or large and amorphous. With increasing numbers of media outlets, there has been more and more targeting of segmented (or specialized) audiences.
6. Social researchers have studied the role of **opinion leaders** in influencing audiences.
7. The media industry is getting more and more concentrated, creating media conglomerates. This concentration raises concerns about how innovative and independent the media can continue to be. In some countries, governments own and control the media.
8. The Internet is the one significant exception to centralization, allowing millions of people to produce their own media content.
9. The media have a global reach, thanks to new communications technology, especially the

Internet. Some people are concerned that this global reach will spread unhealthy influences to other cultures.

10. Sociologists are studying the ways that depiction of violence in the media may promote aggressive behavior or desensitization in viewers.

Critical Thinking Questions

1. What kind of audience is targeted by the producers of televised wrestling? By the creators of a Disney animated film? By a rap group? What kinds of factors determine who makes up a particular media audience?

2. Trace the production process for a new television situation comedy (sitcom). Who do you imagine are the gatekeepers in this process?

3. Use the functionalist, conflict, and interactionist perspectives to assess the effects of global TV programming on developing countries.

Key Terms

Dominant ideology A set of cultural beliefs and practices that help to maintain powerful social, economic, and political interests. (page 154)

Gatekeeping The process by which a relatively small number of people control what material eventually reaches the audience. (154)

Mass media Print and electronic instruments of communication that carry messages to often widespread audiences. (149)

Narcotizing dysfunction The phenomenon in which the media provide such massive amounts of information that the audience becomes numb and generally

fails to act on the information, regardless of how compelling the issue. (153)

Opinion leader Someone who, through day-to-day personal contacts and communication, influences the opinions and decisions of others. (160)

Stereotype An unreliable generalization about all members of a group that does not recognize individual differences within the group. (154)

Surveillance function The collection and distribution of information concerning events in the social environment. (153)

TECHNOLOGY RESOURCES

Internet Connection

*Note: While all the URLs listed were current as of the printing of this book, these sites often change. Please check our website (**www.mhhe.com/schaefer9**) for updates, hyperlinks, and exercises related to these sites.*

1. Bhutan was the last country in the world to legalize television. It has only one homegrown radio and television station. Explore the following site to learn more about the country of Bhutan and its mass media: **www.bbs.com.bt/index.htm.**

2. Media ownership is getting more and more centralized. Even though there continue to be thousands of independent media outlets in every state, the clear trend has been toward centralization. Find out who the Big 10 media owners are in the United States by exploring **www.mediachannel.org/ownership.**

Online Learning Center with PowerWeb

Visit the student center in the Online Learning Center at **www.mhhe.com/schaefer9** and link to "Use Your Sociological Imagination." You will first be asked to become a news junkie, thinking about where you would gather your "facts" or information. Next, you will be asked to imagine yourself as part of an audience for a ballet performance and to think about the similarities you might share with other audience members. Use your sociological imagination to answer the questions.

Reel Society Interactive Movie CD-ROM

Reel Society includes scenes that can be used to spark discussion about the following topics from this chapter:

• Sociological Perspectives on the Media
• The Media Industry

DEVIANCE AND SOCIAL CONTROL

Social Control

Deviance

Crime

Social Policy and Social Control:
Gun Control

Boxes

SOCIAL INEQUALITY:
Discretionary Justice

SOCIOLOGY ON CAMPUS:
Binge Drinking

TAKING SOCIOLOGY TO WORK:
Tiffany Zapata-Mancilla, Victim
Witness Specialist, Cook County
State's Attorney's Office

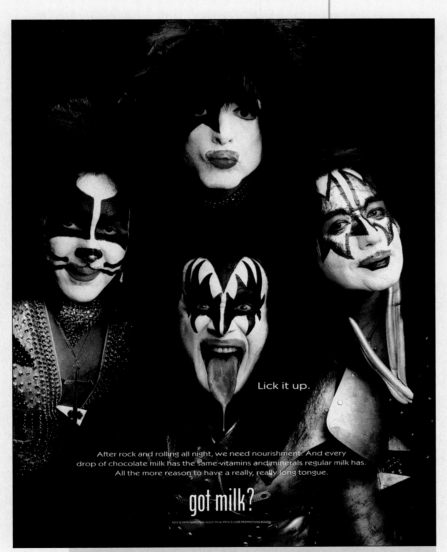

Lick it up.

After rock and rolling all night, we need nourishment. And every
drop of chocolate milk has the same vitamins and minerals regular milk has.
All the more reason to have a really, really long tongue.

got milk?

KISS ©1999 NATIONAL FLUID MILK PROCESSOR PROMOTION BOARD

Deviance and conformity are relative concepts that can change over time.
KISS was a leading example of shock rock in the 1970s, when the band's
theatrical costumes and makeup appeared deviant to some. Today, the group's
well-known image is less shocking, and the milk industry has enlisted the group
to promote its product to young consumers.

Wallbangin' is a gang term that means, roughly, "gangbangin' on a wall." This can be through straightforward writing or through crossing out the writing of others; either activity enforces relationships of power between gangs. Gang members in Los Angeles generally recognize this as a generic term for the activity of wall writing. . . .

Any type of cultural or artistic production forces change on an environment. Most of the time, people abide by well-established rules for culture-producing activities. They do it through consuming certain products in certain ways or by creating symbols of their identity within the scope of what is legal for the entire society. In general, people who write graffiti produce culture in a different manner. No matter what it says, the manner in which graffiti is produced defines the writer's position as an outsider and alienates that person from the rest of society. . . .

Criminal aspects of graffiti free the writers from constraints that laws would place on their creations. Writers force change on an environment, but without recourse or permission. Their marks are like advertising for groups and individuals who may themselves be outside the law already. Graffiti writers usurp public and private property for their own purposes. The graffitists have not been paid, nor do they pay for the space they use for the privilege. Viewed from the larger society's perspective, graffiti is always just wallbangin': it is cultural production through destruction. . . .

The antisocial nature of graffiti makes its analysis an inherently social endeavor. Graffiti is all about people. It's about relationships, and individuals, and motives. As a researcher, you need to get hold of a social situation on the ground in order to understand the story presented on the walls. . . .

A young man from 29th Street in South Central Los Angeles explained it like this:

It all comes down to basically politics, like everything else. . . . Graffiti . . . to us . . . what we write on the walls . . . is to mark our territory. Which you already know. A way of us marking our territory so people know. See right now we might not be here to represent our neighborhood, but they pass through this, "oh look this is where so and so kicks back." See, it does serve a purpose! That's what we use it for. But yet when we try different styles and different things. Because, believe it or not, we try to make our neighborhood look good. . . . We don't want to write on the wall and just leave it all ugly, we want to write on the wall and make it look nice. . . .

Whether in alleys, around hangouts, parks, on main drags, or on major streets, gang members write graffiti for themselves and others who understand their messages as acts of representing. Gang members use graffiti to organize the spaces in which they reside; in the process, they cover the streets with manifestations of their own identity. Like silent sentinels, the graffiti keep watch and inform onlookers of the affiliations and activities that define a certain area. *(S. A. Phillips 1999:21, 23, 134–135)* ■ 🖙

Additional information about this excerpt can be found on the Online Learning Center at **www.mhhe.com/schaefer9**.

SUSAN A. PHILLIPS

Wallbangin'

GRAFFITI and GANGS in L.A.

Anthropologist Susan Phillips studied graffiti writing in Los Angeles neighborhoods over a period of six years. In her book *Wallbangin': Graffiti and Gangs in L.A.* she notes that while graffiti writing is regarded as vandalism in the eyes of the law, it actually serves important social purposes for gang members, from making political statements to identifying home turf and making the "neighborhood look good" (S. A. Phillips 1999:135).

As Phillips makes clear, what should be considered deviant is not always obvious. Wall writing, in fact, has an illustrious history. She begins her book with pages of descriptions of wall writing from such literary sources as the Bible, Mark Twain, Edgar Allan Poe, and George Orwell. Even today, Phillips points out, government authorities sometimes protect graffiti. At Los Angeles harbor, officials do not erase the writing of sailors. Along the Harlem River Parkway in New York City, a playground wall with graffiti by the late artist Keith Haring (who began as a tagger) has been preserved as a work of art.

As another example of the difficulty of determining what is and is not deviant, consider the issue of binge drinking on campus. On the one hand, we can view binge drinking as *deviant,* as violating a school's standards of conduct and endangering one's health. On the other hand, we can see it as *conforming,* or complying with peer culture. In the United States, people are socialized to have mixed feelings about both conforming and nonconforming behavior. The term *conformity* can conjure up images of mindless imitation of one's peer group—whether a circle of teenagers wearing "phat pants" or a group of business executives all dressed in gray suits. Yet the same term can also suggest that an individual is cooperative or a "team player." What about those who do not conform? They may be respected as individualists, leaders, or creative thinkers who break new ground. Or they may be labeled as "troublemakers" and "weirdos" (Aronson 1999).

This chapter examines the relationship between conformity, deviance, and social control. When does conformity verge on deviance? And how does a society manage to control its members and convince them to conform to its rules and laws? What are the consequences of deviance? We will begin by distinguishing between conformity and obedience and then look at two experiments on conforming behavior and obedience to authority. Then we will analyze the informal and formal mechanisms societies use to encourage conformity and discourage deviance. We will pay particular attention to the legal order and how it reflects underlying social values.

The second part of the chapter focuses on theoretical explanations for deviance, including the functionalist approach employed by Émile Durkheim and Robert Merton; interactionist-based theories; labeling theory, which draws on both the interactionist and the conflict perspectives; and conflict theory.

The third part of the chapter focuses on crime, a specific type of deviant behavior. As a form of deviance that is subject to official, written norms, crime has been a special concern of policymakers and the public in general. We will look at various types of crime found in the United States, the ways crime is measured, and international crime rates. Finally, the social policy section considers the controversial topic of gun control and its relation to violent crime. ■

■ SOCIAL CONTROL

As we saw in Chapter 3, each culture, subculture, and group has distinctive norms governing appropriate behavior. Laws, dress codes, bylaws of organizations, course requirements, and rules of sports and games all express social norms.

How does a society bring about acceptance of basic norms? The term **social control** refers to the techniques and strategies for preventing deviant human behavior in any society. Social control occurs on all levels of society. In the family, we are socialized to obey our parents simply because they are our parents. Peer groups introduce us to informal norms, such as dress codes, that govern the behavior of their members. Colleges establish standards they expect of students. In bureaucratic organizations, workers encounter a formal system of rules and regulations. Finally, the government of every society legislates and enforces social norms.

Most of us respect and accept basic social norms and assume that others will do the same. Even without thinking, we obey the instructions of police officers, follow the day-to-day rules at our jobs, and move to the rear of elevators when people enter. Such behavior reflects an effective process of socialization to the dominant standards of a culture. At the same time, we are well aware that individuals, groups, and institutions *expect* us to act "properly." This expectation p. 67 carries with it **sanctions**, penalties and rewards for conduct concerning a social norm. If we fail to live up to the norm, we may face punishment through informal sanctions such as fear and ridicule, or formal sanctions such as jail sentences or fines.

The challenge to effective social control is that people often receive competing messages about how to behave. While the state or government may clearly define acceptable behavior, friends or fellow employees may encourage quite different behavior patterns. Historically, legal measures aimed at blocking discrimination based on race, religion, gender, age, and sexual orientation have been difficult to implement, because many people tacitly encourage the violation of such measures.

Functionalists maintain that people must respect social norms if any group or society is to survive. In their view, societies literally could not function if massive numbers of people defied standards of appropriate conduct. In contrast, conflict theorists contend that the "successful functioning" of a society will consistently benefit the powerful and work to the disadvantage of other groups. They point out that in the United States, for example, widespread resistance to social norms was necessary to win our independence from England, to overturn the institution of slavery, to allow women to vote, to secure civil rights, and to force an end to the war in Vietnam.

Conformity and Obedience

Techniques for social control operate on both the group level and the societal level. People we think of as peers or equals influence us to act in particular ways; the same is true of people who hold authority over us or occupy awe-

Social control, Finnish style. This young man is relaxing in his prison cell, not in his college dorm room. Thirty years ago Finland rejected the rigid Soviet model of imprisonment and adopted a gentler correctional system meant to shape prisoners' values and encourage moral behavior. Today, Finland's rate of imprisonment is less than half that of England's, and one-fourth that of the United States.

inspiring positions. Stanley Milgram (1975) made a useful distinction between these two important levels of social control.

Milgram used the term **conformity** to mean going along with peers—individuals of our own status, who have no special right to direct our behavior. In contrast, **obedience** is compliance with higher authorities in a hierarchical structure. Thus, a recruit entering military service will typically *conform* to the habits and language of other recruits and *obey* the orders of superior officers. Students will *conform* to the drinking behavior of their peers and *obey* the requests of campus security officers.

Conformity to Prejudice

We often think of conformity as being rather harmless, as when members of an expensive health club all don the same costly sportswear. But researchers have found that people may conform to the attitudes and behavior of their peers even when it means expressing intolerance toward others. Fletcher Blanchard, Teri Lilly, and Leigh Ann Vaughn (1991) conducted an experiment at Smith College and found that the statements people overhear others make influence their own expressions of opinion on the issue of racism.

In the experiment, a student who was a confederate (or ally) of the researchers approached 72 White students as each was walking across campus. She said she was conducting an opinion poll for a class. At the same time, she stopped a second White student—actually another confederate working with the researchers—and asked the person to participate in the survey. The first question concerned how Smith College should respond to anonymous racist notes that were sent to four African American students in 1989. The confederate always answered first. In some cases, she condemned the notes; in others, she justified them.

Blanchard and his colleagues (1991:102–103) concluded that "hearing at least one other person express strongly antiracist opinions produced dramatically more strongly antiracist public reactions to racism than hearing others express equivocal opinions or opinions more accepting of racism." When the confederate expressed sentiments justifying racism, subjects were much less likely to express antiracist opinions than were those who heard no one else offer opinions. In this experiment, social control (through the process of conformity) influenced people's attitudes, or at least the expression of those attitudes. In the next section, we will see that social control (through the process of obedience) can alter people's behavior.

Obedience to Authority

If ordered to do so, would you comply with an experimenter's instruction to administer increasingly painful electric shocks to a subject? Most people would say no; yet the research of social psychologist Stanley Milgram (1963, 1975) suggests that most of us *would* obey such orders. In Milgram's words (1975:xi), "Behavior that is unthinkable in an individual . . . acting on his own may be executed without hesitation when carried out under orders."

Milgram placed advertisements in New Haven, Connecticut, newspapers to recruit subjects for a learning experiment at Yale University. Participants included postal clerks, engineers, high school teachers, and laborers. They were told that the purpose of the research was to investigate the effects of punishment on learning. The experimenter, dressed in a gray technician's coat, explained that in each test, one subject would be randomly selected as the "learner," while another would function as the "teacher." However, the experiment was rigged so that the "real" subject would always be the teacher, while an associate of Milgram's served as the learner.

At this point, the learner's hand was strapped to an electric apparatus. The teacher was taken to an electronic "shock generator" with 30 levered switches labeled from 15 to 450 volts. Before beginning the experiment, all subjects received sample shocks of 45 volts, to convince them

In one of Stanley Milgram's experiments, the "learner" supposedly received an electric shock from a shock plate when he answered a question incorrectly. At the 150-volt level, the "learner" would demand to be released and would refuse to place his hand on the shock plate. The experimenter would then order the actual subject (the "teacher") to force the hand onto the plate, as shown in the photo. Though 40 percent of the true subjects stopped complying with Milgram at this point, 30 percent did force the "learner's" hand onto the shock plate, despite his pretended agony.

of the authenticity of the experiment. The experimenter then instructed the teacher to apply shocks of increasing voltage each time the learner gave an incorrect answer on a memory test. Teachers were told that "although the shocks can be extremely painful, they cause no permanent tissue damage." In reality, the learner did not receive any shocks.

In a prearranged script, the learner deliberately gave incorrect answers and expressed pain when "shocked." For example, at 150 volts, the learner would cry out, "Get me out of here!" At 270 volts, the learner would scream in agony. When the shock reached 350 volts, the learner would fall silent. If the teacher wanted to stop the experiment, the experimenter would insist that the teacher continue, using such statements as "The experiment requires that you continue" and "You have no other choice; you *must* go on" (Milgram 1975:19–23).

The results of this unusual experiment stunned and dismayed Milgram and other social scientists. A sample of psychiatrists had predicted that virtually all subjects would refuse to shock innocent victims. In their view, only a "pathological fringe" of less than 2 percent would continue administering shocks up to the maximum level. Yet almost *two-thirds* of participants fell into the category of "obedient subjects."

Why did these subjects obey? Why were they willing to inflict seemingly painful shocks on innocent victims who had never done them any harm? There is no evidence that these subjects were unusually sadistic; few seemed to enjoy administering the shocks. Instead, in Milgram's view, the key to obedience was the experimenter's social role as a "scientist" and "seeker of knowledge."

Milgram pointed out that in the modern industrial world, we are accustomed to submitting to impersonal authority figures whose status is indicated by a title (professor, lieutenant, doctor) or by a uniform (the technician's coat). Because we view the authority as larger and more important than the individual, we shift responsibility for our behavior to the authority figure. Milgram's subjects frequently stated, "If it were up to me, I would not have administered shocks." They saw themselves as merely doing their duty (Milgram 1975).

From an interactionist perspective, one important aspect of Milgram's findings is the fact that subjects in follow-up studies were less likely to inflict the supposed shocks as they were moved physically closer to their victims. Moreover, interactionists emphasize the effect of *incrementally* administering additional dosages of 15 volts. In effect, the experimenter negotiated with the teacher and convinced the teacher to continue inflicting higher levels of punishment. It is doubtful that anywhere near the two-thirds rate of obedience would have been reached had the experimenter told the teachers to administer 450 volts immediately (B. Allen 1978; Katovich 1987).

Milgram launched his experimental study of obedience to better understand the involvement of Germans in the annihilation of 6 million Jews and millions of other people during World War II. In an interview conducted long after the publication of his study, he suggested that "if a system of death camps were set up in the United States of the sort we had seen in Nazi Germany, one would be able to find sufficient personnel for those camps in any medium-sized American town" (CBS News 1979:7–8).

Use Your Sociological Imagination www. mhhe.com /schaefer9

If you were a participant in Milgram's research on conformity, how far do you think you would go in carrying out orders? Do you see any ethical problem with the experimenter's manipulation of the control subjects?

Informal and Formal Social Control

The sanctions that are used to encourage conformity and obedience—and to discourage violation of social norms—are carried out through both informal and formal social control. As the term implies, people use ***informal social control*** casually to enforce norms. Examples include smiles, laughter, a raised eyebrow, and ridicule.

In the United States and many other cultures, adults often view spanking, slapping, or kicking children as a proper and necessary means of informal social control. Child development specialists counter that such corporal punishment is inappropriate because it teaches children to solve problems through violence. They warn that slapping and spanking can escalate into more serious forms of abuse. Yet, despite a 1998 policy statement by the American Academy of Pediatrics that corporal punishment is not effective and can indeed be harmful, 59 percent of pediatricians support the use of corporal punishment, at least in certain situations. Our culture widely accepts this form of informal social control (Wolraich et al. 1998).

Formal social control is carried out by authorized agents, such as police officers, judges, school administrators, employers, military officers, and managers of movie theaters. It can serve as a last resort when socialization and informal sanctions do not bring about desired behavior. An increasingly significant means of formal social control in the United States is to imprison people. During the course of a year, 6 to 7 million adults undergo some form of correctional supervision—jail, prison, probation, or parole. Put another way, almost 1 out of every 30 adult Americans is subject to this very formal type of social control every year (Glaze 2002).

Which behaviors are subject to formal social control, and how severe should the sanctions be? Societies vary. In the nation of Singapore, chewing gum is restricted, feeding birds can lead to fines of up to $640, and there is even a $95 fine for failing to flush the toilet. Singapore deals with serious crimes especially severely. The death penalty is mandatory for murder, drug trafficking, and crimes committed with firearms.

In the aftermath of September 11, 2001, new measures of social control became the norm in the United States. Some of them, such as stepped-up security at airports and high-rise buildings, were highly visible to the public. The federal government has also publicly urged citizens to engage in informal social control by watching for and reporting people whose actions seem suspicious. But many other measures taken by the government have increased the covert surveillance of private records and communications.

Just 45 days after September 11, with virtually no debate, Congress passed the USA PATRIOT Act of 2001. (The phrase USA PATRIOT is an acronym for "Uniting and Strengthening America by Providing Appropriate Tools Required to Intercept and Obstruct Terrorism.") Sections of this sweeping legislation revoked legal checks on the power of law enforcement agencies. Without a warrant or probable cause, the FBI can now secretly access most private records, including medical histories, library accounts, and student registrations. In 2002, for example, the FBI searched the records of hundreds of dive shops and scuba organizations. Agents had been directed to identify every person who had taken diving lessons in the past three years because of speculation that terrorists might try to approach their targets underwater (Moss and Fessenden 2002).

Many people think this kind of social control goes too far. Civil rights advocates also worry that the government's request for information on suspicious activities may encourage negative stereotyping of Muslims and Arab Americans. We will return to this topic in the social policy section of Chapter 23, which addresses the tradeoff between the benefits of new surveillance technology and the right to privacy.

The interplay between formal and informal social control can be complicated, especially if people are encouraged to violate social norms. Box 8-1 (page 177) considers binge drinking among college students, who receive conflicting messages about the acceptability of the behavior from sources of formal and informal social control.

Law and Society

Some norms are so important to a society they are formalized into laws controlling people's behavior. ***Law*** may be defined as governmental social control (Black 1995). Some laws, such as the prohibition against murder, are directed at all members of society. Others, such as fishing and hunting regulations, primarily affect particular categories of people. Still others govern the behavior of social institutions (for instance, corporate law and laws regarding the taxing of nonprofit enterprises).

FIGURE 8-1

The Status of Medical Marijuana

Note: Federal law confers a one-year prison sentence on those convicted of possessing a small amount of marijuana. No exception is made for medical use, even if state law allows it, as it does in California.

Source: Developed by author based on data from Americans for Medical Rights 2003.

Sociologists see the creation of laws as a social process. Laws are passed in response to perceived needs for formal social control. Sociologists have sought to explain how and why such perceptions arise. In their view, law is not merely a static body of rules handed down from generation to generation. Rather, it reflects continually changing standards of what is right and wrong, of how violations are to be determined, and of what sanctions are to be applied (Schur 1968).

Sociologists representing varying theoretical perspectives agree that the legal order reflects the values of those in a position to exercise authority. Therefore, the creation of civil and criminal law can be a most controversial matter. Should it be against the law to employ illegal immigrants in a factory (see Chapter 11), to have an abortion (see Chapter 12), to allow prayer in public schools (Chapter 15), or to smoke on an airplane? Such issues have been bitterly debated, because they require a choice among competing values. Not surprisingly, laws that are unpopular—such as the one-time prohibition of alcohol under the Eighteenth Amendment and the widespread establishment of a 55-mile-per-hour speed limit on highways—become difficult to enforce when there is no consensus supporting the norms.

One current and controversial debate over laws governing behavior is whether people should be allowed to use marijuana legally, for medical purposes. Although the majority of adults polled in national surveys support such use, state governments have been reluctant to grant the right to use marijuana for medical purposes; see Figure 8-1, page 175.

Socialization is actually the primary source of conforming and obedient behavior, including obedience to law. Generally, it is not external pressure from a peer group or authority figure that makes us go along with social norms. Rather, we have internalized p. 84 such norms as valid and desirable and are committed to observing them. In a profound sense, we want to see ourselves (and to be seen) as loyal, cooperative, responsible, and respectful of others. In the United States and other societies around the world, people are socialized both to want to belong and to fear being viewed as different or deviant.

Control theory suggests that our connection to members of society leads us to systematically conform to society's norms. According to sociologist Travis Hirschi and other control theorists, our bonds to family members, friends, and peers induce us to follow the mores and folkways of our society. We give little conscious thought to whether we will be sanctioned if we fail to conform. Socialization develops our self-control so well that we don't need further pressure to obey social norms. While control theory does not effectively explain the rationale for every conforming act, it nevertheless reminds us that while the media may focus on crime and disorder, most members of most societies conform to and obey basic norms (Gottfredson and Hirschi 1990; Hirschi 1969).

DEVIANCE

What Is Deviance?

For sociologists, the term *deviance* does not mean perversion or depravity. **Deviance** is behavior that violates the standards of conduct or expectations of a group or society (Wickman 1991:85). In the United States, alcoholics, compulsive gamblers, and the mentally ill would all be classified as deviants. Being late for class is categorized as a deviant act; the same is true of wearing jeans to a formal wedding. On the basis of the sociological definition, we are all deviant from time to time. Each of us violates common social norms in certain situations.

Is being overweight an example of deviance? In the United States and many other cultures, unrealistic stan-

dards of appearance and body image place a huge strain on people—especially adult women and girls—based on how they look. Journalist Naomi Wolf (1992) has used the term *beauty myth* to refer to an exaggerated ideal of beauty, beyond the reach of all but a few females, which has unfortunate consequences. In order to shed their "deviant" image and conform to unrealistic societal norms, many women and girls become consumed with adjusting their appearances. Yet what is deviant in one culture may be celebrated in another. In Nigeria, for example, being fat is considered a mark of beauty. Part of the coming-of-age ritual calls for young girls to spend a month in a "fattening room." Among Nigerians, being thin at this point in the life course is deviant (Simmons 1998).

Deviance involves the violation of group norms, which may or may not be formalized into law. It is a comprehensive concept that includes not only criminal behavior but also many actions that are not subject to prosecution. The public official who takes a bribe has defied social norms, but so has the high school student who refuses to sit in an assigned seat or cuts class. Of course, deviation from norms is not always negative, let alone criminal. A member of an exclusive social club who speaks out against a traditional policy of excluding women, Blacks, and Jews from admittance is deviating from the club's norms. So is a police officer who blows the whistle on corruption or brutality within the department.

From a sociological perspective, deviance is hardly objective or set in stone. Rather, it is subject to social definition within a particular society and at a particular time. For that reason, what is considered deviant can shift from one social era to another. In most instances, those individuals and groups with the greatest status and power define what is acceptable and what is deviant. For example, despite serious medical warnings against the dangers of tobacco made as long as 30 years ago, cigarette smoking continued to be accepted—in good part because of the power of tobacco farmers and cigarette manufacturers. Only after a long campaign led by public health and anticancer activists did cigarette smoking become more of a deviant activity. Today, many state and local laws limit where people can smoke.

While deviance can include relatively minor day-to-day decisions about our personal behavior, in some cases it can become part of a person's identity. This process is called *stigmatization.*

Deviance and Social Stigma

There are many ways a person can acquire a deviant identity. Because of physical or behavioral characteristics, some people are unwillingly cast in negative social roles. Once they have been assigned a deviant role, they have

Sociology on Campus

8-1   BINGE DRINKING

Scott Krueger was an outstanding high school student, well liked, well rounded, and academically gifted. Courted by the best engineering schools —Penn, Cornell, Michigan, MIT—Scott chose MIT, after an overnight visit convinced him that "they weren't all geeks" there.

One night in September 1997, after Scott had been at MIT a little more than a month, he told his sister over the phone that his fraternity pledge class had a big night ahead. Collectively, they had to drink a large amount of alcohol. Several hours later Scott lay comatose in a hospital emergency room. His blood-alcohol level was 4.1—five times the drunken driving standard in Massachusetts. A few days later he died, another college-age victim of binge drinking.

Scott was not unusual in his behavior. According to a study published by the Harvard School of Public Health in 2002, 44 percent of college students indulge in binge drinking (defined as at least five drinks in a row for men and four in a row for women). For those who live in a Greek fraternity or sorority, the rates are even higher—four out of five are binge drinkers (see the figure). These numbers represent an increase from 1990s data, despite efforts on many campuses across the nation to educate students about the risks of binge drinking. The problem is not confined to the United States—Britain, Russia, and South Africa all report regular "drink till you drop" alcoholic consumption among young people.

Binge drinking on campus presents a difficult social problem. On the one hand, it can be regarded as *deviant*, violating the standards of conduct expected of those in an academic setting. In fact, Harvard researchers consider binge drinking the most serious public health hazard facing colleges. Not only does it cause about 50 fatalities a year and hundreds of cases of alcohol poisoning; it in-

creases the likelihood of falling behind in schoolwork, getting injured, and damaging property.

The other side of this potentially self-destructive behavior is that binge drinking represents *conformity* to the peer culture, especially in fraternities and sororities, which serve as social centers

---

44 percent of college students indulge in binge drinking.

---

on many campuses. Most students seem to take an "everybody does it—no big deal" attitude toward the behavior. Many find that taking five drinks in a row is fairly typical. As one student at Boston University noted, "Anyone that goes to a party does that or worse. If you talk to anyone college age, it's normal."

Some colleges and universities are taking steps to make binge drinking a bit less "normal" by means of *social control*—banning kegs, closing fraternities and sororities, encouraging liquor retailers not to sell in high volume to students, and expelling students after three alcohol-related infractions. Yet many colleges still tolerate spring break organizers who promote "All you can drink" parties as part of a tour package.

Let's Discuss

1. Why do you think most college students regard binge drinking as a normal rather than a deviant behavior?
2. Which do you think would be more effective in stopping binge drinking on your campus, informal or formal social control?

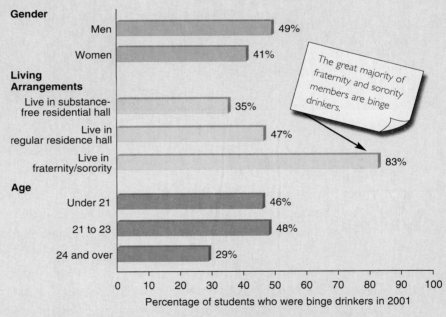

Note: Based on a national survey of more than 10,000 college students in 2001. Binge drinking is defined as one drinking session of at least five drinks for men or four drinks for women during the two weeks prior to the self-administered questionnaire.

Source: Wechsler et al. 2002:208.

Sources: Glauber 1998; Goldberg 1998; Hoover 2002; Leinwand 2003; McCormick and Kalb 1998; Wechsler et al. 2002.

Who Is Deviant?

Customary greeting among residents of the mountainous kingdom of Bhutan

What if your teachers greeted you in class by extending their tongues and hands? What if your girlfriend started to "elongate" her neck by layering it with heavy brass coils? Wouldn't you think that they were behaving in bizarre ways? Certainly by the standards of U.S. society, they would be. But not if you were living in Bhutan, where such greetings are customary, or if you lived among the Kayan tribe in northern Thailand, where females traditionally wear up to 12 pounds of coils around their necks as a mark of beauty and tribal identity. Deviance is socially constructed and is subject to different social interpretations over time and across cultures.

As these photos show, what is deviant in one culture could very well be celebrated in another. In Latin America, Spain, Portugal, and many other countries, bullfighting is a popular sport. But imagine how Hindus, who consider the cow sacred, would react to the dance of death in the bullring. Using sociology to look at other peoples and cultures from their point of view, as well as from our own perspective, helps us to understand deviance as a social construction.

"Long-necked" girls of the Kayan tribe in Thailand

Matador in the bullring, Portugal

◀ p. 86 trouble presenting a positive image to others, and may even experience lowered self-esteem. Whole groups of people—for instance, "short people" or "redheads"—may be labeled in this way. The interactionist Erving Goffman coined the term *stigma* to describe the labels society uses to devalue members of certain social groups (Goffman 1963a; Heckert and Best 1997).

Prevailing expectations about beauty and body shape may prevent people who are regarded as ugly or obese from advancing as rapidly as their abilities permit. Both overweight and anorexic people are assumed to be weak in character, slaves to their appetites or to media images. Because they do not conform to the beauty myth, they may be viewed as "disfigured" or "strange" in appearance, bearers of what Goffman calls a "spoiled identity." However, what constitutes disfigurement is a matter of interpretation. Of one million cosmetic procedures done every year in the United States alone, many are performed on women who would be objectively defined as having a normal appearance. And while feminist sociologists have accurately noted that the beauty myth makes many women feel uncomfortable with themselves, men too lack confidence in their appearance. The number of males who choose to undergo cosmetic procedures has risen sharply in recent years; men now account for 9 percent of such surgeries, including liposuction (Kalb 1999; Saukko 1999).

Often people are stigmatized for deviant behaviors they may no longer engage in. The labels "compulsive gambler," "ex-convict," "recovering alcoholic," and "ex–mental patient" can stick to a person for life. Goffman draws a useful distinction between a prestige symbol that draws attention to a positive aspect of one's identity, such as a wedding band or a badge, and a stigma symbol that discredits or debases one's identity, such as a conviction for child molestation. While stigma symbols may not always be obvious, they can become a matter of public knowledge. Starting in 1994, many states required convicted sex offenders to register with local police departments. Some communities publish the names and addresses, and in some instances even the pictures, of convicted sex offenders on the web.

A person need not be guilty of a crime to be stigmatized. Homeless people often have trouble getting a job, because employers are wary of applicants who cannot give a home address. Moreover, hiding one's homelessness is difficult, since agencies generally use the telephone to contact applicants about job openings. If a homeless person has access to a telephone at a shelter, the staff generally answers the phone by announcing the name of the institution—a sure way to discourage prospective employers. Even if a homeless person surmounts these obstacles and manages to get a job, she or he is often fired when the employer learns of the situation. Regardless of a person's positive attributes, employers regard the spoiled identity of homelessness as sufficient reason to dismiss an employee.

While some types of deviance will stigmatize a person, other types do not carry a significant penalty. Some good examples of socially tolerated forms of deviance can be found in the world of high technology.

Deviance and Technology

Technological innovations such as pagers and voice mail can redefine social interactions and the standards of behavior related to them. When the Internet was first made available to the general public, no norms or regulations governed its use. Because online communication offers a high degree of anonymity, uncivil behavior—speaking harshly of others or monopolizing chat room "space"—quickly became common. Online bulletin boards designed to carry items of community interest became littered with commercial advertisements. Such deviant acts are beginning to provoke calls for the establishment of formal rules for online behavior. For example, policymakers have debated whether to regulate the content of websites featuring hate speech and pornography (see the social policy section of Chapter 23).

Some deviant uses of technology are criminal, though not all participants see it that way. The pirating of software, motion pictures, and music has become a big business. At conventions and swap meets, pirated copies of movies, CDs, and DVDs are sold openly. Some of the products are obviously counterfeit, but many come in sophisticated packaging, complete with warranty cards. When vendors are willing to talk, they say they merely want to be compensated for their time and the cost of materials, or that the software they have copied is in the public domain.

Similarly, the downloading of music from the Internet, which is typically protected by copyright, is widely accepted. But file sharing, like the pirating of CDs and DVDs, has grown to the point that it is threatening the profits of copyright owners. Napster, the renegade website that allowed thousands of people to download from a wide selection of music files for free, has been shut down, the victim of a court challenge by the music industry. Nevertheless, its fleeting success has encouraged imitators, many of them college students who run file-sharing programs from their dorm rooms. The music industry is fighting back by urging law enforcement agents to track the pirates down and prosecute them (see Figure 8-2).

Though most of these black market activities are clearly illegal, many consumers and small-time pirates are proud of their behavior. They may even think themselves smart for figuring out a way to avoid the "unfair" prices charged by "big corporations." Few people see the pirating of a new software program or a first-run movie as a threat to the public good, as they would embezzling from a bank. Similarly, most businesspeople who "borrow" software from another department, even though they lack a site license, do not think they are doing anything wrong. No social stigma attaches to their illegal behavior.

Deviance, then, is a complex concept. Sometimes it is trivial, sometimes profoundly harmful. Sometimes it is accepted by society and sometimes soundly rejected. What accounts for deviant behavior and people's reaction to it? In the next section we will examine four theoretical explanations for deviance.

Explaining Deviance

Why do people violate social norms? We have seen that deviant acts are subject to both informal and formal so-

cial control. The nonconforming or disobedient person may face disapproval, loss of friends, fines, or even imprisonment. Why, then, does deviance occur?

Early explanations for deviance identified supernatural causes or genetic factors (such as "bad blood" or evolutionary throwbacks to primitive ancestors). By the 1800s, substantial research efforts were being made to identify biological factors that lead to deviance, and especially to criminal activity. While such research was discredited in the 20th century, contemporary studies, primarily by biochemists, have sought to isolate genetic factors that lead to a likelihood of certain personality traits. Although criminality (much less deviance) is hardly a personality characteristic, researchers have focused on traits that might lead to crime, such as aggression. Of course, aggression can also lead to success in the corporate world, in professional sports, or in other areas of life.

The contemporary study of the possible biological roots of criminality is p. 62 but one aspect of the larger debate over sociobiology. In general, sociologists reject any emphasis on genetic roots of crime and deviance. The limitations of current knowledge, the possibility of reinforcing racist and sexist assumptions, and the disturbing implications for rehabilitation of criminals have led sociologists to draw largely on other approaches to explain deviance (Sagarin and Sanchez 1988).

Functionalist Perspective

According to functionalists, deviance is a common part of human existence, with positive (as well as negative) consequences for social stability. Deviance helps to define the limits of proper behavior. Children who see one parent scold the other for belching at the dinner table learn about approved conduct. The same is true of the driver who receives a speeding ticket, the department store cashier who is fired for yelling at a customer, and the college student who is penalized for handing in papers weeks overdue.

Durkheim's Legacy Émile Durkheim ([1895] 1964) focused his sociological investigations mainly on

FIGURE 8-2

Catching Music Thieves

Investigators can track down a computer used to swap music files by using the same software used for file sharing. How the tracking process works:

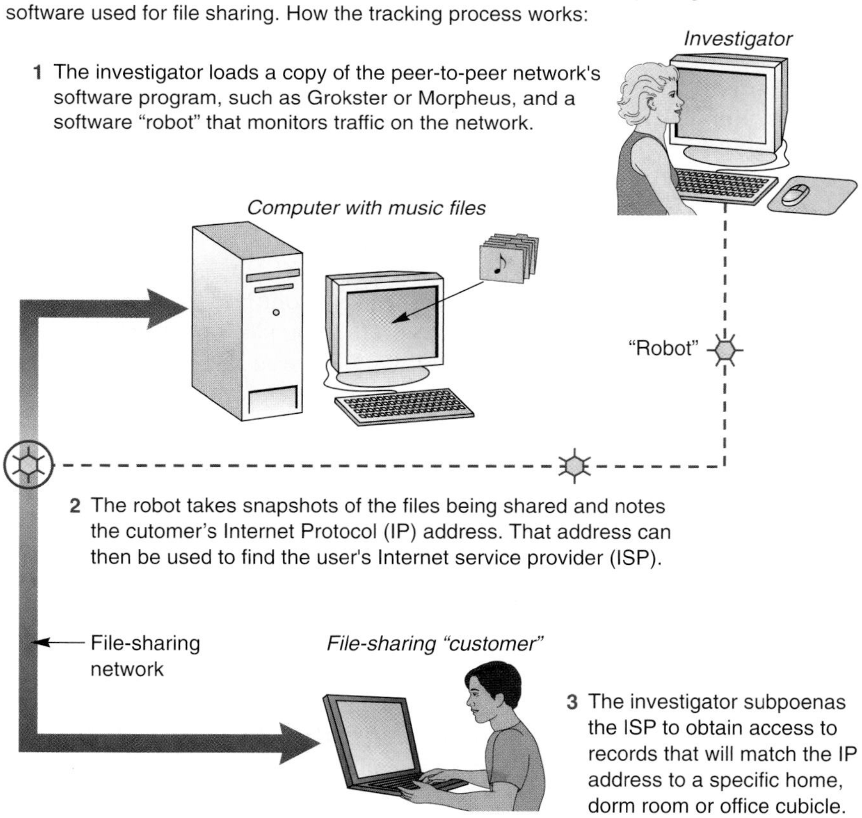

1 The investigator loads a copy of the peer-to-peer network's software program, such as Grokster or Morpheus, and a software "robot" that monitors traffic on the network.

Investigator

Computer with music files

"Robot"

2 The robot takes snapshots of the files being shared and notes the cutomer's Internet Protocol (IP) address. That address can then be used to find the user's Internet service provider (ISP).

File-sharing network

File-sharing "customer"

3 The investigator subpoenas the ISP to obtain access to records that will match the IP address to a specific home, dorm room or office cubicle.

Source: Healey 2003:A21.

At the urging of the music industry, law enforcement agencies have tracked down individuals who set up Internet servers to share music illegally. College students working from computers in their residence halls have been among those prosecuted.

criminal acts, yet his conclusions have implications for all types of deviant behavior. In Durkheim's view, the punishments established within a culture (including both formal and informal mechanisms of social control) help to define acceptable behavior and thus contribute to stability. If improper acts were not sanctioned, people might stretch their standards of what constitutes appropriate conduct.

Kai Erikson (1966) illustrated the boundary-maintenance function of deviance in his study of the Puritans of 17th-century New England. By today's standards, the Puritans placed tremendous emphasis on conventional morals. Their persecution and execution of women as witches represented continuing attempts to define and redefine the boundaries of their community. In effect, their changing social norms created "crime waves," as people whose behavior was previously acceptable suddenly faced punishment for being deviant (Abrahamson 1978; N. Davis 1975).

Durkheim ([1897] 1951) introduced the term *anomie* into sociological literature to describe the loss of direction felt in a society when social control of individual behavior has become ineffective. Anomie is a state of normlessness that typically occurs during a period of profound social change and disorder, such as a time of economic collapse. People become more aggressive or depressed, and this results in higher rates of violent crime and suicide. Since there is much less agreement on what constitutes proper behavior during times of revolution, sudden prosperity, or economic depression, conformity and obedience become less significant as social forces. It also becomes much more difficult to state exactly what constitutes deviance.

Merton's Theory of Deviance What do a mugger and a teacher have in common? Each is "working" to obtain money that can then be exchanged for desired goods. As this example illustrates, behavior that violates accepted norms (such as mugging) may be performed with the same basic objectives in mind as those of people who pursue more conventional lifestyles.

On the basis of this kind of analysis, sociologist Robert Merton (1968) adapted Durkheim's notion of anomie to explain why people accept or reject the goals of a society, the socially approved means of fulfilling their aspirations, or both. Merton maintained that one important cultural goal in the United States is success, measured largely in terms of money. In addition to providing this goal for people, our society offers specific instructions on how to pursue success—go to school, work hard, do not quit, take advantage of opportunities, and so forth.

What happens to individuals in a society with a heavy emphasis on wealth as a basic symbol of success?

Merton reasoned that people adapt in certain ways, either by conforming to or by deviating from such cultural expectations. His *anomie theory of deviance* posits five basic forms of adaptation (see Table 8-1).

Conformity to social norms, the most common adaptation in Merton's typology, is the opposite of deviance. It involves acceptance of both the overall societal goal ("become affluent") and the approved means ("work hard"). In Merton's view, there must be some consensus regarding accepted cultural goals and the legitimate means for attaining them. Without such a consensus, societies could exist only as collectives of people rather than as unified cultures, and might experience continual chaos.

The other four types of behavior represented in Table 8-1 all involve some departure from conformity. The "innovator" accepts the goals of society but pursues them with means that are regarded as improper. For instance, a safecracker may steal money to buy consumer goods and expensive vacations.

In Merton's typology, the "ritualist" has abandoned the goal of material success and become compulsively committed to the institutional means. Work becomes simply a way of life rather than a means to the goal of success. An example would be the bureaucratic official who blindly applies rules and regulations without remembering the larger goals of an organization. Certainly this would be true of a welfare caseworker who refuses to assist a homeless family because their last apartment was in another district.

The "retreatist," as described by Merton, has basically withdrawn (or retreated) from both the goals and the means of a society. In the United States, drug addicts and vagrants are typically portrayed as retreatists. There is also growing concern that adolescents who are addicted to alcohol will become retreatists at an early age.

The final adaptation identified by Merton reflects people's attempts to create a *new* social structure. The "rebel" feels alienated from the dominant means and goals and may seek a dramatically different social order. Members of a revolutionary political organization, such as the Irish Republican Army (IRA) or right-wing militia groups, can be categorized as rebels according to Merton's model.

Merton's theory, though popular, has had relatively few applications. Little effort has been made to determine to what extent all acts of deviance can be accounted for by his five modes. Moreover, while Merton's theory is useful in examining certain types of behavior, such as illegal gambling by disadvantaged "innovators," his formulation fails to explain key differences in crime rates. Why, for example, do some disadvantaged groups have lower rates of reported crime than others? Why do

Table 8-1	**Models of Individual Adaptation**	
Mode	**Institutionalized Means (Hard Work)**	**Societal Goal (Acquisition of Wealth)**
Nondeviant		
Conformity	Accept	Accept
Deviant		
Innovation	Reject	Accept
Ritualism	Accept	Reject
Retreatism	Reject	Reject
Rebellion	Replace with new means	Replace with new goals

Source: Adapted from Merton 1968: 194.

many people in adverse circumstances reject criminal activity as a viable alternative? Merton's theory of deviance does not answer such questions easily (Clinard and Miller 1998).

Still, Merton has made a key contribution to the sociological understanding of deviance by pointing out that deviants such as innovators and ritualists share a great deal with conforming people. The convicted felon may hold many of the same aspirations as people with no criminal background. His theory helps us to understand deviance as a socially created behavior rather than as the result of momentary pathological impulses.

Interactionist Perspective

The functionalist approach to deviance explains why rule violations continue to happen despite pressure to conform and obey. However, functionalists do not indicate how a given person comes to commit a deviant act, or why on some occasions crimes do or do not occur. The emphasis on everyday behavior that is the focus of the interactionist perspective offers two explanations of crime—cultural transmission and routine activities theory.

Cultural Transmission   The graffiti writers described by Susan Phillips in the chapter-opening excerpt learn from one another. In fact, Phillips (1999) was surprised by how stable their focus was over time. She also noted how other ethnic groups built on the models of the African American and Chicano gangs, superimposing Cambodian, Chinese, or Vietnamese symbols.

Humans *learn* how to behave in social situations, whether properly or improperly. There is no natural, innate manner in which people interact with one another. These simple ideas are not disputed today, but such was not the case when sociologist Edwin Sutherland

(1883–1950) first advanced the idea that an individual undergoes the same basic socialization process in learning conforming and deviant acts.

Sutherland's ideas have been the dominating force in criminology. He drew on the **cultural transmission** school, which emphasizes that one learns criminal behavior by interacting with others. Such learning includes not only the techniques of lawbreaking (for example, how to break into a car quickly and quietly) but also the motives, drives, and rationalizations of the criminal. The cultural transmission approach can also be used to explain the behavior of those who habitually abuse alcohol or drugs.

Sutherland maintained that through interactions with a primary group and significant others, people acquire definitions of proper and improper behavior. He used the term **differential association** to describe the process through which exposure to attitudes *favorable* to criminal acts leads to the violation of rules. Research suggests that this view of differential association also applies to noncriminal deviant acts such as smoking, truancy, and early sexual behavior (E. Jackson et al. 1986).

To what extent will a given person engage in activity that is regarded as proper or improper? For each individual, it will depend on the frequency, duration, and importance of two types of social interaction—those experiences that endorse deviant behavior and those that promote acceptance of social norms. People are more likely to engage in norm-defying behavior if they are part of a group or subculture that stresses deviant values, such as a street gang.

Sutherland offers the example of a boy who is sociable, outgoing, and athletic and who lives in an area with a high rate of delinquency. The youth is very likely to come into contact with peers who commit acts of vandalism, fail to attend school, and so forth, and may come to adopt such behavior. However, an introverted boy who lives in the same neighborhood may stay away from his peers and avoid delinquency. In another community, an outgoing and athletic boy may join a Little League baseball team or a scout troop because of his interactions with peers. Thus, Sutherland views improper behavior as the result of the types of groups to which one belongs and the kinds of friendships one has (Sutherland and Cressey 1978).

According to critics, however, the cultural transmission approach may explain the deviant behavior of juvenile delinquents or graffiti artists, but it fails to explain

Under cover of darkness, drag racers await the start signal on a deserted Los Angeles street. Sutherland's concepts of differential association and cultural transmission would both apply to the practice of drag racing on city streets.

the likelihood that such a crime will occur. Campus and airport parking lots, where vehicles may be left in isolated locations for long periods, represent a new target for crime that was unknown just a generation ago. Routine activity of this nature can occur even in the home. If a parent keeps a number of liquor bottles in an easily accessible place, juveniles can siphon off the contents without attracting attention to their "crime." This theory derives its name of "routine" from the fact that the elements of a criminal or deviant act come together in normal, legal, and routine activities. It is considered interactionist because of its emphasis on everyday behavior and micro-level social interactions.

Advocates of this theory see it as a powerful explanation for the rise in crime over the last 50 years. That is, routine activities have changed, making crime more likely. Homes left vacant during the day or during long vacations are more accessible as targets of crime. The greater presence of highly portable consumer goods, such as

the conduct of the first-time impulsive shoplifter or the impoverished person who steals out of necessity. While it is not a precise statement of the process through which one becomes a criminal, differential association theory does direct our attention to the paramount role of social interaction in increasing a person's motivation to engage in deviant behavior (Cressey 1960; E. Jackson et al. 1986; Sutherland and Cressey 1978).

Routine Activities Theory Another, more recent interactionist explanation considers the requisite conditions for a crime or deviant act to occur: there must be, at the same time and in the same place, a perpetrator, a victim, and/or an object of property. *Routine activities theory* contends that criminal victimization increases when motivated offenders and suitable targets converge. It goes without saying that you cannot have car theft without automobiles, but the greater availability of more valuable automobiles to potential thieves *heightens*

These highly desirable consumer electronics, boxed and ready to go, invite shoplifting. Such in-store displays provide an ideal setting for the convergence of a perpetrator (the shoplifter), a victim (the store), and an article of property. According to routine activities theory, crimes are more likely to occur wherever motivated offenders meet vulnerable targets.

video equipment and computers, is another change that makes crime more likely (L. Cohen and Felson 1979; Felson 2002).

Some significant research supports routine activities theory. For example, studies done in the aftermath of Hurricane Andrew in Florida (1992) show that certain crimes increased as citizens and their property became more vulnerable. Studies of urban crime have documented the existence of "hot spots," such as tourist destinations and ATM machines, where people are more likely to be victimized because of their routine comings and goings (Cromwell et al. 1995; Sherman et al. 1989).

Labeling Theory

The Saints and Roughnecks were two groups of high school males who were continually engaged in excessive drinking, reckless driving, truancy, petty theft, and vandalism. There the similarity ended. None of the Saints was ever arrested, but every Roughneck was frequently in trouble with police and townspeople. Why the disparity in their treatment? On the basis of observation research in their high school, sociologist William Chambliss (1973) concluded that social class played an important role in the varying fortunes of the two groups.

The Saints hid behind a facade of respectability. They came from "good families," were active in school organizations, planned on attending college, and received good grades. People generally viewed their delinquent acts as a few isolated cases of sowing wild oats. The Roughnecks had no such aura of respectability. They drove around town in beat-up cars, were generally unsuccessful in school, and aroused suspicion no matter what they did.

We can understand such discrepancies by using an approach to deviance known as **labeling theory.** Unlike Sutherland's work, labeling theory does not focus on why some individuals come to commit deviant acts. Instead, it attempts to explain why certain people (such as the Roughnecks) are *viewed* as deviants, delinquents, bad kids, losers, and criminals, while others whose behavior is similar (such as the Saints) are not seen in such harsh terms. Reflecting the contribution of interactionist theorists, labeling theory emphasizes how a person comes to be labeled as deviant, or to accept that label. Sociologist Howard Becker (1963:9; 1964), who popularized this approach, summed it up with this statement: "Deviant behavior is behavior that people so label."

Labeling theory is also called the **societal-reaction approach,** reminding us that it is the *response* to an act, and not the behavior itself, that determines deviance. For example, studies have shown that some school personnel and therapists expand educational programs designed for learning-disabled students to include those with behav-

ioral problems. Consequently, a "troublemaker" can be improperly labeled as learning-disabled, and vice versa.

Traditionally, research on deviance has focused on people who violate social norms. In contrast, labeling theory focuses on police, probation officers, psychiatrists, judges, teachers, employers, school officials, and other regulators of social control. These agents, it is argued, play a significant role in creating the deviant identity by designating certain people (and not others) as deviant. An important aspect of labeling theory is the recognition that some individuals or groups have the power to *define* labels and apply them to others. This view ties into the conflict perspective's emphasis on the social significance of power.

In recent years the practice of *racial profiling*, in which people are identified as criminal suspects purely on the basis of their race, has come under public scrutiny. Studies confirm the public's suspicions that in some jurisdictions, police officers are much more likely to stop African American males than White males for routine traffic violations, in the expectation of finding drugs or guns in their cars. Civil rights activists refer to these cases sarcastically as DWB violations (Driving While Black). Beginning in 2001, profiling took a new turn as people who appeared to be Arab or Muslim came under special scrutiny.

The labeling approach does not fully explain why certain people accept a label and others manage to reject it. In fact, this perspective may exaggerate the ease with which societal judgments can alter our self-images. Labeling theorists do suggest, however, that the power one has relative to others is important in determining a person's ability to resist an undesirable label. Competing approaches (including that of Sutherland) fail to explain why some deviants continue to be viewed as conformists rather than as violators of rules. According to Howard Becker (1973), labeling theory was not conceived as the *sole* explanation for deviance; its proponents merely hoped to focus more attention on the undeniably important actions of those people who are officially in charge of defining deviance (N. Davis 1975; compare with Cullen and Cullen 1978).

The popularity of labeling theory is reflected in the emergence of a related perspective, called social constructionism. According to the **social constructionist perspective,** deviance is the product of the culture we live in. Social constructionists focus specifically on the decision-making process that creates the deviant identity. They point out that "child abductors," "deadbeat dads," "spree killers," and "date rapists" have always been with us, but at times have become *the* major social concern of the moment because of intensive media coverage (Liska and Messner 1999; E. R. Wright et al. 2000).

In the 1930s, the Federal Bureau of Narcotics launched a campaign to portray marijuana as a dangerous drug rather than a pleasure-inducing substance. From a conflict perspective, those in power often use such tactics to coerce others into adopting a different point of view.

Use Your Sociological Imagination www.mhhe.com/schaefer9

You are a teacher. What kind of labels, freely used in educational circles, might you attach to your students?

Conflict Theory

Conflict theorists point out that people with power protect their own interests and define deviance to suit their own needs. Sociologist Richard Quinney (1974, 1979, 1980) is a leading exponent of the view that the criminal justice system serves the interests of the powerful. Crime, according to Quinney (1970), is a definition of conduct created by authorized agents of social control—such as legislators and law enforcement officers—in a politically organized society. He and other conflict theorists argue that lawmaking is often an attempt by the powerful to coerce others into their own morality (see also Spitzer 1975).

This theory helps to explain why our society has laws against gambling, drug usage, and prostitution, many of which are violated on a massive scale (we will examine these "victimless crimes" later in the chapter). According to conflict theorists, criminal law does not represent a consistent application of societal values, but instead reflects competing values and interests. Thus, marijuana is outlawed in the United States because it is alleged to be harmful to users, yet cigarettes and alcohol are sold legally almost everywhere. Similarly, conflict theorists contend that the entire criminal justice system of the United States treats suspects differently on the basis of their racial, ethnic, or social class background (see Box 8-2).

The perspective advanced by conflict and labeling theorists forms quite a contrast to the functionalist approach to deviance. Functionalists see standards of deviant behavior as merely reflecting cultural norms; conflict and labeling theorists point out that the most powerful groups in a society can shape laws and standards and determine who is (or is not) prosecuted as a criminal. These groups would be unlikely to apply the label "deviant" to the corporate executive whose decisions lead to large-scale environmental pollution. In the opinion of conflict theorists, agents of social control and other powerful groups can impose their own self-serving definitions of deviance on the general public.

Feminist Perspective

For many years any husband who forced his wife to have sexual intercourse—without her consent and against her will—was not legally considered to have committed rape. The law defined rape as pertaining only to sexual relations between people who were not married to each other, reflecting the overwhelmingly male composition of state legislatures at the time.

It took repeated protests by feminist organizations to get changes in the criminal law defining rape. As of 1996, husbands in all 50 states could be prosecuted under most circumstances for the rape of their wives. There remain alarming exceptions: for example, in Tennessee a husband may legally use force or coercion to rape his wife as long as no weapon is present and he has not inflicted "serious bodily harm." Despite such exceptions, the rise of the women's movement has unquestionably led to important changes in societal notions of criminality. For example, judges, legislators, and police officers now view wife battering and other forms of domestic violence as serious crimes (National Center on Women and Family Law 1996).

When it comes to crime and to deviance in general, society tends to treat women in a stereotypical fashion. For example, consider how women who have many and frequent sexual partners are more likely to be viewed with scorn than men who are promiscuous. Cultural views and attitudes toward women influence how they are perceived

8-2 DISCRETIONARY JUSTICE

ace matters in the criminal justice system. Conflict theorists remind us that while the basic purpose of law is to maintain stability and order, it can actually perpetuate inequality. In many cases, criminal justice officials use their *discretionary powers*—decisions made on their own discretion about whether to press charges or drop them, whether to set bail and how much, whether to offer parole or deny it—in biased ways. Researchers have found that discretionary differences in the way social control is exercised put African Americans and Latinos at a disadvantage in the justice system, both as juveniles and adults. In this way, Richard Quinney and other conflict theorists argue, the criminal justice system keeps the poor and oppressed in their deprived positions.

> On average, White offenders receive shorter sentences than comparable Latino and African American offenders.

How do sociologists determine whether suspects and offenders are treated differently based on racial, ethnic, and social class backgrounds? One way is to look at convicted criminals and compare the sentences they receive for equivalent crimes. The task can be complicated, because researchers must take into consideration a number of factors that affect sentencing. For example, in their study of federal court data, sociologists Darrell Steffensmeier and Stephen Demuth examined the severity of the crime and the convict's prior arrest record. Even after taking these and other factors into consideration, they found that on average, White offenders receive shorter sentences than comparable Latino and African American offenders.

Race plays a crucial role in death penalty cases, as the accompanying figure

shows. While White non-Hispanics make up 71 percent of the U.S. population, they constitute only 43 percent of criminals sentenced to death. Conflict theorists point out that the overwhelming majority of prosecutors in death penalty cases are White and non-Hispanic. The victim's race matters a great deal in these cases, as well. Studies have consistently shown that a convicted criminal is much more likely to be sentenced to death if the victim is White and non-Hispanic than if the victim is non-White or Hispanic.

Let's Discuss

1. Do you know anyone who was treated leniently by the criminal justice system? If so, was the person White and non-Hispanic? Why do you think police and/or other officials used their discretionary powers to excuse the person's offense or reduce the penalties?

2. Besides race, what other factors might contribute to the disproportionately severe sentencing of Black and Hispanic defendants? Explain.

Race and the Death Penalty

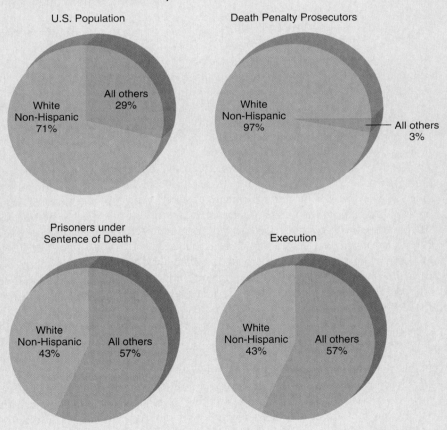

U.S. Population

White Non-Hispanic 71%
All others 29%

Death Penalty Prosecutors

White Non-Hispanic 97%
All others 3%

Prisoners under Sentence of Death

White Non-Hispanic 43%
All others 57%

Execution

White Non-Hispanic 43%
All others 57%

Note: Population data are for 2000; data on prosecutors, for 1998; data on prisoners, for December 30, 2001; and data on executions, for 1977–2001.

Sources: Based on Bureau of the Census 2002a; Dieter 1998:13; Snell and Maruschak 2002:10, 11.

Sources: Butterfield 2000; Hawkins et al. 2000; Quinney 1974; Steffensmeier and Demuth 2000; Texeira 2000.

and labeled. The feminist perspective also emphasizes that deviance, including crime, tends to flow from economic relationships. Traditionally, men have had greater earning power than their wives. As a result, wives may be reluctant to report acts of abuse to the authorities, and lose what may be their primary or even sole source of income. In the workplace, men have exercised greater power than women in pricing, accounting, and product control, giving them greater opportunity to engage in such crimes as embezzlement and fraud. But as women take more active and powerful roles both in the household and in business, these gender differences in deviance and crime will undoubtedly narrow.

In the future, feminist scholarship can be expected to grow dramatically, particularly on topics such as white-collar crime, drinking behavior, drug abuse, differential sentencing rates between the genders, and the whole question of how to define deviance (Maguire and Radosh 1999).

CRIME

Crime is a violation of criminal law for which some governmental authority applies formal penalties. It represents a deviation from formal social norms administered by the state. Laws divide crimes into various categories, depending on the severity of the offense, the age of the offender, the potential punishment, and the court that holds jurisdiction over the case.

Over 1.4 million violent crimes were reported in the United States in 2000, including more than 15,500 homicides. The key ingredients in the incidence of street crime appeared to be drug use and the widespread presence of firearms. According to the FBI, 18 percent of all reported aggravated assaults, 41 percent of reported robberies, and 66 percent of reported murders in 2000 involved a firearm. Even with a recent decline in major crime in the United States, current levels exceed levels experienced in the 1960s (Department of Justice 2001d).

Types of Crime

Rather than relying solely on legal categories, sociologists classify crimes in terms of how they are committed and how society views the offenses. In this section, we will examine four types of crime differentiated by sociologists: professional crime, organized crime, white-collar crime, and victimless crimes.

Professional Crime

Although the adage "Crime doesn't pay" is familiar, many people do make a career of illegal activities. A *profes-*sional criminal* (or career criminal) is a person who pursues crime as a day-to-day occupation, developing skilled techniques and enjoying a certain degree of status among other criminals. Some professional criminals specialize in burglary, safecracking, hijacking of cargo, pickpocketing, and shoplifting. Such people have acquired skills that reduce the likelihood of arrest, conviction, and imprisonment. As a result, they may have long careers in their chosen "professions."

Edwin Sutherland (1937) offered pioneering insights into the behavior of professional criminals by publishing an annotated account written by a professional thief. Unlike the person who engages in crime only once or twice, professional thieves make a business of stealing. They devote their entire working time to planning and executing crimes, and sometimes travel across the nation to pursue their "professional duties." Like people in regular occupations, professional thieves consult with their colleagues concerning the demands of work, becoming part of a subculture of similarly occupied individuals. They exchange information on places to burglarize, on outlets for unloading stolen goods, and ways of securing bail bonds if arrested.

Organized Crime

A 1978 government report devotes three pages to defining the term *organized crime.* For our purposes, we will consider **organized crime** to be the work of a group that regulates relations between various criminal enterprises involved in illegal activities, including prostitution, gambling, and the smuggling and sale of drugs. Organized crime dominates the world of illegal business just as large corporations dominate the conventional business world. It allocates territory, sets prices for goods and services, and acts as an arbitrator in internal disputes. A secret, conspiratorial activity, it generally evades law enforcement. It takes over legitimate businesses, gains influence over labor unions, corrupts public officials, intimidates witnesses in criminal trials, and even "taxes" merchants in exchange for "protection" (National Advisory Commission on Criminal Justice 1976).

Organized crime serves as a means of upward mobility for groups of people struggling to escape poverty. Sociologist Daniel Bell (1953) used the term *ethnic succession* to describe the sequential passage of leadership from Irish Americans in the early part of the 20th century to Jewish Americans in the 1920s and then to Italian Americans in the early 1930s. Recently, ethnic succession has become more complex, reflecting the diversity of the nation's latest immigrants. Colombian, Mexican, Russian, Chinese, Pakistani, and Nigerian immigrants are among those who have begun to play a significant role in organized crime activities (Chin 1996; Kleinknecht 1996).

TIFFANY ZAPATA-MANCILLA **Victim Witness Specialist, Cook County State's Attorney's Office**

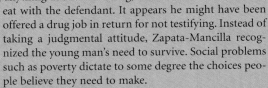

Tiffany Zapata-Mancilla's typical day brings her into contact with all manner of crime victims—those who have survived murder attempts, domestic assault, child abuse, robbery, and other violent crimes—as well as family members who testify on behalf of victims. She works closely with victims who have witnessed a crime, since they are invariably called to testify in a trial. "My job is to make the courtroom experience for them as comfortable as possible," she says. That may mean offering them referral for crisis counseling, a court escort, court orientation, help with impact statements, assistance with restitution, protection services, transportation, child care, emergency financial assistance, or just a hot lunch. Her caseload of 500 cases comes from the four to eight courtrooms to which she is assigned in Chicago's Cook County.

"My sociological background helps me in all situations on a daily basis," Zapata-Mancilla says. In particular, it helps her to recognize the underlying societal issues, even in what seem to be horrendous individual acts, and to help victims to recognize those issues as well. "I do not judge those who come into the courtroom; I can only judge society," she says. According to Zapata-Mancilla, that doesn't mean that individuals have no personal responsibility for their life choices. But it helps to understand that people are conditioned by the environment and society they live in. One of her cases involved a young man who was called to testify to who killed his younger brother in a gang

shootout. At the time of the trial, two years later, he denied knowing anything about the killing, and afterward went out to eat with the defendant. It appears he might have been offered a drug job in return for not testifying. Instead of taking a judgmental attitude, Zapata-Mancilla recognized the young man's need to survive. Social problems such as poverty dictate to some degree the choices people believe they need to make.

Zapata-Mancilla majored in sociology at DePaul University after becoming hooked by her introductory course. She went on to earn her master's degree in sociology there in 2001. "I was very interested in societal issues such as poverty, crime, organized crime, and gang involvement, and how they influenced the lifestyles and psychology of individuals. Sociology, for me, offers reasons, not excuses, for why individuals act and react in certain ways," she says. She also thinks she has gained a greater understanding of herself as a Latina through her studies.

Her advice for students: "Keep an open mind and don't be judgmental of others."

Let's Discuss

1. Why do you think victim witnesses need special attention?
2. What aspect of sociological study do you think best prepared Zapata-Mancilla for her job?

There has always been a global element in organized crime. But law enforcement officials and policymakers now acknowledge the emergence of a new form of organized crime that takes advantage of advances in electronic communications. *Transnational* organized crime includes drug and arms smuggling, money laundering, and trafficking in illegal immigrants and stolen goods, such as automobiles (Office of Justice Programs 1999).

White-Collar and Technology-Based Crime

Income tax evasion, stock manipulation, consumer fraud, bribery and extraction of kickbacks, embezzlement, and misrepresentation in advertising—these are all examples of **white-collar crime,** illegal acts committed in the course of business activities, often by affluent, "respectable" people. Edwin Sutherland (1949, 1983) likened these crimes to organized crime because they are often perpetrated through occupational roles.

A new type of white-collar crime has emerged in recent decades: computer crime. The use of high technology allows criminals to carry out embezzlement or electronic fraud, often leaving few traces, or to gain access to a company's inventory without leaving home. An adept programmer can gain access to a firm's computer by telephone and then copy valuable files. It is virtually impossible to track such people unless they are foolish enough to call from the same phone each time. According to a 2002 study by the FBI and the Computer Security Institute, 90 percent of companies relying on computer systems had detected computer security breaches in the past

"BUT IF WE GO BACK TO SCHOOL AND GET A GOOD EDUCATION, THINK OF ALL THE DOORS IT'LL OPEN TO WHITE-COLLAR CRIME."

year, but only 34 percent reported those attacks to authorities (Power 2002).

Sutherland (1940) coined the term *white-collar crime* in 1939 to refer to acts by individuals, but the term has been broadened more recently to include offenses by businesses and corporations as well. *Corporate crime,* or any act by a corporation that is punishable by the government, takes many forms and includes individuals, organizations, and institutions among its victims. Corporations may engage in anticompetitive behavior, environmental pollution, tax fraud, stock fraud and manipulation, accounting fraud, the production of unsafe goods, bribery and corruption, and health and safety violations (Hansen 2002; Jost 2002).

For many years, corporate wrongdoers got off lightly in court by documenting their long history of charitable contributions and agreeing to help law enforcement officials find other white-collar criminals. In 2003, ten investment firms and two stock analysts collectively paid a $1.4 billion settlement for issuing fraudulent information to investors. While the magnitude of the fine grabbed headlines nationwide, it must be balanced against the millions of investors who were lured into buying billions of dollars worth of shares in companies that the accused knew were either troubled or on the verge of collapse. The bottom line is that no individual served a jail sentence as part of the settlement, and no firm lost its license to do

business. Prosecutors in other investigations into corporate scandals have pledged to pursue jail sentences for white-collar criminals, but to date most defendants have only been fined (Labaton 2003; O'Donnell and Willing 2003).

Conviction for corporate crime does not generally harm a person's reputation and career aspirations nearly so much as conviction for street crime would. Apparently, the label "white-collar criminal" does not carry the stigma of the label "felon convicted of a violent crime." Conflict theorists don't find such differential labeling and treatment surprising. They argue that the criminal justice system largely disregards the white-collar crimes of the affluent, focusing on the crimes committed by the poor. Generally, if an offender holds a position of status and influence, his or her crime is treated as less serious than others', and the sanction is much more lenient (Maguire 1988).

Use Your Sociological Imagination www. mhhe.com /schaefer9

As a newspaper editor, how might you treat stories on corporate crime differently from those on violent crimes?

Victimless Crimes

White-collar and street crimes endanger people's economic or personal well-being against their will (or without their direct knowledge). By contrast, sociologists use the term *victimless crime* to describe the willing exchange among adults of widely desired, but illegal, goods and services, such as prostitution (Schur 1965, 1985).

Some activists are working to decriminalize many of these illegal practices. Supporters of decriminalization are troubled by the attempt to legislate a moral code for adults. In their view, prostitution, drug abuse, gambling, and other victimless crimes are impossible to prevent. The already overburdened criminal justice system should instead devote its resources to "street crimes" and other offenses with obvious victims.

Despite the wide use of the term *victimless crime,* however, many people object to the notion that there is no victim other than the offender in such crimes. Excessive drinking, compulsive gambling, and illegal drug use contribute to an enormous amount of personal and property damage. A person with a drinking problem can become abusive to a spouse or children; a compulsive gambler or drug user may steal to pursue his obsession. And feminist sociologists contend that prostitution, as well as the more disturbing aspects of pornography, reinforce the misconception that women are "toys" who can be treated as objects rather than people. According to critics of decriminalization, society must not give tacit approval to conduct that has such harmful consequences (Flavin 1998; Jolin 1994; National Advisory Commission on Criminal Justice 1976; Schur 1968, 1985).

The controversy over decriminalization reminds us of the important insights of labeling and conflict theorists presented earlier. Underlying this debate are two questions: Who has the power to define gambling, prostitution, and public drunkenness as "crimes"? and Who has the power to label such behaviors as "victimless"? The answer is generally the state legislatures, and in some cases, the police and the courts.

Again, we can see that criminal law is not simply a universal standard of behavior agreed on by all members of society. Rather, it reflects a struggle among competing individuals and groups to gain governmental support for their moral and social values. For example, organizations such as Mothers Against Drunk Driving (MADD) and Students Against Drunk Driving (SADD) have been successful in recent years in modifying public attitudes toward drunkenness. Rather than being viewed as a victimless crime, drunkenness is increasingly associated with the potential dangers of driving while under the influence of alcohol. As a result, the mass media are giving greater (and more critical) attention to people who are found guilty of drunk driving, and many states have instituted severe fines and jail terms for a wide variety of alcohol-related offenses.

Crime Statistics

Crime statistics are not as accurate as social scientists would like. However, since they deal with an issue of grave concern to the people of the United States, they are frequently cited as if they were completely reliable. Such data do serve as an indicator of police activity, as well as an approximate indication of the level of certain crimes. Yet it would be a mistake to interpret these data as an exact representation of the incidence of crime.

Understanding Crime Statistics

Reported crime is very high in the United States, and the public regards crime as a major social problem. However, there has been a significant decline in violent crime nationwide following many years of increases. A number of explanations have been offered, including:

- A booming economy and falling unemployment rates through most of the 1990s.
- Community-oriented policing and crime prevention programs.
- New gun control laws.
- A massive increase in the prison population, which at least prevents inmates from committing crimes outside prison.

It remains to be seen whether this pattern will continue, but even with current declines, reported crimes remain well above those of other nations, and exceed the reported rates in the United States of just 20 years earlier. Feminist scholars draw our attention to one significant variation: the proportion of major crimes committed by women has increased. In a recent five-year period (1995–2000), female arrests for major reported crimes remained virtually the same, while comparable male arrests declined 6 percent (Department of Justice 2001:216).

Sociologists have several ways of measuring crime. Historically, they have relied on police data, but underreporting has always been a problem with such measures. Because members of racial and ethnic minority groups often distrust law enforcement agencies, they may not contact the police. Feminist sociologists and others have noted that many women do not report rape or spousal abuse out of fear they will be blamed for the crime.

Partly because of these deficiencies in official statistics, the National Crime Victimization Survey was initiated in 1972. The Bureau of Justice Statistics, in compiling this annual report, seeks information from law enforcement agencies, but also interviews members of 86,800 households and asks if they have been victims of a specific set of crimes during the preceding year. In general, those who administer *victimization surveys* question ordinary people, not police officers, to determine whether they have been victims of crime.

Unfortunately, like other crime data, victimization surveys have particular limitations. They require that

FIGURE 8-3

Victimization Rates, 1973–2001

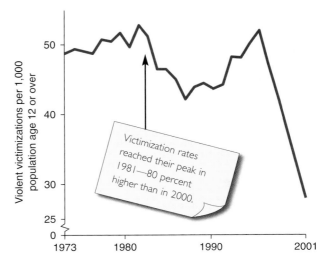

Source: Rennison 2002:12.

victims understand what has happened to them and are willing to disclose such information to interviewers. Fraud, income tax evasion, and blackmail are examples of crimes that are unlikely to be reported in victimization studies. Nevertheless, 93 percent of all households have been willing to cooperate with investigators for the National Crime Victimization Survey. As shown in Figure 8-3 (page 191), data from these surveys reveal a fluctuating crime rate with significant declines in both the 1980s and 1990s (Rennison 2002).

International Crime Rates

If developing reliable crime data is difficult in the United States, making useful cross-national comparisons is even more difficult. Nevertheless, with some care, we can offer preliminary conclusions about how crime rates differ around the world.

During the 1980s and 1990s, violent crimes were much more common in the United States than in Western Europe. Murders, rapes, and robberies were reported to the police at much higher rates in the United States. Yet the incidence of certain other types of crime appears to be higher elsewhere. For example, England, Italy, Australia, and New Zealand all have higher rates of car theft than the United States (International Crime Victim Survey 2003).

Why are rates of violent crime so much higher in the United States? Sociologist Elliot Currie (1985, 1998) has suggested that our society places greater emphasis on individual economic achievement than other societies. At the same time, many observers have noted that the culture of the United States has long tolerated, if not condoned, many forms of violence. Coupled with sharp disparities between poor and affluent citizens, significant unemployment, and substantial alcohol and drug abuse, these factors combine to produce a climate conducive to crime.

However, disturbing increases in violent crime are evident in other Western societies. For example, crime has skyrocketed in Russia since the overthrow of Communist Party rule (with its strict controls on guns and criminals) in 1991. In 1998 there were fewer than 260 homicides in Moscow, but now there are more than 1,000 homicides a year. Organized crime has filled a power vacuum in Moscow since the end of communism; one result is that gangland shootouts and premeditated "contract hits" have become more common. Some prominent reformist politicians have been targeted as well. Russia is the only nation in the world that incarcerates a higher proportion of its citizens than the United States. The country imprisons 580 per 100,000 of its adults on a typical day, compared to 550 in the United States, fewer than 100 in Mexico or Britain, and only 16 in Greece (Currie 1998; Shinkai and Zvekic 1999).

| SOCIAL POLICY and SOCIAL CONTROL | Gun Control | |

Two high school students present themselves at Kmart's national headquarters. They are not looking for jobs. Survivors of the mass murders at Columbine High School in 1999, they still have bullets lodged in their bodies—bullets their attackers bought at Kmart. In a symbolic protest, the two young people ask Kmart's representative if they can return the bullets.

This scene was shown in the Academy Award–winning documentary *Bowling for Columbine*. Producer-director Michael Moore was amazed when the day after he filmed the encounter, Kmart announced that the store would cease to sell the ammunition.

The Issue

While reported crime has declined in recent years, the role of firearms in crime has remained fairly consistent. Over the past 10 years, two-thirds of all murders were committed with firearms. Although handgun owners frequently insist that they need to own firearms to protect themselves and their loved ones from violent crime, over the years, high-profile assassinations of public figures such as President John F. Kennedy, Senator Robert Kennedy, Dr. Martin Luther King Jr., and Beatle John Lennon have forced legislators to consider stricter gun control measures (Department of Justice 2002).

In 1994 Congress passed the Brady Handgun Violence Prevention Act, named after White House press secretary Jim Brady, who was seriously wounded in the 1981 assassination attempt against President Ronald Reagan. John Hinckley, the would-be assassin, had given false information about himself at the pawnshop where he bought the gun he used to shoot Reagan and Brady. The Brady Act mandates that firearms dealers run criminal history background checks on people who wish to purchase handguns. About 2 percent of all purchases are denied as a result of the checks—roughly 400 purchases per day (Bowling et al. 2002).

A customer purchases ammunition at a discount store in a scene from Michael Moore's documentary *Bowling for Columbine*.

group nature flourish across the country. On a national basis, powerful formal organizations promote gun ownership. Clearly, owning a gun is not a deviant act in our society (National Rifle Association 2003; Saad 2002).

Sociological Insights

Since the Brady Act went into effect, support for stricter measures has actually declined (Gallup 2002c). Still, national surveys show that about half of all adults in the United States favor stricter laws covering the sale of firearms; about 1 in 10 favor more lenient laws. Though support for gun control far outweighs sentiment against it, the nation's major anti–gun control lobby, the National Rifle Association (NRA), has been able to use its impressive power to block or dilute such measures (Saad 2002).

Conflict theorists contend that powerful groups like the NRA can dominate the legislative process because of their ability to mobilize resources in opposition to majority will. Founded in 1871, the NRA has 3.8 million members; state rifle associations, with 4 to 5 million members, support many of the NRA's goals. In contrast, Handgun Control, a key organization in the gun control battle, has only 400,000 members. Compared to the NRA's formidable war chest, Handgun Control's resources are limited.

Gun control supporters claim that even stricter legislation is needed, but opponents charge that the Brady Act only hampers honest people who want to buy guns, since those with criminal intent can turn to other sources. Opponents suggest, instead, strengthening and enforcing criminal penalties for the illegal use of guns.

The Setting

Guns and ammunition are big business in the United States, where the Second Amendment to the Constitution guarantees the "right of the people to keep and bear arms." Currently, 30 to 35 million people in the United States own handguns, and about 45 percent of U.S. households have some type of firearm on the premises. Informal gun clubs of both a primary- and secondary-

Policy Implications

Advocates for stricter gun control laws identify a series of measures they would like to see enacted:

- A total ban on assault weapons.
- Tight restrictions on permits to carry concealed weapons.
- Regulation of gun shows, where "private sellers" often trade in firearms unrestricted by the Brady Act.
- Increased penalties for leaving firearms where they are easily accessible to children and others who could misuse them.

Efforts to pass these measures have been made at all levels of government, since towns, states, and the federal government all have the authority to regulate the possession and sale of firearms (Brady Campaign 2003).

Proposed legal restrictions on gun ownership have met strong opposition by both the NRA and firearms manufacturers. The NRA has been particularly successful in defeating political candidates who favor stricter laws, and in backing those who seek to weaken such restrictions. Except in a handful of states, office seekers rarely risk taking an antigun position. Alarmed by the NRA's rhetoric, many voters fear that restricting the sale of firearms will hamper their ability to protect themselves, independent of law enforcement officers. Indeed, in light of growing concern over terrorism on the home front, the handgun debate has turned now to the question of allowing pilots to carry guns in the cockpit (Tumulty and Novak 2002).

Let's Discuss

1. Do you see guns more as weapons that could jeopardize your safety or as protection against those who would harm you? What formal or informal sources of social control may have influenced you to form this attitude?

2. Kmart changed its policy on the sale of ammunition after being visited by survivors of the Columbine High School shootings. Analyze the company's decision as a sociologist would. If retailers' policies on the sale of ammunition had been different in 1999, could the massacre at Columbine High have been prevented?

3. Did the September 11, 2001, terrorist attacks on the United States strengthen or weaken the case for stronger control of firearms? Explain your position.

CHAPTER RESOURCES

Summary

Conformity and *deviance* are two ways in which people respond to real or imagined pressure from others. In this chapter, we examined the relationship between conformity, deviance, and mechanisms of *social control.*

1. A society uses social control to encourage the acceptance of basic norms.

2. Stanley Milgram defined *conformity* as going along with one's peers; *obedience* is defined as compliance with higher authorities in a hierarchical structure.

3. Some norms are so important to a society, they are formalized into *laws.* Socialization is a primary source of conforming and obedient behavior, including obedience to law.

4. Deviant behavior violates social norms. Some forms of deviance carry a negative social *stigma,* while other forms are more or less accepted.

5. From a functionalist point of view, deviance and its consequences help to define the limits of proper behavior.

6. Some interactionists maintain that people learn criminal behavior by interacting with others *(cultural transmission).* To them, deviance results from exposure to attitudes that are favorable to criminal acts *(differential association).*

7. Other interactionists stress that for a crime to occur, there must be a convergence of motivated offenders and suitable targets of crime *(routine activities theory).*

8. An important aspect of *labeling theory* is the recognition that some people are viewed as deviant, while others who engage in the same behavior are not.

9. The conflict perspective views laws and punishments as a reflection of the interests of the powerful.

10. The feminist perspective emphasizes that cultural attitudes and differential economic relationships help to explain gender differences in deviance and crime.

11. *Crime* represents a deviation from formal social norms administered by the state.

12. Sociologists differentiate among *professional crime, organized crime, white-collar crime,* and *victimless crimes* (such as drug use and prostitution).

13. Crime statistics are among the least reliable social data, partly because so many crimes are not reported to law enforcement agencies. Rates of violent crime are higher in the United States than in other Western societies, although they have been dropping.

14. The power of the National Rifle Association (NRA) has been a major factor in preventing the passage of strong gun control legislation.

Critical Thinking Questions

1. What mechanisms of formal and informal social control are evident in your college classes and in day-to-day life and social interactions at your school?
2. What approach to deviance do you find most persuasive: that of functionalists, conflict theorists, interactionists, or labeling theorists? Why do you consider that approach more convincing than the other three? What are the main weaknesses of each approach?
3. Rates of violent crime in the United States are higher than they are in Western Europe, Canada, Australia, or New Zealand. Draw on as many of the theories discussed in this chapter as possible to explain why the United States is such a comparably violent society.

Key Terms

Anomie Durkheim's term for the loss of direction felt in a society when social control of individual behavior has become ineffective. (page 182)

Anomie theory of deviance Robert Merton's theory of deviance as an adaptation of socially prescribed goals or of the means governing their attainment, or both. (182)

Conformity Going along with peers—individuals of our own status, who have no special right to direct our behavior. (172)

Control theory A view of conformity and deviance that suggests that our connection to members of society leads us to systematically conform to society's norms. (176)

Crime A violation of criminal law for which some governmental authority applies formal penalties. (188)

Cultural transmission A school of criminology that argues that criminal behavior is learned through social interactions. (183)

Deviance Behavior that violates the standards of conduct or expectations of a group or society. (176)

Differential association A theory of deviance proposed by Edwin Sutherland that holds that violation of rules results from exposure to attitudes favorable to criminal acts. (183)

Formal social control Social control that is carried out by authorized agents, such as police officers, judges, school administrators, and employers. (174)

Informal social control Social control that is carried out casually by ordinary people through such means as laughter, smiles, and ridicule. (174)

Labeling theory An approach to deviance that attempts to explain why certain people are viewed as deviants while others engaging in the same behavior are not. (185)

Law Governmental social control. (175)

Obedience Compliance with higher authorities in a hierarchical structure. (172)

Organized crime The work of a group that regulates relations between criminal enterprises involved in illegal activities, including prostitution, gambling, and the smuggling and sale of illegal drugs. (188)

Professional criminal A person who pursues crime as a day-to-day occupation, developing skilled techniques and enjoying a certain degree of status among other criminals. (188)

Routine activities theory The notion that criminal victimization increases when there is a convergence of motivated offenders and suitable targets. (184)

Sanction A penalty or reward for conduct concerning a social norm. (172)

Social constructionist perspective An approach to deviance that emphasizes the role of culture in the creation of the deviant identity. (185)

Social control The techniques and strategies for preventing deviant human behavior in any society. (171)

Societal-reaction approach Another name for *labeling theory*. (185)

Stigma A label used to devalue members of certain social groups. (180)

Victimization survey Questionnaire or interview given to a sample of the population to determine whether people have been victims of crime. (191)

Victimless crime A term used by sociologists to describe the willing exchange among adults of widely desired, but illegal, goods and services. (190)

White-collar crime Crimes committed by affluent, "respectable" individuals in the course of business activities. (189)

TECHNOLOGY RESOURCES

Internet Connection

*Note: While all the URLs listed were current as of the printing of this book, these sites often change. Please check our website (**www.mhhe.com/schaefer9**) for updates, hyperlinks, and exercises related to these sites.*

1. Sociologists and government agencies share a need for timely, accurate, and complete data regarding crime rates. The Federal Bureau of Investigation provides an online examination of crime statistics. You can access this data by linking to **www.fbi.gov.**

2. Historically, execution has served as a significant form of punishment for deviance from social norms and criminal behavior. Yet execution has also been, and remains, a controversial issue. To find out how Americans feel about the death penalty, go to Public Agenda Online (**www.publicagenda.org**).

Online Learning Center with PowerWeb

If you are interested in what people in the United States think about the death penalty, visit the student center of the Online Learning Center at **www.mhhe.com/schaefer9.** Link to "How Americans Feel About . . . " You will find colorful graphs showing what percentage of citizens favor the death penalty, what percentage do not feel it is imposed often enough, and what percentage support the death penalty even though they believe innocent people have been executed.

Reel Society Interactive Movie CD-ROM

Reel Society includes scenes that can be used to spark discussion about the following topics in this chapter:

• Conformity and Obedience

• Informal and Formal Social Control
• Deviance
• Discretionary Justice

chapter

9

STRATIFICATION AND SOCIAL MOBILITY IN THE UNITED STATES

Understanding Stratification

Stratification by Social Class

Social Mobility

Social Policy and Stratification: Rethinking Welfare in North America and Europe

Boxes

SOCIOLOGY IN THE GLOBAL COMMUNITY: Under Pressure: The Caste System in India

RESEARCH IN ACTION: When Jobs Disappear

Mark Lawson stuffs a 26th hot dog into his mouth, just enough to win an annual contest held in Beachwood, NJ.

ELSEWHERE IN AMERICA, 12 MILLION CHILDREN ARE FIGHTING HUNGER.

THE SOONER YOU BELIEVE IT, THE SOONER WE CAN END IT. Call 1-800-FEED KIDS, or visit feedingchildrenbetter.org to learn about child hunger in America.

In the United States, some people overindulge while others go hungry, as this public service advertisement reminds us. Social class stratification determines the distribution of resources in our society, from necessities such as food and shelter to relative luxuries such as higher education.

In the early 1990s, the McDonald's Corporation launched a television ad campaign featuring a young black man named Calvin, who was portrayed sitting atop a Brooklyn stoop in his Golden Arches uniform while his friends down on the sidewalk passed by, giving him a hard time about holding down a "McJob." After brushing off their teasing with good humor, Calvin is approached furtively by one young black man who asks, *sotto voce,* whether Calvin might help him get a job too. He allows that he could use some earnings and that despite the ragging he has just given Calvin, he thinks the uniform is really pretty cool—or at least that having a job is pretty cool. . . .

Americans have always been committed to the moral maxim that work defines the person. We carry around in our heads a rough tally that tells us what kinds of jobs are worthy of respect and what kinds are to be disdained, a pyramid organized by the income a job carries, the sort of credentials it takes to secure a particular position, the qualities of an occupation's incumbents—and we use this system of stratification (ruthlessly at times) to boost the status of some and humiliate others. This penchant for ranking by occupation is more pervasive in the United States than in other societies, where there are different ways of evaluating the personal worth of individuals. In these societies, coming from a "good family" counts heavily in the calculus of social standing. Here in America, there is no other metric that matters as much as the kind of job you hold.

Given our tradition of equating moral value with employment, it stands to reason that the most profound dividing line in our culture is that separating the working person from the unemployed. Only after this canyon has been crossed do we begin to make the finer gradations that distinguish white-collar worker from blue-collar worker, CEO from secretary. We attribute a whole host of moral virtues—self-discipline, personal responsibility, maturity—to those who have found and kept a job, almost any job, and dismiss those who haven't as slothful or irresponsible.

We inhabit an unforgiving culture that is blind to the many reasons why some people cross that employment barrier and others are left behind. While we may remember, for a time, that unemployment rates are high, or that particular industries have downsized millions of workers right out of a job, or that racial barriers or negative attitudes toward teenagers make it harder to get a job at some times and for some people, in the end American culture wipes these background truths out in favor of a simpler dichotomy: the worthy and the unworthy, the working stiff and the lazy sloth. *(Newman 1999:86, 86–87)* ■

Additional information about this excerpt can be found on the Online Learning Center at **www.mhhe.com/schaefer9.**

I n this excerpt from her book *No Shame in My Game,* Katherine Newman, an anthropologist and professor of urban studies at Harvard University, examines the role of work in defining a person's status, especially in the United States. *No Shame in My Game* is based on Newman's research, a study of 200 fast-food workers in Harlem, New York. For a year and a half, using interviews, home and school visits, and on-site observation of the workplace, Newman tracked workers as they struggled to get a job and keep it, to balance work with school and family, to tolerate long hours and ill-mannered customers. In the course of her study, she described the workers' social hierarchy.

Newman's goal in researching fast-food work was to highlight a segment of the population often overlooked by social scientists and policymakers. The working poor—Black, White, Latino—are in fact a significant segment of the labor force, yet they are largely invisible to the better-off people who eat at the restaurants and visit the hotels where they work. Moreover, they are virtually nonexistent to the legislators who represent them. Still, as the title of Newman's book suggests, they take considerable pride in the fact that they do work. Socially, they have leapt the deep gulf that separates those who work from those who do not.

Ever since people first began to speculate about the nature of human society, their attention has been drawn to the differences between individuals and groups within a society. The term **social inequality** describes a condition in which members of a society have different amounts of wealth, prestige, or power. Some degree of social inequality characterizes every society.

When a system of social inequality is based on a hierarchy of groups, sociologists refer to it as **stratification:** a structured ranking of entire groups of people that perpetuates unequal economic rewards and power in a society. These unequal rewards are evident not only in the distribution of wealth and income, but even in the distressing mortality rates of impoverished communities. Stratification involves the ways in which one generation passes on social inequalities to the next, producing groups of people arranged in rank order from low to high.

Stratification is a crucial subject of sociological investigation because of its pervasive influence on human interactions and institutions. It inevitably results in social inequality, because certain groups of people stand higher in social rankings, control scarce resources, wield power, and receive special treatment. As we will see in this chapter, the consequences of stratification are evident in the unequal distribution of wealth and income within industrial societies. The term **income** refers to salaries and wages. In contrast, **wealth** is an inclusive term encompassing all a person's material assets, including land, stocks, and other types of property.

Is social inequality an inevitable part of society? How does government policy affect the life chances of the working poor? Is this country still a place where a hardworking person can move up the social ladder? This chapter focuses on the unequal distribution of socially valued rewards and its consequences. We will examine four general systems of stratification, paying particular attention to the theories of Karl Marx and Max Weber, as well as to functionalist and conflict theory. We will see how sociologists define social class and examine the consequences of stratification for people's wealth and income, health, and educational opportunities. And we will confront the question of social mobility, both upward and downward. Finally, in the social policy section, we will address welfare reform, an issue that is complicated by the attitudes that people, particularly those in the United States, hold toward those who do not work. ■

UNDERSTANDING STRATIFICATION

Systems of Stratification

Look at the four general systems of stratification examined here—slavery, castes, estates, and social classes—as ideal types useful for purposes of analysis. Any stratification system may include elements of more than one type. For example, prior to the Civil War, you could find in the southern states of the United States both social classes dividing Whites and the institutionalized enslavement of Blacks.

To understand these systems better, it may be helpful to review the distinction between *achieved status* and *ascribed status*, described in Chapter 5. **Ascribed status** is

| pp. 105–106 | a social position assigned to a person without regard for that person's unique talents or characteristics. In contrast, **achieved status** is a social position attained by a person largely through his or her own efforts. The two are closely linked. The nation's most affluent families generally inherit wealth and status, while many members of racial and ethnic minorities inherit disadvantaged status. Age and gender, as well, are ascribed statuses that influence a person's wealth and social position.

Slavery

The most extreme form of legalized social inequality for individuals or groups is **slavery.** What distinguishes this oppressive system of stratification is that enslaved individuals are *owned* by other people who treat these human beings as property, just as if they were household pets or appliances.

Slavery has varied in the way it has been practiced. In ancient Greece, the main source of slaves consisted of captives of war and piracy. Although succeeding generations could inherit slave status, it was not necessarily permanent. A person's status might change depending on which city-state happened to triumph in a military conflict. In effect, all citizens had the potential of becoming slaves or of being granted freedom, depending on the circumstances of history. In contrast, in the United States and Latin America, where slavery was an ascribed status, racial and legal barriers prevented the freeing of slaves.

Today, the Universal Declaration of Human Rights, which is binding on all members of the United Nations, prohibits slavery in all its forms. Yet around the world, millions of people still live as slaves. In many developing countries, bonded laborers are imprisoned in virtual lifetime employment; in some countries, human beings are owned outright. But slavery also exists in Europe and the United States, where guest workers and illegal immigrants have been forced to labor for years under terrible conditions, either to pay off debts or to avoid being turned over to immigration authorities (Bassiouni 2002).

Castes

Castes are hereditary ranks that are usually religiously dictated, and that tend to be fixed and immobile. The caste system is generally associated with Hinduism in India and other countries. In India there are four major castes, called *varnas*. A fifth category of outcastes, referred to as *untouchables* or the *dalit,* is considered to be so lowly and unclean as to have no place within this system of stratification. There are also many minor castes. Caste membership is an ascribed status (at birth, children automatically assume the same position as their parents). Each caste is quite sharply defined, and members are expected to marry within that caste.

Caste membership generally determines one's occupation or role as a religious functionary. An example of a lower caste in India is the *Dons,* whose main work is the undesirable job of cremating bodies. The caste system promotes a remarkable degree of differentiation. Thus, the single caste of chauffeurs has been split into two separate subcastes: drivers of luxury cars have a higher status than drivers of economy cars.

In recent decades, industrialization and urbanization have weakened India's rigid caste system. Box 9-1 examines the changes that are taking place in this ancient form of stratification.

Estates

A third type of stratification system, called *estates,* was associated with feudal societies during the Middle Ages. The **estate system,** or feudalism, required peasants to work land leased to them by nobles in exchange for military protection and other services. The basis for the system was the nobles' ownership of land, which was critical to their superior and privileged status. As in systems based on slavery and caste, inheritance of one's position

Jacob Lawrence's painting, *Harriet Tubman* Series No. 9, graphically illustrates the torment of slavery as once practiced in the United States. Slavery is the most extreme form of legalized social inequality.

Sociology in the Global Community

9-1 UNDER PRESSURE: THE CASTE SYSTEM IN INDIA

In 2001, the murder of a young Indian man in the small village of Kalvakol became the subject of international outrage. The man, an untouchable, or *dalit,* had been dragged into a field, tortured, and killed by upper-caste villagers. His crime: he had dared to speak his mind in a village where untouchables are not supposed to have opinions. Those arrested for the murder were defiant. Said one, "What do you expect us to do, hand over the whole village to those people?"

The murder was one sign of the tensions that have arisen from the weakening of the traditional Hindu caste system. India's constitution, adopted in 1950, formally abolished discrimination against untouchables, whose status as outcastes excluded them from temples, schools, and most forms of employment. Yet the caste system prevails today, because it is founded not in law but in religious custom. It is strongest in the rural villages, where almost 90 percent of untouchables still live. It is weakest in the fast-growing cities, where low-caste migrants from the country may blend into the crowd unrecognized in public schools, hospitals, and transportation facilities.

Historically, the caste system has not been immune to change. During the Mogul empire, many untouchables escaped their status as outcastes by converting to Islam. And when the British took over during the colonial period, impos-ing Western-style agriculture, industry, and bureaucracy on the country, they opened up new opportunities to caste-bound Indians. In the 20th century, government leaders tried to level the playing field for the lower castes, but with limited success. Government "reservations," a kind of quota system, set aside a certain percentage of government jobs and educational opportunities for the lower castes—a policy that has produced a sharp backlash among the upper castes. The need is greatest among the untouch-

> Urbanization and technological advances have brought more change to India's caste system than the government or politics has.

ables, confined to menial labor at jobs that are fast disappearing, yet barred from training for better employment. Today, these 150 million outcastes, who constitute about a quarter of India's population, have organized and are making their voices heard in electoral politics. In 1997, for the first time in India's history, the symbolic but high-status position of president went to an untouchable, K. R. Narayanan.

On the whole, urbanization and technological advances have brought more change to India's caste system than the government or politics has. Besides the anonymity of city life, which tends to blur caste boundaries, the globalization of high technology has opened up India's social order, bringing new opportunities to those who possess the skills and ability to capitalize on them. Srinivas Rao, a lower-caste Indian who started his own information technology company, is one example of the liberating effects of technological change. Though Rao still suffers in small ways because of his caste, his achievement is a remarkable sign of social change in a country where such upward mobility was unknown a generation ago.

Let's Discuss

1. If you were a government official in India, would you favor the "reservations" system that is aimed at reducing discrimination against people of lower castes? If not, what other solutions would you recommend?

2. Compare India's caste system, which is based on religious custom, to the form of slavery that was once practiced in the United States, which was based on racial differences. How would the experiences of a former slave and an untouchable differ?

Sources: Dugger 1999; Gose 2003; McGivering 2001; National Campaign on Dalit Human Rights 2003; Schmetzer 1999; Seabrook 2002.

---

largely defined the estate system. The nobles inherited their titles and property, whereas the peasants were born into a subservient position within an agrarian society.

As the estate system developed, it became more differentiated. Nobles began to achieve varying degrees of authority. By the 12th century, a priesthood had emerged in most of Europe, along with classes of merchants and artisans. For the first time, there were groups of people whose wealth did not depend on land ownership or agriculture. This economic change had profound social consequences as the estate system ended and a class system of stratification came into existence.

Social Classes

A *class system* is a social ranking based primarily on economic position in which achieved characteristics can influence social mobility. In contrast to slavery and caste systems, the boundaries between classes are imprecisely defined, and one can move from one stratum, or level, of society to another. Even so, class systems maintain stable

FIGURE 9-1

Household Income in the United States, 2001

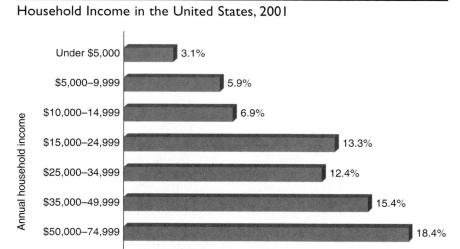

Source: DeNavas-Walt and Cleveland 2002:15.

stratification hierarchies and patterns of class divisions, and they, too, are marked by unequal distribution of wealth and power. Class standing, though it is achieved, is heavily dependent on family and ascribed factors, like race and ethnicity.

Income inequality is a basic characteristic of a class system. In 2001, the median household income in the United States was $42,228. In other words, half of all households had higher incomes in that year and half had lower incomes. Yet this fact may not fully convey the income disparities in our society. As Figure 9-1 shows, there is a broad range around the median household income. Furthermore, considerable numbers of people fall at the extremes. In 1999, about 205,000 tax returns reported incomes in excess of $1 million. At the same time, about 27 million households reported incomes under $10,000 (DeNavas-Walt and Cleveland 2002:1; Internal Revenue Service 2001).

Sociologist Daniel Rossides (1997) uses a five-class model to describe the class system of the United States: the upper class, the upper-middle class, the lower-middle class, the working class, and the lower class. Although the lines separating social classes in his model are not so sharp as the divisions between castes, members of the five classes differ significantly in ways other than just income level.

Rossides categorizes about 1 to 2 percent of the people of the United States as *upper class,* a group limited to the very wealthy. These people associate in exclusive clubs and social circles. In contrast, the *lower class,* consisting of approximately 20 to 25 percent of the population, disproportionately consists of Blacks, Hispanics, single mothers with dependent children, and people who cannot find regular work or must make do with low-paying work. This class lacks both wealth and income and is too weak politically to exercise significant power.

Both these classes, at opposite ends of the nation's social hierarchy, reflect the importance of ascribed status and achieved status. Ascribed statuses such as race clearly influence a person's wealth and social position. Sociologist Richard Jenkins (1991) has researched how the ascribed status of being disabled marginalizes a person in the labor market of the United States. People with disabilities are particularly vulnerable to unemployment, are often poorly paid, and in many cases are on the lower rung of occupational ladders. Regardless of their actual performance on the job, the disabled are stigmatized as not earning their keep. Such are the effects of ascribed status.

Sandwiched between the upper and lower classes in Rossides's model are the upper-middle class, the lower-middle class, and the working class. The *upper-middle class,* numbering about 10 to 15 percent of the population, is composed of professionals such as doctors, lawyers, and architects. They participate extensively in politics and take leadership roles in voluntary associations. The *lower-middle class,* which accounts for approximately 30 to 35 percent of the population, includes less affluent professionals (such as elementary school teachers and nurses), owners of small businesses, and a sizable number of clerical workers. While not all members of this varied class hold degrees from a college, they share the goal of sending their children there.

Rossides describes the *working class*—about 40 to 45 percent of the population—as people holding regular manual or blue-collar jobs. Certain members of this class, such as electricians, may have higher incomes than people in the lower-middle class. Yet even if they have achieved some degree of economic security, they tend to identify with manual workers and their long history of involvement in the labor movement of the United States. Of Rossides's five classes, the working class is declining noticeably in size. In the economy of the United States, service and technical jobs are replacing those involved in the actual manufacturing or transportation of goods.

Social class is one of the independent or explanatory variables most frequently used by social scientists to shed light on social issues. In later chapters, we will analyze the relationships between social class and divorce patterns (Chapter 14), religious behavior (Chapter 15), and formal schooling (Chapter 16), as well as other relationships in which social class is a variable.

Perspectives on Stratification

Sociologists have hotly debated stratification and social inequality and have reached varying conclusions. No theorist stressed the significance of class for society—and for social change—more strongly than Karl Marx. Marx viewed class differentiation as the crucial determinant of social, economic, and political inequality. In contrast, Max Weber questioned Marx's emphasis on the overriding importance of the economic sector, and argued that stratification should be viewed as having many dimensions.

Karl Marx's View of Class Differentiation

Sociologist Leonard Beeghley (1978:1) aptly noted that "Karl Marx was both a revolutionary and a social scientist." Marx was concerned with stratification in all types of human societies, beginning with primitive agricultural tribes and continuing into feudalism. But his main focus was on the effects of economic inequality on all aspects of 19th-century Europe. The plight of the working class made him feel that it was imperative to strive for changes in the class structure of society.

In Marx's view, social relations during any period of history depend on who controls the primary mode of economic production, such as land or factories. Differential access to scarce resources shapes the relationship between groups. Thus, under the feudal estate system, most production was agricultural, and the land was owned by the nobility. Peasants had little choice but to work according to terms dictated by those who owned the land.

Using this type of analysis, Marx examined social relations within **capitalism**—an economic system in which the means of production are held largely in private hands and the main incentive for economic activity is the accumulation of profits (D. H. Rosenberg 1991). Marx focused on the two classes that began to emerge as the feudal estate system declined, the bourgeoisie and the

proletariat. The **bourgeoisie,** or capitalist class, owns the means of production, such as factories and machinery, whereas the **proletariat** is the working class. In capitalist societies, the members of the bourgeoisie maximize profit in competition with other firms. In the process, they exploit workers, who must exchange their labor for subsistence wages. In Marx's view, members of each class share a distinctive culture. Marx was most interested in the culture of the proletariat, but he also examined the ideology of the bourgeoisie, through which it justifies its dominance over workers.

According to Marx, exploitation of the proletariat will inevitably lead to the destruction of the capitalist system, because the workers will revolt. But first, the working class must develop **class consciousness**—a subjective awareness of common vested interests and the need for collective political action to bring about social change. Workers must often overcome what Marx termed **false consciousness,** or an attitude held by members of a class that does not accurately reflect their objective position. A worker with false consciousness may adopt an individualistic viewpoint toward capitalist exploitation ("*I* am being exploited by *my* boss"). In contrast, the class-conscious worker realizes that all work-

Karl Marx would identify these coal miners as members of the *proletariat,* or working class. For generations, miners were forced to spend their meager wages at "company stores," whose high prices kept them perpetually in debt. The exploitation of the working class is a core principle of Marxist theory.

FIGURE 9-2

Around the World: What's a CEO Worth?

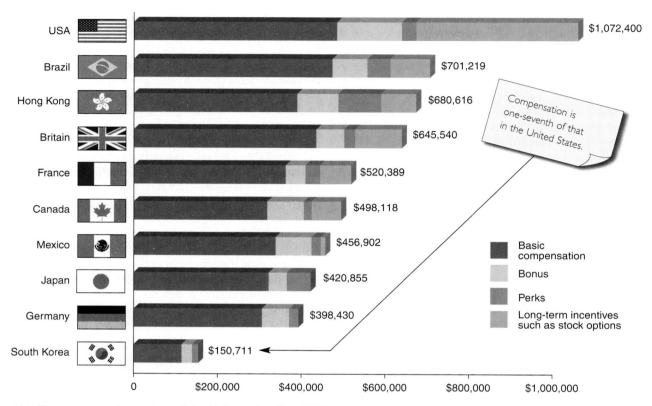

Note: The average annual pay package of the chief executive officer (CEO) of an industrial company with annual revenues of $250 million to $500 million in 10 countries. Figures are from April 1998 and are not weighted to compensate for different costs of living or levels of taxation.

Source: Towers Perrin in A. Bryant 1999:Section 4, p. 1.

> **Think About It**
> Why should CEOs in the United States be worth more than those in other countries?

ers are being exploited by the bourgeoisie, and have a common stake in revolution.

For Karl Marx, class consciousness is part of a collective process in which the proletariat comes to identify the bourgeoisie as the source of its oppression. Revolutionary leaders will guide the working class in its struggle. Ultimately, the proletariat will overthrow the rule of both the bourgeoisie and the government (which Marx saw as representing the interests of capitalists) and will eliminate private ownership of the means of production. In Marx's rather utopian view, classes and oppression will cease to exist in the postrevolutionary workers' state.

How accurate were Marx's predictions? He failed to anticipate the emergence of labor unions, whose power in collective bargaining weakens the stranglehold that capitalists maintain over workers. Moreover, as contemporary conflict theorists note, he did not foresee the extent to which political liberties and relative prosperity could contribute to false consciousness. Many workers have come to view themselves as individuals striving for improvement within free societies that offer substantial mobility, rather than as downtrodden members of a social class who face a collective fate. Finally, Marx did not predict that Communist Party rule would be established and later overthrown in the former Soviet Union and throughout Eastern Europe. Still, the Marxist approach to the study of class is useful in stressing the importance of stratification as a determinant of social behavior and the fundamental separation in many societies between two distinct groups, the rich and the poor.

Max Weber's View of Stratification

Unlike Karl Marx, Max Weber insisted that no single characteristic (such as class) totally defines a person's position within the stratification system. Instead, writing in 1916, he identified three distinct components of stratification: class, status, and power (Gerth and Mills 1958).

Weber used the term **class** to refer to a group of people who have a similar level of wealth and income. For example, certain workers in the United States try to support their families through minimum-wage jobs. According to Weber's definition, these wage earners constitute a class because they share the same economic position and fate. Although Weber agreed with Marx on the importance of this economic dimension of stratification, he argued that the actions of individuals and groups could not be understood *solely* in economic terms.

Weber used the term **status group** to refer to people who have the same prestige or lifestyle. An individual gains status through membership in a desirable group, such as the medical profession. But status is not the same as economic class standing. In our culture, a successful pickpocket may be in the same income class as a college professor. Yet the thief is widely regarded as a member of a low-status group, whereas the professor holds high status.

For Weber, the third major component of stratification has a political dimension. **Power** is the ability to exercise one's will over others. In the United States, power stems from membership in particularly influential groups, such as corporate boards of directors, government bodies, and interest groups. Conflict theorists generally agree that two major sources of power—big business and government—are closely interrelated (see Chapters 17 and 18). For instance, many of the heads of major corporations also hold powerful positions in the government or military.

The corporate executives who head private companies in the United States earn the highest incomes in the nation. They represent the pinnacle not just of U.S. society, but of corporate executives around the world. Figure 9-2 shows how much better heads of U.S. corporations are compensated than chief executive officers (CEOs) in other industrial countries. The compensation these CEOs receive is not necessarily linked to conventional measures of success, however. As the U.S. economy worsened in 2002, an analysis showed that the CEOs who received the highest compensation were generally those who authorized the largest layoffs (Klinger et al. 2002).

To summarize, in Weber's view, each of us has not one rank in society but three. Our position in a stratification system reflects some combination of class, status, and power. Each factor influences the other two, and in fact the rankings on these three dimensions often tend to coincide. John F. Kennedy came from an extremely wealthy family, attended exclusive preparatory schools, graduated from Harvard University, and went on to become president of the United States. Like Kennedy, many people from affluent backgrounds achieve impressive status and power.

At the same time, these dimensions of stratification may operate somewhat independently in determining a person's position. Harry S. Truman owned a clothing store in Kansas City, Missouri, but he used a political power base to work his way up to the presidency of the United States in 1945. A widely published poet may achieve high status while earning a relatively modest income. Successful professional athletes have little power but enjoy a relatively high position in terms of class and status. To understand the workings of a culture more fully, sociologists must carefully evaluate the ways in which it distributes its most valued rewards, including wealth and income, status, and power (Duberman 1976; Gerth and Mills 1958).

Interactionist View

Both Karl Marx and Max Weber looked at inequality primarily from a macrosociological perspective, considering the entire society or even the global economy. Marx did suggest the importance of a more microsociological analysis, however, when he stressed the ways in which individuals develop a true class consciousness.

Interactionists, as well as economists, have long been interested in the importance of social class in shaping a person's lifestyle. The theorist Thorstein Veblen (1857–1929) noted that those at the top of the social hierarchy typically convert part of their wealth into *conspicuous consumption*, purchasing more automobiles than they can reasonably use and building houses with more rooms than they can possibly occupy. Or they may engage in *conspicuous leisure*, jetting to a remote destination and staying just long enough to have dinner or view a sunset over some historic locale (Veblen [1899] 1964).

At the other end of the spectrum, behavior that is judged to be typical of the lower class is subject not only to ridicule but even to legal action. Communities have, from time to time, banned trailers from people's front yards and sofas from their front porches. In some communities, it is illegal to leave a pickup truck in front of the house overnight.

Use Your Sociological Imagination   www.mhhe.com/schaefer9

Refer to the photo essay on pages 4–5. How do you think Thorstein Veblen would answer the question posed in the title? What do you think he would say about the three families pictured in the essay?

Is Stratification Universal?

Must some members of society receive greater rewards than others? Do people need to feel socially and economically

This couple's expensive lifestyle illustrates Thorstein Veblen's concept of conspicuous consumption, a spending pattern common to those at the very top of the social ladder.

superior to others? Can social life be organized without structured inequality? These questions have been debated for centuries, especially among political activists. Utopian socialists, religious minorities, and members of recent countercultures have all attempted to establish communities that to some extent or other would abolish inequality in social relationships.

Social scientists have found that inequality exists in all societies—even the simplest. For example, when anthropologist Gunnar Landtman ([1938] 1968) studied the Kiwai Papuans of New Guinea, he initially noticed little differentiation among them. Every man in the village did the same work and lived in similar housing. However, on closer inspection, Landtman observed that certain Papuans—men who were warriors, harpooners, and sorcerers—were described as "a little more high" than others. In contrast, villagers who were female, unemployed, or unmarried were considered "down a little bit" and were barred from owning land.

Stratification is universal in that all societies maintain some form of social inequality among members. De-

pending on its values, a society may assign people to distinctive ranks based on their religious knowledge, skill in hunting, beauty, trading expertise, or ability to provide health care. But why has such inequality developed in human societies? And how much differentiation among people, if any, is actually essential?

Functionalist and conflict sociologists offer contrasting explanations for the existence and necessity of social stratification. Functionalists maintain that a differential system of rewards and punishments is necessary for the efficient operation of society. Conflict theorists argue that competition for scarce resources results in significant political, economic, and social inequality.

Functionalist View

Would people go to school for many years to become physicians if they could make as much money and gain as much respect working as street cleaners? Functionalists say no, which is partly why they believe that a stratified society is universal.

In the view of Kingsley Davis and Wilbert Moore (1945), society must distribute its members among a variety of social positions. It must not only make sure that these positions are filled but also see that they are staffed by people with the appropriate talents and abilities. Rewards, including money and prestige, are based on the importance of a position and the relative scarcity of qualified personnel. Yet this assessment often devalues work performed by certain segments of society, such as women's work as homemakers or in occupations traditionally filled by women, or low-status work in fast-food outlets.

Davis and Moore argue that stratification is universal and that social inequality is necessary so that people will be motivated to fill functionally important positions. But critics say that unequal rewards are not the only means of encouraging people to fill critical positions and occupations. Personal pleasure, intrinsic satisfaction, and value orientations also motivate people to enter particular careers. Functionalists agree but note that society must use some type of reward to motivate people to enter unpleasant or dangerous jobs and professions that require a long training period. This response does not justify stratification systems in which status is largely inherited, such as slave or caste societies. Similarly, it is difficult to explain the high salaries our society offers to professional athletes or entertainers on the basis of how critical those jobs are to the survival of society (R. Collins 1975; Kerbo 2003; Tumin 1953, 1985).

Even if stratification is inevitable, the functionalist explanation for differential rewards does not explain the wide disparity between the rich and the poor. Critics of the functionalist approach point out that the richest 10 percent of households account for 20 percent of the nation's income in Sweden, 25 percent in France, and 31 percent in the United States. In their view, the level of income inequality found in contemporary industrial societies cannot be defended—even though those societies have a legitimate need to fill certain key occupations (World Bank 2002a:74–76).

Conflict View

The writings of Karl Marx lie at the heart of conflict theory. Marx viewed history as a continuous struggle between the oppressors and the oppressed, which would ultimately culminate in an egalitarian, classless society. In terms of stratification, he argued that under capitalism, the dominant class — the bourgeoisie—manipulates the economic and political systems in order to maintain control over the exploited proletariat. Marx did not believe that stratification was inevitable, but he did see inequality and oppression as inherent in capitalism (Wright et al. 1982).

pp. 11–12

Like Marx, contemporary conflict theorists believe that human beings are prone to conflict over scarce resources such as wealth, status, and power. However, Marx focused primarily on class conflict; more recent theorists have extended the analysis to include conflicts based on gender, race, age, and other dimensions. British sociologist Ralf Dahrendorf is one of the most influential contributors to the conflict approach.

Dahrendorf (1959) has modified Marx's analysis of capitalist society to apply to *modern* capitalist societies. For Dahrendorf, social classes are groups of people who share common interests resulting from their authority relationships. In identifying the most powerful groups in society, he includes not only the bourgeoisie—the owners of the means of production—but also the managers of industry, legislators, the judiciary, heads of the government bureaucracy, and others. In that respect, Dahrendorf has merged Marx's emphasis on class conflict with Weber's recognition that power is an important element of stratification (Cuff et al. 1990).

Conflict theorists, including Dahrendorf, contend that the powerful of today, like the bourgeoisie of Marx's time, want society to run smoothly so that they can enjoy their privileged positions. Because the status quo suits those with wealth, status, and power, they have a clear interest in preventing, minimizing, or controlling societal conflict.

One way for the powerful to maintain the status quo is to define and disseminate the society's dominant ideology. p. 69 The term **dominant ideology** describes a set of cultural beliefs and practices that helps to maintain powerful social, economic, and political interests. For Karl Marx, the dominant ideology in a capitalist society serves the interests of the ruling class. From a conflict perspective, the social significance of the dominant ideology is that not only do a society's most powerful groups and institutions control wealth and property; even more important, they control the means of producing beliefs about reality through religion, education, and the media (Abercrombie et al. 1980, 1990; Robertson 1988).

The powerful, such as leaders of government, also use limited social reforms to buy off the oppressed and reduce the danger of challenges to their dominance. For example, minimum wage laws and unemployment compensation unquestionably give some valuable assistance to needy men and women. Yet these reforms also serve to pacify those who might otherwise rebel. Of course, in the view of conflict theorists, such maneuvers can never entirely eliminate conflict, since workers will continue to demand equality, and the powerful will not give up their control of society.

As popular songs and movies suggest, long-haul truck drivers take pride in their low-prestige job. According to the conflict perspective, the cultural beliefs that form a society's dominant ideology, such as the popular image of the truck driver as hero, help the wealthy to maintain their power and control at the expense of the lower classes.

Table 9-1	Major Perspectives on Social Stratification		
	Functionalist	**Conflict**	**Interactionist**
Purpose of social stratification	Facilitates filling of social positions	Facilitates exploitation	Influences people's lifestyles
Attitude toward social inequality	Necessary to some extent	Excessive and growing	————
Analysis of the wealthy	Talented and skilled, creating opportunities for others	Use the dominant ideology to further their own interests	Exhibit conspicuous consumption and conspicuous leisure

Conflict theorists see stratification as a major source of societal tension and conflict. They do not agree with Davis and Moore that stratification is functional for a society or that it serves as a source of stability. Rather, conflict sociologists argue that stratification will inevitably lead to instability and to social change (R. Collins 1975; L. Coser 1977).

Table 9-1 summarizes and compares the three major perspectives on social stratification.

Lenski's Viewpoint

Let's return to the question posed earlier—Is stratification universal?—and consider the sociological response. Some form of differentiation is found in every culture, from the most primitive to the most advanced industrial societies of our time. Sociologist Gerhard Lenski, in his sociocultural evolution approach, described how economic systems change as their level of technology becomes more complex, beginning with hunting and gathering and culminating eventually with industrial society. In subsistence-based hunting-and-gathering societies, people focus on survival. While pp. 116–118 some inequality and differentiation are evident, a stratification system based on social class does not emerge because there is no real wealth to be claimed.

As a society advances in technology, it becomes capable of producing a considerable surplus of goods. The emergence of surplus resources greatly expands the possibilities for inequality in status, influence, and power and allows a well-defined, rigid social class system to develop. To minimize strikes, slowdowns, and industrial sabotage, the elites may share a portion of the economic surplus with the lower classes, but not enough to reduce their own power and privilege.

As Lenski argued, the allocation of surplus goods and services controlled by those with wealth, status, and power reinforces the social inequality that accompanies stratification systems. While this reward system may once have served the overall purposes of society, as functionalists contend, the same cannot be said for the large disparities separating the haves from the have-nots in current societies. In contemporary industrial society, the degree of social and economic inequality far exceeds what is needed to provide for goods and services (Lenski 1966; Nolan and Lenski 1999).

STRATIFICATION BY SOCIAL CLASS

Measuring Social Class

We continually assess how wealthy people are by looking at the cars they drive, the houses they live in, the clothes they wear, and so on. Yet it is not so easy to locate an individual within our social hierarchies as it would be in slavery or caste systems of stratification. To determine someone's class position, sociologists generally rely on the objective method.

Objective Method

In the **objective method** of measuring social class, class is viewed largely as a statistical category. Researchers assign individuals to social classes on the basis of criteria such as occupation, education, income, and place of residence. The key to the objective method is that the *researcher*, rather than the person being classified, identifies an individual's class position.

The first step in using this method is to decide what indicators or causal factors will be measured objectively, whether wealth, income, education, or occupation. The prestige ranking of occupations has proved to be a useful indicator of a person's class position. For one thing, it is much easier to determine accurately than income or wealth. The term **prestige** refers to the respect and admiration that an occupation holds in a society. "My daughter, the physicist" connotes something very different from "my daughter, the waitress." Prestige is independent of the particular individual who occupies a job, a characteristic that distinguishes it from esteem. **Esteem** refers to the reputation that a specific person has earned within an occupation. Therefore, one can say that the position of president of the United States has high prestige, even though it has been occupied by people with varying degrees of esteem. A hairdresser may have the esteem of his clients, but he lacks the prestige of a corporate executive.

Table 9-2 ranks the prestige of a number of well-known occupations. In a series of national surveys, sociologists assigned prestige rankings to about 500 occupations, ranging from physician to newspaper vendor. The highest possible prestige score was 100; the lowest was 0. Physician, lawyer, dentist, and college professor were the most highly regarded occupations. Sociologists have used such data to assign prestige rankings to virtually all jobs and have found a stability in rankings from 1925 to the present. Similar studies in other countries have also developed useful prestige rankings of occupations (Hodge and Rossi 1964; Lin and Xie 1988; Treiman 1977).

Table 9-2	**Prestige Rankings of Occupations**		
Occupation	**Score**	**Occupation**	**Score**
Physician	86	Secretary	46
Lawyer	75	Insurance agent	45
Dentist	74	Bank teller	43
College professor	74	Nurse's aide	42
Architect	73	Farmer	40
Clergy	69	Correctional officer	40
Pharmacist	68	Receptionist	39
Registered nurse	66	Barber	36
High school teacher	66	Child care worker	35
Accountant	65	Hotel clerk	32
Airline pilot	60	Bus driver	32
Police officer and detective	60	Truck driver	30
Prekindergarten teacher	55	Salesworker (shoes)	28
Librarian	54	Garbage collector	28
Firefighter	53	Waiter and waitress	28
Social worker	52	Bartender	25
Electrician	51	Farm worker	23
Funeral director	49	Janitor	22
Mail carrier	47	Newspaper vendor	19

Note: 100 is the highest and 0 the lowest possible prestige score.

Source: J. Davis et al. 2003.

Gender and Occupational Prestige

For many years, studies of social class tended to neglect the occupations and incomes of *women* as determinants of social rank. In an exhaustive study of 589 occupations, sociologists Mary Powers and Joan Holmberg (1978) examined the impact of women's participation in the paid labor force on occupational status. Since women tend to dominate the relatively low-paying occupations, such as bookkeeper and child care worker, their participation in the workforce has led to a general upgrading of the status of most male-dominated occupations. More recent research conducted in both the United States and Europe has noted the occupations of husbands *and* wives in determining the class positions of families (Sørensen 1994). With more than half of all married women now working

outside the home (see Chapter 12), this approach seems long overdue, but it raises some questions. For example, how is class or status to be judged in dual-career families—by the occupation regarded as having greater prestige, the average, or some other combination of the two?

Sociologists—in particular, feminist sociologists in Great Britain—are drawing on new approaches to assess women's social class standing. One approach is to focus on the individual (rather than the family or household) as the basis for categorizing a woman's class position. Thus, a woman would be classified based on her own occupational status rather than that of her spouse (O'Donnell 1992).

Another feminist effort to measure the contribution of women to the economy reflects a more clearly political agenda. International Women Count Network, a global

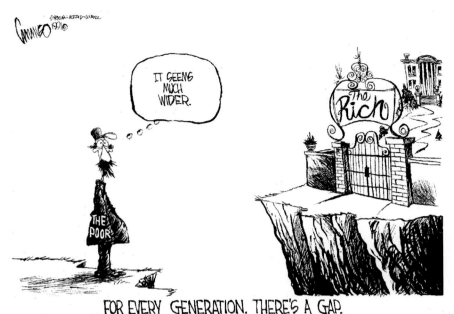

FOR EVERY GENERATION, THERE'S A GAP.

grassroots feminist organization, has sought to give a monetary value to women's unpaid work. Besides providing symbolic recognition of women's role in labor, this value would also be used to calculate pension and other benefits that are based on wages received. The United Nations has placed an $11 trillion price tag on unpaid labor by women, largely in child care, housework, and agriculture. Whatever the figure, the continued undercounting of many workers' contributions to a family and to an entire economy means that virtually all measures of stratification are in need of reform (United Nations Development Programme 1995; Wages for Housework Campaign 1999).

Multiple Measures

Another complication in measuring social class is that advances in statistical methods and computer technology have multiplied the factors used to define class under the objective method. No longer are sociologists limited to annual income and education in evaluating a person's class position. Today, studies use as criteria the value of homes, sources of income, assets, years in present occupations, neighborhoods, and considerations regarding dual careers. Adding these variables will not necessarily paint a different picture of class differentiation in the United States, but it does allow sociologists to measure class in a more complex and multidimensional way.

Whatever the technique used to measure class, the sociologist is interested in real and often dramatic differences in power, privilege, and opportunity in a society. The study of stratification is a study of inequality. Nowhere is this more evident than in the distribution of wealth and income.

Wealth and Income

By all measures, income in the United States is distributed unevenly. Nobel Prize–winning economist Paul Samuelson has described the situation in the following words: "If we made an income pyramid out of building blocks, with each layer portraying $500 of income, the peak would be far higher than Mount Everest, but most people would be within a few feet of the ground" (P. Samuelson and Nordhaus 2001:386).

Recent data support Samuelson's analogy. As Figure 9-3 shows, in 2001, members of the richest fifth (or top 20 percent) of the nation's population earned $150,499 or more, accounting for 50 percent of the nation's total income. In contrast, members of the bottom fifth of the nation's population earned just $17,970 or less, accounting for only 3 percent of the nation's total income.

There has been modest redistribution of income in the United States over the past 70 years. From 1929 through 1970, the government's economic and tax policies shifted income slightly toward the poor. However, in the last three decades—especially during the 1980s—federal tax policies have favored the affluent. The Federal Reserve reported in 2003 that while a rising economic tide lifted the boats of almost all families in the late 1990s, it also sharply increased the gap in wealth between the rich and the rest of society (Aizcorbe et al. 2003).

Survey data show that only 38 percent of people in the United States believe that government should take steps to reduce the income disparity between the rich and the poor. In contrast, 80 percent of people in Italy, 66 percent in Germany, and 65 percent in Great Britain support governmental efforts to reduce income inequality. It is not surprising, then, that many European countries provide more extensive safety nets to assist and protect the disadvantaged. In contrast, the strong cultural value placed on individualism in the United States leads to greater possibilities for both economic success and failure (Lipset 1996).

Wealth in the United States is much more unevenly distributed than income. As Figure 9-3 shows, in 1997, the richest fifth of the population held 85 percent of the nation's wealth. Government data indicate that more than 1 out of every 100 households had assets over $2.4 million, while one-fifth of all households were in debt

FIGURE 9-3

Comparison of Distribution of Income and Wealth in the United States

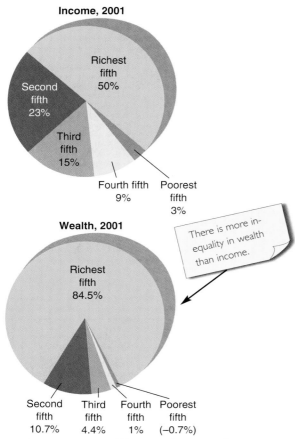

Income, 2001

Richest fifth 50%

Second fifth 23%

Third fifth 15%

Fourth fifth 9%

Poorest fifth 3%

Wealth, 2001

Richest fifth 84.5%

Second fifth 10.7%

Third fifth 4.4%

Fourth fifth 1%

Poorest fifth (–0.7%)

There is more inequality in wealth than income.

Note: Data do not add to 100 percent due to rounding.

Source: Income data (household) are from Bureau of the Census (DeNavas-Walt and Cleveland 2002:19). Data on wealth are from Wolff 1999.

and therefore had a negative net worth. Researchers have also found a dramatic disparity in wealth between African Americans and Whites. This disparity is evident even when educational backgrounds are held constant: the households of college-educated Whites have about three times as much wealth as the households of college-educated Blacks (Oliver and Shapiro 1995; Wolff 2002).

Poverty

Approximately one out of every nine people in this country lives below the poverty line established by the federal government. In 2001, 32.9 million people were living in poverty. The economic boom of the 1990s passed these people by. A recent Bureau of the Census report showed that one in five households has trouble meeting basic

needs—everything from paying the utility bills to buying dinner. In this section, we'll consider just how we define *poverty* and who is included in that category (Bauman 1999; Proctor and Dalaker 2002).

Studying Poverty

The efforts of sociologists and other social scientists to better understand poverty are complicated by the difficulty of defining it. This problem is evident even in government programs that conceive of poverty in either absolute or relative terms. **Absolute poverty** refers to a minimum level of subsistence that no family should be expected to live below. Policies concerning minimum wages, housing standards, or school lunch programs for the poor imply a need to bring citizens up to some predetermined level of existence. For example, in 1997, the federal minimum wage rate was raised to $5.15 an hour. Even so, when one takes inflation into account, this standard is currently *lower* than the wage workers were guaranteed in the 1950s. Today, more than a million workers over the age of 25 are employed at or below the minimum wage (Bureau of the Census 2002a:405).

One commonly used measure of absolute poverty is the federal government's *poverty line,* a money income figure adjusted annually to reflect the consumption requirements of families based on their size and composition. The poverty line serves as an official definition of which people are poor. In 2001, for example, any family of four (two adults and two children) with a combined income of $18,104 or less fell below the poverty line. This definition determines which individuals and families will be eligible for certain government benefits (Proctor and Dalaker 2002:5).

Although by absolute standards, poverty has declined in the United States, it remains higher than in many other industrial nations. As Figure 9-4 (page 212) shows, a comparatively high proportion of U.S. households are poor, meaning that they are unable to purchase basic consumer goods. If anything, this cross-national comparison understates the extent of poverty in the United States, since U.S. residents are likely to pay more for housing, health care, child care, and education than residents of other countries, where such expenses are often subsidized.

In contrast, **relative poverty** is a floating standard of deprivation by which people at the bottom of a society, whatever their lifestyles, are judged to be disadvantaged *in comparison with the nation as a whole.* Therefore, even if the poor of the 1990s are better off in absolute terms than the poor of the 1930s or 1960s, they are still seen as deserving special assistance.

In the 1990s, there was growing debate over the validity of the poverty line as a measure of poverty and a standard for allocating government benefits. Some critics

FIGURE 9-4

Absolute Poverty in Selected Industrial Countries

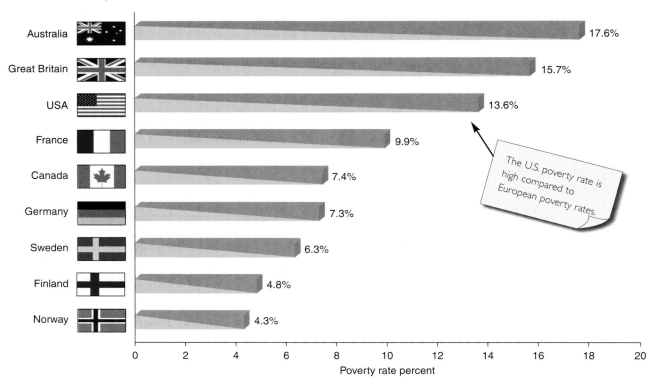

Source: Smeeding et al. 2001:51.

charge that the poverty line is too low; they note that the federal government continues to use 20-year-old nutritional standards in assessing people's level of poverty. If the poverty line is too low, then government data will underestimate the extent of poverty in the United States, and many deserving poor citizens will fail to receive benefits.

Other observers dispute this view. They argue that the poverty line may actually overestimate the number of low-income people because it fails to consider noncash benefits (such as Medicare, Medicaid, food stamps, public housing, and health care and other fringe benefits provided by some employers). In response, the Bureau of the Census has considered several different definitions of poverty; they showed at most a 1.4 percent lower rate. That is, if the official poverty threshold places 13 percent of the population in the category of the poor, the poverty estimate including *all* these noncash benefits would account for about 11.6 percent of the population (Brady 2003; Short et al. 1999).

Who Are the Poor?

Not only does the category of the poor defy any simple definition; it counters the common stereotypes about

"poor people" that Barbara Ehrenreich addressed in her

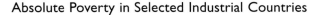 book *Nickel and Dimed* (see the opening excerpt in Chapter 1). For example, many people in the United States believe that the vast majority of the poor are able to work but will not. Yet many poor adults do work outside the home, although only a small portion of them work full-time throughout the year. In 2001, about 11 percent of all poor adults worked full-time, compared to 46 percent of all adults. Of those poor adults who do not work, most are ill or disabled, or are occupied in maintaining a home (Proctor and Dalaker 2002:8).

A sizable number of the poor live in urban slums, but a majority live outside those poverty-stricken areas. Poverty is no stranger in rural areas, from Appalachia to hard-hit farming regions to Native American reservations. Table 9-3 provides additional statistical information regarding these low-income people in the United States.

Since World War II, an increasing proportion of the poor people of the United States have been women, many of whom are divorced or never-married mothers. In 1959, female householders accounted for 26 percent of the nation's poor; by 2001, that figure had risen to 51 percent (see Table 9-3). This alarming trend, known as the *feminization of poverty,* is evident not just in the United States but around the world.

About half of all women living in poverty in the United States are in transition, coping with an economic crisis caused by the departure, disability, or death of a husband. The other half tend to be economically dependent either on the welfare system or on friends and relatives living nearby. A major factor in the feminization of poverty has been the increase in families with women as single heads of the household (see Chapter 14). In 2001, 11.7 percent of all people in the United States lived in poverty, compared to 26.4 percent of households headed by single mothers. Conflict theorists and other observers trace the higher rates of poverty among women to three distinct factors: the difficulty in finding affordable child care, sexual harassment, and sex discrimination in the labor market (Proctor and Dalaker 2002).

pp. 97–98

In 2001, 41 percent of poor people in the United States were living in central cities. These highly visible urban residents are the focus of most governmental efforts to alleviate poverty. Yet according to many observers, the plight of the urban poor is growing worse, owing to the devastating interplay of inadequate education and limited employment prospects. Traditional employment opportunities in the industrial sector are largely closed to the unskilled poor. Past and present discrimination heightens these problems for those low-income urban residents who are Black and Hispanic (Proctor and Dalaker 2002:2–3).

Sociologist William Julius Wilson (1980, 1987, 1989, 1996) and other social scientists have used the term **underclass** to describe the long-term poor who lack training and skills. According to an analysis of Census 2000 data, 7.9 million people live in high-poverty neighborhoods. About 30 percent of the population in these neighborhoods is Black; 29 percent, Hispanic; and 24 percent, White (Jargowsky 2003:4–5). In central cities, about 49 percent of the underclass are African American, 29 percent Hispanic, 17 percent White, and 5 percent "other" (O'Hare and Curry-White 1992).

Conflict theorists, among others, have expressed alarm at the portion of the nation's population living on this lower rung of the stratification ladder and at society's reluctance to address the lack of economic opportunities for these people. Often, portraits of the underclass seem to blame the victims for their own plight, while ignoring other factors that push people into poverty. Box 9-2 (page 214) considers Wilson's latest research into the persistence of urban poverty.

Analyses of the poor in general reveal that they are not a static social class. The overall composition of the poor changes continually, because some individuals and families near the top edge of poverty move above the poverty level after a year or two, while others slip below it. Still, hundreds of thousands of people remain in poverty for many years at a time. African Americans are more likely than Whites to be persistently poor. Over a 20-year period, African Americans were twice as likely as Whites to experience long spells of poverty. Two studies in 1998 documented the fact that Hispanics also suffer chronic or long-term periods of poverty. Both Hispanics and Blacks are less likely than Whites to leave the welfare rolls as a result of

Table 9-3	Who Are the Poor in the United States?	
Group	**Percentage of the Population of the United States**	**Percentage of the Poor of the United States**
Under 18 years old	26%	37%
18 to 64 years old	61	53
65 years and older	13	10
Whites (non-Hispanic)	83	46
Blacks	12	25
Hispanics	11	24
Asians and Pacific Islanders	4	4
Married couples and families with male householders	82	49
Families with female householders	18	51

Note: Data are for 2001, as reported by the Bureau of the Census in 2002.
Source: Proctor and Dalaker 2002:2.

Research in Action
9-2 WHEN JOBS DISAPPEAR

Woodlawn, an urban neighborhood on Chicago's South Side, used to boast more than 800 commercial and industrial establishments. Today, some 50 years later, there are only about 100 left: mostly barber shops, thrift stores, and small catering businesses. One Woodlawn resident described the changes on returning after many years: "I was just really appalled. . . . Those resources are just gone, completely. . . . And . . . everybody has moved, there are vacant lots everywhere" (W. J. Wilson 1996:5). Another South Side resident noted, "Jobs were plentiful in the past. You could walk out of the house and get a job. . . . Now, you can't find anything" (p. 36).

More than 35 years have passed since President Lyndon Johnson launched a series of federal programs known as the "war on poverty," yet poverty is still with us. Using surveys, interviews, and census data from 1987 to the present, sociologist and past president of the American Sociology Association William Julius Wilson has undertaken a major study of poverty, the Urban Poverty and Family Life Study (UPFLS). Increasingly, Wilson and his colleagues have noted, the jobless dominate low-income Chicago neighborhoods, some of which have poverty rates of at least 20 percent. The absence of full-time workers is especially noticeable in African American neighborhoods, which

have become increasingly marginal to the city's economic, social, and cultural life. Wilson sees this trend as a movement away from what historian Allan Spear (1967) termed the institutional ghetto, where viable social institutions served the minority community, toward a new *jobless ghetto*.

What drives the trend toward increasing poverty in urban areas? According to Wilson, it is primarily the exodus of well-paid jobs, especially in the manufacturing sector. Over the last several decades, U.S. manufacturers have relied more and more on improved technology and skilled workers. They no longer hire

> "Jobs were plentiful in the past. You could walk out of the house and get a job."

many unskilled assembly-line workers, who once enjoyed union benefits and some protection from layoffs. A generation ago, the typical ghetto resident might have worked as a machine operator or assembler; today, he is working as a waiter or janitor—if he is working at all.

In Wilson's view, the economy, not the poor, needs to be reformed. He has proposed some initiatives, such as national education standards, to upgrade the skills of youths in poverty-stricken areas. His research also shows a clear need for ex-

William Julius Wilson, a sociologist at Harvard University, specializes in the study of urban poverty.

panded child care and family support services. And he calls for metropolitan solutions that bridge the central cities and the suburbs. Wilson admits these approaches are not likely to meet with easy acceptance. There is no simple solution to reducing poverty when jobs disappear.

Let's Discuss

1. Have jobs disappeared from a community you live in or near? If so, what changes took place in your neighborhood as a result?
2. Where have the assembly-line jobs that once supported inner-city neighborhoods gone?

Sources: Small and Newman 2001; W. J. Wilson 1996, 1999a, 2003.

---

welfare reform, discussed in the social policy section of this chapter (DeParle 1998; Gottschalk et al. 1994; Naifeh 1998).

Explaining Poverty

Why is it that poverty pervades a nation of such vast wealth? Sociologist Herbert Gans (1995) has applied functionalist analysis to the existence of poverty and argues that various segments of society actually *benefit* from the existence of the poor. Gans has identified a

number of social, economic, and political functions that the poor perform for society:

- The presence of poor people means that society's dirty work—physically dirty or dangerous, dead-end and underpaid, undignified and menial jobs—will be performed at low cost.
- Poverty creates jobs for occupations and professions that serve the poor. It creates both legal employment (public health experts, welfare caseworkers) and illegal jobs (drug dealers, numbers runners).

- The identification and punishment of the poor as deviants uphold the legitimacy of conventional social norms and mainstream values regarding hard work, thrift, and honesty.

p. 180

- Within a relatively hierarchical society, the existence of poor people guarantees the higher status of the more affluent. As psychologist William Ryan (1976) has noted, affluent people may justify inequality (and gain a measure of satisfaction) by blaming the victims of poverty for their disadvantaged condition.
- Because of their lack of political power, the poor often absorb the costs of social change. Under the policy of deinstitutionalization, mental patients released from long-term hospitals have been transferred primarily to low-income communities and neighborhoods. Similarly, halfway houses for rehabilitated drug abusers, rejected by more affluent communities, often end up in poorer neighborhoods.

In Gans's view, then, poverty and the poor actually satisfy positive functions for many nonpoor groups in the United States.

Life Chances

Max Weber saw class as being closely related to people's *life chances*—that is, their opportunities to provide themselves with material goods, positive living conditions, and favorable life experiences (Gerth and Mills 1958). Life chances are reflected in measures such as housing, education, and health. Occupying a higher position in a society improves your life chances and brings greater access to social rewards. In contrast, people in the lower social classes are forced to devote a larger proportion of their limited resources to the necessities of life.

In times of danger, the affluent and powerful have a better chance of surviving than people of ordinary means. When the supposedly unsinkable British ocean-liner *Titanic* hit an iceberg in 1912, it was not carrying enough lifeboats to accommodate all passengers. Plans had been made to evacuate only first- and second-class passengers. About 62 percent of the first-class passengers survived the disaster. Despite a rule that women and children would go first, about a third of those passengers were male. In contrast, only 25 percent of the passengers in third class survived. The first attempt to alert them to the need to abandon ship came at least 45 minutes after other passengers had been notified (Butler 1998; Crouse 1999; Riding 1998).

Class position also affects people's day-to-day health. In fact, class and wealth are increasingly being viewed as important predictors of health. As Figure 9-5 (page 216)

In the movie *Titanic,* the romantic fantasy of a love affair that crossed class lines obscured the real and deadly effects of the social class divide. This poster appeared in Japan.

shows, the poorer the social stratum, the greater the percentage of people with less than good health. The affluent avail themselves of improved health services while such advances bypass poor people. Indeed, the chances of a child's dying during the first year of life are much higher in poor families than among the middle class. This higher infant mortality rate results in part from the inadequate nutrition received by low-income expectant mothers. Even when the poor survive infancy, they are more likely than the affluent to suffer from serious, chronic illnesses such as arthritis, bronchitis, diabetes, and heart disease. In addition, the poor are less likely to be protected from the high costs of illness by private health insurance. They may have jobs that do not offer health insurance; may work part-time and not be eligible for employee health benefits; or may simply be unable to afford the premiums (E. Goode 1999; R. Mills 2002).

Like disease, crime can be particularly devastating when it attacks the poor. According to the 2000 National Crime Victimization Survey, people in low-income

FIGURE 9-5

Health Status of the Poor and Nonpoor, 2000

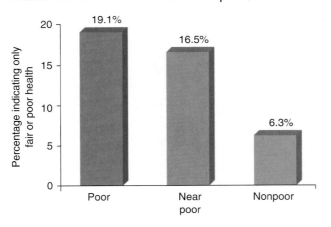

Note: Respondent-assessed in National Health Interview Survey.
Source: National Center for Health Statistics 2002:192.

families were more likely to be assaulted, raped, or robbed than were the most affluent people. Furthermore, if accused of a crime, a person with low income and status is likely to be represented by an overworked public defender. Whether innocent or guilty, the accused may sit in jail for months, unable to raise bail (Rennisson 2002).

Some people have hoped that the Internet revolution would help to level the playing field by making information and markets uniformly available. Unfortunately, however, not everyone can get onto the information highway, so yet another aspect of social inequality has emerged—the *digital divide.* The poor, minorities, and those who live in rural communities and inner cities are not getting connected at home or at work. A recent government study found that despite falling computer prices, the Internet gap between the haves and have-nots has not narrowed. For example, while 52 percent of all households could access the Internet in 2001, about 74 percent of households with family incomes over $50,000 but fewer than 17 percent of households in which families make less than $20,000 had such access. As wealthier people begin to buy high-speed Internet connections, they will be able to take advantage of even more sophisticated interactive services, and the digital divide will grow even larger (Bureau of the Census 2002a:699).

Wealth, status, and power may not ensure happiness, but they certainly provide additional ways of coping with one's problems and disappointments. For this reason, the opportunity for advancement—for social mobility—is of special significance to those who are on the bottom of society looking up. These people want the rewards and privileges that are granted to high-ranking members of a culture.

Use Your Sociological Imagination www.mhhe.com/schaefer9

Imagine a society in which there are no social classes—no differences in people's wealth, income, and life chances. What would such a society be like? Would it be stable, or would its social structure change over time?

SOCIAL MOBILITY

In the movie *Maid in Manhattan,* Jennifer Lopez plays the lead in a modern-day Cinderella story, rising from the lowly status of chambermaid in a big-city hotel to become a company supervisor and the girlfriend of a well-to-do politician. The ascent of a person from a poor background to a position of prestige, power, or financial reward is an example of social mobility. The term *social mobility* refers to the movement of individuals or groups from one position of a society's stratification system to another. But how significant—how frequent, how dramatic—is mobility in a class society such as the United States?

Open versus Closed Stratification Systems

Sociologists use the terms *open stratification system* and *closed stratification system* to indicate the degree of social mobility in a society. An *open system* implies that the position of each individual is influenced by the person's *achieved* status. Such a system encourages competition among members of society. The United States is moving toward this ideal type as the government attempts to reduce the barriers faced by women, racial and ethnic minorities, and people born in lower social classes.

At the other extreme of social mobility is the *closed system,* which allows little or no possibility of moving up. The slavery and caste systems of stratification are examples of closed systems. In such societies, social placement is based on *ascribed* statuses, such as race or family background, which cannot be changed.

Types of Social Mobility

An airline pilot who becomes a police officer moves from one social position to another of the same rank. Each occupation has the same prestige ranking: 60 on a scale ranging from a low of 0 to a high of 100 (see Table 9-2 on page 209). Sociologists call this kind of movement *horizontal mobility.* However, if the pilot were to become a lawyer (prestige ranking of 75), he or she would experience *vertical mobility,* the movement from one social position to another of a different rank. Vertical mobility can also involve moving *downward* in a society's stratification system, as would be the case if the airline pilot became a bank teller (ranking of 43). Pitirim Sorokin ([1927] 1959) was the first sociologist to distinguish between horizontal and vertical mobility. Most sociological analysis, however, focuses on vertical rather than horizontal mobility.

One way of examining vertical social mobility is to contrast intergenerational and intragenerational mobility. *Intergenerational mobility* involves changes in the social position of children relative to that of their parents. Thus, a plumber whose father was a physician provides an example of downward intergenerational mobility. A film star whose parents were both factory workers illustrates upward intergenerational mobility.

Intragenerational mobility involves changes in social position within a person's adult life. A woman who enters the paid labor force as a teacher's aide and eventually becomes superintendent of the school district experiences upward intragenerational mobility. A man who becomes a taxicab driver after his accounting firm goes bankrupt undergoes downward intragenerational mobility.

Social Mobility in the United States

The belief in upward mobility is an important value in our society. Does that mean that the United States is indeed the land of opportunity? Not unless such ascriptive characteristics as race, gender, and family background have ceased to be significant in determining one's future prospects. We can see the impact of these factors in the occupational structure.

Occupational Mobility

Two sociological studies conducted a decade apart offer insight into the degree of mobility in the nation's occupational structure (Blau and Duncan 1967; Featherman and Hauser 1978). Taken together, these investigations lead to several noteworthy conclusions. First, occupational mobility (both intergenerational and intragenerational) has been common among males. Approximately 60 to 70 percent of sons are employed in higher-ranked occupations than their fathers.

Second, although there is a great deal of mobility in the United States, much of it is minor. That is, people who reach an occupational level above or below that of their parents usually advance or fall back only one or two out of a possible eight occupational levels. Thus, the child of a laborer may become an artisan or a technician, but he or she is less likely to become a manager or professional. The odds against reaching the top are extremely high unless one begins from a relatively privileged position.

The Impact of Education

Another conclusion of both studies is that education plays a critical role in social mobility. The impact of formal schooling on adult status is even greater than that of family background (although as we have seen, family background influences the likelihood that one will receive higher education). Furthermore, education represents an important means of intergenerational mobility. Three-fourths of college-educated men in these studies achieved some upward mobility, while only 12 percent of those who received no schooling did (see also J. Davis 1982).

The impact of education on mobility has diminished somewhat in the last decade, however. An undergraduate degree—a B.A. or a B.S.—serves less as a guarantee of upward mobility now than it did in the past simply because more and more entrants into the job market hold such a degree. Moreover, intergenerational mobility is declining, since there is no longer such a stark difference between generations. In earlier decades many high school–educated parents successfully sent their children to college, but today's college students are increasingly likely to have college-educated parents (Hout 1988).

The Impact of Race

Sociologists have long documented the fact that the class system is more rigid for African Americans than it is for members of other racial groups. Black men who have good jobs, for example, are less likely than White men to see their adult children attain the same status. The cumulative disadvantage of discrimination plays a significant role in the disparity between the two groups' experience. Compared to White households, the relatively modest wealth of African American households means that adult Black children are less likely than adult White children to receive financial support from their parents. Indeed, young Black couples are much more likely than young White couples to be assisting their parents—a sacrifice that hampers their social mobility.

The African American middle class has grown over the last few decades, due to economic expansion and the benefits of the civil rights movement of the 1960s. Yet many of these middle-class households have little savings, a fact that puts them in danger during times of crisis. Studies have consistently shown that downward mobility is significantly higher for Blacks than it is for Whites (Oliver and Shapiro 1995; Sernau 2001; W. J. Wilson 1996).

The Impact of Gender

Studies of mobility, even more than those of class, have traditionally ignored the significance of gender, but some research findings are now available that explore the relationship between gender and mobility.

Andrea Jung, president of Avon Corporation, is one of the few women in the United States who have risen to the top of the corporate hierarchy. Despite the passage of equal opportunity laws, occupational barriers still limit women's social mobility.

Women's employment opportunities are much more limited than men's (as Chapter 12 will show). Moreover, according to recent research, women whose skills far exceed the jobs offered them are more likely than men to withdraw entirely from the paid labor force. Their withdrawal violates an assumption common to traditional mobility studies: that most people will aspire to upward mobility and seek to make the most of their opportunities.

In contrast to men, women have a rather large range of clerical occupations open to them. But the modest salary ranges and few prospects for advancement in many of these positions limit the possibility of upward mobility. Self-employment as shopkeepers, entrepreneurs, independent professionals, and the like—an important road to upward mobility for men—is more difficult for women, who find it harder to secure the necessary financing. Although sons commonly follow in the footsteps of their fathers, women are unlikely to move into their fathers' positions. Consequently, gender remains an important factor in shaping social mobility. Women in the United States (and in other parts of the world) are especially likely to be trapped in poverty, unable to rise out of their low-income status (Heilman 2001).

The Intersection of Class, Race, and Gender

We have seen that people's life chances and social mobility are affected by their race, gender, and social class. Women and children, as well as members of racial and ethnic minorities, predominate among the poor and the underclass, the very lowest levels of society. White men predominate at the highest levels.

Max Weber ([1913–1922] 1947) wrote of the privileged class that monopolizes the purchase of high-priced consumer goods and wields the power to grant or withhold opportunity from others. To grasp just how White and male the membership of this elite group is, consider the following: 82 percent of the 11,500 people who serve on the boards of directors of Fortune 1,000 corporations are non-Hispanic White males. For every 82 White men on these boards, there are 2 Latinos, 2 Asian Americans, 3 African Americans, and 11 White women (G. Strauss 2002).

What efforts are being made to assist those at the opposite end of the social scale, the very poor? In the social policy section of this chapter, which follows, we will

Claudio Gonzales, who sits on the board of directors of General Electric Corporation, belongs to a very small group of elites: minority group members who serve as directors of major corporations.

consider the welfare system in the United States and Europe.

So far we have focused on stratification and social mobility in the United States. In Chapter 10, we will broaden our focus to consider stratification from a global perspective.

SOCIAL POLICY and STRATIFICATION

Rethinking Welfare in North America and Europe

www.
mhhe.com
/schaefer9

The Issue

- In Milwaukee, a single mother of six has just lost her job as a security guard. Once considered a success story of the welfare reform program, she has fallen victim to the economic recession that followed the boom years of the 1990s. Because she has been on welfare before, she is ineligible to receive additional assistance from the state of Wisconsin. Yet like many other workers who made the transition from welfare to work in the late 1990s, she does not qualify for unemployment benefits; food stamps are all she can count on (Pierre 2002).

- In Paris, France, Hélène Desegrais, another single mother, waited four months to place her daughter in government-subsidized day care. Now she can seek a full-time job, but she is concerned about government threats to curtail such services to keep taxes down (Simons 1997).

These are the faces of people living on the edge—often women with children seeking to make a go of it amid changing social policies. Governments in all parts of the world are searching for the right solution to welfare: How much subsidy should they provide? How much responsibility should fall on the shoulders of the poor?

The Setting

In the 1990s, there was intense debate in the United States over the issue of welfare. Welfare programs were costly, and there was widespread concern (however unfounded) that welfare payments discouraged recipients from seeking jobs. Both Democrats and Republicans vowed to "end welfare as we know it."

In late 1996, in a historic shift in federal policy, Congress passed the Personal Responsibility and Work Opportunity Reconciliation Act, ending the long-standing federal guarantee of assistance to every poor family that meets eligibility requirements. The law set a lifetime limit of five years of welfare benefits, and required all able-bodied adults to work after receiving two years of benefits (although hardship exceptions were allowed). The federal government would give block grants to the states to use as they wished in assisting poor and needy residents, and it would permit states to experiment with ways to move people off welfare.

Other countries vary widely in their commitment to social service programs. But most industrialized nations devote higher proportions of their expenditures to housing, social security, welfare, health care, and unemployment compensation than the United States does. Data available in 2002 indicated that in Ireland, 76 percent of health expenditures were paid for by the government; in Switzerland, 73 percent; in Canada, 71 percent; but in the United States, only 44 percent (World Bank 2002a:102–104).

Sociological Insights

Many sociologists tend to view the debate over welfare reform throughout industrialized nations from a conflict perspective: the "haves" in positions of policymaking listen to the interests of other "haves," while the cries of the "have-nots" are drowned out. Critics of welfare reform believe that the nation's economic problems are unfairly being blamed on welfare spending and the poor. From a conflict perspective, this backlash against welfare recipients reflects deep fears and hostility toward the nation's urban, predominantly African American and Hispanic underclass.

Those who are critical of the backlash note that "welfare scapegoating" conveniently ignores the lucrative federal handouts that go to *affluent* individuals and families. For example, while federal housing aid to the poor was cut drastically in the 1980s, tax deductions for mortgage interest and property taxes more than doubled. The National Association of Home Builders, an ardent defender of the mortgage-interest deduction, estimates that this subsidy costs the federal government $60 billion a year in lost taxes. The deduction generally benefits affluent taxpayers who own their own homes. According to one study, more than 44 percent of the benefits from this tax break go to the 5 percent of taxpayers with the highest incomes, who together save themselves $22 billion annually (Goodgame 1993; Johnston 1996).

Those who take a conflict perspective also urge policy-makers and the general public to look closely at **corporate welfare**—the tax breaks, direct payments, and grants that the government makes to corporations—rather than to focus on the comparatively small allowances being given to welfare mothers and their children. Yet any suggestion to curtail such corporate welfare brings a strong response from special-interest groups that are much more powerful than any coalition on behalf of the poor. One example of corporate welfare is the airline bailout bill that was passed in the wake of terrorist attacks on the United States in September 2001. Within 11 days the federal government had approved the bailout, whose positive impact was felt largely by airline executives and shareholders. Relatively low-paid airline employees were still laid off, and hundreds of thousands of low-wage workers in airports, hotels, and related industries received little or no assistance. Efforts to broaden unemployment assistance to help these marginally employed workers failed (Hartman and Miller 2001b).

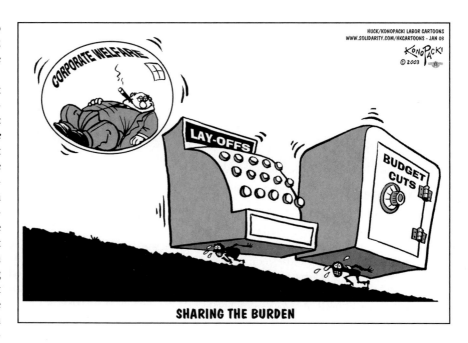

SHARING THE BURDEN

Policy Initiatives

The government likes to highlight welfare reform success stories. It is true that many people who previously depended on tax dollars are now working and paying taxes themselves. But it is much too soon to see if "workfare" will be successful. The new jobs that were generated by the booming economy of the late 1990s were an unrealistic test of the system. Prospects for the hard-core jobless—those people who are difficult to train or are encumbered by drug or alcohol abuse, physical disabilities, or child care needs—have faded as the boom passed and the economy moved into recession.

True, fewer people remained on welfare after enactment of the welfare reform law in August 1996. By September 2002, 7.1 million people had left the system, reducing the rolls to under 5 million people. Yet research showed that most adults who had gone off welfare had taken low-wage jobs that did not offer benefits. As they moved off welfare, their Medicaid coverage ended, leaving them without health insurance. Support has also been lacking for working parents who need high-quality child care. And assistance to immigrants, even those who are legal residents, continues to be limited (Department of Health and Human Services 2003a, 2003b; Ehrenreich and Piven 2002).

European governments have encountered many of the same citizen demands as in North America: Keep our taxes low, even if it means reducing services to the poor. However, nations in eastern and central Europe have faced a special challenge since the end of communism. Though the governments in those nations had traditionally provided an impressive array of social services, they differed from capitalist systems in several important respects. First, the communist system was premised on full employment, so there was no need to provide unemployment insurance; social services focused on the old and the disabled. Second, subsidies for housing and even utilities played an important role. With new competition from the West and tight budgets, some of these countries are beginning to realize that universal coverage is no longer affordable and must be replaced with targeted programs. Even Sweden, despite its long history of social welfare programs, is feeling the pinch. Still, only modest cutbacks have been made in European social service programs, leaving them much more generous than those in the United States (Gornick 2001).

Both in North America and in Europe, people are beginning to turn to private means to support themselves. For instance, they are investing money for their later years rather than depending on government social security programs. But that solution works only if you have a job and can save money. Increasingly, people are seeing the gap between themselves and the affluent grow, with fewer government programs available to assist them. Solutions are frequently left to the private sector, while government policy initiatives at the national level all but disappear.

Let's Discuss

1. How does the level of spending for social services in the United States compare with that of European countries? What accounts for the differences?
2. Do you think welfare recipients should be required to work? What kind of support should they be given?
3. Has the welfare system that went into effect in the United States in 1996 been successful? Why or why not?

CHAPTER RESOURCES

Summary

Stratification is the structured ranking of entire groups of people that perpetuates unequal economic rewards and power in a society. In this chapter, we examined four general systems of stratification, the explanations offered by functionalist and conflict theorists for the existence of *social inequality,* the relationship between stratification and *social mobility,* and the welfare system in North America and Europe.

1. Some degree of *social inequality* characterizes all cultures.
2. Systems of social stratification include *slavery, castes,* the *estate system,* and social classes.
3. Karl Marx saw that differences in access to the means of production created social, economic, and political inequality and distinct classes of owners and laborers.
4. Max Weber identified three analytically distinct components of stratification: *class, status group,* and *power.*
5. Functionalists argue that stratification is necessary to motivate people to fill society's important positions; conflict theorists see stratification as a major source of societal tension and conflict. Interactionists stress the importance of social class in determining a person's lifestyle.

6. One consequence of social class in the United States is that both *wealth* and *income* are distributed unevenly.
7. The category of the poor defies any simple definition, and counters common stereotypes about poor people. The long-term poor, who lack training and skills, form an *underclass.*
8. Functionalists find that the poor satisfy positive functions for many of the nonpoor in the United States.
9. One's *life chances*—opportunities for obtaining material goods, positive living conditions, and favorable life experiences—are related to one's social class. Occupying a high social position improves a person's life chances.
10. *Social mobility* is more likely to be found in an *open system* that emphasizes achieved status than in a *closed system* that focuses on ascribed characteristics. Race, gender, and family background are important factors in social mobility.
11. Today, many governments are struggling with how much tax revenue to spend on welfare programs. The trend in the United States is to put welfare recipients to work.

Critical Thinking Questions

1. Sociologist Daniel Rossides has conceptualized the class system of the United States using a five-class model. According to Rossides, the upper-middle class and the lower-middle class together account for about 40 percent of the nation's population. Yet studies suggest that a higher proportion of respondents identify themselves as middle class. Drawing on the model presented by Rossides, suggest why members of both the upper class and the working class might prefer to identify themselves as middle class.
2. Sociological study of stratification is generally conducted at the macro level and draws most heavily on the functionalist and conflict perspectives. How

might sociologists use the *interactionist* perspective to examine social class inequalities within a college community?

3. Imagine you have the opportunity to do research on changing patterns of social mobility in the

United States. What specific question would you want to investigate, and how would you go about it?

Key Terms

Absolute poverty   A minimum level of subsistence that no family should be expected to live below. (page 211)

Achieved status   A social position that is attained by a person largely through his or her own efforts. (200)

Ascribed status   A social position that is assigned to a person by society without regard for the person's unique talents or characteristics. (199)

Bourgeoisie   Karl Marx's term for the capitalist class, comprising the owners of the means of production. (203)

Capitalism   An economic system in which the means of production are held largely in private hands and the main incentive for economic activity is the accumulation of profits. (203)

Caste   A hereditary rank, usually religiously dictated, that tends to be fixed and immobile. (200)

Class   A group of people who have a similar level of wealth and income. (205)

Class consciousness   In Karl Marx's view, a subjective awareness held by members of a class regarding their common vested interests and need for collective political action to bring about social change. (203)

Class system   A social ranking based primarily on economic position in which achieved characteristics can influence social mobility. (201)

Closed system   A social system in which there is little or no possibility of individual social mobility. (216)

Corporate welfare   Tax breaks, direct payments, and grants that the government makes to corporations. (220)

Dominant ideology   A set of cultural beliefs and practices that help to maintain powerful social, economic, and political interests. (207)

Estate system   A system of stratification under which peasants were required to work land leased to them by nobles in exchange for military protection and other services. Also known as *feudalism*. (200)

Esteem   The reputation that a particular individual has earned within an occupation. (209)

False consciousness   A term used by Karl Marx to describe an attitude held by members of a class that does not accurately reflect their objective position. (203)

Horizontal mobility   The movement of an individual from one social position to another of the same rank. (216)

Income   Salaries and wages. (199)

Intergenerational mobility   Changes in the social position of children relative to their parents. (217)

Intragenerational mobility   Changes in a person's social position within his or her adult life. (217)

Life chances   The opportunities people have to provide themselves with material goods, positive living conditions, and favorable life experiences. (215)

Objective method   A technique for measuring social class that assigns individuals to classes on the basis of criteria such as occupation, education, income, and place of residence. (208)

Open system   A social system in which the position of each individual is influenced by his or her achieved status. (216)

Power   The ability to exercise one's will over others. (205)

Prestige   The respect and admiration that an occupation holds in a society. (208)

Proletariat   Karl Marx's term for the working class in a capitalist society. (203)

Relative poverty   A floating standard of deprivation by which people at the bottom of a society, whatever their lifestyles, are judged to be disadvantaged *in comparison with the nation as a whole*. (211)

Slavery   A system of enforced servitude in which people are legally owned by others and in which enslaved status is transferred from parents to children. (200)

Social inequality   A condition in which members of a society have different amounts of wealth, prestige, or power. (199)

Social mobility   Movement of individuals or groups from one position of a society's stratification system to another. (216)

Status group   People who have the same prestige or lifestyle, independent of their class positions. (205)

Stratification   A structured ranking of entire groups of people that perpetuates unequal economic rewards and power in a society. (199)

Underclass   The long-term poor who lack training and skills. (213)

Vertical mobility   The movement of a person from one social position to another of a different rank. (216)

Wealth   An inclusive term encompassing all a person's material assets, including land, stocks, and other types of property. (199)

TECHNOLOGY RESOURCES

Internet Connection

*Note: While all the URLs listed were current as of the printing of this book, these sites often change. Please check our website (**www.mhhe.com/schaefer9**) for updates, hyperlinks, and exercises related to these sites.*

1. In this chapter you have learned that millions of people still live as slaves today. iAbolish is a project of the American Anti-Slavery Group (AASG), a grassroots organization founded in 1993 to combat slavery around the world. To read more about people who are enslaved in the United States, link to **www.iabolish.com.**

2. The term *social mobility* refers to the movement of individuals or groups from one position of a society's stratification system to another. Dr. John Newmeyer, an epidemiologist at the Haight-Ashbury Free Clinic in San Francisco, has published an essay titled "Seven Paths of Upward Mobility." Go to his website to read the essay (**www.newmeyer.com/main.html**).

Online Learning Center with PowerWeb

When you visit the student center in the Online Learning Center at **www.mhhe.com/schaefer9,** link to Audio Clips. Listen to Richard Schaefer, the author of your textbook, talk about some sociology students he taught and their prestige rankings of various occupations. These so-ciology students were all "lifers" in a maximum-security prison. Professor Schaefer defines prestige, then tells you how these students ranked the prestige of police officers, judges, lawyers, and governors.

10

SOCIAL INEQUALITY WORLDWIDE

This UNICEF poster reminds affluent Western consumers that the brand-name jeans they wear may be produced by exploited workers in developing countries. In sweatshops throughout the developing world, nonunion garment workers—some of them still children—labor long hours for extremely low wages.

Stratification in the World System

Stratification within Nations: A Comparative Perspective

Case Study: Stratification in Mexico

Social Policy and Social Inequality Worldwide: Universal Human Rights

Boxes

SOCIOLOGY IN THE GLOBAL COMMUNITY: The Informal Economy

SOCIAL INEQUALITY: Stratification in Japan

Instantly recognized throughout the world, the *Nike* swoosh sometimes seems to be everywhere—on shirts and caps and pants. The icon is no longer confined to shoes as sponsorship deals have plastered the *swoosh* across jerseys and sporting arenas of all manner, from basketball to football to volleyball to track to soccer to tennis to hockey. *Nike*'s growth strategy is based on penetrating new markets in apparel while making acquisitions in sporting goods. The value of the *swoosh* now runs so deep that visitors to remote, rural, and impoverished regions of the Third World report finding peasants sewing crude *swoosh* imitations onto shirts and caps, not for the world market but for local consumption.... As the *Nike* symbol has grown ascendant in the marketplace of images, *Nike* has become the sign some people love to love and the sign others love to hate....

Nike is a transnational corporation that links national economies into a complex web of global production arrangements.... Almost all production of shoes, apparel and accessories is outsourced to contract suppliers in developing nations while the home office in Beaverton, Oregon, designs, develops, and markets the branded goods....

It is very difficult to compete in today's athletic footwear industry without engaging in the outsourcing of labor to relatively unskilled laborers in impoverished nations. Companies in the athletic footwear industry depend on the existence of poor Asian nations where there is a ready surplus of labor force in need of work and wages, even if those wages are below the poverty line....

During the summer of 1996, *Nike* became the focus of media scrutiny because of questions about the treatment of the laborers who manufacture *Nike* shoes.... The photographic "discovery" of Pakistani children making *Nike* soccer balls at 6¢ an hour precipitated nothing less than a moral hailstorm, stirring up dormant feelings about justice and questions of right and wrong in a global economy....

Nike speaks the language of universal rights, concern for children, transcendence over the categories of age, race, gender, disability or any social stereotype. As moral philosophy, its images speak out against racism, sexism, and ageism. *Nike*'s imagery celebrates sport, athletic activity, and play as universally rewarding categories. Playing makes for healthier, more productive citizens, and better self-actualized human beings. However, no matter what its imagery suggests, *Nike*, like any other capitalist firm, must operate within the relationships and constraints of competitive capitalist marketplaces. No matter how many P.L.A.Y. commercials *Nike* runs on TV, there will still be haunting images of production practices in Pakistan, Indonesia, and Vietnam. As the world grows more unified, it becomes increasingly difficult to suppress entirely those gaps between image and practice, between humanism and capitalism, between moral philosophy and the bottom line of corporate profit growth. *(R. Goldman and Papson 1998:2, 6, 7–9, 184)* ■

Additional information about this excerpt can be found on the Online Learning Center at **www.mhhe.com/schaefer9.**

CORE CULTURAL ICONS

NIKE
CULTURE

Robert Goldman
& Stephen Papson

As sociologists Robert Goldman and Stephen Papson note in their book *Nike Culture,* the Nike symbol (the swoosh) and philosophy ("Just do it") have swept the world. People in all parts of the globe pay up to hundreds of dollars for a pair of Air Jordan shoes, and teams in all kinds of sporting arenas wear the Nike logo. Unfortunately, there is another side to Nike's global dominance. Its products are made in harsh sweatshop conditions for very little compensation, mostly in developing nations. One group critical of Nike's practices claimed in 1996 that the 45 Indonesian workers who participated in making a $70 pair of Air Pegasus shoes shared a total of $1.60. Other stories of Vietnamese and Chinese women who are pitifully underpaid, subjected to health and safety hazards, and physically harassed by shop floor managers have also helped to fuel concern about human rights violations.

Students protesting sweatshop labor in developing countries mock Nike with its own slogan: "Just do it."

Such concerns have recently given rise to a nationwide coalition called United Students Against Sweatshops, based on college campuses across the country. Because this is an issue that combines women's rights, immigrant rights, environmental concerns, and human rights, it has linked disparate groups on campus. Nike is not their only target. Many apparel manufacturers contract out their production to take advantage of cheap labor and overhead costs. The student movement—ranging from sit-ins and "knit-ins" to demonstrations and building occupation—has been aimed at ridding campus stores of all products made in sweatshops, both at home and abroad. Pressed by their students, many colleges and universities have agreed to adopt antisweatshop codes governing the products they make and stock on campus. And Nike and Reebok, partly in response to student protests, have raised the wages of some 100,000 workers in their Indonesian factories (to about 20 cents an hour—still far below what is needed to raise a family) (Appelbaum and Dreier 1999; Fair Labor Association 2003; Global Alliance for Workers and Communities 2001, 2003).

The global corporate culture of the apparel industry focuses our attention on worldwide social stratification—on the enormous gap between wealthy nations and poorer nations. In many respects, the wealth of rich nations depends on the poverty of poor nations. As Figure 10-1 shows, people in industrialized societies benefit when they buy consumer goods made by low-wage workers in developing countries. Yet the low wages workers earn in multinational factories are comparatively high for those countries.

What economic and political conditions explain the divide between rich nations and poor? Within developing nations, how are wealth and income distributed, and how much opportunity does the average worker have to move up the social ladder? How do race and gender affect social mobility in these countries? In this chapter we will focus on stratification around the world, beginning with an examination of who controls the world marketplace. We will consider the impact of colonialism and neocolonialism, of globalization, of the rise of multinational corporations, and of the trend toward modernization. Then we will focus on stratification *within* nations, in terms of the distribution of wealth and income, prestige, and social mobility. In a special case study, we will look closely at social stratification in Mexico, including the social impact of race and gender and the environmental effects of industrialization. The chapter closes with a social policy section on universal human rights. ■

FIGURE 10-1

The Sweat behind the Shirt

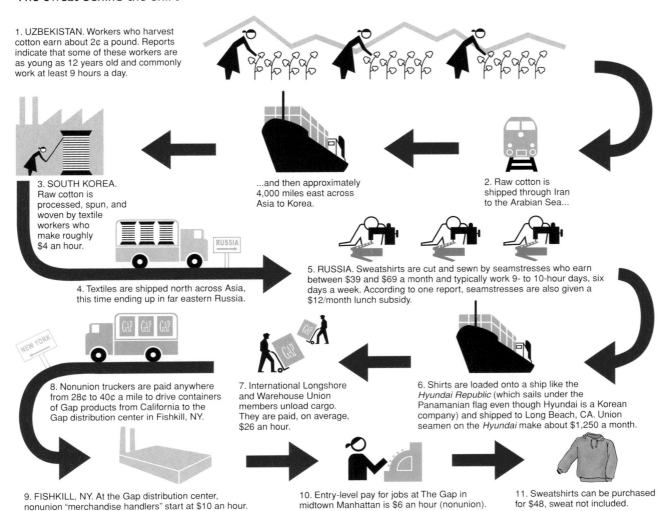

1. UZBEKISTAN. Workers who harvest cotton earn about 2¢ a pound. Reports indicate that some of these workers are as young as 12 years old and commonly work at least 9 hours a day.

3. SOUTH KOREA. Raw cotton is processed, spun, and woven by textile workers who make roughly $4 an hour.

...and then approximately 4,000 miles east across Asia to Korea.

2. Raw cotton is shipped through Iran to the Arabian Sea...

4. Textiles are shipped north across Asia, this time ending up in far eastern Russia.

5. RUSSIA. Sweatshirts are cut and sewn by seamstresses who earn between $39 and $69 a month and typically work 9- to 10-hour days, six days a week. According to one report, seamstresses are also given a $12/month lunch subsidy.

8. Nonunion truckers are paid anywhere from 28¢ to 40¢ a mile to drive containers of Gap products from California to the Gap distribution center in Fishkill, NY.

7. International Longshore and Warehouse Union members unload cargo. They are paid, on average, $26 an hour.

6. Shirts are loaded onto a ship like the *Hyundai Republic* (which sails under the Panamanian flag even though Hyundai is a Korean company) and shipped to Long Beach, CA. Union seamen on the *Hyundai* make about $1,250 a month.

9. FISHKILL, NY. At the Gap distribution center, nonunion "merchandise handlers" start at $10 an hour.

10. Entry-level pay for jobs at The Gap in midtown Manhattan is $6 an hour (nonunion).

11. Sweatshirts can be purchased for $48, sweat not included.

Source: Gordon and Knickerbocker 2001:14.

Think About It
To what extent does the affluence Americans enjoy depend on the labor of workers in less-developed countries?

STRATIFICATION IN THE WORLD SYSTEM

Kwabena Afari is a pineapple exporter in Ghana. For years his customers had to show a great deal of ingenuity to get in touch with him. First a call had to be placed to Accra, the capital city. Someone there would call the post office in Afari's hometown; then the post office would send a messenger to his home. Afari has recently solved his problem by getting a cellular phone, but his longtime dilemma symbolizes the difficulties of the roughly 600 million people who live in sub-Saharan Africa and are being left behind by the trade and foreign investment transforming the global economy. As one African entrepreneur notes, "It's not that we have been left behind. It's that we haven't even started" (Buckley 1997:8).

It is true that technology, the information highway, and innovations in telecommunications have all made the world a smaller and more unified place. Yet while the

FIGURE 10-2

Gross National Income per Capita, 2002

Mapping Life WORLDWIDE

www.
mhhe.com
/schaefer9

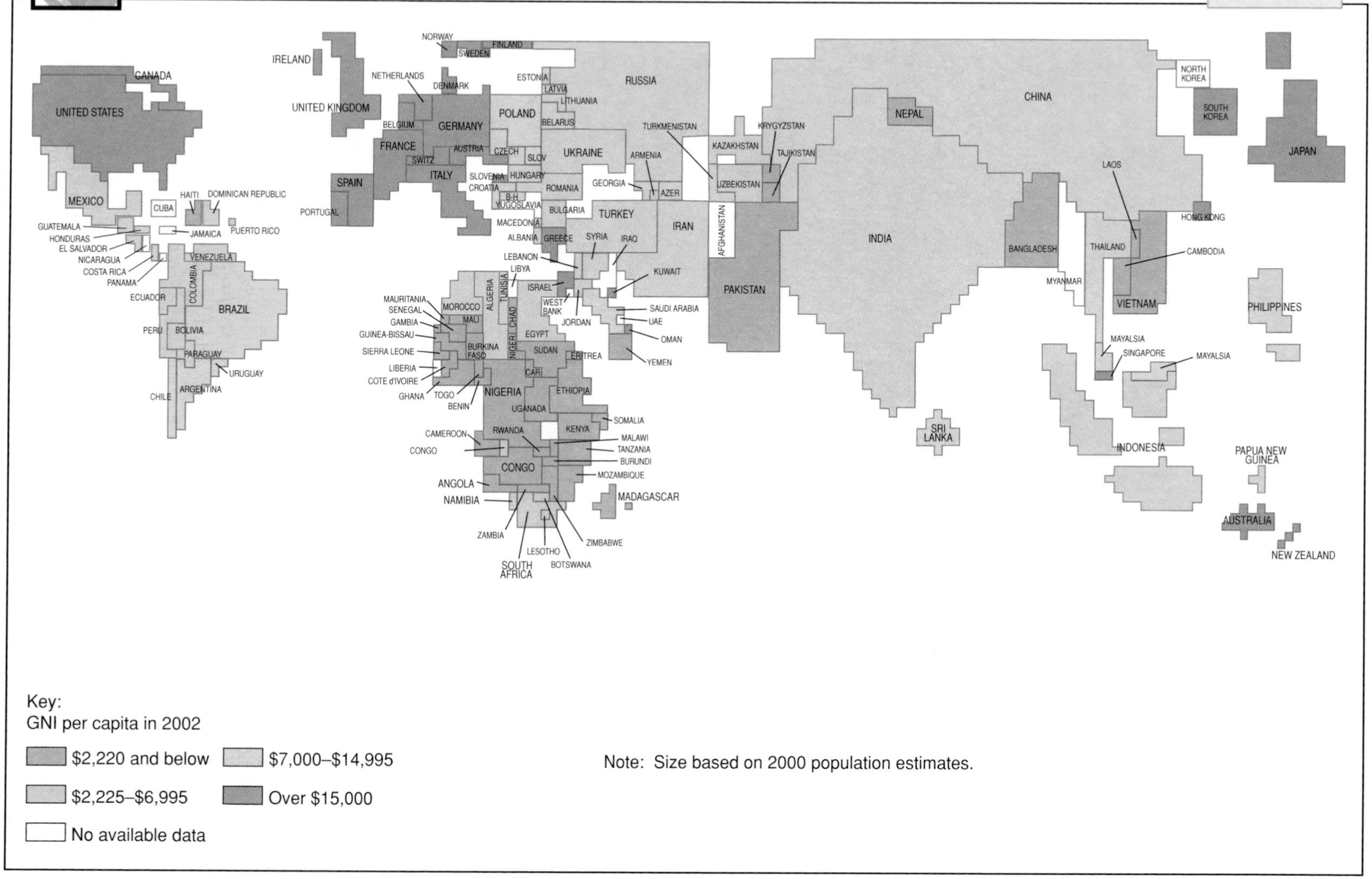

Key:
GNI per capita in 2002

$2,220 and below	$7,000–$14,995
$2,225–$6,995	Over $15,000
No available data	

Note: Size based on 2000 population estimates.

Sources: Haub 2003; Weeks 2002:22–23.

This stylized map reflects the different sizes in population of the world's nations. The color for each country shows the 2001 estimated gross national income (the total value of goods and services produced by the nation in a given year) per capita. As the map shows, some of the world's most populous countries—such as Nigeria, Bangladesh, and Pakistan—are among the nations with the lowest standard of living, as measured by per capita gross national income.

world marketplace is gradually shrinking in space and tastes, business profits are not being shared equally. There remains a substantial disparity between the world's "have" and "have-not" nations. For example, in 2002, the average value of goods and services produced per citizen (per capita gross national income) in the industrialized countries of the United States, Japan, Switzerland, Belgium, and Norway was more than $25,000. In at least 13 poorer countries the value was $800 or less. In fact, the richest 1 percent of the world's population received as much income as the poorest 57 percent. Figure 10-2 illustrates these stark contrasts. Three forces discussed here are particularly responsible for the domination of the world marketplace by a few nations: the legacy of colonialism, the advent of multinational corporations, and modernization (Haub 2002; United Nations Development Programme 2001).

The Legacy of Colonialism

Colonialism occurs when a foreign power maintains political, social, economic, and cultural domination over a people for an extended period. In simple terms, it is rule by outsiders. The long reign of the British Empire over much of North America, parts of Africa, and India is an example of colonial domination. The same can be said of French rule over Algeria, Tunisia, and other parts of North Africa. Relations between the colonial nation and colonized people are similar to those between the dominant capitalist class and the proletariat, as described by Karl Marx.

By the 1980s, colonialism had largely disappeared. Most of the nations that were colonies before World War I had achieved political independence and established their own governments. However, for many of these countries, the transition to genuine self-rule was not yet complete. Colonial domination had established patterns of economic exploitation that continued even after nationhood was achieved—in part because former colonies were unable to develop their own industry and technology. Their dependence on more industrialized nations, including their former colonial masters, for managerial and technical expertise, investment capital, and manufactured goods kept former colonies in a subservient position. Such continuing dependence and foreign domination constitute **neocolonialism.**

The economic and political consequences of colonialism and neocolonialism are readily apparent. Drawing on the conflict perspective, sociologist Immanuel Wallerstein (1974, 1979a, 2000) views the global economic system as being divided between nations that control wealth and nations from which resources are taken. Through his **world systems analysis,** Wallerstein has described the unequal economic and political relationships in which certain in-

dustrialized nations (among them the United States, Japan, and Germany) and their global corporations dominate the *core* of this system (see Figure 10-3). At the *semiperiphery* of the system are countries with marginal economic status, such as Israel, Ireland, and South Korea. Wallerstein suggests that the poor developing countries of Asia, Africa, and Latin America are on the *periphery* of the world economic system. The key to Wallerstein's analysis is the exploitative relationship of core nations toward noncore nations. Core nations and their corporations control and exploit noncore nations' economies. Unlike other nations, they are relatively independent of outside control (Chase-Dunn and Grimes 1995).

The division between core and periphery nations is significant and remarkably stable. A study by the International Monetary Fund (2000) found little change over the course of the *last 100 years* for the 42 economies that were studied. The only changes were Japan's movement up into the group of core nations and China's movement down toward the margins of the semiperiphery nations. Yet Wallerstein (2000) speculates that the world system as we currently understand it may soon undergo unpredictable changes. The world is becoming increasingly urbanized, a trend that is gradually eliminating the large pools of low-cost workers in rural areas. In the future, core nations will have to find other ways to reduce their labor costs. The exhaustion of land and water resources through clear-cutting and other forms of pollution is also driving up the costs of production.

FIGURE 10-3

World Systems Analysis at the Beginning of the 21st Century

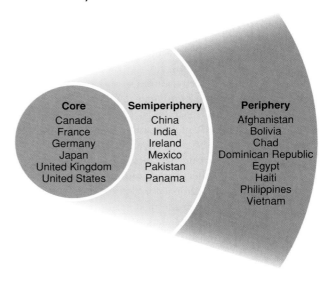

Note: Figure shows only a partial listing of countries.

Wallerstein's world systems analysis is the most widely used version of ***dependency theory.*** According to this theory, even as developing countries make economic advances, they remain weak and subservient to core nations and corporations in an increasingly intertwined global economy. This interdependency allows industrialized nations to continue to exploit developing countries for their own gain. In a sense, dependency theory applies the conflict perspective on a global scale.

In the view of world systems analysis and dependency theory, a growing share of the human and natural resources of developing countries is being redistributed to the core industrialized nations. This happens in part because developing countries owe huge sums of money to industrialized nations as a result of foreign aid, loans, and trade deficits. The global debt crisis has intensified the Third World dependency begun under colonialism, neocolonialism, and multinational investment. International financial institutions are pressuring indebted countries to take severe measures to meet their interest payments. The result is that developing nations may be forced to devalue their currencies, freeze workers' wages, increase privatization of industry, and reduce government services and employment.

Closely related to these problems is ***globalization,*** or the worldwide integration of government p. 60 policies, cultures, social movements, and financial markets through trade and the exchange of ideas. Because world financial markets transcend governance by conventional nation states, international organizations such as the World Bank and the International Monetary Fund have emerged as major players in the global economy. The function of these institutions, heavily funded and influenced by core nations, is to encourage economic trade and development and to ensure the smooth operation of international financial markets. As such, they are seen as promoters of globalization and defenders primarily of the interests of core nations. Critics call attention to a variety of issues, including violations of workers' rights, the destruction of the environment, the loss of cultural identity, and discrimination against minority groups in periphery nations.

Some observers see globalization and its effects as the natural result of advances in communications technology, particularly the Internet and satellite transmission of the mass media. Others view it more critically, as a process that allows multinational corporations to expand unchecked, as we will see in the next section (Chase-Dunn et al. 2000; Feketekuty 2001; Feuer 1989; Pearlstein 2001).

Use Your Sociological Imagination www. mhhe.com /schaefer9

You are traveling through a developing country. What evidence do you see of neocolonialism and globalization?

Multinational Corporations

A key role in neocolonialism today is played by worldwide corporate giants. The term ***multinational corporations*** refers to commercial organizations that are headquartered in one country but do business throughout the world. Such private trade and lending relationships are not new; merchants have conducted business abroad for hundreds of years, trading gems, spices, garments, and other goods. However, today's multinational giants are not merely buying and selling overseas; they are also *producing goods* all over the world, as we saw in the case of Nike (I. Wallerstein 1974).

Moreover, today's "global factories" (factories throughout the developing world that are run by multinational corporations) now have the "global office" alongside them. Multinationals based in core countries are beginning to establish reservations services and centers for processing data and insurance claims in the periphery nations. As service

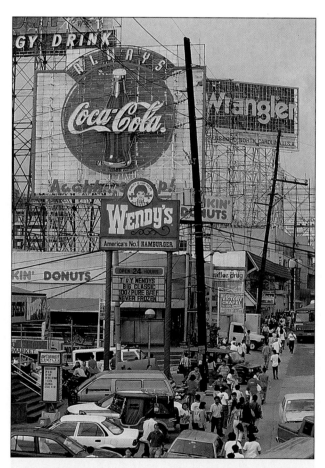

The influence of multinational corporations abroad can be seen in this street scene from Manila, capital of the Philippines.

Table 10-1	Multinational Corporations Compared to Nations		
Corporation	**Revenues ($ millions)**	**Comparable Nation(s)**	**Gross Domestic Product ($ millions)**
1. Wal-Mart (USA)	$246,525	Switzerland	$239,800
2. General Motors (USA)	186,763	Austria	189,000
3. ExxonMobil (USA)	182,466	Venezuela plus Pakistan	182,100
4. Royal Dutch/Shell Group (Netherlands/Britain)	179,431	Egypt plus Philippines	173,400
5. BP–British Petroleum (Britain)	178,721	Saudi Arabia	173,300
6. Ford Motor (USA)	163,871	Norway	161,800
7. DaimlerChrysler (Germany)	141,421	Colombia plus Peru	134,800
8. Toyota Motor (Japan)	131,754	South Africa	125,900
9. General Electric (USA)	131,698	Finland	121,500
13. Citigroup (USA)	100,789	Ireland	93,900
16. Nippon Telephone and Telegraph (Japan)	89,644	Malaysia	89,700

Notes: Revenues are for 2002. GDP data are for 2000, based on local currencies converted to prevailing U.S. dollar equivalents. Corporations are ranked by their placement on the Fortune 500 list of global corporations.

Sources: For corporate data, *Fortune* 2003; for GDP data, United Nations Development Programme 2002:190–193.

Think About It

What happens to society when corporations grow richer than countries and spill across international borders?

industries become a more important part of the international marketplace, many companies are concluding that the low costs of overseas operations more than offset the expense of transmitting information around the world.

Do not underestimate the size of these global corporations. Table 10-1 shows that the total revenues of multinational businesses are on a par with the total value of goods and services exchanged in *entire nations.* Foreign sales represent an important source of profit for multinational corporations, a fact that encourages them to expand into other countries (in many cases, the developing nations). The economy of the United States is heavily dependent on foreign commerce, much of which is conducted by multinationals. Over one-fourth of all goods and services in the United States has to do with either the export of goods to foreign countries or the import of goods from abroad (United States Trade Representative 2003).

Functionalist View

Functionalists believe that multinational corporations can actually help the developing nations of the world.

They bring jobs and industry to areas where subsistence agriculture previously served as the only means of survival. Multinationals also promote rapid development through the diffusion of inventions and innovations from industrial nations. Viewed from a functionalist perspective, the combination of skilled technology and management provided by multinationals and the relatively cheap labor available in developing nations is ideal for a global enterprise. Multinationals can take maximum advantage of technology while reducing costs and boosting profits.

Through their international ties, multinational corporations also make the nations of the world more interdependent. These ties may prevent certain disputes from reaching the point of serious conflict. A country cannot afford to sever diplomatic relations or engage in warfare with a nation that is the headquarters for its main business suppliers or a key outlet for its exports.

Conflict View

Conflict theorists challenge this favorable evaluation of the impact of multinational corporations. They emphasize that multinationals exploit local workers to maximize profits. Starbucks—the international coffee retailer based in Seattle—gets some of its coffee from farms in Guatemala. But to earn enough money to buy a pound of Starbucks coffee, a Guatemalan farmworker would have to pick 500 pounds of beans, representing five days of work (Entine and Nichols 1996).

The pool of cheap labor in the developing world prompts multinationals to move factories out of core countries. An added bonus for the multinationals is that the developing world discourages strong trade unions. In industrialized countries, organized labor insists on decent wages and humane working conditions, but governments seeking to attract or keep multinationals may develop a "climate for investment" that includes repressive antilabor laws restrictive of union activity and collective bargaining. If labor's demands become too threatening, the multinational firm will simply move its plant elsewhere, leaving a trail of unemployment behind. Nike, for example, moved its factories from the United States to Korea to Indonesia to Vietnam in search of the lowest labor costs. Conflict theorists conclude that on the whole, multinational corporations have a negative social impact on workers in *both* industrialized and developing nations.

Workers in the United States and other core countries are beginning to recognize that their own interests are served by helping to organize workers in developing nations. As long as multinationals can exploit cheap labor abroad, they will be in a strong position to reduce wages and benefits in industrialized countries. With this in mind, in the 1990s, labor unions, religious organizations, campus groups, and other activists mounted public campaigns to pressure companies such as Nike, Starbucks, Reebok, Gap, and Wal-Mart to improve the wages and working conditions in their overseas operations (Global Alliance for Workers and Communities 2003; Gonzalez 2003).

Several sociologists who have surveyed the effects of foreign investment by multinationals conclude that although it may initially contribute to a host nation's wealth, it eventually increases economic inequality within developing nations. This conclusion is true for both income and ownership of land. The upper and middle classes benefit most from economic expansion, whereas the lower classes are less likely to benefit. Multinationals invest in limited areas of an economy

and in restricted regions of a nation. Although certain sectors of the host nation's economy expand, such as hotels and expensive restaurants, this very expansion appears to retard growth in agriculture and other economic sectors. Moreover, multinational corporations often buy out or force out local entrepreneurs and companies, thereby increasing economic and cultural dependence (Chase-Dunn and Grimes 1995; Kerbo 2003; I. Wallerstein 1979b).

Modernization

Around the world, millions of people are witnessing a revolutionary transformation of their day-to-day life. Contemporary social scientists use the term *modernization* to describe the far-reaching process by which peripheral nations move from traditional or less developed institutions to those characteristic of more developed societies.

Wendell Bell (1981), whose definition of modernization we are using, notes that modern societies tend to be urban, literate, and industrial. These societies have sophisticated transportation and media systems. Families tend to be organized within the nuclear family unit rather than the extended-family model (see Chapter 14). Members of societies that have undergone modernization shift allegiance from traditional sources of authority such as parents and priests to newer authorities such as government officials.

Many sociologists are quick to note that terms such as *modernization* and even *development* contain an ethnocentric bias. The unstated assumption behind these terms is that "they" (people living in developing countries) are struggling to become more like "us" (in the

core industrialized nations). Viewed from a conflict perspective, these terms perpetuate the dominant ideology of capitalist societies.

A similar criticism has been made of ***modernization theory,*** a functionalist approach proposing that modernization and development will gradually improve the lives of people in developing nations. According to this theory, even though countries develop at uneven rates, the development of peripheral countries will be assisted by innovations transferred from the industrialized world. Critics of modernization theory, including dependency theorists, counter that any such technology transfer only increases the dominance of core nations over developing countries and facilitates further exploitation.

When we see all the Coca-Cola and IBM signs going up in developing countries, it is easy to assume that globalization and economic change are effecting cultural change. But that is not always the case, researchers note.

Distinctive cultural traditions, such as a particular religious orientation or a nationalistic identity, often persist, and can soften the impact of modernization on a developing nation. Some contemporary sociologists emphasize that both industrialized and developing countries are "modern." Current researchers increasingly view modernization as movement along a series of social indicators—among them degree of urbanization, energy use, literacy, political democracy, and use of birth control. Clearly, some of these are subjective indicators; even in industrialized nations, not everyone would agree that wider use of birth control represents an example of progress (Armer and Katsillis 1992; Hedley 1992; Inglehart and Baker 2000).

Current modernization studies generally take a convergence perspective. Using the indicators noted above, researchers focus on how societies are moving closer together, despite traditional differences. From a conflict

FIGURE 10-4

Distribution of Income in Nine Nations

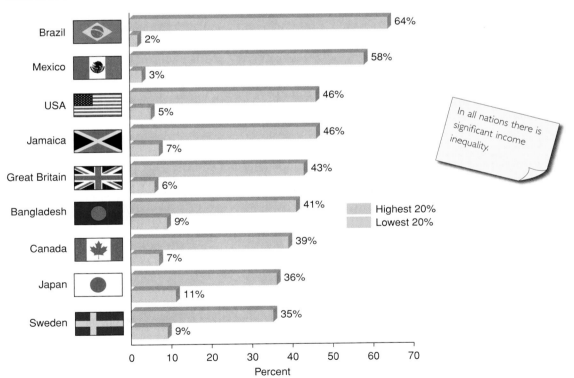

Note: Data are considered comparable although based on statistics covering 1992 to 1997.

Source: World Bank 2003b:64–66.

Think About It
Why is income inequality higher in the United States than in Canada, Japan, and Sweden?

perspective, the modernization of developing countries often perpetuates their dependence on and continued exploitation by more industrialized nations. Conflict theorists view such a continuing dependence on foreign powers as an example of contemporary neocolonialism.

STRATIFICATION WITHIN NATIONS: A COMPARATIVE PERSPECTIVE

At the same time that the gap between rich and poor nations is widening, so too is the gap between rich and poor citizens *within* nations. As discussed earlier, stratification in developing nations is closely related to their relatively weak and dependent position in the global economy. Local elites work hand in hand with multinational corporations and prosper from such alliances. At the same time, the economic system creates and perpetuates the exploitation of industrial and agricultural workers. That's why foreign investment in developing countries tends to increase economic inequality (Bornschier et al. 1978; Kerbo 2003). As Box 10-1 makes clear, inequality within a society is also evident in industrialized nations such as Japan.

Distribution of Wealth and Income

In at least 24 nations around the world, the most affluent 10 percent of the population receives at least 40 percent of all income. The list includes the African nation of Namibia (the leader, at 65 percent of all income), as well as Colombia, Mexico, Nigeria, and South Africa. Figure 10-4 (page 233) compares the distribution of income in selected industrialized and developing nations.

Women in developing countries find life especially difficult. Karuna Chanana Ahmed, an anthropologist from India who has studied women in developing nations, calls women the most exploited of oppressed people. Beginning at birth women face sex discrimination. They are commonly fed less than male children, are denied educational opportunities, and are often hospitalized only when they are critically ill. Inside or outside the home, women's work is devalued. When economies fail, as they did in Asian countries in the late 1990s, women are the first to be laid off from work (E. Anderson and Moore 1993; Kristof 1998).

Surveys show a significant degree of *female infanticide* (the killing of baby girls) in China and rural areas of India. Only one-third of Pakistan's sexually segregated schools are for women, and one-third of those schools have no buildings. In Kenya and Tanzania, it is illegal for a woman to own a house. In Saudi Arabia, women are prohibited from driving, walking alone in public, and socializing with men outside their families (C. Murphy

1993). We will explore women's second-class status throughout the world more fully in Chapter 12.

Prestige

Sociologists have recognized that comparative research is essential in determining whether observed patterns of stratification are unique to a single nation, are restricted to a particular type of society (such as industrial or developing nations), or are applicable to a wide range of societies (Kalleberg 1988). We have seen that societies as different as Brazil, Mexico, the United States, and Japan all share a marked inequality in the distribution of income (refer to Figure 10-4). But a person's class position, defined largely in economic terms and reflecting his or her level of wealth and income, is but one component of stratification.

By ranking the prestige of various occupations, sociologists can gain a deeper understanding of another aspect of inequality. But are perceptions in the United States regarding the prestige of occupations comparable to those held in other societies? In an effort to study stratification from a cross-cultural perspective, sociologist Donald Treiman (1977) examined the reputation that certain jobs had in 53 different nations. He asked people to rate occupations and tabulated the results along a scale ranging from 0 to 100, the higher scores being more prestigious. Treiman found a high degree of correlation or similarity in all contemporary societies, including both industrialized and nonindustrialized nations.

Treiman's pioneering research inspired subsequent efforts to gather and compare data from many societies using the objective method of measuring stratification differences. In one important study, sociologists Nan Lin and Wen Xie (1988) interviewed a random sample of residents of Beijing to study occupational prestige. They found that physicians ranked near the top of the occupational hierarchy, while police officers were near the mid- p. 209 dle, and garbage collectors were close to the bottom—a finding similar to survey results in the United States. Teachers and professors, however, received much lower prestige ratings in China, reflecting the low wages they receive relative to other occupations. The Chinese respondents gave a much higher prestige rating to textile workers than did respondents in the United States. Textile workers evidently fare much better relative to other workers in China than they do relative to other workers in the United States or Europe.

As one part of their analysis, the researchers compared the prestige rankings of male and female respondents. Although China has officially maintained a

10-1 STRATIFICATION IN JAPAN

A tourist visiting Japan may at first experience a bit of culture shock after noticing the degree to which everything in Japanese life is ranked: corporations, universities, even educational programs. These rankings are widely reported and accepted. Moreover, the ratings shape day-to-day social interactions: Japanese find it difficult to sit, talk, or eat together unless the relative rankings of those present have been established, often through the practice of *meishi* (the exchange of business cards).

The apparent preoccupation with ranking and formality suggests an exceptional degree of stratification. Yet researchers have determined that Japan's level of income inequality is among the lowest of major industrial societies (see Figure 10-4 on page 233). The pay gap between Japan's top corporate executives and the nation's lowest-paid workers is about 8 to 1; the comparable figure for the United States would be 37 to 1.

One factor that works against inequality is that Japan is rather homogeneous—certainly when compared with the United States—in terms of race, ethnicity, nationality, and language. Japan's population is 98 percent Japanese. Still, there is discrimination against the nation's Chinese and Korean minorities, and the *Burakumin,* a low-status subculture, encounter extensive prejudice.

Perhaps the most pervasive form of inequality in Japan today is gender discrimination. Overall, women earn only about 64 percent of men's wages. Fewer than 10 percent of Japanese managers are

> Even in developing countries, women are twice as likely to be managers as women in Japan.

female—a ratio that is one of the lowest in the world. Even in developing countries, women are twice as likely to be managers as women in Japan.

In 1985, Japan's parliament—at the time, 97 percent male—passed an Equal Employment bill that encourages employers to end sex discrimination in hiring, assignment, and promotion policies.

However, feminist organizations were dissatisfied because the law lacked strong sanctions. In a landmark ruling issued in late 1996, a Japanese court for the first time held an employer liable for denying promotions due to sex discrimination.

Progress has also been made in terms of public opinion. In 1987, 43 percent of Japanese adults agreed that married women should stay home, but by 2000 the proportion had dropped to 25 percent. On the political front, Japanese women have made progress but remain underrepresented. In a study of women in government around the world, Japan ranked near the bottom of the countries studied, with only 7 percent of its national legislators female.

Let's Discuss

1. What factors might contribute to the relatively low level of income inequality in Japan?
2. Describe the types of gender discrimination found in Japan. Why do you think Japanese women occupy such a subordinate social position?

Sources: French 2001a; Goodman and Kashiwagi 2002; Inter-Parliamentary Union 2003; Magnier 1999; *Migration News* 2002b; Neary 2003; Strom 2000.

national policy of gender equality since 1949, the government has not been able to eliminate occupational segregation by gender. Partly as a result, the prestige rankings of Chinese men and women seemed to reflect the structure of occupational opportunity. Males, for example, gave higher ratings than females to such occupations as natural scientist, athlete, driver, and mechanic—all of which are more likely to be held by males. Respondents of each gender showed a tendency to rate more highly those occupations most open to them.

Treiman's cross-cultural research reminds us that prestige distinctions are universal; the study of China by Lin and Xie underscores this finding. Even a society that has experienced revolutionary movements and decades of Communist party rule stratifies itself in its ranking of prestigious occupations.

Social Mobility

Mobility in Industrial Nations

Studies of intergenerational mobility in industrialized nations have found the following patterns:

1. Substantial similarities exist in the ways that parents' positions in stratification systems are transmitted to their children.
2. As in the United States, mobility opportunities in other nations have been influenced by structural factors, such as labor market changes that lead to the rise or decline of an occupational group within the social hierarchy.
3. Immigration continues to be a significant factor in shaping a society's level of intergenerational mobility (Ganzeboom et al. 1991; Haller et al. 1990; Hauser and Grusky 1988).

In developing countries, people who hope to rise out of poverty often move from the country to the city, where employment prospects are better. The jobs available in industrialized urban areas offer perhaps the best means of upward mobility. This woman works in an electronics factory in Kuala Lumpur, Malaysia.

Cross-cultural studies suggest that intergenerational mobility has been increasing in recent decades, at least among men. Dutch sociologists Harry Ganzeboom and Ruud Luijkx, joined by sociologist Donald Treiman of the United States (1989), examined surveys of mobility in 35 industrial and developing nations. They found that almost all the countries studied had witnessed increased intergenerational mobility between the 1950s and 1980s. In particular, they noted a common pattern of movement away from agriculture-based occupations.

Mobility in Developing Nations

Mobility patterns in industrialized countries are usually associated with intergenerational and intragenerational mobility. However, within developing nations, macro-level social and economic changes often overshadow micro-level movement from one occupation to another. For example, there is typically a substantial wage differential between rural and urban areas, which leads to high levels of migration to the cities. Yet the urban industrial sectors of developing countries generally cannot provide sufficient employment for all those seeking work. When migrants find that they are unable to move upward within the conventional economy, the informal or underground economies described in Box 10-2 become more attractive as a source of employment and financial rewards.

In large developing nations, the most socially significant mobility is the movement out of poverty. This type of mobility is difficult to measure and confirm, however, because economic trends can differ from one area of a country to another. For instance, China's rapid income growth has been accompanied by a growing disparity in income between urban and rural areas, and among different regions. Similarly, in India during the 1990s, poverty declined in urban areas but may have remained static at best in rural areas. Around the world, social mobility is also dramatically influenced by catastrophes such as crop failure and warfare (World Bank 2000c).

Gender Differences and Mobility

Only recently have researchers begun to investigate the impact of gender on the mobility patterns of developing nations. Many aspects of the development process—especially modernization in rural areas and the rural-to-urban migration just described—may result in the modification or abandonment of traditional cultural practices and even marital systems. The effects on women's social standing and mobility are not necessarily positive. As a country develops and modernizes, women's vital role in food production deteriorates, jeopardizing both their autonomy and their material well-being. Moreover, the movement of families to the cities weakens women's ties to relatives who can provide food, financial assistance, and social support.

In the Philippines, however, women have moved to the forefront of the indigenous peoples' struggle to protect their ancestral land from exploitation by outsiders. Having established their right to its rich minerals and forests, members of indigenous groups had begun to feud among themselves over the way in which the land's resources should be developed. Aided by the United Nations Partners in Development Programme, women volunteers established the Pan-Cordillera Women's Network for Peace and Development, a coalition of women's groups dedicated to resolving local disputes. The women mapped boundaries, prepared development plans, and negotiated more than 2,000 peace pacts

Do you know someone who takes in tips and doesn't report the income? Have you traded services with someone—say, a haircut for help with a computer problem? These are aspects of an *informal economy,* the transfer of money, goods, or services that are not reported to the government. Participants in this type of economy avoid taxes, regulations, and minimum wage provisions, as well as expenses incurred for bookkeeping and financial reporting. Anthropologists studying developing nations and preindustrial societies have long acknowledged the existence of informal social networks that make, sell, and trade goods and services. Only recently have these networks been identified as common to all societies.

In industrial societies, the informal economy embraces transactions that are individually quite small but can be quite significant when taken together. One major segment of this economy involves illegal transactions—prostitution, the sale of illegal drugs, gambling, and bribery—leading some observers to describe it as an "underground economy." Yet the informal economy also includes unregulated child care services and the unreported income of craftspeople, street vendors, and employees who receive substantial tips. According to estimates, the informal economy may account for as much as 10 to 20 percent of all economic activity in the United States.

Although these informal economic transactions take place in virtually all societies—both capitalist and socialist—the pattern in developing countries differs somewhat from the informal economy of industrialized nations. In the developing world, governments often set up burdensome business regulations that an overworked bureaucracy must administer. When requests for licenses and permits pile up, holding up business projects, legitimate entrepreneurs find they need to go underground to get anything

> When requests for licenses and permits pile up, holding up business projects, legitimate entrepreneurs find they need to "go underground" to get anything done.

done. In Latin America, for example, the underground economy is estimated to account for one-third to one-half of employment in urban areas. Informal industrial enterprises, such as textile factories and repair shops, tend to be labor-intensive. Underground entrepreneurs cannot rely on advanced machinery, since a firm's assets can be confiscated for failure to operate within the open economy.

Viewed from a functionalist perspective, bureaucratic regulations have contributed to the rise of an efficient informal

economy in certain countries. Nevertheless, these regulatory systems are dysfunctional for overall political and economic well-being. Since informal firms typically operate in remote locations to avoid detection, they cannot easily expand, even when they become profitable. Given the limited protection for their property and contractual rights, participants in the informal economy are less likely than others to save and invest their income.

Informal economies have been criticized for promoting highly unfair and dangerous working conditions. A study of the underground economy in Spain found that workers' incomes were low, there was little job security, and safety and health standards were rarely enforced. Both the Spanish government and the nation's trade unions seemed to ignore the exploitation of participants in the informal economy. Still, especially in the developing world, the existence of a substantial underground economy simply reflects the need for an economic system that is accessible to all residents.

Let's Discuss

1. What conditions contribute to the creation of an informal economy?
2. Describe an informal economy that you have observed or been a part of. Which perspective—functionalist, conflict, or interactionist—do you think best fits the notion of an informal economy?

Sources: Ferman et al. 1987; Hershey 1988; Lemkow 1987; Weigard 1992; World Bank 2003b:68–70.

among community members. They have also run in elections, campaigned against social problems, and organized residents to work together for the common good (United Nations Development Programme 2000:87).

Studies of the distribution of wealth and income within various countries, comparative studies of prestige, and cross-cultural research on mobility consistently reveal that stratification based on class, gender, and other factors shows up within a wide range of societies. Clearly, a

worldwide view of stratification must include not only the sharp contrast between wealthy and impoverished nations but also the layers of hierarchies *within* industrialized societies and developing countries.

Use Your Sociological Imagination www.mhhe.com/schaefer9

Imagine that the United States borders a country with a much higher standard of living. In this neighboring country, the salaries of workers with a college degree start at $120,000 a year. What would life in the United States be like?

> **CASE STUDY:**
> STRATIFICATION IN MEXICO

In May 2003, on a stretch of highway in southern Arizona, the open doors of an abandoned tractor trailer revealed the dead bodies of 19 Mexicans. The truck had been carrying a group of illegal immigrants across the Sonoran Desert when the people hidden inside began to suffer from the intense desert heat. Their story was not unusual. In 2002, almost a hundred illegal immigrants died attempting to traverse the U.S.–Mexican border in the hot, arid corridor that connects the state of Sonora in Mexico to the state of Arizona in the United States.

Why do Mexicans risk their lives crossing the dangerous desert that lies between the two countries? The answer to this question can be found in the income disparity between the two nations—one an industrial giant and the other a partially developed country, still recovering from a history of colonialism and neocolonialism. In this section we will look in some detail at the dynamics of stratification in Mexico, a country of 102 million people. Since the early 20th century there has been a close cultural, economic, and political relationship between Mexico and the United States, but it has clearly been a relationship in which the United States is the dominant party. According to Wallerstein's analysis, the United States is at the core while neighboring Mexico is still on the semiperiphery of the world economic system.

If we compare Mexico to the United States, the overall differences in the standard of living and in life chances are quite dramatic, even though Mexico would be classified as a semiperipheral nation in world systems analysis. The *gross domestic product*—the value of all final goods and services produced within a country—is a commonly used measure of an average resident's economic well-being. In 2003, the gross domestic product per person in the United States came to $34,280; in Mexico, it was a mere $8,240. About 86 percent of adults in the United States have a high school education, compared to only 20 percent of those in Mexico. At birth, people in the United States can expect to live an average of 77 years, whereas life expectancy in Mexico is 75 years (Bureau of the Census 2002a:832; Haub 2003).

Although Mexico is unquestionably a poor country, the gap between its richest and poorest citizens is one of the widest in the world (refer back to Figure 10-4). According to the World Bank, in 2003, 24 percent of the population survived on $2 per day. At the same time, the wealthiest 10 percent of Mexico's people accounted for 42 percent of the entire nation's income. According to a *Forbes* magazine portrait of the world's wealthiest individuals, Mexico had the fourth-largest number of people

on the list—behind only the United States, Germany, and Japan (Castañeda 1995; World Bank 2003b:59).

Political scientist Jorge Castañeda (1995:71) calls Mexico a "polarized society with enormous gaps between rich and poor, town and country, north and south, white and brown (or *criollos* and *mestizos*)." He adds that the country is also divided along lines of class, race, religion, gender, and age. We will examine stratification within Mexico by focusing on race relations and the plight of Mexican Indians, the status of Mexican women, Mexico's economy and environment, and emigration to the United States and its impact on the U.S.–Mexican borderlands.

Race Relations in Mexico: The Color Hierarchy

On January 1, 1994, rebels from an armed insurgent group called the Zapatista National Liberation Army seized four towns in the state of Chiapas in southern Mexico. The rebels—who named their organization after Emiliano Zapata, a farmer and leader of the 1910 revolution against a corrupt dictatorship—were backed by 2,000 lightly armed Mayan Indians and peasants. Zapatista leaders declared that they had turned to armed insurrection to protest economic injustices and discrimination against the region's Indian population. The Mexican government mobilized the army to crush the revolt, but was forced to retreat as news organizations broadcast pictures of the confrontation around the world. A cease-fire was declared after only 12 days of fighting, but 196 people had already died. Negotiations between the Mexican government and the Zapatista National Liberation Army have been shaky ever since.

In response to the crisis, the Mexican legislature enacted the Law on Indian Rights and Culture, which went into effect in 2001. The act allows 62 recognized Indian groups to apply their own customs in resolving conflicts and electing leaders. Unfortunately, state legislatures must give final approval to these arrangements, a requirement that severely limits the rights of large Indian groups whose territories span several states. Tired of waiting for state approval, many indigenous communities in Chiapas have declared self-rule without obtaining official recognition (Boudreaux 2002; J. Smith 2001).

While many factors contributed to the Zapatista revolt, the subordinate status of Mexico's Indian citizens, who account for an estimated 10 percent of the nation's population, was surely important. More than 90 percent of the indigenous population lives in houses without sewers, compared with 21 percent of the population as a whole. And whereas just 10 percent of Mexican adults are illiterate, the proportion for Mexican Indians is 44 percent (Boudreaux 2002; Thompson 2001b).

The subordinate status of Mexico's Indians is but one reflection of the nation's color hierarchy, which links social class to the appearance of racial purity. At the top of this hierarchy are the *criollos,* the 10 percent of the population who are typically White, well-educated members of the business and intellectual elites with familial roots in Spain. In the middle is the large, impoverished *mestizo* majority, most of whom have brown skin and a mixed racial lineage as a result of intermarriage. At the bottom of the color hierarchy are the destitute, full-blooded Mexican Indian minority and a small number of Blacks, some descended from 200,000 African slaves brought to Mexico. This color hierarchy is an important part of day-to-day life—enough so that some Mexicans in the cities use hair dyes, skin lighteners, and blue or green contact lenses to appear more White and European. Ironically, however, nearly all Mexicans are considered part Indian because of centuries of intermarriage (Castañeda 1995; DePalma 1995a).

In 2000, a group of masked women demonstrated outside the Mexican Army's barracks in the state of Chiapas, demanding that the soldiers leave. The women were supporters of the Zapatista National Liberation Army, an insurgent group that protests economic injustices and discrimination against the Indian population in Chiapas.

Many observers take note of widespread denial of prejudice and discrimination against people of color in Mexico. Schoolchildren are taught that the election of Benito Juárez, a Zapotec Indian, as president of Mexico in the nineteenth century proves that all Mexicans are equal. Yet there has been a marked growth in the last decade of formal organizations and voluntary associations representing indigenous Indians. The Zapatista revolt in Chiapas was an even more dramatic indication that those at the bottom of Mexico's color hierarchy are weary of inequality and injustice (DePalma 1995a, 1996; Stavenhagen 1994).

The Status of Women in Mexico

In 1975, Mexico City hosted the first international conference on the status of women, convened by the United Nations. Much of the focus was on the situation of women in developing countries; in that regard, the situation is mixed. Women now constitute 42 percent of the labor force, an increase from 34 percent in the past 20 years, but still behind industrial countries. Unfortunately, Mexican women are even more mired in the lowest-paying jobs than their counterparts in industrial nations. In the political arena, women are rarely seen in top decision-making positions, though they have increased their representation in the national legislature to 16 percent, ranking Mexico at 55th among 181 nations worldwide (Bureau of the Census 2002a:841; Inter-Parliamentary Union 2003).

Feminist sociologists emphasize that even when Mexican women work outside the home, they often are not recognized as active and productive household members, whereas men are typically viewed as heads of households. As one consequence, women find it difficult to obtain credit and technical assistance in many parts of the country, and to inherit land in rural areas. Within manufacturing and service industries, women generally receive little training and tend to work in the least-automated and least-skilled jobs—in good part because there is little expectation that women will pursue career advancement, organize for better working conditions, or become active in labor unions (Kopinak 1995; Martelo 1996; see also Young 1993).

In recent decades, Mexican women have begun to organize to address an array of economic, political, and health issues. Since women continue to serve as the household managers for their families, even when they work outside the home, they are well aware of the consequences of the inadequate public services in their lower-income urban neighborhoods. As far back as 1973, women in Monterrey—the nation's third-largest city—began protesting the continuing disruptions of the city's

Women account for just a small proportion of elected officials and cabinet ministers in Mexico.

water supply. After individual complaints to city officials and the water authority proved fruitless, social networks of female activists began to emerge. These activists sent delegations to confront politicians, organized protest rallies, and blocked traffic as a means of getting media attention. Their efforts brought improvement in Monterrey's water service, but the issue of reliable and safe water remains a concern in Mexico and many developing countries (Bennett 1995).

Mexico's Economy and Environment

Mexico lobbied strongly for acceptance of the North American Free Trade Agreement (NAFTA), ultimately signed in 1993, which provided for the dismantling of almost all trade barriers among the United States, Canada, and Mexico. Officials hoped their struggling economy would receive a major boost from such a favorable linkage to the world's largest consumer market, the United States. Indeed, in 1995, Mexico recorded its first trade surplus with the United States since 1990. Still, any benefit from NAFTA was dramatically undercut in 1994 by the collapse of the *peso,* Mexico's unit of currency. The collapse reflected a widespread loss of confidence as a result of internal political unrest (the Zapatista revolt, discussed earlier) and the assassination of a leading political figure who had spearheaded economic reform. Although U.S. investment in Mexico has increased since the signing of NAFTA, the implementation of the agreement has meant little in the day-to-day economic struggles of the average Mexican (DePalma 1995b; Robberson 1995).

Recession has also hampered efforts to address the nation's environmental problems, which threaten basic resources like air and water. Because much of the nation's water is contaminated, Mexicans consume huge amounts of bottled water. They also drink more Coke per capita than citizens of any other country. Experienced tourists know that even in poor mountain villages, they can often get a Coke from a local distributor's refrigerator case. Unfortunately, not all Mexicans can afford to buy these upscale substitutes for safe drinking water. Especially in poor states like Chiapas, many people suffer from water-borne parasites and diseases, such as hepatitis (*Migration News* 2003a).

At the beginning of the 1990s, air pollutants were hitting emergency levels in Mexico City half the year. Despite opposition from oil companies, the government gradually introduced stronger environmental controls. For example, the "Today You Can't Drive" program took 20 percent of all vehicles without catalytic converters off the road each weekday. But the situation is still dire; by U.S. standards, Mexico City should be under a smog alert 250 days a year. Furthermore, medical research on the children of Mexico City has found that the majority of them show early signs of lung disease, caused, researchers say, by the air pollution (Goering 2001; World Bank 2003a:29–31).

The Borderlands

Air and water pollution are but two of the many ways in which the problems of Mexico and the United States intertwine. Growing recognition of the borderlands reflects the increasingly close and complex relationship between these two countries. The term **borderlands** refers to the area of common culture along the border between Mexico and the United States. Legal and illegal emigration from Mexico to the United States, day laborers crossing the border regularly to go to jobs in the United States, the implementation of the North American Free Trade Agreement, and the exchange of media across the border all make the notion of separate Mexican and U.S. cultures obsolete in the borderlands.

The economic position of the borderlands is rather complicated, as we can see in the emergence of *maquiladoras* on the Mexican side (see Figure 10-5). These are foreign companies that establish operations in Mexico, yet are exempt from Mexican taxes and are not required to provide insurance or benefits for their workers. The *maquiladoras* have attracted manufacturing jobs from other parts of North America to Mexico. As of the fall of 2002, 1.1 million people were employed in the *maquiladoras,* where the daily take-home pay for entry-level workers was $4 to $5. Since many of these firms come from the United States and sell their products to Mexico's vast domestic market, their operations deepen the impact of U.S. consumer culture on Mexico's urban and rural areas (Thompson 2001c).

Ironically, the *maquiladoras* are now experiencing the same challenge from global trade as U.S. manufacturing plants did. Beginning in 2001, some began shifting operations to China. While Mexican labor costs (wages plus benefits) are just $2 to $2.50 an hour, Chinese labor costs are even lower—50 cents to $1 an hour (*Migration News* 2002c).

The *maquiladoras* have contributed to Mexico's economic development, but not without some cost. Conflict theorists note that unregulated growth allows the owners to exploit the workers with jobs that lack security, possibilities for advancement, and decent wages. Moreover, many of the U.S.-owned companies require female job applicants to take a urine test to screen out those who are pregnant—a violation of Mexican law as well as the NAFTA agreement, and the source of numerous cases of sexual discrimination. Social activists also

FIGURE 10-5

The Borderlands

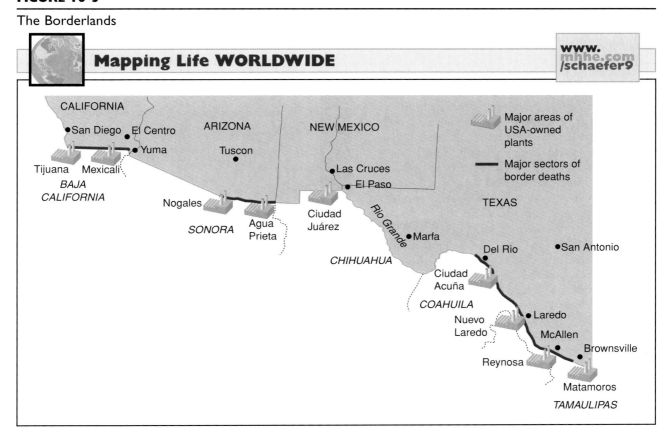

Source: Prepared by the author based on Ellingwood 2001; Thompson 2001a.

Maquiladoras located just south of the U.S.–Mexican border employ uninsured Mexican workers at wages considerably lower than those earned by U.S. workers. In search of higher wages, undocumented Mexicans often attempt to cross the border illegally, risking their lives in the process.

Think About It
How do U.S. consumers benefit from the buildup of factories along the U.S.–Mexican border?

complain that tens of thousands of Mexicans work on *maquiladora* assembly lines for very low wages, such as $1 an hour, raising the issue of sweatshop labor noted earlier in this chapter (Dillon 1998; Dougherty and Holthouse 1999).

When people in the United States think about the borderlands, they generally think about immigration. As we'll see in the social policy section of Chapter 11, immigration is a controversial political issue in the United States—especially immigration across the Mexican border. For its part, Mexico is concerned about the priorities and policies of its powerful northern neighbor. From the Mexican point of view, the United States too often regards Mexico simply as a reserve pool of cheap labor, encouraging Mexicans to cross the border when workers are needed but discouraging and cracking down on immigrants when they are not. Some people, then, see immigration more as a labor market issue than a law enforcement issue. Viewed from the perspective of Immanuel Wallerstein's world systems analysis and dependency theory, it is yet another example of a core industrialized nation exploiting a developing country.

As we saw at the beginning of this case, the risks of immigration are considerable. Following September 11, 2001, when the U.S. government increased surveillance at common entry points along the border, migrants without proper documentation moved to more remote and dangerous locations. In all, several hundred illegal immigrants lose their lives every year while attempting to cross the long border, many of them from dehydration in the intense desert heat (Dellios 2002).

The social impact of emigration to the United States is felt throughout Mexico. According to sociological research, the earliest emigrants were typically married men of working age who came from the middle of the stratification system. They had enough financial resources to afford the costs and risks of emigration, yet were experiencing enough financial strain that entering the United States was attractive to them. Over time, kinship ties to migrants multiplied and emigration became less class-selective, with entire families making the trek to the United States. More recently, the occupational backgrounds of Mexican emigrants have widened further, reflecting not only changes in U.S. immigration policy but the

continuing crisis in the Mexican economy (Massey 1998).

Many Mexicans who have come to the United States send some part of their earnings back across the border to family members still in Mexico. This substantial flow of money, sometimes referred to as **remittances** or *migradollars,* is estimated at a minimum of $10 billion a year, and is surpassed only by oil as a source of income. Sociologist Douglas Massey points out that if these funds went solely into the purchase of consumer goods, they would underscore the view of dependency theory, that Mexico's economy is little more than an extension of the economy of the United States. In fact, however, some of these migradollars are used by Mexicans to establish and maintain small business enterprises, such as handicraft workshops and farms. Consequently, the transfer of migradollars does stimulate the local and national economies of Mexico (Durand et al. 1996; Thompson 2002).

We now turn to an examination of how social inequality takes on an especially ugly face in the form of human rights abuse.

Use Your Sociological Imagination www. mhhe.com /schaefer9

Imagine a day when the border between the United States and Mexico is completely open. What would the two countries' economies be like? What would their societies be like?

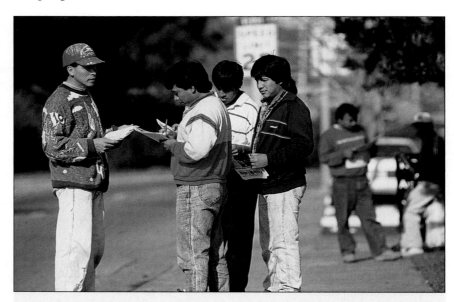

Mexican workers looking for day jobs on a California street. Many Mexican immigrants to the United States send part of their earnings back home to their families in Mexico. Some of these migradollars are used to establish small businesses.

SOCIAL POLICY and SOCIAL INEQUALITY WORLDWIDE

Universal Human Rights

The Issue

Poised on the third millennium, the world seemed capable of mighty feats, ranging from explorations of distant solar systems to the refinement of tiny genes within human cells. Yet at the same time came constant reminders of how quickly people and their fundamental human rights could be trampled. The end of Soviet dominance of Eastern Europe set off bitter and sometimes violent clashes among racial, ethnic, and religious groups in Bosnia, Kosovo, Serbia, and former republics of the Soviet Union itself. In central Africa, Hutus and Tutsis massacred one another in a virulent civil war. Meanwhile, Kurds continued to fight for their rights in both Iraq and Turkey, as did Mexican peasants of Indian heritage. A peace agreement between Israel and the Palestinians did not end hostilities or killings in that troubled area.

Human rights refers to universal moral rights possessed by all people because they are human. The most important elaboration of human rights appears in the Universal Declaration of Human Rights, adopted by the United Nations in 1948. This declaration prohibits slavery, torture, and degrading punishment; grants everyone the right to a nationality and its culture; affirms freedom of religion and the right to vote; proclaims the right to seek asylum in other countries to escape persecution; and prohibits arbitrary interference with one's privacy and the arbitrary taking of a person's property. It also emphasizes that mothers and children are entitled to special care and assistance.

What steps, if any, can the world community take to ensure the protection of these rights? And is it even possible to agree on what those rights are?

The Setting

At first, the United States opposed a binding obligation to the Universal Declaration of Human Rights. The government feared that the declaration would cause international scrutiny of the nation's own domestic civil rights controversies (at a time when racial segregation by law was still common). By the early 1960s, however, the United States had begun to use the declaration to promote democracy abroad (Forsythe 1990).

The 1990s brought the term *ethnic cleansing* into the world's vocabulary. Within the former Yugoslavia, Serbs initiated a policy intended to "cleanse" Muslims from parts of Bosnia-Herzegovina and ethnic Albanians from the province of Kosovo. Hundreds of thousands of people were killed in fighting in this area, while many others were uprooted from their homes. Moreover, there were reports of substantial numbers of rapes of Muslim, Croatian, and Kosovar women by Serbian soldiers. In 1996 a United Nations tribunal indicted eight Bosnian Serb military and police officers for rape, marking the first time that sexual assault was treated as a war crime under international law (Simons 1996; see also Fein 1995).

In the wake of the terrorist attacks of September 11, 2001, increased security and surveillance at U.S. airports and border crossings caused some observers to wonder whether human rights were not being jeopardized at home. In the first few months of 2003 alone, U.S. agents separated out for questioning 130,000 male immigrants and visitors, most of them either Arab or Muslim. About 10,000 were detained, largely because they were in the country illegally. A few were placed in custody, sometimes without access to legal assistance. For the foreseeable future, it seems, the United States and other countries will walk a delicate tightrope between human rights and the need for security (A. Lewis 2003; Swarns and Drew 2003).

Sociological Insights

By its very title, the Universal Declaration of Human Rights emphasizes that such rights should be *universal.* Even so, cultural relativism encourages the understanding and respect for the distinctive norms, values, and customs of each culture. In some situations, conflicts arise between human rights standards and local social practices that rest on alternative views of human dignity. For example, is India's caste system an inherent violation of human rights? What about the many cultures of the world that view the subordinate status of women as an essential element in their traditions? Should human rights be interpreted differently in different parts of the world?

In 1993, the United States rejected such a view by insisting that the Universal Declaration of Human Rights set a single standard for acceptable behavior around the world. However, in the late 1990s, certain Asian and African nations were reviving arguments about cultural relativism in an attempt to block sanctions by the United Nations Human Rights Commission.

p.73

For example, female genital mutilation, a practice that is common in more than 30 countries around the world, has been condemned in Western nations as a human rights abuse. This controversial practice often involves removal of the clitoris, in the belief that its excision will inhibit a young woman's sex drive, making her chaste and thus more desirable to her future husband. Though some countries have passed laws against the practice, they have gone largely unenforced. Immigrants from countries where genital mutilation is common often insist that their daughters undergo the procedure, to protect them from Western cultural norms that allow premarital sex. In this context, how does one define human rights? (Rising Daughters Aware 2003)

It is not often that a nation makes such a bold statement. Policymakers, including those in the United States, more frequently look at human rights issues from an economic perspective. Functionalists would point out how much more quickly we become embroiled in "human rights" concerns when oil is at stake, as in the Middle East, or when military alliances come into play, as in Europe. The United States is less likely to want to interfere in an area where its economic concerns are modest (as in Africa) or where it is seeking to advance an economic agenda (as in China).

This intersection of economics and human rights issues has led to the creation of a Human Rights Index (HRI), using a database that weighs measures of human rights violations in a country against its level of economic development. Human rights abuses include such indicators as the denial of minority and women's rights, the presence of political prisoners, and the use of torture. Because poverty and a position at the periphery of the world economic system make equality difficult to achieve, the HRI is adjusted to reflect the level of a nation's development. Figure 10-6 highlights the best nations and worst offenders in this index of 195 nations. On the list, Mexico ranks 154, and Russia and the

FIGURE 10-6

Human Rights Index

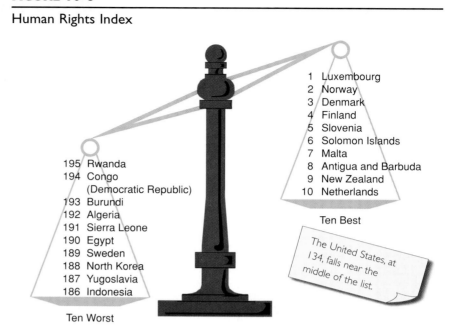

195 Rwanda
194 Congo (Democratic Republic)
193 Burundi
192 Algeria
191 Sierra Leone
190 Egypt
189 Sweden
188 North Korea
187 Yugoslavia
186 Indonesia

Ten Worst

1 Luxembourg
2 Norway
3 Denmark
4 Finland
5 Slovenia
6 Solomon Islands
7 Malta
8 Antigua and Barbuda
9 New Zealand
10 Netherlands

Ten Best

The United States, at 134, falls near the middle of the list.

Notes: Fourteen nations had no abuses. Nations were ranked based on per capita gross domestic product, except for Andorra, Liechtenstein, Monaco, Palau, San Marino, and Tuvalu, for which there were no reliable GDP data.

Sources: Haub 2003; *The Observer* (London) 1999.

Think About It
What do most of the 10 worst countries have in common? The 10 best countries?

United States are tied at 134—closer to the worst offenders than the best nations, despite the United States' avowed advocacy of human rights.

Policy Initiatives

Human rights come wrapped up in international diplomacy. For that reason, many national policymakers hesitate to interfere in human rights issues, especially if they conflict with what are regarded as more pressing national concerns. Stepping up to fill the gap are international organizations such as the United Nations and nongovernmental organizations (NGOs) like Médecins sans Frontières and Amnesty International. Most initiatives come from these international bodies.

Médecins sans Frontières (Doctors without Borders), the world's largest independent emergency medical aid organization, won the 1999 Nobel Peace Prize for its work in countries worldwide. Founded in 1971 and based in Paris, the organization has 5,000 doctors and nurses working in 80 countries. "Our intention is to highlight current upheavals, to bear witness to foreign tragedies and reflect on the principles of humanitarian aid," explains Dr. Rony Brauman, the organization's president (Spielmann 1992:12; also see Daley 1999).

Among the endangered peoples of the world are many indigenous (native or tribal) peoples whose settlement preceded immigration from other countries and colonialism. They include nomadic Bedouins of the Arabic peninsula, the Inuit (Eskimo) of North America, the Sami (or Lapp) of northern Scandinavia, the Ainu of Japan, the Aborigines of Australia, and Brazil's Yanomani Indians. Indigenous peoples are organizing to defend their way of life, assisted by voluntary associations in the core industrialized nations. As one result of their activism, the United Nations has established a working group to draft a Universal Declaration of the Right of Indigenous Peoples (Durning 1993).

Amnesty International monitors human rights violations around the world. Founded in 1961, the organization has chapters in many countries and 400,000 members in the United States alone. AI works for the release of men and women detained for their conscientiously held beliefs, their color, ethnic origin, sex, religion, or language—provided they have neither used nor advocated violence. The winner of the 1977 Nobel Prize for Peace, Amnesty International opposes all forms of torture and capital punishment and advocates prompt trials of all political prisoners.

Women's rights got a boost from the 1995 World Conference on Women. Conference delegates agreed on a "platform of action" calling on governments around the world to improve the status of girls, better the economic situation of women, and protect women from increasing levels of violence.

In recent years, awareness has been growing of lesbian and gay rights as an aspect of universal human rights. In 1994, Amnesty International USA (1994:2) published a pioneering report in which it acknowledged that "homosexuals in many parts of the world live in constant fear of government persecution." The report examined abuses in Brazil, Greece, Mexico, Iran, the United States, and other countries, including cases of torture, imprisonment, and extrajudicial execution. Later in 1994, the United States issued an order that would allow lesbians and gay men to seek political asylum in the United States if they could prove they had suffered government persecution in their home countries solely because of their sexual orientation. We'll look at lesbian and gay rights in more detail in Chapter 22 (Johnston 1994).

Ethnic cleansing in the former Yugoslavia; human rights violations in Iraq, Iran, and the Sudan; persecution of the Aborigines of Australia and other indigenous peoples; increased surveillance in the name of counterterrorism; violence against women inside and outside the family; governmental torture of lesbians and gay men—all these are vivid reminders that social inequality today can have life-and-death consequences. Universal human rights remain an ideal, not a reality.

Human rights abuses are often committed during war. In the bitter struggle between Russia and its breakaway province of Chechnya, both Russian security forces and Chechen rebels have been accused of human rights violations. The Russian special police shown in this photograph are responding to the Chechen takeover of Moscow's Palace of Culture in 2002, in which rebels threatened to kill 600 civilian hostages.

Let's Discuss

1. Why do definitions of human rights vary?
2. Does it surprise you that the United States does not rank very high in human rights? Why do you think that is the case?
3. How have feminist groups broadened the debate over universal human rights?

CHAPTER RESOURCES

Summary

Worldwide, stratification can be seen both in the gap between rich and poor nations and in the inequality within countries. This chapter examined stratification within the world economic system; the impact of globalization, modernization, and multinational corporations on developing countries; and the distribution of wealth and income in various nations.

1. As of 1995, the 140 developing nations accounted for 78 percent of the world's population but only 16 percent of all wealth.
2. Former colonized nations are kept in a subservient position, subject to foreign domination, through the process of **neocolonialism.**
3. Drawing on the conflict perspective, the **world systems analysis** of sociologist Immanuel Wallerstein views the global economic system as being divided between nations that control wealth (*core nations*) and those from which capital is taken (*periphery nations*).
4. According to **dependency theory,** even as developing countries make economic advances, they remain weak and subservient to core nations and corporations within an increasingly integrated global economy.
5. **Globalization,** or the worldwide integration of government policies, cultures, social movements, and financial markets through trade and the exchange of ideas, is a controversial trend that critics blame for contributing to the cultural domination of periphery nations by core nations.
6. **Multinational corporations** bring jobs and industry to developing nations, but they also tend to exploit workers in order to maximize profits.
7. Many sociologists are quick to note that terms such as **modernization** and even *development* contain an ethnocentric bias.
8. According to **modernization theory,** development in peripheral countries will be assisted by innovations transferred from the industrialized world.
9. Social mobility is more limited in developing nations than in core nations.
10. While Mexico is unquestionably a poor country, the gap between its richest and poorest citizens is one of the widest in the world.
11. The subordinate status of Mexico's Indians is but one reflection of the nation's color hierarchy, which links social class to the appearance of racial purity.
12. Growing recognition of the **borderlands** reflects the increasingly close and complex relationship between Mexico and the United States.
13. **Human rights** need to be identified and abuses of those rights corrected in countries throughout the world.

Critical Thinking Questions

1. How have multinational corporations and the trend toward globalization affected you, your family, and your community? List both the pros and the cons. Have the benefits outweighed the drawbacks?
2. Imagine that you have the opportunity to spend a year in Mexico studying inequality in that nation. How would you draw on the research designs (surveys, observation, experiments, existing sources) to better understand and document stratification in Mexico?
3. How active should the U.S. government be in addressing violations of human rights in other countries? At what point, if any, does concern for human rights turn into ethnocentrism by failing to respect the distinctive norms, values, and customs of another culture?

Key Terms

Borderlands The area of common culture along the border between Mexico and the United States. (page 240)

Colonialism The maintenance of political, social, economic, and cultural dominance over a people by a foreign power for an extended period. (229)

Dependency theory An approach that contends that industrialized nations continue to exploit developing countries for their own gain. (230)

Globalization The worldwide integration of government policies, cultures, social movements, and financial markets through trade and the exchange of ideas. (230)

Human rights   Universal moral rights possessed by all people because they are human. (243)

Informal economy   Transfers of money, goods, or services that are not reported to the government. (237)

Modernization   The far-reaching process by which peripheral nations move from traditional or less developed institutions to those characteristic of more developed societies. (232)

Modernization theory   A functionalist approach that proposes that modernization and development will gradually improve the lives of people in developing nations. (233)

Multinational corporation   A commercial organization that is headquartered in one country but does business throughout the world. (230)

Neocolonialism   Continuing dependence of former colonies on foreign countries. (229)

Remittances   The monies that immigrants return to their families of origin. Also called *migradollars*. (242)

World systems analysis   A view of the global economic system as divided between certain industrialized nations that control wealth and developing countries that are controlled and exploited. (229)

TECHNOLOGY RESOURCES

Internet Connection

*Note: While all the URLs listed were current as of the printing of this book, these sites often change. Please check our website (**www.mhhe.com/schaefer9**) for updates, hyperlinks, and exercises related to these sites.*

1. Human rights play an important role in everyday life. Explore the Human Rights Web (**www.hrweb.org**), a website dedicated to promoting human rights, to learn more about this concept.

2. As you have learned in this chapter, social inequality affects many people worldwide. Visit Inequality.org (**www.inequality.org**) to find out more about social inequality.

Online Learning Center with PowerWeb

This chapter has focused on social inequality worldwide. Test your knowledge about the information presented by visiting the student center in the Online Learning Center at **www.mhhe.com/schaefer9** and taking the multiple choice quiz. This quiz will not only test your knowledge; it will give you immediate feedback on the questions that you answered incorrectly.

RACIAL AND ETHNIC INEQUALITY

HAVE YOU EVER SEEN A REAL INDIAN?

AMERICAN INDIAN
COLLEGE FUND
EDUCATION IS STRENGTH

Nearly 60% of our graduates go on to a non-Indian college or university, exceeding the transfer rate of community college students nationwide. For more on tribal colleges, call 800.776.3863 or go to collegefund.org.

Dr. Lori Arviso Alvord, M.D., Navajo. Surgeon, Associate Dean of Student Affairs, Dartmouth Medical School, author of *The Scalpel and the Silver Bear.*

This advertisement for the American Indian College Fund explodes common stereotypes about Native Americans with its photograph of a Navaho surgeon, Dr. Lori Arviso Alvord. Historically, prejudice and discrimination against minority groups has prevented them from reaching their full potential. (To learn more about Dr. Alvord, see her autobiography, *The Scalpel and the Silver Bear* [Alvord and Van Pelt 1999].)

Minority, Racial, and Ethnic Groups

Prejudice and Discrimination

Studying Race and Ethnicity

Patterns of Intergroup Relations

Race and Ethnicity in the United States

Social Policy and Race and Ethnicity: Global Immigration

Boxes

SOCIAL INEQUALITY: The Latino Middle Class

RESEARCH IN ACTION: Prejudice against Arab Americans and Muslim Americans

TAKING SOCIOLOGY TO WORK: Prudence Hannis: Researcher and Community Activist, Quebec Native Women

Ah so. No tickee, no washee. So sorry, so sollee.

Chinkee, Chink. Jap, Nip, zero, kamikaze. Dot-head, flat face, flat nose, slant eye, slope. Slit, mamasan, dragon lady. Gook, VC, Flip, Hindoo.

By the time I was ten, I'd heard such words so many times I could feel them coming before they parted lips. I knew they were meant in the unkindest way. Still, we didn't talk about these incidents at home, we just accepted them as part of being in America, something to learn to rise above.

The most common taunting didn't even utilize words but a string of unintelligible gobbledygook that kids—and adults—would spew as they pretended to speak Chinese or some other Asian language. It was a mockery of how they imagined my parents talked to me.

Truth was that Mom and Dad rarely spoke to us in Chinese, except to scold or call us to dinner. Worried that we might develop an accent, my father insisted that we speak English at home. This, he explained, would lessen the hardships we might encounter and make us more acceptable as Americans.

I'll never know if my father's language decision was right. On the one hand, I, like most Asian Americans, have been complimented countless times on my spoken English by people who assumed I was a foreigner. "My, you speak such good English," they'd cluck.

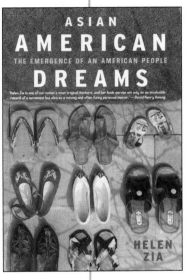

"No kidding, I ought to," I would think to myself, then wonder: should I thank them for assuming that English isn't my native language? Or should I correct them on the proper usage of "well" and "good"?

More often than feeling grateful for my American accent, I've wished that I could jump into a heated exchange of rapid-fire Chinese, volume high and spit flying. But with a vocabulary limited to *"Ni hao?"* (How are you?) and *"Ting bu dong"* (I hear but don't understand), meaningful exchanges are woefully impossible. I find myself smiling and nodding like a dashboard ornament. I'm envious of the many people I know who grew up speaking an Asian language yet converse in English beautifully.

Armed with standard English and my flat New Jersey "a," I still couldn't escape the name-calling. I became all too familiar with other names and faces that supposedly matched mine—Fu Manchu, Suzie Wong, Hop Sing, Madame Butterfly, Charlie Chan, Ming the Merciless—the "Asians" produced for mass consumption. Their faces filled me with shame whenever I saw them on TV or in the movies. They defined my face to the rest of the world: a sinister Fu, Suzie the whore, subservient Hop Sing, pathetic Butterfly, cunning Chan, and warlike Ming. Inscrutable Orientals all, real Americans none. *(Zia 2000)* ■ 🖱

Additional information about this excerpt can be found on the Online Learning Center at **www.mhhe.com/Schaefer9.**

H elen Zia, the journalist and community activist who wrote this reminiscence from her childhood, is the successful daughter of Chinese immigrants to the United States. As her story shows, Zia experienced blatant prejudice against Chinese Americans, even though she spoke flawless English. In fact, all new immigrants and their families have faced stereotyping and hostility, whether they were White or non-White, Asian, African, or East European. In this multicultural society, those who are different from the dominant social group have never been welcome.

Today, millions of African Americans, Asian Americans, Hispanic Americans, and many other racial and ethnic minorities continue to experience the often bitter contrast between the "American dream" and the grim realities of poverty, prejudice, and discrimination. Like class, the social definitions of race and ethnicity still affect people's place and status in a stratification system, not only in this country but throughout the world. High incomes, a good command of English,

and hard-earned professional credentials do not always override racial and ethnic stereotypes or protect those who fit them from the sting of racism.

What is prejudice, and how is it institutionalized in the form of discrimination? In what ways have race and ethnicity affected the experience of immigrants from other countries? What are the fastest growing minority groups in the United States today? In this chapter we will focus on the meaning of race and ethnicity. We will begin by identifying the basic characteristics of a minority group and distinguishing between racial and ethnic groups. Then we will examine the dynamics of prejudice and discrimination. After considering the functionalist, conflict, and interactionist perspectives on race and ethnicity, we'll take a look at common patterns of intergroup relations. The following section will describe the major racial and ethnic groups in the United States. Finally, in the social policy section, we will explore issues related to global immigration. ■

MINORITY, RACIAL, AND ETHNIC GROUPS

Sociologists frequently distinguish between racial and ethnic groups. The term ***racial group*** describes a group that is set apart from others because of obvious physical differences. Whites, African Americans, and Asian Americans are all considered racial groups in the United States. While race does turn on physical differences, it is the culture of a particular society that constructs and attaches social significance to these differences, as we will see later. Unlike racial groups, an ***ethnic group*** is set apart from others primarily because of its national origin or distinctive cultural patterns. In the United States, Puerto Ricans, Jews, and Polish Americans are all categorized as ethnic groups. Table 11-1 lists the major racial and ethnic groups in the United States.

Minority Groups

A numerical minority is any group that makes up less than half of some larger population. The population of the United States includes thousands of numerical minorities, including television actors, green-eyed people,

tax lawyers, and descendants of the Pilgrims who arrived on the *Mayflower*. However, these numerical minorities are not considered to be minorities in the sociological sense; in fact, the number of people in a group does not necessarily determine its status as a social minority (or dominant group). When sociologists define a minority group, they are primarily concerned with the economic and political power, or powerlessness, of that group. A ***minority group*** is a subordinate group whose members have significantly less control or power over their own lives than the members of a dominant or majority group have over theirs.

Sociologists have identified five basic properties of a minority group: unequal treatment, physical or cultural traits, ascribed status, solidarity, and in-group marriage (Wagley and Harris 1958):

1. Members of a minority group experience unequal treatment compared to members of a dominant group. For example, the management of an apartment complex may refuse to rent to African Americans, Hispanics, or Jews. Social inequality may be created or maintained by prejudice, discrimination, segregation, or even extermination.

2. Members of a minority group share physical or cultural characteristics that distinguish them from the dominant group. Each society arbitrarily decides which characteristics are most important in defining the groups.

3. Membership in a minority (or dominant) group is not voluntary; people are born into the group.

◀ p. 105 Thus, race and ethnicity are considered *ascribed* statuses.

4. Minority group members have a strong sense of group solidarity. William Graham Sumner, writing in 1906, noted that people make distinctions between members of their own group (the *in-group*)

◀ pp. 128–129 and everyone else (the *out-group*). When a group is the object of long-term prejudice and discrimination, the feeling of "us versus them" can and often does become extremely intense.

5. Members of a minority generally marry others from the same group. A member of a dominant group is often unwilling to marry into a supposedly inferior minority. In addition, the minority group's sense of solidarity encourages marriages within the group and discourages marriages to outsiders.

Table 11-1	Racial and Ethnic Groups in the United States, 2000	
Classification	**Number in Thousands**	**Percentage of Total Population**
Racial groups		
Whites (includes 16.9 million White Hispanics)	211,461	75.1
Blacks/African Americans	34,658	12.3
Native Americans, Alaskan Native	2,476	0.9
Asian Americans	10,243	3.6
Chinese	2,433	0.9
Filipinos	1,850	0.7
Asian Indians	1,679	0.6
Vietnamese	1,123	0.4
Koreans	1,077	0.4
Japanese	797	0.2
Other	1,285	0.5
Ethnic groups		
White ancestry (single or mixed)		
Germans	46,489	16.5
Irish	33,067	11.7
English	28,265	10.0
Italians	15,943	5.7
French	9,776	3.5
Poles	9,054	3.2
Jews	6,000	2.1
Hispanics (or Latinos)	35,306	12.5
Mexican Americans	23,337	8.3
Central and South Americans	5,119	1.8
Puerto Ricans	3,178	1.1
Cubans	1,412	0.5
Other	2,260	0.8
Total (all groups)	281,422	

Note: Percentages do not total 100 percent and figures under subheadings do not add up to figures under major headings because of overlap among groups (e.g., Polish American Jews or people of mixed ancestry, such as Irish and Italian). Hispanics may be of any race. White ancestry data should be regarded as an approximation. See Yin 2001.

Sources: American Jewish Committee 2001; Bureau of the Census 2001c; Grieco and Cassidy 2001; Therrien and Ramirez 2001.

Race

The term *racial group* refers to those minorities (and the corresponding dominant groups) set apart from others by obvious physical differences. But what is an "obvious" physical difference? Each society determines which differences are important, while ignoring other characteristics that could serve as a basis for social differentiation. In the United States, we see differences in both skin color and hair color. Yet people learn informally that differences in skin color have a dramatic social and political meaning, while differences in hair color do not.

When observing skin color, people in the United States tend to lump others rather casually into such categories as "Black," "White," and "Asian." More subtle differences in skin color often go unnoticed. However, that is not the case in other societies. In many nations of Central America and South America, people recognize color gradients on a continuum from light to dark skin color. Brazil has approximately 40 color groupings, while in other countries people may be described as "Mestizo Hondurans," "Mulatto Colombians," or "African Panamanians." What we see as "obvious" differences, then, are subject to each society's social definitions.

FIGURE 11-1

Racial and Ethnic Groups in the United States, 1500–2100 (Projected)

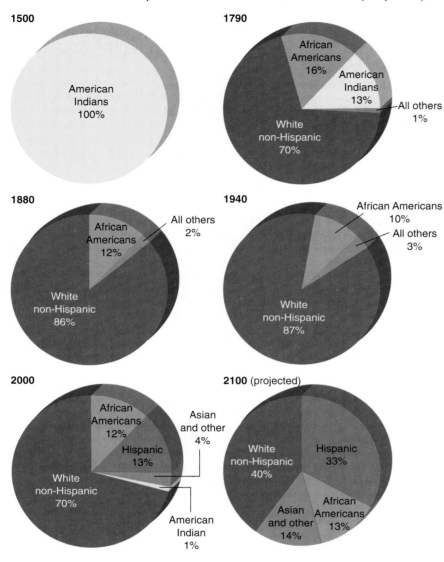

Sources: Author's estimate; Bureau of the Census 1975, 2000c; Grieco and Cassidy 2001; Thornton 1987. Data for 2100 African Americans and Asian and other are for non-Hispanics.

The racial and ethnic composition of what is today the United States has been undergoing change not just for the last 50 years, but for the last 500. Five centuries ago the land was populated only by indigenous Native Americans.

The largest racial minorities in the United States are African Americans (or Blacks), Native Americans (or American Indians), and Asian Americans (Japanese Americans, Chinese Americans, and other Asian peoples). Figure 11–1 provides information about the population of racial and ethnic groups in the United States over the past five centuries.

Biological Significance of Race

Viewed from a biological perspective, the term *race* would refer to a genetically isolated group with distinctive gene frequencies. But it is impossible to scientifically define or identify such a group. Contrary to popular belief, there are no "pure races." Nor are there physical traits—whether skin color or baldness—that can be used to describe one group to the exclusion of all others. If scientists examine a smear of human blood under a microscope, they cannot tell whether it came from a Chinese or a Navajo, a Hawaiian or an African American. There is, in fact, more genetic variation *within* races than across them.

Migration, exploration, and invasion have led to the intermingling of races. Scientific investigations indicate that the percentage of North American Blacks with White ancestry ranges from 20 percent to as much as 75 percent. Recent DNA findings suggest that some Blacks today can even claim Thomas Jefferson as their ancestor. Such statistics undermine a fundamental assumption of life in the United States: that we can accurately categorize individuals as "Black" or "White" (Herskovits 1930; D. Roberts 1975).

Some people would like to find biological explanations to help social scientists understand why certain peoples of the world have come to dominate others (see the discussion of sociobiology in Chapter 3). Given the absence of pure racial groups, there can be no satisfactory biological answers for such social and political questions.

p. 62

Social Construction of Race

In the southern part of the United States, it was known as the "one-drop rule." If a person had even a single drop of "Black blood," that person was defined and viewed as Black, even if he or she *appeared* to be White. Clearly, race had social significance in the South, enough so that White legislators established official standards about who was "Black" and who was "White."

The one-drop rule was a vivid example of the *social construction of race*—the process by which people come to define a group as a race based in part on physical characteristics, but also on historical, cultural, and economic factors. This is an ongoing process subject to some debate, especially in a diverse society such as the United States, where each year increasing numbers of children are born to parents of different racial backgrounds.

In the 2000 census, nearly 7 million people in the United States (or about 2 percent of the population) reported that they were of two or more races. Half the people classified as multiracial were under age 18, suggesting that this segment of the population will grow in the years to come. People who claimed both White and American Indian ancestry were the largest group of multiracial residents (Grieco and Cassidy 2001).

This statistical finding of millions of multiracial people obscures how individuals handle their identity. The prevailing social construction of race pushes people to choose just one race, even if they acknowledge a broader cultural background. Still, many individuals, especially young adults, struggle against social pressure to choose a single identity, and instead openly embrace multiple heritages. Tiger Woods, the world's best-known professional golfer, considers himself both Asian and African American.

A dominant or majority group has the power not only to define itself legally but to define a society's values. Sociologist William I. Thomas (1923), an early critic of theories of racial and gender differences, saw that the "definition of the situation" could mold the personality of the individual. To put it another way, Thomas, writing from the interactionist perspective, observed that people respond not only to the objective features of a situation or person but also to the *meaning* that situation or person has for them. Thus, we can create false images or stereotypes that become real in their consequences. **Stereotypes** are unreliable generalizations about all members of a group that do not recognize individual differences within the group.

In the last 30 years, critics have pointed out the power of the mass media to perpetuate false racial and

Not long ago, these children of a White mother and an African American father would automatically have assumed their father's racial identity. Today, however, some children of mixed-race families identify themselves as biracial.

ethnic stereotypes. Television is a prime example: Almost all the leading dramatic roles are cast as Whites, even in urban-based programs like *Friends* (see Chapter 7). Blacks tend to be featured mainly in crime-based dramas.

Use Your Sociological Imagination www.mhhe.com/schaefer9

Using a TV remote control, how quickly do you think you could find a television show in which all the characters share your own racial or ethnic background? What about a show in which all the characters share a different background from your own—how quickly could you find one?

Ethnicity

An ethnic group, unlike a racial group, is set apart from others because of its national origin or distinctive cultural patterns. Among the ethnic groups in the United States are peoples with a Spanish-speaking background, referred to collectively as *Latinos* or *Hispanics,* such as Puerto Ricans, Mexican Americans, Cuban Americans, and other Latin Americans. Other ethnic groups in this country include Jewish, Irish, Italian, and Norwegian Americans. While these groupings are convenient, they serve to obscure differences *within* ethnic categories (as in the case of Hispanics), as well as to overlook the mixed ancestry of so many ethnic people in the United States.

The distinction between racial and ethnic minorities is not always clear-cut. Some members of racial minorities, such as Asian Americans, may have significant

Research in Action

11-1 PREJUDICE AGAINST ARAB AMERICANS AND MUSLIM AMERICANS

As marginal groups with little political power, Arab Americans and Muslim Americans are vulnerable to prejudice and discrimination. In the first five days after the terrorist attack on the World Trade Center in September 2001, these groups filed more than 300 reports of harassment and abuse, including one death. Six years earlier, when the bombing of a federal office building in Oklahoma City was mistakenly attributed to Middle Eastern terrorism, many Arabic and Islamic schoolchildren in the United States were blamed for the attack. One fifth-grade boy was told, "Go back where you came from!" His mother, an attorney and second-generation Syrian American, asked where her children were supposed to go. One was born in Texas, the other in Oklahoma.

Sociologists have observed two trends in the United States over the last 20 years. First, the numbers of people in the United States who are Arab or who practice the Muslim faith have increased dramatically. Second, the open expression of hostility toward Arab and Muslim people has also increased. This heightened hostility has discouraged many Arab and Muslim Americans from participating in

civic life. In 2002, a year after the attack on the World Trade Center, only 70 Muslims ran for office anywhere in the United States, compared to 700 in the year 2000.

"Profiling" of potential terrorists at airports has put Arab and Muslim Americans under special surveillance. A number of airlines and law enforcement authorities use appearance and ethnic-sounding names to identify and take aside Arab Americans (or those who

> One fifth-grade boy was told, "Go back where you came from!"

match the "profile") and search their belongings. After the terrorist attacks of September 2001, criticism of this practice declined as concern for the public's safety mounted.

Muslim women who choose to don head scarves or *hijbab* in keeping with their tradition of dressing modestly encounter harassment from strangers in the street. Many employers insist that the women shed the covering if they wish to

get a job or expect to be promoted. These women find it difficult to understand such attitudes in a nation founded on religious freedom.

Many people in the United States inaccurately lump together Arab Americans and Muslims. While these groups overlap, many Arab Americans are Christians (as is true of many Arabs living in the Middle East) and many Muslims (such as African Americans, Iranians, and Pakistanis) are non-Arabs. Currently, there are an estimated 870,000 Arab Americans, and their numbers are rising. Many cling to the culture of their nation of origin, which can vary considerably, from nations in North Africa to the Middle East.

At present, perhaps as many as 3 million Muslims live in the United States, of whom about 42 percent are African American, 24 percent are South Asian, 12 percent are Arab, and 22 percent are "other." Muslims are followers of Islam, the world's largest faith after Christianity. Islam is based on the teachings found in the Koran (or Al-Qur'an), by the seventh-century prophet Mohammed. Islamic believers are divided into a variety of faiths and sects, such as Sunnis and Shiites,

Sources: American Civil Liberties Union of Northern California 2002; El-Badry 1994; Henneberger 1995; Lindner 1998; Power 1998; Shaheen 1999; Tom Smith 2001; H. Weinstein et al. 2001.

cultural differences from other racial groups. At the same time, certain ethnic minorities, such as Latinos, may have obvious physical differences that set them apart from other ethnic groups in the United States.

Despite categorization problems, sociologists continue to feel that the distinction between racial groups and ethnic groups is socially significant. In most societies, including the United States, physical differences tend to be more visible than ethnic differences. Partly as a result of this fact, stratification along racial lines is more resistant to change than stratification along ethnic lines. Over time, members of an ethnic minority can sometimes become indistinguishable from the majority—although the process may take generations, and may never include all

members of the group. In contrast, members of a racial minority find it much more difficult to blend in with the larger society and gain acceptance from the majority.

PREJUDICE AND DISCRIMINATION

In recent years, college campuses across the United States have been the scene of bias-related incidents. Student-run newspapers and radio stations have ridiculed racial and ethnic minorities; threatening literature has been stuffed under the doors of minority students; graffiti endorsing the views of White supremacist organizations such as the Ku Klux Klan have been scrawled on university walls. In which are sometimes antagonistic toward one another (just as religious rivalries exist among Christians and Jews).

Today, there are more than 1,200 mosques in this country, of which 80 percent were established in the last 25 years. The largest group of Muslims in the United States, African Americans, is divided between those who follow mainstream Islamic doctrine and those who follow the teachings of the controversial Nation of Islam (headed by Minister Louis Farrakhan). The Muslim population of the United States is growing significantly, owing to high birthrates, substantial immigration rates, and conversion of non-Muslims.

Let's Discuss

1. Do you know an Arab American or Muslim American who has been the subject of ethnic profiling? If so, explain the circumstances. What was the person's reaction?
2. What can be done to promote better understanding of Arab and Muslim Americans and counter prejudice and discrimination against them?

LET'S HOPE WE NEVER RETURN TO THOSE DAYS OF PARANOIA AND SUSPICION.

MCCARTHY HEARING TRANSCRIPTS

MUSLIM AMERICANS

In the 1950s, Senator Joseph McCarthy raised the public's fear of communism to a fever pitch, accusing innocent people of betraying their country. Could fear of terrorism cause a similar hysteria today?

some cases, there have even been violent clashes between groups of White and Black students (Bunzel 1992; Schaefer 2004). What causes such ugly incidents?

Prejudice

Prejudice is a negative attitude toward an entire category of people, often an ethnic or racial minority. If you resent your roommate because he or she is sloppy, you are not necessarily guilty of prejudice. However, if you immediately stereotype your roommate on the basis of such characteristics as race, ethnicity, or religion, that is a form of prejudice. Prejudice tends to perpetuate false definitions of individuals and groups.

Sometimes prejudice results from **ethnocentrism**—the tendency to assume that one's own culture and way of life represent the norm or are superior to all others. Ethnocentric people judge other cultures by the standards of their own group, which leads quite easily to prejudice against cultures they view as inferior.

p. 72

One important and widespread form of prejudice is **racism,** the belief that one race is supreme and all others are innately inferior. When racism prevails in a society, members of subordinate groups generally experience prejudice, discrimination, and exploitation. In 1990, as concern mounted about racist attacks in the United States, Congress passed the Hate Crimes Statistics Act.

FIGURE 11-2

Active Hate Groups in the United States, 2002

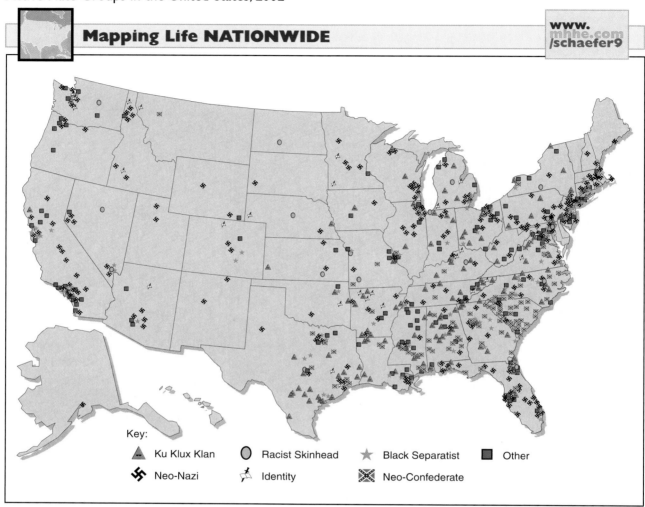

Key:
- ▲ Ku Klux Klan
- ⚡ Neo-Nazi
- ● Racist Skinhead
- ⚐ Identity
- ★ Black Separatist
- ✖ Neo-Confederate
- ■ Other

Source: Southern Poverty Law Center 2003.

Think About It

Why do you think state legislators enacted special hate crime laws covering criminal acts that already were illegal?

This law directs the Department of Justice to gather data on crimes motivated by the victim's race, religion, ethnicity, or sexual orientation. In 2001 alone, more than 7,800 hate crimes were reported to authorities. Some 55 percent of these crimes against persons involved racial bias; another 17 percent, religious bias; 16 percent, sexual orientation bias; and 12 percent, ethnic bias. Most of the crimes were carried out by individuals acting alone or with a few friends (Department of Justice 2002b).

A particularly horrifying hate crime made the front pages in 1998: In Jasper, Texas, three White men with possible ties to race-hate groups tied up a Black man, beat him with chains, and then dragged him behind their truck until his body was dismembered. Numerous groups in the United States have been victims of hate crimes as well as generalized prejudice. In the wake of the terrorist attacks of September 11, 2001, hate crimes against Asian Americans and Muslim Americans escalated rapidly. Box 11-1 (pages 254–255) examines prejudice against Arab Americans and Muslims who live in the United States.

As Figure 11-2 shows, there is a disturbingly large number of hate groups in the United States. Their activity appears to be increasing, both in reality and in virtual reality. Although only a few hundred such groups may exist, there were at least 2,000 websites advocating racial hatred on the Internet in 1999. Particularly troubling were sites disguised as video games for young people, or as "educational sites" about crusaders against prejudice. The technology of the Internet has allowed race-hate groups to expand far beyond their traditional southern base to reach millions (*Intelligence Report* 2003; Sandberg 1999).

Discriminatory Behavior

John and Glenn are alike in almost every way—about the same age, they are both Big Ten college graduates with good jobs. But the two find they have different experiences in everyday routines, such as walking into a store. John gets instant attention from the same sales staff that ignores Glenn, even though he has been waiting five minutes. When Glenn is locked out of his car, passersby ignore him; John receives many offers of help in the same situation. At an employment agency, Glenn is lectured on laziness and told he will be monitored "real close"; John is encouraged.

What accounts for these differences in the everyday life experiences of two men? Very simply, John is White and Glenn is Black. The two were part of an experiment, conducted by the television newsmagazine *Primetime Live,* to assess the impact of race on the day-to-day lives of residents in a typical U.S. city. Over a three-week period reporters closely monitored the two men, who had been trained to present themselves in an identical manner. Not once or twice, but "every single day," said program host Diane Sawyer, John and Glenn were treated differently (ABC News 1992).

Prejudice often leads to *discrimination,* the denial of opportunities and equal rights to individuals and groups because of prejudice or other arbitrary reasons. Say that a White corporate president with a prejudice against Asian Americans has to fill an executive position. The most qualified candidate for the job is a Vietnamese American. If the president refuses to hire this candidate and instead selects an inferior White candidate, he or she is engaging in an act of racial discrimination.

Prejudiced *attitudes* should not be equated with discriminatory *behavior.* Although the two are generally related, they are not identical, and either condition can be present without the other. A prejudiced person does not always act on his or her biases. The White president, for example, might choose—despite his or her stereotypes—to hire the Vietnamese American. This would be prejudice without discrimination. On the other hand, a White corporate president with a completely respectful view of Vietnamese Americans might refuse to hire them for executive posts out of fear that biased clients would take their business elsewhere. In this case, the president's action would constitute discrimination without prejudice.

Discrimination persists even for the most educated and qualified minority group members from the best family backgrounds. Despite their talents and experiences, they sometimes encounter attitudinal or organizational bias that prevents them from reaching their full potential. The term **glass ceiling** refers to an invisible barrier that blocks the promotion of a qualified individual in a work environment because of the individual's gender, race, or ethnicity (Schaefer 2004; Yamagata et al. 1997).

In early 1995, the federal Glass Ceiling Commission issued the first comprehensive study of barriers to promotion in the United States. The commission found that glass ceilings continue to block women and minority group men from top management positions in the nation's industries. While White men constitute 45 percent of the paid labor force, they hold down a much higher proportion of top positions. Even in *Fortune* magazine's 2002 listing of the most diversified corporations, White men held more than 80 percent of both the board of directors seats and the top 50 paid positions in the firms. According to the 1995 report, the existence of this glass ceiling results principally from the fears and prejudices of many middle- and upper-level White male managers, who believe that the inclusion of women and minority group men in management circles will threaten their own prospects for advancement (Bureau of the Census 2001a:367; Department of Labor 1995a, 1995b; Hickman 2002).

The Privileges of the Dominant

One aspect of discrimination that is often overlooked is the privileges that dominant groups enjoy at the expense of others. For instance, we tend to focus more on the difficulty women have getting ahead at work and getting a hand at home than on the ease with which men avoid household chores and manage to make their way in the world. Similarly, we concentrate more on discrimination against racial and ethnic minorities than on the advantages members of the White majority enjoy. Indeed, most White people rarely think about their "Whiteness," taking their status for granted. But sociologists and other social scientists are becoming increasingly interested in what it means to be "White," for White privilege is the other side of the proverbial coin of racial discrimination.

The feminist scholar Peggy McIntosh (1988) became interested in White privilege after noticing that most men would not acknowledge that there were privileges attached to being male—even if they would agree that being female had its disadvantages. Did White people suffer

White people tend to underestimate the value of racial privilege. Employers generally hire those with backgrounds similar to their own, as this all-White committee meeting suggests.

from a similar blind spot regarding their own racial privilege? she wondered. Intrigued, McIntosh began to list all the ways in which she benefited from her Whiteness. She soon realized that the list of unspoken advantages was long and significant.

McIntosh found that as a White person, she rarely needed to step out of her comfort zone, no matter where she went. If she wished to, she could spend most of her time with people of her own race. She could find a good place to live in a pleasant neighborhood, buy the foods she liked to eat from almost any grocery store, and get her hair styled in almost any salon. She could attend a public meeting without feeling that she did not belong, that she was different from everyone else.

McIntosh discovered, too, that her skin color opened doors for her. She could cash checks and use credit cards without suspicion, browse through stores without being shadowed by security guards. She could be seated without difficulty in a restaurant. If she asked to see the manager, she could assume he or she would be of her own race. If she needed help from a doctor or a lawyer, she could get it.

McIntosh also realized that her Whiteness made the job of parenting easier. She did not need to worry about protecting her children from people who did not like them. She could be sure that their textbooks would show pictures of people who looked like them, and that their history texts would describe White people's achievements. She knew that the television programs they watched would include White characters.

Finally, McIntosh had to admit that others did not constantly evaluate her in racial terms. When she appeared in public, she didn't need to worry that her clothing or behavior might reflect poorly on White people. If she was recognized for an achievement, it was seen as her achievement, not that of an entire race. And no one ever assumed that the personal opinions she voiced should be those of all White people. Because McIntosh blended in with the people around her, she wasn't always onstage.

These are not all the privileges McIntosh found she took for granted as a result of her membership in the dominant racial group in the United States. Whiteness *does* carry privileges—to a much greater extent than most White people realize.

Institutional Discrimination

Discrimination is practiced not only by individuals in one-to-one encounters but also by institutions in their daily operations. Social scientists are particularly concerned with the ways in which structural factors such as employment, housing, health care, and government operations maintain the social significance of race and ethnicity. *Institutional discrimination* refers to the denial of opportunities and equal rights to individuals and groups that results from the normal operations of a society. This kind of discrimination consistently affects certain racial and ethnic groups more than others.

The Commission on Civil Rights (1981:9–10) has identified various forms of institutional discrimination:

- Rules requiring that only English be spoken at a place of work, even when it is not a business necessity to restrict the use of other languages.
- Preferences shown by law and medical schools in the admission of children of wealthy and influential alumni, nearly all of whom are White.
- Restrictive employment-leave policies, coupled with prohibitions on part-time work, that make it difficult for the heads of single-parent families (most of whom are women) to obtain and keep jobs.

A recent example of institutional discrimination occurred in the wake of the September 11, 2001, terrorist attack on the United States. In the heat of demands to prevent terrorist takeovers of commercial airplanes, Congress passed the Aviation and Transportation Security Act, which was intended to strengthen airport screening procedures. The law stipulated that all airport screeners must be U.S. citizens. Nationally, 28 percent of all airport screeners are legal residents but not citizens of the United States; as a group, they are disproportionately Latino, Black, and Asian. Many observers noted that other airport and airline workers, including pilots, cabin attendants, and even armed National Guardsmen stationed at airports, need not be citizens. Efforts are now being made to test the constitutionality of the act. At the least, the debate over its fairness shows that even well-meant legal measures can have disastrous consequences for racial and ethnic minorities (Weinstein 2002).

In some cases, even ostensibly neutral institutional standards can turn out to have discriminatory effects. African American students at a midwestern state university protested a policy under which fraternities and sororities that wished to use campus facilities for a dance were required to post $150 security deposits to cover possible damages. The Black students complained that this policy had a discriminatory impact on minority student organizations. Campus police countered that the university's policy applied to all student groups interested in using these facilities. However, since overwhelmingly White fraternities and sororities at the school had their own houses, which they used for dances, the policy indeed affected only African American and other minority organizations.

Attempts have been made to eradicate or compensate for discrimination in the United States. The 1960s saw the passage of many pioneering civil rights laws, including the landmark 1964 Civil Rights Act (which prohibits discrimination in public accommodations and publicly owned facilities on the basis of race, color, creed, national origin, and gender). In two important rulings in 1987, the Supreme Court held that federal prohibitions against racial discrimination protect members of all ethnic minorities—including Hispanics, Jews, and Arab Americans—even though they may be considered White.

For more than 20 years, affirmative action programs have been instituted to overcome past discrimination. *Affirmative action* refers to positive efforts to recruit mi-

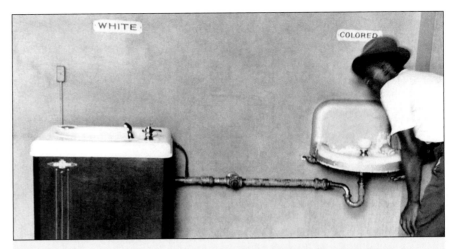

Before passage of the Civil Rights Act (1964), segregation of public accommodations was the norm throughout the South. Whites used the most up-to-date bathrooms, waiting rooms, and even drinking fountains, while Blacks ("Colored") were directed to older facilities in inferior condition. Such separate-but-unequal arrangements are a blatant example of institutional discrimination.

nority group members or women for jobs, promotions, and educational opportunities. Many people, however, resent these programs, arguing that advancing one group's cause merely shifts the discrimination to another group. By giving priority to African Americans in admissions, for example, schools may overlook more qualified White candidates. In many parts of the country and many sectors of the economy, affirmative action is being rolled back, even though it was never fully implemented. The social policy section in Chapter 18 will discuss affirmative action in more detail.

Discriminatory practices continue to pervade nearly all areas of life in the United States today. In part, that is because various individuals and groups actually *benefit* from racial and ethnic discrimination in terms of money, status, and influence. Discrimination permits members of the majority to enhance their wealth, power, and prestige at the expense of others. Less qualified people get jobs and promotions simply because they are members of the dominant group. Such individuals and groups will not surrender these advantages easily. We'll turn now to a closer look at this functionalist analysis, as well as the conflict and interactionist perspectives.

STUDYING RACE AND ETHNICITY

Relations among racial and ethnic groups lend themselves to analysis from the three major sociological perspectives. Viewing race from the macro level, functionalists observe that racial prejudice and discrimination serve positive functions for dominant groups, whereas conflict theorists see the economic structure as a central factor in the exploitation of minorities. The micro-level analysis of interactionist researchers stresses the manner in which everyday contact between people from different racial and ethnic backgrounds contributes to tolerance or leads to hostility.

Functionalist Perspective

What possible use could racial bigotry have for society? Functionalist theorists, while agreeing that racial hostility is hardly to be admired, point out that it indeed serves positive functions for those who practice discrimination.

Anthropologist Manning Nash (1962) has identified three functions that racially prejudiced beliefs have for the dominant group:

1. Racist views provide a moral justification for maintaining an unequal society that routinely deprives a minority of its rights and privileges. Southern Whites justified slavery by believing that Africans were physically and spiritually subhuman and devoid of souls (Hoebel 1949).
2. Racist beliefs discourage the subordinate minority from attempting to question its lowly status, which would be to question the very foundations of society.

3. Racial myths suggest that any major societal change (such as an end to discrimination) would only bring greater poverty to the minority and lower the majority's standard of living. As a result, Nash suggests, racial prejudice grows when a society's value system (one underlying a colonial empire or perpetuating slavery, for example) is threatened.

Although racial prejudice and discrimination may serve the interests of the powerful, such unequal treatment can also be dysfunctional for a society and even for its dominant group. Sociologist Arnold Rose (1951) has outlined four dysfunctions associated with racism:

1. A society that practices discrimination fails to use the resources of all individuals. Discrimination limits the search for talent and leadership to the dominant group.
2. Discrimination aggravates social problems such as poverty, delinquency, and crime, and places the financial burden of alleviating these problems on the dominant group.
3. Society must invest a good deal of time and money to defend its barriers to the full participation of all members.
4. Racial prejudice and discrimination often undercut goodwill and friendly diplomatic relations between nations.

A sign in a shop window in Los Angeles advertises the proprietor's prejudice against immigrants. According to the functionalist perspective, open displays of racial and ethnic bigotry are an attempt to maintain the power of the dominant group in society.

Conflict Perspective

Conflict theorists would certainly agree with Arnold Rose that racial prejudice and discrimination have many harmful consequences for society. Sociologists such as Oliver Cox (1948), Robert Blauner (1972), and Herbert M. Hunter (2000) have used the **exploitation theory** (or *Marxist class theory*) to explain the basis of racial subordination in the United States. As we saw in Chapter 9, Karl Marx viewed the exploitation of the lower class as a basic part of the capitalist economic system. From a Marxist point of view, racism keeps minorities in low-paying jobs, thereby supplying the capitalist ruling class with a pool of cheap labor. Moreover, by forcing racial minorities to accept low wages, capitalists can restrict the wages of *all* members of

PRUDENCE HANNIS **Researcher and Community Activist, Quebec Native Women**

Prudence Hannis is an Abenati First Nations (Native American) woman who works with the organization Quebec Native Women, where she is responsible for the women's health portfolio. Her job entails the organizing and facilitating of various activities such as seminars on sexual abuse in local communities and the production of a resource booklet on the subject for community members. Prudence is also working for the Centre of Excellence on Women's Health, Consortium Université de Montréal, where she focuses on First Nations women's health issues such as HIV and AIDS, prostitution, poverty, sexual discrimination, drug and alcohol abuse, and family violence.

Prudence received her B.A. in sociology from the University of Quebec at Montreal. "Sociology is now, more than it has ever

been, a part of my job," she says. "The purpose of my job is to defend First Nations' women's concerns, to be their spokesperson when needed, to analyze critical situations for our sisters, and mostly, to determine ways in which women can empower themselves, their families, and their communities."

Let's Discuss

1. Explain the connection between Native Americans' ethnicity and their health.
2. In speaking of empowering First Nations women, what sociological perspective do you think Hannis is drawing on?

---

the proletariat. Workers from the dominant group who demand higher wages can always be replaced by minorities who have no choice but to accept low-paying jobs.

The conflict view of race relations seems persuasive in a number of instances. Japanese Americans were the object of little prejudice until they began to enter jobs that brought them into competition with Whites. The movement to keep Chinese immigrants out of the United States became most fervent during the latter half of the 19th century, when Chinese and Whites fought over dwindling work opportunities. Both the enslavement of Blacks and the extermination and removal westward of Native Americans were, to a significant extent, economically motivated.

However, the exploitation theory is too limited to explain prejudice in its many forms. Not all minority groups have been economically exploited to the same extent. In addition, many groups (such as the Quakers and the Mormons) have been victimized by prejudice for other than economic reasons. Still, as Gordon Allport (1979:210) concludes, the exploitation theory correctly "points a sure finger at one of the factors involved in prejudice, . . . rationalized self-interest of the upper classes."

The practice of *racial profiling* fits both the conflict perspective and labeling theory. Generally, profiling occurs when law enforcement of-

▶ p. 185

ficers—customs officials, airport security personnel, and police—assume that people who fit certain descriptions are likely to be engaged in illegal activities. Skin color became a key characteristic of criminal profiles beginning in the 1980s, with the emergence of the crack cocaine market. But profiling can also involve a much more explicit use of stereotypes. For example, the federal antidrug initiative Operation Pipeline encouraged officers to look specifically for people wearing dreadlocks and for Latino men traveling together. In 2003 President George W. Bush banned racial profiling by federal agencies, but specifically exempted security personnel. Thus, immigration officials can continue to require visitors from Middle Eastern countries to register with the government, even though visitors from other countries are not required to register. Conflict theorists point out that in all these cases, it is the powerful and privileged dominant majority that determines who is profiled and for what purposes (Harris 1999; Lichtlau 2003; Ramirez et al. 2000).

Interactionist Perspective

A Hispanic woman is transferred from a job on an assembly line to a similar position working next to a White man. At first, the White man is patronizing, assuming that she must be incompetent. She is cold and resentful; even when she needs assistance, she refuses to admit it. After a week, the growing tension between the two leads to a bitter quarrel. Yet over time, each slowly comes to appreciate the other's strengths and talents. A year after they begin working together, these two workers become respectful friends. This story is an example of what interactionists call the *contact hypothesis* in action.

The **contact hypothesis** states that in cooperative circumstances, interracial contact between people of equal status will cause them to become less prejudiced and to abandon old stereotypes. People begin to see one another as individuals and discard the broad generalizations characteristic of stereotyping. Note the phrases *equal status* and *cooperative circumstances*. In the story above, if the two workers had been competing for one vacancy as a supervisor, the racial hostility between them might have worsened (Allport 1979; Schaefer 2004; Sigelman et al. 1996).

As Latinos and other minorities slowly gain access to better-paying and more responsible jobs, the contact hypothesis may take on even greater significance. The trend in our society is toward increasing contact between individuals from dominant and subordinate groups. This may be one way of eliminating—or at least reducing—racial and ethnic stereotyping and prejudice. Another may be the establishment of interracial coalitions, an idea suggested by sociologist William Julius Wilson (1999b). To work, such coalitions would obviously need to be built on an equal role for all members.

Contact between individuals occurs on the micro level. We turn now to a consideration of intergroup relations on a macro level.

Too often, authorities treat individuals differently based solely on their race or ethnicity. This poster dramatizes the injustice of racial profiling, a practice in which the Reverend Martin Luther King Jr. (left) would be treated with more suspicion than the mass murderer Charles Manson (right).

PATTERNS OF INTERGROUP RELATIONS

Racial and ethnic groups can relate to one another in a wide variety of ways, ranging from friendships and intermarriages to hostility, from behaviors that require mutual approval to behaviors imposed by the dominant group.

One devastating pattern of intergroup relations is **genocide**—the deliberate, systematic killing of an entire people or nation. This term describes the killing of 1 million Armenians by Turkey beginning in 1915. It is most commonly applied to Nazi Germany's extermination of 6 million European Jews, as well as gays, lesbians, and the Romani people ("Gypsies"), during World War II. The term *genocide* is also appropriate in describing the United States' policies toward Native Americans in the 19th century. In 1800, the Native American (or American Indian) population of the United States was about 600,000; by 1850, it had been reduced to 250,000 through warfare

with the cavalry, disease, and forced relocation to inhospitable environments.

The *expulsion* of a people is another extreme means of acting out racial or ethnic prejudice. In 1979, Vietnam expelled nearly 1 million ethnic Chinese, partly as a result of centuries of hostility between Vietnam and neighboring China. In a more recent example of expulsion (which had aspects of genocide), Serbian forces began a program of "ethnic cleansing" in 1991 in the newly independent states of Bosnia and Herzegovina. Throughout the former nation of Yugoslavia, the Serbs drove more than 1 million Croats and Muslims from their homes. Some were tortured and killed, others abused and terrorized, in an attempt to "purify" the land for the remaining ethnic Serbs. In 1999, Serbs again became the focus of worldwide condemnation as they sought to "cleanse" the province of Kosovo of ethnic Albanians.

Genocide and expulsion are extreme behaviors. More typical intergroup relations follow four identifiable patterns: (1) amalgamation, (2) assimilation, (3) segregation, and (4) pluralism. Each pattern defines the dominant group's actions and the minority group's responses. Intergroup relations are rarely restricted to only one of the four patterns, although invariably one does tend to dominate. Think of these patterns primarily as ideal types.

Amalgamation

Amalgamation happens when a majority group and a minority group combine to form a new group. Through intermarriage over several generations, various groups in society combine to form a new group. This pattern can be expressed as $A + B + C \rightarrow D$, where A, B, and C represent different groups in a society, and D signifies the end result, a unique cultural-racial group unlike any of the initial groups (W. Newman 1973).

The belief in the United States as a "melting pot" became compelling in the first part of the 20th century, particularly since that image suggested that the nation had an almost divine mission to amalgamate various groups into one people. However, in actuality, many residents were not willing to include Native Americans, Jews, African Americans, Asian Americans, and Irish Roman Catholics in the melting pot. Therefore, this pattern does not adequately describe dominant–subordinate relations in the United States.

Assimilation

Many Hindus in India complain about Indian citizens who copy the traditions and customs of the British. In Australia, Aborigines who have become part of the dominant society refuse to acknowledge their darker-skinned grandparents on the street. In the United States, some Italian Americans, Polish Americans, Hispanics, and Jews have changed their ethnic-sounding family names to names that are typically found among White Protestant families.

Assimilation is the process through which a person forsakes his or her own cultural tradition to become part of a different culture. Generally, it is practiced by a minority group member who wants to conform to the standards of the dominant group. Assimilation can be described as a pattern in which $A + B + C \rightarrow A$. The majority, A, dominates in such a way that members of minorities B and C imitate it and attempt to become indistinguishable from it (W. Newman 1973).

Assimilation can strike at the very roots of a person's identity. Alphonso D'Abuzzo, for example, changed his name to Alan Alda. The British actress Joyce Frankenberg changed her name to Jane Seymour. Name changes, switches in religious affiliation, and dropping of native languages can obscure one's roots and heritage. However, assimilation does not necessarily bring acceptance to minority group individuals. A Chinese American such as Helen Zia (see the chapter-opening excerpt) may speak English fluently, achieve high educational standards, and become a well-respected professional or businessperson and *still* be seen as different. Other Americans may reject her as a business associate, neighbor, or marriage partner.

You have immigrated to another country with a very different culture. What steps might you take to assimilate?

Segregation

Separate schools, separate seating on buses and in restaurants, separate washrooms, even separate drinking fountains—these were all part of the lives of African Americans in the South when segregation ruled early in the 20th century. *Segregation* refers to the physical separation of two groups of people in terms of residence, workplace, and social events. Generally, a dominant group imposes this pattern on a minority group. Segregation is rarely complete, however. Intergroup contact inevitably occurs, even in the most segregated societies.

From 1948 (when it received its independence) to 1990, the Republic of South Africa severely restricted the movement of Blacks and other non-Whites by means of a wide-ranging system of segregation known as *apartheid.* Apartheid even included the creation of separate homelands where Blacks were expected to live. However, decades of local resistance to apartheid, combined with international pressure, led to marked political changes in the 1990s. In 1994, a prominent Black activist, Nelson Mandela, was elected South Africa's president in the first election in which Blacks (the majority of the nation's population) were allowed to vote. Mandela had spent almost 28 years in South African prisons for his anti-apartheid activities. His election was widely viewed as the final blow to South Africa's oppressive policy of apartheid.

Long-entrenched social patterns are difficult to change, however. In the United States today, despite federal laws that forbid housing discrimination, residential segregation is still the norm, as a recent analysis of living patterns in metropolitan areas shows. Across the nation, neighborhoods remain divided along both racial and ethnic lines. The average White person lives in an area that is at least 83 percent White, while the average African American lives in a neighborhood that is mostly Black. The typical Latino lives in an area that is 42 percent Hispanic. Overall, segregation flourishes at the community and neighborhood level, despite the increasing diversity of the nation as a whole (Lewis Mumford Center 2001).

A policeman stops to chat with three young residents of the Langston Hughes housing project in East New York. Although the United States is a diverse society, U.S. neighborhoods are not. Public housing projects often reinforce the racial segregation in existing neighborhoods, even though the federal government has outlawed discrimination in housing.

Whatever the country, residential segregation directly limits people's economic opportunity. Sociologists Douglas Massey and Nancy Denton (1993), in a book aptly titled *American Apartheid,* noted that segregation separates poor people of color from job opportunities and isolates them from successful role models. This pattern repeats itself the world over, from South Central Los Angeles to Oldham, England, and Soweto, South Africa.

Pluralism

In a pluralistic society, a subordinate group does not have to forsake its lifestyle and traditions. *Pluralism* is based on mutual respect among various groups in a society for one another's cultures. This pattern allows a minority group to express its own culture and still participate without prejudice in the larger society. Earlier, we described amalgamation as A + B + C → D, and assimilation as A + B + C → A. Using this same approach, we can conceive of pluralism as A + B + C → A + B + C. All the groups coexist in the same society (W. Newman 1973).

In the United States, pluralism is more of an ideal than a reality. There are distinct instances of pluralism—the ethnic neighborhoods in major cities, such as Koreatown, Little Tokyo, Andersonville (Swedish Americans), and Spanish Harlem—yet there are also limits to such cultural freedom. To survive, a society must promote a certain consensus among its members regarding basic ideals, values, and beliefs. Thus, if a Romanian migrating to the United States wants to move up the occupational ladder, he or she cannot avoid learning the English language.

Switzerland exemplifies the modern pluralistic state. The absence of both a national language and a dominant religious faith leads to a tolerance for cultural diversity. In addition, various political devices safeguard the interests of ethnic groups in a way that has no parallel in the United States. By contrast, Great Britain has had difficulty achieving cultural pluralism in a multiracial society. East Indians, Pakistanis, and Blacks from the Caribbean and Africa are experiencing prejudice and discrimination within the dominant White British society. Some British advocate cutting off all Asian and Black immigration, and a few even call for expelling those non-Whites currently living in Britain.

 RACE AND ETHNICITY IN THE UNITED STATES

Few societies have a more diverse population than the United States; the nation is truly a multiracial, multiethnic society. Of course, that has not always been the case. The population of what is now the United States has changed dramatically since the arrival of European settlers in the 1600s, as Figure 11-1 (page 252) showed. Immigration, colonialism, and in the case of Blacks, slavery determined the racial and ethnic makeup of our present-day society. (See Figure 11-3, which shows where various racial and ethnic minorities are concentrated in the United States.)

Racial Groups

The largest racial minorities in the United States are African Americans, Native Americans, and Asian Americans.

African Americans

"I am an invisible man," wrote Black author Ralph Ellison in his novel *Invisible Man* (1952:3). "I am a man of substance, of flesh and bone, fiber and liquids—and I might

FIGURE 11-3

Census 2000: The Image of Diversity

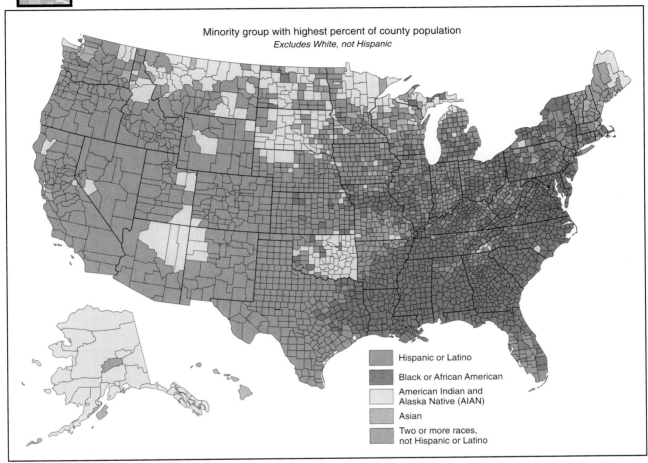

Minority group with highest percent of county population
Excludes White, not Hispanic

- Hispanic or Latino
- Black or African American
- American Indian and Alaska Native (AIAN)
- Asian
- Two or more races, not Hispanic or Latino

Source: C. Brewer and Suchan 2001:20.

Think About It
The United States is a diverse nation. Why, in many parts of the country, can't people see that diversity in their own towns?

even be said to possess a mind. I am invisible, understand, simply because people refuse to see me."

Over five decades later, many African Americans still feel invisible. Despite their large numbers, they have long been treated as second-class citizens. Currently, by the standards of the federal government, more than 1 out of every 4 Blacks—as opposed to 1 out of every 12 Whites—is poor.

Contemporary institutional discrimination and individual prejudice against African Americans are rooted in the history of slavery in the United States. Many other subordinate groups had little wealth and income, but as sociologist W. E. B. Du Bois (1909) and others have noted, enslaved Blacks were in an even more oppressive situation, because by law, they could not own property and could not pass on the benefits of their labor to their children. Today, increasing numbers of African Americans and sympathetic Whites are calling for *slave reparations* to compensate for the injustices of forced servitude. Reparations could include official expressions of apology from governments such as the United States, ambitious programs to improve African Americans'

Table 11-2	**Relative Economic Positions of Various Racial and Ethnic Groups**				
Characteristic	**Whites**	**African Americans**	**Native Americans**	**Asian Americans**	**Hispanics**
Four-year college education, people 25 and over (2002)	27.3%	17.5%	11.5%	43.8%	11.2%
Median household income (2001)	$46,305	$29,470	$32,116	$53,635	$33,565
Unemployment rate (2003)	5.5%	11.1%	——	5.9%	8.2%
People below the poverty line (2001)	7.8%	22.7%	25.7%	10.2%	21.4%

Notes: Data on Whites, where available, are for White non-Hispanics. On reservations, estimated median family income for Native American households is $18,063. Educational and poverty data for Native Americans are for 2000 and 1999, respectively. Unemployment rate for Asian Americans estimated by author.

Sources: Bauman and Graf 2003:5; Bishaw and Ireland 2003; Bureau of the Census 2002a:41–44; DeNavas-Walt and Cleveland 2002:4, 6; Department of Labor 2003; McKinnon 2003; Proctor and Dalaker 2002:3; Ramirez and de la Cruz 2003; Reeves and Bennett 2003.

Think About It

Notice how much higher the rate for college education is among Asian Americans than among Whites. Yet the median income for Asian Americans is only slightly higher than it is for Whites. What might explain this disparity?

economic status, or even direct payments to descendants of slaves (E. Allen Jr. and Chrisman 2001).

The end of the Civil War did not bring genuine freedom and equality for Blacks. The Southern states passed "Jim Crow" laws to enforce official segregation, and the Supreme Court upheld them as constitutional in 1896. In addition, Blacks faced the danger of lynching campaigns, often led by the Ku Klux Klan, during the late 1800s and early 1900s. From a conflict perspective, Whites maintained their dominance formally through legalized segregation and informally by means of vigilante terror and violence (Franklin and Moss 2000).

A turning point in the struggle for Black equality came in 1954 with the unanimous Supreme Court decision in the case of *Brown v. Board of Education of Topeka, Kansas*. The Court outlawed segregation of public school students, ruling that "separate educational facilities are inherently unequal." In the wake of the *Brown* decision, there was a surge of activism on behalf of Black civil rights, including boycotts of segregated bus companies and sit-ins at restaurants and lunch counters that refused to serve Blacks.

During the 1960s, a vast civil rights movement emerged, with many competing factions and strategies for change. The Southern Christian Leadership Conference (SCLC), founded by Dr. Martin Luther King Jr., used nonviolent civil disobedience to oppose segregation. The National Association for the Advancement of Colored People (NAACP) favored use of the courts to press for equality for African Americans. But many younger Black leaders, most notably Malcolm X, turned toward an ideology of Black power. Proponents of **Black power** rejected the goal of assimilation into White middle-class society. They defended the beauty and dignity of Black and African cultures and supported the creation of Black-controlled political and economic institutions (Ture and Hamilton 1992).

Despite numerous courageous actions to achieve Black civil rights, Black and White citizens are still separate, still unequal. From birth to death, Blacks suffer in terms of their life chances. Life remains difficult for millions of poor pp. 215–216 Blacks, who must attempt to survive in ghetto areas shattered by high unemployment and abandoned housing. The economic position of Blacks is shown in Table 11-2. At the beginning of the new century, the median household income of Blacks was only 60 percent that of Whites, and the unemployment rate among Blacks was more than twice that of Whites.

Some African Americans—especially middle-class men and women—have made economic gains over the last 50 years. For example, data compiled by the

Department of Labor show that the number of African Americans in management increased nationally from 2.4 percent of the total in 1958 to 8.3 percent in 2000. Yet Blacks still represent only 7 percent or less of all physicians, engineers, scientists, lawyers, judges, and marketing managers. In another area important to developing role models, African Americans and Hispanics together account for less than 10 percent of all editors and reporters in the United States (Bureau of the Census 2002a:381).

In many respects, the civil rights movement of the 1960s left institutionalized discrimination against African Americans untouched. Consequently, in the 1970s and 1980s, Black leaders worked to mobilize African American political power as a force for social change. Between 1970 and 2000, the number of African American elected officials increased sixfold. Even so, Blacks remain significantly *underrepresented*. This underrepresentation is especially distressing in view of the fact that sociologist W. E. B. Du Bois observed over 90 years ago that Blacks could not expect to achieve equal social and economic opportunities without first gaining political rights (Bureau of the Census 2002a:282; Green and Driver 1978).

Native Americans

Today, 2.5 million Native Americans represent a diverse array of cultures distinguishable by language, family organization, religion, and livelihood. The outsiders who came to the United States—European settlers and their descendants—came to know these native peoples' forefathers as "American Indians." By the time the Bureau of Indian Affairs (BIA) was organized as part of the War Department in 1824, Indian–White relations had already included three centuries of mutual misunderstanding. During the 19th century many bloody wars wiped out a significant part of the nation's Indian population. By the end of the century, schools for Indians—operated by the BIA or by church missions—prohibited the practice of Native American cultures. Yet at the same time, such schools did little to make the children effective competitors in White society.

Today, life remains difficult for members of the 554 tribal groups in the United States, whether they live in cities or on reservations. For example, one Native American teenager in six has attempted suicide—a rate four times higher than the rate for other teenagers. Traditionally, some Native Americans have chosen to assimilate and abandon all vestiges of their tribal cultures to escape certain forms of prejudice. However, by the 1990s, an increasing number of people in the United States were openly claiming a Native American identity. Since 1960, the federal government's count of Native Americans has tripled, to an estimated 2.5 million. According to the 2000 census, there was a 26 percent increase in the Native

American population during the 1990s. Demographers believe that more and more Native Americans who previously concealed their identity are no longer pretending to be White (Grieco and Cassidy 2001).

The introduction of gambling on Indian reservations threatens to become still another battleground between Native Americans and the dominant White society. About one-third of all tribes operate off-track betting, casino games such as blackjack and roulette, slot machines, high-stakes bingo, sports betting, and video gambling. The gamblers—who are overwhelmingly not Native Americans—typically travel long distances to wager money at the new casinos. While gambling on reservations generates $12.7 billion annually, the profits are not evenly spread among tribes. Much of Native America is untouched by casino windfalls. The lopsided nature of these revenues, with huge profits going to just a few tribes and non-Indian investors, is the reason the economic standing of the vast majority of Native Americans has not changed much. Some Native Americans oppose gambling on moral grounds and charge that it is being marketed in a manner incompatible with Native American culture. Yet some reservations have managed profits from gambling well and have invested them in projects for the betterment of the entire reservation. At the same time, established White gambling interests, particularly in Nevada and New Jersey, have pressured Congress to restrict Native American casinos (P. Marshall 2003; Schaefer 2004).

Use Your Sociological Imagination www.mhhe.com/schaefer9

You are a Native American whose tribe is about to open a reservation-based casino. Will the casino further the assimilation of your people into mainstream society or encourage pluralism?

Cabazon men perform a traditional dance during a tribal gathering in California. In recent years, Native Americans have sought to revive customs that Whites once encouraged them to abandon.

FIGURE 11-4

Major Asian American Groups in the United States, 2000

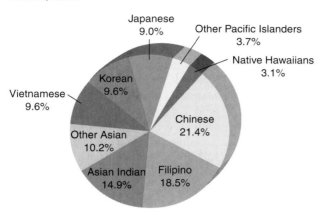

Source: Logan 2001.

> **Think About It**
> Do Asian Americans really have a common identity?

Asian Americans

Asian Americans are a diverse group, one of the fastest-growing segments of the U.S. population (up 69 percent between 1990 and 2000). Among the many groups of Americans of Asian descent are Vietnamese Americans, Chinese Americans, Japanese Americans, and Korean Americans (see Figure 11-4).

Asian Americans are held up as a **model** or **ideal minority** group, supposedly because despite past suffering from prejudice and discrimination, they have succeeded economically, socially, and educationally without resorting to confrontations with Whites. The existence of a model minority seems to reaffirm the notion that anyone can get ahead in the United States with talent and hard work, and implies that those minorities that don't succeed are somehow responsible for their failures. Viewed from a conflict perspective, this attitude is yet another instance of "blaming the victims" (Hurh and Kim 1998).

The concept of a model minority ignores the diversity among Asian Americans: There are rich and poor Japanese Americans, rich and poor Filipino Americans, and so forth. In fact, Southeast Asians living in the United States have the highest rate of welfare dependency of any racial or ethnic group. As Table 11-2 shows, Asian Americans have substantially more schooling than other ethnic groups, but their median income is only slightly higher than Whites' income, and their poverty rate is higher. In 2001, for every Asian American family with an annual income of $100,000 or more, there was another earning less than $25,000 a year. Moreover, even when

Asian Americans are clustered at the higher-paying end of the stratification system, the glass ceiling may limit how far they can rise (DeNavas-Walt and Cleveland 2002:17).

Vietnamese Americans Each Asian American group has its own history and culture. Vietnamese Americans, for instance, came to the United States primarily during and after the Vietnam War—especially after the U.S. withdrawal from the conflict in 1975. Assisted by local agencies, refugees from the communist government in Vietnam settled throughout the United States, tens of thousands of them in small towns. But over time, Vietnamese Americans have gravitated toward the larger urban areas, establishing Vietnamese restaurants and grocery stores in their ethnic enclaves there.

In 1995, the United States resumed normal diplomatic relations with Vietnam. Gradually, the *Viet Kieu,* or Vietnamese living abroad, began to return to their old country to visit, but usually not to take up permanent residence. Today, 30 years after the end of the Vietnam War, sharp differences of opinion remain among Vietnamese Americans, especially the older ones, concerning the war and the present government of Vietnam (Lamb 1997).

Chinese Americans Unlike African slaves and Native Americans, the Chinese were initially encouraged to immigrate to the United States. From 1850 to 1880, thousands of Chinese immigrated to this country, lured by job opportunities created by the discovery of gold. However, as employment possibilities decreased and competition for mining jobs grew, the Chinese became the target of a bitter campaign to limit their numbers and restrict their rights. Chinese laborers were exploited, then discarded.

In 1882, Congress enacted the Chinese Exclusion Act, which prevented Chinese immigration and even forbade Chinese in the United States to send for their families. As a result, the Chinese population steadily declined until after World War II. More recently, the descendants of the 19th-century immigrants have been joined by a new influx from Hong Kong and Taiwan. These groups may contrast sharply in their degree of assimilation, desire to live in Chinatowns, and feelings about this country's relations with the People's Republic of China.

Currently, about 2.7 million Chinese Americans live in the United States. Some Chinese Americans have entered lucrative occupations, yet many immigrants struggle to survive under living and working conditions that belie the model-minority stereotype. New York City's Chinatown district is filled with illegal sweatshops in which recent immigrants—many of them Chinese women—work for minimal wages. Even in legal factories in the garment industry, hours are long and rewards are limited. A seamstress typically works 11 hours per day, 6 days a week, and earns about $10,000 a year. Other workers, such as hemmers and cutters, earn only $5,000 per year (Finder 1995; Lum and Kwong 1989).

Japanese Americans   Approximately 1.1 million Japanese Americans live in the United States. As a people, they are relatively recent arrivals. In 1880, only 148 Japanese lived in the United States, but by 1920 there were more than 110,000. Japanese immigrants—called the *Issei,* or first generation—were usually males seeking employment opportunities. Many Whites saw them (along with Chinese immigrants) as a "yellow peril" and subjected them to prejudice and discrimination.

In 1941, the attack on Hawaii's Pearl Harbor by Japan had severe repercussions for Japanese Americans. The federal government decreed that all Japanese Americans on the West Coast must leave their homes and report to "evacuation camps." Japanese Americans became, in effect, scapegoats for the anger that other people in the United States felt concerning Japan's role in World War II. By August 1943, in an unprecedented application of guilt by virtue of ancestry, 113,000 Japanese Americans had been forced into hastily built camps. In striking contrast, only a few German Americans and Italian Americans were sent to evacuation camps (Hosokawa 1969).

This mass detention was costly for Japanese Americans. The Federal Reserve Board estimates their total income and property losses at nearly half a billion dollars. Moreover, the psychological effect on these citizens—including the humiliation of being labeled "disloyal"—was immeasurable. Eventually, children born in the United States to the *Issei,* called *Nisei,* were allowed to enlist in the Army and serve in Europe in a segregated combat unit. Others resettled in the East and Midwest to work in factories.

In 1983, a federal commission recommended government payments to all surviving Japanese Americans who had been held in detention camps. The commission reported that the detention was motivated by "race prejudice, war hysteria, and a failure of political leadership." It added that "no documented acts of espionage, sabotage, or fifth-column activity were shown to have been committed" by Japanese Americans. In 1988, President Ronald Reagan signed the Civil Liberties Act, which required the federal government to issue individual apologies for all violations of Japanese Americans' constitutional rights, and established a $1.25 billion trust fund to pay reparations to the approximately 77,500 surviving Japanese Americans who had been interned (Pear 1983; Takezawa 1995).

Korean Americans   At 1.2 million, the population of Korean Americans now exceeds that of Japanese Americans. Yet Korean Americans are often overshadowed by other groups from Asia.

Today's Korean American community is the result of three waves of immigration. The initial wave arrived between 1903 and 1910, when Korean laborers migrated to Hawaii. The second wave followed the end of the Korean War in 1953; most of these immigrants were wives of U.S. servicemen and war orphans. The third wave, continuing to the present, has reflected the admissions priorities set up in the 1965 Immigration Act. These well-educated immigrants arrive in the United States with professional skills. Yet because of language difficulties and discrimination, many must settle at least initially for positions of lower responsibility than those they held in Korea, and must suffer through a period of disenchantment. Stress, loneliness, and family strife may accompany the pain of adjustment.

Like many other Asian American women, Korean American women commonly participate in the paid labor force, though in Korea women are expected to serve as mothers and homemakers only. While these roles carry over to the United States, Korean American women are also pressed to support their families while their husbands struggle to establish themselves financially. Many Korean American men begin small service and retail businesses and gradually involve their wives in the ventures. Making the situation even more difficult is the hostility Korean American–run businesses often encounter from their prospective customers (Hurh 1994, 1998; Kim 1999).

In the early 1990s, the apparent friction between Korean Americans and another subordinate racial group, African Americans, attracted nationwide attention. In New York City, Los Angeles, and Chicago, Korean American merchants confronted Blacks who were allegedly threatening them or robbing their stores. Black neighborhoods responded with hostility to what they perceived as the disrespect and arrogance of Korean American entrepreneurs. In South Central Los Angeles, the only shops in which to buy groceries, liquor, or gasoline were owned by Korean immigrants, who had largely replaced White businesspeople. African Americans were well aware of the dominant role that Korean Americans played in their local retail markets. During the 1992 riots in South Central Los Angeles, small businesses owned by Koreans were a particular target. More than 1,800 Korean businesses were looted or burned during the riots (Kim 1999).

Conflict between the two groups was dramatized in Spike Lee's 1989 movie *Do the Right Thing.* The situation stems from Korean Americans' position as the latest immigrant group to cater to the needs of inner-city populations abandoned by those who have moved up the economic ladder. This type of friction is not new; generations of Jewish, Italian, and Arab merchants have encountered similar hostility from what to outsiders seems an unlikely source—another oppressed minority.

Ethnic Groups

Unlike racial minorities, members of subordinate ethnic groups generally are not hindered by physical differences from assimilating into the dominant culture of the United States. However, members of ethnic minority groups still face many forms of prejudice and discrimination. Take the cases of the country's largest ethnic groups—Latinos, Jews, and White ethnics.

Latinos

Together, the various groups included under the general category *Latinos* represent the largest minority in the United States. In 2000 there were more than 35 million Hispanics in this country, including 23 million Mexican Americans, more than 3 million Puerto Ricans, and smaller numbers of Cuban Americans and people of Central and South American origin (see Figure 11-5). The latter group represents the fastest-growing and most diverse segment of the Hispanic community.

According to Census Bureau data, the Latino population now outnumbers the African American population in 6 of the 10 largest cities of the United States: Los Angeles, Houston, Phoenix, San Diego, Dallas, and San Antonio. Hispanics are now the majority of residents in cities such as Miami, Florida; El Paso, Texas; and Santa Ana, California. The rise in the Hispanic population of the United States—fueled by comparatively high birthrates and levels of immigration—could intensify debates over controversial public policy issues such as bilingualism and immigration (S. Roberts 1994).

The various Latino groups share a heritage of Spanish language and culture, which can cause serious problems in their assimilation. An intelligent student whose first language is Spanish may be presumed slow or even unruly by English-speaking schoolchildren, and frequently by English-speaking teachers as well. The labeling of Latino children as underachievers, as learning disabled, or emotionally disturbed can act as a self-fulfilling p. 74 prophecy for some children. Bilingual education aims at easing the educational difficulties experienced by Hispanic children and others whose first language is not English.

The educational difficulties of Latino students certainly contribute to the generally low economic status of Hispanics. In 2001, about 26 percent of all Hispanic households earned less than $25,000, compared to 36 percent of non-Hispanic White households. By 2000, only 11 percent of Hispanic adults had completed college, compared with 28 percent of non-Hispanic Whites. In that same year the poverty rate for people ages 18 to 64 was 17.7 percent for Hispanics, compared to only 7.2 percent for non-Hispanic Whites. Overall, Latinos are not as affluent as White non-Hispanics, but a middle class is beginning to emerge within the Latino community (see Box 11-2) (DeNavas-Walt and Cleveland 2002:17, 19; Proctor and Dalaker 2002:27, 29).

Mexican Americans The largest Latino population is Mexican Americans, who can be further subdivided into those descended from residents of the territories annexed after the Mexican-American War of 1848 and those who have immigrated from Mexico to the United States. The opportunity for a Mexican to earn in one hour what it would take an entire day to earn in Mexico has pushed millions of legal and illegal immigrants north.

Aside from the family, the most important social organization in the Mexican American (or Chicano) community is the church, specifically the Roman Catholic church. This strong identification with the Catholic faith has reinforced the already formidable barriers between Mexican Americans and their predominantly White and Protestant neighbors in the Southwest. At the same time, the Catholic Church helps many immigrants to develop a sense of identity and assists their assimilation into the norms and values of the dominant culture of the United States. The complexity of the Mexican American community is underscored by the fact that Protestant churches—especially those that endorse expressive, open worship—have attracted increasing numbers of Mexican Americans (Herrmann 1994; Kanellos 1994).

FIGURE 11-5

Major Hispanic Groups in the United States, 2000

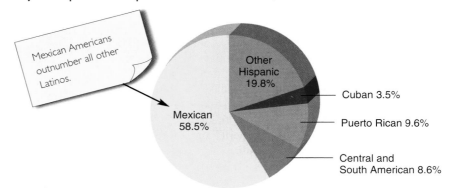

Source: Therrien and Ramirez 2001:1.

11-2 THE LATINO MIDDLE CLASS

No racial or ethnic group belongs to just one social class. Among Latinos, as in society as a whole, there is a social class hierarchy. The recent rapid growth of the Hispanic population, which rose 58 percent in the 1990s, has focused marketers' attention on the burgeoning Latino middle class, which grew 71 percent in the same period. Latino-oriented magazines and advertising, not always published in Spanish, are one sign of this group's growing economic power. Segments of the Mexican American and Cuban American communities have begun to display the typical signs of middle-class status: moderate to high incomes, postgraduate and professional schooling, and substantial assets, including homes in middle- and upper-class neighborhoods.

Mexican Americans were among the first middle-class people in North America. In the 1660s, settlers in San Antonio enjoyed an almost aristocratic status granted by the Spanish crown. Some of these old-line families, as well as Hispanic families in other parts of the Southwest, have been able to retain their elevated status. In the 20th century, well-trained professionals who fled Cuba following the revolution created middle-class Hispanic communities in South Florida.

Among other Latinos, social mobility has created an unmistakable middle class. About one in nine Latinos now has a college degree; one in six U.S.-born Latinos is college educated. A growing number of

> A growing number of Latinos own their own businesses—more than 1.2 million firms nationally.

Latinos own their own businesses—more than 1.2 million firms nationally. Latino-owned businesses account for about one-quarter of all businesses in metropolitan Los Angeles and San Diego, as well as in the state of New Mexico. Women—that is, *Latinas*—are especially prominent in these businesses, most of which are very small family-owned enterprises.

Will these newly affluent Latinos continue to ally themselves with the concerns of lower-income Hispanics? Although many still favor liberalized immigration laws and bilingual education, some affluent Latinos have begun to back more restrictive immigration policies and to question the wisdom of funding bilingual education.

The assimilated children of the Latino middle class, like all children of immigrants, are caught between two worlds. More than one-quarter of the children of Latino immigrants speak only English at home. One sign that they are blending in with mainstream American culture is that many of these young adults are now studying *Español*, either to boost their careers or to become better acquainted with their roots.

Let's Discuss

1. Have you seen signs of Latino affluence on television or in magazine advertisements? What stores or brand names are pitching their wares directly to Latinos?
2. Why do you think marketers aim their promotional materials at specific racial and ethnic groups?

Sources: Bean et al. 2001; Brischetto 2001; Bureau of the Census 2001b; Campo-Flores 2000; Gonzales 1997; J. Moore and Pachon 1985; Romney 1998; Therrien and Ramirez 2001.

Puerto Ricans   The second-largest segment of Latinos in the United States is Puerto Ricans. Since 1917, residents of Puerto Rico have held the status of American citizens; many have migrated to New York and other eastern cities. Unfortunately, Puerto Ricans have experienced serious poverty both in the United States and on the island. Those who live in the continental United States earn barely half the family income of Whites. As a result, a reverse migration began in the 1970s, when more Puerto Ricans were leaving for the island than were coming to the mainland (Lemann 1991).

Politically, Puerto Ricans in the United States have not been as successful as Mexican Americans in organizing for their rights. For many mainland Puerto Ricans—as for many residents of the island—the paramount political issue is the destiny of Puerto Rico itself:

Should it continue in its present commonwealth status, petition for admission to the United States as the 51st state, or attempt to become an independent nation? This question has divided Puerto Rico for decades and remains a central issue in Puerto Rican elections. In a 1998 referendum, voters supported a "none of the above" option, effectively favoring continuing the commonwealth status over statehood or independence.

Cuban Americans   Cuban immigration to the United States dates back as far as 1831, but it began in earnest following Fidel Castro's assumption of power in the Cuban revolution (1959). The first wave of 200,000 Cubans included many professionals with relatively high levels of schooling; these men and women were largely welcomed as refugees from communist tyranny. However, more

Members of the Hispanic sorority Sigma Lambda Gamma smile for the camera at Eastern Michigan University. In the United States, about 11 percent of Hispanic adults are college graduates.

Jewish Americans

Jews constitute almost 3 percent of the population of the United States. They play a prominent role in the worldwide Jewish community, because the United States has the world's largest concentration of Jews. Like the Japanese, many Jewish immigrants came to this country and became white-collar professionals in spite of prejudice and discrimination.

Anti-Semitism—that is, anti-Jewish prejudice—has often been vicious in the United States, although rarely so widespread and never so formalized as in Europe. In many cases, Jews have been used as scapegoats for other people's failures. Not surprisingly, Jews have not achieved equality in the United States. Despite high levels of education and professional training, they are still conspicuously absent from the top management of large corporations (except for the few firms founded by Jews). Until the late 1960s, many prestigious universities maintained restrictive quotas that limited Jewish enrollment. Private social clubs and fraternal groups frequently limit membership to gentiles (non-Jews), a practice upheld by the Supreme Court in the 1964 case *Bell v. Maryland*.

recent waves of immigrants have aroused growing concern, partly because they were less likely to be skilled professionals. Throughout these waves of immigration, Cuban Americans have been encouraged to locate around the United States. Nevertheless, many continue to settle in (or return to) metropolitan Miami, Florida, with its warm climate and proximity to Cuba.

The Cuban experience in the United States has been mixed. Some detractors worry about the vehement anticommunism of Cuban Americans and the apparent growth of an organized crime syndicate that engages in the drug trade and ganglike violence. Recently, Cuban Americans in Miami have expressed concern over what they view as the indifference of the city's Roman Catholic hierarchy. Like other Hispanics, Cuban Americans are underrepresented in leadership positions within the church. Finally—despite many individual success stories—as a group, Cuban Americans in Miami remain behind "Anglos" (Whites) in income, rate of employment, and proportion of professionals (Firmat 1994; Llanes 1982).

The Anti-Defamation League (ADL) of B'nai B'rith funds an annual survey of reported anti-Semitic incidents. Although the number has fluctuated, the 1994 tabulation reached the highest level in the 17 years the ADL has been recording such incidents. The total reported incidents of harassment, threats, vandalism, and assaults came to 1,547 in 1999. Some incidents were inspired and carried out by neo-Nazi skinheads—groups of young people who champion racist and anti-Semitic ideologies. Such threatening behavior only intensifies the fears of many Jewish Americans, who find it difficult to forget the Holocaust—the extermination of 6 million Jews by the Nazi Third Reich during World War II (Anti-Defamation League 2001).

As is true for other minorities discussed in this chapter, Jewish Americans face the choice of maintaining ties to their long religious and cultural heritage or becoming as indistinguishable as possible from gentiles. Many Jews have tended to assimilate, as is evident from the rise in marriages between Jews and Christians. A study conducted in 2000 found that more than half of Jews who married chose to marry a non-Jew. Many people within the Jewish community worry that intermarriage will lead to a rapid decline in those who identify themselves as "Jewish." Yet when asked which was the greater threat to Jewish life in the United States—intermarriage or anti-Semitism—only 41 percent of respondents replied that intermarriage was the greater threat; 50 percent selected anti-Semitism (American Jewish Committee 2001).

White Ethnics

A significant segment of the population of the United States is made up of White ethnics whose ancestors arrived from Europe within the last 100 years. The nation's White ethnic population includes about 58 million people who claim at least partial German ancestry, 39 million Irish Americans, 15 million Italian Americans, and 9 million Polish Americans, as well as immigrants from other European nations. Some of these people continue to live in close-knit ethnic neighborhoods, while others have largely assimilated and left the "old ways" behind (Bureau of the Census 1999:56).

Many White ethnics today identify only sporadically with their heritage. *Symbolic ethnicity* refers to an emphasis on concerns such as ethnic food or political issues rather than on deeper ties to one's ethnic heritage. It is reflected in the occasional family trip to an ethnic bakery, the celebration of a ceremonial event such as St. Joseph's Day among Italian Americans, or concern about the future of Northern Ireland among Irish Americans. Except in cases in which new immigration reinforces old traditions, symbolic ethnicity tends to decline with each passing generation (Alba 1990; Gans 1979).

For practicing Jews, the Hebrew language is an important part of religious instruction. This teacher is showing flashcards of Hebrew alphabetic characters to deaf students.

White ethnics and racial minorities have often been antagonistic to one another because of economic competition—an interpretation that agrees with the conflict approach to sociology. As Blacks, Latinos and Native Americans emerge from the lower class, they must compete with working-class Whites for jobs, housing, and educational opportunities. In times of high unemployment or inflation, any such competition can easily generate intense intergroup conflict.

In many respects, the plight of White ethnics raises the same basic issues as that of other subordinate people in the United States. How ethnic can people be—how much can they deviate from an essentially White, Anglo-Saxon, Protestant norm—before society punishes them for their willingness to be different? Our society does seem to reward people for assimilating. Yet as we have seen, assimilation is no guarantee of equality or freedom from discrimination. In the social policy section that follows, we will focus on immigrants, people who inevitably face the question of whether or not to strive for assimilation.

SOCIAL POLICY and RACE AND ETHNICITY · Global Immigration

www. mhhe.com /schaefer9

FIGURE 11-6

Immigration in the United States, 1820s–1990s

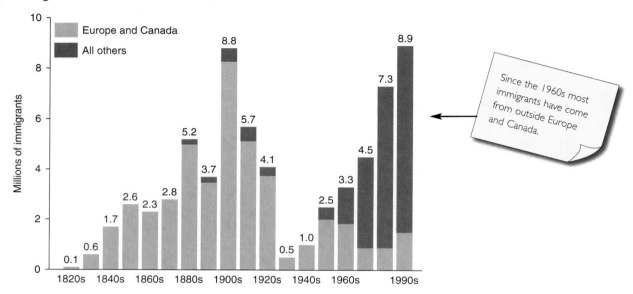

Source: Immigration and Naturalization Service 1999a, 1999b. Projection for the 1990s by the author based on Immigration and Naturalization data.

The Issue

Worldwide, immigration is at an all-time high. Each year, 2 to 4 million people move from one country to another. As of the mid-1990s, immigrants totaled about 125 million, representing 2 percent of the global population (P. Martin and Widgren 1996). Their constantly increasing numbers and the pressure they put on job opportunities and welfare capabilities in the countries they enter raise troubling questions for many of the world's economic powers. Who should be allowed in? At what point should immigration be curtailed?

The Setting

The migration of people is not uniform across time or space. At certain times, war or famine may precipitate large movements of people, either temporarily or permanently. Temporary dislocations occur when people wait until it is safe to return to their home areas. However, more and more migrants who cannot make an adequate living in their home nations are making permanent moves to developed nations. The major migration streams flow into North America, the oil-rich areas of the Middle East, and the industrial economies of western

Europe and Asia. Currently, seven of the world's wealthiest nations (including Germany, France, the United Kingdom, and the United States) shelter about one-third of the world's migrant population, but less than one-fifth of the world's total population. As long as disparities in job opportunities exist among countries, there is little reason to expect this international trend to reverse.

Countries that have long been a destination for immigrants, such as the United States, usually have policies to determine who has preference to enter. Often, clear racial and ethnic biases are built into these policies. In the 1920s, U.S. policy gave preference to people from western Europe, while making it difficult for residents of southern and eastern Europe, Asia, and Africa to enter the country. During the late 1930s and early 1940s, the federal government refused to lift or loosen restrictive immigration quotas in order to allow Jewish refugees to escape the terror of the Nazi regime. In line with this policy, the SS St. Louis, with more than 900 Jewish refugees on board, was denied permission to land in the United States in 1939. The ship was forced to sail back to Europe, where it is estimated that at least a few hundred of its passengers later died at the hands of the Nazis (A. Morse 1967; G. Thomas and Witts 1974).

FIGURE 11-7

Foreign-Born Population of the United States, from 10 Leading Countries, 2000

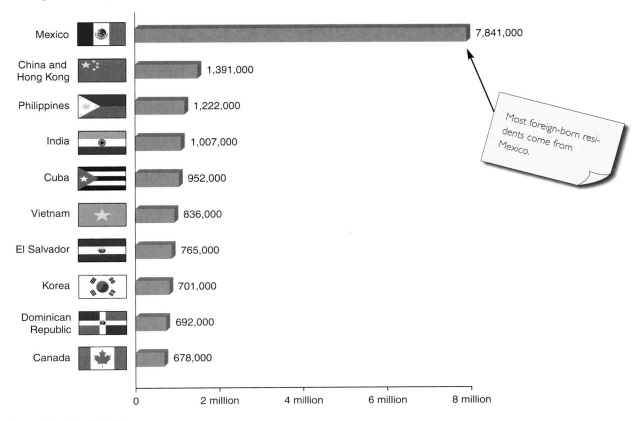

Source: Schmidley 2001:12

Since the 1960s, U.S. policy has encouraged the immigration of relatives of U.S. residents as well as of people who have desirable skills. This change has significantly altered the pattern of sending nations. Previously, Europeans dominated, but for the last 40 years, immigrants have come primarily from Latin America and Asia (see Figure 11-6). Thus, an ever-growing proportion of the United States will be Asian or Hispanic (see Figure 11-7). To a large degree, fear and resentment of growing racial and ethnic diversity is a key factor in opposition to immigration. In many nations, people are concerned that the new arrivals do not reflect their own cultural and racial heritage.

Sociological Insights

Despite people's fears, immigration performs many valuable functions. For the receiving society, it alleviates labor shortages, as it does in health care and technology in the United States. In 1998, Congress debated not whether individuals with technological skills should be allowed into the country, but just how much to increase the annual quota. For the sending nation, migration can relieve an economy unable to support large numbers of people. Often overlooked is the large amount of money, called *remittances,* that immigrants send *back* to their home nations. Worldwide, immigrants send more than $80 billion a year back home to their relatives—an amount that represents a major source of income for developing nations (World Bank 2003c).

Immigration can be dysfunctional as well. Although studies generally show that it has a positive impact on the receiving nation's economy, areas that accept high concentrations of immigrants may find it difficult to meet short-term social service needs. And when migrants with skills or educational potential leave developing countries, their departure can be dysfunctional for those nations. No amount of payments sent back home can make up for the loss of valuable human resources from poor nations (P. Martin and Midgley 1999; Mosisa 2002).

Conflict theorists note how much of the debate over immigration is phrased in economic terms. But the debate is intensified when the arrivals are of a different racial and ethnic background from the host population. For example, Europeans often refer to "foreigners," but the term does not necessarily mean one of foreign birth. In Germany, "foreigners" refers to people of non-German ancestry, even if they were *born* in Germany; it does not refer to people of German ancestry born in another country, who may choose to return to their "mother country." Fear and dislike of "new" ethnic groups divide countries throughout the world.

Policy Initiatives

The long border with Mexico provides ample opportunity for illegal immigration into the United States. Throughout the 1980s, there was a growing public perception that the United States had lost control of its borders. Feeling pressure for immigration control, Congress ended a decade of debate by approving the Immigration Reform and Control Act of 1986. The act marked a historic change in the nation's immigration policy. For the first time, the hiring of illegal aliens was outlawed, and employers caught violating the law became subject to fines and even prison sentences. Just as significant a change was the extension of amnesty and legal status to many illegal immigrants already living in the United States. More than a decade later, however, the act appears to have had mixed results. Substantial numbers of illegal immigrants continue to enter the country each year, with an estimated 8 to 10 million present at any given time (Deardorff and Blumerman 2001).

In part because the law failed to end illegal immigration, pressure has been increasing in several states for further government action. Most dramatically, in November 1994, California's voters overwhelmingly approved Proposition 187, a controversial initiative that among other provisions, called for withholding social services and schooling from illegal immigrants. Constitutional challenges to the law blocked all the measure's provisions, however.

The entire world feels the overwhelming impact of globalization on immigration patterns. The European Union agreement of 1997 gave the governing commission authority to propose Europewide policy on immigration beginning in 2002. However, the policy must be accepted unanimously, which seems unlikely. An EU policy that would allow immigrants to live and work in one EU country would allow them to work anywhere. The issue is expected to complicate efforts by the sending nations (such as Turkey) to become members of the EU (Light 1999; Sassen 1999).

In the wake of the attacks of September 11, 2001, on the World Trade Center and the Pentagon, immigration procedures were complicated by the need to detect potential terrorists. Illegal immigrants especially, but even legal immigrants, have felt increased scrutiny by government officials around the world. For would-be immigrants to many nations, the wait to receive the right to enter a country—even to join relatives—has increased substantially, as immigration officials scrutinize what were once routine applications more closely.

The intense debate over immigration reflects deep value conflicts in the cultures of many nations. One strand of our culture, for example, has traditionally emphasized egalitarian principles and a desire to help people in time of need. At the same time, hostility to potential immigrants and refugees—whether the Chinese in the 1880s, European Jews in the 1930s and 1940s, or Mexicans, Haitians, and Arabs today—reflects not only racial, ethnic, and religious prejudice, but a desire to maintain the dominant culture of the in-group by keeping out those viewed as outsiders.

Let's Discuss

1. Did you or your parents or grandparents immigrate to the United States from another nation? If so, when and where did your family come from, and why?

2. Do you live, work, or study with recent immigrants to the United States? If so, are they well accepted in your community, or do they face prejudice and discrimination?

3. What is your opinion of the backlash against illegal immigrants in California?

CHAPTER RESOURCES

Summary

The social dimensions of race and ethnicity are important factors in shaping people's lives in the United States and other countries. In this chapter, we examine the meaning of race and ethnicity and study the major racial and ethnic groups of the United States.

1. A *racial group* is set apart from others by obvious physical differences; an *ethnic group* is set apart primarily by national origin or cultural patterns.
2. When sociologists define a *minority group,* they are concerned primarily with the economic and political power, or powerlessness, of the group.
3. In a biological sense, there are no "pure races," and no physical traits that can be used to describe one group to the exclusion of all others.
4. The meaning people attach to the physical differences between races gives social significance to race, producing *stereotypes.*
5. *Prejudice* often leads to *discrimination,* but the two are not identical, and each can be present without the other.
6. *Institutional discrimination* results from the normal operations of a society.
7. Functionalists point out that discrimination is both functional and dysfunctional for a society. Conflict theorists explain racial subordination through *exploitation theory.* Interactionists pose the *contact hypothesis* as a means of reducing prejudice and discrimination.
8. Four patterns describe typical intergroup relations in North America and elsewhere: *amalgamation, assimilation, segregation,* and *pluralism.* Pluralism remains more of an ideal than a reality.
9. Contemporary prejudice and discrimination against African Americans are rooted in the history of slavery in the United States.
10. Asian Americans are commonly viewed as a *model* or *ideal minority,* a stereotype not necessarily beneficial to members of that group.
11. The various groups included under the general term *Latinos* represent the largest ethnic minority in the United States.
12. The increase in immigration worldwide has raised questions in many nations about how to control the process.

Critical Thinking Questions

1. Why is institutional discrimination even more powerful than individual discrimination? How would functionalists, conflict theorists, and interactionists study institutional discrimination?
2. Examine the relations between dominant and subordinate racial and ethnic groups in your hometown and your college. Can the community in which you grew up and the college you attend be viewed as genuine examples of pluralism?
3. What are some of the similarities and differences in the position of African Americans and Hispanics in the United States? What are some of the similarities and differences in the position of Asian Americans and Jewish Americans?

Key Terms

Affirmative action   Positive efforts to recruit minority group members or women for jobs, promotions, and educational opportunities. (page 259)

Amalgamation   The process through which a majority group and a minority group combine to form a new group. (263)

Anti-Semitism   Anti-Jewish prejudice. (272)

Apartheid   A former policy of the South African government designed to maintain the separation of Blacks and other non-Whites from the dominant Whites. (263)

Assimilation   The process through which a person forsakes his or her own cultural tradition to become part of a different culture. (263)

Black power   A political philosophy promoted by many younger Blacks in the 1960s that supported the creation of Black-controlled political and economic institutions. (266)

Contact hypothesis   An interactionist perspective which states that in cooperative circumstances, interracial contact between people of equal status will reduce prejudice. (262)

Discrimination   The denial of opportunities and equal rights to individuals and groups because of prejudice or other arbitrary reasons. (257)

Ethnic group   A group that is set apart from others primarily because of its national origin or distinctive cultural patterns. (250)

Ethnocentrism The tendency to assume that one's own culture and way of life represent the norm or are superior to all others. (255)

Exploitation theory A Marxist theory that views racial subordination in the United States as a manifestation of the class system inherent in capitalism. (260)

Genocide The deliberate, systematic killing of an entire people or nation. (262)

Glass ceiling An invisible barrier that blocks the promotion of a qualified individual in a work environment because of the individual's gender, race, or ethnicity. (257)

Institutional discrimination The denial of opportunities and equal rights to individuals and groups that results from the normal operations of a society. (258)

Issei Japanese immigrants to the United States. (269)

Minority group A subordinate group whose members have significantly less control or power over their own lives than the members of a dominant or majority group have over theirs. (250)

Model or ideal minority A minority group that despite past prejudice and discrimination, succeeds economically, socially, and educationally without resorting to confrontations with Whites. (268)

Nisei Japanese children born in the United States to the Issei. (269)

Pluralism Mutual respect for one another's cultures among the various groups in a society, which allows minorities to express their own cultures without experiencing prejudice. (264)

Prejudice A negative attitude toward an entire category of people, often an ethnic or racial minority. (255)

Racial group A group that is set apart from others because of obvious physical differences. (250)

Racism The belief that one race is supreme and all others are innately inferior. (255)

Segregation The physical separation of two groups of people in terms of residence, workplace, and social events; often imposed on a minority group by a dominant group. (263)

Stereotype An unreliable generalization about all members of a group that does not recognize individual differences within the group. (253)

Symbolic ethnicity An ethnic identity that emphasizes concerns such as ethnic food or political issues rather than deeper ties to one's ethnic heritage. (273)

TECHNOLOGY RESOURCES

Internet Connection

*Note: While all the URLs listed were current as of the printing of this book, these sites often change. Please check our website (**www.mhhe.com/schaefer9**) for updates, hyperlinks, and exercises related to these sites.*

1. The Southern Poverty Law Center (**www.splcenter.org**) is a nonprofit organization that combats hate, intolerance, and discrimination through education and litigation. Go to the center's website to learn about hate groups in your home state.

2. Racial and ethnic groups can relate to one another in a wide variety of ways, ranging from friendships and intermarriages to hostility. One devastating pattern of intergroup relations is genocide—the deliberate, systematic killing of an entire people or nation. Genocide Watch is the coordinator for the International Campaign to End Genocide. Visit their website (**www.genocidewatch.org**) to learn more about the stages of genocide.

Online Learning Center with PowerWeb

The Civil Rights movement was a defining sociological event in modern U.S. history. To learn more about this movement, go to the Online Learning Center at **www.mhhe.com/schaefer9** and visit the student center. Link to "Internet Exercises," and scroll down to the third exercise. Through the Papers Project, Stanford University has helped to preserve the words and life of Dr. Martin Luther King Jr., leader of the Civil Rights movement.

Reel Society Interactive Movie CD-ROM

Reel Society includes scenes that can be used to spark discussion about the following topics from this chapter:

- Minority Groups
- Race

- Ethnicity
- Prejudice and Discrimination

chapter

STRATIFICATION BY GENDER

This billboard in Hollywood, California, produced by the feminist advocacy group Guerrilla Girls, points out the gender inequities in the motion picture industry. In all categories, including makeup, the overwhelming majority of Oscars have been awarded to men.

Social Construction of Gender

Explaining Stratification by Gender

Women: The Oppressed Majority

Minority Women: Double Jeopardy

Social Policy and Gender Stratification: The Battle over Abortion from a Global Perspective

Boxes

SOCIOLOGY IN THE GLOBAL COMMUNITY:
The Head Scarf and the Veil: Complex Symbols

RESEARCH IN ACTION: Communication Differences between Male and Female Physicians

At last, after a long silence, women took to the streets. In the two decades of radical action that followed the rebirth of feminism in the early 1970s, Western women gained legal and reproductive rights, pursued higher education, entered the trades and the professions, and overturned ancient and revered beliefs about their social role. A generation on, do women feel free?

The affluent, educated, liberated women of the First World, who can enjoy freedoms unavailable to any women ever before, do not feel as free as they want to. And they can no longer restrict to the subconscious their sense that this lack of freedom has something to do with—with apparently frivolous issues, things that really should not matter. Many are ashamed to admit that such trivial concerns—to do with physical appearance, bodies, faces, hair, clothes—

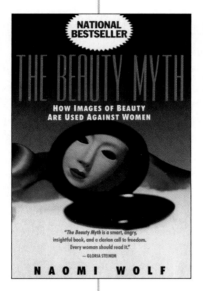

matter so much. But in spite of shame, guilt, and denial, more and more women are wondering if . . . something important is indeed at stake that has to do with the relationship between female liberation and female beauty.

During the past decade, women breached the power structure; meanwhile, eating disorders rose exponentially and cosmetic surgery became the fastest-growing medical specialty. During the past five years, consumer spending doubled, pornography became the main media category, ahead of legitimate films and records combined, and thirty-three thousand American women told researchers that they would rather lose ten to fifteen pounds than achieve any other goal. More women have more money and power and scope and legal recognition than we have ever had before; but in terms of how we feel about ourselves *physically,* we may actually be worse off than our unliberated grandmothers. Recent research consistently shows that inside the majority of the West's controlled, attractive, successful working women, there is a secret "underlife" poisoning our freedom; infused with notions of beauty, it is a dark vein of self-hatred, physical obsessions, terror of aging, and dread of lost control.

It is no accident that so many potentially powerful women feel this way. We are in the midst of a violent backlash against feminism that uses images of female beauty as a political weapon against women's advancement: the beauty myth. . . .

The beauty myth tells a story: The quality called "beauty" objectively and universally exists. Women must want to embody it and men must want to possess women who embody it. This embodiment is an imperative for women and not for men, which situation is necessary and natural because it is biological, sexual, and evolutionary: Strong men battle for beautiful women, and beautiful women are more reproductively successful. Women's beauty must correlate to their fertility, and since this system is based on sexual selection, it is inevitable and changeless.

None of this is true. "Beauty" is a currency system like the gold standard. Like any economy, it is determined by politics, and in the modern age in the West it is the last, best belief system that keeps male dominance intact. (N. Wolf 1992:9–10, 12) ■ ☺

Additional information about this excerpt can be found on the Online Learning Center at **www.mhhe.com/Schaefer9.**

In this excerpt from Naomi Wolf's book *The Beauty Myth,* a feminist confronts the power of a false ideal of womanhood. In recent decades, American women have broken legal and institutional barriers that once limited their educational opportunities and career advancement. But psychologically, Wolf writes, they are still enslaved by unrealistic standards of appearance. The more freedom women have gained, in fact, the more obsessed they seem to have become with the ideal of the ultrathin supermodel—an ideal that few women can ever hope to attain, even if they are willing to jeopardize their health through obsessive dieting and exercise, plastic surgery, anorexia or bulimia.

Wolf asserts that the beauty myth is a societal control mechanism that is meant to keep women in their place—as subordinates to men at home and on the job. But men too are captive to unrealistic expectations regarding their physical appearance. In hopes of attaining a brawny, muscular physique, more and more men are now taking steroids or electing to undergo cosmetic surgery. Today's media bombard both men and women with the need to look good in ads hawking everything from nutrition supplements to hair color formulas to expensive exercise equipment and health club memberships. The latest manifestation of this trend is ABC Television's Extreme Makeover, a show that follows volunteers of both sexes as they undergo a variety of cosmetic surgeries. In screening the 7,000 people who responded to the show's initial casting call, however, producers found that the overwhelming majority were women (P. Thomas and Owens 2000).

The beauty myth is but one example of how cultural norms may lead to differentiation based on one's gender. Such differentiation is evident in virtually every human society about which we have information. We saw in Chapters 9 to 11 that most societies establish hierarchies based on social class, race, and ethnicity. This chapter will examine the ways in which societies stratify their members on the basis of gender.

Do gender roles differ from one culture to another? Are women in the United States still oppressed because of their gender, as Naomi Wolf asserts? How does a woman's race affect her social standing? We will begin to answer these and other questions by looking first at how various cultures, including our own, assign women and men to particular social roles. Then we will consider sociological explanations for gender stratification. Next, we will focus on the unique situation of women as an oppressed majority, and on the double jeopardy women of color face. The chapter closes with a social policy section on the intense and continuing controversy over a woman's right to abortion. ■

SOCIAL CONSTRUCTION OF GENDER

How many air passengers do you think are startled by hearing a female captain's voice from the cockpit? Or what do we make of a father who announces that he will be late for work because his son has a routine medical checkup? Consciously or unconsciously, we are likely to assume that flying a commercial plane is a *man's* job and that most parental duties are, in fact, *maternal* duties. Gender is such a routine part of our everyday activities that we typically take notice only when someone deviates from conventional behavior and expectations.

Although a few people begin life with an unclear sexual identity, the overwhelming majority begin with a definite sex and quickly receive societal messages about how to behave. Many societies have established social distinctions between females and males that do not inevitably result from biological differences between the sexes (such as women's reproductive capabilities).

In studying gender, sociologists are interested in the gender-role socialization that leads females and males to behave differently. In Chapter 4, *gender roles* were defined as expectations regarding the proper behavior, attitudes, and activities of males and females. The application of traditional gender roles leads to many forms of differentiation between women and men. Both sexes are physically capable of learning to cook and sew, yet most Western societies determine that women should perform these tasks. Both men and women are capable of learning to weld and fly airplanes, but these functions are generally assigned to men.

Gender roles are evident not only in our work and behavior but in how we react to others. We are constantly "doing gender" without realizing it. If the father just discussed sits in the doctor's office with his son in the middle of a workday, he will probably receive approving glances from the receptionist and from other patients. "Isn't he a wonderful father?" runs through their minds. But if the boy's mother leaves *her* job and sits with the son in the doctor's office, she will not receive such silent applause.

We socially construct our behavior so as to create or exaggerate male–female differences. For example, men and women come in a variety of heights, sizes, and ages. Yet traditional norms regarding marriage and even casual dating tell us that in heterosexual couples, the man should be older, taller, and wiser than the woman. As we will see throughout this chapter, such social norms help to reinforce and legitimize patterns of male dominance.

In recent decades, women have increasingly entered occupations and professions previously dominated by men. Yet our society still focuses on "masculine" and "feminine" qualities, as if men and women must be evaluated in those terms. Clearly, we continue to "do gender," and our construction of gender continues to define significantly different expectations for females and males (Lorber 1994; Rosenbaum 1996; West and Zimmerman 1987).

Gender Roles in the United States

Gender-Role Socialization

Male babies get blue blankets; females get pink ones. Boys are expected to play with trucks, blocks, and toy soldiers; girls receive dolls and kitchen goods. Boys must be masculine—active, aggressive, tough, daring, and dominant—but girls must be feminine—soft, emotional, sweet, and submissive. These traditional gender-role patterns have been influential in the socialization of children in the United States.

An important element in traditional views of proper "masculine" and "feminine" behavior is **homophobia,** fear of and prejudice against homosexuality. Homophobia contributes significantly to rigid gender-role socialization, since many people stereotypically associate male homosexuality with

femininity and lesbianism with masculinity. Consequently, men and women who deviate from traditional expectations about gender roles are often presumed to be gay. Despite the advances made by the gay liberation movement, the continuing stigma attached to homosexuality in our culture places pressure on all males (whether gay or not) to exhibit only narrow "masculine" behavior and on all females (whether lesbian or not) to exhibit only narrow "feminine" behavior (Seidman 1994; see also Lehne 1995).

It is *adults,* of course, who play a critical role in guiding children into those gender roles deemed appropriate in a society. Parents are normally the first and p. 91 most crucial agents of socialization. But other adults, older siblings, the mass media, and religious and educational institutions also exert an important influence on gender-role socialization, in the United States and elsewhere.

It is not hard to test how rigid gender-role socialization can be. Just try transgressing some gender norm—say, by smoking a cigar in public if you are female, or by carrying a purse if you are male. That was exactly the assignment given to sociology students at the University of Colorado and Luther College in Iowa. Professors asked students to behave in ways that they thought violated norms of how a man or woman should act. The students had no trouble coming up with gender-norm

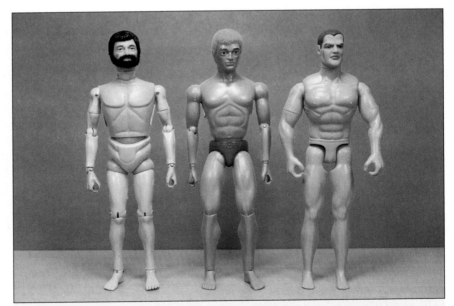

Society often exaggerates male–female differences in appearance and behavior. In 1964, the G.I. Joe doll (left) had a realistic appearance, but by 1992 (middle) it had begun to acquire the exaggerated muscularity characteristic of professional wrestlers (right). The change intensified the contrast with ultrathin female figures, like the Barbie doll (Angier 1998).

Table 12-1	An Experiment in Gender Norm Violation by College Students
Norm Violations by Women	**Norm Violations by Men**
Send men flowers	Wear fingernail polish
Spit in public	Needlepoint in public
Use men's bathroom	Throw Tupperware party
Buy jock strap	Cry in public
Buy/chew tobacco	Have pedicure
Talk knowledgeably about cars	Apply to baby-sit
Open doors for men	Shave body hair

Source: Nielsen et al. 2000:287.

In an experiment testing gender-role stereotypes, sociology students were asked to behave in ways that might be regarded as violating gender norms, and to keep notes on how others reacted. This is a sample of their choices of behavior over a seven-year period. Do you agree that these actions test the boundaries of conventional gender behavior?

transgressions (see Table 12-1), and they kept careful notes on how others reacted to their behavior, ranging from amusement to disgust (Nielsen et al. 2000).

Women's Gender Roles

How does a girl come to develop a feminine self-image, while a boy develops one that is masculine? In part, they do so by identifying with females and males in their families and neighborhoods and in the media. If a young girl regularly sees female television characters working as defense attorneys and judges, she may believe that she herself can become a lawyer. And it will not hurt if women that she knows—her mother, sister, parents' friends, or neighbors—are lawyers. In contrast, if this young girl sees women portrayed in the media only as models, nurses, and secretaries, her identification and self-image will be quite different. Even if she does become a professional, she may secretly regret falling short of the media stereotype—a shapely, sexy young woman in a bathing suit.

Television is far from alone in stereotyping women. Studies of children's books published in the United States in the 1940s, 1950s, and 1960s found that females were significantly underrepresented in central roles and illustrations. Virtually all female characters were portrayed as helpless, passive, incompetent, and in need of a strong male caretaker. Studies of picture books published from the 1970s through the 1990s found some improvement, but males still dominated the central roles. While males were portrayed as a variety of characters, females tended

to be shown mostly in traditional roles, such as mother, grandmother, or volunteer, even if they also held nontraditional roles, such as working professional (Etaugh 2003).

Social research on gender roles reveals some persistent differences between men and women in North America and Europe. Women tend to feel pressure both to marry and to become a mother. Often, marriage is viewed as their true entry into adulthood. And women are expected not only to become mothers but to *want* to be mothers. Obviously, men play a role in marriage and parenthood, but these events do not appear to be as critical in the life course of a man. Society defines men's identity by their economic success. And even though many women today fully expect to have careers and achieve recognition in the labor force, success at work is not as important to their identity as it is for men (Doyle and Paludi 1998; Russo 1976).

Traditional gender roles have restricted females more severely than males. This chapter shows how women have been confined to subordinate roles within the political and economic institutions of the United States. Yet it is also true that gender roles have restricted males.

Men's Gender Roles

Stay-at-home fathers? Until recent decades such an idea was unthinkable. Yet in a nationwide survey done in 2002, 69 percent of respondents said that if one parent stays home with the children, it makes no difference whether that parent is the mother or the father. Only 30 percent thought that the mother should be the one to stay home. But while people's conceptions of gender roles are obviously changing, the fact is that men who stay home to care for their children are still an unusual phenomenon. In 2001, for every stay-at-home dad there were about seven married stay-at-home moms (Bureau of the Census 2002a:374; Robison 2002).

While attitudes toward parenting may be changing, studies show little change in the traditional male gender role. Men's roles are socially constructed in much the same way as women's roles are. Family, peers, and the media all influence how a boy or a man comes to view his appropriate role in society. Robert Brannon (1976) and James Doyle (1995) have identified five aspects of the male gender role:

- Antifeminine element—show no "sissy stuff," including any expression of openness or vulnerability.
- Success element—prove one's masculinity at work and sports.
- Aggressive element—use force in dealing with others.
- Sexual element—initiate and control all sexual relations.
- Self-reliant element—keep cool and unflappable.

No systematic research has established all these elements as necessarily common to all males, but specific studies have confirmed individual elements.

Males who do not conform to the socially constructed gender role face constant criticism and even humiliation, both from children when they are boys and from adults as men. It can be agonizing to be treated as a "chicken" or a "sissy"—particularly if such remarks come from one's father or brothers. At the same time, boys who successfully adapt to cultural standards of masculinity may grow up to be inexpressive men who cannot share their feelings with others. They remain forceful and tough, but as a result they are also closed and isolated (Faludi 1999; McCreary 1994; Sheehy 1999).

A small but growing body of scholarship suggests that for men as well as women, traditional gender roles may be disadvantageous. In many communities across the nation, girls seem to outdo boys in high school, grabbing a disproportionate share of the leadership positions, from valedictorian to class president to yearbook editor—everything, in short, except captain of the boys' athletic teams. Their advantage continues after high school. In the 1980s, girls in the United States became more likely than boys to go to college. By 2000, women accounted for over 56 percent of college students nationwide.

Some of this discrepancy in enrollments can be explained by noting that men can earn good hourly wages with less formal schooling than women. Yet by a number of measures, girls appear to take schooling more seriously than boys. In 2000, for example, female students taking the Advanced Placement (AP) tests outnumbered male students 19 out of 33 subjects. Overall, they accounted for 54 percent of students who took the AP tests. Educational professionals need to look more closely at men's underperformance in school, not to mention their overrepresentation in reported crime and illegal drug use (Bureau of the Census 2002a:161, 164; Conlin 2003; Sommers 2000).

In the last 40 years, inspired in good part by the contemporary feminist movement (examined later in the chapter), increasing numbers of men in the United States have criticized the restrictive aspects of the traditional male gender role. Some men have taken strong public positions in support of women's struggle for full equality, and have even organized voluntary associations such as the National Organization for Men Against Sexism (NOMAS), founded in 1975 to support positive changes for men. Nevertheless, the traditional male gender role remains well entrenched as an influential element of our culture (Messner 1997; National Organization for Men Against Sexism 2003).

Use Your Sociological Imagination

www.mhhe.com /schaefer5

You are living in a society in which there are no gender roles. What is your life like?

Cross-Cultural Perspective

To what extent do actual biological differences between the sexes contribute to the cultural differences associated with gender? This question brings us back to the debate over "nature versus nurture." In assessing the alleged and real differences between men and women, it is useful to examine cross-cultural data.

pp. 81–84

The research of anthropologist Margaret Mead points to the importance of cultural conditioning—as opposed to biology—in defining the social roles of males and females. In *Sex and Temperament*, Mead ([1935] 2001; 1973) describes the typical behaviors of each sex in three different cultures in New Guinea:

> In one [the Arapesh], both men and women act as we expect women to act—in a mild parental responsive way; in the second [the Mundugumor], both act as we expect men to act—in a fierce initiating fashion; and in the third [the Tchambuli], the men act according to our stereotypes for women—are catty, wear curls, and go shopping—while the women are energetic, managerial, unadorned partners. (Preface to 1950 ed.)

If biology determined all differences between the sexes, then cross-cultural differences, such as those described by Mead, would not exist. Her findings confirm the influential role of culture and socialization in gender-role differentiation. There appears to be no innate or biological reason to designate completely different gender roles for men and women.

In any society, gender stratification requires not only individual socialization into traditional gender roles within the family, but the promotion and support of those traditional roles by other social institutions, such as religion and education. Moreover, even with all major institutions socializing the young into conventional gender roles, every society has women and men who resist and successfully oppose the stereotypes: strong women who

Cultural conditioning is important in the development of gender role differences. This sister and brother from Sudest Island in Papua New Guinea expect women to be the honorary heads of the family.

become leaders or professionals, gentle men who care for children, and so forth. It seems clear that differences between the sexes are not dictated by biology. Indeed, the maintenance of traditional gender roles requires constant social controls—and those controls are not always effective.

EXPLAINING STRATIFICATION BY GENDER

Cross-cultural studies indicate that societies dominated by men are much more common than those in which women play the decisive role. Sociologists have turned to all the major theoretical perspectives to understand how and why these social distinctions are established. Each approach focuses on culture rather than biology as the primary determinant of gender differences. Yet in other respects, advocates of these sociological perspectives disagree widely.

The Functionalist View

Functionalists maintain that gender differentiation has contributed to overall social stability. Sociologists Talcott Parsons and Robert Bales (1955) argued that to function most effectively, the family requires adults who specialize in particular roles. They viewed the traditional gender roles as arising out of the need to establish a division of labor between marital partners.

Parsons and Bales contended that women take the expressive, emotionally supportive role and men the instrumental, practical role, with the two complementing each other. *Instrumentality* refers to an emphasis on tasks, a focus on more distant goals, and a concern for the external relationship between one's family and other social institutions. *Expressiveness* denotes concern for the maintenance of harmony and the internal emotional affairs of the family. According to this theory, women's interest in expressive goals frees men for instrumental tasks, and vice versa. Women become anchored in the family as wives, mothers, and household managers; men become anchored in the occupational world outside the home. Of course, Parsons and Bales offered this framework in the 1950s, when many more women were full-time homemakers than is true today. These theorists did not explicitly endorse traditional gender roles, but they implied that dividing tasks between spouses was functional for the family as a unit.

Given the typical socialization of women and men in the United States, the functionalist view is initially persuasive. However, it would lead us to expect girls and women who have no interest in children to become babysitters and mothers. Similarly, males who love spending time with children might be programmed into careers in the business world. Such differentiation might harm the individual who does not fit into prescribed roles, as well as deprive society of the contributions of many talented people who feel confined by gender stereotyping. Moreover, the functionalist approach does not convincingly explain why men should be assigned categorically to the instrumental role, and women to the expressive role.

The Conflict Response

Viewed from a conflict perspective, the functionalist approach masks the underlying power relations between men and women. Parsons and Bales never explicitly presented the expressive and instrumental roles as being of unequal value to society, yet their inequality is quite evident. Although social institutions may pay lip service to women's expressive skills, men's instrumental skills are more highly rewarded, whether in terms of money or prestige. Consequently, according to feminists and conflict theorists, any division of labor by gender into instrumental and expressive tasks is far from neutral in its impact on women.

Conflict theorists contend that the relationship between females and males has traditionally been one of unequal power, with men in a dominant position over women. Men may originally have become powerful in preindustrial times because their size, physical strength, and freedom from childbearing duties allowed them to dominate women physically. In contemporary societies, such considerations are not so important, yet cultural beliefs about the sexes are long established, as anthropologist Margaret Mead and feminist sociologist Helen Mayer Hacker (1951, 1974) both stressed. Such beliefs support a social structure that places males in controlling positions.

Conflict theorists, then, see gender differences as a reflection of the subjugation of one group (women) by another group (men). If we use an analogy to Marx's

pp. 11, 203

analysis of class conflict, we can say that males are like the bourgeoisie, or capitalists; they control most of the society's wealth, prestige, and power. Females are like the proletariat, or workers; they can acquire valuable resources only by following the dictates of their bosses. Men's work is uniformly valued; women's work (whether unpaid labor in the home or wage labor) is devalued.

The Feminist Perspective

A significant component of the conflict approach to gender stratification draws on feminist theory. Although use of that term is

pp. 15–16

comparatively recent, the critique of women's position in society and culture goes back to some of the earliest works that have influenced sociology. Among the most important are Mary Wollstonecraft's *A Vindication of the Rights of Women* (originally published in 1792), John Stuart Mill's *The Subjection of Women* (originally published in 1869), and Friedrich Engels's *The Origin of the Family, Private Property, and the State* (originally published in 1884).

Engels, a close associate of Karl Marx, argued that women's subjugation coincided with the rise of private property during industrialization. Only when people moved beyond an agrarian economy could males enjoy the luxury of leisure and withhold rewards and privileges from women. Drawing on the work of Marx and Engels, contemporary feminist theorists often view women's subordination as part of the overall exploitation and injustice that they see as inherent in capitalist societies. Some radical feminist theorists, however, view the oppression of women as inevitable in *all* male-dominated societies, whether they are labeled capitalist, socialist, or communist (Feuer 1989; Tuchman 1992).

Feminist sociologists would find little to disagree with in the conflict theorists' perspective, but are more likely to embrace a political agenda. Feminists would also argue that the very discussion of women and society, however well meant, has been distorted by the exclusion of women from academic thought, including sociology. We have noted the many accomplishments of Jane

pp. 12, 16

Addams and Ida Wells-Barnett, but they generally worked outside the discipline, focusing on what we would now call applied sociology and social work. At the time their efforts, while valued as humanitarian, were seen as unrelated to the research and conclusions being reached in academic circles, which of course were male academic circles (Andersen 1997; J. Howard 1999).

Feminist theorists today (including conflict theorists) emphasize that in the United States male dominance goes far beyond the economic sphere. Throughout this textbook, we examine disturbing aspects

Conflict theorists emphasize that men's work is uniformly valued, while women's work (whether unpaid labor in the home or wage labor) is devalued. These women are making tents in a factory in Binghamton, New York.

In April 2002, the Congressional Women's Caucus conferred with Kofi Annan, secretary general of the United Nations, at his office in New York.

of men's behavior toward women. The ugly realities of rape, wife battering, sexual harassment, and street harassment all illustrate and intensify women's subordinate position. Even if women reach economic parity with men, even if they win equal representation in government, genuine equality between the sexes cannot be achieved if these attacks remain as common as they are today.

Functionalist, conflict, and feminist theorists acknowledge that it is not possible to change gender roles drastically without making dramatic revisions in a culture's social structure. Functionalists perceive the potential for social disorder, or at least unknown social consequences, if all aspects of traditional gender stratification are disturbed. Yet for conflict and feminist theorists, no social structure is ultimately desirable if it is maintained by oppressing a majority of citizens. These theorists argue that gender stratification may be functional for men—who hold the power and privilege—but it is hardly in the interests of women.

The Interactionist Approach

While functionalists and conflict theorists who study gender stratification typically focus on macro-level social forces and institutions, interactionist researchers tend to examine gender stratification on the micro level of everyday behavior. As an example, studies show that men initiate up to 96 percent of all interruptions in cross-sex (male–female) conversations. Men are more likely than women to change the topic of conversation, to ignore topics chosen by members of the opposite sex, to minimize the contributions and ideas of members of the opposite sex, and to validate their own contributions.

These patterns reflect the conversational (and in a sense, political) dominance of males. Moreover, even when women occupy a prestigious position, such as that of physician, they are more likely to be interrupted than their male counterparts (Ridgeway and Smith-Lovin 1999; Tannen 1990; West and Zimmerman 1983).

These findings regarding cross-sex conversations have been frequently replicated. They have striking implications when one considers the power dynamics underlying likely cross-sex interactions—employer and job seeker, college professor and student, husband and wife, to name just a few. From an interactionist perspective, these simple, day-to-day exchanges are one more battleground in the struggle for gender equality—as women try to get a word in edgewise in the midst of men's interruptions and verbal dominance (Hollander 2002; Okamoto and Smith-Lovin 2001; Tannen 1994a, 1994b).

WOMEN: THE OPPRESSED MAJORITY

Many people, both male and female, find it difficult to conceive of women as a subordinate and oppressed group. Yet take a look at the political structure of the United States: Women remain noticeably underrepresented. In 2003, for example, only 6 of the nation's 50 states had a female governor (Arizona, Delaware, Hawaii, Kansas, Michigan, and Montana).

Women have made slow but steady progress in certain political arenas. In 1981, out of 535 members of Congress, there were only 21 women: 19 in the House of Representatives and 2 in the Senate. In contrast, the Congress that took office in January 2003 had 72 women: 59 in the House and 13 in the Senate. Yet the membership and leadership of Congress remain overwhelmingly male (Center for American Women and Politics 2003).

In October 1981, Sandra Day O'Connor was sworn in as the nation's first female Supreme Court justice. Still, no woman has ever served as president of the United States, vice president, speaker of the House of Representatives, or chief justice of the Supreme Court.

Sexism and Sex Discrimination

Just as African Americans are victimized by racism, women suffer from sexism in our society. *Sexism* is the

12-1 COMMUNICATION DIFFERENCES BETWEEN FEMALE AND MALE PHYSICIANS

When Perry Klass told her four-year-old son she would be taking him to the pediatrician, he replied, "Is she a nice doctor?" Klass, a professor of pediatrics, was struck by his innocent assumption that like his mother, all pediatricians were female. "Boys can be doctors too," she told him.

Not long ago, there would have been little potential for confusion on her son's part. Klass probably would not have been admitted to medical school, no less appointed a professor of medicine. But since the advent of the women's movement, the medical profession has been integrating women into its ranks. Now, more than two dozen studies done over the past three and a half decades indicate that not only are women competent physicians; in some respects they are more effective than their male counterparts.

The female advantage is particularly noteworthy in physician–patient communication. Female primary care physicians spend an extra two minutes talking with patients, or 10 percent more time than male primary care physicians. They also engage in more patient-centered communication, listening more, asking questions about patients' personal well-being, and counseling patients about the

> Not only are women competent physicians; in some respects they are more effective than their male counterparts.

concerns they bring to the doctor's office. Perhaps most important, female physicians tend to see their relationship with patients as an active partnership, one in which they discuss several treatment options with patients rather than recommending a single course of treatment.

From a sociological point of view, these differences between female and male physicians correspond to the gender differences in communication style that interactionist researchers have noted.

In some respects, female and male physicians do not differ. Researchers noted no differences in the quality or amount of time the two groups spend on purely medical matters, or on the length of time they spend conversing socially with patients.

Let's Discuss

1. In your own experience, have you noted a gender difference in the way doctors communicate with their patients? Explain.
2. Why is the quality of a doctor's communication with patients important? What might be the benefit of female physicians' superior communication style?

Sources: Carroll 2003; Klass 2003:319; Roter et al. 2002.

---

ideology that one sex is superior to the other. The term is generally used to refer to male prejudice and discrimination against women. In Chapter 11, we noted that Blacks can suffer from both individual acts of racism and institutional discrimination. *Institutional discrimination* was defined as the denial of opportunities and equal rights to individuals or groups that results from the normal operations of a society. In the same sense, women suffer from both individual acts of sexism (such as sexist remarks and acts of violence) and institutional sexism.

It is not simply that particular men in the United States are biased in their treatment of women. All the major institutions of our society—including the government, armed forces, large corporations, the media, universities, and the medical establishment—are controlled by men. These institutions, in their normal, day-to-day operations, often discriminate against women and perpetuate sexism. For example, if the central office of a na-

tionwide bank sets a policy that single women are a bad risk for loans—regardless of their incomes and investments—that bank will discriminate against women in state after state. It will do so even at branches where loan officers hold no personal biases concerning women, but are merely "following orders." Box 12-1 dispels the sexist myth that women cannot be good doctors, which medical schools used for years to justify their discriminatory admissions policies.

Our society is run by male-dominated institutions, yet with the power that flows to men come responsibility and stress. Men have higher reported rates of certain types of mental illness than women, and a greater likelihood of death due to heart attack or stroke. The pressure on men to succeed, and then to remain on top in the competitive world of work, can be especially intense. That is not to suggest that gender stratification is as damaging to men as it is to women. But it is clear that the power and privilege men enjoy are no guarantee of personal well-being.

The wearing of a veil or head scarf, which is common to many but not all Middle Eastern societies, originated in a verse from the Koran: "Prophet, enjoin your wives, your daughters and the wives of true believers to draw their veils close round them . . . so that they may be recognized and not molested." The injunction to cover one's body in the presence of men to whom one is not closely related is based on a view of women as bearers of the family's honor. To protect their chastity from men's predatory sexual advances, women must keep themselves out of harm's way. Wearing a veil in public is intended to do just that, to signal others that they are not to touch the wearer. A man who ignores that signal does so at his peril, for his action shames not just the woman, but her whole family.

> In effect, the veil represents a rejection of the beauty myth, which is so prevalent in Western societies.

The veil is also a way of maintaining a family's social status. Unlike rich families, poor families depend on their wives' and daughters' presence in the fields and markets, where a veil and robe can hamper a woman's ability to work. Thus in some regions of North Africa, Muslim women have never worn the veil. Nor do women veil themselves in small communities, where everyone knows everyone else. Only in cities in a few countries are women required to wear a veil.

In effect, the veil represents a rejection of the beauty myth, which is so prevalent in Western societies. While a Muslim woman's beauty is valued, it is not to be seen or exploited by the whole world. By covering themselves almost completely, Muslim women assure themselves and their families that their physical appear-

ance will not play a role in their contacts outside the family. Rather, these women will be known only for their faith, their intellect, and their personalities.

In the 20th century, the veil was politicized by modernization movements that pitted Western cultural values against traditional Islamic values. In Turkey, for instance, the rise to power of President Kemal Atatürk in 1923 sparked a process of sweeping social change, in which government officials attempted to subordinate traditional ethnic and religious influences to their nationalistic goals. Though women weren't forbidden to wear the veil, they were not allowed to veil themselves in public places like schools. Not surprisingly, many Muslims resented these forced social changes. In recent decades, strict clergy in countries like Iran and Afghanistan have reinstituted the veil and other Islamic traditions.

In Turkey, however, a modified version of the veil has recently become the symbol of militant feminists. Among educated young women who study at the universities, the new veil signifies an intention to transcend the traditional roles of wife and mother.

Two women from South Yemen wear the traditional garb of the Hadramaut region. Restrictions on Muslim women's clothing vary widely from one region to another; in many places, women are not required to cover their faces.

Women who are professionals, writers, intellectuals, and activists wear it as a public statement of their aspirations.

Westerners may think the Turkish feminists' adoption of the veil is strange. Together with some Muslim feminists, people from the West tend to see the veil as a symbol of women's second-class status. But to many Muslim women it makes sense. The veil allows young women to leave their homes in the countryside and mix with strange men in the great universities of the city, without violating Islamic custom. To many Muslim women, the veil is no less than a means of liberation.

Let's Discuss

1. Consider life in a society in which women wear veils. Can you see any advantages, from the woman's point of view? From the man's?

2. Do you find the Western emphasis on physical beauty oppressive? If so, in what ways?

Sources: Cancel 1997; Fernea 1998; Gole 1997; I. Perlman 2000; Read and Bartkowski 1999.

Sexual Harassment

The courts recognize two kinds of sexual harassment. Formally defined, ***sexual harassment*** is behavior that occurs when work benefits are made contingent on sexual favors (as a quid pro quo), or when touching, lewd comments, or the exhibition of pornographic material creates a hostile environment in the workplace. In 1998, the Supreme Court ruled that harassment applies to people of the same sex as well as the opposite. The quid pro quo type of harassment is fairly easy to identify in a court of law. But the issue of hostile environment has become the subject of considerable debate both in courts and in the general public (L. Greenhouse 1998; Lewin 1998).

Sexual harassment must be understood in the context of continuing prejudice and discrimination against women. Whether it occurs in the federal bureaucracy, in the corporate world, or in universities, sexual harassment generally takes place in organizations in which White males are at the top of the hierarchy of authority, and women's work is valued less than men's. One survey of the private sector found that African American women were three times more likely than White women to experience sexual harassment. From a conflict perspective, it is not surprising that women—and especially women of color—are most likely to become victims of sexual harassment. In terms of job security, these groups are typically an organization's most vulnerable employees (J. Jones 1988).

 Use Your Sociological Imagination   www.mhhe.com/schaefer9

How would Naomi Wolf (author of *The Beauty Myth*) interpret the problem of sexual harassment?

The Status of Women Worldwide

A detailed overview of the status of the world's women, issued by the United Nations in 2000, noted that women and men live in different worlds—worlds that differ in access to education and work opportunities, and in health, personal security, and human rights. The Hindu culture of India, for example, makes life especially harsh for widows. When Hindu women marry, they join their husband's family. If the husband dies, the widow is the "property" of that family. In many cases, she ends up working as an unpaid servant; in others she is simply abandoned and left penniless. Ancient Hindu scriptures portray widows as "inauspicious" and advise that "a wise man should avoid her blessings like the poison of a snake" (Burns 1998:10). Such attitudes die slowly in the villages, where most Indians live.

Though Westerners tend to view Muslim societies as being similarly harsh toward women, that perception is actually an overgeneralization. Muslim countries are exceedingly varied and complex and do not often fit the stereotypes created by the Western media. For a detailed discussion of the status of Muslim women today, see Box 12-2.

It is estimated that women grow half the world's food, but they rarely own land. They constitute one-third of the world's paid labor force, but are generally found in the lowest-paying jobs. Single-parent households headed by women, which appear to be on the increase in many nations, are typically found in the poorest sections of the population. The feminization of poverty has become a global phenomenon. As in the United States, women around the world are underrepresented politically.

While acknowledging that much has been done to sharpen people's awareness of gender inequities, a UN report issued in 2000 identified a number of areas of continuing concern:

- Despite their advances in higher education, women still face major barriers when they attempt to use their educational achievements to advance in the workplace. For example, women rarely hold more than 1 to 2 percent of top executive positions.
- Women almost always work in occupations with lower status and pay scales than men. In both developing and developed countries, many women work as unpaid family laborers. (Figure 12-1 on page 292 shows the paid labor force participation of women in seven industrialized countries.)
- Despite social norms regarding support and protection, many widows around the world receive little concrete support from extended family networks.
- In many African and a few Asian nations, traditions mandate the cutting of female genitals, typically by practitioners who fail to use sterilized instruments. This practice can lead to immediate and serious complications, from infection to long-term health problems. (For a discussion of female genital mutilation as a human rights issue, see Chapter 10.)
- While males outnumber females as refugees, refugee women have unique needs, such as protection against physical and sexual abuse (United Nations 2000).

Despite these challenges, women are not responding passively; they are mobilizing, individually and collectively. Given the significant underrepresentation of women in government offices and national legislatures, however, the task is difficult, as we shall see in Chapter 17.

What conclusions can we draw about women's inequality worldwide? First, as anthropologist Laura Nader

(1986:383) has observed, even in the relatively more egalitarian nations of the West, women's subordination is "institutionally structured and culturally rationalized, exposing them to conditions of deference, dependency, powerlessness, and poverty." While the situation of women in Sweden and the United States is significantly better than that of women in Saudi Arabia and Bangladesh, women nevertheless remain in a second-class position in the world's most affluent and developed countries.

Second, there is a link between the wealth of industrialized nations and the poverty of the developing countries. Viewed from a conflict perspective or through the lens of Immanuel Wallerstein's world systems analysis, the economies of developing nations are controlled and

◀ pp. 229–233 exploited by industrialized countries and multinational corporations based in those countries. Much of the exploited labor in developing nations, especially in the nonindustrial sector, is performed by women. Women workers typically toil long hours for low pay, but contribute significantly to their families' incomes (Jacobson 1993).

Women in the Workforce of the United States

"Does your mother work?" "No, she's just a housewife." This familiar exchange reminds us of women's traditional role in the United States, and reminds us that women's work has generally been viewed as unimportant. The Commission on Civil Rights (1976:1) concluded that the passage in the Declaration of Independence proclaiming that "all men are created equal" has been taken too literally for too long—especially with respect to women's opportunities for employment.

A Statistical Overview

Women's participation in the paid labor force of the United States increased steadily throughout the 20th century (see Figure 12-2). No longer is the adult woman associated solely with the role of homemaker. Instead, millions of women—married and single, with and without

FIGURE 12-1

Percentage of Adult Women in the Paid Labor Force by Country

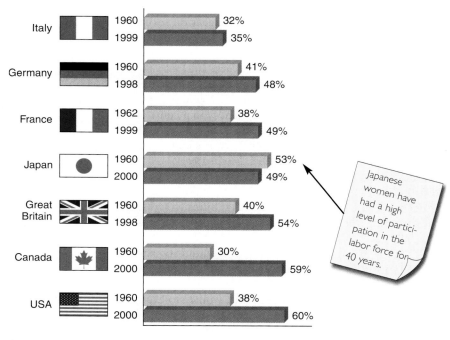

Source: Bureau of Labor Statistics 2001a.

Think About It
In industrialized nations, what appears to be the trend in women's labor force participation?

children—are working in the paid labor force. In 2001, 60 percent of adult women in the United States held jobs outside the home, compared with 38 percent in 1960. A majority of women are now members of the paid labor force, not full-time homemakers. Among new mothers, 58 percent return to the labor force within a year of giving birth. As recently as 1975 only 31 percent went back to work (Bureau of the Census 2002a:372–375).

Yet women entering the job market find their options restricted in important ways. Particularly damaging is occupational segregation, or confinement to sex-typed "women's jobs." For example, in 2001, women accounted for 98 percent of all secretaries and dental assistants and 86 percent of all librarians. Entering such sex-typed occupations places women in "service" roles that parallel the traditional gender-role standard under which housewives "serve" their husbands.

Women are *underrepresented* in occupations historically defined as "men's jobs," which often carry much greater financial rewards and prestige than women's jobs. For example, in 2001, women accounted for approximately 47 percent of the paid labor force of the United

States. Yet they constituted only 10 percent of all engineers, 20 percent of all dentists, 27 percent of all computer systems analysts, and 29 percent of all physicians (see Table 12-2, page 294).

Women from all groups and men from minority groups sometimes encounter attitudinal or organizational bias that prevents them from reaching their full potential. As we saw in Chapter 11, the term *glass ceiling* refers to an invisible barrier that blocks the promotion of a qualified individual in a work environment because of the individual's gender, race, or ethnicity. A study of the Fortune 1,000 largest corporations in the United States showed that less than 15 percent of the seats on their boards of directors were held by women in 2002 (G. Strauss 2002).

One response to the glass ceiling and other types of gender bias in the workplace is to start your own business and work for yourself. This route to success, traditionally taken by men from immigrant and racial minority groups, has become more common among women as they have increasingly sought paid employment outside the home. According to data released in 2001, women own an impressive 5.4 million businesses in the United States. However, many of these operations are very small, self-run firms. Only 16 percent of women-owned businesses have any paid employees (Bureau of the Census 2001c).

The workplace patterns described here have one crucial result: women earn less money than men in the paid labor force. A study done by the General Accounting Office (2002) compared managerial salaries for women and men in the 10 industries that employ 70 percent of women workers, including entertainment, insurance, retailing, public administration, and education. Women

managers came closest to matching men's salaries in education, where those who worked full time earned 91 cents for every dollar received by their male counterparts. But on average, women earned only about 78 cents for every dollar earned by men. Particularly troubling was the finding that in most industries, the male–female earnings gap actually widened between 1995 and 2000. The gap remained even after researchers adjusted their findings for variables such as education, age, and marital status. The glass ceiling is very firm.

While women may well be at a disadvantage in male-dominated occupations, the same is not true for men in female-dominated occupations. Sociologist Michelle Budig (2002) examined a national database containing career information on more than 12,000 men, collected over the course of 15 years. She found that men were uniformly advantaged in female occupations. Though male nurses, grade school teachers, and librarians may experience some scorn in the larger society, they are much more

FIGURE 12-2

Trends in U.S. Women's Participation in the Paid Labor Force, 1890–2001

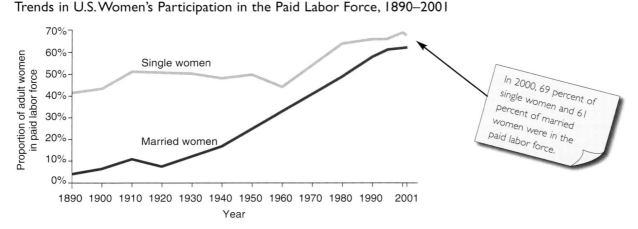

Sources: Bureau of the Census 1975; 2002a:372.

Table 12-2	U.S. Women in Selected Occupations, 2001: Women as Percentage of All Workers in the Occupation		
Underrepresented		**Overrepresented**	
Firefighters	3%	High school teachers	59%
Airline pilots	4	Social workers	72
Engineers	10	Cashiers	77
Police	14	File clerks	82
Clergy	15	Elementary teachers	83
Dentists	20	Librarians	86
Computer systems analysts	27	Registered nurses	93
Lawyers	29	Child care workers	97
Physicians	29	Receptionists	97
Mail carriers	31	Secretaries	98
College teachers	43	Dental hygienists	98

Source: Bureau of the Census 2002a:381–383.

likely than women to be encouraged to become administrators. Observers of the labor force have termed this advantage for men in female-dominated occupations the *glass escalator*—quite a contrast to the glass ceiling (Jerry Jacobs 2003; C. L. Williams 1992, 1995).

Social Consequences of Women's Employment

"What a circus we women perform every day of our lives. It puts a trapeze artist to shame." These words by the writer Anne Morrow Lindbergh attest to the challenge many women face today, trying to juggle work and family. Their situation has many social consequences. For one thing, it puts pressure on child care facilities, public financing of day care, and even the fast-food industry, which provides many of the meals women used to prepare themselves. For another, it raises questions about what responsibility male wage earners have in the household.

Who does the housework when women become productive wage earners? Studies indicate that there is still a clear gender gap in the performance of housework, although it is narrowing. Still, as Figure 12-3 shows, one study found women doing more housework and spending more time on child care than men, whether on a workday or a nonworkday. Taken together, then, a woman's workday on and off the job is much longer than a man's. A recent development over the last 20 years is women's involvement in elder care. According

to a Department of Labor (1998) study, 72 percent of these caregivers are women who typically spend around 18 hours per week caring for a parent.

Sociologist Arlie Hochschild (1989, 1990) has used the phrase **second shift** to describe the double burden—work outside the home followed by child care and housework—that many women face and few men share equitably. On the basis of interviews with and observations of 52 couples over an eight-year period, Hochschild reports that the wives (and not their husbands) drive home from the office while planning domestic schedules and play dates for children—and then begin their second shift. Drawing on national studies, she concludes that women spend 15 fewer hours each week in leisure activities than their husbands. In a year, these women work an extra month of 24-hour days because of the second shift; over a dozen years, they work an extra year of 24-hour days. Hochschild found that the married couples she studied were fraying at the edges, and so were their careers and their marriages. With such reports in mind, many feminists have advocated greater governmental and corporate support for child care, more flexible family leave policies, and other reforms designed to ease the burden on the nation's families.

pp. 97–98

Most studies of gender, child care, and housework focus on the time actually spent by women and men in performing these duties. However, sociologist Susan Walzer (1996) was interested in whether there are gender differences in the amount of time parents spend *thinking* about the care of their children. Drawing on interviews with 25 couples, Walzer found that mothers are much more involved than fathers in the invisible mental labor associated with caring for a baby. For example, while involved in work outside the home, mothers are more likely to think about their babies, and to feel guilty if they become so consumed with the demands of their jobs that they *fail* to think about their babies.

Women: Emergence of a Collective Consciousness

The feminist movement of the United States was born in upstate New York, in a town called Seneca Falls, in the summer of 1848. On July 19, the first women's rights convention began, attended by Elizabeth Cady Stanton, Lucretia Mott, and other pioneers in the struggle for women's rights. This first wave of *feminists*, as they are currently known, battled ridicule and scorn as they fought for legal and political equality for women. They were not afraid to risk controversy on behalf of their cause; in 1872, Susan B. Anthony was arrested for attempting to vote in that year's presidential election.

Ultimately, the early feminists won many victories, among them the passage and ratification of the Nineteenth Amendment to the Constitution, which granted women the right to vote in national elections beginning in 1920. But suffrage did not lead to other reforms in women's social and economic position, and in the early and middle 20th century the women's movement became a much less powerful force for social change.

The second wave of feminism in the United States emerged in the 1960s and came into full force in the 1970s. In part, the movement was inspired by three pioneering books arguing for women's rights: Simone de Beauvoir's *The Second Sex*, Betty Friedan's *The Feminine Mystique*, and Kate Millett's *Sexual Politics*. In addition, the general political activism of the 1960s led women—many of whom were working for Black civil rights or against the war in Vietnam—to reexamine their own powerlessness. The sexism often found within allegedly progressive and radical political circles convinced many women that they needed to establish their own movement for women's liberation (S. Evans 1980; S. Firestone 1970; Freeman 1973, 1975).

As more and more women became aware of sexist attitudes and practices, including attitudes they themselves had accepted through socialization into traditional gender roles, they began to challenge male dominance. A sense of sisterhood, much like the class consciousness that Marx hoped would emerge in the proletariat, became evident. Individual women identified their interests with those of the collectivity *women*. No longer were women happy in submissive, subordinate roles ("false consciousness" in Marxist terms).

National surveys done today, however, show that while women generally endorse feminist positions, they do not necessarily accept the label *feminist*. Close to 40 percent of women considered themselves feminists in 1989; the proportion dropped to about 20 percent in 1998. Feminism as a unified political cause, requiring one to accept a similar stance on everything from abortion to sexual harassment to pornography to welfare, has fallen out of favor. Both women and men prefer to express their views on these complex issues individually, rather than under a convenient umbrella like feminism. Still, feminism is very much alive in the growing acceptance of women in nontraditional roles, and even the basic acknowledgment that a married mother not only can work outside the home but perhaps *belongs* in the labor force. A majority of women say that given the choice, they would prefer to work outside the home rather than stay home and take care of a house and family, and about one-quarter of women prefer *Ms.* to *Miss* or *Mrs.* (Bellafante 1998; Geyh 1998).

The women's movement has undertaken public protests on a wide range of issues. Feminists have endorsed passage of the equal rights amendment, government subsidies for child care (see Chapter 4), affirmative action for women and minorities (see Chapter 18), federal legislation outlawing sex discrimination in education (see Chapter 16), greater representation of women in government (see Chapter 17), and the right to legal abortions (discussed in the social policy section of this chapter).

FIGURE 12-3

Gender Differences in Child Care and Housework, 1997

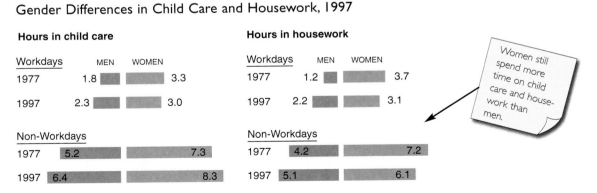

Source: Bond et al. 1998:40–41, 44–45.

Kim Ng is vice president and assistant general manager of the Los Angeles Dodgers. In the virtually all-male world of major league baseball, she has overcome both racial-ethnic and gender bias, winning a reputation as a tough negotiator in player arbitration cases.

MINORITY WOMEN: DOUBLE JEOPARDY

Many women experience differential treatment not only because of gender but because of race and ethnicity. These citizens face a "double jeopardy"—that of subordinate status twice defined. A disproportionate share of this low-status group is also impoverished, so that the double jeopardy effectively becomes a triple jeopardy.

Feminists have addressed the particular needs of minority women. The question for African American women, Latinas, Asian American women, and others appears to be whether they should unify with their "brothers" against racism or challenge them for their sexism. One answer is that in a truly just society, both sexism and racism must be eradicated (Epstein 1999).

The discussion of gender roles among African Americans has always provoked controversy. Advocates of Black nationalism contend that feminism only distracts women from full participation in the Black struggle. The existence of feminist groups among Blacks, in their view, simply divides the Black community, and thus serves the dominant White society. In contrast, Black feminists such as Florynce Kennedy argue that little is to be gained by adopting or maintaining the gender-role divisions of the dominant society. African American journalist Patricia Raybon (1989) has noted that the media commonly portray Black women in a negative light: as illiterate, as welfare mothers, prostitutes, and so forth. Black feminists emphasize that it is not solely Whites and White-dominated media that focus on these negative images; Black men (most recently, some Black male rap artists) have also been criticized for the way they portray African American women.

The plight of Latinas is usually considered part of either the Latino or the feminist movement, ignoring the distinctive experiences of Mexican American, Cuban, Puerto Rican, and Central and South American women. In the past, these women have been excluded from decision making in the two institutions that most directly affect their daily lives: the family and the church. The Hispanic family, especially in the lower class, feels the pervasive tradition of male domination. The Roman Catholic church relegates women to supportive roles while reserving leadership positions for men (Browne 1999; De Andra 1996).

We can see that activists among minority women do not agree on whether priority should be granted to fighting for sexual equality or to eliminating inequality among racial and ethnic groups. Neither component of inequality can be ignored. Helen Mayer Hacker (1974:11), who pioneered research on both Blacks and women, stated before the American Sociological Association, "As a partisan observer, it is my fervent hope that in fighting the twin battles of sexism and racism, Black women and Black men will [create] the outlines of the good society for all Americans" (see also Zia 1993).

SOCIAL POLICY and GENDER STRATIFICATION

The Battle over Abortion from a Global Perspective

The Issue

Few issues seem to stir as much intense conflict as abortion. A critical victory in the struggle for legalized abortion in the United States came in 1973 when the Supreme Court granted women the right to terminate pregnancies. This ruling, known as *Roe v. Wade,* was based on a woman's right to privacy. The Court's decision was generally applauded by pro-choice groups, which believe women should have the right to make their own decisions about their bodies and should have access to safe and legal abortions. It was bitterly condemned by those opposed to abortion. For these pro-life groups, abortion is a moral and often a religious issue. In their view, human life begins at the moment of conception, so that its termination through abortion is essentially an act of murder.

The Setting

The debate that has followed *Roe v. Wade* revolves around prohibiting abortion altogether, or at the very least, putting limits on it. In 1979, for example, Missouri required parental consent for minors wishing to obtain an abortion, and the Supreme Court upheld the law. Parental notification and consent have become especially sensitive issues in the debate. Pro-life activists argue that the parents of teenagers should have the right to be notified about—and to permit or prohibit—abortions. In their view, parental authority deserves full support at a time when the traditional nuclear family is embattled. However, pro-choice activists counter that many pregnant teenagers come from troubled families where they have been abused. These young women may have good reason to avoid discussing such explosive issues with their parents.

Changing technology has had its impact on the debate. "Day-after" pills are now available in some nations; these pills can abort a fertilized egg the day after conception. In 2000, the U.S. government approved RU-486, an abortion-inducing pill that can be used in the first seven weeks of pregnancy. The regime requires doctor visits but no surgical procedures. In addition, doctors, guided by ultrasound, can now end a pregnancy as early as eight days after conception. Pro-life activists are concerned that the use of ultrasound technology will allow people to abort unwanted females in nations where a premium is placed on male offspring.

As of 2003, the people of the United States appeared to support their right to legal abortion, but with reservations. According to a national survey, 60 percent favor a woman's general right to have an abortion. However, only 40 percent feel abortion should be legal if a family is very poor and cannot afford a child (Graham 2003).

Sociological Insights

Sociologists see gender and social class as the defining issues surrounding abortion. The intense conflict over abortion reflects broader differences over women's position in society. Sociologist Kristin Luker (1984) has studied activists in both the pro-choice and pro-life movements. Luker interviewed 212 activists in California, overwhelmingly women, who spent at least five hours a week working for one of the two movements. According to Luker, each group has a consistent, coherent view of the world. Feminists involved in defending abortion rights typically believe that men and women are essentially similar; they support women's full participation in work outside the home and oppose all forms of sex discrimination. In contrast, most antiabortion activists believe that men and women are fundamentally different. In their view, men are best suited to the public world of work, while women are best suited to the demanding and crucial task of rearing children. These activists are troubled by women's growing participation in work outside the home, which they view as destructive to the family, and ultimately to society.

The first major restriction on the legal right to terminate a pregnancy affected poor people. In 1976, Congress passed the Hyde Amendment, which banned the use of Medicaid and other federal funds for abortions. The Supreme Court upheld this legislation in 1980. State laws also restrict the use of public funds for abortions (see Figure 12-4, page 298).

Another obstacle facing the poor is access to abortion providers: In the face of vocal pro-life sentiment, fewer and fewer hospitals throughout the world are allowing physicians to perform abortions, except in extreme cases. As of 2001, only about 6 percent of specialists in obstetrics and gynecology in the United States were trained and willing to perform abortions under any circumstances, and a majority of those physicians were in their 50s and 60s. To avoid controversy, many medical schools have ceased to offer training in the procedure. Moreover, some doctors who work in clinics, intimidated by death threats and actual murders, have stopped performing abortions. For poor people in rural

FIGURE 12-4

Restrictions on Public Funding for Abortion

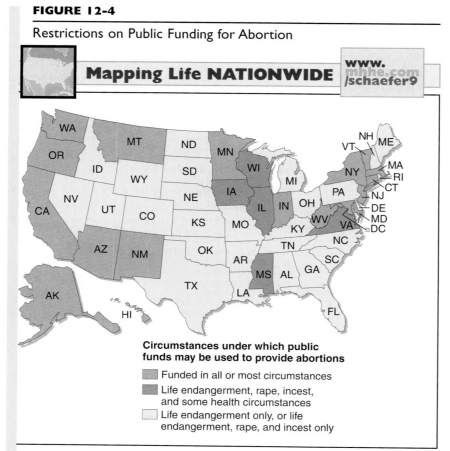

Mapping Life NATIONWIDE www.mhhe.com/schaefer9

Circumstances under which public funds may be used to provide abortions

- Funded in all or most circumstances
- Life endangerment, rape, incest, and some health circumstances
- Life endangerment only, or life endangerment, rape, and incest only

Source: NARAL Pro-Choice America 2003:xxii–xxiii.

areas, this reduction in service makes it more difficult to locate and travel to a facility that will accommodate their wishes. Viewed from a conflict perspective, this is one more financial burden that falls especially heavily on low-income women (T. Edwards 2001; Villarosa 2002).

Policy Initiatives

The Supreme Court currently supports the general right to terminate a pregnancy by a narrow 5–4 majority. Although pro-life activists continue to hope for an overruling of *Roe v. Wade,* they have focused in the interim on weakening the decision through tactics such as limiting the use of fetal tissue in medical experiments and prohibiting certain late-term abortions, which they term "partial-birth" abortions. The Supreme Court continues to hear cases involving such restrictions. In 1998, the Court gave the states the authority (32 have done so) to prohibit abortions at the point where the fetus is viable outside the mother's womb—a point that contin-

ues to be redefined by new developments in medical technology (Biskupic 2000).

What is the policy in other countries? As in the United States, many European nations responded to public opinion and liberalized abortion laws in the 1970s, although Ireland, Belgium, and Malta continue to prohibit abortion. Austria, Denmark, Greece, the Netherlands, Norway, and Sweden have laws that allow a woman to have an abortion on request. Other countries have much more restrictive legislation, especially concerning abortions in the later stages of pregnancy. Inspired by their counterparts in the United States, antiabortion activists have become more outspoken in Great Britain, France, Spain, Italy, and Germany.

The policies of the United States and developing nations are intertwined. Throughout the 1980s and 1990s, antiabortion members of Congress have often successfully blocked foreign aid to countries that might use the funds to encourage abortion. (We will discuss this political tactic in greater detail in Chapter 21.) And yet these developing nations generally have the most restrictive abortion laws. As shown in Figure 12-5, it is primarily in Africa, Latin America, and parts of Asia that women are not allowed to terminate a pregnancy on request. As might be expected, illegal abortions are most common in these nations. An estimated quarter of the world's women live in countries where abortion is illegal or is permitted only if a woman's life is in jeopardy. Hence, 40 percent of abortions worldwide—about 20 million procedures each year—are performed illegally (Joynt and Ganeshananthan 2003).

Let's Discuss

1. Do you know anyone who has undergone an illegal abortion? If so, what were the circumstances? Was the woman's health endangered by the procedure?

2. Do you think teenage girls should have to get their parents' consent before having an abortion? Why?

3. Under what circumstances should abortions be allowed? Explain your reasoning.

FIGURE 12-5

The Global Divide on Abortion

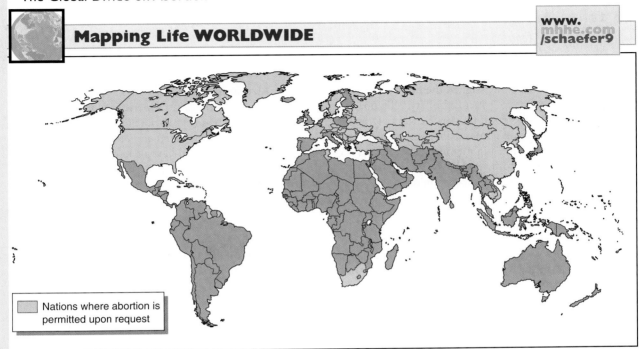

Nations where abortion is permitted upon request

Note: Data current as of June 2001.

Sources: Developed by the author based on United Nations Population Division 1998 and Gonnut 2001.

CHAPTER RESOURCES

Summary

Gender is an ascribed status that provides a basis for social differentiation. This chapter examines the social construction of gender, theories of stratification by gender, women as an oppressed majority group, and the double jeopardy of minority women.

1. In the United States, the social construction of gender continues to define significantly different expectations for females and males.
2. ***Gender roles*** show up in our work and behavior and in how we react to others.
3. Though females have been more severely restricted than men by traditional gender roles, those roles have also restricted males.
4. The research of anthropologist Margaret Mead points to the importance of cultural conditioning in defining the social roles of males and females.

5. Functionalists maintain that sex differentiation contributes to overall social stability, but conflict theorists charge that the relationship between females and males is one of unequal power, with men dominating women. This dominance shows up in people's everyday interactions.
6. As one example of their micro-level approach to the study of gender stratification, interactionists have analyzed men's verbal dominance over women through conversational interruptions.
7. Women around the world suffer from ***sexism, institutional discrimination,*** and ***sexual harassment.***
8. As women have taken on more and more hours of paid employment outside the home, they have been only partially successful in getting their husbands to take on more homemaking duties, including child care.

9. Many women agree with the positions of the feminist movement but reject the label *feminist*.
10. Minority women experience a double jeopardy through differential treatment based on both their gender and their race and ethnicity.
11. The issue of abortion has bitterly divided the United States (as well as other nations), pitting pro-choice activists against pro-life activists.

Critical Thinking Questions

1. Imagine that you are assigned the opposite gender at birth, but that your race, ethnicity, religion, and social class background remain the same. Drawing on the information contained in this chapter, describe how your life as a member of the opposite sex might differ from your life today.
2. In what ways is the social position of White women in the United States similar to that of African American women, Latinas (Hispanic women), and Asian American women? In what ways are women's social positions markedly different, given their racial and ethnic status?
3. Imagine that you have been asked to study political activism among women. How might you employ surveys, observations, experiments, and existing sources to better understand such activism?

Key Terms

Expressiveness   Concern for the maintenance of harmony and the internal emotional affairs of the family. (page 286)

Gender role   Expectations regarding the proper behavior, attitudes, and activities of a male or female. (282)

Glass ceiling   An invisible barrier that blocks the promotion of a qualified individual in a work environment because of the individual's gender, race, or ethnicity. (293)

Homophobia   Fear of and prejudice against homosexuality. (283)

Institutional discrimination   The denial of opportunities and equal rights to individuals and groups that results from the normal operations of a society. (289)

Instrumentality   An emphasis on tasks, a focus on more distant goals, and a concern for the external relationship between one's family and other social institutions. (286)

Second shift   The double burden—work outside the home followed by child care and housework—that many women face and few men share equitably. (294)

Sexism   The ideology that one sex is superior to the other. (288)

Sexual harassment   Behavior that occurs when work benefits are made contingent on sexual favors (as a quid pro quo), or when touching, lewd comments, or the exhibition of pornographic material creates a "hostile environment" in the workplace. (291)

TECHNOLOGY RESOURCES

 ### Internet Connection

*Note: While all the URLs listed were current as of the printing of this book, these sites often change. Please check our website (**www.mhhe.com/schaefer9**) for updates, hyperlinks, and exercises related to these sites.*

1. Women have a huge stake in the current and future job market. Between 1998 and 2008, women's participation in the labor force is expected to increase by 15 percent, while men will only see an increase of about 10 percent. Learn more about women in high-tech jobs and the fastest growing occupations for women in the 21st century by visiting the Women's Bureau of the Department of Labor (**www.dol.gov/wb**).

2. One of the lessons of sociological inquiry is that socially constructed gender roles place limits on both women and men. The National Coalition of Free Men (NCFM) (**www.ncfm.org**) maintains a website focused on the limitations faced by males. Visit the site to learn about this organization.

 ## Online Learning Center with PowerWeb

Few issues seem to stir as much intense conflict as abortion. To find out how Americans feel about abortion, visit the student center at our Online Learning Center (**www.mhhe.com/schaefer9**) and link to "How Americans Feel About. . . ." Read an overview of the abortion issue and then look at the colorful pie charts and graphs. These charts and graphs show what percentage of Americans surveyed consider themselves pro-choice or pro-life, how they feel about the *Roe v. Wade* decision, and how both men and women feel about the legality of abortion.

 ## Reel Society Interactive Movie CD-ROM

Reel Society includes scenes that can be used to spark discussion about the following topics from this chapter:

- Gender Roles in the United States
- Cross-Cultural Perspectives on Gender
- Sexism and Gender Discrimination
- The Status of Women Worldwide

STRATIFICATION BY AGE

Aging and Society

Explaining the Aging Process

Role Transitions Throughout the Life Course

Age Stratification in the United States

Social Policy and Age Stratification: The Right to Die Worldwide

Boxes

SOCIOLOGY IN THE GLOBAL COMMUNITY: Aging Worldwide—Issues and Consequences

SOCIOLOGY ON CAMPUS: Adult Students

TAKING SOCIOLOGY TO WORK: A. David Roberts: Social Worker

This poster promoted 1999 as the United Nations' International Year of Older Persons. In April 2002, recognizing that soon every third person in the world would be over age 60, delegates to the Second World Assembly on Aging focused on ensuring that everyone, regardless of age, will have an active role to play in society.

Later that day, we talked about aging. Or maybe I should say the fear of aging—another of the issues on my what's-bugging-my-generation list. On my ride from the Boston airport, I had counted the billboards that featured young and beautiful people. There was a handsome young man in a cowboy hat, smoking a cigarette, two beautiful young women smiling over a shampoo bottle, a sultry-looking teenager with her jeans unsnapped, and a sexy woman in a black velvet dress, next to a man in a tuxedo, the two of them snuggling a glass of scotch.

Not once did I see anyone who would pass for over thirty-five. I told Morrie I was already feeling over the hill, much as I tried desperately to stay on top of it. I worked out constantly. Watched what I ate. Checked my hairline in the mirror. I had gone from being proud to say my age—because of all I had done so young—to not bringing it up, for fear I was getting too close to forty and, therefore, professional oblivion.

Morrie had aging in better perspective.

"All this emphasis on youth—I don't buy it," he said. "Listen, I know what a misery being young can be, so don't tell me it's so great. All these kids who came to me with their struggles, their strife, their feelings of inadequacy, their sense that life was miserable, so bad they wanted to kill themselves . . .

tuesdays with
Morrie

an old man, a young man,

and life's greatest lesson

Mitch Albom

"And, in addition to all the miseries, the young are not wise. They have very little understanding about life. Who wants to live every day when you don't know what's going on? When people are manipulating you, telling you to buy this perfume and you'll be beautiful, or this pair of jeans and you'll be sexy—and you believe them! It's such nonsense."

Weren't you *ever* afraid to grow old, I asked?

"Mitch, I *embrace* aging."

Embrace it?

"It's very simple. As you grow, you learn more. If you stayed at twenty-two, you'd always be as ignorant as you were at twenty-two. Aging is not just decay, you know. It's growth. It's more than the negative that you're going to die, it's also the positive that you *understand* you're going to die, and that you live a better life because of it."

Yes, I said, but if aging were so valuable, why do people always say, "Oh, if I were young again." You never hear people say, "I wish I were sixty-five."

He smiled. "You know what that reflects? Unsatisfied lives. Unfulfilled lives. Lives that haven't found meaning. Because if you've found meaning in your life, you don't want to go back. You want to go forward. You want to see more, do more. You can't wait until sixty-five. . . ." *(Albom 1997:117–118)* ■ ◉

Additional information about this excerpt can be found on the Online Learning Center at **www.mhhe.com/schaefer9.**

In *Tuesdays with Morrie,* journalist Mitch Albom (1997) recounted his final class with his favorite college professor, the respected Brandeis University sociologist Morrie Schwartz. Albom, who had graduated years before, contacted Schwartz when he learned the professor was dying of amyotrophic lateral sclerosis (ALS), also known as Lou Gehrig's disease. To his surprise, he found that his series of conversations with Morrie, held always on Tuesday, were more about life than death. From this sage he learned that age has its benefits, and that growing old can also mean growing wise.

Age, like race or gender, is socially constructed. It is an ascribed status that dominates people's perceptions of others, obscuring individual differences. Rather than suggesting that a particular elderly person is no longer competent to drive, for instance, we may condemn the entire age group: "Those old codgers shouldn't be allowed on the road." Unless people can begin to look at the life course as a continuum, rather than as a series of finite stages with predictable consequences, such stereotypical attitudes toward age and aging are not likely to change.

What happens in the aging process? How do people's roles change as they age? What are the social implications of the growing number of elderly in the United States? How does ageism affect an older person's employment opportunities? In this chapter we will look at the process of aging throughout the life course. We will examine aging around the world, focusing primarily on older people in the United States. After exploring various theories of the impact of aging, both on the individual and on society, we will discuss the role transitions typical of the major stages in the life course. In the process we will consider the challenges facing the "sandwich generation," middle-aged people who care for both their children and their aging parents. We will pay particular attention to the effects of prejudice and discrimination on older people, and to the rise of a political consciousness among the elderly. Finally, in the social policy section, we will discuss the controversial issue of the right to die. ◼

AGING AND SOCIETY

The Sherpas—a Tibetan-speaking Buddhist people in Nepal—live in a culture that idealizes old age. Almost all elderly members of the Sherpa culture own their homes, and most are in relatively good physical condition. Typically, older Sherpas value their independence and prefer not to live with their children. Among the Fulani of Africa, however, older men and women move to the edge of the family homestead. Since that is where people are buried, the elderly sleep over their own graves, for they are viewed socially as already dead. Like gender stratification, age stratification varies from culture to culture. One society may treat older people with great reverence, while another sees them as unproductive and "difficult" (M. Goldstein and Beall 1981; Stenning 1958; Tonkinson 1978).

It is understandable that all societies have some system of age stratification that associates certain social roles with distinct periods in life. Some of this age differentiation seems inevitable; it would make little sense to send young children off to war, or to expect most older citizens to handle physically demanding tasks, such as loading freight at shipyards. However, as is the case with stratification by gender, in the United States age stratification goes far beyond the physical constraints of human beings at different ages.

"Being old" is a master status that commonly overshadows all others in the United States. The insights of labeling theory can help us in analyzing the consequences of aging. Once people have been labeled "old," the designation has a major impact on how others perceive them, and even on how they view themselves. Negative stereotypes of the elderly contribute to their position as a minority group subject to discrimination, as we will see later in the chapter.

The model of five basic properties of a minority or subordinate group (introduced in Chapter 11) can be applied to older people in the United States to clarify their subordinate status:

1. The elderly experience unequal treatment in employment, and may face prejudice and discrimination.
2. The elderly share physical characteristics that distinguish them from younger people. In addition, their cultural preferences and leisure-time activities often differ from those of the rest of society.

p. 185

pp. 250–251

3. Membership in this disadvantaged group is involuntary.
4. Older people have a strong sense of group solidarity, as is reflected in the growth of senior citizens' centers, retirement communities, and advocacy organizations.
5. Older people generally are married to others of comparable age.

There is one crucial difference between older people and other subordinate groups, such as racial and ethnic minorities or women: *All* of us who live long enough will eventually assume the ascribed status of an older person (Barron 1953; Levin and Levin 1980; Wagley and Harris 1958).

EXPLAINING THE AGING PROCESS

Aging is one important aspect of socialization—the lifelong process through which an individual learns the cultural norms and values of a particular society. There are no clear-cut definitions for different periods of the aging cycle in the United States. *Old age* has typically been regarded as beginning at 65, which corresponds to the retirement age for many workers, but not everyone in the

This elderly Sherpa in Nepal is honored for his age. Not all old people are so lucky—in many cultures, being old is considered next to being dead.

United States accepts that definition. With the increase in life expectancy, writers are beginning to refer to people in their 60s as the "young old," to distinguish them from those in their 80s and beyond (the "old old"). Box 13-1 (page 306) considers some of the consequences of the growth of both these age groups.

The particular problems of the elderly have become the focus for a specialized area of research and inquiry known as gerontology. ***Gerontology*** is the scientific study of the sociological and psychological aspects of aging and the problems of the aged. It originated in the 1930s, as an increasing number of social scientists became aware of the plight of the elderly.

Gerontologists rely heavily on sociological principles and theories to explain the impact of aging on the individual and society. They also draw on psychology, anthropology, physical education, counseling, and medicine in their study of the aging process. Two influential views of aging—disengagement theory and activity theory—can be best understood in terms of the sociological perspectives of functionalism and interactionism, respectively. The conflict perspective also contributes to our sociological understanding of aging.

Use Your Sociological Imagination

Time has passed, and you are now in your 70s or 80s. How does old age in your generation compare with your parents' or grandparents' experience of old age?

Functionalist Approach: Disengagement Theory

After studying elderly people in good health and relatively comfortable economic circumstances, Elaine Cumming and William Henry (1961) introduced their ***disengagement theory,*** which contends that society and the aging individual mutually sever many of their relationships. In keeping with the functionalist perspective, disengagement theory emphasizes that passing social roles on from one generation to another ensures social stability.

According to this theory, the approach of death forces people to drop most of their social roles—including those of worker, volunteer, spouse, hobby enthusiast, and even reader. Younger members of society then take on these functions. The aging person, it is held, withdraws into an increasing state of inactivity while preparing for death. At the same time, society withdraws from the elderly by segregating them residentially (in retirement homes and communities), educationally (in programs designed solely for senior citizens), and recreationally (in senior citizens' centers). Implicit in disengagement theory is the view that society should *help* older

An electric water kettle is wired so that people in another location can determine if it has been used in the previous 24 hours. This may seem a zany use of modern technology, but it symbolizes a change taking place around the globe—the growing needs of an aging population. The Japanese Welfare Network Ikebukuro Honcho has installed these wired hot pots so that volunteers can monitor whether the elderly have used the devices to prepare their morning tea. An unused pot initiates contacts to see if the older person needs help. This technological monitoring system is an indication of the tremendous growth of Japan's elderly population, and particularly significant, the increasing numbers who live *alone*.

Around the world, there are more than 442 million people aged 65 or over, representing about 7 percent of the world's population. In an important sense, the aging of the world's population represents a major success story that unfolded during the latter years of the 20th century. Through the efforts of both national governments and international agencies, many societies have drastically reduced the incidence of diseases and their rates of death. Consequently, these nations—especially the industrialized countries of Europe and North America—now have increasingly higher proportions of older members.

The overall population of Europe is older than that of any other continent. As the proportion of older people in Europe continues to rise, many governments that have long prided themselves on their

> An unused pot initiates contacts to see if the older person needs help.

pension programs have reduced benefits and raised the age at which retired workers can receive benefits. By 2050, Europe's population is projected to have a median age of over 52, compared to 35 in the United States.

In most developing countries, people over 60 are likely to be in poorer health than their counterparts in industrialized nations. Yet few of those nations are in a position to offer extensive financial support to the elderly. Ironically, modernization of the developing world, while bringing with it many social and economic advances, has undercut the traditionally high status of the elderly. In many cultures, the earning power of younger adults now exceeds that of older family members.

Worldwide, governments are beginning to pay attention to population aging and the permanent social transformation it represents. In 1940, of the 227 nations with a population of at least 5,000, only 33 had some form of old-age disability or survivors' program. By 2001 the number stood at 167, or 74 percent of those 227 nations.

Let's Discuss

1. For an older person, how might life in Pakistan differ from life in France?
2. Do you know an aged person who lives alone? What arrangements have been made (or should be made) for the person's care in case of emergency?

Sources: R. Bernstein 2003; Hani 1998; Haub 2003; Kinsella and Velkoff 2001; R. Samuelson 2001.

people to withdraw from their accustomed social roles.

Since it was first outlined more than four decades ago, disengagement theory has generated considerable controversy. Some gerontologists have objected to the implication that older people want to be ignored and put away—and even more to the idea that they should be encouraged to withdraw from meaningful social roles. Critics of disengagement theory insist that society *forces* the elderly into an involuntary and painful withdrawal from the paid labor force and from meaningful social relationships. Rather than voluntarily seeking to disengage, older employees find themselves pushed out of their jobs—in many instances, even before they are entitled to maximum retirement benefits (Boaz 1987).

Although functionalist in its approach, disengagement theory ignores the fact that postretirement employment has been *increasing* in recent decades. In the United States, fewer than half of all employees actually retire from their career jobs. Instead, most move into a "bridge job"—employment that bridges the period between the end of a person's career and his or her retirement. Unfortunately, the elderly can easily be victimized in such "bridge jobs." Psychologist Kathleen Christensen (1990), warning of "bridges over troubled water," emphasizes that older employees do not want to end their working days as minimum-wage jobholders engaged in activities unrelated to their career jobs (Doeringer 1990; Hayward et al. 1987).

Interactionist Approach: Activity Theory

Ask Ruth Vitow if she would like to trade in her New York City custom lampshade business for a condo in Florida, and you will get a quick response: "Deadly! I'd hate it." Vitow, in her 90s, vows to give up her business "when it gives me up." James Russell Wiggins has been working at a weekly newspaper in Maine since 1922. At age 95 he is now the editor. Vitow and Wiggins are among the 9 percent of the men and 3 percent of the women aged 75 years or older who are still participating in the nation's labor force (Himes 2001).

How important is it for older people to stay actively involved, whether at a job or in other pursuits? A tragic disaster in Chicago in 1995 showed that it can be a matter of life and death. An intense heat wave lasting more than a week—with a heat index exceeding 115 degrees on two consecutive days—resulted in 733 heat-related deaths. About three-fourths of the deceased were 65 and older. Subsequent analysis showed that older people who lived alone had the highest risk of dying, suggesting that support networks for the elderly literally help to save lives. Older Hispanics and Asian Americans had lower death rates from the heat wave than other racial and ethnic groups. Their stronger social networks probably resulted in more regular contact with family members and friends (Schaefer 1998a; Klinenberg 2002).

These "silver surfers" still enjoy life to the fullest, just as they did when they were young. Staying active and involved has been shown to be healthy for the older population.

Often seen as an opposing approach to disengagement theory, **activity theory** argues that the elderly person who remains active and socially involved will be best-adjusted. Proponents of this perspective acknowledge that a 70-year-old person may not have the ability or desire to perform various social roles that he or she had at age 40. Yet they contend that old people have essentially the same need for social interaction as any other group.

The improved health of older people—sometimes overlooked by social scientists—has strengthened the arguments of activity theorists. Illness and chronic disease are no longer quite the scourge of the elderly that they once were. The recent emphasis on fitness, the availability of better medical care, greater control of infectious diseases, and the reduction of fatal strokes and heart attacks have combined to mitigate the traumas of growing old. Accumulating medical research also points to the importance of remaining socially involved. Among those who

decline in their mental capacities later in life, deterioration is most rapid in those who withdraw from social relationships and activities. Fortunately, the aged are finding new ways to remain socially engaged, as evidenced by their increasing use of the Internet, especially to keep in touch with family and friends (Korczyk 2002).

Admittedly, many activities open to the elderly involve unpaid labor, for which younger adults may receive salaries. Unpaid elderly workers include hospital volunteers (versus aides and orderlies), drivers for charities such as the Red Cross (versus chauffeurs), tutors (as opposed to teachers), and craftspeople for charity bazaars (as opposed to carpenters and dressmakers). However, some companies have recently begun programs to hire retirees for full-time or part-time work.

Though disengagement theory suggests that older people find satisfaction in withdrawal from society, conveniently receding into the background and allowing the next generation to take over, proponents of activity theory view such withdrawal as harmful to both the elderly

Three generations of this family celebrate their March birthdays together. While we all move through the life course in individual ways, it is possible to identify certain developmental periods, with critical transitions between the stages.

and society. Activity theorists focus on the potential contributions of older people to the maintenance of society. In their opinion, aging citizens will feel satisfied only when they can be useful and productive in society's terms—primarily by working for wages (Civic Ventures 1999; Dowd 1980; Quadagno 2002).

The Conflict Approach

Conflict theorists have criticized both disengagement theorists and activity theorists for failing to consider the impact of social structure on aging patterns. Neither approach, they say, questions why social interaction must change or decrease in old age. In addition, they often ignore the impact of social class on the lives of the elderly.

The privileged upper class generally enjoys better health and vigor and less likelihood of dependency in old age. Affluence cannot forestall aging indefinitely, but it can soften the economic hardships people face in later years. Although pension plans, retirement packages, and insurance benefits may be developed to assist older people, those whose wealth allows them access to investment funds can generate the greatest income for their later years.

In contrast, the working class often faces greater health hazards and a greater risk of disability; aging is particularly difficult for those who suffer job-related injuries or illnesses. Working-class people also depend more heavily on Social Security benefits and private pen-

sion programs. During inflationary times, their relatively fixed incomes from these sources barely keep pace with the escalating costs of food, housing, utilities, and other necessities (Atchley 1985).

Conflict theorists have noted that in the developing world, the transition from agricultural economies to industrialization and capitalism has not always been beneficial to the elderly. As a society's production methods change, the traditionally valued role of older people tends to erode. Their wisdom is no longer relevant in the new economy.

According to the conflict approach, the treatment of older people in the United States reflects the many divisions in our society. The low status of older people is seen in prejudice and discrimination against them, in age segregation, and in unfair job practices—none of which are directly addressed by either disengagement or activity theory.

In sum, the three perspectives considered here take different views of the elderly. Functionalists portray older people as socially isolated, with reduced social roles; interactionists see them as involved in new networks and changing social roles; conflict theorists see them as victimized by social structure, with their social roles relatively unchanged but devalued. Table 13-1 summarizes these perspectives.

ROLE TRANSITIONS THROUGHOUT THE LIFE COURSE

As noted in Chapter 4 and throughout this textbook, socialization is a lifelong process. We simply do not experience things the same way at different p. 88 points in the life course. For example, one study found that even falling in love differs according to where we are in the life course. Young unmarried adults tend to treat love as a noncommittal game or an obsession characterized by possessiveness and dependency. People over the age of 50 are much more likely to see love as involving commitment, and they tend to take a practical approach to finding a partner who meets a set of rational criteria. The life course, then, affects the manner in which we relate to one another (Montgomery and Sorell 1997).

A. DAVID ROBERTS **Social Worker**

Dave Roberts admits to being a "people person," a trait that sociology courses fostered by showing how "everybody has differences; there are little bits of different cultures in all of us." He also had the benefit of "a lot of great teachers" at Florida State University, including Dr. Jill Quadagno in an "Aging" course. It was this class that sparked his interest in aging issues, which led to a certificate in gerontology in addition to a sociology degree in 1998. He realized that there was a good job market in working with the aging baby boom generation.

Volunteer work with the Meals on Wheels program steered him toward working with the elderly. Today Roberts is a social worker in a nursing home, where he is responsible for patients' care plans. In the course of his work, he meets regularly with patients, family members, and medical residents. Roberts finds that the concept of teamwork he learned in group projects in college has helped him in his job. Also, the projects he had to do in school taught him to work on a schedule. Perhaps most important, sociology has helped him "to grow as a person to explore different angles, different theories. . . . I'm a better person."

His advice to sociology students: "Just give it a chance; they throw everything into an intro course. Don't get overwhelmed; take it as it comes."

Let's Discuss

1. What other types of employment might be open to a college graduate with a certificate in gerontology?
2. What might be the special rewards of working with the elderly?

How we move through the life course varies dramatically, depending on the individual. Some people, for instance, finish high school in their 20s, or do not attend college until well into adulthood (see Box 13-2, page 310). Some start their own households in their early 20s, while others are well into their 30s before beginning a permanent relationship. Still, it is possible to identify a series of developmental periods, with critical transitions between the various stages, as shown in the model devised by psychologist Daniel Levinson (Figure 13-1, page 311).

The first transitional period identified by Levinson begins at about age 17 and extends to age 22. It marks the time at which an individual gradually enters the adult world, perhaps by moving out of the parental home, beginning a career, or entering a marriage. The second transitional period, the midlife transition, typically begins at about age 40. Men and women often experience a stressful period of self-evaluation, commonly known as the *midlife crisis,* in which they realize that they have not achieved basic goals and ambitions and have little time left to do so. Thus, Levinson (1978, 1996) found that most adults surveyed experienced tumultuous midlife conflicts within the self and with the external world.

Not all the challenges at this time of life come from career or one's partner. In the next section we will examine a special challenge faced by a growing number of middle-aged adults, caring for two generations at once.

Table 13-1	**Theoretical Perspectives on Aging**		
Sociological Perspective	**View of Aging**	**Social Roles**	**Portrayal of Elderly**
Functionalist	Disengagement	Reduced	Socially isolated
Interactionist	Activity	Changed	Involved in new networks
Conflict	Competition	Relatively unchanged	Victimized, organized to confront their victimization

Picture a college student. Most likely, you will imagine a young adult—someone under age 25. This stereotype reflects the common assumption that education is for the young, something a person undertakes before embarking on a career or starting a family. Recent years, however, have brought a dramatic increase in the number of older students pursuing two-year, four-year, and graduate degrees. In 1970, only one-quarter of all students taking credit courses in colleges in the United States were 25 or older. By the mid-1990s, the figure had risen to more than 40 percent (see the graph).

Obviously, sociological models of the collegiate subculture will need to be revised in light of such changes. Mature

> Recent years have brought a dramatic increase in the number of older students pursuing two-year, four-year, and graduate degrees.

students are more likely to be female and either Black or Latina than the typical 19- or 20-year-old undergraduate. Viewed from a conflict perspective, the fact that women and minorities are overrepresented among older students is not surprising; members of these groups are the most likely to miss out on higher education the first time around. They are also more likely to need support services that traditional college students have not needed in the past. As the age of the typical college student has increased, for example, the need for on-campus child care has grown, especially at community colleges, where the median age of students is now 31.

Another reason for the boom in adult education is that in an age of technological innovation, the economy is changing

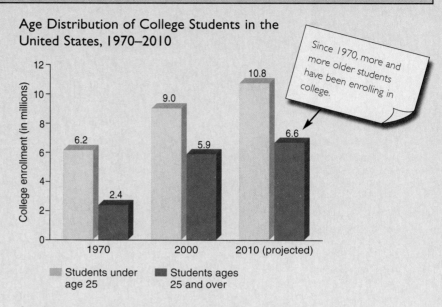

Age Distribution of College Students in the United States, 1970–2010

Since 1970, more and more older students have been enrolling in college.

Source: National Center for Education Statistics 2002a: Table 174.

rapidly. Business firms have come to accept the view of education as a lifelong necessity, and may encourage or require employees to return to the classroom to learn job-related skills. Thus, office assistants take special courses to familiarize themselves with the latest computer software; realtors sign up for classes on alternative forms of financing. In occupation after occupation, longtime workers and professionals are going back to school to adapt to the new demands of their jobs.

Not all adult education is college level or vocationally oriented. Each year, thousands of young adults drop out of high school, sometimes because of family obligations and sometimes out of a desire to enter the workforce or the informal economy. Later, these adults may recognize the desirability of a high school education and decide to pursue a General Educational Development (GED) diploma, which usually means taking preparatory classes followed by a series of exams. In recent years, the proportion of students

who choose this alternative route to finishing high school has grown steadily. During the 1990s, the percentage of high school diplomas awarded to GED students ages 18 to 24 rose from less than 5 percent to over 10 percent. Thus far, researchers have found conflicting evidence on the effects of a GED versus a traditional degree on graduates' employment status and earnings; additional research needs to be done on this topic.

Let's Discuss

1. Do some research on your college or university's student body. How many older students are there on your campus? What is their sex ratio (female to male) and average age? How many belong to ethnic or racial minorities?

2. What are the pros and cons of postponing higher education? Consider the question from both a personal and a societal point of view.

Sources: F. Best and Eberhard 1990; Francese 2003; National Center for Education Statistics 2002b; Population Reference Bureau 2000.

FIGURE 13-1

Developmental and Transitional Periods in Adulthood

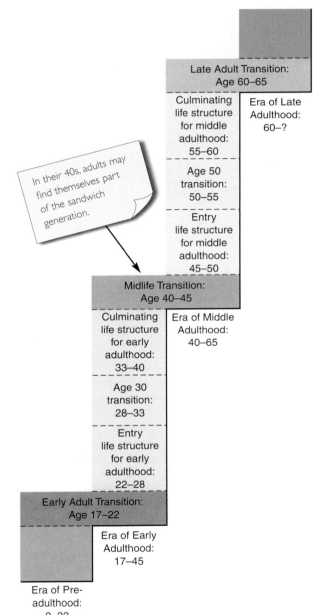

> In their 40s, adults may find themselves part of the sandwich generation.

Late Adult Transition:
Age 60–65

Culminating life structure for middle adulthood:
55–60

Era of Late Adulthood:
60–?

Age 50 transition:
50–55

Entry life structure for middle adulthood:
45–50

Midlife Transition:
Age 40–45

Culminating life structure for early adulthood:
33–40

Era of Middle Adulthood:
40–65

Age 30 transition:
28–33

Entry life structure for early adulthood:
22–28

Early Adult Transition:
Age 17–22

Era of Early Adulthood:
17–45

Era of Pre-adulthood:
0–22

Source: D. Levinson 1996:18.

Think About It
Which developmental periods do you think you will find the easiest? The hardest?

The Sandwich Generation

During the late 1990s social scientists focused on the *sandwich generation*—adults who simultaneously try to meet the competing needs of their parents and their children. That is, caregiving goes in two directions: (1) to children, who even as young adults may still require significant direction, and (2) to aging parents, whose health and economic problems may demand intervention by their adult children. According to a national survey done in 1997, almost one-fourth of all households in the United States are providing informal, unpaid care for an older friend or relative. The average caregiver spends 18 hours a week in this assistance—a significant amount of time for the 40 percent of caregivers who still have children under 18 (Chatzky 1999; National Alliance for Caregiving 1997; Velkoff and Lawson 1998).

A sandwich-generation mom cares for her bedridden parent as her older child feeds the younger one. Increasingly, members of the baby boom generation find themselves caring for two generations at once.

The last major transition identified by Levinson occurs after age 60. This is a time when dramatic changes take place in people's everyday lives, as we will now see.

Adjusting to Retirement

Retirement is a rite of passage that marks a critical transition from one phase of a person's life to another. Typically, symbolic events are associated with this rite of passage, such as retirement gifts, a retirement party, and special moments on the last day on the job. The preretirement period itself can be emotionally charged, especially if the retiree is expected to train his or her successor (Atchley 1976).

Life begins at 65 for these retirees in Georgetown, Texas, checking out a model of Sun City, a full-service retirement community.

From 1950 to the mid-1990s, the average age at retirement in the United States declined, but over the last few years it has reversed direction and begun to climb. In 2000, 12.8 percent of Americans 65 and older were still working—the highest level in more than two decades. A variety of factors explains this reversal: changes in Social Security benefits, an economic shift away from hard manual labor, and workers' concern with maintaining their health insurance and pension benefits. At the same time, longevity has increased, and the quality of people's health has improved with it. According to a study released in 2000, in any given year after age 65, the elderly are now less likely to have a hospital stay or to need nursing services than they were in 1993 (Liao et al. 2000; Walsh 2001).

Gerontologist Robert Atchley (1976) has identified several phases of the retirement experience:

- *Preretirement,* a period of anticipatory socialization as the person prepares for retirement
- *The near phase,* when the person establishes a specific departure date from his or her job
- *The honeymoon phase,* an often euphoric period in which the person pursues activities that he or she never had time for before
- *The disenchantment phase,* in which retirees feel a sense of letdown or even depression as they cope with their new lives, which may include illness or poverty
- *The reorientation phase,* which involves the development of a more realistic view of retirement alternatives

- *The stability phase,* a period in which the person has learned to deal with life after retirement in a reasonable and comfortable fashion
- *The termination phase,* which begins when the person can no longer engage in basic, day-to-day activities such as self-care and housework

As this analysis demonstrates, retirement is not a single transition, but rather a series of adjustments that varies from one person to another. The length and timing of each phase will differ for each individual, depending on such factors as financial and health status. In fact, a person will not necessarily go through all the phases identified by Atchley. For example, people who are forced to retire or who face financial difficulties may never experience a honeymoon phase. A significant number of retirees continue to be part of the paid labor force of the United States, often taking part-time jobs to supplement their pension income. That is certainly the expectation of baby boomers, as Figure 13-2 shows.

Like other aspects of life in the United States, the experience of retirement varies according to gender, race, and ethnicity. White males are most likely to benefit from retirement wages as well as to have participated in a formal retirement preparation program. As a result, anticipatory socialization for retirement is most systematic for White men. In contrast, members of racial and ethnic minority groups—especially African Americans—are more likely to exit the paid labor force through disability than through retirement. Because of their comparatively lower incomes and smaller savings, men and women from racial and ethnic minority groups work intermittently

FIGURE 13-2

Retirement Expectations

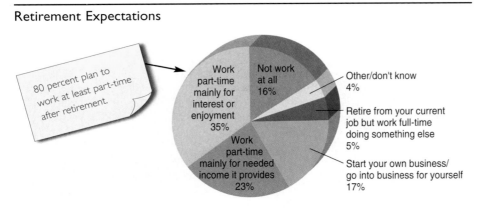

80 percent plan to work at least part-time after retirement.

Work part-time mainly for interest or enjoyment 35%

Not work at all 16%

Other/don't know 4%

Retire from your current job but work full-time doing something else 5%

Start your own business/ go into business for yourself 17%

Work part-time mainly for needed income it provides 23%

Note: Survey of the baby boom generation (people born from 1946 to 1964) conducted in 1998.
Source: AARP 1999.

after retirement more often than older Whites (National Institute on Aging 1999; Quadagno 2002).

Death and Dying

Among the role transitions that typically (but not always) come later in life is death. Until recently, death was viewed as a taboo topic in the United States. However, psychologist Elisabeth Kübler-Ross (1969), through her pioneering book *On Death and Dying,* has greatly encouraged open discussion of the process of dying.

Drawing on her work with 200 cancer patients, Kübler-Ross identified five stages of the experience of dying that a person may undergo:

1. When people finally realize that they are dying, they first *deny* the truth to themselves, their families, and their friends.
2. When they can no longer maintain denial, a period of *anger* follows; the anger can be directed at almost anyone or anything.
3. In the stage of *bargaining*—often relatively brief—people talk about the unfulfilled goals they will pursue if they somehow recover. In effect, they are hoping to bargain with God for additional time.
4. When people realize that these deals are not realistic, they enter a stage of *depression* and experience a pervasive sense of loss.
5. The final stage, *acceptance,* is not reached by every dying patient. Those who accept death are not happy about the prospect, but have come to terms with their fate and are ready to die in peace.

As Kübler-Ross (1969:113) notes: "It is as if the pain had gone, the struggle is over, and there comes a time for 'the final rest before the long journey' as one patient phrased it."

Despite its continued popular appeal, the Kübler-Ross five-stage theory of dying has been challenged. Researchers often cannot substantiate these stages. Moreover, this model relies on an assumption that the dying person clearly recognizes that death is nearing. Yet more than 20 percent of people in the United States age 65 and over die in nursing homes; for them and many others, an array of chronic, debilitative, degenerative diseases can mask death. Finally, critics of Kübler-Ross emphasize that even if this five-stage model is accurate for the United States, it does not apply to other cultures that deal with death quite differently (Marshall and Levy 1990; Retsinas 1988).

Functionalists would see those who are dying as fulfilling distinct social functions. Gerontologist Richard Kalish (1985) lists among the tasks of the dying: completing unfinished business, such as settling insurance and legacy matters; restoring harmony to social relationships and saying farewell to friends and family; dealing with medical needs; and making funeral plans and other arrangements for survivors. In accomplishing these tasks, the dying person actively contributes to meeting society's need for smooth intergenerational transitions, role continuity, compliance with medical procedures, and minimal disruption of the social system, despite the loss of one of its members.

This functionalist analysis brings to mind the cherished yet controversial concept of a "good death." One researcher described a good death among the Kaliai, a people of the South Pacific. In that culture, the dying person calls together all his relatives, settles his debts, disposes of his possessions, and then announces that it is time for him to die (Counts 1977). The Kaliai concept of a good death has a parallel in Western societies, where people may speak of a "natural death," an "appropriate death," or "death with dignity." The practice of **hospice care,** introduced in London, England, in the 1960s, is founded on this concept. Hospice workers seek to improve the quality of a dying person's last days by offering comfort and by helping the person to remain at home, or in a homelike setting at a hospital or other special facility, until the end. Currently there are more than 3,100 hospice programs serving over half a million people a year.

Although the Western ideal of the good death makes the experience of dying as positive as possible, some critics fear that acceptance of the concept of a good death may direct both individual efforts and social resources away from attempts to extend life. Still others argue that fatally ill older people should not just passively accept death, but should forgo further treatment in order to reduce public health care expenditures. As we will see in the social policy section, such issues are at the heart of current debates over the right to die and physician-assisted suicide (Counts 1977; Hospice Foundation of America 2002).

Recent studies in the United States suggest that in many varied ways, people have broken through the historic taboos about death and are attempting to arrange certain aspects of the idealized good death. For example, bereavement practices—once highly structured—are becoming increasingly varied and therapeutic. More and more people are actively addressing the inevitability of death by making wills, leaving "living wills" (health care proxies that explain their feelings about the use of life-support equipment), donating organs, and providing instructions for family members about funerals, cremations, and burials. Given medical and technological advances and a breakthrough in open discussion and negotiation regarding death and dying, it is possible that good deaths may become a social norm in the United States (La Ganga 1999; J. Riley 1992).

Coffins in Ghana sometimes reflect the way the dead lived their lives. This Methodist burial service honors a woman who died at age 85, leaving behind 11 children, 82 grandchildren, and 60 great-grandchildren. Her coffin, designed to resemble a mother hen, features 11 chicks nestling between the wings (Secretan 1995).

 AGE STRATIFICATION IN THE UNITED STATES

The "Graying of America"

When Lenore Schaefer, a ballroom dancer, tried to get on the *Tonight Show,* she was told she was "too young": she was in her early 90s. When she turned 101, she made it. But even at that age, Lenore is no longer unusual in our society. Today, people over 100 constitute, proportionately, the country's fastest-growing age group. They are part of the increasing proportion of the population of the United States composed of older people (Himes 2001; Rimer 1998).

As Figure 13-3 shows, in the year 1900, men and women aged 65 and older constituted only 4.1 percent of the nation's population, but by 2005, that age group is expected to grow to 12.6 percent. According to current projections, the over-65 segment will continue to increase throughout this century, with the "old old" (people who are 85 and older) increasing in numbers at an ever-faster rate.

In 2005, 17.0 percent of non-Hispanic Whites are projected to be older than 65, compared to 9.4 percent of African Americans, 9.3 percent of Asian Americans, and 6.9 percent of Hispanics. These differences reflect the shorter life spans of the latter groups, as well as immigration patterns among Asians and Hispanics, who tend to be young when they enter the country. Yet people of color are increasing their presence among the elderly population of the United States. By 2050, 36 percent of the elderly will be non-White, compared to only 16 percent in 2000 (Bureau of the Census 2002a:20; Graham 2002).

The highest proportions of older people are found in Florida, Pennsylvania, Rhode Island, Iowa, West Virginia, and Arkansas. However, many more states are undergoing an aging trend. In 2000, Florida was the state most populated by the elderly, with 17.6 percent of the population over the age of 65. Yet, as Figure 13-4 shows, in about 25 years, more than half the states will have a greater proportion of elderly than Florida does now.

The graying of the United States is a phenomenon that can no longer be ignored—either by social scientists or by government policymakers. Advocates for the elderly

FIGURE 13-3

Actual and Projected Growth of the Elderly Population of the United States

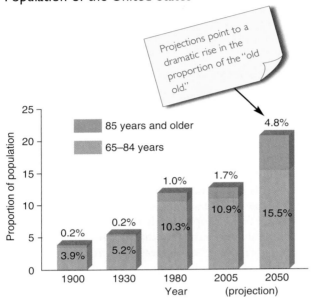

Projections point to a dramatic rise in the proportion of the "old old."

Sources: Bureau of the Census 1975, 2002a:15.

what: Those older people who enjoyed middle-class incomes while younger tend to remain better off after retirement, but less so than before (Denise Smith and Tillipman 2000).

To some extent, older people owe their overall improved standard of living to a greater accumulation of wealth—in the form of home ownership, private pensions, and other financial assets. But much of the improvement is due to more generous Social Security benefits. While modest when compared with other countries' pension programs, Social Security nevertheless provides 40 percent of all income received by older people in the United States. Still, about 10 percent of the nation's elderly population lives below the poverty line. At the extreme end of poverty are those groups who were more likely to be poor at earlier points in the life cycle: female-headed households and racial and ethnic minorities (AARP 2001; Saad and Carroll 2003; Denise Smith and Tillipman 2000).

Viewed from a conflict perspective, it is not surprising that older women experience a double burden; the same is true of elderly members of racial and ethnic minorities. For example, in 2001 the proportion of older Latinos with incomes below the poverty level (21.8 percent) was more than twice as large as the proportion

have spoken out on a wide range of issues, as we will see later in the chapter. Politicians court the votes of older people, since they are the age group most likely to register and vote. In fact, in the 2000 presidential race, people 60 or older made up 22 percent of the total vote (Berke 2001).

Wealth and Income

There is significant variation in wealth and poverty among the nation's older people. Some individuals and couples find themselves poor in part because of fixed pensions and skyrocketing health care costs (see Chapter 19). Nevertheless, as a group, older people in the United States are neither homogeneous nor poor. The typical elderly person enjoys a standard of living that is much higher now than at any point in the nation's past. Class differences among the elderly remain evident, but tend to narrow some-

FIGURE 13-4

Twenty-Six Floridas by 2025

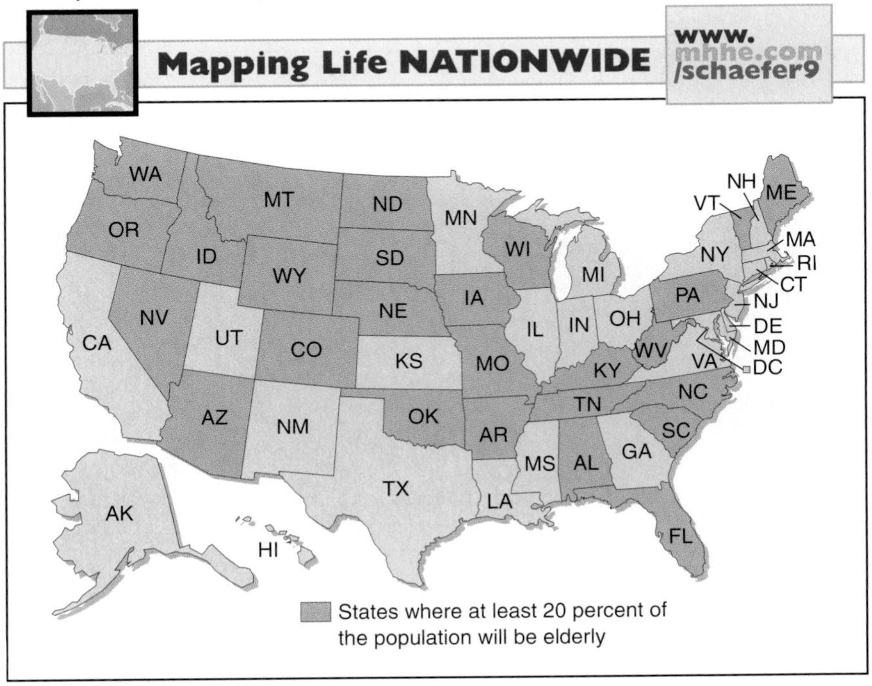

Mapping Life NATIONWIDE

www.mhhe.com/schaefer9

States where at least 20 percent of the population will be elderly

Source: Bureau of the Census in Yax 1999.

of older non-Hispanic Whites (8.1 percent). Moreover, 21.9 percent of older African Americans fell below the federal government's poverty line (Proctor and Dalaker 2002:27–29).

Ageism

Physician Robert Butler (1990) became concerned 30 years ago when he learned that a housing development near his home in metropolitan Washington, D.C., barred the elderly. Butler coined the term *ageism* to refer to prejudice and discrimination based on a person's age. For example, we may choose to assume that someone cannot handle a rigorous job because he is "too old," or we may refuse to give someone a job with authority because she is "too young."

Ageism is especially difficult for the old, because at least youthful recipients know that in time they will be "old enough." For many, old age symbolizes disease. With ageism all too common in the United States, it is hardly surprising that older people are barely visible on television. In 2002, the Senate Special Committee on Aging convened a panel on the media's portrayal of older people and sharply criticized media and marketing executives for bombarding audiences with negative images of the aged. The social consequences of such images are significant. Research shows that older people who have positive perceptions of aging live an average of 7.5 years longer than those who have negative perceptions (M. Gardner 2003; Levy et al. 2002; Ramirez 2002).

Use Your Sociological Imagination www.mhhe.com/schaefer9

It is September and you are channel surfing through the new fall TV series. How likely are you to watch a television show that is based on older characters who spend a lot of time together?

Competition in the Labor Force

Participation in paid work is not typical after the age of 65. In 2001, 31 percent of men ages 65 to 69 and 20 percent of women participated in the paid labor force. While some people view these workers as experienced contributors to the labor force, others see them as "job stealers," a biased judgment similar to that directed against illegal immigrants. This mistaken belief not only intensifies age conflict, but leads to age discrimination (Himes 2001).

While firing people simply because they are old violates federal law, courts have upheld the right to lay off older workers for economic reasons. Critics contend that later the same firms hire young, cheaper workers to replace experienced older workers. When economic growth began to slow in 2001 and companies cut back on their work forces, complaints of age bias grew sharply as older workers began to suspect they were bearing a disproportionate share of the layoffs. According to the Equal Employment Opportunity Commission, between 2000 and 2003, complaints of age discrimination rose more than 24 percent (Puri 2003).

A controlled experiment conducted by the AARP confirmed that older people often face discrimination when applying for jobs. Comparable résumés for two applicants—one 57 years old and the other 32 years old—were sent to 775 large firms and employment agencies around the United States. In situations for which positions were actually available, the younger applicant received a favorable response 43 percent of the time. By contrast, the older applicant received favorable responses less than half as often (only 17 percent of the time). One Fortune 500 corporation asked the younger applicant for more information, while informing the older applicant that no appropriate positions were open (Bendick et al. 1993).

In contrast to the negative stereotypes, researchers have found that older workers can be an *asset* to

About 30 percent of older workers choose to remain on the job past the usual retirement age. Research shows they can be retrained in new technologies and are more dependable than younger workers.

employers. According to a study issued in 1991, older workers can be retrained in new technologies, have lower rates of absenteeism than younger employees, and are often more effective salespeople. The study focused on two corporations based in the United States (the hotel chain Days Inns of America and the holding company Travelers Corporation of Hartford) and a British retail chain—all of which have long-term experience in hiring workers age 50 and over. An official of the private fund that commissioned the study concluded, "We have here the first systematic hard-nosed economic analysis showing older workers are good investments" (Telsch 1991:A16).

Members of SAGE, Senior Action in a Gay Environment, take part in a gay pride demonstration in New York City. This nationwide organization focuses on the special needs of gay seniors.

The Elderly: Emergence of a Collective Consciousness

During the 1960s, students at colleges and universities across the country, advocating "student power," collectively demanded a role in the governance of educational institutions. In the following decade, many older people became aware that *they* were being treated as second-class citizens and turned to collective action.

The largest organization representing the nation's elderly is the AARP, founded in 1958 by a retired school principal who was having difficulty getting insurance because of age prejudice. Many of AARP's services involve discounts and insurance for its 35 million members (44 percent of Americans aged 50 or older), but the organization also functions as a powerful lobbying group. Recognizing that many elderly are still gainfully employed, it has dropped its full name, American Association of *Retired* Persons.

The potential power of AARP is enormous. It is the third-largest voluntary association in the United States (behind only the Roman Catholic church and the American Automobile Association), representing one out of every four registered voters in the United States. The AARP has endorsed voter registration campaigns, nursing home reforms, and pension reforms. In acknowledgment of its difficulties recruiting members of racial and ethnic minority groups, AARP recently began a Minority Affairs Initiative. The spokeswoman for this initiative, Margaret Dixon, became AARP's first African American president in 1996 (AARP 2003).

People grow old in many different ways. Not all the elderly face the same challenges or enjoy the same resources. While the AARP lobbies to protect the elderly in general, other groups work in more specific ways. For example, the National Committee to Preserve Social Security and Medicare, founded in 1982, successfully lobbied Congress to keep Medicare benefits for the ailing poor elderly. Other large special interest groups represent retired federal employees, retired teachers, and retired union workers (Quadagno 2002).

Still another manifestation of the new awareness of older people is the formation of organizations for elderly homosexuals. One such group, Senior Action in a Gay Environment (SAGE), was established in New York City in 1977 and now oversees a nationwide network of community groups, as well as affiliates in Canada and Germany. Like more traditional senior citizens' groups, SAGE sponsors workshops, classes, dances, and food deliveries to the homebound. At the same time, the group must deal with special concerns, such as informing gay people of their rights, supporting gay people with Alzheimer's, and advocating for gays who face eviction (Senior Action in a Gay Environment 2003).

The elderly in the United States are better off today both financially and physically than ever before. Many of them have strong financial assets and medical care packages that will take care of almost any health need. But as we have seen, a significant segment is impoverished, faced with the prospect of declining health and mounting medical bills. And some older people may now have to add being aged to a lifetime of disadvantage. As in all other stages of the life course, the aged constitute a diverse group in the United States and around the world.

The Issue

On August 4, 1993, Dr. Jack Kevorkian, a retired pathologist, helped a 30-year-old Michigan man with Lou Gehrig's disease to commit suicide in a van. The patient died after inhaling carbon monoxide through a mask designed by Dr. Kevorkian; in doing so, he became the 17th person to commit suicide with Kevorkian's assistance. Kevorkian was openly challenging a Michigan law (aimed at him) that makes it a felony—punishable by up to four years in jail—to assist in a suicide. Since then Kevorkian has assisted in numerous other suicides, but not until he did it on television in 1998 did the charges brought against him result in his imprisonment for second-degree murder.

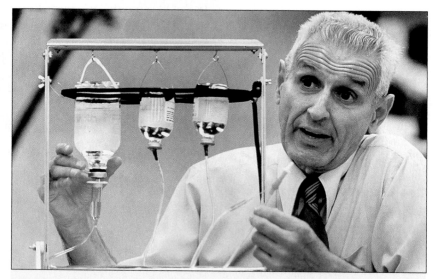

Dr. Jack Kevorkian with the apparatus that administers a lethal injection to those who want assistance in committing suicide.

The issue of physician-assisted suicide is but one aspect of the larger debate in the United States and other countries over the ethics of suicide and euthanasia. The term *euthanasia* has been defined as the "act of bringing about the death of a hopelessly ill and suffering person in a relatively quick and painless way for reasons of mercy" (Council on Ethical and Judicial Affairs, American Medical Association 1992:2, 229). This type of mercy killing reminds us of the ideal of the "good death" discussed earlier in the chapter. The debate over euthanasia and assisted suicide often focuses on cases involving older people, though it can involve younger adults with terminal and degenerative diseases, or even children.

National surveys show that public opinion on this controversial practice is divided. In 2002, 72 percent of respondents said that a physician should be legally permitted to end a patient's life if both the patient and the patient's family make such a request. However, an earlier survey found that only half of respondents could even imagine a situation in which they themselves would request physician-assisted suicide (Gallup 2002c).

The Setting

Many societies are known to have practiced *senilicide*—"killing of the aged"—because of extreme difficulties in providing basic necessities such as food and shelter. In a study of the treatment of the elderly in 41 nonindustrialized societies, Anthony Glascock (1990) found some form of "death-hastening" behavior in 21 of them. Killing of the elderly was evident in 14 of the societies, while abandoning of older people was evident in 8. Typically, death hastening occurs when older people become decrepit and are viewed as already dead. In these nonindustrialized cultures it is open and socially approved. Family members generally make decisions, often after open consultation with those who are about to die.

Currently, public policy in the United States does not permit *active euthanasia* (such as a deliberate injection of lethal drugs to a terminally ill patient) or physician-assisted suicide. Although suicide itself is no longer a crime, assisting suicide is illegal in at least 29 states. There is greater legal tolerance for *passive euthanasia* (such as disconnecting life-support equipment from a comatose patient).

Sociological Insights

Although formal norms concerning euthanasia may be in flux, informal norms seem to permit mercy killings. According to an estimate by the American Hospital Association, as many as 70 percent of all deaths in the United States are quietly negotiated, with patients, family members, and physicians agreeing not to use life-support technology. In an informal poll of internists, one in five reported that he or she had assisted or helped cause the death of a patient. In a period in which AIDS-related deaths are common, an AIDS underground is known to share information and assistance regarding suicide (Gibbs 1993; E. Martinez 1993).

p. 119

Conflict theorists ask questions about the values raised by such decisions. By endorsing physician-assisted suicide, are we devaluing the disabled through an acceptance of their premature death? Critics note that we are all only temporarily able-bodied; disease or a speeding automobile can place any one of us among the disabled. By establishing a precedent for ending the lives of selected disabled people, we may unwittingly contribute to negative social views and labeling of all disabled people. Further reflecting the conflict perspective, gerontologist Elizabeth Markson (1992:6) argues that the "powerless, poor or undesirable are at special risk of being 'encouraged' to choose assisted death."

Critics of euthanasia charge that many of its supporters are guilty of ageism and other forms of bias. In a society that commonly discriminates against the elderly and people with disabilities, medical authorities and even family members may decide too quickly that such people should die "for their own good" or (in a view somewhat reminiscent of disengagement theory) "for the good of society." Some critics fear that society may use euthanasia to reduce health care costs—rather than striving to make life better for those near the end. Older people may even feel compelled to end their lives prematurely, to ease the emotional and financial burdens on family members and friends (Glascock 1990:45; *New York Times* 1993; Richman 1992).

Policy Initiatives

In the industrialized world, euthanasia is widely accepted only in the Netherlands, where physicians perform about 4,000 such procedures each year. According to Dutch law, euthanasia is legal if a patient has voluntarily requested assistance in committing suicide and has received a second medical opinion. National surveys consistently show that 90 percent of the Dutch people, including doctors, accept the practice of euthanasia and physician-assisted suicide (Cloud 2001; Simons 2000).

In the United States, the only state to allow assisted suicide is Oregon, where the Death with Dignity Act became law in 1997. At least 129 terminally ill Oregonians have chosen to end their lives since the law took effect. Similar measures have failed to win support in at least 20 other states, where the issue has encountered sharp opposition. In 2001 and again in 2003 President Bush's administration sought unsuccessfully to stop doctors from prescribing lethal drugs for terminally ill patients (Gorman 2003).

Advances in technology now allow us to prolong life in ways that were unimaginable decades ago. But should people be forced or expected to prolong lives that are unbearably painful, or that are in effect "lifeless"? Unfortunately, medical and technological advances cannot provide answers to these complex ethical, legal, and political questions.

Let's Discuss

1. Why do you think "death-hastening" behavior is common in nonindustrialized countries?

2. In what ways are conflict theory and disengagement theory relevant to the debate over the "right to die"?

3. Do you think someone should be allowed to choose to die? Why or why not?

CHAPTER RESOURCES

Summary

Age, like gender and race, is an ascribed status that forms the basis for social differentiation. This chapter examines theories regarding the aging process, role transitions in the life course, age stratification in the United States, the growing political activism of the nation's elderly population, and the controversy surrounding the right to die.

1. Like other forms of stratification, age stratification varies from culture to culture.
2. In the United States, being old is a master status that seems to overshadow all others.
3. The particular problems of the aged have become the focus for a specialized area of research and inquiry known as *gerontology.*
4. *Disengagement theory* implicitly suggests that society should help older people to withdraw from their accustomed social roles. In contrast, *activity theory* suggests that the elderly person who remains active and socially involved will be better adjusted.

5. From a conflict perspective, the low status of older people is reflected in prejudice and discrimination against them and in unfair job practices.
6. About 40 percent of those who look after their elderly relatives still have children to care for; these people have been dubbed the *sandwich generation.*
7. As we age, we go through role transitions, including adjustment to retirement and preparation for death.
8. An increasing proportion of the population of the United States is composed of older people.
9. *Ageism* reflects a deep uneasiness about growing old on the part of younger people.
10. The AARP is a powerful lobbying group that backs legislation to benefit senior citizens.
11. The "right to die" often entails physician-assisted suicide, a controversial issue worldwide.

Critical Thinking Questions

1. Are there elderly students at your college or university? If so, how are they treated by younger students and by faculty members? Is there a subculture of older students? How do younger students view faculty members in their 50s and 60s?
2. Is age segregation functional or dysfunctional for older people in the United States? Is it functional

or dysfunctional for society as a whole? What are the manifest functions, the latent functions, and the dysfunctions of age segregation?
3. If you were hired to run a senior center where you live, how would you use what you have learned in this chapter to better the lives of your community's seniors?

Key Terms

Activity theory   An interactionist theory of aging that argues that elderly people who remain active and socially involved will be best-adjusted. (page 307)

Ageism   Prejudice and discrimination based on a person's age. (316)

Disengagement theory   A functionalist theory of aging that contends that society and the aging individual mutually sever many of their relationships. (305)

Euthanasia   The act of bringing about the death of a hopelessly ill and suffering person in a relatively quick and painless way for reasons of mercy. (318)

Gerontology   The scientific study of the sociological and psychological aspects of aging and the problems of the aged. (305)

Hospice care   Treatment of the terminally ill in their own homes, or in special hospital units or other facilities, with the goal of helping them to die easily, without pain. (313)

Midlife crisis   A stressful period of self-evaluation that begins at about age 40. (309)

Sandwich generation   The generation of adults who simultaneously try to meet the competing needs of their parents and their children. (311)

Senilicide   The killing of the aged. (318)

TECHNOLOGY RESOURCES

Internet Connection

*Note: While all the URLs listed were current as of the printing of this book, these sites often change. Please check our website (**www.mhhe.com/schaefer9**) for updates, hyperlinks, and exercises related to these sites.*

1. In this chapter we have examined aging around the world, focusing primarily on older people in the United States. To find more useful statistics and profiles of older Americans, visit the homepage of the Administration on Aging (AoA): (**www.aoa.gov**).

2. Every one of us has opinions about older people, and expectations about our own aging process. To examine some of the myths and misconceptions about aging and older people, explore the HelpAge International website (**www.helpage. org/index.htm**).

Online Learning Center with PowerWeb

Aging is a topic that is important to all of us, no matter how old we are. The Administration on Aging (AoA) offers online information of interest to people of all ages. Visit the student center of the Online Learning Center at **www.mhhe.com/schaefer9** and link to "Internet Exercises." Scroll down to exercise 3, link to the AoA, and learn about important issues related to aging, such as elder abuse and age discrimination.

chapter 14

THE FAMILY AND INTIMATE RELATIONSHIPS

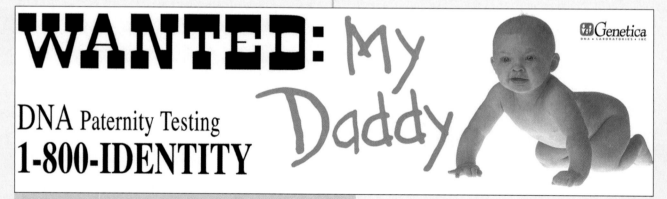

Reproductive technology is changing people's personal lives, raising questions about ethics and social policy in the process. For the first time, mothers can positively identify the fathers of their children, and parents can manipulate their children's genes—a prospect many people find disturbing.

Global View of the Family

Studying the Family

Marriage and Family

Divorce

Diverse Lifestyles

Social Policy and the Family: Reproductive Technology

Boxes

SOCIOLOGY IN THE GLOBAL COMMUNITY: Domestic Violence

RESEARCH IN ACTION: The Lingering Impact of Divorce

From the time of the breakdown of my marriage to Cliff's mother in 1979 to my marriage to Elleni in 1990, I was forced to deal with a difficult but nonetheless standard set of problems. My ex-wife was awarded custody of two-year-old Cliff and then decided to move to Atlanta. I had no recourse, legal or otherwise. And yet in my struggle to build a close relationship with my son, I now had to cope with an almost impossible set of barriers. Hundreds of miles separated me from Cliff, and I had limited visitation rights—a few specified weekends during the year plus three months in the summer. Besides which, what would I do with my son during our precious time together? My bachelor homes did not provide a supportive context for a four-year-old or a nine-year-old—there were no kids on the block, no basketball hoop in the back yard. But I wrestled with these problems and over time developed a strategy that worked, albeit imperfectly.

I hit upon this great solution for the summers. I would take Cliff back to Sacramento, back to the loving, child-centered home that had been so good to me and my siblings a generation ago. It required a lot of stretching and bending of the rules, but I organized life so that I really could take two and a half months out of the year. It meant postponing book deadlines and taming an almost impossible travel schedule, but it was well worth it. Those summers in Sacramento stand out like jewels in my memory. My parents' home turned out to be a profoundly healing place in which Cliff and I could reach out to one another. It provided the deeply needed (and yet so hard to contrive) rhythms and routines of normal family life. Three meals a day; regular bedtimes; clean clothes; a bevy of cousins—Kahnie, Phillip and Phyllis, Cornel and Erika—just around the corner, on tap for casual play; bicycles and baseball gear in the garage all ready to be put to use whenever a grownup was available. And hovering in the backgrounds, loving, eagle-eyed grandparents.... The evening meal was particularly important, as all three generations gathered for a cookout in the back yard. Conversation and laughter flowed, advice was sought and help was freely offered, jokes and stories were traded, and the children, spellbound, hung on the edges, absorbing the spirit and the meaning of family life.

The rest of the year was a struggle. I maintained regular telephone contact with Cliff, calling him several times a week just to hear his voice and shoot the breeze. But in the rushed, tantalizing visits around Thanksgiving, Christmas, and Easter, it was always hard not to lapse into the role of being a "good-time dad," showering gifts on him in an attempt to make up for real time or a deeper agenda. *(Hewlett and West 1998:21–22)* ■ ✎

SYLVIA ANN HEWLETT
& CORNEL WEST

the war against parents

"This splendid book tells more about the crisis our children face today and what we as a nation must do about it than anything I have read."
DORIS KEARNS GOODWIN

MARINER BOOKS

Additional information about this excerpt can be found on the Online Learning Center at **www.mhhe.com/schaefer9**.

In this excerpt from *The War Against Parents* philosophy scholar Cornel West underscores how deeply family life has been altered by divorce, one of many social factors that have gradually but inevitably turned the traditional nuclear family on its head. The family of today is not what it was a century ago or even a generation ago. New roles, new gender distinctions, new child-rearing patterns have all combined to create new forms of family life. Today, for example, more and more women are taking the breadwinner's role, whether married or as a single parent. Blended families—the result of divorce and remarriage—are almost the norm. And many people are seeking intimate relationships outside marriage, whether it be in gay partnerships or in cohabiting arrangements.

This chapter addresses family and intimate relationships in the United States as well as other parts of the world. As we will see, family patterns differ from one culture to another and even within the same culture. Despite the differences, however, the family is universal—found in every culture. A *family* can be defined as a set of people related by blood, marriage or some other agreed-upon relationship, or adoption, who share the primary responsibility for reproduction and caring for members of society.

What are families in different parts of the world like? How do people select their mates? When a marriage fails, how does the divorce affect the children? What are the alternatives to the nuclear family, and how prevalent are they? In this chapter we will look at the family and intimate relationships from the functionalist, conflict, and interactionist points of view. We'll examine variations in marital patterns and family life, including child rearing, paying particular attention to the increasing numbers of people in dual-income and single-parent families. We'll examine divorce in the United States, and consider diverse lifestyles such as cohabitation, lesbian and gay relationships, and marriage without children. In the social policy section we will confront the controversial issues surrounding new reproductive technologies. ■

GLOBAL VIEW OF THE FAMILY

Among Tibetans, a woman may be simultaneously married to more than one man, usually brothers. This system allows sons to share the limited amount of good land. A Hopi woman may divorce her husband by placing his belongings outside the door. A Trobriand Island couple signals marriage by sitting in public on a porch eating yams provided by the bride's mother. She continues to provide cooked yams for a year while the groom's family offers in exchange such valuables as stone axes and clay pots (Haviland 2002).

As these examples illustrate, there are many variations in the family from culture to culture. Yet the family as a social institution is present in all cultures. Moreover, certain general principles concerning its composition, kinship patterns, and authority patterns are universal.

Composition: What Is the Family?

If we were to take our information on what a family is from what we see on television, we might come up with some very strange scenarios. The media don't always present a realistic view of the family. Moreover, many people still think of the family in very narrow terms—as a married couple and their unmarried children living together, like the family in the old *Cosby Show* or *Family Ties* or even *Dawson's Creek*. However, this is but one type of family, what sociologists refer to as a **nuclear family**. The term *nuclear family* is well chosen, since this type of family serves as the nucleus, or core, on which larger family groups are built.

Most people in the United States see the nuclear family as the preferred family arrangement. Yet by 2000, only about a third of the nation's family households fit this model. The proportion of households in the United States composed of married couples with children at home has decreased steadily over the last 40 years, and is expected to continue shrinking. At the same time, the number of single-parent households has increased (see Figure 14-1).

A family in which relatives—such as grandparents, aunts, or uncles—live in the same home as parents and their children is known as an **extended family**. Although not common, such living arrangements do exist in the United States. The structure of the extended family offers certain advantages over that of the nuclear family. Crises such as death, divorce, and illness put less strain on family members, since more people can provide assistance and emotional support. In addition, the extended family constitutes a larger economic unit than the nuclear family. If the family is engaged in a common enterprise—a farm or a small business—the additional family members may represent the difference between prosperity and failure.

In considering these differing family types, we have limited ourselves to the form of marriage that is characteristic of the United States—monogamy. The term *monogamy* describes a form of marriage in which one woman and one man are married only to each other. Some observers, noting the high rate of divorce in the United States, have suggested that "serial monogamy" is a more accurate description of the form that marriage takes in the United States. In *serial monogamy,* a person may have several spouses in his or her lifetime, but only one spouse at a time.

Some cultures allow an individual to have several husbands or wives simultaneously. This form of marriage is known as *polygamy.* In fact, most societies throughout the world, past and present, have preferred polygamy to monogamy. Anthropologist George Murdock (1949, 1957) sampled 565 societies and found that in more than 80 percent, some type of polygamy was the preferred form. While polygamy declined steadily through most of the 20th century, in at least five countries in Africa 20 percent of men still have polygamous marriages (Population Reference Bureau 1996).

There are two basic types of polygamy. According to Murdock, the most common—endorsed by the majority of cultures he sampled—is *polygyny.* Polygyny refers to the marriage of a man to more than one woman at the same time. The wives are often sisters, who are expected to hold similar values and have already had experience sharing a household. In polygynous societies, relatively few men actually have multiple spouses. Most individuals live in monogamous families; having multiple wives is viewed as a mark of status.

The other principal variation of polygamy is *polyandry,* in which a woman can have more than one husband at the same time. This is the case in the culture of the Todas of southern India. Polyandry, however, is exceedingly rare today. It has been accepted by some extremely poor societies that practice female infanticide (the killing of baby girls), and thus have a relatively small number of women. Like many other societies, polyandrous cultures devalue the social worth of women.

Kinship Patterns: To Whom Are We Related?

Many of us can trace our roots by looking at a family tree or by listening to elderly family members talk about their lives—and about the lives of ancestors who died long before we were born. Yet a person's lineage is more than simply a personal history; it also reflects societal patterns that govern descent. In every culture, children encounter relatives to whom they are expected to show an emotional attachment. The state of being related to others is called *kinship.*

FIGURE 14-1

U.S. Households by Family Type, 1940–2000

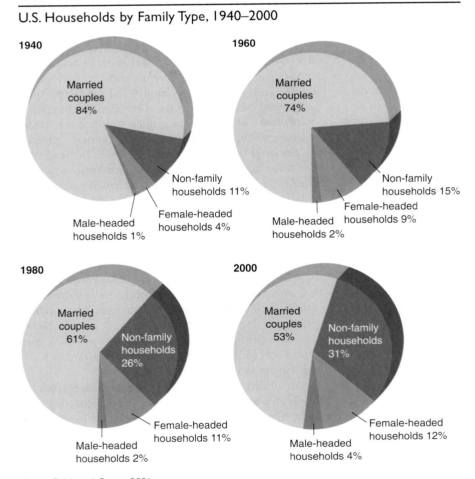

Source: Fields and Casper 2001.

Kinship is culturally learned, however, and is not totally determined by biological or marital ties. For example, adoption creates a kinship tie that is legally acknowledged and socially accepted.

The family and the kin group are not necessarily one and the same. Whereas the family is a household unit, kin do not always live together or function as a collective body on a daily basis. Kin groups include aunts, uncles, cousins, in-laws, and so forth. In a society such as the United States, the kinship group may come together only rarely, for a wedding or funeral. However, kinship ties frequently create obligations and responsibilities. We may feel compelled to assist our kin, and we feel free to call upon them for many types of aid, including loans and baby-sitting.

Smile—it's family reunion time! The state of being related to others is called kinship. Kin groups include aunts, uncles, cousins, and so forth, as shown in this family from Slovakia.

How do we identify kinship groups? The principle of descent assigns people to kinship groups according to their relationship to a mother or father. There are three primary ways of determining descent. The United States follows the system of **bilateral descent,** which means that both sides of a person's family are regarded as equally important. For example, no higher value is given to the brothers of one's father than to the brothers of one's mother.

Most societies—according to George Murdock, 64 percent—give preference to one side of the family or the other in tracing descent. In **patrilineal** (from the Latin *pater,* "father") **descent,** only the father's relatives are important in terms of property, inheritance, and emotional ties. Conversely, in societies that favor **matrilineal** (from the Latin *mater,* "mother") **descent,** only the mother's relatives are significant.

New forms of reproductive technology (discussed in the social policy section) will necessitate a new way of looking at kinship. Today, a combination of biological and social processes can "create" a family member, requiring that more distinctions be made about who is related to whom.

Authority Patterns: Who Rules?

Imagine that you have recently married and must begin to make decisions about the future of your new family. You and your spouse face many questions. Where will you live? How will you furnish your home? Who will do the cook-

ing, the shopping, the cleaning? Whose friends will be invited to dinner? Each time a decision must be made, an issue is raised: Who has the power to make the decision? In simple terms, who rules the family? The conflict perspective examines these questions in the context p. 286 of traditional gender stratification, under which men have held a dominant position over women.

Societies vary in the way that power is distributed within the family. A society that expects males to dominate in all family decision making is termed a **patriarchy.** In patriarchal societies, such as Iran, the eldest male often wields the greatest power, although wives are expected to be treated with respect and kindness. A woman's status in Iran is typically defined by her relationship to a male relative, usually as a wife or daughter. In many patriarchal societies, women find it more difficult to obtain a divorce than a man does (Farr 1999). In contrast, in a **matriarchy,** women have greater authority than men. Matriarchies, which are very uncommon, emerged among Native American tribal societies and in nations in which men were absent for long periods because of warfare or food-gathering expeditions.

In a third type of authority pattern, the **egalitarian family,** spouses are regarded as equals. That does not mean, however, that all decisions are shared in such families. Wives may hold authority in some spheres, husbands in others. Many sociologists believe the egalitarian family has begun to replace the patriarchal family as the social norm in the United States.

Do we really need the family? A century ago, Friedrich Engels ([1884] 1959), a colleague of Karl Marx, described the family as the ultimate source of social inequality because of its role in the transfer of power, property, and privilege. More recently, conflict theorists have argued that the family contributes to societal injustice, denies women opportunities that are extended to men, and limits freedom in sexual expression and mate selection. In contrast, the functionalist perspective focuses on the ways in which the family gratifies the needs of its members and contributes to social stability. The interactionist view considers the intimate, face-to-face relationships that occur in the family.

Functionalist View

The family performs six paramount functions, first outlined more than 65 years ago by sociologist William F. Ogburn (Ogburn and Tibbits 1934):

1. **Reproduction.** For a society to maintain itself, it must replace dying members. In this sense, the family contributes to human survival through its function of reproduction.
2. **Protection.** Unlike the young of other animal species, human infants need constant care and economic security. In all cultures, the family assumes the ultimate responsibility for the protection and upbringing of children.
3. **Socialization.** Parents and other kin monitor a child's behavior and transmit the norms, values, and language of their culture to the child.
4. **Regulation of sexual behavior.** Sexual norms are subject to change both over time (for instance, in the customs for dating) and across cultures (compare Islamic Saudi Arabia to the more permissive Denmark). However, whatever the time period or cultural values of a society, standards of sexual behavior are most clearly defined within the family circle.
5. **Affection and companionship.** Ideally, the family provides members with warm and intimate relationships, helping them to feel satisfied and secure. Of course, a family member may find such rewards outside the family—from peers, in school, at work—and may even perceive the home as an unpleasant or abusive setting. Nevertheless, we expect our relatives to understand us, to care for us, and to be there for us when we need them.
6. **Provision of social status.** We inherit a social position because of the family background and reputation of our parents and siblings. The family presents the newborn child with an ascribed status based on race and ethnicity that helps to determine his or her place within society's stratification system. Moreover, family resources affect children's ability to pursue certain opportunities, such as higher education and special lessons.

Traditionally, the family has fulfilled a number of other functions, such as providing religious training, education, and recreational outlets. But Ogburn argued that other social institutions have gradually assumed many of those functions. Education once took place at the family fireside; now it is the responsibility of professionals working in schools and colleges. Even the family's traditional recreational function has been transferred to outside groups such as Little Leagues, athletic clubs, and Internet chat rooms.

Conflict View

Conflict theorists view the family not as a contributor to social stability, but as a reflection of the inequality in wealth and power that is found within the larger society. Feminist and conflict theorists note that the family has traditionally legitimized and perpetuated male dominance. Throughout most of human history—and in a wide range of societies—husbands have exercised overwhelming power and authority within the family. Not until the first wave of contemporary feminism in the United States, in the mid-1800s, was there a substantial ◀ p. 15 challenge to the historic status of wives and children as the legal property of husbands.

While the egalitarian family has become a more common pattern in the United States in recent decades—owing in good part to the activism of feminists beginning in the late 1960s and early 1970s—male dominance within the family has hardly disappeared. Sociologists have found that women are significantly more likely to leave their jobs when their husbands find better employment opportunities than men are when their wives receive desirable job offers (Bielby and Bielby 1992). And unfortunately, many husbands reinforce their power and control over wives and children through acts of domestic violence. Box 14-1 (page 328) considers cross-cultural findings about violence within the home.

Conflict theorists also view the family as an economic unit that contributes to societal injustice. The family is the basis for transferring power, property, and privilege from one generation to the next. Although the ◀ pp. 217–218 United States is widely viewed as a land of opportunity, social mobility is restricted in important ways. Children inherit the privileged or less-than-privileged social and economic status

Sociology in the Global Community

14-1   DOMESTIC VIOLENCE

"It's the same every Saturday night. The husband comes home drunk and beats her." This is how Tania Kucherenko describes her downstairs neighbors in Moscow, turning a deaf ear to the screams of terror and the sounds of furniture being overthrown and glass breaking. "There's nothing we can do. It's best not to interfere." Contempt for women runs deep in Russia, where women who dare to leave their husbands risk losing their legal status, a place to live, and the right to work (Bennett 1997:A1).

Wife battering and other forms of domestic violence are not confined to Russia. Drawing on studies conducted throughout the world, we can make the following generalizations:

- Women are most at risk of violence from the men they know.
- Violence against women occurs in all socioeconomic groups.
- Family violence is at least as dangerous as assaults committed by strangers.

- Though women sometimes exhibit violent behavior toward men, the majority of violent acts that cause injury are perpetrated by men against women.
- Violence within intimate relationships tends to escalate over time.
- Emotional and psychological abuse can be at least as debilitating as physical abuse.

> The family can be a dangerous place not only for women but also for children and the elderly.

- Use of alcohol exacerbates family violence but does not cause it.

Using the conflict and feminist models, researchers have found that in relationships in which the inequality between men and women is great, the likelihood of assault on wives increases dramatically. This discovery suggests that much of the violence between intimates, even when sexual in nature, is about power rather than sex.

The family can be a dangerous place not only for women but also for children and the elderly. In 2000, public agencies in the United States received more than 3 million reports of child abuse and/or neglect. That means reports were filed on about 1 out of every 25 children. Another national study found that 1 million violent crimes a year are committed by current or former spouses, boyfriends, or girlfriends.

Let's Discuss

1. Do you know of a family that has experienced domestic violence? Did the victim(s) seek outside help, and if so, was it effective?
2. Why might the degree of equality in a relationship correlate to the likelihood of domestic violence? How might conflict theorists explain this finding?

Sources: American Bar Association 1999; Bennett 1997; Gelles and Cornell 1990; Heise et al. 1999; Rennison and Welchans 2000; J. J. Wilson 2000.

of their parents (and in some cases, of earlier generations as well). As conflict theorists point out, the social class of parents significantly influences children's socialization experiences and the degree of protection they receive. This means that the socioeconomic status of a child's family will have a marked influence on his or her nutrition, health care, housing, educational opportunities, and in many respects, life chances as an adult. For this reason, conflict theorists argue that the family helps to maintain inequality.

Interactionist View

Interactionists focus on the micro level of family and other intimate relationships. They are interested in how individuals interact with one another, whether they are cohabiting partners or longtime married couples. For example, in a study of both Black and White two-parent households, researchers found that when fathers are more involved with their children (reading to them, helping

them with homework, or restricting their television viewing) children have fewer behavior problems, get along better with others, and are more responsible (Mosley and Thomson 1995).

Another interactionist study might examine the role of the stepparent. The increased number of single parents who remarry has sparked an interest in those who are helping to raise other people's children. Studies have found that stepmothers are more likely than that stepfathers to accept the blame for bad relations with their stepchildren. Interactionists theorize that stepfathers (like most fathers) may simply be unaccustomed to interacting directly with children when the mother isn't there (Bray and Kelly 1999; Furstenberg and Cherlin 1991).

Feminist View

Because "women's work" has traditionally focused on family life, feminist sociologists have taken a strong interest in the family as a social institution. As we saw in

p. 294 Chapter 12, research on gender roles in child care and household chores has been extensive. Sociologists have looked particularly closely at how women's work outside the home impacts their child care and housework—duties Arlie Hochschild (1989, 1990) has referred to as the "second shift." Today, researchers recognize that for many women, the second shift includes the care of aging parents as well.

Feminist theorists have urged social scientists and social agencies to rethink the notion that families in which no adult male is present are automatically a cause for concern, or even dysfunctional. They have also contributed to research on single women, single-parent households, and lesbian couples. In the case of single mothers, researchers have focused on the resiliency of many such households, despite economic stress. According to

Table 14-1	Sociological Perspectives on the Family
Theoretical Perspective	**Emphasis**
Functionalist	The family as a contributor to social stability Roles of family members
Conflict	The family as a perpetuator of inequality Transmission of poverty or wealth across generations
Interactionist	Relationships among family members
Feminist	Family as a perpetuator of gender roles Female-headed households

Interactionists are particularly interested in the ways in which mothers and fathers relate to each other and to their children. This mother and her two children are expressing a close and loving relationship, one of the foundations of a strong family.

Velma McBride Murray and her colleagues (2001) at the University of Georgia, such studies show that among African Americans, single mothers draw heavily on kinfolk for material resources, parenting advice, and social support. Considering feminist research on the family as a whole, one researcher concluded that the family is the "source of women's strength" (L. Richardson et al. 2001:297).

Finally, feminists stress the need to investigate neglected topics in family studies. For instance, in a small but significant number of dual-income households, the wife earns a higher income than the husband. Sociologist Suzanne Bianchi estimates that in 11 percent of marriages, the wife earns at least 60 percent of the family's income. Yet beyond individual case studies, little research has been done on how these families may differ from those in which the husband is the major breadwinner (Tyre and McGinn 2003:47).

Table 14-1 summarizes the four major theoretical perspectives on the family.

MARRIAGE AND FAMILY

Currently, close to 90 percent of all men and women in the United States marry at least once during their lifetimes. Historically, the most consistent aspect of family life in this country has been the high rate of marriage. In fact, despite the high rate of divorce, there are some indications of a miniboom in marriages of late.

In this part of the chapter, we will examine various aspects of love, marriage, and parenthood in the United States and contrast them with cross-cultural examples. Though we're used to thinking of romance and mate selection as strictly a matter of individual preference, sociological analysis tells us that social institutions and distinctive cultural norms and values also play an important role.

Courtship and Mate Selection

"My rugby mates would roll over in their graves," says Tom Buckley of his online courtship and subsequent marriage to Terri Muir. But Tom and Terri are hardly alone these days in turning to the Internet for matchmaking services. Today, thousands of websites are dedicated to helping people find mates; one service alone claims 2 million subscribers. Though prospective brides and grooms typically expect to find that special someone within a year of signing up, 9 out of 10 admit they have had fewer than five dates during that period. Yet success stories do occur. Tom and Terri carried on their romance via e-mail for a year before they met. According to Tom, "E-mail made it easier to communicate because neither one of us was the type to walk up to someone in the gym or a bar and say 'You're the fuel to my fire'" (Match.com 2003; B. Morris 1999:D1).

Internet romance is only the latest courtship practice. In the central Asian nation of Uzbekistan and many other traditional cultures, courtship is defined largely through the interaction of two sets of parents, who arrange marriages for their children. Typically, a young Uzbekistani woman will be socialized to eagerly anticipate her marriage to a man whom she has met only once, when he is presented to her family at the time of the final inspection of her dowry. In the United States, by contrast, courtship is conducted primarily by individuals who have a romantic interest in each other. In our culture, courtship often requires these individuals to rely heavily on intricate games, gestures, and signals. Despite such differences, courtship—whether in the United States, Uzbekistan, or elsewhere—is influenced by the norms and values of the larger society (Carol J. Williams 1995).

One unmistakable trend in mate selection is that the process appears to be taking longer today than in the past. A variety of factors, including concerns about financial security and personal independence, has contributed to this delay in marriage. Most people are now well into their 20s before they marry, both in the United States and in other countries (see Figure 14-2).

Aspects of Mate Selection

Many societies have explicit or unstated rules that define potential mates as acceptable or unacceptable. These norms can be distinguished in terms of endogamy and exogamy. *Endogamy* (from the Greek *endon,* "within") specifies the groups within which a spouse must be found, and prohibits marriage with others. For example,

in the United States, many people are expected to marry within their own racial, ethnic, or religious group, and are strongly discouraged or even prohibited from marrying outside the group. Endogamy is intended to reinforce the cohesiveness of the group by suggesting to the young that they should marry someone "of our own kind."

In contrast, *exogamy* (from the Greek *exo,* "outside") requires mate selection outside certain groups, usually one's own family or certain kinfolk. The *incest taboo,* a social norm common to virtually all societies, prohibits sexual relationships between certain culturally specified relatives. For people in the United States, this taboo means that we must marry outside the nuclear family. We cannot marry our siblings, and in most states we cannot marry our first cousins.

FIGURE 14-2

Percentage of People Aged 20 to 24 Ever Married, Selected Countries

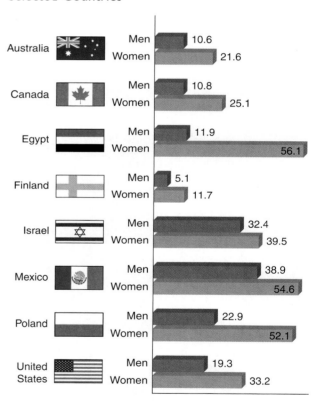

Source: United Nations Population Division 2001.

> **Think About It**
> Why is the percentage of young women who are married particularly high in Egypt, Mexico, and Poland? Particularly low in Finland?

Endogamous restrictions may be seen as preferences for one group over another. In the United States, such preferences are most obvious in racial barriers. Until the 1960s, some states outlawed interracial marriage. Nevertheless, the number of marriages between African Americans and Whites in the United States has increased more than seven times in recent decades, jumping from 51,000 in 1960 to 363,000 in 2000. Moreover, 25 percent of married Asian American women and 12 percent of married Asian American men are married to a person who is not of Asian descent. Marriage across ethnic lines is even greater among Hispanics; 27 percent of all married Hispanics have a non-Hispanic spouse. But while all these examples of racial exogamy are noteworthy, endogamy is still the social norm in the United States (Bureau of the Census 1998a, 2002a:47).

The Love Relationship

Today's generation of college students seems more likely to "hook up" or cruise in large packs than to engage in the romantic dating relationships of their parents and grandparents. Still, at some point in their adult lives, the great majority of today's students will meet someone they love and enter into a long-term relationship that focuses on creating a family.

Parents in the United States tend to value love highly as a rationale for marriage, and they encourage their children to develop intimate relationships based on love and affection. Songs, films, books, magazines, television shows, and even cartoons and comic books reinforce the theme of love. At the same time, our society expects parents and peers to help a person confine his or her search for a mate to "socially acceptable" members of the opposite sex.

Most people in the United States take the importance of falling in love for granted, but the coupling of love and marriage is by no means a cultural universal. Many of the world's cultures give priority in mate selection to factors other than romantic feelings. In societies with *arranged marriages* engineered by parents or religious authorities, economic considerations play a significant role. The newly married couple is expected to develop a feeling of love *after* the legal union is formalized, if at all.

Even within the United States, some subcultures carry on the arranged marriage practices of their native cultures. Among the Sikhs and Hindus who have immigrated from India, and among Islamic Muslims and Hasidic Jews, young people allow their parents or designated matchmakers to find spouses within their ethnic community. As one young Sikh declared, "I will definitely marry who my parents wish. They know me better than I know myself." Young people who have emigrated without their families often turn to the Internet to find partners who

Interracial unions, which are becoming increasingly common and accepted, are blurring definitions of race. Would the children of this interracial couple be considered Black or White?

share their background and goals. Matrimonial ads for the Indian community run on such websites as SuitableMatch.com and Indolink.com. As one Hasidic Jewish woman noted, the system of arranged marriages "isn't perfect, and it doesn't work for everyone, but this is the system we know and trust, the way we couple, and the way we learn to love. So it works for most of us" (R. Segall 1998:48, 53).

Use Your Sociological Imagination

Your parents and/or a matchmaker are going to arrange a marriage for you. What kind of mate will they select? Will your chances of having a successful marriage be better or worse than if you selected your own mate?

Variations in Family Life and Intimate Relationships

Within the United States, social class, race, and ethnicity create variations in family life. Studying these variations will give us a more sophisticated understanding of contemporary family styles in our country.

FIGURE 14-3

Rise of One-Parent Families among Whites, African Americans, Hispanics, and Asians or Pacific Islanders in the United States

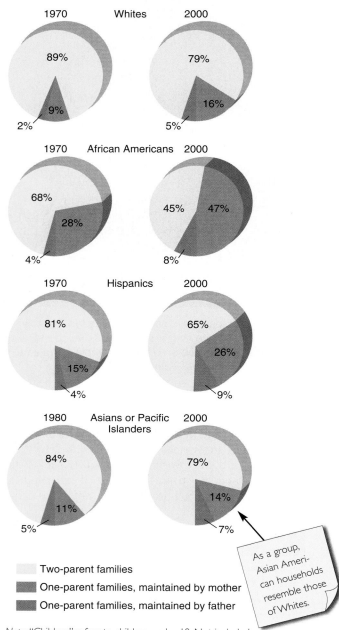

Two-parent families

One-parent families, maintained by mother

One-parent families, maintained by father

As a group, Asian American households resemble those of Whites.

Note: "Children" refers to children under 18. Not included are unrelated people living together with no children present. Early data for Asian Americans are for 1980.

Source: Bureau of the Census 1994:63; Fields and Casper 2001:7.

Social Class Differences

Various studies have documented the differences in family organization among social classes in the United States.

In the upper class, the emphasis is on lineage and maintenance of family position. If you are in the upper class, you are not simply a member of a nuclear family, but rather a member of a larger family tradition (think of the Rockefellers or the Kennedys). As a result, upper-class families are quite concerned about what they see as proper training for children.

Lower-class families do not often have the luxury of worrying about the "family name"; they must first struggle to pay their bills and survive the crises often associated with a life of poverty. Such families are more likely to have only one parent at home, which creates special challenges in child care and financial needs. Children from lower-class families typically assume adult responsibilities—including marriage and parenthood—at an earlier age than children from affluent homes. In part, that is because they may lack the money needed to remain in school.

Social class differences in family life are less striking today than they once were. In the past, family specialists agreed that the contrasts in child-rearing practices were pronounced. Lower-class families were found to be more authoritarian in rearing children and more inclined to use physical punishment. Middle-class families were more permissive and more restrained in punishing their children. However, these differences may have narrowed as more and more families from all social classes turned to the same books, magazines, and even television talk shows for advice on rearing children (Kohn 1970; Luster et al. 1989).

Among the poor, women often play a significant role in the economic support of the family. Men may earn low wages, may be unemployed, or may be entirely absent from the family. In 2001, 26.4 percent of all families headed by women with no husband present were below the government poverty line. The rate for married couples was only 4.9 percent (Proctor and Dalaker 2002:3).

Many racial and ethnic groups appear to have distinctive family characteristics. However, racial and class factors are often closely related. In examining family life among racial and ethnic minorities, keep in mind that certain patterns may result from class as well as cultural factors.

Racial and Ethnic Differences

The subordinate status of racial and ethnic minorities in the United States profoundly affects their family lives. For example, the lower incomes of African Americans, Native Americans, most Hispanic groups, and selected Asian American groups make creating and maintaining successful marital unions a difficult task. The economic restructuring of the last 50 years, described by sociologist p. 214 William Julius Wilson (1996) and others, has especially affected people living in inner cities and desolate rural areas, such as reservations. Furthermore, the immigration policy of the United States has complicated the successful relocation of intact families from Asia and Latin America.

The African American family suffers from many negative and inaccurate stereotypes. It is true that in a significantly higher proportion of Black than White families, no husband is present in the home (see Figure 14-3). Yet Black single mothers often belong to stable, functioning kin networks, despite the pressures of sexism and racism. Members of these networks—predominantly female kin such as mothers, grandmothers, and aunts—ease financial strains by sharing goods and services. In addition to these strong kinship bonds, Black family life has emphasized deep religious commitment and high aspirations for achievement. The strengths of the Black family were evident during slavery, when Blacks demonstrated a remarkable ability to maintain family ties despite the fact that they had no legal protections, and in fact were often forced to separate (Willie and Reddick 2003).

Sociologists have also taken note of differences in family patterns among other racial and ethnic groups. For example, Mexican American men have been described as exhibiting a sense of virility, personal worth, and pride in their maleness that is called *machismo.* Mexican Americans are also described as being more familistic than many other subcultures. *Familism* refers to pride in the extended family, expressed through the maintenance of close ties and strong obligations to kinfolk outside the immediate family. Traditionally, Mexican Americans have placed proximity to their extended families above other needs and desires.

These family patterns are changing, however, in response to changes in Latinos' social class standing, educational achievements, and occupations. Like other Americans, career-oriented Latinos in search of a mate but short on spare time are turning to Internet sites. As Latinos and other groups assimilate into the dominant culture of the United States, their family lives take on both the positive and negative characteristics associated with White households (Becerra 1999; Vega 1995).

Within a racial or ethnic minority, family ties can serve as an economic boost. For example, Korean immigrants to the United States generally begin small service or retail businesses that involve all adult family members. To obtain the funds needed to begin a business, they often pool their resources through a *kye* (pronounced KAY)—an association (not limited to kinfolk) that grants money to members on a rotating basis, so they can gain access to additional capital. The *kye* allows Korean Americans to start small businesses long before other minorities in similar economic circumstances. Such rotating credit associations are not unique to Korean Americans;

other Asian Americans as well as West Indians living in the United States have used them (H. Lee 1999).

Child-Rearing Patterns in Family Life

The Nayars of southern India acknowledge the biological role of fathers, but the mother's eldest brother is responsible for her children. In contrast, uncles play only a peripheral role in child care in the United States. Caring for children is a universal function of the family, yet the ways in which different societies assign this function to family members can vary significantly. Even within the United States, child-rearing patterns are varied. We'll take a look here at parenthood and grandparenthood, adoption, dual-income families, single-parent families, and stepfamilies.

Parenthood and Grandparenthood

The socialization of children is essential to the maintenance of any culture. Consequently, parenthood is one of the most important (and most demanding) social roles in the United States. Sociologist Alice Rossi (1968, 1984) has identified four factors that complicate the transition to parenthood and the role of socialization. First, there is little anticipatory socialization for the social p. 90 role of caregiver. The normal school curriculum gives scant attention to the subjects most relevant to successful family life, such as child care and home maintenance. Second, only limited learning occurs during the period of pregnancy itself. Third, the transition to parenthood is quite abrupt. Unlike adolescence, it is not prolonged; unlike the transition to work, the duties of caregiving cannot be taken on gradually. Finally, in Rossi's view, our society lacks clear and helpful guidelines for successful parenthood. There is little consensus on how parents can produce happy and well-adjusted offspring—or even on what it means to be well-adjusted. For these reasons, socialization for parenthood involves difficult challenges for most men and women in the United States.

One recent development in family life in the United States has been the extension of parenthood, as adult children continue to live at home or return home after college. In 2000, 56 percent of men and 43 percent of women ages 18 to 24 lived with their parents. Some of these adult children are still pursuing an education, but in many instances, financial difficulties lie at the heart of these living arrangements. While rents and real estate prices have skyrocketed, salaries for younger workers have not kept pace, and many find themselves unable to afford their own homes. Moreover, with many marriages now ending in divorce—most commonly in the first seven years of marriage—divorced sons and daughters are returning to live with their parents, sometimes with their own children (Fields and Casper 2001).

What Is a Family?

amiliies change over time. Milton Rogovin (1994) first photographed residents of the Lower West Side, a working-class neighborhood in Buffalo, New York, in the early 1970s. He returned to the neighborhood twice over a 20-year period, photographing many of the same people and documenting their changing lives and families. Rogovin's time-lapse portraits highlight the social dynamics of the family as it forms, grows, and develops from one generation to the next. As a couple makes room for children, then watches them mature and bear children of their own, their relationship with each other and with the larger society changes along with their family.

In 1973 this couple's four children were still young. When Rogovin returned in 1986, the children had grown but were still single. Six years later, in 1992, the original six-member household had become an extended family with four grandchildren.

1973

1986

1992

Table 14-2	Foreign-Born Adoptees by Top Six Countries of Origin, 1989 and 2002				
1989			**2002**		
Number of Children	**Country**	**Rank**	**Number of Children**	**Country**	
3,544	S. Korea	1	5,053	China	
736	Colombia	2	4,939	Russia	
648	India	3	2,219	Guatemala	
465	Philippines	4	1,779	S. Korea	
253	Chile	5	1,106	Ukraine	
252	Paraguay	6	819	Kazakhstan	
Total, all countries 6,654			20,099		

Source: Department of State 2003.

Think About It

Why did so many foreign-born adopted children come from these countries in particular? What accounts for the change in countries of origin from 1989 to 2002?

Is this living arrangement a positive development for family members? Social scientists have just begun to examine the phenomenon, sometimes called the "boomerang generation" or the "full-nest syndrome" in the popular press. One survey in Virginia seemed to show that neither the parents nor their adult children were happy about continuing to live together. The children often felt resentful and isolated, but the parents suffered too: Learning to live without children in the home is an essential stage of adult life, and may even be a significant turning point for a marriage (*Berkeley Wellness Letter* 1990; Mogelonsky 1996).

In some homes, the full nest holds grandchildren. Census data for the year 2000 showed that 5.6 million grandparents lived with their grandchildren, and fully 42 percent of them were responsible for the youngsters. Special difficulties are inherent in such relationships, including legal custodial concerns, financial issues, and emotional problems for adults and youths alike. Little surprise that support groups such as Grandparents as Parents have emerged to provide assistance (Peterson 2001).

Adoption

In a legal sense, *adoption* is a "process that allows for the transfer of the legal rights, responsibilities, and privileges of parenthood" to a new legal parent or parents (E. Cole 1985:638). In many cases, these rights are transferred from a biological parent or parents (often called birth parents) to an adoptive parent or parents.

Viewed from a functionalist perspective, government has a strong interest in encouraging adoption. Policymakers, in fact, have both a humanitarian and a financial stake in the process. In theory, adoption offers a stable family environment for children who otherwise might not receive satisfactory care. Moreover, government data show that unwed mothers who keep their babies tend to be of lower socioeconomic status, and often require public assistance to support their children. Government can lower its social welfare expenses, then, if children are transferred to economically self-sufficient families. From a conflict perspective, however, such financial considerations raise the ugly specter of adoption as a means through which affluent (often infertile) couples "buy" the children of the poor (Bachrach 1986).

Adoption by relatives is still the most common type of adoption in the United States. In most cases, a stepparent adopts the children of a spouse. Adoptions between unrelated persons have been growing in number, however. There are two legal methods of adopting an unrelated person: the adoption may be arranged through a licensed agency, or in some states it may be arranged through a private agreement sanctioned by the courts.

Adopted children may come from the United States or from abroad. In 2002, more than 20,000 children entered the United States as the adopted children of U.S. citizens (see Table 14-2).

In some cases the adopters are not married. In 1995, an important court decision in New York held that a couple does not need to be married to adopt a child. Under this ruling, unmarried heterosexual couples, lesbian couples, and gay male couples can all legally adopt children in New York. Writing for the majority, Chief Justice Judith Kaye argued that by expanding the boundaries of who can be legally recognized as parents, the state may be able to assist more children in securing "the best possible home." With this ruling, New York became the third state (after Vermont and Massachusetts) to recognize the right of unmarried couples to adopt children (Dao 1995).

For every child who is adopted, many more remain the wards of state-sponsored child protective services. At any given time, over half a million children in the United States are living in foster care. These children are often moved from family to family during their childhood and adolescence. Each year about 20,000 of them reach the age of 18 and enter adulthood without the financial or emotional support of a permanent family (Children's Bureau 2002; Carol W. Williams 1999).

Dual-Income Families

The idea of a family consisting of a wage-earning husband and a wife who stays at home has largely given way to the *dual-income household.* Among married people between the ages of 25 and 34, 96 percent of the men and 70 percent of the women are in the labor force.

Why has there been such a rise in the number of dual-income couples? A major factor is economic need. In 2000, the median income for households with both partners employed was 85 percent more than in households in which only one person was working outside the home ($63,816, compared with $34,423). Of course, because of such work-related costs as child care, not all of a family's second wage is genuine additional income. Other factors that have contributed to the rise of the dual-income model include the nation's declining birthrate, the increase in the proportion of women with a college education, the shift in the economy of the United States from manufacturing to service industries, and the impact of the feminist movement in changing women's consciousness (Bureau of the Census 2002a:372; 438).

Single-Parent Families

In the United States during the late 19th century, immigration and urbanization made it increasingly difficult to maintain *Gemeinschaft* communities, where everyone knew one another and shared the responsibility for un-

wed mothers and their children. In 1883, the Florence Crittenton Houses were founded in New York City—and subsequently around the nation—as refuges for prostitutes (then stigmatized as "fallen women"). Within a few years, the Crittenton homes began accepting unwed mothers as residents. By the early 1900s, sociologist W. E. B. Du Bois (1911) had noted that the institutionalization of unwed mothers was occurring in segregated facilities. At the time he was writing, there were seven homes for unwed Black mothers nationwide, as well as one Crittenton home reserved for that purpose.

In recent decades, the stigma attached to unwed mothers and other single parents has significantly diminished. *Single-parent families,* in which only one parent is present to care for the children, can hardly be viewed as a rarity in the United States. In 2000, a single parent headed about 21 percent of White families with children under 18, 35 percent of Hispanic families with children, and 55 percent of African American families with children (see Figure 14-3 on page 332).

The lives of single parents and their children are not inevitably more difficult than life in a traditional nuclear family. It is as inaccurate to assume that a single-parent family is necessarily deprived as it is to assume that a two-parent family is always secure and happy. Nevertheless, life in a single-parent family can be extremely stressful, in both economic and emotional terms. A family headed by a single mother faces especially difficult problems when the mother is a teenager.

Why might low-income teenage women wish to have children and face the obvious financial difficulties of motherhood? Viewed from an interactionist perspective, these women tend to have low self-esteem and limited options; a child may provide a sense of motivation and purpose for a teenager whose economic worth in our society is limited at best. Given the barriers that many young women face because of their gender, race, ethnicity, and class, many teenagers may believe they have little to lose and much to gain by having a child.

According to a widely held stereotype, "unwed mothers" and "babies having babies" in the United States are predominantly African American. However, this view is not entirely accurate. African Americans account for a disproportionate share of births to unmarried women and teenagers, but the majority of all babies born to unmarried teenage mothers are born to White adolescents. Moreover, since 1980, birthrates among Black teenagers have declined steadily (B. Hamilton et al. 2003; J. Martin et al. 2002; Ventura et al. 2001).

Although 82 percent of single parents in the United States are mothers, the number of households headed by single fathers more than quadrupled over the period 1980 to 2000. The stereotypes of single fathers hold that they raise only boys or older children. In fact, however, about 44 percent of children living in such households are girls, and almost one-third of single fathers care for preschoolers. Though single mothers often develop social networks, single fathers are typically more isolated. In addition, they must deal with schools and social service agencies that are more accustomed to women as custodial parents (Fields 2001).

What about single fathers who do not head the household? This is typically a neglected group for research purposes, but one study of low-income unmarried fathers in Philadelphia produced some unexpected findings. When asked what their lives would be like without children, many responded that they would be dead or in jail. This was true even of those fathers who had very little to do with their children. Apparently, the mere fact of fathering children prompts men to get jobs, stay in the community, and stay healthy. Many of these men were upset that they had to hand over money to the mothers without having a say in how it was spent, or in some cases even receiving legal access to their offspring (P. Cohen 1998; Rhodes 2000).

Stepfamilies

Approximately 45 percent of all people in the United States will marry, divorce, and then remarry. The rising rates of divorce and remarriage have led to a noticeable increase in stepfamily relationships. In 1991, 9.4 percent of all children lived with a stepparent, but just five years later, that figure had increased to 16.5 percent (Furukawa 1994:4; Kreider and Fields 2002).

The exact nature of blended families has social significance for adults and children alike. Certainly resocialization is required when an adult becomes a stepparent or a child becomes a stepchild and stepsibling. Moreover, an important distinction must be made between first-time stepfamilies and households where there have been repeated divorces, breakups, or changes in custodial arrangements.

In evaluating the rise of stepfamilies, some observers have assumed that children would benefit from remarriage because they would be gaining a second custodial parent, and would potentially enjoy greater economic security. However, after reviewing many studies of stepfamilies, sociologist Andrew J. Cherlin (2002:476) concluded that "the well-being of children in stepfamilies is no better, on average, than the well-being of children in divorced, single-parent households."

Stepparents can play valuable and unique roles in their stepchildren's lives, but their involvement does not guarantee an improvement in family life. In fact, standards may decline. Studies suggest that children raised in families with stepmothers are likely to have less health

Most households in the United States do not consist of two parents living with their unmarried children.

care, education, and money spent on their food than children raised by biological mothers. The measures are also negative for children raised by stepfathers, but only half as negative as in the case of stepmothers. These results don't mean that stepmothers are "evil"—it may be that the stepmother holds back out of concern for seeming too intrusive, or relies mistakenly on the biological father to carry out parental duties (Lewin 2000).

DIVORCE

"Do you promise to love, honor, and cherish . . . until death do you part?" Every year, people of all social classes and racial and ethnic groups make this legally binding agreement. Yet an increasing number of these promises shatter in divorce.

Statistical Trends in Divorce

Just how common is divorce? Surprisingly, this is not a simple question; divorce statistics are difficult to interpret. The media frequently report that one out of every two marriages ends in divorce. But that figure is misleading, since many marriages last for decades. It is based on a comparison of all divorces that occur in a single year (regardless of when the couples were married) with the number of new marriages in the same year.

In the United States, and many other countries, divorce began to increase in the late 1960s, but then started to level off and has even declined since the late 1980s (see Figure 14-4). This trend is due partly to the aging of the baby boomer population and the corresponding decline in the proportion of people of marriageable age. But it also indicates an increase in marital stability in recent years.

Getting divorced obviously does not sour people on marriage. About two-thirds of divorced women and three-fourths of divorced men eventually remarry.

Women are less likely than men to remarry because many retain custody of their children after a divorce, which complicates a new adult relationship (Bianchi and Spain 1996).

Some people regard the nation's high rate of remarriage as an endorsement of the institution of marriage, but it does lead to the new challenges of a kin network composed of both current and prior marital relationships. Such networks can be particularly complex if children are involved or if an ex-spouse remarries.

Factors Associated with Divorce

Perhaps the most important factor in the increase in divorce over the last hundred years has been the greater social *acceptance* of divorce. It's no longer considered necessary to endure an unhappy marriage. More important, various religious denominations have relaxed their negative attitudes toward divorce, and most religious leaders no longer treat it as a sin.

The growing acceptance of divorce is a worldwide phenomenon. In 1998, a few months after a highly publicized divorce by pop superstar Seiko Matsuda, the prime minister of Japan released a survey showing that 54 percent of those polled supported uncontested divorce, compared to 20 percent in 1979 (Kyodo News International 1998).

A few other factors deserve mention:

- Many states have adopted more liberal divorce laws in the last two decades. No-fault divorce laws, which allow a couple to end their marriage without fault on either side (by specifying adultery, for instance), accounted for an initial surge in the divorce rate after they were introduced in the 1970s, but appear to have had little effect beyond that.
- Divorce has become a more practical option in newly formed families, since families tend to have fewer children now than in the past.
- A general increase in family incomes, coupled with the availability of free legal aid for some poor people, has meant that more couples can afford costly divorce proceedings.
- As society provides greater opportunities for women, more and more wives are becoming less dependent on their husbands, both economically and emotionally. They may feel more able to leave a marriage if it seems hopeless.

FIGURE 14-4

Trends in Marriage and Divorce in the United States, 1920–2002

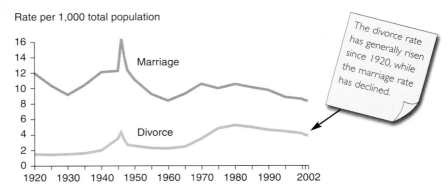

Sources: Bureau of the Census 1975:64, 2000a; National Vital Statistics Reports 2003:3.

Impact of Divorce on Children

Divorce is traumatic for all involved, as Cornel West made clear in the excerpt that opened this chapter. But it has special meaning for the more than 1 million children whose parents divorce each year (see Box 14-2, page 340).

Of course, for some of these children, divorce signals the welcome end to being witness to a very dysfunctional relationship. A national sample conducted by sociologists Paul R. Amato and Alan Booth (1997) showed that in about a third of divorces, the children benefit from parental separation because it lessens their exposure to conflict. But in about 70 percent of divorces, the parents engaged in a low level of conflict; in those cases, the realities of divorce appeared to be harder for the children to bear than living with the marital unhappiness. Other researchers, using differing definitions of conflict, have found greater unhappiness for children living in homes with marital differences. Still, it would be simplistic to assume that children are automatically better off following the breakup of their parents' marriage. The interests of the parents do not necessarily serve children well.

Use Your Sociological Imagination   www.mhhe.com/schaefer9

In a society that maximizes the welfare of all family members, how easy should it be for couples to divorce? How easy should it be to get married?

DIVERSE LIFESTYLES

Marriage is no longer the presumed route from adolescence to adulthood. In fact, it has lost much of its social significance as a rite of passage. The nation's marriage rate has declined since 1960 because people are postponing marriage until later in life, and because more

Research in Action

14-2 THE LINGERING IMPACT OF DIVORCE

What happens to the children of divorce? Early research suggested that the negative effects of divorce on children were confined to the first few years following a breakup. According to these studies, most children eventually adjusted to the change in family structure and went on to live normal lives. But recent studies suggest that the effects of divorce may linger much longer than scholars at first suspected, peaking in the adult years, when grown children are attempting to establish their own marriages and families.

A foremost proponent of this view is psychologist Judith A. Wallerstein, who has been conducting qualitative research on the effects of divorce on children since 1971. Wallerstein has been following the original 131 children in her study for 30 years; her subjects are now ages 28 to 43. She is convinced that these adult children of divorce have had greater difficulty than other adults in forming and maintaining intimate relationships because they have never witnessed the daily give-and-take of a successful marital partnership.

Another researcher, sociologist Paul R. Amato, agrees that divorce can affect children into adulthood, but for a differ-

ent reason. Amato thinks that the parents' decision to end their marriage lies at the root of the higher-than-normal divorce rate among their children. In this study, based on telephone interviews, children whose parents had divorced had a 30 percent divorce rate themselves, which is 12 to 13 percent higher than the divorce rate among children whose parents had *not* divorced. Significantly, chil-

> Recent studies suggest that the effects of divorce may linger much longer than scholars at first suspected.

dren of parents who did not divorce had roughly the same divorce rate regardless of whether the level of conflict in their parents' marriage was low or high. The parental example that a marriage contract can be broken—not the demonstration of poor relationship skills—is what makes an adult child more vulnerable than others to divorce, Amato thinks.

Sociologist Andrew J. Cherlin concedes that divorce can have lingering ef-

fects, but thinks the potential for harm has been exaggerated. Cherlin, who has conducted quantitative analyses of the effects of divorce on thousands of children, finds that parental divorce does elevate children's risk of emotional problems, school withdrawal, and teen pregnancy. But most children, he emphasizes, do not develop those problems. Even Wallerstein admits that the ill effects of divorce do not apply across the board. Some children seem to be strengthened by the crisis, she observes, and go on to lead highly successful lives, both personally and professionally.

Let's Discuss

1. Do you know any adult children of divorce who have had difficulty establishing successful marriages? If so, what seems to be the problem, an inability to handle conflict or a lack of commitment to the marriage?

2. What practical conclusions should we draw from the research on children of divorce? Should couples stay together for the sake of their children?

Sources: Amato 2001; Amato and Sobolewski 2001; Bumiller 2000; Cherlin 2002; J. Wallerstein et al. 2000. For a different view, see Hetherington and Kelly 2002.

couples, including same-sex couples, are deciding to form partnerships without marriage.

Cohabitation

Saint Paul once wrote, "It is better to marry than to burn." However, as journalist Tom Ferrell (1979) has suggested, more people than ever "prefer combustible to connubial bliss." One of the most dramatic trends of recent years has been the tremendous increase in male–female couples who choose to live together without marrying, a practice called *cohabitation.*

About 37 percent of all *currently* married couples in the United States say that they lived together before marriage. This percentage is likely to increase. The number of unmarried-couple households in the United States rose

sixfold in the 1960s and increased another 72 percent between 1990 and 2000. Presently over 8 percent of opposite-sex couples are unmarried. Cohabitation is more common among African Americans and American Indians than among other racial and ethnic groups; it is least common among Asian Americans. Figure 14-5 shows regional variations in the incidence of cohabitation (Fields and Casper 2001; Lyons 2002a; T. Simmons and O'Connell 2003).

In much of Europe, cohabitation is so common that the general sentiment seems to be "Love, yes; marriage, maybe." In Iceland, 62 percent of all children are born to single mothers; in France, Great Britain, and Norway, the proportion is about 40 percent. Government policies in these countries make few legal distinctions between married and unmarried couples or households (Lyall 2002).

People commonly associate cohabitation only with college campuses or sexual experimentation. But according to a study done in Los Angeles, working couples are almost twice as likely to cohabit as college students. And census data show that in 2000, 41 percent of unmarried couples had one or more children present in the household. These cohabitants are more like spouses than dating partners. Moreover, in contrast to the common perception that people who cohabit have never been married, researchers report that about half of all people involved in cohabitation in the United States have been previously married. Cohabitation serves as a temporary or permanent alternative to matrimony for many men and women who have experienced their own or their parents' divorces (Fields and Casper 2001; Popenoe and Whitehead 1999).

Recent research has documented significant increases in cohabitation among older people in the United States. For example, census data indicate that in 1980, 340,000 cohabiting opposite-sex couples were over the age of 45. By 1999, there were 1,108,000 such couples—three times as many. Older couples may choose cohabitation rather than marriage for many reasons: because of religious differences, to preserve the full Social Security benefits they receive as single people, out of fear of commitment, to avoid upsetting children from previous marriages, because one partner or both are not legally divorced, or because one or both have lived through a spouse's illness and death, and do not want to do so again. But some older couples simply see no need for marriage, and report being happy simply living together (Bureau of the Census 2001a:48).

FIGURE 14-5

Unmarried-Couple Households by State

Note: Data are for 2000 and include both opposite-sex and same-sex partners. U.S. average is 9.1 percent.
Source: T. Simmons and O'Connell 2003:4.

Remaining Single

Looking at TV programs today, you would be justified in thinking that most households are composed of singles. Although that is not the case, it is true that more and

This young couple in England are cohabiting, an increasingly popular alternative to marriage in many countries today.

more people in the United States are *postponing* entry into first marriages. As of 2000, one out of every four households in the United States (accounting for over 26 million people) was a single-member household. Even so, fewer than 4 percent of women and men in the United States are likely to remain single throughout their lives (Bureau of the Census 2002a:46, 48).

The trend toward maintaining a single lifestyle for a longer period is related to the growing economic independence of young people. This trend is especially significant for women. Freed from financial needs, women

p. 292

don't necessarily need to marry to enjoy a satisfying life. Divorce, late marriage, and longevity also figure into this trend.

There are many reasons why a person may choose not to marry. Some singles do not want to limit their sexual intimacy to one lifetime partner. Some men and women do not want to become highly dependent on any one person—and do not want anyone depending heavily on them. In a society that values individuality and self-fulfillment, the single lifestyle can offer certain freedoms that married couples may not enjoy.

Remaining single represents a clear departure from societal expectations; indeed, it has been likened to "being single on Noah's Ark." A single adult must confront the inaccurate view that he or she is always lonely, is a workaholic, or is immature. These stereotypes help to support the traditional assumption in the United States and most other societies that to be truly happy and fulfilled, a person must get married and raise a family. To counter these societal expectations, singles have formed numerous support groups, such as Alternative to Marriage Project (www.unmarried.org).

Singlehood—living without a partner and without children—also has social implications for the broader society. According to Robert Putnam of Harvard University, people in the United States are now less active both politically and socially than they were in the 1970s, due in part to the fact that more of them are living the single life. Experts worry about a potential decline in support for local schools, as well as a probable rise in the number of elderly people needing home care (Belsie 2001).

Lesbian and Gay Relationships

We were both raised in middle-class families, where the expectation was we would go to college, we would become educated, we'd get a nice white-collar job, we'd move up and own a nice house in the suburbs. And that's exactly what we've done. (*New York Times* 1998:B2)

Sound like an average family? The only break with traditional expectations in this case is that the "we" described here is a gay couple.

The lifestyles of lesbians and gay men are varied. Some live in long-term, monogamous relationships. Some live with children from former heterosexual marriages or adopted children. Some live alone, others with roommates. Others remain married and do not publicly acknowledge their homosexuality. Based on election exit polls, researchers for the National Health and Social Life Survey and the Voter News Service estimate that 2 to 5 percent of the adult population identify themselves as either gay or lesbian. An analysis of the 2000 Census shows a minimum of at least 600,000 gay households, and a gay and lesbian adult population approaching 10 million (Lauman et al. 1994b:293; David M. Smith and Gates 2001).

Recognition of same-sex partnerships is not uncommon in Europe, including Denmark, Holland, Switzerland, France, Belgium, and parts of Germany, Italy, and Spain. In 2001, the Netherlands converted their "registered same-sex partnerships" into full-fledged marriages, with provisions for divorce. The trend is toward recognition in North America as well. In Canada in 2003, same-sex marriages were upheld as legal in the province of Ontario, with the expectation that proposed legislation would extend the policy to all of Canada. In the United States, as of 2003, 60 local jurisdictions had passed legislation allowing for registration of domestic partnerships, and 110 cities provided employee benefits that extend to domestic partnerships. Under such policies, a **domestic partnership** may be defined as two unrelated adults who share a mutually caring relationship, reside together, and agree to be jointly responsible for their dependents, basic living expenses, and other common necessities. Domestic partnership benefits can apply to couples' inheritance, parenting, pensions, taxation, housing, immigration, workplace fringe benefits, and health care. Even though the most passionate support for domestic partnership legislation has come from lesbian and gay male activists, the majority of those eligible for such benefits would be cohabiting heterosexual couples (American Civil Liberties Union 2001; Daley 2000; Ritter 2003).

Domestic partnership legislation, however, faces strong opposition from conservative religious and political groups. In the view of opponents, support for domestic partnership undermines the historic societal preference for the nuclear family. Advocates of domestic partnership counter that such relationships fulfill the same functions as the traditional family both for the individuals involved and for society, and should therefore enjoy the same legal protections and benefits. The gay couple quoted at the beginning of this section consider themselves a family unit, just like the nuclear family that lives down the street in their West Hartford, Connecticut, suburb. They cannot understand why they have been denied a family membership at their municipal swimming pool (*New York Times* 1998).

Marriage without Children

There has been a modest increase in childlessness in the United States. According to data from the census, about 16 to 17 percent of women will now complete their childbearing years without having borne any children, compared to 10 percent in 1980. As many as 20 percent of women in their 30s expect to remain childless (Clausen 2002).

Childlessness within marriage has generally been viewed as a problem that can be solved through such means as adoption and artificial insemination. More and more couples today, however, choose not to have children, and regard themselves as child-free, not childless. They do not believe that having children automatically follows from marriage, nor do they feel that reproduction is the duty of all married couples. Childless couples have formed support groups (with names like No Kidding) and set up websites on the Internet (Terry 2000).

Economic considerations have contributed to this shift in attitudes; having children has become quite expensive. According to a government estimate made in 2000, the average middle-class family will spend $156,890 to feed, clothe, and shelter a child from birth to age 18. If the child attends college, that amount could double, depending on the college chosen. Aware of the financial pressures, some couples are having fewer children than they otherwise might, and others are weighing the advantages of a child-free marriage (Bureau of the Census 2001a:429).

Childless couples are beginning to question current practices in the workplace. While applauding employers' efforts to provide child care and flexible p. 97 work schedules, some nevertheless express concern about tolerance of employees who leave early to take children to doctors, ballgames, or after-school classes. As more dual-career couples enter the paid labor force and struggle to balance career and familial responsibilities, conflicts with employees who have no children may increase (Burkett 2000).

Meanwhile, many childless couples who desperately want children are willing to try any means necessary to get pregnant. The social policy section that follows ex-

In a backlash against gay and lesbian efforts to legalize same-sex partnerships, some groups have mounted public demonstrations against such legislation.

plores the controversy surrounding recent advances in reproductive technology.

Use Your Sociological Imagination   www. mhhe.com /schaefer9

What would happen to our society if many more married couples suddenly decided not to have children? How would society change if cohabitation and/or singlehood became the norm?

SOCIAL POLICY and
THE FAMILY

Reproductive Technology

www.
mhhe.com
/schaefer9

The Issue

The 1997 feature film *Gattaca* told the story of a future in which genetic engineering enhanced people's genes. Those who were not "enhanced" in the womb—principally those whose parents could not afford the treatments—suffered discrimination throughout their lives. To borrow a line from the movie, "Your genes are your résumé."

Far-fetched? Perhaps, but today we are witnessing reproductive technologies that were regarded as so much science fiction just a generation ago. "Test tube" babies, frozen embryos, surrogate mothers, sperm and

The possibility of cloning humans, eerily foreshadowed in Andy Warhol's *The Twenty Marilyns,* poses major ethical dilemmas.

egg donation, and cloning of human cells are raising questions about the ethics of creating and shaping human life. To what extent should social policy encourage or discourage innovative reproductive technologies?

The Setting

In an effort to overcome infertility, many couples have turned to a recent reproductive advance known as in vitro fertilization (IVF). In this technique, an egg and a sperm are combined in a laboratory dish. If the egg is fertilized, the resulting embryo (the so-called test tube baby) is transferred to the woman's uterus. Combined with drug therapy, IVF increases the likelihood of a successful pregnancy.

The procedure also makes *multiple* births more likely. Between 1980 and 2000, the rate of triplets or even larger multiple births increased more than 500 percent. Obviously, these births result in substantially larger medical and child care expenses for the parents and present unique and difficult parenting challenges (J. Martin et al. 2002).

While using technology to enhance couples' ability to reproduce is a recent phenomenon, the first successful artificial insemination actually took place in 1884, in Philadelphia. However, beginning in the 1970s, the discovery of how to preserve sperm made the process much simpler, since it eliminated the inconvenience of matching ovulation cycles with sperm donations (Rifkin 1998).

Sociological Insights

Replacing personnel is a functional prerequisite that the family as a social institution performs. p. 112 Obviously, advances in reproductive technology allow childless couples to fulfill both personal and societal goals. The new technology also allows opportunities not previously considered. A small but growing number of same-sex couples are using donated sperm or eggs to bear genetically related children and fulfill their desire to have a family (Bruni 1998).

In the future depicted in *Gattaca*, the poor were at a disadvantage: They could not afford to control their lives genetically. Conflict theorists would note that today, the available reproductive technologies are often accessible only to the most affluent. Just as the techniques were being perfected, insurance companies announced that they were terminating coverage of advanced fertility treatments such as in vitro fertilization. For many infertile couples, cost is a major factor, according to a survey conducted by the Centers for Disease Control and Prevention. In vitro fertilization can cost about $10,000 for each procedure, and there is no guarantee that it will succeed (Stephen 1999).

Conflict theorists note further that while lower-class women have broad access to contraceptive coverage, they have limited access to infertility treatments. Sociologists Leslie King and Madonna Harrington Meyer (1997) conclude that class differences in access to reproductive services lead to a dualistic fertility policy in the United States, one that encourages births among the more affluent and discourages births among the poor, particularly those on Medicaid.

It is now becoming possible to *preselect* the sex of a baby. Beginning in 1998, at a cost of about $2,500, couples could purchase the expertise that would select the sperm more likely to produce a baby of a desired sex. Feminist theorists are watching this development closely. They are concerned that in societies in which men enjoy a higher status than women, use of this technology will effectively reduce the presence of women. In the United States initial indications suggest that couples using this procedure are just as likely to try to engineer a girl as a boy, but this development needs to be monitored in the future (Belkin 1999).

Interactionists observe that the quest for information and social support connected with reproductive technology has created new social networks. Like other special-interest groups, couples with infertility problems band together to share information, offer support to one another, and demand better treatment. They develop social networks—sometimes through voluntary associations or Internet support groups—through which they share information about new medical techniques, insurance plans, and the merits of particular physicians and hospitals. One Internet self-help group, Mothers of Supertwins, offers supportive services for mothers and lobbies for improved counseling at infertility clinics, to better prepare couples for the demands of many babies at one time (MOST 2003).

Policy Initiatives

In Japan, some infertile couples have caused controversy by using eggs or sperm donated by siblings for in vitro fertilization. This practice violates an ethical (though not a legal) ban on "extramarital fertilization," the use of genetic material from anyone other than a spouse for conception. While opinion is divided on this issue, most Japanese agree that there should be government guidelines on reproductive technology. Many nations, including England and Australia, bar payments to egg donors, resulting in very few donors in those countries. Even more countries limit how many times a man can donate sperm. Because the United States has no such restrictions, infertile foreigners who can afford the costs view this country as a land of opportunity (Efron 1998; Kolata 1998).

The legal and ethical issues connected with reproductive technology are immense. Many people think we should be preparing for the possibility of a human clone. At this time, however, industrial societies are hard-pressed to deal with present advances in reproductive technology, much less future ones. Already, reputable hospitals are mixing donated sperm and eggs to create embryos that they freeze for future use. This approach raises the possibility of genetic screening, as couples choose what they regard as the most "desirable" embryo—a "designer baby," in effect. Couples could select (some would say adopt) a frozen embryo that matches their requests in terms of race, sex, height, body type, eye color, intelligence, ethnic and religious background, and even national origin (Begley 1999; Rifkin 1998).

Let's Discuss

1. What ethical and legal issues do recent innovations in reproductive technology raise?
2. Do you think the ability to preselect the sex of a baby will result in an imbalance between the sexes? Why or why not?
3. If you were writing legislation to regulate reproductive technology, what guidelines (if any) would you include?

CHAPTER RESOURCES

Summary

The *family,* in its many varying forms, is present in all human cultures. This chapter examines the state of marriage, the family, and other intimate relationships in the United States and considers alternatives to the traditional nuclear family.

1. Families vary from culture to culture and even within the same culture.
2. The structure of the *extended family* can offer certain advantages over that of the *nuclear family.*
3. Societies determine kinship by descent from both parents *(bilateral descent),* from the father only *(patrilineal descent),* or from the mother only *(matrilineal descent).*
4. Sociologists do not agree on whether the *egalitarian family* has replaced the patriarchal family as the social norm in the United States.
5. William F. Ogburn outlined six basic functions of the family: reproduction, protection, socialization, regulation of sexual behavior, companionship, and the provision of social status.
6. Conflict theorists argue that male dominance of the family contributes to societal injustice and denies women opportunities that are extended to men.
7. Interactionists focus on how individuals interact in the family and in other intimate relationships.
8. Feminists stress the need to broaden research on the family. Like conflict theorists, they see the family's role in socializing children as the primary source of sexism.
9. Mates are selected in a variety of ways. Some marriages are arranged; in other societies people choose their own mates. Some societies require mates to be chosen within a certain group *(endogamy)* or outside certain groups *(exogamy).*
10. In the United States, family life varies with social class, race, and ethnic differences.
11. Currently, in the majority of all married couples in the United States, both husband and wife work outside the home.
12. *Single-parent families* account for an increasing proportion of U.S. families.
13. Among the factors that contribute to the rising divorce rate in the United States are greater social acceptance of divorce and the liberalization of divorce laws in many states.
14. More and more people are living together without marrying, a practice known as *cohabitation.* People are also staying single longer, and some married couples are deciding not to have children.
15. While many municipalities in the United States have passed *domestic partnership* legislation, such proposals face strong opposition from conservative religious and political groups.
16. Reproductive technology has advanced to such an extent that ethical questions have arisen about the creation and shaping of human life.

Critical Thinking Questions

1. In an increasing proportion of couples in the United States, both partners work outside the home. What are the advantages and disadvantages of the dual-income model for women, for men, for children, and for society as a whole?
2. Consider the foster care system in the United States. Given the fact that so many children in the United States need caring homes, why do so many couples seek to adopt foreign children? Why do state agencies often deny same-sex couples the right to adopt? What can be done to improve the foster care system?
3. Given the high rate of divorce in the United States, would it be more appropriate to view divorce as dysfunctional or as a normal part of our marriage system? What would be the implications of viewing divorce as normal rather than as dysfunctional?

Key Terms

Adoption   In a legal sense, a process that allows for the transfer of the legal rights, responsibilities, and privileges of parenthood to a new legal parent or parents. (page 336)

Bilateral descent   A kinship system in which both sides of a person's family are regarded as equally important. (326)

Cohabitation   The practice of living together as a male–female couple without marrying. (340)

Domestic partnership   Two unrelated adults who share a mutually caring relationship, reside together, and agree to be jointly responsible for their dependents, basic living expenses, and other common necessities. (342)

Egalitarian family   An authority pattern in which spouses are regarded as equals. (326)

Endogamy   The restriction of mate selection to people within the same group. (330)

Exogamy   The requirement that people select a mate outside certain groups. (330)

Extended family   A family in which relatives—such as grandparents, aunts, or uncles—live in the same home as parents and their children. (324)

Familism   Pride in the extended family, expressed through the maintenance of close ties and strong obligations to kinfolk outside the immediate family. (333)

Family   A set of people related by blood, marriage or some other agreed-upon relationship, or adoption, who share the primary responsibility for reproduction and caring for members of society. (324)

Incest taboo   The prohibition of sexual relationships between certain culturally specified relatives. (330)

Kinship   The state of being related to others. (325)

Machismo   A sense of virility, personal worth, and pride in one's maleness. (333)

Matriarchy   A society in which women dominate in family decision making. (326)

Matrilineal descent   A kinship system in which only the relatives of the mother are significant. (326)

Monogamy   A form of marriage in which one woman and one man are married only to each other. (325)

Nuclear family   A married couple and their unmarried children living together. (324)

Patriarchy   A society in which men dominate in family decision making. (326)

Patrilineal descent   A kinship system in which only the relatives of the father are significant. (326)

Polyandry   A form of polygamy in which a woman may have more than one husband at the same time. (325)

Polygamy   A form of marriage in which an individual may have several husbands or wives simultaneously. (325)

Polygyny   A form of polygamy in which a man may have more than one wife at the same time. (325)

Serial monogamy   A form of marriage in which a person may have several spouses in his or her lifetime, but only one spouse at a time. (325)

Single-parent family   A family in which only one parent is present to care for the children. (337)

TECHNOLOGY RESOURCES

Internet Connection

*Note: While all the URLs listed were current as of the printing of this book, these sites often change. Please check our website (**www.mhhe.com/schaefer9**) for updates, hyperlinks, and exercises related to these sites.*

1. The Family Pride Coalition is a group that is dedicated to educating the public about gay, lesbian, bisexual, and transgender families. Visit their website (**www.familypride.org**) to explore this group's beliefs on gays and lesbians.

2. In 1998, 68.1 percent of children under age 18 in the United States lived with two parents, many of whom were stepparents. To learn more about stepfamilies, visit the website for the Stepfamily Association of America (**www.saafamilies.org**).

Online Learning Center with PowerWeb

Visit the student center in the Online Learning Center at **www.mhhe.com/schaefer9** and link to "Audio Clips." Listen to Richard Schaefer, the author of this text, discuss how chat rooms are playing the role that singles' bars did in the 1980s. Professor Schaefer notes that sociologists are trying to determine whether the Internet is restructuring dating behavior or merely facilitating it.

Reel Society Interactive Movie CD-ROM

Reel Society includes scenes that can be used to spark discussion about the following topics in this chapter:

- Authority Patterns: Who Rules?
- Studying the Family

15

RELIGION

In this billboard, Volkswagen of France compares a secular event, the introduction of a new model ("Rejoice, my friends, for a new Golf is born"), to a sacred event. While such tongue-in-cheek references to religion may offend believers, they indicate the continuing relevance of religion, even in modern, industrialized societies.

Durkheim and the Sociological Approach to Religion

World Religions

The Role of Religion

Religious Behavior

Religious Organization

Case Study: Religion in India

Social Policy and Religion: Religion in the Schools

Boxes

　SOCIAL INEQUALITY:　The Stained Glass Ceiling

　RESEARCH IN ACTION: Doing Religion

Growing up in a small mixed-blood community of seven hundred on the eastern edge of the Pine Ridge Reservation in South Dakota, I uncritically accepted the idea that the old Dakota religion and Christianity were both "true" and in some mysterious way compatible with each other. There were, to be sure, Christian fundamentalists with their intolerance and the old traditional Indians who kept their practices hidden, but the vast majority of the people in the vicinity more or less assumed that a satisfactory blend had been achieved that guaranteed our happiness.

Although my father was an Episcopal priest with a large number of chapels in a loosely organized Episcopal missionary district known (to Episcopalians) as "Corn Creek," he was far from an orthodox follower of the white man's religion. I always had the feeling that within the large context of "religion," which in a border town meant the Christian milieu, there was a special area in his spiritual life in which the old Dakota beliefs and practices reigned supreme. He knew thirty-three songs; some of them social, some ancient, and several spiritual songs used in a variety of ceremonial contexts. Driving to his chapels to hold Christian services he would open the window of the car and beat the side of the door with his hand for the drum beat and sing song after song....

When I went to college I was exposed to a much larger canvas of human experience upon which various societies had left their religious mark. My first reaction was the belief that most of the religious traditions were simply wrong, that a few of them had come close

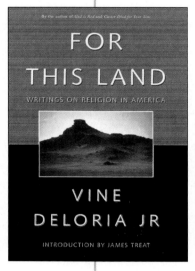

to describing religious reality, but that it would take some intensive study to determine which religious traditions would best assist human beings in succeeding in the world. It was my good fortune to have as a religion and philosophy professor a Christian mystic who was trying to prove the deepest mysteries of the faith. He also had some intense personal problems which emerged again and again in his beliefs, indicating to me that religion and the specific individual path of life were always intertwined.

Over several years and many profound conversations he was able to demonstrate to me that each religious tradition had developed a unique way to confront some problems and that they had something in common if only the search for truth and the elimination of many false paths. But his solution, after many years, became untenable for me. I saw instead religion simply as a means of organizing a society, articulating some reasonably apparent emotional truths, but ultimately becoming a staid part of social establishments that primarily sought to control human behavior and not fulfill human individual potential. It seemed as if those religions that placed strong emphasis on certain concepts failed precisely in the areas in which they claimed expertise. Thus religions of "love" could point to few examples of their efficacy; religions of "salvation" actually saved very few. The more I learned about world religions, the more respect I had for the old Dakota ways. (Deloria 1999:273–275) ■ 🔍

Additional information about this excerpt can be found on the Online Learning Center at **www.mhhe.com/schaefer9.**

In this excerpt from *For This Land*, Vine Deloria—a Standing Rock Sioux—reveals his deep personal ties to the religion of his ancestors, undiluted by the overlays of missionary Christian theology. Even though his father is an Episcopal priest, Deloria is keenly aware of how tribal beliefs intrude and color his father's religious sensibility. He is also aware of the fact that Native American rites and customs have been appropriated by a generation of non-Indians seeking a kind of New Age "magic." For Deloria, Indian spiritual beliefs are an integral part of the Native American culture and help to define that culture. Mixing those beliefs with the beliefs of other religions or systems of thought threatens to undermine the culture's strength.

Religion plays a major role in people's lives, and religious practices of some sort are evident in every society. That makes religion a *cultural universal,* along with other common practices or beliefs found in every

◀ p. 59 culture such as dancing, food preparation, the family, and personal names. At present, an estimated 4 billion people belong to the world's many religious faiths (see Figure 15-1, page 352).

When religion's influence on other social institutions in a society diminishes, the process of *secularization* is said to be under way. During this process, religion will survive in the private sphere of individual and family life (as in the case of many Native American families); it may even thrive on a personal level. But at the same time, other social institutions—such as the economy, politics, and education—maintain their own sets of norms, independent of religious guidance (Stark and Iannaccone 1992).

How do people's religious beliefs and practices differ from one part of the world to the next? What social purposes does religion serve? How do people express their religion, and how do they organize themselves for religious purposes? Has modern communications technology affected religion? In this chapter we will concentrate on religion as it is practiced in modern industrial societies. We will begin with a brief description of the approaches Émile Durkheim introduced, and those later sociologists have used, in studying religion. A brief overview of the world's major religions follows. Next, we will explore religion's role in societal integration, social support, social change, and social control. We'll examine three important dimensions of religious behavior—belief, ritual, and experience—as well as the basic forms of religious organization. We will pay particular attention to the emergence of new religious movements. Finally, the chapter will close with a social policy discussion of the controversy over religion in public schools. ■

DURKHEIM AND THE SOCIOLOGICAL APPROACH TO RELIGION

If a group believes that it is being directed by a "vision from God," sociologists will not attempt to prove or disprove this revelation. Instead, they will assess the effects of the religious experience on the group. What sociologists are interested in is the social impact of religion on individuals and institutions (McGuire 2002).

Émile Durkheim was perhaps the first sociologist to recognize the critical importance of religion in human societies. He saw its appeal for the individual, but more important, he stressed the *social* impact of religion. In

◀ p. 10 Durkheim's view, religion is a collective act that includes many forms of behavior in which people interact with others. As in his work on suicide, Durkheim was not so interested in the personalities of religious believers as he was in understanding religious behavior within a social context.

Durkheim defined *religion* as a "unified system of beliefs and practices relative to sacred things." In his view, religion involves a set of beliefs and practices that are uniquely the property of religion, as opposed to other social institutions and ways of thinking. Durkheim ([1912] 2001) argued that religious faiths distinguish between certain transcending events and the everyday world. He referred to those realms as the *sacred* and the *profane*.

The *sacred* encompasses elements beyond everyday life that inspire awe, respect, and even fear. People become part of the sacred realm only by completing some ritual, such as prayer or sacrifice. Because believers have faith in the sacred, they accept what they cannot understand. In contrast, the *profane* includes the ordinary and commonplace. This concept can be confusing, however, because the same object can be either sacred or profane,

FIGURE 15-1

Religions of the World

Mapping Life WORLDWIDE

Predominant Religions

Christianity (C)*
Roman Catholic
Protestant
Mormon (LDS)
Eastern Churches
Mixed Sects

Islam (M)
Sunni
Shi'a

Buddhism (B)
Hinayanistic
Lamaistic

Hinduism (H)

Judaism (J)

Sikhism

Animism (Tribal)

Chinese Complex
(Confucianism, Taoism, and Buddhism)

Korean Complex
(Buddhism, Confucianism, Christianity, and Chondogyo)

Japanese Complex
(Shinto and Buddhism)

Vietnamese Complex
(Buddhism, Taoism, Confucianism, and Cao Dai)

Unpopulated Regions

* Capital letters indicate the presence of locally important minority adherents of nonpredominant faiths.

Scale: 1 to 180,000,000

0   1000   2000 Miles
0   1000   2000   3000 Kilometers

www.
mhhe.com
/schaefer9

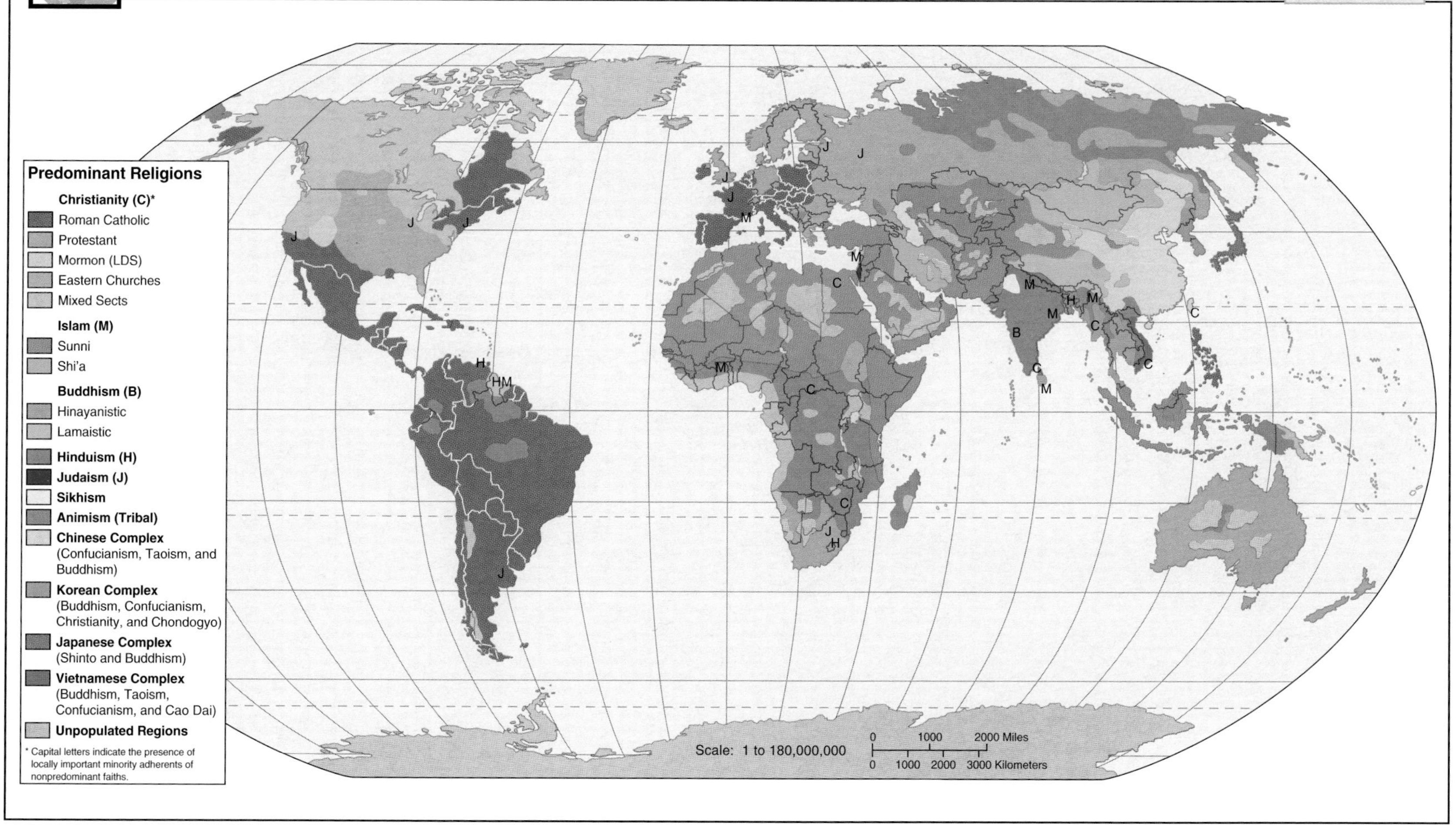

Source: J. Allen 2003:28.

depending on how it is viewed. A normal dining room table is profane, but becomes sacred to some Christians if it bears the elements of a communion. A candelabra becomes sacred to Jews if it is a menorah. For Confucians and Taoists, incense sticks are not mere decorative items, but highly valued offerings to the gods in religious ceremonies that mark the new and full moons.

Following the direction established by Durkheim almost a century ago, contemporary sociologists view religions in two different ways. They study the norms and values of religious faiths by examining their substantive beliefs. For example, it is possible to compare the degree to which Christian faiths interpret the Bible literally, or Muslim groups follow the Qur'an (or Koran), the sacred book of Islam. At the same time, sociologists examine religions in terms of the social functions they fulfill, such as providing social support or reinforcing social norms. By exploring both the beliefs and the functions of religion, we can better understand its impact on the individual, on groups, and on society as a whole.

A military chaplain baptizes a U.S. Marine in the Kuwaiti desert during the 2003 war in Iraq. Chaplains turn secular space into sacred space, bringing comfort to soldiers serving far from home.

WORLD RELIGIONS

Tremendous diversity exists in religious beliefs and practices. Overall, about 87 percent of the world's population adheres to some religion; only about 13 percent is nonreligious. Christianity is the largest single faith; the second largest is Islam (see Table 15-1, page 354). Although news events often suggest an inherent conflict between Christians and Muslims, the two faiths are similar in many ways. Both are monotheistic (that is, based on a single deity); both include a belief in prophets, an afterlife, and a judgment day. In fact, Islam recognizes Jesus as a prophet, though not as the son of God. Both faiths impose a moral code on believers, which varies from fairly rigid proscriptions for fundamentalists to relatively relaxed guidelines for liberals.

The followers of Islam, called *Muslims,* believe that Islam's holy scriptures were received from Allah (God) by the prophet Mohammad nearly 1,400 years ago. They see Mohammad as the last in a long line of prophets, preceded by Adam, Abraham, Moses, and Jesus. Islam is more communal in its expression than Christianity, particularly the more individualistic Protestant denominations. Consequently, in countries that are predominantly Muslim, the separation of religion and the state is not considered necessary or even desirable. In fact, Muslim governments often reinforce Islamic practices through their laws. Muslims do vary sharply in their interpretation of several traditions, some of which—such as the wearing of veils by women—are more cultural than religious in origin.

Like Christianity and Islam, Judaism is monotheistic. Jews believe that God's true nature is revealed in the Torah, which Christians know as the first five books of the Old Testament. According to these scriptures, God formed a covenant, or pact, with Abraham and Sarah, the ancestors of the tribes of Israel. Even today, Jews believe, this covenant holds them accountable to God's will. If they follow both the letter and spirit of the Torah, a long-awaited Messiah will one day bring paradise to earth. Although Judaism has a relatively small following compared to other major faiths, it forms the historical foundation for both Christianity and Islam. That is why Jews revere many of the same sacred Middle Eastern sites as Christians and Muslims.

Two other major faiths developed in a different part of the world, India. The earliest, Hinduism, originated around 1500 B.C. Hinduism differs from Judaism, Christianity, and Islam in that it embraces a number of gods and minor gods, although most worshippers are devoted primarily to a single deity, such as Shiva or Vishnu. Hinduism is also distinguished by a belief in reincarnation, or

Table 15-1	Major World Religions			
Faith	**Current Following, in Millions (and Percent of World Population)**	**Primary Location of Followers Today**	**Founder (and Approximate Birth Date)**	**Important Texts (and Holy Sites)**
Buddhism	364 (5.9%)	Southeast Asia, Mongolia, Tibet	Gautama Siddhartha (563 B.C.)	Triptaka (areas in Nepal)
Christianity	2,039 (33%)	Europe, North America, South America	Jesus (6 B.C.)	Bible (Jerusalem, Rome)
Hinduism	828 (13.3%)	India, Indian communities overseas	No specific founder (1500 B.C.)	Sruti and Smrti texts (seven sacred cities, including Vavansi)
Islam	1,226 (19.8%)	Middle East, Central Asia, North Africa, Indonesia	Mohammad (A.D. 570)	Qur'an or Koran (Mecca, Medina, Jerusalem)
Judaism	14 (0.2%)	Israel, United States, France, Russia	Abraham (2000 B.C.)	Torah, Talmud (Jerusalem)

the perpetual rebirth of the soul after death. Unlike Judaism, Christianity, and Islam, which are based largely on sacred texts, Hindu beliefs have been preserved mostly through oral tradition.

A second religion, Buddhism, developed in the sixth century B.C. as a reaction against Hinduism. This faith is founded on the teachings of Siddhartha (later called Buddha, or "the enlightened one"). Through meditation, followers of Buddhism strive to overcome selfish cravings for physical or material pleasures, with the goal of reaching a state of enlightenment, or *nirvana*. Buddhists created the first monastic orders, which are thought to be the models for monastic orders in other religions, including Christianity. Though Buddhism emerged in India, its followers were eventually driven out of that country by the Hindus. It is now found primarily in other parts of Asia. (Contemporary adherents of Buddhism in India are relatively recent converts.)

Although the differences among religions are striking, they are exceeded by variations within faiths. Consider the differences within Christianity, from relatively liberal denominations such as Presbyterians or the United Church of Christ to the more conservative Mormons and Greek Orthodox Catholics. Similar divisions exist within Hinduism, Islam, and other world religions (Barrett and Johnson 2001; David Levinson 1996).

THE ROLE OF RELIGION

Since religion is a cultural universal, it is not surprising that it plays a basic role in human societies. In sociological terms, it performs both manifest and latent functions. Among its *manifest* (open and stated) functions, religion defines the spiritual world and gives meaning to the divine. It provides an explanation for events that seem difficult to understand, such as what lies beyond the grave. The *latent* functions of religion are unintended, covert, or hidden. Even though the manifest function of a church service is to offer a forum for religious worship, it might at the same time fulfill a latent social function as a meeting ground for unmarried members.

Functionalists and conflict theorists both evaluate religion's impact on human societies. We'll consider a functionalist view of religion's role in integrating society, providing social support, and promoting social change, and then look at religion from the conflict perspective, as a means of social control. Note that for the most part,

p. 14

religion's impact is best understood from a macro-level viewpoint that is oriented toward the larger society. Its social support function is an exception: it is best viewed on the micro, or individual, level.

The Integrative Function of Religion

Émile Durkheim viewed religion as an integrative force in human society—a perspective that is reflected in functionalist thought today. Durkheim sought to answer a perplexing question: "How can human societies be held together when they are generally composed of individuals and social groups with diverse interests and aspirations?" In his view, religious bonds often transcend these personal and divisive forces. Durkheim acknowledged that religion is not the only integrative force; nationalism or patriotism may serve the same end.

How does religion provide this "societal glue"? Religion, whether it be Buddhism, Islam, Christianity, or Judaism, gives meaning and purpose to people's lives. It offers certain ultimate values and ends to hold in common. Although they are subjective and not always fully accepted, these values and ends help society to function as an integrated social system. For example, funerals, weddings, bar and bat mitzvahs, and confirmations serve to integrate people into larger communities by providing shared beliefs and values about the ultimate questions of life.

Religion also serves to bind people together in times of crisis and confusion. Immediately after the terrorist attacks of September 11, 2001, on New York City and Washington, D.C., attendance at worship services in the United States increased dramatically. Muslim, Jewish, and Christian clerics made joint appearances to honor the dead and urge citizens not to retaliate against those who looked, dressed, or sounded different from others. A year later, however, attendance levels had returned to normal (D. Moore 2002).

The integrative power of religion can be seen, too, in the role that churches, synagogues, and mosques have traditionally played and continue to play for immigrant groups in the United States. For example, Roman Catholic immigrants may settle near a parish church that offers services in their native language, such as Polish or Spanish. Similarly, Korean immigrants may join a Presbyterian church that has many Korean American members and follows religious practices like those of churches in Korea. Like other religious organizations, these Roman Catholic and Presbyterian churches help to integrate immigrants into their new homeland.

Yet another example of the integrative impact of religion is provided by the Universal Fellowship of Metropolitan Community Churches, established in the United States in 1968 to offer a welcoming place of worship for lesbians and gay men. This spiritual community is especially important today, given the many organized religions that are openly hostile to homosexuality. The Metropolitan Community Church has 40,000 members in 300 local churches in 18 countries. As part of its effort to support lesbian and gay rights, the church performs same-sex marriages, which it calls "holy union ceremonies" (Stammer 2003).

In some instances, religious loyalties are *dysfunctional;* that is, they contribute to tension and even conflict between groups or nations. During the Second World War, the German Nazis attempted to exterminate the Jewish people; approximately 6 million European Jews were killed. In modern times, nations such as Lebanon (Muslims versus Christians), Israel (Jews versus Muslims, as well as Orthodox versus secular Jews), Northern Ireland (Roman Catholics versus Protestants), and India (Hindus versus Muslims, and more recently, Sikhs) have been torn by clashes that are in large part based on religion. (See the case study near the end of this chapter for a more detailed dicussion of religious conflict in India.)

Religious conflict (though on a less violent level) has been increasingly evident in the United States as well. Sociologist James Davison Hunter (1991) has referred to the "cultural war" taking place in the United States. In many communities, Christian fundamentalists, conservative Catholics, and Orthodox Jews have joined forces in a battle against liberal denominations for control of the secular culture. The battlefield is an array of familiar social issues, among them multiculturalism, child care (Chapter 4), abortion (Chapter 12), home schooling, gay rights (Chapter 22), and government funding for the arts.

pp. 97, 297

Religion and Social Support

Most of us find it difficult to accept the stressful events of life—the death of a loved one, serious injury, bankruptcy, divorce, and so forth. This is especially true when something "senseless" happens. How can family and friends come to terms with the death of a talented college student, not even 20 years old?

Through its emphasis on the divine and the supernatural, religion allows us to "do something" about the calamities we face. In some faiths, adherents can offer sacrifices or pray to a deity in the belief that such acts will change their earthly condition. On a more basic level, religion encourages us to view our personal misfortunes as relatively unimportant in the broader perspective of human history—or even as part of an undisclosed divine purpose. Friends and relatives of the deceased college student may see his death as being "God's will" or as having some ultimate benefit that we cannot understand now.

Why Do Sociologists Study Religion?

Altar assistant at the Roman Catholic cathedral in Miami

Sociologists find religion a fascinating subject of study because it is a cultural universal whose collective expression can be manifested in so many different ways. For example, Christians (above) worship one God and base their beliefs and values on the life and works of Jesus Christ. Jews (next page, top left) are also monotheistic, but they base their beliefs on scriptural revelations about God in the Torah. The Shinto religion in Japan (next page, top right) honors Confucian ethics and personifies aspects of the natural world, such as mountains. Hindus (bottom of the next page) hold many aspects of life sacred, and emphasize the importance of being good in this life in order to advance in the next.

Sociologists are interested in how widely and strongly such beliefs are held, and what influences individuals to adopt religious beliefs. They study the impact of the family, schools, the state, and the predominant culture, among other factors. Also of interest to sociologists are the ways in which people express their faith. Do they do so by attending services? By meditating privately? By performing rituals? At the societal level, sociologists consider what impact religious organizations have on society, and conversely, how a particular culture affects the practice of religion.

Jewish Rabbi in Jerusalem

Shinto priest in Japan

Hindu holy man at the sacred Ganges River in India

357

This perspective may be much more comforting than the terrifying feeling that any of us can die senselessly at any moment—and that there is no divine answer as to why one person lives a long and full life, while another dies tragically at a relatively early age.

Faith-based community organizations have taken on more and more responsibilities in the area of social assistance. In fact, President George W. Bush created the Office of Faith-Based and Community Initiatives to give socially active religious groups access to government funding. Sociologist William Julius Wilson (1999b) has singled out faith-based organizations in 40 communities from California to Massachusetts as models of social reform. These organizations identify experienced leaders and assemble them into nonsectarian coalitions that are devoted to community development.

Religion and Social Change

The Weberian Thesis

When someone seems driven to work and succeed, we often attribute the Protestant work ethic to that person. The term comes from the writings of Max Weber, who carefully examined the connection between religious allegiance and capitalist development. His findings appeared in his pioneering work _The Protestant Ethic and the Spirit of Capitalism_ ([1904] 1958a).

Weber noted that in European nations with both Protestant and Catholic citizens, an overwhelming number of business leaders, owners of capital, and skilled workers were Protestant. In his view, this fact was no mere coincidence. Weber pointed out that the followers of John Calvin (1509–1564), a leader of the Protestant Reformation, emphasized a disciplined work ethic, this-worldly concerns, and a rational orientation to life that have become known as the **Protestant ethic.** One by-product of the Protestant ethic was a drive to accumulate savings that could be used for future investment. This "spirit of capitalism," to use Weber's phrase, contrasted with the moderate work hours, leisurely work habits, and lack of ambition that he saw as typical of the times.

Few books on the sociology of religion have aroused as much commentary and criticism as Weber's work. It has been hailed as one of the most important theoretical works in the field and an excellent example of macro-level analysis. Like Durkheim, Weber demonstrated that religion is not solely a matter of intimate personal beliefs. He stressed that the collective nature of religion has social consequences for society as a whole.

Weber provided a convincing description of the origins of European capitalism. But this economic system has now been adopted by non-Calvinists in many parts of the world. Studies done in the United States today show little or no difference in achievement orientation between Roman Catholics and Protestants. Apparently, the "spirit of capitalism" has emerged as a generalized cultural trait rather than a specific religious tenet (Greeley 1989).

Conflict theorists caution that Weber's theory—even if it is accepted—should not be regarded as an analysis of mature capitalism, as reflected in the rise of multinational corporations. Marxists would disagree with Weber not on the origins of capitalism, but on its future. Unlike Marx, Weber believed that capitalism could endure indefinitely as an economic system. He added, however, that the decline of religion as an overriding force in society opened the way for workers to express their discontent more vocally (R. Collins 1980).

p. 230

Liberation Theology

Sometimes the clergy can be found in the forefront of social change. Many religious activists, especially in the Roman Catholic Church in Latin America, support **liberation theology**—the use of a church in a political effort to eliminate poverty, discrimination, and other forms of injustice from a secular society. Advocates of this religious movement sometimes sympathize with Marxism. Many believe that radical change, rather than economic development in itself, is the only acceptable solution to the desperation of the masses in impoverished developing countries. Activists associated with liberation theology believe that organized religion has a moral responsibility to take a strong public stand against the oppression of the poor, racial and ethnic minorities, and women (C. Smith 1991).

The term _liberation theology_ dates back to the publication in 1973 of the English translation of _A Theology of Liberation._ The book was written by a Peruvian priest, Gustavo Gutiérrez, who lived in a slum area of Lima during the early 1960s. After years of exposure to the vast poverty around him, Gutiérrez concluded that "in order to serve the poor, one had to move into political action" (R. M. Brown 1980:23; Gutiérrez 1990). Eventually, politically committed Latin American theologians came under the influence of social scientists who viewed the domination of capitalism and multinational corporations as central to the hemisphere's problems. One result was a new approach to theology that built on the cultural and religious traditions of Latin America rather than on models developed in Europe and the United States.

Liberation theology may be dysfunctional, however. Some Roman Catholic worshipers have come to believe that by focusing on political and governmental injustice, the clergy are no longer addressing their personal and spiritual needs. Partly as a result of such disenchantment, some Catholics in Latin America are converting to mainstream Protestant faiths or to Mormonism.

Social Inequality

15-1 THE STAINED GLASS CEILING

What is the role of women in organized religion? Most faiths have a long tradition of exclusively male spiritual leadership. Furthermore, most religions are patriarchal, so they tend to reinforce men's dominance in secular as well as spiritual matters. Women do play a vital role as volunteers, staff, and religious educators, but even today, decision making and leadership typically fall to the men. There are exceptions to this rule, such as the Shakers and Christian Scientists, as well as Hinduism with its long goddess heritage, but they are rare.

Nationally, women compose only about 15 percent of U.S. clergy, though they have accounted for at least 20 percent of students enrolled in theological institutions over the last two decades. Women clerics typically have shorter careers than men, often in related fields such as counseling, which do not involve congregational leadership. In faiths that restrict leadership positions to men, women still serve unofficially. For example, about 4 percent of Roman Catholic congregations are led by women who hold nonordained pastoral positions—a

> A stained glass ceiling seems to hover over clergy women, limiting their occupational mobility.

necessity in a church that faces a shortage of male priests.

In the United States, congregations headed by women tend to be smaller and poorer than those headed by men. Consequently, women church leaders are much less likely than men to have any paid full-time staff. They are also more likely to begin and end their careers in positions that do not lead to advancement in their denominations. A stained glass ceiling seems to hover over clergy women, limiting their occupational mobility.

Let's Discuss

1. Does a religious community in your town or city have a female leader? If so, was her calling controversial? What do you think her prospects are for career advancement?
2. From society's point of view, what are the pros and cons of admitting women to religious leadership?

Sources: Bureau of the Census 2002a:381; Chang 1997; Konieczny and Chaves 2000.

 Use Your Sociological Imagination www. mhhe.com /schaefer9

The social support that religious groups provide is suddenly withdrawn from your community. How will your life or the lives of others change? What will happen if religious groups stop pushing for social change?

Religion and Social Control: A Conflict View

Liberation theology is a relatively recent phenomenon that marks a break with the traditional role of churches. It was this traditional role that Karl Marx opposed. In his view, religion *impeded* social change by encouraging oppressed people to focus on otherworldly concerns rather than on their immediate poverty or exploitation. Marx described religion as an "opiate" that was particularly harmful to oppressed peoples. He felt that religion often drugged the masses into submission by offering a consolation for their harsh lives on earth: the hope of salvation in an ideal afterlife. For example, during the period of slavery in the United States, White masters forbade Blacks to practice native African religions, while encouraging them to adopt Christianity, which taught them that obedience would lead to salvation and eternal happiness in the hereafter. Viewed from a conflict perspective, Christianity may have pacified certain slaves and blunted the rage that often fuels rebellion.

Marx acknowledged that religion plays an important role in propping up the existing social structure. The values of religion, as already noted, tend to reinforce other social institutions and the social order as a whole. From Marx's perspective, however, religion's promotion of social stability only helps to perpetuate patterns of social inequality. According to Marx, the dominant religion reinforces the interests of those in power (Harap 1982).

For example, contemporary Christianity reinforces traditional patterns of behavior that call for the subordination of the less powerful. The role of women in the church is an example of this uneven distribution of power. Assumptions about gender roles leave women in a subservient position both within Christian churches and at home. In fact, women find it as difficult to achieve leadership positions in many churches as they do in large corporations. Box 15-1 describes the "stained glass ceiling"

359

that tends to stunt clergywomen's career development even in the most liberal denominations. Like Marx, conflict theorists argue that to whatever extent religion actually does influence social behavior, it reinforces existing patterns of dominance and inequality.

From a Marxist perspective, religion functions as an "agent of depoliticization" (J. Wilson 1978). In simpler terms, religion keeps people from seeing their lives and societal conditions in political terms—for example, by obscuring the overriding significance of conflicting economic interests. Marxists suggest p. 203 that by inducing a "false consciousness" among the disadvantaged, religion lessens the possibility of collective political action that can end capitalist oppression and transform society.

Religious expression can take many forms. This Christian motorcycle club's attire ensures that members will not be mistaken for Hell's Angels, despite their freewheeling lifestyle.

RELIGIOUS BEHAVIOR

All religions have certain elements in common, yet those elements are expressed in the distinctive manner of each faith. These patterns of religious behavior, like other patterns of social behavior, are of great interest to sociologists, since they underscore the relationship between religion and society.

Religious beliefs, religious rituals, and religious experience all help to define what is sacred and to differentiate the sacred from the profane. Let us now examine these three dimensions of religious behavior.

Belief

Some people believe in life after death, in supreme beings with unlimited powers, or in supernatural forces. *Religious beliefs* are statements to which members of a particular religion adhere. These views can vary dramatically from religion to religion.

The Adam and Eve account of creation found in Genesis, the first book of the Old Testament, is an example of a religious belief. Many people in the United States strongly adhere to this biblical explanation of creation, and even insist that it be taught in public schools. These people, known as *creationists*, are worried by the secularization of society, and oppose teaching that directly or indirectly questions biblical scripture. The social policy section at the end of this chapter examines the issue of religion in the schools in depth.

As Figure 15-2 shows, worldwide, the strength of religious beliefs varies dramatically. In general, spirituality is not as strong in industrialized nations as in developing nations. The United States is an exception to the trend toward secularization, in part because the government encourages religious expression (without explicitly supporting it) by allowing religious groups to claim charitable status, and even to receive federal aid for activities such as educational services. And although belief in God is relatively weak in formerly communist states such as Russia, surveys show a growth in spirituality in communist countries over the last 10 years.

Ritual

Religious rituals are practices required or expected of members of a faith. Rituals usually honor the divine power (or powers) worshiped by believers; they also remind adherents of their religious duties and responsibilities. Rituals and beliefs can be interdependent; rituals generally affirm beliefs, as in a public or private statement confessing a sin. Like any social institution, religion develops distinctive norms to structure people's behavior. Moreover, there are sanctions attached to religious rituals, whether rewards (bar mitzvah gifts) or penalties (expulsion from a religious institution for violation of norms).

FIGURE 15-2

Belief in God Worldwide

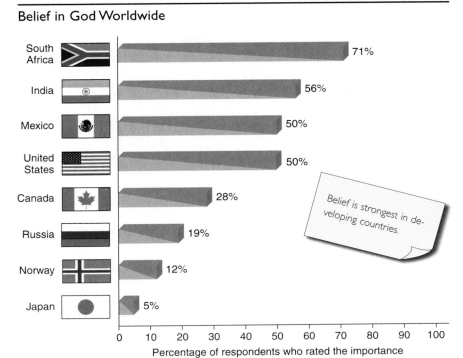

Note: Data are from World Values surveys for 1995–1998, except for Canada, 1990–1991.
Source: Inglehart and Baker 2000:47.

Think About It
Canada and the United States are similar in many ways. Why would faith in God be less important to Canadians than to Americans?

In the United States, rituals may be very simple, such as saying grace at a meal or observing a moment of silence to commemorate someone's death. Yet certain rituals, such as the process of canonizing a saint, are quite elaborate. Most religious rituals in our culture focus on services conducted at houses of worship. Attendance at a service, silent and spoken prayers, communion, and singing of spiritual hymns and chants are common forms of ritual behavior that generally take place in group settings. From an interactionist perspective, these rituals serve as important face-to-face encounters in which people reinforce their religious beliefs and their commitment to their faith (see Box 15-2, page 363).

For Muslims, a very important ritual is the *hajj,* a pilgrimage to the Grand Mosque in Mecca, Saudi Arabia. Every Muslim who is physically and financially able is expected to make this trip at least once. Each year 2 million pilgrims go to Mecca during the one-week period indicated by the Islamic lunar calendar. Muslims from all over the world make the *hajj,* including those in the United States, where many tours are arranged to facilitate the trip.

Some rituals induce an almost trancelike state. The Plains Indians eat or drink peyote, a cactus containing the powerful hallucinogenic drug mescaline. Similarly, the ancient Greek followers of the god Pan chewed intoxicating ivy leaves in order to become more ecstatic during their celebrations. Of course, artificial stimulants are not necessary to achieve a religious high. Devout believers, such as those who practice the pentecostal Christian ritual of "speaking in tongues," can reach a state of ecstasy simply through spiritual passion.

Experience

In the sociological study of religion, the term ***religious experience*** refers to the feeling or perception of being in direct contact with the ultimate reality, such as a divine being, or of being overcome with religious emotion. A religious experience may be rather slight, such as the feeling of exaltation a person receives from hearing a choir sing Handel's "Hallelujah Chorus." But many religious experiences are more profound, such as a Muslim's experience on a *hajj.* In his autobiography, the late African American activist Malcolm X (1964:338) wrote of his *hajj* and how deeply moved he was by the way that Muslims in Mecca came together across race and color lines. For Malcolm X, the color blindness of the Muslim world "proved to me the power of the One God."

Another profound religious experience, for many Christians, is being "born again"—that is, at a turning point in one's life, making a personal commitment to Jesus. According to a 2001 national survey, 40 percent of people in the United States claim they have had a born-again Christian experience at some time in their lives. An earlier survey found that Southern Baptists (75 percent) were the most likely to report such experiences; in contrast, only 21 percent of Catholics and 24 percent of Episcopalians stated that they had been born again. The collective nature of religion, as emphasized by Durkheim, is evident in these statistics. The beliefs and rituals of a particular faith can create an atmosphere either friendly or

Pilgrims on *hajj* to the Grand Mosque in Mecca, Saudi Arabia. Islam requires all Muslims who are able to undertake a pilgrimage to the Holy Land.

indifferent to this type of religious experience. Thus, a Baptist would be encouraged to come forward and share such experiences with others, whereas an Episcopalian who claims to have been born again would receive much less interest (Princeton Religion Research Center 2002).

Use Your Sociological Imagination www.mhhe.com/schaefer9

Choose a religious tradition other than your own. How would your religious beliefs, rituals, and experience differ if you had been raised in that tradition?

RELIGIOUS ORGANIZATION

The collective nature of religion has led to many forms of religious association. In modern societies, religion has become increasingly formalized. Specific structures such as churches and synagogues have been constructed for religious worship; individuals have been trained for occupational roles within various fields. These developments make it possible to distinguish clearly between the sacred and secular parts of one's life—a distinction that could

not be made easily in earlier times, when religion was largely a family activity carried out in the home.

Sociologists find it useful to distinguish between four basic forms of organization: the ecclesia, the denomination, the sect, and the new religious movement or cult. We can see differences among these types of organizations in their size, power, degree of commitment that is expected from members, and historical ties to other faiths.

Ecclesiae

An *ecclesia* (plural, *ecclesiae*) is a religious organization that claims to include most or all members of a society, and is recognized as the national or official religion. Since virtually everyone belongs to the faith, membership is by birth rather than conscious decision. Examples of ecclesiae include Islam in Saudi Arabia and Buddhism in Thailand. However, significant differences exist within this category. In Saudi Arabia's Islamic regime, leaders of the ecclesia hold vast power over actions of the state. In contrast, the Lutheran church in contemporary Sweden holds no such power over the Riksdag (parliament) or the prime minister.

Research in Action

15-2 DOING RELIGION

More than 100 people in a Black congregation are packed into the living room of an old house. Led by the pastor's wife and four dancing women, the worshipers are singing, dancing, waving their arms. The church is rocking, and the pace doesn't stop for three hours. Across town a White congregation is singing the same hymns, but no one is dancing. The mood is mellow and the drummer looks almost embarrassed to be there. Sharon Bjorkman uncovered these contrasting worship styles in the course of her fieldwork on forms of worship in churches in the Chicago area. Her observation research was part of a nationwide study conducted by the Hartford Institute for Religion Research.

Bjorkman was interested in going beyond the doctrinal background of a particular church and observing the physical actions of the people attending services and those conducting them. As Durkheim noted, defining what is sacred in a religion is a collective act. Using the interactionist perspective, Bjorkman took notes on what happened at services, who participated, and what or who motivated them to do so.

The first thing she discovered was the disadvantage of being an outsider. For example, not knowing the ropes, she was unprepared for the strenuous physical activity in the Black church. In other churches she visited she didn't know whether to carry a Bible or what version to use. As Bjorkman notes, you need to be socialized to know what is expected of you in a church service. Depending on the socialization church members receive, usually through example and reprimand, they will be active or passive, loud or quiet, meditative or demonstrative.

> The church is rocking and the pace doesn't stop for three hours.

The church leader plays a key role in shaping the congregation's actions. Leaders decide the format of services, including what songs are sung, what instruments are used, and how much to involve the worshipers. In services that call for testimonies from the congregation, the leader actively solicits certain members and badgers them if need be. The same tactic applies to "altar calls," in which congregants come forward to confess sins or seek blessings.

As important as church leaders are, they would have little influence if individual members chose not to cooperate. Worship styles, then, are jointly developed by leaders and members. Generally, Bjorkman found, leaders take small incremental steps to "train" their members to accept a particular style of service.

This study illustrates the crucial part that human relations play within formal organizations. Religious rituals are not just dry formal procedures dictated by a prescribed program. They evolve out of the active participation of leaders and members "doing religion" together.

Let's Discuss

1. Do you attend a church regularly? If so, what style of worship does the church leader follow? How does it affect your feelings about your religion?
2. What accounts for differing forms of church ritual, even within the same denomination?

Source: Ammerman et al. 1998; Bjorkman 1999.

Generally, ecclesiae are conservative, in that they do not challenge the leaders of a secular government. In a society with an ecclesia, the political and religious institutions often act in harmony and reinforce each other's power in their relative spheres of influence. In the modern world, ecclesiae are declining in power.

Denominations

A *denomination* is a large, organized religion that is not officially linked with the state or government. Like an ecclesia, it tends to have an explicit set of beliefs, a defined system of authority, and a generally respected position in society. Denominations claim as members large segments of a population. Generally, children accept the denomination of their parents, and give little thought to membership in other faiths. Denominations also resemble ecclesiae in that they make few demands on members. However, there is a critical difference between these two forms of religious organization. Although the denomination is considered respectable and is not viewed as a challenge to the secular government, it lacks the official recognition and power held by an ecclesia (Doress and Porter 1977).

The United States is home to a large number of denominations (see Figure 15-3, page 364). In good measure, this diversity is a result of our nation's immigrant heritage. Many settlers brought with them the religious commitments native to their homelands. Some Christian denominations in the United States, such as the Roman Catholics, Episcopalians, and Lutherans, are the outgrowth of ecclesiae established in Europe. New Christian

FIGURE 15-3

Largest Religious Groups in the United States by County, 2000

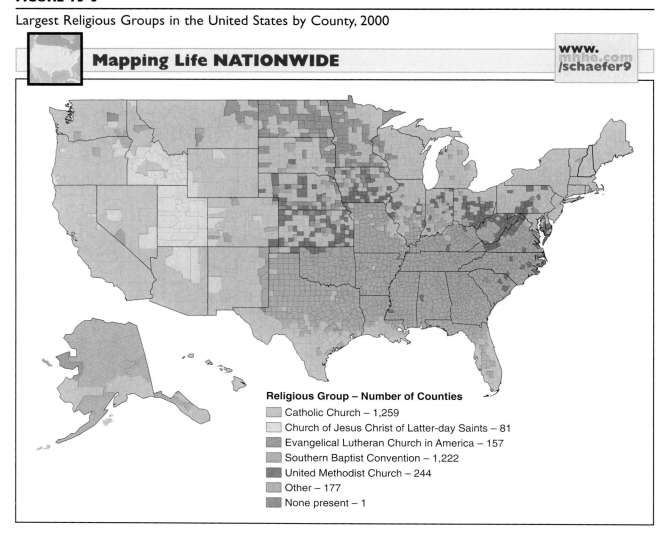

Mapping Life NATIONWIDE

www.mhhe.com/schaefer9

Religious Group – Number of Counties

- Catholic Church – 1,259
- Church of Jesus Christ of Latter-day Saints – 81
- Evangelical Lutheran Church in America – 157
- Southern Baptist Convention – 1,222
- United Methodist Church – 244
- Other – 177
- None present – 1

Source: D. Jones et al. 2002:592.

This map, which shows only the largest participating religious group in each county, nevertheless suggests the large variety of faiths practiced in the United States. A total of 149 religious denominations reported the numbers of their adherents for the study on which this map is based.

denominations also emerged, including the Mormons and Christian Scientists. More recently, immigrants have increased the number of Muslims, Hindus, and Buddhists living in the United States.

Although by far the largest single denomination in the United States is Roman Catholicism, at least 22 other Christian faiths have 1 million or more members. Protestants collectively accounted for about 55 percent of the nation's adult population in 2001, compared with 25 percent for Roman Catholics and 2 percent for Jews. There are also 3 million Muslims in the United States, and large numbers of people adhere to Eastern faiths such as

Buddhism (2 million) and Hinduism (1 million) (Lindner 2002; Princeton Religion Research Center 2002).

Sects

A *sect* can be defined as a relatively small religious group that has broken away from some other religious organization to renew what it considers the original vision of the faith. Many sects, such as that led by Martin Luther during the Reformation, claim to be the "true church," because they seek to cleanse the established faith of what they regard as extraneous beliefs and rituals (Stark and

Bainbridge 1985). Max Weber ([1916] 1958b:114) termed the sect a "believer's church," because affiliation is based on conscious acceptance of a specific religious dogma.

Sects are fundamentally at odds with society and do not seek to become established national religions. Unlike ecclesiae and denominations, they require intensive commitments and demonstrations of belief by members. Partly owing to their outsider status, sects frequently exhibit a higher degree of religious fervor and loyalty than more established religious groups. Recruitment focuses mainly on adults, and acceptance comes through conversion.

Sects are often short-lived. Those that are able to survive may become less antagonistic to society over time and begin to resemble denominations. In a few instances, sects have been able to endure over several generations while remaining fairly separate from society. Sociologist J. Milton Yinger (1970:226–73) uses the term **established sect** to describe a religious group that is the outgrowth of a sect, yet remains isolated from society. The Hutterites, Jehovah's Witnesses, Seventh-Day Adventists, and Amish are contemporary examples of established sects in the United States.

New Religious Movements or Cults

In 1997, 38 members of the Heaven's Gate cult were found dead in Southern California after a mass suicide timed to occur with the appearance of the Hale-Bopp comet. They believed the comet hid a spaceship on which they could catch a ride once they had broken free of their "bodily containers."

Partly as a result of the notoriety generated by such groups, the popular media have stigmatized the word *cult,* associating it with the occult and the use of intense and forceful conversion techniques. The stereotyping of cults as uniformly bizarre and unethical has led sociologists to abandon the term and refer instead to a *new religious movement (NRM).* While some NRMs exhibit strange behavior, many do not. They attract new members just like any other religion, and often follow teachings similar to those of established Christian denominations, though with less ritual.

Sects are difficult to distinguish from cults. A **new religious movement (NRM)** or **cult** is generally a small, secretive religious group that represents either a new religion or a major innovation of an existing faith. NRMs are similar to sects in that they tend to be small and are often viewed as less respectable than more established faiths. Unlike sects, however, NRMs normally do not result from schisms or breaks with established ecclesiae or denominations. Some cults, such as those focused on UFO sight-

The Christian Science Center in Boston, Massachusetts. Christian Scientists believe that all illness can be healed through an understanding of God. The church, which began as a new religious movement, now resembles an established denomination.

ings, may be totally unrelated to existing faiths. Even when a cult does accept certain fundamental tenets of a dominant faith—such as a belief in Jesus as divine or in Mohammad as a messenger of God—it will offer new revelations or insights to justify its claim to being a more advanced religion (Stark and Bainbridge 1979, 1985).

Like sects, NRMs may be transformed over time into other types of religious organizations. An example is the Christian Science Church, which began as a new religious movement under the leadership of Mary Baker Eddy. Today, this church exhibits the characteristics of a denomination. In fact, most major religions, including Christianity, began as cults. NRMs may be in the early stages of developing into a denomination or new religion, or they may just as easily fade away through the loss of members or weak leadership (J. Richardson and van Driel 1997).

Comparing Forms of Religious Organization

How can we determine whether a particular religious group falls into the sociological category of ecclesia, denomination, sect, or NRM? As we have seen, these types of religious organizations have somewhat different relationships to society. Ecclesiae are recognized as national churches; denominations, although not officially approved by the state, are generally widely respected. In contrast, sects and NRMs are much more likely to be at odds with the larger culture.

Still, ecclesiae, denominations, and sects are best viewed as types along a continuum rather than as mutually exclusive categories. Table 15-2 summarizes some of the primary characteristics of these ideal types. Since the United States has no ecclesia, sociologists studying this country's religions have focused on the denomination and the sect. These religious forms have been pictured on either end of a continuum, with denominations accommodating to the secular world and sects protesting against established religions. While NRMs have been included in Table 15-2, they lie outside the continuum, because they generally define themselves in terms of a new view of life rather than in terms of existing religious faiths (Chalfant et al. 1994).

Advances in electronic communications have led to still another form of religious organization: the electronic church. Facilitated by cable television and satellite transmissions, *televangelists* (as they are called) direct their messages to more people—especially in the United States—than are served by all but the largest denominations. While some televangelists are affiliated with religious denominations, most give viewers the impression that they are disassociated from established faiths.

At the close of the 1990s, the electronic church had taken on yet another dimension: the Internet. In one study, researchers estimated that on a typical day in 2000, as many as 2 million people used the Internet for religious purposes. Much of the spiritual content on the Internet is tied to organized denominations. People use cyberspace to learn more about their faith, or even just the activities of their own place of worship (Larsen 2000).

As more and more people are discovering, however, the "church" we locate on the World Wide Web exists only in *virtual* reality. For some purposes, virtual religious experience simply will not do. For example, a minyan, a set quorum for Jewish prayers, requires 10 Jews gathered in one space; cyberspace doesn't count. And while Muslims can view the Kabbah, or Holy Shrine, in Mecca on the Net, they cannot fulfill their religious obligations except by actual pilgrimage there. The Internet, then, isn't

Table 15-2	Characteristics of Ecclesiae, Denominations, Sects, and New Religious Movements			
Characteristic	**Ecclesia**	**Denomination**	**Sect**	**New Religious Movement (or Cult)**
Size	Very large	Large	Small	Small
Wealth	Extensive	Extensive	Limited	Variable
Religious Services	Formal, little participation	Formal, little participation	Informal, emotional	Variable
Doctrines	Specific, but interpretation may be tolerated	Specific, but interpretation may be tolerated	Specific, purity of doctrine emphasized	Innovative, pathbreaking
Clergy	Well-trained, full-time	Well-trained, full-time	Trained to some degree	Unspecialized
Membership	By virtue of being a member of society	By acceptance of doctrine	By acceptance of doctrine	By an emotional commitment
Relationship to the state	Recognized, closely aligned	Tolerated	Not encouraged	Ignored or challenged

Source: Adapted from G. Vernon 1962; see also Chalfant et al. 1994.

suitable for some forms of religious and spiritual expression, but it certainly has added a new dimension to religious behavior (Zelizer 1999).

CASE STUDY:
RELIGION IN INDIA

From a sociological point of view, the nation of India is large and complex enough that it might be considered a world of its own. Four hundred languages are spoken in India, 18 of which are officially recognized by the government. Besides the two major religions that originated there—Hinduism and Buddhism—several other faiths animate this society. Demographically the nation is huge, with over a billion residents. This teeming country is expected to overtake China as the most populous nation in the world in about three decades (Third World Institute 2003; United Nations Population Information Network 2003).

The Religious Tapestry in India

Hinduism and Islam, the two most important religions in India, were described on pages 353–354. Islam arrived in India in the year 1000 A.D., with the first of many Muslim invasions. It flowered there during the Mogul empire (1526–1857), the period when the Taj Mahal was built. Today, Muslims account for 11 percent of India's population; Hindus make up 83 percent.

Another religion, the Sikh faith, originated in the 15th century A.D. with a Hindu named Nanak, the first of a series of *gurus* (prophets). Sikhism shows the influence of Islam in India, in that it is monotheistic (based on a belief in one god rather than many). It resembles Buddhism in its emphasis on meditation and spiritual transcendence of the everyday world. *Sikhs* (learners) pursue their goal of spiritual enlightenment through meditation with the help of a *guru*.

Sikh men have a characteristic mode of dress that makes them easy to identify. They do not cut their beards or hair, and they wrap their heads in turbans. (Because of their distinctive dress, the 400,000 Sikhs who live in the United States are often mistaken—and discriminated against—as Muslims.) Sikhs are highly patriotic. Though their 20 million members make up just 2 percent of India's population, they account for 25 percent of India's army. Their presence in the military gives them a much larger voice in the governance of the country than might be expected, given their numbers (Fausset 2003).

Another faith that has been influential beyond its numbers in India is Jainism (pronounced *Jinism*). This religion was founded six centuries before the birth of

Christ—about the same time as Buddhism—by a young Hindu named Mahavira. Offended by the Hindu caste system, the rigid social hierarchy that reduces some people to the status of outcastes based solely on their birth, and by the numerous Hindu deities, Mahavira left his family and his wealth behind to become a beggar monk. His teachings attracted many followers, and the faith grew and flourished until the Muslim invasions of the 12th century A.D.

According to the Jain faith, there is no god; each person is responsible for his or her own spiritual well-being. By following a strict code of conduct, Jains believe they can ultimately free their souls from the endless cycle of death and rebirth and attain *nirvana* (spiritual enlightenment). Jains are required to meditate; forswear lying and stealing; limit their personal wealth; and practice self-denial, chastity, and nonviolence. Because they will not knowingly harm other living beings, including plants and animals, Jains shun meat, fish, or even vegetables whose harvest kills the entire plant, such as carrots and potatoes. They will not work in the military, in farming

A young Sikh raises a ceremonial sword at a shrine in the holy city of Amritsar, in northern India. The Sikhs' four-hundred-year-old Golden Temple can be seen in the background.

This Hindu temple in Khajuraho was built in the eleventh century A.D. The Hindu faith is enormously influential in India, the country where most Hindus live.

or fishing, or in the manufacture or sale of alcohol and drugs.

Though the Jains are a relatively small group (about 4 million), they exercise considerable influence in India through their business dealings and charitable contributions. Together with Christians and Buddhists, Jains make up 4 percent of India's population (Embree 2003).

Religion and the State in India

Religion was a moving force in India's drive to overturn British colonialism. The great Mohandas K. Gandhi (1869–1948) led the long struggle to regain India's sovereignty, which culminated in its independence in 1947. A proponent of nonviolent resistance, Gandhi persuaded Hindus and Muslims, ancient enemies, to join together in defying British domination. But his influence as a peacemaker could not override the Muslims' demand for a separate state of their own. Immediately after independence was granted, India was partitioned into two states, Pakistan for the Muslims and India for the Hindus. The new arrangement caused large-scale migrations of Indians, especially Muslims, from one nation to the other, and sparked boundary disputes that continue to this day. In many areas Muslims were forced to abandon places they

considered sacred. In the chaotic months that followed, centuries of animosity between the two groups boiled over into riots, ending in Gandhi's assassination in January 1948.

Today, India is a secular state that is dominated by Hindus (see Figure 15-1 on page 352). Though the government is officially tolerant of the Muslim minority, tensions between Hindus and Muslims remain high in some states. Conflict also exists among various Hindu groups, from fundamentalists to more secular and ecumenical adherents (Embree 2003).

Many observers see religion as the moving force in Indian society. That certainly can be said of politics. When Indian political parties align themselves along religious lines, their actions polarize the nation's population. One party in particular, the Bharatiya Janata Party (BJP), is dominated by Hindu nationalists. Members of this party who manage to get elected to local office tend to tolerate anti-Muslim violence. In 2003, the BJP's electoral victories in the state of Guyarat were followed by over 2,000 deaths and the displacement of 220,000 people from their homes. Many commentators see the religious divide in India as being greater now than it has been at any time since the partition of India and Pakistan (*The Economist* 2002; Embree 2003; Mishra 2003).

Religion and Society in India

Though religion provides a great deal of social support for the people of India, many critics charge that it has also impeded the nation's economic progress. For example, the persistence of the Hindu caste system prevents many individuals from reaching their full potential, while favoring less competent people of high birth.

Another way in which religion has hampered social progress is the Hindu custom of the *dowry*, a major transfer of wealth from a bride's parents to the groom's family. Although dowry giving has been illegal in India for several decades, it is still done surreptitiously, as part of the terms that are negotiated when a marriage is arranged. In fact, dowry demands have been escalating recently, along with the flood of consumer goods that has been coming into the country. Indian parents can be deadly serious about dowries. If a groom's family is disappointed in the bride's dowry, they may provoke her suicide or even murder her. In 2000 alone, government statistics show, 6,000 young women died a "dowry death" at the hands of greedy in-laws. The shocking crimes have grabbed the Indian public's attention, and grassroots women's groups are now campaigning to protect young women's lives (Crossette 2003).

Suppose the political landscape in the United States has changed. The two mainstream parties, which once appealed to a broad cross section of U.S. voters, have begun to champion specific religious beliefs. As you prepare to cast

your vote, what are your concerns, both personal and societal? Assuming that one of the parties supports your religious views, would you vote for its candidates on that basis? What would you do if neither party was sympathetic to your beliefs?

SOCIAL POLICY and RELIGION   Religion in the Schools   www.
mhhe.com
/schaefer9

The Issue

Should public schools be allowed to sponsor organized prayers in the classroom? How about reading Bible verses, or just a collective moment of silence? Can public school athletes offer up a group prayer in a team huddle? Should students be able to initiate voluntary prayers at school events? Each of these situations has been an object of great dissension among those who see a role for prayer in the schools and those who want to maintain strict separation of church and state.

Another controversy concerns the teaching of theories about the origin of humans and the universe. Mainstream scientific thinking holds that humans evolved over billions of years from one-celled organisms, and that the universe came into being 15 billion years ago as a result of a "big bang." These theories are challenged by people who hold to the biblical account of the creation of humans and the universe some 10,000 years ago—a viewpoint known as ***creationism.*** Creationists want their theory taught in the schools as the only one, or at the very least, as an alternative to the theory of evolution.

Who has the right to decide these issues, and what is the "right" decision? Religion in the schools is one of the thorniest issues in U.S. public policy today.

The Setting

The issues just described go to the heart of the First Amendment's provisions on religious freedom. On the one hand, the government must protect the right to practice one's religion; on the other hand, it cannot take any measures that would seem to "establish" one religion over another (the separation of church and state).

In the key case of *Engle v. Vitale*, the Supreme Court ruled in 1962 that the use of nondenominational prayer in New York schools was "wholly inconsistent" with the First Amendment's prohibition against government es-

tablishment of religion. In finding that organized school prayer violated the Constitution—even when no student was required to participate—the Court argued, in effect, that promoting religious observance was not a legitimate function of government or education. Subsequent Court decisions have allowed *voluntary* school prayer by students, but forbid school officials to *sponsor* any prayer or religious observance at school events. Despite these rulings, many public schools still regularly lead their students in prayer recitations or Bible reading (D. Firestone 1999).

The controversy over whether the biblical account of creation should be presented in school curricula recalls the famous "monkey trial" of 1925. In that trial, high school biology teacher John T. Scopes was convicted of violating a Tennessee law making it a crime to teach the scientific theory of evolution in public schools. Today, creationists have gone beyond espousing fundamentalist religious doctrine; they are attempting to reinforce their position regarding the origins of humanity and the universe with quasi-scientific data.

In 1987, the Supreme Court ruled that states could not compel the teaching of creationism in public schools if the primary purpose was to promote a religious viewpoint. For a while, this ruling gave priority to the theory of evolution in most public school districts, but especially in the South and Midwest, creationists have been chipping away at the dominance of evolutionary theory in the classroom. Many school districts now require that teachers entertain alternative theories to evolution and the creation of the universe, and some discount evolution altogether.

Sociological Insights

Supporters of school prayer and of creationism feel that strict Court rulings have forced too great a separation between what Émile Durkheim called the *sacred* and the *profane*. They insist that the use of nondenominational prayer can in no way lead to the establishment of an ecclesia in the United States. Moreover, they believe that school prayer—and the teaching of creationism—can provide the spiritual guidance and socialization that many children today do not receive from parents or regular church attendance. Many communities also believe that schools should transmit the dominant culture of the United States by encouraging prayer.

Opponents of school prayer and creationism argue that a religious majority in a community might impose religious viewpoints specific to its faith at the expense of religious minorities. These critics question whether school prayer can remain truly voluntary. Drawing on the interactionist perspective and small-group research, they suggest that children will face enormous social pressure to conform to the beliefs and practices of a religious majority.

Policy Initiatives

School education is fundamentally a local issue, so most initiatives and lobbying have taken place at the local or state level. A significant departure from the local nature of this issue came in 2003, when President George W. Bush declared that schools whose policies prevent constitutionally protected school prayer risk losing their federal education funds. At the same time, federal courts were taking a hard line on religion in the schools. In a decision that is unlikely to be upheld, a federal appeals court ruled that reciting the phrase "under God" during the Pledge of Allegiance that opens each school day violates the U.S. Constitution (Religion News Service 2003).

In a controversial ruling in 2003, the U.S. Ninth Circuit Court of Appeals declared that reciting the phrase "under God" in public schools during the Pledge of Allegiance violates the U.S. Constitution. The ruling, which is under appeal, may well be reversed.

The activism of religious fundamentalists in the nation's public school system raises a more general question: Whose ideas and values deserve a hearing in classrooms? Critics see this campaign as one step toward sectarian religious control of public education. They worry that at some point in the future, teachers may not be able to use books or make statements that conflict with fundamentalist interpretations of the Bible. For advocates of a liberal education who are deeply committed to intellectual (and religious) diversity, this is a genuinely frightening prospect.

Let's Discuss

1. Was there any organized prayer in the school you attended? Was creationism part of the curriculum?
2. Do you think that promoting religious observance is a legitimate function of education?
3. How might a conflict theorist view the issue of organized school prayer?

CHAPTER RESOURCES

Summary

Religion is a cultural universal, found throughout the world in various forms. This chapter examines the major world religions, the functions and dimensions of religion, and the four basic types of religious organization.

1. Émile Durkheim stressed the social impact of religion in attempting to understand individual religious behavior within the context of the larger society.
2. Eighty-seven percent of the world's population adheres to some form of religion. Tremendous diversity exists in religious beliefs and practices, which may be heavily influenced by culture.
3. Religion helps to integrate a diverse society and provides social support in time of need.
4. Max Weber saw a connection between religious allegiance and capitalistic behavior in a religious orientation he termed the **Protestant ethic.**
5. In *liberation theology,* the teachings of Christianity become the basis for political efforts to alleviate poverty and social injustice.
6. From a Marxist point of view, religion serves to reinforce the social control of those in power. It discourages collective political action, which could end capitalist oppression and transform society.
7. Religious behavior is expressed through religious *beliefs, rituals,* and *experience.*
8. Sociologists have identified four basic types of religious organization: the *ecclesia,* the *denomination,* the *sect,* and the *new religious movement (NRM),* or *cult.*
9. Advances in communications have led to a new type of church organization, the electronic church. Televangelists now preach to more people than belong to many denominations, and roughly 2 million people a day use the Internet for religious purposes.
10. India is a secular state that is dominated by a religious majority, the Hindus. The creation of a separate nation, Pakistan, for the Muslim minority following India's independence in 1947 did not end the centuries-old strife between the two groups, which has worsened with their political polarization.
11. Today, the question of how much religion, if any, should be permitted in the U.S. public schools is a matter of intense debate.

Critical Thinking Questions

1. From a conflict point of view, explain how religion could be used to bring about social change. Can you think of an example?
2. What role do new religious movements (or cults) play in the organization of religion? Why are they so often controversial?
3. Do politics and religion mix? Explain your reasoning.

Key Terms

Creationism A literal interpretation of the Bible regarding the creation of humanity and the universe, used to argue that evolution should not be presented as established scientific fact. (page 369)

Cultural universal A common practice or belief found in every culture. (351)

Denomination A large, organized religion that is not officially linked with the state or government. (363)

Ecclesia A religious organization that claims to include most or all members of a society, and is recognized as the national or official religion. (362)

Established sect A religious group that is the outgrowth of a sect, yet remains isolated from society. (365)

Liberation theology Use of a church, primarily Roman Catholicism, in a political effort to eliminate poverty, discrimination, and other forms of injustice from a secular society. (358)

New religious movement (NRM) or **cult** A small, secretive religious group that represents either a new religion or a major innovation of an existing faith. (365)

Profane   The ordinary and commonplace elements of life, as distinguished from the sacred. (351)

Protestant ethic   Max Weber's term for the disciplined work ethic, this-worldly concerns, and rational orientation to life emphasized by John Calvin and his followers. (358)

Religion   A unified system of beliefs and practices relative to sacred things. (351)

Religious belief   A statement to which members of a particular religion adhere. (360)

Religious experience   The feeling or perception of being in direct contact with the ultimate reality, such as a divine being, or of being overcome with religious emotion. (361)

Religious ritual   A practice required or expected of members of a faith. (360)

Sacred   Elements beyond everyday life that inspire awe, respect, and even fear. (351)

Sect   A relatively small religious group that has broken away from some other religious organization to renew what it considers the original vision of the faith. (364)

Secularization   The process through which religion's influence on other social institutions diminishes. (351)

TECHNOLOGY RESOURCES

 www. mhhe.com /schaefer9

Internet Connection

*Note: While all the URLs listed were current as of the printing of this book, these sites often change. Please check our website (**www.mhhe.com/schaefer9**) for updates, hyperlinks, and exercises related to these sites.*

1. Sociologists find it useful to distinguish between four basic forms of religious organization: the ecclesia, the denomination, the sect, and the new religious movement, or cult. The emergence of new religious movements has been the subject of public scrutiny recently. To examine cult group controversies, visit **http://religiousmovements. lib.virginia.edu/cultsect/cultsect.htm.**

2. The American Religion Data Archive (**www.arda.tm**) is a project funded by the Lilly Endowment, Inc., which acts to preserve quantitative data on American religion. Use the interactive maps on this site to learn more about religious congregations and memberships in your home state.

Online Learning Center with PowerWeb

Do you know the difference between a cult and a sect, between the mundane and the sacred? Test your knowledge by doing the crossword puzzle posted at the student center of the Online Learning Center, at **www.mhhe.com/ schaefer9.** This puzzle is not only challenging; it is a valuable learning aid.

Reel Society Interactive Movie CD-ROM

Reel Society includes scenes that can be used to spark discussion about the following topics from this chapter:

• World Religions
• Religious Belief, Ritual, and Experience

EDUCATION

DURHAM COUNTY LITERACY COUNCIL

MY MOM IS
A TERRIFIC STUDENT.
SHE'S LEARNING TO READ.

The need for education isn't limited to school-age youths. This poster recognizes adults who strive to learn a skill most of us take for granted: reading. Nationwide, some 10 million adult Americans cannot read English. Some are immigrants from other countries; others suffer from learning disabilities or a disadvantaged upbringing.

Sociological Perspectives on Education

Schools as Formal Organizations

Trends in Contemporary Education

Social Policy and Education: School Choice Programs

Boxes

RESEARCH IN ACTION: Violence in the Schools

SOCIOLOGY ON CAMPUS: The Debate over Title IX

TAKING SOCIOLOGY TO WORK: Ray Zapata, Business Owner and Former Regent, Texas State University

In order to find Public School 261 in District 10, a visitor is told to look for a mortician's office. The funeral home, which faces Jerome Avenue in the North Bronx, is easy to identify by its green awning. The school is next door, in a former roller-skating rink. No sign identifies the building as a school. A metal awning frame without an awning supports a flagpole, but there is no flag....

Textbooks are scarce and children have to share their social studies books. The principal says there is one full-time pupil counselor and another who is here two days a week: a ratio of 930 children to one counselor. The carpets are patched and sometimes taped together to conceal an open space. "I could use some new rugs," she observes....

Two first grade classes share a single room without a window, divided only by a blackboard. Four kindergartens and a sixth grade class of Spanish-speaking children have been packed into a single room in which, again, there is no window. A second grade bilingual class of 37 children has its own room but again there is no window.

The library is a tiny, windowless and claustrophobic room. I count approximately 700 books. Seeing no reference books, I ask a teacher if encyclopedias and other reference books are kept in classrooms.

"We don't have encyclopedias in classrooms," she replies. "That is for the suburbs."

The school, I am told, has 26 computers for its 1,300 children. There is one small gym and children get one period, and sometimes two, each week. Recess, however, is not possible because there is no playground....

The school, I am told, is 90 percent black and Hispanic; the other 10 percent are Asian, white or Middle Eastern.

In a sixth grade social studies class the walls are bare of words or decorations. There seems to be no ventilation system, or, if one exists, it isn't working.

On the top floor of the school, a sixth grade of 30 children shares a room with 29 bilingual second graders. Because of the high class size there is an assistant with each teacher. This means that 59 children and four grown-ups—63 in all—must share a room that, in a suburban school, would hold no more than 20 children and one teacher. There are, at least, some outside windows in this room—it is the only room with windows in the school—and the room has a high ceiling. It is a relief to see some daylight....

As I leave the school, a sixth grade teacher stops to talk....

I ask her, "Do the children ever comment on the building?"

"They don't say," she answers, "but they know."

I ask her if they see it as a racial message.

"All these children see TV," she says. "They know what suburban schools are like. Then they look around them at their school. This was a roller-rink, you know.... They don't comment on it but you see it in their eyes. They understand." *(Kozol 1991:85, 86, 87, 88)* ■ 🖱

Additional information about this excerpt can be found on the Online Learning Center at **www.mhhe.com/schaefer9.**

In the prosperous 1980s, Jonathan Kozol, the author of this passage from *Savage Inequalities,* toured public schools throughout the United States. He found that while White students in affluent suburban towns enjoyed state-of-the-art science labs, superb music and art programs, and elaborate athletic facilities, inner-city children were crowded into antiquated, decrepit buildings, deprived of even the most basic requirements— textbooks, classrooms, computers, counselors. An educator himself, Kozol challenged his readers to confront the social implications of this stark contrast in educational resources.

Education, like the family and religion, is a cultural universal. As such it is an important aspect of socialization—the lifelong process of learning the attitudes, values, and behavior considered appropriate to members of a particular culture. As we saw in Chapter 4, socialization can occur in the classroom or at home, through interactions with parents, teachers, friends, and even strangers. Exposure to books, films, television, and other forms of communication also promotes socialization. When learning is explicit and formalized—when some people consciously teach, while others adopt the role of learner—the process of socialization is called **education.** But students learn far more about their society at school than what is included in the curriculum.

This chapter focuses in particular on the formal systems of education that characterize modern industrial societies. Do public schools offer everyone a way up the socioeconomic ladder, or do they reinforce existing divisions among social classes? What is the "hidden curriculum" in U.S. schools? And what have sociologists learned about the latest trends in education, such as competency testing? We will begin with a discussion of three theoretical perspectives on education: functionalist, conflict, and interactionist. An examination of schools as formal organizations—as bureaucracies and subcultures of teachers and students—follows. Two contemporary educational trends, testing and homeschooling, merit special mention. The chapter closes with a social policy discussion of controversial school choice programs. ■

SOCIOLOGICAL PERSPECTIVES ON EDUCATION

Education is now a major industry in the United States. In the last few decades, increasing proportions of people have obtained high school diplomas, college degrees, and advanced professional degrees. For example, the proportion of people 25 years of age or over with a high school diploma increased from 41 percent in 1960 to more than 84 percent in 2000. Those with a college degree rose from 8 percent in 1960 to about 27 percent in 1999 (see Figure 16-1, page 376, for international comparisons).

Throughout the world, education has become a vast and complex social institution that prepares citizens for the roles demanded by other social institutions, such as the family, government, and the economy. The functionalist, conflict, and interactionist perspectives offer distinctive views of education as a social institution.

Functionalist View

Like other social institutions, education has both manifest (open, stated) and latent (hidden) functions. The most basic *manifest* function of education is the transmission of knowledge. Schools teach students how to read, speak foreign languages, and repair automobiles. Another important manifest function is the bestowal of status. Because many believe this function is performed inequitably, we will consider it later, in the section on the conflict view of education.

In addition to these manifest functions, schools perform a number of *latent* functions: transmitting culture, promoting social and political integration, maintaining social control, and serving as an agent of change.

Transmitting Culture

As a social institution, education performs a rather conservative function—transmitting the dominant culture. Schooling exposes each generation of young people to the existing beliefs, norms, and values of their culture. In our society, we learn respect for social control and reverence for established institutions, such as religion, the family, and the presidency. Of course, this statement is true of many other cultures as well. While schoolchildren in the United States are hearing about the accomplishments of George Washington and Abraham Lincoln,

FIGURE 16-1

Percentage of Adults Ages 25 to 64 Who Have Completed Higher Education, 1999

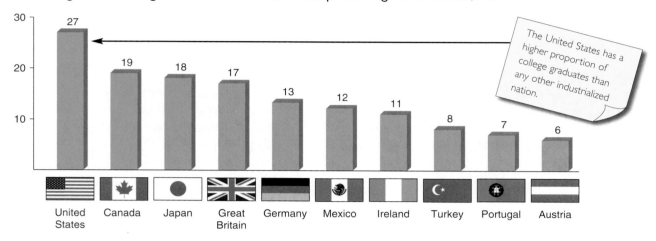

Source: Bureau of the Census 2002a:832.

British children are hearing about the distinctive contributions of Queen Elizabeth I and Winston Churchill.

In Great Britain, the transmission of the dominant culture through schools goes far beyond learning about monarchs and prime ministers. In 1996, the government's chief curriculum adviser—noting the need to fill a void left by the diminishing authority of the Church of England—proposed that British schools should socialize students into a set of core values. The list included honesty, respect for others, politeness, a sense of fair play, forgiveness, punctuality, nonviolent behavior, patience, faithfulness, and self-discipline (Charter and Sherman 1996).

Sometimes nations may reassess the ways in which they transmit culture. Recently South Koreans began to question the content of their school curriculum. South Korean schools teach traditional Confucian values, with a focus on rote memorization. The emphasis is on accumulating facts rather than on reasoning logically. Entrance to college turns on a highly competitive exam that tests students' knowledge of facts. Once in college, students have virtually no opportunity to change their educational programs, and their instruction continues to emphasize memorization. The combination of an economic crisis and growing complaints about the educational process has caused government officials to reevaluate the nation's educational structure. Moreover, growth in juvenile crime, although low by our standards, has led the government to introduce a new civic education program emphasizing honesty and discipline (Woodard 1998).

On the college level in the United States, controversy has been growing over the general education or basic

First-graders in a bilingual class at Acoma Pueblo, New Mexico. These Native American children are holding on to their heritage while learning the English skills they will need to function in mainstream American society.

curriculum requirements. Critics charge that standard academic curricula have failed to represent the important contributions of women and people of color to history, literature, and other fields of study. The underlying questions raised by this debate, still to be resolved, are: Which ideas and values are essential for instruction? Which culture should be transmitted by the schools and colleges of the United States?

Cultural transmission also occurs when students receive their formal schooling in another nation. The United States is a popular destination for college students from abroad: each year, over half a million foreign students enroll at U.S. institutions of higher learning. Typically, only a fourth as many U.S. students choose to study abroad. Of those countries where foreign students originate, Mexico alone receives about as many U.S. students as it sends to the United States, as Table 16-1 shows.

Promoting Social and Political Integration

Many institutions require students in their first year or two of college to live on campus, to foster a sense of community among diverse groups. Education serves the latent function of promoting social and political integration by transforming a population composed of diverse racial, ethnic, and religious groups into a society whose members share—to some extent—a common identity. Historically, schools in the United States have played an important role in socializing the children of immigrants into the norms, values, and beliefs of the dominant culture. From a functionalist perspective, the common identity and social integration fostered by education contribute to societal stability and consensus (Touraine 1974).

In the past, the integrative function of education was most obvious in its emphasis on promoting a common language. Immigrant children were expected to learn English. In some instances, they were even forbidden to speak their native languages on school grounds. More recently, bilingualism has been defended both for its educational value and as a means of encouraging cultural diversity. However, critics argue that bilingualism undermines the social and political integration that education has traditionally promoted.

p. 74

Table 16-1	Foreign Students by Country of Origin or Destination				
Foreign Students in the United States			**U.S. Students Abroad**		
	Country	**Number of Students**		**Country**	**Number of Students**
	India	66,836		Great Britain	30,289
	China	63,211		Italy	16,127
	Korea	49,046		Spain	16,016
	Japan	46,810		France	11,905
	Taiwan	28,930		Mexico	8,360
	Canada	25,279		Australia	8,066
	Mexico	12,518		Germany	5,116
	Total, all countries	582,867			151,168

Note: Data for foreign students are for 2001–2002; data for U.S. students abroad, for 2000–2001.

Source: Institute of International Education, 2003.

Think About It
Why are the statistics for sending nations so different from those for receiving nations?

In response to a high pregnancy rate among adolescent girls, many schools now offer sex education courses that promote abstinence. When schools attempt to remedy negative social trends, they are serving as an agent of social change.

Maintaining Social Control

In performing the manifest function of transmitting knowledge, schools go far beyond teaching skills like reading, writing, and mathematics. Like other social institutions, such as the family and religion, education prepares young people to lead productive and orderly lives as adults by introducing them to the norms, values, and sanctions of the larger society.

Through the exercise of social control, schools teach students various skills and values essential to their future positions in the labor force. They learn punctuality, discipline, scheduling, and responsible work habits, as well as how to negotiate the complexities of a bureaucratic organization. As a social institution, education reflects the interests of both the family and another social institution, the economy. Students are trained for what is ahead, whether it be the assembly line or a physician's office. In effect, then, schools serve as a transitional agent of social control, bridging the gap between parents and employers in the life cycle of most individuals (Samuel Bowles and Gintis 1976; M. Cole 1988).

Schools direct and even restrict students' aspirations in a manner that reflects societal values and prejudices. School administrators may allocate ample funds for athletic programs but give much less support to music, art, and dance. Teachers and guidance counselors may encourage male students to pursue careers in the sciences but steer female students into careers as early childhood

teachers. Such socialization into traditional gender roles can be viewed as a form of social control.

Serving as an Agent of Change

So far, we have focused on the conservative functions of education—on its role in transmitting the existing culture, promoting social and political integration, and maintaining social control. Yet education can also stimulate or bring about desired social change. Sex education classes were introduced in public schools in response to the soaring pregnancy rate among teenagers. Affirmative action in admissions—giving priority to females or minorities—has been endorsed as a means of countering racial and sexual discrimination. Project Head Start, an early childhood program that serves more than 905,000 children annually, has sought to compensate for the disadvantages in school readiness experienced by children from low-income families (Bureau of the Census 2002a:357).

p. 259

Education also promotes social change by serving as a meeting ground where distinctive beliefs and traditions can be shared. In 2002, there were 582,867 foreign students in the United States, of whom 72 percent were from developing nations. Cross-cultural exchanges between these visitors and citizens of the United States ultimately broaden the perspective of both the hosts and their guests. The same is certainly true when students from the United States attend schools in Europe, Latin America, Africa, or the Far East.

Numerous sociological studies have revealed that additional years of formal schooling are associated with openness to new ideas and more liberal social and political viewpoints. Sociologist Robin Williams points out that better-educated people tend to have greater access to factual information, to hold more diverse opinions, and to possess the ability to make subtle distinctions in analysis. Formal education stresses both the importance of qualifying statements (in place of broad generalizations) and the need at least to question (rather than simply accept) established truths and practices. The scientific method, which relies on *testing* hypotheses, reflects the questioning spirit that characterizes modern education (R. Williams et al. 1964).

p. 29

RAY ZAPATA **Business Owner and Former Regent, Texas State University**

Ray Zapata, investor, community activist, and restaurant owner, thinks his degree in sociology was the best preparation he could have received for a life in business and politics. A graduate of Angelo State University in Texas, Zapata finds that his understanding of society and social diversity has given him perspective on his community and helped him to cooperate with others from different backgrounds. "I think that I can pretty much fit anywhere, whether I'm in New York, London, or South Africa, and I think that's very, very important," he remarks.

Zapata was the second Hispanic to be appointed to the Board of Regents of the Texas State University system. As a regent, he was charged with overseeing both the financial and educational management of the system, which includes working with the state legislature to gain funding for new programs and facilities. During his term he presided over a half-billion-dollar construction program, including a major expansion at his alma mater, Angelo State.

More than the buildings that went up during his term, though, Zapata prides himself on the open admissions policy the Board instituted during his tenure. "If you put education out of reach of the working class or poor people in our society, then I think you lose an opportunity for great minds," he says. One of the most wonderful moments for this regent came when he watched a Hispanic woman who had worked as a janitor at Southwest State University graduate at the top of her class. Zapata wants to see more students like her, including senior citizens, on Texas State campuses. "Education will never hurt you at any age," he says.

Let's Discuss

1. How does an open admissions policy benefit society?
2. In what ways do the elderly benefit from education?

Conflict View

Sociologist Christopher J. Hurn (1985) has compared the functionalist and conflict views of schooling. According to Hurn, the functionalist perspective portrays contemporary education as a basically benign institution. For example, it argues that schools rationally sort and select students for future high-status positions, thereby meeting society's need for talented and expert personnel. In contrast, the conflict perspective views education as an instrument of elite domination. Schools convince subordinate groups of their inferiority, reinforce existing social class inequality, and discourage alternative and more democratic visions of society.

Criticizing the functionalist view, conflict theorists argue that the educational system socializes students into values dictated by the powerful, that schools stifle individualism and creativity in the name of maintaining order, and that the level of change they promote is relatively insignificant. From a conflict perspective, the inhibiting effects of education are particularly apparent in the "hidden curriculum" and the differential way in which status is bestowed.

The Hidden Curriculum

Schools are highly bureaucratic organizations, as we will see later. Many teachers rely on rules and regulations to maintain order. Unfortunately, the need for control and discipline can take precedence over the learning process. Teachers may focus on obedience to the rules as an end in itself, in which case students and teachers alike become victims of what Philip Jackson (1968) has called the *hidden curriculum* (see also Freire 1970; Margolis 2001).

The term **hidden curriculum** refers to standards of behavior that are deemed proper by society and are taught subtly in schools. According to this curriculum, children must not speak until the teacher calls on them, and must regulate their activities according to the clock or bells. In addition, they are expected to concentrate on their own work rather than to assist other students who learn more slowly. A hidden curriculum is evident in schools around the world. For example, Japanese schools offer guidance sessions that seek to improve the classroom experience and develop healthy living skills. In effect, these sessions instill values and encourage behavior

379

In this classroom in Tokyo, children take turns serving lunch. Shouldering adult responsibilities is part of the hidden curriculum in Tokyo's public schools.

useful in the Japanese business world, such as self-discipline and openness to group problem solving and decision making (Okano and Tsuchiya 1999).

In a classroom that is overly focused on obedience, value is placed on pleasing the teacher and remaining quiet rather than on creative thought and academic learning. Habitual obedience to authority may result in the type of distressing behavior documented by Stanley Milgram in his classic obedience studies (Leacock 1969).

p. 173

Credentialism

Fifty years ago, a high school diploma was the minimum requirement for entry into the paid labor force of the United States. Today, a college diploma is virtually the bare minimum. This change reflects the process of *credentialism*—a term used to describe an increase in the lowest level of education needed to enter a field.

In recent decades, the number of occupations that are viewed as professions has risen. Credentialism is one symptom of this trend. Employers and occupational associations typically contend that such changes are a logical response to the increasing complexity of many jobs. However, in many cases, employers raise the degree requirements for a position simply because all applicants have achieved the existing minimum credential (R. Collins 1979; Dore 1976; Hurn 1985).

Conflict theorists observe that credentialism may reinforce social inequality. Applicants from poor and minority backgrounds are especially likely to suffer from the escalation of qualifications, since they lack the financial resources needed to obtain degree after degree. In addition, upgrading of credentials serves the self-interest of the two groups most responsible for this trend. Educational institutions profit from prolonging the investment of time and money that people make by staying in school. Moreover, as C. J. Hurn (1985) has suggested, current job-holders have a stake in raising occupational requirements, since credentialism can increase the status of an occupation and lead to demands for higher pay. Max Weber anticipated this possibility as early as 1916, concluding that the "universal clamor for the creation of educational certificates in all fields makes for the formation of a privileged stratum in businesses and in offices" (Gerth and Mills 1958:240–241).

Use Your Sociological Imagination www.mhhe.com/schaefer9

How would you react if the job you have or plan to pursue suddenly required a higher-level degree? If suddenly the requirements were lowered?

Bestowal of Status

Both functionalist and conflict theorists agree that education performs the important function of bestowing status. As noted earlier, an increasing proportion of people in the United States are obtaining high school diplomas, college degrees, and advanced professional degrees. From a functionalist perspective, this widening bestowal of status is beneficial not only to particular recipients but to society as a whole. According to Kingsley Davis and Wilbert E. Moore (1945), society must distribute its members among a variety of social positions. Education can contribute to this process by sorting people into appropriate levels and courses of study that will prepare them for positions within the labor force.

p. 206

Conflict sociologists are far more critical of the *differential* way in which education bestows status. They stress that schools sort pupils according to social class background. Although the educational system helps certain poor children to move into middle-class professional positions, it denies most disadvantaged children the same educational opportunities afforded to children of the affluent. In this way, schools tend to preserve social class inequalities in each new generation (Giroux 1988; Pinkerton 2003).

Even a single school can reinforce class differences by putting students in tracks. The term ***tracking*** refers to the practice of placing students in specific curriculum groups on the basis of their test scores and other criteria. Tracking begins very early, often in reading groups during first grade. Most recent research on such ability groupings raises questions about its effectiveness, especially for low-ability students. Tracks can reinforce the disadvantages that children from less affluent families may face if they haven't been exposed to reading materials, computers, and other forms of educational stimulation during their early childhood years. It is estimated that about 60 percent of elementary schools in the United States and about 80 percent of secondary schools use some form of tracking (Hallinan 2003; Sadker and Sadker 2000).

Tracking and differential access to higher education are evident in many nations around the world. Japan's educational system mandates equality in school funding and insists that all schools use the same textbooks. Nevertheless, only the more affluent Japanese families can afford to send their children to *juku*, or cram schools. These afternoon schools prepare high school students for examinations that determine admission into prestigious colleges (Efron 1997).

Conflict theorists hold that the educational inequalities produced by tracking are designed to meet the needs of modern capitalist societies. Samuel Bowles and Herbert Gintis (1976) have argued that capitalism requires a skilled, disciplined labor force, and that the educational system of the United States is structured with that objective in mind. Citing numerous studies, they offer support for what they call the ***correspondence principle.*** According to this approach, schools promote the values expected

Lunchtime at a high school in Laguna Niguel, California. Schools in affluent suburban communities bestow a special status on their students, most of whom come from White non-Hispanic families. Conflict theorists charge that the U.S. educational system tends to reinforce social class inequality.

Studies conducted since 1987 suggest that the funding inequities between richer and poorer school districts have actually widened in recent years.

of individuals in each social class and perpetuate social class divisions from one generation to the next. Thus, working-class children, assumed to be destined for subordinate positions, are likely to be placed in high school vocational and general tracks, which emphasize close supervision and compliance with authority. In contrast, young people from more affluent families are likely to be directed to college preparatory tracks, which stress leadership and decision making—the skills they are expected to need as adults.

While the correspondence principle continues to be persuasive, researchers have noted that race and gender may overshadow class in their impact on students' educational experiences. In many countries from South Africa to the United States, Black children receive less education than White children, in large part because of an unequal distribution of educational resources. And in many places, such as China, girls still receive less education than boys (M. Cole 1988; Gordon 2002).

Treatment of Women in Education

The educational system of the United States, like many other social institutions, has long been characterized by discriminatory treatment of women. In 1833, Oberlin College became the first institution of higher learning to admit female students—some 200 years after the first men's college was established. But Oberlin believed that women should aspire to become wives and mothers, not lawyers and intellectuals. In addition to attending classes, female students washed men's clothing, cared for their rooms, and served them at meals. In the 1840s, Lucy Stone, then an Oberlin undergraduate and later one of the nation's most outspoken feminist leaders, refused to write a commencement address because it would have been read to the audience by a male student (Fletcher 1943; Flexner 1972).

In the 20th century, sexism in education showed up in many ways—in textbooks with negative stereotypes of women, counselors' pressure on female students to prepare for "women's work," and unequal funding for women's and men's athletic programs. But perhaps nowhere was educational discrimination more evident than in the employment of teachers. The positions of university professor and college administrator, which hold relatively high status in the United States, were generally filled by men. Public school teachers, who earn much lower salaries, were largely female.

Women have made great strides in one area: the proportion of women who continue their schooling. Women's access to graduate education and to medical, dental, and law schools has increased dramatically in the last few decades as a result of the Education Act of 1972.

Box 16-1 examines the far-reaching effects of Title IX, the part of the act that concerns discrimination against women in education.

In cultures in which traditional gender roles remain the social norm, women's education suffers appreciably. For example, in rural China, a school with several hundred students often has only a handful of girls. Although the central government is attempting to address the inequality, the typical five- or six-year-old girl in Chinese villages is engaged in farmwork rather than schoolwork. In 1995, China's State Education Commission estimated that the nation had nearly 10 million school dropouts, most of them girls (P. Tyler 1995).

Interactionist View

In George Bernard Shaw's play *Pygmalion,* later adapted as the hit Broadway musical *My Fair Lady,* flower girl Eliza Doolittle is transformed into a "lady" by Professor Henry Higgins, who changes her manner of speech and teaches her the etiquette of "high society." When Eliza is introduced to society as an aristocrat, she is readily accepted. People treat her as a "lady" and she responds as one.

p. 185 The labeling approach suggests that if we treat people in particular ways, they may fulfill our expectations. Children who are labeled as "troublemakers" may come to view themselves as delinquents. Similarly, a dominant group's stereotyping of racial minorities may limit their opportunities to break away from expected roles.

Can the labeling process operate in the classroom? Because of their focus on micro-level classroom dynamics, interactionist researchers have been particularly interested in this question. Howard S. Becker (1952) studied public schools in low-income and more affluent areas of Chicago. He noticed that administrators expected less of students from poor neighborhoods, and wondered if teachers accepted their view. A decade later, in *Pygmalion in the Classroom,* psychologist Robert Rosenthal and school principal Lenore Jacobson (1968) documented what they referred to as a ***teacher-expectancy effect***—the impact that a teacher's expectations about a student's performance may have on the student's actual achievements. This effect is especially evident in the lower grades (through grade three) (Brint 1998).

Although the Chinese government is attempting to address educational inequalities, girls continue to receive less education than boys—especially in rural areas.

16-1 THE DEBATE OVER TITLE IX

Few federal policies have had such a visible effect on education over the last 30 years as Title IX, which mandates gender equity in education in federally funded schools. Congressional amendments to the Education Act of 1972, together with guidelines for their implementation developed by the Department of Health, Education, and Welfare in 1974–1975, have caused significant changes for both men and women at all levels of schooling. Collectively called Title IX provisions, they require schools to make the following changes or risk losing all federal assistance:

- Eliminate all sex-segregated classes and extracurricular activities. This requirement led to the end of all-girl home economics classes and all-boy shop classes, although single-sex hygiene and physical education classes are still permitted.
- End sex discrimination in admissions and financial aid. This provision forbids admissions officers from inquiring into whether an applicant is married, pregnant, or the parent of a child. Single-sex schools are exempt from the requirement.
- End sex discrimination in the hiring and promotion of faculty.
- Provide more opportunities for women to play sports, both intramural and extramural. All-men's athletic teams are not required to accept women, however.

Today, Title IX is still one of the more controversial attempts ever made by the federal government to promote equality for all citizens. Its consequences for the funding of college athletics programs are hotly debated, while its real and lasting effects on college admissions and employment are often forgotten. Critics charge that men's teams have suffered from proportional funding of women's teams and athletic scholarships, since schools with tight athletic budgets can expand women's sports only at the expense of men's sports. To a certain extent, non-revenue-producing men's sports such as wrestling and golf do appear to have suffered as women's teams have been added. But the high expense of some men's sports, particularly football, would be beyond many schools' means even without Title IX expenditures. And the gains for women have more than made up for the losses to men. In 1971,

> Critics charge that men's teams have suffered from proportional funding of women's teams and athletic scholarships.

when there were few opportunities for women athletes on college campuses, only 300,000 girls participated in high school sports. In 2003, three decades after Title IX opened up college athletics to women, the figure was 2.7 million.

For minority women, however, the results have been less satisfactory. Most of the women's sports that have benefited from increases in scholarships over the last 20 years, like rowing and volleyball, traditionally have not been attractive to minority women. Twenty-five years ago, just 2 percent of female college athletes were African American. Today, the percentage is a disappointing 2.7 percent.

Sociologists note, too, that the social effects of sports on college campuses are not all positive. Michael A. Messner, professor of sociology at the University of Southern California, points to some troubling results of a survey by the Women's Sports Foundation. The study shows that teenage girls who play sports simply for fun have more positive body images than girls who don't play sports. But those who are "highly involved" in sports are more likely than other girls to take steroids and to become binge drinkers and risk takers. "Everyone has tacitly agreed, it seems, to view men's sports as the standard to which women should strive to have equal access," Messner writes. "Missing from the debate is any recognition that men's sports have become sources of major problems on campuses: academic cheating, sexual violence, alcohol abuse, steroid use, serious injuries and other health issues, to name just a few" (Messner 2002:B9). Messner is skeptical of a system that propels a lucky few college athletes to stardom each year while leaving the majority, many of them African American, without a career or an education. Certainly that was not the kind of equal opportunity legislators envisioned when they wrote Title IX.

Let's Discuss

1. Has Title IX had an effect on you personally? If so, explain. On balance, do you think the increase in women's participation in sports has been good for society as a whole?
2. Are the negative social effects of men's sports evident on your campus? If so, what changes would you recommend to address the problem?

Sources: Federal Register, June 4, 1975; V. Gutierrez 2002; H. Mason 2003; Messner 2002.

Between 1965 and 1966, children in a San Francisco elementary school were administered a verbal and reasoning pretest. Rosenthal and Jacobson then *randomly* selected 20 percent of the sample and designated them as "spurters"—children of whom teachers could expect superior performance. On a later verbal and reasoning test, the spurters were found to score significantly higher than before. Moreover, teachers evaluated them as more interesting, more curious, and better-adjusted than their classmates. These results were striking. Apparently, teachers' perceptions that the students were exceptional led to noticeable improvements in their performance.

Studies in the United States have revealed that teachers wait longer for an answer from a student they believe to be a high achiever and are more likely to give such children a second chance. In one experiment, teachers' expectations were even shown to have an impact on students' athletic achievements. Teachers obtained better athletic performance—as measured in the number of sit-ups or push-ups performed—from those students of whom they *expected* higher numbers (R. Rosenthal and Babad 1985).

Despite these findings, some researchers continue to question the accuracy of the teacher-expectancy effect. They claim it is too difficult to define and measure teacher expectancy. Further studies are needed to clarify the relationship between teacher expectations and actual student performance. Nevertheless, interactionists emphasize that ability alone may be less predictive of academic success than one might think (Brint 1998).

SCHOOLS AS FORMAL ORGANIZATIONS

Nineteenth-century educators would be amazed at the scale of schools in the United States as we head into the 21st century. For example, California's public school system, the largest in the nation, currently enrolls as many children as there were in secondary schools in the entire country in 1950 (Bureau of the Census 1975:368; 2002a).

In many respects, today's schools, when viewed as an example of a formal organization, are similar to factories, hospitals, and business firms. Like these organizations, schools do not operate autonomously; they are influenced by the market of potential students. This statement is especially true of private schools, but could have broader impact if acceptance of voucher plans and other school choice programs increases. The parallels between schools and other types of formal organizations will become more apparent as we examine the bureaucratic nature of schools, teaching as an occupation, and the student subculture (Dougherty and Hammack 1992).

Bureaucratization of Schools

It simply is not possible for a single teacher to transmit culture and skills to children of varying ages who will enter many diverse occupations. The growing number of students being served by individual schools and school systems, as well as the greater degree of specialization required within a technologically complex society, have combined to bureaucratize schools.

Max Weber noted five basic characteristics of bureaucracy, all of which are evident in the vast majority of schools, whether at the elementary, secondary, or even college level.

pp. 133–135

1. **Division of labor.** Specialized experts teach particular age levels and specific subjects. Public elementary and secondary schools now employ instructors whose sole responsibility is to work with children with learning disabilities or physical impairments.
2. **Hierarchy of authority.** Each employee of a school system is responsible to a higher authority. Teachers must report to principals and assistant principals, and may also be supervised by department heads. Principals are answerable to a superintendent of schools, and the superintendent is hired and fired by a board of education.
3. **Written rules and regulations.** Teachers and administrators must conform to numerous rules and regulations in the performance of their duties. This bureaucratic trait can become dysfunctional; the time invested in completing required forms could instead be spent in preparing lessons or conferring with students.
4. **Impersonality.** As class sizes have swelled at schools and universities, it has become more difficult for teachers to give personal attention to each student. In fact, bureaucratic norms may actually encourage teachers to treat all students in the same way, despite the fact that students have distinctive personalities and learning needs.
5. **Employment based on technical qualifications.** At least in theory, the hiring of instructors is based on professional competence and expertise. Promotions are normally dictated by written personnel policies; people who excel may be granted lifelong job security through tenure.

Functionalists take a generally positive view of the bureaucratization of education. Teachers can master the skills needed to work with a specialized clientele, since they no longer are expected to cover a broad range of instruction. The chain of command within schools is clear. Students are presumably treated in an unbiased fashion because of uniformly applied rules. Finally, security of position protects teachers from unjustified dismissal. In general, then, functionalists stress that the bureaucratization of education increases the likelihood that students, teachers, and administrators will be dealt with fairly—that is, on the basis of rational and equitable criteria.

In contrast, conflict theorists argue that the trend toward more centralized education has harmful consequences for disadvantaged people. The standardization of educational curricula, including textbooks, will generally reflect the values, interests, and lifestyles of the most powerful groups in our society, and may ignore those of racial and ethnic minorities. In addition, the disadvantaged, more so than the affluent, will find it difficult to sort through complex educational bureaucracies and to organize effective lobbying groups. Therefore, in the view of conflict theorists, low-income and minority parents will have even less influence over citywide and statewide educational administrators than they have over local school officials (Bowles and Gintis 1976; M. Katz 1971).

Sometimes schools can seem overwhelmingly bureaucratic, with the effect of stifling rather than nourishing intellectual curiosity in students. This concern has led many parents and policymakers to push for school choice programs—allowing parents to choose the school that suits their children's needs, and forcing schools to compete for their "customers."

In the United States, another significant countertrend to the bureaucratization of schools is the availability of education over the Internet. Increasingly, colleges and universities are reaching out via the web, offering entire courses and even majors to students in the comfort of their homes. Online curricula provide flexibility for working students and others who may have difficulty attending conventional classes because of distance or disability. Research on this type of learning is just beginning, so the question of whether teacher–student contact can thrive online remains to be settled. Computer-mediated instruction may also have an impact on instructors' status as employees, which we will discuss next, as well as on alternative forms of education like adult education and homeschooling.

Use Your Sociological Imagination

How would you make your school less bureaucratic? What would it be like?

Teachers: Employees and Instructors

Whether they serve as instructors of preschoolers or graduate students, teachers are employees of formal organizations with bureaucratic structures. There is an inherent conflict in serving as a professional in a bureaucracy. The organization follows the principles of hierarchy and expects adherence to its rules, but professionalism demands the individual responsibility of the practitioner. This conflict is very real for teachers, who experience all the positive and negative consequences of working in bureaucracies (see Table 6-2 on page 134).

A teacher undergoes many perplexing stresses every day. While teachers' academic assignments have become more specialized, the demands on their time remain diverse and contradictory. There are conflicts inherent in serving as an instructor, a disciplinarian, and an employee of a school district at the same time. Burnout is one result of these stresses: 20 percent of new teachers quit the profession within three years (*Education Week* 2000). Still, order is needed to establish an environment in which students can actually learn. Many observers sense that the nation's schools have been the scene of increasingly violent misbehavior in recent years, although their concerns may be overblown (see Box 16-2, page 386).

Given these difficulties, does teaching remain an attractive profession in the United States? In 2002, 5.7 percent of first-year college students indicated that they were interested in becoming elementary school teachers and 4.3 percent, high school teachers. Although these figures reflect a modest upturn in the appeal of teaching in recent years, they are dramatically lower than the 13 percent of first-year male students and 38 percent of first-year female students who held these occupational aspirations in 1968 (Astin et al. 1994; Sax et al. 2002:27).

Undoubtedly, economic considerations enter into students' feelings about the attractiveness of teaching. In 2001, the average salary for all public elementary and secondary school teachers in the United States was $43,250, placing teachers somewhere near the average of all wage earners in the nation. (In private industry, workers with professional responsibilities and educational qualifications comparable to those of teachers earn salaries ranging from $52,000 to $75,000.) In most other industrial countries, teachers' salaries are higher in relation to the general standard of living (American Federation of Teachers 2002).

The status of any job reflects several factors, including the level of education required, financial compensation, and the respect given the occupation within society. The teaching profession (see Table 9-2, page 209) is feeling pressure in all three of these areas. First, the amount of formal schooling required for teaching remains high, and the public has begun to call for new competency examinations. Second, the statistics just cited demonstrate that teachers' salaries are significantly lower than those of many professionals and skilled workers. Finally, the overall prestige of the teaching profession has declined in the last decade. Many teachers have become disappointed and frustrated and have left the educational world for careers in other professions.

Student Subcultures

An important latent function of education relates directly to student life: Schools provide for students' social and

16-2   VIOLENCE IN THE SCHOOLS

Littleton, Colorado; Jonesboro, Arkansas; West Paducah, Kentucky; Pearl, Mississippi; Edinboro, Pennsylvania; Springfield, Oregon—these are now more than just the names of small and medium-size cities. They resonate with the sound of gunshots, of kids killing kids on school grounds. As a result, people no longer perceive schools as safe havens. But how accurate is that impression?

Studies of school violence put the recent spate of school killings in perspective:

- A child has less than a one in a million chance of being killed at school.
- Ninety-nine percent of violent deaths of school-aged children in 1992–1999 occurred *outside* school grounds.
- Fewer students are now being found with guns in school.
- With the exception of 1999, school-associated violent deaths declined every year from 1992 through 2000.
- Twenty-three times more children are killed in gun *accidents* than in school killings.

Schools, then, are safer than neighborhoods, but people are still unnerved by the perception of an alarming rise in schoolyard violence generated by heavy media coverage of recent incidents. Some conflict theorists object to the huge outcry about recent violence in schools. Af-

ter all, they note, violence in and around inner-city schools has a long history. It seems that only when middle-class White children are the victims does school violence become a plank on the national policy agenda. When violence hits the middle class, the problem is viewed not as an extension of delinquency, but as a structural issue in need of legislative remedies, such as gun control.

Meanwhile, feminists observe that virtually all the offenders are male, and in some instances, such as the case in Jones-

> A child has less than a one in a million chance of being killed at school.

boro, the victims are disproportionately female. The precipitating factor in the violence is often a broken-off dating relationship—yet another example of the violence of men against women (or in this case, boys against girls).

Increasingly, efforts to prevent school violence are focusing on the ways in which the socialization of young people contributes to violence. For example, the *Journal of the American Medical Association* published a study of Second Step, a violence prevention curriculum for elementary school students that teaches social skills related to anger management,

impulse control, and empathy. The study evaluated the impact of the program on urban and suburban elementary school students and found that it appeared to lead to a moderate decrease in physically aggressive behavior and an increase in neutral and prosocial behavior at school.

Some people believe that a key ingredient in the prevention of violence, in or out of school, is greater parental supervision of and responsibility for their children. In her book *A Tribe Apart*, Patricia Hersch documents the lives of eight teens growing up in a Virginia suburb over a three-year period. Her conclusion: Children need meaningful adult relationships in their lives. And former Secretary of Education Richard Riley cites studies showing that youths who feel connected to their parents and schools are less likely to engage in high-risk behaviors.

Let's Discuss

1. Has a shooting or other violent episode ever occurred at your school? If so, how did students react? Do you feel safer at school than at home, as experts say you are?
2. What steps have administrators at your school taken to prevent violence? Have they been effective, or should other steps be taken?

Sources: Department of Education 1999; Donohue et al. 1998; Hersch 1998; National Center for Education Statistics 2002a.

---

recreational needs. Education helps toddlers and young children to develop interpersonal skills that are essential during adolescence and adulthood. In their high school and college years, students may meet future husbands and wives and establish lifelong friendships.

When people observe high schools, community colleges, or universities from the outside, students appear to constitute a cohesive, uniform group. However, the student subculture is actually complex and diverse. High school cliques and social groups may crop up based on race, social class, physical attractiveness, placement in

courses, athletic ability, and leadership roles in the school and community. In his classic community study of "Elm-town," August B. Hollingshead (1975) found some 259 distinct cliques in a single high school. The cliques, whose average size was five, were centered on the school itself, on recreational activities, and on religious and community groups.

Amid these close-knit and often rigidly segregated cliques, gay and lesbian students are particularly vulnerable. Peer group pressure to conform is intense at this age. Although coming to terms with one's sexuality is difficult

Student subcultures are more diverse today than they were in the past. Many adults are returning to college (left) to obtain further education, advance their careers, or change their line of work. And the practice of *mainstreaming* means that classrooms at all levels are likely to include young people with disabilities (right).

for all adolescents, it can be downright dangerous for those whose sexual orientation does not conform to societal expectations. According to a study by the Massachusetts Department of Education (2000), students who describe themselves as gay, lesbian, or bisexual are significantly more likely than others to attempt suicide, miss classes, and be threatened or injured by other students (see Figure 16-2, page 388).

Teachers and administrators are becoming more sensitized to these issues. Perhaps more important, some schools are creating gay–straight alliances (GSAs), school-sponsored support groups that bring gay teens together with sympathetic straight peers. Begun in Los Angeles in 1984, these programs numbered 1,623 nationwide in 2003; most were founded after the murder of Matthew Shepard, a gay college student, in 1998. In some districts parents have objected to these organizations, but the same court rulings that protect the right of conservative Bible groups to meet on school grounds also protect GSAs. In 2003, the gay–straight movement reached a milestone when the New

York City public schools moved an in-school program for gays, bisexuals, and transgender students to a separate school of their own. The Harvey Milk High School was named in memory of San Francisco's first openly gay city supervisor, who was assassinated in 1978 (Gay Lesbian and Straight Education Network 2003).

We can find a similar diversity of student groups at the college level. Burton Clark and Martin Trow (1966) and, more recently, Helen Lefkowitz Horowitz (1987) have identified four distinctive subcultures among college students:

1. The *collegiate* subculture focuses on having fun and socializing. These students define what constitutes a "reasonable" amount of academic work (and what amount of work is "excessive" and leads to being labeled a "grind"). Members of the collegiate subculture have little commitment to academic pursuits. Athletes often fit into this subculture.

High school students gather in Boston for a Gay/Straight Youth Pride march. An annual event, the march is sponsored by the Governor's Commission on Gay and Lesbian Youth and the Massachusetts Department of Education.

2. The *academic* subculture identifies with the intellectual concerns of the faculty and values knowledge for its own sake.

3. The *vocational* subculture is primarily interested in career prospects, and views college as a means of obtaining degrees that are essential for advancement.

4. Finally, the *nonconformist* subculture is hostile to the college environment, and seeks out ideas that may or may not relate to academic studies. This group may find outlets through campus publications or issue-oriented groups.

Each college student is eventually exposed to these competing subcultures and must determine which (if any) seems most in line with his or her feelings and interests.

The typology used by the researchers reminds us that school is a complex social organization—almost like a community with different neighborhoods. Of course, these four subcultures are not the only ones evident on college campuses in the United States. For ex-

ample, one might find subcultures of Vietnam veterans or former full-time homemakers at community colleges and four-year commuter institutions.

Sociologist Joe R. Feagin has studied a distinctive collegiate subculture: Black students at predominantly White universities. These students must function academically and socially within universities where there are few Black faculty members or Black administrators, where harassment of Blacks by campus police is common, and where the curricula place little emphasis on Black contributions. Feagin (1989:11) suggests that "for minority students life at a predominantly White college or university means long-term encounters with *pervasive whiteness.*" In Feagin's view, African American students at such institutions experience both blatant and subtle racial discrimination, which has a cumulative impact that can seriously damage the students' confidence (see also Feagin et al. 1996).

TRENDS IN CONTEMPORARY EDUCATION

While schools are formal organizations that tend to perpetuate their own cultures, they are also subject to broad-based political and social trends that may run counter to their curricula. In this section we will look at two trends that are reshaping education in the United States: the movement toward basic competency testing and the

FIGURE 16-2

Students at Risk: Gay, Lesbian, and Bisexual

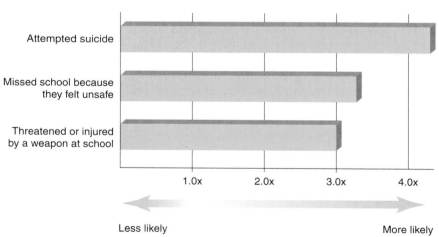

Source: Massachusetts Department of Education 2000.

Students who describe themselves as gay, lesbian, or bisexual are significantly more likely than their straight peers to attempt suicide, miss school, or be threatened or injured at school.

small but growing movement toward schooling children at home.

Testing

Few educational issues receive more attention than testing. From preschool screening through entry-level professional examinations, the practice is always under discussion. On the most basic level, testing raises questions about reliability and validity. *Validity* refers to the degree to which a scale or measure truly reflects the phenomenon under study. Does an admissions test really measure the likelihood of future academic success, for instance? *Reliability* refers to the extent to which a measure provides consistent results. If colleges use an essay exam to measure readiness to enter a first-year composition class, for instance, the process of evaluating the essays should produce consistent results, even if different people grade the essays.

Reliability and validity are major issues

FIGURE 16-3

High School Exit Examination Requirements by State, 2002

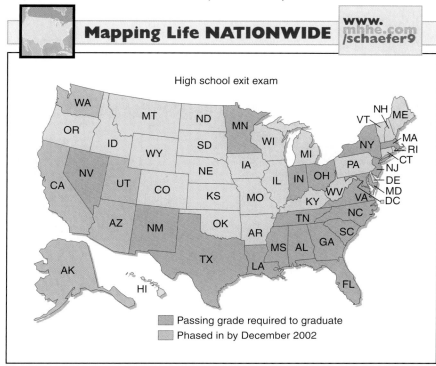

Source: Amrein and Berliner 2002.

in constructing any test; rarely are they totally resolved. Scholars who design standardized tests are constantly tweaking the questions to improve them. Accuracy in testing is becoming even more important in the era of what is termed high-stakes testing. From preschool to graduate and professional programs, testing affects everything from the allocation of funds to admission decisions in highly competitive programs. And as Figure 16-3 shows, almost half the 50 states now require or are in the process of requiring public school students to pass a standardized exam before receiving a high school diploma. The passage of the No Child Left Behind Act in 2001 further expanded the use of testing to make public schools accountable to funding agencies (Hombo 2003).

One danger of putting so much emphasis on testing is that teachers may concentrate too much on what students need to know for an upcoming test. Because the hidden curriculum includes satisfying parents' expectations about their children's test performance, the formal curriculum may narrow to include only the content and skills that are being tested (Abrams 2003).

Even when test scores are shared only with teachers, students, and parents, they can be difficult to accept. One danger is that a child may be labeled a low achiever, both

by teachers and by parents. Yet test results are increasingly being reported publicly, by race and ethnicity, gender, English-language proficiency, disability, and socioeconomic status. When properly used, such results can be employed to identify the best educational practices. Improperly used, they may serve only to stigmatize large groups of young people (Education Commission of the States 2001).

Homeschooling

When most people think of school, they think of bricks and mortar and the teachers, administrators, and other employees who staff school buildings. But for an increasing number of students in the United States, home is the classroom and the teacher is a parent. More than 1.6 million students are now being educated at home. That is about 4 percent of the K–12 school population (R. Cox 2003:27).

Before the establishment of public schools in the 1800s, families that taught their children at home lived in isolated environments or held strict religious views that were at odds with the secular environment of public schools. But today, homeschooling is attracting a broader

At a homeschool in Brunswick, Maine, a mother educates her three children. An estimated 3,500 families home-schooled their children in Maine in 1998.

(ADD) and learning disorders (LDs). Such children often do better in smaller classes, which present fewer distractions to disturb their concentration (National Home-school Association 1999).

Quality control is an issue in homeschooling. While home-schooling is legal in all 50 states, only 37 states regulate homeschools; 29 monitor students' progress through tests or evaluations. Despite the lack of uniform standards, a national study funded by the Home School Legal Defense Association reports that homeschooled students score higher than others on standardized tests, in every subject and every grade. Almost 25 percent of the students who participated in the study were working above grade level for their age (Matthews 1999; Paulson 2000).

range of families not necessarily tied to organized religion. Poor academic quality, peer pressure, and school violence are motivating many parents to teach their children at home. The recent publicity given to school shooting sprees seems to have accelerated the move toward homeschooling.

While supporters of homeschooling believe children can do just as well or better in homeschools as in public schools, critics counter that because homeschooled children are isolated from the larger community, they lose an important chance to improve their socialization skills. But proponents of homeschooling claim their children benefit from contact with others besides their own age group. They also see homeschools as a good alternative for children who suffer from attention deficit disorder

Who are the people who are running homeschools? In general, they tend to have higher-than-average incomes and educational levels. Most are two-parent families, and their children watch less television than average—both factors that are likely to support superior educational performance. The same students, with the same types of family and the same support from their parents, would probably do just as well in the public schools. As research has repeatedly shown, small classes are better than big classes, and strong parental and community involvement is key (R. Cox 2003:28).

In the next section we will look at another alternative to the public schools, school choice programs.

| SOCIAL POLICY and EDUCATION | School Choice Programs | www. mhhe.com /schaefer9 |

The Issue

Imagine a school where every child in kindergarten reads, where third graders read *The Iliad,* children beg to do second drafts of their writing, classes are small, and teachers are chosen by the school, not assigned to it. This was the vision dangled before inner-city parents in

Jersey City, New Jersey, one evening in 1998 by a private company that runs publicly financed charter schools. That night, hundreds of parents signed their children up, even though the school didn't have a location yet and was run by a company with a short track record (Winerip 1998:44).

The Setting

This is the world of the school choice movement, which is increasingly pitting parents against public school proponents. The term **school choice programs** refers to various types of educational experiments under which parents can choose where to send their children. In the 1970s, school choice took the form of *magnet schools,* which were usually centralized public schools that offered special enrichment programs to entice children from their local schools. At first they were part of an attempt to improve racial balance in the schools, but they soon became known primarily as laboratories for experiments in education. Another form of school choice is **school voucher programs,** which provide for the transfer of public funds to the public or private school of the parents' choice. Because the funds follow the child, the intent is that voucher plans will stimulate local schools to perform better and keep their students. The most recent form of school choice is the *charter school movement,* a nationwide effort that allows parents and private educators (or anyone with an idea for a school) to create and control a school that is chartered by the state and funded by public money.

Charter schools in New Jersey, like this one in Newark, have become so popular that some of them must use a lottery to select students. While parents are happy with the educational results, critics are concerned that the most motivated students are being lured away from the public schools.

Proponents of school choice often rely on the work of economists for support (Tucker 1993). The use of school vouchers, for example, was first advanced by Milton Friedman (1955). The idea is to set up a sort of free-market system of education: Parents shop for the school they want, which receives that child's portion of the school budget (a maximum of $5,553 in Milwaukee, for example). The schools that are most popular thrive; those that are not must improve to compete, or else close their doors (Jost 2002b:126).

Sociological Insights

The analogy to business competition in a free-market economy seems deceptive to some observers. While a successful business such as Coca-Cola can expand into new markets across the United States and the world, they argue, an elementary school has a limited customer base. Rather than expanding, an outstanding school will become ever more selective, as parents compete to enroll their children. Most charter schools in New Jersey are so oversubscribed they use a lottery to select their students. There is concern, too, about the state of public schools, whose most motivated students often transfer to school choice programs.

Critics of school choice programs are also troubled by the divisive religious issue underlying the voucher policy. About two-thirds of private school students in the United States attend institutions with religious affiliations; among parents who send their children to private schools, as many as 95 percent identify religion as the number-one criterion in choosing a school. For opponents of vouchers and tuition tax credits, any government aid to parochial education—whether direct or indirect—violates the nation's historic separation of church and state. Moreover, drawing on the functionalist perspective, critics of school choice point out that education in the United States has traditionally promoted social and political integration. Such integration is undermined when students attend private and parochial schools and do not interact with their peers across class, racial, ethnic, and religious lines (Jost 2002b).

Viewed from a conflict perspective, the social class and religious implications of school choice programs are a matter of concern—especially when such programs provide financial support for families to send children to private and parochial schools. Studies of existing school choice programs suggest that the more affluent households and those with highly educated parents are especially likely to take advantage of these experiments, in part because vouchers and tax credits may not cover the full cost of private school. Despite opposition by many Black civil rights groups, public opinion surveys show strong support for school vouchers among African American parents, who tend to see a voucher program, however flawed, as a welcome alternative to the public schools (M. Owens 2002).

Research has just begun on the impact of school choice programs. Thus far, the results are inconclusive: some students do better; others do not. Parents do seem satisfied with the decisions they have made, however. Studies are complicated by the fact that participants in these programs are not necessarily motivated by educational goals. Some parents enroll children in school choice or voucher programs for the sake of convenience—to decrease the distance between the child's school and the parents' workplace or to optimize the parents' work schedules. Clearly, much more research is necessary before a definitive verdict can be made on these programs (General Accounting Office 2001; Gill et al. 2001; Winerip 2003).

Policy Initiatives

As interest in school voucher programs grows, the controversy that surrounds them grows as well. Legal challenges have been mounted against several voucher programs, including those affiliated with religious groups. Plaintiffs charged that these programs violated the tradition of separation of church and state. As we saw in

pp. 369–370 the last chapter, the meaning of that fundamental concept is being redefined, and the case of vouchers is no exception. The Supreme Court ruled 5–4 in 2002 that states may give parents money to send their children to religious schools (Nagourney 2002).

So far, school choice policy decisions have been made only at the local and state levels. Relatively few parts of the country have true tax-supported voucher programs. On the federal level, legislation calling for government subsidy of tuition vouchers for low-income families failed to come to a vote in 2001, despite support from President George W. Bush (Alvarez 2001).

Interest in school choice is not unique to the United States. In Great Britain, New Zealand, and Sweden, policymakers have given parents a measure of freedom in selecting their children's schools, and government financing of schools is based on enrollment figures. In Australia, Denmark, and the Netherlands, governmental financial support for private schools has been increasing (Dijkstra and Dronkers 2003).

Let's Discuss

1. Would you send your child to a private or charter school if the government offered you a tuition voucher? Why or why not?
2. What do you think of the idea that public schools should be able to compete with private schools? What difficulties might they face that private schools do not?
3. Which is more important, maintaining the separation of church and state or fostering educational choice by allowing students to attend religious schools at public expense? Justify your position.

CHAPTER RESOURCES

Summary

Education is a cultural universal found throughout the world, although in varied forms. This chapter examines sociological views of education and analyzes schools as an example of formal organizations.

1. The transmission of knowledge and bestowal of status are manifest functions of education. Among the latent functions are transmitting culture, promoting social and political integration, maintaining social control, and serving as an agent of social change.

2. In the view of conflict theorists, education serves as an instrument of elite domination by creating standards for entry into occupations, bestowing status unequally, and subordinating the role of women.
3. Teacher expectations about a student's performance can sometimes have an impact on the student's actual achievements.
4. Today, most schools in the United States are organized in a bureaucratic fashion. Weber's five basic characteristics of bureaucracy are all evident in schools.

5. Nationwide, the trend toward increased testing of public school students has become controversial. Some people question the *reliability* and *validity* of the tests; others fear the practice may narrow the curriculum or encourage negative labeling of whole groups of students.

6. Homeschooling has become a viable alternative to traditional public and private schools. An esti-mated 1.6 million or more American children are now educated at home.

7. *School choice* and *school voucher* programs are having a direct effect on public education, forcing some schools to compete or go out of business.

Critical Thinking Questions

1. What are the functions and dysfunctions of track-ing in schools? Viewed from an interactionist per-spective, how would tracking of high school stu-dents influence the interactions between students and teachers? In what ways might tracking have positive and negative impacts on the self-concepts of various students?

2. Are the student subcultures identified in this text evident on your campus? What other student sub-cultures are present? Which subcultures have the highest (and the lowest) social status? How might functionalists, conflict theorists, and interactionists view the existence of student subcultures on a col-lege campus?

Key Terms

Correspondence principle   The tendency of schools to promote the values expected of individuals in each social class and to prepare students for the types of jobs typically held by members of their class. (page 381)

Credentialism   An increase in the lowest level of edu-cation required to enter a field. (380)

Education   A formal process of learning in which some people consciously teach while others adopt the social role of learner. (375)

Hidden curriculum   Standards of behavior that are deemed proper by society and are taught subtly in schools. (379)

Reliability   The extent to which a measure provides consistent results. (389)

School choice program   An educational experiment under which parents can choose where to send their children to school. (391)

School voucher program   A form of school choice program in which public funds are transferred to the public or private school of the parents' choice. (391)

Teacher-expectancy effect   The impact that a teacher's expectations about a student's performance may have on the student's actual achievements. (382)

Tracking   The practice of placing students in specific curriculum groups on the basis of test scores and other criteria. (381)

Validity   The degree to which a scale or measure truly reflects the phenomenon under study. (389)

TECHNOLOGY RESOURCES

Internet Connection

*Note: While all the URLs listed were current as of the printing of this book, these sites often change. Please check our website (**www.mhhe.com/schaefer9**) for updates, hyperlinks, and exercises related to these sites.*

1. The National Center for Education Statistics provides the public with statistical information on education. To learn more about the most common college majors, tuition trends, and percentages of degrees conferred on females and African Americans, visit the center at **www.nces.ed.gov.**

2. This chapter has focused on many aspects of education, including tracking and school voucher programs. In his book *Savage Inequalities*, Jonathan Kozol demonstrates just how different school can be for poor and minority-race children versus middle-class and White children. You can read an interview with Mr. Kozol at **www. ascd.org.**

Online Learning Center with PowerWeb

The formation of student subcultures is one of the latent functions of education. You can conduct your own "Cyber Student Organization Fair" by visiting the Online Learning Center at **www.mhhe.com/schaefer9** and link-ing to the student center. While you are in the student center, link to "Internet Exercises." The third exercise will direct you to sites where you can learn about organizations found on university and college campuses.

Reel Society Interactive Movie CD-ROM

Reel Society includes scenes that can be used to spark discussion about the following topic from this chapter:

• Sociological Perspectives on Education

17

GOVERNMENT AND POLITICS

This poster, sponsored by the American Institute of Graphic Arts, urges citizens to overcome their apathy toward politics and vote. In the United States, most eligible voters either are not registered or do not bother to vote.

Power and Authority

Political Behavior

Models of Power Structure in the United States

Political Activism on the Internet

Social Policy and the Government: Campaign Financing

Boxes

SOCIOLOGY IN THE GLOBAL COMMUNITY: Terrorist Violence

SOCIAL INEQUALITY: Gender Quotas at the Ballot Box

RESEARCH IN ACTION: Why Don't Young People Vote?

The power elite and Congress are more diverse than they were before the social movements that emerged in the 1960s brought pressure to bear on corporations, politicians, and government. Although the power elite is still composed primarily of Christian white men, there are now Jews, women, blacks, Latinos, and Asian Americans on the boards of the country's largest corporations; presidential cabinets are far more diverse than was the case forty years ago; and the highest ranks of the military are no longer filled solely by white men. In the case of elected officials in Congress, the trend toward diversity is even greater for women and all of the minority groups that we have studied. . . .

Ultimately we suggest that the increase in diversity at the top contains several ironies, the most important of which is related to what is perhaps the major unresolved tension in American life, between liberal individualism and the class structure. The diversification of the power elite has been celebrated, but this celebration ignores the continuing importance of the class structure. The movements that led to diversity in the power elite have succeeded to some extent, especially for women and minorities from privileged social backgrounds, but there has been no effect on the way the power elite functions or on the class structure itself. . . .

The power elite has been strengthened because diversity has been achieved primarily by the selection of women and minorities who share the prevailing perspectives and values of those already in power. The power elite is not

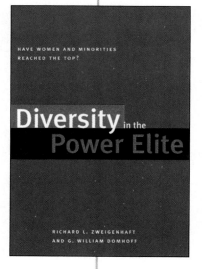

HAVE WOMEN AND MINORITIES REACHED THE TOP?

Diversity in the **Power Elite**

RICHARD L. ZWEIGENHAFT
AND G. WILLIAM DOMHOFF

"multicultural" in any full sense of the concept, but only in terms of ethnic or racial origins. This process has been helped along by those who have called for the inclusion of women and minorities without any consideration of criteria other than sex, race, or ethnicity. Because the demand was strictly for a woman on the Supreme Court, President Reagan could comply by choosing a conservative upper-class corporate lawyer, Sandra Day O'Connor. When pressure mounted to have more black justices, President Bush could respond by appointing Clarence Thomas, a conservative black Republican with a law degree from Yale University. It is yet another irony that appointments like these served to undercut the liberal social movements that caused them to happen. . . .

We therefore have to conclude on the basis of our findings that the diversification of the power elite did not generate any changes in an underlying class system. . . . The values of liberal individualism embedded in the Declaration of Independence, the Bill of Rights, and the civic culture were renewed by vigorous and courageous activists, but despite their efforts the class structure remains a major obstacle to individual fulfillment for the overwhelming majority of Americans. This fact is more than an irony. It is a dilemma. It combines with the dilemma of race to create a nation that celebrates equal opportunity but is, in reality, a bastion of class privilege and conservatism. *(Zweigenhaft and Domhoff 1998:176–177, 192, 194)* ■ 🖱

Additional information about this excerpt can be found on the Online Learning Center at **www.mhhe.com/schaefer9.**

Half a century ago C. Wright Mills ([1956] 2000b), the originator of the phrase *the sociological imagination,* studied the political process in the United States and articulated the concept of the power elite—a White male group of decision makers who in effect ruled the country. Four decades later sociologist G. William Domhoff and psychologist Richard L. Zweigenhaft returned to the question of who rules the United States. As the opening excerpt from their book *Diversity in the Power Elite* (1998) shows, they found only modest changes in the nation's power structure. Today, a few privileged women occupy positions in the power elite, but the majority of the nation's decision makers are still men, and virtually all of them are White.

The power elite operates within the framework of the existing political system, be it local, state, national, or international. By **political system,** sociologists mean the social institution that is founded on a recognized set of procedures for implementing and achieving society's goals, such as the allocation of valued resources. Like religion and the family, the political system is a cultural universal: It is found in every society. In the United States, the political system holds the ultimate responsibility for addressing the social policy issues examined in this textbook: child care, the AIDS crisis, welfare reform, and so forth.

How does the power elite maintain its power? How do other groups attempt to exert theirs? Does our campaign finance system put some groups at a disadvantage? In this chapter we will analyze the impact of government on people's lives from a sociological point of view. We will begin with a macro-level analysis of the sources of power in a political system, and the three major types of authority. We will see how politics works, with particular attention to political socialization, citizens' participation, and the changing role of women. We'll also look at two models of power in the United States: the elite and the pluralist models. Finally, the social policy section will explore the controversy over campaign financing, an issue that vividly illustrates the close relationship between government and the moneyed elite who seek to influence the political process. ▪

POWER AND AUTHORITY

In any society, someone or some group makes important decisions about how to use resources and how to allocate goods, whether it be a tribal chief or a parliament or a dictator. A cultural universal common to all societies, then, is the exercise of power and authority. Inevitably, the struggle for power and authority involves *politics,* which political scientist Harold Lasswell (1936) tersely defined as "who gets what, when, and how." In their study of politics and government, sociologists are concerned with social interactions among individuals and groups and their impact on the larger political and economic order.

ability to exercise one's will over others. To put it another way, whoever can control the behavior of others is exercising power. Power relations can involve large organizations, small groups, or even people in an intimate association.

Alan Greenspan, chairman of the Board of Governors of the Federal Reserve, meeting with some of the other board members. The 12-member Board of Governors is a government body that exerts economic power by controlling key interest rates. Board meetings are held behind closed doors, adding to the influence of these elite decision makers.

Power

◀ p. 205   Power lies at the heart of a political system. According to Max Weber, **power** is the

Sociology in the Global Community

17-1 TERRORIST VIOLENCE

For people in the United States, the moment that a hijacked commercial airliner slammed into the World Trade Center on the morning of September 11, 2001, terrorism became a frightening reality—something that no longer took place only in foreign countries.

It was, of course, not the first terrorist attack on the United States, or even on the World Trade Center. Just six years earlier, the U.S. federal building in Oklahoma City had been truck-bombed by terrorist Timothy McVeigh, who was born and raised in the United States; 168 people died in the blast. And in 1993, terrorists had succeeded in destroying the lower levels of the World Trade Center. But the collapse of the two towers and the loss of more than 3,000 lives in 2001 seared the nation's psyche in a way the earlier attacks had not.

Acts of terror, whether perpetrated by a few or by many people, can also be a powerful political force. Formally defined, **terrorism** is the use or threat of violence against random or symbolic targets in pursuit of political aims. For terrorists, the end justifies the means. They believe the status quo is oppressive and desperate measures are essential to end the suffering of the deprived. Convinced that working through the formal political process will not effect the desired political change, terrorists insist that illegal actions—often directed against innocent people—are needed. Ultimately, they hope to intimidate society and thereby bring about a new political order.

An essential aspect of contemporary terrorism involves use of the media. Terrorists may wish to keep secret their individual identities, but they want their political messages and goals to receive as much publicity as possible. Drawing upon Erving Goffman's dramaturgical approach, sociologist Alfred McClung Lee has likened terrorism to the theater,

where certain scenes are played out in predictable fashion. Whether through calls to the media, anonymous manifestos, or other means, terrorists typically admit responsibility for and defend their violent acts.

Some political commentators have argued that terrorism defies definition because one person's "terrorist" is another person's "freedom fighter." To many people around the world, for example, Osama bin Laden and the terrorists who destroyed the World Trade Center were heroes. In this view of terrorism, we carry our biases into our evaluation of terrorist incidents and criticize only those perpetrated by groups who do not share our political goals.

Sociologists reject this critique, countering that even in warfare there are ac-

> An essential aspect of contemporary terrorism involves use of the media.

cepted rules that outlaw the use of certain tactics. For example, civilian noncombatants are supposedly immune from deliberate attack and are not to be taken prisoner. If we are to set objective standards regarding terrorism, then we should condemn *any and all people* who are guilty of certain actions, no matter how understandable or even admirable some of their goals may be.

Since September 11, 2001, governments around the world have renewed their efforts to fight terrorism. Though the public has generally regarded increased surveillance and social control as a necessary evil, these measures have nonetheless raised governance issues. For example, some citizens in the United States and elsewhere have questioned whether measures such as the USA PA-

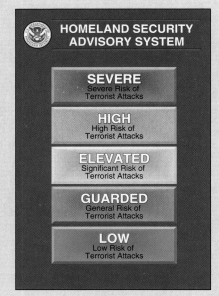

The Homeland Security Advisory system, begun in 2002 to inform the U.S. public of the potential risk of terrorist attacks.

TRIOT Act of 2001 threaten civil liberties. Citizens also complain about the heightened anxiety created by the vague alerts issued by the federal government from time to time. Worldwide, immigration and the processing of refugees have slowed to a crawl, separating families and preventing employers from filling job openings. As these efforts to combat political violence illustrate, the term *terrorism* is an apt one.

Let's Discuss

1. Have you ever lived in a place where the threat of terrorism was a part of daily life, or known someone who did? What was it like?
2. Can any goal, no matter how noble, justify terrorist activity?

Sources: R. Howard and Sawyer 2003; A. Lee 1983; R. Miller 1988.

Because Weber developed his conceptualization of power in the early 1900s, he focused primarily on the nation-state and its sphere of influence. Today scholars recognize that the trend toward globalization has brought new opportunities, and with them new concentrations of power. Power as the ability to exercise one's will over others is now exercised on a global as well as a national stage, as countries and multinational corporations vie to control access to resources and manage the distribution of capital (Sernau 2001).

There are three basic sources of power within any political system: force, influence, and authority. *Force* is the actual or threatened use of coercion to impose one's will on others. When leaders imprison or even execute political dissidents, they are applying force; so, too, are terrorists when they seize or bomb an embassy or assassinate a political leader (see Box 17-1). *Influence,* on the other hand, refers to the exercise of power through a process of persuasion. A citizen may change his or her view of a Supreme Court nominee because of a newspaper editorial, the expert testimony of a law school dean before the Senate Judiciary Committee, or a stirring speech by a political activist at a rally. In each case, sociologists would view such efforts to persuade people as examples of influence. Now let's take a look at the third source of power, *authority.*

Types of Authority

The term *authority* refers to institutionalized power that is recognized by the people over whom it is exercised. Sociologists commonly use the term in connection with those who hold legitimate power through elected or publicly acknowledged positions. A person's authority is often limited. Thus, a referee has the authority to decide whether a penalty should be called during a football game, but has no authority over the price of tickets to the game.

Max Weber ([1913] 1947) developed a classification system for authority that has become one of the most useful and frequently cited contributions of early sociology. He identified three ideal types of authority: traditional, legal-rational, and charismatic. Weber did not insist that only one type applies to a given society or organization. All can be present, but their relative importance will vary. Sociologists have found Weber's typology valuable in understanding different manifestations of legitimate power within a society.

Traditional Authority

Until the middle of the last century, Japan was ruled by a revered emperor, whose absolute power was passed down from generation to generation. In a political system based on *traditional authority,* legitimate power is conferred by custom and accepted practice. A king or queen is accepted as ruler of a nation simply by virtue of inheriting the crown; a tribal chief rules because that is the accepted practice. The ruler may be loved or hated, competent or destructive; in terms of legitimacy, that does not matter. For the traditional leader, authority rests in custom, not in personal characteristics, technical competence, or even written law. People accept the ruler's authority because that is how things have always been done. Traditional authority is absolute when the ruler has the ability to determine laws and policies.

Legal-Rational Authority

The U.S. Constitution gives Congress and our president the authority to make and enforce laws and policies. Power made legitimate by law is known as *legal-rational authority.* Leaders derive their legal-rational authority from the written rules and regulations of political systems, such as a constitution. Generally, in societies based on legal-rational authority, leaders are thought to have specific areas of competence and authority, but are not thought to be endowed with divine inspiration, as in certain societies with traditional forms of authority.

Charismatic Authority

Joan of Arc was a simple peasant girl in medieval France, yet she was able to rally the French people and lead them in major battles against English invaders. How was this possible? As Weber observed, power can be legitimized by the *charisma* of an individual. The term *charismatic authority* refers to power made legitimate by a leader's exceptional personal or emotional appeal to his or her followers.

Charisma lets a person lead or inspire without relying on set rules or traditions. In fact, charismatic authority is derived more from the beliefs of followers than from the actual qualities of leaders. So long as people *perceive* a leader as having qualities that set him or her apart from ordinary citizens, that leader's authority will remain secure and often unquestioned.

Unlike traditional rulers, charismatic leaders often become well known by breaking with established institutions and advocating dramatic changes in the social structure and the economic system. Their strong hold over their followers makes it easier to build protest movements that challenge the dominant norms and values of a society. Thus, charismatic leaders such as Jesus, Joan of Arc, Gandhi, Malcolm X, and Martin Luther King, Jr. all used their power to press for changes in accepted social behavior. But so did Adolf Hitler, whose charismatic appeal turned people toward violent and destructive ends in Nazi Germany.

Observing from an interactionist perspective, sociologist Carl Couch (1996) points out that the growth of the electronic media has facilitated the development of charismatic authority. During the 1930s and 1940s, the heads of state of the United States, Great Britain, and Germany all used radio to issue direct appeals to citizens. In recent decades, television has allowed leaders to "visit" people's homes and communicate with them. In both Taiwan and South Korea in 1996, troubled political leaders facing reelection campaigns spoke frequently to national audiences and exaggerated military threats from neighboring China and North Korea, respectively.

As we noted earlier, Weber used traditional, legal-rational, and charismatic authority as ideal types. In reality, particular leaders and political systems combine elements of two or more of these forms. Presidents Franklin D. Roosevelt, John F. Kennedy, and Ronald Reagan wielded power largely through the legal-rational basis of their authority. At the same time, they were unusually charismatic leaders who commanded the personal loyalty of large numbers of citizens.

Tony Blair works the crowd outside 10 Downing Street in London shortly after his election as Great Britain's prime minister. Blair draws his power from a combination of legal-rational and charismatic authority. Both became important in 2003, when he backed the United States in declaring war on Iraq, despite strong antiwar sentiment.

Use Your Sociological Imagination

What would our government be like if it were founded on traditional rather than legal-rational authority? What difference would it make to the average citizen?

POLITICAL BEHAVIOR

Citizens of the United States take for granted many aspects of their political system. They are accustomed to living in a nation with a Bill of Rights, two major political parties, voting by secret ballot, an elected president, state and local governments distinct from the national government, and so forth. Yet each society has its own ways of governing itself and making decisions. Just as U.S. residents expect Democratic and Republican candidates to compete for public office, residents of Cuba and the People's Republic of China are accustomed to one-party rule by the Communist party. In this section, we will examine a number of important aspects of political behavior within the United States.

Political Socialization

Do your political views coincide with those of your parents? Did you vote in the last election? Did you register to vote, or do you plan to do so? The process by which you acquire political attitudes and develop patterns of political behavior is known as **political socialization.** It involves not only learning the prevailing beliefs of a society but also coming to accept the political system, whatever its limitations and problems.

One of the functional prerequisites that a society must fulfill to survive is teaching recruits to accept the values and customs of the group. In a political sense, this function is crucial; each succeeding generation must be encouraged to accept a society's basic political values and its particular methods of decision making. The principal institutions of political socialization are those that also socialize us to other cultural norms: the family, schools, and the media.

Many observers see the family as playing a particularly significant role in this process. Parents pass on

◄ p. 112

their political attitudes and evaluations to their sons and daughters through discussions at the dinner table and through the example of their political involvement or apathy. Early socialization does not always determine a person's political orientation; changes can occur over time and between generations. Yet parents' views do have an important impact on their children's outlook (Jennings and Niemi 1981).

Schools provide young people with information and analysis of the political world. Unlike the family and peer groups, schools are easily susceptible to centralized and uniform control. That is why totalitarian societies commonly use educational institutions to indoctrinate students in certain political beliefs. Even in democracies, whose local schools are not under the pervasive control of the national government, political education will generally reflect the norms and values of the prevailing political order. Nonetheless, research evidence shows that traditional classroom-based civic education, as well as service learning experiences in the community, can at least encourage future political participation. Service learning generally involves academically supervised work at not-for-profit organizations or in government-affiliated outreach programs (Galston 2001; Jennings and Niemi 1981).

Table 17-1	Political Preferences in the United States
Party Identification	**Percentage of Population**
Strong Democrat	15
Not very strong Democrat	19
Independent, close to Democrat	10
Independent	19
Independent, close to Republican	7
Not very strong Republican	17
Strong Republican	12

Note: Data are for 2002. Numbers do not add to 100 percent because around 1 percent indicated other parties.

Source: J. Davis et al. 2003.

Think About It

Why do so many U.S. voters identify themselves as independents?

Participation and Apathy

In theory, a representative democracy will function most effectively and fairly if an informed and active electorate communicates its views to government leaders. Unfortunately, that is hardly the case in the United States. Virtually all citizens are familiar with the basics of the political process, and most tend to identify to some extent with a political party (see Table 17-1), but only a small minority (often members of the higher social classes) actually participate in political organizations on a local or national level. Studies reveal that only 8 percent belong to a political club or organization. Not more than one in five has *ever* contacted an official of national, state, or local government about a political issue or problem (Orum 2001).

The failure of most citizens to become involved in political parties diminishes the democratic process. Within the political system of the United States, the political party serves as an intermediary between people and government. Through competition in regularly scheduled elections, the two major parties provide for challenges to public policy and an orderly transfer of power. An individual who is dissatisfied with the state of the nation or a local community can become involved in the political process in many ways, such as by joining a political club that supports candidates for public office or by working to change a party's position on controversial issues. If, however, people do not take an interest in the decisions of major political parties, public officials in a "representative" democracy will be chosen from two unrepresentative lists of candidates.

By the 1980s, it had become clear that many people in the United States were beginning to be turned off by political parties, politicians, and big government. The most dramatic indication of this growing alienation came from voting statistics. Today, voters of all ages and races appear to be less enthusiastic than ever about elections, even presidential contests. For example, almost 80 percent of eligible voters in the United States went to the polls in the presidential election of 1896. Yet by the 2000 election, turnout had fallen to less than 51 percent of all eligible voters. Obviously, even modestly higher voter turnout could dramatically change election outcomes, as we saw in the razor-thin margin in the 2000 presidential election.

While a few nations still command high voter turnout, it is increasingly common to hear national leaders of other countries complain of voter apathy. Japan typically enjoyed 70 percent turnout in its Upper House elections through the mid-1980s, but by 2000 turnout was closer to 59 percent. In 2001, only 58 percent of British voters participated in the general elections. More

recently, just 49 percent of Swiss voters went to the polls (Peck 2002:49).

Voter apathy is not the only way to measure citizen participation. Later in this chapter we will consider how people use the Internet to organize themselves for political purposes. And in Chapter 22 we will see how people organize to protest social injustice.

In the end, political participation makes government accountable to the voters. If participation declines, government operates with less of a sense of accountability to society. This issue is most serious for the least powerful individuals and groups in the United States. Voter turnout has been particularly low among members of racial and ethnic minorities. In postelection surveys, fewer African Americans and Hispanics than Whites report that they actually voted. Many more potential voters fail to register to vote. The poor—whose focus understandably is on survival—are traditionally underrepresented among voters as well. The low turnout found among these groups is explained, at least in part, by their common feeling of powerlessness. Yet these low statistics encourage political power brokers to continue to ignore the interests of the less af-

fluent and the nation's minorities. The segment of the voting population that has shown the most voter apathy is the young: see Box 17-2 (Casper and Bass 1998).

Women in Politics

In the United States, women continue to be dramatically underrepresented in the halls of government. In 2003 there were only 73 women in Congress; they accounted for 59 of the 435 members of the House of Representatives and 14 of the 100 members of the Senate. Only six states had female governors: Arizona, Delaware, Hawaii, Kansas, Michigan, and Montana (Center for American Women and Politics 2003).

p. 288
Sexism has been the most serious barrier to women interested in holding office. Women were not even allowed to vote in national elections until 1920. Female candidates have had to overcome the prejudices of both men and women regarding

Judge Charles Burton, chairman of the Palm Beach County, Florida, canvassing board, inspects a contested punch card for signs of the voter's intentions during the manual recount that followed the 2000 presidential election. The public perception that many votes were miscounted may have undermined some Americans' faith in their electoral system, strengthening their suspicions that their votes don't count.

Research in Action

17-2   WHY DON'T YOUNG PEOPLE VOTE?

In 1971, there was great optimism. All through the 1960s, young people in the United States had participated actively in a range of political issues, from pushing civil rights to protesting the Vietnam War. They were especially disturbed by the fact that young men were barred from voting but were being drafted to serve in the military and were dying for their country. In response to these concerns, the 26th Amendment to the Constitution was ratified in 1971, lowering the voting age from 21 to 18 in federal, state, and local elections.

Now, more than 30 years later, we can consider the available research and see what happened. Frankly, what is remarkable is what did *not* happen. First, young voters (those between ages 18 and 21) have not united in any particular political sentiment. We can see in how the young vote the same divisions of race, ethnicity, and gender that are apparent among older age groups.

Second, while the momentum for lowering the voting age came from college campuses, the majority of young voters are not students at all. Many are already part of the workforce and either live with their parents or have established their own households.

Third, and particularly troubling, is their low voter turnout. In the highly competitive 2000 presidential election, only 32 percent of young people cast a vote. Compared to the figure of 50 percent in the 1972 election—the first in which 18-year-olds could vote—this turnout was extremely low.

What lies behind this voter apathy among the young? The popular explanation is that people—especially young people—are alienated from the political system, turned off by the shallowness and negativity of candidates and campaigns. True, studies have documented that young voters are susceptible to cynicism and distrust, but those qualities are not necessarily associated with voter apathy. Numerous studies show that the relationship between how people perceive the

candidates and issues and their likelihood of voting is a very complex one. Young people do vote as they age. Any disaffection with the voting booth is certainly not permanent.

Other explanations for the lower turnout among the young seem more plausible. First, the United States is virtually alone in requiring citizens to vote twice, in effect. They must first *register* to vote, often at a time when issues are not on the front burner and candidates haven't even declared. Then they must vote on election day. Young people, who

> While the momentum for lowering the voting age came from college campuses, the majority of young voters are not students at all.

tend to be mobile and to lead hectic lives, find it difficult to track voting requirements (which vary by state) and to be present where they are legally eligible to vote. In 1995, the motor-voter law went into effect, allowing people to register when they applied for or renewed driver's licenses, but this attempt to simplify the registration process has done little to change voter apathy.

Second, while citizens in the United States tend to be more active than their counterparts in other countries in politics on the community level, young people often feel unmoved by such local issues as public school financing and land use. Many national issues, such as Social Security and health care, also seem far removed from their immediate concerns. Sometimes issues such as landlord policies or student–police relations surface in college towns, mobilizing the youth vote, but their activism often declines as the issue fades from view.

Research does not point to easy solutions for reversing the three-decade pattern of low turnout among the newest voters. Facilitating the registration and

"Rock the Vote" was the theme of this celebrity get-out-the-vote rally during the 2000 presidential election campaign. But neither Sting (at the microphone) nor the other celebrities were very successful in getting out the vote among young people.

voting process, identifying local issues of interest, grassroots campaigning, and more careful evaluation of media campaigns may all help. We also need to continue to research the reasons why more than 11 million people between the ages of 18 and 24 fail to even register to vote, and why another 4 million who take that step fail to vote.

Let's Discuss

1. How often do you vote? If you do not vote, what accounts for your apathy? Are you too busy to register? Are community issues uninteresting to you?
2. Do you think voter apathy is a serious social problem? What might be done to increase voter participation in your age group and community?

Sources: Alwin 2002; Clymer 2000; A. Goldstein and Morin 2002; Jamieson, Shin, and Day 2002; T. Patterson 2002.

FIGURE 17-1

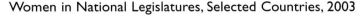

Women in National Legislatures, Selected Countries, 2003

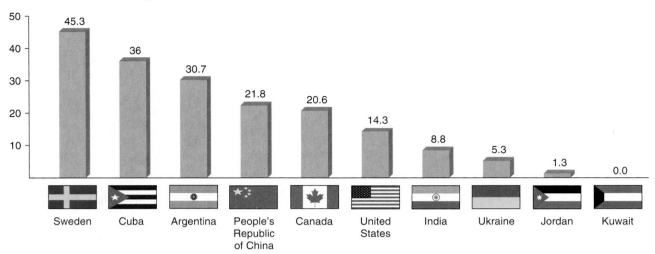

Note: Data are for lower legislative houses only, as of May 31, 2003; data on upper houses, such as the U.S. Senate or the House of Lords (U.K.) are not included.

Source: Inter-Parliamentary Union 2003.

women's fitness for leadership. Moreover, women often encounter prejudice, discrimination, and abuse *after* they are elected. Despite these problems, more women are being elected to political office, and more of them are identifying themselves as feminists.

Women politicians may be enjoying more electoral success now than in the past, but there is evidence that the media cover them differently from men. A content analysis of newspaper coverage of recent gubernatorial races showed that reporters wrote more often about a female candidate's personal life, appearance, or personality than a male candidate's, and less often about her political positions and voting record. Furthermore, when political issues were raised in newspaper articles, reporters were more likely to illustrate them with statements made by male candidates than by female candidates (Devitt 1999).

Figure 17-1 shows the representation of women in selected national legislatures. While the proportion of women has increased in the United States and many other nations, women still do not account for half the members of the national legislature in any country. Sweden ranks the highest, with 42.7 percent. Overall, the United States ranked 47th among 170 nations in the proportion of women serving as national legislators in 2000 (Inter-Parliamentary Union 2003). To remedy this situation, many countries—including the world's largest democracy, India—have reserved a minimum number of legislative seats for women (see Box 17-3).

A new dimension of women and politics emerged beginning in the 1980s. Surveys detected a growing "gen-

der gap" in the political preferences and activities of males and females. Specifically, women were more likely to register as Democrats than as Republicans. According to political analysts, the Democratic Party's support for the right to choose a legal abortion, for family and medical leave legislation, and for governmental action to require insurers to cover a minimum two-day hospital stay for new mothers has attracted women voters.

The gender gap was still evident in the 2000 presidential election. Data from exit polls revealed that Democrat Al Gore received 54 percent of women's votes, compared to 42 percent of men's votes. The 12 percent gap between the sexes indicates that turnout of female voters is a key to Democratic victories. When women did not turn out in the 1994 congressional elections, solid support from White male voters was an important factor in Republican success (Voter News Service 2000).

Use Your Sociological Imagination www.mhhe.com/schaefer9

Imagine a world in which women, not men, held the majority of elective offices. What kind of world would it be?

MODELS OF POWER STRUCTURE IN THE UNITED STATES

Who really holds power in the United States? Do "we the people" genuinely run the country through our elected representatives? Or is it true that behind the scenes, a

17-3 GENDER QUOTAS AT THE BALLOT BOX

Worldwide, women are underrepresented in government. In national legislatures, they make up only 11 percent of the total membership—far below their 49 percent share of the world's population in 2003.

To remedy this situation, many countries have adopted quotas for female representatives. In some, the government sets aside a certain percentage of seats for women, usually from 10 to 30 percent. In others, political parties have decided that 20 to 40 percent of their candidates should be women. Thirty-two countries now have some kind of female quota system.

In sheer numbers, India has seen the biggest gains in female representation. After a third of all village council seats were set aside for women, almost a million Indian women won election to local office. In South Africa, another country with quotas, women now hold 30 percent or more of the seats in both houses of Parliament. Compared with South Africa, the United States, which does not have quotas, has not done nearly as well:

Women hold only 14 percent of seats in the House of Representatives and 13 percent of seats in the Senate.

In Africa, quotas have been particularly popular in countries where women contributed to independence movements. South African women fought hard against apartheid and received constitutional guarantees against discrimina-

> Thirty-two countries now have some kind of female quota system.

tion in return. Ugandan women fought in the National Resistance Army in the 1980s, earning new respect—and new political power—from men. Women now comprise almost 25 percent of Uganda's parliament and form a minimum required percentage of all elected bodies in that country.

With support from President Yoweri Museveni, who appointed a woman,

Wandira Kazibwe, as vice president in 1994, Ugandan women have used their newfound power to enact new privileges for themselves. Married women can now share property ownership with their husbands, and widows can retain property after their husbands' death. Women legislators have also increased educational opportunities for girls in an effort to reduce the harsh poverty in their country. In President Museveni's opinion, the presence of women in government has helped to stabilize politics in Uganda. And in a country where women produce much of the wealth, he notes, they deserve to be empowered.

Let's Discuss

1. Why do you think the United States has so few women in government compared to many other nations?
2. Should the United States adopt a quota system? Why or why not?

Sources: Inter-Parliamentary Union 2003; Simmons and Wright 2000.

---

small elite controls both the government and the economic system? It is difficult to determine the location of power in a society as complex as the United States. In exploring this critical question, social scientists have developed two basic views of our nation's power structure: the power elite and the pluralist models.

Power Elite Models

Karl Marx believed that 19th-century representative democracy was essentially a sham. He argued that industrial societies were dominated by relatively small numbers of people who owned factories and controlled natural resources. In Marx's view, government officials and military leaders were essentially servants of this capitalist class and followed their wishes. Therefore, any key decisions made by politicians inevitably reflected the interests of the dominant bourgeoisie. Like others who hold an *elite model* of power relations, Marx believed that society is

ruled by a small group of individuals who share a common set of political and economic interests.

Mills's Model

Sociologist C. Wright Mills, referred to earlier in this chapter, took this model a step further in his pioneering work *The Power Elite* ([1956] 2000b). Mills described a small group of military, industrial, and governmental leaders who controlled the fate of the United States—the *power elite.* Power rested in the hands of a few, both inside and outside government.

A pyramid illustrates the power structure of the United States in Mills's model (see Figure 17-2a, page 406). At the top are the corporate rich, leaders of the executive branch of government, and heads of the military (whom Mills called the "warlords"). Directly below are local opinion leaders, members of the legislative branch of government, and leaders of special-interest groups. Mills contended that these individuals and groups would

FIGURE 17-2

Power Elite Models

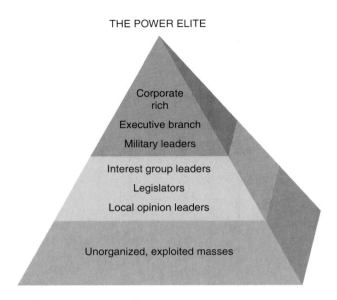

a. C. Wright Mills's model, 1956

Source: Domhoff 2001:96.

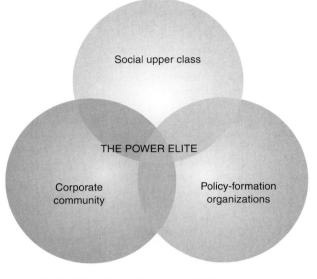

b. G. William Domhoff's model, 1998

basically follow the wishes of the dominant power elite. At the bottom of the pyramid are the unorganized, exploited masses.

The power elite model is, in many respects, similar to the work of Karl Marx. The most striking difference is that Mills believed that the economically powerful coordinate their maneuvers with the military and political establishments to serve their common interests. Yet, reminiscent of Marx, Mills argued that the corporate rich were perhaps the most powerful element of the power elite (first among "equals"). And the powerless masses at the bottom of Mills's power elite model certainly bring to mind Marx's portrait of the oppressed workers of the world, who have "nothing to lose but their chains."

A fundamental element in Mills's thesis is that the power elite not only includes relatively few members but also operates as a self-conscious, cohesive unit. Although not necessarily diabolical or ruthless, the elite comprises similar types of people who regularly interact with one another and have essentially the same political and economic interests. Mills's power elite is not a conspiracy but rather a community of interest and sentiment among a small number of influential people (A. Hacker 1964).

Admittedly, Mills failed to clarify when the elite opposes protests and when it tolerates them; he also failed to provide detailed case studies that would substantiate the interrelationships among members of the power elite. Nevertheless, his challenging theories forced scholars to

look more critically at the democratic political system of the United States.

In commenting on the scandals that have rocked major corporations such as Enron and Arthur Andersen over the last decade, observers have noted that members of the business elite *are* closely interrelated. In a study of the members of the boards of directors of Fortune 1,000 corporations, researchers found that each director can reach *every* other board of directors in just 3.7 steps. That is, by consulting acquaintances of acquaintances, each director can quickly reach someone who sits on each of the other 999 boards. Furthermore, the face-to-face contact directors regularly have in their board meetings makes them a highly cohesive elite. Finally, the corporate elite is not only wealthy, powerful, and cohesive; it is also overwhelmingly White and male (Jerry Davis 2003; Mizruchi 1996; G. Strauss 2002).

Domhoff's Model

Over the last three decades, sociologist G. William Domhoff (2001), coauthor of the chapter-opening excerpt from *Diversity in the Power Elite*, has agreed with Mills that a powerful elite runs the United States. He finds that it is still largely White, male, and upper class, as he wrote in his book with Richard L. Zweigenhaft (1998). But Domhoff stresses the role played both by elites of the corporate community and by the leaders of policy-formation organizations such as chambers of commerce and labor unions. Many of the people in both groups are also members of the social upper class.

While these groups overlap, as Figure 17-2b shows, they do not necessarily agree on specific policies. Domhoff notes that in the electoral arena, two different coalitions have exercised influence. A *corporate-conservative coalition* has played a large role in both political parties, generating support for particular candidates through direct-mail appeals. A *liberal-labor coalition* is based in unions, local environmental organizations, a segment of the minority group community, liberal churches, and the university and arts communities (Zweigenhaft and Domhoff 1998).

Pluralist Model

Several social scientists insist that power in the United States is shared more widely than the elite models indicate. In their view, a pluralist model more accurately describes the nation's political system. According to the **pluralist model,** many conflicting groups within the community have access to government, so that no single group is dominant.

The pluralist model suggests that a variety of groups play a significant role in decision making. Typically, pluralists make use of intensive case studies or community studies based on observation research. One of the most famous—an investigation of decision making in New Haven, Connecticut—was reported by Robert Dahl (1961). Dahl found that although the number of people involved in any important decision was rather small, community power was nonetheless diffuse. Few political actors exercised decision-making power on all issues. One individual or group might be influential in a battle over urban renewal but at the same time have little impact on educational policy.

The pluralist model, however, has not escaped serious questioning. Domhoff (1978, 2001) reexamined Dahl's study of decision making in New Haven and argued that Dahl and other pluralists had failed to trace how local elites who were prominent in decision making were part of a larger national ruling class. In addition, studies of community power, such as Dahl's work in New Haven, can examine decision making only on issues that become part of the political agenda. They fail to address

In 1996, anti-tobacco protesters rallied near the site of the Republican National Convention in San Diego. When public interest groups seek to exert their power through such mass protests, they are demonstrating a belief in the pluralist model of the United States' power structure.

the possible power of elites to keep certain matters entirely out of the realm of government debate.

Dianne Pinderhughes (1987) has criticized the pluralist model for failing to account for the exclusion of African Americans from the political process. Drawing on her studies of Chicago politics, Pinderhughes points out that the residential and occupational segregation of Blacks and their long political disenfranchisement violates the logic of pluralism—which would hold that such a substantial minority should always have been influential in community decision making. This critique applies to many cities across the United States, where other large racial and ethnic minorities, among them Asian Americans, Puerto Ricans, and Mexican Americans, are relatively powerless. The problems encountered by African American voters in Florida in the 2000 election bear out this critique of the pluralist model (American Civil Liberties Union 2001b).

Historically, pluralists have stressed ways in which large numbers of people can participate in or influence governmental decision making. New communications technologies like the Internet are increasing the opportunity to be heard, not just in countries such as the United States but in developing countries the world over. One common point of the elite and pluralist perspectives stands out, however: In the political system of the United States, power is unequally distributed. All citizens may be

The website for Greenpeace, an international organization of environmental activists, encourages interested citizens to get involved in public affairs.

equal in theory, yet those who are high in the nation's power structure are "more equal." New communications technology may or may not change that distribution of power.

POLITICAL ACTIVISM ON THE INTERNET

About one in six people in the United States went online to get the latest vote count during the 2000 presidential election. Not only is the Internet affecting the way people get their news; it is changing the way they think about politics. In one survey, 43 percent of Internet users said the information they received online affected their vote. Modern technology may not eliminate voter apathy, but it is one more way to motivate people to get involved in politics (Pew Research Center for the People and the Press 2001).

On the Internet, political activity is not limited to traditional party politics, and certainly not to domestic politics. In far-flung places including China, Mexico, Indonesia, Kosovo, and Malaysia, citizens are making themselves heard through *cyberactivism* or Net Activism—the use of the Internet for political purposes. In China, 10,000 members of the fast-growing Falun Gong religious sect surprised government officials with a mass rally organized on the web. In Kosovo, the staff of *Koha Ditore*, a dissident newspaper, took to the web after Ser-

bian soldiers closed their office. And in Mexico, the revolutionary Zapatista movement gained support from an online campaign for self-rule in the state of Chiapas.

As these incidents illustrate, organizers find the web especially useful in circumventing the restrictive controls of authoritarian regimes. In fact, groups branded as terrorists in a variety of states have used the web to their advantage. Websites can be established outside a country's borders, beyond the control of government officials yet still accessible to the country's citizens. What is more, government officials who would like to clamp down on such activities are constrained by their desire to reap the commercial benefits of the web. For example, Chinese officials have decided to advance information technology despite the challenges it poses to government control. The technology is simply too important to China's economic modernization for the government to suppress it. From a conflict perspective, then, the Internet seems to have the potential to level the playing field for opposition groups—or at least to minimize the ruling party's clout (Crossette 1999; Hick and McNutt 2002; Piller 2001).

Also growing in importance are borderless organizations that unite people of like mind from around the world. These are very tightly knit communities, notes Professor Juan Enriquez of Harvard University. Labor groups and environmental organizations such as Greenpeace have become particularly adept at using e-mail to mobilize activists quickly, wherever they are needed. The result: a completely new kind of power structure, compared to the more familiar face-to-face approach of Washington lobbyists. "The new people with power are those with credibility and an e-mail list," says political consultant Jennifer Laszlo. "You have no idea who they are, where they are, what color they are" (Engardio 1999:145).

Use Your Sociological Imagination

Imagine a future in which everyone in the United States has access to the Internet, and the Internet is the foremost political medium. How would government in that society differ from government today?

SOCIAL POLICY and THE GOVERNMENT

Campaign Financing

www.
mhhe.com
/schaefer9

The Issue

November 23, 1999

Question: How do you reconcile your position on campaign finance reform with all the money you are spending on television advertisements?

Hillary Rodham Clinton: "I believe we ought to have you know, more public financing of campaigns. We don't have it yet, does that mean I shouldn't raise money?"

(Washington Transcript Service 1999:17).

In her successful bid for election to the U.S. Senate, Hillary Rodham Clinton was not the first politician to criticize campaign financing methods while at the same time raising millions of dollars to pay her expenses. Over the last few decades, many seasoned representatives have left office bemoaning the amount of time they had to spend raising money. Nor, as we shall see, are attempts to regulate campaign financing new.

The Setting

Regulation of campaign contributions has a long history, beginning with efforts to bar the requirement that government employees contribute to their bosses' campaign funds. More recently, the focus on both the state and national levels has been on remedying the shortcomings of the Federal Campaign Act of 1974, which placed restrictions on so-called *hard money,* or donations made to specific candidates for national office. Hard money is now limited to $10,000 per organization or $2,000 per individual donor per election cycle (the primary and election being separate cycles). These limits were intended to keep national candidates or elected officials from being "bought" by the wealthy or by powerful special interest groups.

But soon after passage of the act, contributors and potential recipients—that is, politicians—found loopholes in the new law. In 2002, Congress passed the Bipartisan

Campaign Reform Act (BCRA) to address some of those shortcomings. For the first time, limitations were placed on contributions of *soft money*—donations to the major political parties, leadership committees, and political action committees by corporations and special-interest groups. Now, no soft money is permitted in federal elections, and its use in state and local elections is limited.

Under the BCRA, major political parties are still allowed to spend soft money freely on *independent expenditures,* or purchases made on behalf of a political position rather than an individual candidate. This *issue advocacy money,* as it has been called, has become an important way of supporting a particular candidate while escaping contribution limits. To support a pro-environment, or "green," candidate, for example, donors would purchase television ads expressing concern about the environment and pollution.

Soon after the BCRA was passed, political pundits began to speculate on how politicians might still amass huge campaign war chests, regardless of the new restrictions. Some speculated that the law would encourage political parties and political interest groups to rely more on direct mail, phone banks, voter mobilization drives, and other unregulated activities. Few thought that the massive amounts that had once been raised as soft money would disappear from politics. Indeed, in 2000, the Democratic and Republican parties each raised five times what they did in 1992. Undoubtedly, new ways will be found to channel such huge amounts

of money in a way that conforms to the BCRA. And predictably, these new innovations in spending will be followed by fresh cries for reform (Malbin et al. 2002).

Sociological Insights

Functionalists would say that political contributions keep the public involved in the democratic process and connected to the candidates. Issue advocacy money also offers voters a way to express their views on issues directly, rather than through the candidates. But conflict theorists would counter that since money brings influence, this use of material wealth allows donors to influence government policymakers in ways that tend to preserve their own wealth. In increasing numbers of cases, candidates like the multimillionaires Ross Perot and Steve Forbes have used their own private fortunes to finance their campaigns—an approach that allows them to sidestep public disclosure requirements.

Interactionists would point out the symbolic significance of the public perception that big money drives elections in the United States. Accurate or not, this impression encourages voter apathy, which is reflected in low turnout at the polls. What good does participating in politics do, voters may wonder, when special interests can spend millions to counteract their efforts?

Policy Initiatives

Surveys have regularly shown that the majority of U.S. voters want campaign finance reform, but are unsure how to achieve it. One proposal that has been advanced at the state level is to require that the names of donors be made public through posting on the Internet. Another is to place restrictions on how much money anyone can give to any organization for political purposes.

While these reform proposals have gained much public sympathy, however, the courts have generally ruled that Internet posting may invade donors' privacy, discouraging them from making campaign contributions. Financial limits may also restrict people's freedom to participate in the political process (McDermott 1999; J. Simon 1999).

On the national level, traditional reform groups—Common Cause, the League of Women Voters, and Ralph Nader's organization Public Citizen—continue to call for tighter limits on contributions by both individuals and organizations. But other interest groups, including the American Civil Liberties Union and the Cato Institute, claim that limiting anyone's involvement in the political process is unfair. The BCRA addresses citizens' complaints that politicians are routinely "bought" by wealthy special interests. Yet it also raises the specter of limits on citizens' freedom to support the candidates of their choice. With voter apathy on the rise, such limits may be too high a price to pay for campaign finance reform.

Let's Discuss

1. Did you vote in the most recent election? Does your vote count, or do special interest groups wield more power than voters like you?

2. Do you work for or contribute to political candidates? What about groups that promote special issues, like school prayer, gun control, and free trade? Which is more important to you, the candidate or the issue?

3. Would strict across-the-board spending limits on all candidates for public office help to make the political process more democratic? What about limits on political contributions of all kinds?

CHAPTER RESOURCES

Summary

1. Every society must have a **political system** in order to have recognized procedures for the allocation of valued resources.

2. There are three basic sources of **power** within any political system: **force, influence,** and **authority.**

3. Max Weber identified three ideal types of authority: **traditional, legal-rational,** and **charismatic.**

4. The principal institutions of **political socialization** in the United States are the family, schools, and the media.

5. Political participation makes government accountable to its citizens, but voters display a great deal of apathy in both the United States and other countries.

6. Women are still underrepresented in politics, but are becoming more successful at winning election to public office.

7. Advocates of the **elite model** of the U.S. power structure see the nation as being ruled by a small group of individuals who share common political

and economic interests (a ***power elite***), whereas advocates of a ***pluralist model*** believe that power is shared more widely among conflicting groups.

8. Around the world, the Internet has become a potent political arena, one that dissident groups can use to oppose the power of authoritarian regimes.

9. Despite legislative efforts to reform campaign financing methods, wealthy donors and special interest groups still wield enormous power in U.S. government through their contributions to candidates, political parties, and issue advocacy.

Critical Thinking Questions

1. In many places in the world, the United States is considered a model political system. Drawing on material presented in earlier chapters of this textbook, discuss the values and beliefs on which this political system is founded. Have those values and beliefs changed over time? Has the system itself changed?

2. Who really holds power in the college or university you attend? Describe the distribution of power at your school, drawing on the elite and pluralist models where relevant.

3. Imagine that you have joined your state representative's legislative staff as a summer intern. She has assigned you to a committee that is working on solutions to the problem of school violence. How could you use what you have learned about sociology to conceptualize the problem? What type of research would you suggest the committee undertake? What legislative solutions might you recommend?

Key Terms

Authority   Institutionalized power that is recognized by the people over whom it is exercised. (page 399)

Charismatic authority   Power made legitimate by a leader's exceptional personal or emotional appeal to his or her followers. (399)

Elite model   A view of society as being ruled by a small group of individuals who share a common set of political and economic interests. (405)

Force   The actual or threatened use of coercion to impose one's will on others. (399)

Influence   The exercise of power through a process of persuasion. (399)

Legal-rational authority   Power made legitimate by law. (399)

Pluralist model   A view of society in which many competing groups within the community have access to government, so that no single group is dominant. (407)

Political socialization   The process by which individuals acquire political attitudes and develop patterns of political behavior. (400)

Political system   The social institution that is founded on a recognized set of procedures for implementing and achieving society's goals. (397)

Politics   In Harold Lasswell's words, "who gets what, when, and how." (397)

Power   The ability to exercise one's will over others. (397)

Power elite   A small group of military, industrial, and government leaders who control the fate of the United States. (405)

Terrorism   The use or threat of violence against random or symbolic targets in pursuit of political aims. (398)

Traditional authority   Legitimate power conferred by custom and accepted practice. (399)

TECHNOLOGY RESOURCES

 ## Internet Connection

*Note: While all the URLs listed were current as of the printing of this book, these sites often change. Please check our website (**www.mhhe.com/schaefer9**) for updates, hyperlinks, and exercises related to these sites.*

1. Voting behavior among young people is one of the topics covered in this chapter. Rock the Vote (**www.rockthevote.org**) is among a growing list of organizations trying to involve youths in the political and voting process. Review the material in Box 17-2, then explore the Rock the Vote website to learn more about registering to vote and online polls.

2. Women are still greatly underrepresented in politics. To learn more about women's participation in politics, visit the Center for American Women and Politics at **www.rci.rutgers.edu/~cawp.**

 ## Online Learning Center with PowerWeb

When you visit the student center in the Online Learning Center at **www.mhhe.com/schaefer9,** link to the flash cards. There is a flash card for every key term in your text. The flash cards also have definitions for each term. Flash cards are a valuable study tool: They give you the opportunity to see how familiar you are with important terms in the chapter.

chapter

18

THE ECONOMY AND WORK

Around the world, globalization and the advent of e-commerce are transforming the economy, creating new jobs that workers may not be prepared to perform. Lack of educational opportunities, and of the means to afford new technologies, often prevents people in developing countries from taking advantage of economic change.

Economic Systems

Case Study: Capitalism in China

Aspects of Work

The Changing Economy

Social Policy and the Economy: Affirmative Action

Boxes

SOCIOLOGY IN THE GLOBAL COMMUNITY: The Worldwide Jobs–Skills Mismatch

SOCIAL INEQUALITY: Working Women in Nepal

TAKING SOCIOLOGY TO WORK: Richard J. Hawk, Vice President and Financial Consultant, Smith Barney

413

Percy Barnevik is the chief executive officer of Asea Brown Boveri, a 29-billion-dollar-a-year Swiss-Swedish builder of electric generators and transportation systems, and one of the largest engineering firms in the world. Like other global companies, ABB has recently re-engineered its operations, cutting nearly 50,000 workers from the payroll, while increasing turnover 60 percent in the same time period. Barnevik asks, "Where will all these [unemployed] people go?" He predicts that the proportion of Europe's labor force employed in manufacturing and business services will decline from 35 percent today to 25 percent in ten years from now, with a further decline to 15 percent twenty years down the road. Barnevik is deeply pessimistic about Europe's future: "If anybody tells me, wait two or three years and there will be a hell of a demand for labor, I say, tell me where? What jobs? In what cities? Which companies? When I add it all together, I find a clear risk that the 10% unemployed or underemployed today could easily become 20 to 25%.". . .

For some, particularly the scientists, engineers, and employers, a world without work will signal the beginning of a new era in history in which human beings are liberated, at long last, from a life of back-breaking toil and mindless repetitive tasks. For others, the workerless society conjures up the notion of a grim future of mass unemployment and global destitution, punctuated by increasing social unrest and upheaval. On one point virtually all of the contending parties agree. We

are, indeed, entering into a new period in history—one in which machines increasingly replace human beings in the process of making and moving goods and providing services. . . .

Most workers feel completely unprepared to cope with the enormity of the transition taking place. The rash of current technological breakthroughs and economic restructuring initiatives seem to have descended on us with little warning. Suddenly, all over the world, men and women are asking if there is a role for them in the new future unfolding across the global economy. Workers with years of education, skills, and experience face the very real prospect of being made redundant by the new forces of automation and information. What just a few short years ago was a rather esoteric debate among intellectuals and a small number of social writers around the role of technology in society is now the topic of heated conversation among millions of working people. They wonder if they will be the next to be replaced by the new thinking machines. . . .

The new high-technology revolution could mean fewer hours of work and greater benefits for millions. For the first time in modern history, large numbers of human beings could be liberated from long hours of labor in the formal marketplace, to be free to pursue leisure-time activities. The same technological forces could, however, as easily lead to growing unemployment and a global depression. *(Rifkin 1995a:11–13)* ■

Additional information about this excerpt can be found on the Online Learning Center at **www.mhhe.com/schaefer9.**

I n his book *The End of Work,* social activist Jeremy Rifkin imagines what the economic world will look like after automation and high technology have made human labor more and more obsolete. Economic forces have a huge impact on our lives—from something as basic as whether we can put food on the table to more soul-searching concerns such as "How can I be more productive?" Rifkin's view is that we must be prepared to deal with the inevitable dysfunctions and dislocations that accompany a major transformation of the global economic system.

The term *economic system* refers to the social institution through which goods and services are produced, distributed, and consumed. As with social institutions such as the family, religion, and government, the economic system shapes other aspects of the social order and is in turn influenced by them. Throughout this textbook, you have been reminded of the economy's impact on social behavior—for example, individual and group behavior in factories and offices. You have studied the work of Karl Marx and Friedrich

p. 11 Engels, who emphasized that the economic system of a society can promote social inequality. And you have learned that foreign in- p. 231 vestment in developing countries can intensify inequality among residents.

This chapter will present a sociological analysis of the impact of the economy on people's lives. What makes work satisfying? How has the trend toward deindustrialization changed the work people do? What will the workforce of the 21st century look like? We will begin to answer these questions with a macro-level analysis of two ideal types of economic system, capitalism and socialism. A case study on China, a socialist society that has been moving toward capitalism, follows. Next, we will examine various aspects of work, including the occupations and professions open to people today, worker alienation and its causes, and worker satisfaction. Then we will take a look at the ways in which the economy is changing. Finally, in the social policy section we will explore the controversy over affirmative action, an important issue in the workplace. ∎

ECONOMIC SYSTEMS

The sociocultural evolution approach developed by Gerhard Lenski categorizes preindustrial soci- p. 116 ety according to the way in which the economy is organized. The principal types of preindustrial society, as you recall, are hunting-and-gathering societies, horticultural societies, and agrarian societies.

As noted in Chapter 5, the *industrial revolution*— which took place largely in England during p. 118 the period 1760 to 1830—brought about changes in the social organization of the workplace. People left their homesteads and began working in central locations such as factories. As the industrial revolution proceeded, a new form of social structure emerged: the *industrial society,* a society that depends on mechanization to produce its goods and services.

Two basic types of economic system distinguish contemporary industrial societies: capitalism and socialism. As described in the following sections, capitalism and socialism serve as ideal types of economic system. No nation precisely fits either model. Instead, the economy of each individual state represents a mixture of capitalism

and socialism, although one type or the other is generally useful in describing a society's economic structure.

Capitalism

In preindustrial societies, land functioned as the source of virtually all wealth. The industrial revolution changed all that. It required that certain individuals and institutions be willing to take substantial risks in order to finance new inventions, machinery, and business enterprises. Eventually, bankers, industrialists, and other holders of large sums of money replaced landowners as the most powerful economic force. These people invested their funds in the hope of realizing even greater profits and thereby became owners of property and business firms.

The transition to private ownership of business was accompanied by the emergence of the capitalist economic system. *Capitalism* is an economic system in which the means of production are held largely in private hands, and the main incentive for economic activity is the accumulation of profits. In practice, capitalist systems vary in the degree to which the government regulates private ownership and economic activity (Douglas Rosenberg 1991).

Immediately following the industrial revolution, the prevailing form of capitalism was what is termed ***laissez-faire*** ("let them do"). Under the principle of laissez-faire, as expounded and endorsed by British economist Adam Smith (1723–1790), people could compete freely with minimal government intervention in the economy. Business retained the right to regulate itself and operated essentially without fear of government regulation (Smelser 1963).

Two centuries later, capitalism has taken on a somewhat different form. Private ownership and maximization of profits still remain the most significant characteristics of capitalist economic systems. However, in contrast to the era of laissez-faire, capitalism today features extensive government regulation of economic relations. Without restrictions, business firms can mislead consumers, endanger the safety of their workers, and even defraud the companies' investors—all in the pursuit of greater profits. That is why the government of a capitalist nation often monitors prices, sets safety and environmental standards for industries, protects the rights of consumers, and regulates collective bargaining between labor unions and management. Yet under capitalism as an ideal type, government rarely takes over ownership of an entire industry.

Contemporary capitalism also differs from laissez-faire in another important respect: Capitalism tolerates monopolistic practices. A ***monopoly*** exists when a single business firm controls the market. Domination of an industry allows the firm to effectively control a commodity by dictating pricing, standards of quality, and availability. Buyers have little choice but to yield to the firm's decisions; there is no other place to purchase the product or service. Monopolistic practices violate the ideal of free competition cherished by Adam Smith and other supporters of laissez-faire capitalism.

Some capitalistic nations, such as the United States, outlaw monopolies through antitrust legislation. Such laws prevent any business from taking over so much of the competition in an industry that it controls the market. The U.S. federal government allows monopolies to exist only in certain exceptional cases, such as the utility and transportation industries. Even then, regula-

tory agencies scrutinize these officially approved monopolies and protect the public. The protracted legal battle between the Justice Department and Microsoft, owner of the dominant operating system for personal computers, illustrates the uneasy relationship between government and private monopolies in capitalistic countries.

Conflict theorists point out that although *pure* monopolies are not a basic element of the economy of the United States, competition is much more restricted than one might expect in what is called a *free enterprise system.* In numerous industries, a few companies largely dominate the field and keep new enterprises from entering the marketplace.

As we have seen in earlier chapters, globalization and the rise of multinational corporations have spread the capitalistic pursuit of profits around the world. Especially in developing countries, governments are not always prepared to deal with the sudden influx of foreign capital and its effects on their economies. One particularly striking example of how unfettered capitalism can harm developing nations is found in the Democratic Republic of Congo (formerly Zaire). The Congo has significant deposits of the metal columbite-tantalite—coltan, for short—which is used in the production of electronic

In the movie *Wall Street* (1987), actors Charlie Sheen and Michael Douglas played greedy speculators engaged in insider trading and stock price manipulation. Popular culture often presents capitalists as selfish people who profit unfairly from the labor of others—an image recent corporate scandals have reinforced.

A worker mines for coltan with sweat and a stick. The sudden increase in demand for the metal by U.S. computer manufacturers caused incursions into the Congo by neighboring countries hungry for capital to finance a war. Too often, globalization can have unintended consequences for a nation's economy and social welfare.

circuit boards. Until the market for cell phones, pagers, and laptop computers heated up recently, U.S. manufacturers got most of their coltan from Australia. But at the height of consumer demand, they turned to miners in the Congo to increase their supply.

Predictably, the escalating price of the metal—as much as $400 a kilogram at one point, or more than three times the average Congolese worker's yearly wages—attracted undesirable attention. Soon the neighboring countries of Rwanda, Uganda, and Burundi, at war with one another and desperate for resources to finance the conflict, were raiding the Congo's national parks, slashing and burning to expose the coltan underneath the forest floor. Indirectly, the sudden increase in the demand for coltan was financing war and the rape of the environment. U.S. manufacturers have since cut off their sources in the Congo in an effort to avoid abetting the destruction. But their action has only penalized legitimate miners in the impoverished country (A. Austin 2002; Delawala 2002).

Socialism

p. 11 Socialist theory was refined in the writings of Karl Marx and Friedrich Engels. These European radicals were disturbed by the exploitation of the working class that emerged during the industrial revolution. In their view, capitalism forced large numbers of people to exchange their labor for low wages. The owners of an industry profit from the labor of workers, primarily p. 203 because they pay workers less than the value of the goods produced.

As an ideal type, a socialist economic system attempts to eliminate such economic exploitation. Under *socialism,* the means of production and distribution in a society are collectively rather than privately owned. The basic objective of the economic system is to meet people's needs rather than to maximize profits. Socialists reject the laissez-faire philosophy that free competition benefits the general public. Instead, they believe that the central government, acting as the representative of the people, should make basic economic decisions. Therefore, government ownership of all major industries—including steel production, automobile manufacturing, and agriculture—is a primary feature of socialism as an ideal type.

In practice, socialist economic systems vary in the extent to which they tolerate private ownership. For example, in Great Britain, a nation with some aspects of both a socialist and a capitalist economy, passenger airline service is concentrated in the government-owned corporation British Airways. Yet private airlines are allowed to compete with it.

Socialist societies differ from capitalist nations in their commitment to social service programs. For example, the U.S. government provides health care and health insurance to the elderly and poor through the Medicare and Medicaid programs. But socialist countries typically offer government-financed medical care to *all* citizens. In theory, the wealth of the people as a collectivity is used to provide health care, housing, education, and other key services to each individual and family.

Marx believed that each socialist state would eventually "wither away" and evolve into a *communist* society. As an ideal type, **communism** refers to an economic system under which all property is communally owned and no social distinctions are made on the basis of people's ability to produce. In recent decades, the Soviet Union, the People's Republic of China, Vietnam, Cuba, and nations in Eastern Europe were popularly thought of as examples of communist economic systems. However, this usage represents an incorrect application of a term with sensitive political connotations. All nations known as communist in the 20th century actually fell far short of the ideal type.

By the early 1990s, Communist parties were no longer ruling the nations of Eastern Europe. The first major challenge to Communist rule came in 1980 when Poland's Solidarity movement—led by Lech Walesa and backed by many workers—questioned the injustices of that society. Though martial law forced Solidarity underground, the movement eventually negotiated the end of

Communist Party rule in 1989. Over the next two years, Communist parties were overthrown by popular uprisings in the Soviet Union and throughout Eastern Europe. The former Soviet Union, Czechoslovakia, and Yugoslavia were then subdivided to accommodate ethnic, linguistic, and religious differences within these areas.

As of 2003, China, Cuba, and Vietnam remained socialist societies ruled by Communist parties. Even in these countries, however, capitalism was making inroads. In China, fully 25 percent of the country's production originated in the private business sector. (See the next section, Case Study: Capitalism in China, for a fuller discussion.)

Cuba, in particular, is adjusting to a dual economy. Although the Communist government leader Fidel Castro remains firmly committed to Marxism, the centrally controlled economy has been in ruins because of the end of Soviet aid and the continued trade embargo by the United States. Reluctantly, Castro has allowed small-scale family-managed businesses, such as restaurants and craft shops, to operate and accept dollars rather than the heavily devalued Cuban peso. Ironically, government-employed teachers and doctors now earn less than the small-business operators, taxi drivers, and hotel workers who have access to foreign currency. This situation underscores how difficult it is to understand any nation's economy without considering its position in the global economy (McKinley 1999).

As we have seen, capitalism and socialism serve as ideal types of economic system. In reality, the economy of each industrial society—including the United States, the European Union, and Japan—includes certain elements of both capitalism and socialism. Whatever the differences—whether a society more closely fits the ideal type of capitalism or socialism—all industrial societies rely chiefly on mechanization in the production of goods and services.

The Informal Economy

In many countries, one aspect of the economy defies description as either capitalist or socialist. In the ***informal economy,*** transfers of money, goods, or services take place but are not reported to the government. Examples of the informal economy include trading services with someone—say, a haircut for a computer lesson; selling goods on the street; and engaging in illegal transactions, such as gambling or drug deals. Participants in this type of economy avoid taxes and government regulations.

In developing nations, the informal economy represents a significant and often unmeasured part of total economic activity. Yet because this sector of the economy depends to a large extent on the labor of women, work in the informal economy is undervalued or even unrecognized the world over. p. 237 Box 18-1 describes the informal economy in Nepal.

Functionalists contend that bureaucratic regulations sometimes contribute to the rise of an informal economy. In the developing world, governments often set up burdensome business regulations that overworked bureaucrats must administer. When requests for licenses and permits pile up, delaying business projects, legitimate entrepreneurs find they need to "go underground" to get anything done. Despite its apparent efficiency, this type of informal economy is dysfunctional for a country's overall political and economic well-being. Since informal firms typically operate in remote locations to avoid detection, they cannot easily expand when they become profitable. And given the limited protection for their property and contractual rights, participants in the informal economy are less likely than others to save and invest their income.

Whatever functions an informal economy may serve, it is in some respects dysfunctional for workers. Working conditions in these illegal businesses are often unsafe or dangerous, and the jobs rarely provide any benefits to those who become ill or cannot continue to work. Perhaps more significant, the longer a worker remains in the informal economy, the less likely that person is to make the transition to the regular economy. No matter how efficient or productive a worker, employers expect to see experience in the formal economy on a job application. Experience as a successful street vendor or self-employed cleaning person does not carry much weight with interviewers.

Use Your Sociological Imagination www.mhhe.com/schaefer9

Some of your relatives are working in the informal economy—for example, baby-sitting, lawn cutting, house cleaning—full-time, and are earning all their income that way. What will be the consequences for them in terms of job security and health care? Will you try to persuade them to seek formal employment, regardless of how much money they are making?

CASE STUDY:
CAPITALISM IN CHINA

Today's China is not the China of past generations. In a country where the Communist Party once dominated people's lives, few now bother to follow party proceedings. Instead, after a decade of rapid economic growth, most Chinese are more interested in acquiring the latest

18-1 WORKING WOMEN IN NEPAL

Nepal, a small and mountainous Asian country of about 25 million people, has a per capita gross domestic product (GDP) of just $1,360 per year. (The comparable figure in the United States is $34,280.) But gross domestic product seriously understates the true production level in Nepal, for several reasons. Among the most important is that many Nepalese women work in the informal economy, whose activities are not included in the GDP.

Because women's work is undervalued in this traditional society, it is also underreported and underestimated. Official figures state that women account for 27 percent of GDP and form 40 percent

> Because women's work is undervalued in this traditional society, it is also underreported and underestimated.

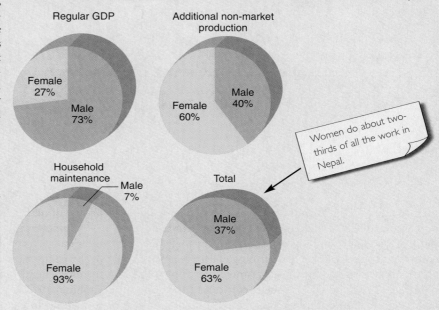

Gender Contributions to GDP and Household Maintenance in Nepal

Regular GDP
- Female 27%
- Male 73%

Additional non-market production
- Male 40%
- Female 60%

Household maintenance
- Male 7%
- Female 93%

Total
- Male 37%
- Female 63%

Women do about two-thirds of all the work in Nepal.

Source: Survey by S. Acharya as cited in Mahbub ul Haq Human Development Centre 2000:54.

of the labor force. But Nepalese women are responsible for 60 percent of additional nonmarket production—that is, work done in the informal economy—and 93 percent of the housework (see figure).

Most female workers cultivate corn, rice, and wheat on the family farm, where they spend hours on time-intensive tasks such as fetching water and feeding livestock. Because much of the food they raise is consumed at home, however, it is considered to be nonmarket production. At home, women concentrate on food processing and preparation, caregiving, and other household tasks, such as clothes making. Childbearing and rear-

ing and elder care are particularly crucial activities. Yet none of these chores are considered part of GDP; instead, they are dismissed as "women's work," both by economists and by the women themselves.

The figures on housework and nonmarket production in Nepal come from an independent economic study. To compile them, researchers had to adapt the conventional accounting system by adding a special account dedicated to household maintenance activities. When they did so, women's "invisible work" suddenly became visible and valuable. Not just in Nepal but in every country, economists need to expand their defini-

tions of work and the labor force to account for the tremendous contributions women make to the world economy.

Let's Discuss

1. In your own family, is "women's work" taken for granted? Have you ever tried to figure out what it would cost your family to pay for all the unpaid work women do?
2. Why is recognizing women's work important? How might life for both men and women change if the true economic value of women's work were recognized?

Sources: Acharya 2000; Haub 2003; Mahbub ul Haq Human Development Centre 2000:54–57.

consumer goods. Ironically, it was party officials' decision to transform China's economy by opening it up to capitalism that reduced the once omnipotent institution's influence (Eckholm 2002).

The Road to Capitalism

When the communists assumed leadership of China in 1949, they cast themselves as the champions of workers and peasants and the enemies of those who exploited

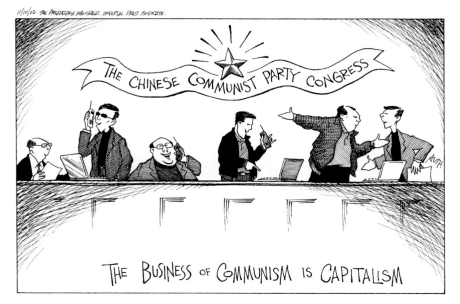

11/10/02 THE PHILADELPHIA INQUIRER. UNIVERSAL PRESS SYNDICATE.

THE CHINESE COMMUNIST PARTY CONGRESS

THE BUSINESS OF COMMUNISM IS CAPITALISM

them, namely landlords and capitalists. Profit making was outlawed, and those who engaged in it were arrested. By the 1960s, China's economy was dominated by huge state-controlled enterprises, such as farming collectives. Workers essentially worked for the government, receiving payment in goods based on their contribution to the collective. In addition, they could receive a small plot of land on which to produce food for their families or for exchange with others. But while the centralization of production for the benefit of all seemed to make sense ideologically, it did not work well economically. The large state-owned farms and factories could not keep up with the needs of a growing population.

In the 1980s, the government eased restrictions against private enterprise somewhat, permitting small businesses with no more than seven employees. But business owners could not hold policymaking positions in the party, at any level. Late in the decade, party leaders began to make market-oriented reforms, revising the nation's legal structure to promote private business. For the first time, private entrepreneurs were allowed to compete with some state-controlled businesses. By the mid-1990s, impressed with the results of the experiment, party officials had begun to hand some ailing state-controlled businesses over to private entrepreneurs, in hopes they could turn them around (Lynch 2002; Pan 2002).

The Chinese Economy Today

Today, the entrepreneurs who weathered government harassment during the Communist Party's early years are among the nation's wealthiest capitalists. Some even hold positions on government advisory boards. By 2001, the Communist Party had extended membership to over 200,000 private business owners. When leaders of the military and government-controlled telecommunications companies need help, they turn to these seasoned executives (Pomfret 2002).

The transition from an economy dominated by state-owned companies to one in which private firms can flourish has been surprisingly rapid. By 2001, six years after the government began turning over troubled state-owned companies to private entrepreneurs, the number of state-owned companies had been cut almost in half. But many of the companies that were privatized turned out to be money losers, a challenge to even the most enterprising of managers (Pan 2002).

Chinese capitalists have also had to compete with multinational corporations, which can operate more easily in China now thanks to government economic reforms. General Motors (GM) first became interested in China in 1992, hoping to use the nation's low-cost labor to manufacture cars for overseas markets. But more and more, foreign-owned enterprises like GM are selling to the Chinese market. By 2003, GM's Chinese operation was producing 110,000 automobiles a year for Chinese consumers, at a profit twice as high as that in the United States (Kahn 2003a).

Chinese Workers in the New Economy

For Chinese workers, the loosening of state control over the economy has meant a rise in occupational mobility, which was severely limited in the early days of Communist Party rule. The new markets created by private entrepreneurs are allowing ambitious workers to advance their careers by changing jobs or even cities. Still, the privately owned factories that churn out lawn chairs and power tools for multinational corporations offer limited opportunities and very long hours. Wages are 40 cents an hour—1/6 what factory workers earn in Mexico, and 1/40 of U.S. workers' wages (Iritani and Dickerson 2002).

Besides low wages, China's new economy has created other problems. In the countryside, incomes lag well behind the modest incomes urban workers earn. This wage differential has prompted a migration to China's urban centers that is well beyond their capability to absorb it. More and more, China's cities suffer from overcrowding and unemployment. Furthermore, in most small businesses, worker safety is not a priority. Just south of Shanghai, in the over 7,000 small, privately owned hardware factories that operate in the region, the unofficial injury rate is 2,500 serious injuries a year. Nationally, China recorded 140,000 workplace deaths in 2002—up 30 percent from the year before (Kahn 2003b; *Migration News* 2003b).

For the average worker, party membership is less important now than in the past. Instead, managerial skill and experience are much in demand. Hong Kong sociologist Xiaowei Zang (2002) surveyed 900 workers in a key industrial city and found that party members still had an advantage in government and state-owned companies, where they earned higher salaries than other workers. But in private businesses, seniority and either managerial or entrepreneurial experience were what counted. As might be expected, being male and well educated also helped.

Women have been slower to advance in the workplace than men. Traditionally, Chinese women have been relegated to subservient roles in the patriarchal family structure. Communist Party rule has allowed them to make significant gains in employment, income, and education, although not as quickly as promised. For rural women in China, the growth of a market economy has meant a choice between working in a factory or on a farm (Bian 2002; Lu et al. 2002; Shu and Bian 2003).

Those Chinese who run small family-owned businesses are prospering in the new economic climate. In a national survey of 3,000 households done in 1996, sociologist Andrew Walder (2002) found that, in general, these mom-and-pop businesses brought in significantly more income than other livelihoods. But in places where workers had the chance to desert the farm for wage work in factories and businesses, they were doing just as well as local businesspeople. As China's economy continues to develop, Walder believes, competition will increase both inside and outside China, and the economic advantages of entrepreneurism will diminish.

ASPECTS OF WORK

As indicated in the chapter-opening excerpt, the workplace has undergone tremendous changes in the last few decades, primarily because of automation and the application of high technology. These changes have affected the types of occupations people enter and their satisfaction (or lack of it) with their jobs. In this section we will examine both these aspects of work.

Occupations and Professions

Whatever we call it—*job, work, occupation, gig, stint, position, duty,* or *vocation*—it is what we do for pay. Our paid labor relates to our social behavior in a number of ways. Preparation for work is a critical aspect of the socialization process. In addition, our work influences our social identities, or what Charles Horton Cooley termed the *looking-glass self.* A person who asks "What do you do?" expects you to indicate your occupation. Thus, we tend to define ourselves by our work. Of course, work has more than a symbolic significance. Our occupations also determine, in large part, our positions in the stratification system.

p. 96

In the United States and other contemporary societies, the majority of the paid labor force is involved in providing services, such as health care, education, banking, and government. Along with the shift toward service industries, there has been a rise in the number of occupations viewed as professions. In popular usage, the term *professional*

A Chinese consumer shops for a television in Beijing. Though multinational corporations have moved factories to China to take advantage of the low wages there, they have discovered they can also sell their products in China.

Table 18-1	Occupations and Professions Compared	
Characteristic	**Occupation**	**Profession**
Systematic body of theory or abstract knowledge	No	Yes
Training	Relatively short; usually informal	Extensive and formalized
Degree of specialization	Little	Extensive
Autonomy	Little	Extensive
Self-regulatory associations	No	Yes
Relationship to public	"Customer is always right"	Client is viewed as somewhat subordinate
Formal certification	Not necessarily	Yes
Sense of community with similar jobholders	Low	High
Code of ethics	Informal	Highly developed; usually formalized

Sources: Author based on Evetts 2003; Greenwood 1957; Leicht and Fennell 1997; Lively 2001; Pavalko 1972, 1988.

is frequently used to convey a positive evaluation of work ("She's a real professional") or to denote full-time paid performance in a vocation (as in "professional golfer").

Sociologists use the term *profession* to describe an occupation requiring extensive knowledge that is governed by a code of ethics. Professionals tend to have a great degree of autonomy. They are not responsible to a supervisor for every action, nor do they need to respond to the whims of a customer. In general, professionals are their own authority in determining what is best for their clients. Table 18-1 summarizes some of the characteristics sociologists use to distinguish professions from other occupations.

It is widely agreed that medicine and law are professions, whereas taxi driving is an occupation. But how do we categorize a paralegal, funeral director, firefighter, or pharmacist? In these cases it's not clear where "occupation" ends and "profession" begins. To some extent, as occupations have become more skill-based and professions tied more and more to large bureaucracies (such as HMOs), the two ideal types have converged. Moreover, a growing number of occupational groups have claimed and even demanded professional status—often in an attempt to gain greater prestige and financial rewards. In certain instances, existing professions may object to the efforts of a related vocation to achieve designation as a profession. They may fear a loss in business or clientele or a downgrade in the status of their profession as still more occupations are included. The hostility of the medical profession toward midwifery is an example of such a con-

flict between an established profession and an occupation that aspires to professional status.

Work and Alienation: Marx's View

"A moron could learn this job, it's so easy," says one Burger King worker in George Ritzer's study of the fast-food industry (2000:137). Doing repetitive tasks that take minimal skills can be demoralizing, leading to a sense of alienation and isolation in the workplace. Jeremy Rifkin, as we saw in the chapter opening excerpt, took this concern a step further: As work becomes more and more automated, human skills become obsolete and workers lose their jobs altogether, or are forced into low-skills service jobs (Rifkin 1996).

All the pioneers of sociological thought were concerned about the negative impact on workers of the changes brought about by the industrial revolution. Émile Durkheim ([1893] 1933) argued that as labor becomes more and more differentiated, individuals experience *anomie*, or loss of direction. Workers can't feel the same fulfillment from performing one specialized task in a factory as they did when they were totally responsible for creating a product. It is clear that the impersonality of bureaucratic organizations can produce a cold and uncaring workplace. But the most penetrating analysis of the dehumanizing aspects of industrialization was offered by Karl Marx.

Marx believed that as the process of industrialization advanced, workers were robbed of any meaningful relationship with their work. In today's terms, consider the telemarketer making a "cold call" to sell someone a credit card. Does he or she feel a part of the financial institution? For Marx, the emphasis on specialization of tasks contributed to a growing sense of alienation among industrial workers. The term *alienation* refers to the situation of being estranged or disassociated from the surrounding society. But it wasn't just the monotonous repetition of the same tasks that concerned Marx. In his view, an even deeper cause of alienation was the *powerlessness* of workers in a capitalist economic system. Workers had no control over their occupational tasks, the products of their labor, or the distribution of profits. Moreover, they were constantly producing property that was owned by others (the members of the capitalist class) (Erikson 1986).

The solution to the problem of workers' alienation, according to Marx, was to give workers greater control over the workplace and the products of their labor. Marx didn't focus on limited reforms of factory life; rather, he envisioned a revolutionary overthrow of capitalist oppression. After a transition to collective ownership of the means of production (socialism), the ideal of communism would eventually be achieved. Yet the trend in capitalist societies has been toward concentration of ownership by giant corporations. Currently, about 49 percent of the paid U.S. labor force is employed in business firms with more than 500 workers. Through mergers and acquisitions, such corporations become even larger, and individual workers find themselves employed by firms of overwhelming size and power (Bureau of the Census 2002a:482).

When Karl Marx wrote about work and alienation in 1844, the physical conditions of labor were much harsher than they are today. Yet his writings inspired research that persists today, even though workers now enjoy safer, more comfortable surroundings. Most studies of alienation have focused on how structural changes in the economy serve to increase or decrease worker satisfaction. In fact, the growth of the size of businesses, the emergence of huge franchise chains, and the dominance of multinational corporations have only increased the isolation of laborers. Large business organizations report an escalation in episodes of "desk rage," in which employees or angry ex-employees act out their frustrations, disrupting the workplace and often raising other workers' alienation in the process (Hodson and Sullivan 1995; Hymowitz and Silverman 2001).

Marx focused on alienation among the proletariat, whom he viewed as powerless to effect change within capitalist institutions. By the 1980s the term *burnout* was increasingly being used to describe the stress experienced by a wide range of workers, including professionals, self-employed persons, and even unpaid volunteers. The concept of work-related anxiety now covers alienation even among more affluent workers, who have a greater degree of control over their working conditions. From a conflict perspective, we have masked the fact that alienation falls most heavily on the lower and working classes by making it appear to be endemic from the boardroom to the shop floor.

Worker Satisfaction

In general, people with greater responsibility for a finished product (such as white-collar professionals and managers) experience more satisfaction than those with less responsibility. For both women and men working in blue-collar jobs, the repetitive nature of work can be particularly unsatisfying. The automobile assembly line is commonly cited as an extreme example of monotonous work. Studs Terkel (1974:159), in his book *Working*, gives a first-person account of a spot welder's labor:

Stocking shelves may help to pay the bills but is unlikely to provide high job satisfaction, especially in a large supermarket where workers have less responsibility and more anonymity.

I stand in one spot, about a two- or three-feet area, all night. The only time a person stops is when the line stops. We do about thirty-two jobs per car, per unit, forty-eight units per hour, eight hours a day. Thirty-two times forty-eight times eight. Figure it out, that's how many times I push that button.

Robert Blauner's (1964) classic research study revealed that printers—who often work in small shops and supervise apprentices—were more satisfied with their work than laborers who performed repetitive tasks on automobile assembly lines.

Factors in Job Satisfaction

A number of general factors can reduce the level of dissatisfaction of contemporary industrial workers. Higher wages give workers a sense of accomplishment apart from the task before them. A shorter workweek is supposed to increase the amount of time people can devote to recreation and leisure, thereby reducing some of the discontent stemming from the workplace. But the number of hours Americans work actually *increased* in the 1990s, by the equivalent of about one workweek. Short staffing because of low unemployment rates may have accounted for part of the increase in hours worked; however, many Americans took a second job during this period, just to make ends meet. At the same time, paid absences rose, and the reasons workers gave for their absenteeism indicated low satisfaction. In 1995, 45 percent of absent workers cited personal illness as a reason, but by 1998, only 22 percent gave that reason. Instead, 16 percent cited stress and another 16 percent indicated a sense of entitlement (Stone 1999; Webb 2001).

Numerous studies have shown that positive relationships with co-workers can make a boring job tolerable or even enjoyable. In his often cited "banana time" study, sociologist Donald Roy (1959) examined worker satisfaction in a two-month participant observation of a small group of factory machine operators. Drawing on the interactionist perspective, Roy carefully recorded the social interactions among members of his work group, including many structured "times" and "themes" designed to break up long days of simple, repetitive work. For example, the workers divided their food breaks into coffee time, peach time, banana time, fish time, Coke time, and lunch time—each of which occurred daily and involved distinctive responsibilities, jokes, and insults. Roy (1959:166) concluded that his observations "seem to support the generally accepted notion that one key source of job satisfaction lies in the informal interaction shared by members of a work group." The patterned conversation and horseplay of these workers reduced the monotony of their workdays.

In Seoul in 2001, protesting employees of the dot-com industry took to the streets to demand job security and better working conditions. The year before, South Korean workers had logged longer hours than those in 199 other countries (Webb 2001).

Sociologist George Ritzer (1977, 2000) has suggested that the relatively positive impression many workers present is misleading. In his view, manual workers are so deeply alienated that they come to expect little from their jobs. Their satisfaction comes from nonwork tasks, and any job-related gratification results from receiving wages. Ritzer's interpretation explains why manual workers—although they say they are satisfied with their occupations—would not choose the same line of work if they could begin their lives over.

Job Satisfaction in Japan

One of the major economic developments of the 1980s was the emergence of Japan as an industrial giant. In earlier decades, many people had attributed Japan's economic accomplishments to low wages combined with the production of inexpensive goods. However, in the 1980s Japanese salaries were comparable to those of other industrial nations. A more likely explanation of Japan's remarkable success at that time focused instead on the unusual pride Japanese workers took in their products. In

Japanese plants and factories, workers are expected to assume the role of quality-control inspector. Although employees are actually involved in specialized tasks of production, they can still identify with the finished product.

For a long time, the collectivist orientation of Japanese culture heavily influenced its economic system. An individual was perceived as an extension of his or her family, business, or community and as bound together with others in a common purpose. In contrast to U.S. firms, most Japanese companies maintained an ideal of "lifetime employment" for some of their employees. They made substantial investments in training workers, and so were reluctant to lay off employees during a business slump. The employer–employee relationship was paramount. Companies even operated reception halls, gymnasiums and swimming pools, mortgage-lending institutions, and cultural programs for the benefit of their workers.

By the close of the 1990s this situation had changed. A severe economic recession had hit Japan, resulting in record unemployment. While joblessness was still low compared to European countries, almost twice as many people were looking for jobs as there were job openings. Companies facing the impact of a lingering recession and increased competition from abroad set aside the notion of lifetime employment. Interactionists observed that Japanese men—accustomed to job security—were so embarrassed over losing a job that they would keep it secret from their families for days, if not weeks (see Chapter 4). Men in their 50s were looking for work along with recent college graduates. As a result of the restructuring, the bonds that link worker and employer are currently weakening. The feelings of worker isolation that Marx and Ritzer wrote about in Europe and North America are becoming increasingly evident in Japan (French 2002).

THE CHANGING ECONOMY

As advocates of the power elite model point out, the trend in capitalist societies has been toward concentration of ownership by giant corporations, especially multinational ones. For example, there were 7,610 mergers in

When job layoffs hit Japan in the 1990s, they caused a stir because the Japanese were accustomed to the idea of lifetime employment with one firm. In this demonstration at Nissan headquarters in Tokyo in 1999, labor activists protested auto plant shutdowns and a 14 percent cut in the workforce. The banners on the bus read: "How can you call the mass dismissal of workers a Renaissance? Stop the closure of five plants in Nissan-Renault's large-sized restructuring."

p. 230 2001 alone, involving $1.7 trillion in business. The U.S. economy is changing in important ways, in part because it is increasingly intertwined with and dependent upon the global economy. In 2001, foreign companies acquired 449 U.S. firms valued together at $132 billion (Bureau of the Census 2002a:487).

In the following sections, we examine developments in the economy that have interested sociologists: the changing face of the workforce, deindustrialization, the impact of new technology, and the rise of a contingent (or temporary) workforce. As these trends show, any change in the economy inevitably has social and political implications that soon become a concern of policymakers.

The Changing Face of the Workforce

The workforce in the United States is constantly changing. During World War II, when men were mobilized to fight abroad, women entered the workforce in large numbers. And with the rise of the civil rights movement in the 1960s, minorities found numerous job opportunities opening to them. The active recruitment of women and minorities into the workplace, known as *affirmative action,* is the subject of this chapter's social policy section.

FIGURE 18-1

Racial and Ethnic Composition of the U.S. Labor Force, 1980 and 2020 (projection)

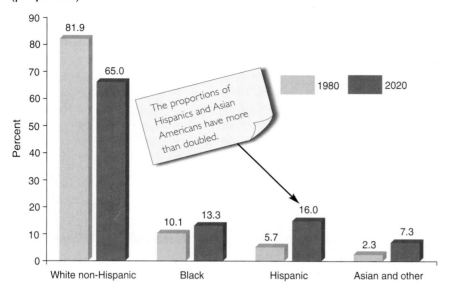

Source: Toossi 2002:24.

While predictions are not always reliable, sociologists and labor specialists foresee a workforce increasingly composed of women and racial and ethnic minorities. In 1960 there were twice as many men in the labor force as women. During the period from 1980 to 2020, three women are expected to enter the labor force for every two men. It's possible that by 2020 the female workforce may be only 3 percent smaller than the male workforce. The dynamics for minority groups in the workforce are even more dramatic. The number of Black, Latino, and Asian American workers continues to increase at a rate faster than the number of White workers, as Figure 18-1 shows (Toossi 2002:24).

More and more, the workforce reflects the diversity of the population, as ethnic minorities enter the labor force and immigrants and their children move from marginal **p. 217** jobs or employment in the informal economy to positions of greater visibility and responsibility. The impact of this changing labor force is not merely statistical. A more diverse workforce means that relationships between workers are more likely to cross gender, racial, and ethnic lines. Interactionists note that people will find themselves supervising and being supervised by people very different from themselves. In response to these changes, 75 percent of businesses had instituted some type of cultural diversity training program as of 2000 (Melia 2000).

Deindustrialization

What happens when a company decides it is more profitable to move its operations out of a long-established community to another part of the country, or out of the country altogether? People lose jobs; stores lose customers; the local government's tax base declines and it cuts services. This devastating process has occurred again and again in the last decade or so.

The term ***deindustrialization*** refers to the systematic, widespread withdrawal of investment in basic aspects of productivity such as factories and plants. Giant corporations that deindustrialize are not necessarily refusing to invest in new economic opportunities. Rather, the targets and locations of investment change, and the need for labor

This photo of a street scene in Columbus, Ohio, could have been taken in almost any American city. The U.S. workforce is becoming increasingly diverse in terms of race, ethnicity, and gender.

When U.S. plants deindustrialize at home, they often move their investment in manufacturing outside the country to take advantage of low wages. Shown here is an AT&T telephone repair plant located across the border in Nuevo Laredo, Mexico.

decreases as technology continues to automate production. First, there may be a relocation of plants from the nation's central cities to the suburbs. The next step may be relocation from suburban areas of the Northeast and Midwest to southern states, where labor laws place more restrictions on unions. Finally, a corporation may simply relocate *outside* the United States to a country with a lower rate of prevailing wages. General Motors, for example, decided to build a multibillion-dollar plant in China rather than in Kansas City or even Mexico (Lynn 2003).

Although deindustrialization often involves relocation, in some instances it takes the form of corporate restructuring, as companies seek to reduce costs in the face of growing worldwide competition. When such restructuring occurs, the impact on the bureaucratic hierarchy of formal organizations can be significant. A large corporation may choose to sell off or entirely abandon less productive divisions and to eliminate layers of management viewed as unnecessary. Wages and salaries may be frozen and fringe benefits cut—all in the name of restructuring. Increasing reliance on automation also spells the end of work as we have known it.

The term *downsizing* was introduced in 1987 to refer to reductions taken in a company's workforce as part of deindustrialization. Viewed from a conflict perspective, the unprecedented attention given to downsizing in the mid-1990s reflected the continuing importance of social class in the United States. Conflict theorists note that job loss among workers has long been a feature of deindustri-

alization. (The social policy section in Chapter 6 describes how trade unions have dealt with job loss and downsizing.) But when large numbers of middle-class managers and other white-collar employees with substantial incomes began to be laid off, suddenly there was great concern in the media over downsizing (Richtel 2000; Safire 1996; R. Samuelson 1996a, 1996b).

p. 141

The social costs of deindustrialization and downsizing cannot be overemphasized. Plant closings lead to substantial unemployment in a community, which can have a devastating impact on both the micro and macro levels. On the micro level, the unemployed person and his or her family must adjust to a loss of spending power. Painting or residing the house, buying health insurance or saving for retirement, even thinking about having another child must be put aside. Both marital happiness and family cohesion may suffer as a result. Although many dismissed workers eventually reenter the paid labor force, they must often accept less desirable positions with lower salaries and fewer benefits (DePalma 2002). Unemployment and underemployment are tied into many of the social problems discussed throughout this textbook, among them the need for child care, the controversy over welfare, and immigration issues.

pp. 97, 219, 274

On the societal, or macro, level, the impact of a plant closing on a community can be as difficult as it is for an individual worker and his or her family. As noted earlier, the community will experience a significant loss of tax revenues. It then becomes more difficult to support police and fire protection, schools, parks, and other public services. Moreover, rising unemployment leads to a reduced demand for goods and services in a community. Sales by retail firms and other businesses fall off, sometimes leading to further layoffs.

Increasingly, job reductions in the United States are accompanied by job expansion overseas. When you speak with a customer service representative over the telephone, the person who assists you may not be located in the United States. Today, the transfer of jobs across national borders is not limited to manufacturing. Office and professional jobs are being exported, too, thanks to advanced telecommunications and the growth of skilled, English-speaking labor forces in nations with relatively low wage

RICHARD J. HAWK **Vice President and Financial Consultant, Smith Barney**

Richard Hawk had no idea what he wanted to do with his life when he entered DePauw University, and no idea what sociology was about when he registered for his first course. But he soon realized that he liked the faculty in the sociology department, and he liked the perspective the subject gave him on other subjects he was studying—economics, history, and communications. In his junior year, Hawk took a course on marriage and the family that helped him to see the "trickle-down effect" of major economic decisions on individuals and communities.

Today, Hawk credits sociology with giving him "a better overall understanding of things," one he uses daily. Asked to elaborate, he replies, "You have to realize that everyone is affected one way or another" by economic and political decisions. He points to the war in Iraq: "Half of the forces are reservists. Look at the social and financial effect on the family, the economic effect on the companies these people work for domestically, not to mention the obvious effects on the Iraqi people." Hawk sees these effects play themselves out in his clients' lives, whether they are physicians or blue-collar workers facing an early retirement. In developing their financial plans, he keeps the big picture in mind.

As a financial consultant, Hawk meets with clients, confers with money managers and financial analysts, and prepares proposals for prospective clients. He applies the same analytical perspective that he uses with clients to the economy and current business issues. "The past few years have not been particularly kind to the equity markets," he observes. "We were in a technology bubble, and as a result, we have been experiencing dramatic changes in accounting methods, compensation issues, and ethics in general."

Hawk advises first-time sociology students to approach the subject with an open mind, to "be willing to look at issues from a different perspective." Doing so, he thinks, will pay off in some valuable insights.

Let's Discuss

1. Pick an economic issue or decision that has been in the news recently and show how it could affect your family.
2. Take the same issue or decision and imagine how it might affect the people you will deal with in your future career.

---

scales. The trend includes even those jobs that require considerable training, such as accounting and financial analysis, claims adjustment, telemarketing, and hotel and airline reservations. Many of these jobs have been moving to countries like India and the Philippines. In 2000, a total of about 102,000 white-collar jobs moved offshore; by 2005, the number is expected to climb to over half a million (Armour and Kessler 2003).

The Contingent Workforce

In the past, the term *temp* typically conjured up images of a replacement receptionist or a worker covering for someone on vacation. However, with deindustrialization and downsizing, a "contingent workforce," in which workers are hired for only as long as they are needed, has emerged in the United States. This trend has been called the "temping of America."

Both unemployed workers and entrants to the paid labor force accept positions as temporary or part-time

workers. Some do so for flexibility and control over their work time, but others accept temporary jobs because they are the only ones available. Young people are especially likely to fill temporary positions. A growing portion of the contingent workforce includes freelancers who work at home via the Internet, or "e-lancers."

Employers favor the shift toward a contingent workforce because it allows them to respond more quickly to workforce demands—as well as to hire employees without having to offer the fringe benefits full-time employees enjoy. All around the United States, large firms have come to rely on part-time or temporary workers, most of whom work part-time involuntarily. Many of these workers feel the effects of deindustrialization and shifts in the global economy. They lost their full-time jobs when companies moved operations to developing nations (Reich 2001).

It is difficult to estimate the size of the contingent workforce in the United States. Heidi Hartmann of the Institute for Women's Policy Research notes that there is no agreement among social scientists on how to define a contingent worker, or even on how many there are. According to one estimate, however, contingent workers constitute about one-fourth of the nation's paid labor force. In 1998, for example, about 28 percent of Microsoft's workforce was temporary. This segment included a large number of long-term temporaries (those who work more than one year), who have come to refer to their awkward status as "perma-temps." In fact, nearly 12,000 long-term temporary workers banded together to sue Microsoft, accusing the company of using their temporary status to deny them benefits. They eventually won a $97 million settlement. Nonetheless, as of the end of 2000, 10 percent of Microsoft workers worldwide were still temps (S. Greenhouse 2000b).

During the 1970s and 1980s, temporary workers typically held low-skill positions at fast-food restaurants, telemarketing firms, and other service industries. Today, the contingent workforce is evident at virtually *all* skill levels and in *all* industries. Clerical temps handle word processing and filing duties; managers are hired on a short-term basis to reorganize departments; freelance writers prepare speeches for corporate executives; and blue-collar workers fill in for a few months when a factory receives an unusually high number of orders. A significant minority of temporary employees are contract workers who are being "rented" for specific periods by the companies that downsized them—and are now working at lower salary levels, without benefits or job security (Kirk 1995; Uchitelle 1996).

The New Economy

Workers in the United States generally blame forces outside their control—indeed, outside the nation—for the problems they experience as a result of deindustrialization and the rise of a contingent workforce. The relocation of factories to other countries has unquestionably contributed to job loss in the United States. But there are growing indications that automation is substantially reducing the need for human labor, in both manufacturing and service industries (Rifkin 1996).

The Impact of New Technology

New technologies can bring wonderful benefits, but they can also have a negative effect on employment and wages. By increasing efficiency, computerization of a company's operations can also reduce the number of workers needed in the production process, resulting in layoffs or reductions in overtime.

New technologies can also increase the gap between the lowest- and highest-paid workers. Sociologist Roberto Fernandez (2001) studied the changes that occurred when a midwestern food processor moved to a new manufacturing plant in the early 1990s. He found that while workers' responsibilities increased, their pay generally did not. In the old plant, for instance, forklift operators needed no special skills other than the ability to operate the equipment. But in the new

An accountant studies a ledger in an office. Increasing numbers of educated, white-collar professionals (such as accountants) have joined low-level temp workers in the contingent workforce.

The want ads go on forever, but even in the best of times, millions are seeking work and even more want a better job. Rich countries still have millions of people living in poverty. What is wrong with this picture? We are seeing a mismatch between the skills people have and the jobs that are available.

The growth of the service and high-tech information-based economy at the expense of manufacturing translates directly into shifts in employment. Economist Jeremy Rifkin has written of the emergence of a *knowledge class* that is responsible for keeping the worldwide high-tech economy going. This kind of expertise calls for workers with high-level skills—skills that are usually difficult to come by among the ranks of the unemployed workers, except during occasional economic downswings, such as the recession that followed the dot-com industry's collapse. At the same time, many unemployed, especially those who have been downsized, are overqualified for low-paying service economy jobs, which call for few skills.

The most visible illustration of this mismatch between jobs available and skills needed can be seen among those who immigrate from developing nations to the cities of industrial countries, where the abilities of the knowledge class are most valued. These new arrivals are attracted by higher standards of living, but their lack of technological skills relegates them to poor-paying service sector jobs, such as food service, custodial work, and support services in hotels and retail establishments.

Foreign labor plays a significant role in many industrial countries, constituting 10 percent or more of the total labor force in the United States, Germany, and Austria, and more than 20 percent in Canada, Australia, and Switzerland. Because these foreign workers send money back home to their families, they are an important source of revenue for their

> A high school education is now considered insufficient for most highly skilled jobs.

homeland, but their generally unskilled jobs make them more vulnerable to unemployment than native-born workers in economic downturns.

The jobs–skills mismatch is spreading to developing nations. For example, the pattern of deindustrialization associated with northern industrial cities in the United States is now beginning to take root in Mexico. Relatively new factories, considered state-of-the-art at the time they were built in the early 1990s by multinational corporations, are already downsizing as they become even more automated. Machines are replacing workers in every developing country, and increasingly, the remaining jobs require the skills associated with the knowledge class. Economic planners in high-tech–oriented Singapore worry that many older workers there will soon face unemployment because of outdated skills.

In the United States, 84 percent of the population has attained at least a high school diploma, but a high school education is now considered insufficient for most highly skilled jobs. Outside Europe, North America, and a few Asian countries, 40 to 60 percent at most have attained that level of education. At the same time that the level of education required for skilled workers worldwide is increasing, there has been little progress to match those needs. Shifting skill requirements and ineffective educational systems have combined to marginalize many immigrant groups around the world, as well as native-born peoples left behind by the information and technological booms and the escalation of skills requirements.

Let's Discuss

1. What is causing the jobs–skills mismatch? Why is the mismatch spreading to developing nations?
2. Do you know someone with skills who was forced to take a low-paying job? What caused this situation?

Sources: Bureau of the Census 2002a:140; Divyanathan 2000; Kasarda 1990; Rifkin 1995b; World Bank 2003b.

plant, they had to record what they moved using a computer—a job that was once done by a clerk. Despite such added skill requirements, workers at the bottom of the wage scale actually earned less than they had in the old factory. The only workers who benefited from the move to the new plant were the specially trained electricians and mechanics who had to be hired to maintain the sophisticated high-tech machinery. These new workers, all of them white males, were paid much better than other laborers, many of whom were women or minority group members. Box 18-2 looks more closely at the jobs–skills mismatch that has arisen from the introduction of high technology.

Another way in which new technology has affected workers can be seen in the emergence of **e-commerce,** the numerous ways in which people with access to the Internet do business from their computers. Today, online retailers like Amazon.com compete for business with more traditional brick-and-mortar establishments. The growth of e-commerce has created jobs both in online retailing and in related industries, such as warehousing, packing, and shipping. However, the industry is volatile, and many e-commerce companies have yet to turn a profit.

Although e-commerce will not immediately overwhelm traditional businesses, it has changed the social dynamics of the retail trade. Consider the impact on traditional retail outlets and on face-to-face interactions with local store owners. On the one hand, companies like Nike, Levi's, and Mattel now have their own online stores, allowing them to bypass the retail outlets they used for years. Cybermalls are replacing megamalls as the place for prospective customers to browse. On the other hand, e-commerce does offer new opportunities

to rural residents and people with disabilities (assuming they have the equipment to take advantage of it). To critics, however, e-commerce means increased social isolation, alienation, and a growing disconnect for the poor and disadvantaged, who are not part of the new Information Age (Drucker 1999; Stoughton and Walker 1999).

Use Your Sociological Imagination www. mhhe.com /schaefer9

What will the U.S. workforce look like in 2050? Consider workers' age, gender, race, and ethnicity. How much education will workers need? Will they work full-time or part-time? What will be the most common occupations?

SOCIAL POLICY and THE ECONOMY — Affirmative Action

www. mhhe.com /schaefer9

The Issue

Jessie Sherrod began picking cotton in the fields of Mississippi when she was eight years old, earning $1.67 for a 12-hour day. Today she is a Harvard-educated pediatrician who specializes in infectious diseases. But the road from the cotton fields to the medical profession was hardly an easy one. "You can't make up for 400 years of slavery and mistreatment and unequal opportunity in 20 years," she says angrily. "We had to ride the school bus for five miles . . . and pass by a white school to get to our black elementary school. Our books were used books. Our instructors were not as good. We didn't have the proper equipment. How do you make up for that?" (Stolberg 1995:A14). Some people think it should be done through affirmative action programs.

The term *affirmative action* first appeared in an executive order issued by President John F. Kennedy in 1961. That order called for contractors to "take affirmative action to ensure that applicants are employed, and that employees are treated during employment, without regard to their race, creed, color, or national origin." In 1967, the order was amended by President Lyndon Johnson to prohibit discrimination on the basis of sex as well, but affirmative action remained a vague concept. Currently, ***affirmative action*** refers to positive efforts to recruit minority group members or women for jobs, promotions, and educational opportunities. But many people think that affirmative action programs constitute reverse discrimination against qualified Whites and males. Does government have a responsibility to make up for past discrimination? If so, how far should it go?

The Setting

A variety of court decisions and executive branch statements have outlawed certain forms of job discrimination based on race, sex, or both, including (1) word-of-mouth recruitment among all-White or all-male workforces, (2) recruitment exclusively in schools or colleges that are limited to one sex or are predominantly White, (3) discrimination against married women or forced retirement of pregnant women, (4) advertising in male and female "help wanted" columns when gender is not a legitimate occupational qualification, and (5) job qualifications and tests that are not substantially related to the job. In addition, the lack of minority (African American, Asian, Native American, or Hispanic) or female employees may in itself represent evidence of unlawful exclusion (Commission on Civil Rights 1981).

In the late 1970s, a number of bitterly debated cases on affirmative action reached the Supreme Court. In 1978, in the *Bakke* case, by a narrow 5–4 vote, the Supreme Court ordered the medical school of the University of California at Davis to admit Allen Bakke, a White engineer who originally had been denied admission. The justices ruled that the school had violated Bakke's constitutional rights by establishing a fixed quota system for minority students. The Court added, however, that it was constitutional for universities to adopt flexible admissions programs that include race as one factor in decision making.

Sociological Insights

Sociologists—and especially conflict theorists—view affirmative action as a legislative attempt to reduce the inequality embedded in the social structure by increasing the opportunities of groups that have been deprived in the past, such as women and African Americans. The gap in earning power between White males and other groups (see Figure 18-2) is one indication of the inequality that needs to be addressed. But even acknowledging the disparity in earnings between White males and others, many people in the United States doubt that everything done in the name of affirmative action is desirable. In a 2003 national survey, 49 percent of respondents favored affirmative action programs for racial minorities; 43 percent opposed them. There was a clear racial difference in the responses. Among Blacks, 70 percent favored affirmative action; among Hispanics, the rate was 63 percent. Only 44 percent of non-Hispanic Whites approved of the programs (D. Moore 2003).

Much less documented than economic inequality are the social consequences of affirmative action policies on everyday life. Interactionists focus on situations in which some women and minorities in underrepresented professions and schools are often mistakenly viewed as products of affirmative action. Fellow students and workers may stereotype them as less qualified, seeing them as beneficiaries of preference over more qualified White males. Obviously, that is not necessarily the case, but such labeling may well affect social rela-

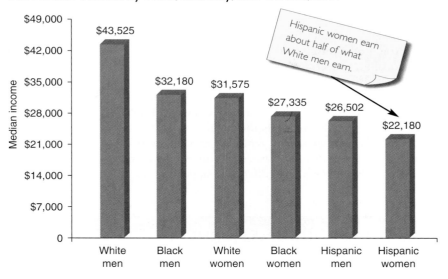

FIGURE 18-2

U.S. Median Income by Race, Ethnicity, and Gender, 2001

Hispanic women earn about half of what White men earn.

Note: Median income includes all financial sources and is limited to year-round, full-time workers over 15 years of age. "White" refers to non-Hispanic.

Source: Bureau of the Census 2002b: parts 78-80, 148-150.

tionships. Sociologist Orlando Patterson (1998) has noted that the workplace isolation experienced by minority workers inhibits their advancement up the corporate ladder; yet if efforts to increase their representation are scaled back, their problems in advancement will persist.

Policy Initiatives

By the early 1990s, affirmative action had emerged as an increasingly important issue in state and national political campaigns. Generally, discussion focused on the use of quotas (or the "Q word," as it came to be known) in hiring practices. Supporters of affirmative action argue that hiring goals (or targets) establish floors for minority inclusion but do not exclude truly qualified candidates from any group. Opponents insist that these "targets" are, in fact, quotas that lead to reverse discrimination. However, affirmative action has caused very few legal claims of reverse discrimination by White people.

In the 1996 elections, California's voters approved by a 54 to 46 percent margin the California Civil Rights Initiative, also known as Proposition 209. This measure amends the state constitution to *prohibit* any program that gives preference to women and minorities in college admissions, hiring, promotion, or government contracts. In other words, it aims to abolish affirmative

action programs. The courts have since upheld the measure. In 1998, voters in Washington state passed a similar anti–affirmative action measure.

In 2003, focusing specifically on college admissions in a pair of decisions involving policies at the University of Michigan, the Supreme Court ruled that colleges may consider race and ethnicity as one factor in their admissions decisions. However, they cannot assign a specific value to being a minority candidate in such a way that race becomes the overriding factor in a decision. The ruling allowed many colleges and universities to continue their existing affirmative action policies. But critics complained that it permits blatant favoritism toward the children of alumni, who are more likely than others to be White, while subjecting programs that favor disadvantaged minority candidates to much greater scrutiny (University of Michigan 2003).

The United States is not alone in its struggle to find acceptable ways of compensating for generations of inequality between racial groups. After dismantling the system of apartheid that favored Whites economically and socially, the Republic of South Africa is now trying to level the playing field by giving Blacks preference in managerial positions. The Malaysian constitution gives preference to Malays to counteract the legacy of colonialism, under which the British gave special protection to the Chinese. And in Brazil, public universities are expected to meet admission quotas for Blacks—a policy that may be extended to government employment. The specifics may be different from one country to the next, but the social concerns are familiar (*The Economist* 2003a; Rohter 2003; Schaefer 2004).

Let's Discuss

1. Would a conflict theorist support the policy of affirmative action? Why or why not?
2. Do you think claims of reverse discrimination have any validity? If so, what should be done about them?
3. If you were to draft legislation either supporting or abolishing affirmative action, what provisions would it include?

CHAPTER RESOURCES

Summary

The *economic system* of a society has an important influence on social behavior and on other social institutions.

1. With the industrial revolution, a new form of social structure emerged: the *industrial society.*
2. Systems of *capitalism* vary in the degree to which the government regulates private ownership and economic activity, but all emphasize the profit motive.
3. The basic objective of *socialism* is to eliminate economic exploitation and meet people's needs.
4. Marx believed that *communism* would evolve naturally out of socialism.
5. In most societies today, the trend is toward an increase in service jobs and a rise in the number of occupations that aspire to be a *profession.*
6. Industrial jobs can lead to a sense of *alienation* in the workplace. Karl Marx expected that powerless workers would eventually overthrow the capitalist system.
7. The nature of the U.S. economy is changing. Sociologists are interested in the changing face of the workforce, the effects of *deindustrialization,* increased use of a contingent workforce, and the impact of new technology.
8. Despite numerous *affirmative action* programs, White males continue to hold the overwhelming majority of prestigious, high-paying jobs in the United States.

Critical Thinking Questions

1. The United States has long been put forward as the model of a capitalist society. Drawing on material in earlier chapters of this textbook, discuss the values and beliefs that have led people in the United States to cherish a laissez-faire, capitalist economy. To what degree have those values and beliefs changed over the past hundred years? What aspects of socialism are now evident in the nation's econ-

omy? Have our values and beliefs changed to support certain principles traditionally associated with socialist societies?

2. Describe some of the service workers in the college or university you attend. Do you see any sign of alienation in the workplace? Does your school make much use of a contingent workforce, especially among students?

3. Imagine that you have been assigned to study possible changes in the economy of the city nearest you. How could you use surveys, observation research, experiments, and existing sources to complete the task?

Key Terms

Affirmative action   Positive efforts to recruit minority group members or women for jobs, promotions, and educational opportunities. (page 431)

Alienation   A condition of estrangement or disassociation from the surrounding society. (423)

Capitalism   An economic system in which the means of production are held largely in private hands, and the main incentive for economic activity is the accumulation of profits. (415)

Communism   As an ideal type, an economic system under which all property is communally owned and no social distinctions are made on the basis of people's ability to produce. (417)

Deindustrialization   The systematic, widespread withdrawal of investment in basic aspects of productivity such as factories and plants. (426)

Downsizing   Reductions taken in a company's workforce as part of deindustrialization. (427)

E-commerce   Numerous ways in which people with access to the Internet do business from their computers. (430)

Economic system   The social institution through which goods and services are produced, distributed, and consumed. (415)

Industrial society   A society that depends on mechanization to produce its goods and services. (415)

Informal economy   Transfers of money, goods, or services that are not reported to the government. (418)

Laissez-faire   A form of capitalism under which people compete freely, with minimal government intervention in the economy. (416)

Monopoly   Control of a market by a single business firm. (416)

Profession   An occupation requiring extensive knowledge that is governed by a code of ethics. (422)

Socialism   An economic system under which the means of production and distribution are collectively owned. (417)

TECHNOLOGY RESOURCES

Internet Connection

*Note: While all the URLs listed were current as of the printing of this book, these sites often change. Please check our website (**www.mhhe.com/schaefer9**) for updates, hyperlinks, and exercises related to these sites.*

1. The workforce in any country changes constantly, reflecting the diversity of its population. Aboriginal (or First Nations) peoples make up one of the fastest-growing segments of the Canadian population, yet their labor force participation is lower, and their unemployment rate higher, than those of other Canadians. Learn what the Canadian government is doing to increase Aboriginals' participation in the labor market by visiting the Aboriginal Workforce Participation initiative (**www.ainc-inac.gc.ca/ai/awpi/index_e.html**).

2. The Bureau of Labor Statistics (**www.bls.gov**) compiles many informative statistics on the U.S. labor force. Explore the site to learn about the current unemployment rate both in the United States and in your home state.

Online Learning Center with PowerWeb

This chapter has focused on the economic system and the important influences it has on social behavior and on other social institutions. Visit the student center in the Online Learning Center at **www.mhhe.com/schaefer9** and link to "Use Your Sociological Imagination." You will be asked to imagine what your life might be like if the United States had a predominantly socialistic economy. You will also be asked to imagine what the U.S. workforce will look like in 2050 in terms of age, gender, race, and ethnicity. Read the questions, think about them, and use your *sociological imagination* to answer them.

chapter 19

HEALTH AND MEDICINE

WELCOME TO AMERICA

the only industrialized country besides South Africa without national healthcare

This billboard protests the lack of a national health care program in the United States. The reference to South Africa was especially pointed when the poster first appeared in 1989, because of the racist apartheid regime that held sway there.

Culture and Health

Sociological Perspectives on Health and Illness

Social Epidemiology and Health

Health Care in the United States

Mental Illness in the United States

Social Policy and Health: Financing Health Care Worldwide

Boxes

SOCIAL INEQUALITY: To Inform or Not to Inform? How Race and Ethnicity Affect Views of Patient Autonomy

RESEARCH IN ACTION: The Nun Study

TAKING SOCIOLOGY TO WORK: Erika Miles, Director, Health Programs, CVS.com

I knew that Navajo people mistrusted Western medicine, and that Navajo customs and beliefs, even Navajo ways of interacting with others, often stood in direct opposition to the way I was trained at Stanford to deliver medical care. I wanted to make a difference in the lives of my people, not only by providing surgery to heal them but also by making it easier for them to understand, relate to, and accept Western medicine. By speaking some Navajo with them, by showing respect for their ways, and by being one of them, I could help them. I watched my patients. I listened to them. Slowly I began to develop better ways to heal them, ways that respected their culture and beliefs. I desired to incorporate these traditional beliefs and customs into my practice. . . .

Navajo patients simply didn't respond well to the brusque and distanced style of Western doctors. To them it is not acceptable to walk into a room, quickly open someone's shirt and listen to their heart with a stethoscope, or stick something in their mouth or ear. Nor is it acceptable to ask probing and personal questions. As I adapted my practice to my culture, my patients relaxed in situations that could otherwise have been highly stressful to them. As they became more comfortable and at ease, something even more remarkable—astonishing, even—happened. When patients were trusting and accepting before surgery, their operations seemed to be more successful. If they were anxious, distrustful, and did not understand, or had resisted treatment, they seemed to have more operative or postoperative complications. Could this be happening? The more I watched, the more I saw it was indeed true. Incorporating Navajo philosophies of balance and symmetry, respect and connectedness into my practice, benefited my patients and allowed everything in my two worlds to make sense.

Navajos believe in *hózhǫ́* or *hózhǫ́ni*—"Walking in Beauty"—a worldview in which everything in life is connected and influences everything else. A stone thrown into a pond can influence the life of a deer in the forest, a human voice and a spoken word can influence events around the world, and all things possess spirit and power. So Navajos make every effort to live in harmony and balance with everyone and everything else. Their belief system sees sickness as a result of things falling out of balance, of losing one's way on the path of beauty. In this belief system, religion and medicine are one and the same. . . .

As I have modified my Western techniques with elements of Navajo culture and philosophy, I have seen the wisdom and truth of Navajo medicine too, and how Navajo patients can benefit from it. In this way I am pulling the strands of my life even closer together. The results have been dazzling—*hózhǫ́ni*. It has been beautiful. *(Alvord and Van Pelt 1999:13–15)* ■ ✍

Additional information about this excerpt can be found on the Online Learning Center at **www.mhhe.com/schaefer9.**

In this excerpt from *The Scalpel and the Silver Bear*, Dr. Lori Arviso Alvord, the first Navajo woman to become a surgeon, describes her effort to bridge the cultural gap between Western medicine and traditional Native American healing. Dropping the impersonal clinical manner she had learned in medical school, Alvord reached out to her Navajo patients, acknowledging their faith in holistic healing practices. Her account communicates the wonder she felt as she watched their health improve. By walking in beauty, Dr. Alvord had become a healer as well as a surgeon.

Dr. Alvord is the physician shown on the poster at the beginning of Chapter 11. Her account illustrates the powerful effect of culture on both health and medicine. Culture affects the way people interact with doctors and healers, the way they relate to their families when they are sick, and even the way they think about health. Are some health problems peculiar to certain cultures? Who defines what illness is? How does health care vary from one social class to another and from one nation to another? In this chapter, we will consider first the relationship between culture and health. Then we will present a sociological overview of health, illness, health care, and medicine as a social institution. We will begin by examining how functionalists, conflict theorists, interactionists, and labeling theorists look at health-related issues. Then we will study the distribution of diseases in a society by social class, race and ethnicity, gender, and age.

We'll look too at the evolution of the health care system of the United States. Sociologists are interested in the roles that people play in the health care system and the organizations that deal with issues of health and sickness. Therefore, we will analyze the interactions among physicians, nurses, and patients; alternatives to traditional health care; and the role of government in providing health services to the needy. The chapter continues with an examination of mental illness that contrasts the medical and labeling approaches to mental disorders. Finally, the social policy section explores the issue of how to finance health care worldwide. ■

CULTURE AND HEALTH

Culture contributes to differences in medical care and even in how health is defined. In Japan, for instance, organ transplants are rare. The Japanese do not generally favor harvesting organs from brain-dead donors. Researchers have shown that diseases themselves are rooted in the shared meanings of particular cultures. The term ***culture-bound syndrome*** refers to a disease or illness that cannot be understood apart from its specific social context (Shepherd 2003; Surgeon General of the United States 1999b).

In the United States, a culture-bound syndrome known as anorexia nervosa has received increasing attention over the last few decades. First described in England in the 1860s, this condition is characterized by an intense fear of becoming obese and a distorted image of one's body. Those suffering from anorexia nervosa (primarily young women in their teenage years or 20s) lose weight drastically through self-induced semistarvation. Anorexia nervosa is best understood in the context of Western culture, which typically views the slim, youthful body as healthy and beautiful, and the fat person as ugly and lacking in self-discipline.

Culture can also influence the relative incidence of a disease or disorder. In *The Scalpel and the Silver Bear*, Dr. Lori Arviso Alvord writes of the depression and alcoholism that attend life on the reservation. These diseases, she says, are born out of "historical grief": "Navajo children are told of the capture and murder of their forefathers and mothers, and then they too must share in the legacy. . . ." Not just for the Navajo, Alvord writes, but for Black Americans as well, the weight of centuries of suffering, injustice, and loss too often manifests itself in despair and addiction. The rate of alcoholism mortality among Native Americans served by the Indian Health Service is five times that of the general population of the United States (Alvord and Van Pelt 1999:12).

SOCIOLOGICAL PERSPECTIVES ON HEALTH AND ILLNESS

If social factors contribute to the evaluation of a person as "healthy" or "sick," how can we define health? We can imagine a continuum with health on one end and death on the other. In the preamble to its 1946 constitution, the World Health Organization defined ***health*** as a "state of complete physical, mental, and social well-being, and not merely the absence of disease and infirmity" (Leavell and Clark 1965:14).

In this definition, the "healthy" end of the continuum represents an ideal rather than a precise condition. Along the continuum, people define themselves as healthy or sick on the basis of criteria established by each individual, relatives, friends, co-workers, and medical practitioners. Because health is relative, we can view it in a social context and consider how it varies in different situations or cultures.

Why is it that you may consider yourself sick or well when others do not agree? Who controls definitions of health and illness in our society, and for what ends? What are the consequences of viewing yourself (or of being viewed) as ill or disabled? Drawing on four sociological perspectives—functionalism, conflict theory, interaction-

ism, and labeling theory—we can gain greater insight into the social context that shapes definitions of health and treatment of illness.

Functionalist Approach

Illness entails breaks in our social interactions, both at work and at home. From a functionalist perspective, then, being sick must be controlled so that not too many people are released from their societal responsibilities at any one time. Functionalists contend that an overly broad definition of illness would disrupt the workings of a society.

Sickness requires that one take on a social role, even if temporarily. The *sick role* refers to societal expectations about the attitudes and behavior of a person viewed as being ill. Sociologist Talcott Parsons (1951, 1975), well

pp. 13–14 known for his contributions to functionalist theory, outlined the behavior required of people who are considered sick. They are exempted from their normal, day-to-day responsibilities and generally do not suffer blame for their condition. Yet they are obligated to try to get well, which may include seeking competent professional care. Attempting to get well is particularly important in the world's developing countries. Modern automated industrial societies can absorb a greater degree of illness or disability than horticultural or agrarian societies, in which the availability of workers is far more critical (Conrad 2000).

According to Parsons's theory, physicians function as "gatekeepers" for the sick role. They either verify a patient's condition as "illness" or designate the patient as "recovered." The ill person becomes dependent on the physician, because the latter can control valued rewards (not only treatment of illness, but also excused absences from work and school). Parsons suggests that the physician–patient relationship is somewhat like that between parent and child. Like a parent, the physician helps the patient to enter society as a full and functioning adult (A. Segall 1976).

The concept of the sick role is not without criticism. First, patients' judgments regarding their own state of health may be related to their gender, age, social class, and ethnic group. For example, younger people may fail to detect warning signs of a dangerous illness, while the elderly may focus too much on the slightest physical malady. Second, the sick role may be more applicable to people experiencing short-term illnesses than to those with recurring, long-term illnesses. Finally, even simple factors, such as whether a person is employed or not, seem to affect willingness to assume the sick role—as does the impact of socialization into a particular occupation or activity. For example, beginning in childhood, athletes learn to define

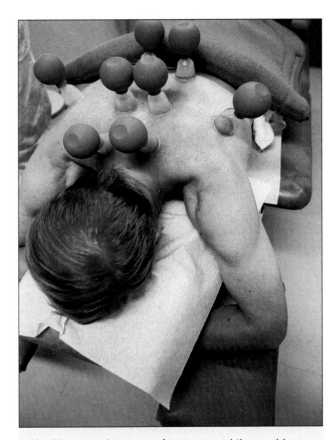

Health care takes many forms around the world. Cupping—a traditional practice used in ancient China, India, Egypt, and Greece—survives in modern Finland. Physiotherapists there use suction cups to draw out blood in order to lower patients' blood pressure, improve their circulation, and relieve muscular pain.

The trend toward the medicalization of society now encompasses obesity, especially among youths. In China, the government has established "fat reduction hospitals" to treat overweight youths like this one, about to have his weight checked. Physicians are concerned about obesity because it is a precursor to heart disease and diabetes.

certain ailments as "sports injuries" and therefore do not regard themselves as "sick." Nonetheless, sociologists continue to rely on Parsons's model for functionalist analysis of the relationship between illness and societal expectations of the sick (Curry 1993).

Conflict Approach

Conflict theorists observe that the medical profession has assumed a preeminence that extends well beyond whether to excuse a student from school or an employee from work. Sociologist Eliot Freidson (1970:5) has likened the position of medicine today to that of state religions yesterday—it has an officially approved monopoly of the right to define health and illness and to treat illness. Conflict theorists use the term *medicalization of society* to refer to the growing role of medicine as a major institution of social control (Conrad and Schneider 1992; McKinlay and McKinlay 1977; Zola 1972, 1983).

The Medicalization of Society

Social control involves techniques and strategies for regulating behavior in order to enforce the distinctive norms and values of a culture. Typically, we think of informal social control as occurring within families and peer groups, and formal social control as being carried out by authorized agents such as police officers, judges, school administrators, and employers. However, viewed from a conflict perspective, medicine is not simply a "healing profession"; it is a regulating mechanism as well.

p. 171

How does medicine manifest its social control? First, medicine has greatly expanded its domain of expertise in recent decades. Physicians now examine a wide range of issues, among them sexuality, old age, anxiety, obesity, child development, alcoholism, and drug addiction. Society tolerates such expansion of the boundaries of medicine because we hope that these experts can bring new "miracle cures" to complex human problems, as they have to the control of certain infectious diseases.

The social significance of this expanding medicalization is that once a problem is viewed using a *medical model*—once medical experts become influential in proposing and assessing relevant public policies—it becomes more difficult for common people to join the discussion and exert influence on decision making. It also becomes more difficult to view these issues as being shaped by social, cultural, or psychological factors, rather than simply by physical or medical factors (Caplan 1989; Conrad and Schneider 1992; Starr 1982).

Second, medicine serves as an agent of social control by retaining absolute jurisdiction over many health care procedures. It has even attempted to guard its jurisdiction by placing health care professionals such as chiropractors and nurse-midwives outside the realm of acceptable medicine. Despite the fact that midwives first brought professionalism to child delivery, they have been portrayed as having invaded the "legitimate" field of obstetrics, both in the United States and Mexico. Nurse-midwives have sought licensing as a way to achieve professional respectability, but physicians continue to exert power to ensure that midwifery remains a subordinate occupation (Friedland 2000).

Inequities in Health Care

The medicalization of society is but one concern of conflict theorists as they assess the workings of health care institutions. As we have seen throughout this textbook, in analyzing any issue, conflict theorists seek to determine who benefits, who suffers, and who dominates at the expense of others. Viewed from a conflict perspective, glaring inequities exist in health care delivery in the United States. For example, poor and rural areas tend to be underserved because medical services concentrate where people are numerous and/or wealthy.

Similarly, from a global perspective, there are obvious inequities in health care delivery. Today, the United States has about 25 physicians per 1,000 people, while African nations have fewer than 1 per 1,000. This situation is only worsened by the **brain drain**—the immigration to the United States and other industrialized nations of skilled workers, professionals, and technicians who are desperately needed in their home countries. As part of this brain drain, physicians and other health care professionals have come to the United States from developing countries such as India, Pakistan, and various African states. Conflict theorists view such emigration out of the Third World as yet another way in which the world's core industrialized nations enhance their quality of life at the expense of developing countries. One way the developing countries suffer is in lower life expectancy. Life expectancy in Africa and much of Latin America and Asia is far lower than in industrialized nations (World Bank 2003b:112–113).

Conflict theorists emphasize that inequities in health care resources have clear life-and-death consequences. From a conflict perspective, the dramatic differences in infant mortality rates around the world (see Figure 19-1) reflect, at least in part, unequal distribution of health care resources based on the wealth or poverty of various communities and nations. Still, despite the wealth of the United States, at least 31 nations have *lower* infant mortality rates, among them Canada, Great Britain, and Japan. Conflict theorists point out that unlike the United States, these countries offer some form of government-supported health care for all citizens, which typically leads to greater availability and use of prenatal care.

Interactionist Approach

From an interactionist point of view, patients are not passive; often, they actively seek the services of a health care practitioner. In examining health, illness, and medicine as a social institution, then, interactionists engage in micro-level study of the roles played by health care professionals and patients. Interactionists are particularly interested in how physicians learn to play their occupational role. According to Brenda L. Beagan (2001), the technical language students learn in medical school becomes the basis for the script they follow as novice physicians. The familiar white coat is their costume—one that helps them to appear confident and professional at the same time that it identifies them as doctors to patients and other staff members. Beagan found that many medical students struggle to project the appearance of competence they think their role demands.

FIGURE 19-1

Infant Mortality Rates, 2002

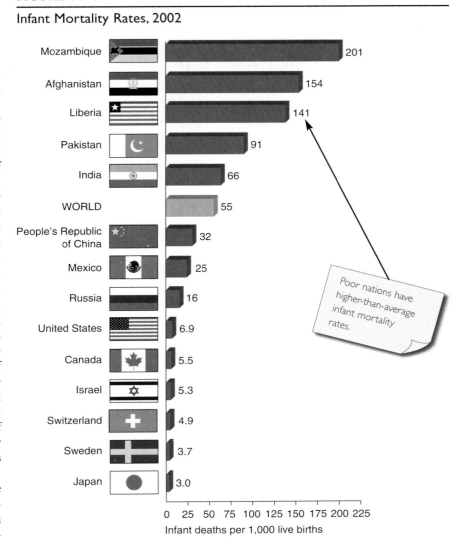

Poor nations have higher-than-average infant mortality rates.

Infant deaths per 1,000 live births

Source: Haub 2003.

19-1 TO INFORM OR NOT TO INFORM? HOW RACE AND ETHNICITY AFFECT VIEWS OF PATIENT AUTONOMY

Should patients be told the seriousness of their illness? Should they be included in the decisions about what medical care they receive? In the last 25 years, the principle of patient autonomy has become a fundamental ideal of medical care in the United States. According to this principle, "people have the right to make informed decisions about their medical care; consequently, they need the truth about their diagnosis, their prognosis, and the risks and benefits of possible treatments." While the ideal of patient autonomy has won wide acceptance from physicians, policymakers, and the general public, some critics argue that the current focus on patient autonomy reflects an ethnocentric cultural bias that ignores other values, such as family integrity and physician responsibility.

The question of how race and ethnicity influence attitudes toward patient autonomy was studied by a team of researchers, including an internal medicine specialist and ethicist, anthropologists, translators, a statistician, and a law professor. At 31 senior centers in Los Angeles County, the researchers administered questionnaires to 800 people of diverse ethnic bckgrounds, all of them age 65 or over. The major finding of the study was that there are marked differences by race

and ethnicity in attitudes toward patient autonomy. While 88 percent of African Americans and 87 percent of White Americans believe that a patient should be informed of a diagnosis of cancer, the same is true of only 65 percent of Mexican Americans and 47 percent of Korean Americans. Moreover, 69 percent of Whites and 63 percent of African Americans believe that a patient should be in-

> Navajos believe that physicians and other healers should never offer a terminal diagnosis or use any negative language that could trouble or hurt a patient.

formed of a terminal prognosis, compared with 48 percent of Mexican Americans and 35 percent of Korean Americans.

One reason why Korean Americans are especially opposed to hearing a terminal prognosis is their belief in the unity of mind and body. Truth-telling is like a death sentence to traditional Koreans, because of their view that the body will react to ominous news received by the mind. Many Korean Americans be-

lieve that physicians should always be optimistic and positive in their communications with patients.

Similarly, a separate study of residents of a Navajo Indian reservation in Arizona revealed that Navajo culture places a high value on thinking and speaking in a positive way. For Navajos, language can shape reality. Consequently, Navajos believe that physicians and other healers should never offer a terminal diagnosis or use any negative language that could trouble or hurt a patient. One highly regarded medicine man notes that the mention of death to a patient "is sharper than any needle" (Carrese and Rhodes 1995:828).

Let's Discuss

1. How has terminal illness been handled in your family? Have relatives who were dying been told the truth about their condition, or has it been withheld from them? Do you think your family's cultural background influenced the decision?

2. Which is more important, the patient's right to know or the patient's faith in the chance of recovery?

Sources: Blackhall et al. 1995; Carrese and Rhodes 1995; Commonwealth Fund 2002; Monmaney 1995.

Sometimes patients play an active role in health care by *failing* to follow a physician's advice. For example, some patients stop taking medications long before they should. Some take an incorrect dosage on purpose, and others never even fill their prescriptions. Such noncompliance results in part from the prevalence of self-medication in our society; many people are accustomed to self-diagnosis and self-treatment. On the other hand, patients' active involvement in their health care can sometimes have very *positive* consequences. Some patients read books about preventive health care techniques, attempt to maintain a healthful and nutritious diet, carefully monitor any side effects of medication, and adjust the dosage based on perceived side effects.

Finally, as Box 19-1 shows, physicians may *change* their approach to a patient based on the patient's wishes.

Labeling Approach

Labeling theory helps us to understand why certain people are *viewed* as deviants, "bad kids," or p. 185 criminals, whereas others whose behavior is similar are not. Labeling theorists also suggest that the designation "healthy" or "ill" generally involves social definition by others. Just as police officers, judges, and other regulators of social control have the power to define certain people as criminals, health care professionals (especially physicians) have the power to define certain people as sick. Moreover, like labels that suggest nonconformity or criminality, labels that are associated with illness commonly reshape how others treat us and how we see ourselves. Our society attaches serious consequences to labels that suggest less-than-perfect physical or mental health (H. Becker 1963; C. Clark 1983; Schwartz 1987).

A historical example illustrates perhaps the ultimate extreme in labeling social behavior as a sickness. As enslavement of Africans in the United States came under increasing attack in the 19th century, medical authorities provided new rationalizations for the oppressive practice. Noted physicians published articles stating that the skin color of Africans deviated from "healthy" white skin coloring because Africans suffered from congenital leprosy. Moreover, the continuing efforts of enslaved Africans to escape from their White masters were classified as an example of the "disease" of drapetomania (or "crazy runaways"). The prestigious *New Orleans Medical and Surgical Journal* suggested that the remedy for this "disease" was to treat slaves kindly, as one might treat children. Apparently, these medical authorities would not entertain the view that it was healthy and sane to flee slavery or join in a slave revolt (Szasz 1971).

By the late 1980s, the power of one particular label—"person with AIDS"—had become quite evident. As we saw p. 106 in our discussion of the late Arthur Ashe, this label often functions as a master status that overshadows all other aspects of a person's life. Once someone is told that he or she has tested positive for HIV, the virus associated with AIDS, that person is forced to confront immediate and difficult questions: Should I tell my family members, my sexual partner(s), my friends, my co-workers, my employer? How will these people respond? People's intense fear of the disease has led to prejudice and discrimination—even social ostracism—against those who have (or are suspected of having) AIDS. A person who has AIDS must deal not only with the serious medical consequences of p. 119 the disease, but with the distressing social consequences associated with the label.

According to labeling theorists, we can view a variety of life experiences as illnesses or not. Recently, premenstrual syndrome, posttraumatic disorders, and hyperactivity have been labeled medically recognized disorders. In addition, disagreement continues in the medical community over whether chronic fatigue syndrome constitutes a medical illness.

Probably the most noteworthy medical example of labeling is the case of homosexuality. For years, psychiatrists classified being gay or lesbian not as a lifestyle but as a mental disorder subject to treatment. This official sanction by the psychiatry profession became an early target of the growing gay and lesbian rights movement in the United States. In 1974, members of the American Psychiatric Association voted to drop homosexuality from the standard manual on mental disorders (Adam 1995; Monteiro 1998).

The four sociological approaches described here share certain common themes. First, any person's health or illness is more than an organic condition, since it is subject to the interpretation of others. The impact of culture, family and friends, and the medical profession mean that health and illness are not purely biological occurrences but sociological occurrences as well. Second, since members of a society (especially industrial societies) share the same health care delivery system, health is a group and societal concern. Although health may be defined as the complete well-being of an individual, it is also the result of his or her social environment, as the next section will show (Cockerham 1998).

SOCIAL EPIDEMIOLOGY AND HEALTH

Social epidemiology is the study of the distribution of disease, impairment, and general health status across a population. Epidemiology initially concentrated on the

In South Africa, the children's television program *Sesame Street* features an HIV-positive Muppet named Kami, created to foster a culture of acceptance for people living with AIDS. Around the world, people who suffer from AIDs must deal with the prejudice, discrimination, and even social ostracism that result from the negative label "person with AIDS."

FIGURE 19-2

Percentage of People without Health Insurance, 2001

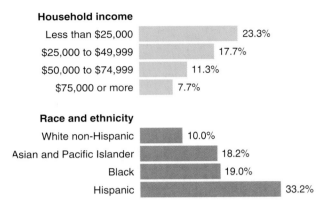

Household income

Less than $25,000   23.3%
$25,000 to $49,999   17.7%
$50,000 to $74,999   11.3%
$75,000 or more   7.7%

Race and ethnicity

White non-Hispanic   10.0%
Asian and Pacific Islander   18.2%
Black   19.0%
Hispanic   33.2%

Source: Mills 2002:23.

scientific study of epidemics, focusing on how they started and spread. Contemporary social epidemiology is much broader in scope, concerned not only with epidemics but also with nonepidemic diseases, injuries, drug addiction and alcoholism, suicide, and mental illness. Epidemiologists draw on the work of a wide variety of scientists and researchers, among them physicians, sociologists, public health officials, biologists, veterinarians, demographers, anthropologists, psychologists, and meteorologists. Box 19-2 examines a recent epidemiological study of the diseases associated with aging.

Recently, the federal government's Centers for Disease Control and Prevention took on the new role of tracking bioterrorism. Epidemiologists mobilized in 2001 to trace the anthrax outbreak and to prepare for any terrorist use of smallpox or other lethal microbes that could lead to an epidemic.

Researchers in social epidemiology commonly use two concepts: incidence and prevalence. **Incidence** refers to the number of new cases of a specific disorder occurring within a given population during a stated period, usually a year. For example, the incidence of AIDS in the United States in 1999 was 41,849 cases. In contrast, **prevalence** refers to the total number of cases of a specific disorder that exist at a given time. The prevalence of AIDS in the United States in January 2000 was about 323,000 cases (Centers for Disease Control and Prevention 2003).

When disease incidence figures are presented as rates, or as the number of reports per 100,000 people, they are called **morbidity rates.** (The term **mortality rate** refers to the incidence of *death* in a given population.) Sociologists find morbidity rates useful because they reveal that a specific disease occurs more frequently among one segment of a population than another. As we shall

see, social class, race, ethnicity, gender, and age can all affect a population's morbidity rates. In 1999, the U.S. Department of Health and Human Services, recognizing the inequality inherent in U.S. morbidity and mortality rates, launched the Campaign for 100% Access and Zero Health Disparities, an ambitious undertaking (Bureau of Primary Health Care 1999).

Social Class

Social class is clearly associated with differences in morbidity and mortality rates. Studies in the United States and other countries have consistently shown that people in the lower classes have higher rates of mortality and disability than others. A study published in 1998 documents the impact of class on mortality. The authors concluded that Americans whose family incomes were less than $10,000 could expect to die seven years sooner than those with incomes of at least $25,000 (Pamuk et al. 1998).

Why is class linked to health? Crowded living conditions, substandard housing, poor diet, and stress all contribute to the ill health of many low-income people in the United States. In certain instances, poor education may lead to a lack of awareness of measures necessary to maintain good health. Financial strains are certainly a major factor in the health problems of less affluent people in the United States.

Another reason for the link between class and health is that the poor—many of whom belong to racial and ethnic minorities—are less able than others to afford quality medical care. As Figure 19-2 shows, the affluent are more likely to have health insurance, either because they can afford it or because they have jobs that provide it.

Another factor in the link between class and health is evident at the workplace: The occupations of people in the working and lower classes of the United States tend to be more dangerous than those of more affluent citizens. Miners, for example, risk injury or death from explosions and cave-ins; they are also vulnerable to respiratory diseases such as black lung. Workers in textile mills who are exposed to toxic substances may contract a variety of illnesses, including one disease commonly known as *brown lung disease.* In recent years, the nation has learned of the perils of asbestos poisoning, a particular worry for construction workers (R. Hall 1982).

In the view of Karl Marx and contemporary conflict theorists, capitalist societies such as the United States care more about maximizing profits than they do about the health and safety of industrial workers. As a result, government agencies do not take forceful action to regulate conditions in the workplace, and workers suffer many preventable job-related injuries and illnesses. Research also shows that the lower classes are

19-2 THE NUN STUDY

At age 93, Sister Nicolette reads, crochets, and plays cards, and until a recent fall walked several miles a day. Her younger sibling, Sister Mary Ursula, is confined to a wheelchair and can barely lift her head or hands: She is a victim of Alzheimer's disease. Both these real-life sisters had a similar family background, and both lived for most of their lives in the same Roman Catholic convent under the same conditions. Why is one so robust and the other so afflicted?

This is one question that Dr. David Snowdon, a scientist at the University of Kentucky, hopes to answer from his long-term study of an order of nuns living in Mankato, Minnesota. Snowdon is particularly interested in detecting causes of Alzheimer's disease and in finding ways to delay or prevent its onset. He began studying the lives of the 678 nuns in 1986, when the sisters ranged in age from 75 to 103. As of 2001, 295 were alive, all over age 85; some were suffering from Alzheimer's and other diseases of the brain, while others were entirely symptom free.

The order of nuns presents an ideal research group for an epidemiological study because the participants lead such similar lives. They eat the same meals, receive the same health care, do not smoke, drink very little alcohol, and have not experienced physical changes associated with pregnancy; most were teachers. These similarities allow the researchers to discount some factors that often contribute to illness, such as diet deficiency or smoking. It is also significant that the entire group is made up of aging women. In the past, most medical research of this type has concentrated on middle-aged men, despite the fact that women constitute the great majority of the elderly population.

Snowdon examines the nuns each year, taking blood samples and testing their cognitive ability to trace the course of their health. He has persuaded the

> The order of nuns presents an ideal research group for an epidemiological study because the participants lead such similar lives.

nuns to donate their brains after they die, because a brain autopsy is the only sure way to diagnose Alzheimer's disease. Although all this information was helpful to Snowdon, he still had to rely on the nuns' memories to establish facts of their background *before* they entered the order, and memories in the elderly can be unreliable, especially among those afflicted with brain disease. Then he ran across a treasure trove of data—archives documenting the births, parentage, and socioeconomic backgrounds of the nuns. These data helped to establish the health risk factors of each nun earlier in life.

Perhaps the most valuable research tools in the archives were the autobiographies written by the applicants to the convent when they were in their 20s. From examining these writings and looking at the current health status of the nuns, Snowdon concluded that an active intellectual life, an ability to express oneself with complex ideas, and a positive outlook all correlate with healthy aging and a long life.

Snowdon has found other factors associated with healthy aging, including a good diet and avoidance of stroke-causing behavior, and he does not discount the value of spiritual and communal living. But he hopes other studies will back up his findings about the importance of early language ability and a positive emotional outlook.

Let's Discuss

1. What are the advantages of using an order of nuns as participants in an epidemiological study? Do you think a similar study should be conducted with men? Why or why not?

2. Among those you know who are healthy in their old age, what in their background has kept them healthy, in your opinion?

Sources: Belluck 2001; Lemonick and Mankato 2001; Nun Study 2003; Snowdon 2001.

more vulnerable to environmental pollution than the affluent, not only where they work but also where they live (see Chapter 21).

Race and Ethnicity

The health profiles of many racial and ethnic minorities reflect the social inequality evident in the United States. The poor economic and environmental conditions of groups such as African Americans, Hispanics, and Native Americans are manifested in high morbidity and mortality rates for these groups. It is true that some afflictions, such as sickle-cell anemia among Blacks, have a clear genetic basis. But in most instances, environmental factors contribute to the differential rates of disease and death.

In many respects, the mortality rates for African Americans are distressing. Compared with Whites, Blacks have higher death rates from heart disease, pneumonia, diabetes, and cancer. The death rate from stroke is twice as high among African Americans. Such epidemiological findings reflect in part the fact that a high proportion of Blacks are found among the nation's lower classes.

A Mexican folk healer, or *curandera,* administers remedies for lack of energy, including herbs, flowers, and an egg. About 20 percent of Hispanics rely on such home remedies to treat their ailments.

According to the National Center for Health Statistics, Whites can expect to live 77.7 years. In contrast, life expectancy for Blacks is 72.2 years (Arias and Smith 2003).

As noted earlier, infant mortality is regarded as a primary indicator of health care. There is a significant gap in the United States between the infant mortality rates of African Americans and Whites. Generally, the rate of infant deaths is more than twice as high among Blacks. African Americans account for 15 percent of all live births in the nation but 30 percent of infant deaths. Puerto Ricans and Native Americans have infant mortality rates that are lower than African Americans' but higher than Whites' (Mathews et al. 2002).

The medical establishment is not exempt from racism. The media often focus on obvious forms of racism, such as hate crimes, while overlooking more insidious forms in social institutions like the medical establishment. One review of more than 100 studies conducted over the last decade concluded that minorities receive inferior care even when they are insured. Despite having access to care, Blacks, Latinos, and American Indians are treated unequally as a result of racial prejudice and differences in the quality of

various health care plans. Furthermore, national clinical studies have shown that even allowing for differences in income and insurance coverage, racial and ethnic minorities are less likely than other groups to receive both standard health care and life-saving treatment for conditions such as HIV infection (Budrys 2003; Caesar and Williams 2002; Smedley et al. 2002).

Drawing on the conflict perspective, sociologist Howard Waitzkin (1986) suggests that racial tensions also contribute to the medical problems of Blacks. In his view, the stress resulting from racial prejudice and discrimination helps to explain the higher rates of hypertension found among African Americans (and Hispanics) compared to Whites. Hypertension—twice as common in Blacks as in Whites—is believed to be a critical factor in Blacks' high mortality rates from heart disease, kidney disease, and stroke (Morehouse Medical Treatment and Effectiveness Center 1999).

Some Mexican Americans as well as many other Latinos adhere to cultural beliefs that make them less likely to use the established medical system. They may interpret

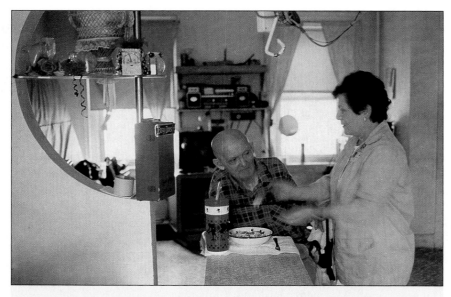

A home health care worker helps an aging man with his meal. Because many older people need assistance in meeting their daily needs, the demand for such services has been rising with the older population, straining the capacity of the U.S. health care system.

their illnesses according to traditional Latino folk practices, or **curanderismo**—a form of holistic health care and healing. *Curanderismo* influences how one approaches health care and even how one defines illness. Most Hispanics probably use folk healers, or *curanderos,* infrequently, but perhaps 20 percent rely on home remedies. Some define such illnesses as *susto* (fright sickness) and *atague* (or fighting attack) according to folk beliefs. Because these complaints often have biological bases, sensitive medical practitioners need to deal with them carefully and diagnose and treat illnesses accurately (Council on Scientific Affairs 1999; Trotter and Chavira 1997).

Gender

A large body of research indicates that in comparison with men, women experience a higher prevalence of many illnesses, though they tend to live longer. There are variations—for example, men are more likely to have parasitic diseases, whereas women are more likely to become diabetic—but as a group, women appear to be in poorer health than men.

The apparent inconsistency between the ill health of women and their greater longevity deserves an explanation, and researchers have advanced a theory. Women's lower rate of cigarette smoking (reducing their risk of heart disease, lung cancer, and emphysema), lower consumption of alcohol (reducing the risk of auto accidents and cirrhosis of the liver), and lower rate of employment in dangerous occupations explain about one-third of their greater longevity than men. Moreover, some clinical studies suggest that the differences in morbidity may actually be less pronounced than the data show. Researchers argue that women are much more likely than men to seek treatment, to be diagnosed as having a disease, and thus to have their illnesses reflected in the data examined by epidemiologists.

From a conflict perspective, women have been particularly vulnerable to the medicalization of society, with everything from birth to beauty being treated in an increasingly medical context. Such medicalization may contribute to women's higher morbidity rates compared to those of men. Ironically, even though women have been especially affected by medicalization, medical researchers have often excluded women from clinical studies. Female physicians and researchers charge that sexism lies at the heart of such research practices, and insist there is a desperate need for studies of female subjects (Bates 1999; McDonald 1999; Vidaver et al. 2000).

Age

Health is the overriding concern of the elderly. Most older people in the United States report having at least one chronic illness, but only some of those conditions are potentially life threatening or require medical care. At the same time, health problems can affect the quality of life of older people in important ways. Almost half of older people in the United States are troubled by arthritis, and many have visual or hearing impairments that can interfere with the performance of everyday tasks.

Older people are also especially vulnerable to certain types of mental health problems. Alzheimer's disease, the

FIGURE 19-3

Availability of Physicians by State

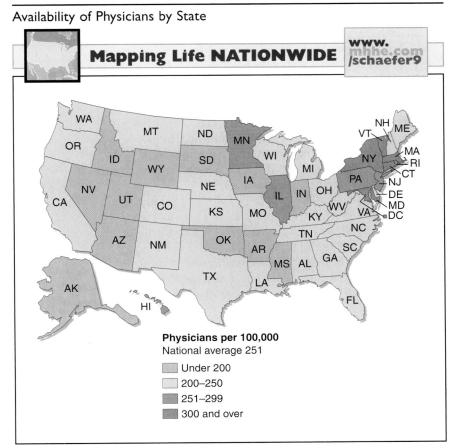

Source: Bureau of the Census 2002a:106.

FIGURE 19-4

Total Health Care Expenditures in the United States, 1970–2010 (projected)

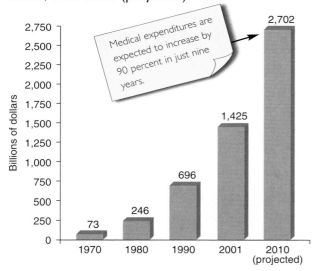

Medical expenditures are expected to increase by 90 percent in just nine years.

Sources: Centers for Medicare and Medicaid Services 2003 (1980–2010 data); Health Care Financing Administration 2001 (1970 data).

Think About It

What social changes in the United States might account for the rise in health care costs from $73 billion in 1970 to almost $1.5 trillion in 2001?

---

leading cause of dementia in the United States, afflicts an estimated 4 million older people. While some individuals with Alzheimer's exhibit only mild symptoms, the risk of severe problems resulting from this disease rises substantially with age (Alzheimer's Association 1999).

Not surprisingly, older people in the United States (ages 75 and older) are three times more likely to use health services and to be hospitalized than younger people (ages 15–24). The disproportionate use of the U.S. health care system by older people is a critical factor in all discussions about the cost of health care and possible reforms of the health care system (Bureau of the Census 2002a).

In sum, to achieve the goal of 100 percent access and zero health disparities, federal health officials must overcome inequities that are rooted not just in age, but in social class, race and ethnicity, and gender. If that were not enough, they must also deal with a geographical disparity in health care resources. Figure 19-3 (page 447) shows the differences in the presence of physicians from one state to another. Dramatic differences in the availability of physicians, hospitals, and nursing homes also exist between ur-

ban and rural areas in the same state. In the next section we will look more closely at issues surrounding the delivery of health care in the United States.

HEALTH CARE IN THE UNITED STATES

As the entire nation is well aware, the costs of health care have skyrocketed in the last 35 years. In 1997, total expenditures for health care in the United States crossed the trillion-dollar threshold—more than four times the 1980 figure (see Figure 19-4). In 2000, the amount spent on health care equaled that spent on education, defense, prisons, farm subsidies, food stamps, and foreign aid combined. By the year 2010, total expenditures for health care in the United States are expected to exceed $2.7 trillion. The rising costs of medical care are especially burdensome in the event of catastrophic illnesses or confinement to a nursing home. Bills of tens of thousands of dollars are not unusual in the treatment of cancer, Alzheimer's disease, and other chronic illnesses requiring custodial care.

The health care system of the United States has moved far beyond the days when general practitioners living in a neighborhood or community typically made house calls and charged modest fees for their services. How did health care become a big business involving nationwide hospital chains and marketing campaigns? How have these changes reshaped the interactions between doctors, nurses, and patients? We will address these questions in the next section of the chapter.

A Historical View

Today, state licensing and medical degrees confer an authority on medical professionals that is maintained from one generation to the next. However, health care in the United States has not always followed this model. The "popular health movement" of the 1830s and 1840s emphasized preventive care and what is termed "self-help." Strong criticism was voiced of "doctoring" as a paid occupation. New medical philosophies or sects established their own medical schools and challenged the authority and methods of more traditional doctors. By the 1840s, most states had repealed medical licensing laws. In response, through the leadership of the American Medical Association (AMA), founded in 1848, "regular" doctors attacked lay practitioners, sectarian doctors, and female physicians in general. (For a different view, see Navarro 1984.) Once their authority had been institutionalized through standardized programs of education and licensing, it was conferred on all who successfully completed the programs. The authority of the physician no longer depended on lay attitudes or on the person occupying the sick role; increasingly, it was built into the structure of the medical profession and the health care system. As the institutionalization of health care proceeded, the medical profession gained control over both the market for its services and the various organizational hierarchies that govern medical practice, financing, and policymaking. By the 1920s, physicians controlled hospital technology, the division of labor of health personnel, and indirectly, other professional practices such as nursing and pharmacy (R. Coser 1984).

Physicians, Nurses, and Patients

Traditionally, physicians have held a position of dominance in their dealings with both patients and nurses. The functionalist and interactionist perspectives offer a framework for understanding the professional socialization of physicians as it relates to patient care. Functionalists suggest that established physicians and medical school professors serve as mentors or role models who transmit knowledge, skills, and values to the passive learner—the medical student. Interactionists emphasize that students are molded by the medical school environment as they interact with their classmates.

Both approaches argue that the typical training of physicians in the United States leads to rather dehumanizing physician–patient encounters. As Dr. Lori Arviso Alvord writes in *The Scalpel and the Silver Bear,* "I had been trained by a group of physicians who placed much more emphasis on their technical abilities and clinical skills than on their abilities to be caring and sensitive" (Alvord and Van Pelt 1999:13). Despite many efforts to formally introduce a humanistic approach to patient care into the medical school curriculum, patient overload and cost-cutting by hospitals have tended to undercut positive relations. Moreover, widespread publicity about malpractice suits and high medical costs has further strained the physician–patient relationship.

Interactionists have closely examined compliance and negotiation between physician and patient. They concur with Talcott Parsons's view that the relationship is generally asymmetrical, with doctors holding a position of dominance and controlling rewards.

Just as physicians have maintained dominance in their interactions with patients, they have controlled interactions with nurses. Despite their training and professional status, nurses commonly take orders from physicians. Traditionally, the relationship between doctors and nurses has paralleled the male dominance of the United States: Most physicians have been male, while virtually all nurses have been female.

Like other women in subordinate roles, nurses have been expected to perform their duties without challenging the authority of men. Psychiatrist Leonard Stein (1967) refers to this process as the *doctor–nurse game.* According to the rules of this "game," the nurse must never openly disagree with the physician. When she has recommendations concerning a patient's care, she must communicate them indirectly, in a deferential tone. For example, if asked by a hospital's medical resident, "What sleeping medication has been helpful to Mrs. Brown in the past?" (an indirect request for a recommendation), the nurse will respond with a disguised recommendation, such as "Pentobarbital mg 100 was quite effective night before last." Her careful response allows the physician to authoritatively restate the same prescription as if it were *his* idea.

Like nurses, female physicians have traditionally found themselves in a subordinate position because of gender. In fall 2002, while 49 percent of all new medical school students in the United States were female, only 29 percent of all faculty members at medical schools were female (Association of American Medical Colleges 2003a, 2003b).

A study of male and female medical residents suggests that the increasing number of women physicians may alter the traditional doctor–patient relationship. Male residents were found to be more focused on the intellectual challenges of medicine and the prestige associated with certain medical specialties. In contrast, female residents were more likely to express a commitment to caring for patients and devoting time to them. In terms of the functionalist analysis of gender stratification offered p. 286 by sociologists Talcott Parsons and Robert Bales, male residents took the *instrumental,* achievement-oriented role, while female residents took the *expressive,* interpersonal-oriented role. As women continue to enter and move higher in the hierarchies of the medical profession, sociological studies will surely be done to see if these apparent gender differences persist. Box 12-1 on page 289 discusses one such difference, the gender difference in doctor–patient communication style.

Patients have traditionally relied on medical personnel to inform them of health care issues, but increasingly they are turning to the media for health care information. Recognizing this change, pharmaceutical firms are advertising their prescription drugs directly to potential customers through television and magazines. The Internet is another growing source for patient information.

Medical professionals are understandably suspicious of these new sources of information. A study published in the *Journal of the American Medical Association* in 2001 found that health information on the Internet is often incomplete and inaccurate, even on the best sites. Nevertheless, there is little doubt that web research is transforming an increasing proportion of patient–physician encounters, as patients arrive for their doctor's appointments armed with the latest printout from the Internet (Berland 2001).

Use Your Sociological Imagination www.mhhe.com/schaefer9

If you were a patient, would you put yourself entirely in the physician's hands? Or would you do some research about your illness on your own? If you were a doctor, would you want your patient checking medical information on the Internet? Explain your positions.

Alternatives to Traditional Health Care

In traditional forms of health care, people rely on physicians and hospitals for the treatment of illness. Yet at least one out of every three adults in the United States attempts to maintain good health or respond to illness through the use of alternative health care techniques. For example, in recent decades interest has been growing in *holistic* (also spelled *wholistic*) medical principles, first developed in China. **Holistic medicine** refers to therapies in which the health care practitioner considers the person's physical, mental, emotional, and spiritual characteristics. The individual is regarded as a totality rather than a collection of interrelated organ systems. Treatment methods include massage, chiropractic medicine, acupuncture (which involves the insertion of fine needles into surface points), respiratory exercises, and the use of herbs as remedies. Nutrition, exercise, and visualization may also be used to treat ailments that are generally treated through medication or hospitalization (Sharma and Bodeker 1998).

The Navajo concept of *hózhó* (Walking in Beauty) is another example of a holistic approach to health (see the chapter introduction). Practitioners of holistic medicine do not necessarily function totally outside the traditional health care system. Some, like Dr. Lori Arviso Alvord, have medical degrees and rely on X-rays and EKG machines for diagnostic assistance. Others who staff holistic clinics, often referred to as *wellness clinics,* reject the use of medical technology. The recent resurgence of holistic medicine comes amid widespread recognition of the value of nutrition and the dangers of overreliance on prescription drugs (especially those used to reduce stress, such as Valium).

The medical establishment—professional organizations, research hospitals, and medical schools—has generally served as a stern protector of traditionally accepted health care techniques. However, a major breakthrough

A street vendor in Indonesia offers bats, used in a folk remedy for asthma. According to the World Health Organization, which is studying such treatments, alternative medicine is far more common than Western-style medicine in the poorer countries of the world.

Taking Sociology To Work

ERIKA MILES **Director, Health Programs, CVS.com**

"Health care has always fascinated me, and I was lucky enough to discover medical sociology," says Erika Miles. Right after graduating from Colgate University in 1992, Miles worked three years for the Robert Wood Johnson Foundation as a quantitative research assistant, doing studies on physician behavior and underserved populations. Just as Miles was starting graduate school, she discovered the Internet and was hooked. She dropped her graduate studies, taught herself web design, and started doing Internet marketing for various pharmaceutical companies. At CVS.com, a nationwide online pharmacy in Seattle, she develops corporate strategies for working with pharmaceutical companies, health care providers, and other Internet companies.

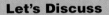

Developing websites in health care has a lot to do with sociology, according to Miles. "Much of the work is really thinking about how people work, act, and react to their surroundings, their families, and their work environments—and how all that relates to their health." She also does "a ton of qualitative and quantitative research," and credits her undergraduate sociology courses with helping her with that aspect of her work.

Miles basically just fell into being a sociology major after starting out with a 200-level course on peace and social change movements, which she loved. "Sociology just made sense, which is more than I can say for a lot of other classes I took." Miles believes that a sociology degree has great potential because it can apply to many different fields. "It is a degree that really helps you learn how to think about the people around you."

Miles's advice to students is to take research classes and write a thesis, whether they are required to or not. "That is really where you get to apply what you've learned."

Let's Discuss

1. What sociological skills might Erika Miles use in developing websites in health care?
2. Are you planning on taking any research classes and/or writing a thesis? How might they be valuable to you in the career of your choosing?

occurred in 1992 when the federal government's National Institutes of Health—the nation's major funding source for biomedical research—opened an Office of Alternative Medicine, empowered to accept grant requests. Possible areas of study include herbal medicine, mind–body control techniques, and the use of electromagnetism to heal bones. A national study published in *The Journal of the American Medical Association* indicates that 46 percent of the general public uses alternative medicine. Most of it is not covered by insurance. In fact, out-of-pocket expenses for alternative medicine match all out-of-pocket expenses for traditional physician services (Eisenberg et al. 1998; Stolberg 2000).

On the international level, the World Health Organization (WHO) has begun to monitor the use of alternative medicine around the world. According to WHO, 80 percent of people who live in the poorest countries in the world use some form of alternative medicine, from herbal treatments to the services of a faith healer. In most countries, these treatments are largely unregulated, even

though some of them can be fatal. For example, Kavakava, an herbal tea used to relieve anxiety in the Pacific Islands, can be toxic to the liver in concentrated form. Yet other alternative treatments have been found to be effective in the treatment of serious diseases, such as malaria and sickle-cell anemia. WHO's goal is to compile a list of such practices, as well as to encourage the development of universal training programs and ethical standards for practitioners of alternative medicine. To date, the organization has published findings on about 100 of the 5,000 plants believed to be used as herbal remedies (McNeil 2002).

The Role of Government

Not until the 20th century did health care receive federal aid. The first significant involvement was the 1946 Hill-Burton Act, which provided subsidies for building and improving hospitals, especially in rural areas. A far more important change came with the enactment in 1965 of

451

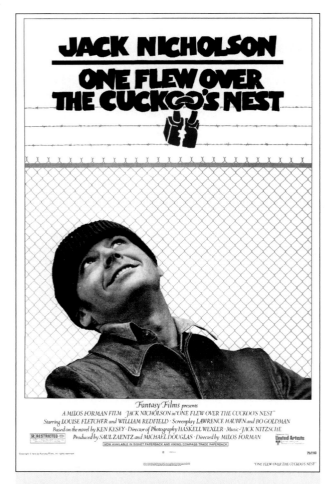

Media emphasis on extreme mental disorders contributes to the stigmatization of mental health issues. This 1975 film featured severe forms of mental illness and portrayed medical practitioners as capable of offering little assistance.

two wide-ranging government assistance programs: Medicare, which is essentially a compulsory health insurance plan for the elderly, and Medicaid, which is a noncontributory federal and state insurance plan for the poor. These programs greatly expanded federal involvement in health care financing for needy men, women, and children.

Given rates of illness and disability among elderly people, Medicare has had a huge impact on the health care system. Initially, Medicare simply reimbursed health care providers such as physicians and hospitals for the billed costs of their services. However, in 1983, as the overall costs of Medicare increased dramatically, the federal government introduced a price-control system. All illnesses were classified into diagnostic-related groups (DRGs); a reimbursement rate was set for each condition, regardless of the individual needs of the patient. In effect, the federal government told hospitals and doctors that it would no longer be concerned with their costs in treating Medicare patients; it would reimburse them only to a designated level (Wynia et al. 2000).

The DRG system of reimbursement has contributed to the controversial practice of "dumping." Under this system, private hospitals transfer patients whose treatment may be unprofitable to public facilities. Many private hospitals in the United States have begun to conduct "wallet biopsies" to investigate the financial status of potential patients. Those judged undesirable are then refused admission or dumped. Though a federal law passed in 1987 made it illegal for any hospital receiving Medicare funds to dump patients, the practice continues. We will look further into the government's role in health care in the social policy section of this chapter (Feinglass 1987; Sherrill 1995).

MENTAL ILLNESS IN THE UNITED STATES

The words *mental illness* and *insanity* evoke dramatic and often inaccurate images of emotional problems. Though the media routinely emphasize the most violent behavior of those with disturbances, mental health and mental illness can more appropriately be viewed as a continuum of behavior that we ourselves move along. Using a less sensational definition, we can consider a person to have a mental disorder "if he or she is so disturbed that coping with routine, everyday life is difficult or impossible." The term **mental illness** should be reserved for a disorder of the brain that disrupts a person's thinking, feeling, and ability to interact with others (Coleman and Cressey 1980:315; National Alliance for the Mentally Ill 2000).

How prevalent is mental illness? The World Bank finds that in industrial economies, mental disorders account for 4 of the 10 leading causes of disability. In the United States, about one out of every five Americans suffers from some form of mental illness. The most common disorders include depression, anxiety disorders, and obsessive-compulsive disorders (Narrow et al. 2002).

People in the United States have traditionally maintained a negative and suspicious view of those with mental disorders. Holding the status of "mental patient" or even "former mental patient" can have unfortunate and undeserved consequences. For example, during the 1972 election campaign, the Democratic vice presidential nominee, Senator Thomas Eagleton of Missouri, admitted to having once received treatment for depression. Public reaction was so strong that presidential nominee George McGovern was forced to drop Eagleton from the Democratic ticket.

Politics is not the only arena in which people viewed as mentally ill experience second-class treatment. Voting rights are denied in some instances, acceptance for jury duty is problematic, and past emotional problems are an issue in divorce and custody cases. Moreover, content analysis of network television programs and films shows that mentally ill characters are uniformly portrayed in a demeaning and derogatory fashion; many are labeled as "criminally insane," "wackos," or "psychos." From an interactionist perspective, a key social institution is shaping social behavior by manipulating symbols and intensifying people's fears about the mentally ill (J. Klein 2003).

Theoretical Models of Mental Disorders

In studying mental illness, we can draw on both a medical model and a more sociological approach derived from labeling theory. Each model offers distinctive assumptions regarding treatment of people with mental disorders.

According to the *medical model,* mental illness is rooted in biological causes that can be treated through medical intervention. Problems in brain structure or in the biochemical balance in the brain, sometimes due to injury and sometimes due to genetic inheritance, are thought to be at the bottom of these disorders. Recently the Surgeon General of the United States (1999a) released an exhaustive report on mental health in which he declared that the accumulated weight of scientific evidence leaves no doubt about the physical origins of mental illness.

That is not to say that social factors do not contribute to mental illness. Just as culture affects the incidence and prevalence of illness in general, its treatment, and the expression of certain culture-bound syndromes, so too it can affect mental illness. In fact, the very definition of mental illness differs from one culture to the next. Mainstream U.S. culture, for instance, considers hallucinations highly abnormal. But many traditional cultures view them as evidence of divine favor, and confer a special status on those who experience them. As we have noted throughout this textbook, a given behavior may be viewed as normal in one society, disapproved of but

tolerated in a second, and labeled as sick and heavily sanctioned in a third.

In contrast to the medical model, *labeling theory* suggests that some behaviors that are viewed as mental illnesses may not really be illnesses, since the individual's problems arise from living in society and not from physical maladies. For example, the Surgeon General's report (1999a:5) notes that "bereavement symptoms" of less than two months' duration do not qualify as a mental disorder, but beyond that they may be redefined. Sociologists would see this approach to bereavement as labeling by those with the power to affix labels rather than as an acknowledgment of a biological condition.

Psychiatrist Thomas Szasz (1974), in his book *The Myth of Mental Illness,* which first appeared in 1961, advanced the view that numerous personality disorders are not diseases, but simply patterns of conduct labeled as disorders by significant others. The response to Szasz's challenging thesis was sharp: The commissioner of the New York State Department of Hygiene demanded his dismissal from his university position because Szasz did not "believe" in mental illness. But many sociologists embraced his model as a logical extension of examining individual behavior in a social context.

In sum, the medical model is persuasive because it pinpoints the causes of mental illness and offers treatment for disorders. Yet proponents of the labeling perspective maintain that mental illness is a distinctively social process, whatever other processes are involved. From

Social factors such as war can jeopardize a person's mental health. Many people who once lived in war zones, like these Rwandans fleeing the horrors of genocide, later suffer from symptoms of severe mental trauma, including depression, nightmares, and flashbacks to violent events.

At a community mental health center, outpatients create a newsletter for their day program. In the 1980s, community-based mental health care replaced hospitalization as the typical form of treatment for people with serious mental illnesses.

a sociological perspective, the ideal approach to mental illness integrates the insights of labeling theory with those of the medical approach (A. Horwitz 2002).

Patterns of Care

For most of human history, those who suffered from mental disorders were deemed the responsibility of their families. Yet mental illness has been a matter of governmental concern much longer than physical illness has. That is because severe emotional disorders threaten stable social relationships and entail prolonged incapacitation. As early as the 1600s, European cities began to confine the insane in public facilities along with the poor and criminals. Prisoners, indignant at being forced to live with "lunatics," resisted this approach. The isolation of the mentally ill from others in the same facility and from the larger society soon made physicians the central and ultimate authority over their welfare.

A major policy development in caring for those with mental disorders came with the passage of the 1963 Community Mental Health Centers Act. The CMHC program, as it is known, not only increased federal government involvement in the treatment of the mentally ill. It also es-

tablished community-based mental health centers to treat clients on an *outpatient* basis, thereby allowing them to continue working and living at home. The program showed that outpatient treatment could be more effective than the institutionalized programs of state and county mental hospitals.

Expansion of the federally funded CMHC program decreased inpatient care. By the 1980s, community-based mental health care had replaced hospitalization as the typical form of treatment. Deinstitutionalization of the mentally ill reached dramatic proportions across the United States. State mental hospitals had held almost 560,000 long-term patients in 1955; by 1998 they had fewer than 63,000 patients. Deinstitutionalization was often defended as a social reform that would effectively reintegrate the mentally ill into the outside world. The authentic humanitarian concern behind deinstitutionalization proved to be convenient for politicians whose goal was simply cost cutting (Bureau of the Census 2002a:117; Grob 1995).

In a marked shift from public policy over the last three decades, several states have recently made it easier to commit mental patients to hospitals involuntarily. These changes have come in part because community groups and individual residents have voiced increasing fear and anger about the growing number of mentally ill homeless people living in their midst, many of them on the streets. All too often, the severely mentally ill end up in jail or prison after committing crimes that lead to their prosecution. Ironically, family members of these mentally ill men and women complain that they cannot get adequate treatment for their loved ones *until* they have committed violent acts. Nevertheless, civil liberties advocates and voluntary associations of mentally ill people worry about the risks of denying people their constitutional rights, and cite horror stories about the abuses people have experienced during institutionalization (Marquis and Morain 1999; Shogren 1994).

The Issue

Cindy Martin died in 1990 at age 26, after four months of surgery and intensive care at Presbyterian Hospital in Pittsburgh. In the aftermath of her death, her husband's insurance company received a bill for $1.25 million. While accountants attempted to untangle the costs of the seven surgical procedures performed on Martin—including heart, liver, and kidney transplants—this case underscored troubling questions regarding the high cost of health care. Who should pay for expensive medical procedures? What role, if any, should government play in providing medical care and health insurance for its citizens? (Freudenheim 1990)

In many developing nations, health care issues concern very basic needs of primary care. The goals established at the UN's World Health Assembly in 1981 were modest by North American standards: safe water in the home or within 15 minutes' walking distance; immunization against major infectious diseases; availability of essential drugs within an hour's walk or travel; and the assistance of trained personnel for pregnancy and childbirth. While some areas have made significant progress in meeting these goals, many developing countries have seen little improvement; in some places, health care has deteriorated (World Bank 1997).

The focus of this social policy section, however, is on those industrialized (or developed) nations where the *availability* of health care is not an issue. The question is more one of accessibility and affordability. What steps are being taken to make the available services reachable and affordable?

The Setting

The United States is now the only Western industrial democracy that does not treat health care as a basic right. According to the Bureau of the Census, in 2000, some 43 million people in the United States had no health insurance the entire year. The uninsured typically include self-employed people with limited incomes, illegal immigrants, and single and divorced mothers who are the sole providers for their families. As we saw in Figure 19-2 earlier, African Americans, Asian Americans, and Hispanics are less likely than Whites to carry private health insurance. Although people with lower incomes are least likely to be covered, substantial numbers of households at all income levels go without coverage for some or most of any given year (Mills 2002).

National health insurance is a general term for legislative proposals that focus on ways to provide the entire population with health care services. First discussed by government officials in the United States in the 1930s, it has come to mean many different things, ranging from narrow health insurance coverage with minimal federal subsidies to broad coverage with large-scale federal funding.

Opponents of national health insurance insist that it would be extremely costly and would lead to significant tax increases. Defenders counter, however, that countries such as Great Britain and Sweden have maintained broad governmental health coverage for decades. Ironically, while these countries offer extensive health coverage for all citizens, the United States has higher health care costs than any other nation: an average annual cost of $4,499 per person, compared to $2,058 in Canada and only $1,747 in Great Britain. As Figure 19-5 (page 456) shows, most industrial nations finance a substantially larger share of health care costs through government than the United States does (World Bank 2003a:92–94).

Sociological Insights

As conflict theorists suggest, the health care system, like other social institutions, resists basic change. In general, those who

UNINSURED WORKING POOR

COFF

FIGURE 19-5

Government Expenditures for Health Care, Selected Countries

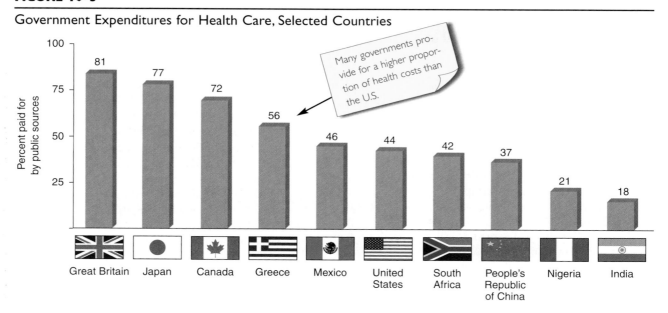

Source: World Bank 2003a:92–94.

receive substantial wealth and power through the workings of an existing institution will have a strong incentive to keep things as they are. In this case, private insurance companies are benefiting financially from the current system, and have a clear interest in opposing certain forms of national health insurance. In addition, the American Medical Association (AMA), one of Washington's most powerful lobbying groups, has been successfully fighting national health insurance since the 1930s.

The health care system is unquestionably undergoing "corporatization," as for-profit health care companies (often linking insurers, hospitals, and groups of physicians) are achieving increasing dominance. Conflict theorists have long argued that an underlying and disturbing aspect of capitalism in the United States is that illness may be exploited for profit. Critics of the corporatization of health care worry that the growing pressures on physicians and other health care providers to make cost-effective decisions may lead to inadequate and even life-threatening patient care (Sherrill 1995).

Policy Initiatives

Early in the 1990s, the U.S. Congress dismissed the idea of any sort of national health insurance. Although virtually everyone agreed that the existing fee-for-service system was too costly, a major move to centralize financing, and hence control, of health care was deemed unacceptable. Yet even without legislative reform, major changes have been occurring.

Today, more and more people are enrolled in managed care plans, which limit patients' choice of physicians and treatments but cover most medical costs. ***Health maintenance organizations (HMOs),*** which provide comprehensive medical services for a preestablished fee, are playing a prominent role in managed care.

Concern is growing about the quality of care people receive through managed care plans such as HMOs—especially the elderly and minorities, who are less likely to be able to afford private insurance plans. According to a national survey, people in managed care feel they spend less time with physicians, find it more difficult to see specialists, and generally sense that the overall quality of health care has deteriorated (Brubaker 2001).

Many industrial countries are paying greater attention than the United States to unequal health care delivery. Addressing this problem, however, often creates difficulties. Great Britain, for example, closed facilities in London and other metropolitan areas in an attempt to reassign medical staff to underserved rural areas. In addition to these concerns about the quality and availability of medical care, Britain's National Health Service remains underfunded (Christie 2001).

Medical services have in the past been delivered according to the ability to pay for services and the availability of facilities and personnel. As governments throughout the world take greater responsibility for health care, and as care becomes increasingly expensive, governments can be expected to pay more and more attention to controlling expenditures. Although the U.S. federal government has not been as heavily involved as other nations, the introduction of payment according to diagnostic-related groups (DRGs) and the institution of managed care plans have created a degree of control previously unknown in the United States (Mechanic and Rochefort 1996).

Let's Discuss

1. Are you and your family covered by a health insurance plan? If not, why aren't you covered? Has anyone in your family ever required a medical procedure he or she couldn't pay for?
2. Have you ever belonged to a health maintenance organization? If so, how satisfied were you with the care you received? Were you ever denied a specific treatment because it was too costly?
3. Should health care be a basic right of all Americans?

CHAPTER RESOURCES

Summary

The meanings of **health,** sickness, and disease are shaped by social definitions of behavior. This chapter considers the relationship between culture and health, several sociological perspectives on health and illness, the distribution of diseases in a society, the evolution of the U.S. health care system, and the sociological dimension of mental health and mental illness. It closes with a discussion of how health care is financed worldwide.

1. The effect of culture on health can be seen in the existence of **culture-bound syndromes,** as well as in cultural differences in medical care and the **incidence** and **prevalence** of certain diseases.
2. According to Talcott Parsons's functionalist perspective, physicians function as "gatekeepers" for the **sick role,** either verifying a person's condition as "ill" or designating the person as "recovered."
3. Conflict theorists use the term *medicalization of society* to refer to medicine's growing role as a major institution of social control.
4. Labeling theorists suggest that the designation of a person as "healthy" or "ill" generally involves social definition by others. These definitions affect how others see us and how we view ourselves.
5. Contemporary **social epidemiology** is concerned not only with epidemics but with nonepidemic diseases, injuries, drug addiction and alcoholism, suicide, and mental illness.
6. Studies have consistently shown that people in the lower classes have higher rates of mortality and disability than others.
7. Racial and ethnic minorities have higher rates of morbidity and mortality than Whites. Women tend to be in poorer health than men but live longer. Older people are especially vulnerable to mental health problems, such as Alzheimer's disease.
8. The preeminent role of physicians in the U.S. health care system has given them a position of dominance in their dealings with nurses and patients.
9. Many people seek alternative health care techniques, such as **holistic medicine** and self-help groups.
10. Mental disorders may be viewed from two different perspectives, the medical model and the sociological model, which is based on labeling theory. In the United States, society has traditionally taken a negative, suspicious attitude toward people with mental disorders.
11. In the developed world, an aging population and technological breakthroughs have made health care both more extensive and more costly. At the same time, developing nations struggle to provide primary care for a burgeoning population.

Critical Thinking Questions

1. Sociologist Talcott Parsons has argued that the doctor–patient relationship is similar to that between parent and child. Does this view seem accurate? Should the doctor–patient relationship be more egalitarian? How might functionalist and conflict theorists differ in their views of the power of physicians in the U.S. health care system?
2. How would the process of classifying a person as mentally ill differ under the medical model and

the sociological model? Draw on Erving Goffman's concept of stigmatization (see Chapter 8).

3. Relate what you have learned about social epidemiology to the question of universal health care coverage. If the United States were to adopt a system of universal coverage, what might be the effect on the incidence and prevalence of disease among Americans of all classes, races and ethnicities, genders, and ages? What might be the ultimate effect of such changes on health care costs?

Key Terms

Brain drain   The immigration to the United States and other industrialized nations of skilled workers, professionals, and technicians who are desperately needed in their home countries. (page 441)

Culture-bound syndrome   A disease or illness that cannot be understood apart from its specific social context. (438)

Curanderismo   Latino folk medicine, a form of holistic health care and healing. (447)

Health   As defined by the World Health Organization, a state of complete physical, mental, and social well-being, and not merely the absence of disease and infirmity. (438)

Health maintenance organization (HMO)   An organization that provides comprehensive medical services for a preestablished fee. (456)

Holistic medicine   Therapies in which the health care practitioner considers the person's physical, mental, emotional, and spiritual characteristics. (450)

Incidence   The number of new cases of a specific disorder occurring within a given population during a stated period. (444)

Mental illness   A disorder of the brain that disrupts a person's thinking, feeling, and ability to interact with others. (452)

Morbidity rate   The incidence of disease in a given population. (444)

Mortality rate   The incidence of death in a given population. (444)

Prevalence   The total number of cases of a specific disorder that exist at a given time. (444)

Sick role   Societal expectations about the attitudes and behavior of a person viewed as being ill. (439)

Social epidemiology   The study of the distribution of disease, impairment, and general health status across a population. (443)

TECHNOLOGY RESOURCES

Internet Connection

*Note: While all the URLs listed were current as of the printing of this book, these sites often change. Please check our website (**www.mhhe.com/schaefer9**) for updates, hyperlinks, and exercises related to these sites.*

1. The National Center for Health Statistics, the federal government's principal health statistics agency, is part of the Centers for Disease Control and Prevention (CDC). To learn more about health trends in the United States, link to Health, United States, at **www.cdc.gov/nchs.**

2. The Substance Abuse and Mental Health Services Administration is an agency of the U.S. Department of Health and Human Services. Learn about mental health services, statistics, and resources in your home state by linking to the administration at **www.samhsa.gov.**

Online Learning Center with PowerWeb

When you visit the student center in the Online Learning Center at **www.mhhe.com/schaefer9,** link to "Flash Cards." There is a flash card for every key term in your text, with a definition for each term. Flash cards are a valuable study tool—they give you the opportunity to see how familiar you are with important terms.

COMMUNITIES AND URBANIZATION

YOU WON'T SEE THEM. THE COLD WILL.
DONATE WARM CLOTHES.
Donate warm clothes to the homeless. Call 0800 126300

CAMPANHA DO
AGASALHO 2001

FUNDO SOCIAL DE SOLIDARIEDADE
DO ESTADO DE SÃO PAULO

Homelessness is a major social problem not just in the United States, but in cities around the world. This poster, published in the city of São Paulo, Brazil, appeals for clothing donations to keep those who sleep on the street warm. As the photograph suggests, whole families, including children, may become homeless.

How Did Communities Originate?

Urbanization

Types of Communities

Social Policy and Communities: Seeking Shelter Worldwide

Boxes

SOCIOLOGY IN THE GLOBAL COMMUNITY:
Squatter Settlements

RESEARCH IN ACTION: Store Wars

It is not hard to understand why Hakim Hasan came to see himself as a public character. Early one July morning, a deliveryman pulled his truck up to the curb behind Hakim's vending table on Greenwich Avenue off the corner of Sixth Avenue [in lower Manhattan] and carried a large box of flowers over to him.

"Can you hold these until the flower shop opens up?" the deliveryman asked.

"No problem," responded Hakim as he continued to set up the books on his table. "Put them right under there."

When the store opened for business, he brought them inside and gave them to the owner.

"Why did that man trust you with the flowers?" I later asked.

"People like me are the eyes and ears of this street," he explained, echoing [sociologist] Jane Jacobs again. "Yes, I could take those flowers and sell them for a few hundred dollars. But that deliveryman sees me here every day. I'm as dependable as any store-owner." . . .

Another day, I was present at the table when a traffic officer walked by to give out parking tickets.

"Are any of these your cars?" she asked Hakim.

"Yes, that one, and that one," said Hakim, pointing.

"What is that all about?" I asked.

"The day I met her, we got into an argument," he explained. "She was getting ready to give the guy across the street a ticket. I say, 'You can't do this!' She said, 'Why not?' I say, ''Cause I'm getting ready to put a quarter in.' She said, 'You can't do that.' I guess that, because of the way I made my argument, she didn't give out the ticket, and from that point onward we became friends. And when she comes on the block, she asks me, for every car on the block that has a violation sign, 'Is that your car?' Meaning, 'Is it someone you know?' And depending on whether I say yes or no, that's it—they get a ticket." . . .

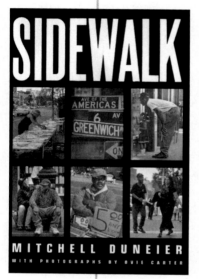

"Are these things part of your job description as a vendor?" I asked him once.

"Let me put it to you this way, Mitch," he replied. "I kind of see what I loosely call my work on the sidewalk as going far, far beyond just trying to make a living selling books. That sometimes even seems secondary. Over time, when people see you on the sidewalk, there is a kind of trust that starts. They've seen you so long that they walk up to you. There have been occasions when I've had to have directions translated out of Spanish into French to get somebody to go someplace!"

It is not only directions and assistance that I have seen Hakim give out. He also tells people a great deal about books—so much so that he once told me he was thinking of charging tuition to the people who stand in his space on the sidewalk. *(Duneier 1999:17–18)* ■ ✎

Additional information about this excerpt can be found on the Online Learning Center at **www.mhhe.com/schaefer9.**

This excerpt from *Sidewalk*, by the sociologist Mitchell Duneier, describes the social position of Hakim Hasan, a sidewalk book vendor in New York City's Greenwich Village. The author, who for two years lived just around the corner from Hasan's table, was so fascinated by street life in the Village that he decided to do observation research on it. As Duneier explains in his book, street vendors like Hasan are just as much a part of the neighborhood as the shopkeepers who occupy the storefronts behind them—even if they don't have a mailing address. In fact, their presence on the street, day in and day out, contributes to the neighborhood's safety and stability (Duneier 1999).

Sociologist Mitchell Duneier *(right)* did participant observation as he worked the tables of sidewalk vendors in Greenwich Village.

This chapter explores communities of all sorts, from rural towns to inner-city neighborhoods and the suburbs that surround them. In sociological terms, a **community** may be defined as a spatial or political unit of social organization that gives people a sense of belonging. That sense of belonging can be based either on shared residence in a particular city or neighborhood, such as Greenwich Village, or on a common identity, such as that of street vendors, homeless people, or gays and lesbians. Whatever the members have in common, communities give people the feeling that they are part of something larger than themselves (Dotson 1991; see also Hillery 1955).

The anthropologist George Murdock (1949) has observed that the community is one of only two truly universal units of social organization (the other being the family). How did communities originate? Why have large cities grown at the expense of small villages in many areas of the world today? And why, even in nations like the United States, are many residents of large and prosperous communities homeless? In this chapter we will begin to answer these questions by tracing the development of communities from their ancient origins to the birth of the modern city and its growth through technological change. In particular, we will examine the rapid and dramatic urbanization that occurred around the world during the 20th century. Then we will study two different sociological views of urbanization, one stressing its functions and the other its dysfunctions. And we'll compare rural, suburban, and urban communities in the United States today. Finally, in the social policy section, we'll analyze the disturbing phenomenon of homelessness, an all-too-familiar feature of community life. ■

HOW DID COMMUNITIES ORIGINATE?

As we noted in the chapter opening, a *community* is a spatial or political unit of social organization that gives people a sense of belonging. The nature of community has changed greatly over the course of history—from early hunting-and-gathering societies to highly modernized postindustrial cities.

Early Communities

For most of human history, people used very basic tools and knowledge to survive. They satisfied their need for an adequate food supply through hunting, foraging for fruits or vegetables, fishing, and herding. In comparison with later industrial societies, early civilizations were much

◄ p. 116

more dependent on the physical environment and much less able to alter that environment to their advantage.

The emergence of horticultural societies, in which people cultivated food rather than merely gathering fruits and vegetables, led to many dramatic changes in human social organization. It was no longer necessary to move from place to place in search of food. Because people had to remain in specific locations to cultivate crops, more stable and enduring communities began to develop. As agricultural techniques became more and more sophisticated, a cooperative division of labor involving both family members and others developed. People gradually began to produce more food than they actually needed for themselves. They could provide food, perhaps as part of an exchange, to others who might be involved in nonagricultural labor. This transition from subsistence to surplus represented a critical step in the emergence of cities.

Eventually, people produced enough goods to cover both their own needs and those of people not engaged in agricultural tasks. At first the surplus was limited to agricultural products, but gradually it evolved to include all types of goods and services. Residents of a city came to rely on community members who provided craft products and means of transportation, gathered information, and so forth (Nolan and Lenski 1999).

With these social changes came an even more elaborate division of labor, as well as greater opportunity for differential rewards and privileges. So long as everyone had been engaged in the same tasks, stratification had been limited to such factors as gender, age, and perhaps the ability to perform the task (a skillful hunter could win unusual respect from the community). But the surplus allowed for the expansion of goods and services, leading to greater differentiation, a hierarchy of occupations, and social inequality. Thus the surplus was a precondition not only for the establishment of cities but for the division of members of a community into social classes (see Chapter 9). The ability to produce goods for other communities marked a fundamental shift in human social organization.

Preindustrial Cities

It is estimated that beginning about 10,000 B.C., permanent settlements free from dependence on crop cultivation emerged. Yet by today's standards, these early communities would barely qualify as cities. The *preindustrial city,* as it is termed, generally had only a few thousand people living within its borders, and was characterized by a relatively closed class system and limited mobility. In these early cities status was usually based on ascribed characteristics such as family background, and education was limited to members of the elite. All the residents relied on perhaps 100,000 farmers and their own part-time farming to provide the needed agricultural surplus. The Mesopotamian city of Ur had a population of about 10,000 and was limited to roughly 220 acres of land, including the canals, the temple, and the harbor.

Why were these early cities so small and relatively few in number? Several key factors restricted urbanization:

- **Reliance on animal power (both humans and beasts of burden) as a source of energy for economic production.** This factor limited the ability of humans to make use of and alter the physical environment.
- **Modest levels of surplus produced by the agricultural sector.** Between 50 and 90 farmers may have been required to support one city resident (K. Davis [1949] 1995).
- **Problems in transportation and the storage of food and other goods.** Even an excellent crop could easily be lost as a result of such difficulties.
- **Hardships of migration to the city.** For many peasants, migration was both physically and economically impossible. A few weeks of travel was out of the question without more sophisticated techniques of food storage.
- **Dangers of city life.** Concentrating a society's population in a small area left it open to attack from outsiders, as well as more susceptible to extreme damage from plagues and fires.

Gideon Sjoberg (1960) examined the available information on early urban settlements in medieval Europe, India, and China. He identified three preconditions of city life: advanced technology in both agricultural and nonagricultural areas, a favorable physical environment, and a well-developed social organization.

For Sjoberg, the criteria for defining a "favorable" physical environment were variable. Proximity to coal and iron helps only if a society knows how to *use* these natural resources. Similarly, proximity to a river is particularly beneficial only if a culture has the means to transport water efficiently to the fields for irrigation and to the cities for consumption.

A sophisticated social organization is also an essential precondition for urban existence. Specialized social roles bring people together in new ways through the exchange of goods and services. A well-developed social organization ensures that these relationships are clearly defined and generally acceptable to all parties. Admittedly,

Sjoberg's view of city life is an ideal type, since inequality did not vanish with the emergence of urban communities.

Industrial and Postindustrial Cities

Imagine how harnessing the energy of air, water, and other natural resources could change a society. Advances in agricultural technology led to dramatic changes in community life, but so did the process of industrialization. The *industrial revolution,* which began in the middle of the 18th century, focused on the application of nonanimal sources of power to labor tasks. p. 118 Industrialization had a wide range of effects on people's lifestyles, as well as on the structure of communities. Emerging urban settlements became centers not only of industry but of banking, finance, and industrial management.

The factory system that developed during the industrial revolution led to a much more refined division of labor than was evident in preindustrial cities. The many new occupations that were created produced a complex set of relationships among workers. Thus, the **industrial city** was not merely more populous than its preindustrial

Detail from a fresco illustrating the effects of good city government; Italian, 14th century A.D. Preindustrial cities had a sophisticated social organization headed by a wealthy nobility.

predecessors; it was based on very different principles of social organization. Sjoberg outlined the contrasts between preindustrial and industrial cities, as summarized in Table 20-1 on page 464.

In comparison with preindustrial cities, industrial cities have a more open class system and more social mobility. After initiatives in industrial cities by women's rights groups, labor unions, and other political activists, formal education gradually became available to many children from poor and working-class families. While ascribed characteristics such as gender, race, and ethnicity remained important, a talented or skilled individual had greater opportunity to better his or her social position. In these and other respects, the industrial city was genuinely a different world from the preindustrial urban community.

In the latter part of the 20th century, a new type of urban community emerged. The **postindustrial city** is a city in which global finance and the electronic flow of information dominate the economy. p. 118 Production is decentralized and often takes place outside of urban centers, but control is centralized in multinational corporations whose influence transcends urban and even national boundaries. Social change is a constant feature of the postindustrial city. Economic restructuring and spatial change seem to occur each decade, if not more frequently. In the postindustrial world, cities are forced into increasing competition for economic opportunities, which deepens the plight of the urban poor (E. Phillips 1996; D. A. Smith and Timberlake 1993).

Sociologist Louis Wirth (1928, 1938) argued that a relatively large and permanent settlement leads to distinctive patterns of behavior, which he called **urbanism.** He identified three critical factors that contribute to urbanism: the size of the population, population density, and the heterogeneity (variety) of the population. A frequent result of urbanism, according to Wirth, is that we become insensitive to events around us and restrict our attention to the primary groups to which we are emotionally attached.

Use Your Sociological Imagination www.mhhe.com/schaefer9

What would the ideal city of the future look like? Describe its architecture, public transportation, neighborhoods, schools, and workplaces. What kinds of people would live and work there?

URBANIZATION

The 1990 census was the first to demonstrate that more than half the population of the United States lived in urban areas of 1 million or more residents. In only three states (Mississippi, Vermont, and West Virginia) do more

Table 20-1	Comparing Types of Cities		
Preindustrial Cities (through 18th century)	**Industrial Cities (18th through mid-20th century)**	**Postindustrial Cities (beginning late 20th century)**	
Closed class system—pervasive influence of social class at birth	Open class system—mobility based on achieved characteristics	Wealth based on ability to obtain and use information	
Economic realm controlled by guilds and a few families	Relatively open competition	Corporate power dominates	
Beginnings of division of labor in the creation of goods	Elaborate specialization in manufacturing of goods	Sense of place fades, transnational networks emerge	
Pervasive influence of religion on social norms	Influence of religion limited as society becomes more secularized	Religion becomes more fragmented; greater openness to new religious faiths	
Little standardization of prices, weights, and measures	Standardization enforced by custom and law	Conflicting views of prevailing standards	
Population largely illiterate, communication by word of mouth	Emergence of communication through posters, bulletins, and newspapers	Emergence of extended electronic networks	
Schools limited to elites and designed to perpetuate their privileged status	Formal schooling open to the masses and viewed as a means of advancing the social order	Professional, scientific, and technical personnel become increasingly important	

Sources: Based on E. Phillips 1996:132–135; Sjoberg 1960:323–328.

than half the residents live in rural areas. Clearly, urbanization has become a central aspect of life in the United States (Bureau of the Census 1991).

Urbanization can be seen throughout the rest of the world, too. In 1900, only 10 percent of the world's people lived in urban areas, but by 2000, that proportion had risen to around 50 percent. By the year 2025, the number of city dwellers could reach 5 billion. During the 19th and early 20th centuries, rapid urbanization occurred primarily in European and North American cities. Since World War II, however, there has been an urban explosion in the world's developing countries; see Figure 20-1 (Koolhaas et al. 2001:3).

Some metropolitan areas have spread so far that they have connected with other urban centers. Such a densely populated area, containing two or more cities and their suburbs, has become known as a *megalopolis.* An example is the 500-mile corridor stretching from Boston south to Washington, D.C., which includes New York City, Philadelphia, and Baltimore and accounts for one-sixth of the total population of the United States. Even when the megalopolis is divided into autonomous political jurisdictions, it can be viewed as a single economic entity. The megalopolis is also evident in Great Britain, Germany, Italy, Egypt, India, Japan, and China. Table 20-2 on page 466 compares the 10 largest megalopolises in the world in 1970 with the projected 10 largest in 2015.

Functionalist View: Urban Ecology

As we will see in Chapter 21, *human ecology* is concerned with the interrelationships between people and their environment. Human ecologists have long been interested in how the physical environment shapes people's lives (for example, how rivers can serve as a barrier to residential expansion) and in how people influence the surrounding environment (for example, how airconditioning has accelerated the growth of major metropolitan areas in the Southwest). *Urban ecology* focuses on such relationships as they emerge in urban areas. Although the urban ecological approach focuses on social change in cities, it is nevertheless functionalist in orientation because it emphasizes how different elements in urban areas contribute to stability.

Early urban ecologists such as Robert Park (1916, 1936) and Ernest Burgess (1925) concentrated on city life but drew on the approaches used by ecologists who study plant and animal communities. With few exceptions,

FIGURE 20-1

Urbanization around the World, 2003

Mapping Life WORLDWIDE

URBAN POPULATION
AS PROPORTION OF
TOTAL POPULATION

Over 80%
Over 60%
Over 40%
Over 20%
Under 20%

No data

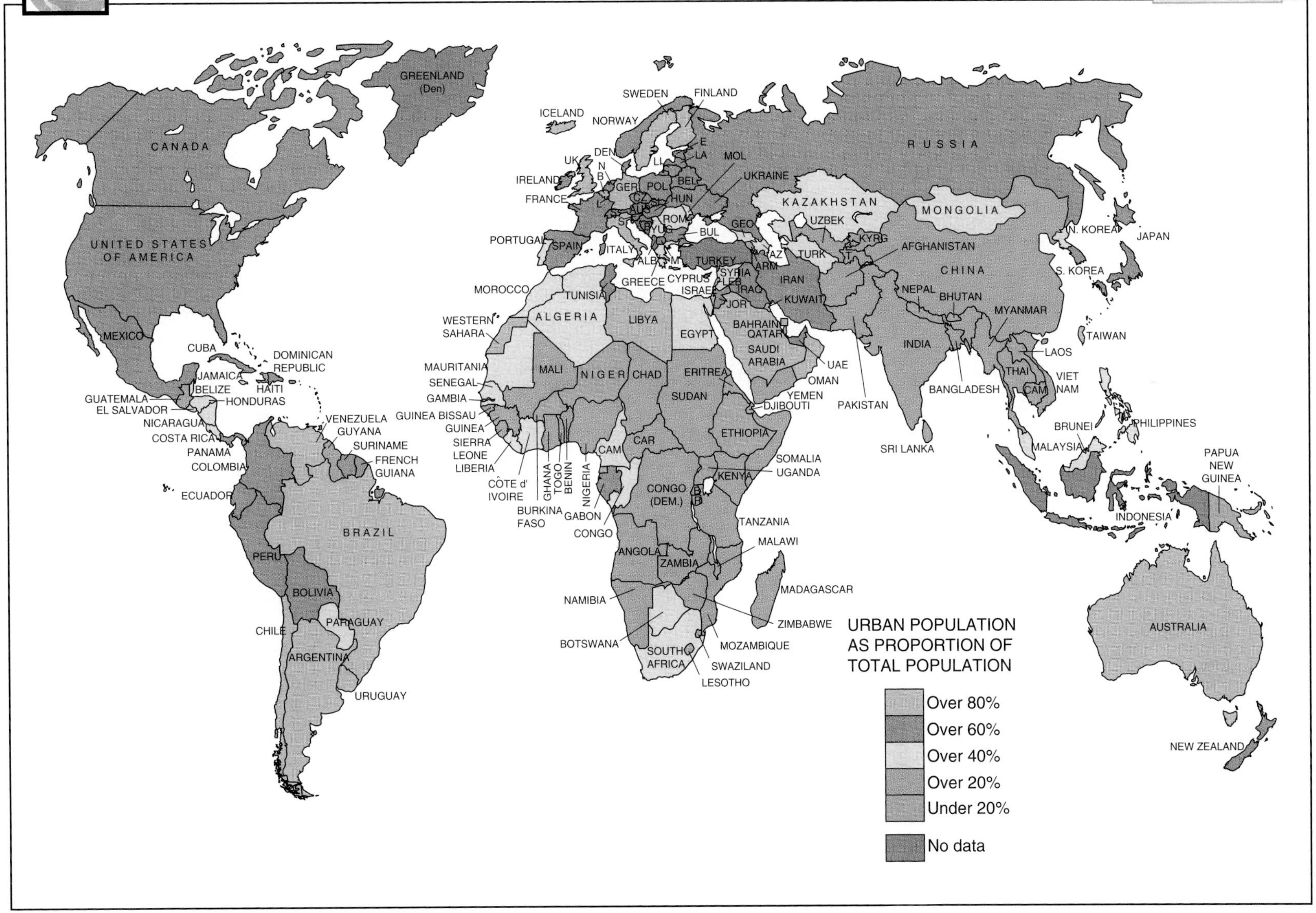

Source: Based on data in Haub 2003.

Table 20-2	The 10 Most Populous Megalopolises in the World, 1970 and 2015 (in millions)		
1970		**2015 (Projected)**	
1. Tokyo	16.5	1. Bombay (India)	28.2
2. New York	16.2	2. Tokyo	26.4
3. Shanghai (China)	11.2	3. Lagos (Nigeria)	23.2
4. Osaka (Japan)	9.4	4. Dhaka (Bangladesh)	23.0
5. Mexico City	9.1	5. São Paulo (Brazil)	20.4
6. London	8.6	6. Karachi (Pakistan)	19.8
7. Paris	8.5	7. Mexico City	19.2
8. Buenos Aires	8.4	8. Delhi (India)	17.8
9. Los Angeles	8.4	9. New York	17.4
10. Beijing	8.1	10. Jakarta (Indonesia)	17.3

Source: United Nations, quoted in Brockerhoff 2000:10.

Think About It
What trend does this table suggest?

urban ecologists trace their work back to the ***concentric-zone theory*** devised in the 1920s by Burgess (see Figure 20-2a). Using Chicago as an example, Burgess proposed a theory for describing land use in industrial cities. At the center, or nucleus, of such a city is the central business district. Large department stores, hotels, theaters, and financial institutions occupy this highly valued land. Surrounding this urban center are zones devoted to other types of land use that illustrate the growth of the urban area over time.

Note that the creation of zones is a *social* process, not the result of nature alone. Families and business firms compete for the most valuable land; those who possess the most wealth and power are generally the winners. The concentric-zone theory proposed by Burgess represented a dynamic model of urban growth. As urban growth proceeded, each zone would move even farther from the central business district.

Because of its functionalist orientation and its emphasis on stability, the concentric-zone theory tended to understate or ignore certain tensions that were apparent in metropolitan areas. For example, the growing use by the affluent of land in a city's peripheral areas was uncritically approved, while the arrival of African Americans in White neighborhoods in the 1930s was described by some sociologists in terms such as *invasion* and *succession.* Moreover, the urban ecological perspective gave little thought to gender inequities,

FIGURE 20-2

Comparison of Ecological Theories of Urban Growth

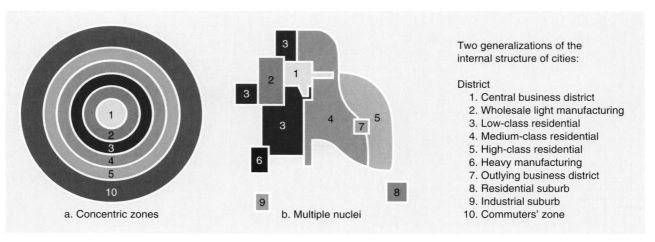

a. Concentric zones   b. Multiple nuclei

Two generalizations of the internal structure of cities:

District
1. Central business district
2. Wholesale light manufacturing
3. Low-class residential
4. Medium-class residential
5. High-class residential
6. Heavy manufacturing
7. Outlying business district
8. Residential suburb
9. Industrial suburb
10. Commuters' zone

Source: Harris and Ullmann 1945:13.

such as the establishment of men's softball and golf leagues in city parks, without any programs for women's sports. Consequently, the urban ecological approach has been criticized for its failure to address issues of gender, race, and class.

By the middle of the 20th century, urban populations had spilled beyond traditional city limits. No longer could urban ecologists focus exclusively on *growth* in the central city, for large numbers of urban residents were abandoning the cities to live in suburban areas. As a response to the emergence of more than one focal point in some metropolitan areas, Chauncy D. Harris and Edward Ullman (1945) presented the **multiple-nuclei theory** (see Figure 20-2b). In their view, all urban growth does not radiate outward from a central business district. Instead, a metropolitan area may have many centers of development, each of which reflects a particular urban need or activity. Thus, a city may have a financial district, a manufacturing zone, a waterfront area, an entertainment center, and so forth. Certain types of business firms and certain types of housing will naturally cluster around each distinctive nucleus (Squires 2002).

The rise of suburban shopping malls is a vivid example of the phenomenon of multiple nuclei within metropolitan areas. Initially, all major retailing in urban areas was located in the central business district. Each residential neighborhood had its own grocers, bakers, and butchers, but people traveled to the center of the city to make major purchases at department stores. However, as major metropolitan areas expanded and the suburbs became more populous, increasing numbers of people began to shop nearer their homes. Today, the suburban mall is a significant retailing and social center in communities across the United States.

In a refinement of the multiple-nuclei theory, contemporary urban ecologists have begun to study what journalist Joel Garreau (1991) has called "edge cities." These communities, which have grown up on the outskirts of major metropolitan areas, are economic and social centers with identities of their own. By any standard of measurement—height of buildings, amount of office space, presence of medical facilities, presence of leisure-time facilities, or of course, population—edge cities qualify as independent cities rather than large suburbs.

Whether metropolitan areas include edge cities or multiple nuclei, more and more of them are characterized by spread-out development and unchecked growth. The metropolitan area of Atlanta, which contains 4.1 million people according to the 2000 census, covers 20 counties—an area nearly the size of Hawaii. Overall, 8 out of every 10 U.S. cities extended over a much greater geographical area in 2000 than they did in 1990. Today's cities are very different from the preindustrial cities of a thousand years ago (El Nasser and Overberg 2001; Glanton 2001).

Conflict View: New Urban Sociology

Contemporary sociologists point out that metropolitan growth is not governed by waterways and rail lines, as a purely ecological interpretation might suggest. From a conflict perspective, communities are human creations that reflect people's needs, choices, and decisions—but some people have more influence over those decisions than others. Drawing on conflict theory, an approach that has come to be called the **new urban sociology** considers the interplay of local, national, and worldwide forces and their effect on local space, with special emphasis on the impact of global economic activity (Gottdiener and Hutchison 2000).

New urban sociologists note that ecological approaches have typically avoided examining the social forces, largely economic in nature, that have guided urban growth. For example, central business districts may be upgraded or abandoned, depending on whether urban policymakers grant substantial tax exemptions to developers. The suburban boom in the post–World War II era was fueled by highway construction and federal housing policies that channeled investment capital into the construction of single-family homes rather than affordable rental housing in the cities. Similarly, while some observers suggest that the growth of sun-belt cities is due to a "good business climate," new urban sociologists counter that the term is actually a euphemism for hefty state and local government subsidies and antilabor policies intended to draw manufacturers (Gottdiener and Feagin 1988; M. Smith 1988).

The new urban sociology draws generally on the conflict perspective and more specifically on sociologist Immanuel Wallerstein's **world systems analysis.** Wallerstein argues that certain industrialized nations (among them the United States, Japan, and Germany) hold a dominant position at the *core* of the global economic system. At the same time, the poor developing countries of Asia, Africa, and Latin America lie on the *periphery* of the global economy, controlled and exploited by core industrialized nations. Using world systems analysis, new urban sociologists consider urbanization from a global perspective. They view cities not as independent and autonomous entities, but as the outcome of decision-making processes directed or influenced by a society's dominant classes and by core industrialized nations. New urban sociologists note that the rapidly growing cities of the world's developing countries were shaped first by colonialism and then by a global economy controlled by core nations and multinational

p. 229

How Do Communities Change?

All communities change over time. Sociologists study communities in terms of their population growth and composition as well as their economic base. How many people, young and old, live there? Which racial and ethnic groups predominate? What economic interests—agriculture, industry, or services—built the community, and how have they developed over the years?

In the 20th century, communities around the United States underwent rapid change. These images of Los Angeles, taken on Hollywood Boulevard, show its transformation from a relatively small city of 1.2 million in 1930 to a city of 2.1 million in 1952 and a major urban center of 3.6 million in 1998—triple its population less than a century before. Over the same period, the U.S. population more than doubled, growing from 122 million in 1930 to 155 million in 1952 and 270 million in 1998.

Los Angeles, 1930

Los Angeles, 1952

Los Angeles, 1998

corporations. The outcome has not been beneficial to the poorest citizens. As Box 20-1 shows, an unmistakable feature of many cities in developing countries is the existence of large squatter settlements just outside city limits (Gottdiener and Feagin 1988; D. A. Smith 1995).

The urban ecologists of the 1920s and 1930s were aware of the role that the larger economy played in urbanization, but their theories emphasized the impact of local rather than national or global forces. In contrast, through their broad, global emphasis on social inequality **pp. 213, 229, 426** and conflict, new urban sociologists concentrate on such topics as the existence of an underclass, the power of multinational corporations, deindustrialization, homelessness, and residential segregation.

For example, developers, builders, and investment bankers are not especially interested in urban growth when it means providing housing for middle- or low-income people. Their lack of interest contributes to the problem of homelessness. These urban elites counter that the nation's housing shortage and the plight of the homeless are not their fault, and insist that they do not have the capital needed to construct and support such housing. But affluent people *are* interested in growth, and they *can* somehow find capital to build new shopping centers, office towers, and ballparks. Why, then, can't they provide the capital for affordable housing, ask new urban sociologists?

Part of the answer is that developers, bankers, and other powerful real estate interests view housing in quite a different manner from tenants and most homeowners. For a tenant, an apartment is shelter, housing, a home. But for developers and investors—many of them large (and sometimes multinational) corporations—an apartment is simply a housing investment. These financiers and owners are concerned primarily with maximizing profit, not with solving social problems (Feagin 1983; Gottdiener and Hutchison 2000).

As we have seen throughout this textbook, in studying such varied issues as deviance, race and ethnicity, and aging, no single theoretical approach necessarily offers the only valuable perspective. As Table 20-3 shows, urban ecology and new urban sociology offer significantly different ways of viewing urbanization, both of which enrich our understanding of this complex phenomenon.

TYPES OF COMMUNITIES

Communities vary substantially in the degree to which their members feel connected and share a common identity. Ferdinand Tönnies ([1887]1988) used **p. 115** the term *Gemeinschaft* to describe a close-knit community where social interaction among people is intimate and familiar. It is the kind of place where people in a coffee shop will stop talking whenever anyone enters, because they are sure to know whoever walks through the door. A shopper at the small grocery store in this town would expect to know every employee, and probably every other customer as well. In contrast, the ideal type of the *Gesellschaft* describes modern urban life, in which people have little in common with others. Social relationships often result from interactions focused on immediate tasks, such as purchasing a product. Contemporary city life in the United States generally resembles a *Gesellschaft*.

The following sections will examine different types of communities found in the United States, focusing on the distinctive characteristics and problems of central cities, suburbs, and rural communities.

Central Cities

In terms of both land and population, the United States is the fourth-largest nation in the world. Yet three-quarters

Table 20-3	**Major Perspectives on Urbanization**	
	Urban Ecology	**New Urban Sociology**
Theoretical perspective	Functionalist	Conflict
Primary focus	Relationship of urban areas to their spatial setting and physical environment	Relationship of urban areas to global, national, and local forces
Key source of change	Technological innovations such as new methods of transportation	Economic competition and monopolization of power
Initiator of actions	Individuals, neighborhoods, communities	Real estate developers, banks and other financial institutions, multinational corporations
Allied disciplines	Geography, architecture	Political science, economics

Sociology in the Global Community
20-1   SQUATTER SETTLEMENTS

arriadas, favelas, bustees, kampungs, and *bidonvilles:* The terms vary depending on the nation and language, but the meaning is the same—"squatter settlements." In **squatter settlements,** areas occupied by the very poor on the fringe of cities, housing is constructed by the settlers themselves from discarded material, including crates from loading docks and loose lumber from building projects. While the term *squatter settlement* has wide use, many observers prefer to use a less pejorative term, such as *autonomous settlements.*

This type of settlement is typical of cities in the world's developing nations. In such countries, new housing has not kept pace with the combined urban population growth resulting from births and migration from rural areas. Squatter settlements also swell when city dwellers are forced out of housing by astronomical jumps in rent. By definition, squatters living on vacant land are trespassers and can be legally evicted. However, given the large number of poor people who live in such settlements (by UN estimates, 40 or 50 percent of inhabitants of cities in many developing nations), governments generally look the other way.

Obviously squatters live in substandard housing, yet that is only one of the many problems they face. Residents do not receive most public services, since their presence cannot be legally recognized. Police and fire protection, paved streets, and sanitary sewers are virtually nonexistent. In some countries, squatters may have trouble voting or enrolling their children in public schools.

Despite such conditions, squatter settlements are not always as bleak as they

> Squatter settlements are not always as bleak as they may appear from the outside.

may appear from the outside. You can often find a well-developed social organization there, rather than a disorganized collection of people. A thriving "informal economy" typically develops: residents establish small, home-based businesses such as grocery stores, jewelry shops, and the like. Local churches, men's clubs, and women's clubs are often established in specific neighborhoods within settlements. In addition, certain areas may

form governing councils or membership associations. These governing bodies may face the usual problems of municipal governments, including charges of corruption and factional splits.

Squatter settlements remind us that respected theoretical models of social science in the United States may not directly apply to other cultures. The various ecological models of urban growth, for example, would not explain a metropolitan expansion that locates the poorest people on the urban fringes. Furthermore, solutions that are logical in a highly industrialized nation may not be relevant in developing nations. Planners in developing nations, rather than focusing on large-scale solutions to urban problems, must think in terms of basic amenities, such as providing water or electrical power to the ever-expanding squatter settlements.

Let's Discuss

1. Do you know of any "squatters" in your own community? If so, describe them and the place where they live.
2. Given the number of homeless people in the United States, why aren't there more squatters?

Sources: Castells 1983; Patton 1988; Rohter 2003; World Bank 2003a; Yap 1998.

---

of the population is concentrated in a mere 1.5 percent of the nation's land area. In 2000 some 226 million people—accounting for 80 percent of the nation's population—lived in metropolitan areas. Even those who live outside central cities, such as residents of suburban and rural communities, find that urban centers heavily influence their lifestyles (Bureau of the Census 2002a:30).

Urban Dwellers

Many urban residents are the descendants of European immigrants—Irish, Italians, Jews, Poles, and others—who came to the United States in the 19th and early 20th centuries. The cities socialized these newcomers to the norms, values, and language of their new homeland

and gave them an opportunity to work their way up the economic ladder. In addition, a substantial number of low-income African Americans and Whites came to the cities from rural areas in the period following World War II.

Even today, cities in the United States are the destinations of immigrants from around the world—including Mexico, Ireland, Cuba, Vietnam, and Haiti—as well as of migrants from the U.S. commonwealth of Puerto Rico. Yet unlike those who came to this country 100 years ago, current immigrants are arriving at a time of growing urban decay. Thus they have more difficulty finding employment and decent housing.

Urban life is noteworthy for its diversity, so it would be a serious mistake to see all city residents as being alike.

Indian American residents of Chicago enjoy an outdoor ethnic festival. Many subordinate racial and ethnic groups in the United States live in close-knit urban neighborhoods.

Sociologist Herbert J. Gans (1991) has distinguished five types of people found in cities:

1. **Cosmopolites.** These residents remain in cities to take advantage of unique cultural and intellectual benefits. Writers, artists, and scholars fall into this category.

2. **Unmarried and childless people.** Such people choose to live in cities because of the active nightlife and varied recreational opportunities.

3. **Ethnic villagers.** These urban residents prefer to live in their own tight-knit communities. Typically, immigrant groups isolate themselves in such neighborhoods to avoid resentment from well-established urban dwellers.

4. **The deprived.** Very poor people and families have little choice but to live in low-rent, and often run-down, urban neighborhoods.

5. **The trapped.** Some city residents wish to leave urban centers but cannot because of their limited economic resources and prospects. Gans includes the "downward mobiles" in this category—people who once held higher social positions, but who are forced to live in less prestigious neighborhoods owing to loss of a job, death of a wage earner, or old age. Both elderly individuals living alone and families may feel trapped in part because they resent changes in their communities. Their desire to live elsewhere may reflect their uneasiness with unfamiliar immigrant groups who have become their neighbors.

These categories remind us that the city represents a choice (even a dream) for certain people and a nightmare for others.

Gans's work underscores the importance of neighborhoods in contemporary urban life. Ernest Burgess, in his study of life in Chicago in the 1920s, gave special attention to the ethnic neighborhoods of that city. Many decades later, residents in such districts as Chinatowns or Greektowns continue to feel attached to their own ethnic communities rather than to the larger unit of a city. Even outside ethnic enclaves, a special sense of belonging can take hold in a neighborhood.

In a more recent study in Chicago, Gerald Suttles (1972) coined the term ***defended neighborhood*** to refer to people's definitions of their community boundaries. Neighborhoods acquire unique identities because residents view them as geographically separate—and socially different—from adjacent areas. The defended neighborhood, in effect, becomes a sentimental union of similar people. Neighborhood phone directories, community newspapers, school and parish boundaries, and business advertisements all serve to define an area and distinguish it from nearby communities.

Issues Facing Cities

People and neighborhoods vary greatly within any city in the United States. Yet all residents of a central city—regardless of social class, racial, and ethnic differences—face certain common problems. Crime, air pollution, noise, unemployment, overcrowded schools, inadequate public transportation—these unpleasant realities and many more are an increasingly common feature of contemporary urban life.

Perhaps the single most dramatic reflection of the nation's urban ills has been the apparent death of entire neighborhoods. In some urban districts, business activity seems virtually nonexistent. Visitors can walk for blocks and find little more than a devastating array of deteriorating, boarded-up, abandoned, and burned-out buildings. Such urban devastation has greatly contributed to the growing problem of homelessness.

Residential segregation has also been a persistent problem in cities across the United States. Segregation has resulted from the policies of financial institutions, the business practices of real estate agents, the actions of home sellers, and even urban planning initiatives (for example, decisions about where to locate public housing). Sociologists Douglas Massey and Nancy Denton (1993) have used the term *American apartheid* to refer to such residential patterns. In their view, we no longer perceive segregation as a problem but rather accept it as a feature of the urban landscape. For subordinate minority groups, segregation means not only limited housing opportunities but reduced access to employment, retail outlets, and medical services.

Another critical problem for the cities has been mass transportation. Since 1950, the number of cars in the United States has multiplied twice as fast as the number of people. Growing traffic congestion in metropolitan areas has led many cities to recognize a need for safe, efficient, and inexpensive mass transit systems. However, the federal government has traditionally

Parishioners gather after a church service. Religious organizations are one of the many resources that form the foundation of asset-based community development.

C stands for "congestion." In 2003, to alleviate gridlock, officials of the city of London began to charge vehicles about $8 a day to enter designated congestion zones. Significant traffic reductions resulted, leading city planners around the world to consider adopting the idea.

given much more assistance to highway programs than to public transportation. Conflict theorists note that such a bias favors the relatively affluent (automobile owners) as well as corporations such as auto manufacturers, tire makers, and oil companies. Meanwhile, low-income residents of metropolitan areas, who are much less likely to own cars than members of the middle and upper classes, face higher fares on public transit along with deteriorating service (Mason 1998).

Asset-Based Community Development

For many people, the words *South Bronx, South Central Los Angeles,* or even *public housing* call forth a variety of negative stereotypes and stigmas. How do communities—whether neighborhoods or cities—that have been labeled as ghettos address the challenges they face? Typically, policymakers have identified an area's problems, needs, or deficiencies and then tried to find solutions. But in the last decade, community leaders, policymakers, and applied sociologists have begun to advocate an approach called **asset-based community development (ABCD),** in which they first identify a community's strengths and then seek to mobilize those assets.

In a distressed community, the ABCD approach helps people to recognize human resources they might otherwise overlook. A community's assets may include its residents' skills; the power of local associations; its institutional resources, whether public, private, or nonprofit; and any physical and economic resources it has. By identifying these assets, planners can help to counter negative images and rebuild even the most devastated communities. The anticipated result is to strengthen the community's capacity to help itself and diminish its need to rely on outside organizations or providers. In fact, one consequence of this approach is to direct assistance to agencies within the community rather than to outside service providers (Asset-Based Community Development Institute 2001; Kretzmann and McKnight 1993; McKnight and Kretzmann 1996).

Tragically, the events of September 11, 2001, have caused many communities both large and small to recognize the ways in which neighbors can depend on one another. Middletown, New Jersey, a suburban community that lost 36 residents in the terrorist attack on the World Trade Center, is one example. In response to the catastrophe, a group of townspeople founded Friends Assisting Victims of Terror (FAVOR) and began canvassing every homeowner and business in the community on behalf of the bereaved families, most of whom had lost a breadwinner. At the end of the first year, the group had collected more than $700,000, along with donations of goods and services ranging from plumbing, car repair, and tree removal to haircuts, karate lessons, and chiropractor's appointments. The town also set up a scholarship fund for the three dozen children who had lost their fathers or mothers. In taking care of their own, the people of Middletown discovered the richness and variety of their resources (A. Jacobs 2001a, 2001b, 2002; G. Sheehy 2003).

Suburbs

The term *suburb* derives from the Latin *sub urbe,* meaning "under the city." Until recent times, most suburbs were just that—tiny communities totally dependent on urban centers for jobs, recreation, and even water.

Today, the term **suburb** defies simple definition. The term generally refers to any community near a large city—or as the Census Bureau would say, any territory within a metropolitan area that is not included in the central city. By that definition, more than 138 million people, or about 51 percent of the population of the United States, live in the suburbs (Kleniewski 2002).

Three social factors differentiate suburbs from cities. First, suburbs are generally less dense than cities; in the newest suburbs, no more than two dwellings may occupy an acre of land. Second, the suburbs consist almost exclusively of private space. For the most part, private ornamental lawns replace common park areas. Third, suburbs have more exacting building design codes than cities, and those codes have become increasingly precise in the last decade. While the suburbs may be diverse in population, their design standards give the impression of uniformity.

Distinguishing between suburbs and rural areas can also be difficult. Certain criteria generally define suburbs: Most people work at urban (as opposed to rural) jobs, and local governments provide services such as water supply, sewage disposal, and fire protection. In rural areas, these services are less common, and a greater proportion of residents is employed in farming and related activities.

Suburban Expansion

Whatever the precise definition of a suburb, it is clear that suburbs have expanded. In fact, suburbanization was the most dramatic population trend in the United States throughout the 20th century. Suburban areas grew at first along railroad lines, then at the termini of streetcar tracks, and by the 1950s along the nation's growing systems of freeways and expressways. The suburban boom has been especially evident since World War II.

Proponents of the new urban sociology contend that initially, industries moved their factories from central cities to suburbs to reduce the power of labor unions. Subsequently, many suburban communities induced businesses to relocate there by offering them subsidies and tax incentives. As sociologist William Julius Wilson (1996) has observed, federal housing policies contributed to the suburban boom by withholding mortgage capital from inner-city neighborhoods, by offering favorable mortgages to military veterans, and by assisting the rapid development of massive amounts of affordable tract housing in the suburbs. Moreover, federal highway and transportation policies provided substantial funding for expressway systems (which made commuting to the cities much easier), while undermining urban communities by building freeway networks through the heart of cities.

All these factors contributed to the movement of the (predominantly White) middle class out of the central cities, and as we shall see, out of the suburbs as well. From the perspective of new urban sociology, suburban expansion is far from a natural ecological process; rather, it reflects the distinct priorities of powerful economic and political interests.

Diversity in the Suburbs

In the United States, race and ethnicity remain the most important factors that distinguish cities from suburbs. Nevertheless, the common assumption that suburbia includes only prosperous Whites is far from correct. The last

20 years have witnessed the diversification of suburbs in terms of race and ethnicity. For example, by 2000, 34 percent of Blacks in the United States, 46 percent of Latinos, and 53 percent of Asians lived in the suburbs. Like the rest of the nation, members of racial and ethnic minorities are becoming suburban dwellers (El Nasser 2001; Frey 2001).

But are the suburban areas re-creating the racial segregation of the central cities? A definite pattern of clustering, if not outright segregation, is emerging. A study of suburban residential patterns in 11 metropolitan areas found that Asian Americans and Hispanics tend to reside in equivalent socioeconomic areas with Whites—that is, affluent Hispanics live alongside affluent Whites, poor Asians near poor Whites, and so on. However, the case for African Americans is quite distinct. Suburban Blacks live in poorer suburbs than Whites, even after taking into account differences in individuals' income, education, and homeownership.

Again, in contrast to prevailing stereotypes, the suburbs include a significant number of low-income people from all backgrounds—White, Black, and Hispanic. Poverty is not conventionally associated with the suburbs, partly because the suburban poor tend to be scattered among more affluent people. In some instances, suburban communities intentionally hide social problems such as homelessness so they can maintain a "respectable image." Soaring housing costs have contributed to suburban poverty, which is rising at a faster rate than urban poverty (Jargowsky 2003).

Some urban and suburban residents are moving to communities even more remote from the central city, or to rural areas altogether. Initial evidence suggests that this move to rural areas is only intensifying the racial disparities in our metropolitan areas (Bureau of the Census 1997b; Holmes 1997).

Rural Communities

As we have seen, the people of the United States live mainly in urban areas. Yet one-fourth of the population lives in towns of 2,500 people or less that are not adjacent to a city. As is true of the suburbs, it would be a mistake to view rural communities as fitting one set image. Turkey farms, coal mining towns, cattle ranches, and gas stations along interstate highways are all part of the rural landscape in the United States.

Today, many rural areas are facing problems that were first associated with the central cities, and are now evident in the suburbs. Overdevelopment, gang warfare, and drug trafficking can be found on the policymaking agenda far outside major metropolitan areas. While the magnitude of the problems may not be as great as in the central cities, rural resources cannot begin to match those that city mayors can marshall in an attempt to address social ills (T. Egan 2002; Osgood and Chambers 2003).

The postindustrial revolution has been far from kind to the rural communities of the United States. Agriculture accounts for only 9 percent of employment in nonurban counties. Moreover, in 1993, the Bureau of the Census calculated that farm residents accounted for only 2 percent of the nation's population, compared to 95 percent in 1790. At the same time that farming has been declining, so have mining and logging—the two nonagricultural staples of the rural economy. When these jobs disappear, the rural poor who want to be economically self-sufficient face problems. Even low-wage jobs are few, distances to services and better-paying jobs are long, and child care options are scarce (Dirk Johnson 1996).

In desperation, residents of depressed rural areas have begun to encourage prison construction, which they once discouraged, to bring in badly needed economic development. Ironically, in regions

The motion picture *American Beauty* (1999) portrayed the suburbs as all-White non-Hispanic communities. Although such communities have not vanished, they are much less typical now than they were in the past.

No organization exists in a vacuum, especially not a corporate giant. Executives of Wal-Mart know that. The epitome of the superstore, Wal-Mart has become the center of controversy in towns and cities across the United States, despite the familiar smiley-face logo and its red, white, and blue corporate image. The reason: A new Wal-Mart can have powerfully negative effects on the surrounding community.

Wal-Mart was founded in 1962 by Sam Walton, whose strategy was to locate new stores in rural communities, where competition from other retailers was weak and unions were not organized. Over the years, as the enormously successful discount chain expanded, Wal-Mart began to move into the fringes of metropolitan areas as well. But the residents of the communities Wal-Mart moved into did not always welcome their new neighbor.

In Ashland, Virginia, a community of 7,200 people, residents worried that Wal-Mart would destroy the small-town atmosphere they treasured. Would their cozy grocery store, known for its personal service, survive the discount giant's competition? Would their quaint and charming Main Street fall into decline? Would full-time jobs with full benefits give way to part-time employment? (Studies have shown that superstores ultimately *reduce* employment.) Ashland's grassroots opposition to Wal-Mart, chronicled in the PBS documentary *Store Wars,* ultimately lost its battle because of Wal-Mart's promised low prices and increased tax revenues. But citizens in many other communities have won, at least temporarily.

On the urban fringes, too, residents have mobilized to stop new superstores. In Bangor, Maine, environmentalists raised an alarm over a proposed Wal-Mart superstore, to be located next to a marsh that sheltered endangered wildlife. Activists in Riverside, California, also challenged Wal-Mart, again on environmental grounds.

But the issue is more complicated in these areas, because communities on the

> In Ashland, Virginia, residents worried that Wal-Mart would destroy the small-town atmosphere they treasured.

urban fringe are hardly untouched by economic development. Wal-Mart's proposed site in Bangor, for instance, is not far from the Bangor mall. And the huge new houses that dot the suburbs surrounding new stores, built on lots carved out of farmland or forest, have had an environmental impact themselves. In fact, the trend toward the superstore seems to parallel the emergence of the megalopolis, whose boundaries push further and further outward, eating up open space in the process. Recognizing the drawbacks of urban sprawl, some planners are beginning to advocate "smart growth"— restoring the central city and its older suburbs rather than abandoning them for the outer rings.

Not all communities reject superstores. In fact, in Canada, some economically depressed rural communities are actively recruiting new Wal-Marts, seeking the jobs and increased traffic they need to reinvigorate themselves. Across Canada, public reaction to the U.S. chain's arrival has been almost universally positive. Canadian shoppers appreciate Wal-Mart's selection and low prices, and Canadian manufacturers have found a huge new outlet for their wares.

Wal-Mart executives are unapologetic about the chain's rapid expansion. They argue that their aggressive competition has lowered prices and raised working people's standard of living. And they say they have given back to the communities where their stores are located by donating money to educational institutions and local agencies.

Let's Discuss

1. Is there a Wal-Mart, Home Depot, or some other superstore near you? If so, was its opening a matter of controversy in your community?

2. What do you think of the "smart growth" movement? Should communities attempt to redirect business and residential development, or should developers be free to build wherever and whatever they choose?

Sources: Leaf 2003; *Maine Times* 2001; PBS 2001; Saporito 2003; B. Simon 2001; Smart Growth 2001; Wal-Mart 2001; Wal-Mart Watch 2003.

where the prison population has declined, communities have been hurt yet again by their dependence on a single industry (Kilborn 2001).

The construction of large businesses can create its own problems, as small communities that have experienced the arrival of large discount stores, such as Wal-Mart, Target, Home Depot, or Costco, have discovered. Although many residents welcome the new employment opportunities and the convenience of one-stop shopping, local merchants see their longtime family businesses endangered by formidable 200,000-square-foot competitors with a national reputation. Even when such discount stores provide a boost to a town's economy (and they do not always do so), they can undermine the town's sense of community and identity. Box 20-2 chronicles the "store wars" that often ensue.

Rural communities that do survive may feel threatened by other changes intended to provide jobs, income, and financial security. For example, the town of Postville, Iowa—with a population of only 1,478—was dying in 1987 when an entrepreneur from New York City bought a run-down meat processing plant. The plant was subsequently transformed into a kosher slaughtering house, and today 150 Postville residents are devout Hasidic Jews from the Lubavitcher sect. The new residents occupy key managerial positions in the slaughtering house, while Lubavitcher rabbis supervise the kosher processing of the meat to ensure that it is acceptable under Jewish dietary laws. Initially, there was distrust between longtime residents of Postville and their new neighbors, but gradually each group came to realize that it needed the other (S. Bloom 2000; B. Simon 2001).

On a more positive note, advances in electronic communication have allowed some people in the United States to work wherever they wish. For those who are concerned about quality-of-life issues, working at home in a rural area that has access to the latest high-tech services is the perfect arrangement. No matter where people make their homes—whether in the city, the suburbs, or a country village—economic and technological change will have an impact on their quality of life.

Observant Jews pray in the locker room at a kosher meat processing plant near Postville, Iowa. When the plant first opened, the rural Christians hired to work there were unfamiliar with Jewish culture and faith, but members of the two groups soon learned to work together.

Use Your Sociological Imagination

You have fast-forwarded to a future in which there are no central cities—just sprawling suburbs and isolated rural communities. What are the economic and social effects of the disappearance of the downtown area?

SOCIAL POLICY and COMMUNITIES

Seeking Shelter Worldwide

The Issue

A chance meeting brought two old classmates together. In late 1997, Prince Charles encountered Clive Harold during a tour of the offices of a magazine sold by the homeless in London. But while Prince Charles can call several palaces home, Harold is homeless. This modern-day version of *The Prince and the Pauper* intrigued many people with its message that "it can happen to anyone." Harold had been a successful author and journalist until his marriage fell apart and alcohol turned his life inside out (*Chicago Tribune* 1997).

The issue of inadequate shelter manifests itself in many ways, for all housing problems can be considered relative. To a middle-class family in the United States, it may mean a somewhat smaller house than they need, because that is all they can afford. For a single working adult in Tokyo, it may mean having to commute two hours to a full-time job. For many people worldwide, however, the housing problem means finding shelter of any kind that they can afford, in a place where anyone would reasonably wish to live. Prince Charles of Buckingham Palace and Clive Harold, homeless person, are extreme examples of a continuum present in all communities and all societies. What can be done to ensure adequate shelter for those who can't afford it?

The Setting

Homelessness is evident in both industrialized and developing countries. According to estimates, the number of homeless persons in the United States was at least 750,000 on any given night in 2001, and as many as 3.5 million Americans may experience homelessness for some period each year. Given the limited amount of space in public shelters, at a minimum, hundreds of thousands of people in the United States are homeless and without shelter (National Alliance to End Homelessness 2001).

In Japan, the problem of homelessness is just as serious. The Japanese usually hide such misfortune, thinking it shameful. But in the past decade, a severe economic downturn has victimized many formerly prosperous citizens, swelling the numbers of the homeless. A chronic space shortage in the heavily populated island nation, together with opposition to the establishment of homeless shelters in residential neighborhoods, has compounded the problem. In 2001, only two homeless shelters served 6,000 to 10,000 homeless people in Tokyo (H. W. French 2001b; Prusher 2001).

In Third World countries, rapid population growth has outpaced the expansion of housing by a wide margin, leading to a rise in homelessness. For example, estimates of homelessness in Mexico City range from 10,000 to 100,000, and do not include the many people living in caves or squatter settlements (see Box 20-1). By 1998, in urban areas alone, 600 million people around the world were either homeless or inadequately housed (G. Goldstein 1998; Ross 1996).

Sociological Insights

Both in the United States and around the world, homelessness functions as a master status that largely defines a person's position within society. In this case, homelessness tends to mean that in many important respects, the individual is *outside* society. Without a home address and

In a story the press dubbed "The Prince and the Pauper," Prince Charles was surprised to run into an old classmate while visiting the office of a magazine sold by the homeless—and was even more surprised to learn that the fellow was himself homeless.

pp. 106, 180

telephone, it is difficult to look for work or even apply for public assistance. Moreover, the master status of being homeless carries a serious stigma and can lead to prejudice and discrimination. Poor treatment of people suspected of being homeless is common in stores and restaurants, and many communities have reported acts of random violence against homeless people.

The profile of homelessness has changed significantly during the last 30 years. In the past, homeless people were primarily older White males living as alcoholics in skid-row areas. However, today's homeless are comparatively younger, with an average age in the low 30s. Overall, an estimated 60 percent of homeless people in the United States are from racial and ethnic minority groups. Moreover, a 25-city survey done in 2002 found that the homeless population is growing faster than the increase in emergency food and shelter space (Burt 2001; U.S. Conference of Mayors 2002).

Changing economic and residential patterns account for much of this increase in homelessness. In recent decades, the process of urban renewal has included a noticeable boom in *gentrification.* This term refers to the resettlement of low-income city neighborhoods by prosperous families and business firms. In some instances, city governments have promoted gentrification by granting lucrative tax breaks to developers who convert low-cost rental units into luxury apartments and condominiums. Conflict theorists note that although the affluent may derive both financial and emotional benefits from gentrification and redevelopment, the poor often end up being thrown out on the street.

There is an undeniable connection between the growing shortage of affordable housing and the rise in homelessness. Yet sociologist Peter Rossi (1989, 1990) cautions against focusing too narrowly on housing shortages while ignoring structural factors, such as the decline in the demand for manual labor in cities and the increasing prevalence of chronically unemployed young men among the homeless. Rossi contends that structural changes have put everyone in extreme poverty at higher risk of becoming homeless—especially poor people with an accumulation of disabilities (such as drug abuse, ill health, unemployment, and a criminal record). Being disabled in this manner forces the individual to rely on family and friends for support, often for a prolonged period. If the strain on this support network is so great that it collapses, homelessness may result. While many researchers accept Rossi's theory, the general public often prefers to blame the victim for becoming homeless (Elliot and Krivo 1991; B. Lee 1992; Twombly et al. 2001).

Homeless women often have additional problems that distinguish them from homeless men. Homeless women report more recent injuries or acute illnesses, as well as more chronic health problems, than homeless men. Moreover, these women have experienced more disruption in their families and social networks than homeless men (Liebow 1993).

Policy Initiatives

Thus far, most policymakers have been content to steer the homeless toward large, overcrowded, unhealthy shelters. Yet many neighborhoods and communities have resisted plans to open large shelters or even smaller residences for the homeless, often raising the familiar cry of "Not in my backyard!" The major federal program intended to assist the homeless is the McKinney Homeless Assistance Act, passed in 1987. This act authorizes federal aid for emergency food, shelter, physical and mental health care, job training, and education for homeless children and adults. Approximately $600 to $800 million in funds are distributed annually to about 100 community-based service organizations (Housing and Urban Development 1999).

According to a report by the National Law Center on Homelessness and Poverty (1996), there was a growing trend in the 1990s toward the adoption of antihomeless public policies and the "criminalization" of homeless people. In 1995 alone, at least 29 cities enacted curbs on panhandling, sitting on sidewalks, standing near automated teller machines, and other behavior sometimes evident among the homeless. At the same time, more and more policymakers—especially conservative officials—have advocated cutbacks in government funding for the homeless and argued that

This biting cartoon from the *Japan Times* acknowledges the plight of the homeless. As of 2001, the city of Tokyo had only two homeless shelters.

voluntary associations and religious organizations should assume a more important role in addressing the problem (J. Davidson 2002).

By 2001, the availability of low-rent housing had reached the lowest levels since surveys began in 1970. Despite the booming economy in much of the 1990s and occasional media spotlights on the homeless, affordable housing has become harder to find. Nearly 5 million low-income households receive no housing allowance, and most spend a disproportionately large share of their income to maintain their shelter. Research shows that this worsening of affordable housing stems from a substantial drop in the number of unsubsidized low-cost rental housing units in the private market and a growing number of low-income renter households. Meanwhile, federally funded rental assistance has failed to keep pace with the need (Housing and Urban Development 2001).

Developing nations have special problems. They have understandably given highest priority to economic productivity, as measured by jobs with living wages. Unfortunately, even the most ambitious economic and social programs may be overwhelmed by minor currency fluctuations, a drop in the value of a nation's major export, or an influx of refugees from a neighboring country. Some of the reforms implemented have included promoting private (as opposed to government-controlled) housing markets, allowing dwellings to be places of business as well, and loosening restrictions on building materials.

All three of these short-term solutions have shortcomings. Private housing markets invite exploitation; mixed residential/commercial use may only cause good housing to deteriorate faster; and the use of marginal building materials leaves low-income residential areas more vulnerable to calamities such as floods, fires, and earthquakes. Large-scale rental housing under government supervision, the typical solution in North America and Europe, has been successful only in economically advanced city-states such as Hong Kong and Singapore (Strassman 1998).

In sum, homeless people both in the United States and abroad are not getting the shelter they need, but they lack the political clout to corral the attention of policymakers.

Let's Discuss

1. Have you ever worked as a volunteer in a shelter or soup kitchen? If so, were you surprised by the type of people who lived or ate there? Has anyone you know ever had to move into a shelter?

2. Is gentrification of low-income housing a problem where you live? Have you ever had difficulty finding an affordable place to live?

3. What kind of assistance is available to homeless people in the community where you live? Does the help come from the government, from private charities, or both? What about housing assistance for people with low incomes, such as rent subsidies—is it available?

CHAPTER RESOURCES

Summary

A ***community*** is a spatial or political unit of social organization that gives people a sense of belonging. This chapter explains how communities originated and analyzes the process of urbanization from both the functionalist and conflict perspectives. It describes various types of communities, including the central cities, the suburbs, and rural communities.

1. Stable communities began to develop when people stayed in one place to cultivate crops; surplus production enabled cities to emerge.

2. Gideon Sjoberg identified three preconditions of city life: advanced technology in both agricultural and nonagricultural areas, a favorable physical environment, and a well-developed social organization.

3. Over time, cities changed and developed with their economies. In the industrial revolution, the ***preindustrial city*** of agricultural societies gave way to the ***industrial city;*** the advent of the Information Age brought with it the ***postindustrial city.***

4. Urbanization is evident not only in the United States but throughout the world; by 2000, 50 percent of the world's population lived in urban areas.

5. The ***urban ecological*** approach is functionalist because it emphasizes how different elements in urban areas contribute to social stability.

6. Drawing on conflict theory, ***new urban sociology*** emphasizes the interplay of a community's political and economic interests as well as the impact of

the global economy on communities in the United States and other countries.

7. Many urban residents are immigrants from other nations who tend to live together in ethnic neighborhoods.

8. In the last three decades, cities have confronted an overwhelming array of economic and social problems, including crime, unemployment, and the deterioration of schools and public transit systems.

9. *Asset-based community development (ABCD)* is a new approach to the revitalization of distressed neighborhoods in which planners first identify an area's resources and then mobilize them, channeling assistance to local agencies based in the community.

10. Suburbanization was the most dramatic population trend in the United States throughout the 20th century. In recent decades, **suburbs** have become more racially and ethnically diverse.

11. Farming, mining, and logging have all been in decline in the rural communities of the United States.

12. Soaring housing costs, unemployment, cutbacks in public assistance, and rapid population growth have all contributed to rising homelessness around the world. Most social policy is directed toward sending the homeless to large shelters.

Critical Thinking Questions

1. How can the functionalist and conflict perspectives be used in examining the growing interest among policymakers in privatizing the public services offered by cities and other communities?

2. How has your home community (your city, town, or neighborhood) changed over the years you have lived there? Have there been significant changes in the community's economic base or its racial and ethnic profile? Have the community's social prob-

lems intensified or lessened? Is unemployment currently a major problem? What are the community's future prospects?

3. Imagine that you have been asked to study the issue of homelessness in the largest city in your state. How might you draw on surveys, observation research, experiments, and existing sources to study this issue?

Key Terms

Asset-based community development (ABCD) An approach to community development in which planners first identify a community's strengths and then seek to mobilize those assets. (page 473)

Community A spatial or political unit of social organization that gives people a sense of belonging, based either on shared residence in a particular place or on a common identity. (461)

Concentric-zone theory A theory of urban growth devised by Ernest Burgess that sees growth in terms of a series of rings radiating from the central business district. (466)

Defended neighborhood A neighborhood that residents identify through defined community borders and a perception that adjacent areas are geographically separate and socially different. (472)

Gentrification The resettlement of low-income city neighborhoods by prosperous families and business firms. (478)

Human ecology An area of study concerned with the interrelationships between people and their environment. (464)

Industrial city A relatively large city characterized by open competition, an open class system, and elabo-

rate specialization in the manufacturing of goods. (463)

Megalopolis A densely populated area containing two or more cities and their surrounding suburbs. (464)

Multiple-nuclei theory A theory of urban growth developed by Harris and Ullman that views growth as emerging from many centers of development, each of which may reflect a particular urban need or activity. (467)

New urban sociology An approach to urbanization that considers the interplay of local, national, and worldwide forces and their effect on local space, with special emphasis on the impact of global economic activity. (467)

Postindustrial city A city in which global finance and the electronic flow of information dominate the economy. (463)

Preindustrial city A city of only a few thousand people that is characterized by a relatively closed class system and limited mobility. (462)

Squatter settlement An area occupied by the very poor on the fringe of cities, in which housing is often constructed by the settlers themselves from discarded material. (471)

Suburb According to the Census Bureau, any territory within a metropolitan area that is not included in the central city. (474)

Urban ecology An area of study that focuses on the interrelationships between people and their environment in urban areas. (464)

Urbanism A term used by Louis Wirth to describe distinctive patterns of social behavior evident among city residents. (463)

World systems analysis Immanuel Wallerstein's view of the global economic system as divided between certain industrialized nations that control wealth and developing countries that are controlled and exploited. (467)

TECHNOLOGY RESOURCES

Internet Connection

*Note: While all the URLs listed were current as of the printing of this book, these sites often change. Please check our website (**www.mhhe.com/schaefer9**) for updates, hyperlinks, and exercises related to these sites.*

1. Homelessness is a serious social problem facing many cities in the United States. The National Law Center on Homelessness and Poverty (**www.nlchp.org**) provides the public with information on homelessness. Explore the site to learn more about homeless families, the causes of homelessness, and suggested solutions to the problem.

2. Asset-based community development (ABCD) is a new approach to the revitalization of distressed neighborhoods in which planners first identify an area's resources and then mobilize them, channeling assistance to local agencies based in the community. Learn more about this new approach by visiting the Asset-Based Community Development Institute's website (**www.northwestern.edu/ipr/abcd.html**).

Online Learning Center with PowerWeb

Chicago is one of the largest urban areas in the United States. Learn more about Chicago by visiting the student center in the Online Learning Center at **www.mhhe.com/schaefer9** and linking to "Internet Exercises." Exercise 2 links you to Don Brown's Chicago Daily Picture Page, which presents interesting photos of life in the Windy City. For contrast, link to the Kentucky Photo File.

21

POPULATION AND THE ENVIRONMENT

Hähnchenbrust hält 2 Tage. Ein Haustier länger. Denken Sie daran. ZENTRALVERBAND ZOOLOGISCHER FACHBETRIEBE DEUTSCHLANDS E.V.

Especially in affluent industrialized countries, population growth puts tremendous pressure on the environment. This German poster, a strong protest against plundering of the environment, shows a wild songbird packaged as if for sale in a supermarket.

Demography: The Study of Population

World Population Patterns

Fertility Patterns in the United States

Population and Migration

The Environment

Social Policy and Population: World Population Policy

Boxes

SOCIOLOGY IN THE GLOBAL COMMUNITY:
Population Policy in China

TAKING SOCIOLOGY TO WORK: Kelsie Lenor
Wilson-Dorsett, Deputy Director, Department of
Statistics, Government of Bahamas

Over the past twenty years, research errands of one kind or another have taken me to a number of communities still stunned by the effects of a recent disaster. These include a valley in West Virginia known as Buffalo Creek, devastated by a fearsome flood; an Ojibwa Indian reserve in Canada called Grassy Narrows, plagued by contamination of the waterways along which members of the band had lived for centuries; a town in South Florida named Immokalee, where three hundred migrant farm workers were robbed of the only money most of them had ever saved; a group of houses in Colorado known as East Swallow, threatened by vapors from silent pools of gasoline that had gathered in the ground below; and the neighborhoods surrounding Three Mile Island.

In one respect, at least, these events were altogether different. A flood. An act of larceny. A toxic poisoning. A gasoline spill. A nuclear accident. My assignment in each of those cases was to learn enough about the people who thought they had been damaged by the blow to appear on their behalf in a court of law, so each was a separate research effort, and each resulted in a separate research report.

In another respect, though, it was clear from the beginning that those scenes of trouble had much in common. I was asked to visit them in the first place, obviously, because the persons who issued the invitations thought they could see resemblances there. And just as obviously, I was drawn to them because they touched a corresponding set of curiosities and preoccu-

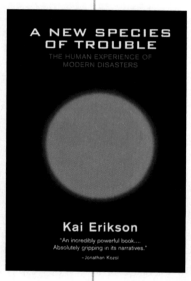

pations in me. Moreover, common themes seemed to come into focus as I moved from one place to another, so that those separate happenings (and the separate stories told of them) began to fuse into a more inclusive whole. One of the excitements of sociological work in general is to watch general patterns—dim and shapeless at first—emerge from a wash of seemingly unconnected details. . . .

In particular: Soon after the black wall of water and debris ground its way down Buffalo Creek, attorneys for the coal company involved called the disaster "an act of God." . . . However people elsewhere may look upon that . . . reasoning, the residents of Buffalo Creek understood it to be blasphemy. They knew that one does not blame God lightly for the wrongdoings of humankind, . . . and they knew, too, that the phrase itself reflected a degree of indifference bordering on contempt. On both of those counts they reacted with fury.

I thought then that the sharpness of the reaction had a lot to do with cultural particulars: the immediacy of Appalachian spirituality, the paternalism of Appalachian coal camps, the communality of Appalachian society. I would suggest now, though, that the people of the valley were drawing on local languages and sensibilities to express feelings that are far more general, for people elsewhere seem to respect a profound difference between those disasters that can be understood as the work of nature and those that need to be understood as the work of humankind. *(Erikson 1994:11–12, 19)* ■ 🔗

Additional information about this excerpt can be found on the Online Learning Center at **www.mhhe.com/schaefer9.**

I n this passage from *A New Species of Trouble,* Kai Erikson explains how he brought his sociological imagination to bear on five seemingly unrelated disasters. Each, he realized, had been caused not by natural forces, but by human disregard for the natural world or for other human beings. But while ignorance or negligence is often thought to be at the bottom of such catastrophes, Erikson saw a larger, more sweeping process at work. Consumerism and rapid increases in population, he thought, lay at the bottom of these calamities. Economically, people and their ever-increasing wants and needs had begun to outstrip the capacity of the environment to tolerate their encroachments. Through overpopulation, overconsumption, overbuilding, and overgrazing, people were beginning to overwhelm their physical environment.

What is the relationship between population and the environment? Are humans in danger of overpopulating the world, causing an environmental catastrophe in the process? How does rapid population growth contribute to the movement of large groups of people from one part of the world to another? What do sociologists have to say about population policy and environmental issues? In this chapter, because we cannot begin to understand the deterioration of our physical environment without grasping the effects of human behavior, we will take a sociological overview of world population and some related environmental issues. We will begin with Thomas Robert Malthus's controversial analysis of population trends and Karl Marx's critical response to it. A brief overview of world population history follows. We'll pay particular attention to the current problem of overpopulation, and the prospects for and potential consequences of stable population growth in the United States. We'll see, too, how population growth fuels the migration of large numbers of people from one area of the world to another.

Later in the chapter, we will examine the environmental problems facing the world as we enter the 21st century, and will draw on the functionalist and conflict perspectives to better understand environmental issues. It is important not to oversimplify the relationship between population and the environment. Rising population, in itself, does not necessarily destroy the environment, while stable population growth alone is no guarantee of healthful air, water, or land. Nevertheless, as will be evident in the second half of the chapter and in the social policy section on world population policy, increases in population can strain our environmental resources and present difficult choices for policymakers. ■

DEMOGRAPHY: THE STUDY OF POPULATION

The study of population issues engages the attention of both natural and social scientists. The biologist explores the nature of reproduction and casts light on factors that affect *fertility,* the level of reproduction in a society. The medical pathologist examines and analyzes trends in the causes of death. Geographers, historians, and psychologists also have distinctive contributions to make to our understanding of population. Sociologists, more than these other researchers, focus on the *social* factors that influence population rates and trends.

In their study of population issues, sociologists are aware that the norms, values, and social patterns of a society profoundly affect various elements of population, such as fertility, *mortality* (the amount of death), and migration. Fertility is influenced by people's age of entry into sexual unions and by their use of contraception—both of which, in turn, reflect the social and religious values that guide a particular culture. Mortality is shaped by a nation's level of nutrition, acceptance of immunization, and provisions for sanitation, as well as its general commitment to health care and health education. Migration from one country to another can depend on marital and kinship ties, the relative degree of racial and religious tolerance in various societies, and people's evaluations of employment opportunities.

Demography is the scientific study of population. It draws on several components of population, including size, composition, and territorial distribution, to understand the social consequences of population change (see Figure 21-1, page 486). Demographers study geographical variations and historical trends in their effort to develop population forecasts. They also analyze the structure of a

FIGURE 21-1

World Population, 2003

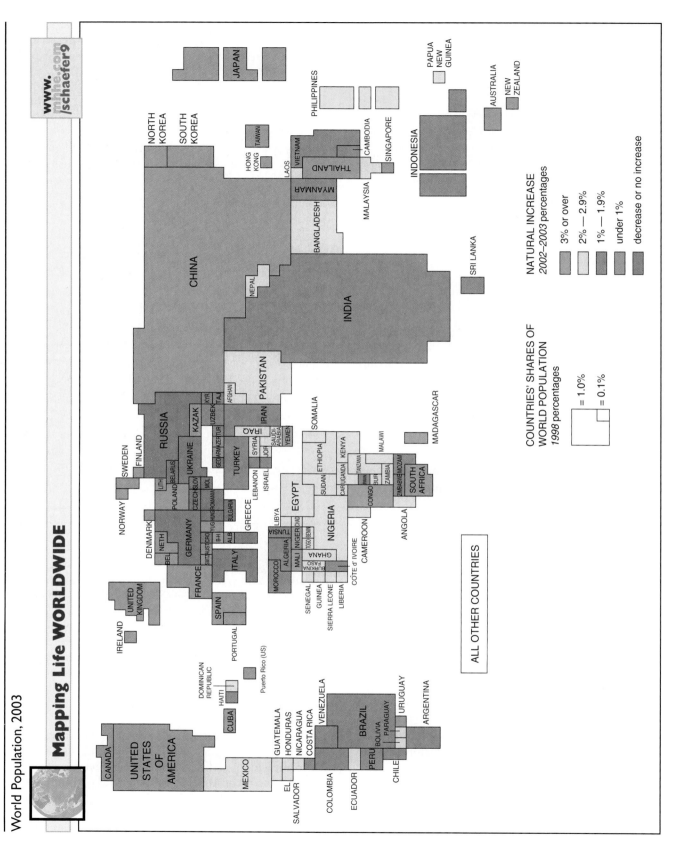

Mapping Life WORLDWIDE

COUNTRIES' SHARES OF
WORLD POPULATION
1998 percentages

☐ = 1.0%

□ = 0.1%

NATURAL INCREASE
2002–2003 percentages

3% or over

2% — 2.9%

1% — 1.9%

under 1%

decrease or no increase

Sources: Haub 2003.

Based on an estimate of population data, this map of the world has been redrawn so that the size of each country is shown in proportion to its population rather than its geographic area. For example, note how India and China are represented on this map.

population—the age, gender, race, and ethnicity of its members. A key figure in this analysis was Thomas Malthus.

Malthus's Thesis and Marx's Response

The Reverend Thomas Robert Malthus (1766–1834), who was educated at Cambridge University, spent his life teaching history and political economy. He strongly criticized two major institutions of his time—the church and slavery—yet his most significant legacy for contemporary scholars is his still-controversial *Essays on the Principle of Population,* published in 1798.

Essentially, Malthus held that the world's population was growing more rapidly than the available food supply. Malthus argued that food supply increases in an arithmetic progression (1, 2, 3, 4, and so on), whereas population expands by a geometric progression (1, 2, 4, 8, and so on). According to his analysis, the gap between food supply and population will continue to grow over time. Even though the food supply will increase, it will not increase nearly enough to meet the needs of an expanding world population.

Malthus advocated population control to close the gap between rising population and food supply, yet he explicitly denounced artificial means of birth control because they were not sanctioned by religion. For Malthus, one appropriate way to control population was to postpone marriage. He argued that couples must take responsibility for the number of children they choose to bear; without such restraint, the world would face widespread hunger, poverty, and misery (Malthus et al. [1824] 1960; Petersen 1979).

Karl Marx strongly criticized Malthus's views on population. Marx pointed to the nature of economic relations in Europe's industrial societies as the central problem. He could not accept the Malthusian notion that rising world population, rather than capitalism, was the cause of social ills. In Marx's opinion, there was no special relationship between world population and the supply of resources (including food). If society were well ordered, increases in population would lead to greater wealth, not to hunger and misery.

Of course, Marx did not believe that capitalism operated under these ideal conditions. He maintained that capitalism devoted its resources to the financing of buildings and tools rather than to the equitable distribution of food, housing, and other necessities of life. Marx's work is important to the study of population because he linked overpopulation to the unequal distribution of resources—a topic that will be taken up again later in this chapter. His concern with the writings of Malthus also testifies to the importance of population in political and economic affairs.

As early as the late 1700s, the Reverend Thomas Robert Malthus suggested that the world's population was growing more rapidly than the available food supply.

The insights of Malthus and Marx regarding population issues have come together in what is termed the *neo-Malthusian view,* best exemplified by the work of Paul Ehrlich (1968; Ehrlich and Ehrlich 1990), author of *The Population Bomb.* Neo-Malthusians agree with Malthus that world population growth is outstretching natural resources. However, in contrast to the British theorist, they insist that birth control measures are needed to regulate population increases. Showing a Marxist bent, neo-Malthusians condemn developed nations, which despite their low birthrates, consume a disproportionately large share of world resources. While rather pessimistic about the future, these theorists stress that birth control and sensible use of resources are essential responses to rising world population (J. Tierney 1990; Weeks 2002; for a critique, see Commoner 1971).

Studying Population Today

The relative balance of births and deaths is no less important today than it was during the lifetime of Malthus and Marx. The suffering that Malthus spoke of

Taking Sociology To Work

KELSIE LENOR WILSON-DORSETT **Deputy Director, Department of Statistics, Government of Bahamas**

Kelsie Wilson-Dorsett was born in the Bahamas, where she received her primary and secondary education. She graduated from McMaster University in Hamilton, Ontario, with a combined honors degree in sociology and political science. Her master's degree in sociology, completed at the University of Western Ontario in London, specialized in demography.

Currently, Wilson-Dorsett holds the positions of Deputy Director, Department of Statistics and Head of the Social Statistics Division, Government of Bahamas, where she oversees the country's census, vital statistics, and other surveys. In this position, she is responsible for the execution of the Bahamas' first Living Conditions Survey (BLCS) which, when completed, will enable the government to establish a poverty line and to measure the incidence and extent of poverty in that country.

Wilson-Dorsett's study of sociology, specializing in demography, is directly related to her current job. She states, "The study of sociology has enabled me to put meaning to the figures which come into my office and has provided me with avenues to interpret these figures and determine the direction of future data collection. The analysis of census data, for instance, allows me to see where my country was several years ago, where it is now, and where it is likely to be in the years ahead."

Let's Discuss

1. What challenges do you think might be part of Wilson-Dorsett's job as she oversees a national census in a country like the Bahamas?
2. What other areas of specialization within the discipline of sociology would be helpful for someone interpreting the results of a project such as the Living Conditions Survey (BLCS)?

---

is certainly a reality for many people of the world who are hungry and poor. Malnutrition remains the largest contributing factor to illness and death among children in developing countries. Almost 18 percent of these children will die before age five—a rate over 11 times higher than in developed nations. Warfare and large-scale migration intensify problems of population and food supply. For example, recent strife in Afghanistan, the Congo, and Iraq have caused maldistribution of food supplies, leading to regional concerns about health. Combating world hunger may require reducing human births, dramatically increasing the world's food supply, or perhaps both at the same time. The study of population-related issues, then, seems to be essential today.

In the United States and most other countries, the census is the primary mechanism for collecting population information. A *census* is an enumeration, or counting, of a population. The Constitution of the United States requires that a census be held every 10 years to determine congressional representation. This periodic investigation is supplemented by *vital statistics,* or records of births, deaths, marriages, and divorces that are gathered through a registration system maintained by govern-

mental units. In addition, other governmental surveys provide up-to-date information on commercial developments, educational trends, industrial expansion, agricultural practices, and the status of groups such as children, the elderly, racial minorities, and single parents.

In administering a nationwide census and conducting other types of research, demographers employ many of the skills and techniques described in Chapter 2, including questionnaires, interviews, and sampling. The precision of population projections depends on the accuracy of a series of estimates that demographers must make. First, they must determine past population trends and establish a current base population. Next, birthrates and death rates must be determined, along with estimates of future fluctuations. In making projections for a nation's population trends, demographers must consider migration as well, since a significant number of individuals may enter and leave a country.

Elements of Demography

Demographers communicate population facts with a language derived from the basic elements of human life—

birth and death. The ***birthrate*** (or more specifically, the *crude birthrate*) is the number of live births per 1,000 population in a given year. In 2002, for example, there were 14 live births per 1,000 people in the United States. The birthrate provides information on the actual reproductive patterns of a society.

One way demography can project future growth in a society is to make use of the ***total fertility rate (TFR).*** The TFR is the average number of children born alive to any woman, assuming that she conforms to current fertility rates. The TFR reported for the United States in 2001 was 2.0 live births per woman, compared to over 8 births per woman in a developing country such as Niger.

Mortality, like fertility, is measured in several different ways. The ***death rate*** (also known as the *crude death rate*) is the number of deaths per 1,000 population in a given year. In 2002, the United States had a death rate of 8.5 per 1,000 population. The ***infant mortality rate*** is the number of deaths of infants under one year of age per 1,000 live births in a given year. This particular measure serves as an important indicator of a society's level of health care; it reflects prenatal nutrition, delivery procedures, and infant screening measures. The infant mortality rate also functions as a useful indicator of future population growth, since those infants who survive to adulthood will contribute to further population increases.

Nations vary widely in the rate of death of newborn children. In 2002, the infant mortality rate for the United States was 6.9 deaths per 1,000 live births, whereas for the world as a whole it was an estimated 55 deaths per 1,000 live births. At the same time, at least 43 nations have lower rates of infant mortality than the United States, including Great Britain, Canada, and Sweden, as we will see later in the chapter.

A general measure of health used by demographers is ***life expectancy,*** the median number of years a person can be expected to live under current mortality conditions. Usually the figure is reported as life expectancy *at birth.* At present, Japan reports a life expectancy

at birth of 81 years, slightly higher than the United States' figure of 77 years. In contrast, life expectancy at birth is less than 45 in several developing nations, including Zambia (see Figure 21-2).

The ***growth rate*** of a society is the difference between births and deaths, plus the difference between *immigrants* (those who enter a country to establish permanent residence) and *emigrants* (those who leave a country permanently) per 1,000 population. For the world as a whole, the growth rate is simply the difference between births and deaths per 1,000 population, since worldwide immigration and emigration must of necessity be equal. In 2001, the United States had a growth rate of 0.6 percent, compared with an estimated 1.3 percent for the entire world (Haub 2003).

FIGURE 21-2

Life Expectancy, 2002

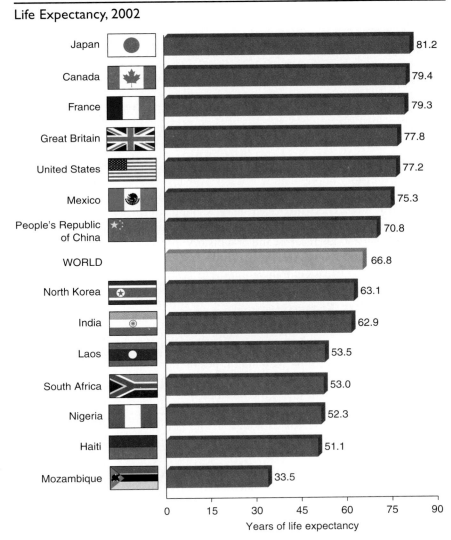

Source: Haub 2003.

Table 21-1	Estimated Time for Each Successive Increase of 1 Billion People in World Population	
Population Level	**Time Taken to Reach New Population Level**	**Year of Attainment**
First billion	Human history before 1800	1804
Second billion	123 years	1927
Third billion	33 years	1960
Fourth billion	14 years	1974
Fifth billion	13 years	1987
Sixth billion	12 years	1999
Seventh billion	15 years	2014
Eighth billion	17 years	2031
Ninth billion	22 years	2053

Source: Author's estimate based on Bureau of the Census 2002c.

WORLD POPULATION PATTERNS

One important aspect of demographic work involves a study of the history of population. But how is that possible? After all, official national censuses were relatively rare before 1850. Researchers interested in early population must turn to archeological remains of settlements, burial sites, baptismal and tax records, and oral history sources. In the next section we will see what such detective work has told us about changes in population over time.

Demographic Transition

On October 13, 1999, in a maternity clinic in Sarajevo, Bosnia-Herzegovina, Helac Fatina gave birth to a son who has been designated the six billionth person on this planet. Until modern times, relatively few humans lived in the world. One estimate places the world population of a million years ago at only 125,000 people. As Table 21-1 indicates, the population has exploded in the last 200 years (World Health Organization 2000:3; for a different view, see Eberstadt 2001).

The phenomenal growth of world population in recent times can be accounted for by changing patterns in births and deaths. Beginning in the late 1700s—and continuing until the mid-1900s—death rates in northern and western Europe gradually decreased. People were beginning to live longer because of advances in food production, sanitation,

nutrition, and public health care. But while death rates fell, birthrates remained high; as a result, this period of European history brought unprecedented population growth. By the late 1800s, however, the birthrates of many European countries had begun to decline, and the rate of population growth had also decreased (O'Neill and Balk 2001).

The changes in birthrates and death rates in 19th century Europe serve as an example of demographic transition. Demographers use the term ***demographic transition*** to describe changes in birthrates and death rates that occur during a nation's development, resulting in new patterns of vital statistics. In many nations today, we are seeing a demographic transition from high birthrates and death rates to low birthrates and death rates. As Figure 21-3 shows, this process typically takes place in three stages:

FIGURE 21-3

Demographic Transition

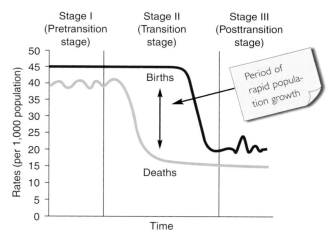

Demographers use the concept of *demographic transition* to describe changes in birthrates and death rates that occur during a nation's development. This graph shows the pattern that took place in presently developed nations. In the first stage, both birthrates and death rates were high, so that there was little population growth. In the second stage, the birthrate remained high while the death rate declined sharply, which led to rapid population growth. By the last stage, which many developing countries have yet to enter, the birthrate had declined as well, reducing population growth.

1. Pretransition stage: high birthrates and death rates with little population growth.
2. Transition stage: declining death rates—primarily the result of reductions in infant deaths—along with high to medium fertility, resulting in significant population growth.
3. Posttransition stage: low birthrates and death rates with little population growth.

The demographic transition should be regarded not as a "law of population growth," but rather as a generalization of the population history of industrial nations. This concept helps us to understand world population problems better. About two-thirds of the world's nations have yet to pass fully through the second stage of the demographic transition. Even if such nations make dramatic advances in fertility control, their populations will nevertheless increase greatly because of the large base of people already at prime childbearing age.

The pattern of demographic transition varies from nation to nation. One particularly useful distinction is the contrast between the rapid transition now occurring in developing nations—which include about two-thirds of the world's population—and that which occurred over the course of almost a century in more industrialized countries. In developing nations, the demographic transition has involved a rapid decline in death rates without adjustments in birthrates.

Specifically, in the post–World War II period, the death rates of developing nations began a sharp decline. This revolution in "death control" was triggered by antibiotics, immunization, insecticides (such as DDT, used to strike at malaria-bearing mosquitoes), and largely successful campaigns against such fatal diseases as smallpox. Substantial medical and public health technology was imported almost overnight from more developed nations. As a result, the drop in death rates that had taken a century in Europe was telescoped into two decades in many developing countries.

Birthrates had little time to adjust. Cultural beliefs about the proper size of families could not possibly change as quickly as the falling death rates. For centuries, couples had given birth to as many as eight or more children, knowing that perhaps only two or three would survive to adulthood. Families were more willing to accept technological advances that prolonged life than to abandon fertility patterns that reflected time-honored tradition and religious training. The result was an astronomical "population explosion" that was well under way by the middle 1900s. By the middle 1970s, however, demographers had observed a slight decline in the growth rate of

FIGURE 21-4

Population Structure of Afghanistan and the United States, 2004

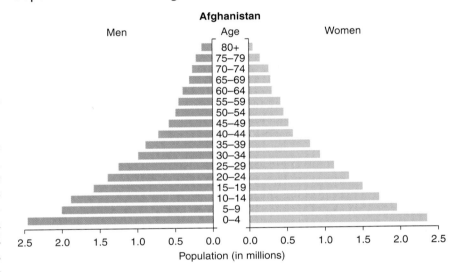

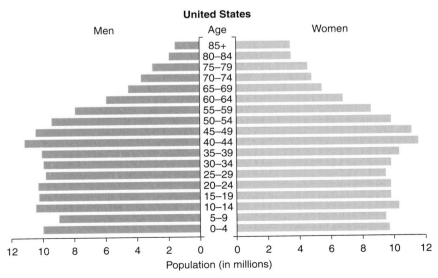

Source: Projections developed by the Census in Bureau of the Census 2002b.

many developing nations, as family planning efforts began to take hold (Crenshaw et al. 2000; McFalls 1998).

The Population Explosion

Apart from war, rapid population growth has been perhaps the dominant international social problem of the past 40 years. Often this issue is referred to in emotional terms as the "population bomb" or the "population explosion." Such striking language is not surprising, given the staggering increases in world population recorded during the 20th century (refer to Table 21-1 on page 490). The population of our planet rose from 1 billion around the year 1800 to 6.1 billion by 2003 (Haub 2003).

Beginning in the 1960s, governments in certain developing nations sponsored or supported campaigns to encourage family planning. In good part as the result of government-sponsored birth control campaigns, Thailand's total fertility rate fell from 6.1 births per woman in 1970 to only 1.7 in 2002. In China, the government's strict one-child policy actually produced a negative growth rate in some urban areas (see Box 21-1). Yet, even if family planning efforts are successful in reducing fertility rates, the momentum toward growing world population is well established. The developing nations face the prospect of continued population growth, since a substantial proportion of their population is approaching the childbearing years (see the top of Figure 21-4, page 491). The social policy section at the end of this chapter takes a look at the challenges policymakers face in developing nations.

A *population pyramid* is a special type of bar chart that shows the distribution of the population by gender and age; it is generally used to illustrate the population structure of a society. As Figure 21-4 shows, a substantial portion of the population of Afghanistan consists of children under the age of 15, whose childbearing years are still to come. Thus, the built-in momentum for population growth is much greater in Afghanistan (and in many other developing countries in other parts of the world) than in western Europe or the United States.

Consider the population data for India, which in 2000 surpassed 1 billion residents. Sometime between the years 2040 and 2050 India's population will exceed China's. The substantial momentum for growth that is built into India's age structure means that the nation will face a staggering increase in population in the coming decades—even if its birthrate declines sharply (Dugger 2001).

Population growth is not a problem in all nations. Today, a handful of countries are even adopting policies that encourage growth. One such country is Japan, where the total fertility rate has fallen sharply. Nevertheless, a global perspective underscores the serious consequences that could result from overall continued population growth.

A tragic new factor has emerged in the last 15 years **p. 119** that will restrict worldwide population growth: the spread of AIDS. As of 2001, 45 countries were severely affected by the disease. About 88 percent of all AIDS cases are concentrated in those 45 countries, most of which are located in sub-Saharan Africa—though Cambodia, India, Thailand, Brazil, the Dominican Republic, and Haiti also are significantly affected. In Botswana, the country with the highest prevalence of HIV, one out of every three adults is HIV positive, and life expectancy has dropped from 60 in 1990 to a projected 36 in 2005 (United Nations Population Division 2001b).

> **Use Your Sociological Imagination** www.mhhe.com/schaefer9
>
> You are living in a country that is so heavily populated, basic resources such as food, water, and living space are running short. What will you do? How will you respond to the crisis if you are a government social planner? A politician?

AIDS has had a dramatic impact on the death rates in many developing countries, particularly in Africa.

Sociology in the Global Community

21-1 POPULATION POLICY IN CHINA

In a residential district in Shanghai, a member of the local family planning committee knocks on the door of a childless couple. Why, she inquires, have they not started a family?

Such a question would have been unthinkable a generation earlier, when family planning officials, in an attempt to avoid a looming population explosion, sometimes resorted to sterilization to enforce the government rule of one child per family. Since then, the birthrate in some areas has fallen so far it is now lower than the death rate—a situation that has left cities short of workers.

To remedy the shortage, the government has quietly begun to grant exceptions to the one-child policy to adults who are only children themselves. In 2002 it extended the privilege to all families, but at a price. A new family planning law imposes "social compensation fees" to cover the cost to society of an additional child. The fee, which is substantial, is equivalent to twenty years' worth of a rural farm family's income.

Chinese families are beset, too, by the unforeseen results of their attempts to circumvent the one-child policy. In the past, in an effort to ensure that their one child would be a male capable of perpetuating the family line, many couples chose to abort female fetuses, or quietly allowed female infants to die of neglect. As a result, China's sex ratio at birth (the ratio of male newborns to female newborns) is now about 117 to 100—well above the normal rate of 106 to 100. This

> The birthrate in some areas has fallen so far it is now lower than the death rate.

difference in birthrates translates into 1.7 million fewer female births per year than normal—and down the line, to many fewer childbearers than normal. In 1993 the Chinese government, alarmed by the long-term implications of sex-selected abortion and infanticide, outlawed gender screening of unborn children except when medically necessary.

Chinese women have borne the brunt not just of the government's population

policy, but of the economic dislocation caused by recent market reforms and the redistribution of rural farmland. In privatized government factories, their need for maternity benefits and child care now limits their employment opportunities. On rural farms, they struggle to cope without their husbands, many of whom have gone to work in city factories. The female suicide rate in rural China is now the highest in the world. Experts think this alarming statistic reflects a fundamental lack of self-esteem among rural Chinese women. The social patterns of centuries, unlike birthrates, cannot be changed in a generation.

Let's Discuss

1. Does any government, no matter how overpopulated a country is, have a right to sterilize people who do not voluntarily limit the size of their families? Why or why not?

2. The Chinese government's one-child policy seems to have backfired. What other policies might have worked better? Explain why.

Sources: Eckholm 2002; *Migration News* 2002d; E. Rosenthal 2003.

FERTILITY PATTERNS IN THE UNITED STATES

During the last four decades, the United States and other industrial nations have passed through two different patterns of population growth—the first marked by high fertility and rapid growth (stage II in the theory of demographic transition), the second marked by declining fertility and little growth (stage III). Sociologists are keenly aware of the social impact of these fertility patterns.

The Baby Boom

The most recent period of high fertility in the United States has often been referred to as the *baby boom*. During World War II, large numbers of military personnel

were separated from their spouses. When they returned, the annual number of births began to rise dramatically. Still, the baby boom was not a return to the large families common in the 1800s. In fact, there was only a slight increase in the proportion of couples having three or more children. Instead, the boom resulted from a striking decrease in the number of childless marriages and one-child families. Although a peak was reached in 1957, the nation maintained a relatively high birthrate of over 20 live births per 1,000 population until 1964. In 2002, the birthrate had fallen to 15 live births per 1,000 population—30 percent lower than in 1964 (Bureau of the Census 1975; Haub 2003).

It would be a mistake to attribute the baby boom solely to the return home of large numbers of soldiers. High wages and general prosperity during the postwar period encouraged many married couples to have children and purchase homes. In addition, several sociologists—as well as feminist author Betty Friedan (1963)—have noted the strong societal pressures on women during the 1950s to marry and become mothers and homemakers (Bouvier 1980).

Stable Population Growth

Although the total fertility rate of the United States has remained low over the last two decades, the nation continues to grow in size because of two factors: the momentum built into our age structure by the postwar population boom and the continued high rates of immigration. Because of the upsurge of births beginning in the 1950s, there are now many more people in their childbearing years than there are in older age groups (in which most deaths occur). This growth of population represents a "demographic echo" of the baby boom generation, many of whom are now parents. Consequently, the number of people born each year in the United States continues to exceed the number who die. In addition, the nation allows a large number of immigrants to enter each year; these immigrants currently account for between one-fourth and one-third of annual growth.

Despite these trends, some analysts in the 1980s and early 1990s projected relatively low fertility levels and moderate net migration over the coming decades. As a result, it seemed possible that the United States might reach *zero population growth (ZPG)*. ZPG is the state of a population in which the number of births plus immigrants equals the number of deaths plus emigrants. In the recent past, although some nations have achieved ZPG, it has been relatively short-lived. Yet 65 countries, 40 of them in Europe, are today actually showing a *decline* in population (Haub 2002).

What would a society with stable population growth be like? In demographic terms, it would be quite different from the United States of the 1990s. There would be relatively equal numbers of people in each age group, and the median age of the population might perhaps be as high as 38 in 2050 (compared to 35 in 2000). As a result, the population pyramid of the United States (as shown in Figure 21-4) would look more like a rectangle (Bureau of the Census 2002a:14–15).

There would also be a much larger proportion of older people, especially age 75 and over. These citizens would place a greater demand on the nation's social service programs and health care institutions. On a more positive note, the economy would be less volatile under ZPG, since the number of entrants into the paid labor force would remain stable. ZPG would also lead to changes in family life. With fertility rates declining, women would devote fewer years to child rearing and to

the social roles of motherhood; the proportion of married women entering the labor force would continue to rise (Spengler 1978; Weeks 2002).

POPULATION AND MIGRATION

Along with births and deaths, migration is one of the three factors that affect population growth or decline. The term *migration* refers to the relatively permanent movement of people, with the purpose of changing their place of residence (Prehn 1991). Migration usually describes movement over a sizable distance, rather than from one side of a city to another.

As a social phenomenon, migration is fairly complex; it results from a variety of factors. The most important tend to be economic—financial failure in the "old country" and a perception of greater economic opportunities and prosperity in the new homeland. Other factors that contribute to migration include racial and religious bigotry, dislike for prevailing political regimes, and desire to reunite one's family. All these forces combine to *push* some individuals out of their homelands and *pull* them to areas believed to be more attractive.

International Migration

International migration—changes of residence across national boundaries—has been a significant force in redistributing the world's population during certain periods of history. For example, the composition of the United States has been significantly altered by immigrants who p. 274 came here in the 19th and 20th centuries. Their entry was encouraged or restricted by various immigration policies.

As noted earlier, immigration into a country can become a significant factor in its population growth. In recent years, immigration has accounted for 20 to 30 percent of growth in the United States, which has led those troubled by population increases to join those opposed to an influx of foreigners in calling for serious restrictions on immigration. In contrast, however, many other countries, especially in Europe, are currently receiving a much higher proportion of immigrants (Martin and Widgren 2002).

In the last decade, immigration has become a controversial issue throughout much of Europe. Western Europe, in particular, has become a desirable destination for many individuals and families from former colonies or former communist-bloc countries who are fleeing the poverty, persecution, and warfare of their native lands. Currently, there are 20 million legal immigrants in western Europe, along with an estimated 2 million illegal immigrants. With the number of immigrants and refugees increasing at a time of widespread unemployment and housing shortages, there has been a striking rise in antiforeign (and often openly racist) sentiment in Germany, France, and other countries. Right-wing forces in Germany (including members of the skinhead counterculture) have mounted more than 3,500 attacks on foreigners in recent years. Immigrants from eastern Europe and Asia are often the targets, and there have been attacks as well on Germany's small Jewish community.

Developing countries in Asia and Africa are also encountering difficulties as thousands of displaced people seek assistance and asylum. For example, at the end of 2000, an estimated 14.5 million people worldwide were refugees or asylum seekers—a number that is equivalent to the population of Michigan or the Netherlands. Half these people came from two areas, Palestine and Afghanistan. Needless to say, the political and economic problems of developing nations (see Chapter 10) are only intensified by such massive migration under desperate conditions (Martin and Widgren 2002).

Within days of the terrorist attack on the World Trade Center in New York, thousands of Afghan refugees had fled to Pakistan in anticipation of U.S. retaliation. Catastrophic conflicts such as war and terrorist attacks often trigger massive international migrations.

Internal Migration

Migratory movements within societies can vary in important ways. In traditional societies, migration often represents a way of life, as people move to accommodate the changing availability of fertile soil and wild game. In industrial societies, people may relocate as a result of job transfers or because they believe that a particular region offers better employment opportunities or a more desirable climate.

Although nations typically have laws and policies governing movement across their borders, the same is not true of internal movement. Generally, residents of a country are legally free to migrate from one locality to another. Of course, that is not the case in all nations; historically, the Republic of South Africa restricted the movement of Blacks and other non-Whites through the system of segregation known as *apartheid* (refer back to Chapter 11).

We can identify three distinctive trends of recent internal migration within the United States:

1. *Suburbanization.* During the period 1980–1990, suburban counties grew in population by 14 percent while the total population of the United States

rose by 10 percent. The proportion of the population living in central cities had stayed constant at about one-third since 1950. Meanwhile, the share of the population living in nonmetropolitan areas declined from 44 percent in 1950 to 20 percent in 1994 (Bureau of the Census 1996:38).

2. *"Sunning of America."* There has been significant internal migration from the "snow belt" of the north central and northeastern states to the "sun belt" in the South and West. Since 1970, the sun belt has absorbed almost two-thirds of the population growth of the United States. Individuals and families move to the sun belt because of its expanding economy and desirable climate. Businesses are attracted by the comparatively inexpensive energy supplies, increased availability of labor, and relative weakness of labor unions. Since 1990, however, while internal migration to the South has remained high, migration to the West has slowed with the job market in that region (see Figure 21-5, page 496).

3. *Rural life rebound.* In the early 1990s, nonmetropolitan counties gained in population, though the trend began to level off in 1998. This migration to rural areas, which reversed a long-standing trend toward urbanization, reflected concerns about the quality of life in the cities and suburbs. It has since dropped off, as the outskirts of metropolitan areas spread out and many downtown areas experienced a rebirth (K. Johnson 1999; Schachter 2001).

FIGURE 21-5

Where Americans Moved in the 1990s

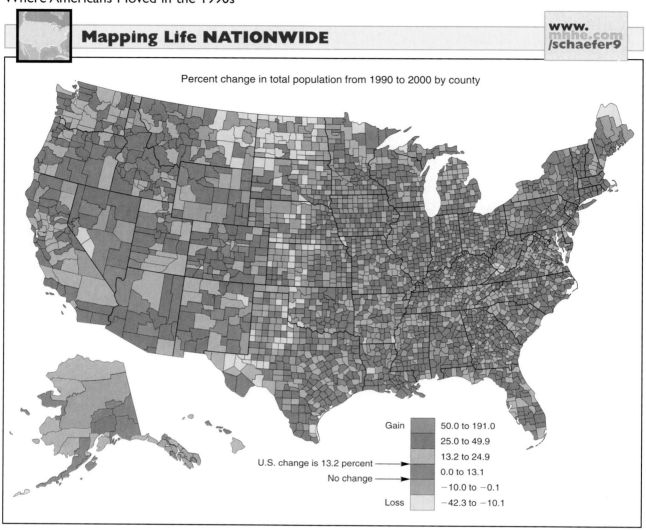

Source: Brewer and Suchan 2001:10.

What would happen if present patterns of migration, both internal and international, reversed themselves? How would your hometown change? What would be the effect on the nation's economy? Would your own life change?

THE ENVIRONMENT

Decisions made in the economic and political spheres often have environmental consequences. We can see signs of despoliation almost everywhere. Our air, our water, and our land are being polluted, whether we live in St. Louis, Mexico City, or Lagos, Nigeria. In the following section, we will survey these problems and see what sociologists have to say about them.

Environmental Problems: An Overview

In recent decades, the world has witnessed serious environmental disasters. For example, Love Canal, near Niagara Falls in New York State, was declared a disaster area in 1978 because of chemical contamination. In the 1940s and 1950s, a chemical company had disposed of waste products on the site where a housing development and a school were subsequently built. The metal drums that held the chemical wastes eventually rusted out, and toxic chemicals with noxious odors began seeping into the residents' yards and basements. Subsequent investigations revealed that the chemical company knew as early as 1958 that toxic chemicals were seeping into homes and a school playground. After repeated protests in the late 1970s, 239 families living in Love Canal had to be relocated.

In 1986, a series of explosions set off a catastrophic nuclear reactor accident at Chernobyl, a part of Ukraine (in what was then the Soviet Union). The accident killed at least 32,000 people. Some 300,000 residents had to be evacuated, and the area became uninhabitable for 19 miles in any direction. High levels of radiation were found as far as 30 miles from the reactor site, and radioactivity levels were well above normal as far away as Sweden and Japan. According to one estimate, the Chernobyl accident and the resulting nuclear fallout may ultimately result in 100,000 excess cases of cancer worldwide (Shcherbak 1996).

While Love Canal, Chernobyl, and other environmental disasters understandably grab headlines, it is the silent, day-to-day deterioration of the environment that ultimately poses a devastating threat to humanity. Examining all our environmental problems in detail would be impossible, but three broad areas of concern stand out: air pollution, water pollution, and contamination of land.

Air Pollution

More than 1 billion people on the planet are exposed to potentially health-damaging levels of air pollution. Unfortunately, in cities around the world, residents have come to accept smog and polluted air as normal. Air pollution in urban areas is caused primarily by emissions from automobiles and secondarily by emissions from electric power plants and heavy industries. Urban smog not only limits visibility; it can lead to health problems as uncomfortable as eye irritation and as deadly as lung cancer. Such problems are especially severe in developing countries. The World Health Organization estimates that up to 700,000 premature deaths *per year* could be prevented if pollutants were brought down to safer levels (Carty 1999; World Resources Institute 1998).

People are capable of changing their behavior, but they are also unwilling to make such changes permanent. For example, during the 1984 Olympics in Los Angeles, residents were asked to carpool and stagger their work hours to relieve traffic congestion and improve the quality of the air athletes would breathe. These changes resulted in a remarkable 12 percent drop in ozone levels. However, when the Olympians left, people reverted to their normal behavior and the ozone levels climbed back up (McCright and Dunlap 2003; Nussbaum 1998).

Water Pollution

Throughout the United States, dumping of waste materials by both industries and local governments has polluted streams, rivers, and lakes. Consequently, many bodies of water have become unsafe for drinking, fishing, and swimming. Around the world, the pollution of the oceans is an issue of growing concern. Such pollution results regularly from waste dumping and is made worse by fuel leaks from shipping and occasional oil spills. In a dramatic accident in 1989, the oil tanker *Exxon Valdez* ran aground in Prince William Sound, Alaska. The tanker's cargo of 11 million gallons of crude oil spilled into the sound and washed onto the shore, contaminating 1,285 miles of shoreline. About 11,000 people joined in a cleanup effort that cost over $2 billion.

Less dramatic than large-scale accidents or disasters, but more common in many parts of the world, are problems with the basic water supply. Worldwide, over a

Rusty barrels leak chemicals into a lake near a city east of Moscow. Throughout the world, industrial pollutants have rendered many water bodies unsafe for fishing, drinking, or swimming.

Vacation in an unspoiled paradise! Increasingly, people from developed countries are turning to ecotourism as an environmentally friendly way to see the world. The new trend bridges the interests of environmentalists and businesspeople, especially in developing countries. These birdwatchers are vacationing in Belize.

billion people lack safe and adequate drinking water, and nearly half the world's population has no acceptable means of sanitation—a problem that further threatens the quality of water supplies. The health costs of unsafe water are enormous (World Health Organization and UNICEF 2000).

Contamination of Land

Love Canal made it clear that industrial dumping of hazardous wastes and chemicals seriously contaminates land. In another noteworthy case of contamination, unpaved roads in Times Beach, Missouri, were sprayed to control dust in 1971 with an oil that contained dioxin. This highly toxic chemical is a by-product of the manufacture of herbicides and other chemicals. After the health dangers of dioxin became evident, the entire community of 2,800 people was relocated (at a cost of $33 million) and the town of Times Beach was shut down in 1985.

A significant part of land contamination comes from the tremendous demand for landfills to handle the nation's waste. Recycling programs aimed at reducing the need for landfills are perhaps the most visible aspect of environmentalism. How successful have such programs been? In 1980, about 10 percent of urban waste was recycled; the proportion increased steadily throughout the 1980s, but started to level off at about 29 percent in 1998. Experts are beginning to revise their goals for recycling campaigns, which now appear overambitious. Still, a new

way to be green has developed: the Internet. For example, over-the-Net commercial transactions allow the downloading of new software, reducing the need for wasteful packaging and shipping materials, including fuel for delivery trucks. And the availability of e-mail and electronic networking encourages people to work at home rather than contribute to the pollution caused by commuting (Belsie 2000; Booth 2000).

What are the basic causes of our growing environmental problems? Some observers, such as Paul Ehrlich and Anne Ehrlich, see the pressure of world population growth as the central factor in environmental deterioration. They argue that population control is essential in preventing widespread starvation and environmental decay. Barry Commoner, a biologist, counters that the primary cause of environmental ills is the increasing use of technological innovations that are destructive to the world's environment—among them plastics, detergents, synthetic fibers, pesticides, herbicides, and chemical fertilizers. In the following sections, we will contrast the functionalist and conflict approaches to the study of environmental issues (Commoner 1971, 1990; Ehrlich 1968; Ehrlich and Ehrlich 1990; Ehrlich and Ellison 2002).

Functionalism and Human Ecology

Human ecology is concerned with interrelationships between people and their environment. Environmentalist Barry Commoner (1971:39) has stated that "everything is connected to everything else." Human ecologists focus on how the physical environment shapes people's lives and on how people influence the surrounding environment.

In an application of the human ecological perspective, sociologist Riley Dunlap suggests that the natural environment serves three basic functions for humans, as it does for the many animal species (Dunlap 1993; Dunlap and Catton 1983):

1. **The environment provides the resources essential for life.** These include air, water, and materials used to create shelter, transportation, and needed products. If human societies exhaust these resources—for example, by polluting the water

supply or cutting down rain forests—the consequences can be dire.

2. **The environment serves as a waste repository.** More so than other living species, humans produce a huge quantity and variety of waste products—bottles, boxes, papers, sewage, garbage, and so on. Various types of pollution have become more common because human societies are generating more wastes than the environment can safely absorb.

3. **The environment "houses" our species.** It is our home, our living space, the place where we reside, work, and play. At times we take this truism for granted, but not when day-to-day living conditions become unpleasant and difficult. If our air is "heavy," if our tap water turns brown, if toxic chemicals seep into our neighborhood, we remember why it is vital to live in a healthful environment.

Dunlap (1993) points out that these three functions of the environment actually compete with one another. Human use of the environment for one of these functions will often strain its ability to fulfill the other two. For example, with world population continuing to rise, we have an increasing need to raze forests or farmland and build housing developments. But each time we do so, we are reducing the amount of land that provides food, lumber, or habitat for wildlife.

The tension between the three essential functions of the environment brings us back to the human ecologists' view that "everything is connected to everything else." In facing the environmental challenges of the twenty-first century, government policymakers and environmentalists must determine how they can fulfill human societies' pressing needs (for example, for food, clothing, and shelter) while at the same time preserving the environment as a source of resources, a waste repository, and our home.

Conflict View of Environmental Issues

In Chapter 10, we drew on world systems analysis to show how a growing share of the human and natural resources of the developing countries is being redistributed to the core industrialized nations. This process only intensifies the destruction of natural resources in poorer regions of the world. From a conflict perspective, less affluent nations are being forced to exploit their mineral deposits, forests, and fisheries in order to meet their debt obligations. The poor turn to the only means of survival available to them: They plow mountain slopes, burn plots in tropical forests, and overgraze grasslands (Livernash and Rodenburg 1998).

Brazil exemplifies this interplay between economic troubles and environmental destruction. Each year more than 5.7 million acres of forest are cleared for crops and livestock. The elimination of the rain forest affects worldwide weather patterns, heightening the gradual warming of the earth. These socioeconomic patterns, with harmful environmental consequences, are evident not only in Latin America but in many regions of Africa and Asia (*National Geographic* 2002).

Conflict theorists are well aware of the environmental implications of land use policies in the Third World, but they contend that such a focus on the developing countries can contain an element of ethnocentrism. Who, they ask, is more to blame for environmental deterioration: the poverty-stricken and "food-hungry" populations of the world or the "energy-hungry" industrialized nations? Conflict theorists point out that Western industrialized nations account for only 25 percent of the world's population but are responsible for 85 percent of worldwide consumption. Take the United States alone: A mere 5 percent of the world's people consume more than half the world's nonrenewable resources and more than one-third of all the raw materials produced. Such data lead conflict theorists to charge that the most serious threat to the environment comes from "affluent megaconsumers and megapolluters" (Bharadwaj 1992; G. T. Miller 1972).

Allan Schnaiberg (1994) further refines this analysis by criticizing the focus on affluent consumers as the cause of environmental troubles. In his view, a capitalist system creates a "treadmill of production" because of its inherent need to build ever-expanding profits. This treadmill necessitates creating an increasing demand for products, obtaining natural resources at minimal cost, and manufacturing products as quickly and cheaply as possible—no matter what the long-term environmental consequences.

Environmental Justice

In a stretch of land along the lower Mississippi River in Louisiana, one factory after another pours its industrial waste into the water, raising pollution counts to dangerous levels. It is no accident that the people who live nearby are African American. Poor and lacking in political clout, the communities that border these industrial sites are no match for the powerful business interests that built them (Bullard 1994).

Observations like this one have given rise to *environmental justice,* a legal strategy based on claims that racial minorities are subjected disproportionately to environmental hazards. The approach has had some success. In 1998 a chemical company called Shintech dropped plans to build a plastics plant in a poor black community in Mississippi after opponents filed a civil rights complaint with the Environmental Protection

Agency (EPA). EPA administrator Carol Browner praised the company's decision: "The principles applied to achieve this solution should be incorporated into any blueprint for dealing with environmental justice issues in communities across the nation" (Associated Press 1998:18).

Following reports from the EPA and other organizations documenting the discriminatory location of hazardous waste sites, President Bill Clinton issued an Executive Order in 1994 that requires all federal agencies to ensure that low-income and minority communities have access to better information about their environment and an opportunity to participate in shaping government policies that affect their communities' health. Initial efforts to implement the policy have aroused widespread opposition because of the delays it imposes in establishing new industrial sites. Some observers question the wisdom of an order that slows economic development in areas that are in dire need of employment opportunities. Others point out that such businesses employ few unskilled or less skilled workers and only make the environment less livable for those left behind (Pellow 2002).

To date, most sociological studies of the problem of industrial waste have focused on the discriminatory nature of the siting process. A new study suggests that not only do these facilities tend to locate near poor minority communities; over time, they tend to increase segregation in the area. The study, done in Hillsborough County, Florida, found that between 1987 and 1999, the student bodies of grade schools located close to hazardous waste sites became more and more heavily Black and Latino. Other schools located farther from the waste sites became more heavily White. A combination of poverty and institutional discrimination may prevent minority group members from moving away from the sites, as Whites might be expected to do. The authors of the study concluded that while the siting of hazardous waste dumps is an important public policy issue, the racial and ethnic segregation that follows may be just as important, if not more so (Stretesky and Lynch 2002).

> **Use Your Sociological Imagination**   www.mhhe.com/schaefer9
>
> Your community has been designated as a site for burial of toxic waste. How will you react? Will you organize a protest? Or will you make sure the authorities carry the project out safely? How can such sites be chosen fairly?

SOCIAL POLICY and POPULATION   World Population Policy   www.mhhe.com/schaefer9

The Issue

Six billion and counting: The world's population is growing as you read, threatening the earth's ability to sustain it. Social planners who have grappled with this problem have suggested a policy that provides for a reasonable amount of population growth. But just what is reasonable growth, and how can it be implemented? Social policies that address population growth touch on the most sensitive aspects of people's lives: sexuality, childbearing, and family relationships. For this reason, reaching a global consensus on population issues has been difficult.

The Setting

Beginning in the 1950s, delegates to international conferences sponsored by the United Nations became concerned about the negative consequences of rapid population growth. As we saw earlier, the introduction of modern medicine in developing countries had caused a rapid fall in death rates, but birthrates remained high. To reduce the birthrates, planners devised programs aimed at encouraging family planning and

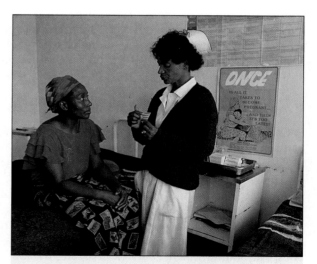

A nurse in Zambia, Africa, instructs a client in how to use birth control pills. Family planning clinics have helped to slow the population growth rate in developing nations.

limiting the number of children couples had through contraception.

But such programs were controversial. In many developing countries, the traditional culture placed great value on large families. Children were seen as a source of support for their aging parents. To compensate for high infant mortality rates, couples generally had more children than they expected to survive to adulthood. Some government officials, reluctant to deny poor people their means of support in old age, hoped instead that rising living standards would eventually allow people to limit the size of their families.

Population planning programs also came under fire in the United States, from antiabortion activists in particular. Public financial aid, they charged, should not be used to support family planning clinics that provided abortion counseling or services. In 1984, under President Ronald Reagan, U.S. delegates to the World Population Conference in Mexico City announced that the United States would no longer support international population planning programs that provided abortion services (Ashford 2001:8; Rayman-Read 2001).

Sociological Insights

Functionalists would note that the best course of action for a community might differ from the best course of action for a society. In developing nations, parents see children as potential laborers, and ultimately, as a means of broadening the family's economic base through the children's marriage. Under such conditions, having fewer children may not appear to be a rational choice. Yet for a country that is struggling to provide clean water, food, and shelter to its people, high population growth *is* dysfunctional. Even so, officials of a developing nation may resent powerful industrial nations that attempt to influence (and may appear to dictate) their population policy.

Because the burden of implementing population policy falls particularly on women, sociologists who take the feminist perspective have focused considerable attention on population policy. Early on, feminists charged that workers in government-funded population control programs were distributing contraceptives without sufficient concern for their health risks. In such programs, they added, women were often pressured to adopt certain contraceptive methods not for their own needs, but so the clinics could meet government quotas. Too often,

feminist critics complained, population control workers ignored sociocultural influences on sexuality and childbearing—influences that often ran counter to the contraceptives they were distributing (Ashford 2001).

Critics who take the conflict perspective have questioned why the United States and other industrialized nations are so enthusiastic about controlling the population of developing countries. In line with Marx's response to Malthus, they argue that neither large families nor population growth is the cause of hunger and misery. Rather, the unjust economic domination of the world by developed states results in an unequal distribution of the world's resources and in widespread poverty in developing nations (Fornos 1997).

Policy Initiatives

The Mexico City policy established during Ronald Reagan's presidency was overturned during President Bill Clinton's administration. However, in 2001, President George W. Bush reinstated it. Today, the Bush administration requires health workers who receive U.S. government funding to refrain from discussing abortion, either publicly or with their patients. To the extent that international family planning services depend on U.S. government funding, they are clearly hampered by this gag rule, which has politicized otherwise nonpartisan public health programs (Purdum 2002).

Setting aside restrictions such as the Mexico City policy, more funding is needed in those countries where government resources are overtaxed. In sub-Saharan Africa, less than 10 percent of women of childbearing age use contraceptives, compared to 83 percent in China. Family planning is still sparse in poverty-stricken rural areas the world over (Haub and Herstad 2002).

Let's Discuss

1. What are the social and cultural attitudes toward family planning in your community? Do people tend to have large families or small ones? What are the reasons they give for their choices?
2. Which perspective on population policy—functionalist, feminist, or conflict—makes the most sense to you? Why?
3. Do you think the U.S. government has a right to dictate abortion policy to other countries? Explain.

CHAPTER RESOURCES

Summary

The size, composition, and distribution of the U.S. population have an important influence on many of the policy issues presented in this book. This chapter examines various elements of population, the current problem of overpopulation, the possibility of *zero population growth,* and the environmental problems facing our planet.

1. Thomas Robert Malthus suggested that the world's population was growing more rapidly than the available food supply, and that the gap would increase over time. However, Karl Marx saw capitalism, rather than rising world population, as the real cause of social ills.
2. The primary mechanism for obtaining population information in the United States and most other countries is the *census.*
3. Roughly two-thirds of the world's nations have yet to pass fully through the second stage of *demographic transition.* Thus they continue to experience significant population growth.
4. Developing nations face the prospect of continued population growth because a substantial portion of their population is approaching childbearing age. Some developed nations, however, have begun to stabilize their population growth.

5. The most important factors in *migration* tend to be economic—financial failure in the "old country" and a perception of greater economic opportunity elsewhere.
6. Three broad areas of environmental concern include air and water pollution and land contamination.
7. Using the human ecological perspective, sociologist Riley Dunlap suggests that the natural environment serves three basic functions: It provides essential resources, serves as a waste repository, and houses our species.
8. Conflict theorists charge that the most serious threat to the environment comes from Western industrialized nations.
9. *Environmental justice* addresses the disproportionate subjection of minorities to environmental hazards.
10. World population policy is controversial both in developing countries, where planners' attempts to limit population growth may run counter to traditional cultural values, and in developed countries such as the United States, where funding of international population programs has been politicized.

Critical Thinking Questions

1. Select one of the social policy issues examined in this textbook and analyze in detail how the size, composition, and distribution of the population of the United States influence that issue.
2. Some European nations are experiencing population declines. Their death rates are low and their birthrates are even lower than in stage III of the demographic transition model. Does this pattern suggest that there is a fourth stage in the demo-

graphic transition? What are the implications of negative population growth for an industrialized nation in the 21st century?
3. Imagine that you have been asked to study the issue of air pollution in the largest city in your state. How might you draw on surveys, observation research, experiments, and existing sources to study the issue?

Key Terms

Birthrate The number of live births per 1,000 population in a given year. Also known as the *crude birthrate.* (page 489)

Census An enumeration, or counting, of a population. (488)

Death rate The number of deaths per 1,000 population in a given year. Also known as the *crude death rate.* (489)

Demographic transition A term used to describe the change from high birthrates and death rates to low birthrates and death rates. (490)

Demography The scientific study of population. (485)

Environmental justice A legal strategy based on claims that racial minorities are subjected disproportionately to environmental hazards. (499)

Fertility The level of reproduction in a society. (485)

Growth rate   The difference between births and deaths, plus the difference between immigrants and emigrants, per 1,000 population. (489)

Human ecology   An area of study concerned with the interrelationships between people and their environment. (498)

Infant mortality rate   The number of deaths of infants under one year of age per 1,000 live births in a given year. (489)

Life expectancy   The median number of years a person can be expected to live under current mortality conditions. (489)

Migration   The relatively permanent movement of people, with the purpose of changing their place of residence. (494)

Population pyramid   A special type of bar chart that shows the distribution of population by gender and age. (492)

Total fertility rate (TFR)   The average number of children born alive to any woman, assuming that she conforms to current fertility rates. (489)

Vital statistics   Records of births, deaths, marriages, and divorces gathered through a registration system maintained by governmental units. (488)

Zero population growth (ZPG)   The state of a population in which the number of births plus immigrants equals the number of deaths plus emigrants. (494)

TECHNOLOGY RESOURCES

Internet Connection

*Note: While all the URLs listed were current as of the printing of this book, these sites often change. Please check our website (**www.mhhe.com/schaefer9**) for updates, hyperlinks, and exercises related to these sites.*

1. Population Connection offers a cyberexamination of the issues raised in this chapter. To learn more about the consequences and issues surrounding population growth, visit the Population Connection website (**www.population connection.org**).

2. Today, environmental activists are working to preserve the environment through organizations such as Greenpeace. Log on to the Greenpeace website to take a virtual tour of this organization's worldwide environmental efforts (**www.greenpeace.org**).

Online Learning Center with PowerWeb

If you are interested in how people feel about the environment, you will want to visit the student center at the Online Learning Center at **www.mhhe.com/schaefer9.** Link to "How Americans Feel About . . ." You will read about three alternative approaches to protecting the environment and view colorful graphs and pie charts showing whether the people surveyed thought the environment would be better, worse, or the same in four years. You will also find out what people your age thought about the long-term future of the environment.

COLLECTIVE BEHAVIOR AND SOCIAL MOVEMENTS

It takes up to 40 dumb animals to make a fur coat.

But only one to wear it.

If you don't want animals gassed, electrocuted, trapped or strangled, don't buy a fur coat.   respect for animals
www.respectforanimals.org

This award-winning poster, created in 1984, garnered international attention for the fledgling animal rights movement. Activists in a wide range of social movements have become adept at using communications technology in their campaigns to promote social change.

Theories of Collective Behavior

Forms of Collective Behavior

Communications Technology and Collective Behavior

Social Policy and Social Movements: Lesbian and Gay Rights

Boxes

SOCIOLOGY IN THE GLOBAL COMMUNITY: A New Social Movement in Rural India

SOCIOLOGY ON CAMPUS: Antiwar Protests

On January 20, 2001, President Joseph Estrada of the Philippines became the first head of state in history to lose power to a smart mob. More than 1 million Manila residents, mobilized and coordinated by waves of text messages, assembled at the site of the 1986 "People Power" peaceful demonstrations that had toppled the Marcos regime. Tens of thousands of Filipinos converged on Epifanio de los Santas Avenue, known as "Edsa," within an hour of the first text message volleys: "Go 2EDSA, Wear blck." Over four days, more than a million citizens showed up, mostly dressed in black. Estrada fell. The legend of "Generation Txt" was born.

Bringing down a government without firing a shot was a momentous early eruption of smart mob behavior. It wasn't, however, the only one.

- On November 30, 1999, autonomous but internetworked squads of demonstrators protesting the meeting of the World Trade Organization used "swarming" tactics, mobile phones, Web sites, laptops, and handheld computers to win the "Battle of Seattle."
- In September 2000, thousands of citizens in Britain, outraged by a sudden rise in gasoline prices, used mobile phones, SMS, email from laptop PCs, and CB radios in taxicabs to coordinate dispersed groups that blocked fuel delivery at selected service stations in a wildcat political protest. . . .

- Since 1992, thousands of bicycle activists have assembled monthly for "Critical Mass" moving demonstrations, weaving through San Francisco streets en masse. Critical Mass operates through loosely linked networks, alerted by mobile phone and email trees, and breaks up into smaller, tele-coordinated groups when appropriate. . . .

Location-sensing wireless organizers, wireless networks, and community supercomputing collectives all have one thing in common: *They enable people to act together in new ways and in situations where collective action was not possible before.* . . .

As indicated by their name, smart mobs are not always beneficial. Lynch mobs and mobocracies continue to engender atrocities. The same convergence of technologies that opens new vistas of cooperation also makes possible a universal surveillance economy and empowers the bloodthirsty as well as the altruistic. Like every previous leap in technological power, the new convergence of wireless computation and social communication will enable people to improve life and liberty in some ways and to degrade it in others. The same technology has the potential to be used as both a weapon of social control and a means of resistance. Even the beneficial effects will have side effects. *(Rheingold 2003:157–158, viii)* ■

Additional information about this excerpt can be found on the Online Learning Center at **www.mhhe.com/schaefer9.**

I n this excerpt from *Smart Mobs*, Howard Rheingold (2003) describes a new phenomenon in which strangers linked by mobile communications devices converge spontaneously to achieve some common goal. Rheingold, an acknowledged authority on the social implications of new technologies, has identified an emergent social behavior, one sociologists would recognize as a form of *collective behavior*. Practically all behavior can be thought of as collective behavior, but sociologists have given distinct meaning to the term. Neil Smelser (1981:431), a sociologist who specializes in this field of study, has defined **collective behavior** as the "relatively spontaneous and unstructured behavior of a group of people who are reacting to a common influence in an ambiguous situation." Rumors are a form of collective behavior; so is public opinion—people's reactions to shared events such as wars and elections.

What guides and governs collective behavior? Why do people participate in fads, and what causes mass panics? How do new social movements spread their message to others? In this chapter we will examine a number of sociological theories of collective behavior, including the emergent-norm, value-added, and assembling perspectives. We will give particular attention to certain types of collective behavior, among them crowd behavior, disaster behavior, fads and fashions, panics and crazes, rumors, public opinion, and social movements. We will also look at the role communications technology plays in collective behavior. Sociologists study collective behavior because it incorporates activities that we all engage in on a regular basis. Moreover, they acknowledge the crucial role that social movements can play in mobilizing discontented members of a society and initiating social change. In the social policy section, we will focus on the role that the social movement for lesbian and gay rights plays in promoting change. ■

THEORIES OF COLLECTIVE BEHAVIOR

In 1979, 11 rock fans died of suffocation after a crowd outside Cincinnati's Riverfront Stadium pushed to gain entrance to a concert by The Who. In 1989, when thousands of soccer fans forced their way into a stadium to see the English Cup semifinals, more than 90 people were trampled to death or smothered. In 2000, fans surged forward at a Pearl Jam concert in Denmark, killing eight men. And in 2003, 100 people died after a pyrotechnics display by Great White ignited a fire at a nightclub in West Warwick, Rhode Island. Many had watched excitedly as flames engulfed the bandstand, thinking they were part of the act.

Collective behavior is usually unstructured and spontaneous. This fluidity makes it more difficult for sociologists to generalize about people's behavior in such situations. Nevertheless, sociologists have developed various theoretical perspectives that can help us to study—and deal with in a constructive manner—crowds, riots, fads, and other types of collective behavior.

Emergent-Norm Perspective

Early writings on collective behavior imply that crowds are basically ungovernable. However, that is not always the case. In many situations, crowds are effectively governed by norms and procedures, including queuing, or waiting in line. We routinely encounter queues when we await service in a fast-food restaurant or bank, or when we enter or exit a movie theater or football stadium. Normally, physical barriers, such as guardrails and checkout counters, help to regulate queuing. When massive crowds are involved, ushers or security personnel may be present to assist in the orderly movement of the crowd. Nevertheless, there are times when such measures prove inadequate, as the examples just given and the one that follows demonstrate.

On December 28, 1991, people began gathering outside the City College gymnasium in New York City to see a heavily promoted charity basketball game featuring rap stars and other celebrities. By late afternoon, more than 5,000 people had arrived for the 6:00 P.M. game, even though the gym could accommodate only 2,730 spectators. Although the crowd was divided into separate lines for ticket holders and those wishing to buy tickets at the door, restlessness and discontent swept through both lines and sporadic fights broke out. The arrival of celebrities only added to the commotion and tension.

Doors to the gymnasium were finally opened one hour before game time, but only 50 people were admitted to the lobby at one time. Once their tickets had been taken, spectators proceeded down two flights of stairs, through a single unlocked entrance and into the gym. Those farther back in the crowd experienced the disconcerting feeling of moving forward, then stopping for a period, then repeating this process again and again. Well past the publicized starting time, huge crowds still stood outside, pressing to gain entrance to the building.

Finally, with the arena more than full, the doors to the gym were closed. As rumors spread outside the building that the game was beginning, more than 1,000 frustrated fans, many with valid tickets, poured through the glass doors into the building and headed for the stairs. Soon the stairwell became a horrifying mass of people surging against locked metal doors to the gym and crushed against concrete walls. The result was a tragedy: 9 young men and women eventually died, and 29 were injured through the sheer pressure of bodies pressing against one another and against walls and doors (Mollen 1992).

Sociologists Ralph Turner and Lewis Killian (1987) have offered a view of collective behavior that is helpful in assessing a tragic event like this one. It begins with the assumption that a large crowd, such as a group of rock or soccer fans, is governed by expectations of proper behavior just as much as four people playing doubles tennis. But during an episode of collective behavior, a definition of what behavior is appropriate or not emerges from the crowd. Turner and Killian call this view the ***emergent-norm perspective.*** Like other social norms, the emergent norm reflects shared convictions held by members of the group and is enforced through sanctions. The new norms of proper behavior

p. 67

may arise in what seem at first to be ambiguous situations. There is latitude for a wide range of acts within a general framework established by the emergent norms (for a critique of this perspective, see McPhail 1991).

Using the emergent-norm perspective, we can see that fans outside the charity basketball game at City College found themselves in an ambiguous situation. Normal procedures of crowd control, such as orderly queues, were rapidly dissolving. A new norm was simultaneously emerging: It is acceptable to push forward, even if people in front protest. Some members of the crowd—especially those with valid tickets—may have felt that their push forward was justified as a way of ensuring that they would get to see the game. Others pushed forward simply to relieve the physical pressure of those pushing behind them. Even individuals who rejected the emergent norm may have felt afraid to oppose it, fearing ridicule or injury. Thus, conforming behavior, which we usually associate with highly structured situations, was evident in this rather chaotic crowd, as it had been at the concerts by The Who, Pearl Jam, and Great White and at the soccer game in England. But it would be misleading to assume that these fans acted simply as a united, collective unit in creating a dangerous situation.

p. 172

Value-Added Perspective

Neil Smelser (1962) proposed a different sociological explanation for collective behavior. He used the ***value-added model*** to explain how broad social conditions are transformed in a definite pattern into some form of collective behavior. This model outlines six important determinants of collective behavior: structural conduciveness, structural strain, a generalized belief, a precipitating factor, mobilization for action, and the exercise of social control.

In Smelser's view, certain elements must be present for an incident of collective behavior to take place. He used the term *structural conduciveness* to indicate that the organization of society can facilitate the emergence of conflicting interests. Structural conduciveness was evident in the former East Germany in 1989, just a year before the collapse of the ruling Communist Party and the reunification of Germany. The government of East Germany was extremely unpopular, and there was growing freedom to publicly

Police arrive at a Pearl Jam concert in Roskilde, Denmark, where eight people died when the crowd surged suddenly toward the outdoor stage.

express and be exposed to new and challenging viewpoints. Such structural conduciveness makes collective behavior possible, though not inevitable.

The second determinant of collective behavior, *structural strain*, occurs when the conduciveness of the social structure to potential conflict gives way to a perception that conflicting interests do, in fact, exist. The intense desire of many East Germans to travel to or emigrate to western European countries placed great strain on the social control exercised by the Communist Party. Such structural strain contributes to what Smelser calls a *generalized belief*—a shared view of reality that redefines social action and serves to guide behavior. The overthrow of Communist rule in East Germany and other Soviet-bloc nations occurred in part as a result of a generalized belief that the Communist regimes were oppressive and that popular resistance *could* lead to social change.

Smelser suggests that a specific event or incident, known as a *precipitating factor*, triggers collective behavior. The event may grow out of the social structure, but whatever its origins, it contributes to the strains and beliefs shared by a group or community. For example, studies of race riots have found that interracial fights or arrests and searches of minority individuals by police officers often precede disturbances. The 1992 riots in South Central Los Angeles, which claimed 58 lives, were sparked by the acquittal of four White police officers charged after the videotaped beating of Rodney King, a Black construction worker.

According to Smelser, the four determinants just identified are necessary for collective behavior to occur. In addition to these factors, the group must be *mobilized for action*. An extended thundershower or severe snowstorm may preclude such mobilization. People are more likely to come together on weekends than on weekdays, and in the evening rather than during the day.

The *manner in which social control is exercised*—both formally and informally—can be significant in determining whether the preceding factors will end in collective behavior. Stated simply, social control may prevent, delay, or interrupt a collective outburst. In some instances, those using social control may be guilty of misjudgments that intensify the severity of an outbreak. Many observers believe that the Los Angeles police did not respond fast enough when the rioting began in 1992, which allowed the level of violence to escalate.

Sociologists have questioned the validity of both the emergent-norm and value-added perspectives because of their imprecise definitions and the difficulty of testing them empirically. For example, some have criticized the emergent-norm perspective for being too vague in defining what constitutes a norm; others have challenged the

value-added model for its lack of specificity in defining generalized belief and structural strain. Of these two theories, the emergent-norm perspective appears to offer a more useful explanation of societywide episodes of collective behavior, such as crazes and fashions, than the value-added approach (M. Brown and Goldin 1973; Quarantelli and Hundley 1975; K. Tierney 1980).

Smelser's value-added model, however, represents an advance over earlier theories that treated crowd behavior as being dominated by irrational, extreme impulses. The value-added approach firmly relates episodes of collective behavior to the overall social structure of a society (for a critique, see McPhail 1994).

Assembling Perspective

A series of football victory celebrations at the University of Texas that had spilled over into the main streets of Austin came under the scrutiny of sociologists (Snow et al. 1981). Some participants had actively tried to recruit passersby for the celebrations by thrusting out open

In spring 2003 antiwar protesters in London rallied against the war in Iraq. According to the assembling perspective, nonperiodic assemblies like this one are relatively spontaneous, loosely organized reactions to galvanizing events.

palms "to get five," or by yelling at drivers to honk their horns. In fact, encouraging further assembling became a preoccupation of the celebrators. Whenever spectators were absent, participants were relatively quiet. As we have seen, a key determinant of collective behavior is mobilization for action. How do people come together to undertake collective action?

Clark McPhail, perhaps the most prolific researcher of collective behavior in the last three decades, sees people and organizations consciously responding to one another's actions. Building on the interactionist approach, McPhail and Miller (1973) introduced the concept of the assembling process. In their **assembling perspective** they sought to examine how and why people move from different points in space to a common location. Before the advent of new technologies, the process of assembling for collective action was slower and more deliberate than it is today, but McPhail's approach still applies.

A basic distinction has been made between two types of assemblies. **Periodic assemblies** include recurring, relatively routine gatherings of people such as work groups, college classes, and season ticket holders in an athletic series. These assemblies are characterized by advance scheduling and recurring attendance of the majority of participants. For example, members of an introductory sociology class may gather for lectures every Monday, Wednesday, and Friday morning at 10 A.M. In contrast, **nonperiodic assemblies** include demonstrations, parades, and gatherings at the scene of fires, accidents, and arrests. Such assemblies, which result from casually transmitted information, are generally less formal than periodic assemblies. One example would be an organized rally held at Gallaudet University in 1988 to back a deaf person for president of the school for deaf students—see the photo of the campaign leaflet, right (D. L. Miller 2000).

These three approaches to collective behavior give us deeper insight into relatively spontaneous and unstructured situations. Although episodes of collective behavior may seem irrational to outsiders, norms emerge among the participants, and organized efforts are made to assemble at a certain time and place.

Gallaudet University in Washington, D.C., is the only four-year liberal arts college for deaf students in the United States. The leaflet shown here was distributed in 1988 as part of an ultimately successful effort by students, faculty, and alumni to force the board of trustees to appoint the university's first deaf president. Political demonstrations, such as the Gallaudet rally, are examples of nonperiodic assemblies (Christiansen and Barnartt 1995).

forms of collective behavior—not only fads and fashions but also crowds, disaster behavior, panics and crazes, rumors, public opinion, and social movements.

Crowds

A **crowd** is a temporary gathering of people in close proximity who share a common focus or interest. Spectators at a baseball game, participants at a pep rally, and rioters are all examples of a crowd. Sociologists have been interested in what characteristics are common to crowds. Of course, it can be difficult to generalize, since the nature of crowds varies dramatically. Think about how hostages on a hijacked airplane might feel, as opposed to participants in a religious revival.

Like other forms of collective behavior, crowds are not totally lacking in structure. Even during riots, participants are governed by identifiable social norms and

FORMS OF COLLECTIVE BEHAVIOR

Do you remember the Ninja Turtles? Did you collect Beanie Babies or Power Ranger toys when you were young? Any grunge clothes or tube tops lurking in your closet? These are all fads and fashions that depend on collective behavior. Using the emergent-norm, value-added, and assembling perspectives along with other aspects of sociological study, sociologists have investigated many exhibit definite patterns of behavior. Sociologists Richard Berk and Howard Aldrich (1972) analyzed patterns of vandalism in 15 cities in the United States during the riots of the 1960s. They found that the stores of merchants who were perceived as exploitative were likely to be attacked, while private homes and public agencies with positive reputations were more likely to be spared. Apparently, looters had reached a collective agreement as to what constituted a "proper" or "improper" target for destruction. Today, this type of information can be shared instantly via text messaging.

The emergent-norm perspective suggests that during urban rioting a new social norm that basically condones looting is accepted, at least temporarily. The norms of respect for private property—as well as norms involving obedience to the law—are replaced by a concept of all goods being community property. All desirable items, including those behind locked doors, can be used for the "general welfare." In effect, the emergent norm allows looters to take what they regard as properly theirs—a scenario that was played out in Baghdad after the collapse of Saddam Hussein's regime in 2003. Yet not everyone participates in the free-for-all. Typically, most community residents reject the new norm, and either stand by passively or attempt to stop the wholesale theft (Couch 1968; Quarantelli and Dynes 1970; see also McPhail 1991, 2003).

Disaster Behavior

Newspapers, television reports, and even rumors bring word of many disasters around the world. The term **disaster** refers to a sudden or disruptive event or set of events that overtaxes a community's resources, so that outside aid is necessary. Traditionally, disasters have been catastrophes related to nature, such as earthquakes, floods, and fires. Yet in an industrial age, natural disasters have been joined by such "technological disasters" as airplane crashes, industrial explosions, nuclear meltdowns, and massive chemical poisonings. The distinction between the two types of disaster is not clear-cut, however. As environmentalists have observed, many human practices either contribute to or trigger natural disasters. Building in flood plains, clear-cutting forests, and erecting rigid structures in earthquake zones all create the potential for disaster (Abramovitz 2001a, 2001b).

Disaster Research

Sociologists have made enormous strides in disaster research, despite the problems inherent in this type of investigation. The work of the Disaster Research Center at the University of Delaware has been especially important. The center has teams of trained researchers prepared to leave for the site of any disaster on four hours' notice. Their field kits include identification material, recording equipment, and interview guidelines for use in various types of disasters. En route to the scene, these researchers try to become informed about the conditions they may encounter. Upon arrival, they establish a communication post to coordinate fieldwork and maintain contact with the center's headquarters.

Since its founding in 1963, the Disaster Research Center has conducted about 600 field studies of natural and technological disasters in the United States, as well as in other nations. Its research has been used to develop effective planning in such areas as delivery of emergency health care, establishment and operation of rumor-control centers, coordination of mental health services after disasters, and implementation of disaster-preparedness and emergency-response programs. The center has also provided training and field research for graduate students, who maintain a professional commitment to disaster research and often go on to work for disaster service organizations such as the Red Cross and civil defense agencies (Disaster Research Center 2003).

Case Study: Collapse of the World Trade Center

The September 11, 2001, terrorist attacks on the Pentagon and New York City's World Trade Center caused the largest civilian death toll of any single day in U.S. history, along with billions of dollars' worth of property damage. As striking as these losses were, however, the public response to the disaster was equally dramatic. The evacuation from the buildings was remarkably orderly, saving thousands of lives. In fact, many of the lifesaving steps that were taken immediately after the terrorist attacks were the outcome of research done after the explosion of a car bomb at the World Trade Center in 1993 (Murphy and Levy 2001).

Researchers have found that disasters are often followed by the creation of an emergency operations group, which coordinates both public services and some private-sector services, such as food distribution. Decision making becomes more centralized during these periods than it is in normal times. Such was the case on September 11, 2001. New York City's well-designed Emergency Management Center, located in the World Trade Center, was destroyed when the building collapsed and all power at nearby City Hall was cut off. Yet within hours, both an incident command post and a new emergency operations center had been established to direct the search and recovery effort at the 16-acre disaster site. Shortly thereafter came a victims' center, information kiosks, and an office for issuing death certificates, staffed around the clock by counselors, as well as facilities for serving meals to rescue

When a terrorist attack destroyed New York City's emergency command center, officials quickly set up a new one to direct the search and recovery effort. Even in times of unimaginable disaster, people respond in predictable ways.

workers. To identify potential hazards to rescuers and survey what had become a gigantic crime scene, police and public safety officials turned to computer maps and aerial photographs. They also designated places where victims could be identified, human resource functions relocated, and charitable contributions collected (Wachtendorf 2002).

Disaster research has shown that even in natural calamities, maintaining and restoring communications is vital not just to directing relief efforts, but to reducing survivors' anxiety. On September 11, most cell phones in Manhattan were rendered useless by the destruction of communications towers and relay stations. To contact loved ones or to plan their escape from a city clogged with emergency vehicles, people stood in line at pay phones. In the days to follow, families seeking information about their loved ones posted fliers at makeshift information centers. Even in the aftermath of an unimaginable disaster, people and organizations responded in predictable ways (Dreifus 2003).

Fads and Fashions

An almost endless list of objects and behavior patterns seems temporarily to catch the fancy of adults and children. Think about Silly Putty, Hula Hoops, the Rubik's Cube, break dancing, *The Simpsons* T-shirts, Nintendo games, and mosh pits. Fads and fashions are sudden movements toward the acceptance of some lifestyle or particular taste in clothing, music, or recreation (Aguirre et al. 1988; R. Johnson 1985).

Fads are temporary patterns of behavior involving large numbers of people; they spring up independently of preceding trends and do not give rise to successors. In contrast, ***fashions*** are pleasurable mass involvements that feature a certain amount of acceptance by society and have a line of historical continuity (J. Lofland 1981, 1985). Thus, punk haircuts would be considered a fashion, part of the constantly changing standards of hair length and style, whereas dancing to the Macarena would be considered a fad of the mid-1990s.

Typically, when people think of *fashions,* they think of clothing, particularly women's clothing. In reality, fads and fashions enter every aspect of life in which choices are not dictated by sheer necessity—vehicles, sports, music, drama, beverages, art, and even the selection of pets.

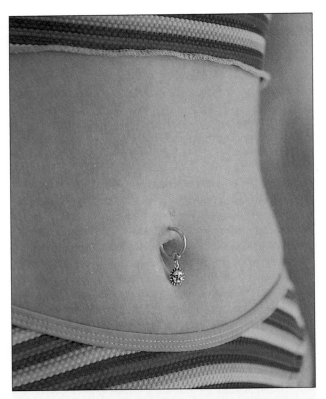

Navel rings can be thought of as a fashion, a new form of body adornment.

Any area of our lives that is subject to continuing change is open to fads and fashions. There is a clear commercial motive behind these norms of collective behavior. For example, in about seven months of 1955, retailers sold over $100 million of Davy Crockett items (worth over $700 million in 2002 dollars), including coonskin caps, toy rifles, knives, camping gear, cameras, and jigsaw puzzles. In 1999 Nintendo took in $5 billion from sales of Pokémon paraphernalia, ranging from virtual pets to compact discs (S. King 1999).

Fads and fashions allow people to identify with something different from the dominant institutions and symbols of a culture. Members of a subculture can break with tradition while remaining "in" with a significant reference group of peers. Fads are generally short-lived and tend to be viewed with amusement or lack of interest by most nonparticipants. Fashions, in contrast, often have wider implications, because they can reflect (or give the impression of) wealth and status.

Panics and Crazes

Panics and crazes both represent responses to some generalized belief. A *craze* is an exciting mass involvement that lasts for a relatively long period (J. Lofland 1981, 1985). For example, in late 1973, a press release from a Wisconsin congressman described how the federal bureaucracy had failed to contract for enough toilet paper for government buildings. Then, on December 19, as part of his nightly monologue, *Tonight Show* host Johnny Carson suggested that it would not be strange if the entire nation experienced a shortage of toilet paper. Millions of people took his humorous comment seriously and immediately began stockpiling the item out of fear that it would soon be unavailable. Shortly thereafter, as a consequence of this craze, a shortage of toilet paper actually did occur. Its effects were felt into 1974 (Malcolm 1974; *Money* 1987).

In contrast, a *panic* is a fearful arousal or collective flight based on a generalized belief that may or may not be accurate. In a panic, people commonly think there is insufficient time or inadequate means to avoid injury. Panics often occur on battlefields, in overcrowded burning buildings, or during stock market crashes. The key distinction between panics and crazes is that panics are flights *from* something, whereas crazes are movements *to* something.

One of the most famous cases of panic in the United States was touched off by a media event: the 1938 Halloween eve radio dramatization of H. G. Wells's science fiction novel *The War of the Worlds*. This broadcast told realistically of an invasion from Mars, with interplanetary visitors landing in northern New Jersey and taking over New York City 15 minutes later. The announcer indicated at the beginning of the broadcast that the account was fictional, but about 80 percent of the listeners tuned in late. Many became frightened by what they assumed to be a news report.

Some accounts have exaggerated the extent of people's reactions to *The War of the Worlds*. One report concluded that "people all over the United States were praying, crying, fleeing frantically to escape death from the Martians." In contrast, a CBS national survey of listeners found that only 20 percent were genuinely scared by the broadcast. Although perhaps a million people *reacted* to the program, many reacted by switching to other stations to see if the "news" was being carried elsewhere. This "invasion from outer space" set off a limited panic rather than mass hysteria (Roger Brown 1954; Cantril 1940; Houseman 1972).

It is often believed that people who are engaged in panics or crazes are unaware of their actions, but that is certainly not the case. As the emergent-norm perspective suggests, people take cues from one another as to how to act during such forms of collective behavior. Even in the midst of an escape from a life-threatening situation, such as a fire in a crowded theater, people do not tend to run in a headlong stampede. Rather, they adjust their behavior on the basis of the perceived circumstances and the conduct of others who are assembling in a given location. To outside observers studying the events, people's decisions may seem foolish (pushing against a locked door) or suicidal (jumping from a balcony). Yet for that individual at that moment, the action may genuinely seem appropriate—or the only desperate choice available (Clarke 2002; Quarantelli 1957).

Rumors

The e-mail carried the subject line "Travelers Beware!" Its message was to warn those planning to go to Mardi Gras in New Orleans in 1997 that a highly organized crime ring there was drugging tourists, removing organs from their bodies, and selling them on the black market. The rumor circulated the country via e-mail and fax, causing an avalanche of calls to the New Orleans Police Department. Of course, an investigation turned up absolutely no evidence of an organ-snatching ring. The department finally set up a website to squash the rumors.

New Orleans wasn't the first city to be struck with this rumor. Similar stories targeted visitors to Houston and Las Vegas. It was said that a visitor to Las Vegas woke up one morning in a bathtub full of ice minus one kidney. Some version of the organ-snatching tale has swept through numerous countries, repeated by thousands of people. No one has ever been able to verify the story or to offer proof of its truth (Emery 1997).

Not all rumors we hear are as astonishing as the one about kidney snatchers. But none of us is immune to hearing or starting rumors. A *rumor* is a piece of information gathered informally that is used to interpret an ambiguous situation. Rumors serve a function by providing a group with a shared belief. As a group strives for consensus, members eliminate those rumors that are least useful or credible. Sociologist Tamotsu Shibutani (1966) sees this process as being akin to the survival of the fittest or strongest rumor. Rumors are also a means of adapting to change. If a business is about to be taken over by another firm, rumors will usually abound as to the significance the move will have for personnel. Gradually, such rumors are either verified or discarded, but the very exchange of rumors allows people to cope with changes over which they have little control. Scary rumors probably spread the fastest, because fear induces stress and stress is reduced by sharing the fear with others. Moreover, some people enjoy provoking fear in others (Berk 1974; Emery 1997; Rosnow and Fine 1976).

The attack on the Pentagon and the World Trade Center produced a flurry of rumors. According to one false account, a police officer "surfed" a steel beam down 86 floors as one of the towers collapsed. Given the role of the media in covering the event, many rumors centered on them. For example, one rumor suggested that a CNN film of Palestinians dancing in the streets after the attack was actually file footage photographed during the Gulf War. In Pakistan, rumors spread that the vivid photos of the hijacked planes crashing into the World Trade Center had actually been staged. Like these examples, rumors often reinforce people's ideologies and their suspicion of the mass media.

Publics and Public Opinion

The least organized and most individualized form of collective behavior is the public. The term *public* refers to a dispersed group of people, not necessarily in contact with one another, who share an interest in an issue. As the term is used in the study of collective behavior, the public does not include everyone. Rather, it is a collective of people who focus on some issue, engage in discussion, agree or disagree, and sometimes dissolve when the issue has been decided (Blumer 1955, 1969; R. Turner and Killian 1987).

The term *public opinion* refers to expressions of attitudes on matters of public policy that are communicated to decision makers. The last part of this definition is particularly important. Theorists of collective behavior see no public opinion without both a public and a decision maker. In studying public opinion, we are not concerned with the formation of an *individual's* attitudes on social and political issues. Instead, we focus on the ways

in which a public's attitudes are communicated to decision makers and on the ultimate outcome of the public's attempts to influence policymaking (R. Turner and Killian 1987).

Polls and surveys play a major role in assessing public opinion. Using the techniques for developing reliable questionnaire and interview schedules, survey specialists conduct studies of public opinion for business firms (market analyses), the government, the mass media (program ratings), and of course, politicians. Survey data have become extremely influential not only in preselecting the products we buy but in determining which political candidates are likely to win election and even which potential Supreme Court nominees should be selected (Brower 1988).

p. 36

Today's political polls are well-constructed surveys based on representative sampling techniques. As a result, their projections of presidential elections often fall within a few percentage points of the actual vote. The "too close to call" projection in the 2000 Bush–Gore–Nader presidential race was quite correct, as the Florida recount proved. In 1996, all eight national polling services accurately predicted that Bill Clinton would win 49 percent of the popular vote, and the Reuters/Zogby poll was exactly on the mark in its prediction of the votes for Clinton, Republican challenger Bob Dole, and independent candidate Ross Perot (Kagay 1996; Mitofsky 1998; Norman 1996).

In marked contrast to these polls, some surveys are downright misleading. Telephone companies have marketed call-in "polls" using 1-900 numbers. Television viewers or newspaper readers are asked to call one number to register an opinion on an issue, or a second number to register an alternative opinion. There are many problems inherent in this type of "polling." The sample that emerges is hardly representative, since it includes only those people who happened to see the commercial or advertisement for the poll and who felt strongly enough about the issue to spend the typical charge of $1 for a 1-900 call.

p. 33

Social Movements

Social movements are the most all-encompassing type of collective behavior, because they may include aspects of other types such as crowds, rumors, publics, and public opinion. Although such factors as physical environment, population, technology, and social inequality serve as sources of change, it is the *collective* effort of individuals organized in social movements that ultimately leads to change.

Sociologists use the term *social movements* to refer to organized collective activities to bring about or resist

Two views on abortion in France: Top, members of the pro-choice movement take to the streets. One sign states "A child if I want it, when I want it." Bottom, a member of the pro-life movement wears a T-shirt that states "To abort is to kill."

Members of each social movement stepped outside traditional channels for bringing about social change and yet had a noticeable influence on public policy. Equally dramatic collective efforts in Eastern Europe helped to topple Communist regimes in a largely peaceful manner, in nations that many observers had felt were "immune" to such social change (Ramet 1991).

Social movements imply the existence of conflict, but we can also analyze their activities from a functionalist perspective. Even when unsuccessful, social movements contribute to the formation of public opinion. Initially, the ideas of Margaret Sanger and other early advocates of birth control were viewed as radical, yet contraceptives are now widely available in the United States. Moreover, functionalists view social movements as training grounds for leaders of the political establishment. Such heads of state as Cuba's Fidel Castro and South Africa's Nelson Mandela came to power after serving as leaders of revolutionary movements. Poland's Lech Walesa, Russia's Boris Yeltsin, and the Czech playwright Vaclav Havel all led protest movements against Communist rule and subsequently became leaders of their countries' governments.

How and why do social movements emerge? Obviously, people are often discontented with the way things are. But what causes them to organize at a particular moment in a collective effort to effect change? Sociologists rely on two explanations for why people mobilize: the relative-deprivation and resource-mobilization approaches.

Relative Deprivation

Those members of a society who feel most frustrated and disgruntled by social and economic conditions are not necessarily worst off in an objective sense. Social scientists have long recognized that what is most significant is how people *perceive* their situation. As Karl Marx pointed out, although the misery of the workers was important to

fundamental change in an existing group or society (Benford 1992). Herbert Blumer (1955:19) recognized the special importance of social movements when he defined them as "collective enterprises to establish a new order of life."

In many nations, including the United States, social movements have had a dramatic impact on the course of history and the evolution of the social structure. Consider the actions of abolitionists, suffragists, civil rights workers, and activists opposed to the war in Vietnam.

their perception of their oppressed state, so was their position *relative* to the capitalist ruling class (Marx and Engels [1847] 1955).

The term ***relative deprivation*** is defined as the conscious feeling of a negative discrepancy between legitimate expectations and present actualities (John Wilson 1973). In other words, things aren't as good as you hoped they would be. Such a state may be characterized by scarcity rather than a complete lack of necessities (as we saw in the distinction between absolute and relative poverty in Chapter 9). A relatively deprived person is dissatisfied because he or she feels downtrodden relative to some appropriate reference group. Thus, blue-collar workers who live in two-family houses on small plots of land—though hardly at the bottom of the economic ladder—may nevertheless feel deprived in comparison to corporate managers and professionals who live in lavish homes in exclusive suburbs.

In addition to the feeling of relative deprivation, two other elements must be present before discontent will be channeled into a social movement. People must feel that they have a *right* to their goals, that they deserve better than what they have. For example, the [p. 229] struggle against European colonialism in Africa intensified when growing numbers of Africans decided that it was legitimate for them to have political and economic independence. At the same time, the disadvantaged group must perceive that it cannot attain its goals through conventional means. This belief may or may not be correct. Whichever is the case, the group will not mobilize into a social movement unless there is a shared perception that members can end their relative deprivation only through collective action (Morrison 1971).

Critics of this approach have noted that people don't need to feel deprived to be moved to act. In addition, this approach fails to explain why certain feelings of deprivation are transformed into social movements, whereas in other similar situations, no collective effort is made to reshape society. Consequently, in recent years, sociologists have paid increasing attention to the forces needed to bring about the emergence of social movements (Alain 1985; Finkel and Rule 1987; Orum 1989).

Resource Mobilization

It takes more than desire to start a social movement. It helps to have money, political influence, access to the media, and personnel. The term ***resource mobilization*** refers to the ways in which a social movement utilizes such resources. The success of a movement for change will depend in good part on what resources it has and how effectively it mobilizes them (see also Gamson 1989; Staggenborg 1989a, 1989b).

Sociologist Anthony Oberschall (1973:199) has argued that to sustain social protest or resistance, there must be an "organizational base and continuity of leadership." As people become part of a social movement, norms develop to guide their behavior. Members of the movement may be expected to attend regular meetings of organizations, pay dues, recruit new adherents, and boycott "enemy" products or speakers. An emerging social movement may give rise to special language or new words for familiar terms. In recent years, social movements have been responsible for such new terms of self-reference as *Blacks* and *African Americans* (used to replace *Negroes*), *senior citizens* (used to replace *old folks*), *gays* (used to replace *homosexuals*), and *people with disabilities* (used to replace *the handicapped*).

Leadership is a central factor in the mobilization of the discontented into social movements. Often, a movement will be led by a charismatic figure, such as Dr. Martin Luther King Jr. As Max Weber described it in 1904, [p. 399] *charisma* is that quality of an individual that sets him or her apart from ordinary people. Of course, charisma can fade abruptly, which helps to account for the fragility of certain social movements (Morris 2000).

Yet many social movements do persist over long periods because their leadership is well organized and ongoing. Ironically, as Robert Michels (1915) noted, political movements that are fighting for social change eventually take on some of the aspects of bureaucracy that they were organized to protest. Leaders tend to dominate the decision-making process without directly consulting followers. The bureaucratization of social movements is not inevitable, however. More radical movements that advocate major structural change in society and embrace mass actions tend not to be hierarchical or bureaucratic (Fitzgerald and Rodgers 2000).

Why do certain individuals join a social movement while others who are in similar situations do not? Some [p. 203] of them are recruited to join. Karl Marx recognized the importance of recruitment when he called on workers to become *aware* of their oppressed status and to develop a class consciousness. Like theorists of the resource-mobilization approach, Marx held that a social movement (specifically, the revolt of the proletariat) would require leaders to sharpen the awareness of the oppressed. They would need to help workers to overcome feelings of ***false consciousness,*** or attitudes that do not reflect workers' objective position, in order to organize a revolutionary movement. Similarly, one of the challenges faced by women's liberation activists of the late 1960s and early 1970s was to convince women that they were being deprived of their rights and of socially valued resources.

aped to the sidewalks and the walls outside classrooms, flyers urged students to join the protest. Soon large groups had gathered at the appointed place, shouting their anger at the government as campus police eyed them nervously. The 1960s? It could have been, but it was 2003. On hundreds of campuses around the United States, students were voicing their opposition to the war in Iraq.

On most campuses, such student activism was a relatively recent development. In the 1990s, observers had noted student apathy toward politics, except for highly local issues such as campus housing policy or financial aid requirements. But gradually, student sentiment had manifested itself in protests against the sweatshop labor used to make the shirts and caps that bore school logos. When U.S. diplomats began to put together a coalition of nations willing to invade Iraq, students organized to question the basis for the action.

Student protests weren't as numerous as those that had occurred during the war in Vietnam, nor as long-lasting. And unlike the protests in the 1960s, the 2003 protests did not necessarily originate with students. Instead, calls to demonstrate and speak out came first from off-campus peace activists.

Most significant, the 2003 protests featured some unprecedented role reversals. Many faculty who had been shaped as students by the movement against war in Vietnam took a strong public stand against war in Iraq. Their students, still

> On campuses such as Brandeis and Yale, some demonstrations were pro-war.

traumatized by the terrorist attacks of September 11, 2001, and not subject themselves to the draft as an earlier generation had been, were less apt to protest. So on campuses such as Brandeis and Yale, some demonstrations were pro-war.

Another difference from the 1960s protests was the reaction of campus officials. In the 1980s, many universities had created "free-speech zones" to contain political demonstrations and prevent

them from interrupting classes. In effect, these zones had limited the constitutional right to free speech to a few small areas on campus, banning students from speaking out everywhere else. But as student protesters geared up in 2003, many colleges dropped the hated restrictions, allowing demonstrations to proceed unhampered by police. Administrators too, it seemed, had learned some lessons from the war in Vietnam.

Let's Discuss

1. Have you ever witnessed a student-led protest in your high school or college? If so, what issues sparked the protest, and how did school administrators respond?

2. Suppose that in 2003 college administrators had attempted to prohibit students from organizing and speaking out against the war. As a practical matter (not a legal one), could such a policy have been easily enforced? What circumstances might make present-day protest movements harder to contain than protest movements of the past?

Sources: Colapinto 2003; Sharp 2002; Zernike 2003.

Even in movements that arise virtually overnight in response to events such as an unpopular war, recruiters play a part. During the 2003 war in Iraq, outside organizers helped to galvanize student protests (see Box 22-1).

Gender and Social Movements

Sociologists point out that gender is an important element in understanding social movements. In our male-dominated society, women find it more difficult than men to assume leadership positions in social movement organizations. While women often serve disproportionately as volunteers in these movements, their work is not always recognized, nor are their voices as easily heard as men's. Moreover, gender bias causes the real extent of women's influence to be overlooked. Traditional examination of the sociopolitical system tends to focus on such

male-dominated corridors of power as legislatures and corporate boardrooms, to the neglect of more female-dominated domains such as households, community-based groups, and faith-based networks. But efforts to influence family values, child rearing, relationships between parents and schools, and spiritual values are clearly significant to a culture and society (Ferree and Merrill 2000; Noonan 1995).

Scholars of social movements now realize that gender can affect even the way we view organized efforts to bring about or resist change. For example, an emphasis on using rationality and cold logic to achieve goals helps to obscure the importance of passion and emotion in successful social movements. It would be difficult to find any movement—from labor battles to voting rights to animal rights—in which passion was not part of the consensus-building force. Yet calls for a more serious study of the role of emotion are frequently seen as applying only to the women's movement, because emotion is traditionally thought of as being feminine (Ferree and Merrill 2000; Taylor 1995).

New Social Movements

Beginning in the late 1960s, European social scientists observed a change in both the composition and the targets of emerging social movements. Previously, traditional social movements had focused on economic issues, often led by people who shared the same occupation or by labor unions. However, many social movements that have become active in recent decades—including the contemporary women's movement, the peace movement, and the environmental movement—do not have the social class roots typical of the labor protests in the United States and Europe over the past century (Tilly 1993).

The term **new social movements** refers to organized collective activities that address values and social identities as well as improvements in the quality of life. These movements may be involved in developing collective identities. Many have complex agendas that go beyond a single issue, and even cross national boundaries. Educated, middle-class people are significantly represented in some of these new social movements, such as the women's movement and the movement for lesbian and

Workers, many of them children, toil in a makeshift cigarette factory in Bangladesh. New social movement theory offers a broad, global perspective on social and political activism, including efforts to deal with the exploitation of child labor in developing nations.

gay rights. Box 22-2 (page 518) describes a new social movement among exploited textile workers in India.

New social movements generally do not view government as their ally in the struggle for a better society. While they typically do not seek to overthrow the government, they may criticize, protest, or harass public officials. Researchers have found that members of new social movements show little inclination to accept established authority, even scientific or technical authority. This characteristic is especially evident in the environmental and anti–nuclear power movements, whose activists present their own experts to counter those of government or big business (Garner 1996; Polletta and Jasper 2001; A. Scott 1990).

The environmental movement is one of many new movements with a worldwide focus. In their efforts to reduce air and water pollution, curtail global warming, and protect endangered animal species, environmental activists have realized that strong regulatory measures within a single country are not sufficient. Similarly, labor union leaders and human rights advocates cannot adequately address exploitative sweatshop conditions in a developing country if a multinational corporation can simply move the factory to another country, where workers earn even less. Whereas traditional views of social movements tended to emphasize resource mobilization on a local level, new social movement theory offers a broader, global perspective on social and political activism.

Table 22-1 summarizes the sociological approaches that have contributed to social movement theory. Each approach has added to our understanding of the development of social movements.

Table 22-1	Contributions to Social Movement Theory
Approach	**Emphasis**
Value-added model	Structural strains and generalized beliefs help to mobilize people for action.
Assembling perspective	Gatherings at social events follow predictable patterns of social behavior.
Relative deprivation approach	Social movements are especially likely to arise when rising expectations are frustrated.
Resource mobilization approach	The success of social movements depends on which resources are available and how effectively they are used.
New social movement theory	Social movements arise when people are motivated by value issues and social identity questions.

In the mid-1980s, 5,000 striking textile workers came home from Bombay to mobilize support in their rural villages and gather food for strikers in the city. As the strike wore on, some remained in their villages and sought employment on governmental drought-relief projects. However, there weren't enough jobs for rural residents, much less for these new migrants from Bombay.

This experience was the origin of a new social movement in rural India. With unemployment threatening an expanded population in rural areas, activists formed what came to be called *Shoshit, Shetkari, Kashtakari, Kamgar, Mukti Sangharsh (SSKKMS)*, which means "exploited peasants, toilers, workers liberation struggle." The initial goal of the movement was to provide drought relief for villagers, but the deeper goal was to bring more power to the rural areas.

The SSKKMS was unusual compared to other social movements in India: about half its participants and many of its leaders were women. This was no accident, for the movement also sought to address gender inequities. At a meeting in 1986, Indutai Patankar—a pioneer in the rural women's movement—declared:

> We have gathered here to discuss our problems as women and a rural poor. . . . Not only do we work twice as hard as men but

we also do not get equal wages, no child care. . . . We have to organize as women with the other oppressed toilers in urban and rural areas (Desai 1996:214).

Women and men from the movement were equally involved in many forms of political activism, including such direct-action tactics as roadblocks.

In addition to addressing issues of gender stratification, the SSKKMS openly confronted the pervasive inequities asso-

> The initial goal of the movement was to provide drought relief for villagers, but the deeper goal was to bring more power to the rural areas.

ciated with the *dalit,* or oppressed people from lower castes (previously called untouchables). Movement activists insisted that both women and landless peasants (most of whom were *dalits*) should have equal access to water once dams were completed. This is a critical issue in the lives of rural Indian women, who typically spend many hours a day in search of good drinking water.

In her analysis of the SSKKMS, sociologist Manisha Desai (1996) emphasizes

that the movement does not have a single focus, but is committed to multiple struggles for social and economic justice. Desai views the SSKKMS as an example of a new social movement because it incorporates concrete, material targets as well as broad ideological goals.

As with any social movement, there are contradictions in the SSKKMS. A middle-class leadership core generally articulates goals for the many exploited villagers in this mass movement. While in one rural area all local assemblies must be at least 30 percent female—a goal rarely achieved in the United States—rural women sometimes serve simply as fronts for the hidden agendas of their male relatives. Nevertheless, Desai's study of the SSKKMS underscores the fact that social movements in general—and new social movements in particular—are found *throughout* the world, not solely in industrialized nations.

Let's Discuss

1. Why do you think so many women participated in the SSKKMS? Describe their goals.
2. What would happen if "powerless" people in the United States formed a similar movement? Would it succeed? Why or why not?

 Use Your Sociological Imagination

Try to imagine a society without any social movements. Under what conditions could such a society exist? Would you want to live in it?

COMMUNICATIONS TECHNOLOGY AND COLLECTIVE BEHAVIOR

Many of the examples that we have used to illustrate collective behavior reflect the impact of communications technology—from radio broadcasts proclaiming that

Martians have landed to the use of text messaging to organize impromptu political protests. Mobile communications devices are only the latest innovation in a wave of new communications technology that has transformed collective behavior.

How might some of the theoretical perspectives we examined earlier in this chapter apply to technology's role in collective behavior? Although Neil Smelser's value-added perspective did not explicitly refer to communications technology, its emphasis on people needing to be mobilized for action takes on new meaning today with text messaging and the Internet. With relatively little effort and expense, we can now reach a large number of people in a short period. Looking at the new technology from the assembling perspective, we could consider the Internet's listservs and chatrooms as examples of nonperiodic assemblies. Without face-to-face contact or even simultaneous interaction, people can develop an identity with a large collective of like-minded people via the Internet (Calhoun 1998).

Sociologists are only beginning to consider the impact of the latest technology on various forms of collective behavior. Technology clearly plays a role in disaster research; moreover, a large number of disasters today are technological in origin. A content analysis of the coverage of disasters by *Time* magazine showed that about 40 percent were technological and 60 percent natural during the 1990s (Bernhardt 1997). (We will consider technological accidents in greater detail in the next chapter.)

We have seen that rumors fly on the Internet. One click of the Send button can forward a message to every person in an address book. Multiply this potential by the millions of e-mail account holders to get an idea of the reach of the Internet in distributing rumors. We have seen, too, how Internet rumors can stir panics. In the same way, people can be exposed almost instantly to the latest crazes, fads, and fashions. And people are constantly being encouraged to call a telephone number or log on to a website to register their public opinion on some policy issue.

Can one be part of a "crowd" via the new communications technology? Television and the Internet, as contrasted with books and newspapers, often convey a false sense of intimacy reinforced by immediacy. We seem to be personally hurt by the death of Princess Diana or moved by the troubles of the Kennedy family. Therefore, the latest technology brings us together to act and to react in an electronic global village (Garner 1999).

This sense of online togetherness extends to social movements, which more and more are being mounted on the web. Through the instantaneous communication that is possible over the Internet, Mexican Zapatistas can transform their cause into an international lobbying effort, and Greenpeace organizers can link environmental activists throughout the world. Sociologists have begun to call such electronic enhancement of established social movements *computer-mediated communication (CMC)*. Elecronic communication strengthens a group's solidarity, allowing fledgling social movements to grow and develop faster than they might otherwise. Thus the face-to-face contact that once was critical to a social movement is no longer necessary (Castells 1996; Diani 2000).

The new communications technology also helps to create enclaves of similarly minded people. Websites are not just autonomous and independent; they are interconnected through a global electronic network. One website, in turn, lists a variety of other sites that serve as links. For example, seeking out information on domestic partnerships may lead you to an electronic enclave that is supportive of cohabitation between men and women, or alternatively to an enclave that is supportive of gay and lesbian couples. New developments in communications technology have clearly broadened the way we interact with one another (Calhoun 1998).

| **SOCIAL POLICY and SOCIAL MOVEMENTS** | Lesbian and Gay Rights | |

The Issue

Despite the large numbers of lesbians and gay men in the United States and around the world, in many societies homosexuality continues to function as a master status that carries a stigma. Amnesty International (1994) published a pioneering report showing that lesbians and gay men suffer from governmental persecution in many parts of the world. In response to such discrimination, a social movement for lesbian and gay rights has emerged across the United States and in many other nations. This movement is putting pressure on policymakers to pass legislation establishing and protecting gay and lesbian rights.

The Setting

The first social movement to advance the civil rights of lesbians and gay men was founded in Germany in 1897 by physician Magnus Hirschfeld and others. The Scientific-Humanitarian Committee fought to abolish legal penalties against homosexual behavior and to educate people about gay rights and women's rights. The committee was eventually crushed by the Nazis in 1933; subsequently, at least 10,000 to 20,000 people identified as homosexuals died in Nazi concentration camps. As a result, one cherished symbol of contemporary gay activists—worn on buttons and patches—is a pink triangle, the very emblem gay prisoners were forced to

Lesbian and gay activism is not confined to large cities like New York and San Francisco. It shows up in diverse communities across the nation, as indicated by the outreach effort of these members of the University of South Dakota's Gay, Lesbian, and Bisexual Alliance.

wear by the Nazis (Lauritsen and Thorstad 1974; Plant 1986).

In the United States, the first homosexual organization was founded in Chicago in 1924, and a number of gay and lesbian groups came into existence in the 1950s. Experience in early gay rights groups gave activists greater organizing ability—an important component of resource mobilization. In addition, their involvement in other social movements of the 1950s and 1960s, such as those for civil rights, against the war in Vietnam, and for women's liberation, had a spillover effect. Many lesbians and gay men were forced to reflect more directly on their own oppression (J. Katz 1992).

Building on earlier homosexual activism and on the growth of lesbian and gay male subcultures in major cities, the contemporary gay movement began publicly in New York City. On June 28, 1969, police raided the Stonewall Inn, an after-hours gay bar, and forced patrons onto the street. But instead of dispersing, the patrons locked police inside the bar and rioted until official reinforcements arrived. For the next three nights, lesbians and gay men marched through the streets of New York, protesting police raids and other forms of discrimination. Within months, gay liberation groups had appeared in cities and on campuses throughout the United States; within two years, similar organizations were evident in Canada, Great Britain, various western European countries, and Australia (B. Adam 1995; B. Adam et al. 1999; Garner 1996).

While many voluntary associations that support lesbian and gay rights are primarily local in focus, a growing number of national organizations address gay issues. In addition, self-help groups—especially in the gay communities of major cities—have been established in response to the AIDS crisis, to care for the sick, educate the healthy, and lobby for more responsive public policies. The most outspoken AIDS activist group has been ACT-UP, which has conducted controversial protests and sit-ins in the halls of government and at scientific conferences. In the view of sociologist Barry Adam (1995), while the rise of such self-help and AIDS activist groups has siphoned away many leaders and participants from gay rights organizations, the broad reach of the AIDS crisis has mobilized new constituencies of gay men and their friends and relatives into AIDS and gay activism.

p. 119

In the private sector, progress in alleviating discrimination has been uneven. Nine out of 10 of the largest Fortune 500 companies in the United States now have rules barring discrimination against gay employees. However, those rules usually do not require the extension of medical benefits to partners of gay employees. Sometimes these corporations can take a step backward. The one major corporation that does not ban discrimination against gays is ExxonMobil. Mobil Corporation once had an antidiscrimination policy that provided full medical benefits to the partners of gay employees. But when Mobil was acquired by Exxon in 1999, the policy was revoked (Kershaw 2003).

Sociological Insights

In 2003, by a 6–3 vote, the Supreme Court reversed a 1986 decision and ruled that laws prohibiting homosexual relations between consenting adults were an unconstitutional invasion of privacy. At the time of the historic ruling, 13 states had such laws on the books. Although they were rarely enforced, the laws had served to stigmatize gay people everywhere, adding the threat of criminal sanctions to the prejudice and widespread discrimination gays suffered. Viewed from a conflict perspective, the dominant ideology encourages such prejudice and discrimination by emphasizing narrow stereotypes and excluding positive images of lesbians and gay men from the media. Despite such biased portrayals, views of gays and lesbians have grown more positive in recent years; see Figure 22-1 (Greenburg 2003).

By the 1990s, lesbian and gay male activists had recognized that encouraging people to "come out" could help to illustrate the diversity of gay life and assist resource mobilization. Many lesbians and gay men had long felt the need to conceal their identities (remain "in the closet") out of fear that they might lose their jobs, be cut off from their families, or fall victim to hate crimes (see Chapter 11). However, the gay movement has given many individuals the support and strength to "come out" and assert their identities publicly and proudly—as new social movements frequently do for those who are challenging dominant social norms.

Among the many lesbian, gay, and bisexual organizations in the United States and Canada, there are gay sports leagues and singing groups; professional associations, such as those for gay doctors and teachers; campus lesbian and gay male organizations; and groups of African American, Asian American, and Latino gays, some of whom have challenged White domination of the lesbian and gay movement (Brelin 1996:34; Tom Lee 2000).

Like all social movements, the movement on behalf of gay and lesbian rights is not unified. Many in the movement see the emphasis on legalizing homosexual marriages as assimilationist. The ideal of sexual fidelity, these critics contend, mimics the heterosexual ideal of monogamy, which is widely violated. According to this view, the recognition of gay rights regardless of one's lifestyle is the only worthy goal (Hequembourg and Arditi 1999; Werum and Winders 2001).

Policy Initiatives

Beginning in the 1990s, opponents of lesbian and gay rights focused on statewide ballot initiatives as a key tactic. In most cases, gay rights supporters have won nar-

FIGURE 22-1

Public Opinion of the Legality of Homosexual Relations, 1977–2003

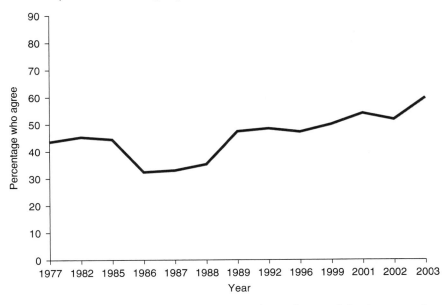

This graph shows the percentage of survey respondents who stated that homosexual relations between consenting adults should be legal.

Source: Newport 2003.

row victories. Gradually, as Figure 22-1 shows, people are coming to accept the idea of homosexual relations between consenting adults.

Resistance to lesbian and gay rights has also been evident in the battle over the proposed legalization of same-sex marriages, and in the continuing controversy over gays in the military. In 1993, President Bill Clinton considered issuing an executive order against antigay discrimination in the military, but was forced to back down because of heated opposition from military leaders and powerful members of Congress. Under a compromise devised in 1994—known as "Don't Ask, Don't Tell"—lesbians and gay men can continue to serve in the military as long as they keep their homosexuality a secret, while commanders are prohibited from asking about a person's sexual orientation. But commanders *can* investigate and dismiss military personnel if there is evidence that they have engaged in homosexual acts. According to a 2000 report, the military is discharging 73 percent *more* gay and lesbian troops today than before the new policy was enacted (Vistica 2000).

A common stereotype is that lesbian and gay organizations are found only in Western industrialized nations. However, the International Lesbian and Gay Association now has about 300 member organizations in 70 countries. In 1995, Japan held its second annual gay pride march, and gay groups were founded in Bolivia, Kenya, Pakistan, South Korea, and Sri Lanka. There are more than 50 gay and lesbian groups in South Africa, more than a dozen in Mexico, and at least 7 lesbian organizations in Brazil. The spread of the Internet has assisted the creation of many pioneering lesbian and gay organizations. In China, where organizing in public is difficult, gays rely heavily on the Internet to maintain a collective identity (B. Adam et al. 1999; Dillon 1997; *The Economist* 1996; Friess 2001).

Let's Discuss

1. Viewed from a conflict perspective, how does the dominant ideology of our society encourage antigay prejudice and discrimination?
2. How has the AIDS crisis affected the movement for lesbian and gay rights?
3. In what ways is the social position of lesbians different from that of gay men?

CHAPTER RESOURCES

Summary

Collective behavior is the relatively spontaneous and unstructured behavior of a group that is reacting to a common influence in an ambiguous situation. This chapter examines sociological theories used to understand collective behavior and forms of collective behavior, with particular attention to *social movements* and their important role in promoting social change.

1. Turner and Killian's *emergent-norm perspective* suggests that new forms of proper behavior may emerge from a crowd during an episode of collective behavior.
2. Smelser's *value-added model* of collective behavior outlines six important determinants of such behavior: structural conduciveness, structural strain, generalized belief, precipitating factor, mobilization of participants for action, and operation of social control.
3. The *assembling perspective* introduced by McPhail and Miller sought to examine how and why people move from different points in space to a common location.
4. In *crowds* people are in relatively close contact and interaction for a period of time and are focused on something of common interest.
5. Researchers are interested in how groups interact in times of *disaster.*
6. *Fads* are temporary patterns of behavior involving large numbers of people; *fashions* have more historical continuity.

7. The key distinction between a *panic* and a *craze* is that a panic is a flight *from* something, whereas a craze is a mass movement toward something.
8. A *rumor* is a piece of information used to interpret an ambiguous situation. It serves a social function by providing a group with a shared belief.
9. *Publics* represent the most individualized and least organized form of collective behavior. *Public opinion* is the expression of attitudes on public policy to decision makers.
10. *Social movements* are more structured than other forms of collective behavior and persist over longer periods of time.
11. A group will not mobilize into a social movement unless there is a shared perception that its *relative deprivation* can be ended only through collective action.
12. The success of a social movement depends in good part on effective *resource mobilization.*
13. *New social movements* tend to focus on more than just economic issues and often cross national boundaries.
14. Advances in communications technology—especially the Internet—have had a major impact on the various forms of collective behavior.
15. A growing number of organizations address national and even international concerns of lesbians and gay men.

Critical Thinking Questions

1. Are the emergent-norm, value-added, and assembling perspectives aligned with or reminiscent of functionalism, conflict theory, or interactionism? What aspects of each of these theories of collective behavior (if any) seem linked to the broader theoretical perspectives of sociology?

2. Without using any of the examples given in the textbook, list at least two examples of each of the following types of collective behavior: crowds, disasters, fads, fashions, panics, crazes, rumors, publics, and social movements. Explain why each example belongs in its assigned category. Distinguish among the types of collective behavior based on the types and degrees of social structure and interaction connected with them.

3. Select one social movement that is currently working for change in the United States. Analyze that movement, drawing on the concepts of relative deprivation, resource mobilization, and false consciousness.

Key Terms

Assembling perspective A theory of collective behavior introduced by McPhail and Miller that seeks to examine how and why people move from different points in space to a common location. (page 509)

Collective behavior In the view of sociologist Neil Smelser, the relatively spontaneous and unstructured behavior of a group of people who are reacting to a common influence in an ambiguous situation. (506)

Craze An exciting mass involvement that lasts for a relatively long period. (512)

Crowd A temporary gathering of people in close proximity who share a common focus or interest. (509)

Disaster A sudden or disruptive event or set of events that overtaxes a community's resources, so that outside aid is necessary. (510)

Emergent-norm perspective A theory of collective behavior proposed by Turner and Killian that holds that a collective definition of appropriate and inappropriate behavior emerges during episodes of collective behavior. (507)

Fad A temporary pattern of behavior that involves large numbers of people and is independent of preceding trends. (511)

False consciousness A term used by Karl Marx to describe an attitude held by members of a class that does not accurately reflect their objective position. (515)

Fashion A pleasurable mass involvement that has a line of historical continuity. (511)

New social movement An organized collective activity that addresses values and social identities, as well as improvements in the quality of life. (517)

Nonperiodic assembly A nonrecurring gathering of people that often results from word-of-mouth information. (509)

Panic A fearful arousal or collective flight based on a generalized belief that may or may not be accurate. (512)

Periodic assembly A recurring, relatively routine gathering of people, such as a college class. (509)

Public A dispersed group of people, not necessarily in contact with one another, who share an interest in an issue. (513)

Public opinion Expressions of attitudes on matters of public policy that are communicated to decision makers. (513)

Relative deprivation The conscious feeling of a negative discrepancy between legitimate expectations and present actualities. (515)

Resource mobilization The ways in which a social movement utilizes such resources as money, political influence, access to the media, and personnel. (515)

Rumor A piece of information gathered informally that is used to interpret an ambiguous situation. (513)

Social movement An organized collective activity to bring about or resist fundamental change in an existing group or society. (513)

Value-added model A theory of collective behavior proposed by Neil Smelser to explain how broad social conditions are transformed in a definite pattern into some form of collective behavior. (507)

TECHNOLOGY RESOURCES

 ## Internet Connection

*Note: While all the URLs listed were current as of the printing of this book, these sites often change. Please check our website (**www.mhhe.com/schaefer9**) for updates, hyperlinks, and exercises related to these sites.*

1. RESULTS is a grassroots citizens lobby working to create the political will to end hunger and the worst aspects of poverty. Visit its website at **http://action. org** to learn more about this organization.

2. Your textbook notes that riots are a form of collective behavior in which people are governed by identifiable social norms and exhibit definite patterns of behavior. The following website links to information about six riots involving African Americans: **http://afroamhistory.about.com/cs/raceriots.**

 ## Online Learning Center with PowerWeb

If you need to review for a test, visit the student center in the Online Learning Center at **www.mhhe.com/schaefer9** and link to the True/False Quiz. It will test your knowledge and give you immediate feedback on incorrect answers.

23

SOCIAL CHANGE
AND TECHNOLOGY

Technological change poses ethical challenges to society. This poster was commissioned by Clonaid, a biotech company that claims to have cloned humans. Though scientists doubt the truth of the company's claim, most find the idea that someone might attempt to clone humans profoundly disturbing.

Theories of Social Change

Resistance to Social Change

Technology and the Future

Technology and Society

Social Policy and Technology: Privacy and Censorship in a Global Village

Boxes

SOCIOLOGY IN THE GLOBAL COMMUNITY: Social Change in South Africa

RESEARCH IN ACTION: The Human Genome Project

Chuck D is an unlikely hero of the digital age. With hit albums such as *Yo! Bum Rush the Show* and *Fear of a Black Planet,* the founder of the rap group Public Enemy would seem to inhabit a world far removed from the more conspicuous pioneers of cyberspace, from the Netscapes and Yahoos! and AOLs. In 1998, however, Chuck D stormed into cyberspace. Rather than giving his latest songs to Def Jam, the label that had produced his music for over a decade, the rap artist instead released his music directly onto the Internet, at www.public-enemy.com. It shouldn't have been such a big deal, really: one artist, a handful of songs, and a funky distribution method that probably reached several thousand fans. But in the music business this was very big news. For Chuck D had taken one of the industry's most sa cred practices and thrown it, quite literally, into space. With just a couple of songs, he challenged how music was sold and, even more fundamentally, how it was owned. "This is the beginning," proclaimed the rapper, "of the end of domination."

As far as Chuck D was concerned, putting music online was a matter of power, of using new technologies to right old wrongs and give recording artists the influence and money that was rightfully theirs. To the recording industry, however, it was heresy. . . .

Had Chuck D been an isolated case, the studios most likely could have looked the other way. They could have dismissed Chuck D as a simple renegade, a rapper gone bad, and forgotten him and his web site. But the problem was that Chuck D, potentially, was everywhere. In cyberspace, any recording artist could distribute his or her music online; any musician could become a ministudio, circumventing the record labels and their complex, clunky rules. . . .

Matters reached a head in 1999, when a nineteen-year-old college dropout named Shawn Fanning joined Chuck D in storming the frontier. Backed by his uncle in Boston, Fanning created Napster, a revolutionary system that allowed thousands—even millions—of users to trade their music online. Within months of its release, Napster had become a social phenomenon and a massive commercial threat. Universities complained that Napster was suddenly consuming huge chunks of their Internet bandwidth, and the music industry condemned it as piracy of the most blatant sort: "STEALING," as one music lawyer described it, "in big letters." Ironic foes such as Prince and the rock band Metallica joined the labels in pursuit of these new pirates, while prophets predicted the death of the recorded music industry. "A revolution has occurred in the way music is distributed," wrote one observer, "and the big record companies are in a state of panic." *(Spar 2001:327–329)* ■

RULING THE WAVES

Cycles of
Discovery, Chaos, and Wealth
from the Compass to the Internet

DEBORA L. SPAR

Additional information about this excerpt can be found on the Online Learning Center at **www.mhhe.com/schaefer9.**

I n this selection from *Ruling the Waves: Cycles of Discovery, Chaos, and Wealth from the Compass to the Internet*, political scientist Debora L. Spar (2001) describes the economic repercussions of a recent change in the way popular music is distributed. To students, the advent of Napster meant that suddenly, free music was available to them over the Internet. But to recording artists and record companies, Napster was a revolutionary new technology with the potential to shift the balance of power from the corporate giants that produced popular music to the artists who created and performed it. The distribution of digitized music via the Internet, then, changed both the way people behaved—how they selected, obtained, and listened to music—and the cultural institution that is the music business.

The invention of the personal computer and its integration into people's day-to-day lives is another example of the social change that often follows the introduction of a new technology. **Social change** has been defined as significant alteration over time in behavior patterns and culture (W. Moore 1967). But what constitutes a "significant" alteration? Certainly the dramatic rise in formal education documented in Chapter 16 represents a change that has had profound social consequences. Other social changes that have had long-term and important consequences include the emergence of slavery as a system of stratification (see Chapter 9), the industrial revolution (Chapters 5 and 20), the increased participation of women in the paid labor forces of the United States and Europe (Chapter 12), and the worldwide population explosion (Chapter 21). In many instances, the social movements covered in Chapter 22 have played an important role in promoting social change.

How does social change happen? Is the process unpredictable, or can we make certain generalizations about it? Why do some people resist social change? What changes are likely to follow the technologies of the future? And what have been the negative effects of the sweeping technological changes of the last century? In this chapter we will examine the process of social change, with special emphasis on the impact of technological advances. Efforts to explain long-term social changes have led to the development of theories of change; we will consider the evolutionary, functionalist, and conflict approaches to change. We will see how vested interests attempt to block changes that they see as threatening. We'll also look at various aspects of our technological future, such as telecommuting, the Internet, biotechnology, and technological accidents. We will examine the effects of technological advances on culture and social interaction, social control, and social stratification and inequality. Taken together, the impact of these technological changes may be approaching a level of magnitude comparable to that of the industrial revolution. Finally, in the social policy section we will discuss the ways in which technological advances have intensified concerns over privacy and censorship. ▪

THEORIES OF SOCIAL CHANGE

A new millennium provides the occasion to offer explanations of *social change*, which we have defined as significant alteration over time in behavior patterns and culture. Such explanations are clearly a challenge in the diverse and complex world we inhabit today. Nevertheless, theorists from several disciplines have sought to analyze social change. In some instances, they have examined historical events to arrive at a better understanding of contemporary changes. We will review three theoretical approaches to change—evolutionary, functionalist, and conflict theory—and then take a look at global change.

Evolutionary Theory

The pioneering work of Charles Darwin (1809–1882) in biological evolution contributed to 19th-century theories of social change. Darwin's approach stresses a continuing progression of successive life forms. For example, human beings came at a later stage of evolution than reptiles and represent a more complex form of life. Social theorists sought an analogy to this biological model and originated *evolutionary theory,* in which society is viewed as moving in a definite direction. Early evolutionary theorists generally agreed that society was inevitably progressing to a higher state. As might be expected, they concluded in ethnocentric fashion that their own behavior and culture were more advanced than those of earlier civilizations.

 August Comte (1798–1857), a founder of sociology, was an evolutionary theorist of change. He saw human societies as moving forward in their thinking from mythology to the scientific method. Similarly, Émile Durkheim ([1893]1933) maintained that society progressed from simple to more complex forms of social organization.

The writings of Comte and Durkheim are examples of **unilinear evolutionary theory.** This approach contends that all societies pass through the same successive stages of evolution and inevitably reach the same end. English sociologist Herbert Spencer (1820–1903) used a similar approach: Spencer likened society to a living body whose interrelated parts were moving toward a common destiny. However, contemporary evolutionary theorists such as Gerhard Lenski are more likely to see social change as being multilinear than to rely on the more limited unilinear perspective. **Multilinear evolutionary theory** holds that change can occur in several ways, and does not inevitably lead in the same direction (Haines 1988; J. Turner 1985).

Multilinear theorists recognize that human culture has evolved along a number of lines. For example, the theory of demographic transition graphically demonstrates that population change in developing nations has not necessarily followed the model evident in industrialized nations. Sociologists today hold that events do not necessarily follow in a single or even several straight lines, but instead are subject to disruptions—a topic we will consider later, in our discussion of global social change.

Functionalist Theory

Functionalist sociologists focus on what *maintains* a system, not on what changes it. This approach might seem to suggest that functionalists can offer little that is of value to the study of social change. Yet as the work of sociologist Talcott Parsons demonstrates, functionalists have made a distinctive contribution to this area of sociological investigation.

Parsons (1902–1979), a leading proponent of functionalist theory, viewed society as being in a natural state of equilibrium. By "equilibrium," he meant that society tends toward a state of stability or balance. Parsons would view even prolonged labor strikes or civilian riots as temporary disruptions in the

status quo rather than as significant alterations in social structure. Therefore, according to his **equilibrium model,** as changes occur in one part of society, adjustments must be made in other parts. If not, the society's equilibrium will be threatened and strains will occur.

Reflecting the evolutionary approach, Parsons (1966) maintained that four processes of social change are inevitable. The first, *differentiation*, refers to the increasing complexity of social organization. A transition from "medicine man" to physician, nurse, and pharmacist is an illustration of differentiation in the field of health. This process is accompanied by *adaptive upgrading*, in which social institutions become more specialized in their

Since 1990, African American golfers like Tiger Woods have been welcome at the most exclusive private golf courses. Their acceptance in previously all-White enclaves like the Augusta National Golf Club, home of the Masters Tournament, illustrates the process of *inclusion* described by Talcott Parsons. Yet the process is far from complete. Women are still barred from joining the Augusta National and other elite clubs, no matter how wealthy or accomplished they are.

purposes. The division of physicians into obstetricians, internists, surgeons, and so forth is an example of adaptive upgrading.

The third process Parsons identified is the *inclusion* of groups that were previously excluded because of their gender, race, ethnicity, and social class background. Medical schools have practiced inclusion by admitting increasing numbers of women and African Americans. Finally, Parsons contends that societies experience *value generalization,* the development of new values that tolerate and legitimate a greater range of activities. The acceptance of preventive and alternative medicine is an example of value generalization: society has broadened its view of health care. All four processes identified by Parsons stress consensus—societal agreement on the nature of social organization and values (B. Johnson 1975; Wallace and Wolf 1980).

Though Parsons's approach explicitly incorporates the evolutionary notion of continuing progress, the dominant theme in his model is balance and stability. Society may change, but it remains stable through new forms of integration. For example, in place of the kinship ties that provided social cohesion in the past, people develop laws, judicial processes, and new values and belief systems.

Functionalists assume that social institutions will not persist unless they continue to contribute to society. This assumption leads them to conclude that drastically altering institutions will threaten societal equilibrium. Critics note that the functionalist approach virtually disregards the use of coercion by the powerful to maintain the illusion of a stable, well-integrated society (Gouldner 1960).

Conflict Theory

The functionalist perspective minimizes the importance of change. It emphasizes the persistence of social life, and sees change as a means of maintaining the equilibrium (or balance) of a society. In contrast, conflict theorists contend that social institutions and practices persist because powerful groups have the ability to maintain the status quo. Change has crucial significance, since it is needed to correct social injustices and inequalities.

Karl Marx accepted the evolutionary argument that societies develop along a particular path. However, unlike Comte and Spencer, he did not view each successive stage as an inevitable improvement over the previous one. History, according to Marx, proceeds through a series of stages, each of which exploits a class of people. Ancient society exploited slaves; the estate system of feudalism exploited serfs; modern capitalist society exploits the working class. Ultimately, through a socialist revolution led by the proletariat, human society will move toward the final stage of development: a classless communist society, or

"community of free individuals," as Marx described it in *Das Kapital* in 1867 (see Bottomore and Rubel 1956:250).

As we have seen, Marx had an important influence

p. 11

on the development of sociology. His thinking offered insights into such institutions as the economy, the family, religion, and government. The Marxist view of social change is appealing because it does not restrict people to a passive role in responding to inevitable cycles or changes in material culture. Rather, Marxist theory offers a tool for those who wish to seize control of the historical process and gain their freedom from injustice. In contrast to functionalists' emphasis on stability, Marx argues that conflict is a normal and desirable aspect of social change. In fact, change must be encouraged as a means of eliminating social inequality (Lauer 1982).

One conflict sociologist, Ralf Dahrendorf (1958), has noted that the contrast between the functionalist perspective's emphasis on stability and the conflict perspective's focus on change reflects the contradictory nature of society. Human societies are stable and long-lasting, yet they also experience serious conflict. Dahrendorf found that the functionalist approach and the conflict approach were ultimately compatible, despite their many points of disagreement. Indeed, Parsons spoke of new functions that result from social change, and Marx recognized the need for change so that societies could function more equitably.

Global Social Change

We are at a truly dramatic time in history to consider global social change. Maureen Hallinan (1997), in her presidential address to the American Sociological Association, asked those present to consider just a few of the recent political events: the collapse of communism; terrorism in various parts of the world, including the United States; major regime changes and severe economic disruptions in Africa, the Middle East, and Eastern Europe; the spread of AIDS; and the computer revolution. Just a few months after her remarks came the first verification of the cloning of a complex animal, Dolly the sheep.

In this era of massive social, political, and economic change on a global scale, is it possible to predict change? Some technological changes seem obvious, but the collapse of communist governments in the former Soviet Union and Eastern Europe in the early 1990s took people by surprise. Yet prior to the Soviet collapse, sociologist Randall Collins (1986, 1995), a conflict theorist, had observed a crucial sequence of events that most observers had missed.

In seminars as far back as 1980, and in a book published in 1986, Collins had argued that Soviet expansionism had resulted in an overextension of resources,

The toppling of Saddam Hussein's totalitarian rule over Iraq in 2003 was one of several regime changes that occurred at the beginning of the 21st century. In a global society, such changes affect people throughout the world, not just those in one nation.

outside pressures. Box 23-1 recounts how international pressure on the all-White government of South Africa forced the end of the racist policy of apartheid.

In her address, Hallinan (1997) cautioned that we need to move beyond the restrictive models of social change—the linear view of evolutionary theory and the assumptions about equilibrium in functionalist theory. She and other sociologists have looked to the "chaos theory" advanced by mathematicians to understand erratic events as a part of change. Hallinan noted that upheavals and major chaotic shifts do occur, and that sociologists must learn to predict their occurrence, as Collins did with the Soviet Union. For example, imagine the dramatic nonlinear social change that will result from major innovations in communications and biotechnology, a topic we will discuss later in the chapter.

including disproportionate spending on military forces. Such an overextension will strain a regime's stability. Moreover, geopolitical theory suggests that nations in the middle of a geographic region, such as the Soviet Union, tend to fragment into smaller units over time. Collins predicted that the coincidence of social crises on several frontiers would precipitate the collapse of the Soviet Union.

And that is just what happened. In 1979, the success of the Iranian revolution had led to an upsurge of Islamic fundamentalism in nearby Afghanistan, as well as in Soviet republics with substantial Muslim populations. At the same time, resistance to Communist rule was growing both throughout Eastern Europe and within the Soviet Union itself. Collins had predicted that the rise of a dissident form of communism within the Soviet Union might facilitate the breakdown of the regime. Beginning in the late 1980s, Soviet leader Mikhail Gorbachev chose not to use military power and other types of repression to crush dissidents in Eastern Europe. Instead, he offered plans for democratization and social reform of Soviet society, and seemed willing to reshape the Soviet Union into a loose federation of somewhat autonomous states. But in 1991, six republics on the western periphery declared their independence, and within months the entire Soviet Union had formally disintegrated into Russia and a number of other independent nations.

Social change does not always follow a period of internal disintegration. Sometimes it can be precipitated by

RESISTANCE TO SOCIAL CHANGE

Efforts to promote social change are likely to meet with resistance. In the midst of rapid scientific and technological innovations, many people are frightened by the demands of an ever-changing society. Moreover, certain individuals and groups have a stake in maintaining the existing state of affairs.

Social economist Thorstein Veblen (1857–1929) coined the term *vested interests* to refer to those people or groups who will suffer in the event of social change. For example, the American Medical Association (AMA) has taken strong stands against national health insurance p. 440 and the professionalization of midwifery. National health insurance could lead to limits on physicians' income, and a rise in the status of midwives could threaten the preeminent position of doctors as deliverers of babies. In general, those with a disproportionate share of society's wealth, status, and power, such as members of the American Medical Association, have a vested interest in preserving the status quo (Starr 1982; Veblen 1919).

Economic and Cultural Factors

Economic factors play an important role in resistance to social change. For example, it can be expensive for

23-1 SOCIAL CHANGE IN SOUTH AFRICA

As recently as 14 years ago, South Africa, a nation of 44 million people, was accurately described as a country where race was the sole determinant of power. Regardless of occupation, education, or family background, White South Africans enjoyed legal rights and privileges that were denied to all people of color. Ever since 1948, when it received its independence from Great Britain, South Africa had maintained this rigid segregationist policy, known as *apartheid.*

During the 1980s, South Africa felt increasing worldwide disapproval and economic pressure to change. At the same time, Black South Africans became more and more vocal about their second-class citizenship. They engaged in many forms of nonviolent and violent protest, including economic boycotts, labor strikes, political demonstrations, and occasional acts of sabotage.

In a dramatic turn of events in 1990, South African prime minister F. W. de Klerk legalized 60 banned Black organizations and freed Nelson Mandela, the leader of the long-outlawed African National Congress (ANC), after 27 years of imprisonment. The following year, de Klerk and Black leaders signed a National Peace Accord, pledging themselves to the establishment of a multiparty democracy.

In 1994, South Africa held its first universal election. Nelson Mandela's ANC received 62 percent of the vote, giving him a five-year term as president.

Mandela and his political party then faced a difficult challenge: making the transition from a liberation movement dedicated to fighting for revolution to a governing party that needed to make political compromises. Moreover, an end to the racist policy of apartheid—while applauded around the world—was not in itself a solution to all of South Africa's problems. At best, one-fifth of the country's Blacks could compete in the nation's economy, while the rest formed a huge underclass.

> An end to the racist policy of apartheid—while applauded around the world—was not in itself a solution to all of South Africa's problems.

Some of the controversial issues facing the government of South Africa today are very familiar to residents of the United States:

- **Affirmative action.** Race-based employment goals and other preference programs have been proposed, yet critics insist that such efforts constitute reverse apartheid.
- **Illegal immigration.** An estimated 2 to 18 percent of South African residents are illegal immigrants, many of whom wish to escape the

poverty and political turmoil of neighboring African states.
- **Medical care.** South Africa is confronting the inequities of private health care for the affluent (usually White) versus government-subsidized care for others (usually people of color).
- **School integration and upgrading.** Multiracial schools are replacing the segregated school system. Still, as of 1999, Whites were four times more likely than Blacks to earn a college degree.

Perhaps the most difficult issue facing the government is land reform. Between 1960 and 1990, the all-White government forced 3.5 million Black South Africans from their land, and frequently allowed Whites to settle on it. By 2001, the government was attempting to resettle 70,000 Black farmers. Though compensation will be offered to current landowners, bitter disputes seem inevitable.

Let's Discuss

1. How would a conflict theorist explain the relatively peaceful revolution in South Africa? What explanation might a functionalist offer?
2. Do you think other nations should use economic pressure to force social change in a country? Why or why not?

Sources: K. Adam 2000; R. Schaefer 2004; Sidiropoulos et al. 1996; South African Institute of Race Relations 2001a, 2001b, 2001c.

---

manufacturers to meet high standards for the safety of products and workers and for the protection of the environment. Conflict theorists argue that in a capitalist economic system, many firms are not willing to pay the price of meeting strict safety and environmental standards. They may resist social change by cutting corners or by pressuring the government to ease regulations.

Communities, too, protect their vested interests, often in the name of "protecting property values." The ab-

breviation *NIMBY* stands for "not in my backyard," a cry often heard when people protest landfills, prisons, nuclear power facilities, and even bike trails and group homes for people with developmental disabilities. The targeted community may not challenge the need for the facility, but may simply insist that it be located elsewhere. The "not in my backyard" attitude has become so common that it is almost impossible for policymakers to find acceptable locations for facilities such as hazardous waste dumps (Jasper 1997).

"Not in my backyard!" say these demonstrators, objecting to the placement of a new incinerator in a Hartford, Connecticut, neighborhood. The NIMBY phenomenon has become so common that it is almost impossible for policymakers to find acceptable locations for incinerators, landfills, and hazardous waste dumps.

Like economic factors, cultural factors frequently shape resistance to change. William F. Ogburn (1922) distinguished between material and nonmaterial aspects of culture. *Material culture* includes inventions, artifacts, and technology; *nonmaterial culture* encompasses ideas, norms, communications, and social organization. Ogburn pointed out that one cannot devise methods for controlling and utilizing new technology before the introduction of a technique. Thus, nonmaterial culture typically must respond to changes in material culture. Ogburn introduced the term **culture lag** to refer to the period of maladjustment when the nonmaterial culture is still struggling to adapt to new material conditions. One example is the Internet. Its rapid uncontrolled growth raises questions about whether to regulate it, and if so, how much (see the social policy section at the end of this chapter).

In certain cases, changes in material culture can strain the relationships between social institutions. For example, new means of birth control have been developed in recent decades. Large families are no longer economically necessary, nor are they commonly endorsed by social norms. But certain religious faiths, among them Roman Catholicism, continue to extol large families and to disapprove methods of limiting family size, such as contraception and abortion. This issue represents a lag between aspects of material culture (technology) and nonmaterial culture (religious beliefs). Conflicts may emerge between religion and other social institutions, such as government and the educational system, over the dissemination of birth control and family-planning information (M. Riley et al. 1994a, 1994b).

Resistance to Technology

p. 118

Technological innovations are examples of changes in material culture that have often provoked resistance. The *industrial revolution,* which took place largely in England during the period 1760 to 1830, was a scientific revolution focused on the application of nonanimal sources of power to labor tasks. As this revolution proceeded, societies came to rely on new inventions that facilitated agricultural and industrial production, and on new sources of energy such as steam. In some industries, the introduction of power-driven machinery reduced the need for factory workers and made it easier for factory owners to cut wages.

Strong resistance to the industrial revolution emerged in some countries. In England, beginning in 1811, masked craft workers took extreme measures: They mounted nighttime raids on factories and destroyed some of the new machinery. The government hunted these rebels, known as **Luddites,** and ultimately banished or hung them. In a similar effort in France, angry workers threw their wooden shoes (*sabots*) into factory machinery to destroy it, giving rise to the term *sabotage.* While the resistance of the Luddites and the French workers was short-lived and unsuccessful, they have come to symbolize resistance to technology.

Are we now in the midst of a second industrial revolution, with a contemporary group of Luddites engaged in resistance? Many sociologists believe that we are living p. 118 in a *postindustrial society.* It is difficult to pinpoint exactly when this era began. Generally, it is viewed as having begun in the 1950s, when for the first time the majority of workers in industrial societies became involved in services rather than in the actual manufacturing of goods (D. Bell 1999; Fiala 1992).

Just as the Luddites resisted the industrial revolution, people in many countries have resisted postindustrial technological changes. The term *neo-Luddites* refers to those who are wary of technological innovations, and

p. 62

who question the incessant expansion of industrialization, the increasing destruction of the natural and agrarian world, and the "throw it away" mentality of contemporary capitalism, with its resulting pollution of the environment. Neo-Luddites insist that whatever the presumed benefits of industrial and postindustrial technology, such technology has distinctive social costs, and may represent a danger to both the future of the human species and our planet (Bauerlein 1996; Rifkin 1995b; Sale 1996; Snyder 1996).

These concerns are worth remembering as we turn to our technological future and its possible impact on social change.

TECHNOLOGY AND THE FUTURE

Technology is information about how to use the material resources of the environment to satisfy human needs and desires. Technological advances—the airplane, the automobile, the television, the atomic bomb, and more recently, the computer, the fax machine, and the cellular phone—have brought striking changes to our cultures, our patterns of socialization, our social institutions, and our day-to-day social interactions. Technological innovations are, in fact, emerging and being accepted with remarkable speed.

p. 116

The technological knowledge with which we work today represents only a tiny portion of the knowledge that will be available in the year 2050. We are witnessing an information explosion: The number of volumes in major libraries in the United States doubles every 14 years. Individuals, institutions, and societies will face unprecedented challenges in adjusting to the technological advances still to come (Cetron and Davies 1991; Wurman 1989).

In the following sections, we will examine various aspects of our technological future and consider their impact on social change, including the social strain they will cause. We will focus in particular on recent developments in computer technology and biotechnology.

Computer Technology

The last decade has witnessed an explosion of computer technology in the United States and around the world. Its effects are particularly noteworthy with regard to telecommuting and the Internet.

Telecommuting

As the industrial revolution proceeded, the factory and the office replaced the home as the typical workplace. But the postindustrial revolution has brought people home

again. In 1999, at least 14 million telecommuters in the United States worked at home at least once a month. *Telecommuters* are employees who work full-time or part-time at home rather than in an outside office. They are linked to their supervisors and colleagues through computer terminals, phone lines, and fax machines. As part of a shift toward postindustrial societies that are linked by a global economy, telecommuting can even cross national boundaries, oceans, and continents (K. Hall 1999).

Telecommuting has many advantages. It facilitates communication between employees who work at different locations, including those who work at home. It also reduces the time and money spent on transportation, and can be helpful in a family's child care arrangements. At the same time, working at home can be isolating and stressful—even more so if a parent must attempt to combine working at home with caring for children. Moreover, companies still need to encourage face-to-face communication in staff meetings and social settings (Marklein 1996).

The rise of telecommuting is especially beneficial to one subordinate group in the United States: people with disabilities. Computer terminals lend themselves to ancillary devices that are adaptable to most types of physical impairments. For example, people who are blind can work at home using word

p. 107

In our postindustrial society, computers are in use almost everywhere imaginable.

processors that read messages in a synthetic voice, or that translate messages into Braille text (J. Nelson 1995).

The Internet

The Internet is the world's largest computer network. Estimates are that by 2005, it will reach 1.1 billion computer users, compared to just 50 million in 1996 (Global Reach 2003).

The Internet evolved from a computer system built in 1962 by the U.S. Defense Department, to enable scholars and military researchers to continue their government work even if part of the nation's communications system was destroyed by a nuclear attack. Until recently, it was difficult to gain access to the Internet without holding a position at a university or a government research laboratory. Today, however, virtually anyone can reach the Internet with a phone line, a computer, and a modem. It is possible to buy and sell cars, trade stocks, auction off items, research new medical remedies, vote, and track down long-lost friends online—to mention just a few of the thousands of possibilities (Reddick and King 2000).

Unfortunately, not everyone can get onto the information highway, especially not the less affluent. Moreover, this pattern of inequality is global. The core nations that

◄ p. 229 Immanuel Wallerstein described in his *world systems analysis* have a virtual monopoly on information technology; the peripheral nations of Asia, Africa, and Latin America depend on these industrial giants both for technology and for the information it provides. For example, North America, Europe, and a few industrialized nations in other regions possess almost all the world's *Internet hosts*—computers that are connected directly to the worldwide network. The same is true for newspapers, telephones, televisions, and even radios. Low-income peripheral nations have an average of only 30 telephone lines per 1,000 people, compared to 593 per 1,000 in high-income nations. The disparity is even greater for cell phones: low-income nations have an average of 10 cell phones per 1,000 people, compared to 609 per 1,000 in high-income nations (World Bank 2003b).

Biotechnology

Sex selection of fetuses, genetically engineered organisms, cloning of sheep and cows—these have been among the significant yet controversial scientific advances in the field of biotechnology in recent years. George Ritzer's

◄ p. 62 concept of McDonaldization applies to the entire area of biotechnology. Just as the fast-food concept has permeated society, no phase of life now seems exempt from therapeutic or medical intervention. In fact, sociologists view many aspects of biotechnology as an extension of the trend toward the medicalization of

society, discussed in Chapter 19. Through genetic manipulation, the medical profession is expanding its turf still further (A. Clarke et al. 2003).

Today's biotechnology holds itself out as totally beneficial to human beings, but it is in constant need of monitoring. As we will see in the following sections, biotechnological advances have raised many difficult ethical and political questions (D. Weinstein and Weinstein 1999).

Sex Selection

Advances in reproductive and screening technology have brought us closer to effective techniques for sex selection. In the United States, the prenatal test called amniocentesis has been used for more than 25 years to ascertain the presence of certain defects that require medical attention prior to birth. Such tests can also identify the sex of the fetus, as can ultrasound scans. This outcome has had profound social implications.

In many societies, young couples planning to have only one child will want to ensure that the child is a boy, because their culture places a premium on a male heir. In such instances, advances in fetal testing may lead to abortion if the fetus is found to be female. Fetal testing clinics in Canada currently advertise that they can tell parents the sex of a fetus. Such advertising is targeted particularly at Asian Indian communities in both Canada and the United States. But in the United States, the preference for a male child is hardly limited to people from India. In one study, when asked what sex they would prefer for an only child, 86 percent of men and 59 percent of women said they wanted a boy. Moreover, through fetal testing, couples today routinely learn the sex of their child (M. Hall 1993; Sohoni 1994).

Sex selection is also possible in connection with a procedure called *in vitro fertilization*. In this procedure, which is intended to help infertile couples conceive a child, an egg is fertilized in a test tube and then implanted in the mother's womb. Couples who use this expensive procedure can now obtain a genetic analysis of the embryo before it is implanted. While the purpose of the analysis is to confirm that an embryo will be free from genetic defects, the results can also be used to select an embryo of the desired sex (Gezari 2002).

From a functionalist perspective, we can view sex selection as an adaptation of the basic family function of regulating reproduction. However, conflict theorists emphasize that sex selection may intensify the male dominance of our society and undermine the advances women have made in entering careers formerly restricted to men.

Genetic Engineering

Even more grandiose than sex selection—and not necessarily improbable—is the possibility of altering human behavior through genetic engineering. Fish and plant genes have already been mixed to create frost-resistant potato and tomato crops; more recently, human genes have been implanted in pigs to provide humanlike kidneys for organ transplants.

One of the latest developments in genetic engineering is gene therapy. Geneticists working with mouse fetuses have managed to disable genes that carry an undesirable trait and replace them with genes carrying a desirable trait. Such advances raise staggering possibilities for altering animal and human life forms. Still, gene therapy remains highly experimental, and must be considered a long, long shot (Kolata 1999).

The debate on genetic engineering escalated in 1997 when scientists in Scotland announced that they had cloned a sheep. After many unsuccessful attempts, they had finally been able to replace the genetic material of a sheep's egg with DNA from an adult sheep, creating a lamb that was a clone of the adult. The very next year, Japanese researchers successfully cloned cows. These developments raised the possibility that in the near future, scientists may be able to clone human beings.

Greenpeace activists dressed in mock safety suits demonstrate against the sale of genetically modified corn flour at a supermarket in Mexico City. The potential health effects of genetic engineering have become the subject of much fear and controversy.

A medical technician inspects the beginnings of several human lives. Advances in biotechnology have made possible not just the artificial conception of test-tube babies, but the selection of a child's sex. Sociologists see these procedures as a sign of the increasing medicalization of society.

In 1997, President Bill Clinton banned any federal support for human cloning and urged private laboratories to abide by a voluntary moratorium until the ethical issues could be carefully considered. Six years later, no federal law on human cloning had been drafted, no less passed. However, state legislatures have grappled with the issue. As of mid-2003, only California specifically allowed human cloning, while Iowa and South Dakota explicitly banned it (Brainard 2003).

William F. Ogburn probably could not have anticipated such scientific developments when he wrote of culture lag 70 years earlier. However, the successful cloning of sheep illustrates again how quickly material culture can change, and how nonmaterial culture moves more slowly in absorbing such changes.

While cloning grabs the headlines, controversy has been growing concerning genetically modified (GM) food. This issue arose in Europe but has since spread to other parts of the world, including the United States. The idea behind the technology is to increase food production and make agriculture more economical. But critics use the term *Frankenfood* (as in "Frankenstein") to refer to everything from breakfast cereals made from genetically engineered grains to "fresh" GM tomatoes. They object to tampering with nature, and are concerned about the possible health effects of GM food. Supporters of genetically modified food include not just biotech companies, but those who see the technology as a way to help feed the

A Hazardous Materials (Hazmat) worker bags dust samples taken from the Associated Press mailroom in October 2001, after letters containing deadly anthrax bacteria were sent to newsrooms in Florida and New York. The threat of bioterrorism has become a matter of increasing concern to governments and organizations throughout the world.

burgeoning populations of Africa and Asia (Golden 1999).

Another form of biotechnology with a potentially wide-ranging impact is the Human Genome Project. This effort involves teams of scientists around the world in sequencing and mapping all the 30,000 to 40,000 human genes in existence, which are collectively known as the *human genome*. Supporters say that the resulting knowledge could revolutionize doctors' ability to treat and even prevent disease. But sociologists worry about the ethical implications of such research. Box 23-2 provides an overview of the many issues the project has raised.

Bioterrorism

Because biotechnology has generally been seen as a benefit to society, critics have been concerned mostly with the possibility of unintended negative consequences. Yet scientists have long recognized that chemical and biological agents can be used intentionally as weapons of mass destruction. Combatants in World War I used mustard gas, and nerve gas was used shortly thereafter. Today as many as 26 nations appear to have stockpiled chemical weapons, and another 10 have developed biological weapons programs.

More disturbing still is the prospect that terrorists might develop their own biological or chemical weapons, which are not difficult or expensive to make. The deaths that occurred as a result of anthrax contamination of the U.S. mails in 2001, shortly after the attack on the Pentagon and World Trade Center, underscored the relative ease with which biotechnology can be used for hostile purposes. In fact, between 1975 and August 2000, terrorists created 342 incidents involving biological or chemical agents. Only about a third of those events were real attacks, and most caused few injuries and even fewer deaths. Yet because chemical and biological weapons are easy to use, these agents, which have come to be known as the poor person's nuclear bomb, are a source of increasing concern to governments the world over (Henry L. Stimson Center 2001; J. Miller et al. 2001; Mullins 2001; White 2002).

Technological Accidents

A carpenter who single-handedly makes a ladder has quite a different investment in the quality of the product than a technician who develops a small part for a space shuttle. Our increasing reliance on technology has led to a growing separation between people and the outcomes of their actions.

Sociologist Charles Perrow (1999) introduced the term ***normal accident*** to refer to a failure that is inevitable given the manner in which human and technological systems are organized. Whether in a hospital or an aerospace program, catastrophes are often caused not by massive errors, but rather by what appear to be (taken in isolation) almost incidental human misjudgments and minor technical flaws. In studying normal accidents, engineers focus on the system design, the physical environment, and the possibility of mechanical failure; social scientists evaluate possible *human* error. Generally, 60 to 80 percent of normal accidents are attributed to human factors (Erikson 1994).

As technology continues to advance at a rapid pace, new possibilities for accidents arise. For example, the disastrous 2003 reentry of the U.S. space shuttle *Columbia*

23-2 THE HUMAN GENOME PROJECT

Together with geneticists, pathologists, and microbiologists, sociologist Troy Duster of New York University has been grappling with the ethical, legal, and social issues raised by the Human Genome Project since 1989. An original member of the oversight committee appointed to deal with such matters, he does not expect that his work will be done anytime in the near future.

Duster, who is also president of the American Sociological Association, has been asked to explain why his committee is taking so long to conclude its work. In reply, he lists the many issues raised by the massive project. First, he is concerned that the medical breakthroughs made possible by the project will not benefit all people equally. He notes that biotechnology firms have used the project's data to develop a test for cystic fibrosis in White Americans, but not for the same syndrome in Zuni Indians. Biotechnology companies are profit-making ventures, not humanitarian organizations. So while the scientists involved in the Human Genome Project hope to map the genes of all the peoples of the world, not everyone may benefit from the project in practical ways.

Duster's committee has also struggled with the question of informed consent—making sure that everyone who donates their genes to the project will do so voluntarily, after being informed of the risks and benefits. In Western societies, scientists commonly obtain such consent from the individuals who participate in their research. But according to Duster, many non-Western societies do not acknowledge the individual's right to make such decisions. Instead, a leader makes the decision for the group as a whole. "When Western-trained researchers descend upon a village," Duster asks, "who should they turn to for consent?" (Duster 2002:69) And what if the answer is no?

Race, too, is a knotty problem for Duster's committee. DNA analysis shows conclusively that there is no genetic difference between the races. Given that analysis, geneticists do not want to invest

> A group's economic and political power helps to determine which diseases scientists study.

more time and effort in research on racial differences. As a sociologist, Duster knows that race is socially constructed. Yet he also knows that for millions of people around the world, race has a significant effect on their health and well-being. More to the point, he knows that a group's economic and political power helps to determine which diseases scientists study. "We may be 99.9 percent alike at the level of DNA," Duster writes, "but if that were the end of the story, we could all pack up and go home" (Duster 2002:70).

Troy Duster, a sociologist at NYU, also teaches and directs the American Cultures Center at the University of California, Berkeley.

Let's Discuss

1. What other criteria besides the power of a racial or ethnic group could be used to determine how much research is done on diseases that affect the group?
2. What should a researcher do if a tribal leader refuses to allow members of the tribe to participate in a research project?

Source: Duster 2002.

---

ended in the deaths of seven astronauts. It has also become apparent that electronic communication devices are vulnerable to failure. In our networked economy, the social consequences of such a failure can be far-reaching. In 1998 the *Galaxy IV* communications satellite malfunctioned, knocking out the paging systems used by 90 percent of people in the United States. Hospitals could not page their doctors, so old-fashioned "phone trees" were established during the week without service. The mal-

function also took several broadcasters off the air, including National Public Radio. Although the foul-up was ultimately corrected, this incident does underscore the possibilities for chaos in an ever-expanding electronic system (Swanson and Kirk 1998; Riding 2002; Vaughan 1996).

System accidents are uncommon, even rare. But like the death of any individual, which occurs only once, their infrequency is not all that reassuring. Given the serious consequences of a systems failure, we can anticipate that social scientists will work even more closely with engineers to explore how better equipment, training, and organization can reduce the likelihood of normal accidents (Perrow 1999; see also L. Clarke 1999; D. W. Miller 2000).

These are but a few instances of technological change, viewed from the vantage point of a new millennium, that raise questions about the future. Sociologists are not fortune-tellers; the focus of their discipline is to examine the society around them rather than to project decades ahead. But sociologists have no problem in asserting that social change (and technological change) is a given in our world. And so, they remind us, is resistance to change. We cannot know what is ahead. But the sociological imagination—with its probing and theorizing and its careful empirical studies—can assist us in understanding the past and present, as well as anticipating and adjusting to the future.

 **Use Your Sociological Imagination** www. mhhe.com /schaefer9

Try to imagine the world 100 years from now. On balance, is it a world in which technology contributes to or threatens people's well-being? In what ways?

 TECHNOLOGY AND SOCIETY

An automated teller machine (ATM) that identifies a person by his or her facial structure; a small device that sorts through hundreds of odors to ensure the safety of a chemical plant; a cell phone that recognizes its owner's voice—these are real-life examples of technology that were so much science fiction a few decades ago. Today's computer chip cannot simply think, but can see, smell, and hear, too (Salkever 1999).

Such technological advances can dramatically transform the material culture. The word processor, pocket calculator, photocopying machine, and compact disc player have largely eliminated the typewriter, adding machine, mimeograph, and turntable—all of which were once technological advances themselves.

Technological change can also reshape *nonmaterial* culture. In the following sections, we will examine the effects of technological advances on culture and social interaction, social control, and stratification and inequality.

Culture and Social Interaction

In Chapter 3, we emphasized that language is the foundation of every culture. From a functionalist perspective, language can bring members of a society together and promote cultural integration. However, from a conflict perspective, the use of language can intensify divisions between groups and societies—just look at the battles over language in the United States, Canada, and other societies.

The Internet has often been lauded as a democratizing force that will make huge quantities of information available to great numbers of people around the world. While the Internet does increase the amount of available information, at least in societies that have access to it, most of that information is presented in English and just a handful of other languages (see Figure 23-1). On the other hand, the technology is helping to preserve dying languages that would otherwise be lost to posterity. Various websites are maintaining the vocabularies, grammars, and audio samples of hundreds of languages that have virtually disappeared from the real world. Among those preserved in virtual reality are rare Aboriginal Australian dialects with no living native speakers (Pollak 2000).

How will social interaction be transformed by the growing availability of electronic forms of communication? Will people turn to e-mail, websites, and faxes rather than to telephone conversations and face-to-face meetings? Certainly, the technological shift to the telephone

FIGURE 23-1

Language Use on the Internet, 1996 and 2005

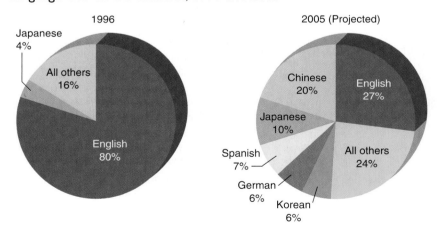

Source: Global Reach 2003.

Think About It
Why do you think Chinese is the second most common language on the Internet?

reduced letter writing as a means of maintaining kinship and friendship ties. For this reason, some people worry that computers and other forms of electronic communication may be socially isolating. Sociologist Sherry Turkle (1999) has warned that some individuals may become so gratified by their online lives that they lose touch with their families, friends, and work responsibilities.

Yet Turkle (1995, 1999) has found positive effects from Internet usage as well. Over a 10-year period, she made anonymous visits to chat rooms and multiuser domains (MUDs), which allow people to assume new identities in role-playing games. She also conducted face-to-face interviews with more than 1,000 people who communicate by e-mail and participate actively in MUDs. Distinguishing between users' on-screen personae and their real identities, Turkle concluded that many MUD users' lives were enhanced by the opportunity to engage in role playing and "become someone else." A new sense of self had emerged, she wrote, that was "decentered and multiple." In making this obser-

Two young patients at a New York City hospital communicate electronically with peers at a hospital in California. Electronic communication has proved useful in promoting social interaction among children who are seriously ill. The new technology, known as Starbright World, was developed with the assistance of director Steven Spielberg.

p. 86 vation, Turkle was expanding on George Herbert Mead's notion of self (Nass and Moon 2000).

One obvious form of online role playing is gender switching. In a 1999 study, researchers found that 40 percent of their subjects had presented themselves online as a member of the opposite sex. Yet gender switching does not appear to dominate online communication. Even among the gender-switched, the majority of subjects spent only about 10 percent of their time online disguised as the opposite sex (L. Roberts and Parks 1999).

If electronic communication can facilitate social interaction within a community—if it can create ties among people in different communities or even countries who "meet" in chat rooms or MUDs—then has it created a new interactive world known as cyberspace? The term *cyberspace* was introduced in 1984 by William Gibson, a Canadian science fiction writer. He came up with the term after he walked by a video arcade and noticed the intensity of the players hunched over their screens. Gibson felt that video game enthusiasts "develop a belief that there's some kind of actual space behind the screen. Some place that you can't see but you know is there" (Elmer-DeWitt 1995:4; see also Shields 1996; Wellman et al. 1996).

The emergence of cyberspace can be viewed as yet another step away from Ferdinand Tönnies's concept of **p. 115** the familiar, intimate *Gemeinschaft* toward the comparatively impersonal *Gesellschaft,* and as yet another way in which social cohesion is being eroded in contemporary society. Critics of electronic communication question whether nonverbal communication, voice inflections, and other forms of interpersonal interaction will be lost as people turn to e-mail and chat rooms (P. Schaefer 1995; Schellenberg 1996).

But while some people think that by opening up the world to cyberspace interaction, we may have reduced face-to-face interaction, others have reached different conclusions. Researchers surveyed more than 2,000 households nationwide to assess the impact of the Internet on the everyday lives of its users. Parents reported that they often surfed the web together with their children, and that the Internet had had little effect on their children's interactions with friends. Researchers concluded that about two-thirds of the people in the United States are using the Internet more than ever, and without sacrificing their social lives (Cha 2000; P. Howard et al. 2001; Nie 2001).

Social Control

A data entry employee pauses to say hello to a colleague. A checker at the supermarket takes a moment to banter with

"Keystroke! ... Keystroke! ... Keystroke!"

trace. One report released in 2000 put cybercrime losses by big businesses at $10 billion in the United States alone. Typically, discussions of computer crime focus on computer theft and on problems caused by "hackers," but widespread use of computers has facilitated many new ways of participating in deviant behavior. Consequently, greatly expanded police resources may be needed to deal with online child molesters, prostitution rings, software pirates, con artists, and other types of computer criminal. There is now a Computer Crime and Intellectual Property section of the Justice Department. The consensus of the heads of the section is that these cases are increasing and becoming more difficult to solve (Piller 2000).

a customer. A telephone representative takes too much time helping callers. Each of these situations is subject to computer surveillance. Given the absence of strong protective legislation, employees in the United States are subject to increasing and pervasive supervision by computers.

Supervisors have always scrutinized the performance of workers, but with so much work now being handled electronically, the possibilities for surveillance have risen dramatically. According to a 2001 study, one-third of the online workforce is under continuous electronic surveillance. With Big Brother watching and listening in more and more, the danger is that electronic monitoring will become a substitute for effective management, or worse, lead to perceptions of unfairness and intrusiveness (T. Levin et al. 2002; Schulman 2001).

In recent years, a new type of corporate surveillance has emerged. A number of Internet sites have been highly critical of the operations of various corporations. On McSpotlight, one could find attacks on nutritional practices at McDonald's; on Up Against the Wal, one could study advice on how to fight plans to open a new Wal-Mart store. The Internet sites of such "anticorporate vigilantes" are generally protected by the First Amendment, but powerful corporations are carefully monitoring them in an attempt to counteract their activities (Neuborne 1996).

Technological advances have also created the possibility of a new type of white-collar crime: computer crime. It is now possible to gain access to a computer without leaving home, and to carry out embezzlement or electronic fraud without leaving a

p. 189

Not all the technological advances relevant to social control have been electronic in nature. DNA data banks have given police a powerful new weapon for solving crimes; they have also opened the way to free wrongfully convicted citizens. From 1993 through 2002, 15 death row inmates were released on the basis of DNA evidence. Efforts are under way to make such testing and other forms of DNA evidence as easily available as fingerprinting. While appropriate safeguards must be devised, the creation of DNA data banks has the potential to revolutionize law enforcement in the United States—especially in the prosecution of sex crimes, for which biological evidence is telling (DPIC 2002).

Another connection between technology and social control is the use of computer databases and electronic verification of documents to reduce illegal immigration to the United States, especially from Muslim nations. While they are concerned about the issue of illegal entry, many Arab Americans, Hispanics, and Asian Americans nevertheless believe that *their* privacy, rather than that of Whites, is most likely to be infringed by government authorities. In the next section we will consider more fully how technological changes can intensify stratification and inequality based on race, ethnicity, and other factors.

Stratification and Inequality

"Today we stand at the brink of becoming two societies, one largely white and plugged in and the other black and unplugged." This is how Black historian Henry Lewis Gates, Jr., starkly describes today's "digital divide" (Gates 1999:A15). Stratification is a continuing theme in sociology. Thus far, there is little evidence to suggest that technology will reduce inequality; in fact, it may only intensify it. Technology is costly, so it is generally impossible to introduce it to everyone simultaneously. Who gets access first? Conflict theorists contend that as we travel further and further along the electronic frontier, through advances such as telecommuting and the Internet, the disenfranchised poor may become isolated from mainstream society in an "information ghetto," just as racial and ethnic minorities have traditionally been subjected to residential segregation (DiMaggio et al. 2001).

Available data show clear differences in the use of computers based on class, race, and ethnicity. A national study released in 2001 estimated that only 14 percent of households earning less than $15,000 had access to the Internet, compared to 79 percent of those with incomes of $75,000 or more. Moreover, 56 percent of Asian American households and 46 percent of White households used the Internet, compared with 24 percent of Hispanic and African American households (see Figure 23-2).

This issue goes beyond individual interest or lack of interest in computers. Accessibility is a major concern. According to a study by the Consumer Federation of America and the National Association for the Advancement of Colored People (NAACP), accessibility to computer networks through fiber-optic corridors (the "information superhighway") may bypass poor neighborhoods and minority populations. The researchers concluded that regional telephone companies' plans for these advanced communications networks target affluent areas, and may lead to an exclusionary "electronic redlining" that resembles discrimination in fields such as banking, real estate, and insurance (Lieberman 1999; Lohr 1994).

Industry executives counter that they have repeatedly stated their intention to deploy the information superhighway to *all* areas. Congress has proposed regulatory

FIGURE 23-2

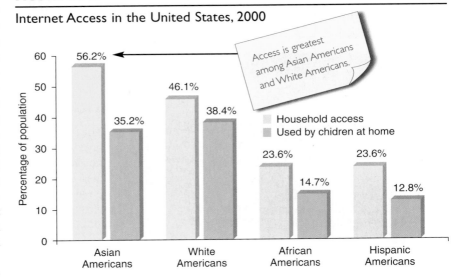

Internet Access in the United States, 2000

Source: Newburger 2001:3–4.

legislation to ensure equal access to the information superhighway by mandating the wiring of schools, libraries, and hospitals. And several communities, such as Manchester, New Hampshire, and Oakland, California, have recently arranged for computer hookups in publicly built low-income housing.

The issue of technology and inequality is especially sensitive when viewed in cross-cultural perspective. Although industrialization has dramatically improved many workers' standard of living, it has allowed elites to amass untold wealth. Moreover, the activities of multinational corporations have increased the inequality between industrialized core nations such as the United States, Germany, and Japan and peripheral developing countries.

Use Your Sociological Imagination

One hundred years from now, how might society have changed? Will people be as free as they are today? Will the differences among social classes be more or less pronounced than they are now? What about the differences among nations, races, religions, and ethnic groups?

Since the terrorist attacks of September 11, 2001, security has grown tighter in public places, and Americans have become accustomed to surveillance they once might have considered invasive.

The Issue

According to BBC News, in 2002, the average city dweller was seen on closed-circuit TV about 300 times a day. Preposterous, you say? Look around you. In train stations and lobbies, on street corners and in elevators, the electronic eye is watching you. In some places, digital cameras may be snapping your picture and sending it to a computer that compares it to the photos of known criminals. You may not want to know about it, but your phone calls, e-mails, credit card purchases, and other forms of electronic communication are all being monitored in some way or other (Rheingold 2003).

Not all these means of surveillance are used for crime prevention. Much of the data organizations gather about you is used for marketing purposes, or compiled for resale to other organizations or individuals. While many people consider such activities an invasion of privacy, at this point in the United States privacy laws have so many loopholes, it is often difficult to distinguish between legally and illegally gathered data. The other side of this coin is censorship—the fear that in an attempt to protect citizens' privacy, government will restrict the flow of electronic information too much. Not everyone is worried about censorship, however; many

people think the government should be allowed to ban pornography on the Internet.

The Setting

The typical consumer in the United States is included in dozens of marketing databases. These lists may seem innocent enough at first. Does it really matter if companies can buy lists of our names, addresses, and telephone numbers? Part of the problem is that computer technology has made it increasingly easy for any individual, business firm, or government agency to retrieve and store more and more information about any of us.

For the average U.S. citizen, the question of how much free expression should be permitted on the Internet relates to the issue of pornography. Pornography websites have proliferated, especially since the Supreme Court struck down federal legislation to regulate "indecent" words and images in 1997. Some of the X-rated material is perfectly legal, if inappropriate for children. Some sites are clearly illegal, such as those that serve the needs of pedophiles who prey on young children. Others are morally and legally ambiguous, such as the sites that post images taken by cameras aimed up the skirts of unsuspecting women in public places.

In other countries, censorship of the Internet is the major issue. On average, the People's Republic of China blocks 50,000 popular web addresses every day, including those of Amnesty International and BBC News. China is not alone in its censorship of the Internet. Myanmar, Cuba, Saudi Arabia, and Vietnam also limit their citizens' access to certain websites (Reporters sans Frontieres 1999; Zittrain and Edelman 2002).

Sociological Insights

In this technological age, the complex issue of privacy versus censorship can be considered an illustration of culture lag. As usual, the material culture (technology) is changing faster than the nonmaterial culture (norms for controlling the use of technology).

Functionalists point to the Internet's manifest function of facilitating communications. They identify its latent function as providing a way for groups with few resources to communicate with tens of millions of people. Poorly financed groups ranging from hate organizations to special interest groups can vie with powerful wealthy interests in this arena. Thus, the functionalist perspective would see technology as fostering communication. The issue of censorship depends on how one views the content of the message; the issue of privacy, on how information is used.

Viewed from a conflict perspective, however, there is an ever-present danger that a society's most powerful groups will use technological advances to invade the privacy of the less powerful. In the past, totalitarian governments have routinely done so, in an effort to stifle dissent and maintain political and social control. Civil liberties advocates remind us that the same abuses can occur in the United States if citizens are not vigilant in protecting their right to privacy.

Interactionists view the debate over privacy and censorship as one that parallels the concerns people have in any social interaction. Just as we may disapprove of some associations that relatives or friends have with other people, we express concern over controversial websites. We may attempt to monitor both. Obviously, the Internet facilitates interactions with a broad range of people, with minimal likelihood of detection compared to face-to-face interactions. Moreover, one can easily move a website from one country to another, avoiding not only detection but also prosecution.

Policy Initiatives

In 1986, the federal government passed the Electronic Communications Privacy Act. Wire communications—defined as use of the human voice in telephone and cordless calls—are highly protected. They cannot be subjected to surveillance unless a prosecutor obtains authorization from both the U.S. attorney general and a federal judge. In contrast, telegrams, faxes, and e-mail can be monitored with the approval of a judge (Eckenwiler 1995).

In 1996, the Communications Decency Act made it a federal crime to transmit "indecent" or "patently offensive" material over the Internet without maintaining safeguards to ensure that children cannot see it. Private e-mail and online chat room communications with anyone under the age of 18 were subjected to the same standard (Fernández 1996; Lappin 1996).

Civil liberties advocates insisted that such governmental action infringes on private communications between consenting adults and inevitably limits freedom of speech. Organizations such as the American Civil Liberties Union (ACLU), the American Library Association, the American Society of Newspaper Editors, and the National Writers Union supported lawsuits challenging the constitutionality of the Communications Decency Act. In 1997, the Supreme Court declared major parts of the act unconstitutional. The Court called government attempts to regulate content on the Inter-

net an attack on the First Amendment guarantee of freedom of speech (Fernández 1996; Harmon 1998).

One month after the terrorist attacks of September 11, 2001, however, Congress passed the Patriot Act, which empowered authorities to move quickly against terrorist threats. As a result, legal checks on surveillance by law enforcement officers have been relaxed. Federal agencies are now freer to gather data electronically on both citizens and resident foreigners.

Both at home and abroad, the U.S. government has been developing a reputation for opposing efforts to protect people's privacy. For example, in 1998 the Center for Public Integrity, a nonpartisan research organization, issued a report that criticized the government for failing to pass legislation protecting the confidentiality

The 1974 motion picture *The Conversation,* in which Gene Hackman eavesdropped on other characters' conversations in their homes and in the park, raised an alarm among viewers concerned about their privacy. A generation later, citizens wonder how much of their electronic communication is monitored, and for what purposes.

of medical records. In another case, a U.S. Navy investigator persuaded America Online to reveal the identity of a sailor who had described himself online as gay. In 1998, both the Navy and America Online were forced to reach settlements for violating the sailor's privacy. At the same time, the United States has been vocal in opposing efforts by the European Union to implement a tough new law designed to protect citizens from computer-age privacy invasions. The U.S. technology industry does not want access to information blocked, since information is vital to global commerce. While a compromise is likely, this case illustrates the fine line between safeguarding privacy and stifling the electronic flow of information (Center for Public Integrity 1998; Perry 1998; Shenon 1998).

The conflict over privacy and censorship is far from over. As technology continues to advance in the twenty-first century, new battles are sure to be fought.

Let's Discuss

1. What are some of the ways that people can obtain information about us? Are you aware of any databases that contain information about your personal life?
2. Do you think corporations and employers have a right to monitor employees' e-mail and phone calls? Why or why not?
3. Are you more concerned about government censorship of electronic communication or about unauthorized invasion of your privacy? As a policymaker, how would you balance these concerns?

CHAPTER RESOURCES

Summary

Social change is significant alteration over time in behavior patterns and culture, including norms and values. *Technology* is information about how to use the material resources of the environment to satisfy human needs and desires. This chapter examines sociological theories of social change, resistance to change, and the impact of technology on society's future and on social change.

1. Early advocates of the *evolutionary theory* of social change believed that society was progressing inevitably toward a higher state.
2. Talcott Parsons, a leading advocate of functionalist theory, viewed society as being in a natural state of equilibrium or balance.
3. Conflict theorists see change as having crucial significance, since it is needed to correct social injustices and inequalities.
4. In general, those with a disproportionate share of society's wealth, status, and power have a *vested interest* in preserving the status quo, and will resist change.
5. The period of maladjustment when a nonmaterial culture is still struggling to adapt to new material conditions is known as *culture lag.*
6. In the computer age, *telecommuters* are linked to their supervisors and colleagues through computer terminals, phone lines, and fax machines.
7. The core industrialized nations have a virtual monopoly on information technology, making the pe-

ripheral nations dependent on them both for technology and for the information it provides.

8. Advances in biotechnology have raised difficult ethical questions about genetic engineering and the sex selection of fetuses.
9. Social scientists focus on human error in the *normal accidents* associated with increasing reliance on technology.
10. Most of the information available on the Internet is written in English and a handful of other languages.
11. Computer and video technology have facilitated supervision, control, and even domination of workers and citizens by employers and the government.
12. Conflict theorists fear that the disenfranchised poor may become isolated from mainstream society in an "information ghetto," just as racial and ethnic minorities have been subjected to residential segregation.
13. Computer technology has made it increasingly easy for any individual, business firm, or government agency to retrieve more and more information about any of us, thereby infringing on our privacy. How much government should restrict access to electronic information is an important public policy issue.

Critical Thinking Questions

1. In the last few years we have witnessed phenomenal growth in the use of cellular phones around the world. Analyze this form of material culture in terms of culture lag. Consider usage, government regulation, and privacy issues.
2. Consider one of the technological advances discussed in the section on technology and the future. Analyze this new technology, focusing on whether it is likely to increase or reduce inequality in the coming decades. Whenever possible, address issues of gender, race, ethnicity, and class, as well as inequality between nations.
3. In what ways has social interaction in your college community been affected by the technological advances examined in this chapter? Are particular subcultures more or less likely to employ new forms of electronic communication?

Key Terms

Apartheid A former policy of the South African government, designed to maintain the separation of Blacks and other non-Whites from the dominant Whites. (page 531)

Culture lag A period of maladjustment when the nonmaterial culture is still struggling to adapt to new material conditions. (532)

Equilibrium model The functionalist view that society tends toward a state of stability or balance. (528)

Evolutionary theory A theory of social change that holds that society is moving in a definite direction. (527)

Luddites Rebellious craft workers in 19th-century England who destroyed new factory machinery as part of their resistance to the industrial revolution. (532)

Multilinear evolutionary theory A theory of social change that holds that change can occur in several ways, and does not inevitably lead in the same direction. (528)

Normal accident A failure that is inevitable, given the manner in which human and technological systems are organized. (536)

Social change Significant alteration over time in behavior patterns and culture, including norms and values. (527)

Technology Information about how to use the material resources of the environment to satisfy human needs and desires. (533)

Telecommuter Employee who works full-time or part-time at home rather than in an outside office and who is linked to supervisor and colleagues through computer terminals, phone lines, and fax machines. (533)

Unilinear evolutionary theory A theory of social change that holds that all societies pass through the same successive stages of evolution and inevitably reach the same end. (528)

Vested interests Those people or groups who will suffer in the event of social change, and who have a stake in maintaining the status quo. (530)

TECHNOLOGY RESOURCES

Internet Connection

*Note: While all the URLs listed were current as of the printing of this book, these sites often change. Please check our website (**www.mhhe.com/schaefer9**) for updates, hyperlinks, and exercises related to these sites.*

1. The field of biotechnology has brought us many scientific advances, some of which, like the sex selection of fetuses, are highly publicized and controversial. But are you aware of the intensifying debate over genetically modified (GM) food crops? Explore the issues surrounding this debate by linking to this PBS website: **www. pbs.org/ wgbh/harvest.**

2. The Internet Economy Indicators website (**www.internetindicators.com/facts.html**) provides basic information about the history and usage of the Internet. Visit the site to find information on such topics as the number of webpages on the Net, the percentage of college graduates who looked for careers online in summer 2001, and the number of adults who go online every month.

Online Learning Center with PowerWeb

Is Big Brother watching? Visit the student center in the Online Learning Center at **www.mhhe.com/schaefer9** and link to "Audio Clips." Listen to Richard Schaefer, the author of this text, discuss how the advent of a new technology has led to a loss of privacy. Professor Schaefer talks about a study of public video cameras conducted by the American Civil Liberties Union in New York City.

Numbers following the definitions indicate pages where the terms were identified. Consult the index for further page references.

A

Absolute poverty A minimum level of subsistence that no family should be expected to live below. (211)

Achieved status A social position that is attained by a person largely through his or her own efforts. (106, 200)

Activity theory An interactionist theory of aging that argues that elderly people who remain active and socially involved will be best-adjusted. (307)

Adoption In a legal sense, a process that allows for the transfer of the legal rights, responsibilities, and privileges of parenthood to a new legal parent or parents. (336)

Affirmative action Positive efforts to recruit minority group members or women for jobs, promotions, and educational opportunities. (259, 431)

Ageism A term coined by Robert N. Butler to refer to prejudice and discrimination based on a person's age. (316)

Agrarian society The most technologically advanced form of preindustrial society. Members are engaged primarily in the production of food, but increase their crop yields through technological innovations such as the plow. (116)

Alienation A condition of estrangement or disassociation from the surrounding society. (133, 423)

Amalgamation The process through which a majority group and a minority group combine to form a new group. (263)

Anomie Durkheim's term for the loss of direction felt in a society when social control of individual behavior has become ineffective. (10, 182)

Anomie theory of deviance Robert Merton's theory of deviance as an adaptation of socially prescribed goals or of the norms governing their attainment, or both. (182)

Anticipatory socialization Processes of socialization in which a person "rehearses" for future positions, occupations, and social relationships. (90)

Anti-Semitism Anti-Jewish prejudice. (272)

Apartheid A former policy of the South African government, designed to maintain the separation of Blacks and other non-Whites from the dominant Whites. (263, 531)

Applied sociology The use of the discipline of sociology with the specific intent of yielding practical applications for human behavior and organizations. (18)

Argot Specialized language used by members of a group or subculture. (69)

Ascribed status A social position that is assigned to a person by society without regard for the person's unique talents or characteristics. (105, 199)

Assembling perspective A theory of collective behavior introduced by McPhail and Miller that seeks to examine how and why people move from different points in space to a common location. (509)

Asset-based community development (ABCD) An approach to community development in which planners first identify a community's strengths and then seek to mobilize those assets. (473)

Assimilation The process through which a person forsakes his or her own cultural tradition to become part of a different culture. (263)

Authority Institutionalized power that is recognized by the people over whom it is exercised. (399)

B

Basic sociology Sociological inquiry conducted with the objective of gaining a more profound knowledge of the fundamental aspects of social phenomena. Also known as *pure sociology*. (20)

Bilateral descent A kinship system in which both sides of a person's family are regarded as equally important. (326)

Bilingualism The use of two or more languages in a particular setting, such as a workplace or schoolroom, treating each language as equally legitimate. (74)

Birthrate The number of live births per 1,000 population in a given year. Also known as the crude birthrate. (489)

Black power A political philosophy promoted by many younger Blacks in the 1960s that supported the creation of Black-controlled political and economic institutions. (266)

Borderlands The area of common culture along the border between Mexico and the United States. (240)

Bourgeoisie Karl Marx's term for the capitalist class, comprising the owners of the means of production. (203)

Brain drain The immigration to the United States and other industrialized nations of skilled workers, professionals, and technicians who are desperately needed in their home countries. (441)

Bureaucracy A component of formal organization that uses rules and hierarchical ranking to achieve efficiency. (133)

Bureaucratization The process by which a group, organization, or social movement becomes increasingly bureaucratic. (135)

C

Capitalism An economic system in which the means of production are held largely in private hands and the main incentive for economic activity is the accumulation of profits. (203, 415)

Caste A hereditary rank, usually religiously dictated, that tends to be fixed and immobile. (200)

Causal logic The relationship between a condition or variable and a particular consequence in which one event leads to the other. (32)

Census An enumeration, or counting, of a population. (488)

Charismatic authority Max Weber's term for power made legitimate by a leader's exceptional personal or emotional appeal to his or her followers. (399)

Class A group of people who have a similar level of wealth and income. (205)

Class consciousness In Karl Marx's view, a subjective awareness held by members of a class regarding their common vested interests and need for collective political action to bring about social change. (203)

Classical theory An approach to the study of formal organizations that views workers as being motivated almost entirely by economic rewards. (136)

Class system A social ranking based primarily on economic position in which achieved characteristics can influence mobility. (201)

Clinical sociology The use of the discipline of sociology with the specific intent of facilitating change by altering social relationships or restructuring social institutions. (20)

Closed system A social system in which there is little or no possibility of individual mobility. (216)

Coalition A temporary or permanent alliance geared toward a common goal. (132)

Code of ethics The standards of acceptable behavior developed by and for members of a profession. (41)

Cognitive theory of development Jean Piaget's theory that children's thought progresses through four stages of development. (88)

Cohabitation The practice of living together as a male–female couple without marrying. (340)

Collective behavior In the view of sociologist Neil Smelser, the relatively spontaneous and unstructured behavior of a group of people who are reacting to a common influence in an ambiguous situation. (506)

Colonialism The maintenance of political, social, economic, and cultural dominance over a people by a foreign power for an extended period. (229)

Communism As an ideal type, an economic system under which all property is communally owned and no social distinctions are made on the basis of people's ability to produce. (417)

Community A spatial or political unit of social organization that gives people a sense of belonging, based either on shared residence in a particular place or on a common identity. (461)

Concentric-zone theory A theory of urban growth devised by Ernest Burgess that sees growth in terms of a series of rings radiating from the central business district. (466)

Conflict perspective A sociological approach that assumes that social behavior is best understood in terms of conflict or tension between competing groups. (14)

Conformity Going along with peers—individuals of our own status, who have no special right to direct our behavior. (172)

Contact hypothesis An interactionist perspective which states that in cooperative circumstances, interracial contact between people of equal status will reduce prejudice. (262)

Content analysis The systematic coding and objective recording of data, guided by some rationale. (40)

Control group The subjects in an experiment who are not introduced to the independent variable by the researcher. (39)

Control theory A view of conformity and deviance that suggests that our connection to members of society leads us to systematically conform to society's norms. (176)

Control variable A factor that is held constant to test the relative impact of an independent variable. (34)

Corporate welfare Tax breaks, direct payments, and grants that the government makes to corporations. (220)

Correlation A relationship between two variables in which a change in one coincides with a change in the other. (32)

Correspondence principle A term used by Bowles and Gintis to refer to the tendency of schools to promote the values expected of individuals in each social class and to prepare students for the types of jobs typically held by members of their class. (381)

Counterculture A subculture that deliberately opposes certain aspects of the larger culture. (71)

Craze An exciting mass involvement that lasts for a relatively long period. (512)

Creationism A literal interpretation of the Bible regarding the creation of humanity and the universe, used to argue that evolution should not be presented as established scientific fact. (369)

Credentialism An increase in the lowest level of education required to enter a field. (380)

Crime A violation of criminal law for which some governmental authority applies formal penalties. (188)

Cross-tabulation A table that shows the relationship between two or more variables. (51)

Crowd A temporary gathering of people in close proximity who share a common focus or interest. (509)

Cult Due to stereotyping, this term has been abandoned by sociologists in favor of *new religious movements.* (365)

Cultural relativism The viewing of people's behavior from the perspective of their own culture. (73)

Cultural transmission A school of criminology that argues that criminal behavior is learned through social interactions. (183)

Cultural universal A common practice or belief found in every culture. (59, 351)

Culture The totality of learned, socially transmitted customs, knowledge, material objects, and behavior. (58)

Culture-bound syndrome A disease or illness that cannot be understood apart from its specific social context. (438)

Culture lag A period of maladjustment when the nonmaterial culture is still struggling to adapt to new material conditions. (62, 532)

Culture shock The feeling of surprise and disorientation that people experience when they witness cultural practices that are different from their own. (72)

Curanderismo Latino folk medicine, a form of holistic health care and healing. (447)

D

Death rate The number of deaths per 1,000 population in a given year. Also known as the *crude death rate.* (489)

Defended neighborhood A neighborhood that residents identify through defined community borders and a

perception that adjacent areas are geographically separate and socially different. (472)

Degradation ceremony An aspect of the socialization process within some total institutions, in which people are subjected to humiliating rituals. (91)

Deindustrialization The systematic, widespread withdrawal of investment in basic aspects of productivity such as factories and plants. (426)

Demographic transition A term used to describe the change from high birthrates and death rates to low birthrates and death rates. (490)

Demography The scientific study of population. (485)

Denomination A large, organized religion that is not officially linked with the state or government. (363)

Dependency theory An approach that contends that industrialized nations continue to exploit developing countries for their own gain. (230)

Dependent variable The variable in a causal relationship that is subject to the influence of another variable. (32)

Deviance Behavior that violates the standards of conduct or expectations of a group or society. (176)

Differential association A theory of deviance proposed by Edwin Sutherland that holds that violation of rules results from exposure to attitudes favorable to criminal acts. (183)

Diffusion The process by which a cultural item spreads from group to group or society to society. (60)

Disaster A sudden or disruptive event or set of events that overtaxes a community's resources, so that outside aid is necessary. (510)

Discovery The process of making known or sharing the existence of an aspect of reality. (60)

Discrimination The denial of opportunities and equal rights to individuals and groups because of prejudice or other arbitrary reasons. (257)

Disengagement theory A functionalist theory of aging introduced by Cumming and Henry that contends that society and the aging individual mutually sever many of their relationships. (305)

Domestic partnership Two unrelated adults who share a mutually caring relationship, reside together, and agree to be jointly responsible for their dependents, basic living expenses, and other common necessities. (342)

Dominant ideology A set of cultural beliefs and practices that help to maintain powerful social, economic, and political interests. (69, 154, 207)

Downsizing Reductions taken in a company's workforce as part of deindustrialization. (427)

Dramaturgical approach A view of social interaction, popularized by Erving Goffman, in which people are seen as theatrical performers. (17, 86)

Dyad A two-member group. (131)

Dysfunction An element or a process of society that may disrupt a social system or lead to a decrease in stability. (14)

E

Ecclesia A religious organization that claims to include most or all members of a society, and is recognized as the national or official religion. (362)

E-commerce Numerous ways in which people with access to the Internet do business from their computers. (430)

Economic system The social institution through which goods and services are produced, distributed, and consumed. (415)

Education A formal process of learning in which some people consciously teach while others adopt the social role of learner. (375)

Egalitarian family An authority pattern in which spouses are regarded as equals. (326)

Elite model A view of society as being ruled by a small group of individuals who share a common set of political and economic interests. (405)

Emergent-norm perspective A theory of collective behavior proposed by Turner and Killian that holds that a collective definition of appropriate and inappropriate behavior emerges during episodes of collective behavior. (507)

Endogamy The restriction of mate selection to people within the same group. (330)

Environmental justice A legal strategy based on claims that racial minorities are subjected disproportionately to environmental hazards. (499)

Equilibrium model Talcott Parsons's functionalist view that society tends toward a state of stability or balance. (528)

Established sect J. Milton Yinger's term for a religious group that is the outgrowth of a sect, yet remains isolated from society. (365)

Estate system A system of stratification under which peasants were required to work land leased to them by nobles in exchange for military protection and other services. Also known as *feudalism*. (200).

Esteem The reputation that a particular individual has earned within an occupation. (209)

Ethnic group A group that is set apart from others primarily because of its national origin or distinctive cultural patterns. (250)

Ethnocentrism The tendency to assume that one's own culture and way of life represent the norm or are superior to all others. (73, 255)

Ethnography The study of an entire social setting through extended systematic observation. (37)

Euthanasia The act of bringing about the death of a hopelessly ill and suffering person in a relatively quick and painless way for reasons of mercy. (318)

Evolutionary theory A theory of social change that holds that society is moving in a definite direction. (527)

Exogamy The requirement that people select a mate outside certain groups. (330)

Experiment An artificially created situation that allows the researcher to manipulate variables. (38)

Experimental group The subjects in an experiment who are exposed to an independent variable introduced by a researcher. (39)

Exploitation theory A Marxist theory that views racial subordination in the United States as a manifestation of the class system inherent in capitalism. (260)

Expressiveness Concern for the maintenance of harmony and the internal emotional affairs of family. (286)

Extended family A family in which relatives—such as grandparents, aunts, or uncles—live in the same home as parents and their children. (324)

F

Face-work A term used by Erving Goffman to refer to the efforts people make to maintain the proper image and avoid public embarrassment. (86)

Fad A temporary pattern of behavior that involves large numbers of people and is independent of preceding trends. (511)

False consciousness A term used by Karl Marx to describe an attitude held by members of a class that does not accurately reflect their objective position. (203, 515)

Familism Pride in the extended family, expressed through the maintenance of close ties and strong obligations to kinfolk outside the immediate family. (333)

Family A set of people related by blood, marriage, or some other agreed-on relationship, or adoption, who share the primary responsibility for reproduction and caring for members of society. (324)

Fashion A pleasurable mass involvement that has a line of historical continuity. (511)

Feminist view A sociological approach that views inequity in gender as central to all behavior and organization. (15)

Fertility The level of reproduction in a society. (485)

Focus group A group of 10 to 15 people assembled by a researcher to discuss a predetermined topic, guided by a moderator. (130)

Folkway A norm governing everyday behavior whose violation raises comparatively little concern. (66)

Force The actual or threatened use of coercion to impose one's will on others. (399)

Formal norm A norm that has been written down and that specifies strict punishments for violators. (66)

Formal organization A group designed for a special purpose and structured for maximum efficiency. (132)

Formal social control Social control that is carried out by authorized agents, such as police officers, judges, school administrators, and employers. (174)

Functionalist perspective A sociological approach that emphasizes the way that parts of a society are structured to maintain its stability. (13)

G

Gatekeeping The process by which a relatively small number of people control what material eventually reaches the audience. (154)

Gemeinschaft A term used by Ferdinand Tönnies to describe a close-knit community, often found in rural areas, in which strong personal bonds unite members. (115)

Gender role Expectations regarding the proper behavior, attitudes, and activities of a male or female. (91, 282)

Generalized other A term used by George Herbert Mead to refer to the attitudes, viewpoints, and expectations of society as a whole that a child takes into account in his or her behavior. (85)

Genocide The deliberate, systematic killing of an entire people or nation. (262)

Gentrification The resettlement of low-income city neighborhoods by prosperous families and business firms. (478)

Gerontology The scientific study of the sociological and psychological aspects of aging and the problems of the aged. (305)

Gesellschaft A term used by Ferdinand Tönnies to describe a community, often urban, that is large and impersonal, with little commitment to the group or consensus on values. (116)

Glass ceiling An invisible barrier that blocks the promotion of a qualified individual in a work environment because of the individual's gender, race, or ethnicity. (257, 293)

Globalization The worldwide integration of government policies, cultures, social movements, and financial markets through trade and the exchange of ideas. (60, 230)

Goal displacement Overzealous conformity to official regulations of a bureaucracy. (134)

Goal multiplication The process through which an organization expands its purpose. (139)

Goal succession The process through which an organization identifies an entirely new objective because its traditional goals have been realized or denied. (139)

Group Any number of people with similar norms, values, and expectations who interact with one another on a regular basis. (109, 127)

Growth rate The difference between births and deaths, plus the difference between immigrants and emigrants, per 1,000 population. (489)

H

Hawthorne effect The unintended influence that observers of experiments can have on their subjects. (39)

Health As defined by the World Health Organization, a state of complete physical, mental, and social well-being, and not merely the absence of disease and infirmity. (438)

Health maintenance organization (HMO) An organization that provides comprehensive medical services for a preestablished fee. (456)

Hidden curriculum Standards of behavior that are deemed proper by society and are taught subtly in schools. (379)

Holistic medicine Therapies in which the health care practitioner considers the person's physical, mental, emotional, and spiritual characteristics. (450)

Homophobia Fear of and prejudice against homosexuality. (283)

Horizontal mobility The movement of an individual from one social position to another of the same rank. (216)

Horticultural society A preindustrial society in which people plant seeds and crops rather than merely subsist on available foods. (116)

Hospice care Treatment of the terminally ill in their own homes, or in special hospital units or other facilities, with the goal of helping them to die easily, without pain. (313)

Human ecology An area of study concerned with the interrelationships between people and their environment. (464, 498)

Human relations approach An approach to the study of formal organizations that emphasizes the role of people, communication, and participation within a bureaucracy and tends to focus on the informal structure of the organization. (136)

Human rights Universal moral rights possessed by all people because they are human. (243)

Hunting-and-gathering society A preindustrial society in which people rely on whatever foods and fibers are readily available in order to survive. (116)

Hypothesis A speculative statement about the relationship between two or more variables. (32)

I

Ideal type A construct or model for evaluating specific cases. (10, 133)

Impression management A term used by Erving Goffman to refer to the altering of the presentation of the self in order to create distinctive appearances and satisfy particular audiences. (86)

Incest taboo The prohibition of sexual relationships between certain culturally specified relatives. (330)

Incidence The number of new cases of a specific disorder occurring within a given population during a stated period. (444)

Income Salaries and wages. (199)

Independent variable The variable in a causal relationship that causes or influences a change in a second variable. (32)

Industrial city A relatively large city characterized by open competition, an open class system, and elaborate specialization in the manufacturing of goods. (463)

Industrial society A society that depends on mechanization to produce its goods and services. (118, 415)

Infant mortality rate The number of deaths of infants under one year of age per 1,000 live births in a given year. (489)

Influence The exercise of power through a process of persuasion. (399)

Informal economy Transfers of money, goods, or services that are not reported to the government. (237, 418)

Informal norm A norm that is generally understood but not precisely recorded. (66)

Informal social control Social control that is carried out casually by ordinary people through such means as laughter, smiles, and ridicule. (174)

In-group Any group or category to which people feel they belong. (129)

Innovation The process of introducing a new idea or object into a culture through discovery or invention. (60)

Institutional discrimination The denial of opportunities and equal rights to individuals and groups that results from the normal operations of a society. (258, 289)

Instrumentality An emphasis on tasks, a focus on more distant goals, and a concern for the external relationship between one's family and other social institutions. (286)

Interactionist perspective A sociological approach that generalizes about everyday forms of social interaction in order to understand society as a whole. (16)

Intergenerational mobility Changes in the social position of children relative to their parents. (217)

Interview A face-to-face or telephone questioning of a respondent to obtain desired information. (37)

Intragenerational mobility Changes in a person's social position within his or her adult life. (217)

Invention The combination of existing cultural items into a form that did not previously exist. (60)

Iron law of oligarchy A principle of organizational life developed by Robert Michels, under which even democratic organizations will develop into bureaucracies ruled by a few individuals. (135)

Issei Japanese immigrants to the United States. (269)

K

Kinship The state of being related to others. (325)

L

Labeling theory An approach to deviance that attempts to explain why certain people are viewed as deviants while others engaged in the same behavior are not. (185)

Labor union Organized workers who share either the same skill or the same employer. (141)

Laissez-faire A form of capitalism under which people compete freely, with minimal government intervention in the economy. (416)

Language An abstract system of word meanings and symbols for all aspects of culture; includes gestures and other nonverbal communication. (63)

Latent function Unconscious or unintended function; hidden purpose. (14)

Law Governmental social control. (66, 175)

Legal-rational authority Max Weber's term for power made legitimate by law. (399)

Liberation theology Use of a church, primarily Roman Catholicism, in a political effort to eliminate poverty, discrimination, and other forms of injustice from a secular society. (358)

Life chances Max Weber's term for the opportunities people have to provide themselves with material goods, positive living conditions, and favorable life experiences. (215)

Life expectancy The median number of years a person can be expected to live under current mortality conditions. (489)

Looking-glass self A concept used by Charles Horton Cooley that emphasizes the self as the product of our social interactions with others. (84)

Luddites Rebellious craft workers in nineteenth-century England who destroyed new factory machinery as part of their resistance to the industrial revolution. (532)

M

Machismo A sense of virility, personal worth, and pride in one's maleness. (333)

Macrosociology Sociological investigation that concentrates on large-scale phenomena or entire civilizations. (13)

Manifest function Open, stated, and conscious function. (14)

Mass media Print and electronic instruments of communication that carry messages to often widespread audiences. (149)

Master status A status that dominates others and thereby determines a person's general position in society. (106)

Material culture The physical or technological aspects of our daily lives. (62)

Matriarchy A society in which women dominate in family decision making. (326)

Matrilineal descent A kinship system in which only the relatives of the mother are significant. (326)

McDonaldization The process by which the principles of the fast-food restaurant industry have come to dominate certain sectors of society, both in the United States and throughout the world. (127)

Mean A number calculated by adding a series of values and then dividing by the number of values. (50)

Mechanical solidarity A collective consciousness that emphasizes group solidarity, characteristic of societies with minimal division of labor. (115)

Median The midpoint or number that divides a series of values into two groups of equal numbers of values. (50)

Megalopolis A densely populated area containing two or more cities and their surrounding suburbs. (464)

Mental illness A disorder of the brain that disrupts a person's thinking, feeling, and ability to interact with others. (452)

Microsociology Sociological investigation that stresses study of small groups and often uses laboratory experimental studies. (13)

Midlife crisis A stressful period of self-evaluation that begins at about age 40. (309)

Migration Relatively permanent movement of people with the purpose of changing their place of residence. (494)

Minority group A subordinate group whose members have significantly less control or power over their own lives than the members of a dominant or majority group have over theirs. (250)

Mode The single most common value in a series of scores. (50)

Model or **ideal minority** A minority group that despite past prejudice and discrimination, succeeds economically, socially, and educationally without resorting to confrontations with Whites. (268)

Modernization The far-reaching process by which peripheral nations move from traditional or less developed institutions to those characteristic of more developed societies. (232)

Modernization theory A functionalist approach that proposes that modernization and development will gradually improve the lives of people in developing nations. (233)

Monogamy A form of marriage in which one woman and one man are married only to each other. (325)

Monopoly Control of a market by a single business firm. (416)

Morbidity rate The incidence of disease in a given population. (444)

Mores Norms deemed highly necessary to the welfare of a society. (66)

Mortality rate The incidence of death in a given population. (444)

Multilinear evolutionary theory A theory of social change that holds that change can occur in several ways, and does not inevitably lead in the same direction. (528)

Multinational corporation A commercial organization that is headquartered in one country but does business throughout the world. (230)

Multiple-nuclei theory A theory of urban growth developed by Harris and Ullman that views growth as emerging from many centers of development, each of which may reflect a particular urban need or activity. (467)

N

Narcotizing dysfunction The phenomenon in which the media provide such massive amounts of information that the audience becomes numb and generally fails to act on the information, regardless of how compelling the issue. (153)

Natural science The study of the physical features of nature and the ways in which they interact and change. (6)

Negotiated order A social structure that derives its existence from the social interactions through which people define and redefine its character. (105)

Negotiation The attempt to reach agreement with others concerning some objective. (104)

Neocolonialism Continuing dependence of former colonies on foreign countries. (229)

New religious movement (NRM) or **cult** A small, secretive religious group that represents either a new religion or a major innovation of an existing faith. (365)

New social movement An organized collective activity that addresses values and social identities, as well as improvements in the quality of life. (517)

New urban sociology An approach to urbanization that considers the interplay of local, national, and worldwide forces and their effect on local space, with special emphasis on the impact of global economic activity. (467)

Nisei Japanese children born in the United States to the Issei. (269)

Nonmaterial culture Ways of using material objects, as well as customs, beliefs, philosophies, governments, and patterns of communication. (62)

Nonperiodic assembly A nonrecurring gathering of people that often results from word-of-mouth information. (509)

Nonverbal communication The sending of messages through the use of posture, facial expressions, and gestures. (16)

Norm An established standard of behavior maintained by a society. (66)

Normal accident A failure that is inevitable, given the manner in which human and technological systems are organized. (536)

Nuclear family A married couple and their unmarried children living together. (324)

O

Obedience Compliance with higher authorities in a hierarchical structure. (172)

Objective method A technique for measuring social class that assigns individuals to classes on the basis of criteria such as occupation, education, income, and place of residence. (208)

Observation A research technique in which an investigator collects information through direct participation and/or closely watching a group, tribe, or community. (37)

Open system A social system in which the position of each individual is influenced by his or her achieved status. (216)

Operational definition An explanation of an abstract concept that is specific enough to allow a researcher to assess the concept. (30)

Opinion leader Someone who, through day-to-day personal contacts and communication, influences the opinions and decisions of others. (160)

Organic solidarity A collective consciousness that rests on mutual interdependence, characteristic of societies with a complex division of labor. (115)

Organized crime The work of a group that regulates relations between criminal enterprises involved in illegal activities, including prostitution, gambling, and the smuggling and sale of drugs. (188)

Out-group A group or category to which people feel they do not belong. (129)

P

Panic A fearful arousal or collective flight based on a generalized belief that may or may not be accurate. (512)

Patriarchy A society in which men dominate in family decision making. (326)

Patrilineal descent A kinship system in which only the relatives of the father are significant. (326)

Percentage A portion of 100. (50)

Periodic assembly A recurring, relatively routine gathering of people, such as a college class. (509)

Personality A person's typical patterns of attitudes, needs, characteristics, and behavior. (81)

Peter principle A principle of organizational life, originated by Laurence J. Peter, according to which each individual within a hierarchy tends to rise to his or her level of incompetence. (135)

Pluralism Mutual respect for one another's cultures among the various groups in a society, which allows minorities to express their own cultures without experiencing prejudice. (264)

Pluralist model A view of society in which many competing groups within the community have access to government, so that no single group is dominant. (407)

Political socialization The process by which individuals acquire political

attitudes and develop patterns of political behavior. (400)

Political system The social institution that is founded on a recognized set of procedures for implementing and achieving society's goals. (397)

Politics In Harold Lasswell's words, "who gets what, when, and how." (397)

Polyandry A form of polygamy in which a woman may have more than one husband at the same time. (325)

Polygamy A form of marriage in which an individual may have several husbands or wives simultaneously. (325)

Polygyny A form of polygamy in which a man may have more than one wife at the same time. (325)

Population pyramid A special type of bar chart that shows the distribution of population by gender and age. (492)

Postindustrial city A city in which global finance and the electronic flow of information dominate the economy. (463)

Postindustrial society A society whose economic system is engaged primarily in the processing and control of information. (118)

Postmodern society A technologically sophisticated society that is preoccupied with consumer goods and media images. (119)

Power The ability to exercise one's will over others. (205, 397)

Power elite A term used by C. Wright Mills for a small group of military, industrial, and government leaders who control the fate of the United States. (405)

Preindustrial city A city of only a few thousand people that is characterized by a relatively closed class system and limited mobility. (462)

Prejudice A negative attitude toward an entire category of people, often an ethnic or racial minority. (255)

Prestige The respect and admiration that an occupation holds in a society. (208)

Prevalence The total number of cases of a specific disorder that exist at a given time. (444)

Primary group A small group characterized by intimate, face-to-face association and cooperation. (127)

Profane The ordinary and commonplace elements of life, as distinguished from the sacred. (351)

Profession An occupation requiring extensive knowledge that is governed by a code of ethics. (422)

Professional criminal A person who pursues crime as a day-to-day occupation, developing skilled techniques and enjoying a certain degree of status among other criminals. (188)

Proletariat Karl Marx's term for the working class in a capitalist society. (203)

Protestant ethic Max Weber's term for the disciplined work ethic, this-worldly concerns, and rational orientation to life emphasized by John Calvin and his followers. (358)

Public A dispersed group of people, not necessarily in contact with one another, who share an interest in an issue. (513)

Public opinion Expressions of attitudes on matters of public policy that are communicated to decision makers. (513)

Q

Qualitative research Research that relies on what is seen in field or naturalistic settings more than on statistical data. (37)

Quantitative research Research that collects and reports data primarily in numerical form. (37)

Questionnaire A printed or written form used to obtain desired information from a respondent. (37)

R

Racial group A group that is set apart from others because of obvious physical differences. (250)

Racism The belief that one race is supreme and all others are innately inferior. (255)

Random sample A sample for which every member of the entire population has the same chance of being selected. (33)

Reference group Any group that individuals use as a standard for evaluating themselves and their own behavior. (130)

Relative deprivation The conscious feeling of a negative discrepancy between legitimate expectations and present actualities. (515)

Relative poverty A floating standard of deprivation by which people at the bottom of a society, whatever their lifestyles, are judged to be disadvantaged *in comparison with the nation as a whole*. (211)

Reliability The extent to which a measure provides consistent results. (33, 389)

Religion According to Émile Durkheim, a unified system of beliefs and practices relative to sacred things. (351)

Religious belief A statement to which members of a particular religion adhere. (360)

Religious experience The feeling or perception of being in direct contact with the ultimate reality, such as a divine being, or of being overcome with religious emotion. (361)

Religious ritual A practice required or expected of members of a faith. (360)

Remittances The monies that immigrants return to their families of origin. Also called *migradollars*. (242).

Research design A detailed plan or method for obtaining data scientifically. (35)

Resocialization The process of discarding former behavior patterns and accepting new ones as part of a transition in one's life. (90)

Resource mobilization The ways in which a social movement utilizes such resources as money, political influence, access to the media, and personnel. (515)

Rite of passage A ritual marking the symbolic transition from one social position to another. (88)

Role conflict The situation that occurs when incompatible expectations arise from two or more social positions held by the same person. (108)

Role exit The process of disengagement from a role that is central to one's self-identity and establishment of a new role and identity. (108)

Role strain The difficulty that arises when the same social position imposes conflicting demands and expectations. (108)

Role taking The process of mentally assuming the perspective of another and responding from that imagined viewpoint. (85)

Routine activities theory The notion that criminal victimization increases when there is a convergence of motivated offenders and suitable targets. (184)

Rumor A piece of information gathered informally that is used to interpret an ambiguous situation. (513)

S

Sacred Elements beyond everyday life that inspire awe, respect, and even fear. (351)

Sample A selection from a larger population that is statistically representative of that population. (33)

Sanction A penalty or reward for conduct concerning a social norm. (67, 172)

Sandwich generation The generation of adults who simultaneously try to meet the competing needs of their parents and their children. (311)

Sapir-Whorf hypothesis A hypothesis concerning the role of language in shaping our interpretation of reality. It holds that language is culturally determined. (63)

School choice program An educational experiment under which parents can choose where to send their children to school. (391)

School voucher program A form of school choice program in which public funds are transferred to the public or private school of the parents' choice. (391)

Science The body of knowledge obtained by methods based on systematic observation. (6)

Scientific management approach Another name for the classical theory of formal organizations. (136)

Scientific method A systematic, organized series of steps that ensures maximum objectivity and consistency in researching a problem. (29)

Secondary analysis A variety of research techniques that make use of previously existing and publicly accessible information and data. (39)

Secondary group A formal, impersonal group in which there is little social intimacy or mutual understanding. (128)

Second shift The double burden—work outside the home followed by child care and housework—that many women face and few men share equitably. (294).

Sect A relatively small religious group that has broken away from some other religious organization to renew what it considers the original vision of the faith. (364)

Secularization The process through which religion's influence on other social institutions diminishes. (351)

Segregation The physical separation of two groups of people in terms of residence, workplace, and social events; often imposed on a minority group by a dominant group. (263)

Self According to George Herbert Mead, a distinct identity that sets us apart from others. (84)

Senilicide The killing of the aged. (318)

Serial monogamy A form of marriage in which a person may have several spouses in his or her lifetime, but only one spouse at a time. (325)

Sexism The ideology that one sex is superior to the other. (288)

Sexual harassment Behavior that occurs when work benefits are made contingent on sexual favors (as a quid pro quo), or when touching, lewd comments, or the exhibition of pornographic material creates a "hostile environment" in the workplace. (291)

Sick role Societal expectations about the attitudes and behavior of a person viewed as being ill. (439)

Significant other A term used by George Herbert Mead to refer to an individual who is most important in the development of the self, such as a parent, friend, or teacher. (86)

Single-parent family A family in which only one parent is present to care for the children. (337)

Slavery A system of enforced servitude in which people are legally owned by others and in which enslaved status is transferred from parents to children. (200)

Small group A group small enough for all members to interact simultaneously—that is, to talk with one another or at least be acquainted. (130)

Social change Significant alteration over time in behavior patterns and culture, including norms and values. (527)

Social constructionist perspective An approach to deviance that emphasizes the role of culture in the creation of the deviant identity. (185)

Social control The techniques and strategies for preventing deviant behavior in any society. (171)

Social epidemiology The study of the distribution of disease, impairment, and general health status across a population. (443)

Social inequality A condition in which members of a society have differing amounts of wealth, prestige, or power. (20, 199)

Social institution Organized patterns of beliefs and behavior centered on basic social needs. (112)

Social interaction The ways in which people respond to one another. (103)

Socialism An economic system under which the means of production and distribution are collectively owned. (417)

Socialization The lifelong process in which people learn the attitudes, values, and behaviors appropriate for members of a particular culture. (81)

Social mobility Movement of individuals or groups from one position of a society's stratification system to another. (216)

Social movement An organized collective activity to bring about or resist fundamental change in an existing group or society. (513)

Social network A series of social relationships that links a person directly to others, and through them indirectly to still more people. (110)

Social role A set of expectations for people who occupy a given social position or status. (106)

Social science The study of various aspects of human society. (6)

Social structure The way in which a society is organized into predictable relationships. (103)

Societal-reaction approach Another name for labeling theory. (185)

Society A fairly large number of people who live in the same territory, are relatively independent of people outside it, and participate in a common culture. (58)

Sociobiology The systematic study of how biology affects human social behavior. (62)

Sociocultural evolution The process of change and development in human societies that results from cumulative growth in their stores of cultural information. (116)

Sociological imagination An awareness of the relationship between an individual and the wider society. (6)

Sociology The systematic study of social behavior and human groups. (3)

Squatter settlement An area occupied by the very poor on the fringe of cities, in which housing is often constructed by the settlers themselves from discarded material. (471)

Status A term used by sociologists to refer to any of the full range of socially defined positions within a large group or society. (105)

Status group A term used by Max Weber to refer to people who have the same prestige or lifestyle, independent of their class positions. (205)

Stereotype An unreliable generalization about all members of a group that does not recognize individual differences within the group. (154, 253)

Stigma A label used to devalue members of certain social groups. (180)

Stratification A structured ranking of entire groups of people that perpetuates unequal economic rewards and power in a society. (199)

Subculture A segment of society that shares a distinctive pattern of mores, folkways, and values that differs from the pattern of the larger society. (69)

Suburb According to the Census Bureau, any territory within a metropolitan area that is not included in the central city. (474)

Surveillance function The collection and distribution of information concerning events in the social environment. (153)

Survey A study, generally in the form of an interview or questionnaire, that provides researchers with information concerning how people think and act. (35)

Symbol A gesture, object, or word that forms the basis of human communication. (85)

Symbolic ethnicity An ethnic identity that emphasizes concerns such as ethnic food or political issues rather than deeper ties to one's ethnic heritage. (273)

T

Teacher-expectancy effect The impact that a teacher's expectations about a student's performance may have on the student's actual achievements. (382)

Technology Information about how to use the material resources of the environment to satisfy human needs and desires. (62, 116, 533)

Telecommuter An employee who works full-time or part-time at home rather than in an outside office and who is linked to supervisor and colleagues through computer terminals, phone lines, and fax machines. (140, 533)

Terrorism The use or threat of violence against random or symbolic targets in pursuit of political aims. (398)

Theory In sociology, a set of statements that seeks to explain problems, actions, or behavior. (8)

Total fertility rate (TFR) The average number of children born alive to any woman, assuming that she conforms to current fertility rates. (489)

Total institution A term coined by Erving Goffman to refer to an institution that regulates all aspects of a person's life under a single authority, such as a prison, the military, a mental hospital, or a convent. (90)

Tracking The practice of placing students in specific curriculum groups on the basis of test scores and other criteria. (381)

Traditional authority Legitimate power conferred by custom and accepted practice. (399)

Trained incapacity The tendency of workers in a bureaucracy to become so specialized that they develop blind spots and fail to notice obvious problems. (133)

Triad A three-member group. (131)

U

Underclass The long-term poor who lack training and skills. (213)

Unilinear evolutionary theory A theory of social change that holds that

all societies pass through the same successive stages of evolution and inevitably reach the same end. (528)

Urban ecology An area of study that focuses on the interrelationships between people and their environment in urban areas. (464)

Urbanism A term used by Louis Wirth to describe distinctive patterns of social behavior evident among city residents. (463)

V

Validity The degree to which a scale or measure truly reflects the phenomenon under study. (33, 389)

Value A collective conception of what is considered good, desirable, and proper—or bad, undesirable, and improper—in a culture. (67)

Value-added model A theory of collective behavior proposed by Neil Smelser to explain how broad social conditions are transformed in a definite pattern into some form of collective behavior. (507)

Value neutrality Max Weber's term for objectivity of sociologists in the interpretation of data. (43)

Variable A measurable trait or characteristic that is subject to change under different conditions. (32)

Verstehen The German word for "understanding" or "insight"; used by Max Weber to stress the need for sociologists to take into account people's emotions, thoughts, beliefs, and attitudes. (10)

Vertical mobility The movement of a person from one social position to another of a different rank. (216)

Vested interests Veblen's term for those people or groups who will suffer in the event of social change, and who have a stake in maintaining the status quo. (530)

Victimization survey A questionnaire or interview given to a sample of the

population to determine whether people have been victims of crime. (191)

Victimless crime A term used by sociologists to describe the willing exchange among adults of widely desired, but illegal, goods and services. (190)

Vital statistics Records of births, deaths, marriages, and divorces gathered through a registration system maintained by governmental units. (488)

Voluntary association An organization established on the basis of common interest, whose members volunteer or even pay to participate. (138)

W

Wealth An inclusive term encompassing all a person's material assets, including land, stocks, and other types of property. (199)

White-collar crime Crimes committed by affluent, "respectable" individuals in the course of business activities. (189)

World systems analysis Immanuel Wallerstein's view of the global economic system as divided between certain industrialized nations that control wealth and developing countries that are controlled and exploited. (229, 467)

X

Xenocentrism The belief that the products, styles, or ideas of one's society are inferior to those that originate elsewhere. (73)

Z

Zero population growth (ZPG) The state of a population in which the number of births plus immigrants equals the number of deaths plus emigrants. (494)

References

A

AARP. 1999. "New AARP Study Finds Boomers Vary in Their Views of the Future and Their Retirement Years." AARP News Release, June 1. Washington, DC.

———. 2001. *Beyond 50—A Report to the Nation on Economic Security.* Washington, DC: AARP.

———. 2003. Home page. Accessed May 12 (www.aarp.org).

ABC News. 1992. *Primetime Live: True Colors.* Transcript of November 26 episode.

Abercrombie, Nicholas, Bryan S. Turner, and Stephen Hill, eds. 1990. *Dominant Ideologies.* Cambridge, MA: Unwin Hyman.

———, Stephen Hill, and Bryan S. Turner. 1980. *The Dominant Ideology Thesis.* London: George Allen and Unwin.

Aberle, David E., A. K. Cohen, A. K. Davis, M. J. Leng, Jr., and F. N. Sutton. 1950. "The Functional Prerequisites of a Society." *Ethics* 60 (January):100–111.

Abrahams, Ray G. 1968. "Reaching an Agreement over Bridewealth in Labwor, Northern Uganda: A Case Study." Pp. 202–215 in *Councils in Action,* edited by Audrey Richards and Adam Kuer. Cambridge: Cambridge University Press.

Abrahamson, Mark. 1978. *Functionalism.* Englewood Cliffs, NJ: Prentice Hall.

Abramovitz, Janet N. 2001a. "Averting Unnatural Disasters." Pp. 123–142 in *State of the World 2001,* edited by Lester R. Brown, Christopher Flavin, and Hilary French. New York: Norton.

———. 2001b. *Unnatural Disasters.* Washington D.C.: Worldwatch Institute.

Abrams, Lisa M., Joseph J. Pedulla, and George F. Madaus. 2003. "Views from the Classroom: Teachers' Opinions of Statewide Testing Progress." *Theory Into Practice* 42 (Winter):18–28.

Acharya, Menna. 2000. *Labor Market Developments and Poverty: With Focus on Economic Opportunities for Women.* Kathmandu, Nepal: Tanka Prasad Acharya Foundation/ FES.

Acosta, R. Vivian, and Linda Jean Carpenter. 2001. "Women in Intercollegiate Sport: A Longitudinal Study: 1977–1998." Pp. 302–308 in *Sport in Contemporary Society: An Anthology.* 6th ed., edited by D. Stanley Eitzen. New York: Worth.

Adam, Barry D. 1992. "Sociology and People Living with AIDS." Pp. 3–18 in *The Social Context of AIDS,* edited by Joan Huber and Beth E. Schneider. Newbury Park, CA: Sage.

———. 1995. *The Rise of a Gay and Lesbian Movement.* Rev. ed. New York: Twayne.

———, Jan Willem Duyvendak, and André Krouwei, eds. 1999. *The Global Emergence of Gay and Lesbian Politics: National Impact of a Worldwide Movement.* Philadelphia: Temple University Press.

Adam, Kanya. 2000. "Affirmative Action and Popular Perceptions: The Case of South Africa." *Society* 37 (February):48–55.

Addams, Jane. 1910. *Twenty Years at Hull-House.* New York: Macmillan.

———. 1930. *The Second Twenty Years at Hull-House.* New York: Macmillan.

Adler, Patricia, and Peter Adler. 2003. "The Promise and Pitfalls of Going into the Field." *Contexts* (Spring): 41–47.

———, Peter Adler, and John M. Johnson. 1992. "Street Corner Society Revisited." *Journal of Contemporary Ethnography* 21 (April): 3–10.

Adler, William M. 2000. *Mollie's Job: A Story of Life and Work on the Global Assembly Line.* New York: Scribner.

AFL-CIO. 2001. *More Workers Are Choosing a Voice at Work.* Accessed April 18 (www. aflcio.org/voiceatwork/morejoin/htm).

Aguirre, Benigno E., E. L. Quarantelli, and Jorge L. Mendoza. 1988. "The Collective Behavior of Fads: The Characteristics, Effects, and Career of Streaking." *American Sociological Review* 53 (August):569–584.

AIDS Alert. 1999. "AIDS Complacency Leads Back to Risk Behavior." November 14, pp. 127–128.

Aizcorbe, Ana M., Arthur B. Kennickell, and Kevin B. Moore. 2003. "Recent Changes in U.S. Family Finances: Evidence from the 1998 and 2001 Survey of Consumer Finances." *Federal Reserve Bulletin* (January):1–32.

Alain, Michel. 1985. "An Empirical Validation of Relative Deprivation." *Human Relations* 38 (8):739–749.

Alba, Richard D. 1990. *Ethnic Identity: The Transformation of White America.* New Haven, CT: Yale University Press.

Albas, Daniel, and Cheryl Albas. 1988. "Aces and Bombers: The Post-Exam Impression Management Strategies of Students." *Symbolic Interaction* 11 (Fall):289–302.

Albiniak, P. 2000. "TV's Drug Deal." *Broadcasting and Cable,* January 17, pp. 3, 148.

Albom, Mitch. 1997. *Tuesdays with Morrie.* New York: Doubleday.

Albrecht, Gary L., Katerine D. Steelman, and Michael Bury. 2001. *Handbook of Disabilities Study.* Thousand Oaks, CA: Sage.

Alexander, Alison, and Janice Hanson, eds. 2001. *Taking Sides: Mass Media and Society.* 6th ed. New York: McGraw-Hill/ Dushkin.

Alexander, Keith L. 2001. "Merged Media Titan's Competitors Gird for Expected Battle." *USA Today,* January 12, p. 3B.

Alfino, Mark, John S. Caputo, and Robin Wynyard. 1998. *McDonaldization Revisited: Critical Essays on Consumer Culture.* Westport, CT: Praeger.

Allen, Bern P. 1978. *Social Behavior: Fact and Falsehood.* Chicago: Nelson-Hall.

Allen, Ernest, Jr., and Robert Chrisman. 2001. "Ten Reasons: A Response to David Horowitz." *The Black Scholar* 31 (Summer):49–55.

Allen, John L. 2001. *Student Atlas of World Geography.* 2d ed. Chicago: McGraw-Hill/ Dushkin.

———. 2003. *Student Atlas of World Geography.* 3rd ed. New York: McGraw-Hill.

Allport, Gordon W. 1979. *The Nature of Prejudice.* 25th anniversary ed. Reading, MA: Addison-Wesley.

Alvarez, Lizette. 2001. "Senate Rejects Tuition and a Key to Bush Education Plan." *New York Times,* June 15, p. A28.

Alvord, Lori Arviso, and Elizabeth Cohen Van Pelt. 1999. *The Scalpel and the Silver Bear.* New York: Bantam.

Alwin, Duane F. 2002. "Generations X, Y, and Z: Are They Changing America?" *Contexts* (Fall/Winter): 42–51.

Alzheimer's Association. 1999. "Statistics/ Prevalence." Accessed January 10, 2000 (www.alz.org/facts/stats.htm).

Amato, Paul, and Alan Booth. 1997. *A Generation at Risk.* Cambridge, MA: Harvard University Press.

Amato, Paul R. 2001. "What Children Learn from Divorce." *Population Today,* January, pp. 1, 4.

————, and Juliana M. Sobolewski. 2001. "The Effects of Divorce and Marital Discord on Adult Children's Psychological Well-Being." *American Sociological Review* 66 (December): 900–921.

American Association of Medical Colleges. 2003a. "FACTS—Applicants, Matriculates and Graduates." Accessed June 14, 2003 (www.aamc.org).

————. 2003b. "Distribution of U.S. Medical School Faculty by Sex and Race/Hispanic Origin." Accessed June 14 (www.aamc.org).

American Association of University Women. 1998. *Gender Gaps: Where Schools Still Fail Our Children.* Washington, DC: AAUW.

American Bar Association. 1999. "Commission on Domestic Violence." Accessed July 20 (www.abanet.org/domviol/stats.html).

American Civil Liberties Union. 2000. "State and Local Laws Protecting Lesbians and Gay Men against Workplace Discrimination." Accessed January 19 (www.aclu.org/issues/gay/gaylaws.html).

————. 2001a. "Domestic Partnerships: List of Cities, States, and Countries." Accessed August 1 (www.aclu.org/issues/gay/dpstate.html).

————. 2001b. "Citing Impact on Minorities, Florida Voting Rights Project Urges DOJ to Object to Electoral Reform Package, July 19, 2001." Accessed June 2, 2003 (www.aclu.org).

American Civil Liberties Union of Northern California. 2002. *Caught in the Backlash: Stories from Northern California.* San Francisco: ACLU of Northern California.

American Federation of Teachers. 2002. "Survey and Analysis of Teacher Salary Trends, 2001." Accessed October 18, 2002 (www.aft.org/research/survey01/statecomparisons.html).

American Jewish Committee. 2001. "2000 Annual Survey of American Jewish Opinion." Accessed October 25 (www.ajc.org/pre/survey2000.htm).

Americans for Medical Rights. 2003. *The State of Medipot.* Washington: Marijuana Policy Project.

American Sociological Association. 1993. *The Sociology Major as Preparation for Careers in Business and Organizations.* Washington, DC: American Sociological Association.

————. 1995. *The Sociological Advantage.* Washington, DC: American Sociological Association.

————. 1997. *Code of Ethics.* Washington, DC: American Sociological Association. Available (www.asanet.org/members/ecoderev.html).

————. 2001. *Data Brief: Profile of ASA Membership.* Washington, DC: American Sociological Association.

————. 2002. *Careers in Sociology.* 6th ed. Washington, DC: American Sociological Association.

————. 2004. *Guide to Graduate Departments of Sociology, 2004.* Washington, DC: American Sociological Association.

Ammerman, Nancy T., Jackson W. Carroll, Carl S. Dudley, and William McKinney, ed. 1998. *Studying Congregations: A New Handbook.* Nashville, TN: Abingdon Press.

Amnesty International. 1994. *Breaking the Silence: Human Rights Violations Based on Sexual Orientation.* New York: Amnesty International.

Amrein, Audrey L., and David C. Berliner. 2002. *The Input of High-Stakes Tests on Student Academic Performance: An Analysis of NAEP Results in States with High-Stakes Tests and ACT, SAT, and AP Test Results in States with High School Graduation Exams.* Tempe, AZ: Education Policy Research Institute.

Amway. 1999. "Amway Asia Pacific Applauds China Commitment to Remove All Restrictions on Direct Selling." News release, April 9. Accessed March 4, 2003 (www.amway.com).

————. 2003. *Our Story.* Accessed March 4 (www.amway.org).

Andersen, Margaret. 1997. *Thinking about Women: Sociological Perspectives on Sex and Gender.* 4th ed. Boston: Allyn and Bacon.

Anderson, Elijah. 1978. *A Place on the Corner.* Chicago: University of Chicago Press.

————. 1990. *Streetwise: Race, Class, and Change in an Urban Community.* Chicago: University of Chicago Press.

————. 1999. *Code of the Streets.* New York: Norton.

————, and Molly Moore. 1993. "The Burden of Womanhood." *Washington Post National Weekly Edition* 10 (March 22–28):6–7.

Angier, Natalie. 1998. "Drugs, Sports, Body Image and G.I. Joe." *New York Times,* December 22, section D. pp. 1, 3.

Anti-Defamation League. 2001. *Audit of Anti-Semitic Incidents.* New York: ADL.

AOL Time Warner. 2003. *About Us.* Accessed July 25, 2003 at (www.aoltimewarner.com).

Appelbaum, Richard, and Peter Dreier. 1999. "The Campus Anti-Sweatshops Movement." *The American Prospect* (September/October):71–78.

Archer, Margaret. 1988. *Culture and Agency: The Place of Culture in Social Theory.* Cambridge: Cambridge University Press.

Argetsinger, Amy, and Jonathan Krim. 2002. "Stopping the Music." *Washington Post National Weekly Edition* 20 (December 2), p. 20.

Arias, Elizabeth, and Betty L. Smith. 2003. "Deaths: Preliminary Data for 2001." *National Vital Statistics Reports* 51 (March 14).

Armer, J. Michael, and John Katsillis. 1992. "Modernization Theory." Pp. 1299–1304 in *Encyclopedia of Sociology,* Vol. 4, edited by Edgar F. Borgatta and Marie L. Borgatta. New York: Macmillan.

Armour, Stephanie, and Michelle Kessler. 2003. "USA's New Money-Saving Export: White Collar Jobs." *USA Today,* August 5, pp. B1, B2.

Aronowitz, Stanley, and William Di Fazio. 1994. *The Jobless Future: Sci-Tech and Dogma of Work.* Minneapolis: University of Minneapolis.

Aronson, Elliot. 1999. *The Social Animal.* 8th ed. New York: Worth.

Ashford, Lori S. 2001. "New Population Policies: Advancing Women's Health and Rights." *Population Bulletin* 56 (March).

Asset-Based Community Development Institute. 2001. *Our Mission.* Accessed September 21 (www.northwestern.edu/IPR/abcd.html).

Associated Press. 1998. "Environmental Test Case Averted." *Christian Science Monitor,* September 21, p. 18.

————. 2001. "Member of the Dwindling Shaker Sect." *Chicago Tribune,* June 20, p. 11.

————. 2003. "House Rejects Attempt to Block Sex-Study Grants." *Seattle Post-Intelligencer,* July 11, p. A13.

Association of American Medical Colleges. 2003a. *Facts-Applicants, Matriculates and Graduates.* Accessed June 14, 2003 (www.aamc.org/data/facts/famg32002.htm).

————. 2003b. *U.S. Medical School Faculty, 2002.* Accessed June 14 (www.amc.org/data/facultyroster/usmsf02/start.htm).

Astin, Alexander, Sarah A. Parrott, William S. Korn, and Linda J. Sax. 1994. *The American Freshman: Thirty Year Trends.* Los Angeles: Higher Education Research Institute.

Atchley, Robert C. 1976. *The Sociology of Retirement.* New York: Wiley.

————. 1985. *The Social Forces in Later Life: An Introduction to Social Gerontology.* 4th ed. Belmont, CA: Wadsworth.

Austin, April. 2002. "Cellphones and Strife in Congo." *Christian Science Monitor* (December 5):11.

Axtell, Roger E. 1990. *Do's and Taboos around the World.* 2d ed. New York: John Wiley and Sons.

Azumi, Koya, and Jerald Hage. 1972. *Organizational Systems.* Lexington, MA: Heath.

B

Bachrach, Christine A. 1986. "Adoption Plans, Adopted Children, and Adoptive Mothers." *Journal of Marriage and the Family* 48 (May):243–253.

Baer, Douglas, James Curtis, and Edward Grabb. 2000. *Has Voluntary Association Activity Declined? A Cross-National Perspective.* Paper presented at the annual meeting of the American Sociological Association, Washington, DC.

Bainbridge, William Sims. 1999. "Cyberspace: Sociology's Natural Domain." *Contemporary Sociology* 28 (November):664–667.

Baker, Therese L. 1999. *Doing Social Research.* 3d ed. New York: McGraw-Hill.

Barr, Cameron W. 2002. "Top Arab TV Network to Hit US Market." *Christian Science Monitor* (December 26):1, 7.

Barrett, David B., and Todd M. Johnson. 2001. "Worldwide Adherents of Selected Religions by Six Continental Areas, Mid-2000." In *Britannica Book of the Year 2001,* p. 302. Chicago: Encyclopedia Britannica.

Barron, Milton L. 1953. "Minority Group Characteristics of the Aged in American Society." *Journal of Gerontology* 8:477–482.

Bassiouni, M. Cherif. 2003. "Sexual Slavery Crosses Moral and National Boundaries." *Chicago Tribune,* February 17, sec. 2, pp. 1, 5.

Basso, Keith H. 1972. "Ice and Travel among the Fort Norman Slave: Folk Taxonomies and Cultural Rules." *Language in Society* 1 (March):31–49.

Bates, Colleen Dunn. 1999. "Medicine's Gender Gap." *Shape,* October.

Bauerlein, Monika. 1996. "The Luddites Are Back." *Utne Reader* (March/April):24, 26.

Bauman, Kurt J. 1999. "Extended Measures of Well-Being: Meeting Basic Needs." *Current Population Reports,* Ser. p. 70, No. 67. Washington, DC: U.S. Government Printing Office.

———, and Nikki L. Graf. 2003. "Education Attainment: 2000." *Census 2000 Brief,* no. C2KBR-24. Washington, DC: U.S. Government Printing Office.

Beagan, Brenda L. 2001. " 'Even If I Don't Know What I'm Doing I Can Make It Look Like I Know What I'm Doing': Becoming a Doctor in the 1990s." *Canadian Review of Sociology and Anthropology* 38:275–292.

Bean, Frank, Steven Trejo, Randy Capps, and Michael Tyler. 2001. *The Latino Middle Class: Myth, Reality and Potential.* Claremont, CA: The Thomás Rivera Policy Institute.

Becerra, Rosina M. 1999. "The Mexican-American Family." Pp. 153–171 in *Ethnic Families in America: Patterns and Variations,* 4th ed., edited by Charles H. Mindel, Robert W. Habenstein, and Roosevelt Wright, Jr. Upper Saddle River, NJ: Prentice Hall.

Becker, Howard S. 1952. "Social Class Variations in the Teacher-Pupil Relationship." *Journal of Educational Sociology* 25 (April): 451–465.

———. 1963. *The Outsiders: Studies in the Sociology of Deviance.* New York: Free Press.

———, ed. 1964. *The Other Side: Perspectives on Deviance.* New York: Free Press.

———. 1973. *The Outsiders: Studies in the Sociology of Deviance.* Rev. ed. New York: Free Press.

Beeghley, Leonard. 1978. *Social Stratification in America: A Critical Analysis of Theory and Research.* Santa Monica, CA: Goodyear Publishing.

Begley, Sharon. 1999. "Designer Babies." *Newsweek* 132 (November 9):61–62.

Belkin, Lisa. 1999. "Getting the Girl." *New York Times Magazine,* July 25, pp. 26–31, 38, 54–55.

Bell, Daniel. 1953. "Crime as an American Way of Life." *Antioch Review* 13 (Summer):131–154.

———. 1999. *The Coming of Post-Industrial Society: A Venture in Social Forecasting.* With new foreword. New York: Basic Books.

Bell, Wendell. 1981. "Modernization." Pp. 186–187 in *Encyclopedia of Sociology.* Guilford, CT: DPG Publishing.

Bellafante, Ginia. 1998. "Feminism: It's All about Me!" *Time* 151 (June 20):54–62.

Belluck, Pam. 2001. "Nuns Offer Clues to Alzheimer's and Aging." *New York Times,* May 7, p. A1.

Belsie, Laurent. 2000. "Strange Webfellows." *Christian Science Monitor,* March 2, pp. 15–16.

———. 2001. "Rise of 'Home Alone' Crowd May Alter US Civic Life." *Christian Science Monitor,* May 24, pp. 1, 2.

Bendick, Marc, Jr., Charles W. Jackson, and J. Horacio Romero. 1993. *Employment Discrimination against Older Workers: An Experimental Study of Hiring Practices.* Washington, DC: Fair Employment Council of Greater Washington.

Bendix, B. Reinhard. 1968. "Max Weber." Pp. 493–502 in *International Encyclopedia of the Social Sciences,* edited by David L. Sills. New York: Macmillan.

Benford, Robert D. 1992. "Social Movements." Pp. 1880–1887 in *Encyclopedia of Sociology,* vol. 4, edited by Edgar F. Borgatta and Marie Borgatta. New York: Macmillan.

Benner, Richard S., and Susan Tyler Hitchcock. 1986. *Life after Liberal Arts.* Charlottesville: Office of Career Planning and Placement, University of Virginia.

Bennett, Claudette E. 1995. "The Black Population in the United States: March 1994 and 1993." *Current Population Reports,* ser. P-20, no. 480. Washington, DC: U.S. Government Printing Office.

Bennett, Vanora. 1997. "Russia's Ugly Little Secret: Misogyny." *Los Angeles Times,* December 6, pp. A1, A9, A10.

Berger, Peter, and Thomas Luckmann. 1966. *The Social Construction of Reality.* New York: Doubleday.

Berk, Richard A. 1974. *Collective Behavior.* Dubuque, IA: Brown.

———, and Howard E. Aldrich. 1972. "Patterns of Vandalism during Civil Disorders as an Indicator of Selection of Targets." *American Sociological Review* 37 (October):533–547.

Berke, Richard L. 2001. "An Older Electorate, Potent and Unpredictable." *New York Times,* March 21, p. D8.

Berkeley Wellness Letter. 1990. "The Nest Refilled." 6 (February):1–2.

Berland, Gretchen K. 2001. "Health Information on the Internet: Accessibility, Quality, and Readability in English and Spanish." *Journal of American Medical Association* 285 (March 23):2612–2621.

Berlin, Brent, and Paul Kay. 1991. *Basic Color Terms: Their Universality and Evolution.* Berkeley, CA: University of California Press.

Bernhardt, Todd. 1997. "Disaster Mythology: A Contest Analysis from 1985 to 1995." Presented at the annual meeting of the Midwest Sociological Society, April, Des Moines, IA.

Bernstein Richard. 2003. "An Aging Europe May Find Itself on the Sidelines." *New York Times,* June 29, p. 3.

Best, Fred, and Ray Eberhard. 1990. "Education for the 'Era of the Adult.' " *The Futurist* 21 (May/June):23–28.

Bharadwaj, Lakshmik. 1992. "Human Ecology." Pp. 848–867 in *Encyclopedia of Sociology,* Vol. 2, edited by Edgar E. Borgatta and Marie L. Borgatta. New York: Macmillan.

Bian, Yanjie. 2002. "Chinese Social Stratification and Social Mobility." Pp. 91–116 in *Annual Review of Sociology,* edited by Karen S. Cook and John Hagan. Palo Alto, CA: Annual Reviews.

Bianchi, Suzanne M., and Daphne Spain. 1996. "Women, Work, and Family in America." *Population Bulletin* 51 (December).

Bielby, Denise D., and William T. Bielby. 2002. "Hollywood Dreams, Harsh Realities: Writing for Film and Television." *Contexts* 1 (Fall/Winter): 21–25.

Bielby, William T., and Denise D. Bielby. 1992. "I Will Follow Him: Family Ties, Gender-Role Beliefs, and Reluctance to Relocate for a Better Job." *American Journal of Sociology* 97 (March):1241–1267.

Billson, Janet Mancini, and Bettina J. Huber. 1993. *Embarking upon a Career with an Undergraduate Degree in Sociology.* 2d ed. Washington, DC: American Sociological Association.

Bishaw, Alemayehu, and John Iceland. 2003. "Poverty: 1999." *Census 2000 Brief* C2KBR-19. Washington, DC: U.S. Government Printing Office.

Biskupic, Joan. 2000. "Abortion Debate Will Continue to Rage." *USA Today*, June 29, p. 9A.

Bjorkman, Sharon. 1999. "Doing Church: The Active Creation of Worship Style." Presented at the Conference of Sociological Ethnography, February 27.

Black, Donald. 1995. "The Epistemology of Pure Sociology." *Law and Social Inquiry* 20 (Summer):829–870.

Blackhall, Leslie J. et al. 1995. "Ethnicity and Attitudes toward Patient Autonomy." *Journal of the American Medical Association* 274 (September 13): 820–825.

Blanchard, Fletcher A., Teri Lilly, and Leigh Ann Vaughan. 1991. "Reducing the Expression of Racial Prejudice." *Psychological Science* 2 (March):101–105.

Blau, Peter M. 1964. *Exchange and Power in Social Life.* New York: Wiley.

———, and Otis Dudley Duncan. 1967. *The American Occupational Structure.* New York: Wiley.

———, and Marshall W. Meyer. 1987. *Bureaucracy in Modern Society.* 3d ed. New York: Random House.

Blauner, Robert. 1964. *Alienation and Freedom.* Chicago: University of Chicago Press.

———. 1972. *Racial Oppression in America.* New York: Harper and Row.

Bloom, Stephen G. 2000. *Postville: A Clash of Cultures in Heartland America.* San Diego, CA: Harcourt Brace.

Blumer, Herbert. 1955. "Collective Behavior." Pp. 165–198 in *Principles of Sociology,* 2d ed., edited by Alfred McClung Lee. New York: Barnes and Noble.

———. 1969. *Symbolic Interactionism: Perspective and Method.* Englewood Cliffs, NJ: Prentice Hall.

Boaz, Rachel Floersheim. 1987. "Early Withdrawal from the Labor Force." *Research on Aging* 9 (December):530–547.

Bok, Sissela. 1998. *Mayhem: Violence as Public Entertainment.* Reading, MA: Addison-Wesley.

Bond, James T., Ellen Galinsky, and Jennifer E. Swanberg. 1998. *The 1997 National Study of the Changing Work Force.* New York: Families and Work Institute.

Booth, William. 2000. "Has Our Can-Do Attitude Peaked?" *Washington Post National Weekly Edition* 17 (February 7):29.

Bornschier, Volker, Christopher Chase-Dunn, and Richard Rubinson. 1978. "Cross-National Evidence of the Effects of Foreign Investment and Aid on Economic Growth and Inequality: A Survey of Findings and a Reanalysis." *American Journal of Sociology* 84 (November):651–683.

Borosage, Robert L. 2003. "Class Welfare: Bush Style." *American Prospect* 14 (March):15–18.

Bottomore, Tom, and Maximilien Rubel, ed. 1956. *Karl Marx: Selected Writings in Sociology and Social Philosophy.* New York: McGraw-Hill.

Boucher, Geoff. 2002. "A Nation Stuck on One Station?" *Los Angeles Times,* October 19, pp. E1, E9.

Boudreaux, Richard. 2002. "Indian Rights Law Is Upheld in Mexico." *Los Angeles Times,* September 7, p. A3.

Bourdieu, Pierre. 1998. *On Television.* New York: The New Press.

Bouvier, Leon F. 1980. "America's Baby Boom Generation: The Fateful Bulge." *Population Bulletin* 35 (April).

Bowles, Samuel, and Herbert Gintis. 1976. *Schooling in Capitalist America: Educational Reforms and the Contradictions of Economic Life.* New York: Basic Books.

Bowling, Michael, Gene Lauren, Matthew J. Hickman, and Devon B. Adams. 2002. "Background Checks for Firearm Transfers, 2001." *Bureau of Justice Statistics Bulletin* (September).

Brady Campaign. 2003. *Brady Campaign—Issue Briefs.* Accessed March 11 (www.bradycampaign.org).

Brady, David. 2003. "Rethinking the Sociological Measurement of Poverty." *Social Forces* 81 (March):715–752.

Brainard, Jeffrey. 2003. "Cloning Debate Moves to the States." *Chronicle of Higher Education* 49 (March 28):A22–A23.

Brannigan, Augustine. 1992. "Postmodernism." Pp. 1522–1525 in *Encyclopedia of Sociology, vo*l. 3, edited by Edgar F. Borgatta and Marie L. Borgatta. New York: Macmillan.

Brannon, Robert. 1976. "Ideology, Myth, and Reality: Sex Equality in Israel." *Sex Roles* 6:403–419.

Braverman, Amy. 2002. "Open Door Sexuality." *University of Chicago Magazine* 95 (October):20–21.

Braxton, Greg, and Dana Calvo. 2002. "Networks Come Under the Gun as Watchdogs Aim for Diversity." *Chicago Tribune,* June 4, sec. 5, p. 2.

Bray, James H., and John Kelly. 1999. *Stepfamilies: Love, Marriage, and Parenting in the First Decade.* New York: Broadway Books.

Brelin, Christa, ed. 1996. *Strength in Numbers: A Lesbian, Gay, and Bisexual Resource.* Detroit: Visible Ink.

Brewer, Cynthia A., and Trudy A. Suchan. 2001. *Mapping Census 2000: The Geography of U.S. Diversity.* Washington, DC: U.S. Government Printing Office.

Brint, Steven. 1998. *Schools and Societies.* Thousand Oaks, CA: Pine Forge Press.

Brischetto, Robert R. 2001. "The Hispanic Middle Class Comes of Age." *Hispanic Business* 23 (December):21–22, 26.

Brockerhoff, Martin P. 2000. "An Urbanizing World." *Population Bulletin* 55 (September).

Brooke, James. 2003a. "The Power of Film: A Bond That Unites Koreans." *New York Times,* January 2.

———. 2003b. "Dowry Too High. Lose Bride and Go to Jail." *New York Times,* May 17, p. 1.

Brower, Brock. 1988. "The Pernicious Power of the Polls." *Money,* March 17, pp. 144–163.

Brown, Michael, and Amy Goldin. 1973. *Collective Behavior: A Review and Reinterpretation of the Literature.* Pacific Palisades, CA: Goodyear.

Brown, Robert McAfee. 1980. *Gustavo Gutierrez.* Atlanta: John Knox.

Brown, Roger W. 1954. "Mass Phenomena." Pp. 833–873 in *Handbook of Social Psychology,* vol. 2, edited by Gardner Lindzey. Reading, MA: Addison-Wesley.

Browne, Irene. 1999. *Latinas and African Women at Work: Race, Gender and Economic Inequality.* New York: Russell Sage Foundation.

Brubaker, Bill. 2001. "A So-So Diagnosis." *Washington Post National Weekly Edition.* September 10, p. 34.

Bruni, Frank. 1998. "A Small-But-Growing Sorority Is Giving Birth to Children for Gay Men." *New York Times,* June 25, p. A12.

Bryant, Adam. 1999. "American Pay Rattles Foreign Partners." *New York Times,* January 17, sec. 6, pp. 1, 4.

Buckley, Stephen. 1997. "Left behind Prosperity's Door." *Washington Post National Weekly Edition,* March 24, pp. 8–9.

Budig, Michelle J. 2002. "Male Advantage and the Gender Composition of Jobs: Who Rides the Glass Escalator?" *Social Problems* 49 (2):258–277.

Budrys, Grace. 2003. *Unequal Health: How In-equality Contributes to Health and Illness.* Lanham, MD: Rowman and Littlefield.

Bullard, Robert. 1983. "Solid Waste Sites and the Black Houston Community." *Sociological Inquiry* 53:273–287.

Bulle, Wolfgang F. 1987. *Crossing Cultures? Southeast Asian Mainland.* Atlanta: Centers for Disease Control.

Bumiller, Elisabeth. 2000. "Resolute Adversary of Divorce." *New York Times,* December 16, pp. A17, A19.

Bunzel, John H. 1992. *Race Relations on Campus: Stanford Students Speak.* Stanford, CA: Portable Stanford.

Bureau of Labor Statistics. 2001a. *Comparative Civilian Labor Force Statistics Ten Countries 1959–2000.* Washington, DC: U.S. Department of Labor, Office of Productivity and Technology.

———. 2001b. *Highlights of Women's Earnings in 2000 Report.* Washington, DC: U.S. Government Printing Office.

———. 2003. *Union Members in 2002.* Accessed February 28 (www.bls.gov).

Bureau of Primary Health Care. 1999. Home page. Accessed January 18, 2000 (www.bphc.hrsa.gov/bphcfactsheet.htm).

Bureau of the Census. 1975. *Historical Statistics of the United States, Colonial Times to 1970.* Washington, DC: U.S. Government Printing Office.

———. 1991. "Half of the Nation's Population Lives in Large Metropolitan Areas." Press release, February 21.

———. 1994. *Statistical Abstract of the United States, 1994.* Washington, DC: U.S. Government Printing Office.

———. 1996. *Statistical Abstract of the United States, 1996.* Washington, DC: U.S. Government Printing Office.

———. 1997. "Geographical Mobility: March 1995 to March 1996." *Current Population Reports,* ser. P-20, no. 497. Washington, DC: U.S. Government Printing Office.

———. 1998. "Race of Wife by Race of Husband." Internet release of June 10.

———. 1999. *Statistical Abstract of the United States, 1996.* Washington, DC: U.S. Government Printing Office.

———. 2000a. *Statistical Abstract of the United States, 2000.* Washington, DC: U.S. Government Printing Office.

———. 2000b. "National Population Projections." Internet release of January 13. Accessed May 11 (www.census.gov/population/ www/projection/natsum-T3html).

———. 2001a. *Statistical Abstract of the United States, 2001.* Washington, DC: U.S. Government Printing Office.

———. 2001b. *Hispanic 1997 Economic Census Survey of Minority-Owned Enterprises.* Series BC97CS-4. Washington, DC: U.S. Government Printing Office.

———. 2001c. *1997 Revenues for Women-Owned Businesses Show Continued Growth.* News release of April 4. Washington, DC: U.S. Government Printing Office.

———. 2001d. *March 2001 Current Population Survey.* From Table PINC-03. Accessed February 1, 2002 (www.census.gov/hhes/ www/income.html).

———. 2001e. *Facts for Features: American/ Alaskan Indian Heritage Month: November 2001.* CB01-FF.15. Accessed October 22 (www.census.gov).

———. 2001a. *Statistical Abstract of the United States, 2002.* Washington, DC: U.S. Government Printing Office.

———. 2002b. *March 2002. Current Population Survey.* From Table PINC-03. Accessed October 18, 2002, (www.census.gov).

———. 2002c. *Historical Estimates of World Population and Total Midyear Population for the World: 1950–2050.* Data updated 10-10-2002. Accessed October 24, 2002 (www.census.gov).

Burgess, Ernest W. 1925. "The Growth of the City." Pp. 47–62 in *The City,* edited by Robert E. Park, Ernest W. Burgess, and Roderick D. McKenzie. Chicago: University of Chicago Press.

Burkett, Elinor. 2000. *The Baby Boom: How Family Friendly America Cheats the Childless.* New York: Free Press.

Burns, John R. 1998. "Once Widowed in India, Twice Scorned." *New York Times,* March 29, p. A1.

Burt, Maritha B. 2001. *What Will It Take to End Homelessness?* Washington, DC: Urban Institute.

Butler, Daniel Allen. 1998. *"Unsinkable": The Full Story.* Mechanicsburg, PA: Stackpole Books.

Butler, Robert N. 1990. "A Disease Called Ageism." *Journal of American Geriatrics Society* 38 (February):178–180.

Butterfield, Fox. 2000. "Racial Disparities Seen as Pervasive in Juvenile Justice." *New York Times,* April 26, pp. A1, A18.

C

Caesar, Lena G., and David R. Williams. 2002. *The ASHA Leader Online: Socioculture and the Delivery of Health Care: Who Gets What and Why.* Accessed December 1 (www.asha.org).

Calhoun, Craig. 1998. "Community without Propinquity Revisited." *Sociological Inquiry* 68 (Summer):373–397.

Campo-Flores, Arian. 2000. "Brown against Brown." *Newsweek* 136 (September 18): 49–51.

Camus, Albert. 1948. *The Plague.* New York: Random House.

Cancel, Cecil Marie. 1997. "The Veil." Accessed October 10, 1999 (http://about.com).

Cantril, Hadley. 1940. *The Invasion from Mars: A Study in the Psychology of Panic.* Princeton, NJ: Princeton University Press.

Caplan, Ronald L. 1989. "The Commodification of American Health Care." *Social Science and Medicine* 28 (11):1139–1148.

Carey, Anne R., and Elys A. McLean. 1997. "Heard It Through the Grapevine?" *USA Today,* September 15, p. B1.

Carrese, Joseph A., and Lorna A. Rhodes. 1995. "Western Bioethics on the Navaho Reservation: Benefit or Harm?" *Journal of the American Medical Association* 274 (September 13):826–829.

Carroll, John. 2003. "The Good Doctor." *American Way* (July 15):26–31.

Carter, Bill, and Jim Rutenberg. 2003. "Shows' Creators Say Television Will Suffer in New Climate." *New York Times,* June 3, pp. C1, C8.

Carty, Win. 1999. "Greater Dependence on Cars Leads to More Pollution in World's Cities." *Population Today* 27 (December): 1–2.

Casper, Lynne M., and Loretta E. Bass. 1998. "Voting and Registration in the Election of November 1996." *Current Population Reports,* ser. P-20, no. 504. Washington, DC: U.S. Government Printing Office.

Castañeda, Jorge G. 1995. "Ferocious Differences." *Atlantic Monthly* 276 (July): 68–69, 71–76.

Castells, Manuel. 1983. *The City and the Grass Roots.* Berkeley: University of California Press.

———. 1997. *The Power of Identity.* Vol. 1 of *The Information Age: Economy, Society and Culture.* London: Blackwell.

———. 1998. *End of Millennium.* Vol. 3 of *The Information Age: Economy, Society and Culture.* London: Blackwell.

———. 2000. *The Information Age: Economy, Society and Culture* (3 vols.). 2d. ed. Oxford and Malden, MA: Blackwell.

———. 2001. *The Internet Galaxy: Reflections on the Internet, Business, and Society.* New York: Oxford University Press.

CBS News. 1979. Transcript of *Sixty Minutes* segment, "I Was Only Following Orders." March 31, pp. 2–8.

Center for Academic Integrity. 2003. *CAI Research.* Accessed February 11 (www.academicintegrity.org).

Center for American Women and Politics. 2003. *Fact Sheet: Women in the U.S. Congress 2003 and Statewide Elective Women 2003.* Rutgers, NJ: CAWP.

Center for Public Integrity. 1998. *Nothing Sacred: The Politics of Privacy.* Washington, DC: CPI.

Centers for Disease Control and Prevention. 2003. *A Glance at the HIV Epidemic.* Accessed February 25 (www.cdc.gov).

Centers for Medicare and Medicaid Services. 2003. *National Health Care Expenditures Projections: 2002–2112, Methodological Summary.* Accessed June 14 (cms.hhs.gov/statistics/nhe/projections-2002/high lights.asp).

Cerulo, Karen A., Janet M. Ruane, and Mary Chagko. 1992. "Technological Ties that Bind: Media Generated Primary Groups." *Communication Research* 19:109–129.

Cetron, Marvin J., and Owen Davies. 1991. "Trends Shaping the World." *Futurist* 20 (September–October):11–21.

Cha, Ariena Eunjung. 2000. "Painting a Portrait of Dot-Camaraderie." *The Washington Post,* October 26, pp. E1, E10.

Chalfant, H. Paul, Robert E. Beckley, and C. Eddie Palmer. 1994. *Religion in Contemporary Society.* 3d ed. Itasca, IL: F. E. Peacock.

Chambliss, Wilham. 1973. "The Saints and the Roughnecks." *Society* 11 (November/December): 24–31.

Chandler, Clay. 2001. "Workers of the World." *Washington Post National Weekly Edition* 19 (December 10):17.

Chang, Leslie. 2003. "Amway in China: Once Banned, Now Booming." *Wall Street Journal,* March 12, pp. B1, B5.

Chang, Patricia M. Y. 1997. "Female Clergy in the Contemporary Protestant Church: A Current Assessment." *Journal for the Scientific Study of Religion* 36 (December): 564–573.

Charter, David, and Jill Sherman. 1996. "Schools Must Teach New Code of Values." *London Times,* January 15, p. 1.

Chase-Dunn, Christopher, and Peter Grimes. 1995. "World-Systems Analysis." Pp. 387–417 in *Annual Review of Sociology, 1995,* edited by John Hagan. Palo Alto, CA: Annual Reviews.

———, Yukio Kawano, and Benjamin D. Brewer. 2000. "Trade Globalization Since 1795: Waves of Integration in the World System." *American Sociological Review* 65 (February):77–95.

Chatzky, Jean Sherman. 1999. "The Big Squeeze." *Money* 28 (October):129, 131–134, 136–138.

Cheng, Wei-yuan, and Lung-li Liao. 1994. "Women Managers in Taiwan." Pp. 143–159 in *Competitive Frontiers: Women Managers in a Global Economy,* edited by Nancy J. Adler and Dafna N. Izraeli. Cambridge, MA: Blackwell Business.

Cherlin, Andrew J. 2002. *Public and Private Families: An Introduction.* 3d ed. New York: McGraw-Hill.

Chesney-Lind, Meda, and Noelie Rodriguez. 1993. "Women under Lock and Key." *Prison Journal* 63:47–65.

Chicago Tribune. 1997. "In London, Prince Meets a Pauper, an Ex-Classmate." December 5, p. 19.

Children Now. 2001. *The Local Television News Media's Picture of Children.* Oakland, CA: Children Now.

Children's Bureau. 2002. *FY 1998, FY 1999, and FY 2000 Foster Care: Entries, Exits and In Care on the Last Day.* Accessed May 19, 2003 (www.acf.dhhs.gov/programs/cb/dis/tables/entryexit.htm).

Chin, Ko-lin. 1996. *Chinatown Gangs: Extortion, Enterprise, and Ethnicity.* New York: Oxford University Press.

Christiansen, John B., and Sharon N. Barnartt. 1995. *Deaf President Now: The 1988 Revolution at Gallaudet University.* Washington, DC: Gallaudet University Press.

Christensen, Kathleen. 1990. "Bridges over Troubled Water: How Older Workers View the Labor Market." Pp. 175–207 in *Bridges to Retirement,* edited by Peter B. Doeringer. Ithaca, NY: IRL Press.

Christie, Brigan. 2001. "Sociological Medicine's Aches and Pains." Pp. 222–223 in *Encyclopedia Britannica Yearbook 2001.* Chicago: Encyclopedia Britannica.

Civic Ventures. 1999. *The New Face of Retirement: Older Americans, Civic Engagement, and the Longevity Revolution.* Washington, DC: Peter D. Hart Research Associates.

Clark, Burton, and Martin Trow. 1966. "The Organizational Context." Pp. 17–70 in *The Study of College Peer Groups,* edited by Theodore M. Newcomb and Everett K. Wilson. Chicago: Aldine.

Clark, Candace. 1983. "Sickness and Social Control." Pp. 346–365 in *Social Interaction: Readings in Sociology,* 2d ed., edited by Howard Robboy and Candace Clark. New York: St. Martin's.

Clarke, Adele E., Janet K. Shim, Laura Maro, Jennifer Ruth Fusket, and Jennifer R. Fishman. 2003. "Bio Medicalization: Technoscientific Transformations of Health, Illness, and U.S. Biomedicine." *American Sociological Review* 68 (April): 161–194.

Clarke, Lee. 1999. *Mission Improbable: Using Fantasy Documents to Tame Disaster.* Chicago: University of Chicago Press.

———. 2002. "Panic: Myth or Reality?" *Contexts* 1 (Fall):21–26.

Clausen, Christopher. 2002. "To Have . . . or Not to Have." *Utne Reader* (July–August): 66–70.

Clawson, Dan, and Mary Ann Clawson. 1999. "What Has Happened to the U.S. Labor Movement? Union Decline and Renewal." Pp. 95–119 in *Annual Review of Sociology 1999,* edited by Karen S. Cook and John Hagan. Palo Alto, CA: Annual Reviews.

Clawson, Dan, and Naomi Gerstel. 2002. "Caring for Our Young: Child Care in Europe and the United States." *Contexts* 1 (Fall/Winter):23–35.

Clinard, Marshall B., and Robert F. Miller. 1998. *Sociology of Deviant Behavior.* 10th ed. Fort Worth: Harcourt Brace.

Cloud, John. 2001. "A License to Kill?" *Time* 157 (August 23):66.

Clymer, Adam. 2000. "College Students Not Drawn to Voting or Politics, Poll Shows." *New York Times.* January 2, p. A14.

Cockerham, William C. 1998. *Medical Sociology.* 7th ed. Upper Saddle River, NJ: Prentice Hall.

Cohen, David, ed. 1991. *The Circle of Life: Ritual from the Human Family Album.* San Francisco: Harper.

Cohen, Lawrence E., and Marcus Felson. 1979. "Social Change and Crime Rate Trends: A Routine Activities Approach." *American Sociological Review* 44:588–608.

Cohen, Patricia. 1998. "Daddy Dearest: Do You Really Matter?" *New York Times,* July 11, p. B7.

Colapinto, John. 2003. "The Young Hipublicans." *New York Times Magazine* (May 25):30–35, 58–59.

Cole, David. 1999. *No Equal Justice: Race and Class in the American Criminal Justice System.* New York: The New Press.

Cole, Elizabeth S. 1985. "Adoption, History, Policy, and Program." Pp. 638–666 in *A Handbook of Child Welfare,* edited by John Laird and Ann Hartman. New York: Free Press.

Cole, Mike. 1988. *Bowles and Gintis Revisited: Correspondence and Contradiction in Educational Theory.* Philadelphia: Falmer.

Coleman, James William, and Donald R. Cressey. 1980. *Social Problems.* New York: Harper and Row.

Collins, Randall. 1975. *Conflict Sociology: Toward an Explanatory Sociology.* New York: Academic.

———. 1979. *The Credential Society: An Historical Sociology of Education and Stratification.* New York: Academic.

———. 1980. "Weber's Last Theory of Capitalism: A Systematization." *American Sociological Review* 45 (December):925–942.

———. 1986. *Weberian Sociological Theory.* New York: Cambridge University Press.

———. 1995. "Prediction in Macrosociology: The Case of the Soviet Collapse." *American Journal of Sociology* 100 (May): 1552–1593.

Commission on Civil Rights. 1976. *A Guide to Federal Laws and Regulations Prohibiting Sex Discrimination.* Washington, DC: U.S. Government Printing Office.

———. 1981. *Affirmative Action in the 1980s: Dismantling the Process of Discrimination.* Washington DC: U.S. Government Printing Office.

Commoner, Barry. 1971. *The Closing Circle.* New York: Knopf.

———. 1990. *Making Peace with the Planet.* New York: Pantheon.

Commonwealth Fund. 2002. *Unequal Treatment: Confronting Racial and Ethnic Disparities in Health Care.* Washington, DC: National Academy of Sciences.

Comstock, P., and M. B. Fox. 1994. "Employer Tactics and Labor Law Reform." Pp. 90–109 in *Restoring the Promise of American Labor Law,* edited by S. Friedman, R. W. Hurd, R. A. Oswald, and R. L. Seeber. Ithaca, NY: ILR Press.

Conlin, Michelle. 2003. "The New Gender Gap." *Business Week,* May 26, p. 74.

Conrad, Peter, ed. 2000. *The Sociology of Health and Illness: Cultural Perspectives,* 6th ed. New York: Worth.

———, and Joseph W. Schneider. 1992. *Deviance and Medicalization: From Badness to Sickness.* Expanded ed. Philadelphia: Temple University Press.

Cooley, Charles. H. 1902. *Human Nature and the Social Order.* New York: Scribner.

Cornfield, Daniel B. 1991. "The US Labor Movement: Its Development and Impact on Social Inequality and Politics." In Scott, W. Richard, and Blake, Judith, eds. *Annual Review of Sociology 1991.* Palo Alto, CA: Annual Reviews.

Corsaro, William A. 1997. *The Sociology of Childhood.* Thousand Oaks, CA: Pine Forge Press.

Cortese, Anthony J. 1999. *Provocateur: Images of Women and Minorities in Advertising.* Lanham, MD: Rowman and Littlefield.

Coser, Lewis A. 1956. *The Functions of Social Conflict.* New York: Free Press.

———. 1977. *Masters of Sociological Thought: Ideas in Historical and Social Context.* 2d ed. New York: Harcourt, Brace and Jovanovich.

Coser, Rose Laub. 1984. "American Medicine's Ambiguous Progress." *Contemporary Sociology* 13 (January):9–13.

Couch, Carl J. 1968. "Collective Behavior: An Examination of Some Stereotypes." *Social Problems* 15:310–322.

———. 1996. *Information Technologies and Social Orders.* Edited with an introduction by David R. Maines and Shing-Ling Chien. New York: Aldine de Gruyter.

Council on Ethical and Judicial Affairs, American Medical Association. 1992. "Decisions Near the End of Life." *Journal of the American Medical Association* 267 (April 22–29): 2229–2333.

Council on Scientific Affairs. 1999. "Hispanic Health in the United States." *Journal of the American Medical Association* 265 (January 9): 248–252.

Counts, D. A. 1977. "The Good Death in Kaliai: Preparation for Death in Western New Britain." *Omega* 7:367–372.

Cox, Oliver C. 1948. *Caste, Class, and Race: A Study in Social Dynamics.* Detroit: Wayne State University Press.

Cox, Rachel S. 2003. "Home Schooling Debate." *CQ Researcher* 13 (January 17): 25–48.

Crenshaw, Edward M., Matthew Christenson, and Doyle Ray Oakey. 2000. "Demographic Transition in Ecological Focus." *American Sociological Review* 65 (June): 371–391.

Cressey, Donald R. 1960. "Epidemiology and Individual Contact: A Case from Criminology." *Pacific Sociological Review* 3 (Fall):47–58.

Cromwell, Paul F., James N. Olson, and D'Aunn Wester Avarey. 1995. *Breaking and Entering: An Ethnographic Analysis of Burglary.* Newbury Park, CA: Sage.

Crossette, Barbara. 1999. "The Internet Changes Dictatorship's Rules." *New York Times,* August 1, sec. 4, p. l.

———. 2003. "The Role of Women." Pp. 137–156 in *Understanding Contemporary India,* edited by Sumit Ganguly and Neil DeVolta. Boulder, CO: Lynne Rienner.

Croteau, David, and William Hoynes. 2003. *Media/Society: Industries, Images, and Audiences.* 3d ed. Thousand Oaks, CA: Pine Forge.

———. 2001. *The Business of the Media: Corporate Media and the Public Interest.* Thousand Oaks, CA: Pine Forge.

Crouse, Kelly. 1999. "Sociology of the Titanic." *Teaching Sociology Listserv.* May 24.

Cuff, E. C., W. W. Sharrock, and D. W. Francis, eds. 1990. *Perspectives in Sociology.* 3d ed. Boston: Unwin Hyman.

Cullen, Francis T., Jr., and John B. Cullen. 1978. *Toward a Paradigm of Labeling Theory,* ser. 58. Lincoln: University of Nebraska Studies.

Cumming, Elaine, and William E. Henry. 1961. *Growing Old: The Process of Disengagement.* New York: Basic Books.

Currie, Elliot. 1985. *Confronting Crime: An American Challenge.* New York: Pantheon.

———. 1998. *Crime and Punishment in America.* New York: Metropolitan Books.

Curry, Timothy Jon. 1993. "A Little Pain Never Hurt Anyone: Athletic Career Socialization and the Normalization of Sports Injury." *Symbolic Interaction* 26 (Fall):273–290.

D

Dahl, Robert A. 1961. *Who Governs?* New Haven, CT: Yale University Press.

Dahrendorf, Ralf. 1958. "Toward a Theory of Social Conflict." *Journal of Conflict Resolution* 2 (June):170–183.

———. 1959. *Class and Class Conflict in Industrial Sociology.* Stanford, CA: Stanford University Press.

Daley, Suzanne. 1999. "Doctors' Group of Volunteers Awarded Nobel." *New York Times,* October 16, pp. A1, A6.

———. 2000. "French Couples Take Plunge that Falls Short of Marriage." *New York Times,* April 18, pp. A1, A4.

Daniels, Arlene Kaplan. 1987. "Invisible Work." *Social Problems* 34 (December): 403–415.

———. 1988. *Invisible Careers.* Chicago: University of Chicago Press.

Daniszewski, John. 2003. "Al-Jazeera TV Draws Flak Outside—and Inside—the Arab World." *Los Angeles Times,* January 5, pp. A1, A5.

Dao, James. 1995. "New York's Highest Court Rules Unmarried Couples Can Adopt." *New York Times,* November 3, pp. A1, B2.

Darwin, Charles. 1859. *On the Origin of Species.* London: John Murray.

Davidson, Joe. 2002. "It's Illegal to Be Homeless." *Focus* (April):3–4.

Davies, Christie. 1989. "Goffman's Concept of the Total Institution: Criticisms and Revisions." *Human Studies* 12 (June): 77–95.

Davis, Darren W. 1997. "The Direction of Race of Interviewer Effects Among African-Americans: Donning the Black Mask." *American Journal of Political Science* 41 (January): 309–322.

Davis, Donald B., and Karen A. Polonko. 2001. *Telework America 2001 Summary.* Accessed March 3, 2003 (www.working fromanywhere.org/telework/twa2001.htm).

Davis, James A. 1982. "Up and Down Opportunity's Ladder." *Public Opinion* 5 (June/July):11–15, 48–51.

Davis, James A., and Tom W. Smith. 2001. *General Social Surveys, 1972–2000.* Storrs, CT: The Roper Center.

Davis, James A., Tom W. Smith, and Peter V. Marsden. 2003. *General Social Surveys, 1972–2002.* Chicago: National Opinion Research Center.

Davis, James A., Tom W. Smith, and Peter V. Marsden. 2003. *General Social Surveys, 1972–2002: Cumulative Codebook.* Chicago: NORC.

Davis, Jerry. 2003. *America's Corporate Banks Are Separated by Just Four Handshakes.* Accessed March 7 (www.bus.umich.edu/ research/davis.html).

Davis, Kingsley. 1937. "The Sociology of Prostitution." *American Sociological Review* 2 (October):744–755.

———. 1940. "Extreme Social Isolation of a Child." *American Journal of Sociology* 45 (January):554–565.

———. 1947. "A Final Note on a Case of Extreme Isolation." *American Journal of Sociology* 52 (March):432–437.

———. [1949] 1995. *Human Society.* Reprint, New York: Macmillan.

———, and Wilbert E. Moore. 1945. "Some Principles of Stratification." *American Sociological Review* 10 (April):242–249.

Davis, Nanette J. 1975. *Sociological Constructions of Deviance: Perspectives and Issues in the Field.* Dubuque, IA: Wm. C. Brown.

De Andra, Roberto M. 1996. *Chicanas and Chicanos in Contemporary Society.* Boston: Allyn and Bacon.

Deardorff, Kevin E., and Lisa M. Blumerman. 2001. "Evaluation Components of International Migration: Estimates of the Foreign-Born Population by Migrant States in 2000." *Working Paper Series,* no. 58. Accessed January 8, 2002 (www.census.gov/population/www/documentation/twps0058.html).

Death Penalty Information Center. 2002. "100th Death Row Exoneree Freed in Arizona." News release, April 9. Accessed June 23, 2003 (www.deathpenaltyinfo.org).

———. 2003. *Black Defendant/White Victim.* Accessed July 5 (www.deathpenalty info.org).

Deegan, Mary Jo, ed. 1991. *Women in Sociology: A Bio-Biographical Sourcebook.* Westport, CT: Greenwood.

Delawala, Imtyaz. 2002. "What Is Coltran?" January 21, 2002 (www.abcnews.com).

Dellios, Hugh. 2002. "Desperate Migrants Accept Risks." *New York Times,* October 20, pp. 1, 7.

Deloria, Vine, Jr. 1999. *For This Land: Writings on Religion in America.* New York: Routledge.

DeNavas-Walt, Carmen, and Robert W. Cleveland. 2002. "Money Income in the United States: 2001." *Current Population Reports,* ser. P-60, no. 218. Washington, DC.

———, Robert W. Cleveland, and Marc L. Raemer. 2001. *Money Income in the United States: 2000.* Washington, DC: U.S. Government Printing Office.

DePalma, Anthony. 1995a. "Racism? Mexico's in Denial." *New York Times,* June 11, p. E4.

———. 1995b. "For Mexico, NAFTA's Promise of Jobs Is Still Just a Promise." *New York Times,* October 10, pp. A1, A10.

———. 1996. "For Mexico Indians, New Voice but Few Gains." *New York Times,* January 13, pp. B1, B2.

———. 2002. "White-Collar Layoffs, Downsized Dreams." *New York Times,* December 5, pp. A1, A38.

DeParle, Jason. 1998. "Shrinking Welfare Rolls Leave Record High Share of Minorities." *New York Times,* July 27, pp. A1 , A12.

Department of Education. 1999. *Report on State Implementation of the Gun-Free Schools Act. School Year 1997–98.* Rockville, MD: Westat.

Department of Health and Human Services. 2003a. *Percent Change in AFDC/TANF Families and Recipients, August 1996–December 2002.* Accessed April 15 (www.acf.dhhs.gov).

———. 2003b. *TANF: Total Number of Recipients Fiscal Year 2002.* Accessed April 15 (www.acf.dhhs.gov).

Department of Justice. 2001. *Crime in the United States 2000. Uniform Crime Reports.* Washington, DC: U.S. Government Printing Office.

———. 2002a. *Firearms and Crime Statistics.* Accessed December 9 (www.ojp.usdoj.gov/bjs/guns.htm).

———. 2002b. *Hate Crime Statistics, 2001.* Accessed April 29, 2003 (www.fbi.gov).

Department of Labor. 1995a. *Good for Business: Making Full Use of the Nation's Capital.* Washington, DC: U.S. Government Printing Office.

———. 1995b. *A Solid Investment: Making Full Use of the Nation's Human Capital.* Washington, DC: U.S. Government Printing Office.

———. 1998. "Work and Elder Care: Facts for Caregivers and Their Employers." Accessed November 20 (www.dol.gov/dol/wb/public/wb_pubs/elderc.htm).

———. 2003. "Labor Force Statistics from the Current Population Survey." Accessed August 3 (http://data.bls.gov/cgi-bin/surveymost).

Department of State. 2003. *Immigrant Visas Issued to Orphans Coming to the U.S.* Accessed May 12 (www.travel.state.gov/orphan_numbers.html).

Desai, Manisha. 1996. "If Peasants Build Their Own Dams, What Would the State Have Left to Do?" Pp. 209–224 in *Research in Social Movements, Conflicts and Change,* vol. 19, edited by Michael Dobkowski and Isidor Wallimann. Greenwich, CT: JAI Press.

Devine, Don. 1972. *Political Culture of the United States: The Influence of Member Values on Regime Maintenance.* Boston: Little, Brown.

Devitt, James. 1999. *Framing Gender on the Campaign Trail: Women's Executive Leadership and the Press.* New York: Women's Leadership Conference.

Diani, Marie. 2000. "Social Movement Networks: Virtual and Real." *Information, Communication and Society.* Accessed October 14, 2001 (www.infosoc.co.uk).

Dieter, Richard C. 1998. *The Death Penalty in Black and White: Who Lives, Who Dies, Who Decides.* Washington, DC: Death Penalty Information Center.

Dijkstra, AnneBert, and Jaap Dronkers. 2003. "Civil Society as 'Equilibrium.'" Pp. 325–341 in *The International Handbook on the Sociology of Education,* edited by Carlos Alberto Torres and Ari Antikainen. Lanham, MD: Rowman and Littlefield.

Dillon, Sam. 1997. "Gay Rights, Prejudice and Politics in Mexico." *New York Times,* January 4, p. 4.

———. 1998. "Sex Bias at Border Plants in Mexico Reported by U.S." *New York Times,* January 13, p. A6.

DiMaggio, Paul, Eszter Hargittai, W. Russell Neuman, and John P. Robinson. 2001. "Social Implications of the Internet." Pp. 307–336 in *Annual Review of Sociology, 2001,* edited by Karen S. Cook and John Hogan. Palo Alto, CA: Annual Reviews.

Directors Guild of America. 2002. *Diversity Hiring Special Report.* Los Angeles: DGA.

Disaster Research Center. 2003. *Who Are We? DRC.* Accessed June 19 (www.vdel.edu/DRC/about.html).

Divyanathan, Denesh. 2000. "Jobs and Skills Mismatch Widens." *The Straits Times* (Singapore), May 20, p. 97.

Dodds, Klaus. 2000. *Geopolitics in a Changing World.* Harlow, England: Pearson Education.

Doeringer, Peter B., ed. 1990. *Bridges to Retirement: Older Workers in a Changing Labor Market.* Ithaca, NY: ILR Press.

Domhoff, G. William. 1978. *Who Really Rules? New Haven and Community Power Reexamined.* New Brunswick, NJ: Transaction.

———. 2001. *Who Rules America?* 4th ed. New York: McGraw-Hill.

Dominguez, Silvia, and Celeste Watkins. 2003. "Creating Networks for Survival and Mobility: Social Capital Among African-American and Latin-American Low-Income Mothers." *Social Problems* 50 (February):111–135.

Dominick, Joseph R. 2002. *The Dynamics of Mass Communication: Media in the Digital Age.* 7th ed. New York: McGraw-Hill.

Donohue, Elizabeth, Vincent Schiraldi, and Jason Ziedenberg. 1998. *School House Hype: School Shootings and Real Risks Kids Face in America.* New York: Justice Policy Institute.

Dore, Ronald P. 1976. *The Diploma Disease: Education, Qualification and Development.* Berkeley: University of California Press.

Doress, Irwin, and Jack Nusan Porter. 1977. *Kids in Cults: Why They Join. Why They Stay, Why They Leave.* Brookline, MA: Reconciliation Associates.

Dornbusch, Sanford M. 1989. "The Sociology of Adolescence." Pp. 233–259 in *Annual Review of Sociology, 1989,* edited by W. Richard Scott and Judith Blake. Palo Alto, CA: Annual Reviews.

Dotson, Floyd. 1991. "Community." p. 55 in *Encyclopedic Dictionary of Sociology.* 4th ed. Guilford, CT: Dushkin.

Dougherty, John, and David Holthouse. 1999. "Bordering on Exploitation." Accessed March 5 (www.phoenixnewtime.com/issies/1998-07-09/feature.html).

Dougherty, Kevin, and Floyd M. Hammack. 1992. "Education Organization." Pp. 535–541 in *Encyclopedia of Sociology,* vol. 2, edited by Edgar F. Borgatta and Marie L. Borgatta. New York: Macmillan.

Douglas, Jack D. 1967. *The Social Meanings of Suicide.* Princeton, NJ: Princeton University Press.

Dowd, James J. 1980. *Stratification among the Aged.* Monterey, CA: Brooks/Cole.

Downie, Andrew. 2000. "Brazilian Girls Turn to a Doll More Like Them." *Christian Science Monitor,* January 20. Accessed January 20 (www.csmonitor.com/durable/2000/01/20/fpls3-csm.shtml).

Doyle, James A. 1995. *The Male Experience.* 3d ed. Dubuque, IA: Brown & Benchmark.

———, and Michele A. Paludi. 1998. *Sex and Gender: The Human Experience.* 4th ed. New York: McGraw-Hill.

Dreifus, Claudia. 2003. "A Conversation with Lee Clarke." *New York Times,* May 20, Science Times Section, p. 2.

Drucker, Peter F. 1999. "Beyond the Information Revolution." *Atlantic Monthly* 284 (October):42–57.

Du Bois, W. E. B. 1909. *The Negro American Family.* Atlanta University. Reprinted 1970. Cambridge, MA: M.I.T. Press.

———. 1911. "The Girl Nobody Loved." *Social News* 2 (November):3.

———. [1940] 1968. *Dusk of Dawn.* New York: Harcourt, Brace. Reprinted New York: Schocken Books.

Duberman, Lucille. 1976. *Social Inequality: Class and Caste in America.* Philadelphia: Lippincott.

Dugger, Celia W. 1999. "Massacres of Low-Born Touch Off a Crisis in India." *New York Times,* March 15, p. A3.

———. 2001. "Relying on Hard and Soft Sells, India Pushes Sterilization." *New York Times,* June 22, pp. A1, A10.

Duneier, Mitchell. 1994a. "On the Job, but Behind the Scenes." *Chicago Tribune,* December 26, pp. 1, 24.

———. 1994b. "Battling for Control." *Chicago Tribune,* December 28, pp. 1, 8.

———. 1999. *Sidewalk.* New York: Farrar, Straus and Giroux.

Dunlap, Riley E. 1993. "From Environmental to Ecological Problems." Pp. 707–738 in *Introduction to Social Problems,* edited by Craig Calhoun and George Ritzer. New York: McGraw-Hill.

———, and William R. Catton, Jr. 1983. "What Environmental Sociologists Have in Common." *Sociological Inquiry* 53 (Spring):113–135.

Durand, Jorge, Emilio A. Parrado, and Douglas S. Massey. 1996. "Migradollars and Developments: A Reconsideration of the Mexican Case." *International Migration Review* 30 (Summer):423–444.

Durkheim, Émile. [1912] 2001. *The Elementary Forms of Religious Life.* A new translation by Carol Cosman. New York: Oxford University Press.

———. [1893] 1933. *Division of Labor in Society.* Translated by George Simpson. Reprint, New York: Free Press.

———. [1897] 1951. *Suicide.* Translated by John A. Spaulding and George Simpson. Reprint, New York: Free Press.

———. [1895] 1964. *The Rules of Sociological Method.* Translated by Sarah A. Solovay and John H. Mueller. Reprint, New York: Free Press.

Durning, Alan B. 1993. "Supporting Indigenous Peoples." Pp. 80–100 in *State of the World,* edited by Lester R. Brown. New York: Norton.

Duster, Troy. 2002. "Sociological Stranger in the Land of the Human Genome Project." *Contexts* 1 (Fall):69–70.

———. 2003. *Backdoor to Eugenics.* 2d ed. New York: Routledge.

E

Ebaugh, Helen Rose Fuchs. 1988. *Becoming an Ex: The Process of Role Exit.* Chicago: University of Chicago Press.

Eberstadt, Nicholas. 2001. "The Population Implosion." *Foreign Policy* (March/April):42–58.

Eckenwiler, Mark. 1995. "In the Eyes of the Law." *Internet World* (August):74, 76–77.

Eckholm, Erik. 2002a. "Desire for Sons Drives Prenatal Scans in China." *New York Times,* June 21, p. A3.

———. 2002b. "As China's Economy Shines, the Party Line Loses Luster." *New York Times,* November 5, pp. A1, A12.

The Economist. 1996. "It's Normal to Be Queer." (January 6):68–70.

———. 2002. "Indian Politics: The Nationalists Dark Victory." *The Economist* (December 19):51–52.

———. 2003. "Race in Brazil: Out of Eden." *The Economist* (July 5):31–32.

Education Commission of the States. 2001. *A Closer Look: State Policy Trends in Three Key Areas of the Bush Education Plan—Testing, Accountability and School Choice.* Accessed July 19 (www.ecs.org/clearing house/).

Education Week. 2000. "Who Should Teach? The States Decide." *Education Week Online.* 19 (18):89. Available (www.edweek.org).

Edwards, Harry. 1973. *Sociology of Sport.* Homewood, IL: Dorsey Press.

Edwards, Tamala M. 2001. "How Med Students Put Abortion Back in the Classroom." *Time* 157 (May 7): 59–60.

Efron, Sonni. 1997. "In Japan, Even Tots Must Make the Grade." *Los Angeles Times,* February 16, pp. A1, A17.

———. 1998. "Japanese in Quandary on Fertility." *Los Angeles Times,* July 27, pp. A1, A6.

Egan, Timothy. 2002. "The Seeds of Decline." *New York Times,* December 8, sec. 4, pp. 1, 3.

Ehrenreich, Barbara. 2001. *Nickel and Dimed: On (Not) Getting By in America.* New York: Metropolitan.

———, and Frances Fox Piven. 2002. "Without a Safety Net." *Mother Jones* 27 (May/June): 34–41.

Ehrlich, Paul R. 1968. *The Population Bomb.* New York: Ballantine.

———, and Anne H. Ehrlich. 1990. *The Population Explosion.* New York: Simon and Schuster.

———, and Katherine Ellison. 2002. "A Looming Threat We Won't Face." *Los Angeles Times.* January 20, p. M6.

Eisenberg, David M. et al. 1998. "Trends in Alternative Medicine Use in the United States, 1990–1997." *Journal of the American Medical Association* 280 (November 11): 1569–1636.

Eitzen, D. Stanley, ed. 2001. *Sport in Contemporary Society: An Anthology.* 6th ed. New York: Worth.

———. 2003. *Fair and Foul: Beyond the Myths and Paradoxes of Sport.* 2d ed. Lanham, MD: Rowman and Littlefield.

El-Badry, Samira. 1994. "The Arab-American Market." *American Demographics* 16 (January): 21–31.

Eller, Claudia, and Lorenza Muñoz. 2002. "The Plots Thicken in Foreign Markets." *Los Angeles Times,* October 6, pp. A1, A26, A27.

Ellingwood, Ken. 2001. "Results of Crackdown and Border Called Mixed." *Los Angeles Times,* August 4, p. B9.

Elliot, Marta, and Lauren J. Krivo. 1991. "Structured Determinants of Homelessness in the United States." *Social Problems* 38 (February):113–131.

Ellison, Ralph. 1952. *Invisible Man.* New York: Random House.

Elmer-DeWitt, Philip. 1995. "Welcome to Cyberspace." *Time* 145 (Special Issue, Spring):4–11.

El Nasser, Haya. 2001. "Minorities Reshape Suburbs." *USA Today,* July 9, p. 1A.

———, and Paul Overberg. 2001. "What You Don't Know about Sprawl." *USA Today,* February 22, pp. 1A, 8A.

Ely, Robin J. 1995. "The Power of Demography: Women's Social Construction of Gender Identity at Work." *Academy of Management Journal* 38 (3): 589–634.

Embree, Ainslie. 2003. "Religion." Pp. 101–220 in *Understanding Contemporary India,* edited by Sumit Ganguly and Neil DeVotta. Boulder, CO: Lynne Rienner.

Emery, David. 1997. "The Kidney Snatchers." Accessed December 21, 1999 (http://urbanlegends.about.com/culture/urban legends/library/blkid.htm).

Engardio, Pete. 1999. "Activists Without Borders." *BusinessWeek,* October 4, pp. 144–145, 148, 150.

Engels, Friedrich [1884] 1959. "The Origin of the Family, Private Property, and the State." Pp. 392–394, excerpted in *Marx and Engels: Basic Writings on Politics and Philosophy,* edited by Lewis Feuer. Garden City, NY: Anchor.

England, Paula. 1999. "The Impact of Feminist Thought on Sociology." *Contemporary Sociology* 28 (May):263–268.

English-Lueck, J. A. 2002. *Cultures@Silicon Valley.* Stanford, CA: Stanford University Press.

Entine, Jon, and Martha Nichols. 1996. "Blowing the Whistle on Meaningless 'Good Intentions.'" *Chicago Tribune,* June 20, Sec. 1, p. 21.

Epstein, Cynthia Fuchs. 1999. "The Major Myth of the Women's Movement." *Dissent* (Fall):83–111.

Ericson, Nels. 2001. "Substance Abuse: The Nation's Number One Health Problem." *OJJDP Fact Sheet* 17 (May):1–2.

Erikson, Kai. 1966. *Wayward Puritans: A Study in the Sociology of Deviance.* New York: Wiley.

———. 1986. "On Work and Alienation." *American Sociological Review* 51 (February):1–8.

———. 1994. *A New Species of Trouble: The Human Experience of Modern Disasters.* New York: Norton.

Etaugh, Claire. 2003. "Witches, Mothers and Others: Females in Children's Books." *Hilltopics* (Winter):10–13.

Etzioni, Amitai. 1964. *Modern Organization.* Englewood Cliffs, NJ: Prentice Hall.

Evans, Sara. 1980. *Personal Politics: The Roots of Women's Liberation in the Civil Rights Movement and the New Left.* New York: Vintage.

Evetts, Julia. 2003. "The Sociological Analysis of Professionalism." *International Sociology* 18 (June):395–415.

F

FAIR. 2001. "Fear and Favor 2000." Accessed December 29, 2001 (www.FAIR.org).

Fair Labor Association. 2003. *Fair Labor Association First Public Report: Towards Improving Workers' Lives.* Washington, DC: Fair Labor.

Faludi, Susan. 1999. *Stiffed: The Betrayal of the American Man.* New York: William Morrow.

Farhi, Paul. 1995. "Selling Is as Selling Does!" *Washington Post,* April 30, p. H1.

———, and Megan Rosenfeld. 1998. "Exporting America." *Washington Post National Weekly Edition* 16 (November 30):6–7.

Farley, Maggie. 1998. "Indonesia's Chinese Fearful of Backlash." *Los Angeles Times,* January 31, pp. A1, A8–A9.

Farr, Grant M. 1999. *Modern Iran.* New York: McGraw-Hill.

Fausset, Richard. 2003. "Sikhs Mark New Year, Fight Post-September 11 Bias." *Los Angeles Times,* April 14, pp. B1, B7.

Feagin, Joe R. 1983. *The Urban Real Estate Game: Playing Monopoly with Real Money.* Englewood Cliffs, NJ: Prentice Hall.

———. 1989. *Minority Group Issues in Higher Education: Learning from Qualitative Research.* Norman, OK: Center for Research on Minority Education, University of Oklahoma.

———. 2001. "Social Justice and Sociology: Agenda for the Twenty-First Century." *American Sociological Review* 66 (February):1–20.

———, Harnán Vera, and Nikitah Imani. 1996. *The Agony of Education: Black Students at White Colleges and Universities.* New York: Routledge.

Featherman, David L., and Robert M. Hauser. 1978. *Opportunity and Change.* New York: Aeodus.

Federal Register, June 4, 1975.

Fein, Helen. 1995. "Gender and Genocide." Paper presented at the annual meeting of the American Sociological Association, Washington, DC.

Feinglass, Joe. 1987. "Next, the McDRG." *The Progressive* 51 (January):28.

Feketekuty, Geza. 2001. "Globalization—Why All the Fuss?" p. 191 in *2001 Britannica*

Book of the Year. Chicago: Encyclopedia Britannica.

Felson, Marcus. 2002. *Crime and Everyday Life.* 3d ed. Thousand Oaks, CA: Pine Forge Press.

Ferman, Louis A., Stuart Henry, and Michael Hoyman, ed. 1987. *The Informal Economy.* Newbury Park, CA: Sage. Published as September 1987 issue of *The Annals of the American Academy of Political and Social Science.*

Fernandez, Roberto M. 2001. "Skill-Biased Technological Change and Wage Inequality Evidence from a Plant Retooling." *American Journal of Sociology* 107 (September):273–320.

Fernández, Sandy. 1996. "The Cyber Cops." *Ms.* 6 (May/June):22–23.

Fernea, Elizabeth. 1998. *In Search of Islamic Feminism: One Woman's Global Journey.* New York: Bantam Books.

Ferree, Myra Marx, and David A. Merrill. 2000. "Hot Movements, Cold Cognition: Thinking about Social Movements in Gendered Frames." *Contemporary Society* 29 (May): 454–462.

Ferrell, Tom. 1979 "More Choose to Live outside Marriage." *New York Times,* July 1, p. E7.

Feuer, Lewis S. 1989. *Marx and Engels: Basic Writings on Politics and Philosophy.* New York: Anchor Books.

Fiala, Robert. 1992. "Postindustrial Society." Pp. 1512–1522 in *Encyclopedia of Sociology,* vol. 3, edited by Edgar F. Borgatta and Marie L. Borgatta. New York: Macmillan.

Fields, Jason. 2003. "Children's Living Arrangements and Characteristics: March 2002." *Current Population Reports,* ser. P-20, no. 547. Washington, DC: U.S. Government Printing Office.

———, and Lynne M. Casper. 2001. "America's Families and Living Arrangements." *Current Population Reports,* Ser. Pp. 20–537. Washington, DC: U.S. Government Printing Office.

Finder, Alan. 1995. "Despite Tough Laws, Sweatshops Flourish." *New York Times,* January 6, pp. A1, B4.

Fine, Gary Alan. 1984. "Negotiated Orders and Organizational Cultures." Pp. 239–262 in *Annual Review of Sociology, 1984,* edited by Ralph Turner. Palo Alto, CA: Annual Reviews.

———. 1987. *With the Boys: Little League Baseball and Preadolescent Culture.* Chicago: University of Chicago Press.

Finkel, Steven E., and James B. Rule. 1987. "Relative Deprivation and Related Psychological Theories of Civil Violence: A Critical Review." *Research in Social Movements* 9:47–69.

Firestone, David. 1999. "School Prayer Is Revived as an Issue in Alabama." *New York Times,* July 15, p. A14.

Firestone, Shulamith. 1970. *The Dialectic of Sex: The Case for Feminist Revolution.* New York: Bantam.

Firmat, Gustavo Perez. 1994. *Life on Hyphen: The Cuban-American Way.* Austin: University of Texas Press.

Fitzgerald, Kathleen J., and Diane M. Rodgers. 2000. "Radical Social Movement Organization: A Theoretical Model." *The Sociological Quarterly* 41 (No. 4):573–592.

Flacks, Richard. 1971. *Youth and Social Change.* Chicago: Markham.

Flavin, Jeanne. 1998. "Razing the Wall: A Feminist Critique of Sentencing Theory, Research, and Policy." Pp. 145–164 in *Cutting the Edge,* edited by Jeffrey Ross. Westport, CT: Praeger.

Fletcher, Connie. 1995. "On the Line: Women Cops Speak Out." *Chicago Tribune Magazine,* February 19, pp. 14–19.

Fletcher, Robert S. 1943. *History of Oberlin College to the Civil War.* Oberlin, OH: Oberlin College Press.

Flexner, Eleanor. 1972. *Century of Struggle: The Women's Rights Movement in the United States.* New York: Atheneum.

Foreman, Judy. 2002. "The Evidence Speaks Well of Bilingualism's Effect on Kids." *Los Angeles Times,* October 7, pp. 51, 56.

Form, William. 1992. "Labor Movements and Unions." Pp. 1054–1060 in *Encyclopedia of Sociology,* vol. 3, edited by Edgar F. Borgatta and Marie L. Borgatta. New York: Macmillan.

Fornos, Werner. 1997. *1997 World Population Overview.* Washington, DC: The Population Institute.

Forsythe, David P. 1990. "Human Rights in U.S. Foreign Policy: Retrospect and Prospect." *Political Science Quarterly* 105(3):435–454.

Fortune. 2002. "Fortune's Global 500." August 12.

———. 2003. "Fortune Global 500." *Fortune* 148 (July 21):97–126.

Fox, Susannah and Lee Rainie. 2001. *Time Online: Why Some People Use the Internet More Than Before and Why Some Use It Less.* Washington, DC: Pew Internet and American Life Project.

Francese, Peter. 2003. "Continuing Education." *American Demographics* 24 (April): 46–47.

Franklin, John Hope, and Alfred A. Moss. 2000. *From Slavery to Freedom: A History of African Americans.* 8th ed. Upper Saddle River, NJ: Prentice Hall.

Freeman, Jo. 1973. "The Origins of the Women's Liberation Movement." *American Journal of Sociology* 78 (January): 792–811.

———. 1975. *The Politics of Women's Liberation.* New York: McKay.

Freidson, Eliot. 1970. *Profession of Medicine.* New York: Dodd, Mead.

Freire, Paulo. 1970. *Pedagogy of the Oppressed.* New York: Herder and Herder.

French, Howard W. 2000. "The Pretenders." *New York Times Magazine,* December 3, pp. 86–88.

———. 2001a. "Diploma at Hand, Japanese Women Find Glass Ceiling Reinforced with Iron." *New York Times,* January 1, p. A4.

———. 2001b. "Brooding Over Its Homelessness, Japan Sees a Broken System." *New York Times,* February 2, pp. A1, A10.

———. 2002. "Teaching Japan's Salarymen to Be Their Own Men." *New York Times,* November 27, p. A4.

Freudenheim, Milt. 1990. "Employers Balk at High Cost of High-Tech Medical Care." *New York Times,* April 29, pp. 1, 16.

Frey, William H. 2001. *Melting Pot Suburbs: A Census 2000 Study of Suburban Diversity.* Washington, DC: The Brookings Institution.

Fridlund, Alan. J., Paul Erkman, and Harriet Oster. 1987. "Facial Expressions of Emotion; Review of Literature 1970–1983." Pp. 143–224 in *Nonverbal Behavior and Communication,* 2d ed., edited by Aron W. Seigman and Stanley Feldstein. Hillsdale, NJ: Lawrence Erlbaum Associates.

Friedan, Betty. 1963. *The Feminine Mystique.* New York: Dell.

Friedland, Jonathon. 2000. "An American in Mexico Champions Midwifery as a Worthy Profession." *Wall Street Monitor,* February 15, pp. A1, A12.

Friedman, Milton. 1955. "The Role of Government in Education." Pp. 123–145 in *Economics and Public Interest,* edited by Robert A. Solo. New Brunswick, NJ: Rutgers University Press.

Friess, Steve. 2001. "Chinese Gays, Slowly Come Out into the Open." *USA Today,* March 9, p. 6A.

Fullerton, Jr., Howard N., and Mitra Toossi. 2001. "Labor Force Projections to 2010: Steady Growth and Changing Compositions." *Monthly Labor Review* (November):21–38.

Furstenberg, Frank, and Andrew Cherlin. 1991. *Divided Families: What Happens to Children When Parents Part.* Cambridge, MA: Harvard University Press.

Furukawa, Stacy. 1994. "The Diverse Living Arrangements of Children: Summer 1991." *Current Population Reports,* ser. P-70., no. 38. Washington, DC: U.S. Government Printing Office.

G

Gale Group. 2003. *Associations Unlimited.* Accessed March 3 (www.galegroup.com).

Gallup. 2001. *Poll Topics and Trends: Race Relations.* Accessed January 28, 2002 (www.gallup.com/poll/topics/race.asp).

Gallup, George H. 2002. "Views on Doctor-Assisted Suicide Follow Religious Lines." *Gallup Tuesday Briefing* (September 10).

Galston, William A. 2001. "Political Knowledge, Political Engagement, and Civic Education." Pp. 217–234 in *Annual Review of Political Science,* 2001, edited by Nelson W. Polsby. Palo Alto, CA: Annual Reviews.

Gamson, Joshua. 1989. "Silence, Death, and the Invisible Enemy: AIDS Activism and Social Movement 'Newness.'" *Social Problems* 36 (October):351–367.

Gans, Herbert J. 1979. "Symbolic Ethnicity: The Future of Ethnic Groups and Cultures in America." *Ethnic and Racial Studies.* 2 (January): 1–20.

———. 1991. *People, Plans, and Policies: Essays on Poverty, Racism, and Other National Urban Problems.* New York: Columbia University Press and Russell Sage Foundation.

———. 1995. *The War against the Poor: The Underclass and Antipoverty Policy.* New York: Basic Books.

Ganzeboom, Harry B. G., Ruud Luijkx, and Donald J. Treiman. 1989. "Intergenerational Class Mobility in Comparative Perspective." Pp. 3–84 in *Research in Social Stratification and Mobility,* edited by Arne L. Kalleberg. Greenwich, CT: JAI Press.

———, Donald J. Treiman, and Woult C. Ultee. 1991. "Comparative Intergenerational Stratification Research." Pp. 277–302 in *Annual Review of Sociology, 1991,* edited by W. Richard Scott. Palo Alto, CA: Annual Reviews.

Garber, Mary K. 2001. "Feds Accused of Initiating Racial Profiling Policy." *Focus* (January):1–2.

Gardner, Carol Brooks. 1989. "Analyzing Gender in Public Places: Rethinking Goffman's Vision of Everyday Life." *American Sociologist* 20 (Spring):42–56.

———. 1990. "Safe Conduct: Women, Crime, and Self in Public Places." *Social Problems* 37 (August):311–328.

———. 1995. *Passing By: Gender and Public Harassment.* Berkeley: University of California Press.

Gardner, Marilyn. 2001. "Media's Eye on Moms." *Christian Science Monitor,* May 30, pp. 12–13.

———. 2003. "This View of Seniors Just Doesn't 'Ad' Up." *Christian Science Monitor,* January 15, p. 15.

Garfinkel, Harold. 1956. "Conditions of Successful Degradation Ceremonies." *American Journal of Sociology* 61 (March): 420–424.

Garner, Roberta. 1996. *Contemporary Movements and Ideologies.* New York: McGraw-Hill.

———. 1999. "Virtual Social Movements." Presented at Zaldfest: A conference in honor of Mayer Zald. September 17, Ann Arbor, MI.

Garreau, Joel. 1991. *Edge City: Life on the New Frontier.* New York: Doubleday.

Garza, Melita Marie. 1993. "The Cordi-Marian Annual Cotillion." *Chicago Tribune,* May 7, sec. C, pp. 1, 5.

Gates, Henry Louis, Jr. 1999. "One Internet, Two Nations." *New York Times,* October 31, p. A15.

Gay, Lesbian, and Straight Education Network (GLSEN). 2003. "Students and GSAs," Accessed August 5 (www.glsen.org/templates/student/index.html/section=49).

Gearty, Robert. 1996. "Beware of Pickpockets." *Chicago Daily News,* November 19, p. 5.

Gecas, Viktor. 1982. "The Self-Concept." Pp. 1–33 in *Annual Review of Sociology,* 1982, edited by Ralph H. Turner and James F. Short, Jr. Palo Alto, CA: Annual Reviews.

———. 1992. "Socialization." Pp. 1863–1872 in *Encyclopedia of Sociology,* Vol. 4, edited by Edgar F. Borgatta and Marie L. Borgatta. New York: Macmillan.

Gelles, Richard J., and Claire Pedrick Cornell. 1990. *Intimate Violence in Families.* 2d ed. Newbury Park, CA: Sage.

General Accounting Office. 2001. *School Vouchers: Publicly Funded Programs in Cleveland and Milwaukee.* Washington, DC: U.S. Government Printing Office.

———. 2002. *A New Look Through the Glass Ceiling: Where Are the Women?* Washington, DC: General Accounting Office.

Gerth, H. H., and C. Wright Mills. 1958. *From Max Weber: Essays in Sociology.* New York: Galaxy.

Geyh, Paul. 1998. "Feminism Fatale?" *Chicago Tribune,* July 26, Sec. 13, pp. 1, 6.

Gezari, Vanessa. 2002. "Sex Testing Used to Call Girls." *Chicago Tribune,* November 10, p. 4.

Ghose, Sagarika. 2003. "The Dalit in India." *Social Research* 70 (Spring):84–109.

Gibbs, Nancy. 1993. "Rx for Death." *Time,* May 31, pp. 34–39.

Giddens, Anthony. 1991. *Modernity and Self-Identity: Self and Society in the Late Modern Age.* Cambridge, UK: Polity.

Gifford, Allen L., et al. 2002. "Participation in Research and Access to Experimental Treatments by HIV-Infected Patients." *New England Journal of Medicine* 346 (May):1400–1402.

Gill, Brian P., Michael Timpane, Karen E. Russ, and Dominic J. Brewer. 2001. *Rhetoric Versus Reality: What We Know and What We Need to Know About Vouchers and Charter Schools.* Santa Monica, CA: RAND.

Giordano, Peggy C., Stephen A. Cernkovich, and Alfred DeMaris. 1993. "The Family and Peer Relations of Black Adolescents." *Journal of Marriage and Family* 55 (May): 277–287.

Giroux, Henry A. 1988. *Schooling and the Struggle for Public Life: Critical Pedagogy in the Modern Age.* Minneapolis: University of Minnesota Press.

Gitlin, Todd. 2001. *Media Unlimited: How the Torrent of Images and Sounds Overwhelms Our Lives.* New York: Henry Holt and Company.

Glanton, Dahleen. 2001. "Sprawl Tests Atlanta's Limits." *New York Times,* August 7, pp. 1, 16.

Glascock, Anthony P. 1990. "By Any Other Name, It Is Still Killing: A Comparison of the Treatment of the Elderly in American and Other Societies." Pp. 44–56 in *The Cultural Context of Aging: Worldwide Perspective,* edited by Jay Sokolovsky. New York: Bergen and Garvey.

Glauber, Bill. 1998. "Youth Binge Drinking Varies Around World." *St. Louis Post-Dispatch,* February 9, p. E4.

Glaze, Lauren. 2002. "Probation and Parole in the United States, 2001." *Bureau of Justice Statistics Bulletin* (August).

Global Alliance for Workers and Communities. 2001. *Workers' Voices: An Interim Report on Workers' Needs and Aspirations in Nine Nike Contract Factories in Indonesia.* Baltimore, MD: Global Alliance.

———. 2003. *About Us.* Accessed April 28 (www.theglobalalliance.org).

Global Reach. 2003. *Global Inuit Statistics (by Language).* Accessed June 20 (www.global-reach.biz/globstats/index.php).

Goering, Laura. 2001. "Mexico City Losing Gains in Air Quality." *Chicago Tribune,* July 5, p. 7.

Goffman, Erving. 1959. *The Presentation of Self in Everyday Life.* New York: Doubleday.

———. 1961. *Asylums: Essays on the Social Situation of Mental Patients and Other Inmates.* Garden City, NY: Doubleday.

———. 1963a. *Stigma: Notes on Management of Spoiled Identity.* Englewood Cliffs, NJ: Prentice Hall.

———. 1963b. *Behavior in Public Places.* New York: Free Press.

———. 1971. *Relations in Public.* New York: Basic Books.

———. 1979. *Gender Advertisements.* Cambridge. MA: Harvard University Press.

Goldberg, Carey. 1998. "Little Drop in College Binge Drinking." *New York Times,* August 11, p. A14.

Golden, Frederic. 1999. "Who's Afraid of Frankenfood?" *Time,* November 29, pp. 49–50.

Goldman, Robert, and Stephen Papson. 1998. *Nike Culture: The Sign of the Swoosh.* London: Sage.

Goldstein, Amy, and Richard Morin. 2002. "The Squeaky Wheel Gets the Grease." *Washington Post National Weekly Edition* 20, October 28, p. 34.

Goldstein, Greg. 1998. "World Health Organization and Housing." Pp. 636–637 in *The Encyclopedia of Housing,* edited by Willem van Vliet. Thousand Oaks, CA: Sage.

Goldstein, Melvyn C., and Cynthia M. Beall. 1981. "Modernization and Aging in the Third and Fourth World: Views from the Rural Hinterland in Nepal." *Human Organization* 40 (Spring):48–55.

Gole, Nilofer. 1997. "Lifting the Veil—Reform vs. Tradition in Turkey—An Interview." *Manushi,* May 1.

Goleman, Daniel, 1991. "New Ways to Battle Bias: Fight Acts, Not Feelings." *New York Times,* July 16, pp. C1, C8.

Gonnut, Jean Pierre. 2001. Interview. June 18, 2001.

Gonzales, John M. 1997. "Relearning a Lost Language." *Los Angeles Times,* May 26, p. A1.

Gonzalez, David. 2003. "Latin Sweatshops Pressed by U.S. Campus Power." *New York Times,* April 4, p. A3.

Goode, Erica. 1999. "For Good Health, It Helps to Be Rich and Important." *New York Times,* June 1, pp. 1, 9.

———. 2002. "A Rare Day: The Movies Get Mental Illness Right." *New York Times,* February 5, p. D6.

Goodgame, Dan. 1993. "Welfare for the Well-Off." *Time* 141 (February 22):36–38.

Goodman, Peter S., and Akiko Kashiwagi. 2002. "In Japan, Housewives No More." *Washington Post National Weekly Edition,* November 4, pp. 18–19.

Google Inc. 2003. *2002 Year-End Google Zeitgeist.* Accessed January 27 (www.google.com/press/zeitgeist.html).

Gordon, Daniel T., ed. 2002. *Minority Achievement.* Harvard Education Letter Focus Series, no. 7. Cambridge, MA: Harvard Graduate School of Education.

Gordon, Jesse, and Knickerbocker. 2001. "The Sweat Behind the Shirt: The Labor History of a Gap Sweatshirt." *The Nation* 273 (September 3/10):14.

Gorman, Tom. 2003. "Clash in Court over Oregon's Law on Suicide." *Chicago Tribune,* May 6, p. A27.

Gornick, Janet C. 2001. "Cancel the Funeral." *Dissent* (Summer):13–18.

Gornick, Vivian. 1979. "Introduction" to *Gender Advertisements.* Cambridge, MA: Harvard University Press.

Gottdiener, Mark, and Joe R. Feagin. 1988. "The Paradigm Shift in Urban Sociology." *Urban Affairs Quarterly* 24 (December):163–187.

———, and Ray Hutchison. 2000. *The New Urban Sociology.* 2d ed. New York: McGraw-Hill.

Gottfredson, Michael, and Travis Hirschi. 1990. *A General Theory of Crime.* Palo Alto, CA: Stanford University Press.

Gottschalk, Peter, Sara McLanahan, and Gary Sandefur. 1994. "The Dynamics and Intergenerational Transmission of Poverty and Welfare Participation." Pp. 85–108 in *Confronting Poverty: Prescriptions for Change,* edited by Sheldon H. Danziger, Gary D. Sandefur, and Daniel H. Weinburg. Cambridge, MA: Harvard University Press.

Gouldner, Alvin. 1960. "The Norm of Reciprocity." *American Sociological Review* 25 (April):161–177.

———. 1970. *The Coming Crisis of Western Sociology.* New York: Basic Books.

Graham, Judith. 2002. "Agencies Adapt to a Less-White Elderly." *Chicago Tribune,* April 11, pp. 1, 16.

———. 2003. "Most Perceive Shades of Gray in Abortion." *Chicago Tribune,* June 20, pp. 1, 18.

Gramsci, Antonio. 1929. *Selections from the Prison Notebooks.* Antonio Gramsci. Edited and translated by Quintin Hoare and Geoffrey Nowell Smith. London: Lawrence and Wishort.

Greeley, Andrew M. 1989. "Protestant and Catholic: Is the Analogical Imagination Extinct?" *American Sociological Review* 54 (August):485–502.

Green, Dan S., and Edwin D. Driver. 1978. "Introduction." Pp. 1–60 in *W. E. B. DuBois on Sociology and the Black Community,* edited by Dan S. Green and Edwin D. Driver. Chicago: University of Chicago Press.

Greenburg, Jan Crawford. 2003. "6–3 Ruling Affects Bans in 13 States." *Chicago Tribune,* June 27, pp. 1, 23.

Greene, Jay P. 1998. "A Meta-Analysis of the Effectiveness of Bilingual Education." Sponsored by the Toms River Policy Initiative. Accessed July 1 (http://data.Fas.harvard.edu/pepg/biling.htm).

Greenhouse, Linda. 1998. "High Court Ruling Says Harassment Includes Same Sex." *New York Times,* March 5, pp. A1, A17.

Greenhouse, Steven. 2000a. "Report Faults Laws for Slowing Growth of Unions." *New York Times,* October 24, p. A14.

———. 2000b. "Temp Workers at Microsoft Win Lawsuit." *New York Times,* December 13, p. C1.

Greenwood, Ernest. 1957. "Attributes of a Profession." *Social Work* 2 (July):45–55.

Grieco, Elizabeth M., and Rachel C. Cassidy. 2001. "Overview of Race and Hispanic Origin." *Current Population Reports Series* CENBR/01–1. Washington, DC: U.S. Government Printing Office.

Grob, Gerald N. 1995. "The Paradox of Deinstitutionalization." *Society* 32 (July/August):51–59.

Grossman, Lew. 2002. "Busjocking for Grownups." *Time,* November 4, p. 80.

Groza, Victor, Daniela F. Ileana, and Ivor Irwin. 1999. *A Peacock or a Crow: Stories, Interviews, and Commentaries on Romanian Adoptions.* Euclid, OH: Williams Custom Publishing.

Guterman, Lila. 2000. "Why the 25-Year-Old Battle over Sociology Is More than Just 'An Academic Sideshow.'" *Chronicle of Higher Education,* July 7, pp. A17–A18.

Gutiérrez, Gustavo. 1990. "Theology and the Social Sciences," in Paul E. Sigmund, *Liberation Theology at the Crossroads: Democracy or Revolution?* New York: Oxford University Press, pp. 214–225.

Gutierrez, Valerie. 2002. "Minority Women Get Left Behind by Title IX." *Los Angeles Times,* June 23, pp. D1, D12.

Gwynne, S. C., and John E. Dickerson. 1997. "Lost in the E-Mail." *Time* 149 (April 21):88–90.

H

Hacker, Andrew. 1964. "Power to Do What?" Pp. 134–146 in *The New Sociology,* edited by Irving Louis Horowitz. New York: Oxford University Press.

Hacker, Helen Mayer. 1951. "Women as a Minority Group." *Social Forces* 30 (October):60–69.

———. 1974. "Women as a Minority Group, Twenty Years Later." Pp. 124–134 in *Who Discriminates against Women?* edited by Florence Denmark. Beverly Hills, CA: Sage.

Haines, Valerie A. 1988. "Is Spencer's Theory an Evolutionary Theory?" *American Journal of Sociology* 93 (March):1200–1223.

Hall, Kay. 1999. "Work from Here." *Computer User* 18 (November):32.

Hall, Mimi. 1993. "Genetic-Sex-Testing a Medical Mine Field." *USA Today,* December 20, p. 6A.

Hall, Robert H. 1982. "The Truth about Brown Lung." *Business and Society Review* 40 (Winter 1981–82):15–20.

Haller, Max, Wolfgang Konig, Peter Krause, and Karin Kurz. 1990. "Patterns of Career Mobility and Structural Positions in Advanced Capitalist Societies: A Comparison of Men in Austria, France, and the United States." *American Sociological Review* 50 (October): 579–603.

Hallinan, Maureen T. 1997. "The Sociological Study of Social Change." *American Sociological Review* 62 (February):1–11.

———. 2003. "Ability Grouping and Student Learning." Pp. 95–140 in *Brookings Papers on Education Policy,* edited by Diane Ravitch. Washington, DC: Brookings Institute Press.

Hamilton, Brady E., Paul D. Sutton, Stephanie J. Ventura. 2003. "Revised Birth and Fertility Rates for the 1990s and New Rates for Hispanic Populations, 2000 and 2001: United States." *National Vital Statistics Reports* 51 (August 4).

Hani, Yoko. 1998. "Hot Pots Wired to Help the Elderly." *Japan Times Weekly International Edition,* April 13, p. 16.

Hank, Karsten. 2001. "Changes in Child Care Could Reduce Job Options for Eastern German Mothers." *Population Today* 29 (April):3, 6.

Hansen, Brian. 2001. "Globalization Backlash." *CQ Researcher* 11 (September 28): 761–784.

———. 2002. "Cyber-Crime." *CQ Researcher* 12 (April 12).

Harap, Louis. 1982. "Marxism and Religion: Social Functions of Religious Belief." *Jewish Currents* 36 (January):12–17, 32–35.

Harlow, Harry F. 1971. *Learning to Love.* New York: Ballantine.

Harmon, Amy. 1998. "The Law Where There Is No Land." *New York Times,* March 16, pp. C1, C9.

Harrington, Michael. 1980. "The New Class and the Left." Pp. 123–138 in *The New Class,* edited by B. Bruce Briggs. Brunswick, NJ: Transaction.

Harris, Chauncy D., and Edward Ullman. 1945. "The Nature of Cities." *Annals of the American Academy of Political and Social Science* 242 (November):7–17.

Harris, David A. 1999. *Driving While Black: Racial Profiling on Our Nation's Highways.* New York: American Civil Liberties Union.

Harris, Judith Rich. 1998. *The Nurture Assumption: Why Children Turn Out the Way They Do.* New York: Free Press.

Hartman, Chris, and Betsy Leondar-Wright. 2001. *Executive Excess 2001: Layoffs, Tax Rebates, the Gender Gap.* Boston: United for a Fair Economy.

———, and Jake Miller. 2001. *Bail Outs That Work for Everyone.* Boston: United for a Fair Economy.

Haub, Carl. 2002. *2002 World Population Report Data Sheet*. Washington, DC: Population Reference Bureau.

———. 2003. *World Population Data Sheet, 2003*. Washington, DC: Population Reference Bureau.

———, and Diana Cornelius. 2001. *2001 World Population Data Sheet*. Washington, DC: Population Reference Bureau.

———, and Britt Herstad. 2002. *Family Planning Worldwide: 2002 Data Sheet*. Washington, DC: Population Reference Bureau.

Hauser, Robert M., and David B. Grusky. 1988. "Cross-National Variation in Occupational Distributions, Relative Mobility Chances, and Intergenerational Shifts in Occupational Distributions." *American Sociological Review* 53 (October):723–741.

Haviland, William A. 2002. *Cultural Anthropology*. 10th ed. Belmont, CA: Wadsworth.

Hawkins, Darnell F., et al. 2000. "Race, Ethnicity, and Serious and Violent Juvenile Offending." *Juvenile Justice Bulletin* (June):107.

Hayward, Mark D., William R. Grady, and Steven D. McLaughlin. 1987. "Changes in the Retirement Process." *Demography* 25 (August):371–386.

Healey, Jon. 2003. "Music Industry Tries Fear as a Tactic to Stop Online Piracy." *Los Angeles Times*, April 23, pp. A1, A21.

Health Canada. 1993. *Gender and Violence in the Mass Media*. Ottawa, Canada: Health Canada.

Health Care Financing Administration. 2001. *National Health Care Expenditures Projections*. Accessed August 10 (www.hefa.gov/stats/NHE-proj/).

Heckert, Druann, and Amy Best. 1997. "Ugly Duckling to Swan: Labeling Theory and the Stigmatization of Red Hair." *Symbolic Interaction* 20 (4):365–384.

Hedley, R. Alan. 1992. "Industrialization in Less Developed Countries." Pp. 914–920 in *Encyclopedia of Sociology*, vol. 2, edited by Edgar F. Borgatta and Marie L. Borgatta. New York: Macmillan.

Heilman, Madeline E. 2001. "Description and Prescription: How Gender Stereotypes Prevent Women's Ascent up the Organizational Ladder." *Journal of Social Issues* 57 (4):657–674.

Heise, Lori, M. Ellsberg, and M. Gottemuelle. 1999. "Ending Violence Against Women." *Population Reports*, ser. L, no. 11. Baltimore: Johns Hopkins University School of Public Health.

Hellmich, Nanci. 2001. "TV's Reality: No Vast American Waistlines." *USA Today*, October 8, p. 7D.

Henly, Julia R. 1999. "Challenges to Finding and Keeping Jobs in the Low-Skilled Labor Market." *Poverty Research News* 3 (1):3–5.

Henneberger, Melinda. 1995. "Muslims Continue to Feel Apprehensive." *New York Times*, April 14, p. B10.

Henrard, Kristin. 2003. "Post-Apartheid South Africa: Transformation and Reconciliation." *World Affairs* 166 (Summer):37.

Henry L. Stimson Center. 2001. "Frequently Asked Questions: Likelihood of Terrorists Acquiring and Using Chemical or Biological Weapons." Accessed December 28, 2001 (www.stimson.org/cwc/acquse.htm#seek).

Hequembourg, Amy, and Jorge Arditi. 1999. "Fractured Resistances: The Debate over Assimilationism and Gays and Lesbians in the United States." *Sociological Quarterly* 40 (4): 663-680.

Herrmann, Andrew. 1994. "Survey Shows Increase in Hispanic Catholics." *Chicago Sun-Times*, March 10, p. 4.

Hersch, Patricia. 1998. *A Tribe Apart: A Journey into the Heart of the American Adolescence*. New York: Fawcett Books.

Hershey, Robert D., Jr. 1988. "Underground Economy Is Not Rising to the Bait." *New York Times*, January 24, p. E5.

Herskovits, Melville J. 1930. *The Anthropometry of the American Negro*. New York: Columbia University Press.

Hetherington, E. Mavis, and John Kelly. 2002. *For Better or For Worse*. New York: Norton.

Hewlett, Sylvia Ann, and Cornel West. 1998. *The War Against Parents*. Boston: Houghton Mifflin.

Hick, Steven F., and John G. McNutt. 2002. *Advocacy, Activism, and the Internet*. Chicago: Lyceum.

Hickman, Jonathan. 2002. "America's 50 Best Corporations for Minorities." *Fortune* 146 (July 8): 110–120.

Hill, Charles W. L. 2003. *International Business: Competing in the Global Marketplace*. 4th ed. New York: McGraw-Hill/Irwin.

Hill, Michael R., and Susan Hoecker-Drysdale, eds. 2001. *Harriet Martineau: Theoretical and Methodological Perspectives*. New York: Routledge.

Hillery, George A. 1955. "Definitions of Community: Areas of Agreement." *Rural Sociology* (2):111–123.

Himes, Vristine L. 2001. "Elderly Americans." *Population Bulletin* 56 (December).

Hirschi, Travis. 1969. *Causes of Delinquency*. Berkeley: University of California Press.

Hirst, Paul, and Grahame Thompson. 1996. *Globalization in Question: The International Economy and the Possibilities of Governance*. Cambridge, UK: Polity Press.

Hochschild, Arlie Russell. 1990. "The Second Shift: Employed Women Are Putting in Another Day of Work at Home." *Utne Reader* 38 (March/April):66–73.

———, with Anne Machung. 1989. *The Second Shift: Working Parents and the Revolution at Home*. New York: Viking Penguin.

Hodge, Robert W., and Peter H. Rossi. 1964. "Occupational Prestige in the United States, 1925–1963." *American Journal of Sociology* 70 (November):286–302.

Hodson, Randy, and Teresa A. Sullivan. 1995. *The Social Organization of Work*. 2d ed. Belmont, CA: Wadsworth.

Hoebel, E. Adamson. 1949. *Man in the Primitive World: An Introduction to Anthropology*. New York: McGraw-Hill.

Hoffman, Adonis. 1997. "Through an Accurate Prism." *Los Angeles Times*, August 8, p. M1.

Hoffman, Lois Wladis. 1985. "The Changing Genetics/Socialization Balance." *Journal of Social Issues* 41 (Spring):127–148.

Holden, Constance. 1980. "Identical Twins Reared Apart." *Science* 207 (March 21): 1323–1328.

———. 1987. "The Genetics of Personality." *Science* 257 (August 7):598–601.

Hollander, Jocelyn A. 2002. "Resisting Vulnerability: The Social Reconstruction of Gender in Interaction." *Social Problems* 49 (4):474–496.

Hollingshead, August B. 1975. *Elmtown's Youth and Elmtown Revisited*. New York: Wiley.

Holmes, Steven A. 1997. "Leaving the Suburbs for Rural Areas." *New York Times*, October 19, p. 34.

Homans, George C. 1979. "Nature versus Nurture: A False Dichotomy." *Contemporary Sociology* 8 (May):345–348.

Hombo, Catherine M. 2003. "NAEP and No Child Left Behind: Technical Challenges and Practical Solutions." *Theory into Practice* 42 (Winter):59–65.

Hondagneu-Sotelo, Pierette. 2001. *Domestica: Immigrant Workers Cleaning and Caring in the Shadows of Affluence*. Berkeley: University of California Press.

Hoover, Eric. 2002. "Binge Thinking." *Chronicle of Higher Education* 49 (November 8):A34–A37.

Horgan, John. 1993. "Eugenics Revisited." *Scientific American* 268 (June): 122–128, 130–133.

Horovitz, Bruce. 2003. "Smile! You're the Stars of the Super Ad Bowl." *USA Today*, January 24, pp. B1, B2.

Horowitz, Helen Lefkowitz. 1987. *Campus Life*. Chicago: University of Chicago Press.

Horwitz, Allan V. 2002. *Creating Mental Illness*. Chicago: University of Chicago Press.

Hosokawa, William K. 1969. Nisei: *The Quiet Americans*. New York: Morrow.

Hospice Foundation of America. 2002. *What Is Hospice?* Accessed January 2 (www.hospicefoundation.org/what_is).

Houseman, John. 1972. *Run Through.* New York: Simon and Schuster.

Housing and Urban Development. 1999. *Stuart B. McKinney Homeless Programs.* Washington, DC: U.S. Government Printing Office.

———. 2001. *A Report on Worst Case Housing Needs in 1999: New Opportunity Amid Continuing Challenges.* Washington, DC: HUD.

Hout, Michael. 1988. "More Universalism, Less Structural Mobility: The American Occupational Structure in the 1980s." *American Journal of Sociology* 91 (May): 1358–1400.

Howard, Judith A. 1999. "Border Crossings between Women's Studies and Sociology." *Contemporary Sociology* 28 (September): 525–528.

Howard, Michael C. 1989. *Contemporary Cultural Anthropology.* 3d ed. Glenview, IL: Scott, Foresman.

Howard, Philip E., Lee Rainie, and Steve Jones. 2001. "Days and Nights on the Internet." *American Behavioral Scientist* 45 (November): 383–404.

Howard, Russell D., and Reid L. Sawyer. 2003. *Terrorism and Counterterrorism: Understanding the New Security Environment.* Guilford, CT: McGraw-Hill/Dushkin.

Huang, Gary. 1988. "Daily Addressing Ritual: A Cross-Cultural Study." Presented at the annual meeting of the American Sociological Association, Atlanta.

Huber, Bettina J. 1985. *Employment Patterns in Sociology: Recent Trends and Future Prospects.* Washington, DC: American Sociological Association.

Huddy, Leonie, Joshua Billig, John Bracciodieta, Lois Hoeffler, Patrick J. Moynihan, and Patricia Pugliani. 1997. "The Effect of Interviewer Gender on the Survey Response." *Political Behavior* 19 (September):197–220.

Huff, Darrell. 1954. *How to Lie with Statistics.* New York: Norton.

Huffstutter, P. J. 2003. "See No Evil." *Los Angeles Times,* January 12, pp. 12–15, 43–45.

Hughes, Everett. 1945. "Dilemmas and Contradictions of Status." *American Journal of Sociology* 50 (March):353–359.

Hunt, Darnell. 1997. *Screening the Los Angeles "Riots": Race, Seeing, and Resistance.* New York: Cambridge University Press.

Hunter, Herbert, ed. 2000. *The Sociology of Oliver C. Cox: New Perspectives: Research in Race and Ethnic Relations,* vol. 2. Stamford, CT: JAI Press.

Hunter, James Davison. 1991. *Culture Wars: The Struggle to Define America.* New York: Basic Books.

Hurh, Won Moo. 1994. *Korean Immigrants in America: A Structural Analysis of Ethnic Confinement and Adhesive Adaptation.* Rutherford, NJ: Fairleigh Dickinson University Press.

———. 1998. *The Korean Americans.* Westport, CT: Greenwood Press.

———, and Kwang Chung Kim. 1998. "The 'Success' Image of Asian Americans: Its Validity, and Its Practical and Theoretical Implications." *Ethnic and Racial Studies* 12 (October):512–538.

Hurn, Christopher J. 1985. *The Limits and Possibilities of Schooling,* 2d ed. Boston: Allyn and Bacon.

Hymowitz, Carol, and Rachel Emma Silverman. 2001. "Can Work Place Stress Get Worse?" *Wall Street Monitor,* January 16, pp. B1, B4.

I

Immigration and Naturalization Service. 1999a. *Legal Immigration, Fiscal Year 1998.* Washington, DC: U.S. Government Printing Office.

———. 1999b. *1997 Statistical Yearbook of the Immigration and Naturalization Service.* Washington, DC: U.S. Government Printing Office.

Inglehart, Ronald, and Wayne E. Baker. 2000. "Modernization, Cultural Change, and the Persistence of Traditional Values." *American Sociological Review* 65 (February):19–51.

Institute of International Education. 2003. *Open Doors: International Students 2002 and U.S. Study Abroad 2002-Data Tables.* Accessed May 22, 2002 (www.opendoors.iienetwork.org).

Intelligence Report. 2003. "Hate Web Site List." *Intelligence Report* (Spring):42–47.

Internal Revenue Service. 2001. *1999 Individual Tax Returns: Introduction and Changes in Law.* IRS Publication 1304. Washington, DC: U.S. Government Printing Office.

International Crime Victim Survey. 2003. *Nationwide Surveys in the Industrialized Countries.* Accessed April 1 (www.ruljis.leidenuniv.nl/group/jfer/www/icvs).

International Monetary Fund. 2000. *World Economic Outlook: Asset Prices and the Business Cycle.* Washington, DC: International Monetary Fund.

Inter-Parliamentary Union. 2003. *Women in National Parliaments.* May 31. Accessed August 6 (www.ipu.org).

Iritani, Evelyn, and Marla Dickerson. 2002. "People's Republic of Products." *Los Angeles Times,* October 20, pp. A1, A10.

J

Jackson, Elton F., Charles R. Tittle, and Mary Jean Burke. 1986. "Offense-Specific Models of the Differential Association Process." *Social Problems* 33 (April): 335–356.

Jackson, Philip W. 1968. *Life in Classrooms.* New York: Holt.

Jacobs, Andrew. 2001a. "A Nation Challenged: Neighbors, Town, Shed Its Anonymity to Confront the Bereaved." *New York Times.* October 14.

———. 2001b. "A Suburb Pulls Together for Its Grieving Families." *New York Times.* November 13, p. B1.

———. 2002. "Emerging from a Cocoon of Grief." *New York Times,* September 9, p. A23.

Jacobs, Jerry. 2003. "Detours on the Road to Equality: Women, Work and Higher Education." *Contexts* (Winter):32-41.

Jacobson, Jodi. 1993. "Closing the Gender Gap in Development." Pp. 61–79 in *State of the World,* edited by Lester R. Brown. New York: Norton.

Jamieson, Arnie, Hyon B. Shin, and Jennifer Day. 2002. "Voting and Registration in the Election of November 2000." *Current Population Reports,* ser. P-20, no. 542. Washington, DC: U.S. Government Printing Office.

Jargowsky, Paul A. 2003. *Stunning Progress, Hidden Problems: The Dramatic Decline of Concentrated Poverty in the 1990s.* Washington, DC: Brookings Institute.

Jasper, James M. 1997. *The Art of Moral Protest: Culture, Biography, and Creativity in Social Movements.* Chicago: University of Chicago Press.

Jenkins, Richard. 1991. "Disability and Social Stratification." *British Journal of Sociology* 42 (December):557–580.

Jennings, M. Kent, and Richard G. Niemi. 1981. *Generations and Politics.* Princeton, NJ: Princeton University Press.

Jobtrak.com. 2000a. "Jobtrak.com's Poll Finds that Students and Recent Grads Only Plan to Stay with Their First Employer No Longer than Three Years." Press release January 6. Accessed June 29 (http://static.jobtrak.com/mediacenter/press_polls/poll_010600.html).

———. 2000b. "79% of College Students Find the Quality of an Employer's Website Important in Deciding Whether or Not to Apply for a Job." Accessed on June 29 (http://static.jobtrak.com/mediacenter/press_polls/polls_061200.html).

Johnson, Anne M., Jane Wadsworth, Kaye Wellings, and Julie Field. 1994. *Sexual Attitudes and Lifestyles.* Oxford: Blackwell Scientific.

Johnson, Benton. 1975. *Functionalism in Modern Sociology: Understanding Talcott Parsons.* Morristown, NJ: General Learning.

Johnson, Dirk. 1996. "Rural Life Gains New Appeal, Turning Back a Long Decline." *New York Times,* September 23, pp. A1, B6.

Johnson, Jeffrey, et al. 2002. "Television Viewing and Aggressive Behavior During Adolescence and Adulthood." *Science* 295 (March 29):2468–2471.

Johnson, Kenneth M. 1999. "The Rural Rebound." *Reports on America* 1 (September).

Johnson, Richard A. 1985. *American Fads.* New York: Beech Tree.

Johnston, David Cay. 1994. "Ruling Backs Homosexuals on Asylum." *New York Times,* June 12, pp. D1, D6.

———. 1996. "The Divine Write-Off." *New York Times,* January 12, pp. D1, D6.

Jolin, Annette. 1994. "On the Backs of Working Prostitutes: Feminist Theory and Prostitution Policy." *Crime and Delinquency* 40 (2):69–83.

Jones, Dale E., Dherri Doty, James E. Horsch, Richard Houseal, Mac Lynn, John P. Marcum, Kenneth M. Sanchagrin, and Richard H. Taylor. 2002. *Religious Congregations and Membership in the United States 2000: An Enumeration by Religion, State and Country Based on Data Reported by 149 Religious Bodies.* Nashville, TN: Glenmary Research Center.

Jones, James T., IV. 1988. "Harassment Is Too Often Part of the Job." *USA Today,* August 8, p. 5D.

Jones, Stephen R. G. 1992. "Was There a Hawthorne Effect?" *American Journal of Sociology* 98 (November):451–568.

Jost, Kenneth. 2002a. "Corporate Crime." *CQ Researcher* 12 (October 11).

———. 2002b. "School Vouchers Showdown." *CQ Researcher* 12 (February 15): 121-144.

Joynt, Jen, and Vasugi Ganeshananthan. 2003. "Abortion Decisions." *Atlantic Monthly* 291 (April):38–39.

Juhasz, Anne McCreary. 1989. "Black Adolescents' Significant Others." *Social Behavior and Personality* 17 (2):211–214.

K

Kagay, Michael R. 1996. "Experts Say Refinements Are Needed in the Polls." *New York Times,* December 15, p. 34.

Kahn, Joseph. 2003a. "Made in China, Bought in China." *New York Times,* January 5, sec. 3, pp. 1, 10.

———. 2003b. "China's Workers Risk Limbs in Export Drive." *New York Times,* April 7, p. A3.

Kaiser Family Foundation. 2001. *Few Parents Use V-Chip to Block TV Sex and Violence.* Menlo Park: Kaiser Family Foundation.

———. 2003. *Sex on TV: 2003.* Santa Barbara, CA: Kaiser Family Foundation.

Kalb, Claudia. 1999. "Our Quest to Be Perfect," *Newsweek* 131 (August 9):52–59.

Kalish, Richard A. 1985. *Death, Grief, and Caring Relationships.* 2d ed. Monterey, CA: Brooks/Cole.

Kalleberg, Arne L. 1988. "Comparative Perspectives on Work Structures and Inequality." Pp. 203–225 in *Annual Review of Sociology,* 1988, edited by W. Richard Scott and Judith Blake. Palo Alto, CA: Annual Reviews.

Kanellos, Nicholas. 1994. *The Hispanic Almanac: From Columbus to Corporate America.* Detroit: Visible Ink Press.

Kang, Mee-Eun. 1997. "The Portrayal of Women's Images in Magazine Advertisements: Goffman's Gender Analysis Revisited." In *Sex Roles* 37(December): 979–996.

Kapner, Suzanne. 2003. "U.S. TV Shows Losing Potency Around World." *New York Times,* January 2, pp. A1, A8.

Kasarda, John D. 1990. "The Jobs-Skills Mismatch." *New Perspectives Quarterly* 7 (Fall):34–37.

Katovich, Michael A. 1987. Correspondence. June 1.

Katz, Jonathan Ned. 1992. *Gay American History: Lesbians and Gay Men in the United States.* Rev. ed. New York: Meridian.

Katz, Michael. 1971. *Class, Bureaucracy, and the Schools: The Illusion of Educational Change in America.* New York: Praeger.

Kelsoe, John R. et al. [12 authors]. 1989. "Reevaluation of the Linkage Relationship between Chromosome LTP Loci and the Gene for Bipolar Affective Disorder in the Old Order Amish." *Nature* 342 (November 16): 238–243.

Kerbo, Harold R. 2003. *Social Stratification and Inequality: Class Conflict in Historical, Comparative, and Global Perspective.* 5th ed. New York: McGraw-Hill.

———, and John A. McKinstry. 1998. *Modern Japan.* Boston: McGraw-Hill.

Kershaw, Sarah. 2003. "Wal-Mart Sets a New Policy That Protects Gay Workers." *New York Times,* July 2, pp. A1, A16.

Kilborn, Peter T. 2001. "Rural Towns Turn to Prisons to Reignite Their Economies." *New York Times,* August 1, pp. A1, A11.

Kilbourne, Jean. 2000a. *Can't Buy My Love: How Advertising Changes the Way We Think and Feel.* New York: Touchstone Book, Simon and Schuster.

———. 2000b. *Killing Us Softly* 3. Videorecording. Northampton, MA: Media Education Foundation (Cambridge Documentary Films).

Kim, Kwang Chung. 1999. *Koreans in the Hood: Conflict with African Americans.* Baltimore: Johns Hopkins University Press.

King, Leslie. 1998. "France Needs Children: Pronatalism, Nationalism, and Women's Equity." *Sociological Quarterly* 39 (Winter): 33–52.

———, and Madonna Harrington Meyer. 1997. "The Politics of Reproductive Benefits: U.S. Insurance Coverage of Contraceptive and Infertility Treatments." *Gender and Society* 11 (February):8–30.

King, Sharon A. 1999. "Mania for 'Pocket Monsters' Yields Billions for Nintendo." *New York Times,* April 26, pp. A1, A18.

Kinkade, Patrick T., and Michael A. Katovich. 1997. "The Driver Adaptations and Identities in the Urban Worlds of Pizza Delivery Employees." *Journal of Contemporary Ethnography* 25 (January):421–448.

Kinsella, Kevin, and Victoria A. Velkoff. 2001. "An Aging World: 2001." *Current Population Reports,* ser. 95, no. 01-1. Washington, DC: U.S. Government Printing Office.

Kinsey, Alfred C., Wardell B. Pomeroy, and Clyde E. Martin. 1948. *Sexual Behavior in the Human Male.* Philadelphia: Saunders.

———, Wardell B. Pomeroy, and Paul H. Gebhard. 1953. *Sexual Behavior in the Human Female.* Philadelphia: Saunders.

Kirk, Margaret O. 1995. "The Temps in the Gray Flannel Suits." *New York Times,* December 17, p. F13.

Kitchener, Richard F. 1991. "Jean Piaget: The Unknown Sociologist." *British Journal of Sociology* 42 (September):421–442.

Klass, Perri. 2003. "This Side of Medicine." In *This Side of Doctoring: Reflection for Women in Medicine* by Eliza Lo Chin (ed.). P. 319 New York: Oxford University Press.

Klein, Julia M. 2003. "Film: Depicting Mental Illness." *Chronicle of Higher Education* 49 (June 27):B15–B16.

Klein, Naomi. 1999. *No Logo: Money, Marketing, and the Growing Anti-Corporate Movement.* New York: Picador (St. Martin's Press).

Kleiner, Art. 2003. "Are You In with the In Crowd?" *Harvard Business Review* 81 (July):86–92.

Kleinknecht, William. 1996. *The New Ethnic Mobs: The Changing Face of Organized Crime in America.* New York: Free Press.

Kleniewski, Nancy. 2002. *Cities, Change, and Conflict: A Political Economy of Urban Life.* 2d ed. Belmont, CA: Wadsworth.

Klinenberg, Eric. 2002. *Heat Wave: A Social Autopsy of Disaster in Chicago.* Chicago: University of Chicago Press.

Klinger, Scott et al. 2002. *Executive Excess 2002: CEOs Cook the Books, Skewer the Rest of Us.* Boston, MA: United for a Fair Economy.

Kohn, Melvin L. 1970. "The Effects of Social Class on Parental Values and Practices." Pp. 45–68 in *The American Family: Dying or Developing,* edited by David Reiss and H. A. Hoffman. New York: Plenum.

Kolata, Gina. 1998. "Infertile Foreigners See Opportunity in U.S." *New York Times,* January 4, pp. 1, 12.

———. 1999. *Clone: The Road to Dolly and the Path Beyond.* New York: William Morrow.

Komarovsky, Mirra. 1991. "Some Reflections on the Feminist Scholarship in Sociology." Pp. 1–25 in *Annual Review of Sociology,* edited by W. Richard Scott and Judith Blake. Palo Alto, CA: Annual Reviews.

Konieczny, May Ellen, and Mark Chaves. 2000. "Resources, Race, and Female-Headed Congregations in the United States." *Journal for the Scientific Study of Religion* 39 (September): 261–271.

Koolhaas, Rem, et al. 2001. *Mutations.* Barcelona, Spain: Actar.

Kopinak, Kathryn. 1995. "Gender as a Vehicle for the Subordination of Women Maquiladora Workers in Mexico." *Latin American Perspectives* 22 (Winter):30–48.

Korczyk, Sophie M. 2002. *Bank to Which Future: The U.S. Aging Crisis Revisited.* Washington, DC: AARP.

Koval, John, Roberta Garner, Judith Bootcheck, Kenneth Fidel, and Noel Barker. 1996. "Motorola in Harvard: A Microcosm of Social Change." Proposal to the National Science Foundation, DePaul University, Chicago.

Kozol, J. 1991. *Savage Inequalities.* New York: Crown.

Krauss, Clifford. 2003. "Quebec Seeking to End Its Old Cultural Divide." *New York Times,* April 13, p. A12.

Kreider, Rose M., and Jason M. Fields. 2002. "Number, Timing, and Duration of Marriages and Divorces: 1996." *Current Population Reports,* ser. P-70. no. 80. Washington, DC: U.S. Government Printing Office.

Kretzmann, John P., and John L. McKnight. 1993. *Building Communities from the Inside Out: A Path Toward Finding and Mobilizing a Communities Assets.* Evanston, IL: Institute for Policy Research.

Kristof, Nicholas D. 1998. "As Asian Economies Shrink, Women Are Squeezed Out." *New York Times,* June 11, pp. A1, A12.

Kübler-Ross, Elisabeth. 1969. *On Death and Dying.* New York: Macmillan.

Kunkel, Dale, et al. 2001. Sex on TV2. Menlo Park, CA: Kaiser Family Foundation.

Kyodo News International. 1998. "More Japanese Believe Divorce Is Acceptable." *Japan Times* 38 (January 12):B4.

L

La Ganga, Maria L. 1999. "Trying to Figure the Beginning of the End." *Los Angeles Times,* October 15, pp. A1, A28, A29.

Labaton, Stephan. 2003. "10 Wall St. Firms Settle with U.S. in Analyst Inquiry." *New York Times,* April 29, pp. A1, C4.

Ladner, Joyce. 1973. *The Death of White Sociology.* New York: Random Books.

Lamb, David. 1997. "Viet Kieu: A Bridge Between Two Worlds." *Los Angeles Times,* November 4, pp. A1, A8.

Landtman, Gunnar. [1938] 1968. *The Origin of Inequality of the Social Class.* New York: Greenwood (original edition 1938, Chicago: University of Chicago Press).

Lang, Eric. 1992. "Hawthorne Effect." Pp. 793–794 in *Encyclopedia of Sociology,* vol. 2, edited by Edgar F. Borgatta and Marie L. Borgatta. New York: Macmillan.

Lappin, Todd. 1996. "Aux Armes, Netizens!" *The Nation* 262 (February 26):6–7.

Larsen, Elena. 2000. *Wired Churches, Wired Temples: Taking Congregations and Missions into Cyberspace.* Washington, DC: Pew Internet and American Life Project.

Lasn, Kalle. 2003. "Ad Spending Predicted for Steady Decline." *Adbusters* (January/February).

Lasswell, Harold D. 1936. *Politics: Who Gets What, When, How.* New York: McGraw-Hill.

Lauer, Robert H. 1982. *Perspectives on Social Change.* 3d ed. Boston: Allyn and Bacon.

Laumann, Edward O., John H. Gagnon, and Robert T. Michael. 1994a. "A Political History of the National Sex Survey of Adults." *Family Planning Perspectives* 26 (February): 34–38.

———, John H. Gagnon, Robert T. Michael, and Stuart Michaels. 1994b. *The Social Organization of Sexuality: Sexual Practices in the United States.* Chicago: University of Chicago Press.

Lauritsen, John, and David Thorstad. 1974. *The Early Homosexual Rights Movement (1864–1935).* New York: Times Change.

Lazarsfeld, Paul, Bernard Beretson, and H. Gaudet. 1948. *The People's Choice.* New York: Columbia University Press.

———, and Robert K. Merton. 1948. "Mass Communication, Popular Taste, and Or-ganized Social Action." Pp. 95–118 in *The Communication of Ideas,* edited by Lymon Bryson. New York: Harper and Brothers.

Leacock, Eleanor Burke. 1969. *Teaching and Learning in City Schools.* New York: Basic Books.

Leaf, Nathan. 2003. "Wal-topia." *The Capital Times* (Madison, WI), May 3, pp. 1A, 4A.

Leavell, Hugh R., and E. Gurney Clark. 1965. *Preventive Medicine for the Doctor in His Community: An Epidemiologic Approach.* 3d ed. New York: McGraw-Hill.

Lee, Alfred McClung. 1983. *Terrorism in Northern Ireland.* Bayside, NY: General Hall.

Lee, Barrett A. 1992. "Homelessness." Pp. 843–847 in *Encyclopedia of Sociology,* vol. 2, edited by Edgar F. Borgatta and Marie L. Borgatta. New York: Macmillan.

Lee, Heon Cheol. 1999. "Conflict Between Korean Merchants and Black Customers: A Structural Analysis." Pp. 113–130 in *Koreans in the Hood Conflict with African Americans,* edited by Kwang Chung Kim. Baltimore: Johns Hopkins University Press.

Lee, Tom. 2000. "The Gay Asian Male—Struggling to Find an Identity." *AsianWeek* 21 (June 22):15–17.

Lehne, Gregory K. 1995. "Homophobia among Men: Supporting and Defining the Male Role." Pp. 325–336 in *Men's Lives,* edited by Michael S. Kimmel and Michael S. Messner. Boston: Allyn and Bacon.

Leicht, Kevin T., and Mary L. Fennell. 1997. "The Changing Organizational Context of Professional Work." Pp. 215–231 in *Annual Review of Sociology 1997,* edited by John Hagan. Palo Alto, CA: Annual Reviews.

Leinwand, Donna. 2000. "20% Say They Used Drugs with Their Mom and Dad." *USA Today,* August 24, pp. 1A, 2A.

———. 2003. "Alcohol-Soaked Spring Break Lures Students Abroad." *USA Today,* January 6, pp. A1, A2.

Lemann, Nicholas. 1991. "The Other Underclass." *Atlantic Monthly* 268 (December):96–102, 104, 107–108, 110.

Lemkow, Louis. 1987. "The Employed Unemployed: The Subterranean Economy in Spain." *Social Science and Medicine* 25 (2):111–113.

Lemonick, Michael D., and Alice Park Mankato. 2001. "The Nun Study." *Time* 157 (May 14):54–59, 62, 64.

Lengermann, Patricia Madoo, and Jill Niebrugge-Brantley. 1998. *The Women Founders: Sociology and Social Theory, 1830–1930.* Boston: McGraw-Hill.

Lenski, Gerhard. 1966. *Power and Privilege: A Theory of Social Stratification.* New York: McGraw-Hill.

———, Jean Lenski, and Patrick Nolan. 1995. *Human Societies: An Introduction to Macrosociology.* 7th ed. New York: McGraw-Hill.

Leo, John. 1987. "Exploring the Traits of Twins." *Time* 129 (January 12):63.

Levin, Jack, and William C. Levin. 1980. *Ageism.* Belmont, CA: Wadsworth.

Levin, Thomas Y., Ursula Frohne, and Peter Weibel, eds. 2002. *Ctrl Space: Rhetorics of Surveillance from Bentham to Big Brother.* Cambridge: MIT Press.

Levinson, Daniel J. 1978. *The Seasons of a Man's Life.* With Charlotte N. Darrow et al. New York: Knopf.

———. 1996. *The Season of a Woman's Life.* With Judy D. Levinson. New York: Knopf.

Levinson, David. 1996. *Religion: A Cross-Cultural Encyclopedia.* New York: Oxford University Press.

Levy, Becca R., Martin D. Slade, Suzanne R. Kunkel, and Stanislav V. Kasl. 2002. "Longevity Increased by Positive Self-Perceptions of Aging." *Journal of Personality and Social Psychology* 83 (2):261–270.

Lewin, Tamar. 1998. "Debate Centers on Definition of Harassment." *New York Times,* March 22, pp. A1, A20.

———. 2000. "Differences Found in Care with Stepmothers." *New York Times,* August 17, p. A16.

Lewis, Anthony. 2003. "The Silencing of Gideon's Trumpet." *New York Times,* April 20, pp. 50–52, 77.

Lewis, David Levering. 1994. *W. E. B. DuBois: Biography of a Race, 1868–1919.* New York: Holt.

———. 2000. *W. E. B. DuBois: The Fight for Equality and the American Century, 1919–1963.* New York: Holt.

Lewis Mumford Center. 2001. *Ethnic Diversity Grows, Neighborhood Integration Is at a Standstill.* Albany, NY: Lewis Mumford Center.

Liao, Youlian, Daniel L. McGee, Guichan Cao, and Richard S. Cooper. 2000. "Quality of the Last Year of Life of Older Adults: 1986–1993." *Journal of American Medical Association* 283 (January 26):512–518.

Lichter, S. Robert, Linda S. Lichter, and Daniel R. Amundson. 1999. *Merchandizing Mayhem: Violence in Popular Media, 1998–1999.* Washington, DC: CMPA.

Lictblau, Eric. 2003. "Bush Issues Racial Profiling Ban but Exempts Security Awareness." *New York Times,* June 18, pp. A1, A14.

Lieberman, David. 1999. "On the Wrong Side of the Wires." *USA Today,* October 11, pp. B1, B2.

Liebow, Elliot. 1993. *Tell Them Who I Am: The Lives of Homeless Women.* New York: Free Press.

Light, Ivan. 1999. "Comparing Incomes of Immigrants." *Contemporary Sociology* 28 (July):382–384.

Liker, Jeffrey K., Carol J. Hoddard, and Jennifer Karlin. 1999. "Perspectives on Technology and Work Organization." Pp. 575–596 in *Annual Review of Sociology 1999,* edited by Karen S. Cook and John Hagen. Palo Alto, CA: Annual Reviews.

Lin, Nan, and Wen Xie. 1988. "Occupational Prestige in Urban China." *American Journal of Sociology* 93 (January):793–832.

———. 1999. "Social Networks and Status Attainment." Pp. 467–487 in *Annual Review of Sociology 1999,* edited by Karen S. Cook and John Hagen. Palo Alto, CA: Annual Reviews.

Lindner, Eileen, ed. 1998. *Yearbook of American and Canadian Churches, 1998.* Nashville: Abingdon Press.

———. 2002. *Yearbook of American and Canadian Churches 2002.* Nashville: Abingdon Press.

Linn, Susan, and Alvin F. Poussaint. 1999. "Watching Television: What Are Children Learning About Race and Ethnicity?" *Child Care Information Exchange* 128 (July):50–52.

Lipset, Seymour Martin. 1996. *American Exceptionalism: A Double-Edged Sword.* New York: Norton.

Lipson, Karen. 1994. "'Nell' Not Alone in the Wilds." *Los Angeles Times,* December 19, pp. F1, F6.

Liska, Allen E., and Steven F. Messner. 1999. *Perspectives on Crime and Deviance.* 3d ed. Upper Saddle River, NJ: Prentice Hall.

Little, Kenneth. 1988. "The Role of Voluntary Associations in West African Urbanization." Pp. 211–230 in *Anthropology for the Nineties: Introductory Readings,* edited by Johnnetta B. Cole. New York: Free Press.

Lively, Kathryn J. 2001. "Occupational Claims to Professionalism: The Case of Paralegal Symbolic Interaction." 24 (no. 3):343–366.

Livernash, Robert, and Eric Rodenburg. 1998. "Population Change, Resources, and the Environment." *Population Bulletin* 53 (March).

Llanes, Jose. 1982. *Cuban Americans: Masters of Survival.* Cambridge, MA: Abt Books.

Lofland, John. 1981. "Collective Behavior: The Elementary Forms." Pp. 441–446 in *Social Psychology: Sociological Perspectives,* edited by Morris Rosenberg and Ralph Turner. New York: Basic Books.

———. 1985. *Protests: Studies of Collective Behavior and Social Movements.* Rutgers, NJ: Transaction.

Lofland, Lyn H. 1975. "The 'Thereness' of Women: A Selective Review of Urban Sociology." Pp. 144–170 in *Another Voice,* edited by M. Millman and R. M. Kanter. New York: Anchor/Doubleday.

Logan, John R. 2001. "From Many Shores: Asians in Census 2000." Accessed November 29, 2001 (http://mumford1.dyndns: org/cen2000/ Asianpop).

Lohr, Steve. 1994. "Data Highway Ignoring Poor, Study Charges." *New York Times,* May 24, pp. A1, D3.

Long, Jeff. 2002. "Harvard Has Plans for Motorola Funds." *Chicago Tribune,* July 6, p. 16.

Lorber, Judith. 1994. *Paradoxes of Gender.* New Haven, CT: Yale University Press.

Lu, Ming, Jianyong Fan, Shejan Liu, and Yan Yan. 2002. "Employment Restructuring During China's Economic Transition." *Monthly Labor Review* (August):25–31.

Lukacs, Georg. 1923. *History and Class Consciousness.* London: Merlin.

Luker, Kristin. 1984. *Abortion and the Politics of Motherhood.* Berkeley: University of California Press.

Lum, Joann, and Peter Kwong. 1989. "Surviving in America: The Trials of a Chinese Immigrant Woman." *Village Voice* 34 (October 31):39–41.

Luster, Tom, Kelly Rhoades, and Bruce Haas. 1989. "The Relation between Parental Values and Parenting Behavior: A Test of the Kohn Hypothesis." *Journal of Marriage and the Family* 51 (February):139–147.

Lyall, Sarah. 2002. "For Europeans, Love, Yes; Marriage, Maybe." *New York Times,* March 24, pp. 1–8.

Lynch, David J. 2002. "China's New Attitude Toward Capitalists Too Late for Some." *USA Today,* December 9, pp. B1, B2.

Lynn, Barry C. 2003. "Trading with a Low-Wage Tiger." *The American Prospect* 14 (February):10–12.

Lyons, Linda. 2002a. "The Future of Marriage: Part II." *Gallup Poll Tuesday Briefing,* July 30.

Lyotard, Jean François. 1993. *The Postmodern Explained: Correspondence, 1982–1985.* Minneapolis: University of Minnesota Press.

M

Mack, Raymond W., and Calvin P. Bradford. 1979. *Transforming America: Patterns of Social Change.* 2d ed. New York: Random House.

Magnier, Mark. 1999. "Equality Evolving in Japan." *Los Angeles Times,* August 30, pp. A1, A12.

Maguire, Brendan. 1988. "The Applied Dimension of Radical Criminology: A Survey of Prominent Radical Criminologists." *Sociological Spectrum* 8 (2):133–151.

————, and Polly F. Radosh. 1999. *Introduction to Criminology.* Belmont, CA: Wadsworth/Thomson Learning.

Mahbub ul Haq Human Development Centre. 2000. *Human Development in South Asia 2000.* Oxford, England: Oxford University Press for Mahbub ul Haq Human Development Centre.

Maine Times. 2001. Article on Wal-Mart's Plan to Build Near the Penja. January 4, 2001.

Maines, David R. 1977. "Social Organization and Social Structure in Symbolic Interactionist Thought." Pp. 235–259 in *Annual Review of Sociology, 1977,* edited by Alex Inkles. Palo Alto, CA: Annual Reviews.

————. 1982. "In Search of Mesostructure: Studies in the Negotiated Order." *Urban Life* 11 (July):267–279.

Malbin, Michael, et al. 2002. "New Interest Group Strategies—A Preview of Post Mc-Cain-Feingold Politics?" Accessed May 7 (www.CFInst.org).

Malcolm, Andrew H. 1974. "The 'Shortage' of Bathroom Tissue: A Classic Study in Rumor." *New York Times,* February 3, p. 29.

Malcolm X, with Alex Haley. 1964. The *Autobiography of Malcolm X.* New York: Grove.

Malthus, Thomas Robert. [1798] 1965. *Essays on the Principle of Population.* New York: Augustus Kelly, Bookseller.

————, Julian Huxley, and Frederick Osborn. [1824] 1960. *Three Essays on Population.* Reprint. New York: New American Library.

Margolis, Eric, ed. 2001. *The Hidden Curriculum in Higher Education.* New York: Routledge.

Marijuana Policy Report. 2003. "Take Action." Accessed April 2 (www.mpp.org).

Marklein, Mary Beth. 1996. "Telecommuters Gain Momentum." *USA Today,* June 18, p. 6E.

Markson, Elizabeth W. 1992. "Moral Dilemmas." *Society* 29 (July/August):4–6.

Marquand, Robert. 2002. "Yule Trees on Buddhist Temples and Handle's Messiah in Beijing." *Christian Science Monitor,* December 23, pp. 1, 10.

Marquis, Julie, and Dan Morain. 1999. "A Tortuous Path for the Mentally Ill." *Los Angeles Times,* November 21, pp. A1, A22, A23.

Marr, Phebe. 2003. "Civics 101, Taught by Saddam Hussein: First, Join the Paramilitary." *New York Times,* April 20.

Marshall, Patrick. 2003. "Gambling in America." *CQ Researcher* 13 (March 7):201–224.

Marshall, Victor W., and Judith A. Levy. 1990. "Aging and Dying." Pp. 245–260 in *Handbook of Aging and the Social Sciences,*

edited by Robert H. Binstock and Linda K. George. San Diego: Academic Press.

Martelo, Emma Zapata. 1996. "Modernization, Adjustment, and Peasant Production." *Latin American Perspectives* 23 (Winter):118–130.

Martin, Joyce A., Melissa M. Park and Paul D. Sutton. 2002. "Births: Preliminary Data for 2001." *National Vital Statistics Reports* 50 (June 6).

————, Brady E. Hamilton, Stephanie J. Ventura, Fay Menacker, Melissa M. Park and Paul D. Sutton. 2002. "Births: Final Data For 2001." *National Vital Statistics Reports* 51 (December 18).

Martin, Marvin. 1996. "Sociology Adapting to Changes." *Chicago Tribune* (July 21), Section 18, p. 20.

Martin, Philip, and Elizabeth Midgley. 1999. "Immigrants to the United States." *Population Bulletin* 54 (June):1–42.

————. "Immigration: Shaping and Reshaping America." *Population Bulletin* 58 (June):1–47.

————, and Jonas Widgren. 1996. "International Migration: A Global Challenge." *Population Bulletin* 51(April).

Martin, Philip, and Jonas Widgren. 2002. "International Migration: A Global Challenge," *Population Bulletin* 57 (No. 1).

Martin, Susan E. 1994. "Outsider Within the Station House: The Impact of Race and Gender on Black Women Politics." *Social Problems* 41 (August):383–400.

Martineau, Harriet. 1896. "Introduction" to the translation of *Positive Philosophy* by Auguste Comte. London: Bell.

————. [1837] 1962. *Society in America.* Edited, abridged, with an introductory essay by Seymour Martin Lipset. Reprint. Garden City, NY: Doubleday.

Martinez, Elizabeth. 1993. "Going Gentle into That Good Night: Is a Rightful Death a Feminist Issue?" *Ms.* 4 (July/August):65–69.

Marx, Karl, and Friedrich Engels. [1847] 1955. *Selected Work in Two Volumes.* Reprint, Moscow: Foreign Languages Publishing House.

Mason, Heather. 2002. "What Do American's See in Title IX's Future?" *Gallup Poll Tuesday Briefing.* Accessed on January 28, 2003 at www.gallup.com.

Mason, J. W. 1998. "The Buses Don't Stop Here Anymore." *American Prospect* 37 (March):56–62.

Massachusetts Department of Education. 2000. *Learning Support Service Progress: Safe Schools Program for Gay and Lesbian Students.* Accessed July 19, 2001 (www. doe.mass. edu/lss/program/ ssch.html).

Massey, Douglas S. 1998. "March of Folly: U.S. Immigration Policy After NAFTA." The *American Prospect* (March/April):22–23.

————, and Nancy A. Denton. 1993. *American Apartheid: Segregation and the Making of the Underclass.* Cambridge, MA: Harvard University Press.

Match.com. 2003. *Match.com Reports Paid Subscribers Exceed 766,000 at End of Q1 2003.* May 7. Accessed May 18 (www. match.com).

Mathews, T. J., Marian F. MacDorman, and Fay Menacker. 2002. "Infant Mortality Statistics from the 1999 Period Linked Birth/Infant Death Data Set." *National Vital Statistics Reports* 50 (January 30).

Matsushita, Yoshiko. 1999. "Japanese Kids Call for a Sympathetic Ear." *Christian Science Monitor,* January 20, p. 15.

Matthews, Jay. 1999. "A Home Run for Home Schooling." *Washington Post National Weekly Edition* 16 (March 29):34.

Maugh, Thomas H., II. 2003. "Number of AIDS Diagnoses on the Rise Again in the United States." *Los Angeles Times,* February 12, p. A36.

Mayer, Karl Ulrich, and Urs Schoepflin. 1989. "The State and the Life Course." Pp. 187–209 in *Annual Review of Sociology, 1989,* edited by W. Richard Scott and Judith Blake. Palo Alto, CA: Annual Reviews.

Mazur, Dennis J. 2003. *The New Medical Conversation.* Lanham, MD: Rowman and Littlefield.

McCormick, John, and Claudia Kalb. 1998. "Dying for a Drink." *Newsweek,* June 15, pp. 30–34.

McCreary, D. 1994. "The Male Role and Avoiding Femininity." *Sex Roles* 31: 517–531.

McCright, Aaron M., and Riley E. Dunlap. 2003. "Defeating Kyoto: The Conservative Movement's Impact on U.S. Climate Change Policy." *Social Problems* 50 (No. 3):348–373.

McDermott, Kevin. 1999. "Illinois Bill Would Repeal Law Requiring Listing of Campaign Donors on Internet." *St. Louis Post-Dispatch,* November 25, p. A1.

McDonald, Kim A. 1999. "Studies of Women's Health Produce a Wealth of Knowledge on the Biology of Gender Differences." *Chronicle of Higher Education* 45 (June 25):A19, A22.

McFalls, Joseph A., Jr. 1998. "Population: A Lively Introduction." *Population Bulletin* 53 (September).

McGivering, Jill. 2001. *Activists Urge Caste Debate.* August 28. Accessed April 15, 2003 (www.news.bbc.co.uk).

McGue, Matt, and Thomas J. Bouchard, Jr. 1998. "Genetic and Environmental Influence on Human Behavioral Differences." Pp. 1–24 in *Annual Review of Neurosciences.* Palo Alto, CA: Annual Reviews.

McGuire, Meredith B. 2002. *Religion: The Social Context.* 5th ed. Belmont, CA: Wadsworth.

McIntosh, Peggy. 1988. "White Privilege and Male Privilege: A Personal Account of Coming to See Correspondence Through Work and Women's Studies." Working Paper No. 189, Wellesley College Center for Research on Women, Wellesley, MA.

McKinlay, John B., and Sonja M. McKinlay. 1977. "The Questionable Contribution of Medical Measures to the Decline of Mortality in the United States in the Twentieth Century." *Milbank Memorial Fund Quarterly* 55 (Summer):405–428.

McKinley, James C., Jr. 1999. "In Cuba's New Dual Economy, Have-Nots Far Exceed Haves." *New York Times,* February 11, pp. A1, A6.

McKinnon, Jesse. 2003. "The Black Population in the United States: March 2002." *Current Population Reports,* ser. P-20, no. 541. Washington, DC: U.S. Government Printing Office.

McKnight, John L., and John P. Kretzmann. 1996. *Mapping Community Capacity.* Evanston, IL: Institute for Policy Research.

McLane, Daisann. 1995. "The Cuban-American Princess." *New York Times Magazine,* February 26, pp. 42–43.

McLuhan, Marshall. 1964. *Understanding Media: The Extensions of Man.* New York: New American Library.

———, and Quentin Fiore. 1967. *The Medium Is the Message: An Inventory of Effects.* New York: Bantam Books.

McNeil, Jr., Donald G. 2002a. "With Folk Medicine on Rise, Health Group Is Monitoring." *New York Times,* May 12, p. A9.

———. 2002b. "W.H.O. Moves to Make AIDS Drugs More Accessible to Poor Worldwide." *New York Times,* August 23, p. D7.

McPhail, Clark. 1991. *The Myth of the Madding Crowd.* New York: De Gruyter.

———. 1994. "The Dark Side of Purpose in Riots: Individual and Collective Violence." *Sociological Quarterly* 35 (January):i–xx.

———, and David Miller. 1973. "The Assembling Process: A Theoretical Empirical Examination." *American Sociological Review* 38 (December):721–735.

———. 2003. *Stereotypes of Crowds and Collective Behavior: Looking Backward, Looking Forward.* Accessible at www.soc.uiuc.edu/faculty/cmcphail/frwrds.htm.

Mead, George H. 1934. In *Mind, Self and Society,* edited by Charles W. Morris. Chicago: University of Chicago Press.

———. 1964a. In *On Social Psychology,* edited by Anselm Strauss. Chicago: University of Chicago Press.

———. 1964b. "The Genesis of the Self and Social Control." Pp. 267–293 in *Selected Writings: George Herbert Mead,* edited by Andrew J. Reck. Indianapolis: Bobbs-Merrill.

Mead, Margaret. 1973. "Does the World Belong to Men—Or to Women?" *Redbook* 141(October):46–52.

———. [1935] 2001. *Sex and Temperament in Three Primitive Societies.* New York: Perennial, HarperCollins.

Mechanic, David, and David Rochefort. 1996. "Comparative Medical Systems." Pp. 475–494 in *Annual Review of Sociology, 1996,* edited by John Hagan. Palo Alto, CA: Annual Reviews.

MediaGuardian. 2001. "Censorship of News in Wartime Is Still Censorship." October 15. Accessed January 25, 2003 (http://media.guardian.co.uk/attack/story/0,1301,57445,00.html).

Melia, Marilyn Kennedy. 2000. "Changing Times." *Chicago Tribune,* January 2, Sec. 17, pp. 12–15.

Mencimer, Stephanie. 2002. "Children Left Behind." *The American Prospect,* December 30, pp. 29–31.

Mendez, Jennifer Bickman. 1998. "Of Mops and Maids: Contradictions and Continuities in Bureaucratized Domestic Work." *Social Problems* 45 (February):114–135.

Menzel, Peter. 1994. *Material World.* Berkeley: University of California Press.

Merton, Robert. 1948. "The Bearing of Empirical Research upon the Development of Social Theory." *American Sociological Review* 13 (October):505–515.

———. 1968. *Social Theory and Social Structure.* New York Free Press.

———. 1987. "The Focused Interview and Focus Groups." *Public Opinion Quarterly* 51:550–566.

———, and Alice S. Kitt. 1950. "Contributions to the Theory of Reference Group Behavior." Pp. 40–105 in *Continuities in Social Research: Studies in the Scope and Methods of the American Soldier,* edited by Robert K. Merton and Paul L. Lazarsfeld. New York: Free Press.

Messner, Michael A. 1997. *Politics of Masculinities: Men in Movements.* Thousand Oaks, CA: Sage.

———. 2002. "Gender Equity in College Sports: 6 Views." *Chronicle of Higher Education.* 49 (December 6):B9–B10.

Meyers, Thomas J. 1992. "Factors Affecting the Decision to Leave the Old Order Amish." Presented at the annual meeting of the American Sociological Association, Pittsburgh.

Michels, Robert. 1915. *Political Parties.* Glencoe, IL: Free Press (reprinted 1949).

Migration News. 2001. "Labor Unions." 8 (April). Accessed March 20 (http://migration.ucdavis.edu).

———. 2002a. "Japan, South Korea." (August). Accessible online at (http://migration.ucdavis.edu).

———. 2002b. "China: Migrants, One-Child, Water." (September). Accessible online at (http://migration.ucdavis.edu).

———. 2002c. "Mexico: Bush, IDs, Remittances." (December). Accessible online at (http://migration.ucdavis.edu).

———. 2003a. "Mexico: Migration, Border, Economy." 10 (April). Accessible online at (http://migration.ucdavis.edu).

———. 2003b. "China: Economy, Migrants." (January). Accessible online at (http://migration.ucdavis.edu).

Milgram, Stanley. 1963. "Behavioral Study of Obedience." *Journal of Abnormal and Social Psychology* 67 (October):371–378.

———. 1975. *Obedience to Authority: An Experimental View.* New York: Harper and Row.

Miller, D. W. 2000. "Sociology, Not Engineering May Explain Our Vulnerability to Technological Disaster." *Chronicle of Higher Education* (October 15):A19–A20.

Miller, David L. 2000. *Introduction to Collective Behavior and Collective Action.* 2d ed. Prospect Heights, IL: Waveland Press.

———, and JoAnne DeRoven Darlington. 2002. *Fearing for the Safety of Others: Disasters and the Small World Problem.* Paper presented at Midwest Sociological Society, Milwaukee, WI.

Miller, G. Tyler, Jr. 1972. *Replenish the Earth: A Primer in Human Ecology.* Belmont, CA: Wadsworth.

Miller, Judith, Stephen Engelberg, and William J. Broad. 2001. *Germs: Biological Weapons and America's Secret War.* New York: Simon and Schuster.

Miller, Reuben. 1988. "The Literature of Terrorism." *Terrorism* 11 (1):63–87.

Mills, C. Wright. [1959] 2000a. *The Sociological Imagination. 40th Anniversary Edition: New Afterword by Todd Gitlin.* New York: Oxford University Press.

———. [1956] 2000b. *The Power Elite.* A New Edition. Afterword by Alan Wolfe. New York: Oxford University Press.

Mills, Robert J. 2002. "Health Insurance Coverage: 2001." *Current Population Reports,* ser. P-60, no. 220. Washington, DC: U.S. Government Printing Office.

Minnesota Twin Family Study. 2001. *What's Special About Twins to Science?* Accessed February 11, 2003 (www.psych.umn.edu/psylabs/mtgs/special.htm).

Mirapaul, Matthew. 2001. "How the Net Is Documenting a Watershed Moment." *New York Times,* October 15, p. E2.

Mishra, Pankaj. 2003. "The Other Face of Fanaticism." *New York Times Magazine,* February 2, pp. 42–46.

Mitofsky, Warren J. 1998. "The Polls-Review. Was 1996 a Worse Year for Polls than 1948?" *Public Opinion Quarterly* 62 (Summer):230–249.

Mizruchi, Mark S. 1996. "What Do Interlocks Do? An Analysis, Critique, and Assessment of Research on Interlocking Directorates." Pp. 271–298 in *Annual Review of Sociology, 1996,* edited by John Hagan and Karen Cook. Palo Alto, CA: Annual Reviews.

Moeller, Susan D. 1999. *Compassion Fatigue.* London: Routledge.

Mogelonsky, Marcia. 1996. "The Rocky Road to Adulthood." *American Demographics* 18 (May):26–29, 32–35, 56.

Mollen, Milton. 1992. *"A Failure of Responsibility": Report to Mayor David N. Dinkins on the December 28, 1991, Tragedy at City College of New York.* New York: Office of the Deputy Mayor for Public Safety.

Monaghan, Peter. 1993. "Sociologist Jailed Because He 'Wouldn't Snitch' Ponders the Way Research Ought to Be Done." *Chronicle of Higher Education* 40 (September 1):A8, A9.

Money. 1987. "A Short History of Shortages." 16 (Fall, special issue):42.

Monmaney, Terence. 1995. "Ethnicities' Medical Views Vary, Study Says." *Los Angeles Times,* September 13, pp. B1, B3.

Monteiro, Lois A. 1998. "Ill-Defined Illnesses and Medically Unexplained Symptoms Syndrome." *Footnotes* 26 (February):3, 6.

Montgomery, Marilyn J., and Gwendolyn T. Sorrell. 1997. "Differences in Love Attitudes Across Family Life Stages." *Family Relations* 46:55–61.

Moore, David W. 2002. "Americans' View of Influence of Religion Settling Back to Pre-September 11 Levels." *Gallup Poll Tuesday Briefing.* December 31.

———. 2003. "Public: Only Merit Should Count in College Admissions." Accessed July 8 (www.gallup.com).

Moore, Joan, and Harry Pachon. 1985. *Hispanics in the United States.* Englewood Cliffs: Prentice Hall.

Moore, Wilbert E. 1967. *Order and Change: Essays in Comparative Sociology.* New York: Wiley.

———. 1968. "Occupational Socialization." Pp. 861–883 in *Handbook of Socialization Theory and Research,* edited by David A. Goslin. Chicago: Rand McNally.

Morehouse Medical Treatment and Effectiveness Center. 1999. *A Synthesis of the Literature: Racial and Ethnic Differences in Access to Medical Care.* Menlo Park, CA: Henry J. Kaiser Family Foundation.

Morin, Richard. 2000. "Will Traditional Polls Go the Way of the Dinosaur?" *Washington Post National Weekly Edition* 17 (May 15):34.

Morris, Aldon. 2000. "Reflections on Social Movement Theory: Criticisms and Proposals." *Contemporary Sociology* 29 (May):445–454.

Morris, Bonnie Rothman. 1999. "You've Got Romance! Seeking Love on Line." *New York Times,* August 26, p. D1.

Morrison, Denton E. 1971. "Some Notes toward Theory on Relative Deprivation, Social Movements, and Social Change." *American Behavioral Scientist* 14 (May/June):675–690.

Morse, Arthur D. 1967. *While Six Million Died: A Chronicle of American Apathy.* New York: Ace.

Morse, Jodie. 1999. "Cracking Down on the Homeless." *Time,* December 2000, pp. 69–70.

Mosisa, Abraham T. 2002. "The Role of Foreign-Born Workers in the U.S. Economy." *Monthly Labor Review* (May):3–14.

Mosley, J., and E. Thomson. 1995. Pp. 148–165 in *Fatherhood: Contemporary Theory, Research and Social Policy,* edited by W. Marsiglo. Thousand Oaks, CA: Sage.

Moss, Michael, and Ford Fessenden. 2002. "New Tools for Domestic Spying, and Qualms." *New York Times,* December 10, pp. A1, A18.

MOST. 2003. Home page of MOST. Accessed May 18 (www.mostonline.org).

Mullins, Marcy E. 2001. "Bioterrorism Impacts Few." *USA Today,* October 18, p. 16A.

Mumola, Christopher J. 2000. *Incarcerated Parents and Their Children.* Washington, DC: U.S. Government Printing Office.

Murdock, George P. 1945. "The Common Denominator of Cultures." Pp. 123–142 in *The Science of Man in the World Crisis,* edited by Ralph Linton. New York: Columbia University Press.

———. 1949. *Social Structure.* New York: Macmillan.

———. 1957. "World Ethnographic Sample." *American Anthropologist* 59 (August): 664–687.

Murphy, Caryle. 1993. "Putting Aside the Veil." *Washington Post National Weekly Edition* 10 (April 12–18):10–11.

Murphy, Dean E. 1997. "A Victim of Sweden's Pursuit of Perfection." *Los Angeles Times,* September 2, pp. A1, A8.

———, and Clifford J. Levy. 2001. "The Evacuation That Kept a Horrible Toll from Climbing Higher." *New York Times,* September 21, p. B10.

Murray, Susan B. 2000. "Getting Paid in Smiles: The Gendering of Child Care Work." *Symbolic Interaction* 23 (No. 2): 135–160.

Murray, Velma McBride, Amanda Willert, and Diane P. Stephens. 2001. "The Half-Full Glass: Resilient African American Single Mothers and Their Children." *Family Focus,* June, pp. F4–F5.

N

Nader, Laura. 1986. "The Subordination of Women in Comparative Perspective." *Urban Anthropology* 15 (Fall/Winter): 377–397.

Nagourney, Adam. 2002. "Supreme Court, 5–4, Upholds Voucher System That Pays Religious Schools' Tuition." *New York Times,* June 28, pp. A1, A17.

Naifeh, Mary. 1998. "Trap Door? Revolving Door? Or Both? Dynamics of Economic Well-Being, Poverty 1993–94." *Current Population Reports,* ser. P-70, no. 63. Washington, DC: U.S. Government Printing Office.

NARAL Pro-Choice America. 2003. *Who Decides? A State-by-State Review of Abortion and Reproductive Rights.* Washington, DC: NARAL Pro-Choice America and NARAL Pro-Choice America Foundation.

Narrow, William E., Donald S. Rae, Lee N. Robbins, and Darrel A. Regier. 2002. "Revised Prevalence Estimates of Mental Disorders in the United States." *Archives of General Psychiatry* 59:115–123.

Nash, Manning. 1962. "Race and the Ideology of Race." *Current Anthropology* 3 (June): 285–288.

Nass, Clifford, and Youngme Moon. 2000. "Machines and Mindlessness: Social Responses to Computers." *Journal of Social Issues* 56 (1):81–103.

National Advisory Commission on Criminal Justice. 1976. *Organized Crime.* Washington, DC: U.S. Government Printing Office.

National Alliance for Caregiving. 1997. *The NAC Comparative Analysis of Caregiver Date for Caregivers to the Elderly, 1987 and 1997.* Bethesda, MD: National Alliance for Caregiving.

National Alliance for the Mentally Ill. 2000. "What Is Mental Illness?" Accessed January 18 (www.nami.org/disorder/whatis. html).

National Alliance to End Homelessness. 2001. *Facts about Homelessness.* Accessed September 23 (www.naeh.org).

National Campaign on Dalit Human Rights. 2003. *Who Are Dalits?* Accessed April 28 (www.dalits.org).

National Center for Education Statistics. 2002a. *Indicators of School Crime and Safety.* Washington, DC: U.S. Government Printing Office.

———. 2002b. *Participation Trends and Patterns in Adult Education 1991 to 1999.*

Washington, DC: U.S. Government Printing Office.

National Center for Health Statistics. 2002. *Health, United States, 2002.* Washington, DC: U.S. Government Printing Office.

National Center on Women and Family Law. 1996. *Status of Marital Rape Exemption Statutes in the United States.* New York: National Center on Women and Family Law.

National Geographic. 2002. "A World Transformed." *National Geographic* (September): map.

National Homeschool Association. 1999. *Homeschooling Families: Ready for the Next Decade.* Accessed November 19, 2000 (www.n-h-a.org/decade.htm).

National Institute on Aging. 1999. *Early Retirement in the United States.* Washington, DC: U.S. Government Printing Office.

National Intelligence Council. 2000. *Global Trends 2015: A Dialogue About the Future with Nongovernment Experts.* Accessed January 2, 2001 (www.cia.gov).

National Law Center on Homelessness and Poverty. 1996. *Mean Sweeps: A Report on Anti-Homeless Laws, Litigation, and Alternatives in 50 United States Cities.* Washington, DC: National Law Center on Homelessness and Poverty.

National Organization for Men Against Sexism. 2003. Home page. Accessed May 11 (www.nomas.org).

National Rifle Association. 2003. *Fact Sheet: Firearm Facts.* Accessed March 11 (www.mraila.org).

National Right to Work Legal Defense Foundation. 2001. *Issue Paper: Employees in Right to Work States.* Accessed April 18 (www. nrtw.org/a/rtwempl.htm).

———. 2003. *Right to Work States.* Accessed February 28 (www.nrtw.org/rtws.htm).

National Vital Statistics Reports. 2003. "Births, Marriages, Divorce, and Deaths. Provisional Data for January–March 2002." *National Vital Statistics Reports* 51 (April 29).

Navarro, Mireya. 2002. "Trying to Get Beyond the Role of the Maid." *New York Times,* May 16, pp. E1, E4.

Navarro, Vicente. 1984. "Medical History as Justification Rather Than Explanation: A Critique of Starr's The Social Transformation of American Medicine." *International Journal of Health Services* 14 (4):511–528.

Neary, Ian. 2003. "Burakumin at the End of History." *Social Research* 70 (Spring): 269–294.

Nelson, Jack. 1995. "The Internet, the Virtual Community, and Those with Disabilities." *Disability Studies Quarterly* 15 (Spring): 15–20.

Neuborne, Ellen. 1996. "Vigilantes Stir Firms' Ire with Cyber-antics." *USA Today,* February 28, pp. A1, A2.

New York Times. 1993. "Dutch May Broaden Euthanasia Guidelines." February 17, p. A3.

———. 1998. "2 Gay Men Fight Town Hall for a Family Pool Pass Discount." July 14, p. B2.

———. 2001. "Sizing Up an Industry and AOL Time Warner's Place in It," December 6, p. C7.

Newburger, Eric C. 2001. "Home Computers and Internet Use in the United States: August 2000." *Current Population Reports,* ser. P-23, no. 207. Washington, DC: U.S. Government Printing Office.

Newman, Katherine S. 1999. *No Shame in My Game: The Working Poor in the Inner City.* New York: Alfred A. Knopf and Russell Sage Foundation.

Newman, William M. 1973. *American Pluralism: A Study of Minority Groups and Social Theory.* New York: Harper and Row.

Newport, Frank. 2003. "Six in Ten Americans Agree that Gay Sex Should be Legal." Accessed June 27, 2003, at www.gallup.com.

Newsday. 1997. "Japan Sterilized 16,000 Women." September 18, p. A19.

Ni, Ching-Ching. 2002. "Chinese Web Surfers Still Face a Backwash." *Los Angeles Times,* September 13, p. A4.

NICHD. 1998. *Early Childhood Care.* Accessed October 19, 2000 (www.nichd.nih.gov/ publications/pubs/ early_child_care.htm).

Nie, Norman H. 2001. "Sociability, Interpersonal Relations, and the Internet." *American Behavioral Scientist* 45 (November): 420–435.

Nielsen, Joyce McCarl, Glenda Walden, and Charlotte A. Kunkel. 2000. "Gendered Heteronormativity: Empirical Illustrations in Everyday Life." *Sociological Quarterly* 41(2): 283–296.

Nixon, Howard L., II. 1979. *The Small Group.* Englewood Cliffs, NJ: Prentice Hall.

Nolan, Patrick, and Gerhard Lenski. 1999. *Human Societies: An Introduction to Macrosociology.* New York: McGraw-Hill.

Noonan, Rita K. 1995. "Women Against the State: Political Opportunities and Collective Action Frames in Chile's Transition to Democracy." *Sociological Forum* 10:81–111.

Norman, Jim. 1996. "At Least 1 Pollster Was Right on Target." *USA Today,* November 7, p. 8A.

The Nun Study. 2003. *The Nun Study: What's New.* Accessed June 14 (www.mcuky.edu/ nunnet).

Nussbaum, Daniel. 1998. "Bad Air Days." *Los Angeles Times Magazine,* July 19, pp. 20–21.

Oberschall, Anthony. 1973. *Social Conflict and Social Movements.* Englewood Cliffs, NJ: Prentice Hall.

The Observer (London). Human Rights Abuses by Country. October 24, 1999. Accessed August 27, 2001 (www.guardian. co.uk).

O'Donnell, Jayne, and Richard Willig. 2003. "Prison Time Gets Harder for White-Collar Crooks." *USA Today,* May 12, pp. A1, A2.

O'Donnell, Mike. 1992. *A New Introduction to Sociology.* Walton-on-Thames, United Kingdom: Thomas Nelson and Sons.

Office of Justice Programs. 1999. "Transnational Organized Crime." *NCJRS Catalog* 49 (November/December):21.

Ogburn, William F. 1922. *Social Change with Respect to Culture and Original Nature.* New York: Huebsch (reprinted 1966, New York: Dell).

———, and Clark Tibbits. 1934. "The Family and Its Functions." Pp. 661–708 in *Recent Social Trends in the United States,* edited by Research Committee on Social Trends. New York: McGraw-Hill.

O'Hare, William P., and Brenda Curry White. 1992. "Is There a Rural Underclass?" *Population Today* 20 (March):6–8.

Okamoto, Dina G., and Lynn Smith-Lovin. 2001. "Changing the Subject: Gender, Status, and the Dynamics of Topic Change." *American Sociological Review* 66 (December):852–873.

Okano, Kaori, and Motonori Tsuchiya. 1999. *Education in Contemporary Japan: Inequality and Diversity.* Cambridge: Cambridge University Press.

Oliver, Melvin L., and Thomas M. Shapiro. 1995. *Black Wealth/White Wealth: New Perspectives on Racial Inequality.* New York: Routledge.

O'Neill, Brian, and Deborah Balk. 2001. "World Population Futures." *Population Bulletin* 56 (September).

Orum, Anthony M. 1989. *Introduction to Political Sociology: The Social Anatomy of the Body Politic.* 3d ed. Englewood Cliffs, NJ: Prentice Hall.

———. 2001. *Introduction to Political Sociology.* 4th ed. Upper Saddle River, NJ: Prentice Hall.

Osgood, D. Wayne, and Jeff M. Chambers. 2003. "Community Correlates of Rural Youth Violence." *Juvenile Justice Bulletin* (May):1–9.

Owens, Michael Leo. 2002. "Why Blacks Support Vouchers." *New York Times,* February 26, p. A27.

P

Page, Charles H. 1946. "Bureaucracy's Other Face." *Social Forces* 25 (October):89–94.

Paik, Haejung, and George Comstock. 1994. "The Effects of Television Violence on Anti-social Behavior: A Meta-analysis." *Communication Research* 21:516–546.

Pamuk, E., D. Makui, K. Heck, C. Reuban, and K. Lochren. 1998. *Health, United States 1998 with Socioeconomic Status and Health Chartbook.* Hyattsville, MD: National Center for Health Statistics.

Pan, Philip P. 2002. "When the Employee-Owner Doesn't Work." *Washington Post National Weekly Edition* 20, December 9, pp. 16–17.

Parents Television Council. 2001a. *What a Difference a Decade Makes.* Los Angeles: PTC.

———. 2001b. *The Sour Family Hour: 8 to 9 Goes from Bad to Worse.* Los Angeles: PTC.

Park, Robert E. 1916. "The City: Suggestions for the Investigation of Human Behavior in the Urban Environment." *American Journal of Sociology* 20 (March):577–612.

———. 1922. *The Immigrant Press and Its Control.* New York: Harper.

———. 1936. "Succession, an Ecological Concept." *American Sociological Review* 1 (April): 171–179.

Parsons, Talcott. 1951. *The Social System.* New York: Free Press.

———. 1966. Societies: *Evolutionary and Comparative Perspectives.* Englewood Cliffs, NJ: Prentice Hall.

———. 1975. "The Sick Role and the Role of the Physician Reconsidered." *Milbank Medical Fund Quarterly Health and Society* 53 (Summer): 257–278.

———, and Robert Bales. 1955. *Family: Socialization, and Interaction Process.* Glencoe, IL: Free Press.

Passero, Kathy. 2002. "Global Travel Expert Roger Axtell Explains Why." *Biography.* July, pp. 70–73, 97–98.

Pate, Antony M., and Edwin E. Hamilton. 1992. "Formal and Informal Deterrents to Domestic Violence: The Dade County Spouse Assault Experiment." *American Sociological Review* 57 (October):691–697.

Patterson, Orlando. 1998. "Affirmative Action." *Brookings Review* 16 (Spring):17–23.

Patterson, Thomas E. 2002. *The Vanishing Voter: Public Involvement in an Age of Uncertainty.* New York: Alfred A. Knopf.

Pattillo-McCoy, Mary. 1999. *Black Picket Fences: Privilege and Peril among the Black Middle Class.* Chicago: University of Chicago Press.

Patton, Carl V., ed. 1988. *Spontaneous Shelter: International Perspectives and Prospects.* Philadelphia: Temple University Press.

Paulson, Amanda. 2000. "Where the School Is Home." *Christian Science Monitor,* October 10, pp. 18–21.

Pavalko, Ronald M., ed. 1972. *Sociological Perspectives on Occupations and Professions.* 2d ed. Itasca, IL: F. E. Peacock.

———. 1988. *Sociology of Occupations and Professions.* Itasca, IL: F. E. Peacock.

PBS. 2001. "Store Wars: When Wal-Mart Comes to Town." Accessed August 24, 2001 (www.pbs.org).

Pear, Robert. 1983. "$1.5 Billion Urged for U.S. Japanese Held in War." *New York Times,* June 17, pp. A1, D16.

———. 1997. "Now, the Archenemies Need Each Other." *New York Times,* June 22, Sec. 4, pp. 1, 4.

Pearlstein, Steven. 2001. "Coming Soon (Maybe): Worldwide Recession." *Washington Post National Weekly Edition* 19 (November 12):18.

Peck, Don. 2002. "The Shrinking Electorate." *The Atlantic Monthly* (November):48–49.

Pellow, David Naguib. 2002. *Garbage Wars: The Struggle for Environmental Justice in Chicago.* Cambridge, MA: MIT Press.

Pelton, Tom. 1994. "Hawthorne Works' Glory Now Just So Much Rubble." *Chicago Tribune,* April 18, pp. 1, 6.

Perlman, Ilene. 2000. "Some Cover; Some Don't." *Christian Science Monitor,* August 11. Accessed August 14 (http://csmonitor.com).

Perrow, Charles. 1986. *Complex Organizations.* 3d ed. New York: Random House.

———. 1999. *Normal Accidents: Living with High Risk Technologies.* Updated edition. New Brunswick, NJ: Rutgers University Press.

Perry, Suzanne. 1998. "U.S. Data Companies Oppose Privacy Laws." Reuters, March 19.

Peter, Laurence J., and Raymond Hull. 1969. *The Peter Principle.* New York: Morrow.

Petersen, William. 1979. *Malthus.* Cambridge, MA: Harvard University Press.

Peterson, Karen S. 2001. "Grandparents' Labor of Love." *USA Today,* August 6, p. D1.

Pew Research Center for the People and the Press. 2001. "Youth Vote Influenced by Online Information." Accessed December 29, 2001 (www.people-press.org/online00rpt,htm).

Phillips, E. Barbara. 1996. *City Lights: Urban—Suburban Life in the Global Society.* New York: Oxford University Press.

Phillips, Susan A. 1999. *Wallbangin': Graffiti and Gangs in L.A.* Chicago: University of Chicago Press.

Pholktales. 2003. *You Know You're a Phishhead When . . .* Accessed February 5 (www.pholktales.com).

Piaget, Jean. 1954. *The Construction of Reality in the Child.* Translated by Margaret Cook. New York: Basic Books.

Pierre, Robert E. 2002. "When Welfare Reform Stops Working." *Washington Post National Weekly Edition,* January 13, pp. 29–30.

Piller, Charles. 2000. "Cyber-Crime Loss at Firms Doubles to $10 Billion." *Los Angeles Times,* May 22, pp. C1, C4.

———. 2001. "Terrorists Taking Up Cyber-space." *Los Angeles Times,* February 8, Pp. A1, A14, A15.

Pinderhughes, Dianne. 1987. *Race and Ethnicity in Chicago Politics: A Reexamination of Pluralist Theory.* Urbana: University of Illinois Press.

Pinkerton, James P. 2003. "Education: A Grand Compromise." *Atlantic Monthly* 291 (January/February):115–116.

Plant, Richard. 1986. *The Pink Triangle: The Nazi War against Homosexuals.* New York: Holt.

Plomin, Robert. 1989. "Determinants of Behavior." *American Psychologist* 44 (February):105–111.

Pollak, Michael. 2000. "World's Dying Languages, Alive on the Web." *New York Times,* October 19, p. D13.

Polletta, Francesca, and James M. Jasper. 2001. "Collective Identity and Social Movements." Pp. 283–305 in *Annual Review of Sociology, 2001,* edited by Karen S. Cook and Leslie Hogan. Palo Alto, CA: Annual Review of Sociology.

Pomfret, John. 2002. "Chinese Capitalists Gain New Legitimizing Ties to State Pay Off for Some Ventures." *Washington Post,* September 29, p. A1.

Poniewozik. 2001. "What's Wrong with This Picture?" *Time* 157 (May 28):80–81.

Popenoe, David, and Barbara Dafoe Whitehead. 1999. *Should We Live Together? What Young Adults Need to Know About Cohabitation Before Marriage.* Rutgers, NJ: The National Marriage Project.

Population Reference Bureau. 1996. "Speaking Graphically." *Population Today* 24 (June/July):b.

———. 2000. "More Youths Take Alternative Route to Finish High School." *Population Today* 28 (January):7.

Power, Carla. 1998. "The New Islam." *Newsweek* 131(March 16):34–37.

Power, Richard. 2002. *2002 CSI/FBI Computer Crime and Security Survey.* San Francisco, CA: Computer Security Institute.

Powers, Mary G., and Joan J. Holmberg. 1978. "Occupational Status Scores: Changes Introduced by the Inclusion of Women." *Demography* 15 (May):183–204.

Prehn, John W. 1991. "Migration." Pp. 190–191 in *Encyclopedia of Sociology,* 4th ed. Guilford, CT: Dushkin.

Princeton Religion Research Center.
———. 2002. *Religion in America* 2002. Princeton, NJ: PRRC.

Proctor, Bernadette D., and Joseph Dalaker. 2002. "Poverty in the United States: 2001." *Current Population Reports* Series P60. No. 219. Washington, DC: U.S. Government Printing Office.

Prusher, Ilene R. 2001. "Well-Ordered Homelessness: Life on Japan's Fringe." *Wall Street Journal,* May 14, pp. 1, 8.

Purdum, Todd S. 2002. "U.S. Blocks Money for Family Clinics Promoted by U.N." *New York Times,* July 23, pp. A1, A6.

Puri, Shaifali. 2003. "As Layoffs Rise, So Do Age-Discrimination Charges." *New York Times,* March 18, p. 4.

Pyle, Amy. 1998. "Opinions Vary on Studies That Back Bilingual Classes." *Los Angeles Times,* March 2, pp. B1, B3.

Q

Quadagno, Jill. 2002. *Aging and the Life Course: An Introduction to Social Gerontology,* 2d ed. New York: McGraw-Hill.

Quarantelli, Enrico L. 1957. "The Behavior of Panic Participants." *Sociology and Social Research* 41 (January):187–194.

———, and Russell R. Dynes. 1970. "Property Norms and Looting: Their Patterns in Continuity Crises." *Phylon* (Summer): 168–182.

———, and James R. Hundley, Jr. 1975. "A Test of Some Propositions about Crowd Formation and Behavior." Pp. 538–554 in *Readings in Collective Behavior,* edited by Robert R. Evans. Chicago: Rand McNally.

Quart, Alissa. 2003. *Branded: The Buying and Selling of Teenagers.* New York: Perseus.

Quinney, Richard. 1970. *The Social Reality of Crime.* Boston: Little, Brown.
———. 1974. *Criminal Justice in America.* Boston: Little, Brown.
———. 1979. *Criminology.* 2d ed. Boston: Little, Brown.
———. 1980. *Class, State and Crime.* 2d ed. New York: Longman.

R

Rainie, Lee. 2001. The *Commons of the Tragedy.* Washington, DC: Pew Internet and American Life Project.
———, and Andrew Kohut. 2000. *Tracking Online Life: How Women Use the Internet to Cultivate Relationships with Family and Friends.* Washington, DC: Pew Internet and American Life League.

Ramet, Sabrina. 1991. *Social Currents in Eastern Europe: The Source and Meaning of the Great Transformation.* Durham, NC: Duke University Press.

Ramirez, Deborah, Jack McDevitt, and Amy Farrell. 2000. *A Resource Guide on Racial Profiling Data Collection Systems. Promising Practices and Lessons Learned.* Washington, DC: U.S. Government Printing Office.

Ramirez, Eddy. 2002. "Ageism in the Media Is Seen as Harmful to Health of the Elderly." *Los Angeles Times,* September 5, p. A20.

Ramirez, Roberta R., and G. Patricia de la Cruz. 2003. "The Hispanic Population in the Current United States: March 2002." *Current Population Reports,* ser. P-20, no. 545. Washington, DC: U.S. Government Printing Office.

Rau, William, and Ann Durand. 2000. "The Academic Ethic and College Grades: Does Hard Work Help Students to 'Make the Grade'?" *Sociology of Education* 73 (January):19–38.

Raybon, Patricia. 1989. "A Case for 'Severe Bias.'" *Newsweek* 114 (October 2):11.

Rayman-Read, Alyssa. 2001. "The Sound of Silence." *The American Prospect* (Fall Special Supplement):A20–A24.

Read, Jen'nan Ghazal, and John P. Bartkowski. 1999. "To Veil or Not to Veil? A Case Study of Identity Negotiations Among Muslim Women in Austin, Texas." Presented at the annual meeting of the American Sociological Association, August, Chicago.

Reddick, Randy, and Elliot King. 2000. *The Online Student: Making the Grade on the Internet.* Fort Worth: Harcourt Brace.

Reeves, Terrance, and Claudette Bennett. 2003. "The Asian and Pacific Islander Population in the United States: March 2002." *Current Population Reports,* ser. P-20, no. 540. Washington DC: U.S. Government Printing Office.

Reich, Robert B. 2001. "Working, but Not 'Employed.'" *New York Times,* January 9, p. H25.

Reinharz, Shulamit. 1992. *Feminist Methods in Social Research.* New York: Oxford University Press.

Religion News Services. 2003. "New U.S. Guidelines on Prayer in Schools Get Mixed Reaction." *Los Angeles Times,* February 15, p. B24.

Remnick, David. 1998a. *King of the World: Muhammed Ali and the Rise of an American Hero.* New York: Random House.
———. 1998b. "Bad Seeds." *New Yorker* 74 (July 20):28–33.

Rennison, Callie. 2002. *Criminal Victimization 2001: Changes 2000–01 with Trends 1993–*
2001. Washington, DC: Bureau of Justice Statistics.
———, and Sarah Welchans. 2000. *Intimate Partner Violence.* Washington, DC: U.S. Government Printing Office.

Reporters San Frontieres. 1999. "The 20 Enemies of the Internet." Accessed June 20, 2003 (www.rferl.org/nca/special/enemies.html).

Retsinas, Joan. 1988. "A Theoretical Reassessment of the Applicability of Kübler-Ross's Stages of Dying." *Death Studies* 12:207–216.

Reuters. 2002. "Few Follow Up on Suicide Request." *Chicago Tribune,* July 3, p. 14.

Rheingold, Howard. 2003. *Smart Mobs: The Next Social Revolution.* Cambridge, MA: Perseus.

Rhodes, Eric Bryant. 2000. "Fatherhood Matters." *The American Prospect,* March 13, pp. 48–52.

Richardson, James T., and Barend van Driel. 1997. "Journalists' Attitudes toward New Religious Movements." *Review of Religious Research* 39 (December):116–136.

Richardson, Laurel, Verta Taylor, and Nancy Whittier, eds. 2001. *Feminist Frontiers.* 5th ed. New York: McGraw-Hill.

Richman, Joseph. 1992. "A Rational Approach to Rational Suicide." *Suicide and Life-Threatening Behavior* 22 (Spring):130–141.

Richtel, Matt. 2000. "www.layoffs.com." *New York Times,* June 22, pp. C1, C12.

Rideout, Victoria J., Ulla G. Foehr, Donald E. Roberts, and Mollyann Brodie. 1999. *Kids & Media @ the New Millennium.* New York: Kaiser Family Foundation.

Ridgeway, Cecilia L., and Lynn Smith-Lovin. 1999. "The Gender System and Interaction." Pp. 191–216 in *The Annual Review of Sociology 1999,* edited by Karen Cook and John Hagan. Palo Alto, CA: Annual Review.

Riding, Alan. 1998. "Why 'Titanic' Conquered the World." *New York Times,* April 26, sec. 2, pp. 1, 28, 29.
———. 2002. "Espousing a New View of Accidents." *New York Times,* December 26, Arts Section, pp. 1–2.

Rifkin, Jeremy. 1995a. *The End of Work; The Decline of the Global Labor Force and the Dawn of the Post-Market Era.* New York: Tarcher/ Putnam.
———. 1995b. "Afterwork." *Utne Reader* (May/June):52–62.
———. 1996. "Civil Society in the Information Age." *The Nation* 262 (February 26):11–12, 14–16.
———. 1998. *The Biotech Century: Harnessing the Gene and Remaking the World.* New York: Tarcher/Putnam.

Riley, John W., Jr. 1992. "Death and Dying." Pp. 413–418 in *Encyclopedia of Sociology,* vol. 1, edited by Edgar F. Borgatta and Marie L. Borgatta. New York: Macmillan.

Riley, Matilda White, Robert L. Kahn, and Anne Foner. 1994a. *Age and Structural Lag.* New York: Wiley InterScience.

———, Robert L. Kahn, and Anne Foner, in association with Karin A. Mock. 1994b. "Introduction: The Mismatch between People and Structures." Pp. 1–36 in *Age and Structural Lag,* edited by Matilda White Riley, Robert L. Kahn, and Ann Foner. New York: Wiley InterScience.

Rimer, Sara. 1998. "As Centenarians Thrive, 'Old' Is Redefined." *New York Times,* June 22, pp. A1, A14.

Rising Daughters Aware. 2003. *The Basics: What Is FGM?* Accessed April 25 (www.fgm.org).

Riska, Elianne. 2001. *Medical Careers and Feminist Agendas: American, Scandinavian, and Russian Women Physicians.* Hawthorne, NY: Aldine de Gruyter.

Ritter, John. 2003. "Canada Gives Gays Hope for Change." *USA Today,* June 30, p. 3A.

Ritzer, George. 1977. *Working: Conflict and Change.* 2d ed. Englewood Cliffs, NJ: Prentice Hall.

———. 1995. *Modern Sociological Theory.* 4th ed. New York: McGraw-Hill.

———. 2000. *The McDonaldization of Society.* New Century Edition. Thousand Oaks, CA: Pine Forge Press.

———. 2002. *McDonaldization: The Reader.* Thousand Oaks, CA: Pine Forge Press.

———. 2004. *The Globalization of Nothing.* Thousand Oaks, CA: Pine Forge Press.

Robb, David. 2001. "Hollywood Wars." *Brill's Content* (Fall):134–151.

Robberson, Tod. 1995. "The Mexican Miracle Unravels." *Washington Post National Weekly Edition,* January 6, p. 20.

Roberts, D. F. 1975. "The Dynamics of Racial Intermixture in the American Negro—Some Anthropological Considerations." *American Journal of Human Genetics* 7 (December): 361–367.

———, Lisa Henriksen, Peter G. Christiansson, and Marcy Kelly. 1999. "Substance Abuse in Popular Movies and Music." Accessible online (www.whitehousedrugpolicy.gov/news/press/042899.html). Washington, DC: Office of Juvenile Justice.

Roberts, Johnnie L. 2001. "All for One, One for AOL." *Newsweek,* January 1, pp. 63–65.

Roberts, Lynne D., and Malcolm R. Parks. 1999. "The Social Geography of Gender-Switching in Virtual Environments on the Internet." *Information, Communication and Society* 2 (Winter).

Roberts, Sam. 1994. "Hispanic Population Now Outnumbers Blacks in Four Major Cities as Demographics Shift." *New York Times,* October 9, p. 34.

Robertson, Roland. 1988. "The Sociological Significance of Culture: Some General Considerations." *Theory, Culture, and Society* 5 (February):3–23.

Robinson, Thomas N., Marta L. Wilde, Lisa C. Navracruz, K. Farish Haydel, and Ann Varady. 2001. "Effects of Reducing Children's Television and Video Game Use on Aggressive Behavior." *Archives of Pediatric Adolescent Medicine* 155 (January):17–23.

Robison, Jennifer. 2002. "Should Mothers Work?" *Gallup Poll Tuesday Briefing,* Accessed August 17 (www.gallup.com).

Roethlisberger, Fritz J., and W. J. Dickson. 1939. *Management and the Worker.* Cambridge, MA: Harvard University Press.

Rogovin, Milton. 1994. *Triptychs: Buffalo's Lower West Side Revisited.* New York: W. W. Norton and Co.

Rohter, Larry. 2003a. "Racial Quotas in Brazil Touch Off Fierce Debate." *New York Times,* April 5, p. A5.

———. 2003b. "Brazil to Let Squatters Own Homes." *New York Times,* April 19, p. A7.

Romero, Mary. 1988. "Chicanas Modernize Domestic Service." *Qualitative Sociology* 11:319–334.

Romney, Lee. 1998. "Latinos Get Down to Business." *Los Angeles Times,* November 11, pp. A1, A20.

Roosevelt, Margot. 2001. "A Setback for Medipot." *Time* 157 (May 28), p. 50.

Rose, Arnold. 1951. *The Roots of Prejudice.* Paris: UNESCO.

Rose, Peter I., Myron Glazer, and Penina Migdal Glazer. 1979. "In Controlled Environments: Four Cases of Intense Resocialization." Pp. 320–338 in *Socialization and the Life Cycle,* edited by Peter I. Rose. New York: St. Martin's.

Rosen, Laurel. 2001. "If U Cn Rd Ths Msg, U Cn B Txtin W/Millions in Europe and Asia." *Los Angeles Times,* July 3, p. A5.

Rosenbaum, Lynn. 1996. "Gynocentric Feminism: An Affirmation of Women's Values and Experiences Leading Us toward Radical Social Change." *SSSP Newsletter* 27 (1):4–7.

Rosenberg, Douglas H. 1991. "Capitalism." Pp. 33–34 in *Encyclopedic Dictionary of Sociology,* 4th ed., edited by Dushkin Publishing Group. Guilford, CT: Dushkin.

Rosenberg, Howard. 2003. "Snippets of the 'Unique' Al Jazeera." *Los Angeles Times,* April 4, pp. E1, E37.

Rosenthal, Elizabeth. 2001. "College Entrance in China: 'No' to the Handicapped." *New York Times,* May 23, p. A3.

———. 2003. "Bias for Boys Leads to Sale of Baby Girls in China." *New York Times,* July 20, p. 6.

Rosenthal, Robert, and Elisha Y. Babad. 1985. "Pygmalion in the Gymnasium." *Educational Leadership* 45 (September):36–39.

———, and Lenore Jacobson. 1968. *Pygmalion in the Classroom.* New York: Holt.

Rosman, Abraham, and Paula G. Rubel. 1994. *The Tapestry of Culture: An Introduction to Cultural Anthropology.* 5th ed. Chapter 1, Map. p. 35. New York: McGraw-Hill.

Rosnow, Ralph L., and Gary L. Fine. 1976, *Rumor and Gossip: The Social Psychology of Hearsay.* New York: Elsevier.

Ross, John. 1996. "To Die in the Street: Mexico City's Homeless Population Booms as Economic Crisis Shakes Social Protections." *SSSP Newsletter* 27 (Summer):14–15.

Rossi, Alice S. 1968. "Transition to Parenthood." *Journal of Marriage and the Family* 30 (February):26–39.

———. 1984. "Gender and Parenthood." *American Sociological Review* 49 (February):1–19.

Rossi, Peter H. 1987. "No Good Applied Social Research Goes Unpunished." *Society* 25 (November/December): 73–79.

———. 1989. *Down and Out in America: The Origins of Homelessness.* Chicago: University of Chicago Press.

———. 1990. "The Politics of Homelessness." Presented at the annual meeting of the American Sociological Association, Washington, DC.

Rossides, Daniel W. 1997. *Social Stratification: The Interplay of Class, Race, and Gender.* 2d ed. Upper Saddle River, NJ: Prentice Hall.

Roszak, Theodore. 1969. *The Making of a Counterculture.* Garden City, NY: Doubleday.

Roter, Debra L., Judith A. Hall, and Yutaka Aoki. 2002. "Physician Gender Effects in Medical Communication: A Meta-analytic Review." *Journal of the American Medical Association* 288 (August 14):756–764.

Roy, Donald F. 1959. "'Banana Time': Job Satisfaction and Informal Interaction." *Human Organization* 18 (Winter):158–168.

Russo, Nancy Felipe. 1976. "The Motherhood Mandate." *Journal of Social Issues* 32:143–153.

Rutenberg, Jim. 2002. "Fewer Media Owners, More Media Choices." *New York Times,* December 2, pp. C1, C11.

Ryan, William. 1976. *Blaming the Victim.* Rev. ed. New York: Random House.

S

Saad, Lydia. 2002. *Sniper Attacks Have Little Impact on Public Attitudes About Guns.* Accessed October 25 (www.gallup.com).

———, and Joe Carroll. 2003. "How Are Retirees Faring Financially?" *Gallup Poll Tuesday Briefing* (May 13) at www.gallup.com.

Sadker, Myra Pollack, and David Miller Sadker. 1985. "Sexism in the Schoolroom of the '80s." *Psychology Today* 19 (March): 54–57.

———. 1997. *Teachers, Schools and Society,* 5th ed. New York: McGraw-Hill.

———. 2000. *Teachers, Schools, and Sociology.* 6th ed. New York: McGraw-Hill.

Safire, William. 1996. "Downsized." *New York Times Magazine,* May 26, pp. 12, 14.

Sagarin, Edward, and Jose Sanchez. 1988. "Ideology and Deviance: The Case of the Debate over the Biological Factor." *Deviant Behavior* 9 (1):87–99.

Sale, Kirkpatrick. 1996. *Rebels against the Future: The Luddites and Their War on the Industrial Revolution* (with a new preface by the author). Reading, MA: Addison-Wesley.

Salem, Richard, and Stanislaus Grabarek. 1986. "Sociology B.A.s in a Corporate Setting: How Can They Get There and of What Value Are They?" *Teaching Sociology* 14 (October):273–275.

Salkever, Alex. 1999. "Making Machines More Like Us." *Christian Science Monitor,* December 20, electronic edition.

Samuelson, Paul A., and William D. Nordhaus. 2001. *Economics.* 17th ed. New York: McGraw-Hill.

Samuelson, Robert J. 1996a. "Are Workers Disposable?" *Newsweek* 127, February 12, p. 47.

———. 1996b. "Fashionable Statements." *Washington Post National Weekly Edition* 13 (March 18):5.

———. 2001. "The Specter of Global Aging." *Washington Post National Weekly Edition* 18 (March 11):27.

Sandberg, Jared. 1999. "Spinning a Web of Hate." *Newsweek* 134 (July 19):28–29.

Saporito, Bill. 2003. "Can Wal-Mart Get Any Bigger?" *Time,* January 13, pp. 38–43.

Sassen, Saskia. 1999. *Guests and Aliens.* New York: The New Press.

Saukko, Paula. 1999. "Fat Boys and Goody Girls." In *Weighty Issues: Fatness and Thinness as Social Problems,* edited by Jeffrey Sobal and Donna Mauer. New York: Aldine de Gruyter.

Savishinsky, Joel S. 2000. *Breaking the Watch: The Meaning of Retirement in America.* Ithaca, NY: Cornell University Press.

Sax, Linda J., Jennifer A. Lindholm, Alexander W. Astin, William S. Korn, and Kathryn M. Mahoney. 2002. *The American Freshman: National Norms for Fall 2002.* Los Angeles: Higher Education Research Institute, UCLA.

Scarce, Rik. 1994. "(No) Trial (But) Tribulations: When Courts and Ethnography Conflict." *Journal of Contemporary Ethnography* 23 (July):123–149.

———. 1995. "Scholarly Ethics and Courtroom Antics: Where Researchers Stand in the Eyes of the Law." *American Sociologist* 26 (Spring):87–112.

Schachter, Jason. 2001. "Geographical Mobility: Population Characteristics." *Current Population Reports,* ser. P-20, no. 538. Washington, DC: U.S. Government Printing Office.

Schaefer, Peter. 1995. "Destroy Your Future." *Daily Northwestern,* November 3, p. 8.

Schaefer, Richard T. 1998a. "Differential Racial Mortality and the 1995 Chicago Heat Wave." Presentation at the annual meeting of the American Sociological Association, August, San Francisco.

———. 1998b. *Alumni Survey.* Chicago, IL: Department of Sociology, DePaul University.

———. 2004. *Racial and Ethnic Relations.* 9th ed. Upper Saddle River, NJ: Prentice Hall.

Scharnberg, Kirsten. 2002. "Tattoo Unites WTC's Laborers." *Chicago Tribune,* July 22, pp. 1, 18.

Schellenberg, Kathryn, ed. 1996. *Computers in Society.* 6th ed. Guilford, CT: Dushkin.

Schlenker, Barry R., ed. 1985. *The Self and Social Life.* New York: McGraw-Hill.

Schmetzer, Uli. 1999. "Modern India Remains Shackled to Caste System." *Chicago Tribune,* December 25, p. 23.

Schmidley, Dianne. 2001. "Profile of the Foreign-Born Population in the United States: 2000." *Current Population Reports* ser. P-23, no. 206. Washington, DC: U.S. Government Printing Office.

Schmidt, William E. 1990. "New Vim and Vigor for the Y.M.C.A." *New York Times,* July 18, pp. C1, C10.

Schnaiberg, Allan. 1994. *Environment and Society: The Enduring Conflict.* New York: St. Martin's.

Schulman, Andrew. 2001. *The Extent of Systematic Monitoring of Employee E-mail and Internet Users.* Denver, CO: Workplace Surveillance Project, Privacy Foundation.

Schur, Edwin M. 1965. *Crimes without Victims: Deviant Behavior and Public Policy.* Englewood Cliffs, NJ: Prentice Hall.

———. 1968. *Law and Society: A Sociological View.* New York: Random House.

———. 1985. "'Crimes without Victims': A 20 Year Reassessment." Paper presented at the annual meeting of the Society for the Study of Social Problems.

Schwartz, Howard D., ed. 1987. *Dominant Issues in Medical Sociology.* 2d ed. New York: Random House.

Scott, Alan. 1990. *Ideology and the New Social Movements.* London: Unwin Hyman.

Scott, Gregory. 2001. "Broken Windows behind Bars: Eradicating Prison Gangs through Ecological Hardening and Symbolic Cleansing." *Corrections Management Quarterly* 5 (Winter):23–36.

Seabrook, Jeremy. 2002. *Class, Caste and Hierarchies.* Oxford, England: New Internationalist Publications.

Secretan, Thierry. 1995. *Going into Darkness: Fantastic Coffins from Africa.* London: Thames and Hudson.

Seelye, Katharine Q. 2002. "When Hollywood's Big Guns Come Right from Source." *New York Times,* June 10, pp. A1, A22.

Segall, Alexander. 1976. "The Sick Role Concept: Understanding Illness Behavior." *Journal of Health and Social Behavior* 17 (June): 163–170.

Segall, Rebecca. 1998. "Sikh and Ye Shall Find." *Village Voice* 43 (December 15):46–48, 53.

Segerstråle, Ullica. 2000. *Defense of the Truth: The Battle for Science in the Sociobiology Debate and Beyond.* New York: Oxford University Press.

Seidman, Steven. 1994. "Heterosexism in America: Prejudice against Gay Men and Lesbians." Pp. 578–593 in *Introduction to Social Problems,* edited by Craig Calhoun and George Ritzer. New York: McGraw-Hill.

Senior Action in a Gay Environment (SAGE). 2003. Home page. Accessed May 11 (www.sageusa.org).

Sernau, Scott. 2001. *Worlds Apart: Social Inequalities in a New Century.* Thousand Oaks, CA: Pine Forge Press.

Shaheen, Jack G. 1999. "Image and Identity: Screen Arabs and Muslims." In *Cultural Diversity: Curriculum, Classrooms, and Climate Issues,* edited by J. Q. Adams and Janice R. Welsch. Macomb, IL: Illinois Staff and Curriculum Development Association.

Shapiro, Joseph P. 1993. *No Pity: People with Disabilities Forging a New Civil Rights Movement.* New York: Times Books.

Sharma, Hari M., and Gerard C. Bodeker. 1998. "Alternative Medicine." Pp. 228–229 in *Britannica Book of the Year 1998.* Chicago: Encyclopaedia Britannica.

Sharp, Deborah. 2002. "Peace Groups to Test National Clout." *USA Today,* December 10, p. 3A.

Shcherbak, Yuri M. 1996. "Ten Years of the Chernobyl Era." *Scientific American* 274 (April): 44–49.

Sheehy, Gail. 1999. *Understanding Men's Passages: Discovering the New Map of Men's Lives.* New York: Ballantine Books.

———. 2003. *Middletown America: One Town's Passage from Trauma to Hope.* New York: Random House.

Shenon, Philip. 1995. "New Zealand Seeks Causes of Suicides by Young." *New York Times,* July 15, p. 3.

———. 1998. "Sailor Victorious in Gay Case on Internet Privacy." *New York Times,* June 12, pp. A1, A14.

Shepherd, Jean. 2003. *Japan Performs First Transplants from Brain-Dead Donor.* Accessed June 14 (www.pntb.org/ff-rndwrld.html).

Sherman, Lawrence W., Patrick R. Gartin, and Michael D. Buerger. 1989. "Hot Spots of Predatory Crime: Routine Activities and the Criminology of Place." *Criminology* 27:27–56.

Sherrill, Robert. 1995. "The Madness of the Market." *The Nation* 260 (January 9–16):45–72.

Shibutani, Tamotshu. 1966. *Improvised News: A Sociological Study of Rumor.* Indianapolis: Bobbs-Merrill.

Shields, Rob, ed. 1996. *Cultures of Internet: Virtual Spaces, Real Histories, Living Bodies.* London: Sage.

Shinkai, Hiroguki, and Ugljea Zvekic. 1999. "Punishment." Pp. 89–120 in *Global Report on Crime and Justice,* edited by Graeme Newman. New York: Oxford University Press.

Shogren, Elizabeth. 1994. "Treatment against Their Will." *Los Angeles Times,* August 18, pp. A1, A14–A15.

Short, Kathleen, Thesia Garner, David Johnson, and Patricia Doyle. 1999. "Experimental Poverty Measures: 1990 to 1997." *Current Population Reports,* ser. P-60, no. 205. Washington, DC: U.S. Government Printing Office.

Shu, Xialing, and Yanjie Bian. 2003. "Marketing Transition and Gender Gap in Earnings in Urban China." *Social Forces* 81 (4):1107–1145.

Shupe, Anson D., and David G. Bromley. 1980. "Walking a Tightrope." *Qualitative Sociology* 2:8–21.

Sidiropoulos, Elizabeth et al. 1996. *South Africa Survey 1995/1996.* Johannesburg: South African Institute of Race Relations.

Sigelman, Lee, Timothy Bledsoe, Susan Welch, and Michael W. Combs. 1996. "Making Contact? Black-White Social Interaction in an Urban Setting." *American Journal of Sociology* 5 (March):1306–1332.

Silicon Valley Cultures Project. 2003. The Silicon Valley Cultures Project Website. Accessed September 8, 2003 (www2.sjsu.edu/depts/anthropology/svcp).

Sills, David L. 1957. *The Volunteers: Means and Ends in a National Organization.* Glencoe, IL: Free Press.

Silver, Ira. 1996. "Role Transitions, Objects, and Identity." *Symbolic Interaction* 10 (1):1–20.

Simmel, Georg. 1950. *Sociology of Georg Simmel.* Translated by K. Wolff. Glencoe, IL: Free Press (originally written in 1902–1917).

Simmons, Ann M. 1998. "Where Fat Is a Mark of Beauty." *Los Angeles Times,* September 30, pp. A1, A12.

———, and Robin Wright. 2000. "Gender Quota Puts Uganda in Role of Rights Pioneer." *Los Angeles Times,* February 23, p. A1.

Simmons, Tavia, and Martin O'Connell. 2003. "Married-Couple and Unmarried-Partner Households: 2000." *Census 2000 Special Reports CENBR-5.* Washington, DC: U.S. Government Printing Office.

Simon, Bernard. 2001. "Canada Warms to Wal-Mart." *New York Times* (November 1), pp. B1, B3.

Simon, Joshua M. 1999. "Presidential Candidates Face Campaign Finance Issue." *Harvard Crimson,* July 2.

Simons, Marlise. 1996. "U.N. Court, for First Time, Defines Rape as War Crime," *New York Times,* June 28, pp. A1, A10.

———. 1997. "Child Care Sacred as France Cuts Back the Welfare State." *New York Times,* December 31, pp. A1, A6.

———. 2000. "Dutch Becoming First Nation to Legalize Assisted Suicide." *New York Times,* November 29, p. A3.

Sjoberg, Gideon. 1960. *The Preindustrial City: Past and Present.* Glencoe, IL: Free Press.

Small, Macio Luis, and Katherine Newman. 2001. "Urban Poverty after 'The Truly Disadvantaged': The Rediscovery of the Family, the Neighborhood, and Culture." Pp. 23–45 in *Annual Review of Sociology 2001.* Palo Alto, CA: Annual Reviews.

Smart, Barry. 1990. "Modernity, Postmodernity, and the Present." Pp. 14–30 in *Theories of Modernity and Postmodernity,* edited by Bryan S. Turner. Newbury Park, CA: Sage.

Smart Growth. 2001. "About Smart Growth." Accessed August 24, 2001 (www.smartgrowth.org.).

Smedley, Brian D., Adrienne Y. Stith, and Alan R. Nelson, eds. 2002. *Unequal Treatment: Confronting Racial and Ethnic Disparities in Health Care.* Washington, DC: Institutional Medicine.

Smeeding, Timothy, Lee Rainwater, and Gary Burtless. 2001. "United States Poverty in a Cross-National Context." *Focus* 21 (Spring):50–54.

Smelser, Neil. 1962. *Theory of Collective Behavior.* New York: Free Press.

———. 1963. *The Sociology of Economic Life.* Englewood Cliffs, NJ: Prentice Hall.

———. 1981. *Sociology.* Englewood Cliffs, NJ: Prentice Hall.

Smith, Christian. 1991. *The Emergence of Liberation Theology: Radical Religion and Social Movement Theory.* Chicago: University of Chicago Press.

Smith, David A. 1995. "The New Urban Sociology Meets the Old: Rereading Some Classical Human Ecology." *Urban Affairs Review* 20 (January):432–457.

———, and Michael Timberlake. 1993. "World Cities: A Political Economy/Global Network Approach." Pp. 181–207 in *Urban Sociology in Transition,* edited by Ray Hutchison. Greenwich, CT: JAI Press.

Smith, David M. and Gary J. Gates. 2001. *Gay and Lesbian Families in the United States: Same-Sex Unmarried Partner Households.* Washington, D.C.: Human Rights Campaign.

Smith, Denise, and Hava Tillipman. 2000. "The Older Population in the United States." *Current Population Reports,* ser. P-20, no. 532. Washington, DC: U.S. Government Printing Office.

Smith, James F. 2001. "Mexico's Forgotten Find Cause for New Hope." *Los Angeles Times,* February 23, pp. A1, A12, A13.

Smith, Kristin. 2000. "Who's Minding the Kids? Child Care Arrangements." *Current Population Reports,* ser. P-70, no. 70. Washington, DC: U.S. Government Printing Office.

Smith, Michael Peter. 1988. *City, State, and Market.* New York: Basil Blackwell.

Smith, Tom. 1999. *GSS News: Trendlets: An Inter-Racial Friendship.* Accessed December 17, 2001 (www.icpsr.uonich.edu/GSS/about/news/trends.htm).

———. 2001. *Estimating the Muslim Population in the United States.* New York: American Jewish Committee.

Snell, Tracy L., and Laura M. Maruschak. 2002. "Capital Punishment 2001." *Bureau of Justice Statistics Bulletin* (December).

Snow, David A., Louis A. Zurcher, Jr., and Robert Peters. 1981. "Victory Celebrations as Theater: A Dramaturgical Approach to Crowd Behavior." *Symbolic Interaction* 4:21–42.

Snowdon, David. 2001. *Aging with Grace.* New York: Bantam.

Snyder, Thomas D. 1996. *Digest of Education Statistics 1996.* Washington, DC: U.S. Government Printing Office.

Sohoni, Neera Kuckreja. 1994. "Where Are the Girls?" *Ms.* 5 (July/August):96.

Sommers, Christina Hoff. 2000. *The War Against Boys.* New York: Touchstone.

Sørensen, Annemette. 1994. "Women, Family and Class." Pp. 27–47 in *Annual Review of Sociology, 1994,* edited by Annemette Sørensen. Palo Alto, CA: Annual Reviews.

Soriano, Cesar G. 2001. "Latino TV Roles Shrank in 2000, Report Finds." *USA Today,* August 26, p. 3D.

Sorokin, Pitirim A. [1927] 1959. *Social and Cultural Mobility.* New York: Free Press.

South African Institute of Race Relations. 2001a. "The Future at your Fingertips." *Fast Facts* 2 (January):2.

———. 2001b. "South Africa Survey 2001/2002." Johannesburg: SA IRR.

———. 2001c. "HIV/AIDS." *Fast Facts* (January):7.

———. 2001d. "Unemployment by Race, Sex and Location: February 2000." *Fast Facts* (May):9.

Southern Poverty Law Center. 2003. "Active Hate Groups in the United States in the Year 2002." *Southern Poverty Law Center* (Spring):36–37.

Spalter-Roth, Roberta M., and Sunhwa Lee. 2000. "Gender in the Early Stages of the Sociological Career." *Research Brief* (American Sociological Association) 1 (2):1–11.

———, Jan Thomas, and Felice J. Levine. 2000. "New Doctorates in Sociology: Professions Inside and Outside the Academy." *Research Brief* (American Sociological Association) 1 (1):1–9.

Spar, Debora. 2001. *Ruling the Waves: Cycles of Discovery, Chaos, and Wealth from the Compass to the Internet.* Harcourt.

Spear, Allan. 1967. *Black Chicago: The Making of a Negro Ghetto.* Chicago, IL: University of Chicago Press.

Spengler, Joseph J. 1978. *Facing Zero Population Growth: Reactions and Interpretations, Past and Present.* Durham, NC: Duke University Press.

Spielmann, Peter James. 1992. "11 Population Groups on 'Endangered' List," *Chicago Sun-Times,* November 23, p. 12.

Spitzer, Steven. 1975. "Toward a Marxian Theory of Deviance." *Social Problems* 22 (June):641–651.

Squires, Gregory D., ed. 2002. *Urban Sprawl: Causes, Consequences and Policy Responses.* Washington: Urban Institute.

Staggenborg, Suzanne. 1989a. "Stability and Innovation in the Women's Movement: A Comparison of Two Movement Organizations." *Social Problems* 36 (February):75–92.

———. 1989b. "Organizational and Environmental Influences on the Development of the Pro-Choice Movement," *Social Forces* 36 (September):204–240.

Stammer, Larry B. 2003. "Evangelical Church Welcomes Gays." *Los Angeles Times,* April 5, p. B22.

Stark, Rodney, and William Sims Bainbridge. 1979. "Of Churches, Sects, and Cults: Preliminary Concepts for a Theory of Religious Movements." *Journal for the Scientific Study of Religion* 18 (June):117–131.

———. 1985. *The Future of Religion.* Berkeley: University of California Press.

———, and Laurence R. Iannaccone. 1992. "Sociology of Religion." Pp. 2029–2037 in *Encyclopedia of Sociology,* vol. 4, edited by Edgar F. Borgatta and Marie L. Borgatta. New York: Macmillan.

Starr, Paul. 1982. *The Social Transformation of American Medicine.* New York: Basic Books.

Stavenhagen, Rodolfo. 1994. "The Indian Resurgence in Mexico." *Cultural Survival Quarterly,* Summer/Fall, pp. 77–80.

Steffensmeier, Darrell, and Stephen Demuth. 2000. "Ethnicity and Sentencing Outcomes in U.S. Federal Courts: Who Is Punished More Harshly?" *American Sociological Review* 65 (October):705–729.

Stein, Leonard I. 1967. "The Doctor-Nurse Game." *Archives of General Psychology* (Volume 16):699–703.

Steinberg, Jacques. 2000. "Test Scores Rise, Surprising Critics of Bilingual Ban." *New York Times,* August 20, pp. 1, 16.

Stenning, Derrick J. 1958. "Household Viability among the Pastoral Fulani." Pp. 92–119 in *The Developmental Cycle in Domestic Groups,* edited by John R. Goody. Cambridge, England: Cambridge University Press.

Stephen, Elizabeth Hervey. 1999. "Assisted Reproductive Technologies: Is the Price Too High?" *Population Today* (May):1–2.

Stevenson, David, and Barbara L. Schneider. 1999. *The Ambitious Generation: America's Teenagers, Motivated but Directionless.* New Haven: Yale University Press.

Stolberg, Sheryl. 1995. "Affirmative Action Gains Often Come at a High Cost." *Los Angeles Times,* March 29, pp. A1, A13–A16.

———. 2000. "Alternative Care Gains a Foothold." *New York Times,* January 31, pp. A1, A16.

Stone, Brad. 1999. "Get a Life?" *Newsweek* 133 (June 7):68–69.

Stoughton, Stephanie, and Leslie Walker. 1999. "The Merchants of Cyberspace." *Washington Post National Weekly Edition* 16 (February 15):18.

Strassman, W. Paul. 1998. "Third World Housing." Pp. 589–592 in *The Encyclopedia of Housing,* edited by Willem van Vliet. Thousand Oaks, CA: Sage.

Strauss, Anselm. 1977. *Negotiations: Varieties, Contexts, Processes, and Social Order.* San Francisco: Jossey Bass.

Strauss, Gary. 2002. "'Good Old Boys' Network Still Rules Corporate Boards." *USA Today,* November 1, pp. B1, B2.

Stretesky, Paul B. and Michael J. Lynch. 2002. "Environmental Hazards and School Segregation in Hillsborough County, Florida, 1987–1999." *Sociological Quarterly* 43 (No. 4):553–573.

Strom, Stephanie. 2000. "Tradition of Equality Fading in New Japan." *New York Times,* January 4, pp. A1, A6.

Sugimoto, Yoshio. 1997. *An Introduction to Japanese Society.* Cambridge, England: Cambridge University Press.

Suid, Lawrence H. 2002. *Guts and Glory: The Making of the American Military Image in Film.* Lexington, KY: University of Kentucky Press.

Suitor, J. Jill, Staci A. Minyard, and Rebecca S. Carter. 2001. "'Did You See What I Saw?' Gender Differences in Perceptions of Avenues to Prestige Among Adolescents." *Sociological Inquiry* 71 (Fall): 437-454.

Sumner, William G. 1906. *Folkways.* New York: Ginn.

Sutherland, Edwin H. 1937. *The Professional Thief.* Chicago: University of Chicago Press.

———. 1940. "White-Collar Criminality." *American Sociological Review* 5 (February):1–11.

———. 1949. *White Collar Crime.* New York: Dryden.

———. 1983. *White Collar Crime: The Uncut Version.* New Haven, CT: Yale University Press.

———, and Donald R. Cressey. 1978. *Principles of Criminology.* 10th ed. Philadelphia: Lippincott.

Suttles, Gerald D. 1972. *The Social Construction of Communities.* Chicago: University of Chicago Press.

Swanson, Stevenson, and Jim Kirk. 1998. "Satellite Outage Felt by Millions." *Chicago Tribune,* May 21, pp. 1, 26.

Swarns, Rachel L., and Christopher Drew. 2003. "Fearful, Angry or Confused, Muslim Immigrants Register." *New York Times,* April 25, pp. A1, A17.

Sweet, Kimberly. 2001. "Sex Sells a Second Time." *Chicago Journal* 93 (April):12–13.

Szasz, Thomas S. 1971. "The Same Slave: An Historical Note on the Use of Medical Diagnosis as Justificatory Rhetoric." *American Journal of Psychotherapy* 25 (April):228–239.

———. 1974. *The Myth of Mental Illness* (rev. ed.). New York: Harper and Row.

T

Takezawa, Yasuko I. 1995. *Breaking the Silence: Redress and Japanese American Ethnicity.* Ithaca, NY: Cornell University Press.

Talbot, Margaret. 1998. "Attachment Theory: The Ultimate Experiment." *New York Times Magazine,* May 24, pp. 4–30, 38, 46, 50, 54.

Tannen, Deborah. 1990. *You Just Don't Understand: Women and Men in Conversation.* New York: Ballantine.

———. 1994a. *Talking from 9 to 5.* New York: William Morris.

———. 1994b. *Gender and Discourse.* New York: Oxford University Press.

Taylor, Verta. 1995. "Watching for Vibes: Bringing Emotions into the Study of Feminist Organizations." Pp. 223–233 in *Feminist Organizations: Harvest of the New Women's Movement,* edited by Myra Marx Ferree and Patricia Yancy Martin. Philadelphia: Temple University Press.

Television Bureau of Advertisers. 2001. "TV Historical Data." Personal correspondence to author, July 13, 2001.

Telsch, Kathleen. 1991. "New Study of Older Workers Finds They Can Become Good Investments." *New York Times,* May 21, p. A16.

Terkel, Studs. 1974. *Working.* New York: Pantheon.

Terry, Sara. 2000. "Whose Family? The Revolt of the Child-Free." *Christian Science Monitor,* August 29, pp. 1, 4.

Texeira, Erin. 2000. "Justice Is Not Color Blind, Studies Find." *Los Angeles Times,* May 22, pp. B1, B8.

Therrien, Melissa, and Roberto R. Ramirez. 2001. "The Hispanic Population in the United States, March 2000." *Current Population Report,* ser. P-20, no. 535. Washington, DC: U.S. Government Printing Office.

Third World Institute. 2001. *The World Guide 2001–2002.* Oxford, England. New Internationalist Publishers.

Thomas, Gordon, and Max Morgan Witts. 1974. *Voyage of the Damned.* Greenwich, CT: Fawcett Crest.

Thomas, Jim. 1984. "Some Aspects of Negotiating Order: Loose Coupling and Mesostructure in Maximum Security Prisons." *Symbolic Interaction* 7 (Fall): 213–231.

Thomas, Pattie, and Erica A. Owens. 2000. "Age Care!: The Business of Passing." Presented at the annual meeting of the American Sociological Association, Washington, DC.

Thomas, R. Murray. 2003. "New Frontiers in Cheating." In *Encyclopedia Britannica 2003 Book of the Year.* Chicago: Encyclopedia Britannica.

Thomas, Robert McG., Jr. 1995. "Maggie Kuhn, 89, the Founder of the Gray Panthers, Is Dead." *New York Times,* April 23, p. 47.

Thomas, William I. 1923. *The Unadjusted Girl.* Boston: Little, Brown.

Thompson, Ginger. 2001a. "Chasing Mexico's Dream into Squalor." *New York Times,* February 11, pp. 1, 6.

———. 2001b. "Why Peace Eludes Mexico's Indians." *New York Times,* March 11, Sect. WK, p. 16.

———. 2001c. "Mexican Rebels' Hopes Meet Hard Indian Reality." *New York Times,* March 3, p. A4.

———. 2001d. "Jobs Are Scarce and the Outlook Becomes Dismal." *New York Times* (December 26), pp. C1, C2.

———. 2002. "Big Mexican Breadwinners: The Migrant Worker." *New York Times,* March 28, p. A3.

Thornton, Russell. 1987. *American Indians Holocaust and Survival: A Population History Since 1492.* Norman: University of Oklahoma Press.

Tierney, John. 1990. "Betting the Planet." *New York Times Magazine,* December 2, pp. 52–53, 71, 74, 76, 78, 80–81.

Tierney, Kathleen. 1980. "Emergent Norm Theory as 'Theory': An Analysis and Critique of Turner's Formulation." Pp. 42–53 in *Collective Behavior: A Source Book,* edited by Meredith David Pugh. St. Paul, MN: West.

Tilly, Charles. 1993. *Popular Contention in Great Britain 1758–1834.* Cambridge, MA: Harvard University Press.

Tolbert, Kathryn. 2000. "In Japan, Traveling Alone Begins at Age 6." *Washington Post National Weekly Edition* 17 (May 15):17.

Tonkinson, Robert. 1978. *The Mardudjara Aborigines.* New York: Holt.

Tönnies, Ferdinand. [1887] 1988. *Community and Society.* Rutgers, NJ: Transaction.

Toossi, Mitra. 2002. "A Century of Change: The U.S. Labor Force, 1050–2050." *Monthly Labor Review* (May):15–28.

Touraine, Alain. 1974. *The Academic System in American Society.* New York: McGraw-Hill.

Treiman, Donald J. 1977. *Occupational Prestige in Comparative Perspective.* New York: Academic Press.

Trotter III, Robert T., and Juan Antonio Chavira. 1997. *Curanderismo: Mexican American Folk Healing.* Athens, GA: University of Georgia Press.

Tuchman, Gaye. 1992. "Feminist Theory." Pp. 695–704 in *Encyclopedia of Sociology,* vol. 2, edited by Edgar F. Borgatta and Marie L. Borgatta. New York: Macmillan.

Tucker, James. 1993. "Everyday Forms of Employee Resistance." *Sociological Forum* 8 (March):25–45.

Tumin, Melvin M. 1953. "Some Principles of Stratification: A Critical Analysis." *American Sociological Review* 18 (August):387–394.

———. 1985. *Social Stratification.* 2d ed. Englewood Cliffs, NJ: Prentice Hall.

Tumulty, Karen, and Viveca Novak. 2002. "Dodging the Bullet." *Newsweek* 160, November 4, p. 45.

Ture, Kwame, and Charles Hamilton. 1992. *Black Power: The Politics of Liberation.* Rev. ed. New York: Vintage Books.

Turkle, Sherry. 1995. *Life on the Screen: Identity in the Age of the Internet.* New York: Simon and Schuster.

———. 1999. "Looking Toward Cyberspace: Beyond Grounded Sociology." *Contemporary Sociology* 28 (November):643–654.

Turner, Bryan S., ed. 1990. *Theories of Modernity and Postmodernity.* Newbury Park, CA: Sage.

Turner, J. H. 1985. *Herbert Spencer: A Renewed Application.* Beverly Hills, CA: Sage.

Turner, Ralph, and Lewis M. Killian. 1987. *Collective Behavior.* 3d ed. Englewood Cliffs, NJ: Prentice Hall.

Twombly, Jennifer, Sheila Crowley, Nancy Ferris, and Cushing N. Dolbeare. 2001. *Out of Reach 2001: American's Growing Wage-Rent Disparity.* Washington, DC: National Low Income Housing Coalition.

Tyler, Patrick E. 1995. "For China's Girls, Rural Schools Fail." *New York Times,* December 31, p. 5.

Tyre, Peg, and Daniel McGinn. 2003. "She Works, He Doesn't." *Newsweek* 141, May 12, pp. 45–52.

U

Uchitelle, Louis. 1996. "More Downsized Workers Are Returning as Rentals." *New York Times,* December 8, pp. 1, 34.

UNAIDS. 2002. *AIDS Epidemic Update: December 2002.* Geneva, Switzerland: UNAIDS.

United Nations. 2000. *The World's Women 2000: Trends and Statistics.* New York: United Nations.

United Nations Development Programme. 1995. *Human Development Report 1995.* New York: Oxford University Press.

———. 2000. *Poverty Report 2000: Overcoming Human Poverty.* Washington, DC: UNDP.

———. 2001. *Human Development Report 2001. Making New Technologies Work for Human Development.* New York: UNDP.

———. 2002. *Human Development Report 2002: Deepening Democracy in a Fragmented World.* New York: Oxford University Press.

United Nations Population Division. 1998. *World Abortion Policies.* New York: Department of Economic and Social Affairs, UNPD.

———. 2001a. *World Marriage Patterns 2000.* Accessed September 13, 2002 (www.undp.org/popin/wdtrends/worldmarriage.patters2000.pdf).

———. 2001b. "World Population Prospects: The 2000 Revision." New York: UNPD.

United Nations Population Information Network. 2003. *World Population Prospects: The 2003 Revision.* Accessed May 20 (www.un.org/popin.data.html).

University of Michigan. 2003. *Information on Admissions Lawsuits.* Accessed August 8 (www.umich.edu/~urel/admissions).

Urbina, Ian. 2002. "Al Jazeera: Hits, Misses and Ricochets." *Asia Times,* December 25.

U.S. Conference of Mayors. 2002. *A Status Report on Hunger and Homelessness in America's Cities, 2002.* Washington, DC: U.S. Conference of Mayors.

U.S. English. 2002. *Official English: States with Official English Laws.* Accessed June 10, 2002 (www.us-english.org/inc/official/states.asp).

U.S. Surgeon General. 1999a. *Surgeon General's Report on Mental Health.* Washington, DC: U.S. Government Printing Office.

———. 1999b. "Overview of Cultural Diversity and Mental Health Services. In Chapter 2 of *Surgeon General's Report on Mental Health.* Washington, DC: U.S. Government Printing Office.

———. 2001. *Youth Violence: A Report of the Surgeon General.* Washington, DC: U.S. Government Printing Office.

U.S. Trade Representative. 2003. *2002 Annual Report.* Washington, DC: U.S. Government Printing Office.

V

Vallas, Steven P. 1999. "Rethinking Post-Fordism: The Meaning of Workplace Flexibility." *Sociological Theory* 17(March): 68–101.

van den Berghe, Pierre. 1978. *Race and Racism: A Comparative Perspective.* 2d ed. New York: Wiley.

Van Slambrouck, Paul. 1999. "Netting a New Sense of Connection." *Christian Science Monitor,* May 4, pp. 1, 4.

van Vucht Tijssen, Lieteke. 1990. "Women between Modernity and Postmodernity." Pp. 147–163 in *Theories of Modernity and Postmodernity,* edited by Bryan S. Turner. London: Sage.

Vaughan, Diane. 1996. *The Challenger Launch Decision: Risky Technology, Culture, and Deviance at NASA.* Chicago: University of Chicago Press.

Veblen, Thorstein. [1899] 1964. *Theory of the Leisure Class.* New York: Macmillan. New York: Penguin.

———. 1919. *The Vested Interests and the State of the Industrial Arts.* New York: Huebsch.

Vega, William A. 1995. "The Study of Latino Families: A Point of Departure." Pp. 3–17 in *Understanding Latino Families: Scholarship, Policy, and Practice,* edited by Ruth E. Zambrana. Thousand Oaks, CA: Sage.

Velkoff, Victoria A., and Valerie A. Lawson. 1998. "Gender of Aging." *International Brief,* ser. IB, no. 98-3. Washington, DC: U.S. Government Printing Office.

Venkatesh, Sudhir Alladi. 2000. *American Project: The Rise and Fall of a Modern Ghetto.* Cambridge, MA: Harvard University Press.

Ventura, Stephanie J., Joyce A. Martin, Sally C. Curtin, Fary Menacker, and Brady Hamilton. 2001. "Trends in Pregnancy Rates for the United States, 1976–1997: An Update." *National Vital Statistics Reports* 49 (June 6).

Vernon, Glenn. 1962. *Sociology and Religion.* New York: McGraw-Hill.

Vidaver, R. M. et al. 2000. "Women Subjects in NIH-Funded Clinical Research Literature: Lack of Progress in Both Representation and Analysis by Sex." *Journal of Women's Health Gender-Based Medicine* 9 (June):495–504.

Villarosa, Linda. 2002. "New Skill for Future Ob-Gyns: Abortion Training." *New York Times,* June 11, p. D6.

Vistica, Gregory. 2000. "One, Two, Three, Out." *Newsweek* 135 (March 20):57–58.

Voter News Service. 2000. "Breaking Down the Electorate." *Time* 156 (November 20):74.

W

Wachtendorf, Tricia. 2002. "A Changing Risk Environment: Lessons Learned From the 9/11 World Trade Center Disaster." Presentation at the Sociological Perspectives on Disasters, Mt. Macedon, Australia, July.

Wages for Housework Campaign. 1999. *Wages for Housework Campaign.* Circular. Los Angeles.

Wagley, Charles, and Marvin Harris. 1958. *Minorities in the New World: Six Case Studies.* New York: Columbia University Press.

Waite, Linda. 2000. "The Family as a Social Organization: Key Ideas for the Twentieth Century." *Contemporary Sociology* 29 (May):463–469.

Waitzkin, Howard. 1986. *The Second Sickness: Contradictions of Capitalist Health Care.* Chicago: University of Chicago Press.

Walder, Andrew G. 2002. "Markets and Income Inequality in Rural China: Political Advantage in an Expanding Economy." *American Sociological Review* 67 (April):231–253.

Waldrop, Judith, and Sharon M. Stern. 2003. *Disability Status: 2000.* Census 2000 Brief C2KBR-17. Washington, DC: U.S. Government Printing Office.

Wallace, Ruth A., and Alison Wolf. 1980. *Contemporary Sociological Theory.* Englewood Cliffs, NJ: Prentice Hall.

Wallerstein, Immanuel. 1974. *The Modern World System.* New York: Academic Press.

———. 1979a. *Capitalist World Economy.* Cambridge, England: Cambridge University Press.

———. 1979b. *The End of the World As We Know It: Social Science for the Twenty-First Century.* Minneapolis: University of Minnesota Press.

———. 2000. *The Essential Wallerstein.* New York: The New Press.

Wallerstein, Judith S., Judith M. Lewis, and Sandra Blakeslee. 2000. *The Unexpected Legacy of Deviance.* New York: Hyperion.

Wallerstein, Michael, and Bruce Western. 2000. "Unions in Decline? What Has Changed and Why." Pp. 355–377 in *Annual Review of Political Science* edited by Nelson Polsby. Palo Alto, CA: Annual Reviews.

Wallis, Claudia. 1987. "Is Mental Illness Inherited?" *Time* 129 (March 9):67.

Wal-Mart. 2001. "Wal-Mart News: Our Commitment to Communities." Accessed August 24, 2001 (www.walmartstores.com).

Wal-Mart Watch. 2003. *Wal-Mart Watch: Breaking News.* Accessed June 14 (www.walmartwatch.com).

Walsh, Mary Williams. 2001. "Reversing Decades-Long Trend, Americans Retiring Later in Life." *New York Times,* November 16, pp. A1, A13.

Walzer, Susan. 1996. "Thinking about the Baby: Gender and Divisions of Infant Care." *Social Problems* 43 (May):219–234.

Washington Transcript Service. 1999. "Hillary Rodham Clinton Holds News Conference on Her New York Senatorial Bid." November 23.

Webb, Cynthia L. 2001. "The Workweek Gets Longer." *Washington Post National Weekly Edition,* September 10, p. 21.

Weber, Max. [1913–1922] 1947. *The Theory of Social and Economic Organization.* Translated by A. Henderson and T. Parsons. New York: Free Press.

———. [1904] 1949. *Methodology of the Social Sciences.* Translated by Edward A. Shils and Henry A. Finch. Glencoe, IL: Free Press.

———. [1904] 1958a. *The Protestant Ethic and the Spirit of Capitalism.* Translated by Talcott Parsons. New York: Scribner.

———. [1916] 1958b. *The Religion of India: The Sociology of Hinduism and Buddhism.* New York: Free Press.

Wechsler, Henry, J. E. Lee, M. Kuo, M. Seib-ring, T. F. Nelson, and H. Lee. 2002. "Trends in College Binge Drinking During a Period of Increased Prevention Efforts: Findings from Four Harvard School of Public Health College Alcohol Surveys: 1993–2001." *Journal of American College Health* 50 (5):203–217.

Weeks, John R. 2002. *Population: An Introduction to Concepts and Issues.* 8th ed. Belmont, CA: Wadsworth.

Weigard, Bruce. 1992. *Off the Books: A Theory and Critique of the Underground Economy.* Dix Hills, NY: General Hall.

Weinstein, Deena, and Michael A. Weinstein. 1999. "McDonaldization Enframed." Pp. 57–69 in *Resisting McDonaldization,* edited by Barry Smart. London: Sage.

Weinstein, Henry. 2002. "Airport Screener Curb Is Regretful." *Los Angeles Times,* November 16, pp. B1, B14.

———, Michael Finnegan, and Teresa Watanabe. 2001. "Racial Profiling Gains Support as Search Tactic." *Los Angeles Times,* September 24, pp. A1, M9.

Weinstein, Michael A., and Deena Weinstein. 2002. "Hail to the Shrub." *American Behavioral Scientist* 46 (December):566–580.

Weisman, Jonathan. 2003. "How Poor Is Poor." *Washington Post National Weekly Edition.* (January 5):29.

Wellman, Barry, et al. 1996. "Computer Networks as Social Networks: Collaborative Works Telework, and Virtual Community." Pp. 213–238 in *Annual Review of Sociology, 1996,* edited by John Hagan. Palo Alto, CA: Annual Reviews.

Wells-Barnett, Ida B. 1970. *Crusade for Justice: The Autobiography of Ida B. Wells.* Edited by Alfreda M. Duster. Chicago: University of Chicago Press.

Werum, Regina, and Bill Winders. 2001. "Who's 'In' and Who's 'Out': State Fragmentation and the Struggle over Gay Rights, 1974–1999." *Social Problems* 48 (August):386–410.

West, Candace, and Don H. Zimmerman. 1983. "Small Insults: A Study of Interruptions in Cross Sex Conversations between Unacquainted Persons." Pp. 86–111 in *Language, Gender, and Society,* edited by Barrie Thorne, Cheris Kramarae, and Nancy Henley. Rowley, MA: Newbury House.

———. 1987. "Doing Gender." *Gender and Society* 1 (June):125–151.

White, Jonathan R. 2002. *Terrorism: An Introduction.* Belmont, CA: Wadsworth.

Whyte, William Foote. 1981. *Street Corner Society: Social Structure of an Italian Slum.* 3d ed. Chicago: University of Chicago Press.

Wickman, Peter M. 1991. "Deviance." Pp. 85–87 in *Encyclopedic Dictionary of Sociol-ogy,* 4th ed., edited by Dushkin Publishing Group. Guilford, CT: Dushkin.

Wilford, John Noble. 1997. "New Clues Show Where People Made the Great Leap to Agriculture." *New York Times,* November 18, pp. B9, B12.

Willet, Jeffrey G., and Mary Jo Deegan. 2000. "Liminality? and Disability: The Symbolic Rite of Passage of Individuals with Disabilities." Presented at the annual meeting of the American Sociological Association, Washington, DC.

Williams, Carol W. 1995. "Taking an Eager Step Back." *Los Angeles Times,* June 3, pp. A1, A14.

———. 1999. *Statement on Meet the Needs of Older Youth in Foster Care by Carol W. Williams.* Accessed May 18, 2003 (www.hhs.gov/asl/testify/t990309a.html).

Williams, Christine L. 1992. "The Glass Escalator: Hidden Advantages for Men in the 'Female' Professions." *Social Problems* 39 (3):253–267.

———. 1995. *Still a Man's World: Men Who Do Women's Work.* Berkeley: University of California Press.

Williams, Robin M., Jr. 1970. *American Society.* 3d ed. New York: Knopf.

———, with John P. Dean and Edward A. Suchman. 1964. *Strangers Next Door: Ethnic Relations in American Communities.* Englewood Cliffs, NJ: Prentice Hall.

Williams, Wendy M. 1998. "Do Parents Matter? Scholars Need to Explain What Research Really Shows." *Chronicle of Higher Education* 45 (December 11):B6–B7.

Willie, Charles Vert, and Reinhard J. Reddick. 2003. *A New Look at Black Families,* 5th ed. Walnut Creek, CA: Alta Mira.

Wilson, Edward O. 1975. *Sociobiology: The New Synthesis.* Cambridge, MA: Harvard University Press.

———. 1978. *On Human Nature.* Cambridge, MA: Harvard University Press.

———. 2000. *Sociobiology: The New Synthesis.* Cambridge, MA: Belknap Press, Harvard University Press.

Wilson, James R., and S. Roy Wilson. 2001. *Mass Media. Mass Culture: An Introduction.* 5th ed. New York: McGraw-Hill.

Wilson, John. 1973. *Introduction to Social Movements.* New York: Basic Books.

———. 1978. *Religion in American Society: The Effective Presence.* Englewood Cliffs, NJ: Prentice-Hall.

Wilson, Jolin J. 2000. *Children as Victims.* Washington, DC: U.S. Government Printing Office.

Wilson, Warner, Larry Dennis, and Allen P. Wadsworth, Jr. 1976. "Authoritarianism Left and Right." *Bulletin of the Psychonomic Society* 7 (March):271–274.

Wilson, William Julius. 1980. *The Declining Significance of Race: Blacks and Changing American Institutions.* 2d ed. Chicago: University of Chicago Press.

———. 1987. *The Truly Disadvantaged: The Inner City, the Underclass and Public Policy.* Chicago: University of Chicago Press.

———, ed. 1989. *The Ghetto Underclass: Social Science Perspectives.* Newbury Park, CA: Sage.

———. 1996. *When Work Disappears: The World of the New Urban Poor.* New York: Knopf.

———. 1999a. "Towards a Just and Livable City: The Issues of Race and Class." Address at the Social Science Centennial Conference, April 23. Chicago, IL: DePaul University.

———. 1999b. *The Bridge over the Racial Divide: Rising Inequality and Coalition Politics.* Berkeley: University of California Press.

———. 2003a. "Introduction to the 2003 Edition." In *Tally's Corner* by Elliot Liebow. Lanham, MD: Rowman and Littlefield.

———. 2003b. "There Goes the Neighborhood." *New York Times,* June 16, p. A23.

Winerip, Michael. 1998. "Schools for Sale." *New York Times Magazine,* July 14, pp. 42–48, 80, 86, 88–89.

———. 2003. "What Some Much-Noted Data Really Showed About Vouchers." *New York Times,* May 7, p. B12.

Winter, J. Alan. 1977. *Continuities in the Sociology of Religion.* New York: Harper and Row.

Wirth, Louis. 1928. *The Ghetto.* Chicago: University of Chicago Press.

———. 1931. "Clinical Sociology." *American Journal of Sociology* 37 (July):49–60.

———. 1938. "Urbanism as a Way of Life." *American Journal of Sociology* 44 (July): 1–24.

Wolf, Naomi. 1992. *The Beauty Myth: How Images of Beauty Are Used Against Women.* New York: Anchor.

Wolff, Edward N. 1999. "Recent Trends in the Distribution of Household Wealth Ownership." In *Back to Shared Prosperity: The Growing Inequality of Wealth and Income in America,* edited by Ray Marshall. New York: M. E. Sharpe.

———. 2002. *Top Heavy.* Updated ed. New York: New Press.

Wolraich, M., et al. 1998. "Guidance for Effective Discipline." *Pediatrics* 101 (April): 723–728.

Wonacott, Peter. 2001. "China Examines Retailers in Fight Against Scams." *Wall Street Journal,* December 12, p. A10.

Wood, Daniel B. 2000. "Minorities Hope TV Deals Don't Just Lead to 'Tokenism.'" *Christian Science Monitor,* January 19.

Wood, Julia T. 1994. *Gendered Lives: Communication, Gender and Culture.* Belmont, CA: Wadsworth.

Woodard, Colin. 1998. "When Rote Learning Fails against the Test of Global Economy." *Christian Science Monitor,* April 15, p. 7.

World Bank. 1995. *World Development Report 1994: Workers in an Integrating World.* New York: Oxford University Press.

———. 1997. *World Development Report 1997: The State in a Changing World.* New York: Oxford University Press.

———. 2000. *World Development Report 2000/2001 Attacking Poverty.* New York: Oxford University Press.

———. 2001. *World Development Report 2002. Building Instructions for Markets.* New York: Oxford University Press.

———. 2002. *World Development Indicators 2002.* Washington, DC: World Bank.

———. 2003a. *World Development Report 2003: Sustainable Development in a Dynamic World.* Washington, DC: World Bank.

———. 2003b. *Development Indicators 2003.* Washington, DC: World Bank.

———. 2003c. "Foreign Investment, Remittances Outpace Debt as Sources of Finance for Developing Countries: World Bank—Middle East and North Africa." News release, April 2. Accessed August 3 (www.worldbank.org).

World Desk Reference. 2001. *Vietnam.* Accessed July 19 (www.dk.com).

World Development Forum. 1990. "The Danger of Television." 8 (July 15):4.

World Health Organization. 2002. *Global Report on Health and Violence.* Geneva: WHO.

———, and UNICEF. 2000. *Global Water Supply and Sanitation Assessment 2000 Report.* Washington, DC: WHO and UNICEF.

World Resources Institute. 1998. *1998–1999 World Resources: A Guide to the Global Environment.* New York: Oxford University Press.

Wright, Charles R. 1986. *Mass Communication: A Sociological Perspective.* 3d ed. New York: Random House.

Wright, Eric R., William P. Gronfein, and Timothy J. Owens. 2000. "Deinstitutionalization, Social Rejection, and the Self-Esteem of Former Mental Patients." *Journal of Health and Social Behavior* (March).

Wright, Erik Olin, David Hachen, Cynthia Costello, and Joy Sprague. 1982. "The American Class Structure." *American Sociological Review* 47 (December):709–726.

Wurman, Richard Saul. 1989. *Information Anxiety.* New York: Doubleday.

Wuthnow, Robert, and Marsha Witten. 1988. "New Directions in the Study of Culture." Pp. 49–67 in *Annual Review of Sociology, 1988,* edited by W. Richard Scott and Judith Blake. Palo Alto, CA: Annual Reviews.

Wynia, Matthew K. et al. 2000. "Physician Manipulation of Reimbursement Rules for Patients: Between a Rock and a Hard Place." *Journal of the American Medical Association* 286 (April 12):1858–1865.

Y

Yamagata, Hisashi, Kuang S. Yeh, Shelby Stewman, and Hiroko Dodge. 1997. "Sex Segregation and Glass Ceilings: A Comparative Statistics Model of Women's Career Opportunities in the Federal Government over a Quarter Century." *American Journal of Sociology* 103 (November): 566–632.

Yap, Kioe Sheng. 1998. "Squatter Settlements." Pp. 554–556 in *The Encyclopedia of Housing,* edited by Willem van Vliet. Thousand Oaks, CA: Sage.

Yax, Laura K. 1999. "National Population Projections." Accessed October 30, 1999 (www.census.gov/population/www/projections/natprog.html).

Yin, Sandra. 2001. "Shifting Identities." *American Demographics* 23 (December):21.

Yinger, J. Milton. 1970. *The Scientific Study of Religion.* New York: Macmillan.

Young, Alford A., Jr., and Donald R. Deskins, Jr. 2001. "Early Traditions of African-American Sociological Thought." Pp. 445–477 in *Annual Review of Sociology, 2001,* edited by Karen S. Cook and John Hagan. Palo Alto, CA: Annual Reviews.

Young, Gay. 1993. "Gender Inequality and Industrial Development: The Household Connection." *Journal of Comparative Family Studies* 124 (Spring):3–20.

Z

Zald, Mayer N. 1970. *Organizational Change: The Political Economy of the YMCA.* Chicago: University of Chicago Press.

Zang, Xiaowei. 2002. "Labor Market Segmentation and Income Inequality in Urban China." *Sociological Quarterly* 43 (1):27–44.

Zelizer, Gerald L. 1999. "Internet Offers Only Fuzzy Cyberfaith, Not True Religious Expression." *USA Today,* August 19, p. 13A.

Zellner, William M. 1978. "Vehicular Suicide: In Search of Incidence." Western Illinois University, Macomb. Unpublished M.A. thesis.

———. 1995. *Counter Cultures: A Sociological Analysis.* New York: St. Martin's Press.

———. 2001. *Extraordinary Groups: An Examination of Unconventional Lifestyles.* 7th ed. New York: Worth.

Zernike, Kate. 2002. "With Student Cheating on the Rise, More Colleges Are Turning to Honor Codes." *New York Times,* November 2, p. A10.

———. 2003. "Professors Protest as Students Debate." *New York Times,* April 4.

Zia, Helen. 1993. "Women of Color in Leadership." *Social Policy* 23 (Summer):51–55.

———. 2000. *Asian American Dreams: The Emergence of an American People.* New York: Farrar, Straus, and Giroux.

Zimbardo, Philip G. 1972. "Pathology of Imprisonment." *Society* 9 (April):4, 6, 8.

———, Craig Haney, W. Curtis Banks, and David Jaffe. 1974. "The Psychology of Imprisonments: Privation, Power, and Pathology." In *Doing Unto Others: Joining, Molding, Conforming, Helping, and Loving,* edited by Zick Rubin. Englewood Cliffs, NJ: Prentice Hall.

———, Ann L. Weber, and Robert Johnson. 2003. *Psychology: Core Concepts.* 4e. Boston: Allyn and Bacon.

Zittrain, Johnathan, and Benjamin Edelman. 2002. *Empirical Analysis of Internet Filtering in China.* Beckman Center for Internet and Society, Harvard Law School. Accessed June 20, 2003 (www.cyber.law.harvard.edu/filtering/china).

Zola, Irving K. 1972. "Medicine as an Institution of Social Control." *Sociological Review* 20 (November):487–504.

———. 1983. *Socio-Medical Inquiries.* Philadelphia: Temple University Press.

Zweigenhaft, Richard L., and G. William Domhoff. 1998. *Diversity in the Power Elite: Have Women and Minorities Reached the Top?* New Haven, CT: Yale University Press.

Acknowledgments

Chapter 1

P. 2: Quotation from Barbara Ehrenreich. 2001. *Nickel and Dimed: On (Not) Getting By in America*: 197–198. © 2001 by Barbara Ehrenreich. Reprinted by permission of Henry Holt & Company, LLC.

P. 7: Figure 1–1 from NAACP Legal Defense Fund. 2003. *Death Row USA,* Spring 2003. Used by permission of NAACP Legal Defense and Education Fund, Inc.

Chapter 2

P. 28: Quotation from Elijah Anderson. 1990. *Streetwise: Race, Class, and Change in an Urban Community*: 208, 220–221. Copyright 1990. Reprinted by permission of University of Chicago Press.

P. 33: Cartoon © The New Yorker Collection 1980 James Stevenson from cartoonbank.com. All rights reserved.

P. 34: Table 2–1—Author's analysis of General Social Survey 2002 in J. A. Davis et al. 2003. Used by permission of National Opinion Research Center.

P. 35: Figure 2–4—Author's analysis of General Social Survey 2002 in J. A. Davis et al. 2003. Used by permission of National Opinion Research Center.

P. 35: Cartoon, DOONESBURY © 1989 G. B. Trudeau. Reprinted with permission of UNIVERSAL PRESS SYNDICATE. All rights reserved.

P. 41: Figure in Box 2–2 from William Rau and Ann Durrand. 2000. "The Academic Ethic and College Grades: Does Hard Work Help Students to 'Make the Grade'?" *Sociology of Education* 2000, **73** (January): 26. Used by permission of the American Sociological Association and the authors.

P. 46: Figure 2–5 from Henry J. Kaiser Family Foundation. 2003. Executive Summary of Sex on TV 3: 38, 40. This information was reprinted with permission of the Henry J. Kaiser Family Foundation. The Kaiser Family Foundation, based in Menlo Park, CA, is a nonprofit, independent national health care philanthropy and is not associated with Kaiser Permanente or Kaiser Industries.

P. 50: Figure in Apdx I—General Social Survey in J. A. Davis et al. 2003. Used by permission of National Opinion Research Center.

Chapter 3

P. 57: Excerpts from J. A. English-Lueck. 2002. *cultures@siliconvalley*. Copyright © 2002 by the Board of Trustees of the Leland Stanford Jr. University. Used with permission of Stanford University Press, www.sup.org.

P. 64: Figure 3–1—Figure from John L. Allen. 2001. *Student Atlas of World Geography,* 2nd edition. Copyright © 2001 by The McGraw-Hill Companies, Inc. Reprinted by permission of McGraw-Hill/Dushkin, a division of the McGraw-Hill Companies, Guilford, CT 06437.

P. 68: Figure 3–2 as reported in Astin et al. 1994. And in Sax et al. 2001. From UCLA Higher Education Research Institute. 2001. *The American Freshman: National Norms for Fall '01.* Reprinted by permission of UCLA.

P. 71: Figure 3–3—Illustration by Jim Willis. 1996. "The Argot of Pickpockets," *New York Daily News* (November 19): 5. © New York Daily News, LP. Reprinted by permission.

P. 72: Quotation from www.pholktales.com (2003). Used by permission of Jeffrey Kauflin, PholkTales.com, Ramsey, NJ. PholkTales.com is an unofficial fan site dedicated to all Phish fans. It has no official affiliation with the band or its website.

P. 72: Cartoon by Sidney Harris. © 2004 by Sidney Harris. Used by permission.

P. 75: Figure 3–4—Figure from U. S. English website www.us-english.org. Copyright, U. S. English, Inc. Used by permission.

Chapter 4

P. 80: Quotation from Mary Pattillo-McCoy. 1999. *Black Picket Fences: Privilege and Peril among the Black Middle Class*: 100–02. Copyright 1999. Reprinted by permission of University of Chicago Press.

P. 87: Quotation from Daniel Albas and Cheryl Albas. 1988. "Aces and Bombers: The Post-Exam Impression Management Strategies of Students." *Symbolic Interaction* 11 (Fall): 289–302. © 1988 by JAI Press. Reprinted by permission of University of CA Press and the authors. UC Press Journals, 2000 Center St., Suite 303, Berkeley, CA 94704-1223, (510) 642-6188.

P. 95: Figure 4–1—Figure adapted from Victoria J. Rideout, Ulla G. Foehr, Donald E. Roberts, and Mollyann Brodie. 1999. *Kids & Media @ the New Millennium* (November): 8. New York: Kaiser Family Foundation. This information was reprinted with permission of the Henry J. Kaiser Family Foundation. The Kaiser Family Foundation, based in Menlo Park, CA, is a nonprofit, independent national health care philanthropy and is not associated with Kaiser Permanente or Kaiser Industries.

P. 95: Table 4–2 adapted from Jill Suitor, Staci A. Minyard, and Rebecca S. Carter, "Did You See What I Saw? Gender Difference in Perceptions of Avenues to Prestige Among Adolescents." *Sociological Inquiry* 71 (Fall 2001): 445, Table 2. University of Texas Press. Reprinted by permission of Blackwell Publishing Ltd.

Chapter 5

P. 102: Quotation from Philip G. Zimbardo. 1972. "Pathology of Imprisonment," *Society,* **9** (April): 4. Reprinted by permission of Transaction Publishers. Copyright © 1972 by Transaction Publishers. And Quotation from Philip G. Zimbardo, C. Haney, W. C. Banks, & D. Jaffe. 1974. "The Psychology of Imprisonment: Privation, Power, and Pathology." In Z. Rubin (Ed.), *Doing Unto Others: Explorations in Social Behavior*: 61–63. Used by permission of Philip G. Zimbardo, Stanford University.

P. 110: Cartoon by TOLES © The Buffalo News. Reprinted with permission of UNIVERSAL PRESS SYNDICATE. All rights reserved.

P. 116: Cartoon by Vietor. © The New Yorker Collection 1986 Dean Vietor from cartoonbank.com. All rights reserved.

P. 120: Figure 5–2—Figure from UNAIDS. 2001. *AIDS Epidemic Update*: 27. Reprinted with permission from UNAIDS, World Health Organization, Geneva, Switzerland.

Chapter 6

PP. 126, 127: Quotations from George Ritzer. 1996–2000. *The McDonaldization of Society,* new century edition: 1–4, 10. Copyright © 1996, 2000. Reprinted by permission of Pine Forge Press, a Division of Sage Publications.

P. 129: Cartoon © The New Yorker Collection 1979 Robert Weber from cartoonbank.com. All rights reserved.

P. 139: Figure 6–1—Published by the Roper Center, Storrs, CT. Reprinted by permission of National Opinion Research Center.

Chapter 7

PP. 148, 149: Quotations from Todd Gitlin. 2001. *Media Unlimited: How the Torrent of Images and Sounds Overwhelms Our Lives*: 176–179. © 2001 by Todd Gitlin. Reprinted by permission of Henry Holt & Company, LLC.

P. 151: Figure 7–2 from Google, Inc. 2003.

P. 155: Quotation from Todd Gitlin. 2001. *Media Unlimited: How the Torrent of Images and Sounds Overwhelms Our Lives*: 176–179. © 2001 by Todd Gitlin. Reprinted by permission of Henry Holt & Company, LLC.

P. 165: Table 7–2 from S. Robert Lichter, Linda S. Lichter, & Daniel R. Amundson. 1999. *Merchandising Mayhem: Violence in Popular Media 1998–1999*. Reprinted with permission from the Center for Media and Public Affairs.

P. 165: Cartoon by Kirk Anderson. Used by permission of Kirk Anderson www.kirktoons.com.

Chapter 8

P. 170: Quotation from Susan A. Phillips. 1999. *Wallbangin': Graffiti and Gangs in L.A.*: 21, 23, 134–35. Copyright 1999. Used by permission of University of Chicago Press and the author.

P. 177: Figure from Henry Wechsler et al. 2002. "Trends in College Binge Drinking During a Period of Increased Prevention Efforts," *Journal of American College Health*, 2002: 208. Copyright © 2002. Reprinted with permission of the Helen Dwight Reid Educational Foundation. Published by Heldref Publications, 1319 18th St. NW, Washington, DC 20036-1802.

P. 181: Figure 8–2 from "How Stuff Works, American Registry for Internet Numbers, Times Research." *Los Angeles Times,* April 30, 2003: A21. Copyright 2003, Los Angeles Times. All rights reserved. Reprinted with permission.

P. 183: Table 8–1 from Robert K. Merton. 1968. *Social Theory and Social Structure*: 194. Copyright © 1967, 1968 by Robert K. Merton. Adapted by permission of The Free Press, a division of Simon & Schuster. All rights reserved.

P. 190: Cartoon by Sidney Harris. © 2004 by Sidney Harris. Used by permission.

P. 193: Cartoon by Dan Wasserman. Copyright, Tribune Media Services, Inc. All Rights reserved. Reprinted with permission.

Chapter 9

P. 198: Quotation from Katherine S. Newman. 1999. *No Shame in My Game* 1999: 86–87. Knopf Publishing Group. Copyright © 1999 by Russell Sage Foundation. Used by permission of Alfred A. Knopf, a division of Random House, Inc.

P. 204: Figure 9–2 from Towers Perrin in Adam Bryant. 1999. "American Pay Rattles Foreign Partners," *New York Times* (January 17): D1. Copyright © 1999 by The New York Times Co. Reprinted by permission.

P. 209: Table 9–2 from James. A. Davis et al. 2003. *General Social Surveys, 1972–2012*. Chicago: National Opinion Research Center. Used by permission of National Opinion Research Center.

P. 210: Cartoon by Frank Cammuso. The Post Standard, Syracuse, NY. Used by permission.

P. 211: Figure 9–3 Data on Income 2001 from Carmen DeNavas-Walt, Robert W. Cleveland, and Marc L. Raemer. 2002. *Money Income in the United States: 2001*. Washington, DC: U.S. Government Printing Office. Data on wealth from Edward N. Wolff. 1999. "Recent Trends in the Distribution of Household Wealth Ownership." In *Back to Shared Prosperity: The Growing Inequality of Wealth and Income in America,* ed. Ray Marshall. New York: M.E. Sharpe. Reprinted by permission of the author.

P. 212: Figure 9–4 from Timothy Smeeding, Lee Rainwater, and Gary Burtless. 2001. "United States Poverty in a Cross-National Context." *Focus,* newsletter of the Institute for Research on Poverty, 21 (Spring): 51. Used by permission of Institute for Research on Poverty.

P. 220: Cartoon used with permission, Mike Konopacki, Huck/Konopacki Labor Cartoons, www.solidarity.com/hkcartoons.

Chapter 10

P. 225: Quotation from Robert Goldman and Stephen Papson. 1998. *Nike Culture: The Sign of the Swoosh*: 2, 6–8, 184. Reprinted by permission of Sage Publications Ltd.

P. 227: Figure 10–1 from Gordon, Jesse, and Knickerbocker. 2001. "The Sweat Behind the Shirt: The Labor History of a Gap Sweatshirt," *The Nation* **273** (September 3/10, 2001): 14. Reprinted with permission of *The Nation*. For subscription information, call 1-800-333-8536. Portions of each week's Nation magazine can be accessed at www.thenation.com.

P. 228: Figure 10–2 adapted in part from John R. Weeks. *Population: An Introduction to Concepts and Issues,* 8th ed.: 22–23. Belmont, CA: Wadsworth © 2002. Reprinted with permission of Wadsworth, a division of Thomson Learning, www.thomsonrights.com. Fax (800) 730-2215. And adapted in part from Carl Haub. 2003. *World Population Data Sheet 2002.* Used by permission of Population Reference Bureau.

P. 231: Table 10–1 adapted in part from *Fortune.* 2002. "Fortune's Global 500" *Fortune,* July 21. © 2003 Time Inc. All rights reserved. And adapted in part from United Nations Development Programme. 2002. *Human Development Report 2002: Deepening Democracy in a Fragmented World*: 190–193. Copyright © 2002 by the United Nations Development Programme. Used by permission of Oxford University Press, Inc.

P. 232: Cartoon by Tony Auth for *Philadelphia Enquirer.* PETT © 2002 Lexington Herald-Leader. Dist. by UNIVERSAL PRESS SYNDICATE. Reprinted with permission. All rights reserved.

P. 233: Figure 10–4 Data from World Bank. 2003b. *2003 World Development Indicators*: 64–66; Table 2–8. © World Bank 2003b. International Bank for Reconstruction and Development/The World Bank. Used by permission.

P. 244: Figure 10–6 adapted in part from *The Observer (London)* 1999. Copyright © 1998 The Observer. Reprinted by permission. And adapted in part from Haub & Cornelius 2001.

Chapter 11

P. 249: Quotation from Helen Zia. 2000. *Asian American Dreams: The Emergence of an American People.* Copyright © 2000 by Helen Zia. Reprinted by permission of Farrar, Straus & Giroux, LLC.

P. 255: Cartoon by Steve Breen, May 9, 2003. Used by permisison of Copley News Service.

P. 256: Figure 11–2 from Southern Poverty Law Center. 2003. "Active Hate Groups in the United States," *2003 Intelligence Report* (Spring): 34–35. Used by permission of Southern Poverty Law Center.

P. 268: Figure 11–4 from John R. Logan. 2001. *From Many Shores: Asians in Census 2000.* Accessed November 29, 2001 at http://mumford1.dyndns.org/cen2000/AsianPop. Used by permission of Lewis Mumford Center for Comparative Urban and Regional Research, SUNY at Albany, NY (www.albany.edu/mumford).

Chapter 12

P. 281: Quotation from Naomi Wolf. *The Beauty Myth.* 1992: 9–10, 12. Used by permission of Abner Stein Literary Agency for Naomi Wolf.

P. 284: Table 12–1 from Joyce McCarl Nielsen, Glenda Walden, and Charlotte A. Kunkel. 2000. "Gendered Heteronormativity: Empirical Illustrations in Everyday Life," *Sociological Quarterly* 41 (No. 2): 287. © 2000 by the Midwest Sociological Society. Reprinted by permission of the author and UC Press Journals, 2000 Center St., Suite 303, Berkeley, CA 94704-1223, (510) 642-6188.

P. 293: Cartoon by Ed Stein. Reprinted by permission of Rocky Mountain News.

P. 295: Figure 12–3 from James T. Bond, Ellen Galinsky, and Jennifer E. Swanberg. 1998. *The 1997 National Study of the Changing Work Force.* New York: Families and Work Institute: 40–41, 44–45. Copyright Families and Work Institute (www.familiesandwork.org). Reprinted by permission.

P. 298: Figure 12–4 from NARAL Pro Choice America Foundation. 2003. *Who Decides? A State-by-State Review of Abortion and Reproductive Rights,* 12th ed., pp. xxii–xxiii. Washington, DC: NARAL Foundation. Used by permission of NARAL.

Chapter 13

P. 303: Quotation from Mitch Albom. 1997. *Tuesdays with Morrie: An Old Man, a Young Man, and Life's Greatest Lesson*: 117–118. Copyright © 1997 by Mitch Albom. Used by permission of Double-day, a division of Random House, Inc.

P. 311: Figure 13–1 from Daniel Levinson with Judy Levinson. 1996. *The Seasons of a Woman's Life.* Copyright © 1996 by Daniel J. Levinson. Used by permission of Alfred A. Knopf, a division of Random House, Inc.

P. 313: Figure 13–2 from AARP. 1999. "New AARP Study Finds Boomers Vary in Their Retirement Years," AARP News Release June 1, Washington, D.C. © AARP 2003. Reprinted by permission of the American Association of Retired Persons.

Chapter 14

P. 323: Quotation from Cornel West and Sylvia Ann Hewlett. 1998. *The War against Parents*: 21–22. Copyright © 1998 by Sylvia Ann Hewlett and Cornel West. Reprinted by permission of Houghton Mifflin Company. All rights reserved.

P. 330: Figure 14–2 from United Nations Population Division. 2001a. *World Marriage Patterns 2000.* Accessed August 2, 2002 at www.undp.org/popin/wdtrends/worldmarriagepatterns2000.pdf. Used by permission of United Nations Population Division, New York.

P. 331: Quotation from Rebecca Segall. 1998. "Sikh and Ye Shall Find," *Village Voice* 43 (December 15): 48; 53. Used by permission of Rebecca Segall.

P. 338: Cartoon by Signe Wilkinson. Used by permission of Signe Wilkinson, Cartoonists & Writers Syndicate/cartoonweb.com.

Chapter 15

P. 350: Quotation from Vine Deloria, Jr. 1999. *For This Land: Writings on Religion in America*: 273–275, 281. Copyright © 1998. Reproduced by permission of the author and Routledge, Inc., part of the Taylor & Francis Group.

P. 352: Figure 15–1 from John L. Allen. 2001. *Student Atlas of World Geography*, 2nd edition. Copyright © 2001 by The McGraw-Hill Companies, Inc. Reprinted by permission of McGraw-Hill/Dushkin, a division of the McGraw-Hill Companies, Guilford, CT 06437.

P. 361: Figure 15–2 from Ronald Inglehart and Wayne Baker. 2000. "Modernization, Cultural Change, and the Persistence of Traditional Values," *American Sociological Review* 65 (February): 19–51; Table 7, p. 47. Used by permission of the American Sociological Association and the authors.

P. 364: Figure 15–3 from D. Jones et al. 2002. *Religious Congregations and Membership in the United States*: 2000: 562. Published by Glenmary Research Center, Nashville. ©Association of Statisticians of American Religious Bodies. Reprinted with permission. All rights reserved.

P. 370: Cartoon by Steve Breen. Used by permission of Copley News Service.

Chapter 16

P. 374: Quotation from Jonathan Kozol. 1991. *Savage Inequalities: Children in America's Schools*: 85–88. Copyright © 1991 by Jonathan Kozol. Reprinted by permission of Crown Publishers, a division of Random House, Inc.

P. 377: Table 16–1 from Institute of International Education. 2003. *Open Doors 2001 Report on International Educational Exchange,* ed. Hey-Kyung Koh, ed. Used by permission of Institute of International Education.

P. 381: Cartoon by Kirk Anderson. Used by permission of Kirk Anderson www.kirktoons.com.

P. 389: Figure 16–3 from Audrey L. Amrein and David C. Berliner, Arizona State University, December 2002. Used by permission of Education Policy Studies Laboratory, Arizona State University.

Chapter 17

P. 396: Quotation from Richard L. Zweigenhaft and G. William Domhoff. 1998. *Diversity in the Power Elite*: 176–77, 192, 194. Copyright 1998. Reprinted by permission of Yale University Press.

P. 401: Table 17.1 from James Allan Davis and Tom W. Smith. 2001. *General Social Surveys, 1972–2000*: 88. Storrs, CT: The Roper Center. Reprinted by permission of National Opinion Research Center.

P. 402: Cartoon by Gary Varvel. Used by permisison of Creators Syndicate.

P. 404: Figure 17–1 from Inter-Parliamentary Union (IPU). 2003. Women in National Parliaments, www.ipu.org/wmn-e/classif.htm. Used by permission of IPU.

P. 406: Figure 17–2 from G. William Domhoff. 2001. *Who Rules America,* 4th ed.: 96. Reproduced with permission of The McGraw-Hill Companies.

P. 408: Web page Copyright Stichting Greenpeace Council. Photos © Greenpeace/Matti Liimatainen, © Greenpeace/Kate Davison, and © Greenpeace/Martin Langer.

P. 409: Cartoon by Bruce Plante/Chattanooga Times.

Chapter 18

P. 414: Quotation from Jeremy Rifkin. 1995a 6. *The End of Work*: 11–13. Copyright © 1995 by Jeremy Rifkin. Reprinted by permission of Putnam Berkley, a division of Penguin Putnam Inc.

P. 419: from S. Acharya. 2000. In Mahbub ul Haq Human Development Centre, *Human Development in South Asia 2000: The Gender Question*: 54. Oxford University Press, Karachi. Reprinted by permission.

P. 420: Cartoon by Tony Auth © 2002 The Philadelphia Inquirer. Reprinted with permission of UNIVERSAL PRESS SYNDICATE. All rights reserved.

P. 429: Cartoon by Toles in *The New Republic*. TOLES © The Buffalo News. Reprinted with permission of UNIVERSAL PRESS SYNDICATE. All rights reserved.

P. 431: Quotation from Sheryl Stolberg. 1995. "Affirmative Action Gains Often Come at a High Cost," *Los Angeles Times* (March 29): A14. Copyright 1995 Los Angeles Times. Reprinted by permission.

P. 432: Cartoon by Mike Peters. Reprinted with special permission of King Features Syndicate.

Chapter 19

P. 437: Quotation from Lori Arviso Alvord & Elizabeth Cohen Van Pelt. 1999. *The Scalpel and the Silver Bear*: 13–14. Copyright © 1999 by Lori Arviso Alvord & Elizabeth Cohen Van Pelt. Used by permission of Bantam Books, a division of Random House, Inc.

P. 441: Figure 19–1 from Carl Haub. 2002. *World Population Data Sheet 2002.* Used by permission of Population Reference Bureau.

P. 448: Cartoon by Sidney Harris. © 2004 by Sidney Harris. Used by permission.

P. 449: Quotation from Lori Arviso Alvord & Elizabeth Cohen Van Pelt. 1999. *The Scalpel and the Silver Bear*: 13. Copyright © 1999 by Lori Arviso Alvord & Elizabeth Cohen Van Pelt. Used by permission of Bantam Books, a division of Random House, Inc.

P. 455: Cartoon by Jim Borgman. Reprinted with special permission of King Features Syndicate.

P. 456: Figure 19–7 from World Bank. 2003a. *World Development Indicators 2003*: 92–94. Published by the World Bank. Used by permission.

Chapter 20

P. 460: Quotation from Mitchell Duneier. 2001. *Sidewalk*: 17–18. Copyright © 1999 by Mitchell Deneier. Reprinted by permission of Farrar, Straus & Giroux, LLC.

P. 464: Table 20–1 based on Gideon Sjoberg. 1960. *The Preindustrial City: Past and Present*: 323–328. Copyright © 1960 by The Free Press; copyright renewed 1968 by Gideon Sjoberg. Adapted with permission of The Free Press, a division of Simon & Schuster Adult Publishing Group. All rights reserved. And based on E. Barbara Phillips. 1996. *City Lights: Urban-Suburban Life in the Global Society*: 132–135. Copyright © 1981 by E. Barbara Phillips and Richard T. LeGates, 1996 by E. Barbara Phillips. Used by permission of Oxford University Press, Inc.

P. 465: Figure 20–1 based on data in Carl Haub 2002. *World Population Data Sheet 2001*. Used by permission of Population Reference Bureau.

P. 466: Figure 20–2 from Chauncy Harris and Edward Ullmann. 1945. "The Nature of Cities," *Annals of the American Academy of Political and Social Science*, 242 (November): 13. Reprinted by permission of American Academy of Political and Social Science, Philadelphia.

P. 466: Table 20–2 data from United Nations, quoted in Brockerhoff. 2000. *An Urbanizing World*: 10. Used by permission of Population Reference Bureau.

P. 479: Cartoon by Roger Dahl, The Japan Times. Used by permission of Roger Dahl.

Chapter 21

P. 484: Quotation from Kai Erikson. 1994. *A New Species of Trouble: The Human Experience of Modern Disasters*: 11–12, 19. Copyright © 1994 by Kai Erikson. Used by permission of W. W. Norton Company, Inc.

P. 486: Figure 21–1 from Carl Haub. 2003c. *World Population Data Sheet 2003.* Used by permission of Population Reference Bureau.

P. 489: Figure 21–2 from Carl Haub. 2003c. *World Population Data Sheet 2003.* Used by permission of Population Reference Bureau.

P. 492: Cartoon by Signe Wilkinson/Philadelphia Daily News. Used by permission of Cartoonists & Writers Syndicate.

Chapter 22

P. 505: Quotation from Howard Rheingold. 2003. *Smart Mobs, The Next Social Revolution: Transforming Cultures and Communities in the Age of Instant Access*: 157, 158, viii. © 2003 Howard Rheingold. Reprinted by permission of Perseus Book Publishers, a member of Perseus Books L.L.C.

P. 509: John B. Christiansen and Sharon N. Barnartt. 1995. *Deaf President Now! The 1988 Revolution at Gallaudet University*: 22. Published by Gallaudet University Press. Copyright 1995 by Gallaudet University. Reprinted by permission of the publisher.

P. 518: Quotation from Manisha Desai. 1996. "If Peasants Build Their Own Dams, What Would the State Have Left to Do?" *Research in Social Movements, Conflicts and Change*, **19**: 214, ed. Michael Dobkowski and Isidor Wallimann. Greenwich, CT: JAI Press. Used with permission from Elsevier.

P. 521: Figure 22–1 from Frank Newport. 2003. Gallup News Service data, issued as poll analyses on May 15, 2003, under the title "Six out of 10 Americans Say Homosexual Relations Should Be Recognized as Legal." © 1977–2003 The Gallup Organization. All rights reserved. Reprinted with permission from www.gallup.com.

Chapter 23

P. 526: Quotation from Debora L. Spar. 2001. *Ruling the Waves: Cycles of Discovery, Chaos, and Wealth from the Compass to the Internet*: 327–329. Copyright © 2001 by Debora L. Spar. Reprinted by permission of Harcourt, Inc.

P. 538: Figure 23–1 from Bill Dunlap www.glreach.com/globstats/. Used by permission.

P. 540: Cartoon © 1985 Carol * Simpson. Reprinted by permission of Carol * Simpson Productions.

Photo Credits

Chapter 1

P. 1 Photo © Barry Dawson, from Street Graphics India (London and New York: Thames & Hudson, 1999)
P. 4 Image © 2000 Peter Menzel/Material World
P. 5 Image © 2000 Peter Menzel/Material World (top)
P. 5 Image © 2000 Peter Menzel/Material World (bottom)
P. 8 AP/Wide World Photos
P. 9 "Harriet Martineau" by Richard Evans. By courtesy of the National Portrait Gallery, London (NPG 1085)
P. 11 Bibliothèque Nationale de France (left)
P. 11 The Granger Collection, New York (center)
P. 11 Archivo Iconografico, S.A./CORBIS (right)
P. 12 Smithsonian Institution
P. 14 A. Ramey/Stock Boston
P. 15 Bettmann/CORBIS
P. 16 Department of Special Collections, The University of Chicago Library
P. 17 Bill Publilano/Getty Images
P. 26 Gary Connor/PhotoEdit, Inc.

Chapter 2

P. 27 ©1990 Erika Rothenberg
P. 30 Van Bucher/Photo Researchers
P. 38 Rex Ziak/Getty Images (top)
P. 38 Courtesy of AT&T(bottom)
P. 39 Everett Collection
P. 42 Mark Reinstein/The Image Works
P. 44 Joe Sohm/The Image Works (top)
P. 44 Bob Daemmrich/The Image Works (bottom)
P. 48 AP/Wide World Photos

Chapter 3

P. 56 © 2000 United Air Lines Inc. All Rights Reserved. By permission of Fallon Minneapolis. Photography by Kevin Peterson/Push, Inc. (left) and Matthew Phillips/PictureQuest (right).
P. 59 Peter Menzel/Stock Boston (top)
P. 59 D. Berbaun/Photo Researchers (bottom)
P. 60 AP/Wide World Photos
P. 65 Pacha/CORBIS
P. 67 AP/Wide World Photos

P. 71 Photofest
P. 75 Pascale Simard/Alpha Press

Chapter 4

P. 79 Setagaya Volunteer Association, Tokyo, Japan
P. 83 Nina Leen/Time Life Pictures/Getty Images
P. 84 Tony Freeman/PhotoEdit, Inc.
P. 85 Richard Hutchings/PhotoEdit, Inc.
P. 88 Thomas S. England/Photo Researchers
P. 89 AP/Wide World Photos
P. 90 A. Ramey/PhotoEdit, Inc.
P. 91 Tom Wagner/CORBIS
P. 93 AP/Wide World Photos
P. 96 Mary Kate Denny/PhotoEdit, Inc.
P. 97 Svenne Nordlov/Tio Photo

Chapter 5

P. 101 interTREND Communications, Inc., Marketing Communications Firm Specializing in Asian American Market
P. 104 Don Murray-Pool/Getty Images
P. 106 Vincent DeWitt/Stock Boston/Picture Quest
P. 108 Richard Lord/PhotoEdit, Inc.
P. 109 Ann Clopet/Getty Images
P. 113 AP/Wide World Photos
P. 114 Charles & Josette Lenars/CORBIS
P. 115 Craig Lovell/CORBIS
P. 118 Sichov/SIPA Press
P. 121 Rachel Epstein/The Image Works

Chapter 6

P. 125 Courtesy of MAGIC International
P. 130 Warner Bros/The Kobal Collection/Claudette Barius
P. 131 AP/Wide World Photos
P. 132 CBS Photo Archive
P. 133 AP/Wide World Photos
P. 136 AP/Wide World Photos
P. 138 Kenneth Jarecke/Woodfin Camp & Associates
P. 140 LWA-JDC/CORBIS
P. 141 Jeff Greenberg/PhotoEdit, Inc.

Chapter 7

P. 147 Courtesy Atlanta Film & Video Festival
P. 151 Universal Studios/Photofest
P. 152 Getty Images (left)
P. 152 PEOPLE Weekly © Time Inc. All Rights Reserved (center)
P. 152 Bettmann/CORBIS (right)
P. 153 Everett Collection
P. 154 Everett Collection
P. 155 Photofest (top)
P. 155 Photofest (bottom)
P. 157 Everett Collection
P. 158 MGM/EON/The Kobal Collection/ Keith Hamshere
P. 159 Reuters NewMedia Inc./CORBIS
P. 160 © CORBIS (top)
P. 160 Dave Benett/Alpha/Globe Photos, Inc. (bottom)
P. 162 Jeffrey Aaronson/Network Aspen
P. 163 Stevens Frederic/SIPA Press

Chapter 8

P. 169 Courtesy of Lowe New York
P. 172 Jussi Nukari/Lehtikuva
P. 173 © 1965 by Stanley Milgram from the film, "Obedience," distributed by Pennsylvania State University, PCR.
P. 178 Fred Ward/STOCKPHOTO
P. 179 Jerry Alexander/Getty Images (top)
P. 179 Bob Krist/CORBIS (bottom)
P. 184 AP/Wide World Photos (top)
P. 184 Park Street/PhotoEdit, Inc. (bottom)
P. 186 Stock Montage, Inc.
P. 193 Alliance Atlantis/Dog Eat Dog/United Broadcasting/The Kobal Collection

Chapter 9

P. 197 feedingchildrenbetter.org/Courtesy Ad Council
P. 200 Hampton University Museum
P. 203 Bettmann/CORBIS
P. 206 Roger Ball/CORBIS
P. 207 Paul A. Souders/CORBIS
P. 214 Courtesy of William Julius Wilson, Harvard University
P. 215 AP/Wide World Photos
P. 218 Suzanne Opton (top)
P. 218 Courtesy of The General Electric Company (bottom)

Chapter 10

P. 224 Agency: Springer & Jacoby Werbung GmbH, Hamburg; creative directors: Bettina Olf, Timm Weber; copyrwriter: Sven Keitel; art director: Claudia Todt; photographer: Jan Burwick
P. 226 Alan Dejacacion/Getty Images
P. 230 Catherine Gupton/Woodfin Camp & Associates
P. 236 Stuart Franklin/Magnum Photos
P. 239 AP/Wide World Photos
P. 240 Cindy Reiman
P. 242 Mark Richards/PhotoEdit, Inc.
P. 245 Rufo/Action Press/ZUMA Press. © 2002 by Action Press

Chapter 11

P. 248 Courtesy of American Indian College Fund
P. 253 Mark Richards/PhotoEdit, Inc.
P. 258 Bob Daemmrich/The Image Works
P. 259 Elliot Erwitt/Magnum Photos
P. 260 Tony Freeman/PhotoEdit, Inc.
P. 262 American Civil Liberties
P. 264 AP/Wide World Photos
P. 267 Spencer Grant/PhotoEdit, Inc.
P. 272 Donna Terek
P. 273 David Bohrer/Los Angeles Times

Chapter 12

P. 280 Photo courtesy www.guerrillagirls.com. ©2002 by Guerrila Girls, Inc.
P. 283 Picture provided by Harrison G. Pope, Jr., adapted from THE ADONIS COMPLEX by Harrison G. Pope, Jr., Katherine Phillips, Roberto Olivardia. The Free Press, ©2000.
P. 286 Maria Lepowsky
P. 287 B. Mahoney/The Image Works
P. 288 AP/Wide World Photos
P. 290 Humbertuss Hanus/Photo Researchers
P. 296 © Los Angeles Dodgers

Chapter 13

P. 302 UN, Programme on Ageing, Division for Social Policy and Development; courtesy Graphic Design Unit, Department of Public Information; designer: Pepe
P. 305 Diane M. Lowe/Stock Boston
P. 307 Catherine Karnow/Woodfin Camp & Associates
P. 308 Rich Frishman Photography
P. 311 Spencer Grant/PhotoEdit Inc.
P. 312 Bob Daemmrich/The Image Works
P. 314 Thierry Secretain /Woodfin Camp & Associates

P. 316 Gabe Palmer/CORBIS
P. 317 Richard Lord/The Image Works
P. 318 Detroit News/Getty Images

Chapter 14

P. 322 Courtesy of Genetica DNA Laboratories Inc.
P. 326 Eastcott/Woodfin Camp & Associates
P. 329 Richard Hutchings/Photo Researchers
P. 331 Diaphor Agency/Index Stock
P. 334 "Buffalo West End, 1973" by Milton Rogovin. Courtesy of the artist, Collection of the Library of Congress
P. 335 "Buffalo West End, 1986" by Milton Rogovin. Courtesy of the artist, Collection of the Library of Congress (top)
P. 335 "Buffalo West End, 1992" by Milton Rogovin. Courtesy of the artist, Collection of the Library of Congress (bottom)
P. 341 Jon Bradley/Getty Images
P. 343 Spencer Grant/PhotoEdit Inc.
P. 344 Photo: The Andy Warhol Foundation for the Visual Arts/Art Resource, NY. © 2003 Andy Warhol Foundation for the Visual Arts /Artists Rights Society (ARS), New York. TM 2003 Marilyn Monroe LLC by CMG Worldwide, Inc. <www.MarilynMonroe.com>

Chapter 15

P. 349 Thomas Coex/Agence France Presse/Getty Images
P. 353 Robert Nikelsberg/Getty Images
P. 356 Tony Savino/The Image Works
P. 357 David Rubinger/CORBIS (top left)
P. 357 Michael S. Yamashita/CORBIS (top right)
P. 357 Linsay Hebberd/CORBIS (bottom)
P. 360 Steve McCurry/Magnum Photos
P. 362 AP/Wide World Photos
P. 365 Spencer Grant/Stock Boston
P. 367 AP/Wide World Photos
P. 368 Lindsay Hebberd/CORBIS

Chapter 16

P. 373 Courtesy Durham County Literacy Council
P. 376 Bob Daemmrich/The Image Works
P. 378 Mary Kate Denny/PhotoEdit, Inc.
P. 380 Joe McNally Photography
P. 381 Photo by Spencer Grant/ZUMA Press. © 2002 by Spencer Grant
P. 382 Marc Riboud/Magnum Photos
P. 387 Bill Bachman/The Image Works (left)
P. 387 Marilyn Humphries/The Image Works (right)

P. 388 Bob Daemmrich/Stock Boston
P. 390 James Marshall/The Image Works
P. 391 Linda Rosier

Chapter 17

P. 395 Charles S. Anderson Design Company <www.csadesign.com>
P. 397 Courtesy of the Board of Governors of the Federal Reserve System
P. 400 AP/Wide World Photos
P. 402 AP/Wide World Photos
P. 403 Robert Matheu/Courtesy Rock the Vote
P. 407 AP/Wide World Photos

Chapter 18

P. 413 David Bartruff/Stock Boston
P. 416 Jerry Ohlinger's Movie Material Store
P. 417 Ramadhan Khamis/Panapress
P. 421 AFP/Getty Images
P. 423 Aaron Haupt/Stock Boston
P. 424 Getty Images
P. 425 AP/Wide World Photos
P. 426 Bill Horsman/Stock Boston
P. 427 Bob Daemmrich/Stock Boston
P. 429 Jim Pickerell/Stock Boston

Chapter 19

P. 436 Gran Fury Collection. Manuscripts and Archives Division, The New York Public Library, Astor, Lenox and Tilden Foundations/Art Resource, NY
P. 439 Stephanie Maze/Woodfin Camp & Associates
P. 440 AFP/Goh Chai Hin/Getty Images
P. 443 "Takalani Sesame's" Kami courtesy of Sesame Workshop.
P. 446 Mark Godfrey/The Image Works (top)
P. 446 AP/Wide World Photos (bottom)
P. 450 Los Angeles Times Photo by Richard C. Paddock
P. 452 © 1975 by Fantasy Films. All Rights Reserved. Jerry Ohlinger's Movie Material Store
P. 453 Betty Press/Woodfin Camp & Associates
P. 454 Rhoda Sidney/Stock Boston

Chapter 20

P. 459 Courtesy of Newcomm Bates, São Paulo
P. 461 Ovie Carter
P. 463 The Art Archive/Palazzo Pubblico Siena/Dagli Orti (A)
P. 468 Security Pacific Collection/Los Angeles Public Library

Page numbers followed by *f* refer to figures
Page numbers followed by *t* refer to tables

A

Abercrombie, Nicholas, 69, 207
Aberle, David F., 112
Abrahams, Ray G., 105, 353
Abrahamson, Mark, 182
Abramovitz, Janet N., 510
Abrams, Lisa M., 389
Acharya, Menna, 419
Acosta, R. Vivian, 19
Adam, Barry D., 443, 520, 522
Adam, Kanya, 531
Adams, Devon B., 192
Addams, Jane, 12, 12–13, 13, 18, 21, 43, 287
Adler, Patricia, 37
Adler, Peter, 37
Aguirre, Benigno E., 511
Ahmed, Karuna Chanana, 234
Aizcorbe, Ana M., 210
Alain, Michel, 515
Alba, Richard D., 273
Albas, Cheryl, 87
Albas, Daniel, 87
Albiniak, P., 151
Albom, Mitch, 303–304, 379
Albrecht, Gary L., 107
Aldrich, Howard E., 513
Alexander, Alison, 166
Alexander, Keith L., 161
Alfino, Mark, 62
Ali, Muhammad, 104, 152
Allen, Bern, 174
Allen, Ernest, Jr., 266
Allen, John L., 352
Allport, Gordon, 261, 262
Alvarez, Lizette, 392
Alvord, Lori Arviso, 248, 437–438, 438, 449, 450
Alwin, Duane F., 403
Amato, Paul R., 339, 340
Amendson, Daniel R., 165
Ammerman, Nancy T., 363
Amrein, Audrey L., 389
Andersen, Margaret, 287
Anderson, Elijah, 28–29, 234
Anderson, Pamela, 148
Angier, Natalie, 283
Annan, Kofi, 288
Anthony, Susan B., 295

Aoki, Yutaka, 289
Appelbaum, Richard, 226
Arafat, Yasir, 154
Archer, Margaret, 69
Arditi, Jorge, 521
Argenti, Paul, 141
Arias, Elizabeth, 446
Armer, J. Michael, 233
Armour, Stephanie, 428
Aronowitz, Stanley, 143
Aronson, Elliot, 171
Ashe, Arthur, 106
Ashford, Lori S., 501
Astin, Alexander, 68, 385
Ataturk, Kemal, 290
Atchley, Robert C., 307, 312
Austin, April, 417
Austin, Erica Weintraub, 61
Avarey, D'Aunn Wester, 185
Axtell, Roger, 85
Azumi, Koya, 132

B

Babad, Elisha Y., 384
Bachrach, Christine A., 336
Baer, Douglas, 138
Bainbridge, William Sims, 46, 364, 365
Baker, Therese L., 38, 233, 361
Bakke, Allen, 431
Bales, Robert, 449–450
Balk, Deborah, 490
Barker, Noel, 20
Barnartt, Sharon N., 509
Barnevik, Percy, 414
Barr, Cameron W., 163
Barrett, David B., 354
Barron, Milton L., 305
Bartkowski, John P., 290
Bass, Loretta E., 402
Bassiouni, M. Cherif, 200
Bates, Colleen Dunn, 447
Bauerlein, Monika, 533
Bauman, Kurt J., 211
Beagan, Brenda L., 441
Beall, Cynthia M., 304
Bean, Frank, 271
Beauvoir, Simone de, 295
Becerra, Rosina M., 333
Becker, Howard S., 185, 382, 443
Beckham, David, 152
Beckley, Robert E., 366

Beeghley, Leonard, 203
Begley, Sharon, 345
Belkin, Lisa, 345
Bell, Daniel, 118–119, 188, 532
Bell, Wendell, 232
Bellafante, Ginia, 295
Belluck, Pam, 445
Belsie, Laurent, 342
Bendick, Marc, Jr., 316
Bendix, B. Reinhard, 43
Benner, Richard S., 25
Bennett, Claudette E., 240, 266
Bennett, Vanora, 328
Berger, Peter, 103, 114
Berk, Richard A., 513
Berke, Richard L., 315
Berland, Gretchen K., 450
Berlin, Brent, 65
Berliner, David C., 389
Bernhardt, Todd, 519
Bernstein, Richard, 306
Berry, Halle, 152, 158
Best, Amy, 180
Best, Fred, 310
Bharadwaj, Lakshmik, 499
Bian, Yanjie, 421
Bianchi, Suzanne, 329, 339
Bielby, Denise D., 326
Bielby, William R., 326
Billig, Joshua, 37
Billson, Janet Mancini, 25
Bishaw, Alemayehu, 266
Biskupic, Joan, 298
Bjorkman, Sharon, 363
Black, Donald, 175
Blackhall, Leslie J., 442
Blair, Tony, 159, 400
Blanchard, Fletcher, 172–173
Blau, Peter, 135, 140, 217
Blauner, Robert, 424
Bledsoe, Timothy, 262
Bloom, Steven G., 477
Blumer, Herbert, 103, 513, 514
Blumerman, Lisa, 276
Boaz, Rachel Floersheim, 306
Bochco, Steven, 157
Bodeker, Gerald C., 450
Bok, Sissela, 165
Bond, James T., 295
Bootcheck, Judith, 20
Booth, Alan, 339
Bornschier, Volker, 234
Borosage, Robert L., 143

Bottomore, Tom, 529
Bouchard, Thomas J., 83
Boudreaux, Richard, 238
Bouvier, Leon F., 494
Bowles, Samuel, 93, 378, 381, 385
Bowling, Michael, 192
Bracciodieta, John, 37
Bradford, Calvin, 112
Brady, David, 212
Brady, Jim, 192
Brainard, Jeffrey, 535
Brannigan, Augustine, 119
Brannon, Robert, 284
Braverman, Amy, 49
Braxton, Greg, 156
Bray, James H., 328
Brelin, Christa, 521
Brewer, Benjamin D., 230
Brewer, Cynthia A., 496f
Brint, Steven, 382, 384
Brockerhoff, Martin P., 466t
Bromley, David G., 38
Brooke, James, 156
Brower, Brock, 513
Brown, Michael, 508
Brown, Robert M., 358
Brown, Roger, 512
Browne, Irene, 296
Browner, Carol, 500
Brubaker, Bill, 456
Bruni, Frank, 344
Bryant, Adam, 204
Buckley, Stephen, 227
Budig, Michelle, 293
Budrys, Grace, 446
Buerger, Michael D., 185, 375
Bullard, Robert, 499
Bulle, Wolfgang F., 65–66
Bumiller, Elisabeth, 340
Bunzel, John H., 255
Burgess, Ernest, 464, 472
Burke, Mary Jean, 183, 184
Burkett, Elinor, 343
Burns, John R., 291
Burt, Maritha B., 478
Burton, Charles, 402
Bury, Michael, 107
Bush, George H. W., 152
Bush, George W., 161, 319, 358, 370, 396, 501
Butler, Daniel Allen, 215
Butler, Robert, 316
Butterfield, Fox, 187

C

Caesar, Lena G., 446
Calhoun, Craig, 519
Calvin, John, 358
Calvo, Dana, 156

Campo-Flores, Arian, 271
Camus, Albert, 119
Cancel, Cecil Marie, 290
Cantril, Hadley, 512
Cao, Guichan, 312
Caplan, Ronald L., 440
Capps, Randy, 271
Caputo, John S., 62
Carey, Anne R., 110
Caroline, Princess of Monaco, 152
Carpenter, Linda Jean, 19
Carrese, Joseph A., 442
Carroll, Diahann, 152
Carroll, Jackson W., 363
Carroll, Joe, 315
Carroll, John, 289, 315
Carson, Johnny, 512
Carter, Bill, 161
Carter, Jimmy, 152
Carter, Rebecca S., 94
Carty, Win, 497
Casper, Lynne, 333, 340, 341, 402
Cassidy, Rachel C., 253, 267
Castells, Manuel, 110, 111, 140, 164, 471, 519
Casteñeda, Jorge, 238, 239
Castro, Fidel, 418, 514
Catton, William R., Jr., 498
Cerulo, Karen A., 158
Cetron, Marvin J., 533
Cha, Ariena Funjung, 539
Chagko, Mary, 158
Chalfant, H. Paul, 366, 366t
Chambers, Jeff M., 475
Chambliss, William, 185
Chandler, Clay, 20
Chang, Leslie, 137
Chang, Patricia M. Y., 359
Charles, Prince of Wales, 477
Charter, David, 376
Chase-Dunn, Christopher, 60, 229, 230, 232, 234
Chatzky, Jean Sherman, 311
Chaves, Mark, 359
Chavira, Juan Antonio, 447
Cheng, Wei-yuan, 21
Cher, 152
Cherlin, Andrew J., 328, 338, 340
Chesney-Lind, Meda, 16
Chin, Ko-lin, 188
Chrisman, Robert, 266
Christensen, Kathleen, 306
Christenson, Matthew, 492
Christiansen, John B., 509
Christie, Brigan, 456
Christopher, Yujio Kawano, 230
Chuck D, 526
Churchill, Winston, 376
Clark, Burton, 387
Clark, Candace, 443
Clark, E. Gurney, 439

Clarke, Adele E., 534
Clarke, Lee, 512
Clausen, Christopher, 343
Clawson, Dan, 98, 142
Clawson, Mary Ann, 141, 142
Clay, Cassius, 104
Cleveland, Robert W., 31, 202, 268, 270
Clinard, Marshall B., 183
Clinton, Bill, 152, 500, 501, 513, 521, 535
Clinton, Hillary Rodham, 409
Clymer, Adam, 403
Cockerham, William C., 443
Cohen, A. K., 112
Cohen, David, 88
Cohen, Lawrence E., 185
Cohen, Patricia, 338
Colapinto, John, 516
Cole, Elizabeth S., 336
Cole, Mike, 381
Coleman, James William, 452
Collins, Randall, 206, 208, 358, 380, 529, 530
Commoner, Barry, 487, 498
Comstock, P., 143, 165
Comte, Auguste, 9, 13, 528, 529
Conlin, Michelle, 285
Conrad, Peter, 439
Cooley, Charles Horton, 12, 13, 17, 18t, 84, 87, 91, 127, 421
Coombs, Michael W., 262
Cooper, Richard S., 312
Cornelius, Diana, 501
Cornell, Claire Pedrick, 328
Cornfield, Daniel B., 142, 143
Corsaro, William A., 91
Cortese, Anthony J., 158
Cosby, Bill, 152
Coser, Lewis, 47, 208
Coser, Rose Laub, 449
Costello, Cynthia, 185, 207
Couch, Carl J., 400, 510
Counts, D. A., 313, 314
Cox, Oliver, 260
Cox, Rachel S., 389, 390
Crenshaw, Edward M., 492
Cressey, Donald R., 183, 184, 452
Cristensen, Kathleen, 306
Crockett, Davy, 512
Cromwell, Paul F., 185
Crossette, Barbara, 368, 408
Croteau, David, 160, 161, 164
Crouse, Kelly, 215
Crowley, Sheila, 479
Cuff, E. C., 207
Cullen, Francis T., Jr., 185
Cullen, John B., 185
Cumming, Elaine, 305
Currie, Elliot, 192
Curry, Timothy Jon, 440
Curry-White, Brenda, 213
Curtis, James, 138

D

D'Abuzzo, Alphonso, 263
Dahl, Robert A., 407
Dahrendorf, Ralf, 15, 207, 529
Dalaker, Joseph, 211, 213, 266, 270, 316, 332
Daley, Suzanne, 245, 342
Daniels, Arlene Kaplan, 139
Daniszewski, John, 163
Dao, James, 337
Darlington, JoAnne DeRoven, 150
Darwin, Charles, 10, 62, 527
Davidson, Joe, 480
Davies, Christie, 90
Davies, Owen, 533
Davis, A. K., 112
Davis, Darren W., 37
Davis, Donald B., 140
Davis, James A., 34, 47, 51, 209, 217
Davis, Jerry, 406
Davis, Kingsley, 14, 82, 206, 380, 462
Davis, Nanette, 182, 185
Davis, Sammy, Jr., 152
Day, Jennifer, 403
De Andra, Roberto M., 296
De Klerk, F. W., 531
De la Cruz, G. Patricia, 266
De Tocqueville, Alexis, 137
Dean, James, 148
Deardorff, Kevin E., 276
Deegan, Mary Jo, 12, 107
Delawala, Imtyaz, 61, 417
Dellios, Hugh, 242
Deloria, Vine, 350–351
Demuth, Stephen, 187
DeNavas-Walt, Carmen, 31, 168, 202, 270
Dennis, Larry, 73
Denton, Nancy, 264, 473
DePalma, Anthony, 239, 240, 427
DeParle, Jason, 214
Desai, Manisha, 518
Deskins, Donald R., Jr., 15
Devine, Don, 68
Devitt, James, 404
Di Fazio, William, 143
Diana, Princess of Wales, 151, 152
Diani, Marie, 519
Diaz, Cameron, 151
Dickerson, John E., 141
Dickerson, Marla, 420
Dickson, W. J., 137
Dieter, Richard C., 187
Dijkstra, AnneBert, 392
Dillon, Sam, 242, 522
DiMaggio, Paul, 140, 541
Divyanathan, Denesh, 430
Dixon, Margret, 317
Dodds, Klaus, 61
Dodge, Hiroko, 257
Doeringer, Peter B., 306

Dolbeare, Cushing N., 479
Domhoff, G. William, 396–397, 406–407
Dominguez, Silva, 111
Dominick, Joseph R., 157, 160
Donato, Paul, 45
Donohue, Elizabeth, 386
Dore, Ronald P., 380
Doress, Irwin, 363
Dornbush, Sanford M., 95
Dorsett, Kelsie Lenor Wilson, 488
Dotson, Floyd, 461
Dougherty, John, 242
Dougherty, Kevin, 384
Douglas, Michael, 416
Dowd, James J., 307
Doyle, James A., 284
Doyle, Patricia, 212
Dreier, Peter, 226
Dreifus, Claudia, 511
Drew, Christopher, 243
Driver, Edwin D., 267
Dronkers, Jaap, 392
Drucker, Peter F., 431
Du Bois, W. E. B., 15, 18, 18t, 21, 43, 265, 267
Duberman, Lucille, 205
Dudley, Carl S., 363
Dugger, Celia W., 201, 492
Duncan, Otis Dudley, 217
Duneier, Mitchell, 114, 460–461
Dunlap, Riley, 498, 499
Durand, Ann, 41
Durand, Jorge, 242
Durkheim, Emile, 3, 8, 10, 12, 13, 18t, 20, 39, 114–115, 119, 181–182, 351, 353, 355, 358, 361, 369, 422, 528
Durning, Alan B., 245
Duster, Troy, 537
Dynes, Russell, 510

E

Eagleton, Thomas, 452
Eason, Yla, 91
Ebaugh, Helen Rose Fuchs, 108–109
Eberhard, Ray, 310
Eberstadt, Nicholas, 490
Ebert, Roger, 65
Eckenwiler, Mark, 543
Eckholm, Erik, 419, 493
Eddy, Mary Baker, 365
Edelman, Benjamin, 542
Edwards, Tamala M., 19, 298
Efron, Sonni, 345, 381
Egan, T., 475
Ehrenreich, Barbara, 2–3, 6, 20, 220
Ehrlich, Ann, 498
Ehrlich, Paul, 487, 498
Eisenberg, David M., 451
Eisenhower, Dwight D., 152

Eitzen, D. Stanley, 19
El-Badry, Samira, 254
El Nasser, Haya, 467, 475
Elizabeth, Queen of England, 376
Eller, Claudia, 156
Ellingwood, Ken, 241
Elliot, Marta, 479
Ellison, Ralph, 264, 498
Ellsberg, M., 328
Elmer-DeWitt, Philip, 539
Ely, Robin J., 132–133
Embree, Ainslie, 368
Emery, David, 512, 513
Eminem, 152
Engardio, Pete, 408
Engels, Friedrich, 11, 12, 15, 60, 133, 287, 326, 415, 417, 514–515
England, Paula, 16
English-Lueck, Jan, 57–58
Enriquez, Juan, 408
Entine, Jon, 232
Epstein, Cynthia Fuchs, 296
Ericson, Nels, 150
Erikson, Kai, 182, 423, 484–485, 536
Etaugh, Claire, 284
Etzioni, Amitai, 140
Evans, Sara, 295
Evetts, Julia, 422

F

Faludi, Susan, 285
Falwell, Jerry, 163
Fan, Jianyong, 421
Fanning, Shawn, 526
Farhi, Paul, 155
Farley, Maggie, 75
Farrell, Amy, 261
Fatina, Helac, 490
Fausset, Richard, 366t
Feagin, Joe R., 21, 388, 467, 470
Featherman, David L., 217
Fein, Helen, 243
Feinglass, Joe, 452
Feketekuty, Guza, 60, 230
Fellini, Federico, 165
Felson, Marcus, 185
Fennell, Mary L., 422
Ferguson, Sarah, 152
Ferman, Louis, 237
Fernandez, Roberto M., 429
Fernandez, Sandy, 543
Fernea, Elizabeth, 290
Ferree, Myra Marx, 516
Ferrell, Tom, 340
Ferris, Nancy, 479
Fessenden, Ford, 175
Feuer, Lewis S., 60, 133, 230, 287
Fiala, Robert, 532

Fidel, Kenneth, 20
Fields, Jason, 97, 325, 333, 338, 340, 341
Finder, Alan, 269
Fine, Gary Alan, 19, 104, 513
Finkel, Steven E., 515
Firestone, David, 369
Firestone, Shulamith, 295
Firmat, Gustavo, 272
Fishman, Jennifer R., 534
Fitzgerald, Kathleen J., 515
Flacks, Richard, 71
Flavin, Jeanne, 190–191
Fletcher, Connie, 108, 382
Flexner, Eleanor, 382
Forbes, Steve, 410
Ford, Gerald R., 152
Foreman, Judy, 74
Fornos, Werner, 501
Forsythe, David P., 243
Foster, Jodie, 165
Fox, M. B., 143, 165
Fox, Susannah, 143, 158
Francese, Peter, 310
Francis, D. W., 207
Frankenberg, Joyce, 263
Franklin, John Hope, 266
Freeman, Jo, 295
Freidson, Eliot, 440
Freire, Paolo, 379
French, Howard W., 86, 235, 425, 478
Freud, Sigmund, 87
Freundenheim, Milt, 455
Frey, William H., 475
Fridlund, Alan J., 65
Friedan, Betty, 295, 494
Friedland, Jonathon, 440
Friedman, Milton, 391
Friess, Steve, 522
Frohne, Ursula, 540
Fukasaku, Kinji, 164
Fullerton, Howard N., Jr., 426
Furstenberg, Frank, 328
Furukawa, Stacy, 338
Fusket, Jennifer Ruth, 534

G

Gagnon, John H., 342
Gale, Elaine, 138
Galinsky, Ellen, 295
Gallup, George H., 193
Gamson, Joshua, 515
Ganeshananthan, Vasugi, 298
Gandhi, Mohandas, K., 368
Gans, Herbert J., 214, 215, 273, 472
Ganzeboom, Harry, 235, 236
Gardner, Carol Brooks, 21
Gardner, Marilyn, 97, 316
Garfinkel, Harold, 91
Garner, Roberta, 20, 517, 519, 520

Garner, Thesia, 212
Garreau, Joel, 467
Gartin, Patrick W., 185, 376
Garza, Melita Marie, 88
Gates, Bill, 141
Gates, Henry Lewis, Jr, 342, 540
Gecas, Viktor, 84, 90
Gelles, Richard J., 328
Gerstel, Naomi, 98
Gerth, H. H., 205, 380
Geyh, Paul, 295
Gezari, Vanessa, 534
Gibbs, Nancy, 319
Gibson, William, 539
Giddens, Anthony, 61
Gifford, Allen L., 121
Gill, Brian P., 392
Gintis, Herbert, 93, 378, 381, 385
Giordano, Peggy C., 86
Giroux, Henry A., 381
Gitlin, Todd, 148–149, 155, 162
Glanton, Dahleen, 467
Glascock, Anthony, 318, 319
Glauber, Bill, 177
Glaze, Lauren, 173–174
Goering, Laura, 240
Goffman, Erving, 17, 18t, 21, 40, 86, 90, 107,
    110, 158, 180, 398
Goldberg, Carey, 177
Golden, Frederic, 536
Goldin, Amy, 508
Goldman, Robert, 225–226
Goldstein, Amy, 403
Goldstein, Greg, 478
Goldstein, Melvyn C., 304
Gole, Nilofer, 290
Goleman, Daniel, 73
Gonnut, Jean Pierre, 570
Gonzales, Claudio, 218
Gonzales, John M., 271
Goode, Erica, 215
Goodgame, Dan, 220
Goodman, Peter S., 235
Gorbachev, Mikhail, 530
Gordon, Daniel T., 381
Gordon, Jesse, 227
Gore, Al, 404
Gorman, Tom, 319
Gornick, Janet C., 158
Gornick, Vivian, 220
Gottdiener, Mark, 467, 470
Gottemuelle, M., 328
Gottfredson, Michael, 176
Gottschalk, Peter, 214
Gouldner, Alvin, 43, 529
Grabarek, Stanislaus, 25
Grabb, Edward, 138
Graham, Judith, 297
Gramsci, Antonio, 69
Greeley, Andrew, 358

Green, Dan S., 267
Greenburg, Jan Crawford, 521
Greene, Jay P., 74
Greenhouse, L., 291
Greenhouse, Steven, 143, 429
Greenspan, Alan, 397
Grieco, Elizabeth M., 253, 267
Grimes, Peter, 229, 232
Grob, Gerald N., 454
Grossman, David C., 164
Grusky, David B., 235
Guterman, Lila, 63
Gutierrez, Gustavo, 358
Gwynne, S. C., 141

H

Hachen, David, 185, 207
Hacker, A., 406
Hacker, Helen Mayer, 287, 296
Hackman, Gene, 543
Hage, Jerald, 132
Haines, Valerie A., 528
Hall, Judith A., 289
Hall, Kay, 533
Hall, Mimi, 534
Hall, Robert H., 444
Haller, Max, 235
Hallinan, Maureen, 381, 529, 530
Hamilton, Brady E., 266
Hamilton, Charles, 266
Hamilton, Edwin, 39
Hammack, Floyd M., 384
Handel, George Frederic, 361
Hani, Yoko, 306
Hank, Karsten, 98
Hannis, Prudence, 261
Hansen, Brian, 61, 190
Hanson, Janice, 166
Harap, Louis, 359
Hargittai, Eszter, 140, 541
Haring, Keith, 171
Harlow, Harry, 82–83
Harmon, Amy, 539, 543
Harnan, Vera, 388
Harold, Clive, 477
Harrington, Michael, 119
Harris, Chauncy D., 466f, 467
Harris, David A., 261
Harris, Judith Rich, 91
Harris, Marvin, 250, 305
Hartman, Chris, 220
Hartmann, Heidi, 428–429
Hasan, Hakim, 460
Haub, Carl, 228, 229, 238, 306, 441, 465f, 486,
    489, 489f, 492, 493, 494, 501
Hauser, Robert M., 217, 235
Havel, Vaclav, 514
Haviland, William A., 324

Hawk, Richard, 428
Hawkins, Darnell F., 187
Hayward, Mark D., 306
Healey, Jon, 181
Heck, K., 444
Heckert, Druann, 180
Hedley, R. Alan, 233
Heilman, Madeline E., 218
Heise, Lori, 328
Hellmich, Nanci, 155
Helms, Jesse, 48
Henneberger, Melinda, 254
Henry, Stuart, 237
Hepburn, Katherine, 152
Hequembourg, Amy, 521
Herrmann, Andrew, 270
Hersch, Patricia, 386
Hershey, Robert D., Jr., 237
Herskovitz, Melville, 252
Herstad, Britt, 501
Hetherington, E. Mavis, 340
Hewlett, Sylvia Ann, 323–324
Hick, Steven F., 408
Hickman, Jonathan, 257
Hickman, Matthew J., 192
Hill, Stephen, 10, 69
Hillery, George A., 461
Himes, Christine L., 306, 314, 316
Hirschfeld, Magnus, 519
Hirschi, Travis, 176
Hirshfeld, Marc, 156, 157
Hitchcock, Susan Tyler, 25, 316
Hitler, Adolf, 399–400
Hochschild, Arlie Russell, 294, 329
Hodge, Robert W., 209
Hodson, Randy, 423
Hoebel, E. Adamson, 260
Hoecker-Drysdale, Susan, 10
Hoeffler, Lois, 37
Hoffman, Adonis, 157
Holden, Constance, 83
Hollander, Jocelyn A., 288
Hollingshead, August B., 386
Holmberg, Joan, 209
Holmes, Steven A., 475
Holthouse, David, 242
Homans, George C., 80–81
Hombo, Catherine M., 389
Hondagneu-Sotelo, Pierrette, 111
Horgan, John, 84
Horne, Lena, 152
Horovitz, Bruce, 153
Horowitz, Helen Lefkowitz, 387
Horwitz, Allan V., 454
Hosokawa, William K., 269
Houseman, John, 512
Houston, Whitney, 152
Hout, Michael, 217
Howard, Judith A., 287
Howard, Michael C., 84

Howard, Philip E., 539
Hoyman, Michael, 237
Hoynes, William, 160, 161, 164
Huang, Gary, 106
Huber, Bettina J., 25
Huddy, Leonie, 37
Huffstutter, P. J., 158
Hughes, Everett, 106
Hull, Raymond, 135
Hundley, James R., Jr., 508
Hunt, Darnell, 160–161, 193
Hunter, Herbert M., 260
Hunter, James Davison, 355
Hurh, Won Moo, 268, 269
Hurn, Christopher J., 378, 380
Hussein, Saddam, 94, 510, 530
Hutchinson, Ray, 467
Hymowitz, Carol, 423

I

Imani, Nikitah, 388
Inglehart, Ronald, 233, 361
Ireland, John, 266
Iritani, Evelyn, 420
Isabelle, 82

J

Jackson, Charles W., 316
Jackson, Elton F., 183
Jackson, Janet, 152
Jackson, Michael, 152
Jackson, Philip, 379
Jacobs, Andrew, 474
Jacobs, Jane, 460
Jacobs, Jerry, 294
Jacobson, Jodi, 292
Jacobson, Lenore, 382, 383
Jamieson, Arnie, 403
Jargowsky, Paul A., 475
Jasper, James M., 517, 531
Jenkins, Richard, 202–203
Jennings, M. Kent, 401
Jesus Christ, 152, 353
Johnson, Benton, 529
Johnson, David, 212
Johnson, Dirk, 475
Johnson, Jeffrey, 165
Johnson, John M., 37
Johnson, Kenneth M., 495
Johnson, Lyndon B., 152
Johnson, Richard A., 511
Johnson, Todd M., 354
Johnston, David Cay, 220, 245
Jolin, Annette, 190–191
Jones, D., 364
Jones, James T., 291

Jones, Stephen R. G., 39
Jones, Steve, 539
Jordan, Michael, 159
Jost, Kenneth, 190, 391
Joynt, Jen, 298
Juarez, Benito, 261
Juhasz, Anne McCreary, 86
Jung, Andrea, 218

K

Kagay, Michael R., 513
Kahn, Joseph, 420, 421
Kalb, Claudia, 177, 180
Kalish, Richard, 313
Kalleberg, Arne L., 234
Kanellos, Nicholas, 270
Kang, Mee-Eun, 40
Kapner, Suzanne, 156
Kasarda, John D., 430
Kashiwagi, Akiko, 235
Kasl, Stanislav V., 316
Katovich, Michael, 128, 174
Katsillis, John, 233
Katz, Jonathan Ned, 520
Katz, Michael, 385
Kay, Paul, 65, 513
Kaye, Judith, 337
Kazibwe, Wandira, 405
Keith, Kenton, 163
Kelly, John, 328, 340
Kelsoe, John R., 84
Kennedy, Florynce, 296
Kennedy, John F., 152, 192, 205, 400, 431
Kennedy, Robert, 192
Kennickell, Arthur B., 210
Kerbo, Harold R., 206, 232, 234
Kershaw, Sarah, 520
Kessler, Michelle, 428
Kevorkian, Jack, 318
Kilborn, Peter T., 476
Kilbourne, Jean, 158
Killian, Lewis, 507, 513
Kim, Kwang Chung, 268, 269
King, Elliot, 534
King, Leslie, 98, 345
King, Martin Luther, Jr., 192, 266, 515
King, Sharon A., 512
Kinkade, Patrick, 128
Kinsella, Kevin, 306
Kinsey, Alfred, 46
Kirk, Jim, 537
Kirk, Margaret O., 429, 537
Kissinger, Henry, 152
Kitchener, Richard F., 88
Kitt, Alice S., 130
Klass, Perry, 289
Klein, Julia M., 453
Klein, Naomi, 162

Kleiner, Art, 138
Kleniewski, Nancy, 474
Klinenberg, Eric, 306
Klinger, Scott, 205
Kohn, Melvin L., 332
Kolata, Gina, 345, 535
Komarovsky, Mirra, 16
Konieczny, May Ellen, 359
Konig, Wolfgang, 235
Koolhaas, Rem, 464
Kopinak, Kathryn, 239
Korczyk, Sophie M., 306
Korn, William S., 68, 385
Koval, John, 20
Kozol, Jonathan, 374–375
Krause, Peter, 235
Krauss, Clifford, 76
Kreider, Rose M., 338
Kretzmann, John P., 474
Krivo, Lauren J., 479
Krueger, Scott, 177
Kubler-Ross, Elisabeth, 313
Kubrick, Stanley, 140
Kucherenko, Tania, 327
Kunkel, Dale, 46
Kunkel, Suzanne R., 316
Kuo, M., 177
Kurz, Karin, 235
Kwong, Peter, 269

L

La Ganga, Maria L., 314
Labaton, Stephan, 190
Lamb, David, 268
Landtman, Gunar, 206
Lang, Eric, 39
Lappin, Todd, 543
Larsen, Elena, 366
Lasn, Kalle, 152
Lasswell, Harold, 397
Laszlo, Jennifer, 408
Lauer, Robert H., 529
Lauman, Edward O., 342
Lauren, Gene, 192
Lauritsen, John, 520
Lawrence, Jacob, 200
Lawson, Valerie A., 311
Lazarsfeld, Paul, 149, 160
Leacock, Eleanor Burke, 380
Leaf, Nathan, 476
Leavell, Hugh R., 439
Lee, Alfred McClung, 398
Lee, Barrett A., 479
Lee, H., 177
Lee, Heon Cheol, 333
Lee, Spike, 269
Lee, Tom, 521
Lehne, Gregory K., 283

Leicht, Kevin T., 422
Leinwand, Donna, 93, 177
Lemann, Nicholas, 271
Lemkow, Louis, 237
Lemonick, Michael D., 445
Leng, M. J., Jr., 112
Lengermann, Patricia Madoo, 12
Lennon, John, 192
Lenski, Gerhard, 62, 114–115, 116, 119, 208, 415, 462
Leo, John, 84
Levin, Jack, 305
Levin, Thomas Y., 540
Levin, William C., 305
Levinson, Daniel, 309, 311, 312
Levinson, David, 354
Levy, Becca R., 316
Levy, Clifford J., 510
Levy, Judith A., 313
Lewin, Tamar, 291
Lewis, David Levering, 15
Liao, Lung-li, 21
Liao, Youlian, 312
Lichter, Linda, 165
Lichter, Robert, 165
Lichtlau, Eric, 261
Lieberman, David, 541
Liebow, Elliot, 479
Light, Ivan, 276
Liker, Jeffrey K., 140
Lilly, Teri, 172–173
Lin, Nan, 110, 209, 235
Lincoln, Abraham, 375
Lindbergh Morrow, Anne, 294
Lindner, Eileen, 254
Linn, Susan, 92
Lipset, Seymour Martin, 210
Lipson, Karen, 82
Little, Kenneth, 138
Liu, Shejan, 421
Lively, Kathryn J., 422
Livernash, Robert, 499
Llanes, Jose, 272
Lockren, K., 444
Lofland, John, 511
Lofland, Lyn H., 38
Logan, John R., 268
Lohr, Steve, 541
Long, Jeff, 20
Lopez, Jennifer, 152, 216
Lorber, Judith, 283
Lu, Ming, 421
Lucas, Wayne, 126
Luckmann, Thomas, 103, 114
Luijkx, Ruud, 236
Lukacs, George, 69
Lum, Joann, 269
Lurker, Kristin, 297
Luster, Tom, 332
Luther, Martin, 364

Lyall, Sarah, 340
Lynch, David J., 420, 500
Lynn, Barry C., 427
Lyons, Linda, 340
Lyotard, Jean Francois, 119

M

MacDorman, Marian F., 446
Mack, Raymond, 112
Madaus, George F., 389
Madonna, 152
Magnier, Mark, 164, 235
Maguire, Brendan, 188, 190
Maines, David R., 105
Makui, D., 444
Malbin, Michael, 410
Malcolm, Andrew H., 512
Malcolm X, 106, 361
Malthus, Thomas Robert, 485, 487
Mandela, Nelson, 263, 514
Mankato, Alice Park, 445
Manson, Charles, 262
Margolis, Eric, 379
Marklein, Mary Beth, 533
Markson, Elizabeth, 319
Maro, Laura, 534
Marquand, Robert, 60
Marquis, Julie, 454
Marr, Phebe, 94
Marsden, Peter V., 34, 47, 209
Marshall, Patrick, 109, 267
Marshall, Victor W., 313
Martelo, Emma Zapata, 239
Martin, Joyce A., 337, 344
Martin, Marvin, 20
Martin, Philip, 7, 274, 275, 494, 495
Martin, Susan E., 108
Martineau, Harriet, 9–10
Martinez, Elizabeth, 319
Maruschak, Laura M., 187
Marx, Karl, 3, 11–12, 13, 14–15, 15, 18t, 21, 60, 69, 119, 133, 143, 199, 203, 204, 205, 229, 260, 261, 287, 295, 326, 327, 358, 359, 360, 405, 406, 415, 417, 422, 423, 425, 487, 514–515, 515
Mason, Heather, 473
Massey, Douglas S., 242, 264, 473
Mathews, T. J., 446
Matsuda, Seiko, 339
Matsushita, Yoshiko, 94
Matthews, Jay, 390
Maugh, Thomas R., 120
Mayer, Karl Ulrich, 96
McCarthy, Joseph, 255
McCormick, John, 177
McCreary, D., 285
McDermott, Kevin, 410
McDevitt, Jack, 261

McDonald, Kim A., 447
McFalls, Joseph A., Jr., 492
McGee, Daniel L., 312
McGinn, Daniel, 329
McGivering, Jill, 201
McGovern, George, 452
McGue, Matt, 83
McGuire, Meredith B., 351
McIntosh, Peggy, 257, 258
McKinlay, John B., 440
McKinlay, Sonja M., 440
McKinley, James C., 418
McKinney, William, 363
McKinnon, Jesse, 266
McKnight, John L., 474
McLanahan, Sara, 214
McLane, Daisann, 88
McLean, Elys A., 110
McLuhan, Marshall, 148, 162
McNeil, Donald G, Jr., 122, 451
McNutt, John G., 408
McPhail, Clark, 507, 508, 509
Mead, George Herbert, 17, 18, 18t, 84, 84–86, 87, 91, 539
Mead, Margaret, 68, 285, 287
Mechanic, David, 457
Melia, Marilyn Kennedy, 426
Menacker, Fay, 446
Mencimer, Stephanie, 98
Mendez, Jennifer Bickman, 135
Mendoza, Jorge L., 511
Merrill, David A., 516
Merton, Robert, 13, 14, 18t, 35, 129, 130, 134, 149, 182–183
Messner, Michael A., 285, 383
Meyer, Madonna Harrington, 345
Meyer, Marshall W., 135
Meyers, Thomas J., 92
Michael, Robert, 342
Michels, Robert, 136, 143, 515
Midgley, Elizabeth, 275
Miles, Erika, 451
Milgram, Stanley, 172, 173–174, 380
Mill, John Stuart, 287
Miller, D. W., 538
Miller, David, 509
Miller, David L., 150
Miller, G. Tyler, 499
Miller, Jake, 220
Miller, Judith, 536
Miller, Robert F., 183
Millett, Kate, 295
Mills, C. Wright, 3–4, 6, 205, 380, 397, 405, 406
Mills, Robert J., 215, 444f, 455
Minyard, Staci A., 94
Mirapaul, Matthew, 150
Mishra, Pankaj, 368
Mitofsky, Warren J., 513
Mizruchi, Mark S., 406

Moeller, Susan D., 153
Mogelonsky, Marcia, 336
Mohammad, 353
Mollen, Milton, 507
Monmaney, Terence, 442
Monteiro, Lois A., 443
Montgomery, Marilyn J., 307
Moon, Youngme, 539
Moore, David W., 355, 432
Moore, Joan, 271
Moore, Kevin B., 210
Moore, Michael, 192, 193
Moore, Molly, 234
Moore, Wilbert E., 95, 206, 208, 234, 380
Morain, Dan, 454
Morin, Richard, 46, 403
Morris, Aldon, 515
Morris, Bonnie Rothman, 330
Morrison, Denton E., 515
Morse, A., 274
Mosely, J., 328
Moses, 353
Mosisa, Abraham T., 275
Moss, Michael, 175, 266
Mott, Lucretia, 295
Moynihan, Patrick J., 37
Mullins, Marcy E., 536
Mumola, Christopher J., 93
Munoz, Lorenza, 156
Murdock, George, 59, 325, 461
Murphy, Caryle, 234
Murphy, Dean E., 107, 510
Murray, Velma McBride, 329
Museveni, Yoweri, 405

N

Nader, Laura, 291
Nader, Ralph, 410
Nagourney, Adam, 392
Narayanan, K. R., 201
Narrow, William E., 452
Nash, Manning, 260
Nass, Clifford, 539
Navarro, Mireya, 156, 449
Neary, Ian, 235
Nelson, Alan R., 446
Nelson, Jack, 534
Nelson, T. F., 177
Neuborne, Ellen, 540
Neuman, W. Russell, 140, 541
Newburger, Eric, 541
Newman, Katherine, 198–199, 214
Newman, William M., 263
Newport, Frank, 521f
Ni, Ching-Ching, 154
Nichols, Martha, 232
Nicholson, Jack, 452
Nicolette, Sister, 445
Nie, Norman H., 539

Niebrugge-Brantley, Jill, 12
Niemi, Richard G., 401
Nixon, Howard L., II, 131
Nixon, Richard M., 152
Nolan, Patrick, 62, 116, 208, 462
Noonan, Rita K., 516
Nordhaus, William, 210
Norman, Jim, 513
Novak, Vivica, 194
Nussbaum, Daniel, 497

O

Oakey, Doyle Ray, 492
Oberschall, Anthony, 515
O'Connell, Martin, 340
O'Connor, Sandra Day, 288, 396
O'Donnell, Jayne, 190
O'Donnell, Mike, 209
Ogburn, William F., 62, 96, 327, 532, 535
O'Hare, William P., 213
Okamoto, Dina, 288
Okano, Kaori, 380
Oliver, Melvin L., 211, 217
Olson, James N., 185
Onassis, Jackie, 152
O'Neill, Brian, 490
Orum, Anthony M., 401, 515
Orwell, George, 171
Osgood, D. Wayne, 475
Ousmane, Sembene, 61
Overberg, Paul, 467
Owens, Erica A., 282
Owens, Michael Leo, 282, 392

P

Pachon, Harry, 271
Page, Charles, 136
Paik, Haejung, 165
Paludi, Michele A., 284
Pamuk, E., 444
Pan, Philip P., 420
Papson, Stephen, 225–226
Park, Robert, 149–150, 464
Parrado, Emilio A., 242
Parrott, Sarah A., 68, 385
Parsons, Talcott, 13, 18t, 68, 439, 449–450, 528
Passero, Kathy, 65–66
Patankar, Indutai, 518
Pate, Anthony, 39
Patterson, Orlando, 432
Patterson, Thomas E., 403
Pattillo-McCoy, Mary, 80–81, 92
Patton, Carl V., 471
Paul, Saint, 340
Paulson, Amanda, 390
Pavalko, Ronald M., 422

Pear, Robert, 132, 269
Pearlstein, Steven, 60, 230
Peck, Don, 402
Pedulla, Joseph J., 389
Pellow, David Naguib, 500
Pelton, Tom, 39
Perlman, Ilene, 290
Perot, Ross, 410, 513
Perrin, Towers, 204
Perrow, Charles, 136, 536, 538
Perry, Suzanne, 544
Peter, Laurence J., 135
Peters, Robert, 508
Petersen, William, 487
Peterson, Karen S., 336
Phillips, E. Barbara, 463, 464
Phillips, Susan A., 170–171, 183
Piaget, Jean, 87–88
Pierre, Robert E., 219
Piller, Charles, 408, 540
Pinderhughes, Dianne, 407
Pinkerton, James P., 381
Piven, Frances Fox, 220
Plomin, Robert, 84
Poe, Edgar Allan, 171
Poitier, Sidney, 152
Pollak, Michael, 538
Polletta, Francesca, 517
Polonko, Karen A., 140
Pomfret, John, 420
Popenoe, David, 341
Porter, Jack Nusan, 363
Poussaint, Alvin F., 92
Power, Carla, 254
Power, Richard, 189–190
Powers, Mary, 209
Prehn, John W., 494
Proctor, Bernadette D., 211, 213, 266, 270, 316, 332
Prusher, Ilene R., 478
Pugliani, Patricia, 37
Purdum, Todd S., 501
Puri, Shaifali, 316
Pyle, Amy, 74

Q

Quadagno, Jill, 88, 307, 313, 317
Quarantelli, Enrico L., 508, 510, 511, 512
Quart, Alissa, 152
Quinney, Richard, 186, 187

R

Radosh, Polly F., 188
Rae, Donald S., 452
Rainie, Lee, 150, 158, 539
Ramet, Sabrina, 514
Ramirez, Deborah, 261

Ramirez, Eddy, 316
Ramirez, Roberta R., 266
Ramirez, Roberto R., 270, 271
Rau, William, 41
Raybon, Patricia, 296
Rayman-Read, Alyssa, 501
Read, Jen'nan Ghazal, 290
Reagan, Ronald, 142, 152, 269, 396, 400, 501
Reddick, Randy, 333, 534
Reddick, Reinhard J., 333
Reeves, Terrence, 266
Regier, Darrel A., 452
Reich, Robert B., 428
Reinharz, Shulamit, 44
Remnick, David, 92, 104
Rennison, Callie, 191, 192, 216, 328
Retsinas, Joan, 313
Reuban, C., 444
Rheingold, Howard, 505–506
Rhodes, Eric Bryant, 338, 442
Rhodes, Lorna A., 442
Richardson, James, 365–366
Richardson, Laurel, 329
Richtel, Matt, 427
Rideout, Victoria J., 95
Ridgeway, Cecilia L., 288
Riding, Alan, 215
Rifkin, Jeremy, 344, 345, 414–415, 422, 429, 430, 533
Riley, John W., Jr., 314
Riley, Matilda White, 532
Rimer, Sara, 314
Ritzer, George, 62, 119, 126–127, 422, 424, 425, 534
Robb, David, 155
Robberson, Tod, 240
Robbins, Lee N., 452
Roberts, D. F., 40
Roberts, David, 252, 308
Roberts, Johnnie L., 161
Roberts, Julia, 152, 154, 165
Roberts, Lynne D., 539
Roberts, Sam, 270
Robertson, Roland, 69, 207
Robinson, John P., 140, 541
Robinson, Thomas N., 165
Robison, Jennifer, 284
Rochefort, David, 457
Rodenburg, Eric, 499
Rodgers, Diane M., 515
Rodriguez, Noelie, 16
Roethlisberger, Fritz J., 137
Rogers, Diane M., 515
Rogovin, Milton, 334
Rohter, Larry, 433, 471
Romero, J. Horacio, 316
Romero, Mary, 111
Romney, Lee, 271
Ronaldo, 152
Roosevelt, Franklin D., 400

Rose, Arnold, 260
Rose, Peter I., 90
Rosen, Laurel, 111
Rosenbaum, Lynn, 283
Rosenberg, Douglas H., 203, 415
Rosenberg, Howard, 163
Rosenfeld, Megan, 155
Rosenthal, Elizabeth, 107, 493
Rosenthal, Robert, 382, 383, 384
Rosnow, Ralph L., 513
Ross, John, 478
Rossi, Alice, 333
Rossi, Peter, 44, 209, 479
Rossides, Daniel, 202–203
Roszak, Theodore, 71
Roter, Debra L., 289
Rowley, Colleen, 133
Roy, Donald, 424
Ruane, Janet M., 158
Rubel, Maximilien, 529
Rubinson, Richard, 234
Rule, James B., 515
Russo, Nancy Felipe, 284
Rutenberg, Jim, 161

S

Saad, Lydia, 193, 315
Sadker, David, 93, 381
Sadker, Myra, 93
Safire, William, 427
Sagarin, Edward, 181
Sale, Kirkpatrick, 119, 533
Salem, Richard, 25
Salkever, Alex, 538
Samuelson, Paul, 210
Samuelson, Robert J., 306, 427
Sanchez, Jose, 181
Sandberg, Jared, 257
Sanger, Margaret, 514
Sapir, Edward, 63, 65
Saporito, Bill, 476
Sassen, Saskia, 276
Saukko, Paula, 180
Sawyer, Diane, 257
Sax, Linda, 68, 385
Scarce, Rik, 43
Schachter, Jason, 495
Schaefer, Lenore, 314
Schaefer, Peter, 539
Schaefer, Richard T., 76, 255, 257, 262, 267, 307, 433, 531, ix
Scharnberg, Kirsten, 17
Schellenberg, Kathryn, 539
Schiraldi, Vincent, 386
Schlenker, Barry R., 86
Schmetzer, Uli, 201
Schmidt, William E., 139
Schnailberg, Allan, 499

Schneider, Barbara, 129
Schneider, Joseph W., 440
Schoepflin, Urs, 96
Schullman, Andrew, 540
Schur, Edwin M., 175, 190, 190–191
Schwartz, Howard D., 443
Schwartz, Morrie, 304
Scopes, John T., 369
Scott, Alan, 517
Scott, Gregory, 14
Seabrook, Jeremy, 201
Seelye, Katherine Q., 155
Segall, Alexander, 439
Segall, Rebecca, 331
Segerstrale, Ullica, 63
Seibring, M., 177
Seidman, Steven, 283
Sernau, Scott, 217, 399
Seymour, Jane, 263
Shaheen, Jack G., 254
Shakira, 152
Shapiro, Joseph P., 107
Shapiro, Thomas M., 211, 217
Sharma, Hari M., 450
Sharp, Deborah, 516
Shaw, George Bernard, 382
Shcherbak, Yuri M., 497
Sheehy, Gail, 285
Sheen, Charlie, 416
Shenon, Philip, 544
Shepard, Matthew, 387
Shepherd, Jean, 438
Sherman, Jill, 376
Sherman, Lawrence W., 185, 376
Sherrill, Robert, 452, 456
Sherrod, Jessie, 431
Shibutani, Tamotshu, 513
Shields, Rob, 539
Shim, Janet K., 534
Shin, Hyon B., 403
Shinkai, Hiroguki, 192
Short, Kathleen, 212
Shu, Xialing, 421
Shue, Elisabeth, 165
Shupe, Anson D., 38
Siddhartha, Guatama, 354
Sidiropolous, Elizabeth, 531
Sigelman, Lee, 262
Sills, David, 140
Silver, Ira, 109
Silverman, Rachel Emma, 423
Simmel, Georg, 131
Simmons, Ann M., 176, 405
Simmons, Tavia, 340
Simon, Bernard, 476, 477
Simon, Joshua, 410
Simons, Marlise, 219, 243
Sjoberg, Gideon, 462, 464
Slade, Martin D., 316
Small, Macio Luis, 214

Smart, Barry, 119
Smedley, Brian D., 446
Smelser, Neil, 416, 506, 518
Smith, Adam, 416
Smith, Betty L., 446
Smith, David A., 463, 470
Smith, David M., 342
Smith, Denise, 315
Smith, James F., 238
Smith, Kristin, 97
Smith-Lovin, Lynn, 288
Smith, Michael Peter, 467
Smith, Tom, 36, 47, 209, 254, 401
Snell, Tracy L., 187
Snow, David A., 508
Snowdon, David, 445
Snyder, Thomas D., 533
Sobowlewski, Juliana M., 340
Sohoni, Neera Kukreja, 534
Sommers, Christina Hoff, 285
Sorensen, Annemette, 209
Soriano, Cesar G., 156
Sorokin, Pitirim, 217
Sorrell, Gwendolyn T., 307
Spain, Daphne, 339
Spalter-Roth, Roberta M., 25, 26
Spar, Debora L., 526–527
Spencer, Herbert, 528, 529
Spengler, Joseph J., 494
Spielmann, Peter James, 245
Spitzer, Steven, 186
Sprague, Joy, 185, 207
Squires, Gregory D., 467
Staggenborg, Suzanne, 515
Stammer, Larry R., 355
Stanton Cady, Elizibeth, 295
Stark, Rodney, 364–365, 365
Starr, Paul, 440
Stavenhagen, Rodolfo, 239
Steelman, Katerine D., 107
Steffensmeier, Darrell, 187
Stein, Leonard I., 449
Stenning, Derrick J., 304
Stephan, Walter, 73
Stephen, Elizabeth Hervey, 345
Stern, Sharon M., 107
Stevenson, David, 129
Stewman, Shelby, 257
Sting, 403
Stith, Adrienne Y., 446
Stohr, Oskar, 83
Stolberg, Sheryl, 431, 451
Stone, Brad, 424
Stone, Lucy, 382
Stoughton, Stephanie, 431
Strassman, W. Paul, 480
Strauss, Anselm, 104, 105
Strauss, Gary, 218, 293, 406
Stretsky, Paul B., 500
Strom, Stephanie, 235

Suchan, Trudy A., 496f
Suid, Lawrence H., 155
Suitor, J. Jill, 94
Sullivan, Theresa A., 423
Sumner, William Graham, 129, 251
Sutherland, Edwin, 183, 184, 188, 189, 190
Suttles, Gerald, 472
Sutton, F. N., 112
Sutton, Paul D., 266
Swanberg, Jennifer E., 295
Swanson, Stevenson, 537
Swarns, Rachel L., 243
Sweet, Kimberly, 48
Szasz, Thomas, 443, 453

T

Takezawa, Yasuko I., 269
Tannen, Deborah, 288
Taylor, Elizabeth, 152
Telsch, Kathleen, 317
Terry, Sara, 343
Texeira, Erin, 187
Therrien, Melissa, 270, 271
Thomas, Clarence, 396
Thomas, Gordon, 274
Thomas, Jim, 105
Thomas, Pattie, 282
Thomas, William I., 104, 253
Thompson, Ginger, 238, 241, 242
Thomson, Elizabeth, 328
Thorstad, David, 520
Tibbits, Clark, 96, 327
Tierney, John, 487
Tierney, Kathleen, 508
Tillipman, Hava, 315
Tilly, Charles, 517
Timberlake, Michael, 463
Tittle, Charles R., 183, 184
Tolbert, Kathryn, 91
Tonkinson, Robert, 304
Tönnies, Ferdinand, 114–116, 119, 470, 539
Toossi, Mitra, 426
Touraine, Alain, 377
Travolta, John, 152
Treiman, Donald, 209, 234
Trejo, Steven, 271
Trotter, Robert T., III, 447
Trow, Martin, 387
Trudeau, Garry, 35
Truman, Harry S., 205
Tsuchiya, Motori, 380
Tubman, Harriet, 200
Tuchman, Gaye, 16, 287
Tucker, James, 391
Tumin, Melvin M., 206
Tumulty, Karen, 194
Ture, Kwame, 266
Turkel, Studs, 423

Turkle, Sherry, 539
Turner, Bryan S., 69, 119
Turner, J. H., 528
Turner, Ralph, 507, 513
Twain, Mark, 171
Twombly, Jennifer, 479
Tyler, Michael, 271
Tyler, Patrick E., 382
Tyre, Peg, 329

U

Uchitelle, Louis, 429
Ullmann, Edward, 466f, 467
Urbana, Ian, 143
Ursula, Sister Mary, 445

V

Vallas, Steven P., 137
Van den Berghe, Pierre, 62
Van Driel, Barend, 365–366
Van Pelt, Elizabeth Cohen, 437–438, 438, 449
Van Slambrouck, Paul, 110
Van Vucht Tijssen, Leiteke, 119
Vaughan, Dianne, 135
Vaughn, Leigh Ann, 172–173, 537
Veblen, Thorstein, 205, 206, 530
Vega, William A., 333
Velkoff, Victoria, 306, 311
Venkatesh, Sudhir Alladi, 131
Ventura, Stephanie J., 266, 337
Vernon, Glenn, 366t
Victoria, Princess of Sweden, 151
Vidaver, R. M., 447
Villarosa, Linda, 298
Vistica, Gregory, 521
Vitow, Ruth, 306

W

Wachtendorf, Tricia, 510
Wadsworth, Allen P., 73
Wagley, Charles, 250, 305
Waitzkin, Howard, 446
Walder, Andrew, 421
Waldrop, Judith, 107
Walesa, Lech, 417, 514
Walker, Leslie, 431
Wallace, Ruth A., 529
Wallerstein, Immanuel, 229, 230, 232, 238, 292, 534
Wallerstein, Judith, 340

Wallerstein, Michael, 141
Walsh, Mary Williams, 312
Walton, Sam, 476
Walzer, Susan, 294
Warhol, Andy, 344
Watkins, Celeste, 111
Webb, Cynthia L., 424
Weber, Max, 3, 10–11, 12, 13, 43, 47, 127, 133, 134, 135, 136, 204–205, 218, 358, 365, 380, 384, 399, 400, 515
Weeks, John R., 487, 494
Weibel, Peter, 540
Weigard, Bruce, 237
Weinstein, Deena, 159, 534
Weinstein, Henry, 254, 259
Weinstein, Michael A., 159, 534
Welch, Susan, 262
Welchans, Sarah, 328
Wellman, Barry, 539
Wells-Barnett, Ida, 16, 18t, 21, 287
Werum, Regina, 521
Weschsler, Henry J. E., 177
West, Candace, 283, 288
West, Cornel, 323–324
Western, Bruce, 141
White, Jonathan R., 536
Whitehead, Barbara Dafoe, 341
Whorf, Benjamin Lee, 63, 65
Wickman, Peter M., 176
Widgren, Jonas, 7, 274, 494, 495
Wiggins Russell, James, 306
Wilford, John Noble, 116
Willet, Jeffrey G., 107
Williams, Carol W., 330, 337
Williams, Christine L., 294
Williams, David R., 446
Williams, Robin, 68, 378, 446
Williams, Wendy M., 91
Willie, Charles Vert, 333
Willig, Richard, 190
Wilson, Edward O., 63
Wilson, J., 360
Wilson, James R., 154
Wilson, John, 515
Wilson, Jolin J., 328
Wilson, S. Roy, 154
Wilson, Warner, 73
Wilson, William Julius, 132, 214, 217, 262, 332, 474
Winders, Bill, 521
Winerip, Michael, 390, 392
Winfrey, Oprah, 162
Wirth, Louis, 20, 463
Witten, Marsha, 69
Witts, Max Morgan, 274
Wolf, Alison, 529

Wolf, Naomi, 176, 281, 291
Wollstonecraft, Mary, 287
Wonacott, Peter, 137
Wood, Daniel B., 156
Wood, Julia T., 157
Woodard, Colin, 376
Woods, Tiger, 253, 528
Wright, Charles R., 149, 160
Wright, Erik Olin, 185, 207
Wright, Robin, 405
Wurman, Richard Saul, 533
Wuthnow, Robert, 69
Wynia, Matthew K., 452
Wynyard, Robin, 62

X

Xie, Wen, 209, 234, 235

Y

Yamagata, Hisashi, 257
Yan, Yan, 421
Yap, Kioe Sheng, 471
Yax, Laura Y., 315
Yeh, Kuang S., 257
Yeltsin, Boris, 514
Yin, Sandra, 156
Yinger, J. Milton, 365
Young, Alford A., 15
Young, Gay, 239
Yufe, Jack, 83

Z

Zald, Mayer N., 139
Zang, Xiaowei, 421
Zapata, Emiliano, 238
Zapata-Mancilla, Tiffany, 189
Zelizer, Gerald L., 367
Zellner, William M., 42–43, 71, 92
Zellweger, Renee, 39
Zernike, Kate, 516
Zia, Helen, 250, 263, 296
Ziedenberg, Jason, 386
Zimbardo, Philip, 102–103, 104, 107, 108
Zimmerman, Don H., 283, 288
Zittrain, Jonathan, 542
Zola, Irving K., 440
Zurcher, Louis A., Jr., 508
Zvekic, Ugljea, 192
Zweigenhaft, Richard L., 396–397, 406–407

Page numbers followed by *f* refer to figures
Page numbers followed by *t* refer to tables

A

AARP (American Association of Retired People), 315*f*
ABC (American Broadcasting Corporation), 282
Aborigines, Australian, 245
Abortion, 48, 175, 297–299
    France, 514
    global divide, 299*t*
    restrictions on public funding, 501
        by state, 298*f*
    for sex selection, 534
Absolute poverty, 211, 212*t*
    definition, 547
Achieved status, 105–106, 202
    definition, 547
ACT-UP, 520
Activists, social. *See* Social activists
Activity theory, of aging process, 306–308
Adaptive upgrading, and social differentiation, 528–529
Addiction, to TV and Internet, 153
Adolescents, 91
    Amish, 92, 93
    peer groups in, 94–95
    popularity, in high school, 94*t*
    and pregnancy, 9
    and sexual harassment, 94
    suicide rates, 9, 267, 387, 388*f*
    working, 95–96
Adoption, 336–337
    definition, 547
Advertising, 169, 349
    functions of, 152–153
Affirmative action, 259, 425, 431–433
    definition, 547
Afghanistan
    collapse of Soviet Union, 529, 530
    gross national income, per capita, 228
    infant mortality rate, 441*f*
    population, 486*f*
        structure, 491*f*
    rise of Islamic Fundamentalism, 530
    urban population, 465*f*
AFL-CIO, 141, 142
Africa
    AIDS in, 120, 121, 492
    civil conflict, 243
    family planning, 500
    and global economy, 227, 228

    place in global economy, 229*f*
    voluntary associations in, 138
    women in politics, 405
African Americans, 252, 264
    cohabitation, 340
    discrimination, 257, 259, 265, 266–267
        in the medical establishment, 446
    economic position, 211, 266–267
    elderly, 316
    family relationships, 329, 332–333
    and health and illness, 445–446
        health beliefs, 442
    homosexual, 521
    infant mortality rate, 446
    and Internet access, 540–541, 541, 541*f*
    interpretation of media, 160–161
    life expectancy, 446
    in the media, 154–155
    median income, U.S., 432
    middle class, 81, 266–267
    as percentage of workforce, 426*f*
    percentage without health insurance, 444*f*, 455
    and political power, 407
    in poverty, 213, 219, 265, 266, 316
        and living conditions, 499, 500
    relative economic position, 266*t*
    religious practices, 363
    and school voucher programs, 392
    single-parent families, 337
        increase over time, 332*f*
    in slavery, 443
    as social activists, 12, 266
    social mobility of, 217
    social status, 106
        and redefining social reality, 104
    socialization, 86, 91
    as sociologists, 15, 16
    stereotypes, 333
    students, 388
    suburban, 475
    urban, 471
    as voters, 401
    women, 291, 296
African National Congress (ANC), 531
African Queen (film), 152
Age, and health and illness, 447–448
Age, stratification by, 302–321. *See also* Age, and health and illness; Elderly
    college students, over 25, 310
    conflict perspective, 308, 309*t*, 315–316
    developmental stages, 309, 311–314, 311*f*
        death and dying, 313–314
        retirement, 312
    functionalist perspective, 305, 306, 309*t*

    interactionist perspective, 306–308, 309*t*
    in the labor force, 316–317
    worldwide, 306
Ageism, 316
    definition, 547
Agrarian societies, 116, 117–118
    definition, 547
AIDS (acquired autoimmune deficiency syndrome), 20, 46–47, 119–122
    in Africa, 120, 121, 492
    and assisted suicide, 319
    incidence, U.S., 444
    medical care for, 121–122
    modes of transmission, 120
    people living with, worldwide, 120*f*
    and social activism, 520
    and social stigma, 121, 443
    worldwide, 492
Ainu people, 245
Air pollution, 497
Airline bailout, after September 11, 220
Al Jazeera news network, 163
Al Qaeda, 163
Alabama
    abortion funding, 298*f*
    elderly population, projected, 315*f*
    high school exit exam requirements, 389*f*
Alaska
    abortion funding, 298*f*
    availability of physicians, 447*f*
    elderly population, projected, 315*f*
    Prince William Sound, 497
Albania, gross national income, per capita, 228
Albanians, as victims of ethnic cleansing, 243
Alcohol use, 447
Alcohol use, in the media, 150
Alcoholism, 176
Algeria
    gross national income, per capita, 228
    and Human Rights Index, 244*t*
    urban population, 465*f*
Alienation, 133
    definition, 423, 547
    and work, 422–423
Alta Vista, 154
Alternative medicine, 450, 451
Alternatives to Marriage Project, 342
Alzheimer's Association, 448
Alzheimer's disease, 447–448
Amalgamation
    definition, 547
America Online, 543
American Academy of Pediatrics, 95, 152, 174
American apartheid, 473

American Association of Aardvark Aficionados, 138

American Association of University Women, 93–94

American Beauty (film), 475

American Civil Liberties Union (ACLU), 254, 407, 410, 543

American Cultures Center, UC Berkeley, 537

American Federation of Teachers, 385

American Indian College Fund, 248

American Institute of Graphic Arts, 395

American Jewish Committee, 273

American Jewish Congress, 138

American Library Association, 543

American Medical Association, 449, 456, 530
   Council on Ethical and Judicial Affairs, 318

American Psychiatric Association, 443

American Society of Newspaper Editors, 543

American Sociological Association, 21, 43, 529, 537
   Code of Ethics, 41–42, 47
   website, 53

American Sociological Society, 12

Amish community, 91, 92

Amnesty International, 244, 245, 519

Amway Corporation, 137

Analysis of data, 33
   content, 40
   secondary, 39–40

Angelo State University, 379

Angola
   gross national income, per capita, 228
   population, 486*f*

Animal rights, 504

Animism, tribal, 352*f*

Anomie, 10, 182, 422
   definition, 547

Anomie theory of deviance, 182–183, 547
   models of individual adaptation, 183*t*

Anthrax, 536

Anthropology, study of, 6

Anti-Defamation League (ADL), 272

Anti-Semitism, 272
   definition, 547

Anticipatory socialization
   definition, 547

Antigua and Barbuda
   and Human Rights Index, 244*t*

AOL Time Warner, 161

Apartheid, 263, 495. *See also* Segregation, racial
   abolishment, 531
   American, 473
   definition, 547

Apollo 13 (film), 155

Appearance, physical, and gender, 176, 180

Applied sociology, 18, 19, 20
   definition, 547

Arab countries, 163

Arab cultures, 109

Arabs, Arab Americans, 540. *See also* Islam; Muslims
   treatment, after September 11, 175, 243, 254

Arapesh people, 286

Argentina
   gross national income, per capita, 228
   population, 486*f*
   urban population, 465*f*
   women in the legislature, 404*f*

Argot, 69, 70
   definition, 547

Aristotle, 7

Arizona
   abortion funding, 298*f*
   availability of physicians, 447*f*
   elderly population, projected, 315*f*
   high school exit exam requirements, 389*f*

Arkansas
   abortion funding, 298*f*
   availability of physicians, 447*f*
   elderly population, projected, 315*f*
   high school exit exam requirements, 389*f*

Arranged marriage, 330, 331

Arunta (Australian tribe), 10

Ascribed status, 105–106, 132, 202
   definition, 547

Asea Brown Boveri company, 414

Asian Americans, 249–250, 252, 268–270, 540
   Chinese, 249–250, 268–269
   cohabitation, 340
   family relationships, 333
   homosexual, 521
   and Internet access, 541, 541*f*
   Japanese, 269
   Korean, 269–270
   as percentage of workforce, 426*f*
   percentage without health insurance, 444*f*, 455
   relative economic position, 266*t*
   single-parent families, increase over time, 332*f*
   suburban, 475
   Vietnamese, 268

Assemblies, periodic vs. nonperiodic, 509

Assembling perspective, 509
   definition, 547
   on social movements, 517*t*
   and the Internet, 519

Asset-Based Community Development (ABCD), 473–474
   definition, 547

Asset-Based Community Development Institute, 474

Assimilation, 263
   definition, 547

Associated Press, 500

Association of American Medical Colleges, 449

Atlantic Monthly (magazine), 52

Attention Deficit Disorder (ADD), 390

Audience, of mass media, 159–161
   behavior, 160–161

opinion leader, 160
   segmented, 160

Augusta National Golf Club, 528

Austin Powers: The Spy Who Shagged Me (film), 153

Australia
   Aborigines, 245
   as host country for U.S. students, 377*t*
   gross national income, per capita, 228
   percentage of people ever married, ages 20-24, 330*f*
   population, 486*f*
   urban population, 465*f*

Austria
   gross national income, per capita, 228
   percentage of college graduates, 376*f*

Authority
   definition, 547
   obedience to, 173–174
   types of, 399–400

"Autocide", 42–43

Autonomous settlements, 471

Aviation and Transportation Security Act, 259

B

Baath Socialist Party, 94

Baby boom, 493–494

Bachelor, The (TV show), 154

Bahamas, 488

Bahrain, 163

Bali, cockfights in, 6

Bangladesh
   Dhaka, 466*t*
   gross national income, per capita, 228
   income distribution, 233*f*
   population, 486*f*
   urban population, 465*f*

Barbie doll, 61

Basic sociology, 20
   definition, 547

Battle of Seattle, 504

BBC (British Broadcasting Company), 162, 542

Beauty myth, 176
   and social stigma, 180

Bedouin people, 245

Beijing, China, 466*t*

Belarus, gross national income, per capita, 228

Belgium
   gross national income, per capita, 228 (map), 229
   population, 486*f*
   same-sex partnership in, 342

Belize, 498
   urban population, 465*f*

Bell v. Maryland, 272

Benin, urban population of, 465*f*

Berkeley Wellness Letter, 336

Beverly Hills 90210 (TV show), 159

Bharatiya Janata Party (BJP), 368

Bhutan, 162
    urban population, 465*f*
Bible, The, 171, 360
Bilateral descent, 326
    definition, 547
Bilingualism, 74–76
    definition, 547
Bill of Rights, 400
Biology, and social behavior, 62–63
    theories of deviance, 181
Biotechnology, 534
Bioterrorism, 536
Bipartisan Campaign Reform Act (BCRA),
    409, 410
Biracial people, 253
Birth control, 297, 487, 488. *See also* Abortion
    policy, in China, 492, 493
    worldwide, 500–501
Birthrate, definition, 489, 547
Bisexuals, teen, 388*f*
Black nationalism, 296
Black power, 15
    definition, 547
Black separatist hate groups, 256
Bolivia
    homosexuals in, 522
    place in global economy, 229*f*
Bombay, India, 466*t*
Borderlands, between U.S. and Mexico,
    240–241, 241*f*
    definition, 547
Bosnia, 243, 490
Bosnia-Herzegovina, 243
Botswana
    AIDS in, 492
    and the disabled, 107
    gross national income, per capita, 228
    urban population, 465*f*
Bourgeoisie, 203
    definition, 547
Bowling for Columbine (film), 192, 193
Brady Campaign 2003, 193
Brain drain, 441
    definition, 547
Brandeis University, 516
Brazil
    affirmative action in, 433
    average pay of CEO, 204*t*
    environmental issues, 499
    gross national income, per capita, 228
    homosexuals in, 522
    human rights abuses, 245
    income distribution, 233*f*
    population, 486*f*
    Sao Paulo, 466*t*
    urban population, 465*f*
Britain
    average pay of CEO, 204*t*
    labor unions in, 141
    media in, 156
    social welfare policies, 210
British Airways, 417

British Broadcasting Company (BBC), 103,
    162
British Elastic Rope Sports Association, 138
Brown v. Board of Education, 266
Brunei
    urban population, 465*f*
Buddhism, 354, 354*t*
    in India, 367
    world wide, 352*f*
Buenos Aires, 466*t*
Bulgaria
    gross national income, per capita, 228
Bullying, 94
Burakumin, 235
Bureau of Indian Affairs, 267
Bureau of the Census, 142–143, 216, 238, 257,
    267, 273, 284, 293, 331, 337, 341, 342, 359,
    475
Bureaucracy, 132, 133–143
    characteristics of, 133–135, 134*t*
    definition, 133, 547
    in educational system, 384–385
    and organizational culture, 136–143
Bureaucracy's other face, 136
Bureaucratization, process of, 135
    definition, 548
Burkina Faso
    population, 486*f*
    urban population, 465*f*
Burundi
    gross national income, per capita, 228
Bush, George W., 121

C

Cable channels, 161
California
    abortion funding, 298*f*
    availability of physicians, 447*f*
    borderlands, between U.S. and Mexico,
        240–241, 241*f*
    cloning in, 535
    elderly population, projected, 315*f*
    high school exit exam requirements, 389*f*
    Riverside, 476
California Civil Rights Initiative, 432
Calvinism, 358
Cambodia
    urban population, 486*f*
Cambridge University, 487
Cameroon
    gross national income, per capita, 228
    population, 486*f*
    urban population, 465*f*
Canada, 75–76
    average pay of CEO, 204*t*
    college students, in U. S., 377*t*
    gross national income, per capita, 228
    health care expenditures, 455, 456*f*
    income distribution, 233*f*
    infant mortality rate, 441*f*
    life expectancy, 489*f*

    percentage of college graduates, 376*f*
    percentage of people ever married, ages
        20-24, 330*f*
    percentage of U.S. immigrants from, 275*f*
    place in global economy, 229*f*
    population, 486*f*
    same-sex partnership in, 342
    welfare system, and healthcare, 219
Capital punishment, 174
Capitalism, 203, 415–417
    in China, 418, 419–421
    definition, 548
Casinos, Native American, 267
Caste, definition, 548
Caste system, 200, 201, 518
Cato Institute, 410
Causal logic, 32–33, 32*f*
    definition, 548
Celebrities, web searches for, 151*t*
Censorship, 165
    Internet, 159
Census, definition, 488, 548
Center for Academic Integrity, 70
Center for American Women and Politics, 401
Center for Public Integrity, 543, 544
Centers for Disease Control and Prevention
    (CDC), 345, 444
Central Americans
    women, 296
Chad
    place in global economy, 229*f*
Challenger space shuttle, 135
Charismatic authority, 399–400, 515
    definition, 548
Chat rooms, chatting, 159
Cheating, in college, 70
Chernobyl nuclear power plant, 497
Chicago Bulls, 159
Chicago Coalition for the Homeless, 44
Chicago Tribune, 477
Chief executive officer (CEO) average pay, by
    country, 204*t*
Child abuse, 328
Child-rearing patterns, 333, 336–338
Childcare, 96–98
Childless couples, 343
Children
    impact of divorce, 339, 340
    and media exposure, 152, 165–166
Chile
    adoptees, U.S., 336*t*
    gross national income, per capita, 228
    population, 486*f*
    urban population, 465*f*
China
    adoptees, U.S., 336*t*
    Amway in, 137
    Beijing, 466*t*
    bilingualism in, 75
    college students, in U.S., 377*t*
    economic system of, 417–418
        capitalism in, 418, 419–421
    education in

China—*Cont.*
　　and women, 382
　　health care expenditures, 456*f*
　　homosexuals in, 522
　　and Human Rights Index, 244*t*
　　infant mortality rate, 441*f*
　　Internet access in, 154
　　involuntary sterilization, 107
　　media in, 161
　　megalopolis, 464
　　occupational prestige, 234, 235
　　place in global economy, 229
　　political system, 400
　　population, 486*f*, 492
　　　　policies, 492, 493
　　　　urban, 465*f*
　　sexual behavior in, 48–49
　　Shanghai, 466*t*
　　State Education Commission, 382
　　sweatshops in, 226
　　women in the legislature, 404*f*
Chinese Americans, 249–250, 268–269, 268*t*
Chinese complex of religions, world wide, 352*f*
Chinese Exclusion Act, 268
Christian Science Church, 365
Christianity, 353, 354*t*
　　creationists, 360
　　denominations of, 363, 364
　　pentecostal, 361
CIA (Central Intelligence Agency), 133, 134
Cigarette smoking, 175, 447
　　in the media, 39
Cities, types of, 464*t*
Citigroup, gross domestic product, 231*t*
City of Angels (TV show), 157
Civil conflicts, 243
Civil Liberties Act, 269
Civil rights, 258–259
　　after September 11, 2001, 175, 243
Civil Rights Act, 1964, 259
Civil Rights Commission, 258–259, 292, 292–294, 431
Civil rights model, of disability, 107
Class consciousness, 203
　　definition, 548
Class, social, 2–3, 81
　　and the family, 331–332
　　and health and illness, 444–445
　　impact in old age, 308
　　and interpretation of media, 160–161
　　measuring, 208–216
　　　　objective method, 208–209
Class system, of stratification, 201–203
　　definition, 548
　　Marxist view, 203, 204
Classical theory, definition, 548
Classical theory, of formal organizations, 136
Clinical sociology, 20
　　definition, 548
Cliques, 386–387
Clonaid, 525
Cloning, 344, 535

Closed system, 548
　　definition, 548
CNN cable station, 161
Coalition, definition, 548
Coalitions, within groups, 131–132
Coca-Cola company, 233
Code of Ethics, American Sociological Association, 41–42, 47
Code of Ethics, definition, 548
Cognitive theory of development, 88
　　definition, 548
Cohabitation, 340–341
　　definition, 548
　　unmarried-couple households, by state, 341*f*
Colgate University, 451
Collective behavior
　　assembling perspective, 508–509
　　and communications technology, 518–519
　　definition, 548
　　forms of, 509–513
　　theories of, 505–509
　　value-added perspective, 507–508
College curriculum, United States, 376–377
College students
　　adult, 310
　　and cheating, 70
　　drinking behavior by GPA, 41
　　foreign, in U.S., 377*t*
　　life goals of, 68–69
　　subcultures, 387–388
　　U.S., abroad, 377*t*
Colombia
　　adoptees, U.S., 336*t*
　　gross national income, per capita, 228
　　population, 486*f*
　　urban population, 465*f*
Colonialism, 229–230
　　definition, 548
Colorado
　　abortion funding, 298*f*
　　availability of physicians, 447*f*
　　elderly population, projected, 315*f*
　　high school exit exam requirements, 389*f*
Columbia space shuttle, 135, 150, 536, 537
Columbine High School, 129, 192, 386
Commission on Civil Rights, 258–259, 292, 292–294, 431
Common Cause, 410
Common sense, and sociology, 7
Communication
　　electronic, 140–141
　　gender differences, 289
　　nonverbal, 16–17, 141
Communication Decency Act, 543
Communism, 400, 417–418
　　definition, 548
Communist countries, 417
　　former, 243
　　　　welfare system, 220
　　media in, 161
Communist Manifesto (Marx), 11, 133
Communist Party, 204, 418

Communities, 459–482
　　early, 461–462
　　industrial, 462–463
　　postindustrial, 463–464
　　preindustrial, 462–463
　　rural, 475, 476–477
Community, definition, 461, 548
Community Mental Health Centers Act (CMHC), 454
Computer-mediated communication (CMC), 519
Computers
　　and crime, 540
　　in the workplace, 140–141
　　　　and telecommuting, 533–534
Computers, in social research, 44, 45–46
Concentric zone theory, of urban growth, 466–467, 466*f*
　　definition, 548
Confidentiality, of research subjects, 43
Conflict perspective, 14–16
　　on affirmative action, 431–432
　　African American view, 15
　　on AIDS, 121
　　on bureaurcracies, 135–136
　　on campaign financing, 410
　　on childcare, 97
　　on communities, 467, 470
　　definition, 548
　　on deviance, 186, 188
　　on education
　　　　bureaucratization of, 386
　　on the environment, 499
　　on the family, 326–327, 327, 328, 329*t*
　　feminist view, 15–16
　　on global economy, 231–232
　　on labor unions, 143
　　Marxist view, 14–15
　　on mass media, 153–157
　　on postindustrial society, 118–119
　　on prejudice and discrimination, 260–261
　　on religion, 359–360
　　on social change, 529–530
　　on social institutions, 113–114
　　on socialization, 93–94
　　on stratification, 205, 207, 208, 208*t*
　　on urbanization, 470*t*
　　on voluntarism, 138
　　on welfare system, 219–220
Conformity, 171–173
　　definition, 172, 548
　　to prejudice, 172–173
Congo
　　gross national income, per capita, 228
　　rites of passage, 88
　　urban population, 465*f*
Connecticut
　　abortion funding, 298*f*
　　availability of physicians, 447*f*
　　elderly population, projected, 315*f*
　　high school exit exam requirements, 389*f*
Conspicuous consumption, 205, 206
Conspicuous leisure, 205, 206

Constitution, United States, 369, 370, 488
Consumer Federation of America, 541
Consumerism, 485
Contact hypothesis, 262
    definition, 548
Content analysis, 39, 40
    definition, 548
Control group, 548
    vs. experimental group, 39
Control theory, 176, 548
Control variable, 34, 548
Conversation, The (film), 543
Copyrights, violation of, 180–181
Core nations, vs. periphery, 229–230, 467
    and Internet access, 534, 541
Cornell University, 70, 94
Corporal punishment, 174
Corporate-conservative coalition, 407
Corporate crime, 190
Corporate mergers, 161
Corporate welfare, 220, 548
Corporations, multinational, 230–232, 425
Correctional system
    Finland, 172
    Singapore, 174
    United States, 174
Correlation, 32, 548
Correspondence principle, 381, 548
Cosby Show, The, 323
Cosmopolitan magazine, 155
Costa Rica
    gross national income, per capita, 228
    population, 486*f*
    urban population, 465*f*
Costco stores, 476
Cote d'Ivoire
    gross national income, per capita, 228
    population, 486*f*
    urban population, 465*f*
Countercultures, 71, 72
    definition, 548
Courtship, online, 330
Cram schools, Japanese, 381
Craze, definition, 548
Crazes, as collective behavior, 512
Creationism, 360, 369, 370, 548
Credentialism, 380, 548
Crime, 188, 189–192
    computer, 540
    definition, 188, 549
    and gender, 188
    organized, 188, 189
    professional, 188
    statistics, 191–192
    victimization rates, 191*t*
        and poverty, 215–216
    victimless, 186, 190–191
    white-collar, 189–190, 540
Crimes, war, 243
Criminal justice system
    and the poor, 216
    racism in, 7, 186–187
"Critical Mass" demonstrations, 504

Croatia, gross national income, per capita,
    228
Croatians, as victims of ethnic cleansing, 243
Crosstabulation, 51, 549
Crouching Tiger, Hidden Dragon (film), 71
Crowd, definition, 509, 549
Crowds, behavior of, 505–506, 509–510
Cuba
    economic system of, 417–418
    media in, 161
    percentage of U.S. immigrants from, 275*f*
    political system, 400
    population, 486*f*
    women in the legislature, 404*f*
Cuban Americans, 270*f*, 271–272
Cults, 365, 549
Cultural domination, 61–62, 69
    and defining social reality, 103, 104
    and language, 74, 75, 76
    and the media, 156
Cultural relativism, 73
    definition, 549
    and human rights, 243–244
Cultural transmission school, and theory of
    deviance, 183–184
Cultural universals, 59, 549
Cultural variation, 69–70
Culture, 56–78
    and countercultures, 71, 72
    and cultural relativism, 73
    and culture shock, 72
    definition, 58, 549
    diffusion of, 60–62
    and the dominant ideology, 69
    East Indian, 57–58
    elements of, 63, 65–68
        language, 63, 64
        nonverbal communication, 64–65
        norms, 66–67
        sanctions, 67
        values, 67–69
    ethnocentrism, 72–73
    and health, 438–439
    and innovation, 60
    material vs. nonmaterial, 62, 532
    organizational, 136–143
    transmission of, 59, 127, 128
    and variation, 69, 70
    xenocentrism, 73
Culture-bound syndrome, 438, 549
Culture lag, 62, 532, 549
Culture shock, 72, 549
Cupping, 439
Curandera, 446
Curanderismo, 447, 549
CVS (Consumer Value Stores), 451
Cyberactivism, 408
Czechoslovakia, 418
    gross national income, per capita, 228

D

DaimlerChrysler, gross domestic product,
    231*t*
Dalit (untouchables), 200, 518
Data
    analysis, 33
    existing sources of, 40*t*
Data collection methods, 33
    experiments, 38–39
    library resources, 52–53
    observation, 37–38
    participant observation, 2–3
    surveys, 35, 36–37
        Internet, 45–46
    use of secondary sources, 39–40
Dawson's Creek (TV show), 324
Days Inns of America, 317
De Paul University, 18, 19, 20
Death and dying, as developmental stages,
    313–314
Death penalty, 7
    in United States, and race, 187
Death rate, 549
Death rate, definition, 489
Death with Dignity Act, 319
Deaths, heat related, 307
Declaration of Independence, 292, 396
Def Jam (recording label), 526
Defended neighborhoods, 471, 549
Defense Intelligence Agency, 134
Degradation ceremony, 91, 549
Deindustrialization, 426–427, 428
    definition, 426, 549
Deinstitutionalization, of the mentally ill,
    215, 454
Delaware
    abortion funding, 298*f*
    availability of physicians, 447*f*
    elderly population, projected, 315*f*
    high school exit exam requirements, 389*f*
Delhi, India, 466*t*
Democratic Party, 138, 404
Demographic transition, 490–491, 490*f*
    definition, 549
Demography, 485–491, 549
    definition, 485
    elements of, 488–489
Denmark
    gross national income, per capita, 228
    and Human Rights Index, 244*t*
    population, 486*f*
    same-sex partnership in, 342
    suicide rate, 8
    urban population, 465*f*
Denomination, definition, 549
Department of Defense, 534
Department of Education, 386
Department of Health and Human Services,
    220, 444
Department of Homeland Security, 143
Department of Justice, 188, 416, 540
Department of Labor, 257, 267, 294

DePauw University, 428
Dependency theory, 230, 549
Dependent variable, 32, 549
Descent, familial, 325–326
Desensitization, through media exposure, 165
Developing nations
    exploitation, 224–227, 230
    homelessness, 480
    modernization, 232–233
    population, 491–492
        control policies, 501
Deviance, 169–196
    definition, 176
    explaining, 181–188
        anomie theory, 182–183
        biological theories, 181
        conflict perspective, 186, 188
        feminist perspective, 186, 188
        functionalist perspective, 181–183
        interactionist perspective, 183–185
        labeling theory, 185
        routine activities theory, 184–185
        social constructionist perspective,
            185–186
        societal-reaction approach, 185
    and social stigma, 176, 180–181
    and technology, 180–181
Dhaka, Bangladesh, 466t
Dharma and Greg (TV show), 156
Die Another Day (film), 155
Differential association, 183, 549
Differentiation, social, 528
Diffusion, cultural, 60, 60–62, 549
Digital divide, and Internet access, 216,
    540–541
Directors Guild of America, 155
Disabled individuals, 212
    and access to public space, 21
    and euthanasia, 319
    and Internet access, 159
    in the media, 154–155
        as victims, 165
    status, 107, 202
        and redefining social reality, 104
Disaster, definition, 549
Disaster Research Center, 510
Disasters, and collective behavior, 7, 8,
    510–511
Discovery, 60
Discovery, definition, 549
Discrimination
    conflict perspective, 260–261
    definition, 257, 549
    and the disabled, 107
    against the elderly, 316
    and euthanasia, 319
    functionalist perspective, 259–260
    gender, 493
    against homosexuals, 520
    institutional, 258–259
    in the medical establishment, 446
    and the mentally ill, 452–453
    and people with AIDS, 443
    racial, 12, 257

Disengagement theory, of aging process,
    307–308, 549
Division of labor, 133
Division of Labor (Durkheim), 115
Divorce, 6, 338–339
Diwaniyas, 109
Djibouti
    urban population, 465f
DNA testing, 322, 540
Do the Right Thing (film), 269
Doctors, and health care system, 449–450
Dolly, the cloned sheep, 535
Domestic partnership
    definition, 549
Domestic partnership, homosexual, 342–343
Domestic violence, 288, 328
    in India, 368
Dominance
    cultural. *See* Cultural domination; Global-
        ization
    male, 66, 287–288, 326
        in religion, 359
Dominant group, privileges of, 257–258, 259
Dominant ideology, 69
    definition, 549
    in the media, 154–155, 156, 157
Domination of world markets, 227–234
Dominican Republic
    AIDS in, 492
    gross national income, per capita, 228
    percentage of U. S. immigrants from, 275f
    place in global economy, 229f
    population, 486f
    urban population, 465f
Dons, in caste system, 200
"Don't ask, don't tell" policy, in the military,
    521
Double jeopardy, of minority women, 296
Downsizing, corporate, 427, 549
Dowry, marriage, 368
Dramaturgical approach, 17, 86, 398
DRGs (diagnostic related groups), 452
Drug abuse, 190–191
Drug use
    intravenous, 121
    in the media, 150–151
    ritual, 361
Drunk driving, 190–191
Duke University, 70
Durkheim, Emile, 20, 39
Dyad, as social group, 131, 549
Dysfunction, social, 14, 549

E

E-commerce, 430–431, 549
E. T.: The Extra-Terrestrial (film), 152
East Indians, in United States, 57–58
Eastern Europe, 243
Eating contests, 197
Eating disorders, 281, 282
Ebay, 154
Ecclesia, definition, 549

Ecclesiae, 362, 363
Economic systems
    definition, 415, 549
    the industrial society, 415
        capitalist, 415–417
        socialist, 417–418
    informal economies, 418
Economics, study of, 6
Economist, The, 368, 433, 522
Economy
    global, 18, 19, 20
    informal, 237
Ecuador
    gross national income, per capita, 228
    urban population, 465f
Edge cities, 467
Education, 373–394
    bilingual/bicultural, 74, 75, 76
    contemporary, trends in, 388–390
        homeschooling, 389–390, 390
        school choice programs, 391, 391–392
        school voucher programs, 390
    definition, 549
    and economic inequality, 373–374
    and gender, 381, 383
    impact on social mobility, 217
    and race, 381
    and schools, as formal organizations,
        384–388
            bureaucratization of, 384–385
            student subcultures, 385, 386–388
            teachers as employees, 385
    and testing, 389, 389f
    theoretical perspectives
        conflict, 379–382
        functionalist, 375–378, 385
        interactionist, 382, 383
Education Act of 1972, 382
Education Commission of the States, 389
Education Week, 385
Educational level, by income, 31, 34t, 35f
Egalitarian family, 326
Egypt
    gross national income, per capita, 228
    and Human Rights Index, 244t
    megalopolis, 464
    percentage of people ever married,
        ages 20-24, 330f
    place in global economy, 229f
    population, 486f
    urban population, 465f
Eighteenth Amendment (prohibition),
    175–176
El Salvador
    gross national income, per capita, 228
    percentage of U. S. immigrants from, 275f
    population, 486f
    urban population, 465f
Elderhostel, 139
Elderly, 139, 302–321. *See also* Aging process
    cohabitation, 341
    and euthanasia, 319
    in Japan, 306

Elderly—*Cont.*
in the media, 154–155
old-old, 314
population, U.S., 314–315
actual and projected, 315*f*
in poverty, 315–316, 317–318
as social activists, 317
status, and redefining social reality, 106
in the workforce, 316–317
Elections, political, 401–402, 403
Electric shock experiment, of Milgram, 173–174
Elementary and Secondary Education Act (ESEA), 76
Elite model, of power relations, 405–407
definition, 549–550
of Domhoff, 406–407, 406*f*
Marxian, 405
of Mills, 405–406, 406*f*
Email, 110–112, 140–141
Emergency Management Center, New York City, 510–511
Emergent-norm perspective, of collective behavior, 505–506
definition, 550
and panics and crazes, 512
Employment, and status, 198
Endogamy, 330, 331
definition, 550
England. *See* Great Britian; United Kingdom
suicide rate, 8
Engle v. Vitale, 369
Environment
conflict perspective, 499
functionalist perspective, 498–499
Environment, and population, 483–503, 496–500
Environmental justice, 20, 499–500
definition, 550
Environmental Protection Agency (EPA), 499–500
Environmental sociology, 20
Epidemiology, social, 443–444
Equal Employment Opportunity Commission, 316
Equatorial Guinea
urban population, 465*f*
Equilibrium model, of social change, 528, 550
ER (TV show), 151
Eritrea
urban population, 465*f*
Essays on the Principle of Population (Malthus), 487
Established sects, 365, 550
Estate system, of stratification, 200, 201
definition, 550
Esteem, 209, 550
Estonia
gross national income, per capita, 228
Ethiopia
gross national income, per capita, 228
population, 486*f*
urban population of, 465*f*

Ethnic cleansing, 243
Ethnic group, definition, 250
Ethnicity, 253–254
and health and illness, 445–446
and median income, U.S., 432*f*
symbolic, 273
Ethnocentrism, 72–73, 255
definition, 550
Ethnography, definition, 550
Europe
cohabitation, 340
labor unions in, 143
population, 494
same-sex partnership in, 342
European Union agreement, 276
Euthanasia, 318–319, 550
Evacuation camps, for Japanese Americans, 269
Evolution, sociocultural, 116
Evolutionary theory, 369, 370
definition, 550
of social change, 527–528
Exogamy, 330, 550
Experiment, definition, 550
Experiment, The (TV show), 103
Experimental group
definition, 550
vs. control group, 39
Experimental research designs, 38–39
Exploitation theory, 260–261
definition, 550
Expressiveness, definition, 550
Extended family, 323–324, 324–325
Extreme Makeover (TV show), 282
Exxon Valdez, 497
ExxonMobil Corporation
discrimination against gays, 520
gross domestic product, 231*t*
"Eye work" study, 28–29

F

Face-work, and presentation of the self, 86, 550
Fads, 511–512, 550
Fair Labor Association, 226
False consciousness, 550
of women, 295
of the working class, 203, 515
Falun Gong, 408
Familism, 333, 550
Family, 322–343
as agent of socialization, 171
authority patterns, 326
childrearing, 333
adoption, 336–337
single-parent, 323–324, 332*f*, 337–338
stepfamilies, 338
composition, 324–325, 325*f*
definition, 324, 550
and divorce, 338–339
dual income, 337

egalitarian, 326
extended, 323–324, 324–325
kinship patterns, 325–326
life, 4–5
variations, by race or ethnicity, 332–333
variations, by social class, 331–332
and marriage, 329–331
alternatives to, 339, 340–343
without children, 343
nuclear, 324
theoretical perspectives
conflict, 327
feminist, 328–329
functionalist, 327
interactionist, 328
violence, 164–165
Family Ties (TV show), 324
Fashion, definition, 550
Fashions, 511–512
Fathers, as single parents, 323–324, 337–338
"Fattening room" , in Nigeria, 176
FBI (Federal Bureau of Investigation), 133, 134, 175
FCC (Federal Communications Commission), 161
Federal Bureau of Narcotics, 186
Federal Campaign Act of 1974, 409
Federal Communications Commission (FCC), 161
Federal Reserve, 210
Board of Governors, 269, 397
Feminine Mystique, The, 295
Feminism, 294–295, 515
in India, 518
Feminist perspective
on beauty standards, 180
on childcare, 98
on deviance, 186, 188
on the family, 327, 328, 329*t*
on mass media, 157–158
and pornography, 158
and violence, 165
on occupational prestige, 209–210
on postmodern society, 119
on stratification by gender, 287–288
on voluntarism, 138
Feminist theory, 15–16
Feminists, 43–44
Muslim, 290
Feminization of poverty, 212–213, 291
Fertility, definition, 485, 550
Feudalism, 200, 201
Film critics, 160
Finland
correctional system in, 172
and Human Rights Index, 244*t*
percentage of people ever married, ages 20-24, 330*f*
population, 486*f*
urban population, 465*f*
Firefighters, in labor unions, 143
First Amendment, 369, 543

Florida
 abortion funding, 298*f*
 availability of physicians, 447*f*
 elderly population, projected, 315*f*
 high school exit exam requirements, 389*f*
Focus groups, 130, 550
Folkways, 66, 550
Football, college, 6
Forbes magazine, 238
Force, as source of power, 399
Ford Motor Company, 153, 231*t*
Foreign citizens, as victims of media violence, 165
Formal norms, 66, 171, 172
 definition, 550
Formal organizations, 132–146
 definition, 132, 550
Formal social control, 174–176
 definition, 550
Fortune 1,000 corporations, 293
Fortune 500 corporations, 316
 and gay employees, 520
Fortune magazine, 257
Foundation for Infantile Paralysis, 139–140
Fox network, 161
France
 abortion, 514
 average pay of CEO, 204*t*
 gross national income, per capita, 228
 as host country for U.S. students, 377*t*
 income inequality in, 206–207
 life expectancy, 489*f*
 place in global economy, 229*f*
 population, 486*f*
 same-sex partnership in, 342
 single mothers, 340
 suicide rate, 8
 urban population, 465*f*
Franchising businesses, 126
Frankenfood, 535–536
Frasier (TV show), 160
Free enterprise system, 416
French Guiana
 urban population, 465*f*
French Revolution, 9
Friends Assisting Victims of Terror (FAVOR), 474
Friends (TV show), 155
Functionalist perspective, 13–14
 on AIDS, 121
 on campaign financing, 410
 on communities, 464, 466–467, 467
 on death and dying, 313
 definition, 550
 on education, 385
 on the environment, 498–499
 on the family, 327, 329*t*
 on global economy, 231
  modernization theory, 233–234
 and health beliefs, 437–438
 on health care system, 449, 449–450
 on informal economies, 418
 on labor unions, 143

on mass media, 149–153
on postindustrial society, 118
on poverty, 214–215
on prejudice and discrimination, 259–260
on social change, 528–529
on social control, 172
on social deviance, 181–183
on social institutions, 112–113
on socialization, 93
on stratification, 206–207, 208*t*
on stratification by gender, 286
on urbanization, 470*t*
Functions, social, manifest vs. latent, 14
Funding, for research, 47–48

G

G. I. Jane (film), 155
Gabon
 urban population, 465*f*
Galapagos Islands
 urban population, 465*f*
Galaxy IV communications satellite, 537
Gallaudet University, 509
Gambia
 gross national income, per capita, 228
 urban population, 465*f*
Gambling, 190–191
 compulsive, 176
Game stage, of socialization, 85
Gangs, and graffiti, 170–171
Gap clothing, 232
Gatekeeping
 definition, 550
 media, 153–154
Gattaca (film), 344
Gay Lesbian and Straight Education Network, 387
Gay-Straight Alliances (GSAs), 387, 388
Gays, 121, 283. *See* Homosexuality; Homosexuals
 and domestic partnership, 342–343
 in high school, 386–387
 human rights, 245
 in the media, 520–521
 as parents, 337
 and religion, 355
 and social stigma, 519
Gemeinschaft, 115–116, 138, 470
 comparison with gesellschaft, 117*t*
 and cyberspace, 539
 and telecommuting, 140
Gemeinschaft
 definition, 550
Gender
 and access to public space, 21
 and deviance, 186, 188
 discrimination, 257, 292–296, 449
 and education, 381, 382
 and health and illness, 447
 and infanticide, 493
 and Internet use, 158

and interpretation of media, 160–161
and median income, U.S., 432*f*
and networking, 110
and occupational prestige, 209–210
 in China, 235
and political preferences, 404
as social construction, 282–286
and social mobility, 217–218
and social movements, 516–517
and socialization, 91, 92, 94–95, 132–133
stereotypes, 157–158, 165
and stratification, 280–301
and suicide, 493
and voluntary associations, 138
and weight issues, 176
Gender differences
 and communication, 289
 and nature vs. nurture, 285–286
 in retirement, 312–313
Gender norms, experiment in violation of, 283–284
Gender quotas, in politics, 405
Gender roles, 92–93, 282–285
 definition, 550
General Accounting Office, 293, 392
General Electric, 138
General Motors, 231*t*, 420, 427
General Social Survey (GSS), 33, 50
Generalized other, 85–86, 551
Genetic engineering, 344, 345, 534–535
Genetically modified food, 535–536
Genetics, 62–63
Genital mutilation, female, 244
Genocide, 243, 262–263
 definition, 551
Gentrification, 478–479, 551
Geopolitical theory, 530
Georgia
 abortion funding, 298*f*
 availability of physicians, 447*f*
 elderly population, projected, 315*f*
 high school exit exam requirements, 389*f*
German Americans, 269, 273
Germany
 average pay of CEO, 204*t*
 gross national income, per capita, 228
 as host country for U. S. students, 377*t*
 megalopolis, 464
 percentage of college graduates, 376*f*
 place in global economy, 229
 population, 486*f*
 same-sex partnership in, 342
 social welfare policies, 210
 urban population, 465*f*
Gerontology, 305
 definition, 551
Gesellschaft, 115–116, 138, 470
 comparison with gemeinschaft, 117*t*
 and cyberspace, 539
 and telecommuting, 140
Gesellschaft
 definition, 551

Ghana
    funerals in, 314
    and global economy, 227, 228
    population, 486*f*
    urban population, 465*f*
Gilmore Girls (TV Show), 161
Girl Scouts of America, 138
Glass ceiling, 257, 268, 293
    definition, 551
    and religion, 359
Glass Ceiling Commission, 257
Glass escalator, 294
Global Alliance for Workers and Communities, 226, 232
Global economy, 18, 19, 20
    gap, between rich and poor nations, 226
    and worker exploitation, 224–227
Global Reach, 534, 538, 538*f*
Global torrent, 162
Global village, 162
Globalization, 61–62
    and cultural domination, 61–62
    definition, 230, 551
    and economic exploitation, 230
    effect on caste system, 201
    and the media, 155, 162–163
    in postmodern societies, 118
    and labor unions, 142
    and Third World nations, 416–417
Goal displacement, in bureaucracy, 134, 551
Goal multiplication, organizational, 139, 551
Goal succession, organizational, 140, 551
Golf Cable Channel, 160
Google (search engine), 151, 154
Governor's Commission on Gay and Lesbian Youth (Massachusetts), 388
Graffiti, 170–171
Grand Theft Auto III (GTA3) (video game), 164
Grandparents as Parents (support group), 337
Grandparents, family role of, 333, 336
Graphs, interpreting, 51
Gray Panthers, 106
Graying of America, 315–316
Great Britain. *See also* United Kingdom
    health care expenditures, 455, 456*f*
    as host country for U. S. students, 377*t*
    life expectancy, 489*f*
    London, 466*t*
    megalopolis, 464
    National Health Service, 456
    percentage of college graduates, 376*f*
    schools, 376
    single mothers, 340
    urban population, 465*f*
    voter turnout in, 401
Great White (band), 505, 506
Greece
    gross national income, per capita, 228
    health care expenditures, 456*f*
    population, 486*f*
    urban population, 465*f*

Greenland
    urban population, 465*f*
Greenpeace, 535
    website, 408
Greenwich Village, New York City, 460–461
Gross national domestic product (GDP), Nepal, 418
Gross national income, per capita, worldwide, 228
Ground Zero, 16–17
Group, definition, 109, 551
Groups, social, 109–110, 125–132, 135
    definition, 127
    small, 130–132
    studying, 130–132
    types of, 127, 128–130
Growth rate, of population, 489
    definition, 551
Guatemala
    adoptees, U.S., 336*t*
    gross national income, per capita, 228
    population, 486*f*
    urban population, 465*f*
Guerrilla Girls, 280
Guinea-Bissau
    gross national income, per capita, 228
Guinea
    population, 486*f*
Gun control, 192–194
Guyana
    urban population, 465*f*

H

Haiti
AIDS in, 492
    gross national income, per capita, 228
    life expectancy, 489*f*
    place in global economy, 229*f*
    population, 486*f*
    urban population, 465*f*
Hajj, 361
HAL (fictional computer), 140
Handgun Control (organization), 193
Harry Potter and the Sorcerer's Stone (film), 161
Hartford Institute for Religion Research, 363
Harvard University, 199, 408
Harvey Milk High School, 387
Hasidic Jews, 331
Hate Crimes Statistics Act, 255, 255–256
Hate Groups, Active, in U.S., 256 (map), 256–257
Hawaii
    abortion funding, 298*f*
    availability of physicians, 447*f*
    elderly population, projected, 315*f*
    high school exit exam requirements, 389*f*
Hawthorne effect, 38, 39
    definition, 551
Hawthorne studies, 137
Hazardous waste, 499–500

HBO cable station, 161
Health and medicine, 436–458
    and culture, 438–439
    functionalist perspective, 439–440
    health beliefs
        of African Americans, 442
        of American Indians, 437–438, 450
        of Hispanics, 446
        Korean Americans, 442
        of Mexican Americans, 442, 446–447
    health care
        expenditures, projected, 448*f*
        nationalized, 436, 455–457
    patient autonomy, 442
    and social epidemiology, 443–448
        age, 447–448
        gender, 444–445, 447
        the poor, 215, 216, 219, 220
        race and ethnicity, 445–447
        social class, 444–445
    theoretical perspectives
        conflict, 440–441
        interactionist, 441–442
        labeling theory, 442–443
    U.S. health care system, 448–454
        costs, 448, 448*f*, 455–457
        functionalist perspective, 449, 449–450
        health status, of poor and nonpoor, 216*t*
        historical view, 449–450
        holistic, 450
        interactionist perspective, 449
        and mental illness, 452–454
        role of government, 451–452
Health Care Financing Administration, 448*f*
Health, defined, 438–439, 551
Health insurance
    nationalized, 455–457
    percentage of people without, U.S., 444*f*
Health maintenance organizations (HMOs), 456, 551
Heirarchy of authority, in bureaucracy, 134
Helping professions, labor unions in, 143
Henry L. Stimson Center, 536
Herbal medicine, 451
Heredity vs. environment, 81, 83–84
Hidden curriculum, 379–380, 551
High school students, cliques, 385, 386–388
Hill-Burton Act, 451
Hindu culture, 291, 368
Hinduism, 353–354, 354*t*, 356, 357
    in India, 367, 368
    world wide, 352*f*
Hispanics, 270–272, 379, 540
    economic position, 266–267
    elderly, 316
    family relationships, 332–333
    and health and illness, 445–446
    health beliefs, 446
    and Internet access, 541, 541*f*
    major groups, 270*f*
    in the media, 154–155

Hispanics—*Cont.*
median income, U.S., 432
percentage without health insurance, 444*f*, 455
in poverty, 213, 214, 219, 315–316
relative economic position, 266*t*
single-parent families, increase over time, 332*f*
suburban, 475
as voters, 401
History, of sociology, 9–13
History, study of, 6
Holistic health care, 450, 551
Hollywood, government cooperation with, 155
Home Depot, 476
Home School Legal Defense Fund, 390
Homeland Security Advisory System, 398
Homeless people, as deviants, 180
Homelessness, 459, 477–480
policy initiatives, 479–480
and urban decay, 472
worldwide, 478
Homeschooling, 389–390
Homophobia, 283, 551
Homosexuality
as master status, 519
medicalization of, 443
policy initiatives, 521–522
public opinion, 521*f*
Homosexuals, 121, 283
and domestic partnership, 342–343
in high school, 386–387
in the media, 154–155, 520–521
in the military, 521
in Nazi Germany, 519–520
as parents, 337
and religion, 355
as social activists, 519–522
and social stigma, 519, 521
teens, at risk, 388*f*
Honduras
gross national income, per capita, 228
population, 486*f*
urban population, 465*f*
Hong Kong
average pay of CEO, 204*t*
gross national income, per capita, 228
population, 486*f*
Honor codes, college, 70
Hopi Indians, marriage, 323
Horizontal mobility, 216–217, 551
Horticultural societies, 116, 551
Hospice care, 313, 551
Hospice Foundation of America, 314
Hotline, for children, 94
Housework, 292, 294
Housing and Urban Development, 479, 480
Hozho, 450
Hull House, 12, 18
Human ecology, 464, 498–499
Human Genome Project, 536, 537
Human Immunodeficiency Virus. *See* AIDS

Human relations approach, to formal organizations, 136, 551
Human rights, 243
definition, 551
violations, after September 11, 243
Human Rights Index, 244, 244*t*
Hungary
gross national income, per capita, 228
Hunger
in United States, 197
world, 488
Hunting-and-gathering societies, 116, 551
Hutus, and Tutsis, 243
Hypothesis
definition, 551
formulating, and scientific method, 32–33

I

IBM corporation, 233
Ice Age (film), 155
Iceland
family, photos, 4–5
single mothers, 340
urban population, 465*f*
Idaho
availability of physicians, 447*f*
elderly population, projected, 315*f*
high school exit exam requirements, 389*f*
Ideal minority, 553
Ideal type, 10–11, 551
Ijime, 94
Ikebukuro Honcho (Japanese welfare network), 306
Iliad, The (Homer), 390
Illinois
abortion funding, 298*f*
elderly population, projected, 315*f*
high school exit exam requirements, 389*f*
Illiteracy, 373
Illness. *See* Health and illness
Imagination, sociological, 3–6
Immigrants, U.S., 269–270, 274–276
Chinese, 268–269
East Indian, 57–58
European, descendants of, 471
illegal, 238, 276
Korean, 269, 333
Mexican, 238, 240–241, 276
Muslim, 540
in organized crime, 188, 189
population of, by nationality, 275*f*
socialization of, 149–150
Immigration, 274–276
conflict perspective, 275–276
functionalist perspective, 275
Immigration Act, 1965, 269
Immigration and Naturalization Service, 274*f*
Immigration Reform and Control Act of 1986, 276
Impersonality, in bureaucracy, 134
Impression management, 86, 551

In-groups and out-groups, 128–129
In vitro fertilization (IVF), 344, 345
Incest taboo, 330, 551
Incidence, of illness, 444, 551
Inclusion, social, 529
Income, definition, 551
Income, household, 199
by educational level, 31, 34*t*, 35*f*
and health insurance coverage, 444*f*
median, by race or ethnicity, U.S., 266*t*
United States, 202
Income, median, U.S., by race, ethnicity and gender, 432*f*
Income, vs. wealth, 199, 210–211
Independent variable, 32, 551
India
adoptees, U.S., 336*t*
belief in God, 361*f*
Bombay, 466*t*
caste system, 200, 201
and human rights, 243
college students, in U.S., 377*t*
Delhi, 466*t*
feminism, 518
gross national income, per capita, 228
health care expenditures, 456*f*
language in, 74
life expectancy, 489*f*
megalopolis, 464
percentage of U.S. immigrants from, 275*f*
population, 486*f*, 492
religion, 367–369
and society, 368
and the state, 368
social movement in, 518
women in, 291
as legislators, 404*f*
Indian Health Service, 438
Indiana
abortion funding, 298*f*
availability of physicians, 447*f*
elderly population, projected, 315*f*
high school exit exam requirements, 389*f*
Indolink.com, 331
Indonesia
gross national income, per capita, 228
and Human Rights Index, 244*t*
Jakarta, 466*t*
population, 486*f*
sweatshops in, 226
urban population, 465*f*
Industrial cities, 464*t*, 551
Industrial revolution, 118, 141, 415, 463, 532
Industrial societies, 118, 463, 551
economic systems of, 415–418
Inequality, social, 2–3, 20–22. *See also* Stratification, social
definition, 199, 556
Infant mortality rate
by country, 441*f*
definition, 489, 551
United States, 446
world wide, 441*f*, 489

Infanticide, female, 493
Infertility, 344–345
Influence, as source of power, 399, 551
Informal economies, 237, 418, 419
    definition, 551
Informal norms, 171, 172
    definition, 552
Informal social control, 174–175, 552
Innovation, cultural, 60, 552
Innovator, in Merton's anomie theory of deviance, 182, 183*t*
Institute for Women's Policy Research, 428–429
Institute of International Education, 377*t*
Institutional discrimination, 258–259, 289
    definition, 552
Instrumentality, 552
Intelligence Report 2003, 257
Inter-Parliamentary Union, 404
Interactionist perspective, 16–17, 47–48
    on affirmative action, 432
    on AIDS, 121
    on campaign financing, 410
    on childcare, 97
    and concept of the self, 84–86
    definition, 552
    on education, 382, 383–384
    on the family, 328–329, 329*t*
    on health and illness, 441, 442
    on health care system, 449
    on mass media, 158–159
    on prejudice and discrimination, 261–262
    and research, 130–131
    on social construction of race, 253
    on social deviance, 183–185
    on social institutions, 114
    on social reality, 103, 104
    on socialization, 92
    on stratification, 205, 208*t*
Interest group, 552
Intergenerational mobility, 217, 236, 552
International Lesbian and Gay Association, 521–522
International Monetary Fund, 229
International Women Count Network, 209–210
Internet, use of, 45–46, 166
    access to, 159
        by the poor, 216, 541
        by race, 541*f*
    celebrity web searches, 151*t*
    chat rooms, chatting, 159
    and collective behavior, 518–519
    and copyright infringement, 70, 526–527
    dating, 330, 331
    deviant behavior, 180
    and education, 385
    gatekeeping, 154
    gender differences, 158
    and globalization, 162–163, 164, 230
    and groups, 110–111
    and language, 538*f*
    and medical information, 450

piracy, 180–181
and political activism, 408
and pornography, 158
on September 11, 2001, 150
and social interaction, 538–539
and social movements, 504
    homosexual, 522
support groups, 345
and the Third World, 534
Interracial marriage, 330, 331
Interview, definition, 552
Interview surveys, 37
Intragenerational mobility, 217, 552
Inuit (Eskimo), 245
Invention, 60, 552
Invisible Man (Ellison), 264
Iowa
    abortion funding, 298*f*
    availability of physicians, 447*f*
    cloning in, 535
    elderly population, projected, 315*f*
    Postville, 477
Iran
    gross national income, per capita, 228
    human rights abuses, 245
    and Human Rights Index, 244*t*
    population, 486*f*
    urban population, 465*f*
Iraq
    2003 war
        in the media, 149
        protests, 516
    gross national income, per capita, 228
    media in, 161
    minorities in, 243
    population, 486*f*
    socialization, 94
    urban population, 465*f*
Ireland
    gross national income, per capita, 228
    percentage of college graduates, 376*f*
    place in global economy, 229
    population, 486*f*
    urban population, 465*f*
    welfare system
        and healthcare, 219
Irish Americans, 273
Irish Republican Army (IRA), 182
Iron Chef (TV show), 156
Iron law of oligarchy, 136, 552
Islam, 11, 243, 254–255, 331, 353, 354*t*, 361, 362
    arranged marriages, 331
    black muslim, 255
    ecclesia, 362
    hajj, 361
    hostility, 254
    human rights, 243
    in India, 201, 367, 368
    monotheistic, 353
    Muslims, 254, 353
    Muslim Americans, 254
    Nation of Islam, 255

prejudice, 254, 255
Qur'an, 254, 354*t*
religious rituals, 254, 353, 354*t*, 360–361
variations, 331
worldwide, 352*f*
Islamic countries, 290, 530
Islamic culture
    marriage practices, 331
Isolation, impact on socialization, 81–83
Israel, 243
    gross national income, per capita, 228
    and Human Rights Index, 244*t*
    infant mortality rate, 441*f*
    percentage of people ever married, ages 20-24, 330*f*
    population, 486*f*
    urban population, 465*f*
Issei, 269, 552
Italian Americans, 269, 273
Italy
    gross national income, per capita, 228
    as host country for U S. students, 377*t*
    megalopolis, 464
    population, 486*f*
    social welfare policies, 210
    urban population, 465*f*

J

Jainism, 367–368
Jakarta, Indonesia, 466*t*
Jamaica
    income distribution, 233*f*
    urban population, 465*f*
Japan
    average pay of CEO, 204*t*
    belief in God, 361*f*
    college students, in U.S., 377*t*
    divorce in, 339
    education in, 381
    elderly, 306
    gross national income, per capita, 228, 229
    health care expenditures, 456*f*
    homelessness, 478, 479
    homosexuals in, 521–522
    income distribution, 233*f*
    infant mortality rate, 441*f*
    infertility treatments, 345
    labor unions in, 141
    life expectancy, 489*f*
    media in, 156
    megalopolis, 464
    Osaka, 466*t*
    percentage of college graduates, 376*f*
    place in global economy, 229
    population, 486*f*, 492
    schools, 379–380
    socialization, 91, 94
    stratification in, 235
    voter turnout in, 401
    workplace, and job satisfaction, 424–425

Japanese Americans, 268*t*, 269
Japanese complex of religions, world wide, 352*f*
Jewish Americans, 272–273
Jim Crow laws, 266
Jordan, 163
    gross national income, per capita, 228
    women in the legislature, 404*f*
Judaism, 353, 354*t*
    Lubavitcher, 477
    world wide, 352*f*
Juku, 381
Jurassic Park (film), 165
Justice, environmental, 20

K

Kaiser Family Foundation, 46
Kansas
    abortion funding, 298*f*
    availability of physicians, 447*f*
    elderly population, projected, 315*f*
    high school exit exam requirements, 389*f*
Kansas State University, 70
Karachi, Pakistan, 466*t*
Kavakava (herb), 451
Kazakhstan
    adoptees, U.S., 336*t*
    gross national income, per capita, 228
    population, 486*f*
    urban population, 465*f*
Kennedy family, 332
Kentucky
    abortion funding, 298*f*
    availability of physicians, 447*f*
    elderly population, projected, 315*f*
Kenya
    and the disabled, 107
    gross national income, per capita, 228
    homosexuals in, 522
    population, 486*f*
    urban population, 465*f*
King of the Hill (TV show), 156
Kinsey Report, 46
Kinship
    definition, 552
    patterns, 325–326
KISS (band), 169
Kiwanis Club, 138
Knowledge class, 430
Koran, 254, 353
Korea
    college students, in U.S., 377*t*
    labor unions in, 141
    percentage of U.S. immigrants from, 275*f*
    population, 486*f*
    urban population, 465*f*
Korean Americans, 268*t*, 269
    health beliefs, 442
Korean complex, of religions, worldwide, 352*f*
Kosovo, 243
Ku Klux Klan, 254, 256 (map), 266

Kurds, 243
Kuwait
    gross national income, per capita, 228
    population, 486*f*
    social groups, 109
    urban population, 465*f*
    women in the legislature, 404*f*
Kye, 333
Kyodo News International, 339

L

Labeling theory, 185
    definition, 552
    and education, 382, 383–384
    and health and illness, 442–443
    and mental illness, 453, 453–454
Labor unions, 138
    declining membership, 141–143
    definition, 552
    in Europe, 143
    post-9/11, 143
    racism and sexism in, 141, 142
    role conflict, for members, 143
Labour Party, Great Britain, 143
Lagos, Nigeria, 466*t*
Laissez-faire capitalism, 416, 552
Land contamination, 498
Language, 59, 63, 64
    bilingualism, 74–75
    definition, 552
    ethnocentric, 232–233
    and prejudice, 65
    and resource mobilization, 515
Languages, by world region, 64
Laos
    gross national income, per capita, 228
    life expectancy, 489*f*
    population, 486*f*
    urban population, 465*f*
Latent function, definition, 552
Latent functions, vs. manifest, 14, 375
Latin America, place in global economy, 229
Latinas, 296
Latinos, 270–272
    discrimination
        in the medical establishment, 446
    homosexual, 521
    in the media, 155, 156
        interpreting, 160–161
    middle class, 271
    in poverty, 500
    women, 296
Law and Order (TV show), 150
Law, definition, 175, 552
League of Women Voters, 138, 410
Learning disorders (LDs), 390
Leaving Las Vegas (film), 165
Lebanon
    gross national income, per capita, 228
    population, 486*f*
    urban population, 465*f*

Legal-rational authority, 399, 552
Leisure, conspicuous, 205, 206
Lesbianism, medicalization of, 443
Lesbians, 283. *See* Homosexuality;
    Homosexuals
    and domestic partnership, 342–343
    in high school, 386–387
    human rights, 245
    in the media, 154–155, 520–521
    as parents, 337
    and religion, 355
    and social stigma, 519
    teens, at risk, 388*f*
Lesotho
    urban population, 465*f*
Levi's corporation, 431
Lewis Mumford Center, 263
Liberal-labor coalition, 407
Liberation theology, 358, 359, 552
Liberia
    infant mortality rate, 441*f*
    population, 486*f*
    urban population, 465*f*
Library of Congress, 150
Library resources, for research, 52–53
Libya
    gross national income, per capita, 228
    and Human Rights Index, 244*t*
    population, 486*f*
    urban population, 465*f*
Life chances, 215–216, 552
Life course, and socialization, 88, 89
Life expectancy
    definition, 489, 552
    by race, 446–447
    worldwide, 489*f*
Lifetime cable station, 161
Lions Club, 138
Literature review, and scientific method, 32
Lithuania
    gross national income, per capita, 228
    population, 486*f*
    urban population, 465*f*
Living Conditions Survey, Bahamas, 488
London, England, 466*t*
    city planning, 473
Looking-glass self, 84, 421, 552
Los Angeles, 466*t*, 468–469
    South Bronx, 473
    South Central, 473
Los Angeles riots, 1992, 160–161
Louisiana
    abortion funding, 298*f*
    elderly population, projected, 315*f*
    environmental issues, 499–500
    high school exit exam requirements, 389*f*
Louisiana State University, 94
Love Canal, 496, 498
Low-income workers. *See also* Sweatshops
    networking, 111
Lower West Side family, photos, 334–335
Luddites, 532–533, 552

Luther College, 283–284
Luxembourg, 244*t*

M

Macedonia
  gross national income, per capita, 228
Machismo, 333, 552
Macrosociology, 13, 159, 259–260
  definition, 552
Madagascar
  gross national income, per capita, 228
  population, 486*f*
  urban population, 465*f*
Magnet schools, 390
Maid in Manhattan (film), 437–438
Maine
  abortion funding, 298*f*
  availability of physicians, 447*f*
  Bangor, 476
  high school exit exam requirements, 389*f*
  homeschooling in, 390
Malagasy, 21
Malawi
  gross national income, per capita, 228
  population, 486*f*
  urban population, 465*f*
Malaysia
  affirmative action in, 433
  population, 486*f*
  urban population, 465*f*
Male dominance, 66, 287–288, 326
  in the media, 157–158
  in religion, 359
Mali
  family, photos, 4–5
  gross national income, per capita, 228
  population, 486*f*
  urban population, 465*f*
Malta
  and Human Rights Index, 244*t*
  urban population, 465*f*
Manifest functions
  definition, 552
Manifest functions, vs. latent, 14, 375
Mankato, Minnesota nun study, 445
Maps
  borderlands, between U.S. and Mexico, 241*f*
  United States, 298*f*, 315*f*, 389*f*, 447*f*
  world, 352*f*, 465*f*, 486*f*
Maquiladoras, 240–241, 242
March of Dimes, 140
Marijuana, medical use of, in United States, 175, 176
Marriage
  alternatives to, 340–343
    cohabitation, 340–341
    homosexual relationships, 342–343
    remaining single, 341–342
  arranged, 330, 331
  childless, 343

and divorce, 338–339, 339*f*
  in India, 368
  interracial, 330, 331
  Jewish Americans, 331
  partner selection, 330–331
  percentage of people ever married, ages 20-24, 330*f*
  Tibetan, 323
  Trobriand Islanders, 323
Marxist perspective
  on the family, 327
  on labor unions, 143
  on prejudice and discrimination, 260–261
  on religion, 358, 359–360
  on stratification, 203, 204, 205
Marxist theory, 14–15
Maryland
  abortion funding, 298*f*
  availability of physicians, 447*f*
  high school exit exam requirements, 389*f*
Masons, 138
Mass media. *See* Media
  definition, 149, 552
Massachusetts
  abortion funding, 298*f*
  high school exit exam requirements, 389*f*
Massachusetts Department of Education, 387, 388, 388*f*
Master status, 106
  definition, 552
  disability as, 107
  homosexuality as, 519
  old age as, 304
  person with HIV as, 121
Masters golf tournament, 528
Match.com, 330
Material culture, 62, 532, 552
Material World: A Global Family Portrait (Menzel), 4–5
Matriarchy, 326, 552
Matrilineal descent, 326, 552
Mattel corporation, 431
Mauritania
  gross national income, per capita, 228
  urban population, 465*f*
McDonaldization, 62, 126–127
  of biotechnology, 534
  definition, 552
McDonald's restaurants, 126, 198
McKinney Homeless Assistance Act, 479
McMaster University, Ontario, 488
McSpotlight, 540
Mean, statistical, 50
Mecca, Saudi Arabia, 361, 362
Mechanical solidarity, 115
Medecins sans Frontieres, 244–245
Media
  addiction to, 153
  advertising, 152–153
  audience, 159–161
  and censorship, 150–151
  in communist countries, 161
  concentration, corporate, 161

conflict perspective, 153–157
    gatekeeping, 153–154
  coverage of Los Angeles riots, 160–161
  developing nations, 156–157
  elderly in, 316
  exposure, of children, 152
  feminist perspective, 157–158
  functionalist perspective, 149–153
  and globalization, 148, 155
  influence on behavior, 164–166
  interpreting, 160–161
  latinos in, 156
  local production, 156
  mass media, defined, 149
  narcotizing dysfunction of, 153, 165
  news, bias in, 163
  and politics, 149, 158–159
  race in, 155–156, 157
  rise of, 150*t*
  role in socialization, 95–96, 149–153, 284
    as agent of socialization, 149–150
    and conferral of status, 151–152
    and social norms, 150–151
    surveillance function, 153
  in schools, 162
  and sexuality, 46
  social functions of, 165
  stereotypes in
    gender, 157–158, 284
    racial, 175, 249
  violence in
    feminist perspective, 165
    increasing, 165*t*
Median, 50–51, 552
Medicaid, 417, 452
Medical care, for AIDS patients, 121
Medical establishment
  and racism, 446
Medical model
  of disability, 107
  of mental illness, 453, 453–454
  of social problems, 440
Medical profession
  justification of slavery, 443
Medical sociology, 20
Medicalization of society, 440–441
Medicare, 417, 452
Megalopolis, 464, 552
Megalopolises, ten most populous, 466*t*
Melting pot, 263
Men. *See also* Gender; Gender differences
  in female-dominated occupations, 293–294
  and physical appearance, 180
Mennonite church, 92, 93
Mental illness, 452–454
  definition, 553
  theoretical models of, 453–454
  treatment, 454
Mentally ill
  deinstitutionalization of, 215
  as deviant, 176
  and discrimination, 452–453

Metallica (band), 526
Metropolitan Community Church, 355
Mexican Americans, 270*f*, 333
　health beliefs, 442, 446–447
Mexico
　average pay of CEO, 204*t*
　belief in God, 361*f*
　college students, in U.S., 377*t*
　and global economy, 427
　gross domestic product, 238
　gross national income, per capita, 228
　health care expenditures, 456*f*
　homelessness, 478
　homosexuals in, 522
　as host country for U.S. students, 377*t*
　human rights abuses, 245
　income distribution, 233*f*, 238
　infant mortality rate, 441*f*
　labor unions in, 141
　life expectancy, 238, 489*f*
　media in, 156
　percentage of college graduates, 376*f*
　percentage of people ever married, ages
　　20-24, 330*f*
　percentage of U.S. immigrants from, 275*f*
　place in global economy, 229*f*
　population, 486*f*
　stratification in, 238–242
　　and gender, 239–240
　　and race, 238–239
　urban population, 465*f*
Mexico City, 466*t*
　homelessness, 478
Michigan
　abortion funding, 298*f*
　availability of physicians, 447*f*
　elderly population, projected, 315*f*
　high school exit exam requirements, 389*f*
Microsociology, 13, 159, 260
　definition, 553
Microsoft corporation
　antitrust case, 141, 416
　temp workers at, 429
Middle Eastern countries, gender in, 21
Middletown, New Jersey, 474
Midlife crisis, 309, 553
Migradollars, 242
Migration, 494, 553
　internal, 495
　international, 494–495
Migration News, 240, 421
Mikes of America, 138
Military, homosexuals in, 521
Minnesota
　abortion funding, 298*f*
　elderly population, projected, 315*f*
　high school exit exam requirements, 389*f*
　Mankato nun study, 445
Minnesota Twin Family Study, 83
Minorities
　and access to public space, 21
　homosexual, 521
　suburban, 475

Minority groups, 74, 250–251
　and affirmative action, 431–433
　and AIDS, 120, 121
　definition, 250, 553
　exploitation, global, 230
　and homelessness, 478
　and Internet access, 540–541
　Internet access for, 216
　in the media, 156
　　as victims, 165
　model or ideal, 268
　as percentage of workforce, 426*f*
　and political power, 407
　retirement from workforce, 312–313
　rural, 477
　status, 106
　　and redefining social reality, 104, 106
　in Turkey, 243
　in the workforce, 425–426
Minority, ideal, 553
Minority women, 296
Mismatch, between skills and jobs, 430
Mississippi
　abortion funding, 298*f*
　availability of physicians, 447*f*
　elderly population, projected, 315*f*
　high school exit exam requirements, 389*f*
Missouri
　abortion funding, 298*f*
　availability of physicians, 447*f*
　elderly population, projected, 315*f*
　high school exit exam requirements, 389*f*
　Times Beach, 498
Mobility, social, 201–202, 216–219
　definition, 556
　in developing nations, 236
　and education, 217
　and gender, 217–218, 236–237
　in industrialized nations, 235–236
　intergenerational, 217, 236, 552
　intragenerational, 552
　and race, 217
　types of, 216–217
Mode, 50, 553
Model minority, 553
Modernization, definition, 553
Modernization theory, 232–233
　and the global economy, 233–234
Money, as social symbol, 182
Mongolia
　urban population, 465*f*
Monogamy, 325, 553
Monopoly, 416, 553
Montana
　abortion funding, 298*f*
　availability of physicians, 447*f*
　elderly population, projected, 315*f*
　high school exit exam requirements, 389*f*
Morbidity, definition, 553
Morbidity rates, 444, 553
Morehouse Medical Treatment and Effective-
　nesss Center, 446

Mores, 66, 553
　and the media, 147
Mormon religion, worldwide, 352*f*
"Morning after" pill, 297
Morocco
　gross national income, per capita, 228
　urban population, 465*f*
Mortality rates, 444, 485, 553
Mothers against drunk driving (MADD), 191
Mothers of Supertwins (MOST) support
　group, 345
Mothers, single, 212–213, 219
Motion picture industry, sexism in, 280
Motor-voter law, 403
Motorola cellular phone plant, 18, 19, 20
Moulin Rouge (film), 155
Movies, 147
　smoking in, 39
Mozambique
　gross national income, per capita, 228
　infant mortality rate, 441*f*
　life expectancy, 489*f*
　population, 486*f*
　urban population, 465*f*
Ms. magazine, 52
MUDs (multiuser domains, Internet),
　538–539
Multilinear evolutionary theory, 528, 553
Multinational corporations, 230, 416, 553
Multiple nuclei theory, of urban growth, 466*f*,
　467, 553
Multiracial people, 253
Multitasking, 96
Mundugumor people, 286
Music industry, 161
Music thieves, 180–181, 526, 527
　catching, 181*f*
Muslim societies, 291
Muslims, 353, 530. *See also* Arab Americans;
　Islam
　in India, 201, 368
　marriage practices, 331
　stereotyping, after September 11, 175
　treatment, after September 11, 243, 254,
　　255
　as victims of ethnic cleansing, 243
　women, 290
"My Heart Will Go On" (song), 161
Myth of Mental Illness (Szasz), 453

N

NAACP (National Association for the
　Advancement of Colored People), 15, 266
NAFTA (North American Free Trade Agree-
　ment), 240, 241
Namibia
　gross national income, per capita, 228
　urban population, 465*f*
Napster, 526, 527
NARAL, 298*f*

Narcotizing dysfunction, of the media, 153, 165, 553

NASA space program, 135, 155

National Advisory Commission on Criminal Justice, 188

National Alliance for Caregiving, 311

National Alliance for the Mentally Ill, 452

National Alliance to End Homelessness, 478

National Association for the Advancement of Colored People (NAACP), 15, 266, 541

National Association of Home Builders, 219

National Center for Education Statistics, 310

National Center for Health Statistics, 446

National Center on Women and Family Law, 186

National Committee to Preserve Social Security and Medicare, 317

National Crime Victimization Survey, 191, 192, 215–216

National Geographic, 499

National Health and Social Life Survey (NHSLS), 48, 342

National Homeschool Association, 390

National Institute of Child Health and Human Development, 47–48, 97, 451

National Institutes of Health (NIH), 48

National Law Center on Homelessness and Poverty, 479

National Opinion Research Center (NORC), 33

National Organization for Men Against Sexism (NOMAS), 285

National Public Radio (NPR), 537

National Reconnaissance Office, 134

National Review (magazine), 52

National Rifle Association (NRA), 193, 194

National Right to Work Legal Defense Foundation, 143

National Writers Union, 543

Nationalized health care, 455–457

Native Americans, 212, 252, 261, 267
cohabitation, 340
discrimination
in the medical establishment, 446
and health and illness, 445–446, 449
relative economic position, 266t
spiritual beliefs, 350–351

Native Hawaiian Americans, 268t

Natural science, 6, 553

Natural selection, 62

Nature vs. nurture, 81
and gender differences, 285–286

Navajo indians, health beliefs, 437–438, 450

Nazis, 274, 399–400
and homosexuality, 519–520

Nebraska
abortion funding, 298f
availability of physicians, 447f
elderly population, projected, 315f
high school exit exam requirements, 389f

Negotiated order, 105, 553

Negotiation, 104–105, 553

Neighborhoods, defended, 472

Nell (film), 81–82

Neo-Confederate hate groups, 256

Neo-Luddites, 532–533

Neo-Malthusian view, of world population, 487

Neo-Nazi hate groups, 256 (map), 272

Neocolonialism, 553

Neocolonialism, definition, 229

Nepal, 304
economic system of, 418
gross national income, per capita, 228
population, 486f
urban population, 465f

Net activism, 408

Netherlands
euthanasia in, 319
gross national income, per capita, 228
and Human Rights Index, 244t
population, 486f
urban population, 465f

Netscape Internet browser, 161

Networking, 110–111

Networks, social, 110–111

Neutrality, political, in research, 43–44

Nevada
abortion funding, 298f
availability of physicians, 447f
elderly population, projected, 315f
high school exit exam requirements, 389f

Nevis
urban population, 465f

New Caledonia
urban population, 465f

New Guinea
gender roles in, 285, 286
gross national income, per capita, 228
population, 486f
urban population, 465f

New Hampshire
abortion funding, 298f
availability of physicians, 447f
elderly population, projected, 315f
high school exit exam requirements, 389f

New Jersey
abortion funding, 298f
availability of physicians, 447f
elderly population, projected, 315f
high school exit exam requirements, 389i
Middletown, 474

New Line Cinema, 161

New Mexico
abortion funding, 298f
availability of physicians, 447f
elderly population, projected, 315f
high school exit exam requirements, 389f

New Orleans Medical and Surgical Journal, 443

New religious movements (NRMs), 365
definition, 553

New social movements, 517, 517t, 518

New urban sociology, 467, 470, 553

New York
abortion funding, 298f

availability of physicians, 447f
elderly population, projected, 315f
high school exit exam requirements, 389f

New York City, 466t
Greenwich Village, 460–461

New York Corset Club, 138

New York State Department of Hygiene, 453

New York University, 537

New Zealand
gross national income, per capita, 228
and Human Rights Index, 244t
population, 486f
suicide rate, 9
urban population, 465f

News media, 162–164
bias in, 163

Nicaragua
gross national income, per capita, 228
population, 486f
urban population, 465f

Niger
gross national income, per capita, 228
population, 486f
urban population, 465f

Nigeria
beauty standards in, 176
health care expenditures, 456f
Lagos, 466t
life expectancy, 489f
population, 486f
urban population, 465f

Nights of Cabiria (film), 165

Nike corporation, 225–226, 232, 431

Nike swoosh, 225

NIMBY (not in my back yard), 531, 532

Nineteenth Amendment, 295

Nintendo, 512

Nippon Telephone and Telegraph
gross domestic product, 231t

Nisei, 269, 553

Nissan corporation, 425

No Child Left Behind Act, 389

No Kidding (support group), 343

Nobel Peace Prize, 244

Nonmaterial culture, 62, 532, 553

Nonperiodic assembly, 509, 553

Nonverbal communication, 16–17, 64–65, 141
definition, 553

NORC (National Opinion Research Center), 33

Normal accident, 536, 553

Norms, 66–67, 171–172
acceptance of, 66–67
bureaucratic, 134
definition, 553
deviation from. See deviance
internalization of, 176
Internet, 159
and the media, 150–151
and social interaction, 103

North American Free Trade Agreement (NAFTA), 240, 241

North Carolina
  abortion funding, 298*f*
  availability of physicians, 447*f*
  elderly population, projected, 315*f*
  high school exit exam requirements, 389*f*
North Dakota
  abortion funding, 298*f*
  availability of physicians, 447*f*
  elderly population, projected, 315*f*
  high school exit exam requirements, 389*f*
North Korea, 161
  gross national income, per capita, 228
  and Human Rights Index, 244*t*
  life expectancy, 489*f*
  population, 486*f*
  urban population, 465*f*
Norway
  belief in God, 361*f*
  gross national income, per capita, 228, 229
  and Human Rights Index, 244*t*
  population, 486*f*
  urban population, 465*f*
NRA (National Rifle Association), 193, 194
Nuclear family, 323, 324, 553
Nun study, 445
Nurse-midwives, 440
Nurses, and health care system, 449–450
Nursing
  and labor unions, 143

O

Obedience, definition, 172, 553
  Milgram's studies of, 173–174, 380
Oberlin College, 382
Objective method, 553
Observation research, 37–38, 553
Occupation, characteristics of, vs. profession, 422*t*
Occupational mobility, 217
Occupational prestige, and gender, 209–210
Occupations, ranked by prestige, 209*t*
Ohio
  abortion funding, 298*f*
  availability of physicians, 447*f*
  elderly population, projected, 315*f*
  high school exit exam requirements, 389*f*
Ojibwa Indians, 484
Oklahoma
  abortion funding, 298*f*
  availability of physicians, 447*f*
  elderly population, projected, 315*f*
  high school exit exam requirements, 389*f*
Oklahoma City bombing, 150, 398
Old age, as master status, 304
Oligarchy, 136
  and labor unions, 143
Oman
  gross national income, per capita, 228
  urban population, 465*f*
One Flew Over the Cookoo's Nest (film), 452

100% Access and Zero Health Disparities program, 444
Open system, 216, 553
Operation Pipeline, 261
Operational definition, of research problem, 30, 553
Opinion leader, audience, 160, 554
Oregon
  abortion funding, 298*f*
  assisted suicide in, 319
  availability of physicians, 447*f*
  elderly population, projected, 315*f*
  high school exit exam requirements, 389*f*
Organic solidarity, 115, 554
Organizational change, 139–140
Organizational culture, classical theory, 136
Organizations, formal, 132–146
  definition, 132
Organized crime, 188, 189, 554
Out-groups
  definition, 554
  and in-groups, 128–129
Overweight people
  as deviant, 176
    and social stigma, 180
  in the media, 154–155

P

Pacific Islanders, 268*t*
  single-parent families, increase over time, 332*f*
Pakistan
  gross national income, per capita, 228
  homosexuals in, 522
  Karachi, 466*t*
  place in global economy, 229*f*
  population, 486*f*
  urban population, 465*f*
Palestine, 243
Pan-Cordillera Women's Network for Peace and Development, 236, 237
Panama
  gross national income, per capita, 228
  place in global economy, 229*f*
  urban population, 465*f*
Panic, definition, 554
Panics, as collective behavior, 512
Papua New Guinea
  gross national income, per capita, 228
  population, 486*f*
  urban population, 465*f*
Paraguay
  adoptees, U.S., 336*t*
  gross national income, per capita, 228
  population, 486*f*
  urban population, 465*f*
Parent, role of, 333, 336
Parents Television Council, 164
Paris, France, 466*t*
Parkers, The (TV show), 157
Participant observation, 2–3
Paternity testing, 322

Patriarchy, 326, 554
Patrilineal descent, 326, 554
PATRIOT Act, 175, 398
Peace Corps, 138
Pearl Harbor attack, 269
Pearl Jam (band), 505, 506
Peer groups
  adolescent, 94–95
  as agents of socialization, 171
Pennsylvania
  abortion funding, 298*f*
  availability of physicians, 447*f*
  elderly population, projected, 315*f*
  high school exit exam requirements, 389*f*
People magazine, 151, 152*t*
People's Republic of China. *See also* China
  gross national income, per capita, 228
  life expectancy, 489*f*
  population, 486*f*
  urban population, 465*f*
Percentage, definition, 50, 554
Periodic assembly, 509, 554
Persian Gulf, 163
Personal Responsibility and Work Opportunity Reconciliation Act, 219
Personality, 81
Personality, definition, 554
Peru
  gross national income, per capita, 228
  population, 486*f*
  urban population, 465*f*
Peter principle, 135, 554
Pew Research Center for the People and the Press, 408
Philippines
  adoptees, U.S., 336*t*
  globalization, 230
  gross national income, per capita, 228
  percentage of U.S. immigrants from, 275*f*
  place in global economy, 229*f*
  population, 486*f*
  social mobility, and gender, 236, 237
  social movements, 504–505
  urban population, 465*f*
Phish (rock band), 70–71
Physicians
  availability, by state, 447*f*
  and health care system, 449–450
Pilgrimage, religious, 361
Piracy, Internet, 180–181, 526
Pizza delivery workers, 128
Place on the Corner, A (Anderson), 29
Plagiarism, 70
Plague, The (Camus), 119
Plastic surgery, 180
Play stage, socialization, 85
Pluralism, social, 264, 554
Pluralist model, of power relations, 407–408, 554
Poland
  gross national income, per capita, 228

Poland—*Cont.*
  percentage of people ever married, ages
    20-24, 330*f*
  population, 486*f*
  solidarity movement, 417–418
  urban population, 465*f*
Policemen, in labor unions, 143
Polish Americans, 273
Political campaign financing, 409–410
Political candidates, and opinion leaders, 160
Political preferences, gender gap, 404
Political socialization, 400–401, 554
Political system, definition, 554
Politics
  definition, 397
  and mass media, 158–159
  and the media, 149, 155
  models of power structure, 404, 405–408
    power elite, 405
  and social movements, 513–514
  women in, worldwide, 405
Polls, public opinion, 513
Pollution, environmental, 496–498
  land contamination, 498
Polyandry, 325, 554
Polygamy, 325, 554
Polygyny, 325, 554
Poor people. *See also* Poverty
  as deviant, 215
  and healthcare, 219, 220
  living conditions, 499, 500
  as victims of media violence, 165
  as voters, 401
  working, 199
Popular health movement, 449
Popularity, in adolescence, 94*t*
Population
  and the environment, 496–500
  and migration, 494–495
Population and the environment, 483–503
Population Bomb, The, 487
Population pyramid, 492, 554
Population Reference Bureau, 325
Population, world, 486*f*
  estimated rate of increase per billion, 490*t*
  explosion, 492–493
  and resources, 487, 488
Pornography, 158
Portugal
  gross national income, per capita, 228
  percentage of college graduates, 376*f*
  population, 486*f*
  urban population, 465*f*
Postindustrial and postmodern societies,
    118–119
  and labor unions, 141–143
Postindustrial cities, 464*t*
Postindustrial city, definition, 463, 554
Postindustrial societies, 463–464, 554
Postmodern society, 119, 554
Postville, Iowa, 477
Poverty, 211–215. *See also* Poor people
  absolute vs. relative, 211

and the elderly, 315–316, 317–318
explaining, 214–216
  functionalist perspective, 214–215
  Weber's view, 215–216
feminization of, 212–213, 291, 332
and healthcare, 215, 216
and Internet access, 216
and life chances, 215–216
minorities in, 213, 214, 265, 266
suburban, 475
Power elite, 396–397, 554
Power Elite, The, 405
Power, social. *See also* Cultural domination
  definition, 397, 554
  and stratification, 205
Practice, The (TV show), 151
Prayer, in the classroom, 369–370
Pregnancy, teenage, 7
Preindustrial cities, 464*t*
Preindustrial societies, 116, 117–118, 554
  voluntary associations in, 138
Prejudice
  conflict perspective, 260–261
  conformity to, 172–173
  definition, 255, 554
  and discrimination, 254, 255, 257
  against the elderly, 316
  functionalist perspective, 259–260
  interactionist perspective, 261–262
  in Japan, 235
  racial, 249–250
Presbyterian Hospital, Pittsburgh, 455
Prestige
  definition, 554
  and social class, 208–209
    rankings of occupations, 209*t*
Pretty Woman (film), 165
Prevalence, of illness, 444, 554
Primary groups, 127, 128, 554
Primate studies, on social deprivation, 82–83
Primetime Live (TV show), 257
Prince (musician), 526
Prince William Sound, Alaska, 497
Princeton Religion Research Center, 362
Prison experiment, of Zimbardo, 102–103,
  104, 107, 108
Privacy, right to, after September 11, 175
Proctor & Gamble, 138
Product placement, 152
Production, music, 161
Profane
  definition, 554
  vs. sacred, 351, 353, 369–370
Profession
  characteristics of, vs. occupation, 422*t*
  definition, 422, 554
Professional criminal, 188, 554
Professional, definition, 421–422
Program, The (film), 165
Prohibition (Eighteenth Amendment),
  175–176
Proletariat, 203, 554
Proposition 209, 432

Prostitutes, portrayal in the media, 165
Prostitution, 190
Protestant denominations, 354
Protestant ethic, 358, 554
Protestant Ethic and the Spirit of Capitalism,
  358
Protestant religion, worldwide, 352*f*
Psychology, study of, 6
Public Citizen (organization), 410
Public, definition, 554
Public Enemy (rap group), 526
Public housing, 473
Public opinion, 554
Public places, access to, and gender, 21
Publics and public opinion, as collective be-
  havior, 513
Publishing industry, 154
Puerto Ricans, 270*f*, 271
  women, 296
Puerto Rico
  gross national income, per capita, 228
  population, 486*f*
  urban population, 465*f*
Pygmalion in the Classroom (Rosenthal and
  Jacobson), 382
Pygmalion (Shaw), 382
Pythagoras, 7

Q

Qatar, 163
Qualitative research, 554
  vs quantitative, 37
Quantitative research
  vs. qualitative, 37
Quebec, 75–76
Questionnaires, 37, 555
Qur'an, 353

R

Race
  biological significance of, 252
  and criminal justice system, 7, 186–187
  discrimination, 12, 257
  and health and illness, 445–446
  impact on social mobility, 217
  impact on socialization, 91
  and interpretation of media, 160–161
  in the media, 155–156, 157
  and median income, U.S., 432*f*
  and public interactions, 28–29
  as social construction, 252–253, 537
  and status, 202
Racial and ethnic groups
  intergroup relations, 262–264
    amalgamation, 263
    assimilation, 263
    expulsion, 262
    genocide, 262
    pluralism, 264

Racial and ethnic groups—*Cont.*
    segregation, 263–264
    relative economic positions, 266*t*
    United States, 251*t*
       projected, 252*t*
Racial group, 250–252
    bi- and multi-racial, 253
    definition, 250, 555
Racial profiling, 254
Racism, 259–261
    and conformity, 172–173
    in criminal justice system, 186–187
    definition, 255, 555
    and language, 65, 76
    in the medical establishment, 446
    in Mexico, 238–239
Random sample, 33, 555
Rape, 21, 186, 188, 288
    as war crime, 243
Rebel, in Merton's anomie theory of deviance,
    182, 183*t*
Recording industry, 154
Red Cross, 510
Reebok, 232
Reference groups, 130, 555
Relative deprivation
    definition, 555
    and social movements, 514–515
Relative deprivation, and social movements,
    517*t*
Relative poverty, 211, 555
Reliability, 33, 555
    of school-based testing, 389
Religion, 349–372, 555
    belief in God worldwide, 361*f*
    conflict perspective, 359–360
    Durkheim defines, 351
    role of, 354–355
       integrative functions, 355
       social support, 355, 358
    sects, 408
    and social change
       liberation theology, 358, 359
       Weberian thesis, 358
    sociological approach, of Durkheim, 351,
       353, 354
    and women, 359
Religion News Service, 370
Religions, world, 352*f*
    American Indians, 350–351
    Buddhism, 354, 354*t*
    Christianity, 353, 354*t*, 356
    Hinduism, 353, 354, 354*t*, 356, 357
       in India, 367, 368
    Islam, 353, 354*t*
       in India, 201, 367, 368
    Jainism, 367–368
    Judaism, 353, 354*t*, 356, 357
    major, 354*t*
    Shintoism, 356, 357
    Sikhism, 367
Religious behavior
    beliefs, 360, 555

experience, 361–362, 555
    rituals, 360–361, 555
Religious conflict, 355
Religious organizations, 362, 363–367
    comparing forms of, 366–367
       characteristics, 366*t*
    cults, 365
    denominations, 363, 364
    ecclesiae, 362, 363
    sects, 364–365
Remittances, 242
    definition, 555
Reparations
    for African Americans, 265, 266, 269
    for Japanese Americans, 269
Reporters sans Frontieres, 542
Reports, writing, 52–53
Reproductive rights, 107
Reproductive technology, 344–345
Republic of Congo, 416–417
Republican Party, 404
Research
    computers in, 44, 45–46
    ethics, 40, 41–44
       and confidentiality, 43
       and neutrality, 43–44, 47
       and right to know vs right to privacy,
        42–43
    on small groups, 130–132
    writing reports, 52–53
Research designs
    definition, 555
    major, 35, 36–39, 40
Research methods. *See also* Scientific method
    focus groups, 130
    importance of understanding, 29–30
    participant observer, 2–3
    qualitative vs quantitative, 37
Resocialization, 89, 90, 555
Resource mobilization
    definition, 555
    and social movements, 515–518, 517*t*
Retirement from workforce, 312–313, 313*f*
Retreatist, in Merton's anomie theory of de-
    viance, 182, 183*t*
Reuters news service, 162
Rhode Island
    abortion funding, 298*f*
    availability of physicians, 447*f*
    elderly population, projected, 315*f*
    high school exit exam requirements, 389*f*
Right-to-work laws, 142, 143
Rising Daughters Aware, 244
Rites of passage, 88, 555
Ritualist, in Merton's anomie theory of de-
    viance, 182
Rock the Vote, 403
Rockefeller family, 332
Roe v. Wade, 297
Role conflict, 108, 555
    of labor union members, 143
Role exit, 108, 555

Role, social
    definition, 556
Role strain, 108, 555
Role taking
    definition, 555
    and development of self, 85
Roles, social, 106, 107–109
Roman Catholic church, 270, 296, 358
    worldwide, 352*f*
Romania, 74
    gross national income, per capita, 228
    orphanages, 82
    population, 486*f*
    urban population, 465*f*
Routine activities theory, of deviance,
    184–185, 555
Royal Dutch/Shell Group
    gross domestic product, 231*t*
RU486 (abortion pill), 297
Rules and regulations, written, in bureau-
    cracy, 134
Rumors
    and collective behavior, 512–513
    definition, 555
Russia
    adoptees, U.S., 336*t*
    belief in God, 361*f*
    domestic violence in, 328
    gross national income, per capita, 228
    infant mortality rate, 441*f*
    population, 486*f*
    urban population, 465*f*

S

Sabrina the Teenage Witch (TV show), 151
Sacred
    definition, 555
    vs. profane, 351, 353, 369–370
Safe sex, 121
SAGE (senior action in a gay environment),
    317
Saint Kitts
    urban population, 465*f*
Saint Lucia
    urban population, 465*f*
Saint Vincent
    urban population, 465*f*
Salk vaccine, 140
Same-sex partnership, 342–343
Sami (Lapp) people, 245
Sample, definition, 555
Samples, random, 33
Sanctions, 67, 172, 555
Sandwich generation, 311–312, 555
Sao Paulo, Brazil, 466*t*
Sapir-Whorf hypothesis, 63, 65
    definition, 555
Saudi Arabia, 163
    gross national income, per capita, 228
    Mecca, 361, 362
    population, 486*f*
    urban population, 465*f*

School choice programs, 391, 555
School voucher programs, 390, 555
Schools
    as agents of change, 378–379
    as agents of socialization, 93–94, 375–380
        and cultural transmission, 375–377
        and social control, 378
        and social integration, 377–378
    bureaucratization, 384–385
    as formal organizations, 384–385
    hidden curriculum in, 379–380
    media in, 162
    and prayer in the classroom, 369–370
    in South Korea, 376
    tracking in, 381
    violence in, 129, 192, 386
Science, definition, 6, 555
Scientific-Humanitarian Committee, 519
Scientific management approach, to formal
    organizations, 136, 555
Scientific method, 29–30, 31–35
    and data analysis, 33
    and data collection, 33
    defining the problem, 30
    definition, 29, 555
    developing the conclusion, 34
    and formulating the hypothesis, 32–33
    and literature review, 32
Screen time, 149
Second Sex, The (Friedan), 295
Second shift, for mothers, 294, 329t, 555
Secondary analysis, of data, 39, 39–40, 555
Secondary groups, 127, 128, 555
Sects, religious, 364–365
    definition, 555
Secularization, definition, 555
Securities and Exchange Commission (SEC),
    132
Segregation
    definition, 555–556
    racial, 259, 263–264, 472–473. See also
        Apartheid
        outlawed, in U.S., 266
Self
    concept of, 84–88
        Mead's stages of development, 84–86
        psychological approaches, 86, 87–88
    definition, 556
    development of
        and gender roles, 284–285
        theoretical approaches to, 89t
    presentation of, 86, 87
Self-esteem, and social stigma, 180
Self-help groups, and AIDS, 121
Senate Judiciary Committee, 133
Senate Special Committee on Aging, 316
Senegal
    population, 486f
    urban population, 465f
Senilicide, 318, 556
September 11, 2001
    airline bailout, 220
    attendance at religious services, 355

and awareness of terrorism, 71, 72, 536
and changing values, 69
and collective behavior, 7, 8, 113, 510–511
and community bonding, 474
in the media, 150
memorabilia, 154
and Muslims and Arab Americans, 6, 63
    stereotyping, 175, 254, 256
national security, breach in, 133, 134
national security, increased, 143, 174–175,
    258–259, 398
    and civil rights, 175, 243, 540, 541
    and racial discrimination, 259
rumors sparked by, 513
and tattoos, 16–17
terrorists, 163
Serbia, ethnic cleansing in, 243
Serial monogamy, 325, 556
Sesame Street (TV show), 159, 443
Sex offenders, registration of, 180
Sex selection, 534
Sexism. See also Gender
    definition, 288, 289, 556
    in education, 93–94, 383
    and language, 65
    in politics, 402, 404
Sexual behavior
    and AIDS, 121
    researching, 46–49
        in China, 48–49
        value neutrality in, 47
Sexual harassment, 21, 288, 291
    and adolescents, 94
    definition, 556
Sexual Politics (Millett), 295
Sexuality, in the media, 46
Shanghai, China, 466t
Sherpas, of Tibet, 304
Shoshit, Shetkari, Kashtakari, Kamgar, Mukti
    Sangharsh (SSKKMS), 518
Sick role, 439–440, 556
Sierra Leone
    population, 486f
    urban population, 465f
Significant others, 86, 556
    peer groups as, 94
Sikh culture, 331
Sikhism
    in India, 367
    worldwide, 352f
Silicon Valley Cultures Project, 95
Simpsons, The (TV show), 511
Singapore
    bilingualism in, 75
    gross national income, per capita, 228
    population, 486f
    social control in, 174
Single-parent families, 332f, 333, 337–338,
    556
    fathers, 323–324, 337–338
Skinhead hate groups, 256 (map), 272
Slavery, 199, 200
    definition, 556

sequelae of, in United States, 265, 266
Slavery, history of, in U.S., 443
Slovenia
    gross national income, per capita, 228
    and Human Rights Index, 244t
Slums, 213
Small groups, 130–132, 556
    bureaucracy in, 135
Smith College, 173
Smoking, 175, 447
    in the media, 39
Social activists
    African Americans as, 12, 18
    elderly as, 317
    homosexuals as, 519–522
    Internet use, 408
    and social movements, 513–514
    sociologists as, 12–13, 18
    against sweatshops, 226
    women as, 239–240, 261, 287
        1900's, 12, 16
        in India, 518
Social change
    definition, 527, 556
    resistance to, 530–532
        and technology, 532–533
    in South Africa, 531
    and technology, 532–546
        biotechnology, 534–536
        computers, 533–534
        culture and social interaction,
            538–539
        social control, 539–540, 542–544
        stratification and inequality, 540–541
        technological accidents, 536, 537–538
    theories of, 527–529
        conflict, 527–528
        evolutionary, 527–528
        functionalist, 528–529
Social class. See Class, social
Social constructionist perspective, 185–186,
    556
Social control
    control theory, 176
    definition, 171, 556
    and education, 378
    formal
        laws, 175–176
        vs informal, 174–175
    functionalist perspective, 172
    and medicine, 440–441
    and technology, 539–540, 542–544
Social epidemiology, 443–444, 556
Social inequality, 2–3, 20, 20–22. See also
    Stratification, social
    definition, 199, 556
Social institutions
    conflict perspective, 113–114
    definition, 556
    functionalist perspective, 112–113
    interactionist perspective, 114
Social interaction, 103, 556
    and reality, 103–105

Social mobility. *See* Mobility, social
Social movements, 513–518
   definition, 513–514, 556
   and gender, 516–517
   new, 517
      in India, 518
   and relative deprivation, 514–515
   and resource mobilization, 515–518
Social networks, 110–111, 556
Social policy issues
   abortion, 297–299
   affirmative action, 431–433
   AIDS, 119–122
   bilingualism, 74–76
   campaign financing, 409–410
   child care, 97–98
   financing health care worldwide, 455–457
   global immigration, 274–276
   gun control, 192–194
   human sexuality, 46–49
   lesbian and gay rights, 519–522
   media violence, 164–166
   privacy and censorship, 538
   population policy, 500–501
   religion in the schools, 369–370
   reproductive technology, 344–345
   right to die worldwide, 318–319
   school choice programs, 390–392
   seeking shelter worldwide, 477–480
   social movements, 519–522
   state of the unions, 141–143
   universal human rights, 243–245
   welfare, 219–221
Social reality, defining, 103–105
Social role, definition, 556
Social science, 6, 556
Social Security, 315
Social stratification. *See* Stratification, social
Social structure, 103, 556
   creating, 104–105
   definition, 556
   elements of, 105–106, 107–110, 111–112
      groups, 109–110
Social worker, profession, 309
Social workers, in labor unions, 143
Socialism, 417–418, 556
Socialization, 79–124
   agents of, 91–96
      family, 91–92, 333, 336–338
      peer groups, 94–95
      schools, 93–94
      the state, 96
   anticipatory, 90, 130
      definition, 547
   definition, 556
   and gender, 91, 92, 94–95
   and gender roles, 283–284
   and heredity vs. environment, 81, 83–84
   impact of isolation on, 81–83
   internalization of social norms, 176
   and the life course, 88, 89
   and the media, 95–96, 149–153
   of physicians, 449–450

political, 400–401
psychological theories of, 87–88
and race, 91, 92
resocialization, 90
and the self, 84–88
and social policy, 119–122
and technology, 95–96
theoretical perspectives
   conflict, 93–94
   functionalist, 93
and total institutions, 90–91
in the workplace, 95–96
Societal-reaction approach, to deviance, 185, 556. *See also* Labeling theory
Societies, early, 461–462
Society
   definition, 58–59, 556
   medicalization of, 440–441
Society for the Psychological Study of Social Issues, 63
Sociobiology, 62–63, 556
   theories of deviance, 181
Sociocultural evolution, 116, 117–119
   definition, 556
   stages of, 116, 117–119, 117*t*
Sociological Abstracts, 52
Sociological imagination, 3–6, 556
Sociological Practice Association, 20
Sociological theory, 7–8
Sociologists, early, 9–13, 18
   American, 12–13
   English, 9–10
   French, 9, 10
   German, 10–12
   as social activists, 12–13, 18
Sociology
   applied, 17, 18, 19, 20
   basic, 20
   careers in, 25, 189, 309, 451, 488
      research, 45, 261
   clinical, 20
   and common sense, 7
   definition, 1, 2, 556
   development of, 9–13
   environmental, 20
   medical, 20
   micro- vs. macro-, 13
   new urban, 467, 470, 553
   study of, 6–7
Software programs, for research, 45
Solomon Islands
   Human Rights Index, 244*t*
Somalia
   gross national income, per capita, 228
   population, 486*f*
   urban population, 465*f*
Sony Corporation, 161
South Africa, 263
   affirmative action in, 433
   AIDS in, 443
   belief in God, 361*f*
   health care expenditures, 456*f*
   homosexuals in, 522

life expectancy, 489*f*
and migration, 495
population, 486*f*
social change in, 531
urban population, 465*f*
women in politics, 405
South Bronx, Los Angeles, 473
South Carolina
   abortion funding, 298*f*
   elderly population, projected, 315*f*
   high school exit exam requirements, 389*f*
South Dakota
   abortion funding, 298*f*
   availability of physicians, 447*f*
   cloning in, 535
   elderly population, projected, 315*f*
   high school exit exam requirements, 389*f*
South Korea
   adoptees, U.S., 336*t*
   average pay of CEO, 204*t*
   gross national income, per capita, 228
   homosexuals in, 522
   place in global economy, 229
   population, 486*f*
   schools, 376
   urban population, 465*f*
South Pacific Islanders, 313
Southeastern Louisiana University, 94
Southern Christian Leadership Conference (SCLC), 266
Soviet Union, former, 243, 418
   collapse of, 529–530
Spain
   gross national income, per capita, 228
   as host country for U.S. students, 377*t*
   population, 486*f*
   urban population, 465*f*
Spider Man (film), 165
Squatter settlements, 471, 556
Sri Lanka, 74
   gross national income, per capita, 228
   homosexuals in, 522
   population, 486*f*
   urban population, 465*f*
St. Louis (ship), 274
Stained glass ceiling, 359
Stanford University prison experiment, 102–103, 104, 107, 108
Star Wars: Attack of the Clones (film), 155
Starbucks, 232
State, the, and socialization, 96
State University of New York at Albany, 94
State University of New York at Stony Brook, 94
Statistical measures, of social class, 210
Statistics, 29–30
   crime, 191–192, 256–257
   interpreting, 50–51
Status, 105–106
   achieved vs. ascribed, 105–106, 132, 199–200, 202
   ascribed
      definition, 547

Status—Cont.
celebrity, 151, 151*t*, 152, 152*t*
definition, 556
and education, 380–381
and gender, 132–133, 239–240
women, worldwide, 291–292
master, 106, 107, 121, 304, 519
measuring, 198
Status group, 205, 556
Stepfamilies, 338
Stereotype, definition, 556
Stereotypes, stereotyping, 154–155
of the elderly, 304
gender, 157–158, 283, 284
of poor people, 212
racial, 253, 333
of Chinese, 249, 249–250
of Muslim and Arab Americans, 175,
256
of single fathers, 337–338
Sterilization, involuntary, 107
Stigma, social
and AIDS, 121
definition, 556
and deviance, 176, 180–181
and homosexuality, 519, 521
and white-collar crime, 190
Stigma symbols, 180
Stonewall Inn, 520
Store Wars (PBS documentary), 476
Stratification, social. *See also* Social inequality
by age, 302–321
among nations, 227–234, 238
and colonialism, 229–230
and multinational corporations,
230–232
caste system, 200, 201
definition, 556
and dependency theory, 230
estates, 200, 201
by gender, 280–301, 286–288
conflict perspective, 286–287
and the family, 326
feminist perspective, 287–288
functionalist perspective, 286
major perspectives, compared, 208*t*
within nations, 234, 234–242
Mexico, 238–242
and prestige, 234–235
and social mobility, 235–236, 237
by wealth and income, 235
and occupation, 421–422
open vs. closed systems, 216
and power, 205
systems of, 199–203
caste, 200, 201
class, 201–203
estate, 200, 201
slavery, 199, 200
theoretical perspectives
conflict, 208*t*
functionalist, 206–207, 208*t*
interactionist, 205, 208*t*

Marxist, 203, 204, 205
universality of, 205–206, 208
Weber's view, 204–205
Students
college. *See* College students
high school, cliques, 385, 386–388
Students against drunk driving (SADD), 191
Subcultures, 69, 70, 70–71
definition, 556
homosexual, 520
student, 385, 386–388
college, 387–388
high school, 385, 385–386
Subjection of Women (Mill), 287
Suburbs, 474–475
characteristics of, 474
definition, 556
diversity in, 474–475
Sudan
gross national income, per capita, 228
population, 486*f*
urban population, 465*f*
Suffrage, women's, 16, 295
Suicide, 7–9, 20, 39
assisted, 318–319
car accidents as, 42–43
female, 493
teenage, 9
homosexual, 387, 388*f*
Native American, 267
theory of, 8–9
SuitableMatch.com, 331
Sum of All Fears (film), 155
Supreme Court, U.S., 291, 298, 369, 370, 543
and affirmative action, 433
Surgeon General of the United States, 438,
453
Suriname
population, 486*f*
urban population of, 465*f*
Surveillance, electronic, 539–540, 542–544
Surveillance function, of media, 153, 556
Survey, 556
Survivor (TV show), 132, 155
Susi doll, 61
Susto, 447*f*
Swaziland
urban population of, 465*f*
Sweatshops, 224–227, 227*f*, 268–269
Sweden
childcare in, 97
gross national income, per capita, 228
(map), 229
health care expenditures, 455
income distribution, 233*f*
income inequality in, 206–207
infant mortality rate, 441*f*
involuntary sterilization, 107
media in, 156
population, 486*f*
social welfare policies, 220
urban population, 465*f*
women in the legislature, 404*f*

Switzerland
gross national income, per capita, 228
infant mortality rate, 441*f*
population, 486*f*
same-sex partnership in, 342
urban population, 465*f*
voter turnout in, 401
welfare system, and healthcare, 219
Symbolic ethnicity, 273, 557
Symbolic interactionist theory. *See* Interactionist theory
Symbols, 85, 557
Syria
gross national income, per capita, 228
population, 486*f*
urban population, 465*f*

T

Tables, interpreting, 51
Taiwan
urban population of, 465*f*
Tanzania
gross national income, per capita, 228
population, 486*f*
urban population, 465*f*
Target stores, 476
Tasmania, 112–113
Tattoos, symbolism of, 16–17, 103–104
Taxi Driver (film), 165
TBS cable station, 161
Tchambuli people, 286
Teacher-expectancy effect, 382, 383–384, 557
Teaching profession, 385
and labor unions, 143
Technical qualifications, for employment in
bureaucracy, 134–135
Technological accidents, 536, 537, 537–538
Technology
biological, 534
and censorship, 159
communications, and collective behavior,
518–519
and crime, 189–190
definition, 533, 557
and the global economy, 227, 228
Lenski's definition, 116
in postmodern societies, 119
in research, 44, 45–46
and resistance to change, 532–533
and social change
biotechnology, 534–536
computers, 533–534
culture and social interaction,
538–539
social control, 539–540, 542–544
stratification and inequality, 540–542
technological accidents, 536, 537–538
and social interaction, 538–539
and social movements, 504–505
and socialization, 95–96
and the workplace, 414–415, 429, 430, 431

Teenagers. *See* Adolescents
Telecommuting, telecommuters, 140, 533–534
    definition, 557
Television, role in socialization, 95
Temporary workers, 428–429
Tennessee
    abortion funding, 298*f*
    availability of physicians, 447*f*
    elderly population, projected, 315*f*
    high school exit exam requirements, 389*f*
Terrorism. *See also* September 11, 2001
    biological, 536
    definition, 398, 557
    and the Internet, 159
Terrorists, 163
Texas
    abortion funding, 298*f*
    availability of physicians, 447*f*
    elderly population, projected, 315*f*
    family, photos, 4–5
    high school exit exam requirements, 389*f*
    state university system, 379
Texting, 111
    lingo, 112*t*
Thailand
    gross national income, per capita, 228
    population, 486*f*
    urban population, 465*f*
Theoretical perspectives, major, 13–18, 19
    comparison of, 18*t*
    conflict, 14–16, 18*t*
    functionalist, 13–14, 18*t*
    interactionist, 16–17, 18*t*
Theory, definition, 8, 557
Third World. *See* Developing nations
    homelessness, 478
Third World Institute, 367
Tibet
    bilingualism in, 75
    marriage in, 323
Tibetan Sherpas, 304
Time magazine, 52, 152, 153
Time Warner Cable, 161
Times Beach, Missouri, 498
Titanic (film), 215
Title XI, 382, 383
TNT cable station, 161
Tobacco use, in the media, 150
Tobago
    urban population, 465*f*
Togo
    gross national income, per capita, 228
    urban population of, 465*f*
Tokyo, 466*t*
    homelessness, 478
Tonga
    urban population, 465*f*
Tonight Show, 314, 512
Total fertility rate (TFR), definition, 489, 557
Total institutions, 90–91, 557
Toyota Motor Company, gross domestic
    product, 231*t*
Tracking, educational, 381, 557

Traditional authority, 399, 557
Trained incapacity, 133, 557
Travelers Corporation, 317
Triad, as social group, 131, 557
Trinidad
    urban population, 465*f*
Trobriand Islanders, marriage, 323
Truck drivers, 207
Tunisia
    gross national income, per capita, 228
    population, 486*f*
    urban population of, 465*f*
Turkey
    gross national income, per capita, 228
    minorities in, 243
    percentage of college graduates, 376*f*
    population, 486*f*
    urban population, 465*f*
    women in, 290
Turkmenistan
    gross national income, per capita, 228
    population, 486*f*
    urban population, 465*f*
Tutsis, and Hutus, 243
Tuvalu
    urban population, 465*f*
TV Guide, 161
26th Amendment, 403
Twins, identical, 83–84
2 Fast 2 Furious (film), 151
2001: A Space Odyssey (film), 140

U

U.S. Conference of Mayors, 478
Uganda
    gross national income, per capita, 228
    urban population of, 465*f*
    women in politics, 405
Ukraine
    adoptees, U.S., 336*t*
    Chernobyl nuclear power plant, 497
    gross national income, per capita, 228
    population, 486*f*
    urban population, 465*f*
Underclass, 213, 219, 557
UNICEF, 498
Unilinear evolutionary theory, 528, 557
Unions, labor, 138. *See* Labor unions
    post-9/11, 143
United Arab Emerates
    urban population, 465*f*
United Farm Workers, 138
United Kingdom. *See also* Great Britain
    gross national income, per capita, 228
    income distribution, 233*f*
    place in global economy, 229*f*
    population, 486*f*
United Nations, 200, 291, 466*t*, 471
    International Year of Older Persons, 302
    population division, 492

Universal Declaration of the Right of In-
    digenous Peoples (United Nations), 245
United Nations Development Programme
    1995, 210
United Nations Development Programme
    2001, 229
United Nations Human Rights Commission,
    243–244
United Nations Partners in Development Pro-
    gramme, 236
United Nations Population Information Net-
    work, 367
United Nations World Health Assembly, 455
United States
    average pay of CEO, 204*t*
    belief in God, 361*f*
    bilingualism in, 74, 75, 76
    birth control policy, 501
    census, 488
    childcare in, 96–98
    corporal punishment in, 174
    correctional system, 174
        sex offender registries, 180
    and the disabled, 107
    education
        college, 376–377
    gender in
        and access to public space, 21
    gross domestic product, 238
    gross national income, per capita, 228,
        229
    health care expenditures, 456*f*
    health care expenditures, projected, 448*f*
    health care in, 448–454
    households, by family type, 325*f*
    human rights abuses, 245
    human rights in, 243
    Human Rights Index, 244*t*
    hunger in, 197
    immigrants, 274–276
    income distribution, 233*f*
        by race or ethnicity, 266*t*
    income inequality in, 206–207
    infant mortality rate, 441*f*, 446, 489
    labor unions in, 141–143
    life expectancy, 238, 489*f*
    marriage, 331–333
        interracial, 331
    materialistic culture of, 182
    measuring social status, 198
    median income by race, ethnicity and
        gender, 432*f*
    medical use of marijuana, by state, 175,
        176
    modern feminism in, 294–295
    and nationalized health care, 455–457
    occupational prestige, 234, 235
    overweight in, 176, 180
    percentage of college graduates, 376*f*
    percentage of people ever married, ages
        20-24, 330*f*
    place in global economy, 229, 229*f*
    political preferences, 401*t*

United States—*Cont.*
poor in, 213*t*
population, 486*f*, 493–494
and internal migration, 495, 496*f*
structure, 491*f*
urban, 465*f*
and population growth, 500
poverty in, 212–213, 214
race and ethnicity in, 264–273
racial and ethnic groups, 251*t*
projected, 252*t*
same-sex partnership in, 342–343
slavery in, 199, 200
suicide rate, 9
union membership in, 142
voluntary associations in, 138
wealth and income, inequality, 210, 211, 211*t*
welfare system, 210, 213, 219–221
women in the legislature, 404*f*
women in the workforce, 292–296
gender bias, 292–293
by occupation, 294*t*
trends over time, 293*f*
workforce, composition of, 426*f*
United Students Against Sweatshops, 226
Universal Declaration of Human Rights (United Nations), 200, 243
Universal Declaration of the Right of Indigenous Peoples (United Nations), 245
Universal Fellowship of Metropolitan Community Churches, 355
University of California at Berkeley, American Cultures Center, 537
University of California at Davis, 431
University of Chicago, 17
University of Colorado, 283–284
University of Georgia, 94
University of Kentucky, 445
University of Michigan, 433
University of New Hampshire, 94
University of South Dakota, 520
University of Wisconsin, 82
Untouchables, in caste system, 200, 201
Up Against the Wal, 540
Urban communities
change over time, 468–469
problems in, 472–473
Urban dwellers, 471–472
Urban ecology, 464, 467, 557
Urban sociology, new, 467, 470
Urbanism, 463, 557
Urbanization, 463, 464
around the world, 465*f*
Uruguay
gross national income, per capita, 228
population, 486*f*
urban population, 465*f*
USA PATRIOT Act, 175, 398
Utah
abortion funding, 298*f*
availability of physicians, 447*f*

elderly population, projected, 315*f*
high school exit exam requirements, 389*f*
Uzbekistan
arranged marriage, 330
gross national income, per capita, 228
population, 486*f*
urban population, 465*f*

V

Validity, 33, 557
of school-based testing, 389
Value-added model, of collective behavior, 507–508, 517*t*
definition, 557
Value, definition, 557
Value generalization, and social change, 529
Value neutrality, in research, 43–44
definition, 557
and sexual behavior, 47
Values, 67–69
Internet, 159
and social interaction, 103
Vanuatu
urban population, 465*f*
Variables, 32
control, 34
independent vs. dependent, 32
Veil, in Middle Eastern cultures, 290
Venezuela
gross national income, per capita, 228
population, 486*f*
urban population, 465*f*
Vermont
abortion funding, 298*f*
availability of physicians, 447*f*
elderly population, projected, 315*f*
high school exit exam requirements, 389*f*
Verstehen, 10, 557
Vertical mobility, 216–217, 557
Vested interests, and resistance to change, 530, 557
VH-1 (cable station), 159
Vice City (video game), 164
Victimization rates, crime, 191*t*
Victimization surveys, 191–192, 557
Victimless crimes, 186, 557
Victims
blaming, 268
of media violence, 165
Video games, violent, 164, 166
Viet Kieu, 268
Vietnam
economic system of, 417–418
gross national income, per capita, 228
percentage of U.S. immigrants from, 275*f*
place in global economy, 229*f*
population, 486*f*
sweatshops in, 226
urban population of, 465*f*
Vietnamese Americans, 268, 268*t*

Vietnamese complex of religions, world wide, 352*f*
Violence
domestic, 164–165, 328
in the media, 157–158
Internet, 164–166
victims of, 165
school-based, 386
against homosexuals, 388*f*
and video games, 164
Virgin Islands
urban population, 465*f*
Virginia
abortion funding, 298*f*
Ashland, 476
availability of physicians, 447*f*
elderly population, projected, 315*f*
high school exit exam requirements, 389*f*
Vital statistics, definition, 488, 557
Voluntarism, definition, 138
Voluntary associations, 138–139
definition, 557
in United States
membership, 138, 139*t*
Voter apathy, 400–401, 403
Voter News Service, 342, 404
Voting, 395
Voting rights, for women, 16, 295

W

Wages for Housework Campaign 1999, 210
Wal-Mart, 232, 476
gross domestic product, 231*t*
Walt Disney company, 161
War crimes, 243
War of the Worlds (radio broadcast), 512
Warner Brothers, 161
Washington, D.C.
abortion funding, 298*f*
elderly population, projected, 315*f*
high school exit exam requirements, 389*f*
on September 11, 2001, 7
Washington State
abortion funding, 298*f*
availability of physicians, 447*f*
elderly population, projected, 315*f*
high school exit exam requirements, 389*f*
Water pollution, 497–498
Wealth
definition, 557
as measure of social class, 210–211
as social symbol, 182
vs income, 199, 210–211
Wealthy, the, and the welfare system, 219–220
Weight issues, for women, 176
Welfare system
in Eastern Europe, 220
United States, 219–221
and illegal immigrants, 276
reform, 219, 220
and the wealthy, 219–220

West Africa, gender in, 21
West Virginia
    abortion funding, 298f
    availability of physicians, 447f
    elderly population, projected, 315f
    high school exit exam requirements, 389f
Western Sahara
    urban population, 465f
Whistleblowing, 133
White-collar crime, 189–190, 557
White ethnics, 273
Whites
    as dominant group, 257–258
    infant mortality rate, 446
    and Internet access, 541f
    life expectancy, 446
    as percentage of workforce, 426f
    percentage without health insurance, 444f
    relative economic position, 266t
    single-parent families, increase over time, 332f
    socialization, 86
Who, The (band), 505, 506
Who Wants to Be a Millionaire (TV show), 155
Wholistic health care, 450
Widows, in India, 291
Will and Grace (TV show), 156
William Shatner Fellowship, 138
Wisconsin
    abortion funding, 298f
    availability of physicians, 447f
    elderly population, projected, 315f
    high school exit exam requirements, 389f
Women
    and access to public space, 21
    and affirmative action, 431–433
    and AIDS, 120, 121
    discrimination. See Gender, discrimination; sexism
    and homelessness, 479
    in the media, 165
    median income, U.S., 432
    minorities, 296
    and networking, 110
    and occupational prestige, 209–210
    in paid labor force
        by country, 292f
        informal economies, 418
        medical professions, 449–450
        U.S., trends over time, 293f

in politics, 401, 403
in poverty, 212–213
and religion, 359
as social activists, 43–44, 239–240, 261, 287
    1900s, 12, 16
    in India, 518
social mobility of, 217–218
as sociologists, 15–16, 43–44
status of, 132–133
    in Mexico, 239–240
    and redefining social reality, 104
    in sweatshops, 226
and unpaid work, 138, 292, 294
    in Nepal, 418
and weight issues, 176
in the workforce, 425–426
Work, unpaid, 138
Workers, exploited, 224–227
Workfare, 220
Workforce, contingent, 428–429
Working class, 202–203, 204
    Marxist view, 203
Working poor, the, 199, 212
Workplace
    alienation, 422–423
    deindustrialization, 426–427, 428
    employee monitoring, 141
    job satisfaction, 423–424
        in Japan, 424–425
    McDonaldization of, 135
    and networking, 110
    socialization in, 95–96
    surveillance, 539–540
    women in, 292–294
World Bank, 154, 452, 455, 534
World Conference on Women, 1995, 245
World Development Forum, 61
World Health Organization (WHO), 8, 438–439, 450, 490, 497, 498
World Population Conference, 501
World Resources Institute, 497
World systems analysis, 229–230, 534
    definition, 557
    and Internet access, of nations, 534, 541
    and new urban sociology, 467, 470
    placement of nations in, 229f
World Trade Center, New York City. See September 11, 2001
World Trade Organization, 504
World Values surveys, 361

World War II, 269, 274
Wyoming
    abortion funding, 298f
    availability of physicians, 447f
    elderly population, projected, 315f
    high school exit exam requirements, 389f

X

Xenocentrism, 73, 557

Y

Yale University, 173–174, 396, 516
Yanomani Indians, 245
Yemen
    gross national income, per capita, 228
YMCA (Young Men's Christian Association), 138, 139
Young people. See also adolescents; College students
    as voters, 403
Yugoslavia, 418
    ethnic cleansing, 243
    gross national income, per capita, 228
    and Human Rights Index, 244t
    population, 486f
    urban population, 465f

Z

Zaire, 416–417
Zambia, 500
    life expectancy, 489
    population, 486f
Zapatistas, 408
Zero population growth (ZPG), 494, 558
Zimbabwe
    gross national income, per capita, 228
    population, 486f
    urban population, 465f
Zoning laws, definition, 558

Applications of Sociology's Major Theoretical Approaches

Sociology provides comprehensive coverage of the major sociological perspectives. The summary table below includes a sample of the topics in this text that have been explored using these approaches. The numbers in parentheses indicate the pertinent chapters.

FUNCTIONALIST PERSPECTIVE

Defined and explained (1)
Adoption (14)
AIDS and social networks (5)
Anomie theory of deviance (8)
Bilingualism (3)
Bureaucratization of schools (16)
Campaign financing (17)
Culture (3, 16)
Davis and Moore's view of stratification (9)
Disengagement theory of aging (13)
Dominant ideology (3)
Durkheim's view of deviance (8)
Dysfunctions of racism (11)
Electronic surveillance (23)
Ethnocentrism (3)
Family (14)
Formal organizations (6)
Functions of dying (13)
Gans's functions of poverty (9)
Gender and stratification (12)
Health and illness (19)
Human ecology (21)
Human rights (10)
Immigration (11)
In-groups and out-groups (6)
Integrative function of religion (15)
Internet (23)
Media and socialization (7)
Modernization theory (10)
Multinational corporations (10)
Narcotizing effect of the media (7)
Population policy (21)
Racial prejudice and discrimination (11)
Rumors (22)
Social change (16, 23)
Social control (8, 16)
Social institutions (5)
Social networks (5)
Socialization in schools (4, 16, 17)
Sports (1)
Subcultures (3)
Urban ecology (20)

CONFLICT PERSPECTIVE

Defined and explained (1)
Abortion (12)
Access to health care (19)
Access to technology (23)
Adoption (14)
Affirmative action (18)
Aging and stratification (13)
AIDS crisis (5)
Bilingualism (3)
Bureaucratization of schools (16)
Campaign financing (17)
Capitalism (15, 18)
Corporate welfare (9)
Correspondence principle (16)
Credentialism (16)
Culture (3)
Day care funding (4)
Deviance (8)
Disability as a master status (5)
Domestic violence (14)
Dominant ideology (3, 7, 9)
Downsizing (18)
Elite model of the U.S. power structure (17)
Environmental issues (21)
Ethnocentrism (3)
Exploitation theory of racial subordination (11)
Family (14)
Gender and stratification (12)
Gender equity in education (16)
Gun control (8)
Hidden curriculum (18)
Immigration (11)
Iron Law of Oligarchy (6)
Labor unions (6)
Lesbian and gay rights (22)
Marx's view of stratification (9)
Media gatekeeping (7)
Media stereotypes (7)
Media violence (7)
Medicalization of society (19)
Model minority (11)
Multinational corporations (10)
New urban sociology (20)
Population policy (21)
Poverty (9)
Privacy and technology (23)
Racism and health (19)
Religion and social control (15)
Reproductive technology (14)
Right to die (13)
School violence (16)
Social change (23)
Social control (8)
Social institutions (5)
Sports (1)
Subcultures (3)
Tracking (16)
Victimless crimes (8)
White-collar crime (8)
World systems analysis (10, 20)

INTERACTIONIST PERSPECTIVE

Defined and explained (1)
Activity theory of aging (13)
Affirmative action (18)
AIDS and its impact (5)
Campaign financing (17)
Charismatic authority (17)
Conspicuous consumption (9)
Contact hypothesis (11)
Differential association (8)
Dramaturgical approach (4, 17)
Electronic communication (7, 23)
Family (14, 17)
Gender stratification (12)
Health and illness (19)
Human relations approach (6)
Media violence (7)
Negotiated order (5)
Privacy and technology (7, 23)
Racial stereotyping (11)
Reproductive technology (14)
Routine activities theory (8)
School prayer (15)
Small groups (6)
Social institutions (5)
Sports (1)
Teacher-expectancy effect (16)
Teenage pregnancy (14)
Unions (6)

FEMINIST PERSPECTIVE

Defined and explained (1)
Day care funding (4)
Domestic violence (14)
Dominant ideology (3)
Ethnographic research (2)
Family (14)
Gender stratification (12)
Language (3)
Media stereotypes (7)
Media violence (7)
Population policy (21)
Pornography (7)
School violence (16)
Sports (1)
Victimless crimes (8)
Women in public (1)

LABELING THEORY

Defined and explained (8)
AIDS and labeling (5, 19)
Disabilities and labeling (5)
Health and illness (19)
Mental illness (19)
Presentation of the self (4)
Societal reaction approach (8)
Teacher-expectancy effect (16)
Victimless crimes (8)